International Handbook of
Underwater Archaeology

The Plenum Series in Underwater Archaeology

Series Editor:
J. Barto Arnold III
Institute of Nautical Archaeology
Texas A&M University
College Station, Texas

International Handbook of Underwater Archaeology
Edited by Carol V. Ruppé and Janet F. Barstad

Iron and Steamship Archaeology: Success and Failure on the SS *Xantho*
Michael McCarthy

Maritime Archaeology: A Reader of Substantive and Theoretical
 Contributions
Edited by Lawrence E. Babits and Hans Van Tillburg

The Material Culture of Steamboat Passengers: Archaeological Evidence
 from the Missouri River
Annalies Corbin

The Persistence of Sail in the Age of Steam: Underwater Archaeological
 Evidence from the Dry Tortugas
Donna J. Souza

International Handbook of Underwater Archaeology

Edited by

Carol V. Ruppé

Librarian Emeritus
Arizona State University
Tempe, Arizona

and

Janet F. Barstad

Prose and Images
Tempe, Arizona

Kluwer Academic/Plenum Publishers
New York   Boston   Dordrecht   London   Moscow

Library of Congress Cataloging-in-Publication Data

International handbook of underwater archaeology/edited by Carol V.
Ruppé and Janet F. Barstad.
     p. cm. — (The Plenum series in underwater archaeology)
    Includes bibliographical references and index.
    ISBN 0-306-46345-8
     1. Underwater archaeology—Handbooks, manuals, etc. I. Ruppé, Carol.
II. Barstad, Jan. III. Series.
    CC77.U5 I55 2001
    930.1′028′04—dc21

                                           2001016493

ISBN: 0-306-46345-8

©2002 Kluwer Academic/Plenum Publishers, New York
233 Spring Street, New York, N.Y. 10013

http://www.wkap.nl/

10 9 8 7 6 5 4 3 2 1

A C.I.P. record for this book is available from the Library of Congress

Printed in the United States of America

To those who have gone before

Willard Bascom
Charles W. Beebe
Howard Chapelle
Jacques-Yves Cousteau
Calvin R. Cummings
S. de Borheghi
Charles H. Fairbanks
Octavio Lixa Filgueiras
Emile Gagnan
John Goggin
Edmund Halley
Donald P. Jewell
Paul Johnstone
Warren G. Kenyon
Per Lindstrom

Eric McKee
Keith Muckleroy
G.P.B. Naish
August Picard
John Rick
Reynold Ruppé
Joel Shiner
Auguste Siebe
John Smeaton
W.E. Suddereth
D.C. Switzer
Joan Du Plat Taylor
Peter Throckmorton
Robert C. Wheeler
Warren Wonka

Contributors

D.K. Abbass, Project Director, Rhode Island Marine Archaeology Project, Newport, Rhode Island 02840

Christian Ahlström, International Congress of Maritime Museums, Helsinki, 00140 Finland

Christopher F. Amer, Deputy State Underwater Archaeologist, South Carolina Institute for Archaeology and Anthropology, University of South Carolina, Columbia, South Carolina 29208

J. Barto Arnold III, Institute of Nautical Archaeology, Texas A&M University, College Station, Texas 77841

Lawrence E. Babits, Program in Maritime Studies, East Carolina University, Greenville, North Carolina 27853

Janet F. Barstad, Prose & Images, Tempe, Arizona 85282

Carlo Beltrame, Dipartmento de Scienze dell' Anticchità e del Vicino Oriente, Universita Ca' di Venezia, S. Polo 1977 30125 Venezia, Italy

Jean-Yves Blot, Archaeologist, Torres Vedras, 2560, Portugal

Colin Breen, Centre for Maritime Archaeology, University of Ulster, Coleraine, Northern Ireland

John D. Broadwater, Manager, Monitor National Marine Sanctuary, National Oceanic and Atmosphere Administration, Newport News, Virginia 23606,

Carl Olof Cederlund, Marine Archaeology Program, University College of South Stockholm, Sweden

Annalies Corbin, Program in Maritime Studies, East Carolina University, Greenville, North Carolina 27853

Kevin J. Crisman, Institute of Nautical Archaeology, Texas A&M University, College Station, Texas 77843

Calvin R. Cummings, Senior Archaeologist, Late of the National Park Service, Golden, Colorado 80401

Glenn P. Darrington, Scottish Institute of Maritime Studies, University of St. Andrews, Fife, Scotland, United Kingdom

Dan Davis, RPM Nautical Foundation, Key West, Florida 33040

James P. Delgado, Executive Director, Vancouver Maritime Museum, Vancouver, British Columbia v63 1A3 Canada

Dolores Carolina Elkin, CONICET, Universidad Nacional del Centro de la Provincia de Buenos Aires, and Instituto Nacional de Antropología, Buenos Aires, Argentina 1378

Jeremy Green, Head, Maritime Archaeology and National Centre of Excellence, Department of Maritime Archaeology, Western Australia Maritime Museum, Fremantle, Western Australia WA 6160

David Gregory, Centre for Maritime Archaeology, National Museum of Denmark, DK-4000, Roskilde, Denmark

John Gribble, South African Resources Agency, Cape Town, 8000, South Africa

Max Guérout, Groupe de Recherche en Archéologie Navale, 75012, Paris, France

Andrew W. Hall, Faculty Associate, Director of Grants and Publications, and Manager, Office for Nursing Research & Scholarship, University of Texas School of Nursing at Galveston, Galveston, Texas 77550

John R. Halsey, Office of the State Archaeologist, Michigan Historical Center, Department of History, Arts, and Libraries, Lansing, Michigan 48918

Edward C. Harris, Director, Bermuda Maritime Museum, Mangrove Bay, Bermuda

Jack Hunter, Underwater Archaeologist, California Department of Transportation District 5, San Luis Obispo, California 93401

Donald H. Keith, Ships of Discovery, Corpus Christi Museum of Science and History, Corpus Christi, Texas 78401

Margaret E. Leshikar-Denton, Archaeologist, Cayman Islands National Museum, Grand Cayman, Cayman Islands

Emad Khalil, Assistant Lecturer, Archaeology Department, Alexandria University, Alexandria, Egypt

Martin Klein, Consultant, Andover, Massachusetts 01810

Susan B.M. Langley, Maryland Historical Trust, Department of Housing and Community Development, Crownsville, Maryland 21032

Pilar Luna Erreguerena, National Institute of Anthropology and History, Subdirreción de Arqueología Aubacuática, Semanario 8, Centro C.P., 06060. Mexico, D.F.

Ian D. MacLeod, Director, Museum Services, Western Australian Museum, Fremantle, Western Australia WA 6160

Colin J.M. Martin, Honorary Reader, Centre for Environmental History, University of St. Andrews, St. Andrews Fife, KY16 9AJ, Scotland, United Kingdom

Victor Mastone, Director, Board of Underwater Archaeological Resources, Executive Office of Environmental Affairs, Boston, Massachusetts 02114

Ian R. Mather, Assistant Professor, Maritime History and Underwater Archaeology, Department of History, University of Rhode Island, Kingston, Rhode Island 02881

Mohamed Mustafa, Archaeology Inspector, Underwater Archaeology Department, Supreme Council of Antiquities, Alexandria, Egypt

Robert S. Neyland, Head, Underwater Archaeology Branch, Naval Historical Center, Washington Navy Yard, Washington, DC 20374

Aidan O'Sullivan, Department for Archaeology, University College, Dublin, Republic of Ireland

Ian Oxley, Department of Civil and Offshore Engineering, Heriot Watt University, Edinburgh, Scotland, United Kingdom

Warren Riess, Historical Marine Sciences, University of Maine, Walpole, Maine 04573

Clifford E. Smith Jr., Bermuda Maritime Museum, Mangrove Bay, MA BX, Bermuda

Roger C. Smith, State Underwater Archaeologist, Florida Bureau of Underwater Archaeology, Division of Historical Resources, Tallahassee, Florida 32399

Sheli O. Smith, Maritime Archaeology Certificate Program, Long Beach City College, Long Beach, California 90808

Bruce G. Terrell, Maritime Archaeologist, National Oceanographic and Atmospheric Administration, Marine Sanctuary Division, Silver Spring, Maryland 20910

Hans Van Tilburg, Marine Option Program, University of Hawaii at Manoa, Hawaii 96822

Shelley Wachsmann, Institute of Nautical Archaeology, Texas A&M University, College Station, Texas 77841

Gordon P. Watts Jr., Institute of International Maritime Research, Inc., Washington, North Carolina 27887

Brian Williams, Senior Inspector, Environmental and Heritage Service, Belfast, BT1 2LA, Northern Ireland

Joseph W. Zarzynski, Beateaux, Inc., Wilton New York 12831

Foreword

Underwater research has long since taken its rightful place as an important subdiscipline in the field of archaeology. Growth has been rapid, both in the prehistoric and historic underwater sites, and has accelerated in the past ten years. However, the published literature has not kept pace with new developments. Comprehensive reports and summaries have been needed to delineate the field's impressive progress.

Carol Ruppé and Janet Barstad have designed the *International Handbook of Underwater Archaeology* to fill the literature gap that has widened so markedly in a decade. The editors take a geographic and topical approach and include perspectives on technology, law, and public and private institutional roles and goals, as well as a look to the future of research and development of technologies and public programs.

The *Handbook* is designed to appeal to a variety of readers: underwater archaeologists, maritime historians, historical archaeologists and archaeologists in general, graduate students, and specialists in auxiliary fields—educators, biologists, environmental scientists, historians, and geographers. The book is also for the public at large, which has developed a voracious appetite for shipwrecks. The editors selected the chapter authors for their depth of knowledge about their locales and for their professional expertise.

The *Handbook* consist of three parts further divided into seven sections of 48 chapters and an Afterword, followed by a glossary and author and subject indexes. Most of the chapters are written by Americans, but other contributors worldwide also share their expertise. Some of the projects are updates, others compilations, and some are just getting their feet wet. Several writers just could not take time away from their research to participate at present. Another volume could be projected at a later time and is certainly encouraged. We owe the present editors a tremendous vote of thanks for the Herculean effort it took to bring the project to fruition. Bravasimas!

Others works of similar structure preceding this one include *Ships and Shipwrecks of the Americas*, edited by George Bass (1988); *The Sea Remembers* with its emphasis on key wreck sites, edited by Peter Throckmorton (1987); *Maritime Archaeology*, edited by Keith Muckelroy (1977); and *Shipwreck Anthropology*, edited by Richard A. Gould (1983).

This volume is written for the wide audience that underwater archaeology attracts, and is dedicated to those who dove before, a number that now includes, the late National Park Service archaeologist Calvin Cummings, who died September 2, 2000. With the dawn of a new century, we wish to acknowledge the previous contributors to the field. There are other introductions to tell the reader the how, why, and where.

Now is the time to update the findings both by area and by subject. Our literature grows from papers presented at meetings, and conferences and published in journals and reference books. The bibliography is there and now an updating, handbook style has its place in the literature of this most special archaeology.

J. Barto Arnold III

Preface

If we go back far enough in human evolution, we find that we humans once lived quite comfortably in the sea. Even when we stepped onto land and lost gills, fins, and other seagoing apparatus, of necessity we lived *near* water—the sea, lakes, rivers, creeks—any little trickle would do. But we learned rather quickly that we could not return to our old home unless we held our breath under water or found something, a log, perhaps, on which to float. It wasn't long before we again began to explore the watery world but on things that floated, then on floating things we made ourselves. We called them boats.

Gradually, we came to take boats for granted. They were a necessary part of our lives. We used them for moving from place to place, for providing food by fishing, for transporting goods, for war (either for attacking or fleeing, depending on which side we were on at the time) and, we can assume, for the simple pleasure of being out on the water.

The word *boat* has become a staple of our vocabulary in odd ways. Two people facing the same problems are said to be "in the same boat." If we fail to take advantage of an opportunity, we have "missed the boat." And in certain circumstances, we really do not want to "rock the boat." *The Random House Dictionary of the English Language* defines a boat as "a vessel for transport by water, constructed to provide buoyancy by excluding water and shaped to give stability and permit propulsion."

This definition has been true since the first days of our somewhat uncomfortable return to water. A boat must be built. It must float. It should be stable. It does not absolutely have to be propelled, but it's almost always nice to be able to push it or pull it in the direction we want to go, flowing rivers notwithstanding. Remove any one of the above elements, and we do not have a boat. Either it does not come into existence, or what we have is a wreck on the bottom of a body of water.

Which brings us to our present endeavor—the *International Handbook of Underwater Archaeology*—by what some might look on as a leap of faith unless we consider the following: Sooner or later, after all the millennia through which we had been "messing about in boats," someone was sure to become curious or greedy enough to want to know what was Down There and would figure out a way to get to it. This happened much sooner than you might think, which is why we introduce this volume with John

Broadwater's excellent timelines, "Timeline for Deepwater Technology and Exploration" and "Timeline of Underwater Archaeology and Salvage." We learn that nearly 2500 years ago the king of Persia sent a diver to recover material from sunken enemy ships, and that a mere one hundred years later Aristotle described the use of a crude diving bell. At the moment Scyllis dove for Xerxes of Persia, the art (or evil) of salvage was born. When Aristotle described a diving bell, the technology needed for underwater exploration was on its way.

From 460 B.C. to 2002 A.D. is indeed a bit of a leap. But we can easily imagine that throughout prehistory and into written history all manner of people peered down into the water and said, "What *is* that down there?" or stood on a pier in Spain and lamented, "Where *is* that galleon? It's been five years since we sent her to New Spain for gold, surely she should be back by now!" And many have argued, "The story of Noah's Ark may be a myth, but myths don't come from nowhere. If we look in the right place, maybe we'll find out what caused the Flood and what it covered."

According to Broadwater's timelines, salvage has been practiced for a long, long time, but underwater archaeology could be said to have begun only in about 1900 A.D., when an archaeologist supervised the recovery of statuary from a Roman wreck carrying Greek art. These last hundred years have been a time of slow development but now underwater archaeology is a solid discipline that uses ultramodern techniques and has high ethical standards. Broadwater's timelines provide a fine long view of that development.

From the perspective of time, the scope of the *International Handbook of Underwater Archaeology* is considerably more limited than the timelines since it covers developments of only the past ten years. Yet, the *Handbook*'s geographic scope could not be broader: We attempted no less than complete coverage of the whole world. Although we did not succeed as well as we would have liked (We were not able to include Canada, Russia, and some other areas in our survey), our chapter authors have covered a huge amount of the earth's surface and waters.

Geography, we felt, was a good place to start our journey through the past decade of developments in underwater archaeology. Our authors take you on a world tour beginning at the northeastern corner of the United States and flowing down through the American South, out west to the Pacific Coast and even farther west to Hawaii, then down into Mexico and South America and out into the Caribbean. Jumping over the Atlantic Ocean, they continue the journey in Sweden, through the Baltic Sea, into the British Isles and back again to northern and southern Europe. From the eastern Mediterranean and Egypt, they head farther east to Asia, the Indian Ocean, and Australia, then down to deepest South Africa.

Wrecks and artifacts abound throughout the tour and, geography being the dynamic process it is, in some weird places: deep under Lisbon, Portugal, in the construction debris of urban works; in abandoned oxbows nearly a mile from the Missouri River's present shore; under a landfill in San Francisco. Testimony of our attachment to water and boats is found eroding out of sand beaches, wedged among coastal rocks, buried in the gravels of the Sea of Galilee, 12,500 feet down in oceans, tossed about in the surf near shore, piled atop one another in a bay on the coast of Israel. We humans have left evidence of our watery travels just about everywhere.

Since underwater archaeology is now a discipline, there are issues to be faced by the discipline's practitioners. In Part III, our authors describe not only how to find, conserve, preserve, and protect wrecks, artifacts, and other objects under water, and what the objects may mean in terms of human history and prehistory; they also tackle the thorny questions of who owns the resources, how best to disseminate information about them and, indeed, whether certain of the resources should be protected at all. The role of some United States government agencies is explored in a separate section. There is also much on the subject of governments' involvement in underwater archaeology in the geography chapters, since many states and nations have in place or are currently devising strategies to deal with their underwater heritage.

Central to the issues is a discussion on ethics, from the development of high standards for finding and dealing with underwater objects to the treating of salvors and sport divers. It is not all smooth sailing, but the various archaeology groups and societies have provided written standards—"lightships," if you will—for keeping the discipline on an ethical course.

The final word on underwater archaeology probably will never be written unless the world runs out of underwater objects to explore. Nonetheless, George Bass provides the last words as he peers down the long rivers and wide seas of the future and speculates what wind the discipline might sail by and what wonders its practitioners might discover. In "Archaeology in the 21st Century," Bass presents an overview of recent findings that he, Robert Ballard, and other archaeologists unearthed in the Black Sea when they discovered freshwater beaches and human habitation on the bottom of that vast inland sea. If this work is an augury of things to come, the journey of underwater archaeology down the rivers and into the seas of human prehistory and history on water will be one of momentous discoveries in the new millenium.

We like to think of the *International Handbook of Underwater Archaeology* as an elegant, well-equipped ship with a highly professional crew, about to set sail on fascinating waters. *Bon voyage!*

CAROL V. RUPPÉ
JANET F. BARSTAD

Contents

Acronyms

AA	Antiquities Act	**AINA**	American Institute for Nautical Archaeology (see INA)
AAA	American Anthropological Association	**ARCH**	National Marine Sanctuary Site Database (NOAA)
ACDO	Australian Cultural Development Office	**ARPO**	Archaeological Resources Protection Act
ACHWS	Advisory Committee on Historic Wrecks, Ireland	**ASA**	Abandoned Shipwreck Act of 1987
ACUA	Advisory Council on Underwater Archaeology	**AST**	Archaeological Service for Teesside (Great Britain)
ADA	Australian Diving Association	**AutoCAD**	Computer-assisted design program (Autodesk)
ADAP	Archaeological Data Acquisition Platform	**AUV**	Autonomous Underwater Vehicle
ADAP III	Electronic state-of-the-art integrated marine remote sensing array	**AWOIS**	Automated Wrecks and Obstruction Information System (NOAA)
ADU	Archaeological Diving Unit (Ireland)		
ADU	Archaeological Diving Unit (United Kingdom)		
AFHRA	Air Force Historical Research Agency (U.S.)	**BAR**	Bureau of Archaeological Research (Florida)
AGM	Museums Association of the Caribbean (See MAC)	**BCA**	Ministry of Beni Culteralie Ambientali (Italy)
AIA	Archaeological Institute of America	**BMI**	Baltimore Museum of Industry
AIA Sub	Associazione degli Archeologi (Italy)	**BSAC**	British Sub Aqua Club
AIC	American Institute for Conservation	**CAD**	Computer-assisted design
AIMA	Australian Institute for Maritime Archaeology	**CADW**	Welsh Historic Monuments Executive Agency

CAHEP	Caesarea Ancient Harbour Excavation Project
CAMM	Council of American Maritime Museums
CAP	Crannog Archaeology Project (Ireland)
CARISUB	Cuba
CCI	Canadian Conservation Institute
CCM	Corpus Christi Museum of Science and History
CDUA	Conservation District Use Application (Hawaii)
CEA	Centre d'Études Alexandrines (Egypt)
CEDAM	Club de Exploraciones y Deportes Acuaticos de Mexico
CINMS	Channel Islands National Marine Sanctuaries (California)
CINP	Channel Islands National Park (California)
CMAR	Coastal Maritime Archaeological Resources (California)
CMAS	Confédération Mondiale des Activitiés Subaquatiques
CMS	Champlain Maritime Society
CMS	Chicago Maritime Society
CMS	Centre for Maritime Studies (Haifa University, Israel)
CNANS	Portuguese Institute of Archaeology, Underwater Branch
CNAS	Civil Navigation Aids System
CNRS	Centre National de la Recherche Scientifique (France)
COE	U.S. Army Corps of Engineers (See also USACE)
CPAS	Portuguese Center of Underwater Activities
CRAS	Comisíon de Rescate Arqueológico Submarino (Dominican Republic)
CRM	Cultural Resource Management
CRT	Cathode ray tube

CTFM	Continuous-transmission-frequency-modulated
DAS	Underwater Archaeology Department (Mexico)
DCMS	Department of Culture, Media, and Sport (United Kingdom)
DGPS	Differential Geographical Positioning System
DLNR	Department of Land and Natural Resources (Hawaii)
DNR	Department of Natural Resources (Maryland)
DOE	Department of the Environment for England
DOE NI	Department of the Environment for Northern Ireland
DOJ	Department of Justice - Civil Division (U.S.)
DOS	Department of State (U.S.)
DRASM	Direction des Recherches Archéologiques Sous-Marines (France)
DRASSM	Départment des Recherches Archéologiques Subaquatiques et Sous-Marines (France)
DRMS	Defense Revitalization and Marketing Service (U.S.)
ECU	East Carolina University
EDA	Exploratory Data Analysis
EDF	Électricité de France
EDM	Electronic distance measurement
EEZ	Exclusive Economic Zone
ESPADAS	Equipos y sistemas de la Plataforma de Adquisición de Datos Arqueológicos Sumergidos (Mexico)
ESRI	Environmental Systems Research Institute, Inc.
FAP	
FDHR	Florida Department of Historic Resources

FFESSM	Fédération Française d'Étude et de Sport Sous-Marin	**ICR**	Central Institute for Restoration (Italy)
FKNMS	Florida Keys National Marine Sanctuary	**ICRMP**	Integrated Cultural Resource Management Plans (U.S.)
		IDAM	Israel Department of Antiquities and Museum (See IAA)
GEOCUBA	Cuba (?)	**IEASM**	Institut Européan d'Archéologie Sous-Marine (France)
GERS	Groupe d'Étude et de Recherche Sous-Marine	**IFA**	Institute of Field Archaeologists (United Kingdom)
GIS	Geographic Information System	**IFREMER**	International French Research Institute for Ocean Utilization
GLSPS	Great Lakes Shipwreck Preservation Society		
GPS	Global Positioning Systems	**IHPA**	Illinois Historic Preservation Agency
GPSLOG	Datalog (Sandia Research Associates)	**IIMR**	Institute for International Maritime Research, Inc. (North Carolina)
GRAN	Groupe de Recherche en Archéologie Navale (France)	**IJNA**	International Journal of Nautical Archaeology
GRULAC	Latin American and Caribbean Group	**IMH**	Institute of Maritime History (York, Maine)
GSA	General Services Administration (U.S.)	**INA**	Instituto Nacional de Antropologia (Argentina)
GTAS	Underwater Archaeology Working Group (Argentina)	**INA**	Institute of Nautical Archaeology (see INA-TAMU)
GTPS	Underwater Heritage Working Group (Argentina)	**INA-TAMU**	Institute of Nautical Archaeology-Texas A&M University
HAPI	Historic Aircraft Preservation, Inc.	**INAH**	National Institute of Anthropological History (Mexico)
HBOI	Harbor Branch Oceanographic Institution	**ISBSA**	International Symposium on Boat and Ship Archaeology
Hypack	Hydrographic data, Coastal Oceanographics	**ISTEA**	Internodal Surface Transportation Efficiency Act (Maryland)
IAA	Israel Antiquities Authority		
ICCROM	International Centre for the Study of the Preservation and the Restoration of Cultural Properties	**JNAPC**	Joint Nautical Archaeology Policy Committee (Great Britain)
ICMM	International Congress of Maritime Museums	**JNHT**	Jamaica National Heritage Trust
ICOM	International Council of Museums		
ICOMOS	International Council on Monuments and Sites	**LAMP**	Lighthouse Archaeological Maritime Program
ICOMOS	International Council on Monuments and Sites (Argentina)	**LCMM**	Lake Champlain Maritime Museum (Vermont)

MAC	Museums Association of the Caribbean	**NHC**	Naval Historical Center (U.S.)
MAHRI	Maritime Archaeological Historic Research Institute (Maine)	**NHPA**	National Historic Preservation Act
		NLP	Navy Legacy Program (U.S.)
MAHS	Maritime Archaeological and Historical Society (Arlington, Virginia)	**NMC**	National Monuments Council (South Africa)
		NMHP	National Maritime Heritage Program (U.S.)
MAHS	Maritime Archaeological and Historical Society (Maryland)	**NMHS**	National Maritime Historical Society (U.S.)
MAHS	Maritime Archaeological and Historical Society (Bermuda)	**NMMA**	National Maritime Museum Association (U.S.)
MARSS	Monitor Archaeological Research and Structural Survey	**NMNA**	National Museum of Naval Aviation
MBUAR	Massachusetts Board of Underwater Archaeological Resources	**NMS**	National Marine Sanctuary (Hawaii)
		NMSP	National Marine Sanctuary Program
MCBH	Marine Corps Base Hawaii		
MDSU	Mobile Diving and Salvage Reserve Unit (U.S. Navy)	**NOAA**	National Oceanic and Atmospheric Administration
MHPC	Maine Historic Preservation Commission	**NOS**	New Old Spaniard (Bermuda)
MHS	Minnesota Historical Society	**NPS**	National Park Service
MHT	Maryland Historical Trust		(U.S.)
MIT	Massachusetts Institute of Technology	**NRL**	Naval Research Laboratory
		NUWC	Naval Undersea Warfare Center (U.S.)
MMAP	Maryland Maritime Archaeology Program	**NUMA**	National Underwater and Marine Agency
MMS	Minerals Management Service (U.S.)		
MOA	Memorandum of Agreement (Maryland)	**OCNMS**	Olympic Coast National Marine Sanctuary
MOP	Marine Option Program (Hawaii)	**OCRM**	Office of Ocean and Coastal Resources Management
MSA	Merchant Shipping Act (United Kingdom)	**OCS**	Outer continental shelf
MSD	Marine Sanctuaries Division (NOAA)	**OCSLA**	Outer Continental Shelf Lands Act
NAS	Nautical Archaeology Society (United Kingdom)	**PADI**	Professional Association of Diving Instructors (U.S.)
NASOH	North American Society for Oceanic History	**PEG**	Polyeurethane glycol
		PIB	Put-It-Back (Minnesota)
NAUI	National Association of Underwater Instructors (U.S.)	**PIMA**	Pan-American Institute of Maritime Archaeology
NCIS	Naval Criminal Investigative Service (U.S.)	**PPR**	Principles of Professional Responsibility

PRIA	Proceedings of the Royal Irish Academy
PRO	Public Records Office (London, England)
QuickSave	Schrieber Instruments
QuickSurf	Contour files (Coastal Oceanographics)
RIHPC/HPC	Rhode Island Historical Preservation Commission
RIMAP	Rhode Island Marine Archaeology Project
ROPA	Register of Professional Archaeologists
ROV	Remotely operated vehicle
RovAnn	Bottom classification equipment
SAA	Society for American Archaeologists (U.S.)
SACHM	South African Cultural History Museum
SAHRA	South African Heritage Resources Agency
SAMA	South African Museums Association
SAS	Subdirección de Arquelogia Subacuática (Mexico)
SCA	Supreme Council of Antiquities (Egypt)
SCDOT	South Carolina Department of Transportation
SCHSSP	South Carolina Historic Ships Supply Program
SCIAA	South Carolina Institute of Archaeology and Anthropology
SCRAN	Scottish Cultural Resources Network
SCRAP	Submerged Cultural Resources Assessment Project
SCRU	Submerged Cultural Resources Unit (National Park Service, U.S.)
SCUBA	Self-contained Underwater Breathing Apparatus

SDAMP	Sport Diver Archaeology Management Program (South Carolina)
SEAC	Southeast Archaeological Center
SEDR	Ships of Exploration and Discovery Research
SHA	Society for Historical Archaeology
SHA	State Highway Administration (Maryland)
SHARP	Ship Analysis and Retrieval Program (U.S. Navy)
SHARPS	Sonic High-Frequency Ranging and Positioning System
SHPO	State Historic Preservation Officer
SHSW	State Historical Society of Wisconsin
SJAEI	St. Johns Archaeological Expeditions, Inc. (Florida)
SMR	Site and Monuments Records (Ireland)
SOEST	School of Ocean and Earth Science and Technology (Hawaii)
SOFRAS	Société Française de Recherche Archéologique Sous-Marine
SONAR	Sound Navigation and Ranging
SOPA	Society of Professional Archaeologists
SRI	Sanctuary Resource Inventory
SSI	Scuba Schools International
SUAS	Southwest Underwater Archaeological Society
SWMAG	South West Marine Archaeological Group
TAMU	Texas A&M University
TAMU-G	Texas A&M University-Galveston
TAR	Tidewater Atlantic Research (Washington, North Carolina)
THC	Texas Historical Commission

UAB	Underwater Archaeology Branch (U.S. Navy)	**UNESCO**	United Nations Educational, Scientific, and Cultural Organization
UAMP	Underwater Antiquities Management Program (South Carolina)	**USACE**	U.S. Army Corps of Engineers
		USFWS	U.S. Fish and Wildlife Service
UASBC	Underwater Archaeological Society of British Columbia	**USGS**	U.S. Geological Survey
UASC	Underwater Archaeological Society of Chicago	**VDHP**	Vermont Division for Historic Preservation
UAU	Underwater Archaeology Unit (North Carolina)	**V/Image**	Hitachi computer application (includes V/Image Plus and Tracer)
UCT	University of Cape Town (South Africa)	**VOC**	Dutch East India Company
UH	University of Hawaii	**WAC**	World Archaeological Congress
UVM	University of Vermont		
UNAM	National Autonomous University of Mexico	**WPA**	Works Progress Administration

Part **I**

Introduction

Chapter 1

Underwater Archaeology in the 20th Century
Filling in the Gaps

JANET F. BARSTAD

MAKING HISTORY

Antikythera

The 20th-century beginnings of modern underwater archaeology were unheralded but auspicious. In 1900 a Greek sponge boat, heading toward its home port of Symi, was caught in a storm and sheltered in the lee of tiny Antikythera Island, midway between Greece and Crete. Taking advantage of the stop, a helmeted diver dove to look for more sponges and found instead a seafloor littered with bronze and marble statuary. As proof of what he had found, the diver hoisted a bronze arm to the surface to show his captain, Demetrios Kondos (Bass, 1966). Kondos sailed home to Symi and asked others what should be done about the find, and it was decided to inform the Greek government. Enlisting the Greek Navy, the government organized an expedition to raise the statues; Director of Antiquities George Byzantinos directed operations from the surface (Muckelroy, 1998).

The recovery was in no way a proper archaeological excavation. The divers never mapped the seabed (Marx, 1975), had no idea what was worth saving, and used only

Janet F. Barstad, Prose & Images, Tempe, Arizona 85282.

International Handbook of Underwater Archaeology, edited by Carol V. Ruppé and Janet F. Barstad. Kluwer Academic/Plenum Publishers, New York, 2002.

ropes to raise the heaviest pieces. Because they worked at dangerous depths, one diver died and two were paralyzed by "the bends" (Bass, 1966).

Nevertheless, the Antikythera operation was successful for several reasons, not least because the expedition was the first to be supervised by an archaeologist and officially sanctioned by a government. Then there were the finds themselves. Among the bronzes was the "Youth of Antikythera," identified as an original sculpted by Lysippos, last of the great Classical Greek masters, and the only large-scale bronze from the first quarter of the 4th century B.C. (Bass, 1966). The marble statuary turned out to be exact copies of Greek antiquities for the voracious Roman art market. A complex bronze mechanism, studied in 1958 by Derek Price, was discovered to be an astromonical "computer." It featured days of the month, signs of the zodiac, and pointers to indicate moon phases and positions of the planets at any given time, all apparently operated by a water-clock. Its setting seemed to indicate that it was made on the island of Rhodes (Faracos, 1995). Writing of the artifact, Paul F. Johnston (1997) says: "By an enormous factor, it is the most complex technological artefact from the ancient world... Its existence...implies an astonishingly sophisticated grasp of science and technology that is otherwise undocumented." Various studies have indicated that the wreck was Roman, sailing around 80–70 B.C. (Johnston, 1997).

Says George Bass (1966), "The story of the discovery and exploitation of the [Antikythera] site deserves a firm place in the history of underwater archaeology, for it was there for the first time in the Mediterranean that divers visited an ancient shipwreck and grappled with the problems of excavating it."

Cape Gelidonya

Now fast-forward to 60 years later.

Grappling with undersea excavation took on new meaning to Bass in 1960, after Peter Throckmorton found a Bronze Age wreck off the coast of Turkey and Bass became part of a team to excavate it (Bass 1966, 1980). The 1942 invention of SCUBA (Self-contained Underwater Breathing Apparatus) by Jacques-Yves Cousteau and Emile Gagnan allowed Bass and others team members to dive freely on the wreck, in 90–95 ft of water. Before leaving for Turkey from Pennsylvania (where he was attached to the University of Pennsylvania Museum), Bass had to learn to dive—at his local YMCA!

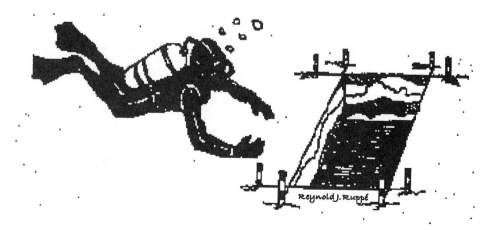

Figure 1.1. Diver and undersea grid. Digitized version of an original drawing by Reynold J. Ruppé.

Work at Cape Gelidonya marked the first time professional land archaeology methods were adapted for work under water, including *in-situ* mapping before excavation took place. It also was the first time pieces were removed from the seabed and "excavated" on land to remove concretions accumulated over the centuries. The artifacts were cleaned, replaced into their original positions (on land this time), and mapped again. At each stage, the team photographed the work.

Bass's comment, "The results of the Cape Gelidonya excavation were both spectacular and of great historical importance" (Bass, 1966) may be something of an understatement. The archaeologists found copper ingots in mat wrappings; scrap metals in baskets; casting waste; a bronze swage block for drawing out pins and hammering sockets on tools; pottery dating to within 50 years of 1200 B.C.; and accurate stone balance-pan weights in ordered sets. By plotting all the objects in the wreck, the team was able to determine which were personal possessions of the ship's crew.

The Gelidonya excavation established that the ship had sailed from Syria to Cyprus and that its artifacts were Syrian, Canaanite, or Phoenician, not Greek. Scholars had supposed that the Syrians hadn't begun their famous sea trade as early as 1200 B.C., and they had dated the writings of Homer much later than the events about which he wrote. Subsequent study of the Cape Gelidonya implements showed that their prototypes were found in Syria or Palestine earlier than in Greece. Homer had written much about the Phoenicians; excavation of the Cape Gelidonya wreck showed that "Phoenician sailors roamed the Mediterranean at the time of Odysseus" (Bass, 1966).

The next year, Bass excavated a Byzantine wreck at Yassi Ada, also off the coast of Turkey, where the team devised new methods for mapping the wreck and handling artifacts. They also saved one crew member from the worst effects of the bends by flying him to a U.S. Navy decompression chamber in Istanbul.

From the Byzantine ship, researchers learned for the first time of the transition between ancient and modern shipbuilding methods. The ship's artifacts of personal possessions, pottery, oil lamps, and coins dated the wreck to the first half of the 7th century A.D. Weighing devices and even the identity of the ship's captain (Greek letters punched into the end of a large steelyard read "George Senior Sea Captain") elucidated a time period in a way never before possible (Bass, 1966).

Even so, even in 1966, Bass still had to say, in *Archaeology Under Water*,

> A defence of underwater archaeology as archaeology might seem unnecessary, but by some it has been considered something special, something just outside the field of true archaeology. Unfortunately, a great deal of nonsense has been written about it. One distinguished archaeologist recently said that underwater archaeology is all rather silly, a view which he does not hold alone. Such a man might take great pains to excavate the drainage systems of an ancient public building, studying the joins and diameters of pipes in detail. Is the study of ancient ship construction less serious? The importance of ships to any maritime people is obvious, yet ships are often completely ignored in archaeology handbooks which cover subjects ranging from roof tiles to clothing, from fortification walls to jewellery, and from coins to furniture (Bass, 1966).

H.L. Hunley

One hundred years after the first "underwater archaeology event," our fast-forward machine carries us to Charleston, South Carolina. A Civil War submarine has been raised after 136 years under 30 ft of water and tons of silt.

At the time of its reappearance in Charleston Harbor in August, 2000, the Confederate submarine *H.L. Hunley* definitely was not ignored, as the Antikythera wreck had been. After the sub was lowered onto the deck of the recovery vessel, a flotilla of small craft, flying the Stars and Stipes as often as the Confederate flag, escorted it into Charleston. News media from around the world touted its discovery and rescue. Its multi-million-dollar funding came from novelist Clive ("Raise the Titanic!") Cussler, the federal government, and the state of South Carolina; the remaining $10 million needed for the project is being raised privately (Pedersen, 2000). The situation could not have been more different from Antikythera and Gelidonya.

After all the media attention, *Hunley*'s story is well-known. On the night of February 17, 1864, the Confederate submarine, 39 ft long with a crew of eight men who propelled the vessel with a crank, torpedoed the Union's *USS Housatonic*, then reversed before the torpedo exploded. *Housatonic* sank within three minutes; *Hunley* itself disappeared the same night.

In 1995, Cussler and his team located the submarine. In 2000, lifted intact in a protective cradle and placed on a barge, *Hunley* was transferred to a state-of-the-art conservation laboratory, the *H.L. Hunley* Research Center at the College of Charleston (Jacobsen, 2001). Work by archaeologists, forensic scientists, and conservators, which will continue for some ten years, already has included X-ray and videoscope examinations to study construction design and fastening patterns. It was also necessary to find a way into the sediment-filled hull to remove the remains of the sub's eight-man crew and excavate artifacts. The *Hunley* conservation team is using digital photogrammetry to record in 3D the hull, machinery, and navigational gear (Jacobsen, 2001). *Hunley* Research Center has had to be equipped with a large viewing area, since people are fascinated with the proceedings and don't want to wait ten years until *Hunley* finally is put on display but want observe its rescue (Thomas Oertling, personal communication). So far has underwater archaeology field that *Hunley* and other undersea discoveries, such as La Salle's *La Belle* in Texas, have their own Internet websites (Hall et al., 1997) and active "Friends of" groups (www.hunley.org and www.thc.state.us/belle).

WRITING HISTORY

The writing of history can be dangerous. A writer's views on some aspect of history can be disproven by subsequent discoveries and, as philosophers of history know so well, a historian's reach often exceeds his grasp. He or she can never tell the whole story about any aspect of history. History by its very nature is never finished.

So it is that *The International Handbook of Underwater Archaeology* always will be a work in progress. Even now the editors feel that certain geographical areas are missing from the text and deserve coverage. So we attempt to fill in some of the gaps in the story of the past decade's accomplishments.

The Arctic

"The long history of exploration and settlement, the rugged conditions, and the loss of many vessels have combined to create a potentially rich underwater archaeological record in the Arctic," says James Delgado (1997a).

Exploration of the world's smallest and most northern body of water centered on the North Pole began with the Vikings in the 10th century; by the 16th century Europeans began to probe along its fringes. Subsequent expeditions sought the Northwest Passage, and Great Britain, its Royal Navy, and Hudson's Bay Company mapped the Arctic and finally found the passage. Expeditions in the 19th century came to grief in the unforgiving Arctic: Sir John Franklin, 128 men, and two ships (*HMS Erebus* and *HMS Terror*) disappeared in 1845; the supply ship *Breadalbane* was crushed by ice during Sir Edward Belcher's expedition of 1853–1854; whalers lost vessels in the 1850s and 1860s; and only a handful of men survived an 1879 U.S. Navy expedition. Norwegian Roald Amundsen was the first to sail through the Northwest Passage in 1903–1905; he took the motor vessel *Maud* through the Passage in 1918–1920. Hudson's Bay Company and the Royal Canadian Mounted Police established outposts in the region in the 1930s, losing some ships in the process, including Amundsen's second ship *Baymaud* (ex-*Maud*) in 1930.

After World War II, air transportation and satellite imaging allowed completion of the mapping of the Arctic Ocean. Still, distance and logistics have kept archaeological work in the Arctic to a minimum (Delgado, 1997a).

The first detailed archaeological documentation of an Arctic shipwreck, undertaken in 1995–1996 by a team led by U.S./Canadian archaeologist James Delgado, studied the intact, mostly submerged hulk of *Baymaud* (ex-*Maud*) near Cambridge Bay and Victoria Island. The work documented the wreck's condition, assessed site formation processes, and compared *Maud*'s construction to that of *Fram* and *St. Roch*, two other Arctic vessels.

Further discoveries in the Arctic will involve high cost and tremendous logistics. Searchers continue to look for *Erebus* and *Terror*; but additional work on other ships and land sites associated with early Arctic expeditions, as well as a better understanding of native maritime practices, is needed first (Delgado, 1997a).

Canada

L'Anse aux Bouleaux Wreck. L'Anse aux Bouleaux is a cove near Baie-Trinité, Province of Québec, on the north shore of the Gulf of St. Lawrence. In 1994, a wreck was discovered by a local sport diver and later identified as a 17th-century New England ship from Sir William Phips's fleet that besieged the city of Québec in 1690. After an unsuccessful attack on Québec during the war between France and the League of Augsburg led by England, Phips was driven back to Boston after four of his ships were sunk. Archival research identified the l'Anse aux Bouleaux wreck as Phips's *Elizabeth and Mary*, a New England-built barque from Massachusetts.

Archaeological work began in 1995. Twenty-one divers trained by the Nautical Archaeology Society helped Parks Canada's archaeologists map the site and recover artifacts. Parks Canada's Marine Section began systematic excavation in 1996. Divers from the Groupe de Préservations des Vestiges Subaquatiques de Manicouagan collaborated.

Archaeologists established that Dorchester Company, under Captain John Wi-thington, traveled on board *Elizabeth and Mary* and that the ship was a victualler as well as a troop carrier. Apart from its importance as part of Canada's most famous episode, the wreck is the oldest found in Canadian waters and could also be a very early example of a New England-built ship (Stevens, 1997).

Montagu Harbour. Between 1989 and 1992, the Montague Harbour Archae-ology Project tested the hypothesis that archaeological remains related to cultural adaptations have been inundated by rising sea-levels during the postglacial period on the

Pacific coast. Montague Harbour, an embayment on the southwest shore of Galiano Island in the Gulf Islands of British Columbia's Georgia Strait, contains deep upper intertidal deposits well stratified below beach gravels with lenses and artifacts related to the Marpole culture period (400 B.C.–400 A.D.). The project used sediment coring to obtain data on the rate and scale of local Holacene sea-level rise; the teams excavated shell middens, indentified Foraminifera and pollen, and found several dozen bones and more than 400 lithic artifacts including projectile points, scrapers, stone beads, net and line sinkers, and an antler harpoon point. Radiocarbon dates range from 400–7000 Y.B.P. Two large earthquakes were found to have taken place close to major culture-type boundaries, one at 3600 Y.B.P., the other at 1900 Y.B.P. (Easton, 1997).

Other projects took Parks Canada's Underwater Archaeology Section to Haida Gwaii, Queen Charlotte Islands, in 1996, where archaeologists searched for remains of people who lived along the North American Pacific coast more than 9,000 years ago, at a time of lower sea levels. On the Rent-Severn Waterway in Ontario, a team investigated an ancient fish weir. In Lake Ontario archaeologists found remains of a coffer dam built in 1846 for the construction of the Market Shoal Tower, the only such fortification to be built in the water. That same year, monitoring activities continued near Sept-Iles on *Corossol*, one of only two 17th-century ships wrecked in Canada whose remains have been identified. The wreck of *Prudent*, a 74-gun French flagship burned and sunk by the British in 1758, was partially excavated in Louisbourg Harbor. A preliminary survey of *Marco Polo*, second most famous ship in Canada after *Bluenose*, was undertaken off Cavendish Beach, Prince Edward Island, where the ship stranded and broke up in 1883 (Carrell, 1997).

In 1997, Parks Canada's Underwater Archaeology Section offered introductory courses in underwater archaeology to avocational groups for the first time. The Section adapted the certification scheme developed by the Nautical Archaeology Society in Britain (Carrell, 1997).

South America

South America is the world's fourth largest continent, with a coastline nearly 32,000 km long and three major fluvial systems: the Orinoco River in Venezuela; the Amazon, America's longest river; and the Parana, navigable for ocean-going vessels as far as Rosario, Argentina. Human activity has been associated with these rivers since about 3000 B.C.

South America's three major lakes are the Maracaibo in Venezuela, the largest body of water on the continent and connected to the Caribbean by a narrow inlet; Lake Titicaca, shared by Bolivia and Peru, at 3,810m above sea level the highest navigable body of water in the world; and salt-water Lake Poopo, in southern Bolivia, 3,700 m above sea level.

The Caribbean is known for its many post-Spanish-conquest shipwrecks dating from the 15th to the 19th centuries, but its high temperatures and salinity are not good for the preservation of cultural remains. The Atlantic coastline, with high temperatures, high salinity, wide submarine platforms, and shallow waters, offers the best potential for underwater archaeological sites in South America. The shores of Uruguay are influenced by cold water from Antarctica, and preservation of archaeological finds is very good. Cape Horn is known for its many wrecks, including one of Magellan's ships in 1520. Pacific coast waters off the Andes, where the smallest number of wrecks have been found, are very deep and cold (Cano, 1997).

Cano says,

There has been little scientific underwater archaeology in South America. There are no official policies on underwater archaeology, nor on the preservation of the submerged cultural heritage. The absence of any legal authority for the protection of archaeological sites, and the promotion of commercial salvage, has encouraged the recovery of material with no scientific aim or methodology... (Cano, 1997).

Bolivia.   In the 1980s, Max Portugal of the National Institute of Archaeology of Bolivia and a team of Japanese divers recovered stone artifacts and ceramics of the Tiwanaku culture from Lake Titicaca. Asahi Television of Tokyo financed the project. Conservation of the ceramics was poor and the material was not stabilized, resulting in much deterioration (Cano, 1997).

Brazil.   In 1990, the government of Brazil created Archenave, a commission to study naval history, archaeology, and ethnography. Archaeologist Gilson Rambelli, at the University of Sao Paulo, is in charge of underwater archaeology. There are few other experienced teams in the country (Cano, 1997).

Chile.   Spanish scientists have conducted underwater archaeology in Chile under the direction of Dr. Manuel Martin Bueno and have concentrated on the search in Antarctic waters for an 18th-century Spanish ship, *San Talmo*, which may have brought the first European settlers to the southern continent. The Chilean Navy provided ships, equipment, and supplies. The last field season to date was in the summer of 1993. Treasure hunting began in the 1990s, the first time the country's underwater heritage was so threatened. The country's laws do not include the preservation of submerged cultural material (Cano, 1997).

Colombia.   With a Caribbean coastline, Colombia has suffered from major treasure hunting. Treasure hunters are regulated only by the contracts they sign with the local government (Cano, 1997).

Peru.   The deep, cold waters off Peru hold great potential for submerged cultural remains, but the country's legislation does not protect such remains. Some treasure hunting has occurred but without much success. Local historians and divers have tried to establish an underwater archaeological program, and historian Dr. Jorge Ortiz Sotelo, with the Association of Ibero-American Maritime and Naval History, is attempting to develop a local team for underwater archaeology (Cano, 1997).

Uruguay.   *HMS Agamemnon*, the famous British warship commanded by Vice-Admiral Viscount Horatio Nelson, met an ignominious end in Uruguay. After serving brilliantly from the time of her launching in 1781 (including at the Battle of Trafalger), she was assigned to the South American station where, in the summer of 1809, she ran aground on a mudbank just inside the mouth of the River Plate; after much effort to free her, she was abandoned.

Two Uruguayan divers discovered *Agamemnon* in the early 1990s. In 1993, Mensun Bound of Oxford University's Maritime Archaeological Research and Excavation (MARE) conducted an archaeological evaluation of the site and in 1997 followed with a complete survey. Finds included the lower hull timbers with a large number of ballast blocks on top, copper bolts marking the keel, fastenings, sheaves, and other fittings and furnishings. Of special interest was a commemorative seal bearing the name of Nelson in reverse. At the same time, the only cannon not salvaged at the time of *Agamemnon*'s loss was raised and studied, then replaced on the seabed (Bound, 1997).

Of all South American countries, Uruguay has suffered the most damage from treasure hunting. One salvage company destroyed two important wrecks, *Nuestra Señora de Loreto* and *Nuestra Señora de la Luz*, and sold their 18th-century artifacts at auction in London. Both the National Museum of Anthropology and the National Commission of Heritage have tried to develop underwater archaeology and stop the destruction of sites (Cano, 1997).

Scandinavia

For more than a millenium, Scandinavia was known for producing the greatest seafarers of Europe. Ship finds in Norway and Denmark have shown that the first known sailing ships, with tightly curved stem- and sternposts, had been developed in the region by the 8th century A.D. The Vikings developed the true keel, flexible hulls, and square sails. Their seaworthy craft allowed them to explore, raid, and colonize lands as far apart as the British Isles, Greenland and Newfoundland, France, Italy, the rivers of eastern Europe, into Russia, and as far south as the Black Sea (Evans, 1980).

Both Norway and Denmark have developed a strong sense for their prehistory and for archaeological remains. They have directed maritime archaeology efforts primarily at prehistoric Iron Age and medieval vessels (Cederlund, 1997).

Norway. Norway's State Antiquary Office in the Ministry of Environment is responsible for the Norwegian law on ancient monuments, which covers shipwrecks older than 100 years and submerged archaeological sites. Five musuems divide the task of enforcing the maritime part of the law: Norsk Sjøfartsmuseum in Oslo; Stavanger Sjøfartsmuseum; Bergen Sjøfartsmuseum, Tromsø Museum, and Vitenskapsmuseet in Trondheim.

In 1994, Vitenskapsmuseet, part of Trondheim University, launched an archaeology course that includes maritime archaeology; this is the first formal training in the field at university level in the country.

During the building of a new main road into Oslo from the south, where the road crosses the silted-up and reclaimed medieval harbor, excavators uncovered the remains of Late Medieval ships abandoned in the harbor, two wood and stone anchors, and several pieces of rope. The best preserved wreck is a small coaster, clinker-built of oak with a keel about 6.6 m long, most of whose starboard side is intact. Researchers have provisionally dated the wreck to the late 15th century.

Also in Olso, The Viking Ship Museum has been cooperating with the Nationalmuseet in Copenhagen to date important Viking material by dendrochronology. As of 1993, the two groups had analyzed burial chambers of the Oseberg, Gokstad, and Tune ship burials and had dated the felling of the timbers for the Oseberg burial chamber to the summer of 834 A.D. (Christensen, 1993).

Denmark. In 1993, the newly founded Danish National Research Foundation provided the means to strengthen maritime archaeology in Denmark by expanding the National Museum's Institute of Maritime Archaeology into a full research center. The Center is focusing on three areas: maritime aspects of archaeology, archaeology of watercraft, and development of tools and methods. It also maintains close ties with the Institute of Archaeology in Copenhagen, which has developed a curriculum in maritime archaeology (Crumlin-Pedersen, 1993).

In the winter of 1996, the Viking Ship Museum in Roskilde, which was expanding, received a remarkable bonus. While clearing a site for a museum-island complex along the foreshore of the original Ship Hall, excavators made the largest ship-find to occur in Europe for 50 years: nine vessels from the Viking Period to the Late Middle Ages, including the largest Viking warship for which there is physical evidence. They had dug into an old coastline and anchorage, which had filled in since the Early Middle Ages (Croome, 1999).

From 1996 to 1997, eight of the nine ships were wholly or partially excavated from the new museum harbor and canal site. The earliest, dated to 1025, is a large Viking longship, the largest example yet recovered of the "Long Serpent" vessel celebrated in the sagas. Its hull was so lightly built and slender that it had a 10:1 length-to-breadth ratio (36:3.5 m), drew only 1 m of water, and accommodated 78 rowers out of a crew of about 100 men. The other ships were cargo-carriers; one was fully rigged when it sank. The eight ships bear a family resemblance, although their dates are spread over 300 years, from 1025–1336 A.D. While all fall within the Nordic shipbuilding tradition, Roskilde 1, built in the 14th century, shows a shift away from Viking ancestry. With straight stem- and stern-posts, it was built far more clumsily and less elegantly than earlier ships (Croome, 1999).

The museum is now exploring a barely recognized but highly important aspect of ancient seafaring. The woolen sail was extremely significant to Viking ships but has been overlooked in modern times, partly, says Croome, because the image of fluffy, hand-knitted woolen sweaters comes to mind. Now interest in the Viking sail has been heightened by the discovery of Viking-period woolen sail-cloth in Norwegian church lofts. Since 1983, the museum has worked to produce woolen sail-cloth of a quality to match that of 1,000 years ago. One of its problems is sheep: in the past, *vildsaur* and *spelsaur* sheep produced the wool needed for such cloth. Today, populations of these sheep exist only on some west-coast islands of Norway.

Since the museum is building a sailing replica of the great ocean trader Skudelev 1, and the creation of an authentic sail requires a multidisciplinary approach, the museum has brought together research groups, held specialized workshops, studied museum collections of ancient textiles, and opened unstudied archives for the ongoing project "Textiles for Seafaring." The production of the sail was part of the museum's 1999 exhibition on seafaring textiles at the museum, and a parallel exhibition on the same subject was held in Trondheim.

The completed sail is to be given some light use to shape it into the familiar "pot-belly," then stabilized by treating it with a mixture of animal fat and tar. This mixture will be worked into one side of the sail to close up the fabric so the wind will not blow through it, to set the shape, and to give a smooth finish to the windward surface (squaresails always present the same side to the wind). Trials on the North Atlantic, set for 2002, will be the real test for the ship and its sail. The Skudelev 1 reconstruction and the production of its sail is the most ambitious project launched by the museum in its 30-year history (Croome, 1999).

One ship remains to be built: Skudelev 2, a 30-m-long oak warship. Tuborg Foundation is financing the 10-million-kroner project, which will take about four years and was scheduled to begin in January, 2000 (Croome, 1999).

Germany

Underwater archaeology has a long tradition in Germany but was a regional effort until 1993, when the German State Archaeologists' Association established the Commission for Underwater Archaeology to bring the regions together. Heads of the five German Councils for Archaeology are members, along with international experts from Switzerland, Denmark, and The Netherlands.

Since 1980, the Viking port of Haithabu (Hedeby), in northern Germany not far from the North Sea, has been under study. In 1993, archaeologists began examining a massive underwater barrier designed to block any approach to Haithabu from the sea, sunk about 740 A.D. The underwater archaeology branch of the Schleswig-Holstein Council for Archaeology is carrying out the operation with backing from the German Federal Ministry of Science and Technology. Schleswig-Holstein also is using advanced side scan and sediment-penetrating sonar to survey the River Elbe, which drains into the North Sea. This project was begun in 1994.

Lake settlements have been known and studied since 1856. Since 1972, low winter water levels, sandbagging, and small coffer dams have been used in the Bodensee (Lake Constance, on the border with Switzerland) to survey five settlements with more than 70 dwellings from the Late and Final Neolithic and Bronze Ages. The German Science Foundation has created a special project to study the archaeology of prehistoric settlements in the Alpine foothills, carrying out two large excavations, "Hornstaad-Hörnle I" on Lake Constance and "Siedlung Forschner" on Federsee, north and east of the Swiss border near the River Donau. The project, which produced fresh insights into this prehistoric economy and environment, has resulted in the establishment of the permanent interdisciplinary Archaeological Council Institution for the study of lake dwellings on Lake Constance and Federsee; the institution has its headquarters in Hemmenhofen.

In the winter of 1981–1982, five Roman ships were revealed in the bank of the Rhine River near Mainz about 70 m from the present riverbed, in what was thought to be an old harbor. The ships were dismantled and stored in water tanks in a warehouse until 1992, when the wood was transferred to the newly established Department for the Conservation of Ancient Ship Remains, part of the Romano-German Central Museum in Mainz. The wood was restored by soaking it in synthetic resin and drying it in a microwave oven. Since 1994, the ships have been on display in an unused market hall in Mainz.

Also in 1994, the Bavarian Council for Archaeology, the Romano-German Commission, and the Romano-German Central Museum have combined to recover several Roman ships from the Danube am Oberstimm near Ingolstadt (Schlicktherle and Kramer, 1996).

Greece

The waters around Greece are full of submerged coastal sites. A long coastline, numerous islands, and fine climate allowed much early and intensive seafaring. The sea was an easier avenue of communications and trade than the rugged land. After some 11,000 years of seafaring in the region, shipwrecks from numerous countries and time periods are abundant.

From about 1100 B.C., Greek civilization spread around the Mediterranean through the use of merchantmen and pentaconters (oared galleys with 50 rowers). Classical

Greece of the 5th century B.C. was dominated by the triremes of city states such as Athens. The following centuries produced a series of cultures in Greece: Roman, Byzantine, Venetian, Ottoman, and others, each competing for control of islands and anchorages. "These conflicts and interactions," says Agouridis (1997), "produced shipwrecks and settlements which have left a rich tapestry of archaeological materials on both land and sea."

Underwater archaeology possibilities were evident early on. In 1884, Greece's Keeper of Antiquities conducted the first systematic underwater survey of the strait between the island of Salamis and Attica, searching for remains of the famous naval battle of 480 B.C. in which Greece defeated Persia.

The 1970s brought home the fact that looting of wrecks was a serious problem. The Hellenic Institute of Marine Archaeology was founded in 1973, and the Ministry of Culture established a Department of Underwater Antiquities in 1976. Since the 1980s, the department has investigated ancient harbors such as Samos, Naxos, Thasos, Toroni, and Phalasarna, some as cooperative projects with foreign groups. Highlights include the excavation by Delaporta and Spondylis of the Early Bronze Age settlement of Platygiali in western Greece, the wreck of Louis XIV's flagship *La Térèse*, and a post-Byzantine wreck off the island of Zakynthos. The most important find to date is a 5th-century B.C. wreck near the island of Alonnesos in the northern Aegean, excavated by Dr. Elpida Hatzidaki from 1992 to 1993. The ship's cargo of more than 3,000 amphorae will illuminate the economic history of the 5th century and provide insights on Classical shipbuilding.

Many areas around Greece have been closed to diving because the government cannot police so many miles of coastline. By 1997, the Department of Antiquities, which was conducting a comprehensive inventory, had received reports of more than 1,000 underwater sites, but few have been adequately surveyed, excavated, or documented since then. Says Agouridis, "There currently exist no scientific criteria for the assignment of research priorities and efforts, and a long-range plan for Greece's underwater heritage yet to be formulated" (Agouridis, 1997). The Department's regular work of providing clearance for construction of harbors, fish-farms, and coastal industrial installations has left little time for purely scientific research.

In 1982, the Department began the ambitious restoration of Niokastro, an Ottoman castle in Pylos, as a national museum and center of maritime archaeological research. The project was still in progress in 1997.

Greek institutions involved in underwater archaeology include the Hellenic Institute for the Preservation of Nautical Tradition, founded in 1981. Since 1985, the institute has organized the biennial International Symposium on Ship Construction in Antiquity, always held in Greece.

The Aegean Maritime Museum, established by private initiative, is based on the island of Mykonos. Its mission is to preserve and promote Greek nautical tradition in the Aegean and beyond. The Piraeus Hellenic Maritime Museum was established under the authority of the Greek Navy at Zea, the ancient harbor of the Athenian triremes. Small local museums around the country, such as Galaxidi, Oinouses, and Hania, focus on regional nautical history (Agouridis, 1997).

Russia and the Former Soviet Union

Russian interest in underwater sites as an integral part of human culture and material activities began in 1718, when Peter the Great signed an edict to collect and protect historical articles found in the ground and under water. Before the 20th century, museums initiated underwater investigations, among them partially submerged ancient towns on the Black Sea: Dioscuria (1876), Feodosiya (1905), and Olbia (1909), as well as examination and measurement of a vessel found in Chudskoye Lake and dating from the 15th century (1902).

Development of modern underwater and maritime archaeology in Russia and the former Soviet Union has taken place in four stages: (1) emergence and formation of investigative techniques (18th century to mid-1930s); (2) elaboration and formation of the foundations of methodology (1930s to mid-1950s); (3) further development of methodology (1950s to 1980s); and (4) acquisition of experience and improvement of scientific methods (1980s to 1990s).

Professor R.A. Orbeli (1880–1943) was first to formulate objectives for the new scientific discipline of underwater historical geography and to develop the concept of an underwater archaeological museum and institute; he also developed new approaches to underwater archaeological investigations using methods of other sciences such as geology and biology.

Investigations from the 1940s to 1980 helped to develop underwater archaeological methods using light diving equipment, geoacoustics, metal detectors, and aerial photography. Avocational underwater expeditions guided by professional underwater archaeologists also began.

At the beginning of the 1990s, the formation of the new state of Russia out of the U.S.S.R. and resulting political and economic changes shifted established attitudes toward history and culture. The Centre for Complex Underwater Studies of the Scientific and Research Institute, founded in 1989, has carried out the most important work, which has included examination of the ancient settlement of Patrei. In cooperation with the Institute of Archaeology, the Centre has revealed the settlement's layout, remains of structures, and ancient vessels (Okorokov, 1997).

CONCLUSION

In the last decades of the 20th century, both archaeologists and nonarchaeologists have realized what a time capsule a shipwreck is—human history in a bottle, so to speak. In *Archaeology and the Social History of Ships*, Richard Gould (2000) notes, "Underwater environments afford us unique opportunities for studying past human behavior, sometimes preserving cultural remains better than they can be preserved on land. Many important issues...may ultimately be resolved by archaeology conducted underwater."

Throughout history, human behavior has been expressed in many ways. It can be inspired, leading to sublime works of art, music, and writing. It can be ferocious, leading to wars. It can be adventurous, leading to discoveries of distant lands, and of the human past and present. And it can be—well, *nutty*.

That human nuttiness actually appears in underwater archaeological investigations may surprise many readers, but it is there. To wit:

In 1971, Robert Sténuit and other French archaeologists excavated the wreck of *Lastdrager*, a Dutch East Indiaman (VOC) lost in 1653 in Shetland waters while on its way out to Batavia. Sténuit couldn't identify four cast-brass artifacts from the wreck; he guessed, and labelled them "cauldron feet." Only in 1978 did he learn what the "cauldron feet" really were, when he was listening to a paper on another VOC ship, *Kennemerland*.

Christopher Dobbs, the paper's author, identified five such artifacts from *Kennemerland* as golf club heads! (Sténuit, 1991).

Sténuit says, "The belated identification of some of the oldest golf club heads now extant has prompted their detailed study as relics of the early days of a game that is practiced worldwide today and is a social and economic element of modern life."

The heads are cast brass (the earliest known in that metal) and hollow. The ends are triangular in section with flat bottoms shorter than the vertical sides. The profiles of the top edges are concave. They look rather like fat putters. The Dutch called them *Colfsloffen*: golf slippers.

The shafts are gone, but still glued inside the shells are small pieces of wood: black locust (*Robinia pseudoacacia*), indigenous to eastern North America, imported to and acclimatized in the Netherlands and Britain in the 17th century because the wood was nearly unbreakable and so prized by Dutch *colfers*. As Sténuit says, "...the choice of the wood for his club shaft was no unimportant matter for a serious Scottish or Dutch player."

It appears that *colf* began in the Netherlands and was widely and enthusiastically played by both men and women, usually outdoors, often on ice in winter. It was played in other countries where expatriate Dutch people were living, hence the presence of *colfsloffen* aboard *Lastdrager* (one wonders if clubs were encased in a special travel bag such as is now used by, say, Chicagoans going to winter in, say, Arizona). Official records document the game's popularity, says Sténuit, "in the form of restrictive laws and decrees to prevent accidents such as broken windows, traffic problems, rows due to trespassing, and injury to passersby." *Colf* was a leisure activity of the Dutch who lived in North America in the 17th century: the Manor Court of Rensselaerswijck in New Netherlands (now in New York State) recorded in 1650 that there was a brawl, a fist-fight, and a *colf* club fight over non-payment of a glass of brandy by the loser of a game.

Until 1700 *colf* was played mostly in the port cities on the west coast of Holland and Zealand. It made its way across the North Sea to Scotland, where it was called *goff*. It spread to Britain and later back to Europe, and in 1890 was taken up again in the Netherlands, where by 1700 it had mutated into a minor, indoor form of miniature *colf*. Says Sténuit (1991), "Golf is played today by many millions of people in the world, many of them influential, and often for deeper reasons than exercise and fresh air."

There you have it: the *supreme nuttiness* of human behavior, illuminated by underwater archaeological finds from the past (this remark is, of course, made by a non-*goffer*). One can only hope that further underwater exploration and advances in 21st-century technology will bring to light many more heart-warming examples.

REFERENCES

Agouridis, Christos S., 1997, Greece. In *Encyclopedia of Underwater and Maritime Archaeology*, edited by James P. Delgado, Yale University Press, New Haven.

Bass, George F., 1966, *Archaeology Under Water*. Frederick A. Praeger Publishers, New York.

Bound, Mensun, 1997. *HMS Agamemnon*. In *Encyclopedia of Underwater and Maritime Archaeology*, edited by James P. Delgado, Yale University Press, New Haven.

Cano, Javier Ferando García, 1997, South America. In *Encyclopedia of Underwater and Maritime Archaeology*, edited by James P. Delgado, Yale University Press, New Haven.

Carrell, Toni L., 1997, Western Hemisphere. *International Journal of Nautical Archaeology* 26(2): 159–168.

Cederlund, Carl Olof, 1997, Baltic Sea. In *Encyclopedia of Underwater and Maritime Archaeology*, edited by James P. Delgado, Yale University Press, New Haven.

Christensen, Arne Emil, 1993, News from the North: Norway. *International Journal of Nautical Archaeology* 22(3): 293–296.

Croome, Angela, 1999, The Viking Ship Museum at Rosilde: expansion uncovers nine more early ships; and advances experimental ocean-sailing plans. *International Journal of Nautical Archaeology* 28(4): 382–393.

Crumlin-Pedersen, Ole, 1993, A centre for maritime archaeology in Denmark. *International Journal of Nautical Archaeology* 22(3): 293.

Delgado, James P., editor, 1997, *Encyclopedia of Underwater and Maritime Archaeology*, Yale University Press, New Haven.

_____, 1997a, The Arctic. In *Encyclopedia of Underwater and Maritime Archaeology*, edited by James P. Delgado, Yale University Press, New Haven.

Easton, Norman A., 1997, Montague Harbour. In *Encyclopedia of Underwater and Maritime Archaeology*, edited by James P. Delgado, Yale University Press, New Haven.

Evans, Angela C., 1980, Keels, sails, and the coming of the Vikings. In *Archaeology under Water: An Atlas of the World's Submerged Sites*, edited by Keith Muckelroy, McGraw-Hill, New York.

Facaros, Dana, 1995, *Greek Islands.* Cadagon Books, London.

Gould, Richard A., 2000, *Archaeology and the Social History of Ships.* Cambridge University Press, Cambridge.

Hall, Rebecca A., Andrew W. Hall, and J. Barto Arnold III, 1997, Presenting Archaeology on the Web: The *La Salle* Shipwreck Project. *International Journal of Nautical Archaeology* 26(3): 247–251.

Jacobsen, Maria, 2001, Excavating an 1864 time capsule, the Civil War submarine *H.L. Hunley.* Paper presented at the 2001 Conference of the Society for Historical Archaeology, Long Beach.

Johnston, Paul F., 1997, Antikythera. In *Encyclopedia of Underwater and Maritime Archaeology*, edited by James P. Delgado, Yale University Press, New Haven.

Marx, Robert F., 1975, *The Underwater Dig: An Introduction to Marine Archaeology.* Henry Z. Walck, Inc., New York.

Muckelroy, Keith, Editor, 1980, *Archaeology under Water: An Atlas of the World's Submerged Sites.* McGraw-Hill Book Company, New York.

_____, 1998, Introducing Maritime Archaeology. In *Maritime Archaeology: A Reader of Substantive and Theoretical Contributions*, edited by Lawrence E. Babits and Hans Van Tilburg, Plenum Press, New York.

Okorokov, Alexander V., 1997, Russia and the ex-Soviet Union. In *Encyclopedia of Underwater and Maritime Archaeology*, edited by James P. Delgado, Yale University Press, New Haven.

Pedersen, Daniel, 2000, The sub finally rises: Civil War submarine *Hunley. Newsweek* 161(8): 61.

Schlichtherle, H., and W. Kramer, 1996, Underwater Archaeology in Germany. *International Journal of Nautical Archaeology* 25(2): 141–151.

Sténuit, Robert, 1191, Some mid 17th-century golfclub heads found during underwater excavations and their significance for the study of the early history of the game of golf. *International Journal of Nautical Archaeology* 20(1): 13–22.

Stevens, Willis, 1997, L'Anse aux Bouleaux Wreck. In *Encyclopedia of Underwater and Maritime Archaeology*, edited by James P. Delgado, Yale University Press, New Haven.

Chapter **2**

Timelines of Underwater Archaeology

JOHN D. BROADWATER

INTRODUCTION

The history of archaeology underwater is inextricably associated with the history of marine technology, for it is through the equipment and techniques of diving and underwater work that archaeology under water is made possible. The following timelines describe a few of the literally hundreds of milestones in the evolution of diving, marine technology, and deepwater archaeology. Undoubtedly, some readers will take issue with one or more of the entries in these timelines. Fortunately, the Historical Diving Society USA (HDS-USA) pointed significant errors in the draft, then helped put things to right. The discipline of underwater archaeology owes a debt of gratitude to the HDS, an international organization of loyal and scholarly volunteers who are preserving the history of the technology of diving. The timelines in this chapter will have served their purpose if they provide the reader with a better understanding of and appreciation for the remarkable inventors and their creations that allow us to confidently venture into the water, seeking evidence of our past that would otherwise never be revealed.

John D. Broadwater, Manager, Monitor National Marine Sanctuary, National Oceanic and Atmospheric Administration, Newport News, Virginia 23606. With significant contributions by Leslie Leaney and Peter Dick, Historical Diving Society USA, and Phil Nuytten, Historical Diving Society Canada. Leslie Leaney deserves particular thanks for recognizing numerous errors in the original draft and for pulling together this team of experts from the HDS to greatly improve the timeline.

International Handbook of Underwater Archaeology, edited by Carol V. Ruppé and Janet F. Barstad. Kluwer Academic/Plenum Publishers, New York, 2002.

TIMELINE FOR DEEPWATER TECHNOLOGY AND EXPLORATION

Major Categories of Diving

Ambient-Pressure Diving

Breathhold Diving

480 B.C.   Greece: Herodotus wrote that Scyllias first becomes rich by collecting treasure for the Persians from the sunken wrecks of Xerxes' ships, then, according to legend, deserts to the Greeks by swimming 9 miles underwater; earliest record of diving for military purposes.

1913 A.D.   Greek diver Stotti Georghios free dives to 200 feet (61 m).

1865   U.S. Navy diver Robert Croft sets a breathhold record of 231 feet (70 m).

1976   Frenchman Jacques Mayol Free dives to 330 feet (100 m).

1998   Gianluca Genoni sets a new world record for "no limits" breathhold dive: 443 feet (135 m), a dive that lasts 3 minutes 3 seconds.

Open Bell

350 B.C.   Greece: Aristotle, in his *Problemata*, describes the use of a crude diving bell.

322 B.C.   Alexander the Great purportedly dives beneath the sea in a bell named *Colimpha*.

1535 A.D.   Italy: Guglielmo de Lorena explores Caligula's barges from Lake Nemi, near Rome; earliest reliable record of diving bell in actual use.

1642   United States: Massachusetts Edward Bendall dives in wooden bell in Charlestown Harbor, Massachusetts.

1691   England: Edmund Halley descends in diving bell and claims to have reached a depth of 60 feet (18.3 m), remaining 1.5 hours; air replenished by air-filled barrels.

1779   England: John Smeaton uses a crude air pump atop a very small diving bell to repair the footings of Hexham Bridge in the shallows.

Surface-Supplied Gas

1715   England: Andrew Becker demonstrates his metal helmet and leather-covered body armor in the River Thames, London, purportedly with air supplied from a bellows.

1754   England: Helmet divers conduct salvage, possibly with an air hose connected to a vacuum pump, allowing air to be pulled down to the helmet.

1773   France: In a dive suit with bellows-supplied air, Freminet dives to 20 feet (6 m) and remains for 3/4 hour.

1823   England: Charles Anthony Deane files a patent for a smoke (fire-fighting) helmet and dress that was soon adapted to diving (see below).

1828   England: Charles Anthony Deane and his brother John adapt the 1823 smoke helmet for underwater use and successfully complete trials in Croydon Canal; the system is referred to as an "open" type.

1829   England: Using their open system diving equipment, the Deane brothers salvage cargo from the wreck of the *Carn Brea Castle*, initiating successful careers as salvage divers.

1834   United States: Leonard Norcross patents and tests what is now believed to be the first successful "closed" (water-tight) diving helmet and dress.

1840   England: Combining his own designs and inventions with those of the Deane brothers and George Edwards, Augustus Siebe constructs a successful "closed" diving helmet and dress; the Siebe equipment sets the standard for practically all surface-supplied helmet equipment.

1905–1907   Britain: The Admiralty Committee for Deep Diving carries out open-water trials using new decompression tables designed by Professor John Scott Haldane, culminating in a world record dive to 211 feet (64 m).

1908   Haldane's decompression tables published.

1915   United States: U.S. Navy prints Stillson's "Report on Deep Diving Tests, 1915;" records diving procedures and equipment and introduces the prototype Mark V helmet and dress.

1916   United States: The Navy Department produces the "Diving Manual, 1916," which standardizes diving procedures and equipment for the U.S. Navy; this manual contains the first appearance of the production Mark V helmet and dress.

1924   United States: U.S. Navy Experimental Diving Unit tests helium-oxygen mixtures as breathing gas for deeper dives.

1930   England: British Admiralty establishes decompression tables to 300 feet (92 m).

1939   United States: Using both air and helium gas mixtures, U.S. Navy divers salvage the sunken submarine *Squalus* from a depth of 240 feet (73 m).

Self-Contained Gas

1811   France: Frederic von Drieberg's "Triton" diving system requires diver to "nod" his head to operate bellows connected to tank on diver's back.

1825   England: William James' dive system was the first self-contained dress with a compressed air supply.

1865   France: Benoît Rouquayrol and Auguste Denayrouze invent a self-contained breathing apparatus with a back-mounted air reservoir and an automatic demand valve.

1879   England: Henry Fleuss patents first oxygen "rebreather," with compressed-oxygen reservoir and carbon dioxide absorbent, permitting breathing gas to be replenished with oxygen, cleaned of carbon dioxide and recirculated.

1926   France: Yves Le Prieur modifies the Fernez surface-supplied apparatus to a self-contained free-flow system, recorded as the Fernez-Le Prieur Apparatus.

1935   France: Yves Le Prieur popularizes self-contained diving by establishing a recreational scuba diving club, Club des Sous l'eau, in Saint-Raphaél.

1935   France: René Commeinhes develops a firefighting apparatus with a demand regulator.

1937   United States: Using self-contained equipment, Max Gene Nohl reaches a world record depth of 420 feet (128 m) in Lake Michigan using a helium-oxygen mixture.

1942   Germany: Austrian free diver Hans Hass and German engineer Herman Stelzner modify a Drager submarine escape oxygen rebreather for scientific diving.

1943   France: Jacques-Yves Cousteau and Emil Gagnan invent the "Aqua-Lung" —the first simple, practical self-contained compressed air breathing apparatus. System's "demand regulator" supplies air to diver as needed; the "Aqua-Lung" opening the underwater world to millions.

1960s–1970s   Other rebreathers develop, including U.S. Navy's MK 15 and MK 16, with computer-controlled electronic gas monitoring and control.

1980s   "Technical diving" techniques and PC-based decompression tables develop, allowing recreational divers to push beyond depth limitations of conventional recreational SCUBA.

Saturation Diving

1938   United States: World's first intentional saturation dive, 27 hours at 101 feet (30.8 m) in Milwaukee, Wisconsin, hyperbaric chamber.

1960   United States: U.S. Navy conducts first extended saturation dives; at 200 ft (61 m) in pressure chamber for 14 days.

1960s   Edwin Link (Man-In-Sea), Jacques Cousteau (Conshelf), and the U.S. Navy (Sealab) conduct first open-water saturation dives.

1962   United States: Hannes Keller and Peter Small, using a diving bell and a gas mixture developed by Keller, reached 1000 feet (m) of Santa Catalina Island, California.

1977   France: COMEX divers conduct deepest working saturation dive, 1510 feet (460 m); later break own record at 1644 feet (501 m).

1980   United States: Duke University divers attain a simulated depth of 2132 feet (650 m) breathing helium-oxygen-nitrogen mixture.

2001   United States: U.S. Navy, Naval Sea Systems Command and Mobile Diving and Salvage Unit Two conduct 45-day saturation diving mission at *Monitor* National Marine Sanctuary.

One-Atmosphere Diving*

Closed Bell

1774   England: In Plymouth Sound, John Day descends in sealed chamber within wooden ship to depth of 30 feet (9 m); dies in later attempt to reach 132 feet (40.2 m).

1831   Italy: Cervo tests closed bell in the form of a wooden sphere; dies in attempt.

1866   Spain: French engineer Ernest Bazin reaches 245 feet (75 m; three times previous record) and stays 1.5 hours without air supplied from surface; bell later supplied with compressed air.

1930   Bermuda: William Beebe descends to 1426 feet (435 m) in 2.5-ton steel bathysphere. reaches 3028 feet (923 m) four years later.

1939   Atlantic Ocean: McCann-Erickson Rescue Chamber rescues men trapped in submarine USS *Squalus* from 243 feet (74 m).

Atmospheric Diving Suit (ADS)

1715   England: John Lethbridge tests rigid diving suit consisting of wooden barrel with glass viewport, arm holes sealed with leather cuffs; reports reaching 70 feet (21 m).

1727   England: A Captain Rowe built and successfully used a system almost identical to the Lethbridge machine (above). The Rowe device is much better documented.

1856   United States/Canada: Canadian ex-patriot Lodner Phillips designs and possibly builds first ADS to provide many of the features found in much later designs.

1882   France: The Carmagnolle brothers design and build an ADS so advanced that certain of its features are still in use more than a century later.

1904   Italy: Two designs are proposed by Restucci: a fully-articulated suit with arms and legs and an ADS with a rigid lower section. The latter may be capable of depths exceeding 400 feet (122 m).

1906–1913   Germany: The salvage firm Kuhnke and Neufeldt patents version of ADS that right up to the middle of the 20th century. The suits are capable of reaching depths up to 600 feet (183 m)—although at that depth the joints become stiff.

1915   United States: Captain Harry Bowdoin of New Jersey, files patent for a new type of oil-filled rotary joint and a design for an ADS; ADS used to salvage precious cargoes.

1919   Mexico/United States: Victor Campos of New York patents ADS with fluid-bearing rotary joints; that Campos tests the ADS to depths exceeding 500 feet (152 m).

1932   United Kingdom: Joseph Salim Peress designs series of suits that culminate in the "Jim" suit of 1969. The first suits are heavy and not as elegant as later models, but all use the ball and socket (or cylinder/piston) approach,supported by a fluid bearing. The design is quite successful to depths of 400 feet (122 m).

1965   United States: Giusta Fonda-Bonardi and Peter Buckley develop the "UX1," a 600 foot (183 m) suit design utilizing a combination of rotary bearings and an accordion-like system called a "rolling convolute." A series of limbs are extensively tested and are successful, but the program (funded by Litton Industries) is cancelled before a complete suit is built.

1969–1980   United Kingdom: Joseph Peress begins to work on ADS systems again, in concert with Michael Humphrey and Mike Borrow; resulting in several advances on original Peress fluid-bearing joint of the 1930s; all rights to are acquired by Oceaneering International before 1980.

1985   Canada: In 1984 Phil Nuytten patents combination of knife-edge seal and fluid bearing that ultimately becomes the 1000-foot (305 m) rated ADS "Newtsuit." Several generations of Newtsuits are produced between 1985 and 1995.

2002   Canada: A lightweight free-swimming ADS called "Exosuit" is in prototype stage. Developed by Phil. Nuytten (Newtsuit), the "Exo" is said to be more flexible and less costly than predecessors. Reported depth is 750 feet (229 m).

---

*Of the many one-atmosphere suits that were proposed, few were actually built; of those, fewer yet were even marginally successful. This list is limited to those units that were used successfully to carry out work underwater.

Submersibles and Submarines

1578 England: William Bourne describes concept for a primitive submarine in his book, *Inventions and Devices.*

1620 England: Cornelius von Drebbel builds two wooden-hulled submarines, reportedly testing them in Thames River; however, according to one report his craft has open bottoms and, if so, do not qualify as submarines.

1776 United States: David Bushnell's wooden submarine, *Turtle*, uses hand-operated screw propellers for moving forward, backward, up and down, and variable ballast for buoyancy control. *Turtle* is first submarine employed in warfare; during the American War for Independence, *Turtle* uses detachable explosive charge in failed attempt to sink HMS *Eagle*.

1800 France: American Robert Fulton launches his copper-hulled submarine *Nautilus.*

1851 Germany: The crew of the submarine *Brandtaucher* performs the world's first submarine escape, from a depth of 60 feet (18.3 m).

1863 France: The French submarine *LePlongeur*, run by compressed air, is launched.

1864 United States: Confederate States Submarine *Hunley* sinks USS *Housatonic* off Charleston, South Carolina; first time in history that a submarine sinks an enemy ship.

1881 United States: John Holland's gasoline-powered submarine *Fenian Ram* is successfully tested; one of first submarines to operate on surface using internal combustion engine.

1886 France: The *Gymnote* becomes the French Navy's first operational submarine; called by some the "world's first modern submarine boat."

1887 France: *Goubet I*, one of the first battery-powered submarines, went into service.

1897 United States: John Holland develops forerunner of conventional military submarines, operating on surface by gasoline engine and underwater by battery-powered electric motor.

1898 United States: Simon Lake's *Argonaut Junior* launched; first submersible built for peaceful purposes.

1948 Belgium: Swiss research scientist Auguste Piccard dives to 4,500 feet (1372 m) in autonomous submersible FRNS (Fonds National de la Recherche Scientifique).

1951 Belgium/France: The third generation FRNS (FRNS-3) launched; George Houot ultimately reaches 13,700 feet (4177 m) in 1954.

1951 Japan: University of Hokkaido launches *Kuroshio*, a large (12.5 ton) research sub with a 600-foot (183 m) operating depth.

1955 United States: U.S. Navy launches world's first nuclear submarine, USS *Nautilus.*

1959 France: Cousteau-developed "Diving Saucer" launched; the small, lightweight, tetherless system with rated working depth of 1000 feet (305 m) uses water jets for steering and propulsion.

1959 United States: *Deep Diver* launched, first small submarine (submersible) with chamber permitting divers to "lock out" to work.

1960 Switzerland/United States: Jacques Piccard and U.S. Navy Lieutenant Don Walsh descend to 35,820 feet (10,916 m) in the bathyscaph *Trieste* (successor to FRNS-3), in Mariana Trench, deepest known spot in the oceans.

1961 France: *Trieste* successor *Archimede* launched; capable of reaching full ocean depth.

1961 United States: *Sportman* 300 built by American Submarine Company; rated at 300 feet (91 m) and one of first commercially-produced sport submarines; more than a dozen built.

1962 United States: John Perry produces the *Cubmarine*, rated at 150 feet (46 m); first of long series of recreational, scientific, and commercial work class subs.

1962 United States: Submaray 2-person, 300-foot (91 m) sub developed by Douglas Privvet; prototype for *Nekton* and *Delta* systems.

1962 United States: Westinghouse Electric announces the *Deepstar* series; several successful subs were built.

1963 Switzerland: First "tourist class" deep submersible, the 1000-foot (305 m) rated *Auguste Piccard* carried thousands of eager tourist to the bottom of a Swiss lake during the Swiss exposition.

1963   United States: The bathyscaph *Trieste* explores sunken submarine USS *Thresher* at 8400 feet (2561 m).

1964   United States: Research submersible *Ashera* launched by General Dynamics; world's first submersible designed specifically for underwater archaeology.

1964   United States: Submersible *Alvin* commissioned at Woods Hole Oceanographic Institution; still in use, it is one of most successful submersibles.

1965   Canada: *Pisces* submersible launched; first class of submersible specifically designed for commercial underwater work; very successful and introduced a number of features that became standard on deep submersibles.

1968   United States: General Dynamics completes U.S. Navy deep submersible *Sea Cliff*, originally rated for 6500 feet (1982 m).

1969   United States: Navy launches NR-1, the world's first nuclear-powered research submersible, capable of diving to 3000 feet (915 m).

1970   United States: Versatile 1000 foot (305 m) submersible *Johnson-Sea-Link* launched; originally with diver lockout capability. This 4-person craft, the brainchild of visionary Edwin Link, is still in use by Harbor Branch Oceanographic Institution.

1971   United States: Navy launches first Deep Submergence Rescue Vehicle (DSRV), able to mate with disabled submarine in 2000 feet (610 m) water.

1985   Canada: Launch of 1000-meter (305 m) rated full acrylic hulled *Deep Rover*, designed by U.K. engineer Graham Hawkes.

1985   France: 20,000 foot (6098 m) rated *Nautile* launched; one of only a few subs capable of reaching that depth.

1987   Russia: 20,000 foot research subs *Mir 1* and *Mir 2* built in Finland for Soviet National Academy of Sciences; gain international prominence for multi-year series of dives on famous sunken liner *Titanic* at nearly 13,000 feet (3963 m).

1989   Japan: Shinkai 6500 launched; at rating of 21,000 foot (6400 m), world's deepest diving piloted submersible.

1996   United States: Graham Hawkes launches *Deep Flight*, a 1000 meter capable, positively buoyant, one-person submersible that breaks with tradition and literally flies underwater using hydrodynamic forces to descend while underway.

1997   Canada: Nuytco Research Ltd. develops *DeepWorker* class "micro-subs," very small (2 ton) single-place units rated to 2000 feet (610 m).

Remote-Controlled (Unmanned) Diving

Remote-Sensing Cabled/Towed Instrumentation

1856   England: William Thompson takes underwater photos in Weymouth Bay at 3 fathoms (5.5 m) with camera lowered from boat.

1890   Patented towed metal detector locates sunken ship *Orinoco* at 126 ft (38 m) by snagging it.

1899   France: Louis Boutan takes underwater photo at 165 ft (50 m) with a remote-operated camera.

1940s   Numerous towed instruments developed during and after World War II.

1960s   Side scan sonar and high-sensitivity magnetometers developed, allowing location of sunken ships, even buried ones.

1990s   Advanced microprocessors bring programmable digital technology to remote-sensing instrumentation.

Remotely-Operated Vehicles (ROVs)

1954   Dimitri Rebikoff designs and builds world's first ROV, *Poodle,* which is able to dive to 700 ft (213 m).

1960   First commercial use of ROV is for oil exploration.

1966   United States Navy's Cable-Controlled Underwater Recovery Vehicle (CURV), one of the world's first ROVs, used to recover hydrogen bomb off coast of Spain.

1977   United States Navy's CURV used to photograph wreck of USS *Monitor*.

1980s–1990s   ROVs become workhorses for many deepwater activities including shipwreck investigations.

Autonomous Underwater Vehicles (AUVs)

1960s   Development begins on unmanned, untethered vehicles designed for very specific tasks.

1970s   Numerous test vehicles are built and operated by University of Washington, University of New Hampshire, the Russian Academy of Sciences, and others.

1980s   Advances in computer technology spur development of prototype AUVs.

1988   The AUV Lab at the Massachusetts Institute of Technology (MIT) builds its first AUV, *Sea Squirt*, and successfully test it in Boston Harbor.

1990s   First generation operational systems emerge; military and commercial markets develop.

1992   MIT's *Odyssey* AUV undergoes successful field trials off of New England.

1995   Autonomous Benthic Explorer (ABE), built by Woods Hole Oceanographic Institution (WHOI), conducts a complete autonomous magnetometer survey over a lava flow along the Juan de Fuca Ridge.

1997   WHOI's REMUS AUV demonstrates impressive hydrographic capabilities to the Navy.

2000   HUGEN is the first AUV sold for commercial operations.

TIMELINE FOR UNDERWATER ARCHAEOLOGY, EXPLORATION AND SALVAGE

17th Century

1663   Sweden: Divers using bell recover cannon from sunken warship *Wasa* at 110 feet (34 m).

1685   Caribbean Sea: Sir William Phips salvages treasure using open bell at Silver Shoals.

18th Century

1775   Italy: First underwater "dig": English antiquarians sponsor expedition to recover artifacts from Tiber River near Rome using open bell; expedition minimally successful.

1716   England: William Tracey dives in leather dress with metal helmet while trying unsuccessfully to raise wreck of *Royal George*, sunk Portsmouth at 65 feet (20 m).

19th Century

1839–1843   England: Using Augustus Siebe's diving equipment, divers of Royal Sappers and Miners successfully remove wreck of *Royal George*.

1844   Sicily: In diving helmet, French/Belgian zoologist Henri Milne-Edwards conducts first documented underwater marine life studies, in Straits of Messina.

20th Century

1900   Greece: Surface-supplied helmet divers work at 180 feet (55 m) to recover statuary from Roman wreck carrying Greek art (c. 75 B.C.) near Antikythera, under supervision of archaeologist.

1907   Tunisia: Helmet divers, under Tunisian Department of Antiquities, investigate 1st-century B.C. Roman wreck near Mahdia, at 150 ft (46 m).

1909   Mexico: First major underwater artifact recovery operation in Western hemisphere: Edward Thompson recovers Mayan artifacts at Chichén Itzá.

1915   Hawaii: Submarine F-4 recovered from 306 ft (93 m), a record for the time.

1917   Northern Ireland: Gold salvaged from *Laurentic* at 132 ft (40 m).

1928   Italy: First disciplined underwater archaeology project is study of two Roman barges lying in Lake Nemi near Rome.

1930   France: Divers in one-atmosphere suits raise gold from *Egypt*, from 426 ft (130 m).

1935   Ireland: Jim Jarratt, in "Iron Man" one-atmosphere suit, locates wreck of *Lusitania* at 330 ft (100 m).

1948   Tunisia: Jacques Cousteau's team excavates at Mahdia site using Aqua-lung and airlift for first time on an underwater shipwreck project.

1954   Dimitri Rebikoff invents one-man diver-operated vehicle *Pegasus*, said to have discovered 50 wrecks in the Mediterranean during first year of operation.

1957–1961   Sweden: 1620 warship *Wasa* raised from 110 ft (34 m) in Stockholm Harbor; this is still considered one of the most significant and successful shipwreck recoveries of all time.

1960   Turkey: First professional underwater archaeological excavation. At Cape Gelidonya, Turkey, on 1300 B.C. wreck at 95 ft (29 m) by George F. Bass, establishing high standards for future underwater archaeological projects.

1962   Varian proton precession magnetometer used to search for sunken submarine USS *Thresher*; magnetometer locates sub in 1963.

1963   First use of side scan sonar, developed by Dr. Harold Edgerton of MIT, to find a wreck.

1964   Turkey: First use of submersible to map a shipwreck; Gerrge Bass mapped ancient wreck in Mediterranean using special-purpose submersible *Ashera*.

1966   Spain: Hydrogen bomb located and recovered at 2500 ft (762 m) with submersible *Alvin* and ROV CURV.

1973   United States: Wreck of USS *Monitor* discovered off Cape Hatteras, North Carolina, at 240 ft (73 m) with remote-sensing equipment; wreck mapped remotely in 1974 by R/V *Alcoa Seaprobe*; photomosaic of entire site published.

1977   United States: Harbor Branch Oceanographic Institution divers and National Oceanic and Atmospheric Administration (NOAA) scientists recover artifacts from *Monitor*.

1977   Straits of Messina: Commercial saturation divers investigate 8th-century B.C. wreck at 193 feet (59 m) with direction from underwater archaeologist.

1979   United States: Archaeologists working with NOAA excavate *Monito*r wreck at 240 ft (73 m), deepest "hands-on" excavation by professional archaeologists to date.

1981   Saturation dives at 800 ft (244 m) to recover gold from HMS *Edinburgh*, (1942).

1985   RMS *Titanic* discovered and photographed at 12,500 ft (3810 m).

1987   *Central America* (1857) discovered at 8000 feet (2439 m).

1989   *Rosario* (1622) discovered at 1476 feet (450 m).

1989   N. Atlantic: German battleship *Bismarck* discovered in deep water.

1989   Sicily: "*Isis*" wreck (4th century B.C.) along with four other ancient shipwrecks discovered at 2950 ft (900 m) on Skerki Banks off Sicily; first wreck located and surveyed with new ROV technology; one of deepest ancient wrecks yet investigated.

1990   United States: Tortugas Project: World's first remote, deepwater excavation, of 1622 Spanish wreck, at 1500 ft (457 m), with ROV *Merlin*.

1991   United States: Six-ton ROV *Nemo* raises gold from wreck of *Central America* (1857) from 8000 ft (2,439 m).

1998   Sicily: Additional investigations of Skerki Banks shipwrecks.

2000   Turkey: Freshwater beaches and signs of human habitation found at 500 ft in Black Sea.

2000   Denmark: Meridan 150 is first autonomous underwater vehicle to conduct an archaeological survey; two shipwrecks and submerged landscapes mapped.

2000   MIT's Odyssey II'c AUV deployed to Greece to search for shipwrecks in Mediterranean Sea.

REFERENCES

Historical Diving Society: For further information on research into various aspects of diving history, consult *Historical Diver Magazine*, the official quarterly publication of the Historical Diving Societies of Canada, Germany, Mexico, Russia, South East Asia and the Pacific, and the U.S.A. For information, see the Historical Diving Society USA Web Site, which has links to all other international historical diving organizations: www.hds.org. Also see References in Chapter 38 for more information.

Part **II**

The Geography of Underwater Archaeology

The United States

Our geographic tour of the United States begins in that vast continent's far northeast corner—Maine. This state's rocky coast, Warren Riess writes, is a dynamic environment that contains large numbers of underwater sites, from a prehistoric fish weir in Sebasticook Lake to early trade and settlement sites, through American Revolution ships. A strict preservation law protects most sites, but funding is the critical need.

In Massachusetts, Victor Mastone elaborates on management of the state's coastal waters. The Massachusetts Board of Underwater Archaeological Resources has developed a permit system that could well be copied by others.

Eastern lakes provide much study for underwater archaeologists. Kevin Crisman and Arthur B. Cohen report on Lake Champlain, a body of water used for several hundred years by many groups of people, American canoes to horse-drawn ferries. What land archaeologists could only know from archival materials, the lake provides. Lake George, says Joseph Zarzinski, was a bustling waterway in New York State. Archival research and appropriate funding so far has produced a replica bateau used for experimental sinking and a submerged preserve.

Kathy Abbass stresses the importance of Rhode Island's inestimable submerged resources, from pre-Columbian artifacts in the shallows to the wreck of *Endeavour* in Newport Harbor. Through cooperation of the Rhode Island Historical Preservation Commission and the Rhode Island Marine Archaeology Project, research is ongoing.

Susan Langley reports that more Maryland sites are being located and reported than ever before. With a new plan in place, Preservation Vision 2000, the state's focus, goals, and priorities are being streamlined. Communication through workshops, establishment of a Friends program, volunteer diver training, partnership with state and federal agencies, and other outreach activities make Maryland's underwater program worthy and viable.

Lawrence Babits reports that marine archaeology is alive and well in North Carolina. Extensive maritime exploration by students and professors of Eastern Carolina University is producing a multitude of publications: papers, theses, and research. Permits, contracts, and grants add to the substance of this state's submerged heritage.

Christopher Amer of South Carolina writes that erosion, beach renourishment, and hurricanes are all in a day's work for the state's archaeological division. Prehistoric, colonial, and Civil War craft abound. The finding of the submarine *H.L. Hunley* has provided a strong incentive, as well as funding, to broaden South Carolina's research into coastal sites.

In Florida, writes Roger Smith, every facet of management and cooperation has been utilized for the preservation of submerged cultural remains with public access and input. The *Marine Atlas of Florida* is a guide others may well duplicate.

The Great Lakes, says John Halsey, is the largest freshwater system in the world, containing every type of vessel from the 1600s to the present as well as the earliest Native American craft. Each state surrounding the system is reviewed: Minnesota, Wisconsin, Michigan, Illinois, Indiana, Ohio, Pennsylvania, and New York. As stated in many other chapters, underwater heritage work is characterized as underfunded, understaffed, and exposed to souvenir-minded divers and commercial salvors.

Riverine archaeology, a specialized part of our historic past, is summarized by Annalies Corbin. States bordering on the Missouri River are just now becoming aware of the river's potential in this regard. Individual state legislation and archaeologists with expertise on innudated sites are needed.

Texas was a pioneer of state programs in nautical archaeology, active in cultural resource management and field research, coordinating sport diving with the professional underwater archaeology, according to J. Barto Arnold. Press coverage and permanent shipwreck museum exhibits help the state's programs continue sucessfully. Arnold provides a lengthy and useful reference list to publications on Texas's underwater treasures.

The Pacific Ocean's 2800-mile coastline provides the backdrop for a rich historic era of fur trading, gold seeking, and lumbering. James Delgado documents ships and sites from southern California to Alaska.

Far out in the Pacific, in Hawaii, Hans Van Tilburg describes the use of oral histories and sailing canoe replicas as a background for the ocean state's underwater resources. After European contact and trade arrived with topsail schooners, brigs, and whalers, the islands became the burial grounds of debris from World War II. Investigations continue with programs at the University of Hawaii but under tight fiscal restraints.

Chapter 3

Maine
The First Twenty-Five Years

WARREN RIESS

INTRODUCTION

Maine is rich in maritime prehistory and history. Blessed with an abundance of sea life for food and navigable waterways for transportation, its coast has attracted people since the glaciers receded more than 10,000 B.P. (Before Present). But for most people, the problems with the area's harsh climate have outweighed the coast's benefits. Long distances from more settled regions, thin soil, and short growing seasons kept people from using agriculture until approximately 150 years before Europeans began to settle in Maine.

The same problems kept historic Mainers from enjoying surpluses to supplement their needs, even with advanced farming tools. Until the mid-19th century, timber, ice, and granite harvesting and small industry were the only nonmaritime activities of any size. Even they were dependent on maritime activities to ship supplies in, and products out of the state until the railroads developed in the late 19th century.

Studies of Maine's prehistory and history have therefore focused mostly on people who lived along the coast, the vast majority of past Mainers. Archaeologists have studied sites on the coastal mainland, the intertidal zone, and lately the subtidal zone to discover much about the prehistoric people and to augment historic archival data. As with many regions of the United States, there were few archaeology investigations in the state until the 1970s, when the number of projects increased dramatically, due partially to changes in federal law.

Warren Riess, History and Marine Sciences, University of Maine, Walpole, Maine 04573.

International Handbook of Underwater Archaeology, edited by Carol V. Ruppé and Janet F. Barstad. Kluwer Academic/Plenum Publishers, New York, 2002.

The University of Maine System, Maine State Museum, and Maine Historic Preservation Commission archaeologists have conducted most maritime archaeological investigations in the state. State law since 1969 reserves all archaeological sites on state property, including state-controlled submerged land, to be the property of the state. The Maine State Museum holds title to artifacts from such sites.

MAINE'S ENVIRONMENT

Geography

The Maine coastline was formed by a series of glaciers that ended approximately 12,000 B.P. It is a coastline dominated by estuaries. Many rivers start in the interior hills and drop through a series of falls until they reach sea level, typically a few miles inland. There, the rivers become brackish-water estuaries and continue until they enter one of the many bays that open into the Gulf of Maine. Typically, the bays are several miles wide and long, with a series of large and small islands spread throughout (Figure 3.1).

The underlying bedrock mostly consists of granite and slate, while the topsoil in most places on land and the sediment underwater is thin. Glaciers formed not only the bays, rivers, and their tributary ponds and streams, but also many adjacent coves. Generally, the coves have filled with silt during the past millennia, becoming intertidal mud flats with minor streams leaving small channels in the sediment.

After the glaciers receded and the land mass rebounded, the water level was approximately 60 m lower than today. The outer banks of the Gulf of Maine kept the gulf quite still by comparison to today. As the water level rose, the banks and outer shores were left underwater. At approximately 6000 B.P., major tidal flows and upwelling of nutrient-rich deep water began, causing the gulf and its estuaries to teem with many species of sea life.

Dynamics

Most of Maine's coastline is open to ocean waves, which have great energy during storms. Each year brings several storms that center off the coast, producing high winds from the northeast with a long fetch. Storm waves are typically 3–6 m along the coast.

Diurnal 3–4-m tides produce a complex and almost constant current system along the coast and throughout the estuaries. Tidal currents are typically 1 knot but approach 4 knots in specific locations.

Rivers and their tributaries drain thousands of square miles of Maine. Watersheds provide the rivers with a great quantity of fresh water that mixes with tidal salt water in the estuaries and bays. There is no particularly dry season in this region; therefore the quantity of fresh water moving down the rivers causes a noticeable balance of flow weighted toward the ebb throughout the year.

Many rivers are experiencing a natural change to a more meandering shape where their course is not determined by granite ledge. This usually causes the outside shore of a turn in the river to erode, while sediment builds at the inside of the turn. Rock outcrops variously resistant to erosion and human intervention keep the rivers from forming classic examples of meandering, but the process proceeds where it can. This process adds shallow areas of low tidal flow to the river basins.

General Environmental Factors Affecting Site Preservation

Natural physical, chemical, and biological forces affect underwater site preservation in Maine's rivers. Physical forces, especially strong currents and moving ice, can dislodge artifacts from a site and scatter them a great distance. If a site is in relatively shallow waters along a river shore, its remains are particularly susceptible to destruction from tidal currents and ice. River currents cause the upper sediment layers to move downstream and be replaced at slack tide by sediment from further upriver. Light artifacts, such as small items made from organics and ceramics, can be carried by the currents unless they are covered and pressed deep into the sediment. Such artifacts could

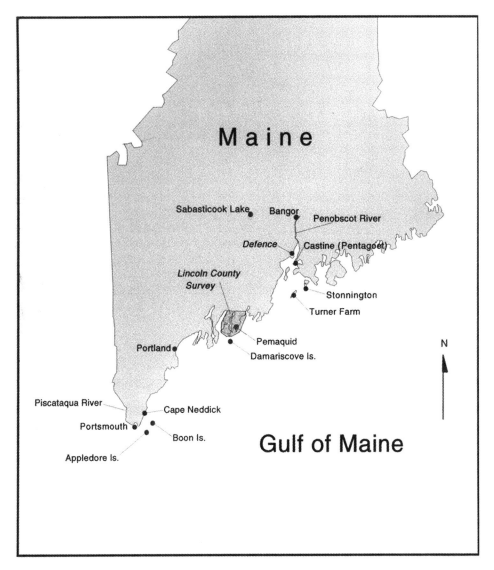

Figure 3.1. Several underwater archaeology sites in Maine.

be carried for many meters during one ebb tide and for many kilometers during the past centuries. This might also be the situation for ship timbers, or sections of timbers, that break away from a ship's hull. The lowest section of the hulls, usually covered by ballast, would not be affected as much by currents or ice.

In the winter, ice forms along sea and river shores, sometimes as much as a meter thick. The weight of the ice can be destructive to sites; its movement is even more destructive. As the water freezes, it forms around objects (such as stones and possibly artifacts), even those usually underwater in the shallows at the riverbank. When the ice breaks during a thaw or a water level change, it moves with the currents, often taking objects with it. Those objects typically are released later down river or at sea when the pieces of ice are further broken by melting and mechanical dynamics. Material in sites deeper than 1 m of water at low tide are not affected by ice flows, while sites in more protected waters, such as that of the privateer *Defence* in Stockton Harbor, are not damaged by ice or normal river currents.

Chemical and biological degradation of underwater sites not only affect individual artifacts but also the relative position of artifacts as they change density and lose integrity at different rates. While both of these processes can be rapid in the water column, both are significantly retarded below the water–sediment interface. Within the sediment (as little as 0.4 cm below the water), the environment is anaerobic (no available oxygen) and relatively still, and oxidizing chemicals are not readily available for chemical or biological degradation within the sediment.

Chemical deterioration of underwater sites is generally related to salinity, amount of dissolved oxygen, and water temperature. The average salinity of Maine's seawater is 31 parts per thousand (ppt), whereas river water varies from 0 ppt to approximately 30 ppt near the ocean. Geographical complexity, 3-m tides, and constant fresh water flow into and out of the estuaries cause the salinity and dissolved oxygen to change almost constantly at various locations and water depths along the coast. Fresh water running downstream usually rides above the salt water mass, mixing mostly in the lower reaches of the rivers. For example, in the Penobscot River at Hampden, the surface water at a particular moment might contain 3.6 ppt dissolved salt, while bottom water (10 m) at the same location might contain 8.5 ppt (Townsend, 1985).

Likewise, bottom temperatures vary from a typical August high of 24 °C (75 °F) at the rivers' falls to 12.5 °C (55 °F) in the ocean. Winter temperatures can reach as low as −0.5 °C (31 °F). Active currents, waves, and irregular underwater geography along the shore and in the estuaries cause turbulence in the water column that keeps the oxygen level high. Bottom dissolved oxygen varies from 2 to 8 parts per million (Townsend, 1985). These conditions allow rapid chemical deterioration of many materials above the sediment. Most metals are especially vulnerable to chemical deterioration, while organics, glass, ceramics, and other materials are effected at a slower rate.

Biological deterioration of underwater artifacts is related to present marine organisms. In Maine's ocean and lower estuary waters, the major species to consider are those that eat or bore into organic material. These include fin fish, shellfish, teredos (ship worms), limnoria (an isopod), and microorganisms. Fish eat organic cargos and other organic material that they can reach above the sediment. Likewise, teredos, limnoria, and oxygen-breathing microorganisms attack organics above the sediment. Wooden ship hulls and other organic artifacts remaining above the sediment are rapidly reduced to weak, honey-combed material and then completely destroyed by the sea life. In the upper estuaries, salinity is generally too low to support teredos and limnoria, the greatest threats to wood in Maine's cold water.

Within the sediment, most artifacts are protected from rapid degradation. The material will be degraded and often chemically changed, requiring intense conservation treatment if recovered. However, artifacts can retain their detailed form and often their relative position in a site through many centuries of burial in underwater sediment.

Some sites may be located where nature continues to deposit more sediment than it removes. This situation often exists on the inside of a curve in a river, where heavier material drops out of the water column as the water slows. A second cause for burial has been the intense use of Maine's rivers as conduits for lumber industry waste material since the early 19th century. Sawdust, log ends, bark, and other timber waste were thrown into the rivers for more than a century. In some places along the estuaries, lumber mill waste deposits are reported to be more than 7 m thick.

PREHISTORIC SITE STUDIES

Professional archaeological investigations began in Maine in the late 1960s. Before that, work was focused primarily on prehistoric Maine, especially the elusive "red paint people." As early as the 1880s, archaeologists used cutting-edge techniques at a few sites while relic hunters excavated and looted some important sites.

Since the mid-1960s, professional archaeologists have studied many small coastal prehistoric sites, including habitation and burial sites along the estuaries, seashore, and islands. Prehistoric people evidently preferred the coastal region, possibly more than people in the historic period. Though they were not "seafaring" in the modern sense, evidence indicates they fished and traveled in dugout canoes for millennia.

Many sites are shell middens, where thousands of empty clam, mussel, or oyster shells are found. Typically, coastal prehistoric people processed the gathered shellfish at their village, where the shells accumulated through the centuries. In the many shell middens, deteriorating shells keep the soil alkaline rather than acidic, allowing the preservation of bone, antler, and tooth artifacts. David Sanger, University of Maine, has conducted extensive coastal and island surveys for the sites and has excavated a number of these artifacts (Sanger, 1979).

Turner Farm, on the shore at North Haven, has been one of the most fruitful maritime prehistoric site investigations in the state. Bruce Bourque, Maine State Museum, directed excavations there between 1971–1980. He found the site was occupied from ±5300 B.P. until the European settlement period, making the Turner Farm site the earliest-dated shell midden in New England. The inhabitants were maritime oriented in the summer months, gathering shellfish and using dugouts canoes to harvest fin fish and sea mammals. In spring and autumn, they hunted and fished in nearby rivers. In winter, there were some who hunted inland for larger game. Data from other archaeological sites and early European observations indicate that these seasonal changes were common for Maine native people (Bourque, 1995).

Underwater prehistoric archaeology studies have been few because of limited resources. In the late 1970s, fishermen dragging an area off Stonnington occasionally brought up stone artifacts in their nets. The subject area was an extension of a present peninsula, probably dry in 6000 B.P. but under 10 m of water today. Steven Cox, Maine State Museum, led two short reconnaissance inspections of the area. He found only two additional stone artifacts in washed gravel and sand. The site probably had been disturbed by storm waves as the sea level slowly rose in the region.

In 1991, two avocational archaeologists located a prehistoric fish weir in Sebasticook Lake. James Peterson, and his team from University of Maine, Farmington, recorded the site and recovered the weir's wooden stakes, which are being conserved and analyzed at the Maine State Museum (Peterson et al., 1994).

Although little prehistoric archaeology has been done underwater, this does not mean it is a futile undertaking. In the many lakes, ponds, rivers, and estuaries, there should be habitation sites that were inundated in peaceful environments. They may contain artifacts that would not survive in a dry terrestrial site, yet finding such sites would be extremely difficult even with today's technology.

Present discussions of future underwater work include high-resolution side scan sonar, which promises the ability to locate more prehistoric fish weirs and possibly sunken dugout and bark canoes in freshwater environments. Their possible proximity to inundated habitation sites could lead archaeologists to even more important discoveries. Shrinking resources during the 1990s have not allowed any such surveying, but optimistic plans exist for the near future.

HISTORIC TERRESTRIAL MARITIME ARCHAEOLOGY

Terrestrial archaeologists have investigated several important coastal historic sites which had a strong maritime function, namely Pentagoet, Pemaquid, Damariscove Island, Stage Island, and Appledore.

Pentagoet, in modern Castine, was on the border between New France and New England. Beginning in 1627, it was variously held by French and English colonists, whose two purposes seemed to have been to fight each other and trade with the Penobscot Indians. Alaric Faulkner's University of Maine work there has exposed much about the trade and life styles of the documented white inhabitants of the trading post (Faulkner and Faulkner, 1987).

Faulkner also conducted two field seasons of reconnaissance at Damariscove Island, where English fishermen had a seasonal base in the early 1600s. The island was permanently settled in the early 1700s, and families lived there until the 1920s (Faulkner, 1985).

Pemaquid, in modern Bristol, was the northernmost coastal English settlement for most of the 1600s. It was a trading settlement, though it included farmers, fishermen, tradesmen, and their families. It was successfully raided by the nearby French and Indians a number of times during the colonial period. In 1974, Helen Camp, a local antiquarian and amateur archaeologist began excavations at the settlement site. Robert Bradley, of the Maine Historic Preservation Commission, eventually joined her and directed the archaeological investigation. Relatively undisturbed below plowing depth, the site continues to reveal much about early colonial trade, fishing, farming, and other aspects of a maritime community. Camp and Bradley have recently died, and Neil DePaoli continues the investigation there as resources permit (Bradley and Camp, 1994).

Faith Harrington, of the University of Southern Maine, directed excavations of the early fishing and trade settlement on Appledore Island, in the Isles of Shoals, during the early 1990s. She was able to confirm the identification of the site, but her excavations yielded few finds in the little topsoil over granite ledge (Harrington, 1990).

In three seasons of field work, a team led by Warren Riess, and Nick Dean, Maritime Archaeological and Historical Research Institute (MAHRI), conducted a shoreline reconnaissance survey of most of Lincoln County in Maine's midcoast region. Centered on the Damariscotta River estuary, the survey extended along the coast of Boothbay, Bremen, Bristol, Damariscotta, Edgecomb, Newcastle, and South Bristol. It included sites along the shore and in the intertidal zone, where the team located 132 prehistoric and historic sites, including aboriginal habitations, temporary brickyards, derelict vessels, piers, quays, dwellings, and shipbuilding yards (Riess and Dean, 1989, 1991, 1992).

UNDERWATER HISTORIC SITES ARCHAEOLOGY

Penobscot Expedition, 1972—1982

History. In 1779, the British Crown and military command decided to build a fortification in Majabagaduce, now Castine, Maine. The new fort would provide protection for Nova Scotia and a possible new colony for American Loyalists made up of Maine's eastern counties. A forward base that commanded the Penobscot Bay and river would also secure an important source of white pine for the British Navy and provide a protected deep-water port for privateers and navy cruisers.

On June 17, 1779, a British force of 700 men on three transports, with three sloops-of-war for protection, left Halifax for Maine. As soon as they arrived, they began clearing an area for Fort Saint George at the top of the hill at Majabagaduce. The Americans knew of the British force while it was being assembled in Halifax, and they reacted swiftly. The Massachusetts Assembly voted to attack the British in Maine before they finished constructing the new fort.

The new Continental Navy could provide only three ships, but Massachusetts assembled transports and warships from both public and private sources (historical records are not clear about the number of vessels in the expedition; archival lists vary from 37 to 42). Although small in size, the many ships carried approximately 400 Continental Marines, 1000 Maine militia, and the artillery and supplies needed for the expedition.

After stopping along the way to pick up the Maine militia units, the Penobscot Expedition arrived before Castine on July 24. Shortly thereafter, the marines led a heroic attack up a defended bluff to take the high ground west of the fort. The combatants soon found themselves embroiled in a siege, with the Americans making slow progress.

In mid-August, American hopes were destroyed by the arrival of a strong British relief squadron at the mouth of Penobscot Bay. Knowing the expedition was lost, the Americans returned to their ships and withdrew up river. The withdrawal was not orderly. The command structure had disintegrated, and most of the crews grounded their ships and set them ablaze. The Penobscot Expedition ended with every surviving crew member walking home. The British captured two warships and a number (5–10) of transports; the American crews had scuttled the rest.

When most of the American fleet retreated up river, Captain John Edmunds sailed his privateer *Defence* west into a large cove to escape the British Navy. That night, as the British approached the brigantine, the crew escaped and set fire to the ship. Shortly thereafter an explosion opened up the ship's stern and *Defence* sank quickly into the shallow water of the cove.

Thirty-five years later, a similar though smaller incident took place on the Penobscot River. In September 1814, during the War of 1812, the crew of USS *Adams* was repairing the bottom of the ship in Hampden, approximately halfway between Castine and Bangor. A strong British force advanced up the river to capture the *Adams*. Unable to maneuver the ship, its crew removed the cannon, set her ablaze, and watched her sink.

USS *Adams* was built in 1799 as a 28-gun frigate. She distinguished herself in the Quasi War with France and fought in the Barbary War. At the outbreak of the War of 1812, she was lowered and extended 15 ft to become a sloop-of-war. She was one of the first sharp-hulled American war ships, yet no plans or drawings of her exist. The discovery of *Adams'* remains would be an extremely significant find.

Archaeology, 1972–present. In 1972, Maine Maritime Academy and Massachusetts Institute of Technology students, guided to an area off the northeast corner of Sears Island by Dean Mayhew, found the remains of *Defence*, using a rudimentary side scan sonar device. They salvaged several artifacts from the site, including two 6-lb iron cannons, before realizing the importance of proper archaeological methods and conservation treatments for the artifacts. Shortly afterward, they contacted the director of the Maine State Museum, who asked George Bass, Ph.D., to survey the site. Bass determined the ship had settled into soft mud, which protected it and its contents from rapid destruction. It appeared to be extant from just above the water line on both sides, down to the keel.

The Maine Maritime Academy, Maine State Museum, Maine Historic Preservation Commission, and the American Institute for Nautical Archaeology (AINA, later INA) soon became partners to investigate the site. David Switzer, of Plymouth State College, directed the investigation for AINA with the help of David Wyman, of the Maine Maritime Academy. Between 1974 and 1980, Switzer's teams excavated the site during eight summer field school sessions, mapping, recovering, and conserving thousands of personal belongings, supplies, and ship items (Ford and Switzer, 1982). All artifacts, field notes, photographs, and other material from the site investigation are curated at the Maine State Museum.

The wonderful preservation environment of the cove's mud allowed the archaeologists to learn much about the era from the site. The hull remains revealed information about the ship's construction and design changes. Much of the weaponry fit accepted norms for the American Revolutionary navies, yet there were some anomalous details, especially with the grapeshot stands.

The artifact assemblage of the *Defence* site includes a medicine chest with two bottles still containing medicines, and a spectrum of foodways artifacts including provision casks, provision bones, potatoes, a cook stove and utensils, mess meat tags, and eating utensils. Some of these parallel foodways artifacts on other sites, while others are anomalous (Switzer, 1981).

The majority of the people on the Penobscot Expedition were landsmen, traveling as militia or temporary crew aboard the warships and transports. One might assume that their belongings would reflect their nonsailor status and, in fact, the three small assemblages of personal artifacts from the *Defence* site do not include any specifically maritime items. They do include items of clothing that offer some information about their owners, such as worn shoes, with wear according to the owner's skeletal and muscular construction. Another collection from the site consists of 23 soft pewter spoons marked by the owners' hands and teeth (Smith, 1986).

Since money to conserve and curate the hull was not available, the partner institutions decided to try a new approach: "preservation through documentation." The archaeologists studied the hull and, in 1981 in order to make the site anaerobic, covered it with large sheets of plastic and buried it in place with many tons of sandbags, loose sand, and mud.

In 1996, as part of the Penobscot Expedition II project, a University of Maine team collected samples of wood from the hull to determine if the remains left at the site were protected by the reburial efforts. They found the upper few centimeters of the hull and main mast protruding from the sediment and rapidly deteriorating. The results of microscopic inspection are not conclusive, but they suggest that the timbers exposed to oxygenated water during the excavation summers were extensively degraded by a number of biota. Wood that was not exposed during the excavation, such as outer planks of the hull, was in much better condition. Further studies have been planned (Riess and Daniel, 1997).

Early Remote Sensing Surveys. While Switzer directed the *Defence* site excavation in the 1970s, Maine State Museum sent two teams with remote sensing equipment to try to locate the remainder of the American ships and provide more information about the *Defence* site.

Armed with historical data from Mayhew, the teams made systematic passes in various places, developed a list of many targets, and dived on some of them, locating much debris and a few possible sites. Survey work was curtailed as diminishing resources were shifted to more immediate needs.

Penobscot Expedition II. In 1995, Warren Riess, of the University of Maine, began a new, long-term project to find and investigate the remaining Penobscot Expedition sites, while beginning a new historical study of the expedition. Assisted by students and faculty from Maine Maritime Academy and funded mostly by two Department of Defense Legacy grants, Riess' team focused on remote sensing surveys to find the flagship *Warren*, ordnance brig *Samuel*, and the three vessels believed lost near Hampden. In addition, they conducted background research, including local interviews and archival searches.

By the end of 1998, the team located five sites which are probably from the Penobscot Expedition, and a more modern wreck in the river. They continue to analyze those sites and collect archival and field data. Plans call for a continued effort of searching and historical research.

Angel Gabriel, 1977—1997

In 1635 the English merchant ship, *Angel Gabriel*, was lost at Pemaquid during a ferocious hurricane. From contemporary accounts, it appears that the ship arrived and anchored on August 14, and the people, with most of the crew, stayed the night ashore in the small Pemaquid trading settlement. The next morning, the strongest hurricane in Maine's history destroyed the ship and almost all of its contents.

Besides ship supplies and hardware, the ship carried settlers' belongings and probably supplies and trading goods for the settlement. If found, the ship itself would be the first of its kind to be studied. Lured by a probably very significant site within four miles of his home, Warren Riess, while a graduate student at Texas A&M University in 1978, gathered a team of fellow students to find the ship's remains. Aided by many people and small grants over the years, Riess led a number of small-scale remote sensing and underwater inspection searches in Inner and Outer Pemaquid Harbor, with no results. The teams systematically searched most of the area without finding one artifact that might be from the ship (Riess, 1999).

Piscataqua—Pemaquid—Damariscove Survey, 1980—1981

For two years, David Switzer, directed a remote sensing and reconnaissance survey of three high-probability areas in Maine and New Hampshire to ascertain the existence of any significant underwater sites. The team found many magnetic and side scan sonar targets, but only two shipwreck sites of merit, both on the New Hampshire side of the Piscataqua River.

These were early days for underwater archaeology remote sensing, and the team was working in environments difficult for sonar and magnetic work: High magnetic background "noise" from iron-rich granite made anomalies difficult to distinguish. In the estuaries, extensive irregular rock outcrops, deep sediments, timber debris, and multiple layers of water with different densities were a problem for side scan sonar. Extensive shallow-water coves were a problem for the subbottom profilers of the day, which "rang" too much to work effectively in less than 2 m of water.

Notified of the latter problem, Harold Edgerton, of the Massachusetts Institute of Technology (MIT) came to visit with his handmade *mud-pinger*, a subbottom profiler he invented to help archaeologists in shallow muddy coves. After a few passes in Hart's Cove, on the New Hampshire side, Edgerton and Switzer discovered the remains of a late 1600s vessel in the mud.

Boon Island

Local sport and commercial divers reported a number of cannon barrels on a ledge at Boon Island, seven miles out to sea in southern Maine. Warren Riess and his team surveyed the ledge and eventually recovered the guns for the Maine State Museum. They are small iron cannon of styles manufactured in England between 1650 and 1720 and found where the English merchantman, *Nottingham Galley*, was lost in 1710. The shipwreck survival story was the basis for *Boon Island*, historical novelist Kenneth Robert's last novel.

The guns were in small crevices where powerful swells sweep the ledge even on the most peaceful days. Below the guns were a number of cannon balls, musket shot, and two grenades. No other artifacts were found on the dynamic ledge. The iron artifacts were extremely corroded, because they were open to the oxidizing salt water for centuries. All the artifacts are being analyzed and conserved at the university's Darling Marine Center before being curated by the Maine State Museum.

Maritime Archaeological and Historical Research Institute, 1984—1998

After working together on the *Defence* site investigation, searching for the *Angel Gabriel* and various other projects in Maine and elsewhere, a number of people formed the Maritime Archaeological and Historical Research Institute (MAHRI) in 1984. MAHRI was a non profit organization "dedicated to discovering, researching, and teaching our maritime past," based in Bristol, Maine. At first, MAHRI concentrated on its own projects but soon found that insurance costs required by workers' compensation and liability laws made it impossible to operate legally as a principal underwater research organization while remaining a small non profit institution.

By 1990, the Institute had shifted to working with larger institutions in maritime research and small educational projects. In 1998, after all the principal researchers were associated with larger institutions, mostly at considerable distance from each other, the group decided to disband the organization. During its 14 years of existence, MAHRI members and staff conducted or supported research and education projects mostly in New England and also in California, Canada, and even Tahiti. Besides conducting its own projects, MAHRI provided seed funds for new projects, professional and volunteer personnel, field equipment, office space and equipment, and supplies for other worthwhile maritime projects. The biannual *Newsletter* included articles on MAHRI and others' projects and a calendar of maritime-related conferences.

Institute of Maritime History, 1995—present

In 1995, a separate group of archaeologists in York started the Institute of Maritime History (IMH), a nonprofit organization with goals similar to MAHRI's. To date, IMH's work in Maine includes the investigation of the *Annabella* site and an intertidal survey of the Cape Neddick River. The *Annabella* site is the intertidal remains of an 18th-century coastal schooner. IMH's meticulous study of the site was the basis for Stefan Claesson's master's thesis at Texas A&M University (Claesson, 1998).

The IMH team, directed by Claesson, discovered the remains of 13 historic sites in their reconnaissance survey along the Cape Neddick River shores, including piers, wharves, and ship remains. This was one of the first of many shoreline surveys the IMH team planned for Maine's coast (Claesson, 1998). In addition, IMH is conducting research in St. Vincent, in the Lesser Antilles.

Snow Squall, 1982—1997

Snow Squall was an American clipper ship built in 1853 in South Portland. After an accident rounding Cape Horn in 1864, she limped into Stanley Harbor, Falkland Islands, for repairs. There she remained in the harbor as support for a wharf until the 1980s, when a group of Americans decided to study her and bring her bow back to South Portland.

During a series of trips to Stanley Harbor, the team studied the ship and placed its bow on the deck of a freighter for its return to Maine. It remained for some time at the Spring Point Museum, within a quarter-mile of the shipway where it was launched, in a special temporary building for conservation. Molly Carlson and Betty Seifert began conservation treatments for the various materials that made up the hull: wood, iron, steel, and copper alloys. Meanwhile, a special team recorded the hull remains, and Nick Dean continued his historical research of the ship and the people associated with her.

Eventually, financial setbacks forced the museum to seek another home for the ship. Luckily, Maine Maritime Museum of Bath was willing to take responsibility. Since the ship required nontraditional conservation treatment, the project directors decided to let the University of Maine try to kiln-dry the bow in a large building used to dry lumber. The experiment was a success. After losing approximately five tons of water, the bow retained its shape and suffered minimal shrinkage. The *Snow Squall* bow and artifacts are now on exhibit at the Maine Maritime Museum.

UNDERWATER CULTURAL RESOURCE MANAGEMENT

Two agencies work together to manage possible archaeology sites in state-controlled waters. The Maine State Museum is responsible for direct management of the sites and curation of all data and artifacts from such sites. The Maine Historic Preservation Commission (MHPC) is responsible for requiring that federally-supported projects conform to federal legislation, such as Section 106 of the National Historic Preservation Act.

Although the state museum began an underwater archaeology program with the *Defence* site in the 1970s, state resources for site management became scarce in the early 1980s. Only recently has the museum been able to conduct some work on the Boon Island site. For several years, the museum and the MHPC have been unable to attain state funding for an underwater management program.

To date, the MHPC has required three underwater remote sensing surveys and no underwater site mitigation in Maine waters. Section 106 allows each state to determine when such work is required. MHPC has required surveys only when there is a high probability that significant sites would be negatively effected. Two of the remote sensing surveys have been in the Bangor–Brewer area of the Penobscot River and one at the mouth of the Piscataqua River.

In addition, MHPC has a database of known shipwrecks in Maine waters, consisting of those found in many primary and secondary sources. It is far from complete, yet it contains more than 1000 reported shipwrecks.

Today, Maine waters contain many known, and probably more unknown, significant archaeological sites. Qualified people and funding have been particularly few in the past, allowing only limited surveys and site investigations. At the same time, a strict preservation law has protected most of the sites from commercial looting. During the next decades, as the public becomes more aware of the need for under water archaeologic investigations, and as funds become available, many significant sites should be found and investigated.

REFERENCES

The following references are only a sample of available material. An extensive bibliography of published and unpublished reports on Maine archaeology and history is maintained by the Maine Historic Preservation Commission, Augusta.

Bourque, Bruce, 1995, *Diversity and Complexity in Prehistoric Maritime Societies, A Gulf of Maine Perspective*. Plenum Press, New York.

Bradley, Robert, 1990, *Shipwrecks Management Plan*, Maine State Plan for Historical Archaeology. Maine Historic Preservation Commission, Augusta.

Bradley, Robert, and Camp, Helen, 1994, *The Forts of Pemaquid, Maine*: *An Archaeological and Historical Study*. Maine Historic Preservation Commission, Augusta.

Claesson, Stefan, 1998, Annabella: *A North American Coasting Schooner*. M.A. thesis, Texas A&M University. College Station.

_____, 1998a, *An Intertidal Archaeological Survey of the Cape Neddick River in Cape Neddick, Maine*. Institute of Maritime History Report to York Historic District Commission.

Faulkner, Alaric, 1985, Archaeology of the Cod Fishery: Damariscove Island. *Historical Archaeology* 10:51–57.

Faulkner, Alaric, and Faulkner, Gretchen, 1987, *The French at Pentagoet 1635–1674*: *An Archaeological Portrait of the Acadian Frontier*. Maine Historic Preservation Commission, Augusta.

Ford, Barbara and David Switzer, 1982, *Under Water Dig*: *The Excavation of a Revolutionary War Privateer*. William Morrow & Co, New York.

Harrington, Faith, 1990, *Preliminary Report on the 1990 Field Season of the Isles of Shoals Archaeology Project*. M.S. thesis, on file, Maine Historic Preservation Commission.

Peterson, James, et al., 1994 Archaeic and Woodlands Period Fish Weir Complex in Central Maine. *Archaeology of Eastern North America* 22:197–222.

Riess, Warren, 1999, Angel Gabriel, *A Seventeenth Century Bristol Ship Wrecked on the Maine Coast*. Redhouse Press, Bristol.

Riess, Warren, and Daniel, Geoffrey, 1997, Evaluation of Preservation Efforts for the Revolutionary War Privateer *Defence*. *International Journal of Nautical Archaeology* 26(4):330–338.

Riess, Warren, and Dean, Nicholas, 1992, *Lincoln County Coastal Survey, Phase I, Part 3: Boothbay, Boothbay Harbor, Southport, and Muscongus Bay*. MAHRI report to Maine Historic Preservation Commission.

_____, 1991, *Lincoln County Coastal Survey, Phase I, Part 2: Lower Damariscotta River, South Bristol, and East Boothbay*. MAHRI report to Maine Historic Preservation Commission.

_____, 1989, *Lincoln County Coastal Survey, Phase I, Part 1: Upper Damariscotta River*. MAHRI report to Maine Historic Preservation Commission.

Smith, Sheli O., 1986, The Defence: *Life at Sea as Reflected in an Archaeological Assemblage from an Eighteenth-Century Privateer*. Ph.D. dissertation, University of Pennsylvania. University Microfilms, Ann Arbor.

Switzer, David, 1981, Provision Stowage and Galley Facilities Onboard the Revolutionary War Privateer Defence. In *Beneath the Waters of Time*: *The Proceedings of the Tenth Conference on Underwater Archaeology, edited by W.A. Cockrell, Fathom Eight, San Marino*.

Townsend, David W., 1985, *Temperature, Salinity, and Dissolved Oxygen Data for the Penobscot River Estuary, Maine, 1963–1977*, Maine Department of Marine Resources, Boothbay Harbor.

Wyman, David, 1981, Developing the Plans for the Revolutionary War Privateer *Defence*. In *Beneath the Waters of Time*: *The Proceedings of the Tenth Conference on Underwater Archaeology*, edited by W.A. Cockrell. Fathom Eight, San Marino.

Chapter 4

Massachusetts
The Devil to Pay and No Pitch Hot!

VICTOR T. MASTONE

INTRODUCTION

Passage of the Abandoned Shipwreck Act of 1987 resulted in three immediate consequences: It recognized the historical value of abandoned shipwrecks; it recognized competing interests in the use of these resources; and it clearly established that ownership and management responsibilities over these resources are vested in the states, which must develop management policies to accommodate a wide range of appropriate uses.

Established in 1973, the Massachusetts Board of Underwater Archaeological Resources is the trustee of the Commonwealth's underwater heritage. Massachusetts addresses these competing interests through program initiatives that promote and protect the public's interest for recreational, economic, environmental, and historical purposes.

Exploitation of shipwrecks is not a new phenomenon. Salvaging shipwrecks and their cargoes is a long tradition that developed out of the need to protect lives and property and maintain highways of commerce and communication. Traditional salvage actions deal with critical concerns in real time, such as the saving of lives and cargoes in immediate peril. Until recently, there was no need to accommodate or even consider alternative natural and cultural uses of historic shipwreck resources (Mastone, 1992).

Changing views of the value of shipwrecks, particularly historic shipwrecks, resulted in the passage of the Abandoned Shipwreck Act of 1987. The act had immediate

Victor T. Mastone, Director, Board of Underwater Archaeological Resources, Executive Office of Environmental Affairs, Boston, Massachusetts 02114.
International Handbook of Underwater Archaeology, edited by Carol. V. Ruppé and Janet F. Barstad. Kluwer Academic/Plenum Publishers, New York, 2002.

consequences for state governments and the resources themselves and implications for neighboring sovereign powers as well: It recognized these resources could possess historical value, that there exists competing interests in these resources, and it guaranteed access to these resources for recreation use. Finally, it established that ownership clearly and management responsibilities over these resources were vested in state governments. While federal government provides advisory guidelines to the states, states are responsible for developing and implementing a management policy that accommodates a wide range of appropriate uses (Mastone, 1992).

Management of cultural resources, including submerged resources such as shipwrecks, involves a sequence of tasks (General Accounting Office, 1987): (1) inventory: discovery and recording; (2) evaluation: scientific and public importance; (3) planning: determining appropriate use; (4) protection: safeguarding resources; and (5) utilization: accommodating proper use. While this sequence of tasks is fairly straightforward, protection and utilization are controversial when they involve shipwreck sites.

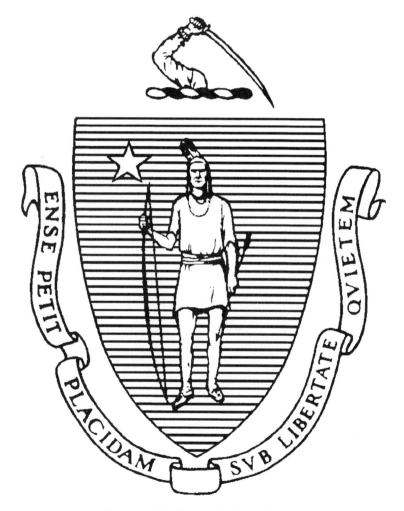

Figure 4.1. The Great Seal of Massachusetts.

HISTORICAL OVERVIEW AND CONTEXT

A comprehensive review is not necessary to establish the local, regional, and national importance of the considerable maritime legacy of New England. The extensive maritime historical literature clearly demonstrates the intensity, interest, and importance of maritime commerce to Massachusetts in the southern Gulf of Maine (Morison, 1979; Albion et al., 1972; Cultural Resources Committee, 1989). Through even the most casual observations, one can easily observe symbols of the region's maritime heritage in the form of the homes of ship captains, fishermen and merchants, customs houses, lighthouses and fortifications, wharves, boat yards, and marine railroads. More than 2000 maritime historical sites have been identified around Massachusetts Bay, and this figure probably under-represents the extent of this resource base (Cultural Resources Committee, 1990).

Land-based components of our maritime heritage demonstrate the importance of maritime activities in our society. These terrestrial resources directly reflect the seaward nature of this heritage, and we must assume a similar intensity in maritime material culture will be found in the region's submerged reaches.

We can anticipate encountering a number of known and potential submerged cultural resources beneath Massachusetts's waters: prehistoric materials and sites, historic and modern shipwrecks, disposal areas, and aircraft. It is estimated that more than 3000 shipwrecks are located in Massachusetts waters, many lost before 1900. Given Massachusetts's long maritime heritage and its leadership in maritime activities, many of these shipwrecks may be historically important.

Potential for Prehistoric Cultural Resources

While no prehistoric cultural resources artifacts or sites have been located under Massachusetts's waters, their potential for existence must be given consideration.

The occasional recovery of megafauna remains (mammoth and mastodon skeletal materials) by fishermen demonstrates environmental conditions were present to support Paleo-Indian populations. Recently, a mastodon or mammoth tooth was recovered by commercial fishermen several miles off Provincetown (H. Arnold Carr, personal communication, 1990). However, these discoveries do not necessarily assume the presence of Amerindian remains. Further, a more diverse subsistence pattern of foraging and hunting (big game and smaller animals) was more likely for Paleo-Indian groups (Funk, 1978; Barber, 1979).

A U.S. Bureau of Land Management study of the outer continental shelf (Barber, 1979) characterizes two possible periods when a considerable portion of Massachusetts's territorial waters were not inundated and could support Amerindian exploitation. Between 12,000 and 9000 B.P., the Stellwagen Bank area was a series of shoals and small islands where seal hunting would have been the major subsistence activity. Between 9000 and 6000 B.P., the bank appears to have been one large, continuous island. It may have supported Amerindians, as did the nearby Provincetown area of Cape Cod (shell middens and habitation). Sites are characterized as small in size and low in frequency.

Some researchers assert that Amerindian populations were exploiting large marine mammals at sea prior to European contact (Proulx, 1986). Erickson (1978) observed that porpoises and seals were hunted in the open ocean. However, exploitation of these resources appears restricted to near-shore or onshore activities such as utilizing beached whales or hunting seals along the shore rather than in the open ocean (Salwen, 1978; Snow, 1978), so it is improbable there is prehistoric cultural materials dating to after

6000 B.P. in much of the submerged coastal bottomlands (Mastone, 1990). A submerged cultural resources management plan for Massachusetts must include the potential for the occurrence of prehistoric materials and sites, habitation or special purpose, and the preservation of these prehistoric archaeological features (Mastone, 1990).

Historic Vessel Traffic and Shipwrecks

Massachusetts Bay can be best described as the gateway to the maritime commerce of Massachusetts. Historically, as today, the main shipping lanes crossed the Stellwagen Bank portion of the bay; until the opening of the Cape Cod Canal, it was the only access to the ports inside Massachusetts Bay, such as Boston, Plymouth, Salem, Gloucester, and Provincetown. Once the canal was opened, vessel traffic using the canal and not destined for Massachusetts Bay ports crossed this area in much higher frequency (Mastone, 1990, 1995), and fishing vessels utilized the area not only as a fishing ground but also as the route to the major fishing grounds of Georges Bank and the South Channel (Mastone, 1990).

The region's fisheries and whaling exploitation is well established. Near-shore fisheries, including whaling from long boats, would have encompassed areas such as Stellwagen Bank at the seaward end of Massachusetts Bay (Stuart Frank, personal communication, 1990). Then a shift from smaller vessels to larger schooners moved the majority of fisheries farther out to sea, to areas such as Georges Bank, South Channel, and Grand Bank. Until the Civil War, near-shore fisheries typically were restricted to a few small open boats engaged in market fisheries, almost exclusively in the winter months (Collins, 1890). It appears that Stellwagen Bank was not heavily exploited by schooner-based fisheries, because the Georges Bank fisheries was more lucrative (Collins, 1889). In this century, the growth of trawler and dragger industries turned attention back to Stellwagen Bank (Mastone, 1990).

A U.S. Bureau of Land Management study of the outer continental shelf (Bourque, 1979) provides a description of historic shipping zones that includes distribution and density of known and expected shipwreck remains. The coastal area of Massachusetts encompasses portions of 14 such zones; unfortunately, the scale of analysis and data presentation in the study provides only a broad sense for sensitivity of site occurrence. Generally, known inventories for most zones are characterized as light; predicted density of shipwreck remains characterized as moderately heavy are clustered along shipping lanes and harbor approaches.

Hamilton (1989) provides a detailed analysis of the extent of waterborne commerce in Massachusetts Bay from 1620 to 1900, research that demonstrates clearly a positive relationship between population growth, volume of vessel traffic, and frequency of shipwrecks. In general terms, shipwreck frequency is 1–3 percent of traffic volume.

Fish (1989) provides insight into the frequency of shipwreck events in the northeast, noting a strong relationship between high shipwreck frequency and major storms such as in 1898. By contrast, collisions and founderings are the major cause for loss during periods of low shipwreck frequency. Further, a strong seasonal distribution of shipwrecks is exhibited for Massachusetts waters, with a peak in November and December (Fish, 1989; Hamilton, 1989). This coincides with the seasonal peak in major storm events, as will be discussed later in this chapter. Interestingly, these months are typified by lower traffic volume, except for fishing.

In the late 19th and early 20th centuries, the Northeast experienced its highest level of coastal shipping (Fish, 1989). The region suffered its greatest number of shipwrecks per year (Fish, 1989) at the turn of the 20th century.

The primary causes of shipwrecks fall into four broad classes: acts of war: naval engagements, piracy, law enforcement; natural forces: storms (gales and hurricanes); human error: poor seamanship, fire, collision; and abandonment: all the above, plus vessel condition and economic conditions.

A bias may exist in the historical and documentary record not to record locational or other information on shipwreck sites that do not pose a hazard to navigation, involve human tragedy, or carry valuable cargo. Government data is aimed at identifying and locating human-made and natural hazards to navigation, not all shipwrecks. In many instances, reported locations of deep-water shipwrecks are approximate but not verified, because they do not pose a hazard to navigation, and because reliable locational information is in private hands (sport divers, researchers, fishermen) whose varying purposes and needs generally preclude sharing this information (Mastone, 1990).

Most available published sources of shipwreck information concentrate on romance of the sea, major calamities, and disasters, and these address an audience that is typically not scholarly. Many works are laundry lists of shipwrecks and are often published without sources or evaluation of sources. Many reflect a certain selective presentation of facts, such as the inclusion of only larger vessels or those carrying "valuable" cargo. Thus, vessel loss is under-recorded (Mastone, 1990).

Ambiguity of location, especially at sea, and types of vessel losses reported for most maritime disasters generally precludes establishing effects on specific resources. Typically, the presumed nearest landfall is used when the shipwreck does not occur at a recognized landmark, on shore, on rocks, or near a buoy marker or lightship. Frequently, the only description given is "off Provincetown," "off Cape Ann," "off the Massachusetts coast," "off New England," or "left port never to be heard of again." For most colonial-period writers, place of loss was less important than who or what was lost. Historically, the precision of location required today was not important to the contemporary recording of vessel losses (Mastone, 1990).

Historically, adverse and unpredictable weather conditions (severe gales and hurricanes) have been identified as the major cause of vessel loss. There were at least 20 major storms in the Massachusetts Bay area before 1900. Luther (1958) identified a number of major storms: August 15, 1695; September, 1676; February 22, 1723; December, 1786; October 9, 1804; September 23, 1815; December 14–15, 17, 22, and 27, 1839 (December, 1839, was a bad period, two weeks of severe storms or hurricanes called "the Triple Hurricanes of 1839"); October 2, 1841; April 14, 1851 (Minots Light destroyed); January 19, 1857 ("the October Gale"); September 8, 1869; December 25, 1873; December 1886; November 25, 1888; September 9, 1896; and November 26, 1898 ("the Portland Gale").

The Triple Hurricanes of December, 1839, and the Portland Gale of November, 1898, were particularly devastating and inspired Longfellow's poem "Wreck of the Hesperus." Contemporary accounts noted more than 200 vessels sunk in Boston Harbor alone, with comparable losses in the ports of Gloucester and Provincetown. Fish (1989) has established that 121 vessels were totally lost and another 218 damaged. By comparison, roughly 400 vessels were lost during the Portland Gale. "[. . .] The largest number of shipwrecks to occur in one year in the entire history of the region happened during 1898. Ninety percent of the shipwrecks that year took place in just three days [November 25–27, 1898]" (Fish, 1989).

Historical records strongly suggest the existence of shipwreck sites across Massachusetts waters. Reliable sources place between 1500–3000 instances of shipwrecks off the Massachusetts coast (Berman, 1972; Hamilton, 1989; Lonsdale and Kaplan, 1964; Luther 1958, 1965; Luther and Weeks, 1967; Marx 1987; Fish, 1989). Casual observation places clusters of shipwrecks in the main shipping lanes along Cape Cod and Cape Ann, and in the approaches to Boston, Salem, Gloucester, and Provincetown harbors.

Loss of SS Portland.   In the waters off Massachusetts is the steamship *Portland*, lost with more than 160 lives in the Portland Gale of 1898; the storm is remembered for that loss. A side-wheeled paddle steamer, *Portland* was built in 1890 by the New England Shipbuilding Company of Bath, Maine. It was 291 ft long, 42 ft wide, and 15 ft in draught, with a gross weight of 2283 tons and a top speed of 15 knots. It served the Boston–Portland Line of Portland Steam Packet Company (Cram, 1980). The remote sensing records of The Historic Maritime Group of New England (HMGNE) place the wreck site in the study area (John Fish, personal communication, 1990).

The loss of *Portland* is one of the most controversial marine mysteries in the history of the region (Fish, 1989). It "marked a change in the practice of coastwise passenger shipping in the region. From that point on, a duplicate passenger list was always left on shore when a passenger vessel left port... It also marked a change in the design of coastal passenger steamers. Paddle-wheel steamers, like the *Portland*, were of shallow draft which, while allowing passage up Maine's rivers, did not make for good handling in heavy seas... [Vessels replacing the *Portland*] were of the propeller type rather than paddle-wheel, had a deeper draft and were more enclosed, thus allowing for more seaworthiness in the unpredictable and often wild waters of the northeast" (Fish, 1989). *Portland* is valuable in historical importance and as a memorial site because of its effect on maritime business and technology (Mastone, 1995).

Aircraft

At least one aircraft "crash" site has been located off Massachusetts. It has been reported that a P-38 Lightning is located on the western edge of Stellwagen Bank (Grey Eagle Charters, personal communication, 1990). At this time, no information is available to explain the reason for the site occurrence or assess possible site importance (Lawrence Webster, personal communication, 1990).

MANAGEMENT OF SUBMERGED CULTURAL RESOURCES

Management of submerged cultural resources resources must incorporate the spirit of the Abandoned Shipwreck Act. This act promotes access to shipwreck sites and encourages citizen involvement in managing these cultural resources in state waters. The incorporation of these two aspects could be accomplished in a number of ways, including cooperative management agreements with those state and federal agencies charged with preservation of the resources.

A wide variety of groups are potentially concerned with historic shipwrecks: dive clubs, dive instructors, sport divers, dive-boat operators, dive shops, and diver certification organizations; commercial and recreational fishermen, boaters, fishing charter boat operators, and marina operators; underwater archaeologists, maritime historians, and historic preservationists; nautical conservators; marine biologists and natural resource specialists; salvors; and government managers.

While these categories represent the major interest groups, they cannot be viewed as mutually exclusive. The type and extent of exploitation varies among the groups with overlap, competition, and conflict. Some can be described as symbiotic while others are parasitic. Use (or exploitation) of shipwrecks can be characterized as destructive or nondestructive. Yet, despite the diversity of interested and affected constituencies, there are really only four groups whose activities regularly have the potential to affect resources adversely: commercial salvors, dive charter operators, sport divers, and archaeologists. The activities over which groups come into to conflict can be viewed broadly in terms of *access* and *possession* (Mastone, 1992, 1999).

There are a number of potential uses and values of shipwrecks: commercial speculation, or traditional salvage; recreational value; ecological or habitat value; cost of replication; educational value; and historical/archaeological value. However, it might be more appropriate to redefine values in terms of the effects of exploitation from activities of the interest groups. Value can be more simply defined in several broad areas: commercial or financial (profit); intellectual (historical–archaeological); public (multiple concerns); and other values yet to be defined. In this way, values and their associated issues could be directly incorporated into a management regime (Mastone, 1992, 1999).

Finally, through processes of structural deterioration and plant and animal colonization, shipwrecks are transformed from their original function into habitats. Their value to the stream of commerce no longer manifests itself in cargoes carried or vessel function but rather in their ability to function as habitat and support the food web. Ancient shipwrecks may achieve historical–archaeological value as well as biological value. Thus, any management of resources must recognize their multifaceted nature and provide adequate consideration to the sometimes competing utilization of these resources (Mastone, 1990, 1995, 1999).

BOARD OF UNDERWATER ARCHAEOLOGICAL RESOURCES

The Massachusetts Board of Underwater Archaeological Resources (MBUAR), established in 1973, is trustee of the Commonwealth's underwater heritage, promoting and protecting the public's interest in these resources for recreational, economic, environmental and historical purposes. MBUAR works to protect the Commonwealth's proprietary, scientific, and historical interest in these resources. The Massachusetts program is a model of the management scheme proposed under the federal guidelines resulting from the Abandoned Shipwreck Act.

MBUAR serves a divergent constituency of sport divers, archaeologists, museums, historical interests, and commercial salvors. Massachusetts has the fifth largest population of active divers in the United States. Based on its membership, the Bay State Council of Divers conservatively estimates that 25,000 sport divers actively utilize Commonwealth waters (active use is eight or more dives per year); casual use estimates exceed 100,000 divers. The state is home to some 200 dive shops, dive charter operators, and sport diving clubs, and these numbers are considered low estimates. MBUAR must maintain a balance between diverse and sometimes conflicting constituencies and Commonwealth interest.

MBUAR's nine-member board is overseen by the Executive Office of Environmental Affairs, which is responsible for the protection and enhancement of the Commonwealth's natural resources through its various departments. One of the agency's missions is to enhance public access to historic and scenic resources.

MBUAR's membership is composed of six statutory appointments: state archaeologist, state archivist, executive director of the Massachusetts Historical Commission, director of Waterways, director of Coastal Zone Management, and director of Environmental Law Enforcement. There are three gubernatorial appointments: a marine archaeologist and two representatives of the diving community. The statutory composition of MBUAR was an early recognition of the need to bring major constituencies and critical technical knowledge into the management process, which focuses on bringing together public and private sectors, recreational and preservation communities, and technical and regulatory expertise.

Under Massachusetts General Laws Chapter 6, Sections 179–180, and Chapter 91, Section 63, MBUAR is charged with encouraging discovery and reporting as well as preserving and protecting underwater archaeological resources. Underwater archaeological resources are a nonrenewable scientific resource, statements left by time to be preserved through their documentation for public study and benefit. Generally, those resources are defined as abandoned property, artifacts, treasure troves, and shipwrecks. Usually these are shipwrecks, but they also could be submerged Native American sites, wharves, or aircraft. The Commonwealth holds title to these resources and retains regulatory authority over their use, and MBUAR's jurisdiction extends over the inland and coastal waters of the state.

Legislation and Legal Challenges

As already noted, the passage of the federal Abandoned Shipwreck Act (Public Law 100–298) affirmed title to these resources and gave regulatory authority over their use to the states.

Like many agencies of her sister states, MBUAR was subject to a number of legal challenges during the 1980s and was a codefendant, with two permittees, in the case of Barry Clifford et al. v. Board of Underwater Archaeological Resources. The case dealt with the MBUAR's regulatory authority over the shipwreck remains of the vessel *White Squall*. Preliminary research strongly suggested the *White Squall* had significant archaeological and historical importance and integrity. The suit was originally brought in 1983 and was decided in MBUAR's favor in February 1991, and the plaintiff withdrew his appeal, an outcome that demonstrated the fairness and appropriateness of MBUAR's administrative actions and resource management scheme.

MBUAR's statute and regulations remained relatively unchanged until the 1990s. Although a complete overhaul of the statute in response to the Abandoned Shipwreck Act was not feasible, some significant changes have taken place. MBUAR's site files are, by state law, not a public record. Board member composition was shifted from gubernatorial appointments to statutory appointments to ensure interagency cooperation, particularly in the key areas of historic preservation and enforcement. MBUAR had the power to designate certain sites of significant archaeological or historical value as preserves. This reserves such properties as permanent public resources not subject to disposition for permittees.

MBUAR Activities

MBUAR's staff undertakes a program of public outreach, project review, resource identification, inventory, and assessment. Public outreach activities include slide shows and presentations to sport diving clubs and school groups. Under MBUAR regulations, priority is given to Massachusetts museums to acquire collections recovered under MBUAR permits. Materials recovered under these permits are on exhibit at Kendall Whaling Museum in Sharon, Springfield Museum, and Maritime and Irish Mossing Museum in Scituate.

In cooperation with the Massachusetts Historical Commission, MBUAR assists in compiling the state's inventory of archaeological and historical assets. In partnership with the Naval Historical Center, MBUAR has undertaken an inventory of naval shipwrecks in Massachusetts water as part of the Department of Defense Legacy Program (Mastone and Trubey, 1996). MBUAR's literature-derived site files suggest a potential for just under 3000 shipwrecks in Massachusetts waters.

As part of the environmental secretariat, MBUAR works closely with other departments in identifying, inventorying, and assessing underwater historical and archaeological sites and provides technical assistance in conducting project reviews (e.g., Massachusetts Environmental Policy Act reviews, CZMA federal consistency reviews, and Section 106 of NHPA reviews). This working relationship has increased the agencies' awareness and has insured consideration for the potential for site occurrence during the project planning and review process.

Permits

No one may remove, displace, damage, or destroy any underwater archaeological resource except in conformity with annual permits issued by MBUAR. There are two types of permits: reconnaissance permits for the nondisruptive inspection and identification of underwater archaeological resources; and excavation permits to uncover and remove underwater archaeological resources. Permits are renewable and the application fee ranges from $10–100 per year, a fee structure unchanged since its inception. Permit requirements and standards are outlined in the MBUAR's regulations (312 CMR 2.0–2.16).

Permit applicants must have demonstrable proof (documentary evidence alone is insufficient) to be granted a permit. Permittees range from individual sport divers and commercial ventures to museums. Most permits are reconnaissance permits, which can be best characterized as nondisruptive research activities aimed at site identification and delineation; excavation activities are prohibited and recoveries are limited to surface finds. Excavation permits are required when any destructive activities are undertaken, ranging from test excavations to mitigation. Permit areas (not to exceed one nautical mile^2) are located along the state's coastline and on inland waters.

Board permittees must provide all necessary resources to complete their projects and must demonstrate their financial ability to carry out their plans. Depending on the nature of the resource and their proposed activities, permittees are required to have a project research team, which could include an archaeologist and a conservator. Work is undertaken in conformance with an approved research design–work plan.

Permittees work with MBUAR to maximize the cultural value of the site while enjoying the board's protection of their proprietary interest in the site. Although the Commonwealth holds title to the resources, it may retain 25 percent and award the permittee 75 percent of the recovered resource's fair market value. To date, there has been no sale or other disposition of resources recovered under board permits.

MBUAR has issued or renewed nearly 100 permits since 1973. Most are renewed multiple times, demonstrating the long-term nature of the projects; several permits have been renewed continuously, five and ten times. As already noted, permits have been issued to a wide variety of applicants and resources: public entities (Massachusetts Water Resources Authority, University of Massachusetts), museums (Kendall Whaling Museum, Scituate Historical Society), utilities (Commonwealth Electric); individuals and groups of sport divers; and commercial salvors.

Resources under investigation have been the whaling ship *Wanderer*, jettisoned cannon from HMS *Nimrod*, the French 74-gun *Le Magnifique*, and the early iron bark *White Squall*. The most controversial permit was issued to Maritime Underwater Surveys on the *Whydah* (1984–1989). That investigation is currently subject to a Memorandum of Agreement between the Advisory Council on Historic Preservation, U.S. Army Corps of Engineers, Massachusetts Historical Commission (SHPO), and MBUAR.

Two permits issued for inland waters are associated with 19th-century canals: Blackstone Canal on the Blackstone River, and South Hadley Canal on the Connecticut River.

Isolated Finds

To deal with certain types of artifact discoveries, MBUAR's regulation's provide an exemption from the permit process for isolated finds and exempted sites. To obtain title to this underwater archaeological resource under the isolated find exemption, an applicant must complete and return the Isolated Find form along with a map (USGS topographic map or NOAA chart), indicating location of the find, and must detail the research undertaken to determine that this resource should be considered an isolated find. Although there is no applicant fee for an isolated find, Isolated Finds applications must be approved by MBUAR at a public board meeting.

MBUAR received only four isolated find requests prior to 1998. Two were for anchors whose recovery location was revealed to be outside state waters and not under MBUAR's jurisdiction; the other two had insufficient documentation to demonstrate these were indeed isolated finds. Both applicants subsequently submitted reconnaissance permit applications. In both cases, no additional resources were identified during field investigations.

In December 1998, MBUAR approved 22 isolated find applications for late-19th century medicine bottles recovered from various locations under the Connecticut River. All finds appeared to be independent random depositional episodes and were not associated with any sites or activities. The applicants donated the bottles to Springfield Museum for incorporation into an ongoing exhibit about the Connecticut River.

List of Exempted Sites

In its enabling legislation, MBUAR was directed to establish and maintain a list of exempted sites composed of previously disturbed (i.e., salvaged) shipwrecks and to preserve such shipwrecks for the continued enjoyment of the recreational diving community in an unregulated setting. Traditional recreational diving activities on exempted sites, such as casual collecting, does not require a permit; however, major disruption of these sites is prohibited. The recreational diving community is encouraged to work with MBUAR to protect these sites.

In 1985, MBUAR assigned 40 shipwrecks to the list of exempt sites, which included vessels flattened by the U.S. Army Corps of Engineers as hazards to navigation, commercially salvaged, or subjected to significant collecting. While this list is open to modification, no additional sites have been approved. This list is not included here but is available from MBUAR.

Underwater Archaeological Preserves

Neighboring states, including Vermont, New York, and Rhode Island, and federal agencies (NOAA's Stellwagen Bank Sanctuary) have established or are planning to establish underwater historic shipwreck parks and preserves. Recognizing the paramount public value of these resources, MBUAR revised its statute in 1995 to allow MBUAR to designate underwater archaeological preserves to provide special protection to those underwater archaeological resources of substantial historical value. Access to underwater archaeological preserves for recreational, historical, and scientific purposes is guaranteed. No permits will be granted to recover underwater archaeological resources from an underwater archaeological preserve except for historical or scientific purposes, and all collected materials remain the permanent property of the Commonwealth. Underwater archaeological preserves will encourage public enjoyment, use, and appreciation of the resource. Regulations were promulgated in 1996, and guidelines are currently being developed. Preliminary investigations of potential preserve sites is underway, including resources identified from inland and coastal permit sites.

CONCLUSION

The Massachusetts program has attempted to bring together various interest groups to manage historic shipwreck properties in state waters. The approach balances traditional uses with contemporary views of the value of these resources. The permit process is an attempt to accommodate conflicting commercial and historical values of these resources. The exempt shipwreck component allows for continuation of traditional recreational activities in an unregulated setting, a major, unanticipated by-product of which is a growing appreciation of the dive community of the adverse affects of collecting. Underwater archaeological preserves will provide a nondestructive recreational outlet, encourage scientific research, and elevate the public's awareness of the state's submerged heritage. The Massachusetts program depends heavily on active involvement of the public, as MBUAR members, permittees, or casual visitors to the state's resources, to identify, evaluate and protect these nonrenewable resources.

REFERENCES

Albion, Robert G., et al., 1972, *New England and the Sea*. Mystic Seaport Museum and Wesleyan University Press, Middletown.

Barber, Russell, 1979, *Archaeology and Palaeontology. Vol. 2: Summary and Analysis of Cultural Resources Information on the Continental Shelf from the Bay of Fundy to Cape Hatteras, Final Report*. Institute for Conservation Archaeology, Harvard University, Cambridge.

Bourque, Bruce, 1979, *Historic Shipping. Vol. 3: Summary and Analysis of Cultural Resource Information on the Continental Shelf from the Bay of Fundy to Cape Hatteras, Final Report*. Institute for Conservation Archaeology, Harvard University, Cambridge.

Berman, Bruce, 1972, *Encyclopedia of American Shipwrecks*. Mariners Press, Boston.

Collins, J.W., 1889, *The Beam-Trawl Fishery of Great Britian*. Government Printing Office, Washington.

_____, 1890, *Suggestions for the Employment of Improved Types of Vessels in Market Fisheries*. Government Printing Office, Washington.

Cram, W. Bartlett, 1980, *Picture History of New England Passenger Vessels*. Burntcoat Corp., Hampden Highlands.

Cultural Resource Committee, 1989, *Maritime Resources of Massachusetts Bay: Guide to Identification and Preservation*. Massachusetts Bay Marine Studies Consortium, Boston.

_____, 1990, *Maritime Cultural Resources of Massachusetts Bay: The Present State of Identification and Documentation*. Massachusetts Bay Marine Studies Consortium, Boston.

Erickson, Vincent O., 1978, Maliseet–Passamaquoddy. In *Handbook of North American Indians, Northeast*, edited by Bruce G. Trigger, Vol. 15, pp. 123–136. Smithsonian Institution, Washington.

Fish, John Story, 1989, *Unfinished Voyages, A Chronology of Shipwrecks in the Northeastern United States*. Lower Cape Publishing, Orleans.

Funk, Robert E. 1978, Post-Pleistocene Adaptations. In *Handbook of North American Indians, Northeast*, edited by Bruce G. Trigger, Vol. 15, pp. 16–27. Smithsonian Institution, Washington.

General Accounting Office, 1987, *Cultural Resources: Problems Protecting and Preserving Archaeological Resources*. General Accounting Office, Washington.

Hamilton, Christopher, 1989, An Analysis of Recorded Shipwrecks and Shipping and Trading Systems of Massachusetts, 1620–1900. *In 1988 Annual Report of Archaeological Data Recovery, The Whydah Project*, edited by Christopher Hamilton et al., pp. 184–219. Report on file with Massachusetts Board of Underwater Archaeological Resources.

Lonsdale, Adrian L., and Kaplan, H.R., 1964, *A Guide to Sunken Ships in American Waters*. Compass Publications, Inc., Arlington.

Luther, Brad W., 1958, *Wrecks Below*. Unpublished manuscript.

_____, 1965, *The Vanishing Fleet—Massachusetts and Rhode Island Shipwrecks*. Unpublished manuscript.

Luther, Brad W., and Weeks Edwin, 1967, *New England Shipwrecks*. Boston Sea Rovers, Boston.

Marx, Robert F., 1987, *Shipwrecks in the Americas*. Dover Publications, New York.

Mastone, Victor T., 1990, Cultural Profile of Stellwagen Bank. In *Proceedings of the 1990 Conference on Stellwagen Bank*, edited by Jack H. Archer, pp. 17–22. Urban Harbors Institute, University of Massachusetts, Boston.

_____, 1992, The Impact of Technology on Shipwrecks: A Management Dilemma. In *Historic Shipwreck Management: Meeting of Experts*, edited by Porter Hoagland III, pp. 9–10. Marine Policy Center, Woods Hole Oceanographic Institution, Woods Hole.

_____, 1995, Vessel Traffic in Sanctuary Waters. In *Stellwagen Bank: A Guide*, edited by Nathalie Ward, pp. 138–141. Center for Coastal Studies, Provincetown.

_____, 1999, In the Same Boat and Learning the Ropes: An Alexandria/Boston Comparison. *Coastal Region and Small Island Papers 5*, pp.173–178. UNESCO, Paris.

Mastone, Victor T., and Hoagland III Porter, 1993, Professional Societies Panel Discussion Summaries 1, Society for Historical Archaeology. *In Historic Shipwreck Management: Meeting of Experts II*, edited by Porter Hoagland III, pp. 18–27. Marine Policy Center, Woods Hole Oceanographic Institution, Woods Hole.

Mastone, Victor T., and Trubey David, 1996, Naval Wreck Sites in Massachusetts Waters: Challenges and Strategies in Site Stewardship. Work in Progress Paper presented at Society for Historical Archaeology Conference on Underwater Archaeology, annual meeting, Corpus Christi.

Morison, Samuel Eliot, 1979, *The Maritime History of Massachusetts 1783–1860*. Northeastern University Press, Boston.

National Ocean Service, 1988, *Automated Wreck and Obstruction Information System, Upper East Coast*. National Oceanic and Atmospheric Administration, Rockville.

Proulx, Jean-Pierre, 1986, *Whaling in the North Atlantic from Earliest Times to the Mid-19th Century*. Parks Canada, Ottawa.

Salwin, Bert, 1978, Indians of Southern New England and Long Island: Early Period. In *Handbook of North American Indians, Northeast*, edited by Bruce G. Trigger, Vol. 15, pp. 160–176. Smithsonian Institution, Washington.

Snow, Dean R., 1978, Eastern Abenaki. In *Handbook of North American Indians, Northeast*, edited by Bruce G. Trigger, Vol. 15, pp. 137–147. Smithsonian Institution, Washington.

Trigger, Bruce G., editor, 1978, *Handbook of North American Indians, Northeast*, Vol. 15. Smithsonian Institution, Washington.

Chapter 5

The Nautical Archaeology of Lake Champlain

KEVIN J. CRISMAN and ARTHUR B. COHN

INTRODUCTION

Lake Champlain is not the largest body of fresh water in North America, but its location has given it an importance in history far beyond its size. The lake extends for 193 km (120 mi) between the border of northeastern New York and western Vermont. At its southern end, the lake is separated from the Hudson River by a relatively short overland distance; at its northern end, it drains into Canada's St. Lawrence River. In the age preceding the railroad, when transportation on the continent relied almost exclusively on waterborne craft, the proximity and orientation of the Hudson, Champlain, and St. Lawrence waterways facilitated the passage of people and goods between the mid-Atlantic seaboard and Canada. Explorers, armies, navies, settlers, merchants, and tourists sailed the length of Lake Champlain for nearly four centuries in an ebb and flow of humanity that has helped to define the course of North American history.

Lake Champlain and its maritime history are of particular significance to nautical archaeologists for two reasons: the diversity of its watercraft, and the spectacular preservation of shipwrecks sunk beneath its waters. The diversity of ship and boat types is

Kevin J. Crisman, Institute of Nautical Archaeology, Texas A&M University, College Station, Texas 77843. **Arthur B. Cohn**, Lake Champlain Maritime Museum Basin Harbour Road, Vergennes, Vermont 05491.

International Handbook of Underwater Archaeology, edited by Carol V. Ruppé and Janet F. Barstad. Kluwer Academic/Plenum Publishers, New York, 2002.

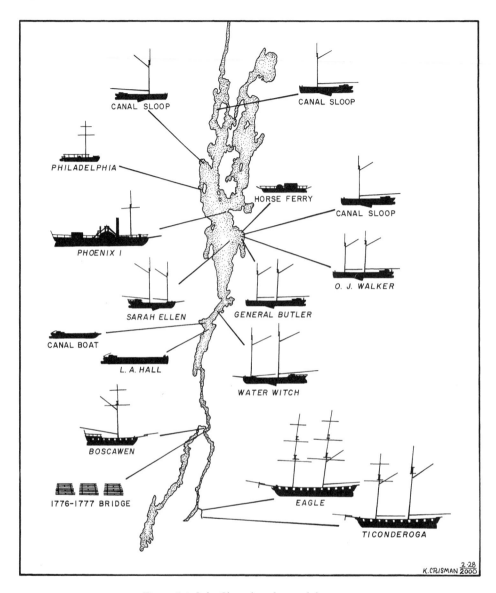

Figure 5.1. Lake Champlain shipwreck locations.

a result of the wide variety of naval, commercial, and recreational activities that have occurred on the lake, and was further increased by the invention of new designs, techniques of construction, and forms of propulsion in the late 18th and 19th centuries. Through the centuries, the lake has floated Native American dugouts and bark canoes, bateaux and scows, warships ranging in size from gunboats to frigates, sloop- and schooner-rigged sailing merchant vessels, canal boats, sidewheel steamships, and ferryboats propelled by sail, oars, poles, or horse power (Figure 5.1).

Wooden ships and boats are highly perishable creations with an average working life span of eight to ten years before decay or accidents send them to the bottom. Unlike most of the world's oceans, Lake Champlain contains no wood-boring mollusks that chew up and digest the fabric of a ship's hull. Vessels that sink in the lake, particularly in waters deeper than 10 m (33 ft), settle into a cold, dark environment ideal for preserving wood and other organic materials for an indefinite period of time. Shipwrecks found in deeper water often retain their original masts, spars, and paint; below-deck spaces yield cargo, tools, galley ware, furniture, and even items of clothing, much of which is lying where the crew stowed it before the ship's final voyage. Recreating the design and appearance of shipwrecks in such excellent condition requires little or no conjecture on the part of the archaeologist, only an ability to observe and record detail.

The lake's history and well-preserved shipwrecks have attracted the attention of antiquarians—souvenir hunters and salvagers—since the early 19th century. Generally, their interest in acquiring relics of the past has lead to adverse consequences for modern archaeologists. Wrecks from famous naval campaigns were dragged from shallow waters, cut up for use in building commemorative furniture, or placed on display until weathering or fire caused their complete destruction. Few of the hulls recovered from the lake have survived, the one significant exception being the Revolutionary War gondola *Philadelphia* (Figure 5.1). In 1935, New York salvage engineer Lorenzo F. Hagglund raised the vessel intact, its single mast still standing and three cannon in their carriages. Unlike other salvors of lake shipwrecks, Hagglund dedicated himself to preserving *Philadelphia* as he found it, and upon his death the gunboat was acquired by the Smithsonian Institution's Museum of American History, where it is still displayed today (Lundeberg, 1995; Bratten, 1996, 2000).

The invention and widespread use of SCUBA in the second half of the 19th century opened many of Lake Champlain's previously inaccessible wrecks to divers, and some sites suffered looting and inadvertent damage. At the same time, however, the states and province bordering the lake enacted legislation designed to protect underwater archaeological sites from salvaging, and professional and avocational archaeologists began to take an interest in systematically locating and recording ships and other archaeological remains on the lake bottom. In 1980, a group of Vermont and New York historians, archaeologists, and sport divers formed the nonprofit Champlain Maritime Society (CMS) to initiate studies of shipwrecks and to aid state and provincial governments in their efforts to preserve Lake Champlain's heritage. The society's inaugural project in August 1980 involved the recording of the earliest known steamboat hull in the world, *Phoenix I* (built in 1815 and sunk after a fire in 1819). Over the following years the CMS recorded the remains of warships from the French and Indian War and the War of 1812, sailing canal schooners and sloops, the piers of a Revolutionary War-era bridge across the lake, and other submerged sites (Cohn, ed., 1984; Crisman, 1986).

A new center for lake research was formed in 1985 at Basin Harbor Maritime Museum in Vergennes, Vermont (renamed Lake Champlain Maritime Museum [LCMM] in 1989). The CMS merged with the museum at Basin Harbor in 1987, and since that time LCMM has sponsored most of the archaeological investigations on and in the lake. Contributing institutions have included the Institute of Nautical Archaeology at Texas A&M University (INA-TAMU), the University of Vermont (UVM), the Vermont Division for Historic Preservation (VDHP), the New York Office of Parks, Recreation and Historic Preservation, and the New York State Education Department's State Museum. Two decades of continuous archaeological survey, excavation, and recording have greatly expanded our knowledge of the people and ships so central to the story of Lake Champlain (Crisman and Cohn, 1994; Crisman, 1996).

LAKE CHAMPLAIN THROUGH THE CENTURIES

Four broadly defined eras of maritime activity can be identified in the 10,000 and more years that humans have occupied the Champlain Valley, navigating its waters. The Prehistoric era began with the arrival of Amerindians at the close of the last ice age around 9300 B.C. and ended with the arrival of French explorer Samuel de Champlain in A.D. 1609 (Haviland and Power, 1994). Archaeological finds in the lake and on its shores indicate fish and waterfowl were an important source of food for prehistoric inhabitants, and that the lake was their primary means of transportation. There is little question watercraft were widely used for most of the Prehistoric era, but only a handful of boats from this period, all dugout canoes, have been located and archaeologically studied (Bazilchuk et al., 1985). Bark canoes also were common in the region during the first two centuries of contact between Native Americans and Europeans and undoubtedly were in use much earlier, but archaeological examples of these lighter, more fragile craft have proved elusive.

The second period of maritime activity on the lake, the era of warfare, began with the appearance of the first Europeans in 1609 and continued until 1815 (Barranco et al., 1999). During these two centuries, Native Americans and Europeans fought for ownership of the valley's resources and, on a wider scale, for control of North America. Beginning in the 1680s, the lake became a focal point of the contest between the English and French for control of North America. After three indecisive wars, their struggle reached a climax during a fourth conflict, the French and Indian War (1755–1760), when French fortifications on the lake shores were overwhelmed by British and colonial armies, and a French flotilla was captured by English warships. Only 15 years later, in 1775, the lake again became an active theater of fighting, this time in the military struggle between Britain and its rebelling colonies known as the Revolutionary War (1775–1783). Rival naval flotillas fought for control of the lake in 1776 at the Battle of Valcour Island; the British emerged victorious, only to see the resulting opportunities vanish the following year in the crushing defeat of their army at Saratoga.

Three decades of relative peace (1783–1812) followed, but a third conflict engulfed the region before lasting peace would return. The War of 1812 (1812–1815) brought American and British armies and naval forces into the Champlain Valley, and again rival naval squadrons met in an engagement that would profoundly affect the outcome of the war. The American naval victory at Plattsburgh Bay in September 1814 turned back a British invasion of the United States and hastened the end of the war.

Widespread settlement of the Champlain Valley and expansion of agriculture, industry, and commerce all began in the 18th century, but the third period on the lake, the Era of Commerce, was not fully underway until the end of the War of 1812. A convergence of social, political, and technological developments in the early decades of the 19th century ushered in a "golden age" of merchant shipping on the lake. The vast increase in the numbers of vessels at this time and the introduction of new types of vessels, new forms of ship construction and propulsion, and an expanded maritime infrastructure of canals, wharves, breakwaters, and lighthouses, are all evident in shipwrecks and other archaeological remains. Commercial traffic on Lake Champlain in the late 18th century and the first quarter of the 19th century was limited mostly to small, poled or rowed craft such as bateaux and scows, and to sloops or schooners under 50 tons.

Sloops and schooners would continue in service far into the 19th century, but new, larger, and often radically different vessel types appeared in the era of commerce. The lake's first steamboat was launched in 1809, the first of many that plied the lake until the mid-20th century. The Champlain Canal, a humanmade waterway connecting the lake and the Hudson River, opened in 1823 and greatly increased the volume of trade throughout the region. A second canal (the Chambly Canal) connecting the lake with the St. Lawrence River to the north opened in 1843 and further contributed to the economic vitality of the Champlain Valley. Hundreds of canal boats navigated the lake in the century that followed the opening of the first canal.

The railroad gradually ended the era of commerce on Lake Champlain. Railroads arrived in the Champlain Valley in the 1840s and at first only contributed to the busy lake traffic. By the 1860s, however, year-round railroads were drawing passengers and freight from the seasonal steamers and canal boats, and at the end of the 19th century the railroad was nearly dominant.

In the early 20th century, the once busy lake and its commercial ports languished, but a new trend, begun in the previous century, continued and became the fourth and most recent phase in the maritime history of Lake Champlain, the era of recreation. In the perception of the public, the long, narrow, mountain-enclosed waterway is no longer an avenue of commerce but a recreational destination, a place for fishing, sailing, diving, and other water-oriented sports and leisure activities. Although vestiges of the previous era remain in ferryboats, barges, and a handful of other working craft, pleasure craft now constitute the great majority of boats that ply the lake annually.

Thus we see that human endeavors on the waters of Champlain have changed over time, beginning with 10,000 years of hunting and gathering by Native Americans, followed by two centuries of intermittent naval and military conflict, a century of active maritime commerce and finally, a century in which the lake has been redefined as a place of recreation. Lake Champlain truly represents a microcosm of life and transportation technology on the inland waterways of North America. Archaeological work has expanded and revised what was previously known about the lake's past and has revealed new information about its people and ships. The recent work has focused especially on the eras of warfare and commerce, because the 18th and 19th centuries have left so many wrecks and sites to find and investigate.

RECENT RESEARCH

Gunboats, Sloops, and Brigs: The Era of Warfare

Because of its strategic location in the interior of North America, Lake Champlain was considered a valuable prize in three major wars between 1755 and 1815. Indeed, one writer has termed it "the key to a continent" (Hill, 1976). Three great naval contests occurred in the lake's history, and each saw the hasty construction of warships and decisive encounters between opposing flotillas. All three contests left shipwrecks on the bottom of the lake, vessels sunk in service or abandoned in the aftermath of war when decay and expense rendered them worthless.

French and Indian War. Archaeological discoveries from the first of the three conflicts, the French and Indian War, have been relatively scant, although this war produced some of the earliest large vessels to sail the lake. Nearby Lake George, a tributary of Champlain, has yielded the hulls of bateaux used to transport British armies and supplies (Crisman, 1988) as well as *Land Tortoise*, a spectacularly preserved floating gun battery or *radeau*, accidentally scuttled in deep water in 1758 (Bellico, 1992; Paine, 1998). A 1983 Champlain Maritime Society-sponsored survey of Lake Champlain waters below Fort Ticonderoga turned up the remains of three warships that rotted and sank a few years after the end of the French and Indian War. One, identified as the British 16-gun sloop *Boscawen* (Figure 5.1), was excavated in a joint CMS–Fort Ticonderoga Museum project in 1984 and 1985 (Krueger, et al., 1985).

Boscawen was abandoned after the war rather than sunk in service but nevertheless yielded a sizeable collection of artifacts: weaponry and munitions (Carter, 1995); crew-related artifacts such as shoes, uniform buttons and buckles, and eating utensils (Erwin, 1994); foraging, entrenching, and blacksmithing tools (Grant, 1996); and rope, blocks, deadeyes, and other rigging elements (Flanigan, 1999). The range of artifacts and their distribution inside the hull provided clues to the sources of supplies and provisions, patterns of stowage below decks, and crew routines and diet. The artifacts also hinted at the widespread use of military equipment, which was either obsolete or obtained from sources other than the usual British Army suppliers. That so many objects were left aboard the sloop at the time of its abandonment also suggested an attitude of indifference toward government property by the soldiers and officers who garrisoned Fort Ticonderoga in the 1760s. Since completing conservation treatments, all of the *Boscawen*'s artifacts have been maintained in the collections of the Fort Ticonderoga Museum.

About 40 percent of *Boscawen*'s hull survived, including the entire keel and keelson, the lower stem and stern assemblies, and the lower frames, planking, and ceiling out to the turn of the bilge on both port and starboard sides. Standards of construction exhibited in the hull were rough, which might be expected since the sloop was built and launched in a matter of weeks in September 1759. Despite the crude assembly, *Boscawen*'s scantlings were substantial in their dimensions and securely fastened with iron bolts, spikes, and treenails. The identification of the wreck as the sloop *Boscawen* was aided by the find of a single saddle-type mast step (a large block of wood that straddled the keelson). The wreck measured 21.33 m (70 ft) in overall length and was estimated to have originally been 22.86 m (75 ft) in length and 7.62 m (25 ft) in beam. Analysis of *Boscawen* is nearly complete, and work has begun on a final publication.

Revolutionary War. The struggle for control of Lake Champlain during the early phases of the Revolutionary War, between 1775 and 1777, left shipwrecks and other archaeological material strewn over the bottom of the lake. The defeat of the American flotilla at the Battle of Valcour Island and its aftermath in October 1776 resulted in the sinking of 10 warships; four more went to the bottom the following year during the American retreat from the lake.

Although most of the wrecks appear to have been destroyed by salvaging and dredging, the Continental gondola *Philadelphia*, salvaged by Lorenzo F. Hagglund in 1935, has survived and is now displayed at the Smithsonian Institution in Washington, D.C. A second Continental gondola was discovered in deep water during a Champlain Maritime Society-directed sonar survey in 1997. Like *Philadelphia*, it is intact, with its single mast still upright and its 12-lb. bow gun still pointing over the stem. The hull has been extensively videotaped by a remotely operated vehicle (ROV), and LCMM is currently preparing a plan for the future study and protection of the warship. Although the identity of the recently discovered gondola is uncertain, it is thought to be either *Connecticut* or *Spitfire* (Cohn and Barranco, in preparation).

A 1983 CMS-sponsored survey of the waters around the Revolutionary War fortification of Mount Independence, Vermont, turned up some timber caissons that anchored a 1.6-km-long (1 mi) floating bridge that connected Independence with Fort Ticonderoga across the lake (Figure 5.1, lower left). The caissons were assembled log-cabin fashion, with the trunks of pine trees spiked and treenailed together and sunk into position with masses of stone ballast. Historical records show the caisson assembly took place on the ice of the frozen-over lake in the winter of 1776–1777. The CMS divers also found cannon shot and other Revolutionary-era artifacts scattered around the lake bottom below Mount Independence (Fischer, 1985).

After their discovery, the Mount Independence materials were left in situ on the lake bottom, but the 1992 arrest and conviction of a looter on the site led the Vermont Division for Historic Preservation to authorize an intensive survey and recovery operation in 1992 and 1993, a project jointly directed as a field school by LCMM, INA-TAMU, and UVM. During the operation, sonar, magnetometer, and diver surveys yielded many new finds: a 12-pounder iron cannon with one of its trunnions broken off by hammer blows (the trunnion was found nearby); mortar bombs, round shot, bar shot, grenades, and two wooden boxes filled with grape shot; bayonets and a complete American-made musket; an extensive collection of entrenching tools; and miscellaneous small finds such as bottles, shoes, deer bones, and a copper ladle.

The bridge caissons underwent more intensive study in 1992, and the 21 surviving structures were located, plotted, and recorded (Crisman, 1992, 1993a, 1995b; Cohn 1995a, 1995b, 1995c). Both contemporary documents and archaeological evidence suggest that most of the war material probably was thrown into the lake by British soldiers who abandoned the captured position and returned to Canada in the winter of 1777 (McLaughlin, 2000).

War of 1812.   The War of 1812, the third and final armed conflict on the lake, was a limited war in the sense that most of the intensive building took place during 1814 and resulted in only one major naval action on the lake, the Battle of Plattsburgh Bay in September 1814. American victory in this battle turned back a British land invasion, undoubtedly hastening the end of the war three months later by negotiation and peace treaty.

Although the opposing squadrons shot each other full of holes at Plattsburgh Bay, no ships sank in the action. The three large American warships, along with the two large Royal Navy ships captured in the battle, were repaired and sailed up the lake to the port of Whitehall, New York, and placed "in ordinary" (today called "mothballing"). The green-timbered hulls, which succumbed to decay within a few years, were moved to an out-of-the-way creek and allowed to sink. They were sold in 1825, but most were never salvaged.

In 1958, Whitehall residents recovered one warship, the 17-gun schooner *Ticonderoga* (Figure 5.1), and placed it on display behind the Skenesboro Museum in downtown Whitehall; a CMS team recorded it in 1981 (Crisman, 1983). A diver search for the rest of the squadron in 1981 turned up three more warship wrecks in the creek's murky waters: the U.S. Navy 20-gun brig *Eagle* (Figure 5.1), the ex-Royal Navy 16-gun brig *Linnet*, and a U.S. Navy 2-gun row galley, probably *Allen*. *Eagle* was a particularly promising wreck for study: The brig had tipped over to port as it sank, and that side of the hull was complete up to the deck level and lower gun ports; the keel and keelson were complete, and the lower stem and stern were well-preserved. The wreck was of interest because it was constructed in just 19 days, from the laying of the keel to launching. A CMS project in 1982 and 1983, supported by the VDHP, succeeded in recording details of *Eagle*'s design and construction and permitted reconstruction of the vessel as it looked in 1814. The *Eagle*'s 35.78-m-long (117 ft, 3 in) hull was noteworthy for obvious construction shortcuts (the use of softwood timber in the frames and the omission of reinforcing knees) and an extremely shallow design that permitted operation in shoal areas of the lake (Crisman, 1987, 1991b; Cassavoy and Crisman, 1988).

Linnet and *Allen*, the two remaining 1812 warships at Whitehall, were the subjects of a 1995 archaeological field school undertaken jointly by LCMM, INA-TAMU, and UVM, with partial funding by a Navy Department legacy grant administered through the Naval Historical Center (Crisman, 1995a). During the project, both hulls were excavated in selected locations for record of their scantlings and design. Like *Eagle* and most other archaeologically studied warships built on Lake Champlain, *Linnet* and *Allen* showed evidence of the fast but adequate assembly typical of many wartime-built naval vessels. The excavations also uncovered small collections of artifacts within each wreck, including buttons, shot, and, from *Allen*, a complete white clay smoking pipe whose bowl is shaped like the head of a bearded and turbaned man with the raised words "United States of America" around its rim (Washburn, 1996a, 1996b, 1998; Emery 1995, 1996).

Schooners, Steamboats, and Canal Boats: The Era of Commerce

Between the late 18th and early 20th centuries, Lake Champlain experienced an explosion of maritime commerce and shipping. During this era, hundreds of cargo- and passenger-carrying vessels of all types—steamboats, canal boats, ferryboats, and sailing merchant craft were built for service on the lake and its canals.

Accidents involving collisions, fires, groundings, and sinking due to storms, squalls, or simply inadequate maintenance of wooden hulls took an annual toll on these ships. Many other ships went to the bottom at the end of their working lives, after they were stripped of useable materials and abandoned in "boneyards" around the lake. Thus there are more archaeological finds from the era of commerce than from any other period in the region's maritime history. Shipwrecks and their contents have told us much about trade and daily life on the lake and its canals in the 19th century.

Small canoes, bateaux, and scows were the earliest forms of merchant vessels on the lake; larger sailing craft, such as sloops and schooners, appeared in the years following the 1759–1760 British conquest of the Champlain Valley. These "lake sailors" were the mainstay of regional trade until the second quarter of the 19th century and hauled cargoes between lake ports even after the opening of the Champlain Canal in 1823 brought large numbers of specialized canal boats to the region. Examples of early "pre-canal" lake sailors have yet to be found and studied, but two examples of post-1823 lake schooners have undergone limited archaeological recording and analysis.

Water Witch. *Water Witch* (Figure 5.2), the first of these schooners, had an unusual career. It was launched as a steamboat in 1832 and competed with the lake's dominant steamboat company until it was bought out in 1835 and converted to a schooner the following year. It sailed for 30 more years, hauling goods and materials around the lake, until an 1866 squall knocked it over and sent it to the bottom with a load of iron ore (Figure 5.3). In 1977, Canadian divers located the wreck, and in 1990 and 1993 the lines were taken off the hull by an LCMM–INA-TAMU team.

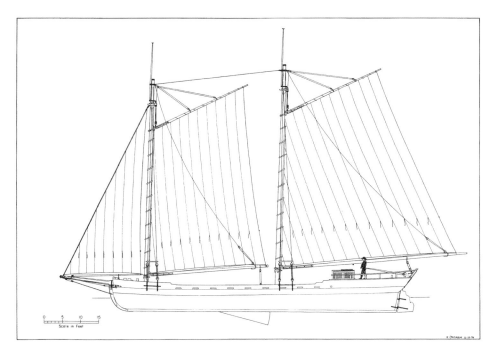

Figure 5.2. *Water Witch*, Lake Champlain, 1832–1866.

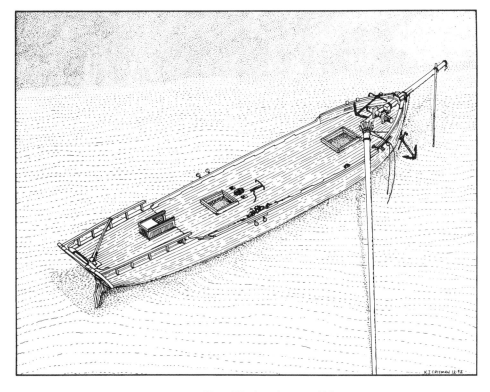

Figure 5.3. *Water Witch* on bottom of lake.

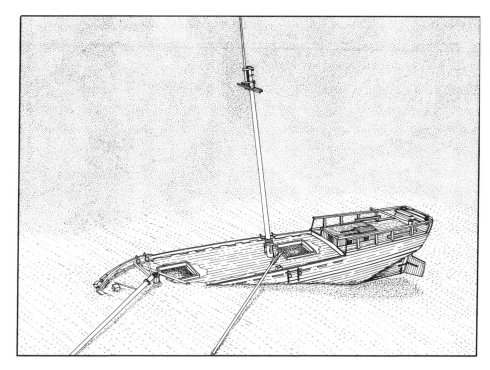

Figure 5.4. Schooner *Sarah Ellen* on the bottom of lake.

Despite its beginning as a steamer, the 24.38-m (80 ft) *Water Witch* bore little resemblance to typical steamboat designs of the time. With a bowsprit, two cargo hatches, slightly raised quarter deck, and small housing over the companionway at the forward end of the quarterdeck, the schooner more closely resembled what we believe to be a typical lake sailor design (Crisman and Cohn, 1993a; Crisman, 1993a).

The *Sarah Ellen*.   The *Sarah Ellen*, the second example of a lake schooner, was built in 1849 and sailed for 21 years until it was overwhelmed in a storm and sunk in deep water in 1860. The wreck was found in 1989 during an LCMM–Woods Hole Oceanographic Institute survey, with the help of archival data provided by lake historian A. Peter Barranco.

The *Sarah Ellen* was found bow down but upright on the bottom. Its mainmast was still standing. The foremast had fallen forward, and may have broken from shock induced by the ship hitting the bottom (Figure 5.4). The excellent condition of the vessel was astounding; even the painted letters spelling out the name and home port were still legible on the stern. Although the 22.25-m-long (73 ft) schooner was shorter than *Water Witch* and built 17 years later, the two vessels were nearly identical in layout and general appearance. The similarity of the two wrecks and their resemblance to photographs and prints of other lake sailors suggest this vessel class was consistent in design and changed little over time.

Vermont I.   Lake Champlain's first steam-powered vessel, *Vermont I*, appeared in 1809, only two years after Robert Fulton's *North River Steamboat* achieved commercial success on the Hudson River. Steamboats profoundly affected travel, commerce, and daily life in the Champlain Valley. During the next century, some 30 were built for service on the lake, and a few continued to operate on its waters until the middle of the 20th century. The period between 1809 and the Civil War was undoubtedly the high point of the lake steamer era: It it was during this time, before railroads really took hold, that these vessels were the principal carriers of passengers and high-value freight between the northern and southern ends of Lake Champlain.

Vermont I sank in an accident in 1815 and was, unfortunately, one of the wrecks pulled from the water in the 20th century and left to rot on land. Some hull measurements were taken, but not much is known about the design except that, like Fulton's *North River*, it appears to have been flat-bottomed and hard-chined in the manner of a canal boat.

Phoenix I.   *Phoenix I* (Figure 5.1), the lake's second steamer, was built in 1815 and sunk four years later after a fire that burned it to the waterline. Discovered by divers in 1979, it became the first CMS project in 1980. The charred remnants of the lower hull were recorded in detail, and offsets were taken from the hull (Davison, 1981; Hadden, 1995). Unlike its predecessor *Vermont I*, *Phoenix I* was built with a somewhat more rounded bottom and more robust construction.

Champlain II.   One other example of a Lake Champlain steamer has undergone intensive archaeological investigation, the wreck of the steamer *Champlain II* (previously known as *Oakes Ames*). This vessel was built in 1868 to serve as a ferryboat for railroad cars passing between Burlington, Vermont, and Plattsburgh, New York. After a subsequent consolidation of railroad lines, the vessel was no longer needed for rail ferrying and in 1873 was converted to passenger service. Two years later, an opium-addicted pilot ran *Champlain II* into a mountainside, completely wrecking the steamer but not injuring passengers or crew.

Champlain II's hull was studied in 1993 and 1994 during a joint LCMM–INA-TAMU–UVM field school when the hull's construction and lines were recorded. The machinery and upperworks were salvaged after the sinking and the bow was missing from the wreck, but the frames and planking of the remaining structure were preserved up to the level of the main deck. Also preserved were the bed timbers for two boilers and two engines (most lake steamers had a single boiler and engine mounted on the centerline of the hull; *Champlain II* had to keep this space free for rail cars and so was built with one power plant on each side).

The steamer had a pattern of framing not seen before, with single frames closely spaced amidships to bear the extra weight of the machinery and cargo and much more widely spaced single frames at either end. Reducing the number and weight of frames in the bow and stern would have lessened the hull's tendency to hog (droop) over time, a problem common in long wooden ships. Brief inspections of the wrecks of two of *Champlain II*'s contemporaries, the steamers *Adirondack* (1867) and *Reindeer* (1882), showed the same framing pattern (Baldwin, 1994a, 1994b, 1996, 1997; Baldwin et al., 1996; Cohn et al., 1994).

Horse-Powered Ferries.   Between 1989 and 1992, joint LCMM–INA-TAMU–UVM nautical archaeology field schools studied the remains of an unusual sidewheel vessel sunk under 15.24 m (50 ft) of water in Burlington Bay on the Vermont side of the lake. The most unusual feature of the wreck was its "engine": two horses walking atop a large wheel (Figure 5.1).

The use of horse power in boat propulsion owed much to Robert Fulton's 1807 commencement of steamboat service on the Hudson River. The advantages of paddle propulsion, safety, speed, and reliability soon became apparent, but the expense of boilers and engines, along with Fulton's 17-year monopoly on steam propulsion in New York waters, limited the ability of ferry owners to use the paddle wheel—until they realized that for short-distance crossings horse power was as effective and cheaper, and did not infringe on Fulton's monopoly. Horse-powered ferries, also known as "team boats," first achieved commercial success at New York City ferryboat crossings in 1814. Soon they were being used throughout North America, and their use continued into the early 20th century (Crisman and Cohn, 1998).

The earliest historical reference to horseboat operation on Lake Champlain dates to 1826, and boats of this type continued to serve the lake's ferry crossings until sometime in the 1860s. Although they were never very numerous (nine horse ferry operations serving seven crossings have been discovered in historical records), during their heyday in the 1830s and 1840s they made a substantial contribution to the traffic of people and goods in the Champlain Valley. Until the discovery of the wreck in Burlington Bay in 1983, almost nothing was known about the design and appearance of the lake's horse-propelled ferries. Lake Champlain's horseboat wreck, complete with machinery, is still the only known example of a once-common type of North American inland watercraft.

Investigation of the horseboat began in 1989 with the documentation of the exposed deck, machinery, frames and hull planking, followed in 1990–1992 with excavation of selected areas within the hull to examine the lower structure and record the lines (Crisman, 1991a, 1992, 1993b). The ferry's hull was double ended and was 19.2 m (63 ft) long. It had a curved stem and straight sternpost. The scantlings were of modest dimensions throughout, no doubt to lessen the hull's weight, reduce its draft, and make its propulsion easier for the horses.

The square frames were constructed in a manner not seen on any other Champlain wreck. Each frame consisted of a floor and two futtocks; the futtocks measured 10.16 cm^2 (4 in) and were not shaped from naturally curved compass timber but from straight pieces of oak by cutting them across their width for half the timber's length and bending them to shape on a mold. They may have been steamed before bending to make them more flexible.

Examination of the ferry's propulsion machinery revealed a simple but ingenious system for harnessing the motion of two horses to rotate the sidewheels. The horses walked in place on top of a large, horizontal wooden wheel called a "treadwheel." The movement of the wheel under the horses' hooves was transmitted to the ferry's axle by gears and a transmission shaft; a gearshift at the axle allowed the boat operators to reverse the motion of the sidewheels without having to turn the horses around.

Although this boat and others like it probably were not fast and their range limited by the endurance of the horses, they were inexpensive and more dependable than the sail ferries they replaced. The name of the ferry sunk in Burlington Bay has not been determined (the lake was too wide and rough at Burlington for this kind of ferry to operate on a regular basis), but there can be no doubt that it was successful at whatever crossing it served; wear and tear on the hull and its machinery indicated that it was at least 10 years old or older when it sank. It appears to have been intentionally scuttled in the bay when worn out and no longer worth repairing (Crisman and Cohn, 1993b, 1998).

Canal Boats.   Canal boats were first built in 1823, when the completion of the Champlain Canal provided a direct water link with the Hudson River. There is no question

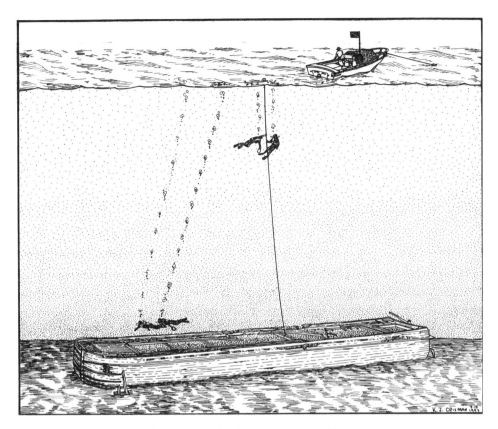

Figure 5.5. Unidentified "standard" canal boat.

that they were the most common type of commercial craft to navigate the lake in the 19th and early 20th centuries; records show that hundreds were built to haul raw materials and finished goods. Their dimensions were dictated by the canal's shallow depth and the narrow dimensions of the locks. Although the canal system was enlarged over time to accommodate larger vessels, canal boats were always relatively shallow in draft and had a high length to beam ratio, generally around 6:1. Besides their distinctively long, narrow form, canal boats are easily recognized by their boxy shape (Figure 5.5). Most were built with a chine (a hard angle where the flat bottom meets the vertical sides), and generally had full ends with blunt bows and nearly square sterns. Some early types were built with the flat bottom angling up to the deck level in the manner of a scow. Capacity was paramount, and the relatively placid waters of the canals permitted shipwrights to build these craft to hold the maximum amount of cargo.

Basic canal boat design may have been well suited for navigating canals and carrying substantial loads, but it lacked the easy lines and robust construction needed for service on the open waters of the lake. Many sank when they were under tow, and today their wrecks litter the bottom of the lake.

The Stove Boat. Despite their ubiquity, or perhaps because of it, only a limited number of canal boat wrecks have undergone archaeological study over the past two decades. One recorded example is known only as the "Stove Boat," a name referring to

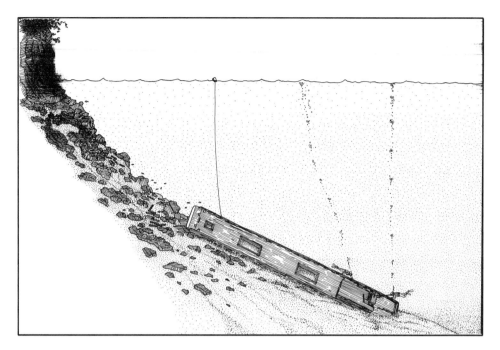

Figure 5.6. The "Stove Boat" on the bottom.

the cargo of cast iron stoves and other ironware still contained in the hold (Figure 5.6). This boat met a dramatic fate when it drifted loose from an anchorage or steamboat tow and crashed into a steep, rocky shore; it settled on a sloping bottom with its bow in 9.14 m (30 ft) of water and its stern in 24.38 m (80 ft). In 1998, the wreck was measured as part of a joint LCMM–INA-TAMU project.

The Stove Boat's dimensions and certain other characteristics indicated that it pre-dated an 1858 enlargement of the canal system. The hull measured 24.38 m (80 ft) long, 3.76 m (12 ft, 4 in) wide, and about 1.6 m (5 ft, 3 in) deep. It had sloping ends and a square-cornered deck ("scow-ended"). The deck was enclosed by a low "toe rail," and a small deckhouse with sliding shutters at the stern provided headroom in the crew's living quarters. The Stove Boat has not been identified, but we determined the approximate date of its demise after we recovered and conserved three items from the cargo: two cast iron cauldrons and a cast iron kettle with a bird's head spout. Cast into the surface of one cauldron and the kettle was the name "Noyes & Hutton," a Troy, New York, iron foundry that seems to have existed for only a few years around 1850 (LCMM, 1998–1999).

L.A. Hall.   Many canal boats that sank in service carried heavy loads of stone, ore, or raw materials that caused or contributed to their demise. One unnamed wreck near Potash Point, Vermont, went down with a weighty cargo of quarried stone blocks and seems to have "exploded" when it hit bottom. On its last voyage in 1878, the canal boat *L.A. Hall* was loaded (or overloaded) with 100 tons of pig iron bars, some stacked on deck. According to contemporary newspaper accounts, the captain and his son were awakened during the night by a mighty crash as the deck collapsed into the hold. *L.A.*

Figure 5.7. Canal boat *L.A. Hall* on the bottom.

Hall sank within seconds, but the crew managed to swim to safety. LCMM found the wreck in 1994, sunk in almost 61 m (200 ft) of water. Like the Potash Point wreck, *L.A. Hall* lies with its sides partially fallen out, yet another victim of the "let's-add-a-little-more-cargo-so-we-can-increase-our-profit'' mentality that seems to have been so prevalent among canal boat owners (Figure 5.7).

Sailing Canal Boats.   The standard canal boat had no means of propulsion and was towed by teams of mules when passing through canals, or towed by steamboats on open water.

A canal boat's inability to navigate the lake independently could have hindered the flow of commerce, particularly for northern ports located far from the canal's entrance at Whitehall. The invention of a new vessel form, ''sailing canal boats,'' was an improvement. Also known as ''lake and canal boats,'' these boats had the long, narrow, shallow hull form of towed canal boats, but were fitted with a retractable centerboard and one or two fore- and aft-rigged masts stepped on the deck in boxes called ''tabernacles.'' Once a sailing canal boat had passed through the canal, the centerboard was lowered to provide stability and lateral resistance to the wind, masts were raised and rigged, and the vessel proceeded to its destination on its own schedule.

Sailing canal boats were introduced when the canal opened in 1823. The first vessel to pass the length of the new waterway was such a craft. These vessels were in widespread use until the 1870s (Cohn and True, 1992).

Troy.   In 1999, LCMM's ongoing sonar survey of the lake turned up the schooner *Troy*, one of the earliest sailing canal boats built for the Champlain Canal. Lost in 1825 when it foundered with a load of iron ore, *Troy* sank in deep water and the ore tumbled into the bow, causing it to hit the lake floor at an extreme angle and stick. The stern still extends nearly 9.14 m (30 ft) above the bottom. An ROV inspection of this curiously

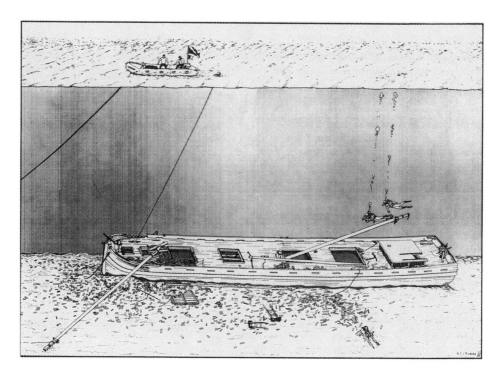

Figure 5.8. Canal schooner *O.J. Walker.*

positioned wreck showed the centerboard extended beneath the hull and mast tabernacles on deck, indicating that these features were part of the earliest sailing canalers.

General Butler and O.J. Walker. Wrecks of five sailing canal boats built between 1840 and 1862 have been discovered in the northern half of the lake. These include three unidentified sailing canal sloops sunk off Isle La Motte, Vermont, Cumberland Bay, New York, and North Beach in Burlington, Vermont, and two schooners, *General Butler* and *O.J. Walker* (Figure 5.8) both sunk in Burlington Bay, Vermont. Earlier sloops averaged fewer than 24.38 m (80 ft) long and 4.11 m (13 ft 6 in) wide; the schooners, built in response to an enlargement in the canal system in the mid-1850s, were slightly under 27.43 m (90 ft) long and 4.4 m (14 ft 6 in) wide (Cozzi, 1996).

Although all five of these sailing canal boats had a centerboard, one or two mast tabernacles, and chine construction they differed significantly in other aspects of construction. The sides of the Cumberland Bay and North Beach sloops were assembled by stacking thick hardwood and softwood planks and fastening them together with long iron bolts inserted through holes drilled in their edges. This "edge-fastened" construction saved timber and increased hold space, and it probably was just as strong as conventionally framed and planked hulls, but replacing rotten or damaged planks would have been difficult. While the three sloops had molded bows, the stern of the Cumberland Bay wreck differed from the other two; instead of a tapering design, it was built with a curving, scow-type stern.

General Butler and *O.J. Walker* were assembled with frames; floors and futtocks met at and were mortised into heavy beams or "chine logs" that ran parallel to the hull's centerline. Both schooners were reinforced longitudinally with a pair of wooden hogging trusses fastened to the interior of the frames on each side of the hull, a feature intended to keep the hull's ends from hogging.

The sloops, however, showed no evidence of hogging trusses; with their edge-fastened construction and shorter length, they might not have needed them. All five of the sailing canal boats were given additional internal reinforcement by the numerous lengths of iron tie-rod that extended both vertically and horizontally between major timbers (Cozzi, 1992, 1993a, 1993b, 1994).

Sailing canal boats were an inspired response to the changes in lake navigation and commerce wrought by the opening of the Champlain Canal. As with all ships, they were a compromise of design, construction, and performance features. Their molded ends, centerboards, and more robust construction reduced their capacity relative to standard canal boats of the same external dimensions, and they were probably challenging vessels to sail, especially in stormy conditions. For 50 years, however, they were a mainstay of lake shipping. Only in the 1870s, when railroads were beginning to bite deeply into the business of the canals, and when steam tugs for towing vessels were becoming more widely available, did owners of existing "lake and canal" boats begin stripping their masts and converting them into towed craft.

CONCLUSIONS

Over the 10,000 years humans have occupied the Champlain Valley, the nature of life and water transportation has changed, sometimes slowly and nearly imperceptibly, sometimes radically and quickly. For most of these millennia, the lake and its surrounding countryside was home to Amerindians who lived by hunting and gathering the land's bounty and who used dugout and bark canoes to travel, trade, hunt, or fish. Their way of life changed forever when the Europeans arrived in the early 17th century.

The following two centuries were unsettled times, as native people and rival European colonists vied for control of the region and its resources. In three wars between 1755 and 1815, naval flotillas were hastily assembled to meet the timetables of invasion and defense; in each instance the clash of rival ships ultimately proved decisive to the political division of North America.

The commercial era on Lake Champlain following the War of 1812 was part of the general expansion of trade and shipping enjoyed by the United States on its inland waterways and on the high seas in the 19th century. It was an era of a worldwide transportation revolution, when invention, industrialization, and economic expansion were providing new methods of propulsion, new or greater quantities of materials construction, and new approaches to ship design and assembly. The lake experienced more than a half-century of intensive commercial use by many types of passenger- and cargo-carrying vessels, but the growth of railroads in the second half of the 19th century drew trade away from the lake. By the beginning of the 20th century, only the bulkiest and cheapest cargoes were still profitable to ship.

Today the lake is a center for recreational activity, the annual destination of thousands of boaters, fishermen, divers, and similar water-sport enthusiasts. Other visitors are attracted to the lake by its aesthetic and historical qualities, the beauty of its waters, the surrounding hills and mountains, and the mystery and drama of its association with the people who shaped the early history of the United States and Canada.

Twenty years of archaeological research on Lake Champlain's shipwrecks has vastly increased our knowledge of the people and ships so central to the lake's history. Studies of sunken hulls has shown us how vessel design and construction changed over the centuries in response to changing conditions of warfare or commerce, to the development of new technologies for vessel construction, and to changes in the availability of resources, principally timber and iron, for shipbuilding. Studies of the contents of sunken ships, their cargoes, equipment, and crews' possessions, have likewise revealed new insights into the material and social culture of Lake Champlain's mariners.

REFERENCES

Baldwin, E., 1994a, My God, How Can It Be? The Wreck of the Steamship *Champlain II*. *The Institute of Nautical Archaeology Quarterly* 21(1–2):3–11.

_____, 1994b, The *Champlain II* Project: A Lake Champlain Sidewheel Steamship. In *Underwater Archaeology Proceedings from the Society for Historical Archaeology Conference*, edited by Robyn P. Woodward and Charles D. Moore. Society for Historical Archaeology.

_____, 1996, The Steamboat Wrecks of Lake Champlain. In *Underwater Archaeology*, edited by Stephen R. James, Jr. and Camille Stanley. Society for Historical Archaeology.

_____, 1997, *The Reconstruction of the Lake Champlain Sidewheel Steamer* Champlain II. Master's thesis, Department of Anthropology, Texas A&M University, College Station.

Baldwin, E., Cohn, A., Crisman, K., and McLaughlin, S., 1996, *Underwater Historic Preserve Feasibility Study of the Lake Champlain Steamboat* Champlain II, *Westport, Essex County, New York*. Lake Champlain Maritime Museum, Basin Harbor.

Barranco, A., Cohn, A., Crisman, K., Lewis, D., and Titus, T., 1999, *Lake Champlain, Lake George, and the Upper Richelieu River Naval and Military Vessel Inventory, 1742–1836*. Lake Champlain Maritime Museum, Basin Harbor.

Bazilchuk, N., Fastie, C., Heise, A., Kasmer, J., Naumann, T., Paul, R., Publicover, D., Savonen, C., Whidden, S., and Zimmerman, K., 1985, *The Physical Characteristics, Site of Discovery, and Method of Preservation of a Dugout Canoe Found at Shelburne Pond, Vermont.* Manuscript report, Department of Botany, University of Vermont, Burlington.

Bellico, R., 1992, Ghost from the Depths. *American History Illustrated* 27(1):44–49, 70.

Bratten, J., 1996, The Continental Gondola *Philadelphia*: A New Look at America's Oldest Surviving Warship. In *Underwater Archaeology*, edited by Stephen R. James, Jr. and Camille Stanley. Society for Historical Archaeology.

Bratten, J., 2000, *The Continental Gondola* Philadelphia. Texas A&M University Press, College Station.

Carter, B., 1995, *Armament Remains from His Majesty*'s Sloop Boscawen. Master's thesis, Department of Anthropology, Texas A&M University, College Station.

Cassavoy, K., and Crisman, K., 1988, The War of 1812: Battle for the Great Lakes. In *Ships and Shipwrecks of the Americas*, edited by George F. Bass. Thames and Hudson, London.

Cohn, A., 1995a, Archaeology, History, and Public Policy: The Results of the Submerged Cultural Resource Project at Lake Champlain's Fort Ticonderoga and Mount Independence, 1992–1993. In *Underwater Archaeology Proceedings*, edited by Paul F. Johnston. Society for Historical Archaeology.

_____, 1995b, *The Great Bridge: From Ticonderoga to Independant Point.* Demonstration Report No. 4C, Lake Champlain Basin Program Publication Series.

_____, 1995c, *The Fort Ticonderoga–Mount Independence Submerged Cultural Resources Survey.* Executive summary, Lake Champlain Basin Program Publication Series.

_____, editor, 1984, *A Report on the Nautical Archaeology of Lake Champlain: Results of the 1982 Field Season of the Champlain Maritime Society.* The Champlain Maritime Society, Burlington.

Cohn, A., and True, M., 1992, The Wreck of the *General Butler* and the Mystery of Lake Champlain's Sailing Canal Boats. *Vermont History* 60(1):29–45.

Cohn, A., Crisman, K., and Baldwin, E., 1994, *Underwater Historic Preserve Feasibility Study of the Lake Champlain Steamboat* Champlain II. Manuscript on file, Division for Historic Preservation, Montpelier.

Cohn, Arthur and Barranco, A. Peter, in preparation, American Gunboats on Lake Champlain in 1776. Draft chapter in preparation for Gunboat Wreck Management Report to the Naval Historical Center, U.S. Navy, Washington, DC.

Cozzi, J., 1992, The North Beach Wreck: A Solid Wall of Timber. *Institute of Nautical Archaeology Quarterly* 19(2):14–16.

_____, 1993a, The North Beach Wreck: A Modern Example of Edge-fastened Construction. In *Underwater Archaeology Proceedings*, edited by Sheli O. Smith. Society for Historical Archaeology.

_____, 1993b, *North Beach Wreck: Report of the 1992 Field Season.* Manuscript on file, Division for Historic Preservation, Montpelier.

_____, 1994, Chine Construction on Sailing Canal Boats of Lake Champlain. In *Underwater Archaeology Proceedings from the Society for Historical Archaeology Conference*, edited by Robyn P. Woodward and Charles D. Moore. Society for Historical Archaeology.

_____, 1996, The Lake Champlain Sailing Canal Boat. In *Underwater Archaeology*, edited by Stephen R. James Jr. and Camille Stanley. Society for Historical Archaeology.

Crisman, K., 1983, *The History and Construction of the United States Schooner* Ticonderoga. Eyrie Publications, Alexandria.

_____, 1986, *Of Sailing Ships and Sidewheelers.* Division for Historic Preservation, Montpelier.

_____, 1987, *The* Eagle: *An American Brig on Lake Champlain During the War of 1812.* The New England Press and the Naval Institute Press, Shelburne and Annapolis.

_____, 1988, Struggle for a Continent: Naval Battles of the French and Indian War. In *Ships and Shipwrecks of the Americas*, edited by George F. Bass, pp. 129–148. Thames and Hudson, London.

_____, 1991a, Horsepower on the Water: The Burlington Bay Horse Ferry Project. *Institute of Nautical Archaeology Newsletter* 18(4):12–15.

_____, 1991b, The Lake Brigs *Jefferson* and *Eagle*. *Seaways* II(4):5–9.

_____, 1992, Horseboat, Canal Boat, and Floating Bridge: The 1992 Field Season on Lake Champlain. *Institute of Nautical Archaeology Quarterly* 19(4):17–20.

_____, 1993a, Relics of the Revolution and a Schooner Called *Water Witch*. *Institute of Nautical Archaeology Quarterly* 20(4):22–30.

_____, 1993b, The Design and Construction of a Horse-powered Sidewheel Ferry Sunk in Burlington Bay, Lake Champlain. In *Underwater Archaeology Proceedings*, edited by Sheli O. Smith. Society for Historical Archaeology.

_____, 1995a, Coffins of the Brave: A Return to Lake Champlain's War of 1812 Ship Graveyard. *Institute of Nautical Archaeology Quarterly* 22(1):4–8.

_____, 1995b, *The 1992 Mount Independence Phase One Underwater Archaeological Survey*. Demonstration Report No. 4B, Lake Champlain Basin Program Publication Series.

_____, 1996, The Nautical Archaeology of Lake Champlain: Research from 1980 to 1995. In *Underwater Archaeology*, edited by Stephen R. James and Camille Stanley. Society for Historical Archaeology.

Crisman, K., and Cohn, A., 1993a, *The Lake Champlain Schooner* Water Witch. Manuscript on file, Division for Historic Preservation, Montpelier.

_____, 1993b, *The Burlington Bay Horse Ferry Wreck and the Era of Horse-powered Watercraft*. Manuscript on file, Division for Historic Preservation, Montpelier, Vt.

_____, 1994, Lake Champlain Nautical Archaeology Since 1980. *The Journal of Vermont Archaeology*: 153–166.

_____, 1998, *When Horses Walked on Water: Horse-powered Ferries in Nineteenth-Century America*. Smithsonian Institution Press, Washington.

Davison, R., editor, 1981, *The* Phoenix *Project*. Champlain Maritime Society, Burlington.

Emery, E., 1995, Whitehall Project 1995: A Preliminary Report on the Excavation and Study of the U.S.N. Row Galley *Allen*. *Institute of Nautical Archaeology Quarterly* 22(4):9–14.

_____, 1996, Gallies are Unquestionably the Best Description of Vessels for the Northern Parts of this Lake: The Excavation and Study of the USN Row Galley *Allen* on Lake Champlain. In *Underwater Archaeology*, edited by Stephen R. James and Camille Stanley. Society for Historical Archaeology.

Erwin, G., 1994, *Personal Possessions from the HMS* Boscawen: *Life on Board a Mid-Eighteenth-Century Warship during the French and Indian War*. Master's thesis, Department of Anthropology, Texas A&M University, College Station.

Fischer, R., editor, 1985, *A Report on the Nautical Archaeology of Lake Champlain*. Champlain Maritime Society, Burlington.

Flanigan, A., 1999, *The Rigging Material from the* Boscawen: *Setting the Sails of a Mid-Eighteenth-Century Warship during the French and Indian War*. Master's thesis, Department of Anthropology, Texas A&M University, College Station.

Grant, D., 1996, *Tools from the French and Indian War Sloop* Boscawen. Master's thesis, Department of Anthropology, Texas A&M University, College Station.

Hadden, J., 1995, *Ceramics from the American Steamboat* Phoenix *(1815–1819), and Their Role in Understanding Shipboard Life*. Master's thesis, Department of Anthropology, Texas A&M University, College Station.

Haviland, W., and Power, M., 1994, *The Original Vermonters*. University Press of New England, Hanover.

Hill, R., 1976, *Lake Champlain: Key to a Continent*. The Countryman Press, Woodstock.

Krueger, J., Cohn, A., Crisman, K., and Miksch, H., 1985, The Fort Ticonderoga King's Shipyard Excavation. *Bulletin of Fort Ticonderoga Museum* 14(6):335–436.

Lake Champlain Maritime Museum, 1998–1999, *LCMnews*, Fall & Winter.

Lundeberg, P., 1995, *The Gunboat* Philadelphia *and the Defense of Lake Champlain in 1776*. Lake Champlain Maritime Museum, Basin Harbor.

McLaughlin, S., 2000, *History Told from the Depths of Lake Champlain: 1992–1993 Fort Ticonderoga-Mount Independence Submerged Cultural Resource Survey*. Master's thesis, Department of Anthropology, Texas A&M University, College Station.

Paine, G., 1998, Ord's Arks: Angles, Artillery and Ambush on Lakes George and Champlain. *American Neptune* 58(2):105–122.

Washburn, E., 1996a, The Story of HMS *Linnet*, A Brig from the War of 1812. In *Underwater Archaeology*, edited by Stephen R. James and Camille Stanley. Society for Historical Archaeology.

_____, 1996b, *Linnet*: A Brig from the War of 1812. *Institute of Nautical Archaeology Quarterly* 23(1):14–19.

_____, 1998, Linnet: *The History and Archaeology of a Brig from the War of 1812*. Master's thesis, Department of Anthropology, Texas A&M University, College Station.

Chapter 6

Lake George, New York
Recent Archaeological Investigations at a Mountain Waterway

JOSEPH W. ZARZYNSKI

INTRODUCTION

Lake George is 51.2 km (32 mi.) long and located in the Adirondack Mountains of New York State (Figure 6.1). It is part of the historic Hudson River–Lake George–Lake Champlain corridor, noteworthy as the scene of significant frontier battles during the French and Indian War (1755–1763) and the American Revolution (1775–1783). During the 19th and 20th centuries, the lake attracted tourists and boaters to visit its historic sites and enjoy its great natural beauty. The lake was a well traveled "road" of commerce, too, as work barges transported products of the region. Thus, it is no coincidence that the cold mountain waters of the "Queen of American Lakes" hold a collection of historical watercraft that offers great potential for archaeological study.

One colonial incident on Lake George, which would later become a catalyst for underwater archaeology, was a little-known but eventful British naval action, the deliberate sinking of more than 260 British and provincial warships in 1758. Placed into cold and wet storage to prevent capture by marauding French and their Indian allies, these wooden ghosts of the deep are today referred to as the Sunken Fleet of 1758.

Joseph W. Zarzynski, Bateaux Below, Inc., Wilton, New York 12831.

International Handbook of Underwater Archaeology, edited by Carol V. Ruppé and Janet F. Barstad. Kluwer Academic/Plenum Publishers, New York, 2002.

Figure 6.1. Lake George, New York. A historic waterway located in the Adirondack Mountains of New York. (Bateaux Below, Inc.)

This chapter gives a brief account of Lake George's French and Indian War history as background for understanding the public and scholarly interest in the lake's colonial shipwrecks. It also will examine recent archaeological investigations, especially the study of the Sunken Fleet of 1758, discuss public access to shipwrecks through the establishment of shipwreck preserves, and give details of underwater heritage inventory projects.

THE FRENCH AND INDIAN WAR

The French and Indian War (1755–1763) was the culmination of several colonial wars fought between the French and English. These included King William's War (1689–1697), Queen Anne's War (1702–1713), and King George's War (1744–1748).

During the decisive French and Indian War, Lake George was a major theater of conflict. In 1755, British and provincial troops built Fort William Henry at the south end of this long and narrow frontier waterway. Fort William Henry's wood and earth stronghold was opposed by two nearby French forts, St. Frédéric and Carillon (the latter later known as Ticonderoga), both situated on Lake Champlain.

During the war's early stages, both sides launched offensives to push the other from the region. In March 1757, the French sent 1600 soldiers to destroy Fort William Henry. After crossing ice-covered Lake George, the French could not overwhelm the fortification, but they burned 350 British bateaux and several other larger warships that lay ashore near the fort. In August of that year, however, a second French siege was successful, and the fort surrendered (Bellico, 1992). The capitulation of Fort William Henry and a reputed massacre were immortalized in James Fenimore Cooper's 1826 novel, *The Last of the Mohicans.*

In July 1758, 15,000 British and provincial troops were ferried north over Lake George in 900 bateaux, 135 whaleboats, and several other warships to fight the French at Lake Champlain's Fort Carillon. This was the largest army and naval armada ever assembled in North America. Though they outnumbered the French, the British forces were defeated, and they withdrew to their base at the south end of the lake and undertook a massive boat-building campaign, planning to return to Carillon before the end of 1758.

As winter approached, it became obvious that General Abercromby's army and mountain navy could not besiege Fort Carillon again that year, and the decision was grudgingly made to sink the fleet. King George II's soldiers had learned a painful lesson during the March 1757, French attack at Fort William Henry. Therefore, without a defensible fortification at Lake George and with memories of 350 warships burned during the March 1757 French offensive, British regulars and their provincial allies began sinking their naval squadron. Two 12.2 m (40 ft) row galleys were sunk at Lake George on October 16, 1758. (Bellico, 1992).

Captain Samuel Cobb, a 39-year-old shipwright who commanded Massachusetts soldiers, wrote in his journal that on October 22, 1758, only two days after their launching, "Working on the Raddows Sinking them in the lake" (Cobb, 1981). By the time the process was complete, before the end of October 1758, the British had put down the *Land Tortoise* radeau plus a second smaller radeau, numerous whaleboats, two row galleys, the sloop *Halifax*, and 260 bateaux (Bellico, 1992). Furthermore, according to British Colonel John Bradstreet, 30 bateaux were also "hid in the woods near Lake George. . . " (Public Records Office).

After visiting the abandoned British encampment, the French reported finding "the location of the bark [sloop *Halifax*], fifty sunken barges [bateaux], and several other caches in a neighboring swamp" (Bourgainville, 1964). Nonetheless, the British fleet would be safe in the cold lake waters. Retrieval was scheduled for 1759, when British regulars and provincials returned to Lake George.

Fortunately for archaeology today, the British war effort of 1759 moved quickly and decisively from Lake George to Lake Champlain. British General Jeffery Amherst, General Abercromby's replacement, launched a triumphant military invasion against the two French fortresses at Lake Champlain, so that he and his forces never recovered many of the warships of the Sunken Fleet of 1758. Yet, before leaving Lake George, Amherst's troops raised the sloop *Halifax,* though it was a 10-day effort (Bellico, 1992). Lemuel Wood, a Massachusetts provincial, also reported that "a Row galley that had been sunk Last fall was found and got up to shoer" (Wood, 1882). Other wrecks of the Sunken Fleet of 1758 had to await modern-day explorers with the technology and willingness to learn more about these historic warships.

EARLY INTEREST IN SHIPWRECKS

Renewed interest in the Sunken Fleet of 1758 and other colonial shipwrecks of Lake George began as early as 1893. On June 10, 1893, the *Lake George Mirror*, a local newspaper, printed an article that described four sunken bateaux visible in the clear lake waters and speculated that one "could be successfully brought to land and placed on exhibition."

On July 2, 1903, a 13.4 m (44 ft) × 4.27 m (14 ft) colonial shipwreck, one of the British warships destroyed during the French raid of March 1757, was raised from 4.57 m (15 ft) of water from the south end of Lake George. The wooden skeleton yielded several colonial artifacts, including a 1743 Spanish coin, before the hulk was eventually cut up for souvenirs (Bellico, 1992). Today, both the Lake George Historical Association and Fort William Henry museums have timbers in their collections thought to be from the 1757 warship.

Decades later, some Lake Georgians touted a more preservationist ethic toward the lake's shipwrecks. On August 18, 1934, the *Lake George Mirror* published a short article suggesting that a "war bateaux [sic]" be raised and properly housed in a museum.

MODERN INTEREST IN SHIPWRECKS

In 1953, W. Carleton Dunn, a young scuba diver, made several dives in the shallows of Lake George's south basin and recovered artifacts for the Fort William Henry Corporation, a businessman's group restoring Fort William Henry as a location for heritage tourism. During one dive, Dunn reported seeing mounds of rocks sitting on sunken warships, apparently put there to help sink them (Dunn, 1997).

In 1960, two teenage divers, Fred Bolt and Dick LaVoy, unexpectedly discovered 10–15 bateaux lying in shallow waters off the southeast corner of the lake. The bateaux were believed to come from the Sunken Fleet of 1758 (Barr, 1960). A few months after the Bolt and LaVoy find, three bateaux were raised from the lake bottom. After conservation, one bateau was exhibited at the Adirondack Museum, Blue Mountain Lake, New York; the other two were put into archival storage by the State of New York. The 1960 discovery of these sunken bateaux was indeed the spark for today's fascination in Lake George's colonial shipwrecks.

The years 1963 and 1964 were benchmark dates in the underwater archaeology of Lake George. Under an archaeological permit issued by the State of New York, archaeological diver Terry Crandall conducted dozens of searches for sunken colonial warships. His project, dubbed "Operation Bateaux," located, mapped, and photographed several clusters of the sunken craft. Crandall's attention to detail and his scientific methodology set a standard for the time and is admired by archaeologists even today.

On July 27, 1965, the *New York Times* published an article entitled "Lake George Divers Find 1758 Battle Craft." The account outlined what were called "salvage operations" by more than 30 state police divers who planned to raise "the remains of at least eight bateaux" scuttled in 1758 (Johnston, 1965). Unfortunately, no detailed written reports of this so-called salvage operation exist except a few contemporary newspaper stories.

Since the 1960s, many divers visiting Lake George have explored those waters, looking for remains from the Sunken Fleet of 1758 and other historic wrecks. Unfortunately, some discoveries have resulted in vandalism at many sites. In 1987, however, a group of divers, trained in basic underwater archaeology techniques and sensitive to historic preservation, revived serious interest in studying the lake's historic shipwrecks. Several of the divers later founded a nonprofit educational corporation,

Bateaux Below, Inc., whose goals were to locate and study Lake George wrecks, to complete a lakewide underwater heritage inventory, and to nominate historic shipwrecks to the National Register of Historic Places.

BATEAUX

Wiawaka Bateaux

Bateaux Below's first project was a study of seven 1758 wrecks known as the Wiawaka bateaux, named after the Wiawaka Holiday House near the shipwrecks' location. The Wiawaka bateaux, each approximately 9.15 m (30 ft) long, lie in 6.1–12.2 m (20–40 ft) of water on a gradual, soft-sediment slope. Rocks used to help sink the ships were found inside or adjacent to the wrecks and holes drilled in the bottom planking to facilitate sinking were still noticeable.

In 1991, Bateaux Below completed its four-year survey of the Wiawaka bateaux. In 1992, the seven bateaux were nominated and listed on the National Register of Historic Places, a noteworthy event since only one other shipwreck in New York state, the Revolutionary War 74-gun British frigate HMS *Culloden* off Long Island, was listed (Shaver, 1993).

Bateaux: Their Construction

The colonial bateau (plural: *bateaux*) was the utilitarian watercraft of its era. Though the word "bateau" is French for "boat," its construction shows some Dutch influence. Generally, bateaux were 7.62–10.67 m (25–35 ft) long and pointed at bow and stern. Rather simple in construction, they were fashioned from pine planks and had oak frames and metal fasteners. Bottom planks were held in place by plank battens or cross-pieces, which were caulked to minimize leaking. Bateaux had axe-hewn oak frames about 0.61 m (2 ft) apart. The curved stempost and rather straight sternpost were made of oak or another local hardwood.

Bateaux were powered by rowing, poled in shallow water, and sometimes rigged with a crude mast and sail (Hager, 1987). They were rowed with four to six oars for power, and an additional oar, rather than a rudder, was latched off the stern for steerage. In 1963 and 1964, Crandall found structural evidence of wooden thole pins and thole pin blocks used to hold oars. Historical accounts indicate that six colonial soldiers could build a bateau in two days, including sawing the planks (Hamilton, 1964).

Mark L. Peckham of New York's Office of Parks, Recreation, and Historic Preservation and an amateur boat builder constructed a 7.01 m (23 ft) colonial bateau replica. Peckham noted that "handling the bateau on land can only be described as miserable. . . A 30-foot [9.15 m] bateau of the kind found sunken in Lake George would have been almost impossible to carry overland without the use of a special carriage. Perhaps that is why many of Lake George's sunken bateaux of 1758 were never recovered" (Peckham, 1996).

THE 1758 RADEAU *LAND TORTOISE*

On June 26, 1990, members of Bateaux Below, Inc., used a Klein 595 side scan sonar to discover another member of the Sunken Fleet of 1758 (see Martin Klein, Chapter 39, this volume, for details on side scan sonar). While searching for colonial bateau shipwrecks, the five-person remote sensing team (Bob Benway, Vincent J. Capone, John Farrell, David Van Aken, and Joseph W. Zarzynski) discovered the *Land Tortoise*, an intact 15.85 m (52 ft) × 5.49 m (18 ft) radeau, now recognized by the Smithsonian Institution as "the oldest intact war vessel in North America" (Lundeberg, 1995). The strange seven-sided vessel sits upright in 32.62 m (107 ft) of water in the middle of the lake, well preserved by its cold freshwater environment.

Radeau is a French word meaning "raft," a type of floating gun battery or small floating fort. Historian Russell P. Bellico described a radeau as flat-bottomed with "the lower sides. . . inclined slightly outward while the upper sides or bulwarks curved inward at a steep angle over the interior of the vessel. The upper sides, fitted with cannon ports, fully enclosed and protected 'ye men's Bodys & Heads' and 'contrived so that its impossible for the Enemy to board her'" (Bellico, 1995).

Bateaux Below, Inc., and other volunteers studied the *Land Tortoise* from 1991 to 1994 under the direction of D. K. Abbass, a Rhode Island archaeologist. Since the *Land Tortoise* is the only existing radeau-class vessel, much was learned from the investigation.

The *Land Tortoise* is seven-sided, with an oak hull and upper pine bulwarks (Figure 6.2). It is undecked, with 16 oak frames per side. Every hull frame has a corresponding stanchion to support the upper bulwarks. Two view holes are located in the bow, one port and one starboard. The hull is caulked and tarred. It has four mooring rings, two forward and two aft, and is fastened together with wooden treenails and iron nails or drifts.

The *Land Tortoise* has 26 sweep holes, 13 port and 13 starboard. Mast steps were found inside the vessel, but no rigging. The warship's sides were pierced for seven

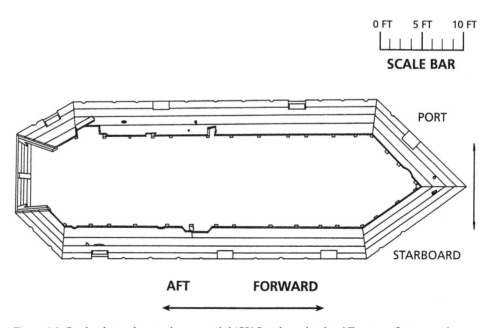

Figure 6.2. Overhead view showing the seven-sided 1758 British warship *Land Tortoise*, a floating gun battery shipwreck lying in Lake George, New York. (SOURCE: Bateaux Below, Inc. and K. Norton. © 1993 Bateaux Below, Inc.)

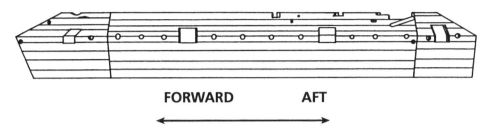

Figure 6.3. Drawing of the 1758 *Land Tortoise* radeau shipwreck, showing its great structural integrity. (SOURCE: Bateaux Below, Inc.)

cannons (four on the port and three on the starboard), and its cannon port positions were offset to accommodate cannon recoil (Abbass et al., 1992). Because the *Land Tortoise* had a short career, and because she was apparently stripped of her armament before sinking, no colonial artifacts were found. The true treasure of this warship is its unusual naval design and its structural integrity (Figure 6.3).

In 1993–1994, Bateaux Below's Bob Benway, a photographer, and Kendrick McMahan, a computer technician, created a photomosaic of the entire wreck, a project partially funded by the Lake Champlain Basin Program. After photographing each section of the wreck, they assembled the resultant 200 photographs into a photomosaic, which they photographed and digitally removed the seams. This photographic map documented the wreck, created baseline data for future cultural resource management strategies, and provided a single image that showed the entire wreck from an overhead perspective.

The *Land Tortoise* was listed on the National Register of Historic Places in 1995. In 1998, the radeau was listed as a National Historic Landmark, only the sixth shipwreck so designated, testimony to its historic significance and uniqueness.

SUBMERGED HERITAGE PRESERVES

To share these submerged cultural resources with the public, the State of New York, in partnership with several local government agencies and nonprofit corporations, created the state's first shipwreck preserves. In September 1993, two shipwreck sites, one a 1906 gasoline-powered launch named the *Forward*, and the other the seven Wiawaka bateau shipwrecks dubbed "The Sunken Fleet of 1758," opened as an underwater park or shipwreck museum for diving enthusiasts. Each site is marked by both a mooring buoy and a navigation buoy. Underwater trail lines and signs guide divers around each preserve. A state-produced brochure gives background on the two preserves and includes site histories, suggested reading lists, regulations, emergency information, preserve location map, and a diagram explaining mooring procedures. The *Forward* and colonial bateaux preserves are open from Memorial Day weekend (last weekend and Monday in May) into October and can be visited on a first-come, first-served basis.

The *Land Tortoise*: A 1758 Floating Gun Battery

In August 1994, the *Land Tortoise* was added to the shipwreck preserve park. However, due to the wreck's fragile structure, and because it is a deep dive (32.62 m/107 ft), visitation is by registration only. Three time slots a day from the second weekend in June to Labor Day (first Monday of September) allow divers to visit the radeau, restricted to no more than eight divers per time slot.

Before the opening of the preserve, Bateaux Below constructed a "ring-around-a-radeau," a plastic perimeter around the vessel to discourage divers from touching this fragile French and Indian War icon. Supports for the protective barrier were 3.66–4.57 m (12–15 ft) tall × .1 m (4 in.) diameter white polyvinyl chloride (PVC) pipes, each of which was driven ±2.13 m (7 ft) into the soft-sediment lake bottom. The pipes serve as stanchions to support a white plastic chain erected around the wreck forming the "ring," and the chain is attached to each PVC stanchion with breakaway ties in case it gets snagged by a wayward anchor or fishing gear. This barrier allows divers to view the radeau from 1.22–1.52 m (4–5 ft) away but discourages touching of the one-of-a-kind wreck. At regular intervals around the wreck, signs are attached to the stanchions, informing divers where they are on the site and providing safety advice (Zarzynski et al., 1996).

Replica Bateau

On September 7, 1997, "The Sunken Fleet of 1758" preserve (also known as Wiawaka bateaux) was enhanced by the addition of a colonial bateau replica that was a third smaller than the original. Bateaux Below and state officials deliberately sank the replica bateau to test hypotheses about colonial sinking techniques and to provide visiting divers with an example of how an intact bateau would look.

Prior to sinking the replica, rocks were weighed, and it was determined that 1491 pounds of rocks would provide the necessary weight to put and keep the vessel down. This amount was calculated from the weight of rocks used to keep the 7.01 m (23 ft) replica sunk in 1.22 m (4 ft) of water while the vessel's planks swelled to minimize the openings between planks. Then the rocks were removed, the replica refloated, and the rocks and bateau transported to the Wiawaka bateaux site for the September 7 scuttling.

Planning for the deliberate sinking involved studying historic journals to gain insight into how British military forces of 1758 scuttled their fleet with the intention of raising the ships the following year. The journals offered few details. Therefore a plan, based upon conjecture and the limited journal entries, was devised to sink the replica in a manner we believed the British might have used in 1758.

Before the sinking, a line was tied to the bateau's bow, run ashore, and wrapped around a tree. Another line, tied to an anchor, was rigged from the stern and the anchor sunk. There is no evidence that a stern anchor was used by the soldiers in 1758, but this strategy provided an easy way to orient the vessel in the desired direction. Thus, the replica bateau was pointed perpendicular to shore and designed to sink onto a gradual slope, an orientation that would match that of six of the seven 1758 bateaux at the Wiawaka site and be in the direction to pull them toward shore during the retrieval process. Small circular holes, like those found on some of the Wiawaka bateaux, were drilled into the replica to facilitate sinking.

As the replica bateau sank, it came to rest on a slight slope in more than 12.2 m (40 ft) of water, first hitting bottom in shallow water, then sliding down the slope.

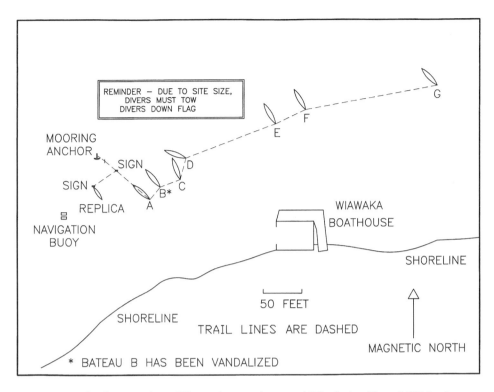

REMINDER — DUE TO SITE SIZE,
DIVERS MUST TOW
DIVERS DOWN FLAG

MOORING
ANCHOR

SIGN

SIGN

REPLICA

NAVIGATION
BUOY

A

B*   C

D

E

F

G

WIAWAKA

BOATHOUSE

SHORELINE

50 FEET

SHORELINE

TRAIL LINES ARE DASHED

MAGNETIC NORTH

* BATEAU B HAS BEEN VANDALIZED

Figure 6.4. Replica bateau sunk in 1997 near the seven bateaux of "The Sunken Fleet of 1758," enhancing this shipwreck preserve in Lake George, New York. (SOURCE: Bateaux Below, Inc.)

We learned several things from that scuttling exercise. First, more rocks than originally anticipated were needed to sink and hold down the replica; it required about 1800 to 1850 pounds of rocks to sink. Second, it must have been a major effort for the British to collect rocks, place them in bateaux, row out to the locations selected for sinking, and scuttle more than 260 warships. Third, the vessels sunk in 1758 ended up at a depth, location, and vessel orientation from which they could easily be raised the following year. After it was sunk, the replica bateau's centerline axis was approximately 325 degrees, an angle that matched well with six of the seven 1758 Wiawaka bateaux (Figure 6.4), whose centerlines ranged from 310 to 340 degrees. Fourth, the replica bateau came to rest in moderately deep water, more than 12.2 m (40 ft), quite possibly like the Wiawaka bateaux of 1758. In 1759, this would have prohibited free divers from swimming down to the bateaux, removing the sinking rocks, and refloating the sunken warships or pulling them in to shore. Did Wiawaka's colonial bateaux, found today on a slope in 6.1–12.2 m (20–40 ft) of water, sink in water deeper than anticipated, thus contributing to the reason British forces never retrieved them?

The 1997 bateau sinking probably replicated rather closely the procedures used and the placement of the Wiawaka bateaux. Following this experiment, there was greater admiration for the engineering skills of those colonial British regulars and provincials for their skill in sinking and retrieving their warships.

In addition to the knowledge gained from the sinking replica, the replica itself will be examined over the years to study its rate of deterioration in a cold freshwater environment, a process that is little understood (Zarzynski, 1997).

THE "*FORWARD* UNDERWATER CLASSROOM"

In June 1998, Bateaux Below, Inc., completed a two-year conversion of the *Forward* preserve into "The *Forward* Underwater Classroom." The site transformation was financed by a grant from The Fund for Lake George, Inc., a local environmental watchdog group. The remodeled preserve was designed not only to provide recreation for divers but to also promote stewardship of the lake's environmental and cultural resources.

"The *Forward* Underwater Classroom" lies in 6.1–13.72 m (20–45 ft) of water. A 152.43 m (500 ft) trail leads divers to stations near the 13.72 m (45 ft)-long *Forward* wreck. New features added to the existing 1906-era gasoline motor launch wreck include a wooden cabin cruiser that was deliberately sunk in 1997 (which created a simulated underwater archaeological laboratory for divers), and a fish observation zone. Other site stations explain color loss underwater at depth, describe site geology and vegetation, include a secchi disk where divers measure horizontal water transparency, direct divers along a navigation course, have thermometers for divers to record water temperature patterns, and include a zebra mussel monitoring station. This site has become a favorite of divers interested in the diversity offered by the underwater classroom.

Lake George's Submerged Heritage Preserves are an experiment in public access for shipwrecks. Most divers have treated these cultural resources with great respect. Unfortunately, there has been vandalism at all three sites. Thus the experiment is still on trial. Nevertheless, the New York State Divers Association received a 1998 Maritime Heritage Grant from the National Park Service for "Diving Historical Sites in New York," which funded a program to educate recreational divers about shipwreck preservation concerns when diving historic sites. Such programs help instill a shipwreck preservation mentality among divers.

SUBMERGED CULTURAL RESOURCES INVENTORY

In 1995, Bateaux Below initiated a systematic inventory of Lake George's submerged cultural resources, which covered a 7.2 km (4.5 mi.) × ±1.6 km (1 mi.) zone from the south end of Lake George to Canoe Island. The one-year inventory was funded by a grant from the Preservation League of New York State. It involved four days of remote sensing using a Klein side scan sonar, operated by Vincent J. Capone, and searches by divers to ground-truth sonar targets and revisit previously known underwater heritage sites. All site locations were noted and videographed, and basic data about each resource were recorded.

The result of the project was that 35 submerged cultural resources were studied and added to the inventory list, including 32 wreck sites, one possible wreck whose classification is pending, one submerged marine rail ballasted with marble, and one old, L-shaped dock cribbing.

The total wrecks in the 32 wreck sites numbered at least 60 and included approximately 35 colonial bateaux, one 1758 radeau, one submarine, seven rowboats, two skiff-like vessels, one wooden cruiser, three runabouts, four launches, one modern canoe,

Figure 6.5. A research submarine, brought to Lake George to photograph 18th century shipwrecks, stolen from its dock and sunk in 1960. The vessel was found during a shipwreck inventory in 1995. (SOURCE: Bateaux Below, Inc.)

one guideboat, one excursion steamboat, one sailboat, one inflatable boat, and one motor-sailor. Since 1995, two more wrecks—a modern work boat and a colonial bateau—have been found in the inventory area.

A 4.57 m (15 ft) yellow research submarine (Figure 6.5) was a unique find. Built in 1960 to photograph bateaux of the Sunken Fleet of 1758, it was stolen from its dock in 1960 and was one of the lake's great mysteries until its 1995 discovery.

Recently, Scott Padeni of Bateaux Below completed an archaeological survey and shipwreck inventory of the northern end of Lake George at an area known as the "Landing," at Ticonderoga, New York, where water depths in the area do not exceed 3.05 m (10 ft). Survey techniques consisted of scuba and free-swimming searches, and ground-penetrating radar remote sensing. When submerged cultural resources were found, their location, type of vessel or resource, general dimensions, and depths were noted and photographs and videotapes were made at each site. The survey was funded in part by the Lake Champlain Basin Program with assistance from the Lake Champlain Maritime Museum and Bateaux Below, Inc.

Padeni's inventory resulted in the discovery of "over 15 watercraft and other archaeological sites...within the search area. (Padeni, 1998). Of the 15 shipwrecks, two were colonial warships, seven were barges, three were steamboats, one was a naptha- or gasoline-powered vessel, one was a rowboat, and one was a sailboat. The barges, the most prevalent wreck type found, carried graphite, iron ore, coal, timber, and other products. The identity of the two colonial wrecks is still to be determined, but future archaeological investigations planned for these wrecks will undoubtedly classify their type and origin (Padeni, 1998).

ZEBRA MUSSELS

In 1996, Bateaux Below, assisted by a grant from The Fund for Lake George, Inc., began monitoring Lake George's shipwreck preserves for the presence of zebra mussels, since nearby lakes are infested with this exotic species, a thumbnail-sized mollusk that came into the United States from Europe in 1988. When zebra mussels colonize a waterway, they attach to hard substrate surfaces such as rocks, docks, water intake pipes—and shipwrecks. Their weight can collapse fragile structures, which makes them one of the greatest threats to historic wrecks.

In 1999, zebra mussels were discovered in Lake George. However, quick action by Rensselaer Polytechnic Institute's Darrin Fresh Water Institute has minimized the infestation of this species. So far, less than one acre of the lake's bottomlands have adult zebra mussels. Thus, Lake George offers archaeologists wonderful opportunities to study pristine, zebra-mussel-free shipwrecks.

CONCLUSION

Through programs such as those detailed in the chapter, we hope Lake George's underwater heritage will continue to be a time capsule, providing scubaphiles with exciting "dives into history" while also allowing researchers and scholars opportunities to study history's footprints.

REFERENCES

Abbass, D.K., Cembrola, Robert, and Zarzynski, Joseph W., 1992, The Lake George Radeau: An Intact Vessel of 1758. In *Underwater Archaeology Proceedings from the Society for Historical Archaeology Conference*, edited by Donald H. Keith and Toni L. Carrell, pp. 142–147. Society for Historical Archaeology, Kingston, Jamaica.

Barr, Dan, 1960, Teenage Scuba Divers Discovered Lake George Relics: Historical Boat Finds Authenticated. *Times-Union*, Albany, New York, July 25.

Bellico, Russell P., 1992, *Sails and Steam in the Mountains—A Maritime and Military History of Lake George and Lake Champlain*. Purple Mountain Press, Fleischmanns.

——————, 1995, *Chronicles of Lake George—Journeys in War and Peace*. Purple Mountain Press, Fleischmanns.

Bourganville, Louis Antoine de, 1964, *Adventure in the Wilderness. The American Journals of Louis Antoine de Bourgainville* 1756–1760. Translated and edited by Edward P. Hamilton. University of Oklahoma Press, Norman.

Cobb, Samuel, 1981, The Journal of Captain Samuel Cobb. *Bulletin of the Fort Ticonderoga Museum* 14, Summer:12–31.

Dunn, W. Carleton, 1997, Conversations with W. Carleton Dunn.

Hager, Robert E., 1987, *Mohawk River Boats and Navigation before 1820*. Canal Boat Society of New York State, Syracuse.

Hamilton, Edward P., 1964, *Fort Ticonderoga—Key to a Continent*. Little, Brown & Company, Boston.

Johnston, Richard J.H., 1965, Lake George Divers Find 1758 Battle Craft. *New York Times*, July 27.

The Lake George Mirror. 1893, 1934. Lake George, New York: p. 8, 3.

Lundeberg, Philip K., 1995, Letter to Dr. D.K. Abbass, April 17.

Padeni, Scott, 1998, *Sunken Barges in Northern Lake George*. Paper presented at Heritage Tourism in the Adirondacks Conference, October 31, 1998, Lake George.

Peckham, Mark L., 1996, Insights Gained from a Replica Lake George Bateau. *Lake George Nautical Newsletter* 5(2), pp. 1, 7. Bateaux Below, Inc., Wilton, New York.

Public Records Office. London, 160, 34, 57–58, Folio 21, British Museum War Office.

Shaver, Peter D., 1990, *National Register of Historic Places in New York State*. Compiled for the Preservation League of New York State. Rizzoli International Publications, Inc., New York.

Wood, Lemuel, 1882, Diaries Kept by Lemuel Wood, of Boxford. In *The Essex Institute Historical Collections* 19 (1882), pp. 61–80, 143–192.

Zarzynski, Joseph W., Abbass, D.K., Benway, Bob, and Farrell, John, 1996, Ring-Around-A-Radeau, or, Fencing in a 1758 Shipwreck for Public Access and Preservation. In *Underwater Archaeology*, edited by Stephen R. James, Jr. and Camille Stanley, pp. 35–40, Society for Historical Archaeology, Tucson.

Chapter 7

Underwater Archaeology in Rhode Island

D.K. ABBASS

INTRODUCTION

What is now the state of Rhode Island has always been dominated by its great water features, Narragansett Bay and Rhode Island Sound. The sound provides access to the bay from the North Atlantic Ocean, and the bay provides access to the whole interior of New England via the state's northern river valleys.

The region's resources have supported human economies dependent on maritime assets from pre-Columbian times to the present. Although no securely identified inundated terrestrial Native American site has been found in Rhode Island, the potential for such exists. Certainly, ship-building and maritime trade were pivotal in the development of colonial Rhode Island, and those industries have continued into modern times. Much of this material is to be found in the state's waters.

EARLY RHODE ISLAND SHIPWRECK "STUDIES"

Study of the state's submerged cultural resources has had a checkered past. Early shipwreck studies were fraught with the limitations of all such similar attempts at the time. With the development of modern methodologies and technology, the state of Rhode

D.K. Abbass, Project Director, Rhode Island Marine Archaeology Project, Newport, Rhode Island 02840.

International Handbook of Underwater Archaeology, edited by Carol V. Ruppé and Janet F. Barstad. Kluwer Academic/Plenum Publishers, New York, 2002.

Island has seen a more controlled approach to such work and, since 1992, the Rhode Island Marine Archaeology Project (RIMAP) has sponsored professionally managed field investigations using trained volunteer sport divers to execute the research.

Early "Marine Archaeology" in Rhode Island

Marine salvage has always been an important part of the Rhode Island economy, especially the retrieval of cargos and ships' equipment from lost vessels. Most salvaged material was recycled into the maritime economy, but some passed into private hands or into museum collections. In those early days, however, there were few professional divers and, in the beginning of scuba (self-contained underwater breathing apparatus) diving, there were few who practiced the sport. This meant the pressure on locating historic submerged cultural resources in Rhode Island was limited to a few individuals who were interested in collecting artifacts.

"Marine Archaeology" in the 1950s and 1960s

With the advent of scuba technology, early divers in the state practiced what was called "marine archaeology," but their focus was collecting of artifacts for private and public display. These attempts paid varying degrees of attention to the need for scientific documentation and conservation of the removed waterlogged artifacts.

High-profile "archaeological" activities in the 1950s included removal of the periscope, propellers, and personal property from the U-853, the last German submarine sunk during World War II, and removal of equipment and ship's structure from the *Gem*, a reputed slaver in Newport's Brenton Cove. These projects were reported in the local press, and some artifacts were displayed in a small Newport maritime museum. Although the museum is now well remembered by local residents, it was disbanded in the late 1970s, and the current location of its artifacts is unknown.

RIMAP has tried with limited success to document those early activities and to locate the removed artifacts. Interviews with former divers, who now are in their 60s, 70s, and 80s, indicate these "archaeologists" were well intentioned but kept no detailed records of their retrievals. Most of what is now known about those early years comes from unevenly reliable newspaper accounts.

Marine Archaeology in the 1970s

In the early 1970s, University of Rhode Island ocean engineering graduate student Al Davis found HMS *Lark*, HMS *Orpheus*, and HMS *Cerberus*, three Revolutionary War British frigates sunk in 1778 along the west coast of Aquidneck Island. The excavation of these sites then became a bicentennial project sponsored by the university.

With federal and private support, university students excavated *Orpheus* and removed a number of small artifacts, including crew members' personal effects. They also removed a number of cannons and bits of ship's structure from the *Cerberus* debris field. After four years of collecting, the university cancelled this program because of lack of proper conservation facilities and fading financial support. Many of the artifacts that had been assembled, however, were placed on display during the bicentennial.

In preparation for RIMAP's further study of the British Revolutionary War frigates, we revisited what the University of Rhode Island students did in the 1970s, located the extant artifacts, evaluated the collection for conservation needs, and documented it. Al

Davis shared his miscellaneous notes and photographs from the project, and we interviewed some of the university staff involved at the time. These materials indicate there are no extant field notes, site maps, or other documentation from the field research.

Artifact inventories reveal most of the small pieces are now in the Rhode Island Historical Preservation Commission (RIHPC) storage in Providence, although some that had been on display at the National Maritime Museum in Greenwich were stolen, and most of the recovered cannons have not survived. As RIMAP volunteer Kerry Lynch catalogued the remaining collection, she discovered that the two hand grenades in the collection had not been defused (Lynch, 1999). The Newport Navy Explosive Demolition Unit arranged for these artifacts to be rendered inert and returned to the RIHPC.

Since there was no conservation information for the artifacts, RIMAP volunteer Jonathan Faucher evaluated the collection and made recommendations for its future care. Charlotte Taylor of the RIHPC is implementing those recommendations, and RIMAP volunteer Gregory DeAscentis has photographed the collection to document its current condition. Despite the lack of data analysis and interpretation, the 1970s artifacts may provide useful information as the frigate sites are restudied.

Marine Archaeology in the 1980s

Diving became wildly popular in the 1970s and 1980s, and more individuals began to dive Rhode Island's waters. Today, the state is the premier dive destination of all New England. Divers come to see submerged geological features, to see tropical fish swept north along the Gulf Stream in the summer, and to see our shipwrecks, more per square mile than any other state. This interest, although an overlooked benefit to the Rhode Island economy, creates a situation in which the state's historic shipwrecks have been increasingly vandalized.

At the same time diving became more accessible to the public, the state of Rhode Island began to respond to the need to protect its submerged cultural resources. Most marine archaeological activities of the 1980s were associated with Phase I surveys required by federal and state preservation laws. A major event in this decade was the discovery, during a remote sensing survey in 1988, of a British Revolutionary War transport sunk in Newport harbor in 1778. This site was immediately stripped of all portable artifacts by divers when notice of its discovery was published in a statewide newspaper.

THE RHODE ISLAND MARINE ARCHAEOLOGY PROJECT

In 1992, we created RIMAP to document the state's shipwrecks and especially to educate the public about the importance of protecting the state's submerged cultural heritage. Now an incorporated, nonprofit membership organization, RIMAP research has been sponsored by the Rhode Island Historical Preservation Commission, Rhode Island Sea Grant, Navy Legacy Program, National Maritime Heritage Program, and National Park Service. Individuals and RIMAP memberships also support this work. By far the major contributions have been the in-kind donations of time and equipment from the many volunteers who participate in the fieldwork.

RIMAP is organized with professional archaeologists acting as "site managers" to conduct research on selected sites and leading teams of RIMAP-trained volunteer divers to execute field research. RIMAP's 1999 site managers and their sites are: Jonathan Faucher of Texas A&M University (unidentified British Revolutionary War transport),

John Hoagland formerly of Polaroid Corporation and RIMAP vice president (World War II marine railway at Fort Adams), Kerry Lynch of the University of Massachusetts/ Amherst (19th-century Barrington Brickyard Barge), I. Roderick Mather of the University of Rhode Island (British Revolutionary War frigate HMS *Cerberus* and miscellaneous unidentified shore wrecks), Donna Souza of Brown University (unidentified 19th century vessel and Naval Torpedo station targets), and Joe Zarzynski of Bateaux Below, Inc. (19th century reputed slave ship *Gem*). Project Director D.K. Abbass coordinates all administrative and research activities, and all RIMAP work is done under permit from the RIHPC and with the guidance of Rhode Island State Underwater Archaeologist Charlotte Taylor. For those sites with a naval history, RIMAP works with the Naval Historical Center in Washington, D.C.

Over the course of the past eight years, RIMAP instructors have trained more than 400 volunteers in the organization's basic philosophy through a series of classes. More than 200 of these individuals have participated in the fieldwork. The educational program is open to all members of the interested public, but RIMAP's "Introduction to Underwater Archaeology" course is required of all RIMAP volunteers. Optional classes include "Site Mapping in Underwater Archaeology," "Ship Construction for Underwater Archaeologists," "Remote Sensing," "Conservation Theory," "Museum Theory," and "Artifact Management," and a panel session, "Meet the Underwater Archaeologists."

RIMAP Field Studies

RIMAP efforts have succeeded to the extent that our teams have documented a number of submerged sites. We have delivered papers at the annual meetings of the Society for Historical Archaeology (SHA) and the North American Society for Oceanic History. We have published in the Proceedings of the SHA and have produced our own inhouse publications. More important for local site protection, however, is an aggressive program of local press contact and presentations focused on public education, especially to divers, on the legalities and preservation ethic of historic shipwreck protection. The following site descriptions will sketch some RIMAP projects.

Potential Inundated Native American Site.   Narragansett Bay was formed as the result of scouring during the last glacial period. Moving sheets of ice gouged out the original river bed, which still exists as the deepest part of the Bay. As the glacier melted, the shoreline expanded to the present footprint of the bay. Native Americans who lived nearby used the natural resources found along the shore, especially fish and shellfish, and left archaeological deposits. As the pre-Columbian shoreline was covered by the rising waters, these terrestrial sites were covered by shallow waters.

When a shell fisherman discovered a lithic embedded in what appears to be a bison, or possibly cow, knee joint in Warick Cove, it indicated the potential for a prehistoric site nearby (Turnbaugh, 1998). Although the joint cannot be securely identified, if it is bison, the lithic is prehistoric; if it is modern cow, it is no earlier than the European Colonial period. In either case, the presence of Native American sites in the swamps and shore nearby suggests the strong possibility that there may be an inundated site in the cove.

In 1997, RIMAP documented an indigenous dugout canoe reportedly found in a marsh by a local waterman. Although this canoe was clumsily made, it appears to be genuine; certainly the possibility exists that similar material culture will emerge from the state's wetlands and shallow waters.

RIMAP's long-range goals include further investigation of inundated pre-Columbian terrestrial sites, but to date most of its work has focused on colonial and later maritime activities.

Colonial Sites.   What later became the state of Rhode Island was first visited by Europeans when Verrazano dropped anchor in the West Passage of Narragansett Bay and explored the area for two weeks in 1524. Stories of supposed earlier visits by the Vikings have nourished local lore about a Norse connection, especially with Newport, but so far there has been no undisputed evidence found to support this relationship.

More likely to leave evidence of their presence, however, were 17th-century Dutch traders, and this is most prominently found at Fort Ninigret on the southwestern shore of Rhode Island Sound (Taylor, no date). Dutch Island in the West Passage of Narragansett Bay was named thus because a Dutch trading post supposedly was there in the 17th century. To date, there has been no terrestrial evidence found of this post, and remote sensing of the waters off the island revealed no evidence of such a colonial association.

Roger Williams, a dissident Massachusetts bay colonist, was the first European to settle the Rhode Island area permanently, when he established Providence at the head of Narragansett bay in 1636. The largest island in the bay was called Aquidneck by the Native Americans, and Rhode Island by the Europeans. The colony was named Rhode Island and Providence Plantations to indicate the total geographic area.

In 1638, more dissidents from Massachusetts, under the leadership of Anne Hutchinson, settled Portsmouth at the north end of Aquidneck Island. In 1639, members of the Portsmouth group split off to establish Newport at the south end of the island, near the mouth of Narragansett Bay.

Newport quickly became a major maritime depot, building ships for merchants throughout New England and Europe. Providence, Warren, Bristol, East Greenwich, and Warwick also were early to build vessels for sale. Secondary colonial maritime businesses included sparmakers and riggers, block and pump makers, caulkers, sailmakers, blacksmiths and anchor forges, and rope–walks.

In the 17th and 18th centuries, Rhode Island ships and crews openly traded with the English colonies in the Caribbean, but "sly" trade with Dutch and French colonies was common. Rhode Island also was known as a haven for piracy and privateers, although the recurring local lore about buried treasure in the state is not supported by historical facts. There has been no firm identification of a colonial shipwreck in the state's waters as yet, although the presence of a great number of Revolutionary War vessels indicates that this may only be a matter of attribution.

The Revolutionary War in Rhode Island.   For a brief period during the American Revolution (1776–1781), control of Rhode Island was a focus of conflict between the British, French, and Americans. Newport, the best harbor between Boston and Philadelphia, was ideally located for large fleets of warships. In addition, Rhode Island had always been known as a place for dissidents, home of privateers, and "scofflaws" who avoided paying duty on imports. British efforts to control these activities were generally unsuccessful. Therefore, in December 1776, British troops occupied Newport, and their ships blockaded Narragansett Bay to bottle up the Americans in Providence. In unsuccessful attempts to run the blockade, the Americans lost a number of their vessels along the bay shores, including the frigate *Columbus* in the West Passage and a number of smaller vessels in the Sakonnet River.

Following an aborted attempt to oust the British from Rhode Island in the fall of 1777, the Americans assembled a fleet of 150 small vessels to carry their troops to Newport for a second try the following year. To forestall this possibility, the British attacked Bristol and Warren in May 1778, and destroyed the American vessels in those harbors and on the ways, and all small craft in the Kickemuit River. British troops also burned a sawmill and some small vessels at Fall River. Although contemporary Fage charts give the location of these events, today no visible remains are found on the shore.

In July 1778, a French fleet arrived at the mouth of Narragansett Bay to assist the American army in another planned assault on the British in Newport. This was the first attempt at American–French cooperation following the formal alliance between the two countries in the spring of 1778.

When the French fleet arrived, the Americans put the city of Newport and its British occupiers under siege. To keep their Royal Navy vessels from falling into enemy hands, the British burned and sank a sloop-of-war, *Kingsfisher*, and two small armed galleys, *Alarm* and *Spitfire*, in the Sakonnet River. Four frigates, *Lark*, *Orpheus*, *Cerberus*, and *Juno*, were on guard in Narragansett bay to blockade the rebel American fleet in Providence in 1778; these frigates were also burned and sunk along the west coast of Aquidneck Island north of Newport to avoid capture by the French.

At Newport itself, the British sank *Falcon*, a sloop-of-war, the frigate *Flora*, and about 30 small craft in the harbor. To protect Newport from the French fleet's cannonade, they also sank as many as 13 transports to act as a blockade.

Many of these vessels had significant histories prior to their loss. The frigates were used as couriers to carry news and orders between the various centers of the campaign, acted as convoy for transports and other lesser armed vessels, patrolled the coasts of southern New England to capture rebel vessels (which then were sold and the proceeds divided among the crew members), and were involved in minor skirmishes. One of the transports had been HMB *Endeavour*, which went around the world with Captain James Cook (Abbass, 1999).

The British fleet from New York arrived shortly after the British sank their vessels in Narragansett Bay. When the French fleet sailed out to meet it in the North Atlantic, both were overtaken by a hurricane that severely damaged all ships; the British returned to New York for repairs, and the French returned to Newport but immediately departed for Boston. When the French ships left Narragansett Bay, the American army then investing Newport retreated from the city. The British caught the Americans at the north end of Aquidneck Island, and a skirmish, called the Battle of Rhode Island, ensued. But the Americans successfully completed their escape to their mainland stronghold (Deardon, 1980).

Intermittent attempts by others have failed to find the British sloop-of-war *Kingsfisher* and galleys *Alarm* and *Spitfire* in the Sakonnet River. In Newport's inner harbor, the small craft and the frigate *Flora* were raised, but the sloop-of-war *Falcon* had quickly filled with silt and, despite repeated attempts, could not be raised. The area where the *Falcon* was sunk probably has been dredged, and RIMAP has devoted no resources to the search for these vessels.

However, with remote sensing and ground-truthing, RIMAP has located the potential sites of *Lark*, *Orpheus*, and *Juno*, three of the frigates sunk north of Newport. RIMAP also completed a predisturbance site map of the fourth frigate, HMS *Cerberus*, in three field seasons of research.

HMS *Cerberus*.   HMS *Cerberus* was a British frigate that had a particularly illustrious Revolutionary War history prior to her loss in Rhode Island. She carried the three British generals—Clinton, Burgoyne and Howe—to Boston in 1775 to replace General Gage; she was at the Battle of Bunker Hill; and in 1777, American inventor David Bushnell tested mines against her when she visited New London, Connecticut.

Since 1997, RIMAP has studied the *Cerberus* debris field and determined that it is scattered over an area at least 300×600 ft. This large area is due to the explosion when the vessel was fired, and the dynamic nature of the shore where she is now found. Included in the site are a classic ballast pile, embedded wooden structure, at least two cannons, and miscellaneous small artifacts. In 1998, the Naval Undersea Warfare Center Engineering Support Unit (NUWC), under the direction of Roy Manstan, joined the RIMAP team in its effort to document the site. In 1999, site manager Roderick Mather led RIMAP and NUWC teams to complete this study. That same year, RIMAP and NUWC sponsored an educational demonstration of underwater archaeology for National Maritime Historical Society-sponsored cadets aboard the Revolutionary War frigate replica HMS *Rose*. (Figure 7.1)

Revolutionary War Transports.   Of growing interest is the RIMAP study of the Revolutionary War transports sunk in the two square miles of Newport's outer harbor during the Siege of Newport in 1778. Of all the vessels used and lost in the Revolutionary War, transports have been the most overlooked. Journals and eye-witness accounts usually note the number and names of the Royal Navy ships, but the hard-working, unglamorous transports are commonly ignored.

These vessels were privately owned but chartered to the Royal Navy and used for moving men and material between stations. Little is known about most of the transports, although at least one, *Lord Sandwich* in Newport harbor, was used as a prison ship. Archival research at the Public Records Office (PRO) in London has identified the names

Figure 7.1. Rod Mather explains the HMS *Cerberus* site to cadets on board "HMS" *Rose*, July 29, 1999 (Photo by Walter Foster).

of twelve transports. These were *Betty, Bristol, Britannia, Earl of Oxford, Good Intent, Grand Duke of Russia, Lord Sandwich, Malaga, Peggy, Rachel and Mary, Susannah*, and *Union*. Other archival information includes vessel surveys, acceptance into the transport service, valuations, some of their movements on the North American station during the Revolutionary War, and payoff records of their loss.

One of these transports was found during a cable survey in 1988, and local news reports gave its location. Unfortunately, when RIMAP dived this site in 1994, all portable artifacts reportedly scattered on the surface of the site in 1988 were missing. Detailed study of this site began in 2001 and continues to date.

Another transport site, located just 325 feet from shore in front of the Naval Hospital in Newport, has been the subject of intense RIMAP study. Since 1997, site manager Jonathan Faucher has led RIMAP teams in the creation of a predisturbance site map that shows a classic ballast pile and a partially exposed timber. Two small-caliber cannons are embedded in the ballast pile (Abbass and Faucher, 1998). The site appears to have been stripped of portable artifacts, and a portion of the ballast pile has been mined. We now know that this ship is too small to be *HMB Endeavour*.

In an attempt to find more of the transports, RIMAP has completed side scan and subbottom profile imaging of Newport's outer harbor, where the transports are known to have been lost. The southern portion of this area has been greatly disturbed by large commercial and naval vessels anchoring there, and it is also littered with the debris of vessels used for target practice by the Naval Torpedo Station. Ground-truthing sonar images in this area is a meticulous process.

Yet, the northern section of the area has been disturbed mainly by the construction of the Pell Bridge, which connects Aquidneck Island with Conanicut Island to the west, so that the potential to find existing transport sites is greater in here than to the south.

HMB *Endeavour in Newport.*   Newport has long been thought to be the final port of call for HMB (His Majesty's Bark) *Endeavour*, the vessel that carried Captain James Cook on his first circumnavigation of the earth (1768–1771). In 1828, a Mr. Gibbs of the Newport firm Gibbs and Channing was quoted as having identified *La Liberte*, a vessel abandoned on Newport's waterfront in 1793, as the vessel that went around with world with Captain Cook. Gibbs stated that it was to his firm that the vessel's last cargo had been consigned.

The identification of *La Liberte* as *Endeavour* is now known to have been mistaken. In 1997, two Australian amateur historians, Mike Connell and Des Liddy, published evidence that *La Liberte* was in fact HMS *Resolution*, Cook's vessel from his second (1772–1775) and third (1776–1780) voyages. Because the area where *La Liberte* was abandoned is known to have been severely damaged in the hurricane of 1815, and because the area is now covered with land fill and condominium structures, RIMAP has committed no resources to the search for *La Liberte*.

Connell and Liddy did note that *Endeavour*'s name had been changed to *Lord Sandwich*, as posted in the 1777–1778 "Lloyd's Register," where the vessel is listed as in service as a "transport of troops, prisoners or convicts, out of London." *Lord Sandwich* ex *Endeavour* then drops from Lloyd's records.

RIMAP's research into the transports scuttled in Newport's outer harbor in 1778 had found that the *Lord Sandwich* transport was one of the vessels sunk during the Siege of Newport. It carried German mercenaries to North America in 1776 and was used as a prison ship in Newport Harbor in 1777 and 1778. British admiralty materials in the PRO in

London revealed that Newport's local lore is absolutely correct: Captain Cook's *Endeavour* certainly ended her days in Newport. She had been the *Lord Sandwich* transport sunk in 1778 in the Siege of Newport, not the whaler *La Liberte* abandoned in 1793 (Abbass, 1999).

RIMAP now has the task of locating as many of the transports as possible and determining which had been HMB *Endeavour* prior to coming to North America. Continued remote sensing and ground-truthing will establish the total number of transports still existing in Newport's outer harbor. Identification of the *Endeavour* from among these transports will depend on a comparison of existing ship's timbers with information from original drafts and surveys of the *Endeavour* as she was taken into the Royal Navy, her repair history (especially those repairs done in the southern hemisphere), and comparison with artifacts and structural members jettisoned on the Great Barrier Reef in Australia when she ran aground there on Cook's first circumnavigation. It may be easier to identify the vessel as the *Lord Sandwich* from cultural materials associated with her use as a transport, since there may be artifacts left behind when she moved German mercenaries to North America. There also may be evidence from her use as a prison ship in Newport harbor. At this writing, RIMAP has determined that the Naval Hospital site is too small to be the *Endeavour*, but work continues on the second site, found in 1988.

As the search for *Endeavour* has unfolded, we have incorporated another organization devoted to the administration and fundraising necessary to the study of the *Endeavour* and *Resolution*: the "Foundation for the Preservation of Captain Cook's Ships." RIMAP teams will continue their archaeological study of all shipwrecks and submerged cultural resources in Rhode Island, but the Cook Foundation will have a tighter focus on the *Endeavour* and the *Resolution*, both now known to have ended their days in Newport.

The Cook Foundation is organized to sponsor councils of advisors to provide technical input and public outreach. Individuals from around the world have provided further advice and guidance and, since 1999, one group of three underwater archaeologists from Australian National Maritime Museum, under the leadership of Paul Hundley, participates in the RIMAP-sponsored fieldwork.

The state of Rhode Island has taken particular interest to protect the potential site of HMB *Endeavour*. RIHPC, in its capacity as the state historic preservation office, has moved aggressively to protect the transport vessels by taking them into formal custody, using the federal Abandoned Shipwreck Act, the Rhode Island Historic Preservation Act, and the international Law of Finds and Law of Salvage. By a Memorandum of Agreement, RIHPC has awarded to RIMAP the archaeological study of the vessels thus under its custody. Although, as of this writing, the state has not closed the site to divers, publicity surrounding this action has put divers on notice that the target area is not to be disturbed.

The Slave Trade. Newport, Bristol, and Warren were involved from earliest times in the slave trade, importing molasses to make rum and exporting the rum to Africa in trade for slaves, who were taken to the Caribbean and exchanged for more molasses. Only South Carolina was a more active participant than Rhode Island in this "triangular trade."

The Rhode Island slave trade lasted from 1696 until 1774, when importation of slaves into the state was prohibited. On March 1, 1784, the state decreed that all children born of slave mothers would be free. Despite this progressive stance, local merchants continued in the trade, taking their human cargo to southern ports, especially to Charleston between 1804 and 1807, after which the trade there was banned.

Local lore in Newport has long insisted that the *Gem*, a ship abandoned in Brenton Cove at the southern end of the inner harbor, had been a slaver. Newport newspaper reports of February 3, 1856, stated that *Gem* had come from the West Coast of Africa bound for New York with a load of ivory, palm oil, ebony, and other exotic wood when she ran hard aground on the west side of Block Island in Rhode Island Sound. In the early descriptions of the vessel's loss, there is no mention that she was carrying slaves or that she had been in the slave trade.

Her cargo was salvaged and, by November, 1856, *Gem* was abandoned at a dock along Newport's waterfront, where she stayed for the next 13 years. In 1870, she was towed to Brenton Cove at the south end of Newport harbor, where she was abandoned again. Following the hurricane of 1938, she disappeared from view and was forgotten by everyone except divers, who could visit her remains and collect her bronze fastenings. In 1959, amateur archaeologists removed pieces of *Gem* for display in a local museum.

Because of Newport's historical association with the slave trade, and because local lore surrounding *Gem* identified her as a slaver, RIMAP spent four field seasons, under the direction of site manager Joseph W. Zarzynski, to determine which vessel in Brenton cove could be *Gem* and if she really had been a slaver.

Review of historical materials indicates that prominent abolitionist Thomas Higginson was the first to identify her as a slaver. Higginson used incendiary descriptions of the vessel as a political tool in the abolitionist movement (Zarzynski and Abbass, 1997). Because of the confusion about the vessel's past, RIMAP hoped that archaeological study of *Gem* would identify diagnostic features to identify her securely and confirm or refute her history as a slaver.

RIMAP documented many interesting features of the site such as bronze fastenings, treenails, and massive and closely-spaced futtocks, but nothing on the site allows us to conclude that the vessel had been in the slave trade.

The 19th Century. Following the American Revolution, the shipping centers of New York and Boston overshadowed the cities of Rhode Island. In the late 18th and early 19th centuries, the United States underwent an Industrial Revolution, and water-powered mills developed in the Blackstone River valley to the north of Narragansett Bay. By the late 19th century, Fall River, at the northeast corner of the bay, had a greater number of spindles working in its textile mills than any other city in the country.

At this time, sailing vessels transported most of the bulk and heavy material, including coal, lumber, and quarry products, and the vessels were used until the early 20th century. But rail and steamboat transport eventually changed the economic complexion of Narragansett Bay. The easiest travel from Boston to New York was by train to Fall River or Newport, where overnight passage to New York could be gained on one of the grand "floating palaces."

The steamship industry continued to serve passengers until the late 19th century. One, the *Empire State*, can still be found in Bristol harbor, where it burned and sank in 1887. Although this site has been nearly stripped of portable artifacts, RIMAP has begun a simple predisturbance site map to aid in management planning for the site.

Another industrial site of interest is the Barrington Brickyard and its adjacent canal that feeds into Narragansett Bay. When the brickyard was closed in the early 20th century, a canal barge was abandoned in what appears to be a basin in the canal system. RIMAP has been documenting this area with the intent of interpreting the local industry's importance to the state's 19th century economy.

Military and Naval Installations.   In the early 19th century, the entrance to Newport harbor was protected by construction of a major star fort in stone, named Fort Adams. This installation was in use, although with diminishing intensity, until after the Korean War.

During World War II, the Army built a large shipyard on the grounds to the north of Fort Adams to service its vessels stationed in the area. The yard included two marine railways, the larger of which goes into Newport harbor nearly 400 ft. The railway engine house and the adjacent shipyard have long since disappeared, but the submerged rails and the wooden structure supporting them are still in place 50 years after construction (Figure 7.2). Over the course of two years, RIMAP volunteers, under the direction of site manager John Hoagland, documented the submerged portion of the marine railway and conducted interviews with some employees of the shipyard still living in the area (Hoagland, 1999).

The U.S. Navy established a torpedo development and testing station on Goat Island in the 1860s. This program eventually created a facility that expanded its manufacturing activities throughout World War II. In its early days, the station tested its experimental torpedos on vessels in Newport's outer harbor. Much of the debris on the bottom of the harbor today is the result of late 19th- and early 20th-century torpedo explosions. RIMAP site manager Donna Souza is conducting a study of a large, as yet identified vessel found where the test explosions took place; she warns that the torpedo station's later explosions in these waters may have severely damaged earlier Revolutionary War vessels sunk in the area (Souza, 1999).

Figure 7.2. The Fort Adams Marine Railway (Photo by Greg DeAscentis).

SUMMARY

It is the philosophy of the Rhode Island Historical Preservation Commission that the state's many historical submerged cultural resources deserve study and protection. The Rhode Island Marine Archaeology Project was organized to provide a means to study these resources, to educate the diving public in the preservation ethic, and to incorporate that diving public into professionally- directed underwater archaeology projects. This cooperative program appears to have achieved at least modest success.

REFERENCES

Abbass, D.K., 1997, *Newport and Slavery*: *History, Archaeology and Steven Spielberg.* Paper delivered at the Annual Meeting of the New York Archaeological Society, May 3, Lake George, NY.

_____, 1999, *Endeavour* and *Resolution* Revisited: Newport and Captain James Cook's Vessels. *Newport History*: *Journal of the Newport Historical Society*: Summer.

Abbass, D.K., and Faucher J., 1998, *The Newport "Cannon" Site*: *A Possible Revolutionary Transport.* Paper delivered at the Annual Meeting of the Society for Historical Archaeology, Vol. 70, Part 1, pp. 1–200.

Beaglehole, J.C., 1955, *The Voyage of the Endeavour, 1768–1771*. University Press, Cambridge.

Connell, Mike, and Liddy Des, 1997, Cook's Endeavour Bark: Did This Vessel End Its Days in Newport, Rhode Island? *The Great Circle, Journal of the Australian Association for Maritime History* 19(1):40–49.

Deardon, Paul F., 1980, *The Rhode Island Campaign of 1778*: *Inauspicious Dawn of Alliance.* Rhode Island Bicentennial Foundation, Providence.

Faucher, Jonathan, 1999, *The Navy Hospital Cannon Site.* Paper Presented at the Annual Meeting of the North American Society for Oceanic History, 6 May, Lake George, NY.

_____, 1999, The 1998 Season on the Naval Hospital Site. *Ground Truth: The Newsletter of the Rhode Island Marine Archaeology Project.* Spring, (4): 2.

Hoagland, John, 1999, The Fort Adams Marine Railway. *Ground Truth*: *The Newsletter of the Rhode Island Marine Archaeology Project.* The Spring, (5): 4–5.

Lynch, Kerry, 1999, *Revolutionary War Artifacts from the Rhode Island Frigates*: *A New Study.* Paper presented at the Annual Meeting of the North American Society for Oceanic History, May 6, Lake George, NY.

Mackenzie, Frederick, 1930, *Diary of Frederick Mackenzie.* 2 Vols. Harvard University Press, Cambridge.

Mather, I. Roderick, 1999, *Rhode Island*'s Shoreline Shipwrecks. Paper presented at the Annual Meeting of the North American Society for Oceanic History, May 6, Lake George, NY.

Schroder, W.K., 1980, *Defenses of Narragansett Bay in World War II.* Minuteman Press, East Greenwich.

Souza, Donna, 1999, *The Naval Torpedo Station at Goat Island.* Paper Presented at the Annual Meeting of the North American Society for Oceanic History, May 6, Lake George, NY.

Syrett, David, 1970, *Shipping and the American War, 1775–83*: A Study of British Transport Organization. The Athlone Press, London.

Zarzynski, Joseph W., and Abbass, D.K., 1997, The Rhode Island Slave Ship *Gem*: Slaver or Propaganda? *Underwater Archaeology*: 74–78.

Chapter 8

The Maryland–Chesapeake Region

SUSAN B.M. LANGLEY

INTRODUCTION

Sixteen of the 23 counties that make up Maryland, along with Baltimore City, have tidal waters (Figure 8.1). Chesapeake Bay, the Atlantic Ocean, and their tributaries provide the state with more than 4430 miles of shoreline on the bay alone, accounting for 1726 square miles of water. State waters include all tidal waters from the mean high tide mark to three miles offshore, and all nontidal waters to the normal high water mark, which were navigable as of April 28, 1788, when Maryland ratified the United States Constitution. By this definition, state waters cover almost a fourth of Maryland's total area of 12,327 square miles.

This chapter examines the development of underwater archaeology in Maryland since the advent of the Abandoned Shipwreck Act in 1988 (ASA) (43 USCS Ch. 39). To provide a perspective for the achievements of the past decade, the chapter outlines the activities and circumstances that provided impetus for the creation of the Maryland Maritime Archeology Program (MMAP), as well as the program's role in submerged heritage resource management. This is followed by discussion of a number of specific sites and projects that exemplify the diversity of Maryland's cultural assets. Finally, it summarizes the current state of underwater archaeology in Maryland and delineates the course charted for its progress.

Susan B.M. Langley, Maryland Historical Trust, Department of Housing and Community Development, Crownsville, Maryland 21032.

International Handbook of Underwater Archaeology, edited by Carol V. Ruppé and Janet F. Barstad. Kluwer Academic/Plenum Publishers, New York, 2002.

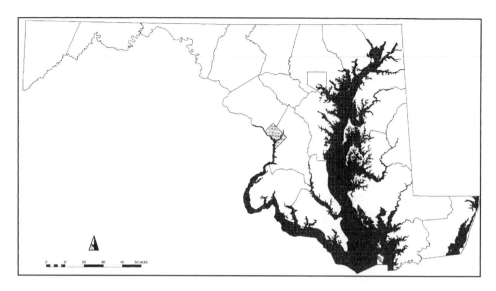

Figure 8.1. Maryland with county lines and major waterways.

BACKGROUND

Creation of the Maryland Maritime Archeology Program

The MMAP is housed in the Maryland Historical Trust's Office of Archeology, an agency of the Maryland Department of Housing and Community Development. That the 10th anniversary of MMAP coincides with that of the ASA is not coincidental. The need for structured management of the state's submerged cultural resources had long been recognized by the preservation community. It found a champion in Maryland Governor William Donald Schaefer, who appointed a Governor's Advisory Committee on Maritime Archeology composed of underwater archeologists, conservators, and representatives of the commercial and recreational diving sectors. The committee helped create the Maryland Submerged Archaeological Historic Property Act (Annotated Code of Maryland, Article 83B, §§ 5-601, 5-611.1, 5-620, 5-621, 5-630), which became law one month after the ASA was passed.

The drafting of implementing regulations and a comprehensive preservation–management plan began in 1989; these were adopted and in effect by January 1993 (Annotated Code of Maryland, Title 05, Subtitle 08, Chapter 03). The preservation plan drafts now are being retooled in light of a new comprehensive state plan, Preservation Vision 2000 (Maryland Historical Trust, 1998), and new strategic planning processes that will permit greater flexibility in addressing changing goals and priorities.

The drafting and passage of state legislation on submerged heritage resources was not as simple as the previous paragraphs suggest. As in other states—and other nations, for that matter—impetus was provided by the wholesale collecting on a potentially significant submerged site. In Maryland, that site was the wreck of the propeller-driven steamboat *New Jersey* (18TA210).

Built and registered in 1862 in Federal Hill, Baltimore, the freighter *New Jersey* initially was chartered by the Union army for a return trip from New York to Washington,

D.C., but it was not until mid-1866 that the vessel was returned to its owners. In the interim, the *New Jersey* hauled troops, cargo, and prisoners as required. It was traded to the Baltimore Steam Packet Company in 1867, becoming the famed Old Bay Line's first propeller-driven vessel. Three years later, enroute between Baltimore and Norfolk, it caught fire and sank off Sharps Island in the Chesapeake Bay, with no loss of life but with a full load of merchandise.

The wreck was relocated in 1973. In 1975, maritime author Donald Shomette, under the auspices of his company Nautical Archaeological Associates, Inc., visited and confirmed the wreck's identity. He provided other documentation to the Maryland Geological Survey, then the entity responsible for archaeology in the state. According to Shomette (1996), divers from the Hydrographic Survey Branch of the National Oceanographic and Atmospheric Administration (NOAA) examined the wreck, sketched the vessel, and submitted a site report. Even though it was more than 50 years old and eligible for inclusion in the National Register of Historic Places, the site was wire-dragged in 1978 as a possible navigational hazard because section 106 of the National Historic Properties Act of 1966 was not widely applied at that time to submerged cultural resources. Information about the remains was published in NOAA's Automated Wrecks and Obstacles Information System (AWOIS) records and by 1979 on navigational charts. A group of Washington, D.C. divers correctly identified the site and reported the information to NOAA, so that the information was added to the public record. Collecting increased exponentially.

Although the state claimed jurisdiction over the site via the Wetlands and Water Resources Acts and cited current antiquities regulations at public meetings in an effort to engender a preservation ethic among the diving community, it lacked a means of enforcing its claim beyond good will and the honor system. A variety of proposals were made to protect the *New Jersey* but were untenable or fiscally impractical, leaving no means to protect the wreck effectively. State claims were untested and faced unfavorable precedents in federal salvage and admiralty courts (the latter were reversing state of Florida decisions on submerged archaeological sites at that time).

NOAA did robotic surveys of the site in 1985, and over the next two years did more with the help of the National Geographic Society and a cadre of other organizations and agencies. The partnership documented the site, advanced the application of remote-operated vehicles (ROVs) to underwater archaeology, and focused attention on the plight of the site and others like it. Donald Shomette made a presentation at the Society for Historical Archaeology meetings (Shomette 1996). Senator Bill Bradley of New Jersey used the site as an example of the need to pass the Abandoned Shipwreck Act. A judiciously coordinated site visit by the newly elected Maryland Governor, William Schaefer, obtained support from him and the Maryland congressional delegation for a state underwater archaeology program. The need for adequate conservation facilities resulted in the construction of the Maryland Archaeological Conservation Laboratory, which opened May 1998.

The Role of MMAP

In 1988, the Office of Archaeology was transferred from the Maryland Geological Survey to the Maryland Historical Trust (MHT). The newly passed Submerged Archaeological Historic Property Act provided financial support and a legislative mandate to implement the federal Abandoned Shipwreck Act at the State level through MMAP.

The Program's duties are myriad and include survey, inventory and management of submerged heritage resources, review of permit and license applications from federal and state agencies and private citizens for dredging and water-related construction, and underwater archaeological research and commercial salvage activities. These endeavors require administrative management and on-site monitoring, even more so if any are funded with an MHT grant. The trust is empowered to enforce its implementing regulations either directly or through any law enforcement agency including the Department of Natural Resources Marine Police. The program also is directed to identify, document, and nominate all properties eligible for the Maryland Register of Historic Properties and the National Register of Historic Places. It may engage in direct fundamental research, synthesize existing research data, and encourage archaeological research and investigation by any scientific or historical institution or organization, museum, or institution of higher education in the state.

Educational outreach is a significant component of program planning—from providing field opportunities to the public to lecturing and instructing at all school levels and museums, other state and federal agencies, and organizations with specialized interests. MMAP actively participates in conferences, workshops, festivals, and symposia to disseminate information. The program cooperates with colleges, universities, and national organizations such as the Maritime Archaeological and Historical Society (MAHS) and dive shops offering specialty certification through the Professional Association of Diving Instructors to provide training in underwater archaeology.

MMAP cooperates and coordinates with other state and federal agencies, including the State Highway Administration, Maryland Department of the Environment, U.S. Army Corps of Engineers, National Park Service, U.S. Fish and Wildlife Service, and, especially, the U.S. Navy Department of Defense Legacy Resource Management Program. Not only does the program assist and cooperate in the excavation or other study of significant sites, either under the control of any of these agencies or those affected by their actions, it also coordinates and aids in the retrieval of objects of archaeological significance that are threatened or removed from such sites. MMAP submits an annual research design for its scheduled activities to the Maryland Board of Public Works and requires its approval to effect the delineated field work. It reports quarterly to the Governor's Maryland Advisory Committee on Archeology and to the Trust's board of directors periodically, at the request of the board or the State Historic Preservation Officer.

A DECADE OF ACHIEVEMENTS

Field work tends to sort out into survey and site-specific activities, with further subdivision into compliance-generated, management or research projects. As in most states, survey receives the greatest emphasis because of the provision of federal funding for compliance review and response. Site-specific and research-driven undertakings face budgetary constraints because extensive excavation and subsequent conservation are costly; these activities are generally possible only as partnership projects with other organizations.

This section examines MMAP's most recent survey and research endeavors, which have focused more on the Chesapeake Bay and its tributaries than on the Atlantic shore and more interior regions of the state because of the nature and extent of threats to these resources. Sites in the bay are imperiled by erosion, dredging, and collecting. Atlantic shore research began in 2000 and will continue through 2003.

Survey

Any cursory review of the geological history of the Chesapeake Bay, from its nascence as an extension of the Susquehanna River valley to its present form as the world's largest estuary, reveals the significant roles played by erosion and rise in sea level, both of which have combined to drown innumerable prehistoric sites and some of Maryland's earliest historic settlements. Erosion still whittles away at island and shoreside sites at a rate of about 1 ft/year but at rates as high as 12 ft/year episodically (Mountford, 1998: personal communication). Whole islands and the settlements they supported, such as Poplar, Three Sisters, and Sharps Islands, have crumbled into the bay (Leatherman et al., 1995).

The quantity of eroded materials deposited in the bay is an astonishing annual average of 6.8 million tons, most of which is bank erosion from the bay's rivers (Mountford 1998: personal communication). The average accumulation on the bay floor is 3 mm/year. Although sea level rise and general land subsidence in this area also amounts to 3 mm/year, the effects do not cancel each other out. Because of regional topography, the bay spreads further horizontally with these rises, covering more land and further exacerbating shoreline erosion. The effects on cultural remains are significant.

As the population around the bay increases, so does the demand for waterfront development, bringing with it the need to protect real estate investments, construct piers, and obtain navigational dredging permit applications against erosion. Erosion protection measures generally utilize additive methods in which rip-rap or wetland fill is placed over filter cloth. Projects involving grading, dredging, or pile-driving require greater scrutiny.

The Maryland Maritime Archeology Program has reviewed more than 3000 water-related applications since 1988. It is in the program's best interests to undertake its mandated survey work first adjacent to areas with high development potential, which not only augments the state's cultural resource inventory but also streamlines the review process. Given this survey strategy, it is not surprising that the vast majority (more than 95 percent) of sites inventoried fall within 15.25 m of a shoreline.

Of the 24 rivers flowing into the bay, 17 have had portions surveyed. Combinations of side scan sonar, magnetometer, diving, shallow-water probing, and pedestrian shoreline surveys have been used to investigate more than 780 miles of Maryland's waterways and record 237 prehistoric and 209 historic sites recorded (Figures 8.2 and 8.3); 217 remote sensing targets are scheduled for further study (Thompson, 1997). Remote sensing equipment tend to pick up only those sites and anomalies that either stand up from the bottom or contain sufficient ferrous materials to produce a detectable signal. Because of heavy silt loads of these rivers, buried sites, and sites including little or no metal or metal too degraded to register have not been inventoried. This causes some concern about sites to which dredging or other development may pose a threat. At this time, MMAP does not have regular access to subsediment imaging equipment. Resolving this lack is of critical importance.

A second and related issue is the increasing significance of survey in light of court findings pertaining to the case of the California shipwreck *Brother Jonathan*. The courts say a state must demonstrate clearly its possession of a wreck beyond the fact that the wreck rests on state-owned lands (Jones, 1998). While this applies technically only to shipwrecks, the implications are far reaching. The state must lay specific claim to

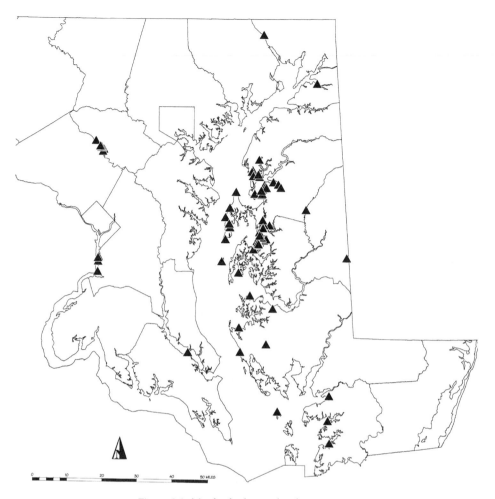

Figure 8.2. Maryland submerged prehistoric sites.

heritage resources lying on its bottomlands. These must be located and recorded—no mean feat in a clear-water environment but even more onerous in the relatively black waters of Maryland's rivers and the low visibility of the Chesapeake Bay. Hence the critical nature of adequate remote sensing equipment, a strongly proactive educational outreach program, and a positive rapport with the businesses, agencies, and individuals who interact with the bay such as watermen, dredging/construction companies, and the sport diving community.

Site-Specific Projects

Projects focusing on a single site generally have been activated either in response to a threat to the resource (compliance with Section 106 of the NHPA, for example), or have been fortunate to have a number of favorable factors converge in a timely manner (Figure 8.4). The latter include management studies undertaken at the request of other

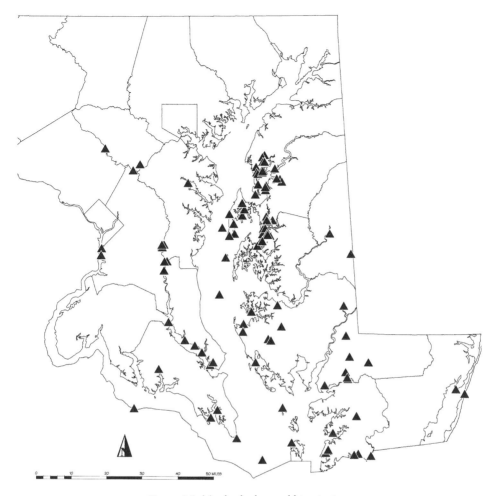

Figure 8.3. Maryland submerged historic sites.

agencies. Only occasionally has it been possible to expend time and resources on a single site to pursue research interests.

This section outlines several projects which fall into each of the previous categories. The MMAP played different roles in each project.

Compliance Projects.   As a matter of policy, the Maryland Historical Trust (MHT) does not undertake compliance-mandated archaeological research, surveys, or investigations to keep the state from competing with private-sector businesses. MMAP simply does not have the resources to undertake this work on a large scale; to do so even once would set a precedent they could not repeat. Because MMAP is the entity that determines whether compliance work is necessary and assesses the acceptability of the completed work, their involvement in such work could be perceived as conflict of interest. Therefore, participation in compliance-generated projects tends to be advisory; MMAP can assist with the development of scopes of work, monitor field work, and determine adequacy of effort. Occasionally MMAP takes on a more active role, providing assessment of a site's significance or rendering assistance to another agency.

Figure 8.4. Maryland's site-specific project locations.

This assistance usua!ly a reciprocal arrangement involving sharing of equipment and expertise.

Stephen Steward Shipyard (18AN817). The Stephen Steward Shipyard is an 18th-century industrial site that served as a supplier of vessels to the Continental Congress during the American Revolution but was burned by the British in 1781. It was located in 1991 during regular MMAP survey activities. During the Archaeological Society of Maryland's (ASM) 1993 field session, the shipyard was selected for archaeological study. About half the site was on property slated to be developed as the recreational parcel for a new housing development and the rest was on private property protected on the National Register site of Norman's Retreat, an 18th-century dwelling. The owner of Norman's Retreat was in favor of archaeological investigations, and the site provided the opportunity for a combined terrestrial–maritime project, since the site's ship ways and other portions extended into the West River.

The project was undertaken cooperatively by MMAP, ASM, University of Maryland, College Park, Baltimore County, and Maritime Archaeological and Historical

Society (MAHS), Inc. (Thompson and Seidel, 1993). At that time, the property scheduled for development was not excavated, but MMAP had surveyed the remains below the mean high tide mark. Once an easement was drawn up with the developers, the program helped locate areas for water-related activities that would not affect submerged cultural resources. Terrestrial concerns were addressed by archaeological consultants via the easement. At present, no development has taken place.

Governor Robert M. McLane (18BC110). When the Baltimore Museum of Industry (BMI) purchased the adjacent Hercules shipyard property, it acquired several submerged and semisubmerged vessels as well as the remains of several wharves. Since the museum grounds formed the southern end of Baltimore's harborwalk, numerous agencies were involved in planning and development. Also, the Maryland State Highway Administration (SHA) played an active role, because the project used monies from the federal Intermodal Surface Transportation Efficiency Act (ISTEA). The museum wanted to clear its waterfront of all remains, reconstruct an existing bulkhead, and develop a revenue-generating marina facility. Because of a technicality, the state does not own the bottomland in that location, and the museum acquired it with the shipyard. Compliance with section 106 could be required only because of the federal funding.

MMAP and SHA archaeologists examined the site and determined that one vessel might be significant, so that the museum was required to do an archaeological survey. Research by SHA archaeologists confirmed the identity of the vessel as the *Governor Robert M. McLane*, flagship of the Maryland State Fishery Force from 1884 to 1931 (Ervin, 1994). This once famed and feared iron ship played a significant role in the Oyster Wars of the late 19th and early 20th centuries (Wennersten, 1982).

The vessel and wharf remains were documented by the consulting firm Tidewater Atlantic Research, Inc., and all hulls except the *McLane* were approved for removal. At present, the museum is exploring alternatives for treatment of the *McLane*, ranging from thorough documentation and destruction to partial physical preservation. All proposals include interpretation as part of larger development plans.

SS *Columbus.* A 1989 U.S. Army Corps of Engineers undertaking, the "Baltimore Harbor and Channels 50 Foot Project" (Morrison et al., 1992; Goodwin, 1995) called for deepening the harbor, its approaches, and the main channel through the Chesapeake to 60 ft, to accommodate vessels drawing 50 ft. In compliance with section 106, the Corps contracted with R. Christopher Goodwin and Associates, Inc. to undertake a cultural resources survey. Two of the numerous documented resources lay at the mouth of the Potomac River near the Maryland–Virginia boundary, and both were 19th-century steamboats. One, the *City of Annapolis,* was in good condition with several decks intact; the second had burned to the waterline and contained mainly the remnants of its engine and paddlewheel. A comparison of documentary sources with archaeological remains eliminated most contenders, and an examination of the engine, known as a crosshead engine and built by Charles Reeder in Baltimore, confirmed the ship as the SS *Columbus* (18ST625). No other examples of this engine are known.

Avoidance of both wrecks was not possible; difficult choices were necessary. Although in a sounder state, the *City of Annapolis* was not unusual; better examples of its genre are known, and its condition made it a navigational hazard. Despite the poor condition of *Columbus'* hull, its unique engine was declared significant enough to be worth raising and conserving. MHT drafted a memorandum of agreement with the corps and the consultant to help coordinate the project and the subsequent curation of the artifact. MMAP staff were involved in the scope of work but played no active role in the field.

The trust had negotiated with the appropriately named Columbus Center, a marine-oriented research and educational facility under construction at Baltimore's inner harbor, to incorporate the artifact into its planned exhibition facility. After the engine was raised and was undergoing conservation treatment, Columbus Center changed its orientation to biological marine studies and no longer wanted the engine. It subsequently went into receivership. Now the Trust and MMAP staff are charged with locating a suitable facility to house the artifact, whose size has eliminated most small museums and others disqualified by their research foci. The Baltimore Museum of Industry is the most satisfactory choice, a good fit technologically and located in blocks of the site where Reeder built the engine. Even so, BMI must construct a suitable facility to house the engine, and the costs of transport, installation, and conservation treatments before final exhibition are formidable. At present, the engine has undergone stabilization and basic conservation and is being curated at the Maryland Archaeological Conservation Laboratory. MMAP staff worked with the consultant, the laboratory staff and the Corps of Engineers to continue treatments and to provide transitional interpretation and exhibition until BMI is able to accept it.

Martin Refuge Burial.   A final example of a cooperative project is a salvage effort in nature and, although not specifically compliance-related, involves the retrieval of eroding human remains. In Martin Refuge, a U.S. Fish and Wildlife Service (USFWS) property, skeletal remains were found. They were extremely friable and located within an equally fragmentary coffin. Based on corroded hardware, fabric, and buttons, the burial dates to around the first quarter of the 19th century. USFWS and MMAP staff removed the remains, which were analyzed by Smithsonian Institution staff (Kollman and Owsley, 1997), and returned to Smith Island for reburial. A MMAP student intern, Mechelle Kerns-Nocerito, from the University of Maryland studied the burial area, using a conductivity survey to determine if more graves were present.

This project is important because it opened the door for development of a federal–state programmatic agreement between USFWS and MMAP to permit an efficient and cost-effective means of dealing with archaeological emergencies on these federal lands in Maryland. Maryland legislation provides concurrent jurisdiction over all National Park Service properties in the state but not yet over other branches of the Department of the Interior or other federal agencies.

Management Projects.   The Martin Refuge project provides an appropriate point to segue into MMAP activities to locate or assess sites in order to determine how best to manage these resources. These projects have been carried out mostly in partnership with the U.S. Naval Historical Center (NHC) through generous funding from the Department of Defense Legacy Resource Management Program.

U-1105 *(the Black Panther) (18ST636).*   Since 1993, both terrestrial and underwater archaeology had been ongoing on naval and army bases in Maryland through the Legacy Program, in compliance with sections 106 and 110 of the NHPA. The state's first maritime project involved creating Maryland's first historic shipwreck preserve around the German submarine U-1105 in the Potomac River. The preserve was opened May 5, 1995.

One of fewer than 10 submarines constructed, the U-1105 is the only known example of an early application of stealth technology. Its hull was sheathed in rubber tiles to evade sonar detection, which lead to its nickname the "Black Panther." Built in 1944, the Black Panther did not enter the war until 1945, and the only action it saw was on April 27 of that year, when it torpedoed and damaged but did not sink the HMS *Redmill*. The Black Panther's captain claims the rubber tiles prevented its destruction by the rest of the 21st Escort Group after it submerged. Within two weeks, the Black Panther received orders to surrender. The war was over.

The submarine was turned over to the U.S. Navy for further study and taken first to Portsmouth, New Hampshire, then to Point No Point, Maryland, where it was sunk and raised as practice for salvage vessels. Finally, it was raised and towed to the Potomac River off Piney Point. On September 19, 1949, it was the subject for testing a new high explosive detonated below the vessel. The pressurized hull cracked, and the Black Panther sank in 20 seconds.

Sport diver Uwe Lovas located it in 1985. In 1987 the Black Panther garnered attention when a popular journal identified its location. The Maryland dive community requested a dive preserve based on recommendations in the guidelines for the Abandoned Shipwreck Act (CFR 55.233). The U.S. Navy, owner of the vessel, entered into an memorandum of agreement with the state to document and assess the vessel to determine the feasibility of a preserve, and it funded both the study and the creation of the preserve. The navy, MMAP staff, contract personnel, along with volunteers with expertise in commercial diving and photography, carried out the work (Pohuski and Shomette, 1994; Pohuski and Kiser, 1995). Ongoing management of the preserve is the responsibility of the State Historic Preservation Office through MMAP and the Department of Recreation and Parks for St. Mary's County via another memorandum of agreement. MMAP volunteers, most from MAHS, continue to monitor the preserve and undertake annual deployment and retrieval of the mooring buoy.

USS *Tulip (18ST644)*.   A second navy-affiliated project was the investigation of the Civil War gunboat USS *Tulip*. Built in 1863 as a river patrol boat for the Chinese government, the *Chih Kiang* was purchased by the North when China defaulted on payment. Modified from sail and steam to steam only, the propeller-driven vessel saw constant service through October 1864. When it was finally granted permission to proceed upriver to the navy yard for repairs, its starboard boiler was considered too unsafe to be functional and was not fired. However, when it took three hours to steam the few miles from St. Inigoes coaling station to the lighthouse at Piney Point, the frustrated captain ordered the faulty boiler fired, a task the engineer had already taken upon himself to do. Shortly thereafter, Confederate prisoners at Point Lookout at the mouth of the Potomac (considerably downstream), heard the explosion. Only 10 of the vessel's 69 personnel survived and were rescued by the tug *Hudson*; of these, two later died.

Farther upriver from the site of the Black Panther, the USS *Tulip* was located in the late 1960s when a waterman asked local divers to untangle nets he had fouled on what he believed was the wreck of a tug. The divers raised items that were quickly recognized as Civil War vintage, and the site was extensively collected by a number of dive teams during the next decade.

The MHT project was undertaken between 1996 and 1998 by MMAP staff and volunteers with financial support from the navy's Legacy Program through NHC. In addition to assessing the site and making recommendations for its future management, the project recovered more than 1500 artifacts from the sport divers who the earlier activities (Thompson, 1998). The artifacts, in surprisingly good condition despite no conservation treatments, are now being stabilized at NHC at the Washington, D.C., Navy Yard. MMAP and MAC Laboratory staff are involved in the conservation of the *Tulip*'s artifact assemblage.

Chesapeake Flotilla. A third project was the search for and study of the War of 1812 Chesapeake flotilla, a small fleet of shallow-draft gunboats or row galleys. The flotilla was assembled at the suggestion of Revolutionary War hero Commodore Joshua Barney, who came out of retirement to command it.

In June 1814, while convoying merchant vessels to the mouth of the Chesapeake Bay, Barney ran afoul of the British off Cedar Point. Escaping up the Patuxent River, the flotilla and other ships retreated up St. Leonard's Creek. After two battles, Barney escaped farther up the Patuxent, scuttling his two slowest gunboats and possibly leaving a few merchantmen at the town of St. Leonard's. Forced to scuttle the remainder of the fleet in the upper reaches of the Patuxent, he marched overland in an effort to aid Washington, D.C. He arrived in August in time for the U.S. rout at Bladensburg, where he was wounded. Washington was burned, and feeble postwar efforts to salvage the flotilla resulted in the raising of only two vessels and about half the guns.

In 1979 and 1980, the Trust sponsored limited test excavation of one vessel (18PR226) through the private, nonprofit Nautical Archaeological Associates, Inc. in cooperation with the Calvert Marine Museum, which maintains a War of 1812 exhibit. Statewide interest in the War of 1812 has been renewed as the war's bicentennial approaches and has led to Trust sponsorship of further investigation through remote sensing surveys. The surveys were carried out in 1997 with MMAP supervision and participation under a contract with the University of Baltimore, and through a field school with East Carolina University's (ECU) graduate program in maritime history and nautical archaeology. Promising vessel remains were located at the head of St. Leonard's Creek at the end of that season.

The 1998 field season, funded by the navy legacy program and MHT, permitted further field work by ECU. Testing produced sufficient evidence for the tentative identification of gunboats 137 and 138 (18CV414). Since the gunboats are considered navy property, continued investigation and management needs will be determined in concert with the NHC. Study was completed in 1999 and confirmed the identification (Enright 1999).

Further remote sensing to locate the rest of the flotilla and any associated merchant vessels was planned for winter months, since shifting channels appear to have placed the areas of highest potential beneath wetlands protected and administered by the Maryland–National Capital Park and Planning Commission. It is probable that some merchant vessels in the convoy (state-owned, nonmilitary vessels) were scuttled, but it is not clear whether this was done to prevent their capture or was done by the British after the ships' capture (Shomette, 1995, Pitch, 1998). While much could be learned from investigation of such remains, they would be ineligible for federal legacy funding, and, without state funds, excavation and conservation endeavors are greatly restricted.

Research Projects. Although the flotilla project was initiated as a research endeavor by the Trust, it evolved into a partnership effort with other organizations.

Research projects executed through the Trust generally are undertaken on sites located during regular MMAP survey activities.

Eastern Shore Vessels.   On Maryland's eastern shore, a survey of the Chester and Choptank River systems produced several sites meriting further study. A keelson (18QU612) in Tilghman Creek off the Chester may date as early as the 17th century, and an 18th century wreck (18KE339) was located in Bungay Creek, also off the Chester.

The public has initiated the investigation of some sites. The Black Dog Marina on the Choptank reported an obstruction that turned out to be a small 19th century steamboat (18CA90). Another individual called to warn of a log canoe (18TA303) eroding from a beach. In Chesapeake parlance, "log canoe" does not connote a prehistoric dugout but historic vessels in which a single log to as many as five logs were shaped and joined to form the hull of a larger craft. The canoe in question was found on La Trappe Creek and dated to the late 18th or early 19th century. It was removed to the Chesapeake Bay Maritime Museum for initial conservation and is now undergoing final treatments at the MAC Laboratory.

Wharves.   Another call resulted in the relocation of the remains of the Troost Alum Plant and its related wharf structure (18AN1090) on the Magothy River between Annapolis and Baltimore (Bilicki, 1998). This early industrial site was the sole source of America's alum during the first quarter of the 19th century (alum is used as a mordant in dyeing, and in tanning; as a medicine, it staunches bleeding and is still used in styptic pencils; in a form called *copperas*, it was used to clean privies).

Other wharf studies have been carried out by MAHS in Back Creek adjacent to Hancock's Resolution (18AN169) (Hammill et al., 1998), and by MMAP at Mulberry Landing (18WC63) at Pemberton Hall on the Wicomico River near Salisbury. Both sites date back to the 18th century. Dendrochronological analysis at Mulberry dates it to no later than 1747, making it the second earliest wharf in America and the earliest known bulkhead-style wharf in the country (Heikkenen and Egan, 1996).

Mallows Bay.   One final site, Mallows Bay on the Potomac River, was documented through an MHT grant to the St. Clements Island–Potomac River Museum. This half-mile-wide embayment contains the remains of more than 150 vessels dating from as early as the Revolutionary War to post-World War II. The majority are World War I wooden steam freighters brought to the area to be scrapped for recovery of their metal fasteners. Although this small-scale recovery effort failed, other such efforts during the Great Depression provided 15 percent of the county's per capita income (Shomette, 1996). In a renewed attempt to salvage metal during World War II, Bethlehem Steel Corp. constructed an artificial basin at the back of the bay to burn the ships, but this also proved not to be cost effective.

Lands surrounding the bay contain a broad spectrum of site types, from prehistoric remains, to those of Civil War Camp McGaw, to a late 19th-century sturgeon caviar cannery (Shomette, 1996). Maryland plans to designate this bay as its second historic shipwreck preserve. Although public land access is lacking at present, Charles County is developing plans to remedy the lack, in partnership with the Department of National Resources Federal Bureau of Land Management.

SUMMARY

As noted, early drafts of a management plan for submerged cultural resources are being reworked in light of Maryland's new comprehensive plan, "Preservation Vision 2000." Strategic planning provides flexibility in addressing the challenges of changing goals and priorities. Short-term aims and needs include renewed focus on survey and inventory requirements, particularly in light of the *Brother Jonathan* case, and in a continuing effort to streamline compliance review and response. This necessitates addressing the need for additional equipment in the form of subsediment imaging apparatus, and for improved interagency communication, specifically with Maryland's Department of the Environment (MDE). MDE includes among its water-related duties the overseeing of state park management, dredging for oyster restoration programs, fisheries reef creation projects, and derelict boat removal. This last responsibility has been delegated to the individual counties. The communication issue is being resolved through workshops tailored for MDE staff, although other agencies including federal organizations have asked to attend. This approach will acquaint the branches of county governments, now charged with removal of derelict vessels, with heritage legislation requirements.

Equipment deficits may be resolved through the establishment, now taking place, of a "friends" group, a nonprofit program support group external to the state. This group will facilitate fundraising and expedite cash flow for special or emergency projects. It can maintain long-term and revolving accounts with greater ease than can the state's financial departments.

Midrange plans involve the pursuit and completion of studies currently underway, which fall into a number of the thematic categories of the comprehensive plan and which synthesize data at regional and state levels. Three examples of statewide recording projects in progress are (1) wharves and landings, being carried out both by river and by county; (2) shipyards from all periods; and (3) the War of 1812, a multi-agency initiative.

Beyond archaeology, historic sites and landmarks as well as museums are involved, and plans are being laid for driving tours, hiker, biker, and canoe trails, and maps and brochures. Maryland aims to do for the War of 1812 what Virginia did for the Civil War.

These projects lead into long-range plans and considerations, the most significant of which is the problem of locating submerged prehistoric sites in the low-visibility, heavily silted bottomlands of the Chesapeake Bay and its rivers. Research has begun in this area, with Blanton's work in Virginia's Chesapeake (1996) and a Corps of Engineers project on the Lower Maurice River, New Jersey (Schuldenrein et al., 1996). The Maryland SHA will cooperate with the MMAP on a pilot project focusing on submerged prehistoric remains, especially on the eastern shore. This region has extensive wetlands and a rapidly growing population with attendant development, which is greatly increasing the demand for roads and concomitant effects on these sites.

Other long-term plans include expanding survey and inventory activities away from the bay and into western and interior Maryland. Such an expansion would include industrial sites such as gold mine remains on the Potomac River in Montgomery County west of Washington D.C., and sites drowned by reservoir construction that can provide a variety of taphonomic data (Langley, 1994).

The National Park Service has recently founded a survey of Atlantic waters adjacent to Assateague National Seashore. MMAP has done limited survey in Sinepuxent Inlet between these barrier islands and the mainland and plans to do more work in this area. Since the passage of the agreement granting the concurrent jurisdiction of Maryland over the state's NPS properties (Agreement, 1996), MMAP has assisted in assessing and documenting cultural remains deposited or exposed by storm action at the National Seashore. Cooperative projects of greater scope are anticipated.

The establishment of more dive preserves, and more research projects focusing on state-owned resources (such as the merchant ships accompanied by Barney's 1812 flotilla or the hunt for Revolutionary War ships *Cato* and *Hawke*) are desirable. However, since the merchantmen were not military, and *Cato* and *Hawke* were the property of the Maryland State Navy and not vessels of the Continental Congress, none are eligible for Legacy funding, and the costs are prohibitive for MMAP alone. Faced with diminishing budgets and increasing administrative duties, the program could easily reach a plateau. The quickest route to increased funding is the location of an exciting and important site with a high public interest profile. However, unless one is found fortuitously, this poses the teleological argument that, while such a site does generate funding, funds are generally first required to find the site. So revitalization usually requires creative solutions. Development of a "friends" support group is one step; educational outreach is another. Thanks to the media the public has a ready appetite for underwater archaeology. MMAP staff members devote a significant amount of time to outreach and public relations activities. Educating the public, especially the sport diving public, is viewed as the best bet to promote site preservation. This perspective, coupled with the realization that "tourism is a $6 billion-a-year industry in Maryland, and visiting historic sites is one of the top three activities of visitors throughout the state" (Gearhart, 1998), brings the value of heritage tourism into sharp focus. Yet, despite fiscal benefits, an inherent danger lurks: "Heritage" can be subsumed by "tourism," causing the final product to degenerate into flimsy "edutainment." So far, MMAP has successfully integrated fundamental research into education via positive partnerships with agencies such as the U.S. Navy, National Park Service, U.S. Fish and Wildlife Service, and Maryland State Highway Administration. Using these experiences as a base, MMAP's will work with MHT's Exhibit Services Program and the Maryland Department of Business and Economic Development and, through regional Heritage Areas, explore the aspects of Maryland's submerged cultural resource base that have beneficial heritage tourism linkages.

Finally, there is the role of the volunteer. A most effective means of education and outreach is to provide opportunities for volunteer field experience. While this can be more complex for maritime situations than terrestrial sites, MMAP works to ensure that participation by any interested volunteer is possible, including nondivers and individuals with disabilities. For MMAP, volunteer involvement goes beyond outreach: It is a fiscal and logistical imperative. In this, the program is fortunate to have access to the talent pool of MAHS. Many MAHS members have received extensive training in underwater archaeology from professionals, and they have wide field experience. They form the core of volunteer participation, undertaking site monitoring and survey work on behalf of the state and providing an effective voice in the diving community. Shops and clubs, with which the MMAP enjoys a positive rapport, do the same. Chief among these is Sea Colony Aqua Sports, whose owner, John Kiser, played a key role during the Program's creation by acting as liaison with the diving community at large and even testifying on behalf of the state during the legislative process.

These groups are active in education and outreach activities. MAHS annually trains 20–30 divers through a 12-week underwater archaeology course that would be acceptable in an undergraduate program and is recognized by national scuba certification agencies.

Through an MHT grant, the lecture series has been videotaped and an instructor's manual developed for wider distribution to universities, government agencies, dive clubs, and libraries, ensuring dissemination of sound information and a consistent preservation message.

The Internet provides a whole new venue for outreach activities. MHT is developing a "virtual classroom" for archaeology. The web site address is www.MarylandHistorialTrust.net.

A crucial aspect of all education, outreach, and heritage tourism is the building of a feeling of proprietorship, of being a stakeholder in heritage preservation. This is not just warm, fuzzy rhetoric. In a state that is almost a fourth water and which has a small, underfunded professional underwater archaeological staff, proprietorship is a necessity.

This chapter provides only the broadest of brushstroke images. Overall, however, MMAP's achievements over the past decade have been impressive (Flanagan, 1996). Not only have more sites been located and even more are being reported. Through judicious partnerships and creative solutions to funding challenges, Maryland should prove equal to the task ahead.

ACKNOWLEDGMENTS. I am grateful and deeply indebted to Melanie Grim, Global Information System Analyst of the Office of Research, Survey and Registration, for researching, creating, and editing the figures in this chapter. I also wish to express my appreciation to Kent Mountford, senior scientist of the Evironmental Protection Agency, for providing erosion data on the Chesapeake, and to James Embrey for suggesting some references and sources that proved most helpful. As always, I want to thank all of MMAP's staff, volunteers, and project partners for their ongoing and tireless support.

REFERENCES

Abandoned Shipwreck Act. 43 USCS. Chapter 39. *Agreement to Establish Concurrent Jurisdiction Over Lands Administered by the National Park Service within the State of Maryland*, 1996, filed September 6, 1996, with the Clerk of the Court, Worcester County, Maryland. *In Liber* R.H.O. No. 2311. Folios 67–77.

Bilicki, Stephen, 1998, Historical Alum Works Uncovered. *In Context* 6(4):3.

Blanton, Dennis B., 1996, Accounting for Submerged Mid-Holocene Archaeological Sites in the Southeast: A Case Study from the Chesapeake Bay, Virginia. In *Archaeology of the Mid-Holocene Southeast*, edited by K.E. Sassaman and D.G. Anderson, pp. 200–217. University Press of Florida, Gainesville.

Enright, Jeffrey, 1999, An Archaeological and Historical Survey of a Jeffersonian Gunboat, Unpublished M.A. Thesis, Eastern Carolina University. On File at Maryland Historical Trust, Crownsville, MD.

Ervin, Richard G., 1994, *Archaeological Investigation and Archival Research Associated with the Harborwalk Southern Terminus, Property Acquisition at 1425–1435 Key Highway, Baltimore City, Maryland*. SHA Contract Number AW 628–201 N. Maryland State Highway Administration. Project Planning Division. Environmental Evaluation Section, Archaeological Report Number 117, Baltimore.

Flanagan, Joseph, 1996, The Art of the Possible. *Common Ground* 1(3/4):34–41.

Gearhart, Tyler, 1998, Historic Preservation's Payoff. Letter to the Editor, *The Washington Post*. October 13, A14.

Goodwin, R. Christopher, Irion, Jack B., and Beard, David V., 1995, *Data Recovery on the Wreck of the Steamship* Columbus, *18ST625, St. Mary's County, Maryland*. Delivery Order 0016. Contract No. DACW31-89-D-0059. U.S. Army Corps of Engineers, Baltimore District, Baltimore.

Hammill, Tom, Hayes, Ray, Henderson, Jaime, Howard, Brenda, Kerr, David, Berkey, Tom, and Gibb, James, 1998, *Limited Underwater Investigation of a Wharf and Pier at Hancock's Resolution (18AN169) and Phase I Underwater Reconnaissance of Marsh Cove*. Prepared by MAHS and James Gibb for the Friends of Hancock's Resolution Advisory Board, Anne Arundel County and the Maryland Historical Trust. On file at Maryland Historical Trust, Crownsville.

Heikkenen, H.J. and Egan, P.J.J., 1996, *Final Report: The Last Year of Tree Growth for Selected Timbers Used in the Construction of Pemberton Wharf as Derived by Key-Year Dendrochronology.* Dendrochronology, Inc. Submitted to the Pemberton Hall Foundation Inc. and the Maryland Historical Trust. On file at Maryland Historical Trust, Crownsville.

Jones, John Paul, 1998, *Treasure Salvage and the U.S. Supreme Court: Issues Remaining after the* Brother Jonathan. Paper presented at Sunken Treasure: Law, Technology & Ethics, 1998 Maritime Law Symposium. Roger Williams University School of Law. August 13–15, Bristol, Rhode Island.

Kollman, Dana D. and Owsley, Douglas W., 1997, *Examination of a Human Skeleton Recovered from Martin Refuge, Crisfield, Maryland.* On file at Maryland Historical Trust, Crownsville, and U.S. Fish & Wildlife Service, Hadley.

Langley, Susan B.M., 1994, *Inundation Taphonomy of Selected Submerged Heritage Resources in Alberta.* Ph.D. dissertation, University of Calgary. Canadian National Archives, Microfilm Division, Ottawa.

Leatherman, Stephen P., Chalfont, Ruth, Pendleton, Edward C., McCandless, Tamara L., and Funderburk, Steve, 1995, *Vanishing Lands: Sea Level, Society and Chesapeake Bay.* U.S. Fish & Wildlife Service, Chesapeake Bay Field Office. Annapolis.

Maryland Historical Trust, 1998, *Preservation Vision 2000: The Maryland Plan.* Maryland Historical Trust Press, Crownsville.

Maryland Submerged Archaeological Historic Property Act. Annotated Code of Maryland. Article 83B.

Maryland Submerged Archaeological Historic Property Regulations. Annotated Code of Maryland. Title 05, Subtitle 08, Chapter 03.

Morrison, Peter H., James, Stephen R., Goodwin, R. Christopher, and Pohuski, Michael, 1992, *Phase II Archaeological Investigations of Three Shipwreck Sites in the Baltimore Harbor and Channels Federal Navigation 50 FT Project, Chesapeake Bay, Maryland and Virginia.* Report submitted to the Baltimore District, U.S. Army Corps of Engineers, Baltimore.

Mountford, Kent, senior scientist, Environmental Protection Agency, 1998, E-mail correspondence regarding rates of erosion and deposition in the Chesapeake Bay, October 5.

Pitch, Anthony S., 1998, *The Burning of Washington.* Naval Institute Press, Annapolis.

Pohuski, Michael, and Kiser, John W., 1995, *Buoy Maintenance, Status Reports, and Safety Guidelines on the U-1105 Black Panther Historic Shipwreck Preserve.* Prepared for Maryland Historial Trust, Naval Hisorical Center, and St. Clements Island-Potomac River Museum. On file at Maryland Historical Turst, Crownsville.

Pohuski, Michael, and Shomette, Donald G., 1994, *The U-1105 Survey, A Report on the 1993 Archaeological Survey of 18ST636, A Second World War German Submarine in the Potomac River, Maryland.* Prepared for Maryland Historial Trust, Naval Historical Center, and St. Clements Island-Potomac River Museum. On file at Maryland Historical Trust, Crownsville.

Schuldenrein, Joseph, Cox, Jr., J. Lee, and Hunter, Richard, 1996, *Phase I Cultural Resources Investigations, Lower Maurice River, Cumberland County, New Jersey.* Delivery Orders 7, 11 & 21. Contract No. DACW61-94-D-0010. U.S. Army Corps of Engineers, Philadelphia District, Philadelphia.

Shomette, Donald G., 1996, *Ghost Fleet of Mallows Bay and Other Tales of the Lost Chesapeake.* Tidewater Publishers, Centreville.

_____, 1995, *Tidewater Time Capsule, History Beneath the Patuxent.* Tidewater Publishers, Centreville.

Thompson, Bruce F., 1997, *Maryland Maritime Archeology Program (MMAP) Statistics and Data Summary 1988–1997.* On file at Maryland Historical Trust, Crownsville.

_____, 1998, *The Terrible Calamity on the Lower Potomac: An Historical and Archaeological Assessment of the Shipwreck USS* Tulip *(18ST644), Potomac River, St. Mary's County, Maryland.* Public Version. Prepared for the Naval Historical Center. On file at Maryland Historical Trust, Crownsville, and U.S. Naval Historical Center, Washington Navy Yard, Washington, D.C.

Thompson, Bruce F., and Seidel, John, 1993, *Field Procedures for the Twenty-Third Annual Field Session in Maryland Archeology: The Stephen Steward Shipyard (18AN817).* Archaeological Society of Maryland, Inc., and the Maryland Historical Trust. On file at Maryland Historical Trust, Crownsville.

U.S. Federal Register, 1990, *Abandoned Shipwreck Act: Final Guidelines; Notice.* Vol. 55, No. 233.

Wennersten, John R., 1982, *The Oyster Wars of Chesapeake Bay.* Tidewater Publishers, Centreville.

Chapter 9

Maritime Archaeology in North Carolina

LAWRENCE E. BABITS

INTRODUCTION

There have been more than 5000 shipwrecks along the North Carolina coast since 1584. This figure does not include even more abandoned vessels. These sites have initiated not only a wide range of exploration as both amateurs and professionals have sought to acquire knowledge of the past but also exploitation as local watermen and salvors sought to recycle boats and their parts.

North Carolina maritime archaeology concentrated on ship remains and cargo between 1962 and 1975 and initially was concerned with wrecks buried on shore. The introduction of self-contained underwater breathing apparatus (SCUBA) greatly expanded accessibility to underwater sites after 1955, and North Carolina was no exception. In the past 30 years, a great many individual sites have been subjected to both archaeological investigation and looting.

A slight shift to regional surveys and modeling occurred in the last 15 years, but site-specific research continues to draw the state's effort. In part, the emphasis on ships is due to funding for research on specific vessels (*Monitor* and *Queen Anne's Revenge*), emergency recording of finds exposed by weather or excavation (Gunboat 140, CSS *Neuse*, *Modern Greece*), and funding limitations on time and equipment. Regional

Lawrence E. Babits, Program in Maritime Studies, East Carolina University, Greenville, North Carolina 27853.

International Handbook of Underwater Archaeology, edited by Carol V. Ruppé and Janet F. Barstad. Kluwer Academic/Plenum Publishers, New York, 2002.

surveys were limited to riverine segments rather than entire drainage systems. Even with these caveats, North Carolina's rich maritime archaeological heritage has been the object of a great deal of research, and publication of results reaches a worldwide audience.

SINGLE SITES IN THE EARLY YEARS

Gunboat 140

The first work in maritime archaeology took place in 1939, when a storm uncovered the remains of a vessel on Bodie Island. Investigated by National Park Service historian Thor Borreson, the vessel was tentatively identified as a Jeffersonian gunboat. Gunboat 140 exploded and burned off the coast in the early 19th century (Borreson, 1939). More recent work on another gunboat (Babits and Enright, 1998) suggests that the identification might be erroneous, but Borreson's report represents a model for preliminary reporting and interpretation in a phase I wreck survey.

Modern Greece

In 1962, another storm uncovered *Modern Greece*, a Civil War blockade runner that ran aground and sank on June 27, 1862 (Bright, 1977). U.S. Navy divers discovered the vessel and recovered some cargo the same year. The indiscriminate recovery of artifacts without provenance controls, and the obvious need for conservation, resulted in the funding of a modest conservation facility at Fort Fisher. Artifacts from *Modern Greece* were stored at the facility, and conservation and research continued until at least 1975. A partial inventory with illustrations was published by the Department of Cultural Resources in 1977 (Bright, 1977). Following work on *Modern Greece*, exploratory dives were made on other Civil War era wreck sites in the Cape Fear area.

CSS *Neuse*

Even before *Modern Greece* was located, another vessel was being explored by North Carolina citizens. The ram CSS *Neuse* was one of some 22 ironclad gunboats commissioned by the Confederate States during the Civil War. Scuttled in 1865, it attracted the attention of local residents in 1961. A private effort to raise the vessel in conjunction with the Civil War centennial attracted widespread attention, but dragline excavation severely damaged the ship's casemate, decking, and interior. Eventually the vessel was raised, cut apart, and moved to a permanent site in Kinston, North Carolina (Bright et al., 1981). Approximately three-quarters of the hull remained. Yet the gunboat's story does not end here. Protected by an overhead roof at a state historic site, the vessel was damaged by flooding in 1996. It was moved to higher ground and underwent a new episode of study and conservation in 1998 and 1999.

   As a result of the *Neuse* and *Modern Greece* situations, North Carolina reevaluated its position regarding underwater resources on the coast and in waterways. Appropriations made by the state legislature provided for a conservation facility at Fort Fisher State Historic Site. Eventually this lab grew into the base for the Underwater Archaeology Unit (UAU) (modern designations for various state agencies are used in this chapter).

CREATION OF NORTH CAROLINA'S UNDERWATER ARCHAEOLOGY LAW

In 1967, North Carolina's legislature passed an underwater archaeology law that declared the state was the owner of all historical and archaeological material that had been lying unclaimed in state waters for 10 years. This law made the Department of Cultural Resources custodian of underwater archaeological resources.

The General Assembly funded the UAU in 1971 (Figure 9.1), and professional staffing began in 1972. Since that time, the UAU has conducted research on individual sites, offshore areas, harbors, and river systems, and has monitored federally permitted activity in North Carolina waters. UAU staff has run a series of field schools cooperatively with local universities to educate students in underwater archaeology (Watts and Bright, 1973).

The office of state archaeologist was created at about the same time. The original state representative for underwater archaeology was Samuel P. Townsend, in the Division of Archives and History, Department of Cultural Resources. In June 1973, North Carolina hired Stephen J. Gluckman, as its first state archaeologist. Three other archaeologists were also hired, and a separate office was established in Raleigh, which included several certified divers. The group continued to work closely with UAU personnel.

A major effect of the Raleigh office was its implementation of federal and state laws, including provisions for cultural resource assessment. The office issued federal and state permits only after archaeological review to ensure that cultural resources were not adversely affected by construction allowed by the permit. Permits were issued by several agencies for a bewildering array of projects including bulkheads, piers, dredging, and marina construction. Accurate record-keeping established that some permits were being issued without accounting for cultural resources and a system for inspecting sites was successfully implemented.

Under North Carolina's underwater archaeology law, the state issues permits to individuals and companies who want to explore sites. Permits are divided into two classes. A short-term sport and hobby permit allows amateur individuals and groups to explore and recover a limited number of artifacts and, since 1968, a special annual permit has been issued to the North Carolina Skin Diving Council to encourage sport diver participation and generate information about wreck sites. The second class of permit allows groups to conduct archaeological exploration of sites, and for commercial salvage under state supervision. Several companies have recovered artifacts and documented sites

Figure 9.1. Logo of Underwater Archaeology Unit, Fort Fisher, North Carolina.

under these permits. Sites involved include the blockade runners *Ella* and *Ranger* and Union gunboats *Pickett* and *Underwriter*. Since 1982, 104 permits have been issued. Only a few have included stipulations for a divison of artifacts between the permittee and the state (Lawrence, 1985, 1989).

INDIVIDUAL SITES

Fort Branch Cannon

The first test and legal proof of North Carolina's underwater archaeology law came in a case involving the Fort Branch cannon. Fort Branch was a Civil War earthwork abandoned in 1865. Its armament was thrown into the Roanoke River when the garrison left. When Alabama divers recovered three cannons in 1972, outraged local residents notified the Department of Cultural Resources. Once informed of the 1967 law, county sheriff's deputies detained the guns until subsequent legal tests validated the law. Later survey and recovery operations at the fort and in the river yielded four additional cannons, shot, and other Civil War materials. Fort Branch remains the only Confederate earthwork with most of its weaponry still on site (Watts et al., 1979).

USS *Monitor*

The USS *Monitor* sank off Cape Hatteras on December 31, 1862. In 1973, after a great deal of research, the site was located by a combined group that included UAU personnel, Duke University, and a host of contributing agencies and groups. The enthusiasm for learning about *Monitor* allowed the generation of considerable funding involving sophisticated technology to examine the wreck site. Since that time, numerous expeditions have visited, and the site is now a National Marine Sanctuary (Arnold et al., 1991; Watts, 1975).

Queen Anne's Revenge

In November 1996, the remains of a wreck believed to be *Queen Anne's Revenge*, flagship of celebrated pirate Edward "Blackbeard" Teach, were found off Beaufort Inlet, North Carolina, by Intersal, a salvage firm operating under a permit from the UAU. Preliminary identification was based on the number of cannons, the early date on a bell, and proof marks on other artifacts. Since the initial discovery, the site has been explored through the combined efforts of the UAU, Maritime Research Institute, North Carolina Maritime Museum, and several North Carolina universities. Nothing found to date indicates that the vessel is not of the right time period and, since there is no other heavily armed vessel known to have sunk off Beaufort during the first third of the 18th century, it seems probable that the vessel is indeed *Queen Anne's Revenge* (Wilde-Ramsing, 1997, 1998, 1999).

REGIONAL SURVEYS

The first regional consolidation of sites occurred when the UAU nominated a number of Cape Fear wreck sites dating to the Civil War era as a National Register District (Wilde-Ramsing and Angley, 1985). This effort led to consideration of the Eastern North

Carolina Civil War Shipwreck District. This widely dispersed district covers 15 sites in the northeastern coastal region above Cape Lookout including the sounds (Lawrence, 1993).

Cape Fear and Northeast Cape Fear Rivers

Regional surveys first began in the lower Cape Fear and Northeast Cape Fear Rivers (Jackson, 1996) partly because of ongoing channelization and heavy industrial development around Wilmington, North Carolina. Consisting of both documentary and field research and secondary testing, this effort is still underway. Under the aegis of a National Park Service battlefield survey grant, wreck locations offshore from Fort Fisher were surveyed during the 1990s.

Pamlico and Pungo Rivers

Portions of the Pamlico River shoreline were systematically explored between 1993 and 1995. The survey located more than 50 vessels, submerged and afloat. A second survey located more than 50 vessels in the creek systems running from the western shore of the Pungo River (Babits et al., 1995; Babits and Kjorness, 1995). Most were found in the creek systems rather than on the main river shoreline. Distribution of the abandoned vessels clustered in certain predictable locations.

Two major documentary searchers, David Stick and Bill Reaves, collected hundreds of references to vessels lost on North Carolina's coast. Since the late 1970s, North Carolina Archives researcher Wilson Angley has compiled numerous additional references to ships sinking along the North Carolina inland waters and coast (Angley, 1991, 1995, 1998a, 1998b), work that is updated when additional information is found. These irregular papers are distributed to other researchers and comprise a basic research tool for assessing the realm of North Carolina's sunken vessels and providing a starting point for areal research. Two problems with shipwreck references are their lack of specific location, especially for the earlier years, and the usual absence of references about whether the vessel was later saved, salvaged, or otherwise disposed of.

During the 1980s, East Carolina University professors William N. Still and Richard Stephenson created a database of North Carolina-built ships, drawing from enrollments, registrations, newspapers, and personal accounts. The database includes vessel dimensions and references to original source material. Not widely publicized, student researchers at East Carolina University have made extensive use of it, and it is still being compiled.

Mattamuskeet Tribe

In 1975, Patrick Garrow completed a preliminary study of a maritime-oriented community in Hyde County, a study concerning a remnant American Indian population and its reservation on Pamlico Sound. During the study, Garrow identified one original town in the reservation area. Survivors of the Mattamuskeet tribe remain in the area on isolated creeks, continuing a maritime lifestyle that, if modern material culture is not considered, has changed little from prehistoric times (Garrow, 1975). Although the study remains a lone example in North Carolina maritime research, its import was recognized at the time of publication.

Harbor Surveys

Several harbor surveys have been conducted by the UAU, Tidewater Atlantic Research, and East Carolina University. The surveys include Bath, Edenton, Wilmingon, and New Bern harbors, where a great many abandoned vessels and several wrecks were reported. In addition to the harbor surveys, a detailed survey of Lake Phelps provided extensive data on prehistoric and historic log canoes (Lawrence, 1989).

WHERE IS IT LEADING?

Results from maritime archaeological work conducted since 1962 demonstrate the important resources available in North Carolina waters. Given the increased utilization of coastal waters and shorelines for recreational housing and activity, permitting activity is likely to generate tremendous amounts of additional information. The real question lies in how to assess these resources to allow nonarchaeological use (such as commercial and domestic construction, and recreational and avocational diving) while conserving them.

Regional surveys that provide a baseline for what remains of the resource are only the starting point. Funding for systematic survey work and its testing should be increased to alleviate pressures both on the sites and on those wanting to use places where they are found. Only by documenting site numbers, to determine what remains, can an accurate assessment of significant resources be attempted. Once significant resources are identified, they can be protected, while other sites are either monitored or recorded prior to other uses.

Students and researchers undoubtedly will use the systematic surveys, as well as individual sites found through research, uncovered by storms, or located by amateurs and sport divers, as resources for learning more about the past. Student theses on individual sites are more manageable than surveys or major excavations. Identifying endangered sites, as the UAU already is doing, allows the state to support limited student excavations. One of a kind sites, such as *Queen Anne's Revenge* and others, will continue to draw attention and funding for their examination.

In retrospect, it is clear that some individuals and agencies have played major roles in recovering, preserving, and publicizing information about North Carolina's maritime heritage. In the early years, Samuel P. Townsend and Stephen J. Gluckman, North Carolina Department of Cultural Resources, were instrumental in administering underwater activities. During Gluckman's tenure as state archaeologist, effective monitoring of permitting activities came of age and ensured compliance with federal and state legislation.

Richard Lawrence and Mark Wilde-Ramsing, senior staffers at UAU, continue to monitor, inspect, and research activities in North Carolina waters. They work closely with East Carolina University faculty, staff, and students to complete studies of numerous site reports and surveys.

Leslie Bright served as archaeological conservator for more than 34 years under UAU's aegis. His pragmatic and innovative approach to conservation set guidelines for other conservators around the world. He also worked to resolve the backlog of materials dating to 1962, all the while responding to a never-ending series of new materials.

Finally, the role of Gordon P. Watts Jr. cannot be over-stated. From working at the UAU to his later roles as faculty member at East Carolina University, and owner of Tidewater Atlantic Research (TAR), a contract research firm, Watts has explored North

Carolina's waters for more than 30 years. Watts, his staff at TAR, and students at East Carolina generated fully a third of the North Carolina underwater bibliography.

The continual production of student papers, theses, and other research at East Carolina, the ongoing permit monitoring, and contract or grant-financed research bodes well for the future of North Carolina's maritime archaeology. A slow shift from site-specific research to regional studies and interpretive research involving a more holistic maritime environment is underway but will never totally supplant research on single sites. Nevertheless, steps beyond artifact and site reporting have been underway for some 35 years. These more inclusive and wider ranging studies will lead to new information about changes over time in the use of the maritime environment.

REFERENCES

Angley, Wilson, 1991, North Carolina Shipwreck References from Newspapers of the Late Eighteenth, Nineteenth, and Early Twentieth Centuries. Manuscript on file, North Carolina State Archives, Raleigh.

_____, 1995, North Carolina Shipwreck References from New York Shipping and Commercial List, 1815–1873. Manuscript on file, North Carolina State Archives, Raleigh.

_____, 1998a, North Carolina Shipwreck References from the Boston News-Letter (1704–1736), Maryland Gazette (1745–1751), and New York Weekly Journal (1733–1751). Manuscript on file, North Carolina State Archives, Raleigh.

_____, 1998b North Carolina Shipwreck References from the Providence Gazette, 1762–1825. Manuscript on file, North Carolina State Archives, Raleigh.

Arnold, J. Barto, III, G. Michael Fleshman, Dina B. Hill, Curtiss E. Peterson, W. Kenneth Stewart, Stephen R. Gegg, Gordon P. Watts, Jr., and Clark Weldon, 1991, The 1987 Expedition to the MONITOR National Marine Sanctuary: Data Analysis and Final Report. Sanctuaries and Reserves Division, National Oceanic and Atmospheric Administration, Washington, D.C.

Babits, Lawrence E., and Jeffrey M. Enright, 1998, Preliminary Report—Flotilla Project Site 18CV414. Manuscript on file, Program in Maritime Studies, East Carolina University, Greenville.

_____, 1995a, A Survey of the Pungo River, Wade's Point to Woodstock Point, Beaufort Country, North Carolina. Report on File, Office of State Archaeologist, Raleigh, (with Annalies C. Kjorness).

_____, 1995b, A Survey of the North Shore Pamlico River: Batch Creek to Wade's Point. Report on File, Office of State Archaeologist, Raleigh NC. (with Jeff Morris and Annalies C. Kjorness).

Borreson, Thor, 1939, Final Report on the Remains of an Old Ship Found on Bodie Island, Dare County, North Carolina. Manuscript on file, National Park Service, Manteo.

Bright, Leslie S., 1977, The Blockade Runner Modern Greece and Her Cargo. North Carolina Department of Cultural Resources, Raleigh.

Bright, Leslie S., William H. Rowland, and James C. Bardon, 1981, CSS Neuse: A Question of Iron and Time. North Carolina Department of Cultural Resources, Raleigh.

Brooks, Barbara L., Ann M. Merriman, and Mark Wilde-Ramsing, 1996, Bibliography of North Carolina Underwater Archaeology. North Carolina Department of Cultural Resources, Raleigh.

Garrow, Patrick H., 1975, The Mattamuskeet Documents: A Study in Social History. North Carolina Department of Cultural Resources, Raleigh.

Jackson, Claude V., III, 1996, A Maritime History and Marine Archaeological Survey of the Cape Fear and Northeast Cape Fear Rivers, Wilmington Harbor, North Carolina. Manuscript on file, Underwater Archaeology Unit, Kure Beach.

Lawrence, Richard, 1993, The Eastern North Carolina Civil War Shipwreck District. Underwater Archaeology Proceedings of the Society for Historical Archaeology Conference, edited by Sheli O. Smith, pp. 107–114. Society for Historical Archaeology, Tucson.

Watts, Gordon P., Jr., 1975, The Location and Identification of the Ironclad USS Monitor. International Journal of Nautical Archaeology and Underwater Exploration 4(2):301–330.

Watts, Gordon P. Jr., and Leslie S. Bright, 1973, Progress in Underwater Archaeology in North Carolina 1962–72. International Journal of Nautical Archaeology and Underwater Exploration 2(1):131–136.

Watts, Gordon P. Jr., Leslie S. Bright, James A. Duff, Dina B. Hill, Richard W. Lawrence, James A. Jr. Pleasants, and J. Reed Whitesell, 1979, *The Fort Branch Survey and Recovery Project.* North Carolina Department of Cultural Resources, Raleigh.

Wilde-Ramsing, Mark and Angley Wilson, 1985, *Cape Fear Civil War Period Shipwreck District, National Register of Historic Places nomination.* Manuscript on file, National Register, U.S. Department of the Interior, Washington.

_____, 1997, *Management Plan.* Underwater Archaeology Unit, Kure Beach.

_____, 1998, *Preliminary Report on the 1997 Test Excavations.* Underwater Archaeology Unit, Kure Beach, DC.

_____, 1999, *Preliminary Report on the 1998 Test Excavations.* Underwater Archaeology Unit, Kure Beach.

Chapter 10

South Carolina
A Drop in the Bucket

CHRISTOPHER F. AMER

INTRODUCTION

In 1998, the South Carolina Institute of Archaeology and Anthropology (SCIAA), celebrated 35 years of advocating and conducting archaeology in the state. For most of those 25 years, the state has had an underwater archaeology program within the SCIAA, which conducts and monitors archaeology conducted on the state's bottomlands. From 1973 to 1987, South Carolina's underwater archaeology was directed by Alan Albright, who headed the SCIAA's Underwater Archaeology Division. With Albright's retirement in 1987, Christopher Amer was hired as the new division head. Under his leadership, emphasis was placed on: (1) inventorying and assessing a wide variety of submerged cultural resources; (2) public education and appropriate public recreational access to sites; and (3) drafting and implementing appropriate legislation to support and guide these strategies—in other words, management of the state's maritime cultural heritage.

It is especially appropriate for South Carolina that *The International Handbook of Underwater Archaeology* emphasize advances in underwater archaeology during the past 10 years. This chapter focuses on the development and implementation of strategies for forming a comprehensive statewide research design, and advances within the state that have made such development possible.

Christopher F. Amer, State Underwater Archaeologist, South Carolina Institute for Archaeology and Anthropology, University of South Carolina, Columbia, South Carolina 29208.

International Handbook of Underwater Archaeology, edited by Carol V. Ruppé and Janet F. Barstad. Kluwer Academic/Plenum Publishers, New York, 2002.

South Carolina Institute of Archaeology and Anthropology (SCIAA)

The South Carolina Institute of Archaeology and Anthropology is an administrative unit of the University of South Carolina. Under two state legislative acts, the SCIAA Enabling Act of 1963 (SCCL 60-13-210, 2000) and the South Carolina Underwater Antiquities Act of 1991 (SCCL 54-7-610 *et seq.*, 1991), SCIAA is the main state agency concerned with South Carolina's material cultural heritage. SCIAA manages the state's cultural resources, creates and maintains the South Carolina site files, and serves as the curation repository for the state's archaeological collections. SCIAA also manages one of the country's largest waterlogged wood conservation facilities. In their facility's 60-foot-long tank, the 18th-century Brown's Ferry vessel was conserved, and several hundred tons of timbers from the Groeneur Lock, part of the Erie–Wabash canal system, have been undergoing treatment.

The Underwater Archaeology Division is an administrative unit of SCIAA. The division head is also the State Underwater Archaeologist. From a staff of two in 1987, the division roster rose to eight in 1989, when the underwater antiquities management program was incorporated into the division and a position was added to manage the sport diver archaeology management program. In the early 1990s, statewide cutbacks reduced the division to its current staffing level of five. Two staff members are based at the Fort Johnson Marine Resources Center in Charleston.

In the late 1980s, the Underwater Archaeology Division identified and set as its primary goals the research and management of submerged cultural resources beneath the state's waters, and the preservation of the archaeological, historical, and recreational values of those resources. Before that could be accomplished, several pressing issues needed to be addressed. These included fulfilling unfinished commitments, enhancing agency–public interaction, revising and updating the legislation, and initiating an aggressive research program.

Completing unfinished commitments, sometimes referred to as "putting out old fires," has occupied much of the division's time and resources during the early days of the last decade of the millennium. Conservation and documentation of the Brown's Ferry vessel, recovered in 1976 from a river near Georgetown, was completed in 1993; the vessel is currently on the top floor of Georgetown's Rice Museum, awaiting the refurbishing of the museum and completion of the exhibition.

Another project is the Little Landing Survey (or 2-Cannon Wreck, as it was formerly known). This project began in 1986 when two sport divers found the remains of a vessel offshore of Lewisfield Plantation on the Cooper River and illegally raised two cannons from the Revolutionary period site. The division completed fieldwork on the site in the late 1980s.

ENHANCING AGENCY–PUBLIC INTERACTION AND EDUCATION

Through the 1970s and 1980s, much of the division's research strategies centered around the hobby diver licensing program and the issuance of search and salvage licenses, which began in 1976. At the time, the program was innovative if somewhat controversial in its concept and unique to North America in its implementation. Unfortunately, little useful research data were recorded from the program's more than 40 search and salvage licenses issued between 1976 and 1986, all but one of which was commercially based (Amer, 1994). This left the maritime resource base, located beneath 300 square miles of territorial waters, largely a mystery. Many of the state's submerged cultural resources lie along approximately 758 miles of Atlantic coastline and under the more than 11,000 linear miles of rivers.[*]

Sport Diver Archaeology Management Program (SDAMP)

In 1988, in a drive to protect the state's submerged cultural resources from damage caused by collecting, we decided to revise the hobby diver program. Driving the change was the understanding that sport divers and avocationalists could provide useful research information and could play an active role in the management of those resources. The following year, Lynn Harris was hired to head the new Sport Diver Archaeology Management Program (SDAMP). The program stepped up enforcement of the legal requirements and developed a broad-based public education program. This strategy has allowed the state to build public support for the protection and nondestructive use of the state's submerged cultural resources.

State law allows licensed sport divers to collect artifacts and fossils lying on state bottomlands, provided those items are neither embedded in sediments nor are components of an archaeological site. The SDAMP enlisted the help of local law enforcement officers, initiated public lectures and school programs, developed underwater archaeology field training courses for sport divers and avocationalists, and provided opportunities for public involvement in the research and management of the state's submerged cultural heritage. In return for this privilege, divers provide the state with quarterly reports of their finds and collecting activities.

A primary result of the program has been a dramatic increase in the quality of hobby-diving reports to the SCIAA. An analysis of these reports and the state's shipwreck files, which recently were committed to a digital database, indicates that almost half (43 percent) of shipwrecks in the state files initially were located through sport diver reports, the majority in the Charleston area. This is not surprising; more than half the state's hobby-diving licenses (61 percent) were issued to Charleston divers.

Over the years, several groups of graduates from the division's training courses have surveyed the state's rivers, recorded historic sites, and provided logistical support on countless state projects. Many students have gone on to produce reports, present their findings at conferences and other public venues, and some have been gone on to underwater archaeology graduate programs at Texas A&M and East Carolina Universities. One such survey initiated the creation a heritage diving trail along the Cooper River near Charleston (Harris, Moss, and Naylor, 1993).

Opened in 1998, the Cooper River Heritage Trail provides recreational and educational opportunities for both the diving and nondiving public. The trail was set up around six historic sites located along a three-mile stretch of the river: a 1705 ferry landing, three shipwrecks ranging in dates from the Revolutionary period through the 19th century, a barge, and an 18th-century dock. Pamphlets and waterproof slates provide history, descriptions, and diving information about the trail, and two of the sites can be viewed at low tide. Residents living along its banks monitor the trail, and local divers and companies working with SCIAA maintain the sites and mooring systems (Harris, 1998).

---

[*] 758 miles includes the foreshore of all bays, estuaries, and harbors in the state, which otherwise has a linear coastline from Georgia to North Carolina of 187 miles.

In 1997, SCIAA opened another heritage trail on the Ashley River, also near Charleston, that provided public access to wrecked and abandoned watercraft along the upper reaches of this historic river. Thirteen vessels dating from the late 18th through the early 20th centuries are visible at low tide and accessible primarily by canoe. The trail is meant to combine recreational opportunities with heritage tourism and thereby boost the economy of the surrounding area (Maritime Heritage Homepage).

BEEFING UP THE LEGISLATION

As SDAMP was being created, an internal evaluation of the state's underwater legislation forced a complete retooling of the laws governing management of the state's underwater material culture. While this was underway, two other events took place that emphasized the need to revise South Carolina's underwater legislation: a test of the strength of the state's Underwater Antiquities Act, and the passage of the federal Abandoned Shipwreck Act.

In 1989, the U.S. District Court in Charleston made a landmark decision regarding jurisdiction of a historic shipwreck site in South Carolina waters. SS *William Lawrence* was a 576-ton cargo steamer carrying a cargo of domestic goods that included South Carolina Dispensary bottles. On February 11, 1899, while enroute from Baltimore to Savannah, the ship went ashore in a storm and sank off Hilton Head, South Carolina. The wreck was a popular dive site for individual divers and charter tours and was known as a site where divers could retrieve souvenirs. In 1988, the site was the subject of an admiralty claim, the salvors asserting in federal court that the wreck was outside South Carolina's territorial sea. A two-year court battle ensued when two different interest groups began fighting for control of the site for commercial recovery of the wreck and its contents. The state intervened and ultimately regained jurisdiction over the site, establishing that it was within South Carolina's territorial sea (Amer, 1994).

While this drama was unfolding—but too late to be applied to the case of SS *Lawrence*—the Abandoned Shipwreck Act of 1987 was signed into law (United States Congress, 1988). The act asserts U.S. title to certain abandoned shipwrecks in state waters. It also transfers title to the state in or on whose submerged lands the shipwrecks are located, clarifies the state's management responsibility of those shipwrecks, and provides an appropriate juncture to revise state underwater legislation. Using National Park Service guidelines, which were then being developed under authority of the act, South Carolina's underwater antiquities legislation was amended and passed to law in 1991. The South Carolina Antiquities Act of 1991 (SCCL 54-7-610 *et seq.*, 1991) rectifies ambiguities in the previous legislation, outlines the state's responsibility toward the cultural and paleontological resources found beneath state waters, and prescribes a licensing system that governs public access and usage of the state's submerged cultural heritage.

Among other advances, including stiffer penalties for violations as well as provisions for the discovery of human remains, the law mandates the educational program set up under SDAMP. Since the bill's passage, there has been no commercial recovery of underwater archaeological sites; the last commercial salvor in the state withdrew to his home state shortly before the bill became law, saying he would not be able to meet the standards in the new law.

Discovery of the Confederate submarine *H.L. Hunley*, which was found to contain the skeletal remains of eight crew members, off Charleston harbor provided an opportunity for the legislature again to amend the act. Harsh penalties were established for anyone who violates warships that might contain human remains. Shortly after the law came into effect, the SCIAA also set up agency rules for arbitrating disputes.

RESEARCH AND MANAGEMENT

A trained avocational base can greatly assist state underwater archaeologists in locating and recording the state's submerged cultural resources. However, it is ultimately up to state cultural resource managers to develop tools to manage those vestiges of our past. To be effective, managers must thoroughly understand the resource base as well as the various threats to, and pressures on, that resource. This means inventorying and assessing all cultural resources in state jurisdiction to provide efficient strategies.

Yet funding is the overriding factor that conditions and dictates our ability to pursue any management course. As with other states, not to mention the federal government, funding for submerged antiquities management and research in South Carolina has not increased enough to support our expanding mandated role. For this reason, grants affect the direction and focus of our research. The low level of financial support for underwater archaeology in this country is probably one of our biggest disappointments, as we have seen one state underwater program on the East Coast disappear and others to drastically decrease their activities. Ironically, this is a time when states desperately need to increase their management roles as coastal development flourishes and rapidly advancing technologies provide treasure hunters with tools to loot sites more efficiently than ever.

Throughout the last dozen years, many of our research questions and directions were generated through the division's compliance role: its response to public notices for activities that could adversely affect the state's bottomlands, such as dredging for marinas, as well as bridge replacements and realignments. Threatened bottomlands are assessed for the presence of cultural resources by using literature and state site file searches and, if appropriate, by conducting reconnaissance surveys of the areas. Comments and recommendations are made to the state historic preservation office and other permitting agencies. Ongoing investigations by the division of historic wharves and causeways are often initiated after reconnaissance surveys of areas under public notice. Likewise, public notices led to investigations of two colonial shipyard sites near Charleston and a more complete investigation of the Pritchard Shipyard. Located on a creek near Charleston, Pritchard is the earliest and largest known existing shipyard in South Carolina, having operated continuously from the 1750s well into the 19th century (Amer and Naylor, 1994).

South Carolina does enough funding for an all-inclusive statewide submerged cultural resource survey. Thus, much of the division's research has focused on small but systematic investigations of sites in the river systems and shipwreck sites both offshore and onshore that have been reported to us by the public, located on navigational and historic charts, or have become exposed through environmental conditions such as hurricanes, droughts, and erosion. The level of documentation of these sites is geared toward establishing good locational and observational information for state site files with a view toward potential nomination to the National Register of Historic Places. While many ocean sites are associated with the Civil War (including steamers and other oceangoing vessels), South Carolina's rivers contain prehistoric sites, prehistoric and historic aboriginal watercraft, small colonial craft, steamboats, canals, landings and causeways, historic shipyards, and the like.

SAMPLING THE RESOURCES

A brief survey of submerged archaeological sites investigated by the SCIAA during the last dozen years will illustrate the range of South Carolina's significant historic sites, as well as an equally broad scope of funding sources and opportunities that allowed us to locate and record them. Funding for projects break down into four categories: agency funding, grants, contracts, and partnerships.

Most investigations of archaeological sites exposed by natural occurrences are funded by internal sources or through partnerships. While internal funding sources appear to decrease each year, and the demands placed on our basically static budget increase, internal funding remains one of the most viable options for these short-term opportunistic projects.

Opportunities

Jonathan May and *Freda Wiley.* When Hurricane Hugo, a category-four hurricane, hit the state in September 1989, it exposed cultural resources along the South Carolina coast. This presented, several research opportunities for the division. Shortly after the hurricane decimated the Myrtle Beach area, the city's mayor asked the division's archaeologists to examine a shipwreck that was exposed when the dunes were dragged out to sea during the immense tidal surge associated with the storm. Scattered along a three-block area centered around 81st Avenue North, the vessel's remains were identified as the *Jonathan May*, a lumber carrier driven ashore during the "Great Storm" of 1893. The *Freda Wiley*, which suffered the same fate, also was investigated by the archaeologists; her remains lay exposed from the keelson to the turn of the bilge on the foreshore 39 blocks to the south. The remains of a third lumber carrier, one of a trio cast ashore in the same storm, was investigated the previous year, when its timbers were exposed and removed by a developer excavating footings for condominiums on an adjacent barrier island south of Myrtle Beach.

The Mulberry Site. The situation left by Hurricane Hugo clearly was a case of catastrophic and rapid erosion. We encounter many sites along rivers and barrier islands that have become exposed because of a much slower, but nevertheless devastating, process of erosion. One such case was a prehistoric Native American site. During the summer of 1988, Dr. Chester DePratter and the division completed archaeological work at the Mulberry site, location of the chiefdom of "Cofitachequi," visited by Hernandez DeSoto during the 16th century. Located on the outside of a bend in the river and containing numerous burial urns, the mound lost more than half its structure to erosion by the mid-20th century.

The project, begun in 1985 under a grant from the University of South Carolina Venture Fund, centered on systematically recording and collecting prehistoric materials that had eroded from the village–mound complex into the adjacent Wateree River and creek. During three weeks in July, this goal was accomplished, as was a survey of a 5.5-km stretch of the Wateree River to ascertain if other mounds on the river exhibited a similar erosional deposition pattern. Funding received for this project also supports an ongoing inquiry into DeSoto's movements through the Southeast and the Native American presence in the state (DePratter and Amer, 1988).

Parris Island Canoe. Also during 1985, work was conducted to record and excavate a prehistoric canoe located on the foreshore of Parris Island. In this case, the craft was being eroded by wave action caused by boats passing the island enroute to the intercoastal waterway. In partnership with the U.S. Marine Corps on whose property the canoe resided, the division excavated the craft. The marines became the canoe's custodian and took responsibility for its conservation and curation.

A year later, the division recovered a historic-period canoe, another victim of Hurricane Hugo, from the foreshore of South Myrtle Beach, in partnership with the Horry County Museum. Division archaeologists, museum staff, and Horry County firefighters battled the rising tide and cold weather to excavate the canoe and deliver it safely to the Horry County Museum in Conway, where it is undergoing conservation.

Slow but inevitable erosion is a problem all along the South Carolina coastline. The state's beaches periodically require sand replenishment to maintain their grade and to slow the erosion process. When significant sites have become exposed, the division has had to act quickly to mitigate the adverse effects on the sites.

Hunting Island Fishing Vessel.   One such case involved a 19th-century fishing vessel eroding on the foreshore of Hunting Island near Beaufort, South Carolina. The vessel's remains initially had been discovered during beach replenishment activities in 1969 and was monitored periodically by SCIAA staff. The 7-m-long wreck, containing the only known live well in an archaeological context in the state, gave us a unique opportunity to study this vessel type, which played an important role in the southeast Atlantic fisheries industry during the late 18th and early 19th centuries. After the South Carolina Department of Archives and History (SCDAH) rejected a grant proposal, the division chose internal funding to excavate and record this important vessel. Unfortunately, before anything could be accomplished, a storm demolished much of the vessel's exposed structure, leaving only the lower hull to be recorded. Subsequent beach replenishment has once again covered the site, protecting it for the moment (Amer, 1992).

Folly Island Midden.   A similar scenario played out on Folly Island, a barrier island located near Charleston. In 1990, a Folly Beach resident reported a shipwreck eroding out of the beach on the north end of the island. Division archaeologists determined the site was not a shipwreck but rather a large sheet midden probably associated with Union occupation during the Civil War. The division partnered with The Charleston Museum to recover a large collection of Civil War artifacts including several dozen shoes, all of which was conserved and curated at the museum.

Malcolm Boat **and** *Clydesdale Vessel.*   A fifth site, the Malcolm Boat (Figure 10.1), was discovered eroding out of the bank of the Ashley River near Charleston. With the help of SCDAH funding, the division partially excavated the site in 1992. For several years, the division had attempted to stabilize and protect the eroding hull structure, but river currents and boat wake took their toll on such efforts. The grant allowed the division to excavate and document the site and attempt a longer term stabilization regime. Plans were made to completely excavate the starboard side of the vessel. This enabled us to reconstruct the boat's shape by mirroring the starboard side to port. This strategy also left half the site for further research and allows us to evaluate the effectiveness of site stabilization using the unexcavated port side as a control.

After the site was recorded, the hull was reburied and stabilized with alternating layers of hundreds of mudbags, sandbags, mud, and more than 10 cubic yards of sand donated and delivered to the site by Charleston County Public Works. Polyethylene

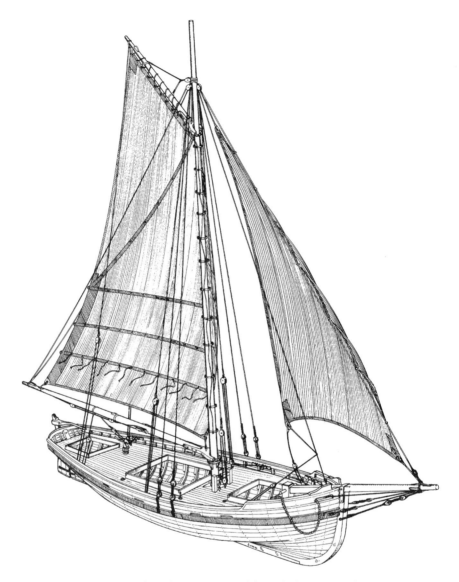

Figure 10.1. Hypothetical reconstruction of the Malcolm Boat, South Carolina.

Geoweb confinement fabric was placed on the exposed slope to contain the sediments and serve as an anchorage for returning flora. Several months were allowed the backfill to settle, and then a final layer of sand and sandbags was added. The site was terraced and planted with grass (*Spartina* sp.) to retard erosion from runoff and boat wake (Amer et al., 1993).

The discovery of the Malcolm Boat was significant on a number of levels. Its abandonment and location, along with other boats found in a similar situation, helped to confirm an emerging pattern of small craft disposal in the many small creeks and sloughs of the state's Low Country (Amer et al., 1993).

Following excavation of the Malcolm Boat, a second 18th-century sloop was excavated in the Savannah River. The Clydesdale Vessel hull evidently was used to plug a blowout in a dike. Excavation and recording of the vessel was conducted as a field school by a partnership of Texas A&M University's Nautical Archaeology Program and the division (Hocker, 1992).

The design and construction of both the Malcolm Boat and Clydesdale Vessel is consistent with contemporary boat-building practices imported to the New World from Europe and developed during the Colonial Period, which utilized abundant colonial woods ideally suited for shipbuilding. They also confirm the extensive use of transoms noted in historical sources (Amer and Hocker, 1998).

Other partnerships have proved equally rewarding. In 1993, the division partnered with the National Park Service to survey the Rembert Mound, the submerged remains of a Mississippian mound group in the Savannah River. The survey's purpose was to predict the potential effects of increasing outflow from a dam upstream on the site (Anderson, Amer, and Elliot, 1994).

A second partnership, this time with a family on whose property is located the state's oldest and largest colonial shipyard, allowed the division to investigate this historic site. The Pritchard Shipyard was in perpetual use as a shipbuilding and repair facility from the mid-18th century until the 1830s. What started as a response to a public notice for a marina being built adjacent to the property became an ongoing investigation of the 7.5-acre site, with encouragement and logistical assistance of the landowners (Amer and Naylor, 1997).

Steamboat SS **Columbia.**   Droughts provide a unique opportunity to investigate formerly submerged sites that are not necessarily in imminent danger. During a drought in 1988, when the water level in the Congaree River was exceptionally low, division staff conducted a nondisturbance survey of the wreck of the steamboat SS *Columbia*, whose remains, including frames and hull planks below the boat's waterline, were abandoned in 1920 across from the state capital. Built in Columbia in 1900, with her sister ship *Highlander*, *Columbia* plied the river systems between Columbia and Georgetown, providing much-needed cargoes and commercial profit for the merchants of South Carolina's capital. Today, the hull lies beneath and partially buried by part of the riverbank historically used as a garbage disposal area throughout the 20th century.

During a one-day survey, the exposed hull was mapped and photographed and its location triangulated for inclusion in the state site files. Further work awaited another fortuitous lowering of the water. A subsequent visit to the site in 1999, when the water was again low, indicated that the site had suffered very little loss of its structure during the intervening 11 years.

Conway Waterfront and Santee Canal.   The awarding of two contracts to the division (one to the Underwater Antiquities Management Program (UAMP) prior to its integration into the division), allowed the division to conduct detailed investigation of the submerged waterfront of a booming 19th century river town and a late 18th century canal.

In 1991, the city of Conway, South Carolina, planned to develop its waterfront area on the Waccamaw River. The proposed work would have affected two historic warehouses and known submerged sites associated with steamboat trade at this busy 19th-century port. With a contract from the city, the division surveyed the waterfront area where pilings for an extensive walkway were to be installed. The survey found nothing worthy of National Register nomination, although the remains of several small craft and an industrial cart or trolley were documented (Newell and Amer, nd.)

Four years earlier, with a contract from the South Carolina Parks, Recreation and Tourism and site owner, Santee Cooper Public Service Authority, division and UAMP archaeologists surveyed the entire length of the 1300-m section of the Santee Canal. Built between 1793 and 1800, the canal is the oldest summit-level canal in the United States. Survey of the site, which was placed on the National Register of Historic Places in 1982, revealed much of the canal's structure, including the terminal tide-lock chamber, a tide-lock, and two wooden flood gates. Also investigated on the site were the remains of two ship-built sailing vessels, a flat or barge, and a possible canal boat (Newell, 1989; Simmons and Newell, 1989).

PROVIDING THE RESOURCES

South Carolina Historic Ships Supply Program (SCHSSP)

An innovative aspect of the South Carolina program involves the opposite end of the spectrum: supplying raw materials for ship construction and repair, not recording the broken end-products. In 1993, during restoration of USS *Constitution* ("Old Ironsides"), staff at the South Carolina Department of Transportation (SCDOT) and SCIAA were contacted about supplying live oak timbers for the effort. The request initiated a partnership between the two agencies to save live-oak trees slated for unavoidable destruction for bridge and road construction and to provide valuable and scarce timber to a historic ship restoration project. So was born the South Carolina Historic Ships Supply Program, or SCHSSP (Amer, 1998).

Earliest evidence of live-oak water craft construction in North America comes from the Brown's Ferry Vessel, discovered in the Black River, South Carolina, in 1976 (Albright and Steffy, 1979). Built during the 1740s, the vessel had frames, posts, and knees fashioned from live oakwood.

Historically, many British and American ships built during the 18th and 19th centuries were framed with South Carolina live-oak. This is attested to by the names of vessels being produced in South Carolina shipyards: two ships named *Live Oak* and one *Heart of Oak* were launched from a Charleston shipyard in the middle years of that century.

USS Constitution *Restoration.*   For the 1992–1995 restoration of USS *Constitution*, a readily available source of live oak had to be located to replace Old Ironsides' rotted timbers. The navy looked to states that previously had supplied them with live oak: Texas, Georgia, and South Carolina, from which they had received some live-oak courtesy of Hurricane Hugo. Appropriate trees were selected from highway projects and from private sources. With the assistance of local contracting firms, the trees were cut to the necessary dimensions and shipped to Charlestown Navy Yard near Boston, where they were seasoned and finished to size before replacing timbers in the vessel's upper works (Amer, 1998).

Amistad *Restoration.*   The latest and by far most ambitious project utilizing live oak during modern times began several years ago at Mystic Seaport Maritime Museum in Connecticut, where shipwrights built a full-size working replica of the schooner *Amistad*.

More than 100 tons of live oak were needed to construct the 77-ft, hand-hewn schooner. *Amistad* featured in the battle against slavery in 1839, when 53 Africans were kidnapped from their homes in Western Africa, smuggled into Cuba, and sold as slaves. Forced aboard the cargo ship *Amistad*, the Africans were enroute to a plantation in eastern Cuba when they rebelled and attempted to sail back to their homeland. They were captured and tried in federal court. Former U.S. President John Quincy Adams, elderly and nearly blind, successfully argued their case before the U.S. Supreme Court, and the Africans were returned to their homeland near modern-day Sierra Leone. The mission of the *Amistad* project is to teach lessons of history, cooperation, and leadership illustrated by the incident, and its legacy (Mystic Seaport Museum, Inc., nd). The *Amistad* was successfully completed in 2000 and visited South Carolina a year later, stopping in Georgetown on its maiden goodwill cruise.

South Carolina live-oak timber continues to be stockpiled for this and other restoration projects, including the next restoration of USS *Constitution* in 2015, which will require some 500 trees to complete.

EXPERIMENTAL ARCHAEOLOGY

Construction of Historic Watercraft

During the first half of the 1990s, the division set up an experimental archaeology program that focused on construction of two historic vessels based on archaeological evidence. Program goals were to learn about the crafts' original appearance, to compare replicas with craft in an archaeological context, to observe changes resulting from normal wear and use with the original appearance of tool and construction marks on the replicas, and to observe the crafts' handling characteristics. The project also proposed to compare modern construction methods with those of the past and to determine how study of these modern methods facilitate interpretation of historic techniques.

The first vessel was a plantation flat, or barge, built in a manner similar to one of the early 19th century at Magnolia Plantation near Charleston (Newell, nd. a). The second was a replica of a boat type called Petersburg or fall boats, used on the Savannah River from the 1790s to the early 1900s. These wooden craft were 70–80 ft long with a 7-1/2-ft beam and drawing some 1-1/2 ft when fully loaded with cotton bales and other cargo. After completion, the replica was tested by rowing it 187 miles down the Savannah River from Augusta to Savannah, Georgia; the trip allowed researchers to evaluate how well the construction methods, fastenings, and construction elements stood up under operating conditions, and to gain some understanding of the craft's life expectancy (Newell, nd. b).

H.L. HUNLEY TURNS THE TIDE IN SOUTH CAROLINA

Discovery of the submarine *H.L. Hunley* was probably the single event that drove South Carolina to systematically survey all state waters and develop a true statewide research design. *H.L. Hunley* is recognized as the first successful submarine in history and the first submersible that actually sank a ship. Built in Mobile, Alabama, in 1863, *Hunley* was the last of three designs built and tested by James McClintock, Horace Hunley, and the Singer Submarine Corps.

Until the submarine was recovered in 2000 and its interior excavated the following year, little was known about the sub's internal design. No plans are known to exist, and contemporary depictions of the submarine are contradictory. A contemporary painting by Conrad Wise Chapman, painted in 1863 and evidently taken from a photograph, shows a fairly accurate representation of the exterior. A drawing made 40 years after the sinking by Lt. William Alexander, one of the builders, and an 1872 drawing by James McClintock are the only known representations of the interior design and inner workings of the boat. The majority of what we know about the *Hunley* is coming from archaeology conducted on and in the boat.

Hunley's History

In August 1863, Confederate Gen. P.G.T. Beauregard arranged to have the submarine shipped to Charleston to operate against Rear Admiral Dahlgren's blockading fleet. After twice sinking while on trials, killing 13 men including the boat's namesake (Horace Hunley), the *Hunley* sank for the third and last time on the night of February 17, 1864, after successfully torpedoing and sinking the Union blockade steam sloop USS *Housatonic* (Ragan, 1995). For 131 years, the *Hunley's* final resting place remained unknown. Then in May 1995, the submarine was discovered (Hall and Wilbanks, 1995).

How did the finding of this small, unobtrusive submarine help state archaeologists fulfill the desire to inventory and assess all submerged cultural resources in the nearly 3000 square miles of South Carolina's bottomlands?

The *Hunley* is considered by many to be the most significant cultural find in the state. Some have even heralded it as, arguably, the most significant archaeological find of our time. In 1996, while the *Hunley* was being assessed for possible recovery, a programmatic agreement was forged between the federal government and South Carolina; simply stated, the federal government retains ownership of the boat, while South Carolina, represented by the South Carolina *Hunley* Commission, is its custodian. Regardless of ownership issues, early on in the process all stakeholders agreed that the boat would be afforded the very best treatment. This commitment was to be borne out during the five years between discovery of the sub in May 1995 to its recovery from the murky waters off Charleston on August 8, 2001. At 8:45 AM, a 300-ton crane mounted atop a jack-up barge with the unlikely name Karlissa B. lifted the *Hunley* in its protective metal truss from its watery grave and gently deposited its precious cargo on a barge. In a five-and-one-half hour trip, the *Hunley* was conveyed through Charleston Harbor to the Old Charleston Naval Base, where the boat would remain for 10 years (Figure 10.2).

The *Hunley* currently resides in a computerized conservation tank in a no less impressive facility. The Warren Lasch Conservation Center contains state-of-the-art equipment wielded by a staff dedicated to probing and studying the mysteries of this impressive little submarine. As of this writing the crew's compartment has been excavated and the remains of the eight crew members recovered. Of the numerous artifacts excavated from the interior of the sub, none can evoke the power of the 20-dollar gold piece found in the left pocket of the sub's commander, Lieutenant George Dixon. That coin, given to Dixon by his fiance, saved his life at the battle of Shiloh when it deflected a bullet. Thereafter, he carried it as a good luck charm, and carried it to his death in the *Hunley*.

While the *Hunley's* artifacts are being recorded and conserved, and the 206 bones of each crewmember are being analyzed and faces and identities ascribed to each sailor, the

Figure 10.2. The port bow of the *Hunley* during the boat's transfer from the lift site to the Warren Lasch Conservation Center (Photo courtesy Christopher F. Amer, SCIAA).

South Carolina *Hunley* Commission is scrutinizing three proposals for museums in which to exhibit the *Hunley* and tell its story. The hull of this intrepid submarine, the little sub that could, will eventually become the centerpiece of a museum in the Charleston area—the place from where the sub was deployed and to where it was returned after each of its three sinkings. The crew will be buried at nearby Magnolia Cemetery along with the remains of the two other crews who died during trials of this innovative submarine.

The 1996 assessment of the *Hunley* site teamed the SCIAA's Underwater Archaeology Division with the NHC and the National Park Service's Submerged Cultural Resource Unit (NPS-SCRU), and it brought experts and state-of-the-art equipment from all over the country. The NPS-SCRU team conducted a remote sensing survey of the battlefield, which included *Hunley* and *Housatonic*. Survey results, along with historic charts and other relevant data, were digitized in a GIS platform as themes to be used for management of the site, and on which to base future survey work (Lenihan et al., 1998). However, the state lacked its own survey equipment and GIS platform to use to display the post-processed data and coverages.

Remote Sensing. The state legislature provided the funding to purchase an integrated marine remote sensing package. Custom designed by Sandia Research Inc., the equipment allowed the division to monitor the Confederate submarine and to implement underwater archaeological surveys in state waterways. The package, called ADAP III, is a combination of diverse electronic components arranged into a state-of-the-art, integrated, marine remote sensing array. The ensemble consists of a cesium magnetometer, high-resolution digital side scan sonar, digital fathometer, and differentially corrected Global Positioning System (DGPS). Three on-board computers are used to gather the diverse data, along with a helmsman's digital guide to maintain straight transects over a targeted area.

Much of the drive behind obtaining the equipment came from members of the *Hunley* Commission. The division head met with commission members to explain that the *Hunley* was not the only vestige of the Confederacy locked beneath state waters and that to manage and protect all the Confederate vessels (and other state watercraft), the state needed to verify their presence and assess their condition and potential threats to each site.

Protective Legislation.   The commission wisely added teeth to South Carolina's underwater antiquities legislation by passing strong penalties for anyone disturbing any military wreck that may contain human remains. NHC, which maintains a database of known ship and aircraft wrecks under navy purview, also viewed this as an opportunity to reassert its authority over naval wrecks in South Carolina waters. According to the Navy's shipwreck database, there are 96 wrecks in South Carolina waters, more than half dating to the Civil War. This latter fact alone added conviction to the commission's resolve to obtain remote sensing equipment for the state. Funding from the Department of Defense legacy grant program permitted historical research on the 96 vessels in the database and search of the archives for information on other naval vessels lost in state waters. The end product of the South Carolina U.S. Naval Wrecks Survey is to provide as much information as possible to complete NHC's database and to draft a management plan for those wrecks lying on state bottomlands. The second phase of this project which began in 1998 is remote sensing surveys to locate and verify the presence of these wrecks, followed by assessment of the remains. In the fall of 2001, remote sensing operations were completed on the normal wrecks around Charleston Harbor and the management plan will be completed by Summer 2002.

DEVELOPING A STATEWIDE RESEARCH DESIGN-SYSTEMATIC SURVEY

Port Royal Sound Survey

In 1998, the Underwater Archaeology Division conducted a comprehensive intertidal and submerged cultural resource survey of Port Royal Sound, South Carolina. Funded in part by a National Park Service historic preservation survey and planning grant and administered through the state's Department of Archives and History, the project included contribution of a local maritime historical researcher specializing in the fishery industry of Port Royal Sound. The project was supported by local institutions and groups, as well as by individuals interested in the maritime history of Port Royal Sound.

The Port Royal Sound Survey is studying and developing the historical, archaeological, and geographical context of the region's prehistoric and historic maritime past. Research methods include locating archival documents and historical references, reviewing archaeological site files and hobby diver reports for previously documented sites, and studying maps and remote imagery to build a database of known and potential archaeological sites in the project area. Division staff have interviewed local watermen, divers, and others who are familiar with underwater and intertidal features such as unrecorded obstructions, snags, rock piles, pilings, landings, shipwrecks, and other items of interest. The research provides baseline information by which to plan and conduct field work to record archaeological sites in and along the periphery of the sound.

Fieldwork for the project's first phase included aerial reconnaissance of the sound's shoreline and a pedestrian survey along the shoreline, both accomplished during low tide. During the three-week pedestrian survey, more than 60 archaeological sites were located for the first time or revisited. Previously unrecorded sites were documented, i.e., measured drawings and photographs, for inclusion in the state site files; latitude and longitude of individual sites were recorded with a hand-held GPS unit. This information is transferred into a GIS database to document on each site.

Based on research and field data, the project team demarcated areas for marine remote-sensing operations to locate and prioritize submerged archaeological sites, and to ground-truth the anomalies. Construction was begun on a comprehensive inventory of the sound's intertidal and underwater archaeological sites that include shipwrecks or abandoned watercraft, landing and wharf remnants, prehistoric sites, and other materials on state-owned bottomlands. In 2001 the operation was expanded to include a search for a French corsair that sank at the entrance to the sound in 1574, as well as identification a number of known wrecks from the Civil War.

The data is being used for analysis, management, and development of guidelines for preservation of these cultural resources—for example, addressing issues concerning access and suitability of a site's recreational, educational, or scientific benefit to South Carolina's citizens and tourists. Other management issues include possible or ongoing effects of development, erosion, and artifact collecting. Eligibility for nomination to the National Register of Historic Places or Areas will be determined for those sites bearing historical or archaeological significance to the maritime history of South Carolina (Spirek, 1997).

The Port Royal Sound Survey, along with the U.S. Naval Wrecks Survey, initiated a program of long-term and comprehensive regional surveys throughout South Carolina, under the direction of the Underwater Archaeology Division of SCIAA and with the support of local organizations and volunteers. Survey results will provide archaeologists with information and tools to manage the state's submerged cultural heritage for the benefit of the citizens of South Carolina and, we hope, will provide a model for state's management of its submerged cultural resources.

REFERENCES

Albright, Alan B. and Steffy, J. Richard, 1979, The Brown's Ferry Vessel, South Carolina: Preliminary Report. In *The International Journal of Nautical Archaeology and Underwater Exploration*. 8(2): 121–142.

Amer, Christopher F.,1992, The Hunting Island Vessel: Now You See It, Now You Don't. In *Underwater Archaeology*: Proceedings from the Society for Historical Archaeology Conference, Kingston, Jamaica, pp. 14–19.

_____, 1994, Legislation and the Management of South Carolina's Historic Shipwrecks and Submerged Cultural Resource. In *Underwater Archaeology*: *Proceedings from the Society for Historical Archaeology Conference*, Vancouver, Canada, pp. 119–125.

_____, 1998, The South Carolina Historic Ships Supply Program. In *Underwater Archaeology*, edited by Lawrence Babits, Catherine Fach and Ryan Harris, pp. 20–24. Society for Historical Archaeology.

Amer, Christopher F. and Hocker, Frederick M., 1995, A Comparative Analysis of Three Sailing Merchant Vessels from the Carolina Coast. In William C. Fleetwood, Tidecraft: *The Boats of South Carolina, Georgia and Northeastern Florida*, 1550–1950. WGM Press, Tybee Island.

Amer, Christopher F., and Naylor, Carleton A., 1997, Pritchard's Shipyard: Investigation at South Carolina's Largest Colonial Shipyard. In *Mount Pleasant's Archaeological Heritage, Proceedings of A Symposium Held At Lynch Hall, Dunes West, Mount Pleasant*, The Town of Mount Pleasant, SC.

Amer, Christopher F., Barr, William B., Beard, David V., Collins, Elizabeth L., Harris, Lynn B., Judd, William R., Naylor, Carl A., and Newell, Mark M., 1993, The Malcolm Boat (38CH803): Discovery, Stabilization, Excavation, and Preservation of an Historic Sea-Going Small Craft in the Ashley River, Charleston County, South Carolina. *Research Manuscript Series* No. 217, South Carolina Institute of Archaeology and Anthropology, Columbia.

Amer, Christopher F., Leader, Jonathan M., and Hocker, Frederick M., 1997, Browns Ferry Vessel. In *Underwater and Maritime Archaeology*, an Encyclopedia, edited by J.P. Delgado. British Museum Press, London.

Anderson, David C., et al., 1994, *Archaeological Survey along the Upper Savannah River including Underwater Investigations at the Rembert Mound Group*. Technical Reports No. 1, Interagency Archaeological Services Division, National Park Service, Atlanta, GA.

DePratter, Chester B. and Amer, Christopher F., 1989, Underwater Archaeology at the Mulberry Site (38KE12) and Adjacent Portions of the Wateree River. Submitted.

Hall, Wes, and Wilbanks, Ralph, 1995, *Search for the Confederate Submarine* H.L. Hunley *off Charleston Harbor*, South Carolina. Final Report prepared for Clive Cussler and National Underwater and Marine Agency. On file at Naval Historical Center, Washington.

Harris, Lynn, 1998, Cooper River Heritage Trail. *Legacy*(2): 27.

Harris, Lynn, Moss, Jimmy, and Naylor, Carl, 1993, The Cooper River Survey: An Underwater Reconnaissance of the West Branch. *Research Manuscript Series 218.* South Carolina Institute of Archaeology and Anthropology, Columbia.

Hocker, Frederick M., 1992, The Clydesdale Plantation Vessel Project: 1992 Field Report. *Institute of Nautical Archaeology Quarterly* 19(4): 12–16.

Lenihan, Daniel, Amer, Christopher F., Murphy, Larry, Russell, Matthew A., Neyland, Robert S., Wills, Richard, Harris, Scott, Askins, Adriane, Smith, Timothy G., and Shope, Steven M., 1998, H.L. Hunley *Site Assessment.* Cultural Resources Management Professional Papers, Number 62, Submerged Cultural Resources Unit, Intermountain Region, National Park Service, Santa Fe.

Maritime Heritage Homepage, http://www.cla.sc.edu/sciaa/staff/amerc/index.html.

Mystic Seaport Museum, Inc., 1997, *Amistad*: *Building the Freedom Schooner.* Publicity Packet, Mystic Seaport, New Haven.

Newell, Mark M., 1989, The *Santee Canal Sanctuary*, Part I. South Carolina Institute of Archaeology and Anthropology, Columbia.

Newell, Mark M., nd.a, *Construction of a Plantation Barge on the Ashley River.* Unedited manuscript on file, South Carolina Institute of Archaeology and Anthropology, Columbia.

Newell, Mark M., nd.b, History, *Ethnology and Design Research on Eastern American Mountain Boats*: *Experimental Archaeology on the Savannah River.* Unedited manuscript on file, South Carolina Institute of Archaeology and Anthropology, Columbia.

Newell, Mark M. and Amer, Christopher, nd., Intensive Underwater Archaeological Survey of a Section of the Historic Waterfront District City of Conway, S.C. *Cultural Resource Management Series No. 12.* South Carolina Institute of Archaeology and Anthropology, Columbia.

Ragan, Mark K., 1995, *The Hunley*: *Submarines, Sacrifice, and Success in the Civil War.* Narwhal Press Inc., Charleston.

Simmons III, Joe J. and Newell, Mark M., 1989, The *Santee Canal Sanctuary*, Part I. South Carolina Institute of Archaeology and Anthropology, Columbia.

South Carolina Institute of Archaeology and Anthropology Enabling Act of 1963. Section 210 of Chapter 13 of Title 60 of the *Code of Laws of South Carolina Ann.* (1963 & 1990 Cum. Supp.).

South Carolina Underwater Antiquities Act of 1991. Sections 610 through 850 of Chapter 7 of Title 54 of the *Code of Laws of South Carolina* Ann. (1976 & 1991 Cum. Supp.).

Spirek, James D., and Amer, Christopher F., 1997, SCIAA's Underwater Archaeology Division Completes First Phase of the Port Royal Sound Survey. *Legacy* 2(3): 24–25.

United States Congress, 1988, Abandoned Shipwreck Act of 1987. Public Law 100–298; 43 *United States Congress*. Sections 2101 through 2106.

Chapter 11

Florida Frontiers
From Ice Age to New Age

ROGER C. SMITH

INTRODUCTION

No part of Florida is far from water. With more than 8500 miles of coastline including rivers, streams, and lakes, the peninsula contains as many, if not more, archaeological sites that are wet as are dry. Many represent terrestrial sites gradually inundated by sea levels that began to rise with the melting of glaciers at the end of the last Ice Age. Others are human deposits that were found at the land–water interface—a key location for subsistence, transportation, commerce, and recreation. Florida's submerged archaeological resources span thousands of years and reflect many different cultures and activities.

In the last decade, underwater archaeology has accelerated in Florida's waters, as it has elsewhere. An increase in site discoveries, notable research projects, and public awareness can be attributed to a number of factors. These include passage of the Abandoned Shipwreck Act; expanded development requiring compliance with federal and state cultural resource regulations; establishment of a proactive underwater program within the Florida Bureau of Archaeological Research (BAR); improved private and public sponsorship of historic preservation; establishment of the Florida Keys National Marine Sanctuary; new partnerships between government agencies, private enterprise, and academic institutions; creative use of funding opportunities for underwater research and resource interpretation; and implementation of programs in underwater archaeology at Florida universities.

Roger C. Smith, State Underwater Archaeologist, Florida Bureau of Archaeological Research, Division of Historical Resources, Tallahassee, Florida 32399.

International Handbook of Underwater Archaeology, edited by Carol V. Ruppé and Janet F. Barstad. Kluwer Academic/Plenum Publishers, New York, 2002.

The following are brief descriptions of several underwater archaeological projects that have been undertaken in Florida during the past 15 years. Each fits within a management context that gradually has evolved with efforts to broaden public understanding of and access to underwater sites of all types in Florida. Each has made use of management tools developed through trial and error on paper and in the field. For example, experimentation in 1987 with the concept of a shipwreck preserve at the site of a 1715 Spanish galleon has expanded into a formal program with seven underwater archaeological preserves throughout the state. Exploration of cooperative relationships between agencies, institutions, and individuals made possible a long-term program of survey and excavation projects, in Pensacola and elsewhere, that have highly visible public education components. A continuation and refinement of private sector exploration and salvage activities under federal court jurisdiction, as well as state authority, has been accompanied by expanded archaeological guidelines and reporting requirements. Grant funding enabled new survey horizons, such as in St. Augustine, and cooperative excavation efforts, such as on the *Maple Leaf* steamship. Aside from technical research reports, publications in more popular formats, such as the *Atlas of Maritime Florida*, have helped share resource management issues with a wider audience. Ultimately, public outreach efforts led to a number of increasingly popular World Wide Web pages (http://dhr.dos.state.fl.us/bar/site_index.html). Development of a Submerged Cultural Resource Management Plan for Florida (Florida Bureau of Archaeological Research, 1994) was followed by a progressive agreement between federal and state agencies for the Florida Keys National Marine Sanctuary (National Oceanic and Atmospheric Administration, 1997). Academic partnerships and research support helped stimulate the establishment of active underwater archaeology programs at the University of West Florida, Florida State University, and the University of Miami.

SURVEYS

1733 Flota Survey

Following a 1977 survey of shipwrecks from the New Spain fleet of 1733 along the Florida Keys (Smith and Dunbar, 1977), a second survey was conducted in 1988 to establish a state underwater archaeological preserve at one of the wreck sites of the fleet. Eleven sites were relocated and studied by students attending a field school sponsored jointly by the Florida Bureau of Archaeological Research, Indiana University, Florida State University, and Quiescence Diving Services, Inc. Criteria for evaluating each site to become an underwater park were developed for colonial shipwrecks in a shallow, subtropical marine environment: water conditions, such as visibility and currents; aquatic sea life and coral formations; structural features and ballast; intrusive features such as fishtraps and trash; site location and public accessibility; and further research potential. Each shipwreck was rated on a point system; the site of *San Pedro* near Indian Key received the highest overall rating (Smith et al., 1990).

A public proposal was disseminated to promote *San Pedro* as the second state preserve and to encourage cooperation between state and local government, waterfront businesses, and the Florida Keys community. To prepare the site for its new status, the wreck was given replica cannons to replace those removed long ago; a brochure was printed; and a laminated underwater guide was prepared to help divers explore the

Figure 11.1. *Nuestra Señora de Balvaneda (El Infante)*, part of the New Spain fleet of 1733, off the Florida Keys.

shipwreck. Mooring buoys were installed to protect the site from anchors, and a bronze plaque officially recognizing *San Pedro* was placed on the wreck site in 1989.

Pensacola Shipwreck Survey

Beginning in 1988, BAR focused its attention on Pensacola Bay's submerged cultural resources to create a regional model for inventory, assessment, and public interpretation. Pensacola was chosen because of its obvious nautical attributes as well as its wide range of environments—from freshwater rivers and brackish estuaries to the muddy bottom of the bay and clear waters of the Gulf. One of the first sites to be investigated was a well-preserved, two-masted coastal schooner abandoned in a back bayou of the Blackwater River. A team of volunteers thoroughly documented the Blackwater schooner, which was placed on the National Register of Historic Places (Baumer, 1990). During the first phase of the survey, more than 30 sites of wrecked or abandoned vessels, ranging from colonial to modern in age, were located, recorded, and assessed. A survey report with classifications of sites and recommendations was published by the BAR (Franklin et al., 1992). Included in the recommendations for further work were additional remote sensing surveys, and a formal survey of the USS *Massachusetts* (BB-2), which had been nominated by a local diver to become Florida's fourth underwater archaeological preserve (Smith, 1991). Systematic mapping of the battleship produced site plans with which to compare 1910 refit drawings. These archaeological data, combined with historical and archival materials, helped survey staff to produce a formal proposal for the new preserve, which was dedicated in 1993.

Elsewhere in the bay, electronic remote sensing operations were conducted in areas associated with colonial maritime activities in Pensacola, especially those relating to the First and Second Spanish periods (1513–1763; 1784–1821). Magnetometry and side-scan sonar sweeps done during the second phase of the survey yielded many targets, both natural and cultural. However, the majority of targets that could be verified were revealed to be modern, ranging from metal cables and pizza ovens, to car bodies and construction debris, as well as dumped military and commercial trash (Spirek et al., 1993). Many of these objects were part of artificial reefs, intentionally deposited by fishermen to attract fish. Despite the preponderance of these byproducts of industrial Pensacola, the electronic tools also detected early shipwrecks, bringing the total number of recorded sunken ships to more than forty-five. These include two 18th-century British cutters or sloops and the remains of a 16th-century Spanish galleon, called the Emanuel Point Ship, which is the earliest shipwreck to be found in Florida.

A classification scheme for the Pensacola Bay shipwrecks was developed based on type, condition, location, age, and significance of sites. These factors helped to determine which management policies may best be suited to particular sites. Coordination with federal and state agencies helped to identify specific resource needs and how they could be met through public-oriented activities. Programs that were tested in Pensacola included public conferences and lectures, sport diver workshops, museum and university involvement, as well as the establishment of a shipwreck preserve by a local support group in response to local nominations. Additionally, coordination with the local press proved to be invaluable in promoting public interest and support of the project. The survey of Pensacola Bay resumed in 1998, under a cooperative agreement with the University of West Florida and the U.S. Navy Meteorology and Oceanography Command to conduct additional remote sensing in the bay. In addition a summer field school focused on the exploration of an 18th-century Spanish shipwreck and a 19th-century Norwegian lumber ship named *Catharine* (Bratten et al., 1999; Burns, 1999). The 18th-century Spanish vessel, dubbed the Santa Rosa Island Wreck, also was investigated during a 2000 field school. This large ship probably was built in the Americas, and may have been in Pensacola to take on a load of lumber when it was wrecked during a hurricane (Hunter, 2001).

Building on the Pensacola project, a statewide overview of environmental, archaeological, and historical data about Florida's maritime heritage was published in *An Atlas of Maritime Florida* (Smith et al., 1997). As a tool for understanding the breadth and scope of the state's resources, research for the atlas also proved useful for the creation of a statewide plan for their management. A draft of this plan, which included comprehensive reviews of existing national, state, and international laws, policies, and programs pertaining to submerged cultural resource management, was completed and disseminated for public review (Florida Bureau of Archaeological Research, 1994). The plan focuses on the various kinds of statewide resources, explores ways in which they are threatened, and makes recommendations for their protection, preservation, and interpretation for the public benefit.

Oklawaha River Survey

Discovery in 1985 of a prehistoric burial eroding from an exposed bank of the Oklawaha River revealed that Early Archaic artifacts and human remains were being threatened along this major tributary of the St. Johns River on Florida's east coast. Concerned professional and avocational archaeologists and volunteer divers undertook a survey in 1991 to locate and record eroding sites along nine miles of the river (Denson, 1992). Working in near-zero visibility and strong currents, the survey team located eleven new sites, provided updates for three previously-recorded sites, and obtained additional information on river geomorphology and the effects of riverine erosion and transformation on archaeological sites. The project also demonstrated the value of a cooperative working relationship between scientists and members of Florida's sport diving community. Aside from resource data and recommendations, other products included an educational booklet produced in conjunction with the local school system (Payne, 1992).

Florida Navy Legacy Shipwreck Project

In 1994, BAR began a study of U.S. Navy and Confederate ship losses in Florida's waters. The project was initiated upon request from the Naval Historical Center in Washington, D.C., for assistance in the identification and inventory of naval shipwrecks in Florida, and in the development of management strategies for them. The study was divided into two phases: (1) gathering primary and secondary historical documentation on Navy and Confederate ship losses; and (2) researching and making field assessments of selected sites in Florida.

During the study's first phase, existing primary and secondary documentation of ships and their losses was examined, and a range of additional data from other sources, such as local fishing and diving guides, was collected. A series of portfolios, containing copies of documents and other written and graphic materials was assembled and imported into a computer database compatible with the existing U.S. Navy database. A status report on each ship included information about what is known or not known about the vessel's history, the condition of its remains, previous or present threats to the site, current needs for management, and future options for public use. This research increased fourfold the number of entries in the existing navy inventory of ship losses in Florida.

A two-volume report entitled "U.S. Navy and Confederate Shipwrecks in Florida" was submitted to the Naval Historical Center (Florida Bureau of Archaeological Research, 1996). The report contains a chronological summary of naval activities and installations throughout the state and an inventory of 306 vessels that are considered to have been commissioned fighting ships, private vessels contracted for naval service, or vessels operating in support of the Confederacy. Data on these vessels were explored through analyses of vessel service, the range of vessel categories, the historical periods of sinkings, causes of losses, geographical locations of losses, and potential threats to wreck sites. The report also contains an electronic database that follows the established format of the navy's shipwreck inventory. Each record in the database contains 83 fields of specific data, including vessel particulars, historical and archaeological information, and source identification. The report includes recommendations for additional archival research, and limited field assessment of selected shipwreck sites, and suggests that a formal agreement between Florida and the U.S. Navy be developed to pursue management and public interpretation.

Field assessments of one site, believed to the remains of the armed schooner USS *Alligator* were made during a joint research effort conducted by BAR, the Naval Historical Center (NHC), the National Oceanic and Atmospheric Administration's (NOAA) Sanctuaries and Reserves Division, the National Center for Shipwreck Research, Ltd., Bateaux Below, Inc., and volunteers (Neyland, 1996). Grounded on a reef in the Florida Keys while on patrol for pirates in 1822, *Alligator* was the first U.S. Navy ship lost in Florida's waters. Known to local divers for many years, the site consists of two coral-encrusted mounds of ballast stones in 3 m of water, adjacent to Alligator Light on a reef named after the ship. Timbers of the vessel's lower hull and remnants of copper sheathing can be seen at the periphery of the largest mound of ballast stones, which may be the primary wreck deposit. The second mound may be stones that were off-loaded in an attempt to lighten the grounded schooner and pull her off the reef. Field and archival research activities have resulted in a detailed historical and archaeological analysis of this early naval vessel, and its nomination to the National Register of Historic Places (McMahan and Zarzynski, 1997).

Florida Keys Submerged Resource Inventory

The management plan for the Florida Keys National Marine Sanctuary recommended the establishment of a submerged cultural resource inventory. An all-volunteer team began to systematically survey the upper Keys in 1994. Local divers developed a database of more than 200 sites in 18 reef zones under the technical guidance of NOAA's Sanctuaries and Reserves Division archaeologist (Hayes, 1996). Their efforts periodically were assisted by students from Indiana University's Underwater Science and Educational Resources program (Indiana University, 1997). In the middle Keys, a similar all-volunteer survey began to document submerged sites using state records, visual searches under water, and a helicopter. Results were compiled in reports to NOAA and the State and then incorporated into the ongoing database maintained by the Sanctuary in cooperation with the Florida site file at the Florida Division of Historical Resources.

St. Augustine Shipwreck Survey

St. Augustine has been the location of extensive terrestrial archaeological investigations, especially those dealing with it's early colonial Spanish occupation, which began in 1565. However, the town's prime importance as a fortified port situated at the edge of the Florida straits also offers a potential wealth of archaeological data concerning several centuries of maritime commerce and naval activities. In 1995, Southern Oceans Archaeological Research, Inc. began a systematic investigation of St. Augustine's maritime history and submerged cultural resources. Funding and permits for the project were obtained from the Florida Division of Historical Resources. Initial research focused on a collection of cartographic data showing geomorphological changes to St. Augustine's inlet and surrounding coastline over time. Historic charts of the area's waterways were digitized and placed in an overlapping format to display the nature and locations of natural and cultural alterations. Archival documents with details of shipping activities, including vessel losses, were consulted to determine likely areas of undisturbed submerged cultural resources or shipping losses of historic significance. Two areas were selected for field survey: an offshore stretch of coastline south of the present-day inlet, and an inshore area near the old channel (Franklin and Morris, 1996).

Magnetometer and side scan sonar sweeps revealed submerged anomalies that may be remains of historic shipwrecks. Several targets were selected for further investigation; most appeared to have been buried by accretion of sediments over time and required probing and test trenching to identify their nature. A second phase of the survey continued in 1997 with the discovery of three significant maritime sites located in the offshore survey area (Morris et al., 1998). The most intriguing was an assemblage of eight cannon, three anchors, iron bar stock, and two grindstones situated on top of an articulated wooden structure partially buried in the sand. The cannon and anchors were in a stowed position, alternating muzzle to cascabel. A second site investigated was the remains of a wooden steamship which had bronze alloy fasteners and articulated steam machinery, including a single-cylinder engine, horizontal boiler, reduction gears, and a shaft with a four-bladed iron propeller. A third site consisted of the lower wooden hull remains of a ship associated with two large piles of cut stone, anchor chain, iron pipes, and a capstan head.

A sand-encrusted cannon was raised from the first site and when cleaned, was found to be decorated with the British crest of George II (1727–1760). Also recovered were iron cannon shot, lead musket shot, a grindstone, a bundle of iron files, and a shovel handle. Archival research suggested a likely candidate for this shipwreck: the British sloop *Industry*. Enroute to Florida from New York in 1764, *Industry* carried subsistence money and ammunition, and "artificers tools" as requested to supply several of the outposts and settlements 1763, when she wrecked on the bar near St. Augustine (Morris et al., 1998; Franklin et al., 1999). The recovered cannon is receiving conservation treatment but is on public display in front of the St. Augustine Lighthouse. A scale model of the steamship machinery and propulsion remains from the second site has been prepared for exhibit in the museum.

In 1999, the St. Augustine Lighthouse and Museum created the Lighthouse Archaeological Maritime Program (LAMP) to conduct long-term archaeological and historical investigations, educate students, and provide a role for public participation. Staff worked with students from two local high schools on the steamship site, and employed two graduate student interns from the University of North Florida (Morris, 2000). The following year, a conservator was hired and a laboratory facility, dedicated to the treatment of waterlogged artifacts, was provided by the Lighthouse and Museum.

Bay County Shipwreck Survey

In 1994, members of the Panama City waterfront community nominated five shipwrecks to be considered as candidates for a new state underwater archaeological preserve. The nominations included USS *Strength*, a World War II minesweeper used to train navy divers; *Chickasaw*, a 1908 steel tugboat built in Pensacola; *E.E. Simpson*, an 1877 tugboat that sank in 1926; *Tarpon*, an 1887 steamer serving the Gulf coast and lost in 1937; and *Vamar*, a 1919 steamer that supplied Richard Byrd's Antarctic base and sank in 1942. In partnership with Bay County government and the Museum of Man in the Sea, BAR responded to the nominations in 1996 by assembling a team of archaeologists and volunteers to relocate, explore, map, and assess each site. Ship histories were researched extensively through national, regional, and local sources.

Criteria used in the formation of previous preserves, and a growing public consensus, helped to select the site of *Tarpon*, a well-known steamer that sank in 95 feet of water during a storm while eight miles off Panama City. A formal proposal for the new preserve was prepared and presented to the public, and a civic support group called Friends of Tarpon was organized to steer its development. To prepare the site, moorings were installed to accommodate boating visitors yet would prevent damage to the ship's remains, and volunteers placed a bronze plaque next to the wreck to officially designate it as a preserve (Florida Bureau of Archaeological Research, 1997).

Santa Fe River Survey

During the summer of 1997, a team of state underwater archaeologists and volunteers conducted a survey of portions of the Santa Fe River in north central Florida. The survey's primary goals were to relocate and assess underwater locations of artifact and fossil discoveries made by river divers in the past, identify the nature and source of any artifacts remaining at the location, develop avenues of communication with other management agencies and river divers in regard to the state's policy on isolated finds, and pursue cooperative strategies for better understanding of the submerged cultural resources in Florida's rivers.

Locational data from past and current collectors were used to select 16 target areas in the lower Santa Fe River for investigation (Smith et al., 1997). Side scan sonar helped to develop digital images of riverbed morphology and to identify submerged features for further examination. Visual survey and sampling were conducted at each of the selected locations. Displaced artifacts and fossils were found in areas of the river channel where current diminishes. Locations of undisturbed ancient sediments likely to contain archaeological deposits were noted, as were areas of erosion. A general lack of stone and bone tools was encountered at locations where previous reports of abundant artifacts were made by river divers. Moreover, many of river locations examined had been looted.

The Santa Fe River Survey demonstrated the feasibility of an active partnership between management agencies, professionals, and amateurs to address basic questions about the nature, condition, and extent of a river's submerged cultural resources. A workshop that oriented river divers to the state's policy on isolated finds also demonstrated a willingness on the part of divers, archaeologists, resource managers, and law enforcement officers to cooperate in programs for cultural and environmental preservation.

Newnan's Lake Canoes

During drought conditions in spring 2000, the largest collection of preshistoric watercraft in North America was discovered in a lake just east of Gainesville, Florida. Embedded in the drying lakebed is an extensive scattering of complete and partial prehistoric dugout canoes and associated artifacts. More than 93 canoes have been mapped at the site, although limited test excavations and local information suggest that this number may only represent a fraction of the watercraft buried in the lakebed (Memory et al., 2000).

Historically, Newnan's Lake was known as Lake Pithlachocco ("place of the long boats" in the Miccosukee language) into the 19th century, then renamed for Colonel Daniel Newnan, a U.S. Army officer during the Second Seminole War (1835–1842). The canoe site may have been associated with a large prehistoric village site along the northern shore of the lake; the canoes, many of which are broken and degraded, probably are boats that were abandoned along the shoreline adjacent to the village. Found near the canoes, some artifacts possibly associated with this village suggest that the area was occupied from the Early Archaic to Alachua cultural periods (7500 B.C.–A.D. 1500).

Wood samples taken from 53 canoes in a study group were submitted for radiocarbon dating and wood species analysis. Radiocarbon dating revealed that the canoes range in age from 500 to 5000 years old. The broad range of dates demonstrates a long tradition of canoe manufacture and use that extends from 5000 years ago to the present. The majority of the wood samples were identified as *Pinus* sp., a southern hard pine, while others appear to be cypress.

The Newnan's Lake canoes are similar in shape and construction to other prehistoric canoes known from Florida (Newsom and Purdy, 1990). Each was hewn from one tree trunk, by stone or shell tools, as well as had fire charring to remove the bulk of the wood from the center of the trunk. A number of the canoes have both stem and stern present; they feature two rounded ends (reflecting the oldest traditions), two pointed ends with overhanging platforms, and others with a combination of each. One interesting feature found on many of the canoes is a thwart, or bulkhead, partition in either the center or the stern of the hull. The function of this feature is unclear.

Although more than 200 canoes had been recorded in Florida prior to the Newnan's Lake discovery, few had been recorded in situ. The Lake Pithlachocco site is significant since it affords the opportunity to document and study preshistoric watercraft in the context in which they were used (Memory et al., 2000). In addition, the large number of canoes and their wide temporal range offers the chance to address their stylistic and functional features and their potential cultural affiliations.

St. Marks River Survey

A survey to re-evaluate known sites and discover new ones was conducted along a five-mile stretch of the St. Marks River in northwest Florida during summer 1998 by students from Florida State University (Meide, 2000a). Side scan sonar was employed with limited success, due to aquatic plant growth masking potential targets along the river's banks. The team inspected the previously documented remains of the old wharf and marine railways adjacent to the historic fort of San Marcos de Apalache. Farther upriver, wreckage of a wooden vessel, thought to be the Confederate gunboat *Spray*, was documented as was an early- to mid-20th-century sunken vessel.

Dog and St. George Islands Shipwreck Survey

Since 1999, Florida Sate University students have conducted remote sensing survey work off Dog Island and St. George Island, which are adjacent to Apalachee Bay in the Big Bend portion of Florida's Gulf Coast. The purpose of the survey is to inventory submerged cultural resources, and in particular to search for the remains of *Le Tigre*, a French merchant brig wrecked in 1766, and HMS *Fox*, an armed schooner lost in 1799 (Meide 2000b).

Magnetometer survey transects were conducted in the waters around St. George in 2000, and a terrestrial magnetometer survey was made on the eastern portion of the island for the purpose of investigating whether the wreck of HMS *Fox* might be located there. St. George Island is a barrier island that has accreted a considerable distance since the 1799 wrecking of *Fox*. Because of this growth, it is possible that the island has migrated over the remains of this vessel and covered the wreck with a substantial amount of sediment. By exploring the geological record of this island through historic records and maps, researchers propose to trace the island's movement over time and predict where the vessel might lie. Off Dog Island, one site which was discovered in 1999 and investigated in 2000, is the remains of a wooden vessel at a location called Ballast Cove. Limited induction dredge testing was conducted to expose some of the wreckage, and a large-scale map was begun (Damour and Horrell 2001). A GIS database of the research area is being developed and is intended to incorporate historic shipwrecks in the area, as well as ballast pile features and other structures related to Apalachee Bay's maritime history.

EXCAVATIONS

Maple Leaf

A wooden side-wheel steamer built in 1851, *Maple Leaf* served as a supply vessel and troop transport for the federal government when she struck a floating Confederate mine (torpedo) and sank in the St. Johns River near Jacksonville in 1864. The ship quickly settled on the muddy river bottom, but local Confederates prevented recovery of the hull and its cargo. In the 1880s, portions of the vessel's superstructure, paddle wheels, and walking beam assembly were reduced as a navigational hazard; local charts continued to feature its location in 20 ft of water off Mandarin Point. In 1984, a Jacksonville group, St. Johns Archaeological Expeditions, Inc. (SJAEI), confirmed *Maple Leaf*'s remains and their excellent state of preservation under several feet of mud (Holland et al., 1994). The vessel apparently still was loaded with tons of cargo—the personal effects of a Union infantry brigade, engineer troops, passengers, and crew, as well as sutlers' stores—all sealed in an anaerobic environment (Duncan, 1994).

SJAEI filed an admiralty claim to the shipwreck, and negotiations began with the federal government and the state of Florida. An out-of-court settlement, allowing a share of artifacts to be received by both federal and state governments, was reached. The agreement stated that activities on the site would be conducted by a private corporation under federal court jurisdiction, but there would not be commercial salvage and the project would receive public funding. As a site of national importance, *Maple Leaf* not only deserved the support and assistance of professional archaeologists, but also to have her recovered materials properly conserved, interpreted, and displayed. For the first few years site exploration was conducted by SJAEI volunteers who funded themselves and donated professional services and equipment. The group's dedication, sincerity, and public relations skills soon garnered regional and national attention, ultimately leading to state historic preservation grants and the involvement of the U.S. Army Center for Military History as well as professors and students from the Maritime Studies Program at East Carolina University.

During early investigations of the buried vessel, the river bottom was probed to determine the extent and orientation of remains. Test excavations were conducted in the aft cargo hold, where personal belongings had been stowed (Cantelas, 1992). These early excavations brought up camp equipment and personal effects of officers and enlisted men that had been packed in wooden boxes. Six of these contained artifacts associated with identifiable individuals serving in the Union army. These materials were treated in a conservation lab established by SJAEI with assistance from professional conservators.

By 1991, structural elements of *Maple Leaf*'s bow, stern, and midships machinery area had been explored, and a profile of the vessel's port side had been obtained by probing. The following year, with funding from the Jacksonville Historical Society through a grant from the Florida Division of Historical Resources, East Carolina University joined the project to help develop a site management plan and to conduct further field investigations. Students documented the forward deck from the bow to the forward cargo hatch, and volunteers penetrated the forward cargo space, discovering extensive damage caused by the torpedo that sank *Maple Leaf* (Cantelas, 1993). A silt barrier constructed around the bow excavation diverted sediment and trash away from the work. Divers gained underwater visibility and were able to accurately map in the current-free structure (Cantelas and Rodgers, 1994). In 1993, documentation of the midships engineering spaces, including paddle-wheels and shaft, walking beam, connecting rod, and boiler, revealed evidence of damage caused by channel clearance work in the 1880s. Excavation in the aft cargo hold revealed intact containers of cargo in their original packing arrangement.

Mapping inside the ship was complicated by zero visibility and the three-dimensional aspect of the cargo. Using the direct survey method, the provenience of boxes, barrels, bags, and other artifacts was recorded, and plans of the packing arrangement were reconstructed by computer (Cantelas, 1994). During the 1994 season, the aft main deck was explored, revealing the layout of passenger cabins and entrance to the aft cargo hold. A site plan of features encountered during these investigations, augmented by historical sources, allowed a preliminary reconstruction of the *Maple Leaf*'s main deck and associated equipment (Babits, 1994).

Maple Leaf is a world-class shipwreck site, with an intact hull containing tons of personal belongings and camp equipment of three Civil War regiments in a remarkable state of preservation. In 1995, the vessel became a National Historic Landmark, the first underwater site to be so designated in Florida. SJAEI donated the artifact collection to the state of Florida. A major exhibit is housed at the Jacksonville Museum of Science and History, and portions of the collection have traveled to other museums. A documentary video, produced by SJAEI, is a centerpiece for the Civil War gallery in the Museum of Florida History in Tallahassee. An illustrated book and interactive computer module also were privately produced. As a model of cooperation involving private entrepreneurship, government responsiveness, public funding and interpretation, and academic research, the *Maple Leaf* project remains a milestone in underwater archaeology.

Little Salt Spring

Little Salt Spring, located five miles from the Gulf of Mexico in southwest Florida, is a spring-fed sinkhole containing the remains of Paleo-Indian and archaic Native American cultures. It was first explored by sport divers in the 1950s, but in the 1970s, the spring was investigated by archaeologists who recovered organic and stone artifacts, human and faunal remains, and fossils (Clausen et al., 1979). The remnants of a large land tortoise and the sharpened wooden stake used to kill it were discovered on a submerged ledge. The stake was radiocarbon-dated to 12,030 B.P.

Archaeological investigations were resumed in the late 1980s by the Rosenstiel School of Marine and Atmospheric Science at the University of Miami, and Florida State University students have been involved since 1994. Of particular note is the 1986 discovery of a 7000-year-old skull containing preserved neural tissue from which DNA was extracted. Latest investigations used coring to examine stratigraphy and to conduct paleoenvironmental analysis, and high-band, 8-mm-video integrated with GIS software to record underwater features (Gifford, 1993).

East Coast Shipwreck Project

The East Coast Shipwreck Project came about as a result of an out-of-court agreement in 1983 between the state of Florida and a commercial salvage firm, Cobb Coin, Inc., putting an end to lengthy legal disputes over management of historic shipwrecks containing treasure. Formal archaeological guidelines for the continuation of salvage activities on the Spanish 1715 fleet shipwrecks under joint federal admiralty court jurisdiction and state authority were drafted by a committee of archaeologists and historians representing the state, salvors, the academic community, and the private sector. The guidelines were intended to establish minimum standards for the recording of archaeological provenience and mapping of wrecksites; the tagging, handling, and conservation of recovered artifacts; and compilation of reports detailing each season's activities and recoveries. They also required that salvors provide a professional archaeologist and sufficiently trained assistants to supervise exploration and salvage activities under contract with the state.

Relying on the sale of subcontracts to part-time salvors in return for a share of artifacts or proceeds from the sale of artifacts, the East Coast Shipwreck Project, under various corporate names, has continued to mine the sites of the 1715 fleet shipwrecks that were grandfathered under the Abandoned Shipwreck Act of 1987 due to prior admiralty arrest. The project has complied with most of the guidelines, employing a succession of archaeologists to collect data and to compile reports of recoveries (Mathewson, 1984; Sinclair and Mathewson, 1990; Gibbs, 1992, 1993; Peebles, 1994, 1995; Gaither, 1996, 1997; Gaither and Essig, 1998). A storage and conservation facility was established near the salvage operations to inventory and process recoveries, which are annually divided between the salvor and the state. The artifact division has been based on various arrangements to satisfy salvors and investors, with the state normally requesting unique or display-quality items to augment its public collection and museum exhibit. Over the years, many significant and historically important artifacts have been retained for the public under state-managed salvage contracts, insuring that they would be available for study, display, and publication. For instance, a unique collection of Spanish colonial coins had been accumulated by the state and was documented in a scholarly format (Craig, 2000a; Craig, 2000b).

Deadman's Island Shipwreck

In 1988, remains of a wooden ship eroding from a small island in Pensacola Bay were brought to the attention of University of West Florida archaeologists, who were conducting a survey for the nearby city of Gulf Breeze (Joy, 1988). On nautical charts, Deadman's Island was called Old Navy Cove. Protected against prevailing winds during the summer months, with deep water close to shore and nearby sources of wood and fresh water, the cove made an ideal careenage where ships could be hauled over and their hulls cleaned and repaired. With assistance from BAR, initial mapping revealed well-preserved remains of one side of a vessel's hull, articulated from stem to stern and from the keel to the turn of the bilge. Its construction appeared to be colonial, with ceiling planking fastened with treenails to hand-hewn frames. Test excavations unearthed English wine bottle glass, gunflints, lead pistol shot, cast-iron swivel gun shot, and a pewter uniform button with the insignia of the 60th Regiment of Foot (Bense, 1988). These clues suggested that the ship was British, had been armed as a naval vessel, and was associated with an infantry regiment stationed at Pensacola between 1776 and 1781 to protect the colony from Spanish forces in Louisiana.

The threat of further erosion and the site's exposed condition necessitated further investigation of the vessel. It was realized this was an ideal opportunity to train students, while at the same time develop public appreciation of local maritime cultural resources. Accordingly, a project was developed in summer 1989 to accomplish three objectives: (1) excavate and recover data from the site; (2) train college students in field and laboratory methods; and (3) develop public involvement in marine archaeology (Smith,

1990). The project was sponsored by BAR, the University of West Florida, and the City of Gulf Breeze. Florida's first undergraduate field school in underwater archaeology attracted ten students from various universities in Florida and elsewhere, who spent 12 weeks in the field and laboratory. The field school headquarters also served as a public reception and interpretation center. With assistance from members of the Gulf Breeze Historical Society, visitors could interact with staff and students and view artifacts and data from the site.

Investigation revealed that the ship at Deadman's Island was a merchantman. It had been built of oak, fastened with iron and wood, and partially sheathed in copper to protect its hull from shipworms (Finegold, 1990). Evidence of prior repairs to the outside of the hull were found: at a critical place near the keel, one of the garboard planks had been replaced by a graving piece after rotten planking had been cut out. The absence of a mast step assembly on the keelson, rigging components, and other hardware, and the lack of ballast stones, suggested that the vessel had been stripped, abandoned, and left to lie on its port side in the shallow waters of a careening area. An organic deposit of natural vegetation surrounded the lower portion of the hull, around the keel, and lay under the port side. This layer contained peat, leaves, cut branches, wooden hull debris, blobs of tar and pitch, burned sticks, and ballast stones. Small slats of wood appeared to have been placed purposefully beneath the port side of the hill, perhaps to cushion the hull where it came into contact with the sand during the process of hauling the ship over for cleaning and repair.

A large section of a tree trunk was discovered perpendicular to the keel and outboard of the hull. Its location and appearance suggested that it may have been a skid placed beneath the keel to haul the vessel over and secure it to the beach for cleaning (Smith, 1999). Sections of rope found at each end of the keel may have helped in this process. Close examination of the filler plank, or graving piece, in the garboard strake on the starboard side of the hull revealed a large crack that ran through a treenail, effectively breaking the garboard in two. The section of abraded tree trunk associated with this feature may have caused stress to the weakened part of the hull and could have been sufficient to cause its failure, making the entire ship unseaworthy.

Historical research on Royal Navy vessels in British West Florida turned up two likely candidates for the identity of the Deadman's Island shipwreck: HMS *Stork* and HMS *Florida*. *Stork* was a 14-gun sloop stationed at Pensacola. Damaged in a gale while trying to enter the harbor, she was condemned as unseaworthy in 1779. Early the next year, her pig-iron ballast and rudder were salvaged for use in a frigate that was being careened at Old Navy Cove (Rea and Servies, 1982). *Florida* served as a patrol schooner, but while careening at Gulf Breeze in 1778, she suddenly filled with water. She could not be pumped out and was condemned on the spot (Ware and Rae, 1982).

Town Point Vessel

In 1991, remains of a second abandoned vessel turned up at Deadman's Island only a few hundred yards north of the first, at a location known as Town Point (Smith, 1999). Initial testing of the site in less than 1 m of water suggested that its well-preserved lower hull and contents also dated from Florida's British Period (1763–1781). A subsequent study of the site by Southern Oceans Archaeological Research, Inc. confirmed that this vessel also had been brought ashore for repairs and abandoned by the British during the last quarter of the 18th century. The archaeologists concluded that the Town Point vessel was a small sloop or cutter built for coastwise, interisland service with unconventional construction techniques that included the use of tropical hardwoods (Morris and Franklin, 1995). Yet they found insufficient evidence to positively identify the site as that of either *Stork* or *Florida*. While the Deadman's Island shipwreck and the Town Point vessel may not be the only craft remains to have been abandoned at this careenage, they remain the most likely candidates for the two vessels described in British accounts of naval activity in the bay.

Brodie's Wharf

During dredging in Pensacola Bay in 1990 for construction of a new pier at the naval air station, a massive submerged object was encountered. The dredge operator, after pulling up several copper-sheathed timbers, personally dived in the bay, and with the assistance of navy divers determined the object was over 40 m long and 15 m wide. The State Historic Preservation Office requested that dredging cease until an archaeological determination of the object's identity and significance was obtained. Panamerican Consultants, Inc. was contracted to assess the submerged structure, which was partially excavated to reveal a large wooden container filled with stone, clay, and sand. Concurrent archival research in government records revealed details of a large caisson constructed and intentionally sunk by the U.S. Navy in the early 1830s. After being sufficiently documented and historically researched, the structure was removed in 1991. The mitigation project was completed after the caisson remains were recorded, artifacts were collected and conserved, and a scale model of the structure was constructed for public exhibit (Mistovich et al., 1991).

Emanuel Point Ship

In the central portion of Pensacola Bay, the remains of another early colonial vessel were discovered in 1992 by the underwater staff of the Florida Bureau of Archaeological Research (Spirek et al., 1993). Apparently a violent storm had grounded the ship on a shallow sandbar off Emanuel Point near the mouth of a bayou. Initial inspection of the site revealed a low mound of ballast stones overgrown with oysters. The ship's mainmast step and associated architecture were discovered beneath shell and stones in the center of the mound. These structural components and a nearby anchor were strikingly similar to those of early Iberian shipwrecks recorded in Europe and the New World. Field specimens of organic materials such as rope, leather, and botanical remains gathered during initial testing provided the first glimpses of the site's unusual state of preservation. A growing collection of clues suggested this had been a Spanish ship that wrecked sometime in the 16th century (Smith, 1995). Lying undisturbed for centuries, the shipwreck was an unprecedented find.

Evidence gathered during two multiyear campaigns of excavation, sponsored by BAR, the University of West Florida, and the Historic Pensacola Preservation Board, suggests that the ship was one of the larger vessels in Tristán de Luna's fleet, which brought the first European colonists to Florida in 1559 (Smith et al., 1995; Smith et al., 1998). Under Luna's command, 11 ships embarked from Mexico to establish a colony and secure the northern frontier of New Spain for the Spanish crown. On board were 1000 settlers and servants, 500 cavalry and foot soldiers, and 240 horses. Clergymen and Aztec

Figure 11.2. A mastadon tusk in the Ichetucknee River, Florida.

mercenaries accompanied the expedition (Priestley, 1928; Scott-Ireton, 1998, 2000). Equipped with agricultural and construction tools as well as livestock, the colonists disembarked at Pensacola, only to suffer a hurricane that destroyed all but three of the anchored ships, some of which had not yet been unloaded. This catastrophe doomed the Luna colony, which eventually was abandoned in 1561.

The shipwreck's remarkable degree of preservation is due to a compact stratigraphy of shells and silt that built up for centuries around the lower hull and ballast. Artifacts and other remains associated with the demise and collapse of the ship were beneath this layer, while those that accumulated in the bottom of the vessel during its sailing career were trapped in a dense, but soft, organic deposit between the ship's frames and in its bilge. This deposit has produced a surprising array of floral and faunal remains, and other organic debris.

Excavations at the central and stern portions of the hull revealed the articulated framework of the ship and its associated fasteners and fittings (Spirek, 1995). The ship's rudder, fashioned of two large oak planks bolted together, was found lying near the sternpost. In the bow, a surprising amount of hull fabric was found preserved on the starboard side, which appears to have quickly collapsed, perhaps under the weight of the anchor during or just after the ship hit a sand bar (Cozzi, 1998). The port bow appears to have quickly disarticulated and is not as well preserved. To help seal the vessel and to prevent shipworm damage, hull planking seams had been covered with strips of sheet lead tacked in place below the water line.

Although the Emanuel Point Ship must have been salvaged by survivors after its sinking, a broad spectrum of materials was left behind. Below ballast and between frames, bilge sediments have preserved a surprising array of organic debris that accumulated throughout the vessel's sailing career. These include wooden tool handles and pegs, fragments of leather shoes, and bits of cordage and rope of all sizes. Deep in the bilge among scraps of wood and other carpenters' debris, the small carved silhouette of a ship was found. Fashioned from fir, the classic features of a typical 16th-century Spanish galleon were faithfully reproduced in miniature by someone who was familiar with contemporary hallmarks of naval architecture (Smith, 1998b).

Among the food remains in the bilge were both European and American fruit seeds and nuts, including olive pits, cherry seeds, and almond, hickory, acorn, and coconut shell fragments. Tropical zapote and papaya remains also have been identified. Hundreds of faunal specimens represent the remains of shipboard provisions, as well as the remains of organisms that died in or near the ship (Bratten, 1995). They include the bones of domestic pig, cow, chicken, and sheep or goat; fragments of fish may be intrusive to the site, having been deposited after the initial wrecking. In addition, the remains of stowaways were found: black rats, mice, cockroaches, and beetles, which inhabited the ship before it anchored at its last port of call.

Ceramic wares were recovered throughout the shipwreck and included coarse earthenwares, lead-glazed earthenwares, tin-glazed enamelwares, and aboriginal wares. The latter are represented by a post-classic Aztec tradition that included effigy containers or ceramic masks. One sherd displays a molded grimacing mouth with painted teeth; another is a partial forehead with painted eyes and facial decorations. In the forward part of the ship were copper galley utensils: a heavy pitcher, cooking couldrons, a skillet, a bucket, a saucepan, a funnel, and a bronze pestle and mortar (Bratten, 1998). Although no artillery pieces or firearms have been found at the wrecksite, a variety of ammunition provides clues to the types of ordnance carried aboard the ship. Stone cannon balls and cast-iron shot were used in the heavy gun batteries, while solid lead and composite lead and iron shot were fired from lighter swivel guns. Musket shot and copper crossbow bolt heads represent the complement of available shoulder arms. An iron breast plate was discovered adjacent to the rudder. Heavily encrusted and extremely fragile, the object is a rare find, although little of the parent metal has survived. Nonetheless, careful examination of the plate's concretion with the aid of computer-assisted tomography scanning and comparison with other examples of European armor, have revealed it to be of munition quality made for a man of larger than average size and probably manufactured in northern Italy around 1510 (Smith, 1999).

The Emanuel Point Ship was a large vessel compared to other 16th-century Iberian shipwrecks reported in the professional literature (Smith, 1993). The hull appears to have been well constructed, with substantial timbers and fastenings. At the time of its last voyage as a "moving van" for settlers and their supplies, the ship must have been a veteran of the Atlantic trade. Extensive use of lead to cover planking seams and to patch leaks, as well as apparent repairs at both bow and stern, indicate the vessel was quite old at its time of sinking. This is supported by analysis of several thousand artifacts and field specimens recovered from in and around the hull (Smith, 1998a). Although its official name and prior history have yet to be determined, the Emanuel Point Ship, as the earliest shipwreck yet found in Florida's waters, has provided new perspectives on the shipbuilding and seafaring traditions that helped to establish the Iberian seaborne empires.

San Felipe

In 1992 and 1993, Indiana University's Office of Underwater Science and Educational Resources conducted an underwater archaeological field school on the site of a Spanish merchant ship wrecked off the Florida Keys in the 1733 flota disaster. Originally discovered in the 1960s, the wreck was worked by commercial salvors who named it "El Lerri" based on a contemporary Spanish salvage map. Although they recovered more than 3000 artifacts, including iron cannon and a large anchor, little treasure was discovered. The unconserved anchor now resides at a local marine shop. In 1977, the site was examined by state of Florida archaeologists during a survey of the 1733 shipwrecks. A preliminary site plan noted much in situ ballast and little additional disturbance (Smith and Dunbar, 1977). Due to the well-preserved nature of the shipwreck, it was ranked as one of the most significant of the 1733 wrecks evaluated by a 1988 joint Indiana University and Florida State University field school (Smith, 1990a). However, later that year, the El Lerri site was looted.

Research in 1992 and 1993 focused on recording extant features of the wreck site, including mapping of timbers exposed by the 1988 looting. A detailed site plan and report of investigations included architectural studies, biological assessments, and an examination of available artifacts (Indiana University and Panamerican Consultants, 1996). The vessel's identity was researched through archival records revealing that its actual name was probably *San Felipe*, and was an English-built merchantman of just over 485 *toneladas* that carried cochineal and indigo dye, sugar, chocolate, vanilla beans, snuff, and medicines.

Aucilla River Prehistory Project

Between 1983 and 1999, the Aucilla River Prehistory Project conducted annual underwater research into the archaeological, paleontological, and paleoenvironmental aspects of the Pleistocene–Holocene transition in Florida. Sponsored by the Florida Museum of Natural History, with support from the Florida Division of Historical Resources, The National Geographic Society, and private benefactors, the project focused on the Aucilla River drainage basin, located in the coastal lowlands of Florida's Big Bend area. The first report of this project featured a bison kill site in the Wacissa River (Webb et al., 1984). The largest underwater excavation is the Page–Ladson Site, which spans 6 m of continuous deposition from about 15,000 to about 9000 years ago. Following a preliminary report on the association of extinct megafauna and Paleo-Indian artifacts (Dunbar et al., 1989), additional discoveries of international significance include the presence of deposits of mastodon digesta and butchered bones (Webb et al., 1992). These digesta include the earliest records of bottle gourds and serve as a basis for comparison of gourds later domesticated in Mesoamerica (Newsom et al., 1993). These same deposits, carbon-dated to 12,200 years B.P., produced a mastodon tusk with numerous lithic cut marks at its base. This represents one of the oldest butchering sites in North America and has caused scientists to rethink existing theories about the migration patterns of early humans in North America. The Aucilla River Project proved to be a successful model of cooperation between private landowners, amateur and professional archaeologists, and sport divers.

Another formal excavation, located four miles downriver, is Sloth Hole, which is notable for the large quantity of Paleo-Indian tools it has yielded, including Clovis, Suwannee, and Bolen points, Aucilla adzes, and the largest concentration of ivory shafts in the New World (Webb et al., 1990; Dunbar and Webb, 1996). Carbon dates from Sloth Hole also place extinct megafauna in association with Paleo-Indian cultural remains at more than 12,000 years B.P.

Boca Chica Channel Wreck

A small, late-18th-century shipwreck, located in a channel adjacent to Naval Air Station Key West, was investigated by a team of federal, state, and local archaeologists. The existance of the site had been known for nearly two decades; local research suggested that the ship might date to the late 16th century or early 17th century. However, test excavations conducted in 1997 produced artifacts that placed the site in a late 18th-century Spanish or French colonial context. The ship appears to have been a small trading or fishing vessel of Caribbean or Central American construction lost in the narrow channel between Boca Chica Key and Stock Island. Although the vessel's identity and function have yet to be firmly established, the shipwreck is important to the early history of the Florida Keys prior to their permanent settlement and may offer new information about regional maritime activities of the period (Neyland, in press).

San Marcos Shipwreck

The remains of a mid-19th-century merchant sailing vessel were investigated by Florida State University students during a 1998 summer field school. Situated in the St. Marks River, near the historic Fort San Marcos de Apalache in northwest Florida, the ship appeared to have been lost or abandoned and showed evidence of having burned to the waterline. Well preserved and articulated hull timbers, some 31 m in length were uncovered, studied, and recorded (Meide, 2000a). Fastened with iron, copper, and wooden fastenings, the ship was estimated to have weighed more than 250 tons, and was likely built to ply the waters of the Gulf of Mexico, the Caribbean, and the east coast of North America. Recovery of more than 200 artifacts and field specimens included elements of the vessel's running rigging and hardware, cargo and stores, a collection of diagnostic ceramic sherds and glass fragments, as well as leather and textile remains.

PaleoAucilla Prehistory Project

Underwater research by Florida State University on inundated prehistoric sites on the continental shelf in Apalachee Bay has focused on a submerged rocky rise located 3.5 miles offshore in 12–15 feet of water on the margins of the ancient bed of the Aucilla River (Faught and Latvis 2000). The site has produced evidence for late Paleo-Indian, Early Archaic, and Middle Archaic activities. More than 30 test pits have revealed that

Figure 11.3. Gun turret on the USS *Massachusetts* off Pensacola, Florida.

sediment basins are filled with both marine, brackish, fresh water, and terrestrial sediments in and around the large rocky rise. Fragmented pieces of mastodon cranium and teeth were found in an intact, terrestrially altered sediment bed in one test pit in 1999. These remains included chipped stone artifacts, but only at the contact of the marine and terrestrial sediments; there were no artifacts in the fully terrestrial sediments. Additional target areas were located by reviewing GPS-based side scan sonar data and investigation by divers. More than 40 new locations, 3–9 miles offshore have been visited; 13 of these have tested positive for artifacts, and seven were designated as sites in the state master site files.

UNDERWATER ARCHAEOLOGICAL PRESERVES

Underwater archaeological preserves, or "shipwreck parks," are relatively new tools for historic preservation and public education. A combination of heritage, recreational, and ecological tourism at a single location makes these parks attractive destinations for residents and visitors. In Florida, there are seven underwater preserves in place, and additional sites are being considered. The success of this program has depended on public participation at each step.

Candidates for preserves are nominated by local residents to the Florida Bureau of Archaeological Research, which responds by working with the waterfront community to evaluate a site's suitability (Smith, 1991). Factors such as public accessibility, archaeological integrity, historical value, biological diversity, and recreational potential are used. If the site meets these criteria, a public proposal is made for the creation of a new preserve through a cooperative partnership between the public and private sectors (Smith, 1990b). Interested organizations and individuals then work together with state and local agencies to prepare the preserve and to maintain it as a historical attraction. An on-site bronze plaque designates each preserve, which is interpreted with brochures and laminated waterproof site guides, as well as museum exhibits. In this way, publicly owned resources become part of a process of education, interpretation, and preservation, and a local community assumes stewardship of each preserve with a broader understanding of its place in their past and future (Smith, 1997).

Florida's Preserves, each of which has been listed on the National Register of Historic Places, include:

Urca de Lima, a 1715 Spanish galleon cast ashore near Fort Pierce, became Florida's first preserve in 1987 through partnership with St. Lucie County and local dive shops.

San Pedro, a 1733 Spanish galleon that sank in the Florida Keys, was designated in 1989 after assistance from the Islamorada Chamber of Commerce and a local community support organization called *San Pedro* Trust.

The late 19th-century steamboat *City of Hawkinsville*, lying on the bottom of the Suwannee River, became the state's third shipwreck park in 1992. The site was nominated by the principal of Bronson High School, whose students helped to map and evaluate it.

In 1993, USS *Massachusetts* (BB-2), the nation's oldest surviving battleship, became a preserve. The vessel was nominated by a local Pensacola diver and sponsored by a citizen group, Friends of *Massachusetts*, who dedicated the new preserve on the 100th anniversary of the battleship's launching.

A fifth preserve, the English steamer *Copenhagen*, which wrecked off Pompano Beach in 1900, was designated in 1994 after being nominated by a local boat captain.

In 1996, the steamer *Tarpon*, was selected from five candidates nominated by Panama City's waterfront community to become Florida's sixth preserve. A partnership between Bay County and the Museum of Man in the Sea made this possible.

Half Moon, a German-built ocean racing yacht with a long and interesting history, wrecked off Miami in 1930. It is Florida's latest preserve, established through the support of the Friends of *Half Moon*.

FLORIDA'S MARITIME HERITAGE TRAIL

To promote public access to Florida's natural and cultural coastal resources, the Bureau of Archaeological Research developed the Florida Maritime Heritage Trail. The project was designed to develop a conceptual trail incorporating heritage locations, including historical, natural, and community resources around Florida's coastline that are open to the public. Six trail themes—coastal communities, coastal environments, coastal forts, lighthouses, historic ports, and historic shipwrecks—are identified and interpreted with a series of narratives and illustrations. The trail, on the model of the already established Florida's Black Heritage Trail and Cuban Heritage Trail, consists of information rather than a marked route; visitors can access any sites on the trail in any order. There is no marker or sign system on the ground that supplies directions or identification. Information about the trail is supplied in two formats: (1) a series of six poster/ brochures presents each theme; and (2) an Internet web site incorporates the same information plus additional materials and offers other Internet links. The six doubled-sided poster/brochures are designed to be used either as a large-format poster (the front side) to reflect trails themes, or as a folded brochure (the back side) that features examples of theme resources and a map of their locations. The web site (http://www.flheritage.com/maritime) has more than 270 pages featuring heritage resources, in addition to illustrations, maps, and additional Internet links.

CONCLUSION

Underwater archaeology is alive and well in Florida. In a state that has a large and varied number of submerged cultural resources, an active regimen of survey and planning, inventory and assessment, and interpretation and exhibition has greatly expanded the archaeological and historical record during the last 15 years. Cooperation between professional and amateur investigators has enabled several important surveys and excavations, providing tantalizing glimpses of Florida's enormous resource base. The general public's interest in historic preservation has been demonstrated by its active participation at every step of the establishment of underwater archaeological preserves. Close coordination between regulatory agencies, private and public entities, and the media has helped protect and preserve Florida's heritage as well as bring it to the public's attention. A growing commitment by academic institutions to the training of students, as demonstrated by the University of West Florida, Florida State University, University of Miami, East Carolina University, and Indiana University, has emerged in large part due to the tremendous potential for archaeological research in Florida's waters. It is hoped that these trends in resource assessment and management will continue into the 21st century.

REFERENCES

Babits, Lawrence, 1994, The *Maple Leaf* Shipwreck. *Archaeology* 47(5):48–50.
Baumer, David R., 1990, *Bethune Blackwater Schooner Report*. Florida Archaeological Reports 21. Florida Bureau of Archaeological Research, Tallahassee.
Bense, Judith A., 1988, *Deadman's Shipwreck, Gulf Breeze; Florida. Preliminary Investigation and Evaluation*. Reports of Investigations No. 18, Institute of West Florida, University of West Florida, Pensacola.
Bratten, John R., 1995, Olive Pits, Rat Bones, and Leather Shoe Soles: A Preliminary Report on the Organic Remains from the Emanuel Point Shipwreck, Pensacola, Florida. In *Underwater Archaeology Proceedings from the Society for Historical Archaeology Conference*, edited by Robyn Woodward, pp. 49–53. Washington, D.C.
Bratten, John R., 1998, Recent Finds from the Emanuel Point Ship. In *Underwater Archaeology*, edited by Lawrence Babits, Catherine Fach, and Ryan Harris, pp. 38–44. Society for Historical Archaeology, Tucson.
Bratten, John R., Burns, Jason M., Hunter III, James W., and Cozzi J., 1999, *Underwater investigations 1998*. Reports of Investigations #70, Archaeology Institute, University of West Florida, Pensacola.
Burns, Jason Mac, 1999, The Life and Times of a Merchant Sailor: History and Archaeology of the Norwegian Ship Catherine. M.A. thesis, Department of History, University of West Florida, Pensacola.
Cantelas, Frank J., 1992, Maple Leaf: *Future Management and Past Field Investigations*. Report prepared for St. Johns Archaeological Expeditions, Inc., by the Program in Maritime History and Nautical Archaeology, East Carolina University, Greenville.
Cantelas, Frank J., 1993, *The 1992* Maple Leaf *Field Investigation*. Report prepared for St. Johns Archaeological Expeditions, Inc., by the Program in Maritime History and Nautical Archaeology, East Carolina University, Greenville.

Cantelas, Frank J., 1994, Maple Leaf: *The 1993 Field Investigations*. Report prepared for St. Johns Archaeological Expeditions, Inc., by the Program in Maritime History and Nautical Archaeology, East Carolina University, Greenville.

Cantelas Frank J., 1995, *An Archaeological Investigation of the Steamboat* Maple Leaf. M.A. thesis, Department of History, East Carolina University, Greenville.

Cantelas, Frank J. and Rodgers, Bradley A., 1994, The *Maple Leaf:* A Case Study in Cost-effective Zero-Visibility Riverine Archaeology. *Internatioanl Journal of Nauthical Archaeology* 23(4): 271–282.

Clausen, C.J., Cohen A.D., Emiliania, C., Holman, J.A., and Stipp, J.J., 1979, Little Salt Spring, Florida: A Unique Underwater Site. *Science* 203:609–614.

Cozzi, J., 1998, Hull Remains of the Emanuel Point Ship. In *Underwater Archaeology*, edited by Lawrence Babits, Catherine Fach, and Ryan Harris, pp. 31–37. Society for Historical Archaeology, Tucson.

Craig, Alan K., 2000a, *Spanish Colonial Silver Coins in the Florida Collection. University Press of Florida*, Gainesville.

Craig, Alan K., 2000b, *Spanish Colonial Gold Coins of the Florida Collection.* University Press of Florida, Gainesville.

Damour, Melanie, and Christopher E. Horrell, 2001, Dog Island Shipwreck Survey. Report of Field Operations: June 26–August 4. Underwater Archaeology Research No. 9, Program in Underwater Archaeology, Florida State University, Tallahassee.

Denson, Robin L., 1992, *The Oklawaha River Survey.* Report prepared for the Florida Bureau of Archaeological Research by the Florida Museum of Natural History, Department of Anthropology, Gainesville.

Dunbar, James, Webb, S. David, and Cring, Dan, 1989, Culturally and Naturally Modified Bones from a Paleoindian Site in the Aucilla River, North Florida. In *Bone Modification*, edited by Robson Bonnichsen and Marcella H. Sorg, pp. 473–497. Center for Study of the First Americans, University of Maine, Orono.

Dunbar, J.S. and Webb, S.D., 1996, Bone and Ivory Tools from Submerged Paleoindian Sites in Florida. In *The Paleoindian and Early Archaic Southeast*, edited by D.G. Anderson and K.E. Sassaman, pp. 331–353 University of Alabama Press, Tuscaloosa.

Duncan, Stanley, 1994, *Site Formation Processes: An Environmental History of the* Maple Leaf *Site, 1864–1993.* M.A. thesis, Department of History, East Carolina University, Greenville.

Faught, Micheal and Latvis, Joseph, 2000, PaleoAucilla Prehistory Project: Report of Offshore Field Operations 1999. Report prepared for the Florida Bureau of Archaeological Research by the Program in Underwater Archaeology, Florida State University, Tallahassee.

Finegold, Robert, 1990, *The Deadman's Sloop: Excavations of a Colonial Careenage.* M.A. thesis, University of St. Andrews, Fife.

Florida Bureau of Archaeological Research, 1994, *Draft Management Plan for Florida's Submerged Cultural Resources.* Florida Bureau of Archaeological Research, Tallahassee.

Florida Bureau of Archaeological Research, 1996, *U.S. Navy and Confederate Shipwrecks in Florida.* 2 vols. Report prepared for the U.S. Naval Historical Center, Washington, D.C., by the Florida Bureau of Archaeological Research, Tallahassee.

Florida Bureau of Archaeological Research, 1997, *Development of State Underwater Archaeological Preserves.* Report prepared for Coastal Management Program, Florida Department of Community Affairs, by the Florida Bureau of Archaeological Research, Tallahassee.

Franklin, Marianne, Morris, John W., and Smith, Roger C., 1992, *Submerged Historical Resources of Pensacola Bay, Florida.* Florida Archaeological Reports, No. 27. Florida Bureau of Archaeological Research, Tallahassee.

Franklin, Marianne and Morris, John W., 1996, *The St. Augustine Shipwreck Survey: Phase One. Southern Oceans Archaeological Research Survey Report No. 1.* Report prepared for the Florida Bureau of Archaeological Research by Southern Oceans Archaeological Research, Inc., Pensacola.

Gaither, Catherine M., editor, 1996, *Florida East Coast Shipwreck Project, 1995 Season.* With contributions from Pat Clyne, William Moore, Taffi Fisher, Lynda Mathews, and Steve Shouppe. Report prepared for the Florida Bureau of Archaeological Research by Salvors, Inc., Sebastian.

Gaither, Catherine M., editor, 1997, *Florida East Coast Shipwreck Project, 1996 Season.* With contributions from William Moore and Lynda Mathews. Report prepared for the Florida Bureau of Archaeological Research by Salvors, Inc., Sebastian.

Gaither, Catherine M. and Essig, H. Michael, editors, 1998, *Florida East Coast Shipwreck Project, 1997 Season.* With contributions from William Moore and Ken Nehiley. Report prepared for the Florida Bureau of Archaeological Research by Salvors, Inc., Sebastian.

Gibbs, Heather, editor, 1992, *Florida East Coast Shipwreck Project, Archaeological Report, 1989–1991*. With contributions from Scott Nierling, Melanie Griffith, Charles Myer, Katherine Amundson, Walter Zackarchuck, Karen Fisher, and R. Duncan Mathewson. Report prepared for the Florida Bureau of Archaeological by Salvors, Inc., Sebastian.

Gibbs, Heather, editor, 1993, A Summary of the East Coast Shipwreck Project, 1992 Season. With contributions from Scott Nierling, Charles Myer, Dave Simmons, Cruise Simmons, Douglas R. Armstrong, Bob Rousseau, and Karen Fisher. Report prepared for the Florida Bureau of Archaeological Research by Salvors, Inc., Sebastian.

Gifford, J.A., 1993, Videography and Geographical Information Systems for Recording the Excavation of a Prehistoric Underwater site. *International Journal of Nautical Archaeology* 22(2):167–172.

Hayes, Chuck, 1996, Underwater Resources of the Florida Keys National Marine Sanctuary, Northeast Region. With contributions by Denis Trelewicz and Paul Caputo. 3 Vols. Report prepared for National Oceanic and Atmospheric Administration, Florida Keys National Marine Sanctuary.

Holland, Keith V., Manley, Lee B., and Towart, James W., 1994, *The Maple Leaf: An Extraordinary American Civil War Shipwreck*. St. Johns Archaeological Expeditions, Inc., Jacksonville.

Hunter, James W. III, Bratten, John R., and Cozzi, J., 2000, *Underwater Field Investigations 1999: The Santa Rosa Island Wreck and Hamilton*'s Shipwreck. Report of Investigation #81. Archaeology Institute, University of West Florida, Pensacola.

Hunter, James W. III, 2001, *A Broken Lifeline of Commerce, Trade, and Defense on the Colonial Frontier: Historical Archaeology of the Santa Rosa Island Wreck, An 18th-Century Spanish Shipwreck in Pensacola Bay*. M.A. thesis, Department of History, University of West Florida, Pensacola.

Indiana University, 1997, *Upper Keys Region, Florida Keys National Marine Sanctuary, Hayes Cultural Resource Report*. Report prepared for the National Oceanic and Atmospheric Administration by Underwater Science and Educational Resources Program, Indiana University, Bloomington.

Indiana University and Panamerican Consultants, Inc., 1996, *Underwater Archaeological Investigations at the Site of the 1733 Spanish Fleet Shipwreck Tentatively Identified as the* San Felipe: An Indiana Field School. Report prepared for the Florida Bureau of Archaeological Research by Indiana University, Department of Recreation and Park Administration, Bloomington.

Joy, Deborah, 1988, *Archaeological Evaluation of Deadman*'s Island, *Gulf Breeze, Florida*. Report of Investigations No. 17, Archaeology Institute, University of West Florida, Pensacola.

Mathewson, R. Duncan, editor, 1984, East Coast Shipwreck Project Report. With contributions by David D. Moore, Kelly Bernard, Janet A. Fittipaldi, Steve Taylor, Richard Brantly, Kim Elmore, Tom Ingram, Pat Clyne, Bob Marx, Jim Sinclair, Deborah Smith, and John Brandon. 4 Vols. Report prepared for the Florida Bureau of Archaeological Research by Cobb Coin Inc., Key West.

McMahan, Frederick B. and Zarzynski, Joseph W., 1997, *A Warship of the "Era of Good Feelings": Recent Archaeology on the United States Schooner* Alligator *Shipwreck*. Paper presented at the 1997 Society for Historical Archaeology Conference, Corpus Christi.

Meide, Chuck, 2000a, An Archaeological Investigation of the San Marcos Shipwreck (8WA501) and a Submerged Cultural Resources Survey of the St. Marks River, 29 June to 07 August 1998. Underwater Archaeology Research Report No. 2, Program in Underwater Archaeology, Florida State University, Tallahassee.

Meide, Chuck, 2000b, Dog Island Shipwreck Survey 1999: Report of Historical and Archaeological Investigations. Underwater Archaeology Research Report No. 4, Program in Underwater Archaeology, Florida State University, Tallahassee.

Memory, Melissa, Swann, Brenda, Staunton, William, Ruhl, Donna, 2000, *Lake Pithlachocco Canoe Site*. Proposal of properties in Florida for Nomination to the National Register of Historic Places. Division of Historical Resources, Tallahassee.

Mistovich, Tim S., Agranat, Brina J., and James Stephen R., 1991, *Brodie's Wharf: Maritime Archaeological Investigation of an Early Nineteenth Century Sunken Caisson at the Pensacola Naval Air Station, Florida*. Report prepared for U.S. Naval Air Station, Pensacola by Panamerican Consultants, Inc., Tuscaloosa.

Morris, John W., 2000, *Site 8SJ3478, The Tube Site: 1999 Field Season Report*. Report prepared for the Florida Bureau of Archaeological Research by the Lighthouse Archaeological Maritime Project, St. Augustine.

Morris, John W. and Franklin Marianne, 1995, *An Archaeological Assessment of the Vessel Remains at Town Point, Site 8SR983.* Report prepared for the Florida Bureau of Archaeological Research by Southern Oceans Archaeological Research, Inc., Pensacola.

Morris, John W., Franklin, Marianne, and Carroll, Norine, 1998, *The St. Augustine Maritime Survey, Southern Oceans Archaeological Research Survey Report No. 2.* Report prepared for the Florida Bureau of Archaeological Research by Southern Oceans Archaeological Research, Inc., Pensacola.

Morris, John W., Franklin, Marianne, Caroll, Norine, Bumpass, Kelly, and White, Andrea P., 1998, *Report on the Tube Site 8SJ3478: Southern Oceans Archaeological Research Site Report No. 2.* Report prepared for the Florida Bureau of Archaeological Research by Southern Oceans Archaeological Research, Inc., Pensacola.

National Oceanic and Atmospheric Administration, 1997, *Programmatic Agreement among The National Oceanic and Atmospheric Administration, The Advisory Council on Historic Preservation, and The State of Florida for Historic Resource Management in the Florida Keys National Marine Sanctuary.* On file at Bureau of Archaeological Research, Tallahassee.

Newsom, Lee A. and Purdy, Barbara A., 1990, Florida Canoes: A Maritime Heritage From the Past, *The Florida Anthropologist* 43(3):164–180.

Newsome, Lee A., Webb S., David, and Dunbar, James S., 1993, History and Geographic Distribution of *Cucurbita pepo* Gourds in Florida. *Journal of Ethnobiology* 13(1):75–97.

Neyland, Robert, 1996, *Survey of USS Alligator: 15–24 July 1996.* Observation Report. Prepared for the Florida Bureau of Archaeological Research by U.S. Naval Historical Center, Washington, D.C.

Neyland, Robert S., editor, in press, *An Investigation of the Boca Chica Channel Wreck, Key West, Florida.* U.S. Naval Historical Center, Washington, D.C.

Payne, Claudine, 1992, *Archaeology Underwater, Surveying Florida*'s Past. Booklet prepared by Marion County School System and the Florida Museum of Natural History. On file at Florida Bureau of Historic Preservation, Tallahassee.

Peebles, Dennis C., editor, 1994, *Florida East Coast Shipwreck Project, 1993 Season.* With contributions from Karen Fisher and Katherine Admunson. Report prepared for the Florida Bureau of Archaeological Research by Salvors, Inc., Sebastian.

Peebles, Dennis C., editor, 1995, *Florida East Coast Shipwreck Project, 1994 Season.* With contributions from Lynda Mathews, William Moore, Katherine Admunson, Mary Moylan, Bob Fullerton, Charles Myer, and Ed Martin. Report prepared for the Florida Bureau of Archaeological Research by Salvors, Inc., Sebastian.

Priestley, Herbert Ingram, editor, 1928, *The Luna Papers.* 2 Vols. Florida State Historical Society, Deland.

Rea, Robert R. and Servies, James A., 1982, *The Log of H.M.S. Mentor 1780–1781. A New Account of the British Navy at Pensacola.* University Press of Florida, Pensacola.

Scott-Ireton, Della, 1998, *An Analysis of Spanish Colonization Fleets in the Age of Exploration Based on the Historical and Archaeological Investigation of the Emanuel Point Shipwreck in Pensacola Bay, Florida.* M.A. thesis, Department of History, University of West Florida, Pensacola.

Scott-Ireton, Della, 2000, Secrets in the Sea: The Emanuel Point Shipwreck. *Florida History and the Arts Magazine* 8(4):16–19.

Sinclair, James and Mathewson, R. Duncan, editors, 1990, *The Florida East Coast Shipwreck Project, 1715 Spanish Plate Fleet, Archaeological Report, 1989.* With contributions from Taffi Fisher, Scott Nierling, Deborah Smith, John Brandon, and John De Bry. Report prepared for the Florida Bureau of Archaeological Research by Cobb Coin Inc., Key West.

Smith, Roger C., 1990a, *A Proposal to Establish an Underwater Archaeological Preserve in the Florida Keys. Florida* Archaeological Reports, No. 7. Florida Bureau of Archaeological Research, Tallahassee.

Smith, Roger C., 1990b, Marine Archaeology Comes of Age in Florida: Excavation of Deadman's Shipwreck, A Careened British Warship in Pensacola Bay. In *Underwater Archaeology Proceedings: Society for Historical Archaeology Conference 1989*, edited by Toni L. Carrell, pp. 110–116. Society for Historical Archaeology, Tucson.

Smith, Roger C., 1991, "Florida's Underwater Archaeological Preserves." In *Underwater Archaeology Proceedings: Society for Historical Archaeology Conference 1991*, edited by John D. Broadwater, pp. 43–46. Society for Historical Archaeology, Richmond.

Smith, Roger C., 1993, *Vanguard of Empire: Ships of Exploration in the Age of Columbus.* Oxford University Press, New York.

Smith, Roger C., 1995, The Ship at Emanuel Point: An Examination of Florida's Earliest Shipwreck. In *Underwater Archaeology Proceedings: Society for Historical Archaeology Conference 1994*, edited by Robyn Woodward, Society for Historical Archaeology, Vancouver.

Smith, Roger C., 1997, Public Stewardship of Shipwrecks: An Example From Florida. *Archaeology and Public Education* 7(2):3–12.

Smith, Roger C., 1998a, Pensacola's Tristán de Luna Shipwreck: A Look at the Archaeological Evidence. *Gulf Coast Historical Review* 14(1):21–30.

Smith, Roger C., 1998b, Discovery, Development, and Interpretation of Florida's Earliest Shipwreck: A Partnership in Research and Historic Preservation. In *Underwater Archaeology*, edited by Lawrence Babits, Catherine Fach, and Ryan Harris, pp. 115–121. Society for Historical Archaeology, Tucson.

Smith, Roger C., 1999, Pensacola's Colonial Maritime Resources. In *Archaeology of Colonial Pensacola*, edited by Judy Bense, pp. 91–120. University Press of Florida, Gainesville.

Smith, Roger C. and Dunbar, James S., 1977, *An Underwater Archaeological Survey of Eight Spanish Merchant Naos of the 1733 New Spain Fleet*. Florida Bureau of Archaeological Research, Tallahassee.

Smith, Roger C., Finegold Robert, and Stephens, Eric, 1990, Establishing an Underwater Archaeological Preserve in the Florida Keys: A Case Study. *APT Bulletin, The Journal of Preservation Technology* 22(3):11–18.

Smith, Roger C., Spirek, James, Bratten, John, and Scott-Ireton, Della, 1995, *The Emanuel Point Ship: Archaeological Investigations, 1992–1995*. Florida Bureau of Archaeological Research, Tallahassee.

Smith, Roger C., Dunbar, James S., and Faught, Michael, 1997, *An Underwater Archaeological Survey in the Santa Fe River, Florida*, July 1997. Florida Archaeological Reports No. 36. Florida Bureau of Archaeological Research, Tallahassee.

Smith, Roger C., Miller, James J., Kelley, Sean M., and Harbin, Linda G., 1997, *An Atlas of Maritime Florida*. University Press of Florida, Gainesville.

Smith, Roger C., Bratten, John, Cozzi, J., and Plaskett, Keith, 1998, *The Emanuel Point Ship: Archaeological Investigations, 1997–1998*. Florida Bureau of Archaeological Research, Tallahassee.

Spirek, James, 1995, Pinned to the Bottom: Emanuel Point Hull Remains. In *Underwater Archaeology Proceedings from the Society for Historical Archaeology Conference 1995*, edited by Paul Johnson, pp. 43–48. Society for Historial Archaeology, Washington, D.C

Spirek, James, Scott, Della, Hughson, Charles, Williamson, Mike, and Smith, Roger C., 1993, *Submerged Historical Resources of Pensacola Bay, Florida*, Phase Two. Report prepared for Coastal Management Program, Florida Department of Community Affairs, by the Florida Bureau of Archaeological Research, Tallahassee.

Stoltman, Thomas and Cantelas, Frank, 1993, Investigation of the Maple Leaf: A Civil War Transport. In *Underwater Archaeology Proceedings from the Society for Historical Archaeology Conference 1993*, edited by Sheli O. Smith, pp. 83–90. Society for Historical Archaeology, Kansas City.

Ware, John D. and Rea, Robert R., 1982, *George Gauld: Surveyor and Cartographer of the Gulf Coast*. University Press of Florida, Gainesville.

Webb, S. David, Milanich, J.T., Alexon, R., and Dunbar, J.S., 1984, A *Bison antiquus* Kill Site, Wacissa River, Jefferson County, Florida. *American Antiquity* 49(2):384–392.

Webb, S. David, Dunbar, James S., and Waller, Benjamin, I., 1990, Ecological Implications of Ivory Foreshafts From Underwater Sites in Florida. *Abstracts of the 6th International Conference for Archaeozoology*, p. 62. Smithsonian Institution, Washington, D.C

Webb, S. David, Dunbar, James S., and Newsome, Lee A., 1992, Mastodon Digesta From North Florida. *Current Research in the Pleistocene* 9:114–116.

Chapter 12

The Great Lakes States

JOHN R. HALSEY

INTRODUCTION

The Great Lakes lie at the heart of the North American continent and comprise the largest freshwater system in the world. They stretch from Duluth at the western end of Lake Superior to Kingston at the eastern end of Lake Ontario and drain into the north Atlantic via the St. Lawrence River. Formed by the advance and retreat of continental glaciers, the lakes did not settle into their present shapes and approximate elevations until about 4000 years ago (Larsen, 1987), long after the first people had entered the region. Hugging the shores in frail craft of wood and bark, prehistoric inhabitants eventually exploited the waters of the Great Lakes, their tributaries, and interior lakes.

The St. Lawrence–Great Lakes system offered a convenient route of entry for European explorers. At first, they used the vessels that brought them from the Old World, but eventually adopted and modified the watercraft of the natives. They developed new vessel types responsive to the unique conditions of the Great Lakes, ocean-sized bodies of fresh water but without tides, capable of throwing up violent storms on short notice, and laced with rocks, sandbars, and uncharted reefs. This experimentation continued through the 18th and 19th centuries, as merchants and shipbuilders struggled to develop the optimum combinations of wood, iron, steel, sail, steam, and crews to carry the products of fields, forests, lakes, and mines (Barry, 1996;

John R. Halsey, Office of the State Archaeologist, Michigan Historical Center, Department of History, Arts, and Libraries, Lansing, Michigan 48918.

International Handbook of Underwater Archaeology, edited by Carol V. Ruppé and Janet F. Barstad.
Kluwer Academic/Plenum Publishers, New York, 2002.

Cooper, 1993; Cooper and Labadie, 1997; Labadie, 1992; Martin, 1993; Peters, 1993; Wilson, 1990). In the 20th century, this experimentation has produced the 1000-ft leviathan iron ore carriers we see today.

Through the years, the lakes exacted their toll, leaving on their bottoms a sample of virtually every type of vessel that traversed them, an unparalleled museum of naval architecture, propulsion and cargoes, from *Griffin* (1679) to USCG *Mesquite* (1989), and countless pleasure craft. Nevertheless, the historical and archaeological record has suffered major alterations over time due to formal salvage of vessels and cargo, and depredations by divers, alterations well under way by the 1850s. One has only to read the incredible autobiographical exploits of the celebrated submarine diver, John Green, to appreciate what divers and salvors in the Great Lakes and big rivers were able to accomplish with primitive, homemade equipment (Green, 1990; Hunter, 1969: 117–120).

PREHISTORY, PROTOHISTORY, AND EUROPEAN EXPLORERS

Habitation Sites

The quantity, distribution, and physical integrity of prehistoric archaeological sites on the bottomlands of the Great Lakes are great unknowns. George Quimby early promoted the concept that important sites lay beneath the waves, perhaps as deep as 100 m (300 ft) (Quimby, 1959, 1965a, 1965b), but only now are we beginning to see significant movement toward identifying probable locations of prehistoric sites through careful study of historic documents and modern remote sensing technology. However, some current researchers note that "sampling for the discovery and recovery of submerged archaeological sites in Saginaw Bay will not be a straightforward process, but will of necessity have to rely on refined bottom sampling technologies" (Lovis et al., 1996). This is especially true of Saginaw Bay in Lake Huron, which has received an enormous load of sediment from upstream agricultural activities. Practical matters such as the fact that few prehistoric archaeologists have been divers, and the costs and dangers of doing prehistoric archaeology under water, have restricted development of such technologies.

Fishing Sites and Artifacts

There must have been many durable interior riverine sites such as fish weirs, but most have undoubtedly been destroyed by dredging and other improvements. The Dyreson Fish Weir in Wisconsin is one of the few documented archaeologically (Barton, 1996).

Recovery of artifacts from lakes and river bottoms has been rare, and it is not surprising that most are related to fishing. Large copper artifacts known as gaff hooks have been discovered from time to time, some in fishermens' nets, but none recently (Bell, 1928; Quimby and Griffin, 1961; Steinbring, 1967). Steinbring's article presents a convincing case for gaff hooks as components of a *leister*, three-part fish spear.

Beginning in the Late Archaic, an inland shore fishery developed in the northern Great Lakes (Cleland, 1982, 1989; Martin, 1985, 1989). All evidence used to build its chronology came from excavation of terrestrial sites or analysis of their distribution, although fishing activities, by definition, took place in the water. Nevertheless, a large number of copper artifacts taken from terrestrial sites, were used to spear, harpoon, and hook fish large and small (e.g., Beukens et al., 1992; Hruska, 1967; Interesting Wisconsin Specimens, 1956, 1957, 1958; Papworth, 1967; Pleger, 1992).

Dugouts and Birchbark Canoes

Activity that took place on the water required some mode of transportation. Principal vehicles were the bark canoe (birch, elm, hickory, chestnut, cottonwood, and spruce) and the wooden log dugout. There is no archaeological or ethnographical evidence of skin boats in the Great Lakes area, but they would have been the only craft available to Paleoindians, who undoubtedly would have found some kind of watercraft useful in their cold, waterlogged environment (Engelbrecht and Seyfert, 1994). Dugouts may be older than bark canoes, but the sample is skewed because large, heavy dugouts have survived, whereas the extremely fragile bark canoes have disappeared completely.

The technology for building a dugout was simple but laborious: Select a tree, fell the tree, cut the tree trunk to the desired length and hollow it out using fire, axe, and adze. The earliest known dugout in the Great Lakes area is the Ringler dugout, accidentally recovered during commercial dredging of Savannah Lake, Ashland County, Ohio (Brose, 1978; Brose and Greber, 1982). Two other dugouts, apparently identical to the Ringler specimen, had been found earlier in Savannah Lake. The white oak dugout, nearly 7 m (22 ft) long and weighing (dry) between 385 and 410 kg (850 and 900 lbs), yielded a radiocarbon date of 3550 ± 70 B.P. Its role in transportation was probably confined to the larger rivers, coastal and interisland regions, and seasonally to connecting waterways (Brose and Greber, 1982).

Many other dugouts have been discovered in the greater Great Lakes region (Baker, 1998; Gibson, 1960; Johnston, 1962; Kidd, 1960; Lemmer, 1955; McCracken, 1962), but few have been reported at this time. An ongoing study by Timothy Kent shows at least 80 from Michigan alone (Pott, 1992). Rogers' (1965) summary of 18 Ontario dugouts shows that all but one came from interior lakes. His assessment of their temporal position is that most postdate European contact and some, based on oral tradition, were made by Europeans. Crane and Griffin (1962) report a date of 275 ± 150 years B.P. on a dugout canoe from Madeline Island, Wisconsin. The dugouts recovered from Pickerel Lake in Allegan County, Michigan, and the Pere Marquette River in Mason County, Michigan, date to the mid-17th and mid-19th centuries respectively (Pott, 1992). Presently, the known time span for dugouts covers nearly 4,000 years. However, the forests were in place and the necessary tools were at hand at least 2,000 years before the Ringler dugout was built. Perhaps even earlier dugouts lie at the bottoms of other lakes in the midwestern United States. It seems unlikely that any will be found in the open Great Lakes themselves.

It would be nice to know more about the antiquity of bark canoes, especially birchbark because, at the time of European contact, it was clearly the preeminent mode of water transport wherever the paper birch tree grew. Birchbark canoes were indispensable to aboriginal peoples long before they became the principal vehicle of commerce and exploration of the North American fur trade (Adney and Chapelle, 1983; Kent, 1997). At the time of first contact, Europeans found native peoples using canoes to set fishing nets (Thwaites, 1959b), to carry cargo (Wrong, 1939), to hunt deer by driving them into water (Biggar, 1929), and to carry war parties (Biggar, 1929; MacLeod, 1995). In skirmishes on water, the birchbark canoe apparently had a significant advantage over other canoes because of its speed, maneuverability, and light weight (Thwaites, 1959a). As much as they loved their canoes, their paddlers tended to stay close to shore (Biggar, 1929). Bark canoes were fragile, leaky, and easily damaged (Wright, 1991). Undoubtedly, there were many tragedies on the open water in these fragile craft: The nearly intact prehistoric ceramic vessel recovered from the bottom of the Rock Harbor Channel at Isle Royale (Carrell, 1987) almost certainly fell from a capsized canoe.

Native American concerns about accidents that might befall on stormy seas are documented in prehistory by small slate amulets or charms (Cleland, 1985; Cleland et al., 1984), and in the Historic Period by offerings at shrines (McKenney, 1972) and drawings of an early schooner and other craft, some possibly in distress, on birchbark and blackboard slate (Birmingham, 1982). Native American fascination with early sailing vessels was also manifested in rock art and a small toy boat from eastern Lake Superior (Agassiz, 1850).

Native American rock art in Canada provides another perspective on canoes. As important as they were for earthly journeys, ". . . canoes on rock art may not always refer to the crafts for traveling through this world. Paintings from across the Shield depict canoes possibly entering or leaving the cliffs, taking the medicine men on their important [spirit] journeys" (Rajnovich, 1994).

DEVELOPMENTS IN THE GREAT LAKES STATES

In the Great Lakes region, individual states have ownership and management responsibilities for abandoned shipwrecks on state-owned bottomlands. There is no basin-wide plan, although there have been efforts to familiarize the various lake states with each others' problems and seek mutually agreeable solutions (Vrana and Mahoney, 1993). Ownership of cultural remains on interior lake and river bottoms varies. In some cases, the state has ownership; in others, the owner of the adjacent upland has ownership rights.

With the passage of the National Historic Preservation Act of 1966 and the Abandoned Shipwreck Act of 1987, states have taken a more active role in attempting to manage the shipwreck resources, since they are technically the "owners." Even with this federal legislative support, legal disputes have consumed thousands of hours and dollars that might have been used to manage and interpret the resource. Because few states employed professionally-trained maritime archaeologists in a permanent capacity, most have made do with prehistorians or historical archaeologists to lead their maritime archaeological efforts. Virtually all states have entered into formal or informal agreements with avocationalists (see Cooper, 1994a, for an excellent outline of responsibilities and expectations) but a few states have trained sport divers in nondestructive documentation techniques (Harrington, 1990). All Great Lakes states have benefited from direct or indirect contacts with colleagues Peter Engelbert and Phillip Wright in Ontario.

Most states have undertaken literature search inventories; some have been more aggressive in assessing and documenting individual wrecks or groups of wrecks. Actual fieldwork has been done by avocational divers on their own initiative or under professional supervision, university-sponsored projects, and even the Submerged Cultural Resources Unit of the National Park Service (Lenihan, 1997b).

The following section is a review of what has been accomplished in maritime archaeology in the various Great Lakes states.

Minnesota

Minnesota lies at the northwestern end of the Great Lakes system. Its main port of Duluth has been a major debarkation point especially for ships carrying iron ore from the Mesabi Range and grain from the prairie states. Of all the Great Lakes states, Minnesota has done the most in placing its 52 reported shipwrecks into firm historical contexts (Anfinson, 1993, 1997; Labadie et al., 1993). The Minnesota Historical Society also has sponsored a series of shipwreck assessments to locate sites, determine site integrity (Agranat et al., 1993; James, 1993; Tidewater Atlantic Research, Inc., 1993a, 1993b, 1993c), and National Register of Historic Places eligibility (Delgado, 1997b), and has developed a submerged cultural resource preservation plan (Marken et al., 1997). An innovative survey was National Register-level evaluation of underwater and water's-edge cultural resources in Duluth Harbor (Ward and McCarthy, 1997), and a similar but smaller-scale project was conducted at Knife River and Two Harbors (Watts et al., 1997). Minnesota is a state with many interior lakes and rivers, and a wide-ranging inventory has revealed a remarkable variety and number of wrecks on these water bodies (Birk and Newell, 1997).

Unique among Minnesota's shipwrecks is USS *Essex* (1876–1931), one of the United States's last sail-powered, wooden fighting ships. A Donald McKay-built sloop of war, it lies today on the beach at Duluth's Minnesota Point (Anfinson, 1996).

Wisconsin

Since 1988, Wisconsin has developed the most fully-formed maritime archaeology program of any of the Great Lakes states, largely through the efforts of State Underwater Archaeologist David Cooper to establish partnerships with a wide variety of agencies, groups, and individuals (Cooper, 1992, 1996). Sadly, budgetary cutbacks and Cooper's move to another position have made the future of the Wisconsin program uncertain.

Prior to the development of a formal program, there had been two shipwreck documentation projects: the Submerged Cultural Resources Unit's study of the schooner barge *Noquebay* (1872–1905) at Stockton Island in Apostle Islands National Lakeshore (Carrell, 1985), and the schooner *Fleetwing* (1867–1888) in Garrett Bay, Door County (Cooper, 1988b). Once Cooper was on board, an early effort was an inventory of shipwreck losses—a total of 61—at the northern end of the Door Peninsula in Lake Michigan (Cooper, 1988a), followed in 1988 by fieldwork on five of the wrecks, including the archetypal Great Lakes bulk carrier, *R.J. Hackett* (1869–1905) (Cooper, 1989). In 1989, the state conducted a marine magnetometer survey in the Death's Door Passage (Cooper and Rodgers, 1990a, 1990b).

In 1990, the State Historical Society of Wisconsin was part of a joint effort to survey submerged cultural resources at Apostle Islands National Lakeshore (Cooper et al., 1991). The survey team located and evaluated 11 wreck sites and made recommendations for management and National Register of Historic Places eligibility. Fieldwork between 1990–1992 resulted in the documentation of the wooden steamer *Frank O'Connor* (ex-*City of Naples*) (1892–1919) and the enormous 338-foot schooner–barge *Pretoria* (1900–1905), one of the largest wooden vessels ever to sail the Great Lakes (Cooper and Jensen, 1995). Both were creations of famed West Bay City, Michigan shipbuilder, James Davidson (Jensen, 1994; Swayze, 1991).

Gordon Watts Jr. located and conducted limited testing on the wreck of *Light Vessel #57*, one of the Great Lakes' first three self-propelled light vessels and a veteran of three decades of service. Since no plans and few contract specifications survived, the wreck represents the most important surviving source of information concerning the design and construction of the vessel (Ebersol, 1993; Watts, 1992). Of the nearly two dozen lightships that served on the Great Lakes for more than a century, the sole survivor is *Huron*, built in 1920 and now a dry-berthed museum ship in Port Huron, Michigan (Schmitt, 1996).

One of the partner groups encouraged by Cooper is the Wisconsin Underwater Archaeology Association which, between 1990 and 1993, conducted a survey of the Leathem and Smith limestone quarry near Sturgeon Bay and the associated remains of the wooden steamers *Joseph L. Hurd* (1869–1913) and *Mueller* (ex-*Edwin S. Tice*) (1887–1935) (Aerts, 1994).

The Mississippi River forms much of the western border of Wisconsin and has been the artery of maritime trade and exploration since the mid-17th century. In 1985, the St. Paul district of the Corps of Engineers did limited testing on the Civil War-era steamer *War Eagle*, burned and sunk at La Crosse in 1870 in the Black River, a tributary of the Mississippi (Berwick, 1992; Jensen, 1992). John Jensen's historical research and analysis suggest a high probability of significant wrecks in the northern Mississippi River (Jensen, 1992).

Michigan

As proclaimed on its automobile license plates, Michigan is "The Great Lakes State." It has 124 lighthouse sites, the most of any state in the country (Hyde 1986), some of whose locations contain significant archaeological remains related to earlier structures on the site (Franzen, 1988; James and Day, 1995). The state once had 34 lifesaving stations, by far the most in the Great Lakes (Stonehouse, 1994), virtually all of which are now archaeological sites. Nearly 40 percent of the territory within Michigan's boundaries, 99,725 km (38,504 mi), lies beneath Great Lakes waters. In 1998, the state had more than 900,000 registered boaters. Because of its vast Great Lakes area and large number of shipwrecks (more than 1300), Michigan has assumed an unofficial leadership role in the areas of shipwreck legislation, management and underwater parks and preserves (Halsey, 1989, 1990a, 1990b, 1992, 1994, 1996; Halsey and Martindale, 1987; Harrington, 1993; Vrana, 1997b; Vrana and Halsey, 1991, 1992; Vrana and Mahoney, 1995).

The first important professional shipwreck excavation in Michigan waters was the Smithsonian Institution's work on *Indiana* (1848–1858), one of the earliest propeller-driven steamboats on Lake Superior. The Smithsonian initiated work in 1979, but the project carried on at intervals until 1993 (Johnston, 1993, 1995, 1997; Johnston and Robinson, 1993; Smith et al., 1980; Wolff, 1979; Wright, 1979, 1980). Early efforts were directed at recovery of the the vessel's propulsion machinery and associated gear, and later work emphasized documentation of the rest of the vessel. Some of the artifacts recovered are on display in the Hall of American Maritime Enterprise at the National Museum of American History.

Another important excavation in Michigan waters was the Michigan Maritime Museum's work on *Rockaway* (1866–1891) off South Haven in southern Lake Michigan (Pott, 1985, 1993, 1997). *Rockaway* was a scow schooner, a ship type often characterized by flat bottoms, square bilges, and bluff bows but embracing an enormous range of variation. Comparative study of *Rockaway* with other scow schooners "is beginning to suggest several different classes of scows, patterns of change in their development . . . and a more thorough understanding of the cultural and environmental factors which influenced these changes" (Pott, 1993). A major benefit of the *Rockaway* project was the publication of a manual on the conservation of artifacts from a freshwater environment (Singley, 1988).

In 1990, local residents discovered the bow of a wooden vessel projecting from the river bank near the mouth of the Millecoquins River (Figures 1 and 2) at the extreme northern end of Lake Michigan (Cantelas, 1991). It is a classic example of the "buoyant hull" type of beached shipwreck site (Delgado, 1997a). Preliminary excavations and historical research led to a faulty identification of the vessel (Halsey, 1991), and extensive excavation over two seasons and exhaustive historical research has failed to identify this vessel conclusively. Probably built in 1833—a large 1833 United States penny was found in the foremast step—(Barkhausen, 1995, 1996), it may have been lost in 1839 or shortly thereafter, a guess based on the name and employment period of New York salt inspector J.M. Allen (Mitchell, 1996) and the shipping label on a box of Chinese tea (Cantelas, 1993:15). Structural integrity of the hull, excellent organic preservation, assemblage of ship's equipment, personal items, cargo, and stowage, all from an early trading vessel, mark the Millecoquins wreck as one of the most significant excavated to date in the Great Lakes.

Other major projects have documented shipwreck structure rather than artifact recovery. Preliminary documentation reports exist for schooner barge *Newell A. Eddy* (1890–1893) (Meadows, 1992); schooner *Goshawk* (1866–1920) (Harrington, 1998:31–32; Olson, 1995); and wooden steamer *Three Brothers* (1888–1911) (Ashlee, 1996; Halsey and Peters, 1996; Vrana, 1996a, 1997a).

Figure 12.1. Stern cabin area of the Millecoquins shipwreck, Lake Michigan, 1991. (Photo courtesy of J.R. Halsey)

Figure 12.2. Hull outline of the Millecoquins shipwreck, Lake Michigan, 1991. (Photo courtesy of J.R. Halsey)

Isle Royale National Park and Pictured Rocks National Lakeshore on Lake Superior, and Sleeping Bear Dunes National Lakeshore on Lake Michigan, lie within Michigan's borders. Each has a complete shipwreck inventory.

The Submerged Cultural Resources Unit of the National Park Service (Lenihan, 1987) conducted Isle Royale's inventory, a massive 568-page document and the result of five seasons of work. It included not only shipwrecks but also an analysis of the development of Lake Superior's maritime tradition, the lake's major vessel types, underwater components of land-based sites, and shipwreck management in the park. All 11 shipwrecks reported were nominated to the National Register of Historic Places. The 1987 report was published in edited form for a lay audience (Lenihan, 1994), which reflects Isle Royale's reputation as one of the premier dive destinations in the Great Lakes. Isle Royale and its shipwrecks also served as the setting for a popular mystery novel, *A Superior Death* (Barr, 1995).

Patrick Labadie's inventory at Pictured Rocks documented the remains of 23 wrecks (1989). This report provides a regional maritime historical context, a developmental sequence of commercial ships on Lake Superior, and shipwreck plans and historic photographs of the vessels. Peter Lindquist, diver and charter boat operator out of Munising on Lake Superior, has expanded his business to include a glass-bottom-boat shipwreck tour of shallow-water wrecks around Munising Bay and Grand Island. Because of the clarity of Lake Superior's water and the high popularity of adjacent Pictured Rocks National Lakeshore, in 1998 12,000 visitors, most of whom had never been close to a submerged shipwreck, were given an "almost-diver's" view of a variety of wooden shipwrecks.

The State of Michigan's Manitou Passage Underwater Preserve lies within the water boundaries of Sleeping Bear Dunes National Lakeshore on Lake Michigan. Making use of years of survey and documentation done by local divers, Ken Vrana of Michigan State University's Center for Maritime and Underwater Resource Management drew together a report that included the maritime history and commerce of the Manitou Passage area, land-associated underwater sites, recreation resources, information and recommendations for comprehensive planning, and vessel and site profiles for 58 ships known or believed to have been lost in the study area (Vrana, 1995).

The National Oceanic and Atmospheric Administration (NOAA) has carried out planning studies preparatory to designating the proposed Thunder Bay National Marine Sanctuary in northern Lake Huron. Volume I of the draft environmental impact statement and draft management plan includes a description of the sanctuary setting, which contains an inventory of 160 ships known or believed to have been lost in the project area (National Oceanic and Atmospheric Administration, 1997). This document also contains a comparative and theme study of national historic landmark potential and a summary of Alcona County maritime history (Martin, 1997).

A unique undertaking was the placement of an official Michigan historical marker at the wreck of the tug *Sport* (1873–1920), thought to be the earliest steel-hulled vessel on the Great Lakes (Peters and Ashlee, 1992; Schmitt, 1989). This marker, telling of the working life and the wreck, was placed next to the National Register-listed, largely intact and easily divable wreck and has been very popular with divers (Stayer and Stayer 1995).

A wreck was forever lost in 1994, when the remains of the schooner *Alvin Clark* (1846–1864) were bulldozed into a landfill to make way for a marina parking lot. The vessel, a magnificently intact two-masted schooner, had been raised with great fanfare in 1969 (Avery, 1974). However, without adequate conservation planning and funding, the ship and its artifacts began to deteriorate and finally became both a physical and emotional eyesore (O'Donnell, 1994). Thus its last owners disposed of it. It has become the classic example of why large vessels should not be raised.

Like Illinois, Michigan has had to deal with legal challenges to state ownership of shipwrecks. The *Captain Lawrence* case (Creviere, 1997; O'Donnell, 1995; Teter and Halsey, 1997) has gone all the way to the United States Supreme Court. Still the question of ownership has not been resolved, and the case has been remanded to the Sixth Circuit Court of Appeals.

As noted by Carrell (1997), the known or suspected presence of human remains on shipwrecks is a contentious issue and an even more delicate problem if there are surviving relatives, as in the case of *Edmund Fitzgerald* (1957–1975) (MacInnis, 1998). After human remains from this most famous of Great Lakes wrecks were videotaped and publicized, the Michigan legislature passed and the governor signed Public Acts 62 and 63 of 1997. This made it a felony to photograph knowingly or display publicly a photograph of all or a portion of a body located in a grave or on or near a shipwreck.

Michigan's Great Lakes shipwrecks continue to be the inspiration for a regular flow of books by avocational diver and historians who tell mainly of (as one title aptly puts it) *Wild Gales and Tattered Sails* (Creviere, 1997). In the past, such books dealt primarily with the drama, pathos, and mystery of the shipwreck. More recently, serious scholars of Great Lakes maritime history have provided more context for the significance of vessels and information on vessel locations, and wreck conditions and features. The best is *Shipwrecks of the Straits of Mackinac* (Feltner and Feltner, 1991). Dennis Hale (1996) provided his own unique version of undergoing and surviving the 1966 Lake Huron sinking of the *Daniel J. Morrell* (1906–1966).

Illinois

Despite its position as an interior prairie state, Illinois has a long maritime history on its rivers, canals, 3952 km (1526 mi) of Lake Michigan shores, and its great port of Chicago. In the mid-1980s, because of a lack of inhouse expertise and funding, the Illinois Historic Preservation Agency began cooperative activities with the Chicago Maritime Society (CMS) and the Underwater Archaeological Society of Chicago (UASC). The group's first project was the 1987 documentation of the shallow-water, 278-foot, five-masted schooner *David Dows* (1881–1889). It was chosen as the site of Illinois' first formal shipwreck project because "it was a large wreck site of an extremely famous ship, well-known to the sport diving community, thus providing appeal to the media and preservation community" (Emerson, 1996).

In 1989, UASC mapped, photographed, and videotaped the wreck of the 200-foot *Wells Burt* (1873–1883) and attached permanent plastic tags to 325 artifacts to serve (they hoped) as deterrents to removal. The wreck's location became known to the local dive community and, for two years, no artifacts were taken. By May 1989, ten deadeyes had disappeared and an interpretive sign had been vandalized. All remaining loose artifacts were removed or securely fastened with chains. Through 1996, no additional thefts or vandalism had taken place (Emerson, 1996).

The discovery of the wrecks of *Lady Elgin* (1851–1860) and *Seabird* (1859–1868) threw Illinois into a continuing legal controversy, when the salvager who discovered them attempted to claim ownership (Emerson, 1996; Erwin, 1994). *Lady Elgin* was a 252-foot, luxurious, sidewheel "palace steamer" that could carry hundreds of passengers, cargo, and even livestock. When it collided with the lumber schooner *Augusta* during a gale, *Lady Elgin* broke up, and nearly 300 passengers and crew died. Through UASC, IHPA conducted preliminary documentation in 1992 (Olson, 1993). Documentation was difficult, since the debris field was strung out over eight miles. Legal disagreements between the salvor, IHPA and UASC prevented recovery of a representative sample of artifacts during the 1993 field season; in the meantime, many portable artifacts disappeared from the site, leaving mostly hull-related equipment. In any case, the work accomplished (Erwin, 1994) has shown that, despite the high standard of workmanship that went into palace steamers, there were fatal design flaws.

Illinois has been the site of at least 20 recoveries, for restoration, of U.S. Navy World War II planes (mostly SBD Dauntless dive bombers) lost in training exercises on the pseudoaircraft carriers USS *Sable* (ex-*Greater Buffalo*) and USS *Wolverine* (ex-*Seeandbee*) (Cooper, 1994b; Emerson, 1996; McHaney, 1992). Some estimates indicate that there may be 300 more planes still on the lake bottom (Association for Great Lakes Maritime History, 1998).

Indiana

Indiana has one of the smallest Great Lakes areas, 583 km (225 mi). Archival and documentary evidence suggests that as many as 50 shipwrecks lie on Indiana bottomlands, 14 of which have been located (Ellis, 1989). Former state archaeologist Gary Ellis developed an excellent working relationship with members of the scuba team of the Indiana Department of Natural Resources Division of Law Enforcement. With their assistance, he was able to document the 14 located wrecks. He produced three final reports (Ellis, 1985a, 1985b, 1987), draft reports, and a National Register of Historic Places nomination for the *Muskegon* (1872–1911) (ex-*Peerless*), a wooden passenger freighter.

Ohio

Ohio was the home of many early shipyards, and its Lake Erie waters contain many early and significant wrecks. The state has a large and active sport diving community, but only within the last decade has the State of Ohio has passed protective legislation and begun to assess its maritime resources. One significant project was the study of the steamer *Adventure* (1875–1903) sunk at Kelleys Island not far from the Kelleys Island Lime & Transport Company's North Bay quarry complex, from which it had hauled lime and limestone for years (Labadie and Herdendorf, 1998). The report contains a concise summary of the Kelleys Island limestone industry which helps to put the ship into context.

The Institute for Great Lakes Research at Bowling Green State University has published an annotated list of vessels built by the American Ship Building Company and its predecessors, a most useful document (Institute for Great Lakes Research, 1988).

Pennsylvania

Pennsylvania is a large state, but it owns only a tiny amount of Lake Erie bottomland. Archaeologist Kurt Carr (personal communication, 1998) reports very little activity in maritime archaeology and no significant discoveries since 1988.

New York

Mark Peckham of New York's State Historic Preservation Office reports little significant activity in the state's Great Lakes waters. Survey and limited excavation in the Niagara River offshore from Fort Niagara revealed an intact, inundated shoreline dating from

1762 to the early 1780s, and a wealth of artifacts (Knoerl, 1991). Additional survey work at Old Fort Niagara has defined the dimensions and condition of an unfinished elliptical bastion (Richardson, 1995). See also Crisman on Lake Champlain and Zarzinski on Lake George in this volume.

MODERN VERNACULAR CRAFT

Due to its isolation and its long history as an important fishery, Isle Royale in western Lake Superior has served as an important reservoir of small vernacular craft. Building on research originally done in the early 1980s, Toni Carrell (1987, 1989) and Hawk Tolson (1991, 1998) have demonstrated the evolution of various small, vernacular craft types and the significance of oral history to the understanding of variation, change and, perhaps most important, the intensely personal commitment of a fisherman to his means of livelihood. Speaking of Stanley and Clara Sivertson, the last commercial fisherfolk with a permit to work the waters around Isle Royale, Tolson notes, "Their fishery at the island and the grounds surrounding their business on the mainland are filled with the hulks of now unusable but still treasured old hulls." However, because of the feeling that "boats were my friends," Stanley had trouble getting rid of any of them. He said, "It was like getting rid of your wife" (Tolson, 1998:201). Because of the availability of this oral evidence, we are parties to what may have been a much more prevalent attitude between sailor and craft than has been suspected.

The work of Carrell and Tolson is especially important, because few small vernacular craft are identified in the Great Lakes shipwreck record. Even vessels as large as fish tugs are nearly invisible in the record because of their relatively small size and the lack of significant publicity when they were lost. Nevertheless, these vessels and those who sailed them have not been forgotten (Oikarinen 1991; Prothero and Prothero 1990; Sivertson, 1992). They have been remembered with at least two memorials: at Grand Marais and Naubinway, Michigan. Resort boats such as gas-powered launches that once plied every lake and river of any size have received much less attention than their big laker cousins (Birk and Newell, 1997; Cowles, 1997; Jensen, 1992).

CANALS

Despite the big lakes and numerous navigable rivers, canals and canal boats were a vital means of transport to and within the Great Lakes area, especially during the first half of the 19th century (Aitken, 1954; Gillham, 1996; Goodrich, 1961; Shaw, 1953; Waggoner, 1958; Wilcox, 1969). Cleland and Stone (1967) pointed out the importance of archaeology in understanding the Erie Canal (Shaw, 1966). More recent work on canals has resulted from review and compliance research and excavation, such as that done on a segment of the Wabash and Erie Canal in Lafayette, Indiana (Dunham and Branstner, 1995).

Pennsylvania's state archaeologist Kurt Carr (personal communication, 1998) reports frequent discoveries of canal remains in construction projects. In these cases, archaeologists document wood or stone structural remains and the canal's prism cross-section.

The United States Congress agreed to the designation of the Cuyahoga Valley National Recreation Area (National Park Service, 1995) and the Illinois & Michigan

Canal National Heritage Corridor (Conzen and Carr, 1988), both featuring canals as a focal feature (Noble, 1991). In 1996, the destruction of a dam across the DuPage River at Channahon, Illinois by flood waters drained a large section of the Illinois and Michigan Canal, exposing the remains of seven oak-hulled canal boats at a place known as Morris Wide Water. The preserved sections were about 4.5 m (15 ft) wide by 30 m (100 ft) long and, although similar in size, varied greatly in construction. The vessels appear to have been tethered together at the time of their abandonment. Harness hardware, personal items, furniture remains, and cooking utensils were found in the hulls. This is a particularly important find because, although there were hundreds of boats on the Illinois & Michigan Canal, not one has survived intact to the present day (Mansberger and Stratton, 1998).

TECHNOLOGY AND ADVANCES

The most significant advance in maritime archaeology undoubtedly has been the ability to discover wrecks through the use of side scan sonar (Klein, 1997), although wrecks continue to be found discovered by fish-finders, depth finders, snagging by anchor, and by visual sightings on beaches and shallow waters. Proton magnetometers have not been used as much in the Great Lakes, because shipwreck preservation is generally so good that side scan sonar gives more immediate and satisfying results. In addition, shipwreck hunters are seldom interested in shipwrecks buried in bottom sediments, a situation more amenable to the capabilities of the magnetometer. However, proton magnetometers have been used in Wisconsin (Cooper and Rodgers, 1990a; Cooper et al., 1991).

Drawn measurement of shipwrecks continues to be done principally through baseline trilateration (Lenihan, 1997a). The photomosaic technique (Broadwater, 1997) has been used only on the *Rockaway* project. Videomosaic imaging has been used successfully on some shallow, flattened wrecks such as *Alva Bradley* (1870–1894) (Stoltmann, 1991). "It is, in a nutshell, a photomosaic technique substituting video images instead of film and a computer rather than a darkroom" (Seeley, 1992; Wright, 1992). Advances in computer technology have already taken this technique well beyond what was described in the references cited above (K. Vrana, personal communication, 1998). There have also been experiments in combining 3-D videotape, survey sled, ROV, and the SHARPS positioning system (Vrana and Schwartz, 1989).

The availability of video cameras and high quality still cameras with complementary light systems has made these tools the standard for recording shipwrecks remains, especially for baseline documentation of new wrecks after their discovery. Presentation of the history of a particular vessel, with historical photographs and a dive tour of its wrecked remains in videotape format, is becoming an increasingly popular alternative mode of publication (Ertel and Turchi, 1997; Out of the Blue Productions 1997a, 1997b), as opposed to the more traditional printed form.

CONTINUING ISSUES IN GREAT LAKES MARITIME ARCHAEOLOGY

Despite having a world-class resource of shipwreck sites, the Great Lakes states have been slow to develop maritime archaeology. Because of their high degree of integrity, many sites would appear to be ideal laboratories for the practice of maritime archaeology, yet until recently little interest has been shown by state historical or recreational resource agencies or university history and archaeology programs. The major reason at the state agency level may be that, after the *Edmund Fitzgerald*, few "name" vessels engaged the public's interest and few cargoes were worth salvaging. So why would anyone care about them? Why should anyone develop a program? At the university level, most archaeologists have been trained as prehistorians; they suspected that underwater archaeology was just dressed-up salvage or that there no significant research questions posed by shipwrecks. In addition, despite the high quality of the recreational shipwreck diving experience, few state travel agencies have understood the tourism potential. Diving in dark, cold water does not have the allure of Cozumel or the Virgin Islands, but the Great Lakes arguably provide the best shipwreck diving in the world.

The growth and availability of technology, specifically side-scan sonar, has put the ability to discover virgin shipwrecks within the range of anyone who can afford it, and the price is dropping all the time. Locational devices such as Loran-C have insured that a site can be relocated once it has been found, even by someone who has never been to the site before. Most shipwreck hunters appear to be interested only in the adrenalin thrill of discovery and ego satisfaction of newspaper coverage rather than unpermitted salvage. Their slide shows with multiple lap-dissolve projectors and New Age background music are elegant productions that take weeks to put together but that are directed principally at a peer group audience of fellow divers interested in the search and discovery and the object itself. These productions only incidentally provide information on the significance of the ship that became a wreck or the research potential of the sites.

Historic shipwrecks in the Great Lakes offer opportunities for interdisciplinary research between archaeologists, divers, and many academic disciplines because of the broad spectrum of ship types represented and the often pristine quality of preservation. Perhaps the first, but by no means the most important, connection is with historians and problems of historical interpretation of shipwreck incidents. Recent discoveries, such as *Titanic* and *Lusitania*, have shown that detailed examination of surviving ship remains and cargo are the only true source of information that can alter long-held positions on how and why ships sank or were sunk. While satisfying no current, pressing "need to know," these questions are certainly ones an interested public most wants answered.

Related to such questions is the ability to visit, revisit, and repeatedly examine specimens of notable technological advancement and failure. Did *W.H. Gilcher* sink in 1892 because of hull plates or rivets made brittle by cold? Where do the pin-crank dual oscillating engines of the *New York* (built 1856) fit into the phylogeny of Great Lakes marine propulsion systems? Interdisciplinary research could help answer these and many other questions of interest to maritime historians and naval architects.

Discovery, documentation, and excavation of certain vessels could provide answers to questions raised on excavation of upland sites. Excavation of La Salle's ship *La Belle* in the Gulf of Mexico has provided new vistas on the quantity, variety, and quality of early trade goods brought to the New World. It is hard to imagine that discovery and excavation of LaSalle's *Griffin* (1679), lost in northern Lake Michigan or Lake Huron, would not have a comparable effect on the archaeology of the French period in the Upper Great Lakes.

Certain ship types are unique. Examples may exist nowhere else on earth except the Great Lakes, and they may have considerable symbolic power beyond their inherent historical significance. Just such vessels are the World War I minesweepers *Inkermann* and *Cerisoles*, built in 1918 at ort William, Ontario, for the French Navy, and lost on their maiden voyages across Lake Superior, each with their entire crew of 38. These two ships offer the additional complicating factor of being foreign-flag ships lost in time of war, and they cannot be salvaged under the internationallyagreed upon doctrine of sovereign immunity (Roach, 1997). Who would have thought that our diplomatic colleagues would have to become involved with shipwrecks!

Shipwrecks lost in the cold, fresh water of the Great Lakes become time capsules of their own structure, crew possessions, and cargoes. A number of vessels still contain substantial portions of their bulk cargoes, and although coal, limestone, and iron ore may be of relatively little interest, cargoes of wheat and corn may preserve genetic material that otherwise may have been lost to contemporary agricultural researchers. Package freighters such as *Regina* (lost 1913) and *Florida* (lost 1897) contain broad-spectrum cargoes exhibiting typical period modes of product packaging, which may not have been breached by corrosion. The product and its packaging can be studied and evaluated for period standards of purity and constituents. These factors are especially useful for research, because the exact date of loss is usually known, as well as the conditions in which the remains have been kept (e.g., 90 years at 100 feet at 40 degrees Fahrenheit).

Certain vessels contain unique cargoes or materials that could be used to assess quality, or variation in quality, such as the Fairport, Ohio, steel billets left on the schooner *Alva Bradley* (lost 1894) after salvage attempts were abandoned. Where else might such pristine examples of the raw product of steel-manufacturing still exist? On the *Morning Star* (lost 1868) is the propulsion system originally installed on the *Ocean*. The walking beam for this engine may contain iron from the first bloom of iron made at the Carp River forge, the first forge built to exploit the immense iron riches of the Marquette Range, a landmark in American history.

CONCLUSIONS

The Great Lakes area of the United States and Canada contains an incomparable collection of shipwreck remains and submerged prehistoric and historic sites that reflect human usage of the lakes over almost 10,000 years. The states surrounding the lakes have made various attempts to inventory, evaluate, study, and protect these resources, but all such efforts may be characterized as underfunded, understaffed, and often in direct competition for staff and funding with more powerful, established environmental and historic preservation programs (Goss, 1998). The ability of private individuals to find and dive wrecks unhindered has put all but the very deepest sites in jeopardy. While there has been a major change in the habits of modern divers in taking souvenirs from wrecks, high-visibility items such as bells and other artifacts carrying a vessel's name are in danger. Given the size of the lakes, the only hope is to continue to work with concerned ethical divers to insure that private profit and collections do not strip these public resources of their ability to illuminate the past for scholar and layman alike.

ACKNOWLEDGMENT. This paper could not have been written without the generous cooperation of the following individuals in providing documents and their thoughts. Minnesota: Scott F. Anfinson and C. Patrick Labadie; Wisconsin: Robert A. Birmingham and John O. Jensen; Michigan: Peter Lindquist, Kenneth R. Pott, Kenneth J. Vrana, and Pat and Jim Stayer; Illinois: Mark Esarey, Floyd Mansberger, and Valerie Olson Van Heest; Indiana: Sean Dunham and Rick Jones; Ohio: Franco Ruffini; Pennsylvania: Kurt

Carr; and New York: Mark Peckham. Of course, any errors of interpretation or statements of fact are the sole responsibility of the author.

REFERENCES

Aerts, D., 1994, *Report on Leathem & Smith Quarry Site, 1990–1993*. Wisconsin Underwater Archeology Association, Madison.

Adney, E.T., and Chapelle, H.I., 1983, *The Bark Canoes and Skin Boats of North America*. Smithsonian Institution Press, Washington, D.C.

Agassiz, L., 1850, *Lake Superior: Its Physical Character, Vegetation, and Animals, Compared with Those of Other and Similar Regions*. Gould, Kendall and Lincoln, Boston.

Aitken, H.G.J., 1954, *The Welland Canal Company: A Study in Canadian Enterprise*. Harvard University Press, Cambridge.

Agranat, B., James Jr., S.R., and Foster, K.J., 1993, Submerged Cultural Resources Investigation: Shipwrecks *Madeira* and *Thomas Wilson*, Lake Superior, Minnesota. In *Archaeological and Historical Studies of Minnesota's Lake Superior Shipwrecks*, edited by S.F. Anfinson. Minnesota State Historic Preservation Office, Minnesota Historical Society, St. Paul.

Anfinson, S.F., 1997, Minnesota's Submerged Cultural Resources. In *History Underwater: Studies of Submerged Cultural Resources in Minnesota*, edited by S.F. Anfinson. Minnesota State Historic Preservation Office, Minnesota Historical Society, St. Paul.

_____, 1996, The Wreck of the USS *Essex*. *Minnesota History 55:94–103*.

_____, 1993, Underwater Cultural Resources in Minnesota: Shipwrecks of Lake Superior. In *Archaeological* and *Historical Studies of Minnesota's Lake Superior Shipwrecks*, edited by S.F. Anfinson. Minnesota State Historic Preservation Office, Minnesota Historical Society, St. Paul.

Ashlee, L.R., 1996, *Three Brothers*, a Lady and a Crayfish. *Michigan History Magazine* 80(6):26–27.

Association for Great Lakes Maritime History, 1998, Historic Planes from Lake Michigan. *Association for Great Lakes Maritime History Newsletter* 15(4):8.

Avery, T., 1974, *The Mystery Ship from 19 Fathoms*. Avery Color Studios, Au Train, MI.

Baker, J., 1998, *The Curtis Pond Canoe: The Identification, Recovery, and Context of a Dugout Vessel from the Pocono Highlands*. Commonwealth Archaeology Program Report No. 2. Bureau for Historic Preservation, Pennsylvania Historical and Museum Commission, Harrisburg.

Barkhausen, H., 1996, *The Riddle of the Naubinway Sands: Updated Report on the Millecoquins River Wreck from the Association for Great Lakes Maritime History*. Association for Great Lakes Maritime History, Bowling Green, OH.

_____, 1995, Second Expedition to Naubinway Gathers New Evidence and Clues. *Association for Great Lakes Maritime History Newsletter* 12(3):1–5.

Barr, N., 1995, *A Superior Death*. Avon Books, New York.

Barry, J., 1996, *Ships of the Great Lakes: 300 Years of Navigation*. Thunder Bay Press, Holt.

Barton, D., 1996, *The Dyreson Fish Weir on the Yahara River*: A Preliminary Report. *Wisconsin Archeologist* 77:78–81.

Bell, C.N., 1928, An Implement of Prehistoric Man. In *Thirty-sixth Annual Archaeological Report*, Ontario, 1928 (including 1926–1927), pp. 51–54.

Berwick, D.E., 1992, Wisconsin's Underwater Archaeological Resources: A Federal Perspective. *Wisconsin Archeologist* 73:7–10.

Beukens, R.P., Pavlish, L.A., Hancock, R.G.V., Farquhar, R.M., Wilson, G.C., Julig, P.J., and Ross, W., 1992, Radiocarbon Dating of Copper-Preserved Organics. *Radiocarbon* 34:890–897.

Biggar, H.P., 1929, *The Works of Samuel de Champlain*. Vol. III. The Champlain Society, Toronto.

Birk, D., and S. Newell, 1997, Shipwrecks of Minnesota's Inland Lakes and Rivers: A Submerged Cultural Resources Survey. In *History Underwater: Studies of Submerged Cultural Resources in Minnesota*, edited by S.F. Anfinson. Minnesota State Historic Preservation Office, Minnesota Historical Society, St. Paul.

Birmingham, R.A., 1982, Art on Blackboard Slates and Birchbark from Archaeological Contexts on Madeline Island, Wisconsin. *Wisconsin Archeologist* 63:239–245.

Broadwater, J.D., 1997, Photomosaic. In *Encyclopaedia of Underwater and Maritime Archaeology*, edited by J.P. Delgado, pp. 313–314. British Museum Press, London.

Brose, D.S., 1978, Archaic Dugout Canoe Found in Northern Ohio. *Explorer* 20(2):13–17.

Brose, D.S., and Greber, I., 1982, The Ringler Archaic Dugout from Savannah Lake, Ashland County, Ohio: With Speculations on Trade and Transmission in the Prehistory of the Eastern United States. *Midcontinental Journal of Archaeology* 7:245–282.

Cantelas, F.J., 1993, A Portrait of an Early 19th-Century Great Lakes Sailing Vessel. In *Underwater Archaeology Proceedings from the Society for Historical Archaeology Conference*, edited by S.O. Smith, pp. 13–17. Kansas City, MO.

_____, 1991, Michigan Field School. *Stem to Stern: Program in Maritime History and Underwater Research* 7: 8. East Carolina University, Greenville, NC.

Carrell, T., 1997, Human Remains. In *Encyclopaedia of Underwater and Maritime Archaeology*, edited by J.P. Delgado, pp. 198–199. British Museum Press, London.

_____, 1989, In All Things Remembered: An Oral History Approach to Understanding Small Craft Remains. In *Underwater Archaeology Proceedings from the Society for Historical Archaeology Conference*, edited by J.B. Arnold III, pp. 76–80. Baltimore, MD.

_____, 1987, Underwater Components of Land-Based Sites and Other Submerged Cultural Resources. In *Submerged Cultural Resources Study: Isle Royale National Park*, edited by D.J. Lenihan, pp. 335–473. Professional Paper No. 8. Southwest Cultural Resources Center, National Park Service, Santa Fe.

_____, 1985, *Submerged Cultural Resources Site Report: Noquebay, Apostle Islands National Lakeshore.* Professional Paper No. 7, Southwest Cultural Resources Center, National Park Service, Santa Fe.

Cleland, C.E., 1989, Comments on "A Reconsideration of Aboriginal Fishing Strategies in the Northern Great Lakes Region" by Susan R. Martin. *American Antiquity* 54:605–609.

_____, 1985, *Naub-cow-zo-win* Discs and Some Observations on the Origin and Development of Ojibwa Iconography. *Arctic Onthropology* 22(2):131–140.

_____, 1982, The Inland Shore Fishery of the Northern Great Lakes: Its Development and Importance in Prehistory. *American Antiquity* 47:761–784.

Cleland, C.E., Clute, R.D., and Haltiner, R.E., 1984, *Naub-cow-zo-win* Discs from Northern Michigan. *Midcontinental Journal of Archaeology* 9:235–249.

Cleland, C.E., and Stone, L.M., 1967, Archaeology as a Method for Investigating the History of the Erie Canal System. *Historical Archaeology* 1:63–70.

Conzen, M.P., and Carr, K.J., editors, 1988, *The Illinois and Michigan Canal National Heritage Corridor: A Guide to Its History and Sources.* Northern Illinois University Press, DeKalb.

Cooper, D.J., 1996, Building Bridges in the Badger State: Partnerships in Wisconsin Underwater Archaeology. In *Underwater Archaeology*, edited by S.R. James Jr. and C. Stanley, pp. 152–156. Society for Historical Archaeology, Tucson, AZ.

_____, 1994a, "Come All Ye Gentlemen Volunteers": Perspectives on Avocationalists in Underwater Archaeology. In *Underwater Archaeology Proceedings from the Society for Historical Archaeology Conference*, edited by R.P. Woodward and C.D. Moore, pp. 145–149. Vancouver, British Columbia.

_____, 1994b, In the Drink: Naval Aviation Resources and Archaeology. In *Underwater Archaeology Proceedings from the Society for Historical Archaeology Conference*, edited by R.P. Woodward and C.D. Moore, pp. 134–139. Vancouver.

_____, 1993, Synthesizing the Archaeological and Historical Record of Great Lakes Maritime Transportation. In *Underwater Archaeology Proceedings from the Society for Historical Archaeology*, edited by S.O. Smith, pp. 7–12. Kansas City.

_____, 1992, Wisconsin Underwater Archaeology: An Introduction. *Wisconsin Archeologist* 73: 1–6.

_____, 1989, *Survey of Submerged Cultural Resources in Northern Door County: 1988 Field Season Report.* State Historical Society of Wisconsin, Madison.

_____, 1988a, *Inventory of Vessel Losses in Death's Door, Door County, Wisconsin, and Surrounding Waters, 1837–1938.* State Historical Society of Wisconsin, Madison.

_____, 1988b, *1986–1987 Archaeological Survey of the Schooner* Fleetwing, *47DR168, Garrett Bay, Wisconsin.* ECU Research Report No. 6. Program in Maritime History and Underwater Research, East Carolina University, Greenville, NC.

Cooper, D.J., and Jensen, J.O., 1995, *Davidson's Goliaths: Underwater Archeological Investigations of the Steamer* Frank O'Connor *and the Schooner-Barge* Pretoria. State Historical Society of Wisconsin, Madison.

Cooper, D.J., and Labadie, C.P., 1997, Great Lakes. In *Encyclopaedia of Underwater and Maritime Archaeology*, edited by J.P. Delgado, pp. 176–180. British Museum Press, London.

Cooper, D.J., Partlow, M.A., Rodgers, B.A., Smith, G.T., and Watts, G.P., Jr., 1991, *By Fire, Storm, and Ice*: *Underwater Archeological Investigations in the Apostle Islands*. State Historical Society of Wisconsin, Madison.

Cooper, D.J., and Rodgers, B.A., 1990a, Probing Wisconsin's "Door of Death": A Preliminary Report on 1989 Marine Magnetometer Survey in Northern Lake Michigan. In *Underwater Archaeology Proceedings from the Society for Historical Archaeology Conference 1990*, edited by T.L. Carrell, pp. 101–105. Tucson.

_____, 1990b, *Report on Phase I Marine Magnetometer Survey in Death's Door Passage, Door County, Wisconsin, 1989*. State Historical Society of Wisconsin, Madison.

Cowles, W.C., 1997, *Antrim Steamers*: *A Brief History of Steam Navigation on the Inland Lakes of Antrim County, Michigan*. Privately published by the author.

Crane, H.R., and Griffin, J.B., 1962, University of Michigan Radiocarbon Dates VII. *Radiocarbon* 4:183–203.

Creviere, P.J. Jr., 1997, *Wild Gales and Tattered Sails: The Shipwrecks of Northwest Lake Michigan from Two Creeks, Wisconsin to Dutch Johns Point, Michigan and All of the Bay of Green Bay*. Privately published by the author. DePere, WI.

Delgado, J.P., 1997a, Beached Shipwreck Sites. In *Encyclopaedia of Underwater and Maritime Archaeology*, edited by J.P. Delgado, pp. 57–59. British Museum Press, London.

_____, 1997b, National Register of Historic Places. In *Encyclopaedia of Underwater and Maritime Archaeology*, edited by J.P. Delgado, p. 291. British Museum Press, London.

Dunham, S.B., and Branstner, M.C., 1995, The Life and Death of a Canal: The Wabash and Erie Canal in Lafayette, Indiana. Paper presented at 28th Annual Meeting of the Society for Historical Archaeology, Washington, D.C.

Ebersol, J.C., 1993, *Light Ship #57*——Grays Reef. *Telescope* 41:87–91.

Ellis, G.D., 1989, Historic Context: Marine Cultural Resources, Indiana Territorial Waters of Lake Michigan. In *Overview of Archaeological Resource Planning*, Chapter 20. Division of Historic Preservation and Archaeology, Indiana Department of Natural Resources, Indianapolis.

_____, 1987, *Preliminary Evaluation of the Muskegon, Marine Cultural Resource Site No. 2, LaPorte County, Indiana*. Marine Cultural Resources Report No. 3. Division of Historic Preservation and Archaeology, Indiana Department of Natural Resources, Indianapolis.

_____, 1985a, *Preliminary Evaluation of the Unknown No. 2, Marine Cultural Resources Site No. 5, Hammond, Indiana*. Marine Cultural Resources Report No. 2. Division of Historic Preservation and Archaeology, Indiana Department of Natural Resources, Indianapolis.

_____, 1985b, Underwater Archaeological Investigations at the *J.D. Marshall* Shipwreck Site, Indiana Dunes State Park, Porter County, Indiana. *Marine Cultural Resources Report No. 1*. Division of Historic Preservation and Archaeology, Indiana Department of Natural Resources, Indianapolis, IN.

Emerson, T.E., 1996, Preserving the Shipwrecks of the Prairie State. *Illinois Archaeology* 8:1–22.

Engelbrecht, W.E., and Seyfert, C.K., 1994, Paleoindian Watercraft: Evidence and Implications. *North American Archaeologist* 15:221–234.

Ertel, D., and Turchi, M., 1997, *A Cold Dark Hart*. A Turchi/Ertel Production, Flint, MI. Video.

Erwin, T., 1994, The *Lady Elgin*: A Nineteenth-Century Palace Steamer in Lake Michigan. In *Underwater Archaeology Proceedings from the Society for Historical Archaeology Conference*, edited by R.P. Woodward and C.D. Moore, pp. 90–95. Vancouver.

Feltner, C.E., and Feltner, J.B., 1991, *Shipwrecks of the Straits of Mackinac*. Seajay Publications, Dearborn, MI.

Franzen, J., 1988, Lighthouse Archaeology: Another Key to the Past. *The Beacon*: *Official Publication of the Great Lakes Lighthouse Keepers Association* 6(3):6.

Gibson, E.P., 1960, That Dugout Canoe. *The Coffinberry News Bulletin* 7:91.

Gillham, S., 1996, The Marvelous Welland Canal. *Inland Seas* 52:88–99.

Goodrich, C., editor, 1961 *Canals and American Economic Development*. Columbia University Press, New York.

Goss, H., 1998, Shipwrecks: Coastal Managers Search for Solutions. *Coastal Services* 1(4):4–5.

Green, J.B., 1990, *Diving with & without Armor*: *Containing the Submarine Exploits of J.B. Green, the Celebrated Submarine Diver*. Atlantic Diving Equipment, Inc., Bowie, MD. Revised from the 1859 edition published by Faxon's Steam Power Press, Buffalo, NY.

Hale, D., 1996, *Sole Survivor*: *Dennis Hale's Own Story*, as told to T. Juhl, P. Stayer, and J. Stayer. Lakeshore Charters & Marine Exploration, Inc., Lexington, MI.

Halsey, J.R., 1996, Twenty Years On: Shipwreck Preservation in Michigan. *Common Ground* 1(3–4): 26–33.

_____, 1994, Freshwater Refractions. In *Underwater Archaeology Proceedings from the Society for Historical Archaeology Conference*, edited by R.P. Woodward and C.D. Moore, pp. 108–113. Vancouver.

_____, 1992, Sea Changes. *Michigan History Magazine* 76(6):55–61.

_____, 1991, "The Reeck of a Small Vessel". *Michigan History Magazine* 75(2):30–36.

_____, 1990a, *Beneath the Inland Seas*: *Michigan's Underwater Archaeological Heritage*. Bureau of History, Michigan Department of State, Lansing.

_____, 1990b, Michigan's Great Lakes Shipwrecks: Save, Salvage, or Excavate? In *Underwater Archaeology Proceedings from the Society for Historical Archaeology Conference*, edited by T.L. Carrell, pp. 2–6. Tucson.

_____, 1989, Nine Years before the Mast: Shipwreck Management in Michigan since 1980. In *Underwater Archaeology Proceedings from the Society for Historical Archaeology Conference*, edited by J.B. Arnold, pp. 43–48. Baltimore.

Halsey, J.R. and Martindale, J.L., 1987, Sacking the Inland Seas: Shipwreck Plundering in the Great Lakes. *Michigan History Magazine* 71(6):32–38.

Halsey, J.R. and Peters, S.M., 1996, Resurrection of a Great Lakes Steamer. *Michigan History Magazine* 80(6):22–25.

Harrington, S., 1998, *Divers Guide to Michigan*. Maritime Press in association with the Great Lakes Diving Council, Inc., St. Ignace, MI. Revised edition.

_____, 1993, *Intentional Vessel Sinking Guidelines*: *Final Report*. Maritime Research Associates, Inc., St. Ignace, MI.

_____, 1990, *Diving into St. Ignace Past*: *An Underwater Investigation of East Moran Bay*. Maritime Press, Mason, MI.

Howland, J., 1997, Video Mosaic. *In Encyclopaedia of Underwater and Maritime Archaeology*, edited by J.P. Delgado, pp. 458–459. British Museum Press, London.

Hruska, R., 1967, The Riverside Site: A Late Archaic Manifestation in Michigan. *Wisconsin Archeologist* 48: 145–260.

Hunter, L.C., 1969, *Steamboats on the Western Rivers*: *An Economic and Technological History*. Octagon Books, New York. Reprint of 1949 edition.

Hyde, C.K., 1986, *The Northern Lights*: *Lighthouses of the Upper Great Lakes*. TwoPeninsula Press, Lansing.

Institute for Great Lakes Research, 1988, *American Ship Building Company and Predecessors*, *1867–1920*. Bowling Green State University, Perrysburg, OH.

Interesting Wisconsin Specimens, 1958, Copper Necklace; Copper Harpoon. *Wisconsin Archeologist* 39: 274.

_____, 1957, Copper Punch; Copper Fishhook. *Wisconsin Archeologist* 38:32.

_____, 1956, Copper Harpoon; Copper Bannerstone. *Wisconsin Archeologist* 37:49.

James, B., and Day, G., 1995, *History and Archaeology of the First Copper Harbor Lighthouse*. Report of Investigations No. 21. Archaeology Laboratory, Department of Social Sciences, Michigan Technological University, Houghton.

James, S.R. Jr., 1993, National Register Assessment of Four Great Lakes Shipwrecks: The *Essex, Hesper, Amboy* and *George Spencer*, Lake Superior, Minnesota. In *Archaeological and Historical Studies of Minnesota's Lake Superior Shipwrecks*, edited by S.F. Anfinson. Minnesota State Historic Preservation Office, Minnesota Historical Society, St. Paul.

Jensen, J.O., 1994, Oak Trees and Balance Sheets: James Davidson, Great Lakes Shipbuilder and Entrepreneur. *American Neptune* 54:99–114.

_____, 1992, Gently down the Stream: An Inquiry into the History of Transportation on the Northern Mississippi River and the Potential for Submerged Cultural Resources. *Wisconsin Archeologist* 73:61–110.

Johnston, P.F., 1997, *Indiana*. In *Encyclopaedia of Underwater and Maritime Archaeology*, edited by J.P. Delgado, pp. 204–205. British Museum Press, London.

_____, 1995, Downbound: The History of the Early Great Lakes Propeller *Indiana*. *American Neptune* 55:323–355.

_____, 1993, Downbound: Exploring the Wreck of the *Indiana*. *Michigan History Magazine* 77(5):24–30.

Johnston, P.F., and Robinson, D.S., 1993, The Wreck of the 1848 Propeller *Indiana*: Interim Report. *International Journal of Nautical Archaeology* 22:219–235.

Johnston, R.B., 1962, Another Dugout Canoe from Ontario. *American Antiquity* 28:95–96.

Kent, T.J., 1997, *Birchbark Canoes of the Fur Trade*, 2 vols. Silver Fox Enterprises, Ossineke, MI.

Kidd, K.E., 1960, A Dugout Canoe from Ontario. *American Antiquity* 25:417–418.

Klein, M., 1997, Side Scan Sonar. In *Encyclopaedia of Underwater and Maritime Archaeology*, edited by J. P. Delgado, pp. 384–385. British Museum Press, London.

Knoerl, T.K., 1991, On the Shores of Fort Niagara: Archaeological Evidence of an Inundated 18th-Century Shoreline. *Underwater Archaeology Proceedings from the Society for Historical Archaeology Conference*, edited by J.D. Broadwater, pp. 103–107. Richmond.

Labadie, C.P., 1992, Ships of the Great Lakes. *Michigan History Magazine* 76(6):40–43.

_____, 1989, *Submerged Cultural Resources Study: Pictured Rocks National Lakeshore*. Professional Paper No. 22. Southwest Cultural Resources Center, National Park Service, Santa Fe.

Labadie, C.P., Agranat, B., and Anfinson, S.F., 1993, Minnesota's Lake Superior Shipwrecks A.D. 1650–1945:Historical Contexts and Property Types. In *Archaeological and Historical Studies of Minnesota's Lake Superior Shipwrecks*, edited by S.F. Anfinson. Minnesota State Historic Preservation Office, Minnesota Historical Society, St. Paul.

Labadie, C.P., and Herdendorf, C.E., 1998, *The Steamer Adventure and the Kelleys Island, Ohio, Limestone Industry*. Ohio Lake Erie Commission, Toledo and Ohio Historic Preservation Office, Columbus.

Larsen, C.E., 1987, *Geological History of Glacial Lake Algonquin and the Upper Great Lakes*. Bulletin No. 1801. U.S. Geological Survey, Washington, D.C.

Lemmer, V.F., 1955, Indian Dugout Canoe Discovered on Thousand Island Lake in Gogebic County, Michigan. *Telescope* 4(3):14–16.

Lenihan, D.J., 1997a, Baseline Trilateration. In *Encyclopaedia of Underwater and Maritime Archaeology*, edited by J.P. Delgado, pp. 54–55. British Museum Press, London.

_____, 1997b, Submerged Cultural Resources Unit. In *Encyclopaedia of Underwater and Maritime Archaeology*, edited by J. P. Delgado, pp. 408–409. British Museum Press, London.

_____, 1994, *Shipwrecks of Isle Royale National Park: The Archaeological Survey*. Lake Superior Port Cities Inc., Duluth.

_____, 1987, *Submerged Cultural Resources Study: Isle Royale National Park*. Professional Paper No. 8. Southwest Cultural Resources Center, National Park Service, Santa Fe.

Lovis, W.A., Holman, M.B., Holley, M.W., and Vrana, K.J. 1996, *Saginaw Bay Archaeological Project: Pilot Technology Assessment*. Report submitted to Coastal Zone Management Program, Michigan Department of Environmental Quality (Contract No. 95D-0.07), Lansing.

MacInnis, J., 1998, *Fitzgerald's Storm: The Wreck of the Edmund Fitzgerald*. Thunder Bay Press, Holt, MI.

MacLeod, D.P., 1995, Naval History of the Ojibwa of Lake Superior. *American Neptune* 55:301–307.

Mansberger, F., and Stratton, C., 1998, *Canal Boats along the Illinois and Michigan Canal: A Study in Archaeological Variability*. Fever River Research, Springfield.

Marken, M.W., Ollendorf, A., Nunnally, P., and Anfinson, S., 1997, Beneath Minnesota Waters: Minnesota's Submerged Cultural Resources Preservation Plan. In *History Underwater: Studies of Submerged Cultural Resources in Minnesota*, edited by S.F. Anfinson, Minnesota State Historic Preservation Office, Minnesota Historical Society, St. Paul.

Martin, J.R., 1997, Preliminary Comparative and Theme Study of National Historic Landmark Potential for Thunder Bay, Michigan. In *Proposed Thunder Bay National Marine Sanctuary: Draft Environmental Impact Statement/Draft Management Plan*, Vol. II. National Oceanic and Atmospheric Administration, Appendix G.

_____, 1993, The Vernacular Lakescape: The Changing Nature of Life Aboard Great Lakes Sailing Craft, 1815–1925. In *Underwater Archaeology Proceedings from the Society for Historical Archaeology Conference*, edited by S.O. Smith, pp. 23–27. Kansas City.

Martin, S.R., 1989, A Reconsideration of Aboriginal Fishing Strategies in the Northern Great Lakes Region. *American Antiquity* 54:594–604.

_____, 1985, *Models of Change in the Woodland Settlement of the Northern Great Lakes Region*. Ph.D. dissertation, Michigan State University. University Microfilms, Ann Arbor.

McCracken, G., 1962, An "Indian" Dugout Canoe from Wyoming County, Pennsylvania. *Pennsylvania Archaeologist* 32:35–38.

McHaney, S.E., 1992, Michigan Goes to War. *Michigan History Magazine* 76(6):22–25.

McKenney, T.L., 1972, *Sketches of a Tour to the Lakes*. Imprint Society, Barre, MA.

Meadows, G.A., 1992, *Investigation of the Sunken Schooner Barge*, Newell A. Eddy, *in Lake Huron, Michigan*. Report No. OEL-9204-OVPR, Ocean Engineering Laboratory, Department of Naval

Architecture and Marine Engineering, College of Engineering, University of Michigan, Ann Arbor.

Mitchell, A., 1996, Interim Report of Casks Excavated from the Millecoquins Shipwreck. In *Underwater Archaeology*, edited by S.R. James, Jr. and C. Stanley, pp. 140–144. Society for Historical Archaeology, Tucson.

National Oceanic and Atmospheric Administration, 1997, *Proposed Thunder Bay National Marine Sanctuary*: *Draft Environmental Impact Statement/Draft Management Plan*. Ann Arbor, MI. 2 vols.

National Park Service, 1995, *Cuyahoga Valley National Recreation Area, Ohio*: *Official Map and Guide*. Washington, D.C.

Noble, V.E., 1991, The Archaeology of American Canals. In Great Lakes Archaeology: Submerged Sites. *Michigan Archaeologist* 37:35–44.

O'Donnell, R.M., 1995, The Last Word. *Association for Great Lakes Maritime History Newsletter* 12(5):1–7.
_____, 1994, Sad Saga of Schooner *Alvin Clark* Finally Came to End This Summer. *Association for Great Lakes Maritime History Newsletter* 11(4):1–7.

Oikarinen, P., 1991, *Armour*: *A Lake Superior Fisherman*. Manitou Books, Calumet, MI.

Olson, V., 1995, *The* Goshawk *Project: A Reconnaissance Survey of the Great Lakes Oldest Schooner*. Underwater Archaeological Society of Chicago, Chicago.
_____, 1993, The *Lady Elgin*: *A Report on the 1992 Reconnaissance Survey by the Underwater Archaeological Society of Chicago*. Underwater Archaeological Society of Chicago, Chicago.

Out of the Blue Productions, 1997a, *Canisteo*. Video. Lexington, MI.
_____, 1997b, Pewabic: *The Death Ship of Lake Huron*. Video. Lexington, MI.

Papworth, M.L., 1967, *Cultural Traditions in the Lake Forest Region during the Late High-Water Stages of the Post-Glacial Great Lakes*. Ph.D. dissertation, University of Michigan. University Microfilms, Ann Arbor.

Peters, S.M., 1993, Michigan Shipyards, 1850–1900: An Evolution In *Underwater Archaeology Proceedings from the Society for Historical Archaeology Conference*, edited by S.O. Smith, pp. 18–22. Kansas City.

Peters, S.M., and Ashlee, L.R., 1992, Working for a Living. *Michigan History Magazine* 76(6):47–51.

Pleger, T.C., 1992, A Functional and Temporal Analysis of Copper Implements from the Chautauqua Grounds Site (47-MT-71), a Multi-Component Site near the Mouth of the Menominee River. *Wisconsin Archaeologist* 73:160–176.

Pott, K.R., 1997, *Rockaway*. In *Encyclopaedia of Underwater and Maritime Archaeology*, edited by J.P. Delgado, pp. 348–349. British Museum Press, London.
_____, 1993, The Wreck of the *Rockaway*: The Archaeology of a Great Lakes Scow Schooner. In *Underwater Archaeology Proceedings from the Society for Historical Archaeology Conference*, edited by S.O. Smith, pp. 28–33. Kansas City.
_____, 1992, The Dugout: Michigan's Early Maritime Traditions. *Michigan History Magazine* 76(6):58.
_____, 1985, Investigating a Lake Michigan Shipwreck. *Michigan History Magazine* 69(4):36–42.

Prothero, F., and Prothero, N., 1990, *The Lone Survivor*: *The* Katherine V *of Rogers City*. Nan-Sea Publications Ltd., Port Stanley, Ontario.

Quimby, G.I., 1965a, Exploring an Underwater Indian Site. *Chicago Natural History Museum Bulletin* 36(8):2–4.
_____, 1965b, Underwater Archaeology in Lake Michigan. *Chicago Natural History Museum Bulletin* 36(6):2–3, 8.
_____, 1959, Lanceolate Points and Fossil Beaches in the Upper Great Lakes Region. *American Antiquity* 24:424–426.

Quimby, G.I., and Griffin, J.B., 1961, Various Finds of Copper and Stone Artifacts in the Lake Superior Basin. In *Lake Superior Copper and the Indians*: *Miscellaneous Studies of Great Lakes Prehistory*, edited by J.B. Griffin, pp. 103–117. Anthropological Papers No. 17. Museum of Anthropology, University of Michigan, Ann Arbor.

Rajnovich, G., 1994, *Reading Rock Art*: *Interpreting the Indian Rock Paintings of the Canadian Shield*. Natural Heritage/Natural History Inc., Toronto.

Richardson, S.K., 1995, Preliminary Report on the 1993–1994 Submerged Cultural Resource Survey at Old Fort Niagara, New York. In *Underwater Archaeology Proceedings from the Society for Historical Archaeology Conference*, edited by P.F. Johnston, pp. 144–146. Washington, D.C.

Roach, J.A., 1997, Sovereign Immunity. In *Encyclopaedia of Underwater and Maritime Archaeology*, edited by J.P. Delgado, pp. 398–399. British Museum Press, London.

Rogers, E.S., 1965, The Dugout Canoe in Ontario. *American Antiquity* 30:454–459.

Schmitt, P.J., 1996, The Last Lightship on the Great Lakes. *Michigan History Magazine* 80(4):38–42.

_____, 1989, The Little Tug *Sport*. *Telescope* 37:87–92.

Seeley, H.J., 1992, *Video Mosaic Imaging: Technical Guideline Report*. Great Lakes Visual/Research, Lansing, Michigan.

Shaw, R.E., 1966, *Erie Water West: A History of the Erie Canal, 1792–1854*. University of Kentucky Press, Lexington.

_____, 1953, Michigan Influences upon the Formative Years of the Erie Canal. *Michigan History Magazine* 37:1–18.

Singley, K., 1988, *The Conservation of Archaeological Artifacts from Freshwater Environments*. Lake Michigan Maritime Museum, South Haven.

Sivertson, H., 1992, *Once upon an Isle: The Story of Fishing Families on Isle Royale*. Wisconsin Folk Museum, Mount Horeb.

Smith, M.J., Howard-Filler, S.R., and Orser, C.E., 1980, Bringing up the *Indiana*. *Michigan History Magazine* 64(6):21–23.

Stayer, P. and Stayer, J., 1995, *Shipwrecks of Sanilac*. Out of the Blue Productions. Lexington, MI.

Steinbring, J., 1967, Copper 'Gaff Hook' from Ontario. *Wisconsin Archeologist* 48:345–358.

Stoltmann, T., 1991, Video-Mosaic Imaging of the *Alva Bradley*. *Stem to Stern: Program in Maritime History and Underwater Research* 7:11–12. East Carolina University, Greenville, NC.

Stonehouse, F., 1994, *Wreck Ashore: The United States Life-Saving Service on the Great Lakes*. Lake Superior Port Cities Inc., Duluth.

Swayze, D., 1991, The Giant Wooden Barges of the Davidson Yard. *Inland Seas* 47:104–108.

Teter, K.L. Jr., and Halsey, J.R., 1997, The *Captain Lawrence* Decision. *Michigan Historic Preservation Network News* 4.

Thwaites, R.G., 1959a, *The Jesuit Relations and Allied Document, Quebec: 1637*. Vol. 12. Pageant Book Company, New York.

_____, 1959b, *The Jesuit Relations and Allied Document, Quebec and Hurons: 1642*. Vol. 23. Pageant Book Company, New York.

Tidewater Atlantic Research, Inc., 1993a, A Cultural Resources Survey along the North Shore of Lake Superior between East Beaver Bay and Castle Danger, Minnesota. In *Archaeological and Historical Studies of Minnesota's Lake Superior Shipwrecks*, edited by Scott F. Anfinson. Minnesota State Historic Preservation Office, Minnesota Historical Society, St. Paul.

_____, 1993b, An Underwater Archaeological Assessment of the Steam Tug *A. C. Adams* and Bulk Freighter *Onoko* and Surveys for the Bulk Freighter *Benjamin Noble* and Schooner *Charlie* in Lake Superior near Duluth, Minnesota. In *Archaeological and Historical Studies of Minnesota's Lake Superior Shipwrecks*, edited by S.F. Anfinson. Minnesota State Historic Preservation Office, Minnesota Historical Society, St. Paul.

_____, 1993c, Underwater Documentation at Grand Marais Harbor, Minnesota, of the Schooner *Elgin* and the Steamer *Liberty* and Nomination of the Steamer *Lafayette* and Rafting Tug *Niagara* to the National Register of Historic Places. In *Archaeological and Historical Studies of Minnesota's Lake Superior Shipwrecks*, S.F. Anfinson. Minnesota State Historic Preservation Office, Minnesota Historical Society, St. Paul.

Tolson, H., 1998, The Boats That Were My Friends: The Fishing Craft of Isle Royale. In *"A Fully Accredited Ocean": Essays on the Great Lakes*, edited by V. Brehm, pp. 199–222. University of Michigan Press, Ann Arbor.

_____, 1991, Vernacular Watercraft of Isle Royale National Park. In *Underwater Archaeology Proceedings from the Society for Historical Archaeology Conference*, edited by J.D. Broadwater, pp. 132–133. Richmond, VA.

Vrana, K.J., 1997a, Revisiting the *Three Brothers*. *Michigan History Magazine* 81(4):50–51.

_____, 1997b, Shipwreck Protected Areas. In *Encyclopaedia of Underwater and Maritime Archaeology*, edited by J.P. Delgado, pp. 380–382. British Museum Press, London.

_____, 1996, *Reconnaissance and Preliminary Assessment of the Shipwreck* Three Brothers *at South Manitou Island*. Center for Maritime and Underwater Resource Management, Department of Park, Recreation and Tourism Resources. Michigan State University, East Lansing.

_____, editor, 1995, *Inventory of Maritime and Recreation Resources of the Manitou Passage Underwater Preserve*. Center for Maritime and Underwater Resource Management, Department of Park, Recreation and Tourism Resources, Michigan State University, East Lansing.

Vrana, K.J., and Halsey, J.R., 1992, Shipwreck Allocation and Management in Michigan: Review of Theory and Practice. In Advances in Underwater Archaeology. *Historical Archaeology* 26(4):81–96.

_____, 1991, Why 5% Wasn't Enough. In *Underwater Archaeology Proceedings from the Society for Historical Archaeology Conference*, edited by J.D. Broadwater, pp. 40–42., Richmond.

Vrana, K.J. and Mahoney, E., 1995, Impacts on Underwater Cultural Resources: Diagnosing Change and Prescribing Solutions. In *Underwater Archaeology Proceedings from the Society for Historical Archaeology Conference*, edited by P.F. Johnston, pp. 176–180. Washington, D.C.

_____, editors, 1993, *Great Lakes Underwater Cultural Resources: Important Information for Shaping Our Future*. Department of Park and Recreation Resources, Michigan State University, East Lansing.

Vrana, K.J., and Schwartz, J., 1989, Instrumented Sled, ROV Join to Provide Enhanced Images of *Edmund Fitzgerald*. *Sea Technology* 30(12):17–21.

Waggoner, M.S., 1958, *The Long Haul West: The Great Canal Era, 1817–1850*. Putnam, New York.

Ward, J.A., and McCarthy, J.P., 1997, A National Register Evaluation of Underwater and Water's-Edge Cultural Resources, Duluth Harbor, Minnesota. In *History Underwater: Studies of Submerged Cultural Resources in Minnesota*, edited by S.F. Anfinson. Minnesota State Historic Preservation Office, Minnesota Historical Society, St. Paul.

Watts, G.P. Jr., 1992, Identification and Assessment of *Light Vessel Number 57*, South Shore Park, Milwaukee, Wisconsin. *Wisconsin Archaeologist* 73:11–60.

Watts, G.P. Jr., Neville, J., and Labadie, C.P., 1997, Lake Superior Shoreline Survey at Knife River and Two Harbors, Minnesota. In *History Underwater: Studies of Submerged Cultural Resources in Minnesota*, edited by S.F. Anfinson. Minnesota State Historic Preservation Office, Minnesota Historical Society, St. Paul.

Wilcox, F.N., 1969, *The Ohio Canals*, selected and edited by M.A. McGill. Kent State University Press, Kent, OH.

Wilson, G., 1990, The Evolution of the Great Lakes Ship. *FreshWater* 5(2):4–15.

Wolff, J.F. Jr., 1979, Salvaging the Engine of the *Indiana*. *Inland Seas* 35:293–294.

Wright, P.J., 1992, *An Evaluation of the Video Mosaic Imaging System and Other Techniques Used on the* Alva Bradley *Site*. Great Lakes Visual/Research, Inc., Lansing, MI.

_____, 1991, Great Lakes Prehistoric Activities: A Freshwater Maritime Perspective. *Ottawa Archaeologist* 18(2):3–10.

Wright, R.J., 1980, The Indiana Salvage: Part II. *Detroit Marine Historian* 33(5):2–4.

_____, 1979, The Indiana Salvage: Part I. *Detroit Marine Historian* 33(4):1–3.

Wrong, G.M., editor, 1939, *The Long Journey to the Country of the Hurons* [by Father Gabriel Sagard]. The Champlain Society, Toronto.

Chapter 13

Steamboat Archaeology on the Missouri River

ANNALIES CORBIN

INTRODUCTION: AN UNFORTUNATE ACCIDENT

Our trip in 1882 was made on the *Red Cloud.* There were nine in our party besides my father, mother, my brother and myself. There were Mrs. Sharp, her aunt, Miss Lees, son and daughter, and John Luke. It was on this trip on a very windy day that the steamer struck a snag at Wright Point, tearing a hole in her side forty feet long. The Captain was at the wheel. He put on full steam ahead and made two lengths of the boat running on to a sand bar where we stuck fast. All passengers were taken off and as much freight as was on the decks, nothing out of the hold. This happened at 9:00 a.m. The boys and men were up on the deck trying to shoot buffalo. Another boat was sighted by her smoke at a far distance around a bend in the river. Deck hands were sent in a row boat to tell them of our disaster. At 4:00 p.m. the boat came to our rescue. We were taken aboard and carried down the river until we met a boat going up the river to Fort Benton, twenty-four hours later (Flanagan, 1940).

On July 11, 1882, the steamboat the *Red Cloud* (Figure 13.1) sank in the Missouri River a few miles above old Fort Peck, Montana Territory. The *Benton Weekly Record* (1882) confirmed the account quoted above and added that the steamer sank in three short minutes after first hitting a snag and then settling on a sandbar. Although all of the passengers and deck cargo were saved, the boat carried 3000 bags of flour into the mud,

Annalies Corbin, Program in Maritime Studies, East Carolina University, Greenville, North Carolina 27853.

International Handbook of Underwater Archaeology, edited by Carol V. Ruppé and Janet F. Barstad. Kluwer Academic/Plenum Publishers, New York, 2002.

Figure 13.1. The steamboat *Red Cloud*, c. 1880.

which, with the vessel, were a total loss. This river disaster is significant as a representative example of a common event in the larger narrative of the westward movement.

The sinking of the *Red Cloud* was an important event in the history of both the Missouri River drainage and the American West. The Fort Benton mercantile firm of I.G. Baker & Company owned the steamer and designated it the flagship of the Baker Line of steamboats. Like the company that owned her, the *Red Cloud* represented business ventures, sustained newly-developed and exploited forms of communication and commerce, and contributed to shaping the land through which she passed. Yet for all of its success and despite its last unfortunate mishap, the *Red Cloud* was just another Missouri River steamer and important only for its individual role in a much larger piece of American river history.

The wreck of the *Red Cloud* is one of an estimated 1000 steamboat wrecks on the Missouri River (Corbin, 1998). Using it as a case study, this analysis suggests that archaeologists and historians have an important role in the assessment of the maritime history of the American West. Three questions shape the discussion: How is the tale of the steamboat the *Red Cloud* linked to a broader understanding of a developing interior region? What, if any, of that history is left for archaeologists to find, preserve, and protect? Finally, who is responsible for lost or forgotten cultural river resources today, and what is the direction of underwater archaeology in the nation's interior? American westward expansion was directly dependent on the opening of the Missouri River, which quickly became not only the gateway to the West but the lifeline of an emerging nation.

THE MISSOURI RIVER: GATEWAY TO THE WEST

President Thomas Jefferson sent the first organized contingent of Euro-Americans up the Missouri River in 1804. However, long before Lewis and Clark's "Corps of Discovery" returned to St. Louis in 1806, the Missouri River was already recognized as a gateway to the nation's deepest interior. The Spanish settled the first European post on the Missouri River when they established Fort Orleans in 1720 (Chittenden, 1902). By 1807, St. Louis merchant and fur trader Manuel Lisa established the first American upper-river fur trade post on the banks of the Missouri's Big Horn River, in what would become Montana Territory (Oglesby, 1963). The development of the American west had begun.

The first Euro-Americans to fully utilize the Missouri River were fur traders. British, French Canadians, Spanish, and American trappers and traders flocked to the pelt-rich Missouri River valley. Through the 1820s and 1830s, small boats navigated the Missouri River system. An adaptation of the native American bull boats was first put to work, but soon canoes, mackinaws, and keelboats were used to transport people, supplies, and furs along the river (Baldwin, 1941).

Steamboat operations on the upper Missouri were directly related to developments such as the upper-river fur trade, military operations, mining in the Rockies and Montana, and settlement in the various plains regions along the river. Steamboating began in May 1819, when the 98-ton *Independence* ascended 250 miles to Chariton, Missouri (Corbin, 1998; Hunter, 1949; Peterson, 1945; Winther, 1964). Major Steven H. Long of the Corps of Topographical Engineers also traveled up the Missouri by steamboat in 1819. His steamer, *Western Engineer*, transported troops and military supplies as far as Fort Lisa, a small trading post a few miles above present-day Omaha (Jackson, 1985; Peterson, 1945). Despite grand beginnings, the 1820s and 1830s were a lackluster time for lower Missouri River steamboating (the lower river was the 660 miles between St. Louis and Council Bluffs). Few boats were in operation, the journey was both dangerous and arduous, and the schedules of the boats that did operate were irregular at best, due to a lack of settlement and limited commerce (Corbin, 1999).

The next landmark came in 1831, when the Western Department of the American Fur Company's steamboat *Yellow Stone* ascended the Missouri as far as present-day Pierre, South Dakota. The next year the vessel reached Kenneth McKenzie's Fort Union, the staging post for expansion into the northern Plains and Rockies at the mouth of the Yellowstone River (Corbin, 1999; Hunter, 1949; Jackson, 1985; Peterson, 1945; Winther, 1964). Almost three decades later, in 1859, the American Fur Company's steamer *Chippewa* steamed to within walking distance of Fort Benton, the effective head of steamboat navigation on the Missouri. Fort Benton, established in 1847 by the American Fur Company, was strategically placed approximately 2500 miles above St. Louis and 500 miles from Fort Union, the central depot of the American Fur Company. In 1860, the *Chippewa* again churned up the Missouri, tying up at Fort Benton and off-loading 250 tons of cargo. This trip set a new distance record in the history of steamboat navigation and established Fort Benton as the steamboat capital of the upper northwest region (Chittenden, 1903; Corbin, 1998; Lass, 1962; Overholser, 1987).

Figure 13.2. Missouri River Valley, with dredge boat and quartersboat, 1889.

The discovery of gold in Montana in 1862 was a major factor in the dramatic rise in upper Missouri River steamboat traffic (Figure 13.2). Gold fever drove a rush of miners, speculators, and suppliers to the Fort Benton area. From 1860 to 1867, and again from 1875 to 1883, Fort Benton experienced a boom in steamboat activity (Corbin, 1996). Joseph LaBarge, a long-time steamboat captain, estimated that approximately 1000 passengers and 6000 tons of freight traveled up the Missouri in 1865. In 1866, 31 boats arrived at Fort Benton and discharged 4686 tons of freight, and 39 boats landed in 1867 (Chittenden, 1903; Corbin, 1999; Lass, 1962; Peterson, 1945; Petsche, 1974). As Paul Sharp (1952) observed:

> This boom in upper-river steamboating subsided within a decade. The short freighting season, long, slow journeys, low water, and frequent accidents drove up freighting costs and escalated insurance rates. When the gold rush lost force, a collapse in river traffic occurred, hitting bottom in 1871 when . . . only six steamboats reached the head of navigation. Declining activity in the gold fields, the completion of the Union Pacific railway, and a disastrously low water level in 1869 paralyzed traffic. When the depression of 1873 cast its dark shadow over the High Plains, steam-boating on the Missouri seemed a thing of the past.

However, by 1875, Fort Benton was again a busy place, with steamboats at the landing and freight wagons waiting to carry cargoes overland toward new markets for companies such as I.G. Baker & Co. and their rival, T.C. Power & Brother.

Principal economic players in the founding of Fort Benton were the Baker and Power mercantile companies, which dominated regional trade because of the wide scope of their trading operations. I.G. Baker & Co. chose the steamboat the *Red Cloud* as the flagship for its diverse interests. The history of Fort Benton and the upper Missouri Region is indelibly linked to the history of I.G. Baker & Co.'s enterprises, both in the formative years of Fort Benton history (1847–1865), and in the region's resurgence in the mid-1870s.

After the region recovered from the collapse of 1873, T.C. Power, I.G. Baker & Co., and a few remaining independent operators found new markets in supplying the Judith Basin, the mines at Maiden and Barker, Lewistown, Sun River, the Blackfeet and Assiniboine agencies, and the Canadian Northwest Mounted Police. When the Canadian government established mounted police at Forts McLeod, Walsh, Lethbridge, Medicine Hat, and Calgary, I.G. Baker & Co. was quick to realize the potential profit for supplying the remote Canadian Northwest region via the Whoop-Up Trail from Fort Benton to Fort McLeod (Sharp, 1978). The upper Missouri River was the most economical and practical way to move goods in the region and to revive Fort Benton's trade (Oviatt, 1957). During the boom years of 1874–1883, the Whoop-Up Trail carried a third of the freight handled through Fort Benton, and I.G. Baker & Co. was one of the most prolific suppliers.

The economic impact of river commerce on Fort Benton was clear. Sharp (1952) argued that Fort Benton's transition from a gold town of the 1860s to a commercial center in the 1870s changed Benton from a "squaw town" and home to horse thieves to a town of "merchants' account books and manifest lists." The lifeblood of Fort Benton, then, flowed via the Missouri River and the Whoop-Up Trail. The chief controllers of this extensive trade were the Baker and Power firms, because their operations were supplied by their own steamboats. The fortunes of these companies are intertwined with the growth of Fort Benton and the steamboating enterprise on the upper Missouri in the post Civil War era (Sharp, 1952). The singular importance of the *Red Cloud* and all other Missouri River steamboats was their role in the broader history of the Missouri River region.

THE BAKER LINE AND STEAMBOAT THE *RED CLOUD*: A NEW PRESENCE ON THE RIVER

In 1875, T.C. Power & Brother and I.G. Baker & Co. purchased the steamer *Benton*, first of eight vessels to carry the new Benton Packet Line's "Block P" insignia. A new era in upper-river steamboating began as Block P boats (and shortly thereafter I.G. Baker & Co.'s Baker Line boats) took control of the upper river shipping which, decades before, had been held by lower river companies such as Durfee and Peck, Kountz, and the Coulson Lines (Oviatt, 1957).

I.G. Baker & Co. sold its interests in the *Benton* and the Benton Packet Line in early 1877, and in April of that year the mercantile company bought the *Red Cloud* for $25,000, thus inaugurating the Baker Line of steamboats (Flanagan, 1940; Overholser, 1987). The *Red Cloud* was built in 1873 for the Evansville & Tennessee River Packet Company by the famed Howard boatyard in Jeffersonville, Indiana (Fishbaugh, 1970). The steamer was a stern-wheel, wooden-hull packet, a combination passenger and freight hauler, originally 178 ft long by 34.5 ft wide, with a 5.2 ft mean depth of hold and rated at 324 tons (Fishbaugh, 1970; Ways, 1983). The *Evansville Journal* (1873) advertised that the *Red Cloud* had an elegant cabin and stateroom appointments, and that her officers ranked among the "best boatmen of the age." In 1877, the steamer was sold to I.G. Baker & Co. of Fort Benton, Montana Territory, where the boat played a vital role in the resurgence of the upper Missouri Mountain trade (Ways, 1983).

On June 22, 1877, the steamboat made its first appearance at the Fort Benton levee. The boat was hailed as a success for bringing in 320 tons of freight and 22 passengers to Fort Benton. When the vessel left port, it carried another 240 tons of freight back down the river, along with 46 passengers anxious to ride the new boat. The *Red Cloud* completed two additional trips to Fort Benton that year. The final trip that season was from Bismarck to Fort Benton in 8 days and 17 hours, an all-time record for speed. From that time on, the *Red Cloud* was noted as one of the fastest mountain packets on the river and a favorite with passengers because of her speed (Overholser, 1987; Ways, 1983).

Despite her early success in the mountain trade, the *Red Cloud* was not well adapted to the shallows of the upper Missouri River. She was long and narrow and drew too much water for late season freighting (Benton Weekly Record, 1882). During the winter of 1877–1878, Baker & Co. had her lengthened by 50 ft, and some modifications may have been made to her bow structure (National Archives, 1877).

The newly-lengthened the *Red Cloud* appeared for the first time at the Fort Benton levee on May 17, 1878, carrying 250 tons of freight and 120 passengers. Captain William Massie reported her buoyancy was much improved. By the time the 1878 freighting season was over, she had off-loaded 981 tons of freight near Fort Benton and had brought 360 passengers into the Fort Benton area (Overholser, 1987).

The *Red Cloud* continued in active service on the Missouri River through 1882. During the freighting seasons of 1879–1882, the steamer came to Fort Benton at least twice each year. She carried a variety of freight over those years, including mercantile and farming supplies, horses, sheep, mules, cattle, large contingents of Canadian Mounties and their supplies, and thousands of passengers, among them Stanley Huntley, the notorious newspaper man who interviewed Sitting Bull (Saum, 1982).

Steamboat traffic on the upper Missouri River reached its highest point in 1879, when 47 steamboat arrived at Fort Benton. Together, these vessels carried approximately 9444 tons of freight upriver. Of this total, I.G. Baker & Co.'s *Red Cloud* brought in more than 2015 tons of freight (almost 25 percent of the total) to Fort Benton in 1879 (*Benton Weekly Record* 1878; Flanagan, 1940; Oviatt, 1957). Between 1877 and 1882, the *Red Cloud* delivered more than an estimated 6000 tons of freight to the Fort Benton levee and brought more than 3000 passengers into Montana Territory. On June 25, 1882, she delivered her last cargo to the then bustling river town of Fort Benton.

LOSS OF *RED CLOUD* AND THE END OF AN ERA

The *Fort Benton Record* reported that the *Red Cloud* struck a snag on July 11, 1882, about 200 miles below Benton, and sank in three minutes. Crew and passengers were saved and later transferred to the steamer the *Rosebud*, which brought them to Fort Benton. None of the hold cargo was saved before the vessel sank into the muddy bottom of the river (*Benton Weekly Record*, 1882). Isaac G. Baker and several members of his family were on board when the disaster happened. Notorious steamboat Captain John A. Williams, who lost several steamboats during his career, was master of the *Red Cloud* at the time of loss. The steamboat and her remaining cargo were not salvaged. The insurance underwriter paid off all claims. The location of the wreck was later called Red Cloud Bend and was labeled as such on several Missouri River survey maps following the loss (Corbin, 1998; Ways, 1983).

The sinking of the *Red Cloud* was an omen. After the 1882 freighting season, Block P Line and Coulson boats handled most of I.G. Baker & Co.'s river freighting needs. The year 1883 would prove to be a hard season for many boats and steamboat companies. I.G. Baker & Co. was disappointed when the *Butte* (a Block P boat) slipped off her ways at Bismarck and smashed another Baker company boat, the *Col. McLeod*, in eight feet of water (Ways, 1983). On August 1, 1883, the *Butte* burned and was lost a few miles above old Fort Peck. The old downriver company of Durfee and Peck no longer operated on the upper Missouri by 1883, and in 1885, the Power Line's Block P bought the *Rosebud* from the Coulson Line. The *Rosebud* was Coulson's last operating boat on the upper Missouri. With the sale, Power's Block P became the last steamboat line serving Fort Benton (Flanagan, 1940).

In 1883, 35 boats came to Fort Benton, but by 1884 only 15 boats made it to the Fort Benton levee (Flanagan, 1940). Numerous steamboat disasters in the preceding years were a presage of the changing times ahead. Financial adjustments of the early 1880s drastically altered the economic role of Fort Benton in the region. When the Canadian Pacific and Northern Pacific railways both bypassed Fort Benton in 1883 (the town was left in a 400-mile gap between the two lines), the once thriving steamboat hub slowly died of "commercial malnutrition." In July 1883, the last major shipment for Fort MacLeod left for Fort Benton, thus ending a 21-year commercial era (Sharp, 1955).

The sinking of the *Red Cloud* and the *Col. McLeod* marked the end of I.G. Baker & Co.'s interest in river steamboating. In 1885, Isaac G. Baker retired from active management of the business, and business partners William and Charles Conrad became the company's active executives. They too felt the pressure of a declining market and sinking economy. In 1891, both I.G. Baker & Co. and T.C. Power & Brother sold their Canadian interests at Forts MacLeod and Walsh to the Hudson's Bay Company, and the Conrads sold their holdings in I.G. Baker & Co. to the Strain Brothers of Great Falls, Montana (Sharp, 1955; Flanagan, 1940). With the loss of its economic base and the subsequent departure of its founding merchants, Fort Benton passed from a bustling steamboat town into a sleepy rural Montana community.

REDISCOVERING *RED CLOUD* AND A THOUSAND OTHER MISSOURI RIVER STEAMBOAT WRECKS

The passing of the steamboat era at Fort Benton did not mean the end of steamboat history on the upper Missouri. At least twice this century the *Red Cloud* has been remembered. On June 8, 1926, the *Helena Independent* (1926) reported from Eight Point, Montana, that Elmer Werner, a local man, had found the wreck of *Red Cloud*. Werner stated he discovered it on May 29 near a camp he established on the south side of the river opposite Eight Point, and that the boat was approximately 20 feet below the surface in an island formed as the river meandered around the wreck. He apparently was attempting to salvage the wreck for any remaining cargo although, after this brief news note, there is no additional mention of the salvage attempt in local newspapers (Corbin, 1996; Corbin, 1998).

In the 1930s, Franklin Roosevelt's New Deal came to the American West. It has been estimated that the federal government spent more than $381,000,000 in Montana alone. One of the most notable New Deal projects was the construction of Fort Peck Dam by the Works Progress Administration (WPA). The WPA began work on the dam—the largest earth-filled dam in the world—in 1933. When completed, it stood 242 feet above the riverbed, was 9000 feet across, and backed up nearly 20,000,000 acre-feet of water (Malone et al., 1976), that protects the *Red Cloud* today.

The Red Cloud still lies in Red Cloud Bend of the 1880s Missouri River. Long before Elmer Werner believed that he had found the wreck, the river had shifted and left the wreck behind. The remains of the vessel and the bend that bore its name were absorbed into the surrounding landscape. Thus, when Werner claimed to have found the wreck, he was searching not in the river, but on the island that formed around the wreck and then became part of the riverbank (Corbin, 1998). The *Red Cloud* has not been in the Missouri River proper since about 1900. When the Fort Peck Dam was completed in 1937, the wreck was again inundated and today lies in more than 130 ft of water.

The *Red Cloud* is one of more than an estimated 800 steamboats wrecked on the Missouri River between 1819 and about 1920 (Corbin, 1998). For 100 years, steamboats navigated the river, carrying supplies and people across the American West. Like the *Red Cloud*, each of those vessels has its place in the story of the Missouri River West. Each carved a niche in that history, and each has the potential to retell its tale.

There have been many collectors of steamboat information over the years. Whether for romantic notions about a bygone era or an honest desire to preserve a piece of the past, steamboat history on the Missouri River has had a wide following in the 20th century. In the 1940s, steamboat historian and collector Dr. E.B. Trail, a dentist and schoolteacher by training, handed out business cards that noted his penchant for steamboat history. On the back of his card was printed the following:

> "Mountain Steamboating" was the greatest steamboating that this country ever knew. This Missouri River was the greatest highway that the world has ever known. Up this river passed a ceaseless stream of people and materials to build a vast empire from the Mississippi to the Pacific Ocean. In all history perhaps no migration ever covered so great an area in so short a time. To the steamboats go the credit of being the prime movers in this great spectacle. Their work is done but romance ever lingers with "Mountain Steamboats." Will you help me save this fine old history before it is forever too late? Please drop me a line if you know of any parts, photographs, or records of these old boats. (Trail, 1940).

As a representative of the cadre of amateur historians, Trail collected all kinds of information regarding the steamboat history of the Missouri River. He estimated that, from the mouth of the Missouri to Fort Benton, a steamboat wreck could be found every seven miles (Trail, 1940). This notion must be the new anthem for recognizing lost river resources in the American West. Trail's estimate challenges historians and archaeologists to reconsider and most likely discard Hiram Chittenden's 1897 estimate of 295 wrecks on the river. Based on Trail's estimates and on research currently underway, the steamboat the *Red Cloud* is one of a host of Missouri River history bits that ended up scattered across the landscape.

WHO LOOKED FOR STEAMBOATS IN THE PAST, AND WHO IS LOOKING NOW?

Captain Chittenden's 1897 report of steamboat wrecks along the Missouri River was a byproduct of the Missouri River Commission's 1878–1895 survey of the river and one of the first published lists of steamboat wrecks (Chittenden, 1897; Corbin, 1998; National Archives, 1892–1897). In his report, Chittenden (1897) estimated there were no more than 295 steamboat wrecks on the whole of the river, a figure repeated by Phil Chappell in 1906. Despite a recognized discrepancy by today's research, the list was groundbreaking in that it tracked inland river wreck resources.

In 1927, W.J. McDonald, an agent of the Steamboat Inspection Service in St. Louis, produced a more comprehensive list, and from then on, more and more published lists, statistics, and comprehensive texts on Missouri River steamboating began to appear as the steamboat era became more of a historical memory. Louis C. Hunter (1949), William Lass (1962), William Lytle and Forrest Holdcamper (1975), Frederick Ways, Jr. (1983), and Joel Overholser (1987) each produced key volumes related to remembering the river's steamboat era. These authors tried to preserve a fast-fading portion of Missouri River history and to fill in the already missing pieces of that history. Central to their efforts was the establishment of an accurate list of wrecks to highlight the magnitude of the river traffic.

In 1949, Louis Hunter recognized the problem of counting wrecks when he published the first comprehensive modern history on western river steamboating. He noted that the available statistics of accidents and the resulting loss of property were ". . . far from satisfactory." He reminded his readers that prior to the establishment of the steamboat inspection system in 1852, the government did not keep official statistics on river accidents. Hunter's work was a notable achievement, because he chronicled every aspect of western river steamboating, not just accidents.

So Trail was not alone in gathering information about the steamboat era. At the turn of the century, several enthusiasts and old steamboat captains were doing the same. Trail and a host of others gathered old photographs, newspaper clippings, and steamboat paraphernalia and conducted numerous interviews with aging steamboat captains and pilots. The massive variety of unpublished manuscript collections, diaries, and letters held in state historical society collections and private collections represent the most comprehensive and influential collection of steamboat information today. Using these sources, Missouri River State Historic Preservation Offices, the Corps of Engineers, and university researchers are gathering information for shipwreck databases, cultural resources management plans, and the drafting of new legislation to protect sites.

Not only has it been steamboat enthusiasts, historians, and archaeologists who have looked for wrecks such as I.G. Baker & Co.'s the *Red Cloud*. Missouri River steamboats have also been the object of numerous salvage attempts in modern times. Elmer Werner, who attempted to salvage the *Red Cloud* in 1926, was not only a local Montanan but also a professional salvor. In a letter dated February 11, 1928, Werner explained to Ralph Arnold, a geologist with the Engineers Office, that many wrecks on the Missouri (295 in the government records) still had valuable cargoes aboard (Werner, 1928).

Werner estimated that of the 295 government-recorded wrecks, only 11 were raised and returned to service, and that some 200 were still full of valuable cargo such as clothing, dry goods, jewelry, and liquors on upbound trips, and furs or gold on downbound vessels. He estimated that the salvage of the steamer *Kate Swinney*, which went down in 1855 loaded with furs belonging to the American Fur Company, were worth millions at the time of loss and were worth at least 25 times more in 1928 (an extreme exaggeration). Werner continued with a list of "salvageable" boats and ultimately proposed to Arnold that an expenditure of "twenty-five hundred dollars would enable me to recover" any of the listed vessels (Werner, 1928). Werner seemed anxious to provide this service for the government. The *Red Cloud* got lucky; Werner apparently decided 3000 bags of flour were not worth his time or his $2500 fee.

The *Red Cloud* was among the first Missouri River steamboat wrecks subjected to salvage. In 1968, two Omaha salvors, Jesse Pursell and Sam Corbino, began salvage operations on the steamboat *Bertrand*, which sank in 1865 about 25 miles north of Omaha. The *Bertrand* was a sternwheel mountain boat on its way to Fort Benton with mining supplies and passengers when it sank at DeSoto Bend. Since it was found on federal land (DeSoto National Wildlife Refuge), it was subject to provisions specified within the "Act for the Preservation of American Antiquities." The act specified that recovered artifacts and valuable items would remain the property of the United States government (Corbin, 1999; Petsche, 1974). As a result, the *Bertrand* was more than just a salvage attempt.

Jerome E. Petsche, an archaeologist with the National Park Service's Midwest Archaeological Center, supervised the total excavation of the *Bertrand*. Pursell and Corbino remained involved with the project through the completion of field work, but neither found a fortune; the United States government kept the artifacts and valuables. After the 1968–1969 excavation, the *Bertrand*'s hull was reburied, and artifacts recovered from the site were conserved at DeSoto National Wildlife Refuge's conservation facility. The collection is now on public display at the refuge museum (Corbin, 1999; Petsche, 1974). Steamboat-era history was the benefactor when it came to the *Bertrand*. History and archaeological integrity won out over the salvor's drive for profit.

Circumstances were different in 1988, when River Salvage, Inc., of Independence, Missouri, began salvage operations on the steamboat *Arabia*, a side-wheel steamer that struck a snag and sank in 1856. The salvage team located the vessel under 45 ft of earth in a Kansas soybean field, a half-mile from the present river channel (Hawley, 1998). Unlike the *Bertrand*, the *Arabia* was not found on federal or state land, and the only legal protection the site received was from Kansas state statutes. River Salvage, Inc., was required to hire an archaeologist to oversee its operation, although there were no specifications as to the qualifications or credibility of the assisting archaeologist. Unfortunately, the *Arabia* was done a disservice by the hired specialist: No excavation records were kept, and the mountains of information such as were preserved in the *Bertrand* excavation were lost in the *Arabia* salvage.

The *Arabia*, however, had a lucky break. The Hawley and Mackey families, who made up River Salvage, Inc., had a change of heart: Initially, the project was a for-profit venture, but at some point, the work crew recognized the true value of the vessel and cargo could be maintained only by keeping the artifact collection together. Instead of reaping a quick profit, the group chose to go hundreds of thousands of dollars into debt to build a museum and conservation facility. Today, *Arabia*'s collection is on public display at the fabulous *Arabia* Steamboat Museum in downtown Kansas City (Hawley, 1998).

CONCLUSION: SEARCHING FOR A NEW DIRECTION IN WESTERN RIVER ARCHAEOLOGY

Past experience with the *Bertrand* and *Arabia* excavations makes us ask the question: What now? Doug Scott (1998) argued that the most ambitious historical archaeology project on the Great Plains to date was the *Bertrand*. Its excavation and subsequent preservation yielded almost two million artifacts from the 19th-century West. More important, the project should be valued most as a baseline for establishing parameters concerning future steamboat excavations or salvage attempts. Both the *Bertrand* and *Arabia* provide excellent planning opportunities.

Now is the time to start asking serious questions about inland river wreck sites. In what direction is Missouri River archaeology headed, and what, if any, measures are being taken to preserve the integrity and history of these sites? Unfortunately, the answer to these questions is neither simple nor positive. Indeed, a crisis exists for cultural sites associated with the Missouri River system.

The author asked the states of Montana, North Dakota, South Dakota, Nebraska, Iowa, Kansas, and Missouri about each state's plan for dealing with embedded riverine or inundated historic sites, and also asked for information about the types and frequency of historic river sites investigated in each state. The inquiry was directed at more than steamboats. The goal was to determine how each state might process a request for, or an outright attempt to salvage, historic shipwreck or related site.

The results of the inquiry were unsettling. Unlike coastal states, inland-river states do not have a long-established history of dealing with wreck sites. The reality is that Missouri River states are only now recognizing the need to preserve their river history.

The two states best able to protect river heritage sites are Missouri and Iowa. Missouri has both a shipwreck coordinator and a state law on the books to protect these sites. Its law, "Historic Shipwrecks, Salvage, or Excavation Regulations" (Missouri State Statutes, 1991), specifies that permits for excavation or salvage can be granted only to professional archaeologists or to groups with an archaeologist as consultant. The heart of the law rests in the fact that the State of Missouri has classified all embedded shipwrecks, whether on private or state land, as eligible for the National Register of Historic Places. This prevents salvors from digging up a wreck on private land with just the owner's permission; state permit procedures must be met first. The weak point in the law is that it does not require the archaeologist applying for a permit to have special training or experience in dealing with wet terrestrial sites, shipwreck sites, or inundated historic sites. These sites often need different excavation procedures and considerations than traditional terrestrial historic sites and call for expertise not possessed by most applicants.

Iowa is unique. Its State Historic Preservation Office (SHPO) has a full-time underwater archaeologist on staff, who specializes in pre-historic archaeology and is well aware of the need to deal with historic sites. The SHPO office is currently assisting the state in drafting legislation to handle its inundated cultural resources (Association of Iowa Archaeologists et al., 1998; Kaufmann, 1998).

North and South Dakota fall between the two extremes, of states having no plan and those with a plan or a plan in progress. South Dakota's cultural resources plan acknowledges river transportation sites including warehouses, river boats, wreck sites, quays, and shoreline facilities. There are no plans to inventory these sites systematically, but the sites are at least recognized as part of the state's archaeological resources. In 1982, South Dakota did investigate a suspected steamboat site and publish a report (Putz, 1983; South Dakota Historical Preservation Center, 1989). North Dakota, although without laws to protect shipwreck sites, has a historical society that actively promotes its river heritage. Nebraska, Montana, and Kansas have no plans for handling inundated or embedded riverine sites. This is particularly unfortunate in Montana, where two known, undocumented shipwreck sites are exposed at extreme low water, and are reportedly disintegrating. One such site is the *Baby Rose* at the Fort Benton levee (Figure 13.3).

The results of this survey suggest that many of the estimated 800 historic Missouri River steamboat sites have the potential to be destroyed. In fact, several sites are currently experiencing a crisis. Missouri recently lost a battle to prevent the salvage of the steamboat *Twilight*. Reports suggest that another Missouri salvage group may petition for

Figure 13.3. Remains of steamboat *Baby Rose* at Fort Benton levee.

right to salvage a very early vessel. In both cases, not only is the right to salvage being questioned but also the credentials of the archaeologist involved with the efforts.

There also may be attempts to excavate wrecks in two other Missouri River states. In both cases, this author speculates about the qualifications and the motives of the archaeologists involved. Perhaps we need not only to protect sites from salvors and those who may cater to their wishes, but also from those in our own profession.

As professional historical and underwater archaeologists, we have the responsibility to point out that there is no longer a shortage of qualified underwater archaeologists to work shipwreck sites on our coasts and in our rivers. As historical archaeologists, we all stretch the limits of our training and abilities; this is a reality of our jobs. But it is irresponsible to pursue the excavation of shipwreck sites without the proper qualifications. Uncovering Missouri River history is an admirable goal but one that could be seriously compromised if it is not handled by those best qualified in archaeological method and theory.

Steamboats such as the *Red Cloud, Bertrand, Arabia*, and others are valuable cultural and historical resources. They constitute the "maritime" history of the inland American West. They are not important as individual shipwreck sites. Their greatest value lies in the history in which they participated. The best way to preserve Western river steamboat history is by reviving the history itself, by encouraging states to enact legislation to protect sites, and by public education. As stated previously, the *Red Cloud* is not unique, yet it is an essential part of the history of the American West.

ACKNOWLEDGMENTS. The author would like to thank the John Calhoun Smith Memorial Committee of the University of Idaho for providing funds for this research. Additional funds were provided by the Gamble Fund, administered by Sons and Daughters of Pioneer Rivermen, and by the Charles Redd Center for Western Studies at Brigham Young University. Without their financial support, this research could not have been completed. The author also wishes to acknowledge Carlos Schwantes, Roderick Sprague, and Kent Hackmann of the University of Idaho; Douglas Scott of the National Park Service's Midwest Archaeological Center, Ann Johnson of Yellowstone National Park, and Janet LaCompte, Anna Williams, Edward Corbin, and John Elam for providing comments and guidance regarding this manuscript.

REFERENCES

Association of Iowa Archaeologists, Office of State Archaeologist, State Historical Society of Iowa (State Historic Preservation Office), 1998, *Guidelines for Archaeological Investigations in Iowa*. State Historical Society of Iowa, Des Moines.

Baldwin, Leland D., 1941, *The Keelboat Age on Western Waters*. University of Pittsburgh Press, Pittsburgh.

Benton Weekly Record. Fort Benton, Montana, November 22, 1878; July 20, 1882.

Chappell, Phil E., 1906, River Navigation: A History of the Missouri River. *Transactions of the Kansas State Historical Society 1905–1906* 9:226–231.

Chittenden, Hiram Martin, 1897, *List of Steamboat Wrecks on the Missouri River from the Beginning of Steamboat Navigation to the Present Time*. Annual Report of the Chief of Engineers, U. S. Army, Serial Set 3631–3636. Government Printing Office, Washington, D.C.

_____, 1902, 1954, *The American Fur Trade of the Far West*. Academic Reprints, Stanford, CA.

_____, 1903, *History of Early Steamboat Navigation on the Missouri River*: Life and Adventures of Joseph LaBarge. The Arthur H. Clark Company, Cleveland.

Corbin, Annalies, 1996, I.G. Baker & Co.'s Steamboat Red Cloud: *Rediscovering a Forgotten Piece of Upper Missouri River History*. Manuscript on file, University of Idaho, Department of History, Moscow, Idaho.

_____, 1998, Shifting Sand and Muddy Water: Historic Cartography and River Migration as Factors in Locating Steamboat Wrecks on the Far Upper Missouri River. *Historical Archaeology* 32(4):IP.

_____, 1999, *The Material Culture of Steamboat Passengers*: Archaeological Evidence from the Missouri River. Plenum Press, New York.

Evansville Journal, Evansville, Indiana, January 3, 1873.

Fishbaugh, Charles Preston, 1970, *From Paddle Wheels to Propellers*. Indiana Historical Society, Indianapolis.

Flanagan, May G., [1940s], A Perspective on the Life and Times of I.G. Baker. May G. Flanagan Papers, Small Collection 1236, Montana Historical Society, Helena. Tms photocopy.

Hawley, Greg, 1998, *Treasure in a Cornfield*: The Discovery and Excavation of the Steamboat Arabia. Paddle Wheel Publishing, Arabia Steamboat Museum, Kansas City.

Helena Independent, Helena, Montana. June 8, 1926.

Hunter, Louis C., 1949, *Steamboats on Western Rivers*: An Economic and Technological History. Harvard University Press, Cambridge.

Jackson, Donald, 1985, *Voyages of the Steamboat* Yellow Stone. Ticknor and Fields, New York.

Kaufmann, Kira E., 1998, *Letter from Des Moines, Iowa to Annalies Corbin, September 15*, 1998. In possession of the author, Bozeman, Montana.

Lass, William E., 1962, *A History of Steamboating on the Upper Missouri*. University of Nebraska Press, Lincoln.

Lytle, William M. and Holdcamper, Forrest R., 1975, *Merchant Steam Vessels of the United States 1790–1868*. Steamship Historical Society of America, New York.

McDonald, W.J., 1927, The Missouri River and Its Victims. *Missouri Historical Review* 21:215–242, 455–480, 581–607.

Malone, Michael P., Roeder, Richard B. and Lang, William L., 1976, *Montana: A History of Two Centuries*. University of Washington Press, Seattle.

Missouri State Statutes, 1991, 1993, 1995, *Historic Shipwrecks, Salvage, or Excavation Regulations* (L. 1991 S. B. 75 1, A.L. 1993 S.B. 52, A.L. 1995 S.B. 3). State of Missouri.

Oglesby, Richard Edward, 1963, *Manuel Lisa and the Opening of the Missouri Fur Trade*. University of Oklahoma Press, Norman.

Overholser, Joel, 1987, *Fort Benton*: World's Innermost Port. Falcon Press Publishing Co., Helena.

Oviatt, Alton B., 1957, Fort Benton, River Capital. In *A History of Montana*, edited by Merrill G. Burlingame and K. Ross Toole, pp. 137–155. Lewis Historical Publishing Company, Inc., New York.

Peterson, William J., editor, 1945, The Log of the Henry M. Shreve to Fort Benton. *Mississippi Valley Historical Review* 31:537–578.

Petsche, Jerome E., 1974, *The Steamboat* Bertrand: *History, Excavation, and Architecture.* Government Printing Office, Washington, D.C.

Putz, Paul M., 1983, Missouri Riverboat Wreckage Downstream from Yankton, South Dakota. *Nebraska History* 64(4):521–541.

Saum, Lewis O., 1982, Stanley Huntley Interview of Sitting Bull: Event, Pseudo-Event or Fabrication? *Montana: The Magazine of Western History* 32(2):2–15.

Scott, Douglas D., 1998, Euro-American Archaeology. In *Archaeology on the Great Plains,* edited by Lawrence W. Raymond Wood, pp. 481–510. University of Kansas Press.

Sharp, Paul F., 1952, Whoop-Up Trail: International Highway on the Great Plains. *Pacific Historical Review* 21(May):129–144.

_____, 1955, Merchant Princes of the Plains. *Montana: The Magazine of Western History* 5(1):2–20.

_____, 1978, *Whoop-Up Country: The Canadian-American West, 1865–1885.* University of Oklahoma Press, Norman.

South Dakota Historical Preservation Center, 1989, *Historic Contexts for Historical and Architectural Resources in South Dakota.* South Dakota State Historical Society, Vermillion.

Trail, Dr. E.B., [1940], *Scrapbooks. E.B. Trail Collection* (#2071), Vol. 41, Western Historical Manuscript Collection, Joint Collections of the University of Missouri and the State Historical Society of Missouri, University of Missouri, Columbia.

U.S. National Archives, 1877, *Public Enrollments from February 12, 1877 to June 29, 1878.* Record Group 41, PE 105, Port of St. Louis. General Service Administration, Washington, D.C.

_____, 1892–1897, *Map of the Missouri River from its Mouth to Three Forks, Montana,* in Eighty-four Sheets and Nine Index Sheets, Missouri River Commission. Record Group 77, Civil Works Map File, 930 Portfolio Map. Washington, D.C.

Ways, Frederick, Jr., 1983, *Way's Packet Directory, 1848–1994.* Ohio University Press, Athens.

Werner, Elmer, 1928, *Letter from Great Falls, Montana to Ralph Arnold, February 11, 1928.* Vertical File-Steamboats-Montana, Montana Historical Society Archives, Montana Historical Society, Helena.

Winther, Oscar O., 1964, *The Transportation Frontier, Trans-Mississippi West 1865–1890.* Holt, Rinehart, and Winston, New York.

Chapter 14

Texas Shipwrecks
Progress in the Decade
1988–1998

J. BARTO ARNOLD III

INTRODUCTION

Texas has long been a focus of activity in nautical archaeology. This chapter summarizes the State's last ten years of shipwreck research and management. Nautical archaeology studies began in Texas because of the Platoro treasure-hunting incident in 1967; therefore, the context is actually a longer period. In all this time, the Texas Historical Commission was the principal state agency concerned with and a leader in underwater archaeology. There were few projects in the state that were not related to the state's in-house research or conducted at its behest under cultural resource management regulations.

In addition to a narrative on the broad themes of the last 10 years, of as much interest are the references presented here. This chapter attempts to present a comprehensive listing of reports on underwater archaeology in Texas waters for the recent decade, from both published and gray literature.

STATE ARCHAEOLOGISTS AND THEIR TERMS

Texas has had three state marine archaeologists: Carl J. Clausen, 1972–1975; J. Barto Arnold III, 1975–1997; and Steven D. Hoyt, 1998–present. Under their leadership, the program in Texas has undergone several shifts in emphasis, dictated principally by

J. Barto Arnold III, Institute of Nautical Archaeology, Texas A&M University, College Station, Texas 77841.

International Handbook of Underwater Archaeology, edited by Carol V. Ruppé and Janet F. Barstad. Kluwer Academic/Plenum Publishers, New York, 2002.

available funding. From 1970 through 1980, the state conducted several major field projects, including excavation of *San Esteban* (1554) (Arnold, 1978a, 1976; Arnold and Clausen, 1975; Arnold and Weddle, 1978; McDonald and Arnold, 1979) as well as a number of large-scale marine magnetometer surveys and test excavations (Arnold, 1987a, 1982a, 1982c, 1981, 1974; Arnold and Nordby, 1987; Nordby and Arnold, 1988). Cultural resource management (CRM or review and compliance) duties also received attention.

Major cuts in agency budgets shifted the emphasis to cultural resource management during 1981–1994. In this period, attention was devoted to achieving the passage of the federal Abandoned Shipwreck Act of 1987 (ASA). The state and several individual Texas archaeologists were key players in initiating and striving for enactment of this vital historic preservation legislation. The need was critical because of the state's experience with the 18-year-long lawsuit spawned by the Platoro incident (Arnold, 1978b, 1989a, 1986a, 1986b, 1984a, 1984b). Many other states had similar experiences with the antipreservation decisions of the federal district courts.

Short-term field projects were conducted throughout the period since 1970, as was the building of a file of shipwreck references to support cultural resource management activities.

In 1994, a new emphasis on major field research was made possible by funding from foundations, corporations, and individuals, leading to the discovery and excavation of La Salle's ship (1686) in Matagorda Bay.

Texas was fortunate when George Bass relocated the Institute of Nautical Archaeology (INA) to Texas A&M University (TAMU) in the mid-1970s (Figure 14.1). The nautical archaeology program at TAMU and INA's world-spanning projects added a parallel focus of shipwreck research. INA was a jewel in the Texas crown but, until 1997, it conducted little fieldwork within the state (INA, 1997, 1998; Adams, 1980; Lang, 1986).

Figure 14.1. Logo of the Institute of Nautical Archaeology.

1988–1998 SUMMARY

Reenergized by the passage of the ASA, the period since about 1988 was at least in part a response to the impetus of the ASA's accompanying guidelines. The ASA removed historic shipwrecks from the purview of the federal courts sitting in admiralty and assigned those sites to the states to manage under their antiquities codes. In return, the states were required to have active programs of shipwreck research and management and to provide appropriate private sector access to historic shipwrecks.

Texas Field Projects, Old and New

Texas responded by stepping up field projects, first with small- to medium-scale projects and, more recently, with a landmark large-scale project (Arnold, 1996a, 1996b, 1993; Arnold and Oertling, 1995; Arnold, Hall, and Hall, 1997; Smith, Arnold, and Oertling, 1987). Active research and management is also demonstrated by reports stemming from analysis of artifacts from wrecks (Arnold, 1992a, 1992b, 1989b, 1987b; Arnold and Godwin, 1990; Arnold, Watson, and Keith, 1995, Rosloff and Arnold, 1984) and from analysis of the substantial shipwreck reference file. Over the years, the author built up the file, established under Clausen, to a level of more than 2200 entries (Arnold, 1982b, 1982d; Arnold, Mallouf, Simons, Wilson, Andrews, and Moore, 1981).

U.S. Army Corps of Engineers

Review and compliance under both state and federal preservation laws and regulations had been pursued vigorously all along. By far the most important agency with which the state interacted was the Galveston District of the U.S. Army Corps of Engineers (COE), the federal agency that issued permits for all construction in navigable waters and itself conducted vast dredging and construction projects. By the current decade, the COE has become a cooperative partner in managing and protecting historic shipwrecks in Texas.

Under COE requirements, industry conducted many surveys in order to avoid damage to historic shipwrecks (Booth, Moye, Groveman, and Moore, 1993; Espey, Hutson & Assoc., Inc., 1987; Gagliano, 1979; Gearhart, 1989; Heartfield, Price, and Green, 1988; Hoyt and Schmidt 1993a; Hudson, 1979; Institute for Underwater Reaserch, 1971; James, 1991b, 1989; Miller and Howell, 1997; Moore, Díaigle, and Winton-Moss, 1996; Neurauter, 1996; Pearson, 1994, 1993, 1992a, 1992b, 1987a, 1987b, 1986; Schmidt, 1998; Schmidt and Gearhart, 1998; Warren, 1988). The COE itself sponsored substantial field research (Bond, 1989; Bond, Gearhart, Hoyt, Glander, Johnson and Myers, 1990; Espey, Hutson and Assoc., Inc., 1981; Fairfield Industries, 1979; Freeman and Prewitt, 1994; Gearhart and Hoyt, 1990, 1989; Gearhart, Hoyt, and Bond, 1990; Gearhart, Neville, Hoyt, and Bond, 1990; Hoyt, 1998, 1993, 1992; Hoyt and Gearhart, 1992; Hoyt, Foster, and Schmidt, 1997; Hoyt, Gearhart, and Myers, 1991; Hoyt and Schmidt, 1997, 1996a, 1996b, 1993b; Hoyt, Foster, and Schmidt, 1998; Hoyt, Schmidt, Nash, and Rogers, 1998; Hoyt, Schmidt, and Gearhart, 1995, 1994; James, 1992, 1991a; James and Pearson, 1993, 1991; Kibler, Freeman, Aten, Hoyt, and Gardner, 1996; Neville, Hoyt, Bond, and Gearhart, 1990; Pearson, 1988a; Pearson and Duff, 1993; Pearson and Hudson, 1990; Pearson and James, 1997; Pearson and Perrault, 1993; Pearson and Simmons, 1994; Pearson and Wells, 1995; Pearson, Baguer, and Duff, 1994; Pearson, James, Hudson, and Duff, 1993; Perrault, 1995; Rogers, Hoyt, Bond, Voellinger, and James, 1990; Schmidt and Hoyt, 1995; Schmidt, Hoyt, and Gearhart, 1995;

Voellinger, Hammond, and Voellinger, 1991; Voellinger, Rogers, Hoyt, Bond, and James, 1990; Weinstein, 1994; Weinstein, Pearson, Whelan, and Kelly, 1988). Both use the services of environmental engineering firms and archaeological contracting firms to carry out the work. The most active companies in Texas were Espey, Huston & Associates, Inc., (now PBS&J Corp.), Coastal Environments, Inc., and Panamerican Consultants, Inc.

Among the most important contributions of COE research are excellent historic background studies of the dredged entrance channels from the Gulf of Mexico, and most of the gulf intracoastal waterway. These studies focus on maritime history and shipwrecks and provide vital context for cultural resource management in the areas of highest shipwreck probability (Foster, Gilver, and Hoyt, 1993; Hoyt, 1994; Hoyt, Foster, and Gilver, 1993; McGuff and Ford, 1974; McGuff and Roberson, 1974; McIntire, 1982; Pendergrass and Pendergrass, 1990; Schmidt, Foster, and Hoyt, 1997; Voellinger and Nash, 1989).

Two important CRM lessons were learned from shipwreck examples in Texas. First, construction projects in zones of high probability for shipwreck occurrence would result in accidental finds in the course of the work if there were insufficient attention to survey and testing prior to beginning the projects. *Comstock* and the wreck called "303 Hang" were encountered during construction (James, 1991b; James, Pearson, Hudson, and Hudson, 1991; Pearson, 1989b). Both cases resulted in work stoppage, delays, and associated high costs. In both cases, the state marine archaeologist previously had warned that cultural resource work was inadequate.

Second, SS *Mary*, located on the edge of the channel between the jetties at Port Aransas, showed that wrecks located in, or on the edge of, a dredged channel could not be ignored. As with CSS *Georgia* in Savannah, *Mary* illustrated that years of dredging did not necessarily obliterate a historic shipwreck (Hoyt, 1990; Pearson and Simmons, 1995; Pearson, Hudson, and James, 1992). In these cases, it was clear that the wrecks were a hazard to the dredge.

Minerals Management Service

Another major federal agency with shipwreck responsibility was Minerals Management Service (MMS), part of the U.S. Department of the Interior. The Gulf of Mexico office of MMS and the state developed an ongoing partnership to monitor and map the wreck of USS *Hatteras*, an important Civil War-period wreck (Arnold and Anuskiewicz, 1995). The wreck is located on the Outer Continental Shelf (OCS), outside state waters. The MMS produced important studies of shipwrecks on the OCS in support of its CRM responsibilities (Arnold and Anuskiewicz, 1995).

Museums

Museums partner with archaeologists to help bring the results of field research to the public. In this regard, the Corpus Christi Museum of Science and History (CCM) is a national leader. The CCM exhibit of the Padre Island 1554 shipwrecks was among the best nautical archaeology exhibits anywhere, and the CCM provided the curation and ongoing conservation for most of the shipwreck artifacts excavated in Texas (Arnold, 1992c). The Austin Children's Museum also produced a popular traveling exhibit on the 1554 wrecks (Arnold and Alsup, 1992).

AN ACTIVE STATE PROGRAM OF RESEARCH AND MANAGEMENT

The AS Act required each state to actively manage and research its shipwrecks. One low-cost response was to increase research based on the shipwreck reference file, existing artifact collections, and short- and medium-term field projects. Federal requirements also provided the impetus to gear up to large field projects, which required the devotion of time and resources to outside fund-raising. The success of funding efforts led to the 1995 survey and resulted in the discovery of La Salle's shipwreck of 1686. In its wake that project brought much public attention and approbation, leading to a favorable atmosphere for continued high levels of activity in shipwreck research.

Today, the state continues its CRM activities and, at the time of this writing, was conducting a search for La Salle's other lost ship, *l'Aimable*, in partnership with the National Underwater and Marine Agency (NUMA), Clive Cussler's private, nonprofit organization.

APPROPRIATE PRIVATE-SECTOR ACCESS

Pre-disturbance mapping

The ASA also required states to provide appropriate, private-sector access to shipwrecks. States were not required to allow commercial treasure salvage, a necessarily destructive process (Arnold, 1996c, 1978b), but they did have to provide some sort of private-sector access. In Texas, this requirement has been satisfied by insisting on nondestructive private-sector access, which includes predisturbance mapping by an avocational group, Southwest Underwater Archaeological Society (SUAS), which was formed specifically to involve the recreational dive community (Arnold, Landry, Roseberry, and Hauser, 1994; Hedrick, 1998; Hole, 1974). Museum exhibits of shipwreck artifacts provided access to the greatest number of persons.

Liberty Ships

World War II liberty ships, used in the 1970s to establish artificial reefs, provided another opportunity for private-sector access to historic shipwrecks. The ships originally were intended as a natural resource for fishermen and divers. Historic research on the ships was conducted and is now offered on the sites, which have become heritage resources as well as natural resources (Arnold, Goloboy, Hall, and Hall, in press: Shively, Arnold, and Goloboy, 1998).

The state issued antiquities permits to NUMA for searches to locate Texas Navy wrecks from the Republic of Texas period (Arnold, Cussler, and Gronquist, 1990; Arnold, Gronquist, Briggs, and Oertling, 1992). NUMA's commitment to survey level projects makes its activities appropriate and nondestructive in nature.

Other new developments occurred in the fall of 1997. J. Barto Arnold joined the Institute of Nautical Archaeology staff at Texas A&M University, after serving more than 20 years as state marine archaeologist, and INA embarked upon a new program of shipwreck investigation in Texas and adjoining areas. A major new INA project began with the excavation of the famous Civil War blockade-runner *Denbigh*, located at Galveston (Arnold, Oertling, Hall, and Hall, 1999).

Texas A&M University-Galveston (TAMU-G) recently added a faculty position in nautical archaeology, which was filled by Cheryl Ward in the fall of 1998. TAMU-G's new interdisciplinary undergraduate program in maritime studies should lead to additional shipwreck research in Texas.

CONCLUSION

Texas was a pioneer of state programs in nautical archaeology. In the late 1990s, several factors came together to comprise a critical mass that led to even higher levels of activity. The state continues to be very active in both CRM and field research. Both NUMA and SUAS have successfully involved the sport diver community in projects with professional underwater archaeologists. Intense and ongoing press coverage of the La Salle shipwreck project and, currently, the *Denbigh* project are keeping shipwrecks in the public eye. This has produced an increased appreciation of history and heritage. Two new nautical archaeology positions were recently established, one a research position at INA and the other a faculty position at TAMU-G. In a few years, there will be another major, permanent museum exhibit for the La Salle shipwreck, joining the 1554 shipwrecks exhibit. Later, we can expect a third large-scale exhibit for the blockade-runner *Denbigh*.

The future of nautical archaeology in this region looks very bright indeed.

REFERENCES

Adams, Robert M., 1980, *The* Black Cloud *Survey, Liberty County, TX*. Archaeological Investigation and Underwater Reconnaissance. Principal Investigator George F. Bass. Texas A&M University Sea Grant College Program, College Station.

Arnold, J. Barto III, 1996a, Magnetometer Survey of La Salle's ship the *Belle*. *International Journal of Nautical Archaeology* 25(3):243–249.

_____, 1996b, The Texas Historical Commission's Underwater Archaeological Survey of 1995 and the Preliminary Report on the *Belle*, La Salle's Shipwreck of 1686. *Historical Archaeology* 30(4):66–87.

_____, 1996c, A Tool for Fighting Treasure Hunting. *Review of Archaeology* 17(2):40–43.

_____, 1993, Matagorda Bay Surveys: Applications of Inexpensive Satellite Navigation. *International Journal of Nautical Archaeology* 22(1):79–87.

_____, 1992a, A Further Note on a Hilt from the 1554 Flota. *International Journal of Nautical Archaeology* 21(1):78.

_____, 1992b, Texas Shipwrecks: A Statistical Characterization. *Underwater Archaeology Proceedings from the Society for Historical Archaeology Conference*, edited by Donald H. Keith and Toni L. Carrell, pp. 111–131. The Society for Historical Archaeology.

_____, 1992c, Shipwreck! The 1554 Flota Exhibit. *International Journal of Nautical Archaeology* 21(4):343–350.

_____, 1989a, The Platoro Lawsuit: Episode III, Including the Appeals Court Decision, New Legislation, Permission to Sue the State, and the Supreme Court Appeal. In *Search of our Maritime Past*: *Proceedings of the Fifteenth Conference on Underwater Archaeology*, edited by Jonathan W. Bream, et al., pp. 20–81. East Carolina University, Greenville.

_____, 1989b, *Texas Shipwrecks: Overview of Historic Contexts*. Texas Antiquities Committee, Austin.

_____, 1987a, Marine Magnetometer Survey of Archaeological Materials Near Galveston, Texas. *Historical Archaeology* 21(1):18–47.

_____, 1987b, Resolution of Unidentified Anomalies and Related Matters. *Proceedings: Seventh Annual Gulf of Mexico Information Transfer Meeting*, pp. 237–239. Minerals Management Service, Outer Continental Shelf Office, New Orleans.

_____, 1986a, The Platoro Lawsuit Revisited. *Underwater Archaeology: Proceedings of the Fourteenth Conference on Underwater Archaeology*, edited by Calvin R. Cummings, pp. 7–30. Fathom Eight, San Marino.

_____, 1986b, The Platoro Lawsuit: The Final Chapter. *Proceedings of the Sixteenth Conference on Underwater Archaeology*, edited by Paul F. Johnston, pp. 1–8. Society for Historical Archaeology, Special Publication Series No. 4.

_____, 1984a, Platoro Limited, Inc. vs. The Unidentified Remains of a Vessel: U.S District Court Proceedings in a Treasure Hunting Case. *Underwater Archaeology: Proceedings of the Thirteenth Conference on Underwater Archaeology*, edited by Donald H. Keith, pp. 59–66. Fathom Eight, San Marino.

_____, 1984b, *The Platoro Lawsuit: Episode III Including the Appeals Court Decision, New Legislative Permission to Sue the State, and Supreme Court Appeal.* Paper presented to the 15th Conference on Underwater Archaeology, Williamsburg, Virginia.

_____, 1982a, *A Matagorda Bay Magnetometer Survey and Site Test Excavation Project.* Texas Antiquities Committee Publication No. 9, Austin.

_____, 1982b, Underwater Cultural Resource Management: The Computerized Shipwreck Reference File. *Underwater Archaeology: The Proceedings of the Eleventh Conference on Underwater Archaeology*, edited by Calvin R. Cummings, pp. 85–95. Fathom Eight, San Marino.

_____, 1982c, Concerning Underwater Remote Sensing Surveys, Anomalies, and Ground Truthing. *Underwater Archaeology: The Proceedings of the Eleventh Conference on Underwater Archaeology*, edited by Calvin R. Cummings, pp. 155–182. Fathom Eight, San Marino.

_____, 1982d, Cultural Resource Management Factors for the OCS. *Proceedings: Third Annual Gulf of Mexico Information Transfer Meeting*, pp. 173–175. Minerals Management Service, Outer Continental Shelf Office, New Orleans.

_____, 1981, Remote Sensing in Underwater Archaeology. *International Journal of Nautical Archaeology* 10(1):51–62.

_____, 1978a, *1977 Underwater Site Test Excavations off Padre Island, Texas.* Texas Antiquities Committee Publication No. 5, Austin.

_____, 1978b, Some Thoughts on Salvage Law and Historic Preservation. *International Journal of Nautical Archaeology* 7(3):173–176.

_____, 1976, *An Underwater Archaeological Magnetometer Survey and Site Test Excavation Project off Padre Island, Texas.* Texas Antiquities Committee, Publication No. 3, Austin.

_____, 1974, A Magnetometer Survey of the Nineteenth-Century Steamboat *Black Cloud. Bulletin of the Texas Archaeological Society* 45:225–230.

Arnold, J. Barto III, and Alsup, Rebecca, 1992, A Children's Museum Exhibit on the 1554 Flota Wrecks. *International Journal of Nautical Archaeology* 21(4):350–353.

Arnold, J. Barto III, and Anuskiewicz, Ric, 1995, USS *Hatteras*: Site Monitoring and Mapping. *Underwater Archaeology Proceedings from the Society for Historical Archaeology Conference*, edited by Paul Forsythe Johnston, pp. 82–87. Society for Historical Archaeology.

Arnold, J. Barto III, and Clausen, Carl J., 1975, A Radar Position-fixing System for Marine Magnetometer Surveys. *Archaeometry* 17(2):237–239.

Arnold, J. Barto III, and Godwin, Molly, 1990, A Hilt From the 1554 Flota. *International Journal of Nautical Archaeology* 19(3):221–224.

Arnold, J. Barto III, and Nordby, Larry, 1987, The Padre Island Archaeological Survey for 1986. *Underwater Archaeology Proceedings from the Society for Historical Archaeology Conference*, edited by Alan B. Albright, pp. 14–20. Society for Historical Archaeology.

Arnold, J. Barto III and Oertling, Tom, 1995, Upper Texas Coast Underwater Archaeological Reconnaissance Project: Galveston, Chambers, and Jefferson Counties. *International Journal of Nautical Archaeology* 24(3):199–204.

Arnold, J. Barto III, and Weddle, Robert, 1978, *The Nautical Archaeology of Padre Island: The Spanish Shipwrecks of 1554.* Academic Press, New York, Texas Antiquities Committee Publication No. 7, Austin.

Arnold, J. Barto III, Cussler, Clive and Gronquist, Wayne, 1990, The Survey for the Zavala, A Steam Warship of the Republic of Texas. *Underwater Archaeology Proceedings from the Society for Historical Archaeology Conference*, pp. 105–109. Society for Historical Archaeology.

Arnold, J. Barto III, Goloboy, Jennifer, Hall, Andrew and Hall, Rebecca in press, *Liberty Ship Wrecks: Working-Class Heroes of World War II off the Texas Coast.* Report prepared for Artificial Reef Program of the Texas Parks and Wildlife Department. Texas Historical Commission, Austin.

Arnold, J. Barto III, Hall, Rebecca, and Hall, Andrew, 1997, Presenting Archaeology on the Web: The *La Salle* Shipwreck Project. *International Journal of Nautical Archaeology* 26(3):247–251.

Arnold, J. Barto III, Watson, David, and Keith, Donald, 1995, The Padre Island Crossbows. *Historical Archaeology* 29(2):4–19.

Arnold, J. Barto III, Gronquist, Wayne, Briggs, Alton K., and Oertling, Thomas, 1992, *Survey for the Texas Navy Warship Invincible, Galveston County, Texas.* Texas Antiquities Committee and National Underwater and Marine Agency, Austin.

Arnold, J. Barto III, Landry, Laura, Roseberry, George, and Hauser, Jim, 1994, Preliminary Mapping of the Caney Creek Wreck: A Model of Appropriate Private Sector Access to an Historic Shipwreck. *International Journal of Nautical Archaeology* 23(2):109–113.

Arnold, J. Barto III, Oertling, Tom, Hall, Andy, and Hall, Rebecca, 1999, *The* Denbigh *Project: Nautical Archaeology of a Civil War Blockade Runner.* Paper presented to Society for Historical Archaeology Conference on Historical and Underwater Archaeology, January 6–9, 1999, Salt Lake City.

Bond, Clell L., 1989, *Cultural Resources Survey of Proposed Corps of Engineers Disposal Areas 182A and 187A, Corpus Christi Bay to Baffin Bay, Padre Island, Texas.* Espey, Huston, & Associates, Inc., Austin.

Bond, Clell L., Gearhart, Robert, Hoyt, Steven, Glander, Wayne P., Johnson, Roger W., and Myers, Teresa Lee, 1990, *Remote Sensing Survey, Diver Verification and Archaeological Testing, Brownsville Ship Channel Entrance and Vicinity, Cameron County, Texas.* Espey, Huston, & Associates, Inc., Austin.

Booth, Robert, Moye, Misty, Groveman, Melissa, and Moore, Roger G., 1993, *Archaeological Investigations of 41GV112 for the Pier 21 Project, City of Galveston, Galveston County, Texas.* Report of Investigations No. 76, Moore Archaeological Consulting, Houston.

Coastal Environments, Inc., 1977, *Cultural Resources Evaluation of the Northern Gulf of Mexico Continental Shelf.* 3 vols. Cultural Resources Management Studies, Office of Archaeology and Historic Preservation, National Park Service, Washington.

Espey, Huston & Associates, Inc., 1987, *A Baseline Assessment of Cultural Resources within the Proposed Playa Del Rio Development Including an Archaeological Survey of Phases I-A and I-B.* Espey, Huston & Associates, Inc., Austin.

_____, 1981, *Final Environmental Report: Proposed Deepwater Channel and Multipurpose Terminal Construction and Operation Near Brownsville, Texas, Volume 8: Appendices N–P (Cultural Resources, Air Quality, Noise).* Espey, Huston & Associates, Inc., Austin.

Fairfield Industries, 1979, *Mouth of Colorado River, Texas Project Cultural Resources Assessment.* Fairfield Industries.

Foster, Eugene, Gilver, John, and Hoyt, Steven D., 1993, *Archival Research, Houston–Galveston Navigation Channels, Texas Project, Galveston, Harris, Liberty and Chambers Counties, Texas.* Prepared for the U.S. Army Corps of Engineers, Galveston District. Espey, Huston & Associates, Inc., Doc. No. 920918, Austin.

Freeman, Martha Doty, and Prewitt, E.L., 1994, *Sargent Beach Project: A History of Confederate Defense at the Mouth of Caney Creek, Matagorda County, Texas.* Report No. 98, Prewitt and Associates Inc., Austin.

Gagliano, Sherwood M., 1979, *Cultural Resources Survey of Four Proposed Pipeline Routes in West Cameron Area, Offshore Louisiana, and High Island Area, East Addition, South Extension, Offshore Texas.* Coastal Environments, Inc., Baton Rouge. Marine Survey Report submitted to Odom Offshore Survey, Inc., Baton Rouge.

Gagliano, Sherwood M., Pearson, Charles E., Weinstein, Richard A., Wiseman, Diane E., and McClendon, Christopher M., 1982, *Sedimentary Studies of Prehistoric Archaeological Sites: Criteria for the Identification of Submerged Archaeological Sites on the Northern Gulf of Mexico Continental Shelf.* Coastal Environments, Inc., Baton Rouge. Preservation Planning Services, National Park Service, U.S. Department of Interior, Washington.

Garrison, Ervan G., Giammona, Charles P., Kelly, Frank J., Tripp, Anthony R., and Wolff, Gary A., 1989, *Historic Shipwrecks and Magnetic Anomalies of the Northern Gulf of Mexico: Reevaluation of Archaeological Resource Management Zone 1.* Texas A&M Research Foundation, College Station.

Gearhart, Robert L., 1989, *Magnetometer Survey and Diver Investigations in Big Cypress Bayou for a Proposed L&A Railway Trestle in Jefferson, Marion County, Texas.* Doc. No. 890058. Espey, Huston & Associates, Inc., Austin.

Gearhart, Robert L., and Hoyt, Steven D., 1990, *Channel to Liberty Underwater Archaeological Investigations, Liberty County, Texas.* Espey, Huston & Associates Inc., Austin.

_____, 1989, *Summary Report: Relocation and Ground Truthing of Magnetic Anomalies in Port Isabel Disposal Area No. 239, Cameron County, Texas.* Espey, Huston & Associates, Inc., Austin.

Gearhart, Robert L., Hoyt, Steven D., and Bond, Clell L., 1990a, *Remote-Sensing Survey, Diver Verification and Cultural Resources Assessment Port Mansfield Entrance Channel and Vicinity, Willacy County, Texas.* Espey, Huston & Associates, Inc., Austin.

Gearhart, Robert L., Neville, John C., Hoyt, Steven D., and Bond, Clell L., 1990, *Ground Truthing Anomalies Port Mansfield Entrance Channel, Willacy County, Texas.* Espey, Huston and Associates Inc., Austin.

Heartfield, Price and Green, Inc., 1988, *A Cultural Resources Survey of Terrestrial Portions of the Proposed Transco 20-inch Tomcat Pipeline, Calhoun and Matagorda Counties, Texas.* (Also includes magnetometer survey of Matagorda Bay State Tracts 139 to 20 and Block 558 to shore.)

Hedrick, David Layne, 1998, *The Investigation of the Caney Creek Shipwreck Archaeological Site 41MG32.* MA thesis, Texas A&M University, College Station.

Hole, Frank, 1974, *The Acadia: A Civil War Blockade Runner.* Technical Report No. 1, Department of Anthropology, Rice University, Texas Antiquities Committee Permit No. 17.

Hoyt, Steven D., 1998, *Initial Investigations: Archival Research, Remote Sensing, and Terrestrial Survey, Neches River Saltwater Barrier, Beaumont, Texas, Jefferson, Orange and Hardin Counties.* Espey, Huston & Associates, Inc., Austin.

_____, 1994, *Reconnaissance Level Investigations of Historic Period Resources Sabine-Neches Waterway: Channel to Orange, Orange and Jefferson Counties, Texas.* Espey, Huston, and Associates Inc., Austin.

_____, 1993, *Offshore Underwater Investigations, Houston–Galveston Navigation Channels, Texas Project, Galveston, Harris, Liberty and Chambers Counties, Texas.* Espey, Huston, and Associates Inc., Austin.

_____, 1992, *Underwater Investigations, Houston–Galveston Navigation Channels, Texas Project, Galveston, Harris, Liberty and Chambers Counties, Texas.* Espey, Huston & Associates, Inc., Austin.

_____, 1990, *National Register Assessment of the SS* Mary, *Port Aransas, Nueces County, Texas.* Espey, Huston and Associates, Austin.

Hoyt, Steven D., and Gearhart, Robert, 1992, *Underwater Investigations, Brazos Island Harbor Navigation Project, Cameron County, Texas.* Espey, Huston & Associates, Inc., Austin.

Hoyt, Steven D., Foster, Eugene, and Schmidt, James S., 1997, *Archival Research, Remote Sensing, and Terrestrial Survey, Neches River Salt Water Barrier at Beaumont, Texas, Jefferson, Orange, and Hardin Counties.* Doc. No. 980006. Prepared for U.S. Army Corps of Engineers, Galveston District. Espey, Huston & Associates, Inc., Austin.

Hoyt, Steven D., Foster, Eugene, and Gilver, J., 1993, *Archival Research, Houston–Galveston Navigation Channels, Texas Project, Galveston, Harris, Liberty and Chambers Counties, Texas.* Espey, Huston, and Associates Inc., Austin.

Hoyt, Steven D., Gearhart, Robert, L., and Myers, Teresa Lee, 1991, *Submerged Historical Resources Investigations, Brownsville Channel and Brazos Santiago Depot (41CF4) Cameron County, Texas.* Espey, Huston & Associates, Inc., Austin.

Hoyt, Steven D., and Schmidt, James S., 1997, *Diving Assessments for Twenty-six Localities, Sabine Pass Channel, Jefferson County, Texas, Cameron Parish, Louisiana.* Doc. No. 960983. Prepared for U.S. Army Corps of Engineers, Galveston District. Espey, Huston & Associates Inc., Austin.

_____, 1996a, *Inundated Site Investigations, Houston–Galveston Navigation Channels, Texas Project, Galveston, Harris, Liberty and Chambers Counties, Texas, Galveston Bay.* Doc. No. 960393. Prepared for U.S. Army Corps of Engineers, Galveston District. Espey, Huston & Associates, Inc., Austin.

_____, 1996b, *National Register Testing in the Lynchburg Townsite, Harris County Texas: Lynchburg Pumpstation Feasibility Study.* Espey, Huston, and Associates Inc., Austin.

_____, 1993a, *Cultural Resources Survey, Proposed 4-Inch Pipeline, Lease Blocks 91 and 92, Live Oak Peninsula, Aransas Bay, Aransas County, Texas.* Doc. No. 930652. Prepared for Wainoco Oil and Gas Company, Houston. Espey, Huston & Associates, Inc., Austin.

_____, 1993b, *Bay Ground Truthing: Phase I and Phase II, Houston–Galveston Navigation Channels, Texas Project, Galveston, Harris, Liberty and Chambers Counties, Texas.* Doc. No. 930440. Prepared for U.S. Army Corps of Engineers, Galveston District. Espey, Huston & Associates, Inc., Austin.

Hoyt, Steven D., Foster, Eugene, and Schmidt, James S., 1998, *Intensive Archival Research, Close-Order Magnetometer Survey, Dating, and Offshore Diving, Houston–Galveston Navigation Channels, Texas Project, Galveston, Harris, Liberty and Chambers Counties, Texas, Offshore, Galveston Bay, and Houston Ship Channel.* Doc. No. 970571, Prepared for U.S. Army Corps of Engineers, Galveston District. Espey, Huston & Associates, Inc., Austin.

Hoyt, Steven D., Schmidt, James S., Nash, M., Aranow, Saul, and Rogers, R., 1998, *Initial Investigations, Archival Research, Remote Sensing, and Terrestrial Survey, Neches River Saltwater Barrier, Beaumont, Texas; Jefferson, Orange, and Hardin Counties.* Espey, Huston, and Associates Inc., Austin.

Hoyt, Steven D., Schmidt, James S., and Gearhart, Robert L., 1995, *Beneficial Use Areas Survey, Houston–Galveston Navigation Channels, Texas Project, Galveston, Harris, Liberty and Chambers Counties, Texas, Galveston Bay*. Doc. No. 950504. Prepared for U.S. Army Corps of Engineers, Galveston District. Espey, Huston & Associates, Inc., Austin.

_____, 1994, *Magnetometer Survey of Sabine Pass Channel and Assessment of the Clifton, 41JF65, Jefferson County, Texas, Cameron Parish, Louisiana*. Doc. No. 940510, Prepared for U.S. Army Corps of Engineers, Galveston District. Espey, Huston & Associates, Inc., Austin.

Hudson, Jack C., 1979, *Second Supplement of Appendix M-History and Archaeology, Proposed Multipurpose Deepwater Port and Crude Oil Distribution System, Galveston, Texas*. Cultural Resource Services, Inc., Seabrook.

Institute for Underwater Research, 1971, *Archaeological Survey for Shipwreck Sites in Northwestern Matagorda Bay, June 1–12, 1971*. Institute for Underwater Research, Inc., Dallas.

Institute of Nautical Archaeology, 1997, Listings of Dissertations and Theses. *INA Quarterly*:24(2).

_____, 1998, Issue Summarizing 25 Years of INA Research. *INA Quarterly*:25(1).

James, Stephen R., Jr., 1992, *Diving Reconnaissance in the Port Mansfield Entrance Channel, Willacy County, Texas*. Coastal Environments, Inc., Baton Rouge, Louisiana. Letter report prepared for Galveston District, U.S. Army Corps of Engineers.

_____, 1991a, *Magnetometer Survey and Ground Truthing Anomalies, Corpus Christi Ship Channel, Aransas and Nueces Counties, Texas*. Coastal Environments, Inc., Baton Rouge.

_____, 1991b, *The 303 Hang: Archaeological Investigations of a Two-Masted Schooner Wrecked Offshore Freeport, Brazoria County, Texas*. Panamerican Consultants, Inc., Tuscaloosa.

_____, 1989, General C.B. Comstock: A Late 19th Century Hopper Dredge. *Underwater Archaeology Proceedings from the Society for Historical Archaeology Conference*, edited by J. Barto Arnold III, pp. 129–134. Society for Historical Archaeology.

James, Steven R., Jr., and Pearson, Charles E., 1993, *Submerged Cultural Resource Investigations of the Steamboat J.D. Hinde (41LB85), Channel To Liberty, Liberty County, Texas*. Coastal Environments, Inc., Baton Rouge.

_____, 1991, *Magnetometer Survey and Ground Truthing Anomalies, Corpus Christi Ship Channel, Aransas and Nueces Counties, Texas*. Submitted to Galveston District, U.S. Army Corps of Engineers. Coastal Environments, Inc., Baton Rouge.

James, Stephen R. Jr., Pearson, Charles E., Hudson, Kay, and Hudson, Jack, 1991, *Archaeological and Historical Investigations of the Wreck of the* General C. B. Comstock, *Brazoria County, Texas*. Coastal Environments, Inc., Baton Rouge.

Kibler, Karl W., Freeman, Martha Doty, Aten, Lawrence E., Hoyt, Steven D., and Gardner, K.M., 1996, *Comprehensive Historic Preservation Plan for the Houston–Galveston Navigation Channels, Chambers, Galveston, and Harris Counties, Texas*. Prewitt and Associates, Inc., Austin.

Lang, Shelley Ruby, 1986, *The* Mittie Stephens: *A Sidewheel Steamboat on the Inland Rivers, 1863–1869*. MA thesis, Texas A&M University, College Station.

Mallouf, Robert J., Simons, Helen, Wilson, Robert L., Andrews, Susan L., Arnold III, J. Barto, and Moore, David, 1981, *Texas Heritage Conservation Plan Computerization Program Manual*. Texas Historical Commission, Austin.

McDonald, David, and Arnold III, J. Barto, 1979, *Documentary Sources for the Wreck of the New Spain Fleet of 1554*. Texas Antiquities Committee Publication No. 8, Austin, Texas (winner of the 1979 Presidio La Bahia Award, presented by Sons of the Republic of Texas, for best publication on Spanish colonial history or archaeology).

McIntire, William G., 1982, Cultural Elements. In *Galveston Bay Area, Texas, Final Interim Feasibility Report and Environmental Impact Statement, Texas City Channel, Vol. III, Appendix 6:1–36*. U.S. Army Corps of Engineers, Galveston.

McGuff, Paul R., and Ford, M., 1974, *Galveston Bay Area, Texas: A Study of Archaeological and Historical Resources in Areas under Investigation for Navigation Improvement*. Texas Archaeological Survey, The University of Texas at Austin.

McGuff, Paul R., and Roberson, Wayne, 1974, *Lower Sabine and Neches Rivers-Texas and Louisiana: A Study of the Prehistoric and Historic Resources in Areas Under Investigation for Navigation Improvement*. Research Report No. 46, Texas Archaeological Survey, The University of Texas at Austin.

Miller, Kevin A., and Howell, Chris, 1997, *An Archaeological Survey of Two Proposed Dredge Disposal Sites Near De Zavala Point, Channelview, Harris County, Texas*. Archaeological Report No. 97–95, SWCA Inc., Environmental Consultants.

Minerals Management Service, 1989, *Archaeology on the Gulf of Mexico Outer Continental Shelf, A Compendium of Studies.* Prepared for First Joint Archaeological Congress, Baltimore.

Moore, Roger G., D'aigle, Robert, and Winton-Moss, Sue, 1996, *An Archaeological and Historical Investigation of a Proposed 5-acre Petroleum Fuel and Terminal Corporation Dredge Disposal Area, Quintana and Brazoria Counties, Texas.* Report of Investigations No. 124, Moore Archaeological Consulting, Houston.

Neurauter, Thomas W., 1996, *A High Resolution Geophysical Report and Cultural Resources Assessment of a Proposed Pipeline Route from Galveston Area Block 150L to High Island Area, Block 179.* NCS International, Inc.

Neville, John C., Hoyt, Steven D., Bond, Clell L., and Gearhart, Robert L., 1990, *Ground Truthing Anomalies, Port Mansfield Entrance Channel, Willacy County, Texas.* Espey, Huston & Associates, Inc., Austin.

Nordby, Larry, and Arnold III, J. Barto, 1988, Preliminary Report on the Padre Island Archaeological Research Project of 1985. In *Archaeology in Solution: Proceedings of the Seventeenth Annual Conference on Underwater Archaeology,* edited by John W. Foster and Sheli O. Smith, pp. 90–94. Coyote Press, Salinas.

Pearson, Charles E., 1994, *Cultural Resources Remote-Sensing Survey, Offshore Borrow Areas For Beach Replenishment Project, 10th Street to 103rd Street, Galveston County, Texas.* Submitted to the City of Galveston. Coastal Environments, Inc., Baton Rouge, Louisiana.

_____, 1993, *Cultural Resources Remote-Sensing Survey for Beach Replenishment Project, 10th Street to 103rd Street, Galveston County, Texas.* Submitted to the City of Galveston. Coastal Environments, Inc., Baton Rouge.

_____, 1992a, *Diver Examination of a Magnetic Target along the Formasa Plastics Corporation Wastewater Pipeline, Lavaca Bay, Calhoun County, Texas.* Submitted to Engineering-Science, Inc., Houston. Coastal Environments, Inc., Baton Rouge, Louisiana.

_____, 1992b, *Magnetometer Survey and Target Evaluation of a Pipeline Construction Area on Matagorda Peninsula, Matagorda County, Texas.* Prepared for Enserch Production Operators, Houston. Coastal Environments, Inc., Baton Rouge, Louisiana.

_____, 1989a, *Evaluation of Prehistoric Site Preservation on the Outer Continental Shelf: The Sabine River Area, Offshore Texas and Louisiana.* Paper presented at First World Anthropological Conference, Baltimore.

_____, 1989b, *Phase 2 of Emergency Investigation of Submerged Historic Property, Freeport Harbor, 45-Foot Project, Brazoria County, Texas.* Submitted to the Galveston District, U.S. Army Corps of Engineers. Coastal Environments, Inc., Baton Rouge, Louisiana.

_____, 1988a, *Laboratory Analysis of Geologic Cores from Texas City Channel, Galveston Bay, Texas.* Coastal Environments, Inc., Baton Rouge.

_____, 1988b, Evaluation of Prehistoric Site Preservation on the Outer Shelf: The Sabine River Area, Offshore Texas. *A Collection of Papers Reviewing the Archaeology of Southeast Texas,* edited by Patricia Wheat and Richard L. Gregg, pp. 26–34. Houston Archaeological Society, Report No. 5.

_____, 1987a, *Cultural Resources Survey of the Placid Oil Company Pipeline Tow Project Area, Matagorda County, Texas.* Marine Survey Report submitted to Placid Oil Company, Houston. Coastal Environments, Inc., Baton Rouge.

_____, 1987b, *Assessment of Cultural Resources Impacts, Placid Oil Company's Pipeline Bottom Tow Route, Matagorda Peninsula, Texas to Green Canyon Block 29, Offshore Louisiana.* Marine Survey Report submitted to Placid Oil Company, Houston. Coastal Environments, Inc., Baton Rouge.

_____, 1986, *Magnetometer Survey of a Pipeline Construction Area on Matagorda Peninsula, Matagorda County, Texas.* Baton Rouge. Submitted to Gulf Comap, Inc., Houston. Coastal Environments, Inc.

_____, 1985, Evaluation of Prehistoric Site Preservation on the Outer Continental Shelf: The Sabine River Area, Offshore Texas. *Proceedings of the Sixth Annual Gulf of Mexico Information Transfer Meeting.* Minerals Management Service, U.S. Department of Interior, New Orleans.

_____, 1983, Archaeology and Paleogeography of the McFaddin Beach Site, Jefferson County, Texas. *Proceedings of the Fourth Annual Gulf of Mexico Information Transfer Meeting,* p. 380. Minerals Management Service, U.S. Department of Interior, New Orleans.

Pearson, Charles E. and Duff, James, 1993, A 19th-Century, Iron-Hulled Steamer Wreck in the Navidad River, Texas. *Underwater Archaeology Proceedings from the Society for Historical Archaeology Conference,* edited by Sheli O. Smith, pp. 63–70. Society for Historical Archaeology.

Pearson, Charles E., and Hudson, Kay G., 1990, *Magnetometer Survey of the Matagorda Ship Channel: Matagorda Peninsula to Point Comfort, Calhoun and Matagorda Counties, Texas.* Submitted to Galveston District, U.S. Army Corps of Engineers. Coastal Environments, Inc., Baton Rouge.

Pearson, Charles E., and James, Steven R., 1997, *Diving Assessment for Target No. 1, Located at Port Ingleside, Gulf Intracoastal Waterway, Corpus Christi Bay, Nueces County, Texas.* Submitted to Galveston District, U.S. Army Corps of Engineers. Coastal Environments, Inc., Baton Rouge.

Pearson, Charles E. and Perrault, Stephanie L., 1993, *Cultural Resources Remote-Sensing Survey, Discharge Area No. 1B, Galveston Entrance Channel, Galveston County, Texas.* Submitted to Galveston District, U.S. Army Corps of Engineers. Coastal Environments, Inc., Baton Rouge.

Pearson, Charles E., and Simmons III, Joe J., 1995, *Underwater Archaeology of the Wreck of the Steamship Mary (41NU252) and Assessment of Seven Anomalies, Corpus Christi Entrance Channel, Nueces County, Texas.* Coastal Environments, Inc., Baton Rouge.

_____, 1994, *Magnetometer Survey of the Gulf Intercoastal Waterway (GIWW), Port Aransas to Live Oak Point, Aransas and Calhoun Counties, Texas.* Coastal Environments, Inc., Baton Rouge.

Pearson, Charles E., and Wells, Tom, 1995, *Magnetometer Survey of the Gulf Intracoastal Waterway (GIWW), Corpus Christi Bay to Point Penascal, Nueces, Kleberg and Kenedy Counties, Texas.* Submitted to Galveston District, U.S. Army Corps of Engineers. Coastal Environments, Inc., Baton Rouge.

Pearson, Charles E., Baguer, Jaques, and Duff, James, 1994, *Identification and Analysis of Historic Watercraft in the Shreveport, Louisiana, to Daingerfield, Texas, Navigation Project.* Submitted to Vicksburg District, U.S. Corps of Engineers, Contract No. DACW38-91-D-0014, Delivery Order No. 007. Coastal Environments, Inc., Baton Rouge.

Pearson, Charles E., James Stephen R., Jr., Hudson, Kay, and Duff, James, 1993, *Underwater Archaeology along the Lower Navidad and Lavaca Rivers, Jackson County, Texas.* Submitted to Galveston District, U.S. Army Corps of Engineers. Coastal Environments, Inc., Baton Rouge.

Pearson, Charles E., Hudson, Kay G., and James, Stephen R., 1992, *Data-Recovery Plan for the* SS Mary *(41NU252) Port Aransas, Nueces County, Texas.* Prepared for Galveston District, U.S. Army Corps of Engineers. Coastal Environments, Inc., Baton Rouge.

Pearson, Charles E., Weinstein, Richard A., and Kelley, David B., 1989, Evaluation of Prehistoric Site Preservation on the Outer Continental Shelf: The Sabine River Area, Offshore Texas and Louisiana. *Underwater Archaeology Proceedings from the Society for Historical Archaeology Conference*, edited by J. Barto Arnold III, pp. 6–11. Society for Historical Archaeology, Baltimore.

Pearson, Charles E., Kelley, David B., Weinstein, Richard A., and Gagliano, Sherwood M., 1986a, *Archaeological Investigations on the Outer Continental Shelf: A Study within the Sabine River Valley, Offshore Louisiana and Texas.* Coastal Environments, Inc., Baton Rouge. Minerals Management Service, U.S. Department of Interior, Reston.

Pendergrass, Bonnie B., and Pendergrass, Lee F., 1990, *In the Era of Limits: A Galveston District History Update, 1976–1986.* Pensec, Inc., Edmonds.

Perrault, Stephanie L., 1995, *Cultural Resources Survey of Proposed Disposal Area 1A, Colorado River, Matagorda County, Texas.* Coastal Environments, Inc., Baton Rouge.

Rogers, Robert, Hoyt, Steven D., Bond, Clell L., Voellinger, Leonard, and James, Stephen, 1990, *Cultural Resources Investigations, Virginia Point, Galveston County, Texas.* Doc. No. 890735. Prepared for U.S. Army Corps of Engineers, Galveston District. Espey, Huston & Associates, Inc., Austin.

Rosloff, Jay and Arnold III, J. Barto, 1984, The Keel of the *San Esteban* (1554): Continued Analysis. *International Journal of Nautical Archaeology* 13(4):287–296.

Schmidt, James S., 1998, *Archaeological and Hazards Survey, Proposed 12-Inch Pipeline Route in Galveston Bay, Texas.* Document No.980788. Prepared for SWCA, Inc. Espey, Huston & Associates, Inc., Austin.

Schmidt, James S., and Gearhart, Robert L., 1998, *Marine Remote Sensing Survey, SH35, Lavaca Bay Causeway, Calhoun County, Texas.* Doc. No. 980889. Prepared for Texas Department of Transportation, Environmental Affairs Division. Espey, Huston & Associates, Inc.

Schmidt, James S., and Hoyt, Steven D., 1995, *Mapping of the Utina (41NU264), Corpus Christi Entrance Channel, Nueces County, Texas.* Doc. No. 941204. Prepared for U.S. Army Corps of Engineers, Galveston District. Espey, Huston & Associates, Inc., Austin.

Schmidt, James S., Foster, Eugene, and Hoyt, Steven D., 1997, *Archival Research and Historic Sites Testing, Houston–Galveston Navigation Channels, Texas Project, Galveston, Harris, Liberty, And Chambers Counties, Texas.* Doc. No. 971726. Prepared for U.S. Army Corps of Engineers, Galveston District. Espey, Huston & Associates, Inc., Austin.

Schmidt, James S., Hoyt, Steven D., and Gearhart, Robert L., 1995, *Magnetometer Survey and Diving, Gulf Intracoastal Waterway and Houston Ship Channel Intersection, Galveston County, Texas.* Doc. No. 950777. Prepared for U.S. Army Corps of Engineers, Galveston District. Espey, Huston & Associates, Inc., Austin.

Shively, Dale, Arnold III, J. Barto, and Goloboy, Jennifer 1998, Liberty Ships: Where Heritage and Habitat Meet. *Texas Parks & Wildlife Magazine* 56(1):14–21.

Smith, Herman, Arnold III, J. Barto and Oertling, Tom 1987, Investigation of a Civil War Anti-torpedo Raft on Mustang Island, Texas. *International Journal of Nautical Archaeology* 16(2):149–157.

Voellinger, Leonard R., and Nash, Michael A., 1989, *Mouth of the San Bernard River: National Register Testing Four Sites, Brazoria County, Texas.* Espey, Huston & Associates, Inc., Austin.

Voellinger, Leonard R., Hammond, W., and Voellinger, M.W., 1991, *Cultural Resources Survey of Proposed Disposal Areas Near the Mouth of Baffin Bay, Kenedy and Kleberg Counties, Texas.* Espey, Huston & Associates, Inc., Austin.

Voellinger, Leonard R., Rogers, Robert, Hoyt, Steven, Bond, Clell, and James, Stephen, 1990, *Cultural Resources Investigations at Virginia Point, Galveston County, Texas.* Prepared for Texas Copper Corporation, Espey, Huston & Associates, Inc., Austin.

Warren, James E., 1988, *A Cultural Resources Survey of the Packery Channel Reopening Project. Nueces County, Texas.* Permit Application No. 18344.

Weinstein, Richard A., 1994, *Archaeological Investigations along the Lower Lavaca River, Jackson County, Texas: The Channel to Red Bluff Project.* Coastal Environments, Inc., Baton Rouge.

Weinstein, Richard A., Pearson, Charles E., Whelan Jr., James P., and Kelley, David B., 1988, *Archaeological investigations along the Lower Trinity River, Chambers and Liberty Counties, Texas.* Submitted to Galveston District, U.S. Army Corps of Engineers. Coastal Environments, Inc., Baton Rouge.

Chapter 15

Maritime and Underwater Archaeology on the Pacific Coast

JAMES P. DELGADO

INTRODUCTION

The Pacific shores of North America are a 2800-mile-long, rugged section of coast running between latitudes 32°–60°. The coast is largely rocky, but has occasional sand or gravel beaches; some of the sand beaches are long spectacular stretches with impressive dune formations. The coastline is broken by a number of islands, notably the Channel Islands of southern California, Vancouver Island, and the Queen Charlotte Islands in British Columbia, the Alexander Archipelago and the Aleutians in Alaska, and an impressive archipelago of hundreds of islands that dot the northern coast from Puget Sound to Alaska. Many form the intricate waterways of the Inside Passage of British Columbia and Alaska. A number of natural harbors are found on the coast, the four largest and most protected at San Francisco, Seattle (Puget Sound), Vancouver (Burrard Inlet), and Anchorage (Cook Inlet). Several rivers flow to the coast and into the sea, some penetrating deep into the interior and connecting to intricate drainage systems. The major watercourses are the Sacramento and San Joaquin in California, Columbia in Oregon, and Fraser and Nass in British Columbia.

James P. Delgado, Executive Director, Vancouver Maritime Museum, Vancouver, British Columbia V6J 1A3 Canada.

International Handbook of Underwater Archaeology, edited by Carol V. Ruppé and Janet F. Barstad. Kluwer Academic/Plenum Publishers, New York, 2002.

This rugged and exposed coast, with its offshore rocks, shoals, and bars, has combined with weather, human error, and misdeeds to wreck or damage thousands of ships and boats for more than 400 years, forming a rich maritime archaeological record. The majority of wreck sites date to a relatively recent period, since the bulk of coastal settlement did not occur until after 1850.

Significant work has been accomplished on earlier sites, as well as thematic research on vessel types, vessels associated with larger socioeconomic events or activities (the California Gold Rush), and specific types of sites and site formation processes (shipwreck remains on beaches). Successful development of avocational archaeology in British Columbia also has been notable.

SITES: 1595–1800

European exploration of the Pacific Coast north of Baja, California commenced soon after the Spanish conquest of Mexico. The California coastline was partially surveyed in 1542, when it was "discovered" by Juan Rodriguez Cabrillo, who sailed under the flag of Spain. Between 1542 and 1792, several expeditions, mostly Spanish, probed and explored the coast. During this period, a number of harbors were discovered and charted, such as San Francisco Bay. Explorers from other nations also examined the coast, including Vitus Bering for Russia, James Cook and George Vancouver for Great Britain, and Jean Francois de Galaup, Comte de La Perouse, for France.

The coast was first settled by a European power in 1769, when a Spanish land and sea expedition pushed into California. By 1776, Spanish settlements had reached San Francisco Bay; San Francisco remained the northernmost permanent outpost of Imperial Spanish power, although temporary settlement was achieved (and ultimately abandoned) on the coast of British Columbia at Nootka Sound. This period of exploration and early settlement resulted in a number of documented wrecks; however, the locations of only two ships from this period have been determined.

Beginning in 1573, Spanish vessels regularly crossed the Pacific between the Philippines and Mexico. The "Manila" trade encouraged Spanish trade and commerce and created major trade centres on the Pacific coast at Panama and Acapulco. The coast of North America was examined for suitable harbors and anchorages for transpacific trading vessels, and several expeditions periodically explored the coasts of California, Oregon, Washington, and British Columbia from the 16th century to the end of the 18th century.

San Agustin

The oldest recorded shipwreck on the Pacific Coast is in California. The Spanish "Manila galleon" and exploration vessel *San Agustin*, under the command of Juan Rodriguez Cermeño, was driven ashore on November 25, 1595. It had been ordered to turn aside from its usual course and examine the California coast near the "Punta de los Tres Reyes," a prominent landmark used by the Spanish as they made landfall after crossing the Pacific. Arriving in what is now known as Drakes Bay, in the lee of the Point Reyes peninsula, the *San Agustin* anchored off the beach, and the crew made contact with the indigenous Coastal Miwok people. When the crew began to chart the bay they named *bahia de San Francisco, a* winter storm caught them unprepared. *San Agustin* drifted ashore in heavy surf, breaking up and killing 16 crew members. Cermeno and the other survivors strengthened and expanded the ship's launch and made a daring open water passage along the California coast to reach Mexico and safety.

Archaeological traces of the *San Agustin* and its porcelain cargo have been recovered during the excavation of Late Horizon prehistoric sites and middens on the shores of Drakes Bay and its adjoining estero. Most, if not all, of these sites were abandoned in the 17th century, providing a *terminus ante quem*. Beginning in 1940 and continuing through the early 1950s, archaeologists Robert Heizer, Richard Beardsley, Adan E. Treganza, and Clement Meighan recovered 125 fragments of Ming white-on-blue porcelain, 59 hand-wrought iron ship's spikes, 6 iron drifts, and 11 pieces of stoneware. Since then, excavations within the sites and ceramic fragments found on the beach have increased the collection to more than 700 pieces of porcelain, additional ship's fastenings, and the tip of a Javanese halberd.

Underwater searches for the main body of the wreck began in 1965, when a group organized by John Huston of San Francisco conducted a magnetometer survey of inshore portions of the bay. Other unauthorized searches are rumored to have followed in the waters of the bay designated first as Point Reyes National Seashore and later as part of Gulf of the Farallones National Marine Sanctuary.

The first comprehensive underwater archaeological survey on the Pacific Coast was conducted in Drakes Bay in 1982 by the U.S. National Park Service's (NPS) Submerged Cultural Resources Unit, under the direction of Daniel J. Lenihan and Larry Murphy. The survey sought to locate the wreck of *San Agustin* and more than a dozen other wrecks known to have occurred in the bay between 1841 and 1940. A total area of 6.5 km^2 was surveyed with a magnetometer, which yielded a number of anomalies. Another 26 km^2 was surveyed with side scan sonar and a number of wrecks pinpointed and documented. A series of low-yielding anomalies close inshore and adjacent to the estero entrance, that appear to be the wreck of *San Agustin,* lay under layers of sand and in heavy surf, denying access for test excavation.

A mid-1980s legal challenge from treasure hunter Robert F. Marx, who claimed he had located the wreck and sought to excavate it as a commercial venture, halted the archaeological work of the National Park Service and National Oceanic and Atmospheric Administration (NOAA). They did not return to excavate Drakes Bay until 1997 and 1998, when a resurvey and test excavation was conducted under the direction of Larry Murphy. The wreck's location remains close to shore despite shoreline changes.

Diving was limited to selected periods because of heavy surf and the fact that the bay is a spawning ground for the Great White Shark. Nonetheless, the National Park Service intends to pursue a test program until the main body of the wreck of *San Agustin* is located. They will then make plans for more detailed excavation and analysis.

San Francisco Xavier

The remains of a vessel of considerable age and a cargo of beeswax were periodically exposed on the beach near Nehalem, Oregon, between the late 18th and early 20th centuries. Besides beeswax, which was recovered by the indigenous peoples and traded to arriving Europeans, fragments of porcelain and stoneware and various ship's fittings including a large wooden block, were taken from the beach by collectors. A number of these items, including large sections of beeswax evidently stowed in large packages, are now in various museums and historical societies, notably the nearby Tillamook County

Museum in Tillamook, Oregon. The large block is in Columbia River Maritime Museum in Astoria, Oregon.

Analysis of the beeswax pollen and the ceramics suggest that a Spanish vessel in the "Manila" trade wrecked at Nehalem in the 18th century. While Spanish records do not record a loss on the coast other than *San Agustin*, a number of ships in the trade did go missing. A likely candidate for the "Nehalem Beeswax Wreck" is the galleon *San Francisco Xavier*, which failed to arrive in Mexico in 1715.

Shoreline accretion may have covered the wreck in the early 20th century, which was the last time periodic winter storms exposed the buried hulk on the beach. Occasional searches of the beach have failed to reveal the site to date. Oregon archaeologists Charles Hibbs and Alison Stanger have formulated a detailed research design to survey the beach and inshore portions of the area to relocate the wreck and conduct test excavations. When it is found, should it prove to be not *San Francisco Xavier* but another Spanish "Manila" trade ship, it and the unexcavated *San Agustin* would be the only ships from the beginnings of transpacific trade and international trade and commerce in the Pacific available for study. They would also be the two oldest wrecks discovered on the Pacific Coast.

SITES: 1800–1849

Following a period of European settlement dominated by Spain in California and Russia in Alaska, scattered centers of trade developed along the coast. Maritime trade played an important role in this development, especially on the Northwest Coast where the maritime fur trade employed large numbers of ships and started a trade war between British and American interests. The trade war led to British settlement under the auspices of the Hudson's Bay Company (H.B.C.), which built several forts on the coast between Oregon and Alaska. The H.B.C. employed a regular fleet of vessels in coastal trade and in 1836 introduced the first steamship to the coast, the small sidewheeler *Beaver*.

In addition to the trade in sea otter and other pelts, large numbers of American ships began trade with Spanish (later Mexican) California, trading China trade goods for hides and tallow from California's huge cattle herds. The presence of these ships and those of Russian fur traders in Alaska (and after 1814 in California), inaugurated a coastal trade between the European settlements along the Pacific Coast with each other, as well as with Central and South America and Hawaii. This period also saw the development of shipyards and ship repair facilities at Fort Ross in California, Fort Vancouver in Washington, and Sitka in Alaska. There were number of wrecks caused by many factors, including several incidents in which the native peoples of the Northwest Coast seized and destroyed fur trade vessels as acts of revenge as well as piracy. Other significant wrecks include early 19th century exploration and trading vessels from Russia, the United States, and Britain, and at least one documented loss of a Japanese junk, with surviving crew, that drifted across the Pacific and crashed ashore in the 1830s. However, the remains of only one shipwreck from this period have been located and studied by archaeologists.

Isabella

A two-masted brig of the Hudson's Bay Company, *Isabella* was an English merchant vessel built in 1825 at Shoreham, Sussex, on the channel coast of England. She was exactly like hundreds of other British brigs built in the early 19th century, a carrier of bulk cargoes such as coal and grain. After the loss of its supply ship *William and Ann* on the Columbia River bar in 1829, the H.B.C. purchased *Isabella* to carry supplies to the company's Pacific Coast fur trading outpost at Fort Vancouver.

Sailing from London in November 1829, *Isabella* carried a varied cargo that reflected the needs of Fort Vancouver's growing agricultural and industrial community: tools, medicines, stationery supplies, preserved foods, lead, pig-iron, and paint, as well as the commodities of the fur trade: guns, ammunition, blankets, beads, copper cooking pots, candles, mirrors, tinware, buttons, combs, tobacco, and tea. Because of the captain's inexperience, *Isabella* stranded on the Columbia River Bar on May 2, 1830, and was a total loss. H.B.C. salvaged two-thirds of the cargo before the brig broke up on a sandbar.

The vessel's remains were rediscovered in September 1986, by a local fisherman, who snagged his nets on the wreck. In 1987, a cooperative effort to study the wreck was made by NPS, led by Daniel J. Lenihan, with assistance from the Columbia River Maritime Museum and the U.S. Coast Guard and several local sport divers. The Maritime Museum conducted another survey in 1994; in 1997, the Underwater Archaeological Society of British Columbia (UASBC), conducted dives at the museum's invitation.

Isabella's hull was nearly perfectly preserved by the fresh water of the river and a constant burial by shifting sand; its hull had split open at the bilges. Its port side has yet to be located, but the starboard side is exposed on the bottom and is intact from the bilge to the waterway, the original deck level (Figure 15.1). The hull is lined with a series of six cargo or ballast ports below the sheerstrake; closed and caulked during voyages, the ports were opened to salvage the cargo when the brig wrecked.

Another indication of salvage was found on the underside of the starboard hull. Below the ports, on the starboard side, a small square hole was cut into the hull. The brig's log entry for May 9, six days after the wreck, noted that the carpenter "cut a hole in

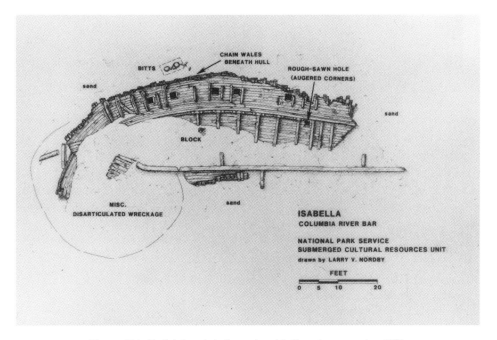

Figure 15.1. English brig *Isabella*, starboard hull, as documented in 1987.

the side to let the water out, so that we could better get at the cargo." The hole was one of the conclusive pieces of evidence in identifying the wreck.

The well-preserved wreck of *Isabella* is the oldest known fur trade vessel ever found on the Pacific Coast of North America, and the oldest wreck on the coast to be discovered and documented by archaeologists. Ongoing study of the brig is yielding important information about the little documented but once common British merchant brigs of the early 19th century and the maritime fur trade of the Northwest Coast.

SITES: 1849–1855

Patterns of settlement and trade on the Pacific Coast were radically changed by the 1848 discovery of gold in California. War between the United States and Mexico was ending; in October 1848, under the provisions of the Treaty of Guadalupe Hidalgo, Mexico surrendered half its territory, including California, to the United States.

California was still a small sleepy land of several thousand people, on a distant frontier, with an unsettled coast between it and the scattered forts of the H.B.C. in "British America" and the Russian settlements in Alaska, "Russian America." The discovery of gold and the resulting Gold Rush brought large numbers of ships from the United States and many other ports from around the world to San Francisco. In 1849, clearances for California from U.S. ports numbered 762 vessels. By 1850, several hundred ships lay at anchor off San Francisco, propelling a small town into a major metropolis as its bay became the principal port on the coast. A number of other towns and ports, on the interior rivers, and along the coast, also sprang up.

Small ocean-going ships could sail up San Francisco Bay to reach the Sacramento and San Joaquin Rivers and the towns of Sacramento and Stockton, jumping-off points for the gold mines. Neither of these towns nor the dozens of mining camps in the mountains had existed before the Gold Rush. Because of the large number of ships carrying people and goods, California changed from a frontier to a heavily populated state with major industries in a matter of a few years.

This period saw a dramatic increase in maritime activity on the coast. The rush to the coast by ship gave way in short order to regular passenger service. Coastal trade developed in agricultural produce and lumber to feed the needs of San Francisco and other rapidly growing urban centers. Merchants on the north coast, including the H.B.C., American settlers in Oregon, and at the new city of Seattle on Washington's Puget Sound, hurried to meet the needs of a booming, gold-inspired economy. Regular steam transportation between Panama, San Francisco, and Oregon, a substantial transpacific and coastal commodities trade, and the rise of large industrial facilities such as shipyards, factories and foundries, were the direct result of the rush to California.

The dangers of a roughly surveyed but not intimately known coast led to a number of wrecks. Many vessels, either no longer needed for trade or had worn out, were pressed into other uses and ultimately sunk, scuttled, or partially scrapped in California, especially at San Francisco. Between 1849 and 1852, more than 150 ships were converted into beached or floating warehouses, hotels, and other buildings.

Wrecks and maritime remains from the Gold Rush years of 1849–1855 constitute the largest group of sites documented by archaeologists on the coast, all of them in California with the exception of one wreck in British Columbia.

Frolic

The oldest Gold Rush wreck discovered to date in California is the clipper brig *Frolic*, wrecked on July 25, 1850, on the Mendocino coast north of San Francisco. Built in Baltimore for the opium trade, *Frolic* was packed with a speculative cargo of Chinese trade goods in response to the news of the Gold Rush in California. She sailed from Canton with bottles of food, chests of tea, alcohol, Chinese furniture, jewelry, guns, and a prefabricated house. Many prefabricated houses were shipped to California from the United States, Great Britain, and China during the period.

When *Frolic* wrecked, only the local Mitom Pomo Indians lived nearby. The ship's crew rowed south in a small boat to reach help, leaving the wreck to break apart in the sea, and the Pomo salvaged blankets, silk rolls, bottles, and ceramics from the stranded vessel. Projectile points made from the bottle glass, bead blanks manufactured from the ceramics, and pieces of the brass straps from tea chests were excavated by archaeologist Thomas N. Layton in historic period Mitom Pomo sites near the wreck. Layton's inquiries led him to wreck divers who had discovered *Frolic* and were salvaging from it.

Only one Chinese prefabricated house has survived to the present day: the house carried by *Frolic*. Layton was able to convince the divers, some of whom had worked the wreck for years, to return the artifacts they had found, and he combined a study of the salvaged material with the remains of the ship. His research also led him to a well-documented written record of the ship's construction, career, final cargo and wreck, providing the most detailed study to date of a Gold Rush trading voyage from China. Artifacts from the wreck include examples of nearly every item listed in the manifest and, although compromised by their nonarchaeological recovery, nonetheless provide a detailed material look at a Gold Rush China trade cargo. At this time, the *Frolic* collection is the only more or less intact Gold Rush cargo currently available for study.

Frolic lies in a small cove in shallow water. The ship's bottom, filled with iron kentledge, the remains of the windlass, and three anchors, mark the site. Much of the cargo was ceramics, and concreted masses of broken plates and bowls lie in the ballast mound. Broken and scattered ceramic pieces fill the cove. Ongoing survey of the wreck continues, undertaken by contractors under the auspices of the state of California.

Niantic

Niantic was built in 1835 for the China Trade. With trade disrupted by the Opium Wars, the ship was converted to a whaler after 1840. She was in the midst of a South Pacific whaling cruise when her crew received news of the discovery of gold in California. Captain Henry Cleaveland sailed to Panama, loaded 249 passengers, and proceeded to San Francisco, arriving in July 1849. The crew quickly deserted for the gold fields, and Captain Cleaveland sold *Niantic* to a group of speculators. They converted the whaler into a beached "storeship," pulling out the masts, hauling it up on the beach, surrounding it with pilings and a wharf, and covering the decks with a substantial barn or cover. The interior of the hull was divided into warehouses, and the structure on the decks was sublet for offices.

Much Gold Rush merchandise from arriving ships was stored in *Niantic*. A major fire May 3–4, 1851, burned the ship along with 2000 other buildings, but the lower hull, embedded in mud, sand, and water, sank and was covered over by landfill as the city rebuilt.

Niantic's remains, filled with thousands of burned and unharmed artifacts, was periodically rediscovered, in 1872 and 1907. In 1978, the San Francisco Maritime Museum performed an emergency excavation under the supervision of archaeologist Isabel Bullen during a few days' lull in construction on the site. Several thousand artifacts were recovered, indicative of a wide range of cargo: miner's tools, weapons, building materials, ceramics, and luxury items such as champagne, pate, and other preserved foodstuffs. The bottom of the hull was cleared, photogrametrically documented, and demolished. A 10-foot section of the midship's hull and the stern were retained for detailed analysis and preservation.

The *Niantic* collection was analyzed by archaeologist Mary Hilderman Smith in 1979–1980, and the vessel's career, construction, and conversion were studied by naval architect William Avery Baker and archaeologist James Delgado. A typical, bluff-bowed merchantman of the 1830s, *Niantic*'s significance lay more in its conversion to a storeship and the range of materials stored in the hull. The variety of goods, many of them luxuries or expensive tools and equipment from Europe and the eastern seaboard of the United States, demonstrated the powerful economies of the Gold Rush and the readiness of supply in the face of an incredible, gold-fueled demand on a distant frontier, a frontier served by well-established maritime routes of trade.

Hoff's Store

The 1851 fire that claimed *Niantic*, also burned a two-story store and office building known as Hoff's Store, erected on pilings over the bay. William C. Hoff and his business partner, Henry Owner, operated a ship's chandlery on the building's first floor and leased the second floor to the San Francisco harbor master. After the fire, the site, like others on the waterfront, was covered with clean sand fill, and new buildings were constructed on what was now dry land.

The remains of Hoff's Store were rediscovered in 1986 during preconstruction archaeological testing at the southwest corner of Sacramento and Battery streets. A detailed excavation, supervised by archaeologist Allen Pastron and assisted by other archaeologists including maritime archaeologist James Delgado, cleared the store's collapsed first floor, which had fallen into the bay as the fire consumed the building. The pilings, foundations, and badly burned remains of the walls and upper story revealed details of construction of a waterfront city termed a "Venice built of pine" in contemporary accounts.

Even more revealing were more than a million artifacts, many of a maritime nature— not surprising given the use of the store as a ship's chandlery. A level of preservation was exceptional, because the store had fallen into mud and water and was immediately buried under fill. Bottled preserves, casks of hardtack and salt pork, chests of tea, bags of coffee and rice, cordage, tools, and boxes of ammunition with powder intact, were among the discoveries. Among the more interesting finds were the Harbor Master's navigational instruments, surplus arms and equipment from the Mexican War (1846–1848), and many items ideally suited not only for mariners but for miners in isolated gold camps.

Analysis of the collection added substantially to the understanding of market dynamics and the role of maritime trade in Gold-Rush San Francisco, augmenting and refining conclusions reached by Smith in her analysis of the *Niantic* collection and demonstrating the potential for significant archaeological returns from other waterfront sites now buried under landfill in the heart of modern San Francisco.

Rome

In December 1994, crews constructing a subway along San Francisco's Embarcadero Street encountered the largely intact remains of a buried Gold Rush vessel that had been scuttled to fix title to a submerged "water lot" and subsequently buried by landfill. Working below ground in a cofferdam on the part of the wreck encountered by the digging, archaeologist James Allan documented the vessel's construction before the section in the path of the project was cleared. Allan's research has determined that the vessel, whose other remains lie buried at the site, was the hulk of the ship *Rome*, built in 1820 and scuttled in 1851.

General Harrison

Another victim of the May 3–4, 1851 fire, the storeship *General Harrison*'s remains were discovered one block east of the *Niantic* site in late August 2001. *General Harrison*, built at Newburyport, Massachusetts in 1840, served as both a coastal packet and a China trader before sailing to California with cargo, but no passengers, in response to the Gold Rush. Arriving in February 1850, the ship was sold to her agents, E. Mickle & Company, beached, and converted into a storeship in late May.

The *General Harrison* storeship remained in business for only a year, as it was destroyed along with *Niantic* and the neighboring *Apollo* storeships in the May 1851 fire that ravaged the Gold Rush waterfront. Chinese laborers under the supervision of "shipbreaker" Charles Hare cleared the hull of burned debris and began to systematically dismantle the unburned bottom portion of the ship, but abandoned their efforts in September 1851. The vessel's remains were buried beneath sand and left untouched until building construction on the site in 1912.

Three-quarters of the hull, from stern to the approximate area of the foremast, was completely uncovered in 2001 under the direction of Allen Pastron, whose firm, Archeo-Tec, had documented the probable presence of the buried hulk and initiated detailed archaeological documentation with the City of San Francisco and the property owner and developer. Final clearing and documentation of the vessel was supervised by James Delgado and yielded significant information on the vessel's construction and the reverse-construction process of dismantling employed by Hare's workers. Excavation of the redeposited "cargo" of the storeship along the sides of the hulk yielded tens of thousands of artifacts, included burned portions of the vessel's upper works, crates of wine and liquor, wheat, red glass beads from Italy, and hardware.

Work on the *General Harrison* site has provided considerable material culture and data for a comprehensive analysis of the Gold Rush waterfront of San Francisco along with the previously excavated Hoff's Store and *Niantic* sites, as well as the best documented look at a Gold Rush storeship in its original context.

Lord Western

Another significant discovery from the Gold Rush was a wreck in British Columbia first discovered by divers in 1957 and later identified as the Gold Rush ship *Lord Western*. Built in Aberdeen, Scotland in 1840, *Lord Western* was employed in trade with India. Condemned at Calcutta in 1842, the "leaky ship" gained a bad reputation which, nonetheless, did not preclude a voyage to California in 1852 with nearly 300 Chinese immigrants. Unable to return to China for more passengers when it developed a bad leak, *Lord Western* was patched up and sent north to British Columbia to load a cargo of logs intended for the San Francisco market; the building boom caused by the Gold Rush had made lumber for houses, docks and piers a valuable commodity. *Lord Western* received her log cargo in early December 1853, and headed south for San Francisco. A storm pushed the half-flooded ship ashore on Vancouver Island on December 4, 1853, where it was abandoned.

The wreck was surveyed and partially excavated in 1987 by the UASBC. Excavation beneath the surviving log cargo revealed substantial hull remains, the captain's telescope, and a Chinese ceramic bowl left behind by one of the immigrants. To date the oldest wreck located in British Columbia, *Lord Western*, like *Frolic*, represented patterns of trade generated by the Gold Rush, the opening of the coast to wider commercial enterprise, and the range of vessels, some ill-equipped or poorly maintained, in the boom economy of that time and place.

William Gray

This buried Gold Rush ship was converted to a storeship and then scuttled to form a stable platform for a dock at the foot of Telegraph Hill in late June or early July 1852. The dock and ship were buried by landfill after 1854. Preconstruction archaeological testing at the site in 1979 revealed the presence of the intact hulk more than 10 feet below the modern street level. Test excavation of the site in February 1980, by archaeologist Allen G. Pastron, assisted by naval architects William Avery Baker and Raymond Aker and historians Roger and Nancy Olmsted, disclosed part of the starboard hull near the bow, with intact bulwarks, chainplates, and deck on which the excavators could walk. The ship had been filled with mud and rock and buried in more of the same, and the level of preservation was exceptional.

After the test excavation, the ship was reburied and a new office complex, Levi's Plaza, erected on the site. The ship now rests below the plaza's courtyard and an ornamental fountain. Research by the Olmsteds revealed that it was the ship *William Gray*, built in 1827 at Medford, Massachusetts, apparently for the Southern packet trade. Its owners sent it to California in August 1849, with a speculative cargo and 12 passengers. The ship arrived at San Francisco on June 15, 1850 and was shortly thereafter sold for use as a storeship. Its buried hull is the most intact example of a ship known from the California Gold Rush and the best preserved remains of an American merchant ship from the first quarter of the 19th century.

Tennessee

Regular steamship service between the eastern seaboard of the United States and California and Oregon was mandated by Congress in 1848 and realized during the California Gold Rush when two companies, the United States Mail Steamship Company and the Pacific Mail Steamship Company, began operation. Running on the Atlantic and Caribbean between New York and Chagres and later Aspinwall, Panama, and between Panama City and San Francisco, the steamers of the two companies opened the "Panama Route" to regular travel and provided the impetus for the Panama Railroad and, later, the Panama Canal.

Both companies operated fleets of steamships, and "opposition lines" of competitors introduced other steamers to the two coasts. The Panama Route steamers also connected other ports in Mexico, California, and Oregon at the same time they ran from Panama to San Francisco. They formed a regular coastal service from the beginning of the Gold Rush, facilitating travel and, ultimately, the development of other ports and urban centers.

Several steamships were wrecked on the Panama Route. The remains of five have been located by divers, two of which have been studied by archaeologists. The first, the steamer *Tennessee*, was built in 1848 to run between New York and Savannah. It was diverted to the Panama Route in late 1849, arriving at San Francisco on April 14, 1850. For the next three years, it ran between San Francisco and Panama, carrying up to 550 passengers and one million dollars in gold specie each voyage. The steamer also transported high-commodity freight and mail.

Tennessee missed the Golden Gate Bridge on the foggy morning of March 6, 1853. The baggage, mail, and specie were salvaged, and the 636 persons on board were rescued, but the steamer broke apart in the heavy surf and was a total loss. Portions of *Tennessee*'s machinery were exposed on the beach of Tennessee Cove by periodic winter storms, and San Francisco Maritime Museum curator Harlan Soeten identified the wreck site in 1965. Between 1980 and 1981, and again in 1982, a National Park Service team led by James Delgado and assisted by volunteers from the Miwok Archaeological Preserve of Marin and the College of Marin, documented the site, excavated several units on the beach, and surveyed the scattered machinery from the steamer's engines.

Although much of the wreck was broken up by violent surf, considerable remains, albeit scattered, were plotted and recovered on the beach, and a site formation process ascertained. Smaller pieces of machinery, ship's fastenings and copper sheathing, ceramics, glassware, and a single Spanish one-*reale* coin were among the finds. The wreck of *Tennessee* is protected within the boundaries of the Golden Gate National Recreation Area. The site has been regularly monitored since 1982, but no additional excavation or recovery has taken place.

Winfield Scott

The Pacific Mail Steamship Company purchased the steamer *Winfield Scott* to replace the wrecked *Tennessee* in the summer of 1853. Ironically, *Winfield Scott* wrecked on a voyage to Panama on December 2, 1853, running aground and sinking off Anacapa Island in Southern California while enroute to Panama. Passengers and some baggage and mail were saved, but the steamer was a total loss. Sport divers rediscovered the wreck after World War II and actively collected artifacts despite the inclusion of the area in Channel Islands National Monument (later National Park) in 1935.

National Park Service archaeologists began work on the wreck in 1981, under the supervision of James Delgado. The work continued in the mid-1980s under Daniel Lenihan of the NPS. Archaeological survey and monitoring of the wreck continued through the mid-1990s under park archaeologist Don Morris and NOAA cultural resources specialist Robert Schwemmer.

The wreck is partially buried in the sand and is often obscured by thick kelp, but many portions of the ship and its machinery have survived the surf, souvenir hunters, and time. It is amazing that so much of the wreck has survived in such a high-energy environment, and it suggests that some notions, such as "shipwrecks completely disintegrate in shallow water," do not always hold true.

The midship portion of the hull, the area where the engine room was located, is exposed. Scattered around it are the remains of the ship's engines and two paddlewheels. The cylindrical base of an engine cylinder remains atop the hull, its sides blasted away in 1894 to extract the pistons. The cylinder base is sometimes mistakenly referred to as a base for one of the ship's two iron flue boilers, but the rectangular boilers actually were located in an area of the hull that appears to have wedged into some large rocks and been broken up.

On either side of the hull are the remains of the two paddlewheels. One, which may be the port side paddlewheel, rests on its side, with its arms and some of its rims rising up from the bottom. Farther away, on the other side, the broken rims and arms of what may be the starboard wheel lie flat in the sand. A number of fragments of the diagonal bracing in the hull, and parts of machinery lie on the wreck site, including two crossheads or crosstails from the engines, and the saddle and supports for a paddlewheel.

There has been some excavation of the wreck, and many artifacts are in the collection of Channel Islands National Park. Some of the artifacts were returned to the park by history-minded divers who had collected them in the years before archaeological work began on the wreck, and before NPS, NOAA, and the state of California began active protection of shipwrecks and natural resources in Channel Islands National Park and the National Marine Sanctuary.

Artifacts in the collection include baggage tags, firearms, glasswares, ceramics, ship's fastenings, machinery parts including broken steam gauges, coal (which was analyzed and determined to be an expensive British import), coins, and personal items such as uniform items from military officers on board as passengers. Some artifacts were comparable to the collection from the wreck of *Tennessee,* as would be expected. The visible remains of *Winfield Scott* join the artifacts in the park's collection as a tangible reminder of a pioneer steamship on the Pacific Coast and of the role steamers played in opening up the coast during and immediately after the Gold Rush.

Sacramento River Wrecks

Archaeologists diving in the Sacramento River have discovered the wrecks of four sailing ships that came to California in 1849. These ships were converted to storeships or other building uses on the river bank, and in time deliberately sunk to clear the waterfront or, in two cases, caught and sunk by the occasional floods that sweep the river. The most intact or complete wreck is the small brig (a two-masted ship) *Sterling*, an older ship used like many others in the Gold Rush. Built in Massachusetts in 1833, the tiny brig sailed to California in 1849 with seven passengers and a cargo of building supplies. While some Gold Rush ships were larger vessels with a greater capacity for passengers and cargo, the average Gold Rush arrival was a small vessel with a limited cargo and a small number of passengers. Large numbers of people arrived in California simply because there were so many ships.

Sterling and a nearby wreck, later determined to be the bark *LaGrange*, were discovered during a remote sensing survey of the Sacramento River near Old Town Sacramento State Historic Park by archaeologist Jack Hunter in 1984. Hunter and state archaeologist John Foster conducted the first examination of the site; Foster subsequently continued the investigation of the wreck, pursuing its identification as *Sterling*. In the latter phase, he was assisted by National Park Service archaeologists James Delgado and Martin Mayer. The ship had been refitted to go to California, the hull covered with new copper sheathing; a bower anchor stamped with the date "1844" (11 years after *Sterling* was built) was found on the wreck. Penetration into the intact forecastle revealed that the stub of the foremast and a few broken pieces of pottery remained inside, because *Sterling* had been stripped after it arrived in Sacramento. Used as a storeship, it sank in a flood in 1855.

The bark *LaGrange*, another 49er, sailed upriver to Sacramento and was converted into the city's prison ship. Pushed onto a sandbar and sunk by a flood in 1863, the wreck was partially broken up before it sank. A detailed study of *LaGrange* was made in 1987 by Jack Hunter, Stephen James, Sheli Smith, and James Delgado. Fragmentary remains of the bark indicated construction similar to *Niantic*. One timber with unusual fittings may have been a prison feature.

A side scan sonar survey of the river, conducted in 1986 by Stephen James for Espey, Huston & Associates, expanded on the earlier survey done by Hunter and located the fragmented remains of two other Gold Rush vessels off the Sacramento riverfront. The remains were identified by James and Delgado as the barks *Ninus* and *Dimon*, 1849 arrivals also converted to storeship use at Sacramento.

SITES: 1855–1870

Rincon Point Chinese Fishing Village

Archaeologist Allen Pastron, working under contract in 1988 to mitigate construction impacts in a development near San Francisco's Rincon Point, discovered the remains of California's first Chinese fishing village and the nearby site of Charles Hare's post-Gold Rush shipbreaking yard, both dating from 1854 with a *terminus ante quem* of 1857–1859. Among the more interesting finds at the village site were carved wood and bamboo models of fishing junks, presumably childrens' toys.

Excavation of the shipbreaking yard disclosed the remains of a number of vessels, all Gold Rush arrivals, which had been systematically dismantled for scrap metal and wood. More than 500 vessels lay idle off San Francisco by 1850; many were converted to storeship or other building uses, but others were left moored off Rincon Point, which gradually became the collection ground for unwanted vessels. Beginning in 1854, Charles Hare, employing laborers from the nearby fishing village, began to break up the old ships.

Analysis of the piles of ship's timbers by archaeologist James Delgado, Pastron's associate, showed a meticulous pattern of careful dismantling, recovery of the smallest metal components, and the subsequent breaking of the timbers into smaller, more manageable parts for firewood. The remains of several vessels, most dating to the first quarter of the 19th century, were present at the site, and were represented for the most part by sections of keel, floors, and frames, as well as a single-bar-style chainplate and pieces of copper sheathing. Tools used in the shipbreaking found on the site included chain "come-alongs" and a large breaking bar.

Brother Jonathan

The steamship *Brother Jonathan*, built for Atlantic service on the Panama Route, arrived in the Pacific in 1852 to run between Nicaragua and San Francisco. In 1856, she was sold and began a new career as one the region's first coastal passenger and freight steamers. The development of San Francisco and other Pacific coast ports between California and Puget Sound was made possible by regular steam service after the Gold Rush. *Brother Jonathan* played a significant role in the development of trade and commerce on the coast, carrying all commercial and agricultural goods between growing population centers in California, Oregon, Washington, and British Columbia. She was lost on the northern California coast on July 30, 1865. The wreck was, and remains, the worst maritime disaster in California waters, and one of the worst maritime disasters on the Pacific Coast.

The loss of a $200,000 U.S. Army payroll and $80,000 in specie inspired searches from 1865 until 1993, when a treasure-hunting consortium discovered the steamer in 250 ft of water. The lower hull, machinery, paddlewheel hubs, and scattered artifacts on the sand bottom are prominent features on the site. No published archaeological survey or research has been conducted on the wreck, which was the subject of a protracted legal battle between the state of California and the salvors over the ownership of the wreck and the disposition of finds. The state of California lost the case and salvage proceeded, recovering approximately 1000 coins and other artifacts in 1997–1998.

SITES: 1870–1900

King Philip

Severe winter storms battered the California coast in 1983, exposing the outline of a vessel on San Francisco's Ocean Beach. Continued beach erosion revealed the intact lower portion, from the 'tween deck to the keel of the medium clipper *King Philip*, built in 1856 at Alna, Maine, for the general carrying trade. After a global career, *King Philip* stranded on Ocean Beach in 1878 and sanded in. The upper works were blasted and scrapped, but the lower hull remained in place. The high level of preservation revealed the lines of the vessel and builder's marks in the timbers. Medium clippers were a transitional hull form between the extreme clippers of the California Gold Rush and the "Downeaster" or generic American wooden-hulled, deep-water cargo carrier of the late 19th century.

King Philip's hull provided the first detailed look at a medium clipper. Continual erosion removed the need for excavation, allowing teams led by James Delgado to document the vessel (Figure 15.2). Erosion also exposed the scattered remains of the Pacific lumber schooner *Reporter*, which stranded atop the wreck of *King Philip* in 1901. Rigging elements from *Reporter* were recovered for conservation and display at the National Maritime Museum, San Francisco.

A magnetometer survey of the beach revealed buried portions of *Reporter*. Subsequent magnetometer surveys were conducted by Robert L. Gearhart II of Espey, Huston & Associates, delineating the by-then reburied *King Philip* and *Reporter* and the supposed nearby site of the 1886 wreck of the whaling bark *Atlantic*. A more detailed survey of all of Ocean Beach was completed in the 1990s under the supervision of Larry Murphy of the NPS.

Beaver

The paddle steamer *Beaver* was built to order in London in 1835 for the Hudson's Bay Company, for fur trading on the Pacific northwest coast of North America. It arrived on the Pacific coast in 1836. *Beaver* was the first steamship to operate on the Pacific coast and enjoyed a 53-year career there, serving as a fur trader, survey vessel for the Royal Navy, passenger steamer, and tugboat. She ran ashore and wrecked July 26, 1888, at the entrance to Burrard Inlet at the site of the modern city of Vancouver.

Figure 15.2. Wreck of *King Philip*, Ocean Beach, San Francisco.

Salvage of the steamer was not economical, and *Beaver*'s owners left the steamer to disintegrate on the rocks. Over the next four years, as it fell apart, *Beaver* was subjected to intensive stripping by souvenir hunters. Local divers rediscovered the wreck in 1960 and until 1974 removed artifacts from the site. The wreck became the subject of a detailed archaeological survey by UASBC and the Vancouver Maritime Museum between 1991 and 1998.

Considerable remains, such as the bottom of the hull in the engine room area, base plates and lower castings for the engines and other machinery, and brass and copper artifacts such as drifts, spikes, copper pipe and valves, remain untouched on the site. The hull and most of the artifacts lie exactly where the ship wrecked in 1888 and have not been disturbed by human activity.

Archaeological survey of the site, documentation of site materials, and previously recovered vessel remains have provided a more detailed view of the pioneer steamship on the Pacific Coast of North America. Working from archaeological data and a large, diverse historic record that included machinery plans, John McKay of Langley, British Columbia, completed more than 80 sheets of plan drawings for *Beaver*; this corpus is probably the most extensive and detailed analysis of an early 19th century merchant steamship. Of particular significance, and worthy of study and analysis, is the social process that transformed *Beaver* from wreck to relic, a process ably reflected in a rich and diverse material record. Also of note are the dynamics of the site formation process. Despite strong tides, deposition on an exposed steep, rocky bottom, and intensive salvage operations between 1888–1892 and 1960–1973, a substantial, articulated, and well-preserved archaeological record survived.

Goldenhorn and *Aggi*

More than a decade of archaeological survey and documentation of wrecks at Channel Islands National Park in Southern California has provided a basic reference for a number of vessel types and trades on the Pacific Coast in the last quarter of the 19th century and the first half of the 20th century. This includes coastal lumber schooners, passenger steamers, smaller craft, and the remains of two metal-hulled "windjammers" involved in the California grain trade, *Aggi* and *Goldenhorn*.

The wreck of *Goldenhorn* is particularly illustrative. Built in 1883 at Greenock, Scotland, *Goldenhorn* was a three-masted ship (later a bark) representative of the typical British deepwater iron- and steel-hulled ships of the time. Built at the end of the sailing era, these larger-capacity ships were the general cargo carriers of the period, gradually declining as steam became paramount. Built to carry coal and other bulk cargoes to California, *Goldenhorn* was returning with grain and was lost September 12, 1891, when she ran aground on Santa Rosa Island.

The remains of *Goldenhorn* were well-known to local divers. National Park Service archaeologists began to study and map the wreck in 1985; resurveys in 1993 and 1994 provided a detailed plan of the vessel's construction and an assessment of the site formation process.

Ericsson

A shipwreck with a long and unique history was located and surveyed in 1985 off the entrance to Barkley Sound on the west coast of Vancouver Island in British Columbia. The sailing ship *Ericsson* was built as an experimental, hot-air-driven "caloric" ship in 1852. The vessel's machinery was the invention of John Ericsson, who later gained fame as the builder of USS *Monitor*. *Ericsson*'s caloric machinery was removed and replaced with steam engines in 1854. After serving as a troop ship in the Civil War, in 1868 it was converted to sail. By the 1880s, the ship was working out of San Francisco and was bound for Nanaimo, British Columbia, when it was lost November 19, 1892.

The wreck was rediscovered during a shipwreck survey of the Barkley Sound area by the UASBC. This avocational group, then headed by David Griffiths, mapped the site and recovered the ship's bells and other artifacts on behalf of the province of British Columbia. Because of its unique history, the wreck of *Ericsson* was declared a protected site by British Columbia. Its remains offer a detailed look at the vessel's construction, similar to contemporary mid-19th-century ocean-going steamships. Diagonal iron strapping, heavy floors, extensive fastenings, and expensive brass fittings including ornate deadlights, were among the features noted.

The UASBC has located a large number of wrecks in the waters of British Columbia, most of them late 19th- and early 20th-century sites. A highly successful avocational or "amateur" group, the UASBC has been responsible for an extensive, government- and member-donation sponsored program of survey, research, some excavation, documentation, preservation and interpretation, which is unrivaled on the Pacific Coast. Preliminary site surveys have been followed by a number of continued, nondestructive documentation projects. A detailed maritime history of British Columbia vessel types, and examples of the various trades including foreign vessels (notably U.S.), could be prepared based on UASBC's work.

The UASBC has raised and conserved artifacts for the province, nearly all of which are housed in either the Vancouver Maritime Museum or the Maritime Museum of British Columbia in Victoria; others are in smaller local museums and historical societies. The UASBC only major excavation project was the previously mentioned *Lord Western*, although large sandstone blocks and columns, quarried near Nanaimo for the U.S. Branch Mint in San Francisco and lost on the bark *Zephyr* in 1873, were raised and placed ashore for display.

Turner Robertson Shipyard

The only detailed archaeological work conducted on a Pacific Coast shipyard site was undertaken in 1986–1987 by a volunteer team led by James Delgado at the San Francisco Bay site of the Matthew Turner–James Robertson Shipyard in Benicia. Established in 1886 by the prodigious Turner, who built 228 vessels in his career, the yard operated until 1918.

Substantial remains on the beach and in the water were mapped. Among these were the ways, foundations for yard buildings, steam machinery, dock and wharf pilings, a sunken barge and, buried in the mud, the substantially intact remains of the former whaler *Stamboul*, which Turner used as a sheer hulk to mast and rig his ships.

Built in 1843, *Stamboul* had a long career before being retired, dismasted, and converted to shipyard use by Turner. Among the most archaeologically intact known remains of an American whaler of the early 19th century, *Stamboul* was partially excavated and documented before being reburied in the mud. Wire rope and other rigging equipment was found stowed on the 'tween deck level, where it had been abandoned when the vessel sank toward the end of the yard's active life. Other discoveries included glassware, notably medicine bottles, and many abandoned timbers for shipbuilding including a number of rough-cut knees and braces for a wooden vessel. These materials were found close in to shore, preserved by the thick mud of the beach. After documentation, the site was registered as a state historic landmark, and the wreck was listed in the National Register of Historic Places. The area is now the City of Benicia's Turner Shipyard Park.

City of Ainsworth

In 1990, the UASBC, working with a local dive club, discovered the intact remains of the sternwheel lake steamer *City of Ainsworth* in 111 m of clear, cold water on British Columbia's Kootenay Lake. A typical interior-waters sternwheeler of the late 19th century, *City of Ainsworth* foundered in 1898.

Using a remotely-operated vehicle, the UASBC documented the wreck in place with a video camera. Dives were made to shallow portions of the wreck to assess scatter from the sinking; this included a handcart and crates of preserves with intact, sealed bottles. The site is protected by provincial designation and, although further research has not been done, the wreck of *City of Ainsworth* has demonstrated the potential for other similarly preserved sites in the many fresh water lakes of interior British Columbia.

Canada

The remains of the bark *Canada* were recorded by the Alaska Heritage Resources Survey in 1978, on the beach where it wrecked in 1898 during the Klondike Gold Rush. Built in

1859 at Bath, Maine, *Canada* entered the Klondike Gold Rush as a lumber- and passenger-carrying vessel. She was blown ashore on February 24, 1898, while delivering a cargo of lumber, shingles, doors, windows, passengers, and horses, to Dyea, Alaska.

The initial survey disclosed the bottom of the hull, with keelson and floors articulated. The site is exposed at extreme low tides. The wreck of *Canada* was listed in the National Register of Historic Places because of its association with the Klondike Gold Rush. No additional archaeological work has been conducted on the site.

SITES: 1900–1940

Neptune

Winter storm erosion on San Francisco's Ocean Beach in December 1982, exposed the midship portion of the starboard side of a small vessel lodged against the face of a cliff. The partially exposed hull section was excavated and documented by a team directed by James Delgado, and the vessel was reconstructed with the assistance of naval architect and historian Raymond Aker. The remains proved to be those of the two-masted lumber schooner *Neptune*, built in 1882 and wrecked at the site on August 10, 1900.

The remains of *Neptune* provided the first archaeological look at a Pacific Coast lumber schooner, and the first opportunity to assess shipwreck remains on a beach. Two significant research projects, one examining the development of the lumber schooner as a type, and the site formation and preservation processes inherent in beached shipwrecks, were inaugurated as a result of the *Neptune* project.

Pomona

Work by archaeologists John Foster and Jack Hunter in Fort Ross Cove (part of Fort Ross State Historic Park) on the northern California coast revealed a number of submerged resources. Beginning in 1981, the two archaeologists documented the remains of the coastal steamship *Pomona*. The steel-hulled *Pomona*, built in 1884 and wrecked in 1908, was a typical Pacific Coast steamer of the late 19th-, early 20th century. Heavily salvaged at the time of her loss and subsequently battered by wave action on an exposed coast, *Pomona*'s remains nonetheless provided a detailed picture of a ship whose regular service and style made her the "Pride of the Coaster Fleet."

Lydia and Whaling on the Pacific Coast

On June 12, 1978, workers digging a sewer outfall on San Francisco's southern Embarcadero struck the buried remains of a wooden-hulled sailing vessel. Consulting archaeologist Allen Pastron, working with historians Roger and Nancy Olmsted and naval architect and historian Raymond Aker, supervised the excavation and removal of the cross-section of the ship from the sewer trench.

Aker's detailed reconstruction, aided by later excavation of the ship's well-preserved stern with intact bulwarks and chainplates, assisted the Olmsteds in a careful archival search. Ultimately the wreck was determined to be the whaler *Lydia*. Built in 1840 at Rochester, Massachusetts, *Lydia* whaled out of New Bedford until 1885. Even

Figure 15.3. Excavation of whaler *Lydia* from a San Francisco sewer trench.

as *Lydia* was launched, the declining whale fishery on the eastern seaboard induced many whalers to seek better fishing elsewhere, and much of her career was spent in the Pacific.

Increased use of the Pacific whale fishery ultimately led to the rise of San Francisco as the United States' principal whaling port and, after 1865, many whale ships were home-ported on San Francisco Bay. The introduction of whaling in the western Arctic after 1865 also played a major role in the shift of the fleet to the Pacific Coast. *Lydia* whaled out of San Francisco until 1897. In 1901, now idle and laid up, she was moored off the San Francisco waterfront near China Basin when a fire damaged her. *Lydia* sank, her bow sticking out of the water. In March 1907, the bow was broken down and the ship forgotten. Soon afterward, a new seawall extended the waterfront, burying the ship until its rediscovery in 1978.

Discovery of *Lydia* provided a detailed look at a mid-19th-century American whaler; only one other whaling vessel, *Stamboul,* has been archaeologically documented on the Pacific Coast. Work on the two whalers complements the 1987 excavation and documentation of an 1857–1873 tryworks oven at a former shore whaling station site at Ballast Point in San Diego. The Ballast Point station, and the research implications of shore whaling sites in California, have been the subject of detailed study by archaeologist Ronald May, adding considerably to the scholarly record on Pacific Coast whaling activities.

The wreck of *Lydia*, now separated into two sections, remains buried at the site on King Street where it was discovered (Figure 15.3). A large body of historical, architectural, and archaeological documentation is available, and the site is listed in the National Register of Historic Places.

Pomo and *Munleon*

In 1982–1983, a NPS team, directed by Daniel Lenihan, undertook a detailed survey of Point Reyes National Seashore in northern California. Many vessels have wrecked at Point Reyes and in adjacent Drakes Bay. The NPS team discovered the remains of the steam schooner *Pomo*, wrecked on the beach in 1913; steam schooner *Hartwood*, wrecked in 1936; tanker *Richfield*, wrecked in 1930; freighter *Munleon*, wrecked in 1930; and steam schooner *Shasta*, scuttled in or around 1940.

Detailed mapping of the wreck of *Munleon* in the [1930] season, directed by archaeologist Toni Carrell, disclosed many details about the construction and loss of this World War I, emergency-built, Frederickstad-type freighter. Its remains, including triple expansion engine, large sections of the hull, and decks, were located on the beach of Limantour Spit on Drakes Bay and were mapped in 1983–1984 under the direction of archaeologist James Delgado. The first steam schooner to be archaeologically mapped, *Pomo*'s remains were plotted over a three-mile section of coast, ascertaining and reconstructing the site formation process. Further refinement of the archaeological data on steam schooners came with later projects to document the wrecks of *Daisy Gadsby*, whose fragmented remains were unearthed in San Francisco during a dredging project, and *Gray*'s *Harbor*, a steam schooner pulled up on the beach near Candlestick Park and burned for her metal in the 1930s.

Monte Carlo

Between 1985 and 1986, a team led by archaeologist Roy Pettus documented the remains of the concrete ship *Monte Carlo*, which lies on the beach near Coronado, California. Built in 1921 in Wilmington, North Carolina, as a late production of the World War I "emergency fleet" type concrete ship, *Monte Carlo* was laid down as *McKittrick*, an oil tanker for the Associated Oil Company of San Francisco. Converted to use as a floating gambling ship just outside the legal limit at San Diego, *Monte Carlo* began operation in 1936. The ship's career was short: It stranded on the beach and broke up January 5, 1937. Gambling equipment and other fittings were salvaged, leaving the hulk to sink slowly into the sand and disappear. The largely buried and submerged wreck is a more or less intact example of a now rare type, although a more intact and visible concrete ship, *Palo Alto*, rests farther north on the beach near Capitola, California, and another concrete ship, *Peratig*, forms part of a floating breakwater on Powell River, British Columbia.

SITES: 1941–1945

In 1989, a NPS team, led by Daniel Lenihan and assisted by the U.S. Navy, U.S. Air Force and the U.S. Fish and Wildlife Service, conducted a submerged cultural resources assessment of Kiska Harbor in Alaska's Aleutian Islands. Occupied and fortified in June 1942, by the Imperial Japanese Navy, the Aleutians were a major World War II campaign on the Pacific Coast of North America. The islands were retaken in 1943 by United States and Canadian forces.

The survey of Kiska Harbor and the nearby shoreline yielded major discoveries of Japanese vessels and craft, including armed transports, landing craft, submarine chasers, and submarines. The transports included the beached, partially sunk and intact *Nissan Maru*. Two landing craft lay off the beach in deeper water, and may be craft used by

Japanese forces to withdraw secretly from Kiska before the allied invasion. Occupying forces met with no opposition at Kiska but faced determined Japanese forces dug in for a fight at nearby Attu. The harbor also yielded the well- preserved and bomb-damaged Vickers-class submarine RO65, sunk by aerial bombing. Dives by the NPS team uncovered evidence of post sinking repair and salvage attempts.

Work on the shore documented the remains of two Type A Japanese midget submarines. Kiska was a base for several of these small, two-person submersibles. One, damaged by a scuttling charge, rests in its launching cradle on the shore; the broken-up remains of another lie partially buried on the beach below it.

The documentation of war remains in the Aleutians was part of a larger NPS–U.S. Navy cooperative effort (Project SEAMARK), which earlier included projects in the Pacific at Pearl Harbor, Guam, Palau, and other locales in the United States. In particular, the extensive underwater survey at Kiska added to the documentation of the island as a National Historic Landmark and showed the way for additional work in the Aleutians, a unique Pacific Coast World War II battlefield.

RESEARCH THEMES, RESOURCE MANAGEMENT, AND LEGAL CHALLENGES

The history of underwater and maritime archaeological research on the Pacific Coast is similar to that of other regions of the United States, Canada, and the world. A post-World War II interest in new scuba diving technology led to the discovery of a number of wrecks, some salvage and souvenir hunting and, occasionally, treasure hunting. The relatively recent nature of most sites on the coast, and a lack of large numbers of wrecks with documented or suspected treasure, has kept treasure hunting to a minimum. The wrecks of greatest interest by treasure hunters, both organized professionals and individual divers, have been *San Agustin* and the Gold Rush steamship wrecks, *Winfield Scott* and *Brother Jonathan*.

The history of site investigation is dominated largely by resource management concerns and mitigation of potential or actual impacts. This is especially the case on land with the buried ships and sites such as *Niantic* in San Francisco, and also holds true for submerged sites such as the ships in the Sacramento River. Shipwreck surveys by and for managing agencies have revealed a number of sites. The most notable work has been conducted by the National Park Service at its California units, Point Reyes National Seashore, Golden Gate National Recreation Area, and Channel Islands National Park, as well as survey work at the Malaspina Foredunes of Wrangell-St. Elias National Park in Alaska. NPS also provided survey and documentation support to California, Oregon, and Alaska, including the extensive field survey in conjunction with the U.S. Navy and others in the Aleutians at the World War II battle sites of Attu and Kiska. NOAA has conducted collaborative surveys with NPS, as well as done its own surveys. California has done the same, under the auspices of the State Lands Commission and the Department of Parks and Recreation. In British Columbia, extensive resource management surveys have been undertaken on behalf of the province, with provincial funding support, by the UASBC, and Parks Canada has conducted submerged cultural resource surveys and assessments in two British Columbia national parks: Pacific Rim (on the west coast of Vancouver Island) and Haida Gwaii (Queen Charlotte Islands). Overviews of potential sites, not yet located through surveys, have been conducted by the state of California, the National Park Service, NOAA, and the state of Washington.

One result of this work has been the listing of a number of sites in the National Register of Historic Places. National Register sites include a thematic group of Gold Rush vessels: *Apollo* (discovered in 1913 and known to exist as a buried vessel in downtown San Francisco), *Niantic, William Gray, Frolic, Tennessee, Winfield Scott, Yankee Blade* (discovered but not yet archaeologically studied), and individual sites such as *San Agustin, Isabella, Lydia, Brother Jonathan, Stamboul*, the steamer *City of Rio de Janeiro*, and the bark *Canada*. In British Columbia, a number of wrecks have been provincially designated as significant, protected sites, including *Lord Western, Beaver, Ericcson*, and *City of Ainsworth*. The site of *Beaver's* wreck is also recognized as being of exceptional national significance by the Historic Sites and Monuments Board of Canada.

Research-oriented work, as opposed to specific site-oriented or resource management-driven work, has been rare on the Pacific Coast. Research conducted to date has focused on the maritime aspects of the California Gold Rush, Pacific Coast lumber trade vessels, shore whaling, and the dynamics of site formation process and preservation of vessel remains on beaches. Gold Rush sites have provided the richest level of detail, both on vessel types, construction, and adaptations to local conditions (e.g., storeships) as well as cargo and merchandise introduced into an unusual, gold-inflated market. The most extensive research with individual sites' material culture has been Thomas Layton's work with the cargo of *Frolic*, Allen Pastron and his associates' work with the Hoff's Store collection, and Mary Smith's analysis of the *Niantic* collection. The most detailed analysis of vessel construction has been undertaken by naval architect and historian Raymond Akeron on the remains of *William Gray*, and the analysis of *LaGrange* by Stephen James, Sheli Smith, James Delgado, and Jack Hunter.

Work on shore whaling has been conducted by Ronald V. May of San Diego, focusing primarily on activities in that area. May's whaling research, if combined in the future with work on the whaling wrecks *Lydia* and *Stamboul*, and unsurveyed, unexcavated sites up the coast as far as British Columbia, will add a material dimension to the scholarship of the whaling industry and the ships and technologies employed in it.

Ultimately, research in this area may also close the file on a unique and controversial site at Palos Verdes, California. The 1975 discovery of a group of stone anchors led to a series of conclusions, debated both in the press and in scholarly circles, that they represented a Pre-Columbian Chinese shipwreck. Although the probability of such a wreck was not debated, the identification of the anchors as empirical evidence of such a wreck has been the topic of heated discussion. Alternate identifications have suggested that they are 19th-century anchors used by Chinese fishermen in California, or that they are whale carcass mooring weights employed by 19th century Portuguese shore whalers. No definitive conclusions have been reached, although the lack of any other type of remains on the site suggests that they are not evidence of a Pre-Columbian Chinese shipwreck.

Work on Pacific Coast lumber vessels was suggested by the late Karl Kortum, founding director of the San Francisco Maritime Museum, and was carried on for several years by James Delgado with the guidance of naval architect Raymond Aker. This work has examined the origins and development of locally designed and built two- and three-masted schooners, and the transition to a Pacific Coast unique type, the "steam schooner." Work on the wrecks of *Neptune, Reporter, Point Arena, Pomo, Gray's*, and *Daisy Gadsby* was most illustrative. This work was continued successfully by NPS archaeologist Matthew Russell, assisted by archaeologist Don Morris, on the beached shipwreck remains of the lumber schooner *Comet, Dora Bluhm, Jane L. Stanford*, and *J.M. Colman* at Channel Islands National Park. As a result of more than a decade of field work, a large body of information on the Pacific Coast lumber schooner is now available, making it one of the best archaeologically documented vessel types in the United States.

A number of lumber vessel wrecks were examined on beaches after they were exposed by winter storms. At times, these exposures are seasonal and the result of geomorphological processes, while at other times they are occasional, the result of exceptional winter storms. The scientific study of this type of wreck site (as compared to vessel sites) began in California in the early 1980s under the direction of James Delgado and coincided with the study of lumber-trade wrecks.

This research successfully challenged the notion that shallow water and littoral deposition shipwrecks disintegrate and are scattered into jumbles that make provenience data unnecessary because it would be meaningless. The "scatter pattern" of disintegrated wooden ships on a beach was discerned first with the *King Philip/Reporter* site, then with the 1913 *Pomo* wreck at Point Reyes National Seashore. This research included the integratation of archaeological data with an interdisciplinary assessment of wave and current patterns, beach erosion and accretion, and other natural processes. Exceptional levels of preservation of detail was also documented, first at the wreck of *King Philip* and again with another site, represented by the starboard bow of the steamer *Point Arena* (lost in 1913), which was exposed in 1983 on the beach south of San Francisco, with intact carvings, including the vessel's name, and paint.

CONCLUSION

Thanks to extensive survey work by the NPS in California and the UASBC, along with reported finds by divers and fishermen, a large number of shipwreck sites has been located, and many have been surveyed or assessed even if they have not been excavated or exhaustively documented. This is particularly true for the area surrounding the entrance to San Francisco Bay, where assessment and surveys have documented the presence of more than 150 shipwrecks with tangible material remains, and the coast and interior waters of British Columbia, with more than one hundred surveyed sites out of a probable population of 1000 shipwrecks. As study collections, all the wrecks in these areas and others have the strong potential not only to provide a means for studying vessel types or specific themes. As a collection, the wrecks also are regional economic indicators that reflect the intricacies of trade, commerce, transportation, and cultural connections both on the coast and across the Pacific. Future assessments that move beyond the detailed study of individual sites, examined in isolation and taking a broader contextual look, will ultimately yield the most significant results.

REFERENCES

Beasley, Thomas F., 1991, The *City of Ainsworth*: An ROV Analysis of a 19th Century Lake Sternwheeler. In *Underwater Archaeology Proceedings from the Society for Historical Archaeology Conference, Richmond, Virginia*, edited by John D. Broadwater. Society for Historical Archaeology, Ann Arbor.

Black, Lydia T., 1983, Record of Maritime Disasters in Russian America, Part One: 1741–1799. In *Proceedings of the Alaskan Marine Archaeology Workshop*, May 17-19, 1983 Sitka, Alaska.

Brooks, Charles Wolcott, 1964, *Japanese Wrecks Stranded and Picked Up Adrift in the North Pacific Ocean*. Ye Galleon Press, Fairfield, Washington. Reprint edition.

Bullen, Isabel, 1979, A Glimpse into the *Niantic*'s Hold. *California History* LXIII(4): Winter.

Cardone, Bonnie J., and Smith, Patrick, 1989, *Shipwrecks of Southern California*. Menasha Ridge Press, Birmingham, Alabama.

Carrell, Toni L., 1984, *Submerged Cultural Resources Inventory, Portions of Point Reyes National Seashore and Point Reyes Farallon Islands National Marine Sanctuary: Field Research results, Session 1, 1983*. National Park Service, Santa Fe.

Chace, Paul, 1988, Chinese Stone Anchors: Research Design Validation. Paper presented at the Fourteenth Annual Conference on Underwater Archaeology, 1983, Denver.

DelCioppo, Nicholas J., 1988, Protecting California's Sunken History: Senate Bill 2199. In *Underwater Archaeology Proceedings from the Society for Historical Archaeology Conference, Reno, Nevada*, edited by James P. Delgado. Society for Historical Archaeology, Ann Arbor.

Delgado, James P., 1979, No Longer a Buoyant Ship: Unearthing the Gold Rush Storeship *Niantic*. *California History* LXIII(4).

_____, 1981, What Becomes of the Old Ships? Dismantling the Gold Rush Fleet of San Francisco. *Pacific Historian* XXV(4).

_____, 1983, Underwater Archaeological Investigations of Gold Rush Era Steamships on the California Coast. In *Proceedings of the First Biennial Conference on Scientific Research in California's National Parks*. University of California (Davis) Cooperative Parks Studies Unit and National Park Service.

_____, 1983, Water Soaked and Covered with Barnacles: The Wreck of S.S. *Winfield Scott*. *Pacific Historian* XXVII(2).

_____, 1984, Shipwreck Archaeology in California: New Discoveries, New Directions. In *Proceedings of the Joint Workshop New Frontiers*. California State Park Rangers Association, Park Rangers Association of California, and Western Interpreters' Association, Santa Cruz.

_____, 1985, Skeleton in the Sand: Documentation of the Environmentally Exposed 1856 Ship *King Philip*. In *Proceedings of the Sixteenth Annual Conference on Historical Archaeology*, edited by Paul F. Johnston. Society for Historical Archaeology, Ann Arbor.

_____, 1986, Documentation and Identification of the Two Masted Schooner *Neptune*. Historical Archaeology XX.

_____, 1990, Ships Were Constantly Arriving: The Hoff Store Site and the Business of Maritime Supply and Demand in Gold Rush San Francisco. In *The Hoff Store Site and Gold Rush Merchandise from San Francisco, California*, edited by Allen G. Pastron and Eugene M. Hattori. Society for Historical Archaeology, Ann Arbor.

_____, 1990, *To California by Sea: A Maritime History of the Gold Rush*. University of South Carolina Press, Columbia.

_____, 1993, *The* Beaver: *First Steamer on the West Coast*. Horsdal and Schubart, Victoria, British Columbia.

_____, 1994, The Wreck of the *SS Tennessee*. Journal of the West XXXIII(4).

_____, 1995, The Brig *Isabella*: A Hudson's Bay Company Shipwreck of 1830. *American Neptune* LV(4):

_____, editor, 1998, *Encyclopedia of Maritime and Underwater Archaeology*. Yale University Press, New Haven.

Delgado, James P., and Haller, Stephen A., 1989, *Submerged Cultural Resources Assessment: Golden Gate National Recreation Area, Point Reyes National Seashore, and Gulf of the Farallones National Maritime Sanctuary*. National Park Service, Washington, D.C.

_____, 1989, *Shipwrecks at the Golden Gate*. Lexicos, San Francisco.

Delgado, James P., Murphy Larry E., and Kelly, Roger E., 1984, Shipwreck Survey of a Portion of Ocean Beach, San Francisco, for the Revenue Cutter *C.W. Lawrence*. National Park Service, San Francisco.

Foster, John W., 1984, Schooners, Steamers and Spilled Cargo: A Preliminary Underwater Survey of Fort Ross Cove. In *Underwater Archaeology: Proceedings of the 13th Conference on Underwater Archaeology*, edited by Donald H. Keith. Fathom Eight, San Marino.

Frost, Frank J., 1982, The Palos Verdes Chinese Anchor Mystery. *Archaeology* XXXV(1).

Gearhart II, Robert L., 1988, *Cultural Resources Magnetometer Survey and Testing Great Highway/Ocean Beach Seawall Project, San Francisco, California*. Espey, Huston & Associates, Inc., Austin.

Gibbs Jr., James A., 1950, Pacific Graveyard. Binfords & Mort, Portland.

_____, 1957, *Shipwrecks of the Pacific Coast*. Binfords & Mort, Portland.

_____, 1968, *Shipwrecks off Juan de Fuca*. Binfords & Mort, Portland.

_____, 1981, *Disaster Log of Ships: A Pictorial Account of Shipwrecks, California to Alaska*. Bonanza Books, New York.

_____, 1986, *Peril at Sea: A Photographic Study of Shipwrecks in the Pacific*. Schiffer Publishing, Ltd., West Chester.

Grant, David, Denfield, Colt, and Schalk, Randall, 1996, *U.S. Naval Shipwrecks and Submerged Aircraft in Washington: An Overview*. International Archaeological Research Institute, Seattle.

Hanable, William S., 1983, Sources for Alaska Shipwreck Research after 1867. In *Proceedings of the Alaskan Marine Archaeology Workshop*, May 17–19, 1983, Sitka, Atlaska.

James Jr., Stephen R., 1984, *Spatial Limits of Two Historic Shipwrecks: J Street Area, Sacramento, California*. Espey, Huston & Associates, Inc., Austin.

_____, 1986, *Submerged Cultural Resources Survey, Sacramento Embarcadero, Sacramento, California*. Espey, Huston & Associates, Inc., Austin.

_____, 1986a, *Underwater Archaeological Investigations, "Docks Area," Sacramento, California*. Espey, Huston & Associates, Inc., Austin.

_____, 1987, The Barks *LaGrange* and *Ninus*: Two Recent Additions to the Growing Number of Gold Rush Era Shipwreck Sites. In *Underwater Archaeology Proceedings from the Society for Historical Archaeology Conference, Savannah, Georgia*, edited by Alan B. Albright. Society for Historical Archaeology, Ann Arbor.

Layton, Thomas N., 1997, *Drug Runner: The Story of the Brig Frolic*. Stanford University Press, Palo Alto.

McKay, John, Leonard McCann, and James P. Delgado, 2001, *The Hudson's Bay Company's 1835 Steam Ship Bearer*. Vonwell Publishing Co. Ltd., Toronto.

Marc, Jacques F., 1988, *A Report on the Sydney Inlet Mystery Wreck*. Underwater Archaeological Society of British Columbia, Vancouver.

_____, 1989, *Exploring the Lord Western*. Underwater Archaeological Society of British Columbia, Vancouver.

_____, 1990, *Historic Shipwrecks of Southern Vancouver Island*. Underwater Archaeological Society of British Columbia, Vancouver.

_____, 1997, *The Underwater Heritage of Friendly Cove: Results of a Submerged Cultural Resources Study Completed in 1994*. Underwater Archaeological Society of British Columbia, Vancouver.

Marshall, Don, 1984, *Oregon Shipwrecks*. Binfords & Mort, Portland.

_____, 1978, *California Shipwrecks: Footsteps in the Sea*. Superior Publishing Company, Seattle.

McCaslin, D.E. and Orzech, J.L., 1988, Romancing the Stones: The Worked Stone Objects off the Palos Verdes Peninsula, Los Angeles, California. *In Archaeology in Solution*, edited by John W. Foster and Sheli O. Smith. Coyote Press, Salinas.

Mauger, Jeffrey E., and Wessen, Gary, 1983, Submerged Archaeological Resources in the Continental Shelf of Northwestern North America. In *Proceedings of the Alaskan Marine Archaeology Workshop*, May 17–19, 1983, Sitka, Alaska.

May, Ronald V., 1990, Discovery at the Ballast Point Whaling Station: Archaeological Exposure of a Tryworks Oven in California. In *Underwater Archaeology Proceedings from the Society for Historical Archaeology Conference, Tucson, Arizona*, edited by Toni L. Carrell. Society for Historical Archaeology, Ann Arbor.

_____, 1985, Schooner, Sloops, and Ancient Mariners: Research Implications of Shore Whaling in San Diego. *Pacific Coast Archaeological Society Quarterly XXI* (4).

_____, 1988, Schooners, Sloops and Devil Fish: Research Implications at 19th Century Shire Whaling Stations. In *Archaeology in Solution*, edited by John W. Foster and Sheli O. Smith. Coyote Press, Salinas.

Morris, Don P., and Lima, James, 1996, *Channel Islands National Park and Channel Islands National Marine Sanctuary Submerged Cultural Resources Assessment*. National Park Service, Santa Fe.

Murphy, Larry, editor, 1984, *Shipwreck Survey of a Portion of Point Reyes National Seashore and Point Reyes/Farallone Islands National Marine Sanctuary, California*. Unpublished manuscript.

Newell, Gordon R., 1955, *SOS North Pacific*. Binfords & Mort, Portland.

Nordby, Larry V., 1988, *Modelling Isabella: Behavioral Linkages Between Submerged and Terrestrial Sites. In Underwater Archaeology Proceedings from the Society for Historical Archaeology Conference, Reno, Nevada, 1988*, edited by James P. Delgado. Society for Historical Archaeology, Ann Arbor.

Olmsted, Roger, Olmsted, Nancy, and Pastron, Allen, 1977, *San Francisco Waterfront: Report on Historical Cultural Resources*. Wastewater Management Program, San Francisco.

Pastron, Allen G., and Pritchett, Jack, 1981, *Behind the Seawall: Historical Archaeology along the San Francisco Waterfront*. 3 Vols. Wastewater Management Program, San Francisco.

Pastron, Allen G., and Delgado, James P., 1991, Archaeological Investigations at a Mid-19th Century Shipbreaking Yard, San Francisco, California. *Historical Archaeology XXV*(2).

Pierce, Richard A., 1983, Record of maritime disasters in Russian America, Part two: 1800–1867. In *Proceedings of the Alaskan Mariner Archaeology Workshop*, May 17–19, 1983, Sitka, Alaska.

Pierson, Larry J., and Moriarty, James R., 1980, Stone Anchors: Asiatic Shipwrecks off the California Coast. *Anthropological Journal of Canada* XVIII.

_____, 1981, New Evidence of Asiatic Shipwrecks off the California Coast. In *Underwater Archaeology: The Challenge Before Us: Proceedings of the Twelfth Conference on Underwater Archaeology*, edited by Gordon P. Watts Jr., Fathom Eight, Inc., San Marino.

Robertson, Thomas Herrick, and Mertz, Douglas K., 1983, The Alaska Historic Preservation Act and Submerged Cultural Resources. In *Proceedings of the Alaskan Marine Archaeology Workshop*, May 17–19, Sitka, Alaska.

Schwartz, Steven J., 1989, Evaluation and Documentation of the Steam Propulsion System of the Wrecked Ferryboat Sierra Nevada. In *Underwater Archaeology Proceedings from the Society for Historical Archaeology Conference*, Baltimore, Maryland, edited by J. Barto Arnold III. Society for Historical Archaeology, Ann Arbor.

Self, Associates, William, 1996, *Historic Archaeology of the Muni Metro Turnback project, San Francisco, California*. 3 Vols. William Self Associates, Orinda, California.

Smith, Mary Hilderman, 1981, *An Interpretive Study of the Collection Recovered from the Storeship* Niantic. M.A. thesis, San Francisco State University, California.

Smith, Sheli O., James Jr., Stephen R., Delgado, James P., Hunter, Jack, and Reed, Monica, 1988, LaGrange: *A California Gold Rush Legacy*. Underwater Archaeological Consortium, Sacramento.

Stickel, Gary E., 1983, The Mystery of the Prehistoric Chinese Anchors: Toward Research designs for Underwater Archaeology. In *Shipwreck Anthropology*, edited by Richard Gould. University of New Mexico Press, Albuquerque.

Stone, David Leigh, 1994, Vancouver's Underwater Heritage: Shipwrecks and Submerged Cultural Sites. In *Burrard Inlet and Howe Sound*. Underwater Archaeological Society of British Columbia, Vancouver.

Tornfelt, Evert E., and Burwell, Michael, 1992, *Shipwrecks of the Alaska Shelf and Shore*. Minerals Management Service, Anchorage.

Wells, R.E., 1984, *A Guide to Shipwrecks Cape Beale to Cox Point Including Barkley Sound*. Morriss Printing Company, Victoria.

_____, 1989, *A Guide to Shipwreck Sites along the Washington Coast*. Morriss Printing Company, Victoria.

Chapter 16

Underwater Archaeology, Hawaiian Style

HANS VAN TILBURG

INTRODUCTION

It would be hard to imagine a spot on the globe more intimately involved with maritime history and associated technologies than the islands of Hawaii. From their original discovery and settlement by voyaging Polynesians, their importance in the sandalwood and whaling trades, and the more recent remains left behind by World War II in the Pacific, the Hawaiian Island chain has accumulated a material record of at least 1500 years of maritime activity. Of course, much has decayed, turned into reef through biological processes, floated away, or otherwise smashed against solid rock cliffs and broken into unrecognizable pieces. What remains of the submerged material record testifies to Hawaii's uniquely diverse maritime traditions. The investigation of this record is relatively new but, most assuredly, there is more than just surfing in the islands of Hawaii.

BACKGROUND

The Hawaiian islands are approximately 2400 miles from the North American west coast, 3800 miles from Japan, 4300 miles from Papua New Guinea, and surrounded by the Pacific

Hans Van Tilburg, Marine Option Program, University of Hawaii at Manoa, Hawaii 96822.

International Handbook of Underwater Archaeology, edited by Carol V. Ruppé and Janet F. Barstad. Kluwer Academic/Plenum Publishers, New York, 2002.

ocean, which occupies a one third of the planet's total surface area. Eight main islands, all volcanic in nature, are most familiar to visitors: Niihau, Kauai, Oahu, Maui, Lanai, Molokai, Kahoolawe, and Hawaii, all occupying a stretch of ocean some 300 miles long. The extended Hawaiian Archipelago stretches some 1200 miles further northwest and includes the lower atolls and islands of Kaula, Nihoa, Necker, French Frigate shoals, Gardner Pinnacles, Laysan, Lisianski, Pearl and Hermes reef, Midway, and Kure (Ocean Island).

Prevailing trade winds from the northeast can raise large ocean swells, and since the Hawaiian islands have no continental shelf, coastlines are often high-energy environments bordered by volcanic rocks and cliffs. Waves generated from distant disturbances crash against all shores of the islands, breaking apart many shallow wreck sites. While coral substrate does not present much interference to magnetometer surveys, the iron content in basaltic lava flows introduces additional signals. Clear, warm water adds to the attraction of working (and playing) in the ocean, but large swells and strong currents in the channels between the islands can present challenges. Hawaiian island shores are a high-energy environment with few natural, consistently sheltered coves or anchorages.

As is common with many locations, most historical and archaeological work in the past has focused on terrestrial material. Only in more recent years has underwater investigation earned more general attention, somewhat surprising given the diversity of submerged cultural resources and the numerous and popular diving sites found throughout the islands. The University of Hawaii's Marine Option Program (MOP) became the first local institution to pioneer scientific investigation of coastal and underwater cultural remains beginning in 1989, and it is still the only institution dedicated to nautical archaeology in the islands. A relatively small program within the School of Ocean and Earth Science and Technology, the nautical archaeology program is currently training a pool of local maritime talent, chiefly through a graduate certificate course in maritime archaeology and history. This chapter is an informal summary of maritime archaeology in Hawaii's past, followed by an outline of the marinetime program's development at the University of Hawaii to the present day. Detailed information of the two most well-known projects, work at Pearl Harbor and at Hanalei Bay in Kauai, has been published in other sources and will be presented here only in outline form (Lenihan, 1989; Johnston, 1988).

PREHISTORY AND HISTORY, PROJECTS AND POTENTIAL

Early Navigation

Sometime between 0 and A.D. 500 (rough dating that remains the subject of continuing debate), the first of many seagoing canoes from the South Pacific (Figure 16.1) encountered the uninhabited islands of Hawaii (Finney, 1994). What followed was a long period of intentional two-way communication between Hawaii in the North Pacific and the original point of departure in either or both the Marquesas and the Society Island area (Tahiti) in the South Pacific, trips of more than 2250 nautical miles. Marquesan-style stone adzes, recovered from underwater locations in the Hawaiian islands, have played a large part in formulating the voyaging chronology.

For westerners, such navigational accomplishment was initially hard to accept and in the mid-1960s led to a debate of intentional voyaging versus accidental voyaging. Subsequent archaeological discoveries revealed more about the complex process of

Figure 16.1. Polynesian voyaging canoes (source: Illustration by Joseph Feber. Photo courtesy of the Bishop Museum)

colonization and importation of changing cultural practices as well as tools, hunting and fishing implements, dogs, pigs, chickens, coconuts, taro, and other basic elements of survival that made settlement possible. Current theories now are more in accord with the oral traditions Hawaiians have always held as fact, that their Polynesian ancestors were extremely skilled navigators, quite capable of building suitable vessels and making long-distance voyages (Figure 16.1). These voyages most likely went from southeast Asia eastward into the Pacific, against the equatorial easterly winds that shift seasonally to the northwest. Virtually all habitable islands of the Pacific had been discovered and settled long before Europeans made their way across the relatively narrow Atlantic Ocean, let alone into the Pacific.

Physical remains of such voyaging canoes are extremely rare. To date, there are no known elements of ocean-going voyaging canoes from any underwater site. Outrigger or double-hulled canoes with no need for ballast simply don't seem to sink very often. The most likely areas for such finds include swamps and ancient occupation sites on land, long since filled with mud. The best known terrestrial site was discovered by Yosihiko Sinoto, chairman of the Anthropology Department of Hawaii's Bernice P. Bishop Museum. In the early 1970s, Sinoto uncovered a canoe production site in French Polynesia. Excavations were initiated by the construction of Hotel Bali Hai on the small island of Huahine, 110 mi northwest of Tahiti (Te Rangi Hiroa, 1964). The partially waterlogged site contained shell, bone, wooden artifacts, and stone tools. Inundated by a tsunami, everything had been quickly covered by a thick layer of sand and silt and preserved in wet-site conditions for hundreds of years. The most critical discoveries relevant to Hawaii were a large wooden steering paddle, an outrigger boom, and two wooden canoe planks 23 long, found in 1977. Such boards would have been upper splash-boards for the bow section of a canoe under construction. These were apparently meant for a large double-hulled sailing canoe. Though found in French Polynesia, these remains helped shape the direction of experimental archaeology and the revival of voyaging culture in Hawaii.

Such evidence for the truly large size of ancient vessels, as well as contemporary examples and academic investigation into the sailing qualities of Pacific vessels, led to the first traditional voyaging canoe replica, *Hokulea*, launched in Hawaii in 1974 (Finney, 1994).

Modern Replicas of Sailing Canoes. Though it is not strictly underwater archaeology, voyaging is so significant in Hawaii that it deserves special mention. Using nontraditional materials, Ben Finney of the University of Hawaii, Herb Kane, and Tommy Holmes led the movement to create a performance-accurate replica of a sailing canoe for the investigation of sailing characteristics to further the study of the oceanic migration of the ancestors of the Polynesians. Since then, the experimental archaeology of voyaging-canoe construction has blossomed throughout the island Pacific, tied closely to a transpacific cultural revival surrounding not just the physical form of the *vaka* or sailing canoe, but also around the social organization of a voyaging society and the continuing transmission of traditional navigating techniques. The Polynesian Voyaging Society, formed in 1973, successfully makes the connection between experimental archaeology, cultural revival, and popular education.

Hokulea was followed in 1994 by another replica of a traditional voyaging canoe, *Hawaiiloa*, a vessel carved from the solid trunks of enormous trees. Both are now two of more than 20 ocean-going voyaging canoes throughout the Pacific Islands, still making traditional long-distance, round-trip journeys, relying on the ancient skills of their navigators, i.e., without charts, modern directional aids, or satellite navigation (Finney, 1994). In the past, the Festival of the Pacific Arts, sponsored by South Pacific Forum, has focused on voyaging themes, and it continues to provide an opportunity for various traditional canoes and cultures of Hawaiians, Maoris, Tahitians, Cook Islanders, and Marshallese to assemble. Experimental maritime archaeology has thus been transformed in Hawaii and other Pacific islands, becoming again long-distance ocean voyaging in true traditional style and leading to an increased awareness of all types of maritime cultural resources. The significance of these journeys goes beyond the academic discipline, for the vessels, voyages, and sailors are a proud revival of an ancient Pacific lifestyle. The canoes themselves are symbols of this reawakening (Jonassen, 1994).

Fish Ponds and Fish Traps

Actual remains of original voyaging canoes are scarce, although for hundreds of years the Hawaiians lived in close relation to the sea (Figure 16.2), and the cultural resources associated with this lifestyle are still much in evidence throughout the main islands. Structures such as seawalls for fish ponds, tools, and fishing implements speak of an advanced maritime culture and a sustainable form of food production. Today, of course, most of the necessities of life are shipped to Hawaii from any number of distant locations.

Stone walls for fish ponds and fish traps once were prominent features in the Hawaiian landscape. Prior to Western contact, there may have been between 400–500 stone fish ponds in the Hawaiian islands, producing around two million pounds of fish annually (Joseph Farber, personal communication, February 11, 1997; Kelly, 1975). Today only a handful of ponds are in condition to produce some fish. Stone canoe houses and canoe launching ramps also can be found in certain locations. Such lithic remains can endure hundreds of years in relatively good shape. MOP maritime archaeology students mapped a stone fish trap at Koloko Honokahau National Park on the Big Island during the 1997 field school, and found compartments that seemed to be traps or holding areas surrounded by a larger seawall; more research will help determine the presence or absence of a traditional gate or *makaha*. Such structures are examples of an advanced and efficient food production system. If restoration is to take place, accurate surveys should be completed before the sites are altered further.

Temples

While terrestrial *heiau* (temples) have been investigated, possible submerged *heiau* and other structures may represent an almost untouched cultural resource. One university

Figure 16.2. "A Canoe of the Sandwich Islands ... " (SOURCE: Engraving by Grignon after a drawing by John Webber, 1784. Photo courtesy of Bishop Museum).

researcher is studying Hawaiian oral histories and chants in an effort to locate further underwater sites (Tom Stone, personal communication, August 27, 1998).

Understanding the cultural significance of such places can be quite challenging to the traditionally trained researcher. In Hawaiian culture, as in other Pacific cultures, the land itself possesses a special connection with the remembered history of the ancestors; sites are a direct link to historical genealogies and events. This cultural difference adds a layer of significance to, and demands a greater sensitivity from, what in the past has often been a strictly Western interpretation of artifacts (Hviding, 1996).

Artifacts

Shell fishhooks and scattered basalt artifacts such as octopus-lure weights, fishtrap weights, and canoe anchors are abundant on specific sites near shore reefs, even in developed areas on the island of Oahu near Honolulu. In 1996, MOP's field school focused on one such site: a scattered collection of lithic artifacts, sinkers, and octopus lures directly off the Waikiki shoreline. Michael Pfeffer, a Ph.D. candidate in anthropology at the University of Washington, hypothesized that near-shore raised reefs, with their greater density of marine life, would identify a greater density of fishing artifacts, which seems to be the case (Pfeffer, 1995). Distribution patterns were recorded, though the artifacts themselves had been weathered by hundreds of years in the near-surf zone (students had a first-hand experience in site formation processes when a strong surge rocked the shallow site; 16-ft waves temporarily postponed field operations). Care must be taken in this line of research, for other sources of basalt, such as dredging and beach enrichment, cannot be completely ruled out. This research also involves the relationship of fishing sites to navigational markers on shore and the distribution of marine resources.

Other artifact locations may be more random in nature. Near Kualoa, on the windward side of Oahu, such artifacts are being eroded out of the river bank and deposited onto the seabed. At least 14 other submerged locations, where prehistoric artifacts have been recovered from the surface of the seabed around the islands (mainly on Oahu and Maui), reflect the greater popularity and easier access for swimmers and divers there (Yosihiko Sinoto, personal communication, August 1998). Shell and bone fishhooks also have been recovered in other locations. Yosihiko Sinoto, Ph.D. has spent years creating a Polynesian fishhook chronology, an important tool for dating sites given the scarcity of ceramic remains in the Pacific. Currently, many traditional Hawaiian fishing sites, where both lithic remains and bone and shell artifacts can be found, are threatened by modern shoreline development. Many traditional fish ponds (an extremely efficient method of nurturing and gathering protein) have been lost to siltation or landfill, though there has been some effort to restore such marine systems to their original operating state on both Oahu and Molokai islands (Farber, 1997). As is often the case, nautical archaeology remains an important tool for locating, investigating, and protecting these culturally significant coastal and underwater sites.

European Contact

By the late 18th century, the time of Captain Cook's third voyage into the Pacific and first substantiated European contact with the islands, Hawaiian voyaging canoes had long since ceased to make regular passages to the South Pacific. Cook encountered an advanced maritime society existing in isolation. Whether he was actually the first European to make contact with the Hawaiians, or whether a stray Spanish galleon making one of the many annual Pacific crossings between New Spain and Manila had first sighted and perhaps even wrecked on the Hawaiian islands, remains a matter of some contention. Areas of Kealakekua Bay, which some feel may contain traces of a Spanish shipwreck, were surveyed in 1997 during remote sensing training by MOP students. This information is currently being processed and interpreted. It is not unfeasible that Japanese or Chinese ships, perhaps disabled and adrift on the currents, may have made early contact with the Hawaiian islands. Documents record disabled junks making exactly this type of landfall in historic times and survivors of several disabled junks being rescued in near-island waters: In 1832, a Japanese junk wrecked on Oahu's north shore, an event covered by local newspapers (Connell, 1933). Nautical archaeology may be the only method to pursue such questions of early outside contact.

For many reasons, Cook's 1779 encounter and death at Kealakekua Bay on the island of Hawaii remain etched in European narratives as a turning point in the island's maritime history. Archaeological investigation in Kealakekua Bay has begun only recently. A small handful of objects associated with 18th-century European encounters are stored at Kona Historical Society. Students in the MOP's 1997 summer maritime archaeology field course conducted a magnetometer survey of a significant portion of the inner bay, and a diving survey of the inshore perimeter but discovered only traditional Hawaiian stone artifacts, as well as more contemporary remains such as 19th- and 20th-century anchors and railroad tracks. They also located several anomalous magnetic targets in the bay for future investigation, and historic and prehistoric cultural materials from a variety of sources along the shore.

No distinct cultural line existed between what was traditionally Hawaiian and what was imported from the West; each style existed and adapted to the other. Western ships did begin to introduce changes in the Hawaiian maritime scene. At first, few European vessels actually reached Hawaii; yet their uses, especially in war, soon became apparent. Kamehameha I, a chief from the island of Hawaii, was the first to unify the Hawaiian islands into one kingdom in the first years of the 19th century. Swivel guns and cannon, as well as a captured vessel, *Fair American*, contributed to his military campaign at sea and on land. Following the successful unification, Kamehameha I promoted the purchase and construction of western-style vessels, until there were more than 30 western ships in his inventory (Kuykendall, 1938). The discovery of the profitability of sandalwood, one of the few commodities accepted in exchange at Canton, had granted the *alii* (chiefs) increased purchasing power. Topsail schooners and brigs, some in advanced stages of rot, went immediately into the interisland trade, and some were outfitted by Hawaiians for trading ventures to China or the South Pacific (Kuykendall, 1938). Many were lost around the islands, grounding onto reefs.

The maritime scene in Hawaii quickly became culturally mixed, as Hawaiian men found employment on board European vessels, as Western ships purchased by Hawaiians sailed between islands, and as missionaries, whalers, and sandalwood hunters increasingly altered local society (Chappell, 1997). David Chappell, Ph.D. history professor at University of Hawaii, refers to this period as a "second diaspora": renewed Hawaiian travel throughout the Pacific on European ships (the first diaspora consists of the initial discovery by Polynesians, the third of modern migrations on airliners). At one point, Hawaiian and other Polynesian sailors comprised a-fifth of the American whaling fleet. Some local researchers suggest that there are at least 33 Western shipwrecks on the Big Island alone (Rick Rogers, Sandwich Island Shipwreck Museum, personal communication, August, 19, 1998). Archaeologists might expect the physical record of these wrecks to reflect these dynamic social changes. This is exactly the case.

In 1995, Paul F. Johnston, curator of maritime history at Smithsonian Institution's National Museum of American History in Washington, D.C., began his first season of survey work in Kauai's Hanalei Bay, searching for the remains of *Cleopatra's Barge*, an American hermaphrodite brig built as a luxury yacht by George Crowninshield Jr. at Salem, Massachusetts in 1816. The ship, 100 ft long on deck and lavishly fitted out, was eventually sold to Kamehameha II in 1820 for 8000 piculs of sandalwood and renamed *Haàheo o Hawaii*, or *Pride of Hawaii*. As often happened, the brig soon went into interisland service, conducting the royal court between locations in the kingdom. Members of the Sandwich Island Shipwreck Museum and Steve James of Panamerican Maritime Ltd., based in Memphis, Tennessee, assisted Dr. Johnston in his search and subsequent excavations. A magnetometer survey located a promising area close inshore, where test trenches confirmed the contemporary historical account of the presence of the wreck by Boston missionary Hiram Bingham. Hydraulic removal of the sand overburden preceded the recovery of remains. After four seasons, collected artifacts portray a Pacific–Western mixed culture on board (Paul Johnston, personal communication, July 23, 1998). Dr. Johnston has published a series of reports on *Pride of Hawaii* in the *Underwater Archaeology* series of the Society for Historical Archaeology.

Common goods of French, British, and Chinese origin, as well as local Hawaiian stone, bone, shell and gourd artifacts and what may be the King's royal *puu* (conch-shell trumpet) are currently undergoing conservation at the Smithsonian Institution in Washington D.C., and Texas A&M University in Austin; all will be returned to the state of Hawaii following conservation.

Exactly why *Haàheo* struck the reef is unclear, although, according to project members, the ship may have been sunk by natives on Kauai in retaliation for the forced removal of their king, Kaumualii, to Oahu (Paul Johnston, personal communication). Contemporary accounts of Reverend Bingham and others attribute the loss of the storied yacht to alcoholic spirits, the presence of which is confirmed in the archaeological record (Paul Johnston, personal communication).

Dr. Johnston's *Haàheo* project adds an important multicultural dimension to traditionally one-sided maritime studies, giving a special Hawaiian significance to these 170-year-distant events. Often the history made available by maritime archaeology cannot be claimed solely by any single national entity. Ever since Hawaii's initial encounter with Europeans, such culturally mixed phenomena have become a hallmark of the islands. Pacific, Asian, and Western cultures continue to coexist in uniquely cooperative style in Hawaii.

Johnston's work represents the first full-scale maritime archaeology excavation in the islands (so far, there have been no applications for any commercial shipwreck excavations). Consequently, bureaucratic processes proved to be a learning experience for various state institutions and no easy task for Johnston. His experience is an example of what happens when various state and federal regulatory agencies are brought into unfamiliar terrain, precisely the situation in Hawaii.

Land development in Hawaii takes up most of the State Historic Preservation Office's resources, with little left over for investigation of what are seen as lower priority underwater sites. The question here really deals with the implementation of the federal Abandoned Shipwreck Act at the state level, which has yet to be perfected in Hawaii. The permitting process for small-scale archaeological work in Hanalei Bay was identical to that faced by large commercial developers, since there was no other model for such a new project. The survey alone involved six separate permits: Army Corps of Engineers, Coastal Zone Management, Department of Health Clean Water Board, Department of Land and Natural Resources Master Permit CDUA (Conservation District Use Application), the U.S. Coast Guard, and a "non-permit" from the office of Conservation and Environmental Affairs, Kauai County. Ultimately, some 26 state and federal agencies were involved in the project review (Johnston, 1994). Each office had to be approached separately in the permit application process.

Other considerations about state procedures for granting survey and excavation rights are relatively familiar: The principal investigator must have at least a master's degree in archaeology; a full description/research plan must be submitted for review; a commitment must be made to complete a full inventory survey report; and an agreement must be reached on curation of objects recovered, with the encouragement for these to be returned to the islands (there are no conservation facilities for marine cultural objects on the islands... yet). It is hoped that this process will become more streamlined in the future.

Whalers

The importance of the Hawaiian islands to whalers needs no special emphasis (Langdon, 1978). Pacific whaling grounds became more and more dominated by American vessels in the mid-19th century. There is not much indication that Hawaiians took whales at sea, though beached whales provided important resources. Soon after the crew of *Balaena* and *Equator* harpooned the first whales off the coast of Maui in 1819, Hawaii won its place on the maps of whale ships. Grog shops and brothels soon made their appearance in

Honolulu on the island of Oahu, and in Lahaina on the island of Maui. Some of Hawaii's present residents can trace their lineage to a deserter from a whaling ship. Lahaina, once known as "one of the breathing holes of hell," now hosts a whaling museum, though no underwater survey of the anchorage there has yet been completed. Hawaii's Maritime Center on Oahu also features a whaling exhibit at the museum: the trypots, whaleboats and implements of a truly global industrial pursuit. Offshore of Honolulu harbor are the remains of brickworks from a yet to be identified whaler, the bricks broken apart following a successful voyage. Local researchers allude to 18 other documented wrecks of whalers in and around the Hawaiian island chain (Rick Rogers, personal communication, August 15, 1998).

Additionally, the burned remains of *Harvest*, a whaler of Hawaiian registry, along with three other ships, have been tentatively located on Pohnpei in the Caroline Islands of Micronesia (Carrell, 1991). In 1865, the four vessels were burned and sunk by CSS *Shenandoah*, the infamous Confederate raider that captured more than 37 prizes in the Pacific during and after the American Civil War. Suzanne Finney, of the Marine Option Program, has received funding for a reconnaissance survey of the whalers in Pohnpei. Ironically, while local Hawaiian museums display whaling-era artifacts, there has been little emphasis on underwater survey for any other remains in nearby historic Hawaiian whaling ports.

Vessels of every description making the long passage across the Pacific, perhaps bound for the rich trading port of Canton, found it expedient to call on Hawaii. The fur trade really got underway in the 1780s (Gibson, 1992). Boston traders, circumnavigating the globe in search of profits, often traded guns and liquor for seal skins, salmon, and lumber from the Pacific Northwest.

Russian explorers competed for the same kinds of resources in the North Pacific and also laid claim to a share of the islands, albeit for a brief period. In 1816, three Russian forts were constructed on the island of Kauai; the remains of two can still be seen. In 1993 and 1994, James Allen, nautical archaeologist and director of the Western Institute of Nautical Archaeology at the University of California, Berkeley, participated in a visual survey for the rudder and associated remains of a Russian vessel wrecked at Fort Elizabeth off the Waimea River. Historic accounts describe the loss of a cannon. Unfortunately, no magnetometer was available for survey. Researchers did inspect a bronze pintle and gudgeon recovered earlier, estimating their age to the 18th or 19th century (Jim Allen, personal communication, August 2, 1998).

Iron Ships

At the turn of the century, what had been a sailing trade between the islands became the domain of iron ships and steam navigation. Companies such as Wilder Steam Navigation Company and the Hawaiian Inter Island Steam Navigation Company operated many locally well-known and well-loved vessels in the cargo and passenger trades in the early decades of the 20th century (Figure 16.3). Sugar and cattle were major concerns in Hawaii, and steamers often were required to moor in small, exposed ports near hazardous reefs. Some 60 sugar mills were scattered around five main islands in 1884, serviced by dozens of small private landings (Mifflin, 1983). The MOP has recorded two such sites. SS *Kauai*, lost at Mahukona Port in 1913, has long been a popular dive and snorkeling destination. The wooden-hulled ship went onto the reef while carrying railroad parts and bags of sugar between islands. Remains of the steamer (boiler, engine, propeller,

Figure 16.3. Inter Island Steam Navigation Co. ship and fishermen laying nets, Kailua-Kona, 1924 (SOURCE: Photo by R.J. Bakery, courtesy of Bishop Museum).

scattered cargo) and the ruins of the port itself combine to record a major era of Hawaii's economic and social development, particularly since the days of Hawaii's commercial sugar industry have ended. Recent storms have since swept the boiler ashore and destroyed the old government wharf at Mahukona.

SS *Maui*, an iron-hulled wreck located further south on the Kona coast of the island of Hawaii, was also employed in the sugar industry when it broke its back on the lava reef in 1917. Built in 1898 by Union Iron Works of San Francisco, its triple-expansion steam engine, boiler, hull plates, and stern section remain scattered atop an underwater lava field. Plans are in the works for a more thorough investigation of the ship's extensive remains, a vessel that was once such an integral part of life among the islands. Remains of other landings and associated shipwrecks tell the same story of this once-prevalent industry. MOP has begun a long-term inventory project for these locations, the first of its kind for Hawaii. In 1999, field school students documented the remains of the 19th century Waiminalo Plantation landing on Oahu. The 2001 field school took place on Shipwreck Beach, Hawaii's "rotten row" for interisland vessels.

Sampans

Just as anthropologists and historians become more aware of non-Western perspectives, nautical archaeologists, too, must appreciate a more complex world. Not all cultural influence came from the West: As new visitors to Hawaii quickly discover, Asians have made up a significant proportion of the islands' population for a long while. For maritime historians and nautical archaeologists, this cultural influence takes the form of a unique style of fishing vessel known today as the Hawaiian sampan, celebrated locally in restaurants, on cocktail napkins, in books and on film.

In fact, the origins of the Hawaiian sampan are purely Japanese. In 1899, a Japanese fishing craft was imported to Hawaii on the deck of a steamer by Gorokichi Nakasugi (Bowman, 1973). Such fishing boats retained features of ancient Yamato-gata-style vessels as recorded in a study by Basil Greenhill (Greenhill, 1995). Mr. Nakasugi, a fisherman and shipwright, was soon employed in the *aku* (tuna) fishing industry, and design elements of Japanese fishing vessels were thus imported "across the beach," as it were, to Hawaii.

Eastern and Western construction methods truly blended in the small boatyards on Oahu, Maui, and the Big Island. Such vessels continued to be built by Japanese shipwrights in Hawaii throughout the 1920s and 1930s, the same shipwrights who repaired many Western vessels visiting from the mainland (Nakashima, 1934). Diesel engines and prominent deckhouses replaced the traditional square sail of Japanese design. Prior to World War II, there were hundreds of large and small sampans throughout the islands. Sometimes students were sent to Japan to study traditional ship construction, then returned to their homes in Hawaii. Today, the remains of these far-ranging vessels might be found anywhere in the long Hawaiian island chain, stretching from the main Hawaiian islands to the northwest.

In the years before World War II, Americans, especially the U.S. Navy, became increasingly suspicious of sampans and their operations. Such feelings reflected the growing apprehension about Pacific relations with Japan. United States Customs officials seized many sampans after discovering some of the domestic fleet were operated by Japanese nationals. The U.S. Navy, facing a critical shortage of boats, purchased many sampans, which were outfitted for harbor salvage and inshore patrol duty. Many were operated by the U.S. Coast Guard during the war years. After 1945, however, the Japanese tuna fishing industry never recovered its prewar levels, and today only a handful of wooden pre-war sampans are left in operation (Chenoweth, 1990). These can still be seen motoring in and out of Kewalo Basin—oil-stained, paint-flaking workhorses in a continual state of fly-by-night repair, crewed by Korean, Micronesian, and local Hawaiian fishermen, and not without their own kind of dogged, salt-laden charm.

Wreckage on reefs, beaches, and lava flows throughout the islands marks the final resting spots of these unique vessels, sampans endemic to the Hawaiian islands. Students from the University of Hawaii's Marine Option Program documented one such wreck site, the remains of *Fuji Maru*, aka YP-183, at Mahuiala Bay on the Kona Coast. Built by Japanese shipwrights and operated in the tuna industry, it was purchased by the U.S. Navy before World War II and was eventually lost in a storm. Portions of its deck lie scattered on a lava flow, while the engine and fuel tanks remain underwater.

Another locally-famous sampan, *Bluefin*, which even appeared in Elvis Presley's 1962 movie "Girls! Girls! Girls!", was a candidate for official preservation. Unfortunately, due to a lack of funds, only her stern now resides at the Hawaiian Maritime Center museum. Many other such locations, such as Lanai's shipwreck beach, harbor the remains of these once-popular yet underdocumented craft, a favorite with islanders and a symbol of prewar days in Hawaii. As a class of vessels, the sampans are unique, associated with the origins of commercial fishing in Hawaii as well as World War II.

World War II

Although the events of December 7, 1941, have been relatively well-documented, with few exceptions almost no underwater survey has been done in Hawaii on submerged World War II cultural resources. Only slowly are the state and the military becoming more cognizant of underwater resources and the legacy of World War II remains, some of which lie in shallow water directly off local beaches.

Some of the finest work, certainly the best-known report on underwater archaeology of World War II in Hawaii, was completed in 1989 by the National Park Service in partnership with the U.S. Navy Mobile Diving Salvage Unit. Entitled *A Submerged Cultural Resource Study of the* USS Arizona *and Pearl Harbor National Historic Landmark* (Lenihan, 1989), the project began in 1988 with a survey of mooring quays and Japanese plane crash sites in the harbor, and a deep water search for Japanese midget submarines. Both the USS *Arizona* and USS *Utah* sites were well-documented, and a side scan and magnetometer survey was conducted of major areas of Pearl Harbor. Other events, such as the West Loch explosion in 1944, also contributed significant amounts of debris to the material record. Archaeologists Dan Lenihan and Jim Adams of the National Park Service briefly inspected the remains of landing craft, several of which are intact, at the bottom of the Loch. Most of what was discovered still lies at the bottom of Pearl Harbor, although one artifact, an Imperial Japanese Navy type-91 torpedo, is currently on display.

USS Arizona. The initial survey of USS *Arizona* proved to be particularly important. The battleship, which had been topped off with fuel before the attack, has since become a well-known memorial visited annually by more than 1.5 million people (more than 1000 per day). Following the survey, which noted artifacts associated with the salvage as well as the initial destruction, a monitoring program for *Arizona* was initiated, an effort that continues to this day, since the amount of biofouling and corrosion continue to change the integrity of the ship and its rate of decay. Photo stations were set up on the ship, allowing consistent recording from a number of locations. Information from depth measurements of the sediments on the deck and a species count of bio-fouling organisms contribute to the evolving model of the whole structure's corrosion potential. An unknown amount of oil remains within the structure, prompting a certain degree of urgency to understand what is happening to *Arizona* (and USS *Utah*, which lies in the harbor as well, slowly leaking oil). Of course, this is in addition to its significance as a symbol of an era, its importance as a war grave, and its interpretive value (Slackman, 1984).

Recently, USS *Missouri* has taken its place alongside *Arizona*, adding to the importance of Pearl Harbor National Monument as a whole.

Japanese Midget Submarines. The story of the Japanese midget submarines in Hawaii is typical of involved archaeological recovery efforts. Of the five midget submarines participating in the December 7, 1941 attack, one was beached at Bellows Airfield, three were sunk by the U.S. Navy, and one remains missing. Three of the submarines have been recovered (the deep-water target discovered during the 1988 survey turned out to be World War II-era Douglass-built flying boats.) Two submarines remain unaccounted for.

In 1992, a private group, working in conjunction with the Hawaii Undersea Research Laboratory operated by University of Hawaii and the National Oceanic and

Atmospheric Administration, conducted a survey for the Douglass aircraft. Surprisingly, they located what was thought to be a midget submarine off Pearl Harbor, at 1500 feet deep. They determined from the visible portion of the submarine that the vessel was not involved in the attack on Pearl Harbor (Slackman, 1984). Nonetheless, ownership claims were filed in federal court. In 1993, the federal court ruled that Japan owned the submarine, which was then turned over to the U.S. State Department, allowing the U.S. government to assert its ownership of the vessel and end the legal battle temporarily. The search still continues for the midget submarine.

Aircraft

Besides this work, there are many places around the islands where downed World War II aircraft and other material are rumored to exist but have yet to be fully investigated. One such contact led to a 1994 Marine Option Program field school in conjunction with East Carolina University's program in maritime history and nautical archaeology, which focused on a PBY-5 wreck in Kaneohe Bay. This aircraft, still connected to its mooring cable, was one of several strafed and destroyed December 7, 1941. Wing, tail section, and fuselage settled together on the bottom of the bay, where teams of divers later produced measured sketches from the murky waters. Positions of the throttle levers, as well as historical documents and oral reports from survivors, suggest that the crew was hastily attempting to get the PBY into the air in the moments before the explosion sent the craft to the bottom. An NPS American Battlefield Protection Program grant enabled the 2000 field school to do a remote sensing survey of the rest of the historic mooring area.

Other significant aircraft wrecksites are coming to light as well. Archaeologist June Cleghorn at Marine Corps Base Hawaii (MCBH) is preparing to investigate a P-40K Warhawk that crashed in 1943 in shallow waters off the windward side of the island of Oahu, one of 211 downed in the Hawaiian islands (June Cleghorn, personal communication).

Midway Atoll

Although not part of the main island group and not under Hawaii's legal or administrative jurisdiction, Midway atoll is the second most northerly island location in the greater Hawaiian archipelago. Currently managed by U.S. Fish and Wildlife Service (USFWS), Midway is jointly operated by the USFWS and a private group, Phoenix Air Incorporated.

Most people associate Midway with the World War II naval battle of the same name, most of which actually occurred on the open ocean hundreds of miles north of the atoll. From the perspective of nautical archaeology, the waters and resources immediately around Midway remain untouched. In 1998, MOP was invited to make a brief initial survey of its submerged cultural resources. It is now possible for a maximum of 100 visitors to visit Midway at any one time, a splendid opportunity to appreciate the natural setting and abundant wildlife and the location's historical significance. USFWS preserves and manages the extensive historic resources, which include pre- and post-war-era artifacts. Sailing barks from the 19th century and shipwrecks from the 1950s lie alongside wartime vessels and aircraft (Casserley, 1998). The island was also an important way station for the early Pan Am Clipper flying boats, one of four important fueling stops (besides Honolulu, Wake Island, and Guam) between San Francisco and Manila (Cohen, 1985).

Known underwater sites within and around the atoll include the wreck of the bark *Carrollton*, a wooden British collier that went aground in 1906. Copper fasteners are scattered over a wide reef area, along with the donkey boiler and windlass and assorted pieces of twisted rigging. A tangle of anchor chain leads to an admiralty-style anchor still projecting above the surf. An F4U Corsair World War II fighter aircraft lies in deeper water, its fuselage and wings separated from its engine and propeller. A U.S. Navy submarine rescue vessel, *Macaw*, is at the bottom of the channel entrance. Apparently involved in the rescue of USS *Trigger*, *Macaw* became a total loss and a navigational hazard and had to be destroyed in place. A large portion of a wrecked water barge projects from the same channel, and a U.S. Navy garbage scow and two landing craft are in shallow waters near the runway, as well as another boiler, barrels, and assorted debris. The incident as well as the remains of *Macaw* are currently the topic of study for MOP students. Historical documentation suggests that several other World War II-vintage aircraft may be nearby, and the lagoon and reef areas adjacent to the ends of runways are prime candidates for survey (Rob Shallenberger, USFWS refuge manager, personal communication). The popularity of aviation wreck sites and successful management of other underwater resources make some kind of maritime survey of the waters closer to Midway itself an important task for the future.

The Northern Islands

Little historical or archaeological work has been conducted in the northern island chain to date. Tane Casserley's report on shipwrecks in this area is the first of its kind (Casserley, 1998). The inventory records 26 vessels wrecked in the northern island reefs and atolls. One specific potential project that continues to tempt researchers is the wreck of USS *Saginaw*. The mission of *Saginaw*, a side-wheel, sail-assisted steamer, was to carry supplies to Midway, where a coaling station was being established. Enroute to San Francisco, *Saginaw* passed by Kure atoll in order to confirm its position, since the atoll was a navigational hazard. Indeed it was: on May 30th, 1870, *Saginaw* went aground on a reef (Robertson, 1956), and its remains still lie there on distant Kure. No one is stationed at the small island since the U.S. Coast Guard abandoned its LORAN station, though Midway as a possible base of operations is nearby.

MARITIME ARCHAEOLOGY AT THE UNIVERSITY OF HAWAII

Stone tools and lures, fish ponds and fish traps, traditional voyaging canoes, parts of Hawaiian-owned American-built brigs, Western merchant vessels, scattered whalers and whaling implements, wreck of Russian ships and Japanese fishing vessels, traditional Japanese junks, boilers and engines from inter island steamers, ruined landings, midget submarines, and World War II aircraft: These are only part of the underwater material record representative of the history of the islands of Hawaii. With this legacy in mind, and with the passage of the 1987 Abandoned Shipwreck Act, MOP at the University of Hawaii, under the direction of Sherwood Maynard, Ph.D. committed itself to expanding its vision and taking on an historical and archaeological role in the Pacific. The system-wide Program at the University of Hawaii School of Ocean and Earth Science and Technology (SOEST), currently offers interdisciplinary certificate curricula to under-graduate and unclassified graduate students at four of the 10 Hawaii campuses: University of Hawaii Manoa, University of Hawaii Hilo, Maui Community College, and

Windward Community College. Before 1989, the program had focused primarily on topics in the marine sciences. Thousands of students have participated in marine education through the program, which features a hands-on approach to field work. The program currently awards an undergraduate certificate, a graduate ocean policy certificate, and a graduate certificate in maritime archaeology and history.

Although graduate certificates document specialized training within a certain field, and may serve as minor topics for double majors or stand alone as independent specialties, they are not equivalent to individual academic degrees. Mentors and associated professionals are available to assist students both on and off campus, in academia and in marine-related industries. The University of Hawaii system is fortunate to have access to some of the best sources of Pacific archival information in the world. The Manoa campus houses Hamilton Library, Hawaiian and Pacific collections, and government documents collection. Hawaii's East–West Center is also located on campus, and nearby are the Hawaiian Historical Society collection, Hawaiian Mission Children's Society archives, Hawaiian State Archives, Hawaiian Maritime Center archives, and the Bernice P. Bishop Museum, a preeminent institutions for anthropological work in the Pacific.

The initial workshop and symposium on maritime history and archaeology was held in 1989, the first of its kind in Hawaii. A number of organizations, community members, and professionals in the field contributed to this inaugural effort. A two-day, in-water skills workshop for 26 MOP students initiated the first field training in Hawaii. A shoreline tower that had been blown into the ocean at Kahe Point by Hurricane Iwa provided a training site for the class. The four-day symposium, open to the public, featured 20 speakers and a wide array of Pacific topics. Nainoa Thompson from the Polynesian Voyaging Society introduced traditional open-ocean navigation, and Yoshi Sinoto from the Bishop museum and Ben Finney of the University of Hawaii addressed aspects of Hawaiian maritime culture and voyaging. Other speakers presented current research on sunken whaling ships at Lahaina, excavation and conservation of Spanish galleon remains, Hawaiian fish pond construction, USS *Arizona* memorial, recreational use of shipwrecks at Chuuk (Truk) lagoon, and technical aspects of survey and underwater recording. Excellent meeting facilities for the first and all subsequent symposiums were made available at the newly-completed Hawaii Maritime Center on Oahu (in Hawaiian, "Oahu" means "the gathering place") located on Honolulu Harbor, with the historic downeaster *Falls of Clyde* immediately alongside. From the beginning, contributions from local businesses, such as Atlantis Submarines and Unitech Environmental Consultants, provided additional support for students to travel from neighboring islands and attend the symposium.

For the following three years, MOP continued to adopt the combined workshop–symposium model, featuring three or four days of training dives either at Kahe Point or on a landing craft and modern shipwreck near Coconut island in Kaneohe Bay, and multiday conferences open to the public (some may recall viewing scenic Coconut Island in the title sequence to the classic television sitcom "Gilligan's Island"). In addition to previous topics, new information included federal and state submerged cultural resource legislation, conservation at the National Museum of the Philippines, maritime archaeology at Bikini Atoll, wrecks at Rapanui (Easter Island), Hawaiian sampans, *Cleopatra's Barge* or *Haàheo o Hawaii*, interisland shipping, Pacific fishing strategies, Dauntless SBD aircraft wreck sites, and the wreck of SS *Empire* (interisland steamer) off the Kona coast. Featured speakers included Marion Kelly, University of Hawaii specialist in Hawaiian fish ponds; William Lee, the director of Los Angeles Maritime Museum; James

Delgado of the Vancouver Maritime Museum; Peter Gesner, of the Queensland Museum of Australia; and Myrna Clamor, conservator of the National Museum of the Philippines. James Delgado and Peter Gesner also were involved in teaching the in-water workshops. The symposia were successful and the diving workshop was popular although quite limited, being compressed into a narrow time frame of just a few days.

In 1993, the in-water workshop was expanded to 11 days. The MOP contracted with East Carolina University to bring Bradley Rodgers, staff conservator there, and a magnetometer and surveying transit out to the Big Island of Hawaii, to begin documenting the wreck of the SS *Kauai*, the steamer wrecked at Mahukona port (one of four official ports of entry for the Kingdom of Hawaii). The longer field project attracted students from the University of Colorado, Texas A&M, and all over the Hawaiian islands to work with Steve Russell, MOP's staff educational specialist. At nearby Hapuna beach, a shoreline map and plan view drawing of the site were completed, along with lectures presented at beachside cabins. Accommodations were primitive (blowing sand, constant wind), but the most difficult obstacle seemed to be the lack of trained assistants or experienced crew chiefs. Nonetheless, the session was successful; two television stations picked up on the story and aired an interview with Dr. Maynard. Pete Hendricks, aquatic resource specialist from the state's Department of Land and Natural Resources (DLNR) who is familiar with much of the Kona coast's cultural and physical history, played an important role in assisting with the project.

The annual symposium continued to attract new faces from throughout the maritime field. Dan Lenihan of the National Parks Service Submerged Cultural Resource Unit addressed the topic of resource management in Hawaii and the Western Pacific. Michael Halpern of the Institute of Nautical Archaeology and Mark Staniforth of the Australian Maritime Museum also participated. Later symposia included Kevin Foster of the National Park Service and William Dudley, Ph.D. U.S. Navy Director of Naval History. As always, the symposium included field trips to several locations: Hawaiian fish ponds, USS *Arizona* museum and memorial, *Bowfin* Submarine Museum, coral reef sinkholes, historic tours of the port of Honolulu, and Bishop Museum. With every passing year, the MOP steadily extended its network, contacting more professionals and learning more about the field as a whole.

In 1994, the University of Hawaii and East Carolina University again collaborated on an expanded workshop, now a true summer field school offering six university credits to enrolled students. Bradley Rodgers returned to Hawaii, this time assisted by Hans Van Tilburg and three East Carolina University crew chiefs, graduate students working toward professional degrees in nautical archaeology. Through Jim Adams, National Park Service employee at the USS *Arizona* memorial, University of Hawaii made contacts with Kaneohe Marine Corps Station (now Marine Corps Base Hawaii). A PBY-5 in Kaneohe Bay had been located previously by military divers but never documented. The six-week course brought students from as far away as Chuuk (Truk) island in the Federated States of Micronesia and New York State and included introductory lectures in a classroom setting, weeks spent diving in the field, and extensive drawing and report production, capped by a public presentation by the students themselves. The class's text was *Archaeology Underwater: The NAS Guide*, edited by Jeremy Green. Still photography, videotape, and measured drawings accompanied historical background, methodology, and research design were included in the report. In addition to work in Kaneohe Bay, Mr. Adams led students on a dive on *Arizona*, where they participated in collecting information at the many biofouling and corrosion monitoring stations on the ship. The class later was awarded the Western Association of Summer Session Exemplary Program Award for 1994. Local newspapers and television coverage and a portion of the "Hawaiian Moving Company" television series publicized the Kaneohe Bay work.

This successful field experience was followed in 1996 by a survey of lithic artifacts off of Waikiki beach, a traditional Hawaiian fishing site hundreds of years old. Hans Van Tilburg, an M.A. graduate from East Carolina University, relocated to the islands and became the instructor for the summer maritime archaeology course and later the world maritime history course. Again, classroom sessions for the maritime archaeology course were followed by field work and report writing. Students came from the United States and the Pacific region. Representatives of the State Historic Preservation Office of Micronesia also participated in the class. The documentation of the scattered stones was the first of its kind in the islands. Site selection was assisted by Michael Pfeffer, an anthropology student from University of Washington. A number of issues were raised by the report on the scattered basalt artifacts, highlighting the complexity of this type of prehistoric underwater research.

This was followed in 1997 by a field school survey of three selected locations on the Kona coast of the Big Island: Mahukona Port (where further documentation and final completion of the report finished the work begun in 1994 on SS *Kauai*); Maihuala Bay (Kona Coast State Park), where teams of students documented the wreckage of the sampan *Fuji Maru* (YP-183); and the diving and remote sensing survey of Kealakekua Bay. Local researcher Rick Rogers also participated in the remote sensing survey, being particularly interested in the possibility of a shipwreck of Spanish origin in or near the bay. Mike Tuttle, survey technician from Panamerican Maritime Ltd. in Memphis, assisted the course with side scan sonar and magnetometer equipment. Crew chiefs were selected from MOP's maritime archaeology and history certificate candidates, who had been through the field course previously. Slowly, a pool of local maritime talent was developing in Hawaii that would prove, as it always has proved elsewhere, to be the true resource for any program's future. In recent years, field students have investigated the steam equipment and structure of 19th century landings (Waimmalo, 1999), and the scattered remains of historic U.S. Navy PBYs in Kameohe Bay (Kameohe, 2000).

Not all years featured in-water field schools, due mainly to budgetary constraints: Hawaii's economy is far from self-sufficient and depends greatly on Asian tourism. Nonetheless, the experiential course has become a permanent feature in the Marine Option Program curriculum. Plans for future investigations include the SS *Maui* on the Kona coast, submerged aircraft wreck sites around Oahu, a general survey of multiple steamship and sailing schooner wrecks on Lanai's north shore (locally known as "Shipwreck Beach"), and the possibility of multiple field schools to be held at Midway Atoll. A long term survey of turn-of-the-century Hawaiian private landings and associated shipwrecks has begun. Certificate students also are involved in continuing work on USS *Arizona*; several MOP certificate students are pursuing M.A. degrees at East Carolina University, and one is currently teaching maritime archaeology at the high school level by surveying wreck sites in Chuuk lagoon, where three aircraft have been investigated so far (Clark Graham, Director of Society for Historic Investigation and Preservation, personal communication; Lanouette, 1998). The program itself has developed connections with the U.S. Navy Historical Center, National Park Service, Smithsonian Institution, USFWS, and a wide variety of local museums and agencies.

Naturally, there are obstacles to the program's progress. Given the current economic state in the islands, MOP, a relatively small entity compared to regular academic departments, is under the same tight fiscal restraints as all academic projects. The University of Hawaii has been operating under a hiring freeze, so the program still has no permanent position for a staff underwater archaeologist or maritime historian. Competition for students for field schools has been increasing. Still, steady progress in the integration of maritime archaeology and history into the MOP curriculum, has been the pattern from the very beginning, as well as the acceptance of helpful input from numerous professionals in the field. The program has a variety of connections and an academic steering committee and, so far, a monopoly on the study of underwater archaeology in the Hawaiian islands.

The maritime symposium continues to offer a variety of topics to professionals, specialists, and the general public. Published proceedings are available. Several options exist for future field schools. From the initial symposium and brief workshops, to extended workshops, to full summer field schools and a recognized graduate certificate course, MOP under Sherwood Maynard has made step-by-step progress toward the eventual goal of a graduate degree program in maritime archaeology and history. In conjunction with Hawaii's Undersea Research Laboratory, maritime archaeology in Hawaii is aptly situated for future projects involving side scan sonar, laser technology, and deep-water archaeological investigations.

CONCLUSION

Generalization is dangerous and is always best restricted to conclusions. Maritime archaeology in Hawaii might be summed up in a few phrases: a chronologically ancient and culturally diverse resource base; a vast potential for further work with only a few significant projects as yet completed; a cooperative network of professionals from near and far ("far" meaning *very* far); and a major commitment to the field by a system-wide, marine-related academic program. Maritime archaeology is in its infancy in the Hawaiian islands, which is why it is possible to include in a brief summary so many seemingly minor details about the handful of projects so far attempted. Much survey work needs to be done in Hawaii, and underwater archaeology must become the focus of more serious institutional attention. The small amount of effort being put into submerged cultural resources does not correspond to the much larger amount of development and construction on the coastlines, let alone answer the needs of resource managers at the state and federal level.

It has been said of many places in the Pacific, and it is certainly true of Hawaii in particular, that maritime archaeology seems wide open to further expansion in a number of different and promising directions. Finally (this surely doesn't need any special emphasis), Hawaii continues to be a beautiful and special place to work and live. If you have to do underwater archaeology, there are certainly less agreeable places in which to do it. *Aloha* and *mahalo*!

REFERENCES

Bennett, Elisa, editor, 1998, *Maritime Archaeology Techniques Course: 1997*. Draft report, Marine Option Program, University of Hawaii, Honolulu.

Bowman, Jesse, 1973, The Trouble with Aku, *Beacon* 13(11):16.

Carrell, Toni, editor, 1991, *Micronesia: Submerged Cultural Resources Assessment*, p. 286. National Park Service, Santa Fe, New Mexico.

Casserley, Tane Renata, 1998, *A Maritime History of the Northwestern Hawaiian Islands from Laysan to Kure*. Graduate certificate technical report. Marine Option Program, University of Hawaii, Honolulu.

Chappell, David A., 1997, *Double Ghosts*: *Oceanian Voyagers on Euroamerican Ships*. M.E. Sharpe, New York.

Chenoweth, Robert P., 1990, *Hawaii's Aku Sampans*: *Historic Treasures Still at Work*. Unpublished report, Anthropology Department, University of Hawaii, Honolulu.

Cohen, Stan, 1985, *Wings to the Orient*. Pictorial Histories Publishing Company, Missoula.

Connell, John Harden, 1933, Typhoon and Shipwreck Brought First Japanese to Hawaii over Century Ago; Old Records Tell of Arrival on Junk. *Honolulu Advertiser*, June 20.

Delgado, James P., editor, 1998, *Encyclopedia of Underwater and Maritime Archaeology*. Yale University Press, New Haven.

Elspeth, Sterling P. and Summers, Catherine C., 1978, *Sites of Oahu*. Bishop Museum Press, Honolulu.

Farber, Joseph, 1997, *Ancient Hawaiian Fishponds*: *Can Restoration Succeed on Molokai*? Neptune House Publishers, Encinitas.

Finney, Ben R., 1979, *Hokuleà*: *The Way to Tahiti*. Dodd, Mead and Company, New York.

_____, 1994, *Voyage of Rediscovery*: *A Cultural Odyssey through Polynesia*. University of California Press, Berkeley.

Gibbs, Jim, 1977, *Shipwrecks in Paradise*: *An Informal Marine History of the Hawaiian Islands*. Superior Publishing Company, Seattle.

Gibson, James R., 1992, *Otter Skins, Boston Ships, and China Goods*: *The Maritime Fur Trade of the Northwest Coast*. University of Washington Press, Seattle.

Greenhill, Basil, 1995, *The Archaeology of Boats and Ships*, p. 107. Naval Institute Press, Maryland.

Hviding, Edvard, 1996, *Guardians of Marovo Lagoon*: *Practice, Place, and Politics in Maritime Melanesia*, University of Hawaii Press, Honolulu.

Hommon, Robert J., 1986, *Historical Resources Study*: *Kealakekua Bay State Historical Park*, Vols. 1 and 2. Technical report prepared for Department of Land and Natural Resources, Division of State Parks, Outdoor Recreation and Historic Sites. Scientific Management Incorporated, Honolulu.

Johnston, Paul F., 1994, *Environmental Assessment for Archaeological Research in Hanalei Bay, Kauai, Hawaii*. Technical report for Department of Land and Natural Resources, Office of Conservation and Environmental Affairs. Smithsonian Institution, Washington, D.C.

_____, 1996, The Wreck of America's First Yacht: Cleopatra's Barge (*Haàheo o Hawaii*): 1995 Survey. In *Underwater Archaeology 1996*, edited by Stephen R. James Jr. and Camille Stanley, pp. 61–66. Society for Historical Archaeology, Cincinnati.

_____, 1997, Preliminary Report on the 1996 Excavations of the Wreck of *Haàheo o Hawaii* (ex-*Cleopatra*'s Barge) in Hanalei Bay, Kauai. In *Underwater Archaeology 1997*, edited by Denise C. Lakey, pp. 113–120. Society for Historical Archaeology, Corpus Christi.

_____, 1998, 1997 Excavations of the Royal Hawaiian Yacht *Haàheo o Hawaii* in Hanalei Bay, Kauai: Preliminary Report. In *Underwater Archaeology 1988*, edited by Lawrence F. Babits, Catherine Fach, and Ryan Harris, pp. 96–103. Society for Historical Archaeology.

Jonassen, Jon, 1994, The Politics of Culture: The Case of the Voyaging Canoes. In *New Politics in the South Pacific*, edited by Werner vom Busch et al., pp. 305–318. University of the South Pacific, Suva.

Kelly, Marion, 1975, *Loko Iá O Heèia*: *Heeia Fishpond*, Bernice Pauahi Bishop Museum, Honolulu.

Kirch, Patrick Vinton, 1985, *Feathered Gods and Fishhooks*: *An Introduction to Hawaiian Archaeology and Prehistory*. University of Hawaii Press, Honolulu.

Koontz, Michelle, 1998, SS *Maui*: *Preliminary Research for an Underwater Archaeological Survey*. Draft report, Marine Option Program, University of Hawaii, Honolulu.

Kuykendall, Ralph S., 1938, *The Hawaiian Kingdom*: 1778–1854, pp. 86–97. University of Hawaii, Honolulu.

Langdon, Robert, 1978, *American Whalers and Traders in the Pacific*: *A Guide to Records on Microfilm*. Australian National University, Canberra.

Langdon, Robert, 1984, *Where the Whalers Went*: *An Index to the Pacific Ports and Islands Visited by American Whalers (and Some Other Ships) in the 19th Century*. Australian National University, Canberra.

Lanouette, JoAnne, 1998, High School Maritime Archaeology Program, *Anthronotes* 20(1):17.

Lenihan, Daniel J., editor, 1989, *Submerged Cultural Resources Study*: USS Arizona *Memorial and Pearl Harbor National Historic Landmark*. Southwest Cultural Resources Center Professional Papers No. 23. National Park Service, Sante Fe.

Lovington, Al, 1998, *Lithics in a Marine Context*: *Methodologies and Issues*. Draft report, Marine Option Program, University of Hawaii, Honolulu.

Maui Historical Society (Wailuku), 1964, *Lahaina Historical Guide*. Star Bulletin Printing Company, Honolulu.

Maynard, Sherwood D., 1994, The University of Hawaii Marine Option Program: Case Study of a Unique Approach to Interdisciplinary, Experiential Ocean Education. In *Ocean Yearbook 11*, edited by Borgese, Elisabeth Mann, Norton Ginsburg, and Joseph R. Morgan, pp. 218–226. University of Chicago Press, Chicago.

Maynard, Sherwood D., Van Tilburg, H.K., Pence, D and Kumab, E., 1998, *University of Hawaii Site Team Visit to Midway Atoll National Wildlife Refuge.* Technical report, Marine Option Program, University of Hawaii at Manoa, Honolulu.

Nakashima, Leslie, 1934, Sampan Boat Building. *Advertiser*, March 10.

Nakayama, Mona, 1987, Maritime Industries of Hawaii: A Guide to Historical Resources (Whaling, Commercial Fishing, Shipping). Hawaiian Historical Society, Honolulu.

Pfeffer, Michael T., 1995, Distribution and Design of Pacific Octopus Lures: The Hawaiian Octopus Lure in Regional Context. *Hawaiian Archaeology* 4:47–56.

Robertson, Kieth,1956, *The Wreck of the Saginaw.* Viking Press, New York.

Sinoto, Yosihiko H., 1983, The Huahine Excavation: Discovery of an Ancient Polynesian Canoe. *Archaeology* 36(2):10–15.

Slackman, Michael, 1984, *Remembering Pearl Harbor: The Story of the USS* Arizona *Memorial.* Arizona Memorial Museum Association, Honolulu.

_____, 1983a, *Archaeological Excavations of the Vaitoòtia and Faàhia Sites on Huahine Island, French Polynesia.* National Geographic Society Research Reports, Vol. 15, pp. 583–599. National Geographic Society, Washington.

Te Rangi Hiroa (Peter Buck), 1964, *Arts and Crafts of Hawaii section VI: Canoes,* Bishop Museum Press, Honolulu.

Thomas, Mifflin, 1982, *Hawaiian Interisland Vessels and Hawaiian Registered Vessels.* Seacoast Press, Santa Barbara.

_____, 1983, *Schooner from Windward: Two Centuries of Hawaiian Interisland Shipping.* University of Hawaii Press, Honolulu.

Van Tilburg, Hans K., 1997, *Maritime Asia Pacific: The Hawaiian Sampan.* Report, Marine Option Program, University of Hawaii at Manoa, Honolulu.

Van Tilburg, H.K. and Adams, J., editors, 1994, *The History and Archaeology of PBY Flying Boats and Kaneohe Naval Air Station.* Technical report, Marine Option Program, University of Hawaii at Manoa, Honolulu.

Mexico, the Caribbean, Bermuda, and South America

The four chapters of Section 2 describe the islands of the Caribbean, as well as Mexico and Argentina. Each author writes of the tribulations of working with local governments and other nations.

Pilar Luna Erreguena stresses the need for Mexico to preserve its patrimony and the need for international cooperation.

Margaret Leshikar-Denton reports on the conditions of the Caribbean Islands with the most significant maritime sites. Support is needed from local, regional, and international organizations to combat ongoing commerical salvage.

Clifford Smith and Edward Harris write of the extraordinary collection of underwater sites in Bermuda waters that date from at least the early 16th century. This patrimony was squandered by treasure hunters until the late 1990s. Little has been published, much less recorded. New legislation and new leadership is sorely needed.

Marine archaeology is fairly new in Argentina. Dolores Elkins's chapter concerns the resources and potential for development with which this nation of coasts and rivers has begun to work. So far there has been significant progress. The need for better legislation goes hand in hand with the need for more skilled underwater archaeologists.

Chapter 17

Mexico
A Country with a Rich Underwater Legacy

PILAR LUNA ERREGUERENA

INTRODUCTION

Mexico is known around the world for its immense and diverse cultural past. Pyramids such as Teotihuacan, Chichen-Itzá, and Monte Albán are only some of its more famous archaeological sites. However, few people are aware of Mexico's vast underwater cultural legacy, which dates from pre-Hispanic times as well as from the colonial period.

Bordered on the north by the United States and on the south by Guatemala, the Mexican Republic has more than 10,000 km of coastline and has jurisdiction over 200 nautical miles, a stretch known as the Economic Exclusive Zone. On the west coast is the Pacific Ocean, and on the east coast the Gulf of Mexico and the Mexican Caribbean.

In inner waters—rivers, lakes, lagoons, springs, and *cenotes* or sink holes—there are pre-Hispanic remains. However, Mexican seas contain the legacy of vessels that have navigated from different parts of the world to America throughout five centuries, especially ships involved in exploration, discovery and conquest of the "new continent."

This submerged cultural patrimony, essentially ignored until recently, has become noticeable for two main reasons: archaeologists' and government's new awareness regarding the importance and value of this legacy, and the growing interest of treasure hunters.

Pilar Luna Erreguerena, National Institute of Anthropology and History, Subdirección de Arqueología Subacuática, Seminario 8, Centro C.P., 06060, México, D.F.

International Handbook of Underwater Archaeology, edited by Carol V. Ruppé and Janet F. Barstad. Kluwer Academic/Plenum Publishers, New York, 2002.

Pre-Hispanic Sites

Civilizations as important as the Olmec, Maya, and Zapotec left behind a rich heritage buried in the same land that witnessed their bloom and decline. These groups, and others, such as the Mixtecs, Otomies, and Totonacas, offered their most valuable objects (semiprecious stones, gold, ceramic, copper, and bone artifacts) to the deities of the water. Sometimes, the offerings included human beings. These groups believed they had to please their gods in order to have a good harvest or to keep evil spirits away.

Besides places used for sacred purposes, other places contain the remains of daily life, since these groups, like any other human group, looked for water to establish temporary or permanent homes. One may find evidence of trading activities in rivers, lakes, lagoons, springs, and *cenotes*, and of pre-Hispanic coastal navigation at sites such as Tulum at Quintana Roo in southeast Mexico.

Other likely sites of pre-Hispanic objects are submerged cave systems along the peninsula of Yucatan and islands in the state of Quintana Roo, such as Cozumel. In the past, some of these systems were connected to the surface through holes that served as entrances, or as holes in which to throw or deposit artifacts. Now, many are completely covered by jungles.

Even if many archaeological sites near these inner waters have been extensively investigated, little or no attention has been paid to the submerged cultural patrimony. Unfortunately, in cases such as the Spring of the Half Moon in Central Mexico, unauthorized divers have been removing pre-Hispanic treasures. There is still much underwater archaeological work to do in continental waters.

Shipwrecks of the Colonial Period

Colonial shipwrecks are the most significant cultural riches in the seas of Mexico. For several centuries, the oceans were the only mean of communication between Europe and the New World. First there were exploration trips, then discovery and conquest voyages, and finally journeys that transported European settlers to new homes in their search for better lives and fortunes.

In the mid-16th century, to protect its interests from pirate attacks and other dangers of the sea, the Spanish Crown established a unique navigational system for its moment: fleets. Several types of vessels sailed together from the Old to the New World, headed by two main ships known as the *Capitana* and the *Almiranta*, where the most valuable cargo was placed. Each year, Spain sent two fleets to America, one called the "New Spain Fleet," whose final destination was the Mexican port of Veracruz, and the "Tierra Firme Fleet," directed to Central and South America.

On their way back to Europe, these ships carried the vast richness produced by the new colonies and collected by the king's ministers, along with goods sent by merchants. On board were daily utensils for such a long journey, and weapons and heavy artillery needed to fight against enemies.

The number of colonial shipwrecks in Mexican waters is high due to different causes. Besides the afore-mentioned pirate attacks shipwrecks were caused by inexperienced pilots, inadequate vessels, inaccurate maps and instruments, fires, and natural disasters.

Historical records show that many of these ships carried significant quantities of precious metals as gold and silver, as well as other treasures. Because of this, treasure hunters have tried to reach these shipwrecks and have even created enterprises dedicated to convincing local authorities to negotiate a legacy that belongs to the country in which it remains.

FIRST SALVAGE WORKS

As in the rest of the world, in Mexico there were accidental recoveries of pieces lying underwater, especially in the Gulf of Mexico and the Caribbean. There were also salvages in inner waters. The first, in the Sacred Well of Chichen-Itzá, occurred at the end of the 19th century. The next sections describe the most notorious salvages in Mexican waters.

Sacred Well of Chichen-Itzá

Cenotes are natural, water-filled limestone sinkholes existing mainly in the Mayan zone of southeastern Mexico. In the past, cenotes were used as sources of fresh water and as sacred sites where offerings to the gods were thrown or deposited. The Cenote of Chichen-Itzá, also called the Sacred Well, is considered the most important in the area. It is about 400 m north of the main plaza of Chichen-Itzá, an ancient Mayan religious center in the northwestern part of the peninsula of Yucatan. The well is connected to the plaza by a *sacbé*, or white path, a typical Mayan road.

The first time someone tried to recover objects at the bottom of the 14-m-deep cenote was in 1882. French antiquarian Desiré Charnay used a dredge, but he was not successful. Then in 1894, Edward Herbert Thompson, the first United States consul in Yucatan, bought the Hacienda of Chichen-Itzá, which included Mayan ruins and the cenote, for a small amount of money. Like Charnay, he used a dredge to try to retrieve artifacts. Between 1904 and 1907, he recovered many significant archaeological artifacts. From 1910 to 1911, he hired U.S. helmet divers, but low visibility prevented their success, so Thompson went back to the dredge system. Most of the recovered pieces were taken to the Peabody Museum at Harvard University and to the Field Museum of Natural History of Chicago.

Material recovered by Thompson included jade figurines, stone sculptures, gold and copper disks, *copal* (a pre-Hispanic resin used as incense), human bones, fragments of textile, and assorted artifacts made of metal, obsidian, wood, bone, stone, gold, and rubber.

It was not until 1960–1961 that the first official recovery work took place, with the participation of the National Institute of Anthropology and History (INAH) through archaeologist Román Piña Chan, Club de Exploraciones y Deportes Acuáticos de México (CEDAM), National Geographic Society, and Norman Scott, a professional diver. The group used an airlift and worked for several months until INAH cancelled the work: Many objects broke as they passed through the airlift, and proper stratigraphical data was not being obtained. The last field season took place 1967–1968. INAH, CEDAM, and Expeditions Unlimited, Inc., worked almost three months, lowering the water level 4 m and using chemicals to increase visibility. Again, divers used an airlift.

Among the pieces recovered were five sculpted stone jaguars, snake-shaped stones, gold and copper bells, jade beads, turquoise fragments, wooden benches and buckets, about 100 ceramic vases and bowls of different sizes and eras, small objects made of shell and obsidian, and animal and human bones. Many of these reside at the National Museum of Anthropology in Mexico City.

X-Coton, X-Lacah, and Agua Azul Cenotes

Between 1952 and 1968, American specialists worked in these three cenotes in southeastern Mexico, two in Yucatan and one in Chiapas, and recovered many artifacts and shards. It was confirmed that these sacred sites were where the Mayas made offerings to Chaac, their god of rain. In 1970, a year after American researcher Stephan F. de Borhegyi died, Mexican archaeologist Roberto Gallegos continued recoveries in Agua Azul Cenote, in Chinkultic. The X-Coton project included mapping and stratigraphical studies. The other two works consisted only of the recovery of objects.

The Nevado of Toluca

The Nevado of Toluca, is the fourth highest mountain in Mexico. At its peak are two lagoons which have been popular sites for high-altitude sport divers. The Sun Lagoon is 400×200 m, and the Moon Lagoon is 200×75 m, with a depth of 14 m; both are 4200 m above sea level. The first dives were made in 1954–1955.

The most recovered objects from these lagoons were ceramic vases, spheres and cones made of copal (incense), and pieces of wood sculpted in the shape of rays. Copal and rays were used for ceremonial purposes.

The Matancero Shipwreck

This Matancero wreck was discovered by Robert Marx in 1957 in a reef located at Punta Matancero, off the coast of Quintana Roo in southeastern Mexico. Marx and journalist Clay Blair found glass bottles, wood crates, and pewter buckles. In 1958, they dove with hookah equipment and worked with hammers and chisels and, in some cases, used dynamite to free small objects found in huge coral concretions. Thousands of pieces were recovered: small brass crucifixes, brass and silver spoons, glass beads, and pewter plates. Mexican police stopped both divers and confiscated the material.

Some time later, CEDAM was authorized to continue the recovery works, and Marx and Blair were invited to participate. On this occasion, large pieces, such as cannons and anchors, also were taken from the sea. Some can still be seen, in a very deteriorated state, in a museum in Puerto Aventuras, Quintana Roo.

Marx and Blair asked the Smithsonian Institution for advice, and they traveled to Spain to consult the Archivo General de Indias, but they never could establish the true identity of the shipwreck. Some believed it was the Spanish merchant ship *Nuestra Señora de los Milagros*, sunk in 1741 in that part of the Mexican Caribbean; others believed it was a British merchant ship. Today, it is still known as the Matancero shipwreck.

UNDERWATER ARCHAEOLOGY IS BORN

In 1980, INAH created the Underwater Archaeology Department (DAS), which was promoted to a vice-directorate (Subdirección de Arqueología Subacuática [SAS]) in 1995. Since its beginnings, the department has undertaken several research projects in inner and marine waters, especially in the Gulf of Mexico and the Caribbean. One of Mexico's main underwater archaeology policies has been to work with experts in other disciplines and with national and international institutions, as well as to raise national consciousness so that Mexicans can understand the importance and value of the submerged cultural patrimony and its future possibilities.

The following sections describe significant underwater archaeology projects Mexico has undertaken in the past 20 years.

Cayo Nuevo Reef

In 1979, two American divers discovered two shipwrecks in the Cayo Nuevo Reef, which is located at the Sonda of Campeche in the Gulf of Mexico. After they notified Mexican authorities, a series of field seasons were held until 1983. These shipwrecks, dating from the 16th and 18th centuries, were registered, and the oldest bronze cannon in America was recovered.

Media Luna Spring

The Media Luna spring, a pre-Hispanic offering site and a place where prehistoric fauna has been found, is located in the state of San Luis Potosí in central Mexico. It has been an ideal site for divers for many years. Unfortunately, most divers, both national and foreign, go home with souvenirs. In 1981 and 1982, DAS archaeologists held field seasons and recovered Pleistocene animal bones and ceramics. The Chichimecan groups had used the

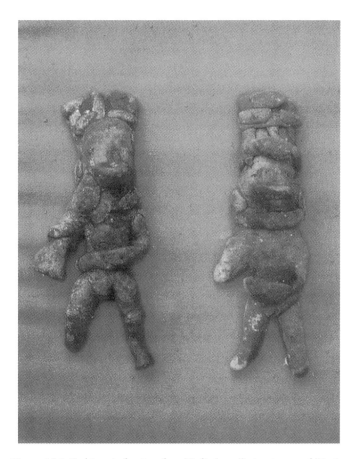

Figure 17.1. Prehispanic figurines from Media Luna Spring in central Mexico.

spring as a sacred place between the years A.D. 600–900. Two infant burials were discovered in a wall of the spring.

An important aspect of this study was to determine the correlation between archaeological sites near the spring and offerings deposited in it. Some of the recovered pieces can be admired at the National Museum of Anthropology in Mexico City.

Coast of Quintana Roo

Between 1984 and 1990, research was conducted along the coast of Quintana Roo, which is in southeastern Mexico, to locate pre-Hispanic structures that may have served as navigational aids or lighthouses for the Maya and other indigenous groups trading in the area. Many of these structures coincide with natural reef openings, or seem to signal harbor entrances or rocky places that would be dangerous for navigators. In fact, local sailors still use some of the structures as points of reference, and modern lighthouses were built near them.

Chitales Reef at Bahía de Mujeres

In 1990 a joint archaeological–biological study took place on Chitales reef, located between Cancun and Isla Mujeres in the state of Quintana Roo. This was the site of a 16th century shipwreck. Before archaeologists could begin their research, marine biologists from the National Autonomous University of Mexico (UNAM) registered and removed the living corals, replanting them afterwards and monitoring the area for one year until the reef had completely recovered. Mexico's underwater archaeologists try to study Mexico's archaeological and historical legacy while doing as little as possible to change the natural environment.

The shipwreck had been visited in the late 1950s and early 1960s by a group of divers who believed that it was *La Nicolasa*, one of Francisco de Montejo's ships. They recovered important artillery pieces dating from the 16th century, some of which were taken out of Mexico, and some that were put in a local museum. However, the pieces never received proper conservation treatment and they deteriorated. In 1984, archaeologists from DAS, the Institute of Nautical Archaeology, and Ships of Discovery relocated, surveyed, and partially excavated the site. Through archival research and field work, they determined that the ship was not *La Nicolasa*.

A NEW GENERATION OF UNDERWATER ARCHAEOLOGISTS

Mexico's first underwater archaeologists had to learn the specialty by working on national or international projects in which they had been invited. Some decided to resume their work on land projects, thus there became an urgent need to acquire experience to prepare a new generation of underwater archaeologists.

Mexico's first diplomate in underwater archaeology was given for a master's level course, in 1994. For six months, 30 professors from Mexico, the United States, and Canada taught 20 students, mainly archaeologists and curators.

As part of the diplomate, the students attended a field session held in Isla Mujeres. For three weeks, students relocated and mapped a shipwreck between Isla Mujeres and Isla Contoy in the Mexican Caribbean. Using information from local fishermen, the students found cannons and anchors that had been previously removed from their original sites and placed near shore for exhibiting in a sort of underwater "museum." The students cleaned away the sand covering the objects, moved them by using balloons, and deposited them in a nearby area that had a more solid bottom. All objects were recorded on maps, photo mosaics, and video before and after the move.

While some of the students worked underwater, others cleaned, inventoried, and catalogued the pieces at the local museum. They also made classification tags and rearranged the museography.

Most of the students who graduated in 1994 have worked or collaborated on the 1630–1631 New Spain's Fleet project, the main underwater archaeological research currently taking place in Mexico. The students also have gone on to train in different areas.

THE 1630–1631 NEW SPAIN'S FLEET RESEARCH PROJECT

Among the fleets with one of the most important cargoes during the Colonial period was the New Spain Fleet that departed from the Spanish port of Cadiz on July 29, 1630, and sank one year later in the Gulf of Mexico. According to information found in manuscripts, the main ships of this fleet were the galleons *Nuestra Señora del Juncal* and *Santa Teresa*.

The fleet left Veracruz on Tuesday, October 14, 1631, for Havana, Cuba, with Spain as its final destination. A few days later, a storm forced the ships to disperse. *Nuestra Señora del Juncal* apparently held out one week until it sank. There were only 36 survivors from among more than 330 people on board. The loss had a dramatic effect on the kingdom of Spain, which was experiencing a severe crisis because of its constant wars against other European countries, especially the Netherlands.

Figure 17.2. Participants in *1630–1631 New Spain's Fleet Research Project*–second field season.

Since 1995, INAH's SAS, supported by trustee Fideicomiso para el Rescate de Pecios, has operated the 1630–1631 New Spain's Fleet Research Project, considered one of the most important in Latin America.

Thank to intense archival research undertaken in Mexico, Spain, and Cuba, and the study of maps and plans dating mainly from the 17th century, researchers now have a more complete idea of the context of this fleet before, during, and after the tragedy. This information is also of great value in widening existing knowledge about navigation in American waters during the 16th–19th centuries.

For many years, treasure hunters have been searching for the *Nuestra Señora del Juncal*, trying by any means to obtain from local authorities permission for its salvage. In 1993, several Mexican official institutions, including the INAH, undertook a field season on board the oceanographic ship *Akademik Mstislav Keldysh* of the Russian Science Academy's Oceanology Institute, in an attempt to find the vessel's remains. They did not reach their goal.

In 1997–1999, three field seasons were undertaken in the Gulf of Mexico, two at the Sonda de Campeche and one in Veracruz. Researchers of different disciplines, institutions, and countries participated and started an inventory of the submerged cultural resources in the Gulf of Mexico. A local fisherman acted as guide and informant in the first two seasons.

During the first season, archaeologists surveyed using towing boards and advanced Differential Geographical Positioning System (DGPS) equipment. This system allowed for accurate positioning of each site. In only 18 days, 532 nautical miles were covered, and 24 sites containing vestiges dating from the 16th century to the present were located and recorded. Many sites showed clear evidence of looting, including the use of dynamite.

During the second field season, the oceanographic research ship *Justo Sierra*, owned by the National Autonomous University of Mexico, was the project's main operational base. Two sophisticated geographical information systems were used: Equipos y Sistemas de la Plataforma de Adquisición de Datos Arqueológicos Sumergidos (ESPADAS), owned by the project, and Archaeological Data Acquisition Platform (ADAP), provided by the U.S. National Park Service's Submerged Cultural Resources Unit. These systems are considered the most advanced for remote detection of underwater cultural remains.

There were 77 anomalies detected at the bottom of Sonda de Campeche. All were checked out by divers. They found modern shipwrecks and some ancient ones, including one dating from the 16th century. Besides underwater archaeological exploration, biological, sedimentological, and physiochemical studies were made at many of the sites.

An important aspect of this research is the aforementioned inventorying and cataloging of submerged cultural sites in the Gulf of Mexico. Perhaps in the future some of the sites discovered and recorded in this atlas will lead to important projects.

One achievement of the second field season was the recovery of 40 lead ingots, apparently the largest collection ever recovered in America. The ingots have been cleaned and treated for proper conservation, and research is continuing to discover the origin and date of the ship carrying them.

During the third field season, the following goals were reached: the testing of the new components of the ESPADAS system, especially designed for this project; the location and registration of several sites containing cultural resources; relocation of the remains of the 19th century American warship USS *Somers*; the training of seven Mexican students; and the making of a video that later won a prize in an international contest.

The 1630–1631 News Spain's Fleet Research Project is a long-term study that includes the eventual creation of the first Museum of Navigation in Mexico.

PROTECTING MEXICO'S SUBMERGED CULTURAL PATRIMONY

Mexico has subscribed to and ratified international treaties. In the domestic arena, the law that applies is the *Ley Federal sobre Monumentos y Zonas Arqueológicos, Artísticos e Históricos*, whose latest version dates from 1972. The law states that the National Institute of Anthropology and History is the guardian of the nation's cultural patrimony. Another important regulation is the *Disposiciones Reglamentarias para la Investigación Arqueológica en México*, approved in 1977 and modified in 1982, in which underwater archaeology was specifically included. These regulations establish the norms that any archaeological or historical project should follow.

Shipwrecks that occurred in Mexican waters between the 16th and 19th centuries are considered national monuments. In the case of shipwrecks belonging specifically to the Colonial period, a principle known as *reversion* applies, meaning that all goods and properties that belonged to Spain and were not negotiated when Spain recognized Mexico's independence are now the property of Mexico.

INAH consults with an archaeological council in charge of reviewing and approving any archaeological project, terrestrial or underwater, that is to be done in Mexican territory. Each project must follow the requirements of the aforementioned regulations, which include three main points: (1) The project must be scientific research; (2) the project's director must be an experienced archaeologist supported by an academic institution; and (3) all recovered objects belong to and will remain in Mexico.

TREASURE HUNTERS: AN ETERNAL STRUGGLE

For centuries, Mexico's underwater history remained relatively protected. However, after the invention of the Scuba diving system at the end of World War II and the development of technology that enables divers to reach almost any depth, the security of these archaeological and historical remains all over the world became a risk. Mexico is no exception.

Part of Mexico's submerged cultural patrimony was looted during those years, even taken out of the country, although this has changed to some extent in the last two decades. INAH's Archaeology Council and SAS often receive applications from treasure hunters or even companies whose only purpose is commercial. Several attempts, disguised as projects, have been detected and stopped in time; however, minor ravages go on.

Treasure hunters pressure and constantly try to obtain permits from local authorities, often offering a percentage of the recovered treasure. This is a trap which Mexico has avoided, being aware that this legacy is not for sale or auction. It belongs not only to the Mexican people but to humankind itself.

FUTURE OF MEXICAN UNDERWATER ARCHAEOLOGY

Mexico is developing better ways to preserve its submerged cultural heritage and has undertaken important projects, such as the 1630–1631 New Spain's Fleet study. All this should evolve in the future according to the possibilities and priorities of the country in general and the corresponding authorities and specialists in particular.

A position that has characterized Mexico's underwater archaeology is the conviction that this heritage should be studied in the context of scientific research, by specialized underwater archaeologists, with the collaboration of experts and institutions of different disciplines and countries, as well as with the support of qualified divers.

In recent years, it has become evident that international cooperation is needed to help protect and manage this important cultural heritage. Since 1992, Mexico has been invited to participate in forums on underwater archaeology in Argentina, Chile, Honduras, Uruguay, and Puerto Rico. Since then, researchers and institutions of these places have maintained constant contacts. However, even if Mexico shares some aspects with other Latin American countries, each nation has its own idiosyncrasies and must find its own way to protect and manage its underwater cultural legacy, in accordance with a general code of ethics and principles.

Mexico has fought many battles to protect its submerged cultural patrimony and has reached a strong and firm attitude regarding "no negotiability" of this part of its national riches. At present, the country counts on the recognition of the international underwater archaeological community. This position should be maintained in the future, especially because of the constant threat of treasure hunters, and also as an important achievement that must be proudly preserved.

The 1630–1631 New Spain's Fleet Research Project, including the inventory of submerged cultural resources in the Gulf of Mexico, will be an important part of Mexican underwater archaeology's future. At the same time, other projects will be developed, especially on Mayan cenotes and inundated caves of the Yucatan Peninsula.

There also is a strong commitment to prepare new generations of underwater archaeologists capable of understanding and recognizing the value of their patrimony, and of devoting themselves to its investigation, protection, conservation and dissemination, in order to share it with the people of Mexico and the world.

REFERENCES

Andrews, Anthony P. and Corletta, Robert, 1995, A Brief History on Underwater Archaeology in the Maya Area. In *Ancient Mesoamerica*, pp. 101–117. Cambridge University Press, New York.

García-Bárcena, Joaquín and Erreguerena, Pilar Luna, 1987, El Patrimonio Cultural Submarino. In *Antropología Documentos*, Nueva Época 17:1–12. Instituto Nacional de Antropología e Historia, México, D.F.

Instituto Nacional de Antropología e Historia, 1975, *Ley Federal sobre Monumentos y Zonas Arqueológicos, Artísticos e Históricos*. México, D.F.

_____, 1985, *Disposiciones Legales del Patrimonio Cultural*. México, D.F.

_____, 1990, *Reglamento del Consejo de Arqueología y Disposiciones reglamentarias para la Investigación Arqueológica en México*. México, D.F.

Luna Erreguerena, Pilar, 1982, *La Arqueología Subacuática*. Manuscript on file, Tesis profesional, Maestría en Ciencias Antropológicas, ENAH-UNAM, México, D.F.

_____, 1997, *Informe de actividades del Proyecto de Investigación de la Flota de la Nueva España de 1630–1631*. Manuscript on file, Instituto Nacional de Antropología e Historia,

Subdirección de Arqueología Subacuática, México, D.F., 1998, *Informe de Actividades del Proyecto de Investigación de la Flota de la Nueva España de 1630–1631*. Manuscript on file, Instituto Nacional de Antropología e Historia, Subdirección de Arqueología Subacuática, México, D.F.

Olivé Negrete, Julio César, 1992, Legislación sobre Arqueología Subacuática. In *Arqueología*, Segunda época, 8:137–145. Coordinación Nacional de Arqueología del Instituto Nacional de Antropología e Historia, México, D.F.

Serrano Mangas, Fernando, 1992, *Naufragios y Rescates en el Tráfico Indiano en el siglo XVII*. Colección Encuentros, Serie Textos, Sociedad Estatal Quinto Centenario, Madrid.

Chapter 18

Problems and Progress in the Caribbean

MARGARET E. LESHIKAR-DENTON

INTRODUCTION

The Caribbean is rich in maritime history (Leshikar-Denton, 1997b; Leshikar-Denton, 1998). Between the 15th and 19th centuries, it was a crossroads of shifting colonial power and waterborne commerce among European nations, particularly Spain, England, France, and the Netherlands. In the Caribbean are hundreds of maritime archaeological sites: prehistoric and historical coastal settlements, forts, lighthouses, shipbuilding sites, ports, and harbors, as well as shipwrecks and contemporary salvage sites. The sites contain remains of ships of exploration and discovery, treasure galleons, slave ships, craft of pirates and privateers, merchantmen, warships, and local vessels.

Countries bordering the Caribbean Sea (Figure 18.1) share a common history, although they are separated by the water and by a variety of cultures, languages, and legal traditions. The apparent isolation and lack of centralized government has been a factor in the area's exploitation of its underwater heritage by treasure hunters. But there is hope that the common heritage of the region will not be lost to profiteers: In our modern world of global communication, Caribbean countries are poised to share their experiences dealing with commercial salvage and legitimate archaeology. They can participate in and

Margaret E. Leshikar-Denton, Archaeologist, Cayman Islands National Museum, Grand Cayman, Cayman Islands.

International Handbook of Underwater Archaeology, edited by Carol V. Ruppé and Janet F. Barstad. Kluwer Academic/Plenum Publishers, New York, 2002.

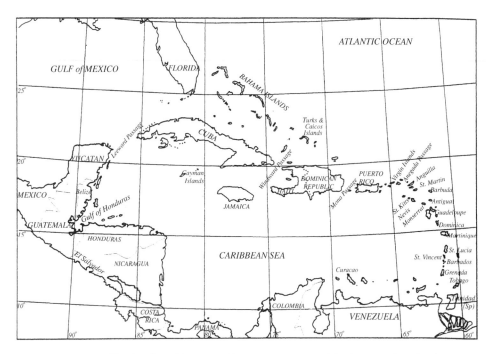

Figure 18.1. The Carribean (Courtesy of Roger Craig, Cayman Islands National Archive).

benefit from international initiatives to protect world maritime heritage. Still, it is a great challenge to implement national, regional, and international programs for the preservation and management of underwater cultural heritage in the Caribbean.

Caribbean island countries giving consideration to underwater cultural heritage are highlighted in the following pages. Although not covered in this section, the Latin American countries of Mexico, Honduras, Panama, and Columbia, all bordering the Caribbean Sea, are participating in the recent Latin American and Caribbean initiatives to address the protection and management of underwater cultural heritage. The South American countries of Argentina, Uruguay, and Ecuador have also joined these initiatives.

THE PROBLEM: SPANISH TREASURE

After Columbus' 1492 encounter with the New World until the late 17th century, Spain claimed a monopoly on all New World territories sighted during Spanish voyages. When gold and silver resources were exhausted in the West Indies, Spanish interests shifted to Mexico, Bolivia, and Peru. Still, vessels inward-bound to Vera Cruz, or homeward-bound to Spain, navigated through the Caribbean, taking advantage of prevailing wind and ocean currents to leave the region, often via the Leeward Passage, out into the Gulf Stream. Ships bound for Mexico navigated west into the Gulf of Mexico, while those enroute to Spain sailed through the Straits of Florida and northeast toward Bermuda for the return passage across the Atlantic. Along the route, Spanish merchantmen, organized from 1537 into regularly scheduled convoys protected by armed vessels and loaded with precious metals and pearls, occasionally foundered in storms or wrecked on perilous reefs.

The greatest problem facing the Caribbean's underwater cultural heritage remains the lure of this Spanish treasure. It is no surprise that early diving entrepreneurs, followed by treasure hunters, ventured into the Caribbean to seek their fortunes, or that island-governments, dazzled by the belief that they would receive percentages of profits from the sale of shipwreck artifacts, were persuaded to permit treasure-hunting schemes. As early as the mid-1800s, hard-hat diver Jeremiah Murphy explored and salvaged Caribbean shipwrecks, harbors, and the sunken city of Port Royal, Jamaica (Keith, 1997). Since the advent of Scuba diving in the mid-20th century, underwater heritage sites have been threatened, particularly shipwrecks located in the warm clear waters of the Caribbean.

Investigations of Spanish merchantmen have been conducted by archaeologists and by treasure hunters (Bass, 1988; Delgado, 1997; Keith, 1988; Smith, 1988b, 1993; Throckmorton, 1987). Archaeologists from the Texas Antiquities Committee excavated the 1554 Fleet located off Padre Island, Texas (Arnold and Weddle, 1978). The Cayo Nuevo Wreck was documented by Texas A&M University's Institute of Nautical Archaeology (INA) and Mexico's *Instituto Nacional de Antropología e Historia* (INAH), in the Gulf of Mexico. The state of Louisiana undertook excavations on the 1766 wreck of *El Nuevo Constante* off the Louisiana coastline (Pearson and Hoffman, 1995). Mapping and recording occurred on *Urca de Lima,* which became Florida's first underwater archaeological preserve in 1987 (Smith, 1991). Archaeologists also have been involved in the investigation of a post-1554 Spanish ship known as the St. John's Bahamas Wreck (Smith, 1993). In the 1990s, the Emanuel Point Ship, a mid-16th-century galleon discovered in the waters of Pensacola Bay, Florida, was excavated (Bratten, 1998; Cozzi, 1998; Scott-Ireton, 1998; Smith, 1994; Smith et al., 1995; Smith et al., 1999).

The majority of discovered sites have been salvaged by treasure hunters. Salvors excavated *San Pedro* and *San Antonio* off Bermuda, *Nuestra Señora de Atocha* and ships of the 1733 Spanish Plate Fleet in the Florida Keys, the 1715 Spanish Plate Fleet off the east coast of Florida, *Concepción* on the Silver Bank of Hispaniola, *Nuestra Señora de Guadalupe* and *Conde de Tolosa* off the northeast coast of Hispaniola, and *Nuestra Señora de las Maravillas* in the Bahama Islands. Countries permitting treasure-hunting ventures are learning that profits are seldom achieved and that irreplaceable cultural resources can be lost forever.

PROGRESS

Archaeology and Museums

Although some Caribbean countries long ago took steps to preserve and interpret terrestrial heritage sites, interest in underwater sites developed as did improvements in the technology used to explore them. By the 1950s, the Institute of Jamaica began to sponsor underwater research at Port Royal. But scientific underwater archaeology did not begin in the Caribbean until the late 1970s. In the past two decades, archaeological projects have been conducted by academic institutions such as Texas A&M University and East Carolina University, and by nonprofit organizations such as INA, Ships of Exploration and

Discovery Research (SEDR) and the Pan-American Institute of Maritime Archaeology (PIMA), working in cooperation with island governments, institutions, or museums. The groups have undertaken projects in the Cayman Islands, Turks and Caicos Islands, Bahama Islands, Jamaica, Anguilla, the Dominican Republic, Puerto Rico, Sint Maarten, Curacao, and other Caribbean countries. Archaeological projects resulting in museum exhibitions, or in the interpretation of sites in situ as underwater preserves, are influencing some countries to take responsibility for protecting their underwater heritage. Preservation benefits the public through education and national identity, and has the important financial effect of benefiting tourism, upon which many Caribbean economies rely.

Regional and International Initiatives

At the ninth meeting of the Forum of Ministers of Culture and Officials Responsible for Cultural Policy of Latin America and the Caribbean, held in Colombia May 28–30, 1997, the ministers decided to establish the Technical Commission on Underwater Cultural Heritage (Forum of Ministers, 1998) which first met June 14–17, 1998, in Santo Domingo, Dominican Republic. Attending were participants from Argentina, Barbados, Columbia, Cuba, Dominican Republic, Ecuador, Haiti, Honduras, Jamaica, Mexico, Panama, Trinidad and Tobago, and Uruguay. Highlighted were each country's experiences, legislation, and regulations regarding salvage, research, and protection of the country's underwater cultural heritage. Each participant commented on their country's national institutions related to underwater cultural heritage and whether these were effective in research and conservation. A representative of UNESCO distributed a notebook, *Protecting Underwater Cultural Heritage* (revised version of a document by the Cayman Islands National Museum for the 1995 Museums Association of the Caribbean AGM). The reference tool, containing articles, documents, and laws, was intended to assist the countries present in developing strategies and legal frameworks to protect underwater cultural heritage. The meeting also recognized the International Council on Monuments and Sites' (ICOMOS) *International Charter on the Protection and Management of Underwater Cultural Heritage*. Ratified by ICOMOS in 1996, the charter sets professional standards for the international community regarding underwater cultural heritage.

A primary objective of the first meeting of the Technical Commission on Underwater Cultural Heritage was to review the draft *UNESCO Convention on the Protection of Underwater Cultural Heritage*. This document was discussed at a meeting of governmental experts at UNESCO Headquarters in Paris from June 29–July 2, 1998. The Latin American and Caribbean Group (GRULAC) examined the draft *UNESCO Convention* and submitted collective regional recommendations and conclusions to the Paris meeting. A report of the Santo Domingo Meeting, including recommendations, also was submitted and approved at the tenth meeting of the Forum of Ministers of Culture and Officials Responsible for Cultural Policy of Latin America and the Caribbean, held December 4–5, 1998, in Bridgetown, Barbados (Forum of Ministers, 1998).

The chief objective of the second meeting of the Technical Commission, convened on March 12, 1999, in Santo Domingo, was to prepare for the second meeting of governmental experts to be held in Paris April 19–24, 1999, to continue review of the draft *UNESCO Convention*. A document known as the *Santo Domingo Declaration* (1998), signed by participants on June 16, 1998, resulted from the first meeting of the Technical Commission on Underwater Cultural Heritage.

At the second meeting of the Technical Commission, participants agreed to call upon all Latin American and Caribbean countries to ratify its terms:

- Underwater Cultural Heritage is the property of the State in which it is found and through this it is the heritage of Humanity.
- Survey, investigation and intervention in this heritage must be carried out only by specialists and for scientific purposes.
- Participating countries agree on the assessment made of their economic and technical limitations, to effect the appropriate management of this heritage and therefore consider it necessary to have recourse to mutual co-operation to mitigate these circumstances.
- It is necessary, therefore, for the cultural authorities in the countries to begin as soon as possible to promote and subscribe to agreements on this issue.
- Similarly, organizations such as UNESCO and ICOMOS are called upon to play a fundamental role in the transfer of technical assistance and logistical support so that these countries may develop underwater archaeological knowledge under the best conditions.
- Approval is expressed concerning the imminent ratification of the *Convention on the Protection of Underwater Cultural Heritage*, and the wish that proposals arising from these proceedings will be considered by said *Convention*.
- Finally, we acknowledge that our countries will modify current legislation so that arising from such, survey and shipwreck recovery operation contracts may be formulated and adopted, provided such meets with the approval of the *Convention*.

Establishment of the Technical Commission on Underwater Cultural Heritage by the Forum of Ministers of Culture and Officials Responsible for Cultural Policy of Latin America and the Caribbean suggests that these countries are prepared to cooperate in information-sharing and decision-making on a regional level. The Forum of Ministers gave approval to the recommendation "that we intensify our efforts to establish common legislative ground so as to modernize our national laws and statutes in order to better support the cause of preservation, restoration and salvage (recovery), conservation and display of our rich underwater heritage for the benefit and enjoyment of our peoples and the whole of mankind" (Forum of Ministers, 1998). The Latin American and Caribbean Group also support the decision of the UNESCO General Conference, made during its 29th session held in 1997, that the protection of the world's underwater cultural heritage should be regulated at the international level and that an international convention should be adopted to that effect (UNESCO, 1997).

UNDERWATER HERITAGE IN THE CARIBBEAN ISLANDS

Cayman Islands

The Cayman Islands are an Overseas Territory of the United Kingdom. The Cayman Government first invited assistance from professional archaeologists in 1978 (Leshikar-Denton, 1996; Leshikar-Denton, 1997a). Between 1979 and 1980, INA conducted a survey of Little Cayman, Cayman Brac, and Grand Cayman to locate and evaluate the islands' shipwrecks. According to project director Roger Smith (1981), members of INA initiated the Cayman Islands Project, their first archaeological research in the Caribbean, because of the apparent need and "because they believed the survey might provide an example to other West Indian nations of how scientific scrutiny, rather than the hunt for treasure, can bring aspects of national heritage to light." There were 77 archaeological sites recorded, including the 17th-century Turtle Wreck, an English turtle-fishing vessel thought to have been burned in 1670 by Spanish privateer, Manuel Rivero Pardal; the Careening Place, a site in use from at least the early 18th century; remains of the 1794 Wreck of the Ten Sail; as well as 19th and 20th-century wrecks. Archival research turned up the names of ships still to be found, such as Dutch West Indiaman *Dolphijn*, lost in 1629; British sloop-of-war *Jamaica*, wrecked in 1715; pirate ship *Morning Star*, run aground in 1722; and Spanish brigantine *San Miguel*, lost in 1730.

In 1979, the Cayman Islands passed a law to establish the Cayman Islands National Museum, and in 1984 Anita Ebanks was appointed director. Located in a historical building on the waterfront, the museum opened to the public in 1990. Between 1990 and 1993, Texas A&M University and the museum helped support archival, folklore, and archaeological investigations conducted by this author on the Wreck of the Ten Sail (Leshikar, 1992; Leshikar 1993; Leshikar-Denton, 1994). The disaster involved HMS *Convert* and nine vessels of a 58-ship merchant convoy, homeward-bound to Great Britain from Jamaica. All were lost on Grand Cayman's eastern reefs on February 8, 1794, during the French Revolutionary War (1792–1802). The frigate *Convert*, formerly *l'Inconstante* of France, had been captured in November 1793, and remained outfitted with much original equipment, including the primary ordnance of French 12-pounder cannons. In 1994, the museum opened an exhibit to commemorate the 200th anniversary of the Wreck of the Ten Sail, bringing archaeology into the public eye. Government officials were proud to bring Britain's Queen Elizabeth II and Prince Philip to see the exhibit during a visit to Grand Cayman. The museum also assisted in a Philatelic Bureau stamp issue, Currency Board commemorative coin, National Archive Publication, Visual Arts Society art competition, public lectures, and radio and television appearances to increase public awareness. Also in 1994, the Cayman Islands Government acknowledged the importance of historical wrecks when a land-based park was created at East End, providing a view of the reefs where the Wreck of the Ten Sail occurred.

During the 1990s, faced with applications from shipwreck salvors, the Ministry of Culture formed the Marine Archaeology Committee to advise them and to review and comment on bringing the Abandoned Wreck Law (1966) up to date. The committee reviewed the law, conducted detailed inquiry into current international experience, ethics and legislation, and concluded that it was inadequate. In 1996, the government instructed the Islands' legal draftsman to create new legislation. Meanwhile, the Marine Archaeology Committee has been successful in influencing the government not to issue permits to salvagers under the existing law.

In 1993, the museum employed an archaeologist. The inventory the INA team had compiled ten years earlier formed the core of a national shipwreck inventory that is being enlarged. The Wreck of the Ten Sail research resulted in documentation of 30 underwater sites and eight terrestrial sites within a three-mile zone at Grand Cayman's East End, expanding INA's work. Another late 17th-century wreck was located in the shallow reefs of Little Cayman. An 18th-century Spanish wreck, a mid-18th-century British merchantman, probable remains of the 1715 wreck of HMS *Jamaica*, and remains of a late 17th-century turtle-butchering station or shipwreck survivor's camp were discovered in Grand Cayman, among other sites. By 1999, the national shipwreck inventory included

80 sites on Grand Cayman, 20 sites on Little Cayman, and nine sites on Cayman Brac. At that date, the terrestrial site inventory included over 200 sites recorded on land in the Cayman Islands.

In 1999, the National Museum and Department of Environment collaborated in a brief but intensive field project to verify locations of shipwrecks first documented in Little Cayman by INA in 1979 and other sites discovered since that date. Original members of the INA survey team provided invaluable assistance in the assessment of 13 shipwrecks. A program to patrol these historical sites was permanently incorporated into the Little Cayman Marine Parks Officer's regular schedule. Among the wrecks are at least five early and archaeologically sensitive sites where public access should be controlled or limited. Little Cayman, however, is an ideal location to initiate a program for wider knowledge and awareness of less sensitive sites that can be interpreted for the education and enjoyment of the public. Thus, steps are being taken to involve the Little Cayman community in stewardship of the island's shipwrecks.

University College London and the museum conducted cooperative projects in 1992 and 1995, surveying for prehistoric sites on all three islands and testing on Cayman Brac (Drewett, 1992; Drewett, 1996). The Florida Museum of Natural History conducted an intensive prehistoric survey of Grand Cayman in 1993 (Stokes and Keegan, 1993). Both groups had negative results, which may mean the Cayman Islands, like Bermuda but unlike most Caribbean islands, were not occupied prehistorically by indigenous people. It is possible Columbus may have discovered the Cayman Islands in 1503.

The museum wants to attract cooperative projects with nonprofit organizations and graduate-level academic institutions to investigate and conserve materials from Cayman's shipwreck sites. At present, archival and nonintrusive archaeological research is being conducted by an undergraduate field school from Ball State University on the 1930 wreck of the schooner *Geneva Kathleen*. Along with oral history studies undertaken by a museum volunteer, the studies should result in an exhibition and publication in 2000. Locally, the museum is developing cooperative projects with watersports operators. In 1996, a brochure on the wreck of *Cali* was developed and a maritime history lesson was given to students who snorkeled over the site.

To increase awareness in protecting underwater heritage sites in the Caribbean, the Cayman Islands National Museum has provided information to individuals and governments from other countries. At the 1995 Museums Association of the Caribbean (MAC) meeting, a workshop entitled, "Protecting Archaeological Sites Underwater: Tools for the Caribbean" was conducted. Each participant received a reference notebook to use. To keep participants abreast of developments affecting underwater cultural heritage in the region, a network of information exchange has been opened among MAC, International Association for Caribbean Archaeology, and Caribbean Conservation Association.

Turks and Caicos Islands

In 1974, the Turks and Caicos Islands, an Overseas Territory of the United Kingdom, enacted the Historic Wrecks Ordinance. This law is based on the U.K.'s Protection of Wrecks Act (1973), although there were some additions and some of the language was adjusted. The authoritative body is the governor rather than the secretary of state. Notable differences from the U.K. law include the following additions: definitions of "historic wreck," "Receiver," and "restricted area"; historic wrecks are vested in the Crown and deemed to be in the possession of the Receiver; a person who commits an offense is liable to a fine of $1000 or imprisonment for six months, or both fine and imprisonment; a person in unlawful possession of part of a wreck or object therefrom is liable to a fine of $500 or imprisonment for three months or both, although the Receiver may release to a salvor part of a historic wreck; restriction on the use of explosives, a pressure hose or vacuum hose on a historic wreck without permission from the Receiver, carrying a fine of $500 or imprisonment for six months for violations; and, the Governor can make regulations for carrying into effect the provisions of the *Ordinance* that prescribe the forms or procedures to be employed in granting licenses, fees, royalties, or other sums to be paid under conditions of the license.

Archaeologist Donald Keith (1997c) relates that in the 1980s, Turks and Caicos Islands allowed groups to salvage shipwrecks in their waters, including the team of Peter Benchley, Stan Waterman and Teddy Tucker, Turks and Caicos Marine and Archaeological Recoveries, Ltd., and Nomad Treasure Seekers, with the resulting loss of shipwreck resources. Government became concerned, however, when a group called Caribbean Ventures discovered a site on Molasses Reef, which, in a 1980 *Miami Herald* article, they claimed was Columbus' *Pinta*. The historical significance of such a find prompted the Turks and Caicos Governor to call upon Colin Martin of the Scottish Institute of Maritime Studies, who verified the site's antiquity and recommended that the governor contact INA to request an archaeologist to work with Caribbean Ventures. In 1980, INA sent Donald Keith to determine if the site could be saved for archaeology. The treasure hunters eventually fell by the wayside, and INA began to excavate the Molasses Reef Wreck (Keith, 1987, 1988, 1997b). Though not *Pinta*, this pre-1520s wreck is thought to be the earliest shipwreck discovered in the Western Hemisphere (Figure 18.2).

The Molasses Reef Wreck was excavated between 1982 and 1985 and the conservation of artifacts undertaken by INA at Texas A&M University. In 1988, responsibility for the materials passed to a new, nonprofit institute, Ships of Exploration and Discovery Research, founded by Donald Keith and other graduate students who had carried out the project. The Molasses Reef Wreck provided a wealth of answers to mysteries surrounding the caravel. Since only two percent of the hull survived, however, the archaeologists decided to investigate the remains of two similar early-16th-century ships to fill in gaps in the analysis. Previously salvaged of most of its artifacts, the Highborn Cay Wreck in the Bahamas was located and test-excavated in the mid-1980s (Keith, 1988, 1997a; Smith, 1993). The early salvors had neglected the hull, so that archaeologists were able to study a well-preserved portion, including the main mast step carved out of the keelson. The second site, the Bahía Mujeres Wreck located off the northeast coast of Mexico's Yucatan Peninsula and surveyed in cooperation with INAH, provided further details (Keith, 1988; Luna Erreguerena, 1997, 1998; Smith, 1993).

By the late 1980s, conservation of the Molasses Reef Wreck artifacts neared completion. Between 1988–1990, through the efforts of private individuals in the Turks and Caicos Islands and Ships of Discovery, the Turks and Caicos Islands National Museum, was created. Fully sanctioned and recognized by the government and situated in a historical building, the museum opened in 1991. The Molasses Reef Wreck, a world-class exhibit, forms the central exhibition, complemented by other displays of cultural and natural history. Since 1991, a museum support facility has been built next to the National Museum, housing an exhibit workshop, conservation lab for messy wet-site work, lab for clean, controlled conservation, curatorial facility, lecture room, and combination office/library.

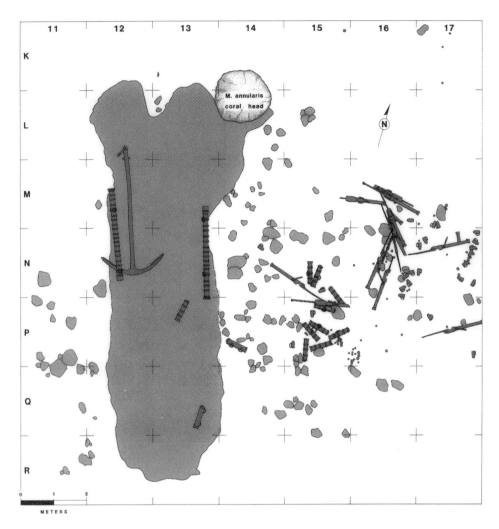

Figure 18.2. Molasses Reef Wreck site plan (Courtesy of Donald Keith, Institute of Nautical Archaeology).

The museum also has achieved progress in facilitating archaeological field surveys, excavations, and research projects, establishing a review process for proposals to conduct shipwreck salvage or archaeological excavations, initiating research projects in U.S., Bahamian, British, and French archives, and locating, examining, and recording collections of artifacts removed from the islands in the last century and now residing in U.S. museums. But problems still lurk on the horizon. The Turks and Caicos Government is considering proposals for a cruise ship port in an area of rich prehistoric and historical resources, and local inhabitants have applied for a permit to salvage shipwrecks.

Jamaica

Jamaica has long been concerned with preservation of historical resources by establishing, as early as 1879, the Institute of Jamaica, and by enactment of the Jamaica

National Trust Commission Act in 1958 and Jamaica National Heritage Trust Act of 1985 (Gray, 1997). In the mid-20th century, the Institute of Jamaica began sponsoring work at Port Royal, site of the thriving English colonial city that subsided into Kingston Harbor during an earthquake on June 7, 1692. Port Royal remains the only sunken city in the New World. The first efforts on underwater portions of the site were lacking in scientific method. They were accomplished in the late 1950s by Edwin Link and the National Geographic Society, who produced a pre-1692 map of Port Royal. From 1966 to 1968, Robert Marx excavated caches of artifacts with little archaeological control. In 1969, Philip Mayes conducted terrestrial work that included the involvement of Jamaicans and resulted in creation of the Jamaican Archaeological Research Center in the Old Naval Hospital.

The most scientific underwater archaeological work at Port Royal was undertaken between 1981 and late 1990 by Texas A&M University in association with INA and the Jamaica National Heritage Trust (JNHT), under the direction of archaeologist Donny Hamilton (1991; 1997). The 10-year project included professional excavation of eight substantial buildings and a ship that rammed through one of the buildings during the 1692 earthquake (Clifford, 1991) (Figure 18.3). The project has resulted in reports, theses, and dissertations that provide a large body of significant data on all aspects of life in 17th-century Port Royal. Hamilton's conservation program and analysis of artifacts from the site are ongoing. Meanwhile, Jamaica has established museums at Port Royal. Today, all activities affecting historical Port Royal must be approved by the Jamaica National Heritage Trust. Enforcement is facilitated by the Jamaica Defense Force Coast Guard based at Port Royal.

In the 1980s and early 1990s, INA launched a series of projects in Jamaica to locate remains of Columbus's two caravels, *Capitana* and *Santiago de Palos*, which were run aground in St. Ann's Bay during his fourth voyage (Geddes, 1992; Neville et al., 1992; Smith 1988a). The ships have not been found but, during the search, INA archaeologists discovered six 18th-century merchantmen. This is not surprising, since Jamaica was Britain's most important outpost in the Western Caribbean, posting naval squadrons there to protect the colony and its extensive merchant trade throughout the 18th century. One British sloop of this era, the Reader's Point Wreck, was investigated in detail by archaeologists from the JNHT and INA in the 1990s, under the direction of Greg Cook (1997). The vessel appeared to have been scuttled at the site around the time of the American Revolutionary War, after a long career as a merchant trader in the West Indies and Central America.

In the 1980s, INA assisted the Jamaican Government in survey work on the treacherous Pedro Banks. Shipwrecks of several nationalities and time periods were located, but the Pedro Cays are geographically far from the Jamaican mainland. Since work there requires much logistical support, limited funding has precluded development of projects. Shipwrecks on Pedro Banks have been affected by the illegal salvaging of treasure hunters.

Sponsored by the Institute of Jamaica, this author documented the construction of a traditional dugout canoe in the summer of 1983 (Leshikar, 1985; Leshikar, 1988). The vessel, made entirely with hand tools in six weeks, is typical of canoes constructed on the north coast of Jamaica. The canoe-makers were concerned that the skill to build such craft would be lost when the current generation of canoe-makers dies. If they are correct, the study thus served a useful purpose in documenting canoe construction methods linked to Jamaica's past.

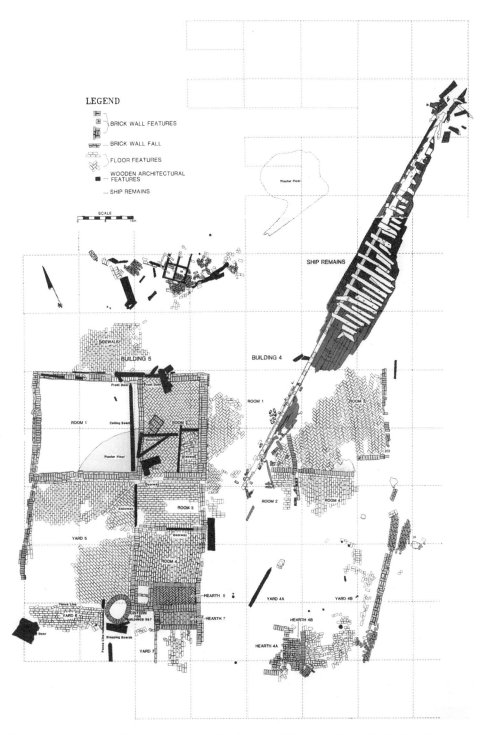

Figure 18.3. Buildings 4, 5 and shipwreck, Port Royal, Jamaica (Courtesy of Donny L. Hamilton, Institute of Nautical Archaeology, Texas A&M University).

Archaeological sites in Jamaica require identification to become part of the protected heritage. There is a recognized need to create a national inventory and to educate the public. Furthermore, Dorrick Grey (1997) of the Jamaica National Heritage Trust suggests that "the multifaceted nature of Caribbean society requires the research and preservation of not only the Spanish galleons but also the British, French and Dutch slavers scattered on our ocean floor."

Jamaica is a member of the Forum of Ministers of Culture and Officials Responsible for Cultural Policy of Latin America and the Caribbean. A representative of the island participated in the 1998 meeting of the Technical Commission on Underwater Cultural Heritage held in Santo Domingo.

Cuba

Representatives of Cuba attended, as observers, the 1998 and 1999 meetings of the Technical Commission on Underwater Cultural Heritage, formed by the Forum of Ministers of Culture and Officials Responsible for Cultural Policy of Latin America and the Caribbean. Eddy Fernández González and Francisco Escobar Guio (1998) related that while underwater archaeology is relatively new in Cuba, scientific archaeology is important. Activities affecting this heritage are controlled within the Ministry of Culture under laws No. 1 and No. 2 of August 4, 1977, *Ley de Protección al Patrimonio Cultural* and *Ley de los Monumentos Nacionales y Locales* respectively. A legal and executive structure exists for companies working there. In 1998, two entities were authorized to conduct investigations. CARISUB had undertaken underwater work for about 18–20 years, while GEOCUBA *Estudios Marinos* had been involved in underwater archaeology for about five years. In the near future, information about various projects that have been undertaken in Cuba, a Caribbean island with an extremely rich history, may be more readily available outside of Cuba.

Haiti

Harold Gaspar (1998) believes there are more than 200 known shipwrecks in the waters of Haiti. Although legal measures dating from the 1940s address terrestrial archaeological sites, access to underwater cultural heritage has not been properly regulated. In an attempt to fill an institutional gap, the decree of September 26, 1995 was issued to create the National Office of Marine Archaeology. The office's principle missions are to establish a national policy on marine archaeology; maintain an inventory of sites; control and manage prospecting activities; establish rules; promote scientific investigation; encourage international cooperation; and create and administer marine archaeological reserves and parks with a view toward increasing museum and tourism activities.

As of 1998, the National Office of Marine Archaeology still had not been instituted. In 1996, however, developments were occurring in the Ministry of Culture that may be favorable for Haitian cultural heritage. Gaspar encouraged development of a legal framework and concluded that Haitian underwater heritage is threatened if nothing is done locally or internationally to protect it.

In 1998, Haiti signed an agreement with the French nongovernmental organization, Nautical Archaeological Research Group (GRAN), whose intent is to verify and document slave routes in Haiti and the Dominican Republic (Forum of Ministers, 1998). Principal investigator Max Guérout included slave ships in the project design.

Haiti participates in the Forum of Ministers of Culture and Officials Responsible for Cultural Policy of Latin America and the Caribbean, and the Island was represented at the 1998 and 1999 meetings of the Technical Commission on Underwater Cultural Heritage held in Santo Domingo.

Dominican Republic

In June 1998, the Dominican Republic hosted the first meeting of the Technical Commission on Underwater Cultural Heritage in Santo Domingo, heralding a new age in Caribbean underwater archaeology (Forum of Ministers, 1998). The country asked for and received approval to head this commission because of its wealth of experience and extensive work in the area of underwater cultural heritage for two decades.

During the meeting, Dominican Republic representatives noted that more than 400 shipwrecks are located in the waters of Hispaniola and suggested that, although cooperative agreements with commercial salvage interests had occurred in the past, they now preferred to work with universities. They expressed a desire to keep 100 percent of recovered artifacts in the country. As a leader in this new awareness of the cultural value of underwater cultural heritage to humanity, the Dominican Republic was chosen to represent the Latin American and Caribbean Group at the 1998 meeting in Paris, to review the draft UNESCO Convention on the Protection of Underwater Cultural Heritage.

A compendium of the Dominican Republic's cultural heritage legislation was published (Brea-Franco and Victoriano M., 1998). In 1979, the Comisión de Rescate Arqueológico Submarino (CRAS) was created by executive order, "with the main objective of salvaging, conserving and exhibiting all cultural heritage goods found in the territorial waters and maritime jurisdictions falling under the economic influence of the country" (Forum of Ministers, 1998). Under the auspices of the navy, the agency identifies archaeological sites, grants exploration permits, and supervises exploratory activities. CRAS developed a specialized laboratory to catalogue and inventory all salvaged items, ensuring that they receive appropriate conservation using scientific methods, so that they may be put on public display. The intent is "to ensure that these artifacts be available for heritage/cultural tourism, for the enjoyment of the citizens of the Dominican Republic and visitors." CRAS administers the Museo de las Reales Atarazanas (Royal Shipyards Museum) and the Museo de Arqueología Submarina del Faro a Colón (Columbus Lighthouse Underwater Archaeology Museum). The agency has loaned exhibits to the Museo de las Casas Reales (Royal Houses Museum) among other Dominican Republic museums, and the National Aquarium. CRAS exhibits are also on tour in Spain, Portugal, and the United States. The agency has been involved in the publication of books about the excavated ships (Borrell B., 1983a; Borrell B., 1983b; Borrell et al., 1997; Santiago, 1990).

Dominican officials consider work on the following projects conducted in the Dominican Republic over the past 19 years to be particularly relevant (Forum of Ministers, 1998): *Nuestra Señora de Guadalupe* and *Conde de Tolosa*, lost in 1724 in Samaná Bay with a large cargo of mercury used in the process of precious metals extraction; *Nuestra Señora de la Pura y Limpia Concepción*, lost in 1641 on the Silver Bank with a cargo of gold and silver ingots, coins and other artifacts destined for the Spanish Crown; French warship *Scipión*, lost in Samaná Bay in 1782 after a battle with several British vessels; French ships *Diómedes* and *Imperial*, lost in 1806 in an area known as Palenque, also after a battle with British ships; excavations on Saona Island to locate the fleet of Hispaniola's conquistador, Frey Nicolás de Ovando; a search for shipwrecks in Monte Cristi Bay (where 20 vessels were found) and in the Isabela area; investigations of the 17th-century "Pipe Wreck" in Monte Cristi Bay; and a new project, currently being carried out by the French organization GRAN, to verify and document slave routes.

To highlight several scientific archaeological projects in progress, in the 1980s INA searched for Columbus' ships lost off the north coast of Hispaniola, including the nao *Santa María*, wrecked during his first voyage, and the caravels *Mariagalante*, *Gallega*, *San Juan*, and *Cardera*, lost during his second trip. Surveys and test excavations in Bahía de Isabela and Bahía de Caracol were unsuccessful. In the 1990s, Indiana University and PanAmerican Consultants cooperated in the continued search for Columbus' ships (James and Beeker, 1994) and investigated prehistoric sites. Of particular importance is research undertaken at Manantial de la Aleta, East National Park, where, in addition to a prehistoric plaza, a cenote containing well-preserved Taino artifacts is under study (Foster and Beeker, 1997). This site has been identified as one of the most significant archaeological sites in the Dominican Republic, because it has the potential to reveal details about Taino ceremonial life and culture.

Finally, the Pan-American Institute of Maritime Archaeology, under the direction of Jerome Hall, has researched a 17th-century interloper into the Spanish colonies off the north coast of Hispaniola, apparently enroute from Europe to North America via the Caribbean when it was lost (Hall, 1991, 1992, 1993, 1994, 1997a). It is hypothesized that the Monte Christi Shipwreck, also known as the "Pipe Wreck," was an English-built merchantman carrying a Dutch cargo of clay tobacco pipes of Amsterdam manufacture. The artifacts suggest that the ship wrecked between 1652 and 1656.[1]

Puerto Rico

Puerto Rico enacted legislation to establish the Consejo para la Conservación y Estudio de Sitios y Recursos Arqueológicos Subacuáticos in 1987. The Consejo created the Office of Underwater Archaeology to register sites, investigate illegal salvage, issue permits and evaluate the effect of coastal development on underwater resources (Hall, 1997b). Two Spanish steamships, *Alicante* (lost in 1881) and *Antonio López* (wrecked in 1898 during the Spanish–American war), and a 17th-century site, the Rincón Astrolabe Wreck, have been investigated. Plans are underway for compiling an inventory of Puerto Rico's underwater archaeological sites and creating a conservation facility. According to Richard Fontánez Aldea (1997), archival research has revealed more than 200 shipwrecks in the waters of Puerto Rico, 12 of which have been archaeologically recorded.

Anguilla

Since 1994, the Government of Anguilla, an Overseas a Dependent Territory of the United Kingdom, has received proposals from people who wish to work commercially on the 1772 Spanish inbound merchantmen *El Buen Consejo* and *Jesús, María y Jos*é. They

---

[1] By the president's decree of June 26, 1999, the Dominican Republic created the National Office for the Protection of the Underwater Cultural Heritage, which replaces all previous authorities responsible for underwater cultural heritage in the country. The decree, mindful of UNESCO and ICOMOS initiatives, is an important development for the protection and management of underwater heritage in the Caribbean.

formed the Historic Wrecks Advisory Committee to advise them on how to proceed. In 1995, when members of the ICOMOS International Committee on Underwater Cultural Heritage became aware of Anguilla's situation, information on protecting underwater cultural heritage was sent to the government. Later, Bob Conrich, a member of the Advisory Committee, attended the 1996 Society for Historical Archaeology Conference and a meeting of the Advisory Council on Underwater Archaeology in the United States. His contact with archaeologists resulted in assistance from East Carolina University and the Washington, D.C., volunteer group MAHS under the direction of Bradley Rodgers, whose team produced a map and site analysis for the Anguilla Government. Plans are underway for archaeologists from Texas A&M University and Florida State University to work in Anguilla in the future. Nonetheless, Government is still entertaining a commercial proposal, so the ultimate disposition of *El Buen Consejo* and *Jesús, María y José* remains uncertain. At the 1997 SHA Conference, Bob Conrich (1997) related his views and experiences in working for the protection of underwater cultural heritage in Anguilla.

Martinique and Guadeloupe

Retired navy Officer Max Guérout, of the French organization GRAN, related at the 1998 meeting of the Technical Commission on Underwater Cultural Heritage in Santo Domingo that, over the past seven years, he has been involved in a project to inventory the shipwrecks of Martinique. Both Martinique and Guadeloupe are considered departments of France and are subject to the laws of that country. At this writing, however, little more can be reported.

Netherlands Antilles

The Netherlands Antilles includes Curacao and Bonaire, located near the coast of Venezuela, and Sint Maarten/St. Martin, St. Eustatius, and Saba, east of Puerto Rico. The 1992 Treaty of Malta, which applies to European archaeological heritage, also applies to the Netherlands Antilles. Thus, the government is currently reviewing existing legislation and working to amend it so that it will come into agreement with the Treaty of Malta (Nagelkerken and Ayubi, 1997).

St. Eustatius. Between 1982 and 1988, the Archaeological–Anthropological Institute of the Netherlands Antilles, in cooperation with the College of William and Mary, undertook archaeological research in the historical anchorage of St. Eustatius at Orange Bay, (Nagelkerken, 1985; Nagelkerken and Ayubi, 1997), a significant anchorage for European seafarers during the 17th and 18th centuries. Size and location of the historical anchorage were identified, and Dutch, French, and English ceramics and wine bottle glass, as well as bricks, tiles, and beads were noted.

Sint Maarten/St. Martin. Between 1994 and 1995, the Sint Maarten National Heritage Foundation, Ministry of Culture, Department of Planning and Environment, and Maritime Archaeology and Research cooperated in the investigation of HMS *Proselyte*, a captured Dutch frigate (ex-*Jason*), which wrecked in 1801 in Sint Maarten (Bequette, 1996). Previously, little attention had been placed on protection and management of underwater cultural heritage in the island. Recent discoveries, however, have focused the attention of sport divers, salvage operators, Sint Maarten's National Heritage Foundation, and the Ministry of Culture on shipwrecks. Archaeologists have mapped and identified the extent of the *Proselyte* site, with a view to developing a management plan to protect it from further looting or salvage. Kathryn Bequette suggests that any further artifacts recovered from the site should be preserved and displayed at the Sint Maarten Museum in Philipsburg and in the archival collection.

Curacao. Since 1987, the Archaeological–Anthropological Institute of the Netherlands Antilles has worked on two major underwater projects in the island of Curacao (Haviser, 1997). The first involved the Dutch frigate *Alphen*, which exploded and sank in 1778 in Santa Anna Bay (Nagelkerken, 1989). Survey work in the 1980s was followed by archaeological excavation at the site between 1994–1998. *Alphen* is currently the only underwater archaeological site on the official Curacao monuments list. The second project was undertaken in 1993. Dredging during repair work on the quay wall of the Handelskade (the main commercial wharf area at the entrance to Santa Anna Bay) revealed 17th-, 18th-, and 19th-century artifacts (Nagelkerken, 1998). Subsequently, the Archaeological–Anthropological Institute of the Netherlands Antilles conducted a survey and limited surface collection prior to the construction of a new sheet pile wall by the Port Authority.

Barbados

The Barbados Museum and Historical Society has long been respected for its contributions to preserving the cultural heritage of Barbados. Much emphasis has been placed on the archaeological heritage, including a rich prehistoric and historical legacy, which is evident in displays in the Barbados Museum. Until recently, underwater cultural heritage has received little attention. In the 1990s, however, the Government of Barbados received several applications from organizations that wanted permits to survey and salvage shipwrecks located in the waters of Barbados. But Barbados has been cautious and has yet to issue such a permit.

Barbados is a member of the Forum of Ministers of Culture and Officials Responsible for Cultural Policy of Latin America and the Caribbean, and has sent representatives to the 1998 and 1999 meetings of the Technical Commission on Underwater Cultural Heritage. According to the museum's director (Cummins, personal communication, 1999), Barbados has conducted a recent intensive examination to delimit its Exclusive Economic Zone in accordance with the 1982 United Nations Convention on the Law of the Sea. On advice from the Barbados Museum and Historical Society during these discussions, the government is considering recommendations for a professional underwater archaeological survey to be conducted, to evaluate the extent and nature of cultural remains existing in the waters surrounding the island. In addition, Barbados has completed a draft of the proposed Preservation of Antiquities and Relics Bill, 1997, which has been under development for several years and which includes underwater heritage. While the bill is not yet law, Barbados, is making great strides towards protection of its cultural heritage.

Trinidad and Tobago

Claire Broadbridge, former director of Trinidad National Museum and Art Gallery, succeeded in influencing the Government of Trinidad and Tobago to enact legislation to protect several French Louis XIV period shipwrecks discovered buried in harbor sediments of the island of Tobago, vessels lost when the Dutch and French fought there in 1677. The potential of these sites is great, when one considers a Wreck of the same nationality and era recently excavated off the coast of Texas, French explorer La Salle's *La Belle*.

In 1998, Vel Lewis (1998), current director of Trinidad National Museum & Art Gallery, described the state of affairs in the twin republic at the First Meeting of the Technical Commission on Underwater Cultural Heritage in Santo Domingo. He related that the 17th-century wrecks were accidentally discovered during harbor dredging, and, as a result of the find, the government introduced the United Kingdom-based Protection of Wrecks Act (1994) to safeguard them and other historical shipwrecks. Key points of the law provide that authority is given to the Minister for Shipping; specific sites can be designated as restricted areas, where it is an offense for anyone to enter or tamper; wrecks are the property of the state; it is mandatory for people to report wrecks to the Receiver of Wrecks; there is provision for licenses to be issued by the Minister of Works & Transport; power is given to declare a dangerous Wreck a prohibited area; and penalties can be imposed for illegal activity.

Little regarding shipwrecks occurred between 1994 and 1997, when the government began to receive calls regarding proposals to work the 1677 sites. A technical advisory committee was appointed to advise the minister on sites to be designated, to approve the issue of licenses by named individuals with conditions attached, and to deal with problems of conservation and the disposition of artifacts. The committee met once before the retirement of its chair, Claire Broadbridge, in 1997. Vel Lewis succeeded her as chair in 1998. The committee is working on compiling an inventory of sites with the help of the local Military Museum, reviewing the 1994 legislation, and developing a set of guidelines to approve requests from international bodies that want to work in Trinidad and Tobago.

Admirably, Trinidad and Tobago took quick action to protect and manage the irreplaceable 1677 Dutch and French shipwrecks in their waters. These well-preserved sites are the legacy not only of the Island but also of the Caribbean region and the world.

CONCLUSION

The Caribbean contains some of the world's most significant maritime heritage sites. The underwater cultural heritage is particularly endangered. Scientific archaeological projects of the past 20 years, and resulting museum exhibitions, are setting precedents for the future, but commercial salvage continues at an alarming rate. The future of Caribbean underwater cultural heritage depends not only on archaeologists, museum professionals and concerned citizens, but also on governments. Local, regional and international initiatives should be promoted to gain their support.[2]

---

[2] This chapter is an adapted and significantly enlarged version of a paper presented at a meeting of the ICOMOS International Committee on Underwater Cultural Heritage on September 7, 1997, in Fremantle, Australia. The original paper was published in *Indian Ocean Week 1997 Proceedings* by the Western Australian Museum in May 1998.

REFERENCES

Arnold III, J. Barto, and Weddle, Robert, 1978, *The Nautical Archaeology of Padre Island, The Spanish Shipwrecks of 1554*. Academic Press, New York.

Bass, George F., editor, 1988, *Ships and Shipwrecks of the Americas*. Thames and Hudson, London.

Bequette, Kathryn E., 1996, The HMS *Proselyte* Project: Survey of an Eighteenth-Century British Frigate in Great Bay, Sint Maarten. In *Underwater Archaeology*, edited by S.R. James, Jr. and C. Stanley, pp. 73–75. Society for Historical Archaeology.

Borrell B., Pedro J., 1983a, *Arqueología Submarina en La República Dominicana*. Comisión de Rescate Arqueológico Submarino, Santo Domingo.

_____, 1983b, *Historia y Rescate del Galeon Nuestra Senora de la Concepción*. Comisión de Rescate Arqueológico Submarino, Santo Domingo.

Borrell, Pedro, Montás, Eugenio Pérez, and Apestegui, Cruz, 1997, *La Aventura del Guadalupe*. Lunwerg, Barcelona.

Bratten, John R., 1998, Recent Artifact Finds from the Emanuel Point Ship. In *Underwater Archaeology*, edited by L.E. Babits, C. Fach, and R. Harris, pp. 38–44. Society for Historical Archaeology.

Brea Franco, Luis O., and Victoriano M., Ramón A., 1998, *Hacia un Programa de Desarrollo Cultural para la República Dominicana, Informes sobre el Diagnóstico Participativo del Sector Cultural, Tomo I, Compendio de Legislación Cultural*. Consejo Presidencial de Cultura, Santo Domingo.

Cayman Islands Government, 1966, *Abandoned Wreck Law*.

Clifford, Sheila A., 1991, A Preliminary Report on a Possible 17th-Century Shipwreck at Port Royal, Jamaica. In *Underwater Archaeology Proceedings from the Society for Historical Archaeology Conference*, edited by J.D. Broadwater, pp. 80–83. Richmond.

Conrich, Bob, 1997, Neocolonialism in Anguilla. In *Underwater Archaeology*, edited by D.C. Lakey, pp. 44–49. Society for Historical Archaeology.

Cook, Gregory D., 1997, Reader's Point Wreck. In *Encyclopaedia of Underwater and Maritime Archaeology*, edited by J.P. Delgado, p. 334. British Museum Press, London.

Cozzi, J., 1998, Hull Remains of the Emanuel Point Ship. In *Underwater Archaeology*, edited by L.E. Babits, C. Fach, and R. Harris, pp. 31–37. Society for Historical Archaeology.

Cummins, Alissandra, 1999, Personal Communication.

Delgado, James P., editor, 1997, *Encyclopaedia of Underwater and Maritime Archaeology*. British Museum Press, London.

Drewett, Peter L., 1992, *The Cayman Islands: Their Potential in Prehistoric Research*. Institute of Archaeology Report. University College, London.

_____, 1996, *An Archaeological Survey of Cayman Brac and Little Cayman Together with a Test Excavation in Great Cave, Cayman Brac, 1995*. Institute of Archaeology Report, University College, London.

Fernández González, Eddy and Escobar Guio, Francisco, 1998, *Cuba*. Presentations at the First Meeting of the Technical Commission on Underwater Cultural Heritage, June 15, 1998. Forum of Ministers of Culture and Officials Responsible for Cultural Policy of Latin America and the Caribbean.

Fontánez Aldea, Richard, 1997, Puerto Rico. In *Encyclopaedia of Underwater and Maritime Archaeology*, edited by J.P. Delgado, p. 330. British Museum Press, London.

Forum of Ministers of Culture and Officials Responsible for Cultural Policy of Latin America and the Caribbean, 1998a, *Santo Domingo Declaration*. First Meeting of the Technical Commission on Underwater Cultural Heritage.

_____, 1998b, *Report on the Status of the Convention for Safeguarding Underwater Cultural Heritage*. Tenth Meeting, December 4–5, 1998 Bridgetown, Barbados.

Foster, John W. and Beeker, Charles D., 1997, The Conquest of a Sinkhole: Initial Archaeological Investigations at El Manantial de la Aleta, East National Park, Dominican Republic. In *Underwater Archaeology*, edited by D.C. Lakey, pp. 27–32. Society for Historical Archaeology.

Gaspar, Harold, 1998, *Haiti*. Presentation at the First Meeting of the Technical Commission on Underwater Cultural Heritage, June 15, 1998. Forum of Ministers of Culture and Officials Responsible for Cultural Policy of Latin America and the Caribbean.

Geddes III, Donald G., 1992, Archival Research: The Search for the Columbus Caravels at St. Ann's Bay, Jamaica. In *Underwater Archaeology Proceedings from the Society for Historical Archaeology Conference*, Kingston, Jamaica, edited by D.H. Keith and T.L Carrell, pp. 148–151.

Gray, Dorrick E., 1997, *Managing Underwater Archaeological Resources: The Jamaican Experience*. Paper presented at the Society for Historical Archaeology Conference, Corpus Christi, Texas.

Hall, Jerome L., 1991, The 17th-Century Merchant Vessel at Monte Cristi Bay, Dominican Republic. In *Underwater Archaeology Proceedings from the Society for Historical Archaeology Conference*, edited by John D. Broadwater, pp. 84–87. Richmond.

_____, 1992, A Brief History of Underwater Salvage in the Dominican Republic. In *Underwater Archaeology Proceedings from the Society for Historical Archaeology Conference*, Kingston, Jamaica, edited by D.H. Keith and T.L. Carrell, pp. 35–40.

_____, 1993, The 17th-Century Merchant Shipwreck in Monte Cristi Bay, Dominican Republic: The Second Excavation Season Interim Report. In *Underwater Archaeology Proceedings from the Society for Historical Archaeology Conference*, Kansas City, edited by S.O. Smith, pp. 95–101.

_____, 1994, Spanish Coins, Dutch Clay Pipes, and an English Ship: The 1993 Monte Cristi Shipwreck Project Interim Report. In *Underwater Archaeology Proceedings from the Society for Historical Archaeology Conference*, Vancouver, edited by R.P. Woodward and C.D. Moore, pp. 32–39.

_____, 1997a, Monte Cristi Wreck. In *Encyclopaedia of Underwater and Maritime Archaeology*, edited by J.P. Delgado, pp. 283–284. British Museum Press, London.

_____, 1997b, *Puerto Rico: Island of Enchantment?* Paper presented at the Society for Historical Archaeology Conference, Corpus Christi.

Hamilton, D.L., 1991, A Decade of Excavations at Port Royal, Jamaica. In *Underwater Archaeology Proceedings from the Society for Historical Archaeology Conference*, edited by J.D. Broadwater, pp. 90–94.

_____, 1997, Port Royal. In *Encyclopaedia of Underwater and Maritime Archaeology*, edited by J.P. Delgado, pp. 316–318. British Museum Press, London.

Haviser, Jay B., 1997, Curacao. In *Encyclopaedia of Underwater and Maritime Archaeology*, edited by J.P. Delgado, p. 121. British Museum Press, London.

James, Stephen R. and Beeker, Charles, 1994, The Fifteenth-century Shipwrecks of La Isabela: Current Investigations. In *Underwater Archaeology Proceedings from the Society for Historical Archaeology Conference*, edited by R.P. Woodward and C.D. Moore, pp. 3–7.

Keith, Donald H., 1987, *The Molasses Reef Wreck*. Ph.D dissertation, Texas A&M University. University Microfilms, Ann Arbor.

_____, 1988, Shipwrecks of the Explorers. In *Ships and Shipwrecks of the Americas*, edited by G.F. Bass, pp. 45–68. Thames and Hudson, London.

_____, 1997a, Highborn Cay Wreck. In *Encyclopaedia of Underwater and Maritime Archaeology*, edited by J.P. Delgado, pp. 192–193. British Museum Press, London.

_____, 1997b, Molasses Reef Wreck. In *Encyclopaedia of Underwater and Maritime Archaeology*, edited by J.P. Delgado, pp. 279–281. British Museum Press, London.

_____, 1997c, Problems and Progress in Underwater Archaeology in the Turks and Caicos Islands. In *Underwater Archaeology*, edited by D.C. Lakey, pp. 38–43. Society for Historical Archaeology.

Leshikar, Margaret E., 1985, Construction of a Dugout Canoe in the Parish of St. Ann, Jamaica. In *Proceedings of the Sixteenth Conference on Underwater Archaeology*, edited by P.F. Johnston, pp. 48–51. Society for Historical Archaeology.

_____, 1988, The Earliest Watercraft: From Rafts to Viking Ships. In *Ships and Shipwrecks of the Americas*, edited by G.F. Bass, pp. 13–32. Thames and Hudson, London.

_____, 1992, Investigation of the Wreck of the Ten Sail, Cayman Islands, British West Indies. In *Underwater Archaeology Proceedings from the Society for Historical Archaeology Conference*, Kingston, Jamaica, edited by D.H. Keith and T.L. Carrell, pp. 30–34.

_____, 1993, *The 1794 Wreck of the Ten Sail, Cayman Islands, British West Indies: A Historical Study and Archaeological Survey*. Ph.D. dissertation, Texas A&M University. University Microfilms, Ann Arbor.

Leshikar-Denton, Margaret E., 1994, *Our Islands Past, Volume II, The Wreck of the Ten Sail*. Cayman Islands National Archive and Cayman Free Press.

_____, 1996 Underwater Cultural Resource Management in Mexico and the Caribbean. In Underwater Archaeology, edited by S.R. James, Jr. and C. Stanley, pp. 57–60. Society for Historical Archaeology.

_____, 1997a, Underwater Cultural Resource Management: A New Concept in the Cayman Islands. In *Underwater Archaeology*, edited by D.C. Lakey, pp. 33–37. Society for Historical Archaeology.

_____, 1997b, Caribbean. In *Encyclopaedia of Underwater and Maritime Archaeology*, edited by J.P. Delgado, p.86–89. British Museum Press, London.

_____, 1998, Maritime Archaeology in the Caribbean. In *Indian Ocean Week 1997 Proceedings*, edited by G. Henderson, pp. 62–72. Western Australian Museum.

Lewis, Vel, 1998, *Trinidad and Tobago*. Presentation at the First Meeting of the Technical Commission on Underwater Cultural Heritage, June 15, 1998. Forum of Ministers of Culture and Officials Responsible for Cultural Policy of Latin America and the Caribbean.

Luna Erreguerena, Pilar, 1997, Stepping Stones of Mexican Underwater Archaeology. In *Underwater Archaeology*, edited by D.C. Lakey, pp. 50–53. Society for Historical Archaeology.

_____, 1998, Aspects of Mexican Underwater Archaeology. In *Indian Ocean Week 1997 Proceedings*, edited by G. Henderson, pp. 36–41. Western Australian Museum.

Nagelkerken, Wil, 1985, Preliminary Report on the Determination of the Location of the Historical Anchorage at Orange Bay, St. Eustatius, Netherlands Antilles. In *Proceedings of the Sixteenth Conference on Underwater Archaeology*, edited by P.F. Johnston, pp. 60–76. Society for Historical Archaeology.

_____, 1989, Survey of the Dutch Frigate *Alphen*, which Exploded and Sank in 1778 in the Harbor of Curacao. In *Proceedings of the Thirteenth International Congress for Caribbean Archaeology*, edited by E. Ayubi and J. Haviser, pp. 771–792. Archaeological–Anthropological Institute of the Netherlands Antilles.

_____, 1998, Nineteenth-Century Dutch Pearlware Recovered in the Harbor of Curacao, Netherlands Antilles. In *Underwater Archaeology*, edited by L.E. Babits, C. Fach, and R. Harris, pp. 104–110. Society for Historical Archaeology.

Nagelkerken, Wil and Ayubi, Edwin, 1997, *Underwater Cultural Resource Management in the Netherlands Antilles*. Paper presented at the Society for Historical Archaeology Conference, Corpus Christi.

Neville, John C., Neyland, Robert S., and Parrent, James M., 1992, The Search for Columbus's Last Ships: The 1991 Field Season. In *Underwater Archaeology Proceedings from the Society for Historical Archaeology Conference*, edited by D.H. Keith and T.L Carrell, pp. 148–151.

Pearson, Charles E., and Hoffman, Paul E., 1995, *The Last Voyage of El Nuevo Constante: The Wreck and Recovery of an Eighteenth-Century Spanish Ship off the Louisiana Coast*. Louisiana State University Press, Baton Rouge.

Santiago, Pedro J., 1990, *Estudios sobre Comercio Maritimo, Naufragios y Rescates Submarinos en la Republica Dominicana*. Comisión de Rescate Arqueológico Submarino and Museo de las Casas Reales, Santo Domingo.

Scott-Ireton, Della A., 1998, An Examination of the Luna Colonization Fleet. In *Underwater Archaeology*, edited by L.E. Babits, C. Fach, and R. Harris, pp. 25–30. Society for Historical Archaeology.

Smith, Roger C., 1981, *The Maritime Heritage of the Cayman Islands: Contributions in Nautical Archaeology*. M.A. thesis, Texas A&M University, College Station.

_____, 1988a, The Voyages of Columbus: The Search for His Ships. In *Ships and Shipwrecks of the Americas*, edited by G.F. Bass, pp. 33–44. Thames and Hudson, London.

_____, 1988b, Treasure Ships of the Spanish Main: The Iberian-American Maritime Empires. In *Ships and Shipwrecks of the Americas*, edited by G.F. Bass, pp. 85–106. Thames and Hudson, London.

_____, 1991, Florida's Underwater Archaeological Preserves. In *Underwater Archaeology Proceedings from the Society for Historical Archaeology Conference*, edited by J.D. Broadwater, pp. 43–46.

_____, 1993, *Vanguard of Empire*. Oxford University Press, Oxford, UK.

_____, 1994, The Ship at Emanuel Point: An Examination of Florida's Earliest Shipwreck. In *Underwater Archaeology Proceedings from the Society for Historical Archaeology Conference*, edited by R.P. Woodward and C.D. Moore, pp. 14–18.

Smith, Roger C., Spirek, James, Bratten, John, and Scott-Ireton, Della, 1995, *The Emanuel Point Ship: Archaeological Investigations, 1992–1995*. Bureau of Archaeological Research, Division of Historical Resources, Florida Department of State, Tallahassee.

Smith, Roger C., Bratten, John R., Cozzi, J., and Plaskett, Keith, 1999, *The Emanuel Point Ship: Archaeological Investigations, 1997–1998*. Report of Investigations No. 68. Archaeology Institute, University of West Florida.

Stokes, A.V., and Keegan, W.F., 1993, *A Settlement Survey for Prehistoric Archaeological Sites on Grand Cayman*. Department of Anthropology Miscellaneous Project Report 52. Florida Museum of Natural History, Gainesville.

Throckmorton, P., editor, 1987, *The Sea Remembers*. Mitchell Beazley International Ltd., London.

Trinidad and Tobago Government, 1994, *Protection of Wrecks Act*.

Turks and Caicos Government, 1974, *Historic Wrecks Ordinance*.

United Kingdom Government, 1973, *Protection of Wrecks Act*.

UNESCO, 1997, *Report by the Director-General on Action Taken Concerning the Desirability of Preparing an International Instrument for the Protection of the Underwater Cultural Heritage*. General Conference, Twenty-ninth Session, Paris.

Chapter 19

Underwater Cultural Heritage in Bermuda

CLIFFORD EARLE SMITH JR. AND EDWARD CECIL HARRIS

INTRODUCTION

The first recorded encounter of Bermuda was between 1503 and 1505 by Spaniard Juan Bermúdez on a return trip to Europe, on the eastern side of the Gulf Stream at 64°40' West and 32°20' North. In the centuries before the invention of the Harrison chronometer, which allowed for the routine determination of longitude, Bermuda served as a navigational beacon for shipping bound for Europe from the Caribbean (Bream, 1990). Surrounded by extensive reefs, Bermuda became the burial ground for vessels of many nations and types, forming an underwater cultural resource of several hundred sites.

In the 1950s, treasure was discovered, and the shipwrecks of Bermuda have been degraded or destroyed by salvage and pilfering since. Legislation enacted in 1959 protected the rights of license-holders but afforded little protection for shipwrecks or other artifacts. Work by the Smithsonian Institution in the 1960s did not lead to archaeological approaches but rather gave a false validity to later salvage activity.

Not until the establishment of the Bermuda Maritime Museum in 1974 would this view toward the salvage of the island's underwater cultural resources be called into

Clifford E. Smith Jr., Bermuda Maritime Museum, Mangrove Bay, Bermuda   **Edward Cecil Harris**, Director, Bermuda Maritime Museum, Mangrove Bay, Bermuda.

International Handbook of Underwater Archaeology, edited by Carol V. Ruppé and Janet F. Barstad. Kluwer Academic/Plenum Publishers, New York, 2002.

question. Starting in 1981, the director of the museum began to develop long-term associations with the Program of Maritime History and Underwater Research at East Carolina University, the Department of Anthropology at Brown University, and volunteer groups such as the Maritime Archaeological and Historical Society, to assist in the survey, recording, excavation and conservation of shipwrecks and related artifacts. The continued commitment by the museum to protect and conserve Bermuda's maritime cultural resource is best illustrated through an examination of the projects undertaken in the second part of this chapter.

Besides leading by example, the museum's underwater archaeological research undertaken in the last ten years has provided a currency and interest in Bermuda's maritime history that otherwise might not have been possible given the limited artifact holdings presently in the public domain. In addition, the museum, along with the Bermuda National Trust, has led the fight to bring about changes in legislation affecting shipwrecks; however, by late 1998 no alterations to the 1959 law had been implemented by the government. The effect of this lack of vision on Bermuda's cultural heritage is discussed in the fourth part of this chapter, through an examination of salvage versus underwater archaeology.

UNDERWATER ARCHAEOLOGY IN BERMUDA: 1988 TO PRESENT

HMS *Vixen*: 1986–1988

Richard A. Gould has described HMS *Vixen* as "one of those anonymous ships found in most world navies" (1989). Launched in 1867, the 160-ft *Vixen* was the first Royal naval vessel to be built as an iron-framed, iron-hulled, twin-screw ship. Its hull was covered in 5.5″ thick teakwood cladding. This type of composite construction "was not unusual for

Figure 19.1. Logo of the Bermuda Maritime Museum.

commercial ships during the 1860s" (Gould, 1989). Thus, an archaeological investigation of the *Vixen* would provide important data on the technology and engineering developed by the British during the 1860s.

With support from the Bermuda Maritime Museum and EarthWatch, Gould directed EarthWatch volunteers on a nondestructive survey of the wreck site. The first stage of the investigation, in 1986, was a reconnaissance of the wreck. Based on their preliminary findings, Gould said it was clear that the ship should be recorded, for there was still structural and engineering details in evidence. In 1987, the survey continued with the mapping and photographing of the wreck site, to provide a deck plan and side elevations of the ship. The final field season, in 1988, completed the mapping and the photographic record of the ship by recording the interior structures and elements of the wreck that had been detached (Gould, 1988; Gould, 1989).

Historically, *Vixen* is described as an ironclad gunboat. However, archaeological findings showed that the ship was not a gunboat but an armored ram. The vessel has a ram bow with a main armor belt to drive the ram. Gould also found longitudinal stiffeners in the lower deck areas of the bow and stern, which would be hard to account for "except in relation to stresses imposed by the ram design" (1989). The *Vixen* is a ram, which would make this wreck the only known surviving example of a first-generation ironclad ram (Gould, 1988; Gould, 1989).

New Old Spaniard Shipwreck: 1987–1988

First identified by Teddy Tucker and Mendel Peterson in the 1960s as the "New Old Spaniard" (NOS), this shipwreck dates to about 1560–1580. Since there are no written records on ship construction from this historic period, reexamination of this site would offer researchers new data on the details employed to build these early vessels. In 1987, the Bermuda Maritime Museum, East Carolina University, and an international team of volunteers decided to reexpose and map the remains of the NOS (Hoyt, 1888a; Watts, 1993a).

The team used water-powered induction dredges to remove the 4–5 ft of sand overburden from the wreck site. Once the hull was uncovered, they established a baseline along the keelson. Mapping grids of 3 m^2 were positioned over the wreck and horizontal bars set in place on the grids. To-scale measurements were recorded on mylar of the hull's timbers, fasteners, and associated artifacts, using a system of x, y, and z coordinates (Hoyt, 1988a; Watts, 1993a).

Analysis of the hull and artifacts suggested the remains were not Spanish but a Dutch-built ship from the 17th century (Watts, 1993a). In addition, Steven D. Hoyt reports that the details of hull construction did not fit into a frame-first or a shell-first pattern. Instead, the results suggest that the NOS is an example of transitional construction (Hoyt, 1988b). Hence, the archaeological reexamination of this site dispelled a previous notion that this was a 16th-century Spanish vessel and provided important new data on a little-understood type of ship construction.

Underwater Construction Features at the Royal Naval Dockyard: 1985–1988

Underwater archaeology in Bermuda is not confined to shipwrecks. In 1985, Gould undertook an investigation of the submerged features in the waters adjacent to the tip of Ireland Island. What began as a reconnaissance of the Royal Naval dockyard became a systematic underwater survey to map and record the reef wall and the reef breakwater. During the 1986 and 1987 field seasons, two teams of EarthWatch volunteers directed by Gould were to define these features as artificial instead of what had been believed to be a natural part of Bermuda's reef (Gould, 1990).

Their survey of the reef wall found a base course of rocks resting in their original positions, with the uppermost rocks dislodged toward the shore. In addition, they recorded a 1.5-m-long iron beam that appears to be part of a retaining structure at the western end of the reef wall. Based on its construction and location, Gould argues that this artificial reef was built during the late 19th century as a defensive barrier offshore from Bastions E and F, to impede the approach of small boats.

The larger and better-constructed reef breakwater was found to have a straight seaward-facing outer wall 196 m long. The inner, shore-facing wall has three well-defined, equal projections spaced to form embayments. There was also evidence of iron attachment points embedded into the stones, suggesting moorings for small boats or barges. Based on these findings, Gould believed this "feature served as a breakwater and mooring basin for shallow draft barges, which were involved in the dockyard's construction" (1990). These barges, Gould hypothesized, transported the hard limestone used to build the dockyard from nearby Moresby Plain.

To test Gould's hypothesis and complete the research, in 1988 Nan Godet and EarthWatch volunteers conducted a volumetric survey to calculate the approximate volume of hard Bermuda limestone used from 1824 to 1843 to build the existing dockyard structures and found that an estimated 24,632 yds^3 of hard stone was totaled for these structures. Moving this large volume of material provides indirect support for the use of barges and the construction of an artificial basin as the simplest way to move the large stones from the quarry to the dockyard (Gould, 1990). Thus, a combination of underwater archaeology and a land-based volumetric experiment combined to add weight to Gould's hypothesis.

Western Ledge Reef Wreck, Santa Lucia: 1988–1991

In September 1988, East Carolina University and Bermuda Maritime Museum initiated a random shipwreck survey to locate early shipwreck sites among the reefs northeast of Chubb Head. With only days remaining before hurricane Emily ended their field season, they discovered a 16th-century Spanish shipwreck in a large sand hole by using towed divers and a proton precession magnetometer. The site showed evidence of previous salvage, but a small section of undisturbed ballast and hull timbers remained. Exposed structural elements of the hull were photographed and recorded and a few ceramic samples recovered to facilitate the dating of the site. The wreck was then covered with sand to minimize deterioration (Morris, 1990; Watts, 1993a; Watts, 1993b).

Recording the site began in 1989 with a predisturbance site survey by museum staff and Canadian volunteers, followed by a systematic visual and metal-detector survey of the areas surrounding the site. Controlled excavation was used to determine the construction of the hull. The small stern section was mapped and six test excavations dug to ascertain if the salvaged areas of the wreck remained intact (Bermuda Maritime Quarterly, 1989; Watts, 1993a; Watts, 1993b). Kaea J. Morris reports that "no articulated wreck remains were uncovered" in these six areas (1990). Still, there was a considerable amount of the hull left to investigate.

In 1990, volunteers from the United States, United Kingdom, and Canada worked with museum staff to complete the excavation of the undisturbed ballast pile and the small stern knee section of the hull. In the fall, the major element of the hull was exposed by students from East Carolina University, Brian Malpas, and staff from the museum. A detailed map of the site was recorded using baselines and underwater grid frames subdivided into 10 cm squares by string. The wreck was photographed with a PVC photo tower at 1-m stations to produce a mosaic of the site. Almost 300 hours of bottom time was logged to complete that season's work (Watts, 1990, 1993a, 1993b).

In 1991, the project shifted to the recovery of the hull. Volunteers from the United States, United Kingdom, Canada, and Spain, under the guidance of Watts and the museum staff, disassembled the upper structures of the shipwreck (Malpas, 1991; Watts, 1993a). Hydraulic jacks were used "to separate the futtocks and floors from the exterior planking" (Watts, 1993a). Ship timbers were palliated on the seabed before being brought to the surface by the divers; hoisted onto a small boat equipped with a lifting frame, they were transported to the museum's conservation laboratory. All recovered timbers were catalogued and documented by project staff and the students and staff from East Carolina University (Watts, 1993a).

Guns from HMS *Irresistible*: 1991

An investigation into historic guns of Bermuda developed into an underwater archaeology project when an underwater survey located the wreck of HMS *Irresistible* in Granaway Deep south of Marshall's Island. Launched in 1859, *Irresistible* was one of the last wooden ships built by the Royal Navy. Historically, it was known that *Irresistible* was deemed unstable after a hurricane struck Bermuda in the late 1870s; to correct this problem, four large rifled muzzle-loaders, described as eight-ton guns, were loaded aboard the ship as ballast (Carpenter, 1993; Harris, 1991).

The underwater survey established that the guns were of the Victorian era, with bores of 8–10″ diameter. Artillery pieces from this period are rare, and the effort was made to raise the guns. With the generosity of Correia Construction, their construction barge, and the tug *Clevelander*, three of the guns were recovered. When raised to the surface, they proved to be 12-ton Mark I model, wrought iron, nine-inch rifled muzzle-loaders made in 1867 by the Royal Gun Factory at Woolwich (Carpenter, 1993; Harris, 1991).

El Galgo: 1991–1992

The wreck of *El Galgo* was worked in the 1960s by Edmund Downing. It was lost again until a team of divers from the Museum rediscovered the site, now designated as IMHA 4, in August 1991. Museum diver Jonathan Bream with British divers Brian Furniss, Ed Sykes, and David Slade conducted a nondestructive survey of the site, which included a visual search of the reef area, mapping the wreck, and photographing the site. Two detailed site maps resulted from their survey: a site plan and a contour map (Bermuda Maritime Museum Quarterly, 1992).

In 1992, students from East Carolina University dug four test pits on the site to determine if enough of the wreck remained to warrant full excavation (Askins, 1992). No further excavations were conducted. In 1994, Jonathan Bream stated in a letter to Edward Harris that "the shipwreck does NOT appear to be that of the *Galgo*," basing his statement on his analysis of the artifacts recovered by Downing in the 1960s and by the museum in 1992. He suggested a 1580s date for this shipwreck (Bream letter, 5 October 1994).

HM Floating Dock *Bermuda*: 1986–1993

HM Floating Dock *Bermuda* was the largest vessel of its type when it was launched September 13, 1868. *Bermuda* serviced ships in the dockyard from 1869 to 1906, then was sold to German ship breakers in 1906 and abandoned by 1907. Faced with this abandoned hulk, authorities had dockyard tugs *Powerful* and *Gladisfen* tow the remains to Spanish Point in 1908 (Gould and Souza, 1985; Knepper, 1993).

When *Bermuda* was built, it had an overall length of 381 ft and a beam of 123 ft 9 in. It was the "first and only [floating dock] ever to be made entirely of iron" (Gould and Souza, 1995). The floating dock's U-shaped cross-section would set it apart from any other floating drydock ever built, for it was designed to be self-careening. This was accomplished by differentially filling and emptying the air chambers, balance chambers, and load chambers inside the dock (Gould and Souza, 1995; Knepper, 1993).

As part of an investigation into the history and archaeology of Royal Naval Dockyard, archaeological work on the floating dock was conducted intermittently between 1986 and 1991. Day trips to the site by EarthWatch volunteers and staff from the Bermuda Maritime Museum provided photographs and documentation of the overall dimensions and condition of the wreck. During this period, extensive research into the historic record was completed in the local archives. Thus, by 1992, Gould and Donna J. Souza could say "it was apparent that HM Floating Dock *Bermuda* was one of the best-documented historic structures in Bermuda" (1995). With the historic information in hand, the program to record the site archaeologically was undertaken that summer (Gould and Souza, 1995).

In four weeks, with volunteers from the Bermuda Sub Aqua Club and museum staff, Gould and Souza were able to develop a comprehensive site plan showing the basic elements of the wreck. In 1993, a second four-week field season was conducted with volunteers from the Maritime Archaeological and Historical Society and the museum. A complete site plan and engineering drawings of the important components of the wreck were produced as a result of their field work. To accomplish this task, they used the baseline trilateration method (Gould and Souza, 1995). Dennis Knepper reports that much of the wreck was mapped by "clambering over the wreckage, most of which lay at or only a few feet below the waterline" (1993). Through research, they determined that 77 percent of the overall length and 92 percent of the lower hull structure survives. However, most of the above-water hull was destroyed due to salvage, blast, and storm damage. What remains represents only about one-sixth of the original structure (Gould and Souza, 1995).

Nola Wreck: 1985, 1988, 1993

Underwater archaeology on the *Nola* was an outgrowth of an interdisciplinary investigation of the maritime heritage Bermuda and America shared during the American Civil War. Bermuda was an important center for Confederate blockade-runners. One of these was *Nola*, built by Caird and Sons, Glasgow. The ship was a 750-ton vessel, 236 ft long, with a 25-ft beam (Watts, 1988; Watts, 1993a).

On January 5, 1864, *Nola* grounded on the reefs, ending her maiden voyage. Even with extensive historic records, many questions remain on how these ships were constructed. At the moment, details can be documented only by an archaeological investigation on shipwrecks such as *Nola*. Thus, in 1985 and 1986, students from East Carolina University under Watts's leadership joined with staff from the Bermuda Maritime Museum to complete an underwater reconnaissance survey of the ship (Watts,

1988, 1993a). Their goal was to document the exposed vessel structure. In his reconnaissance of the wreck, Watts found there was no need to excavate, since there was little sediment within the hull, and *Nola* was almost entirely exposed. After the initial reconnaissance, mapping of the wreck began by establishing baselines, and major features of the ship were mapped by trilateration from these baselines. Photographs also were taken of construction details (Watts, 1988, 1993a).

Investigation of the wreck showed that 80 percent of the ship remained; however, *Nola* had been the target of salvage activity. Damage included the engineering space, port side of the forward boiler, and both paddle wheels. Still, many important interior features remained: ash pits, fire boxes, and fire tubes (Watts, 1988, 1993a), so that underwater archaeological investigation of this ship could document construction details not shown in the historic plans of this type of British-built blockade runner.

Seven years later, in 1993, *Nola* would again be the focus of an underwater investigation by the museum, this time with divers from the Canadian Forces Sub Aqua Club and marine archaeologist Eric Sharp. The project's purpose was to develop an interpretative diver's guide and slate for the site. To accomplish their goal, they shot an extensive underwater video that involved almost 200 hours of bottom time to acquire more than 15 hours of video tape suitable for editing (Fuller, 1993).

Castle Island and HMS *Cerberus*: 1993

In 1993, an investigation of the waters surrounding Castle Island and the wreck of HMS *Cerberus* was undertaken as part of the Bermuda Maritime Museum and the College of William and Mary field season in advanced archaeological field methods. A three-member team conducted the underwater reconnaissance of Castle Island to document a number of modern glass bottles, a few small pieces of concreted iron, ironstone plate dating to A.D. 1813–1900, and a heavily concreted iron cannon. The team's conclusions on this assemblage was that the artifacts represented the disposal of trash, as even cannon once judged to be useless were just tipped overboard (Walker, 1993).

Location of the wreck took several days but once it was found, mapping of the site proceeded with three datum points established. No artifacts were recovered, but distinguishing features of the wreck site were recorded, including a concentration of iron bars, each 1 m long × 20 cm wide. The iron bars identified the wreck as *Cerberus*, a fifth rate built in 1799: Iron ballast was commonly carried aboard British warships during the mid- to late 18th-century (Walker, 1993; Walker. 1996).

In addition to the survey work, the team dug five test pits on the site and found musket balls adjacent to the iron bars. They discovered copper nails and pieces of copper sheathing in three test pits west of the iron bars. Of the five test pits, only the test pit outside the wreck site area produced no cultural materials (Walker, 1993).

An 18th-century Collier: 1992–1993

In 1992, a remote-sensing and visual survey was undertaken to locate shipwreck sites along the reefs northeast of Chub Head. Methods employed to find sites included divers on towboards and a proton precession magnetometer. When a shipwreck was located, its position was established using a Navstar Differential Global Positioning System. Almost 30 sites were recorded that year by Watts and the students of East Carolina University. Each wreck was examined and data collected to date the ships. An initial assessment was made of each site to determine its significance and research potential (Watts and Krivor, 1995).

Based on its preservation, the wreck of the 18th-century ship was chosen for further investigation the next year. To record the collier's remains, a baseline was put down adjacent to the wreck. Simultaneous to setting the baseline, the overburden was removed from the extremities of the hull with a water-induction dredge (Watts and Krivor, 1995).

Once the wreck was cleared, "a series of interlocking 1- and 2-m rigid grid frames were positioned over those exposed portions of the wreck" (Watts and Krivor, 1995). The hull structure was mapped and photographed, and artifacts were recorded, photographed in situ, and recovered for further analysis at the Bermuda Maritime Museum conservation laboratory. Based on an analysis of the surviving hull structure, artifacts, and historical evidence, a preliminary identification of the shipwreck was a modest-sized English collier brig lost in the last quarter of the 18th century. A comparative analysis to the English-built *Betsy*, excavated at Yorktown, Virginia, supports this finding, since both ships have similarities of design and construction (Watts and Krivor, 1995).

The *L'Herminie* Wreck: 1994–1995

Launched in 1824, the French First Class Frigate *L'Herminie* was 54 m long, with a beam of 14.1 m. The ship was carrying 60 guns and a crew of 495 officers and men when it struck the coral reef December 3, 1838. Discovered in 1958, the shipwreck has been heavily disturbed over the years by salvors and other divers (Cook, undated manuscript; Waters, 1996).

In 1994, the site was visited by students and staff from East Carolina University. Due to the obvious disturbance of the wreck by human activity, the site was reported to the Bermuda Receiver of Wreck. A research proposal was put forth to do a reevaluation of the site as a project of the next year (Waters, 1996).

There is no site plan of the wreck in existance, despite the numerous articles mentioning *L'Herminie*. Thus, in 1995, volunteers from the Maritime Archaeological and Historical Society (MAHS), graduate students from East Carolina University, and staff from The Bermuda Maritime Museum came together to assess the wreck's research potential. Goals for the project were to locate the site, examine its exposed cultural remains, and create a preliminary site plan (Waters, 1996).

The site was located using a global positioning system. To define the extent of the wreck and the area's exposed remains, divers on aqua-scooters conducted a visual search of the wreck. The artifact scatter extended to 150 m (Waters, 1996).

Once the site's perimeters were defined, "a baseline was established, connecting large artifact concentrations throughout the area" (Waters, 1996). A detailed map was made of major artifact concentrations, the hull structures, cannons, and other items were recorded using underwater video and photographs, and the data was transferred to a master site plan (Waters, 1996).

Stonewall Wreck: 1992, 1994–1996

This wreck was discovered first by Harry Cox in the 1950s, then excavated in 1975 by Edwin S. Dethlefsen of Franklin Pierce College. Dethlefsen, Ellen Davidson, and D. Lynn Buchman published a report on Dethlefsen's investigation in the *International Journal of Nautical Archaeology* (*International Journal of Underwater Archaeology*, 1977) suggesting that there was an important site of an early shipwreck with an extensive amount of lower hull remaining that should be investigated. Armed with this information, the "Stonewall Wreck" was targeted for reevaluation in 1992 (Watts and Bumpass, unpublished manuscript).

A preliminary examination was undertaken that year by Watts and graduate students from East Carolina University, which confirmed Dethlefsen's report. In 1994, Bermuda Maritime Museum was granted a license from the Receiver of Wreck to investigate and document the Stonewall Wreck. Between 1994 and 1996, students from East Carolina University, under Watts's leadership, focused their field research on the wreck (Lusardi, 1996; Watts and Bumpass, unpublished manuscript; Watts, 1994).

During these three years, the wreck was systematically excavated and documented. This was done annually by establishing a baseline adjacent to the hull. The overburden was cleared from a section of the hull, and grid frames were positioned over the exposed sections. The grid squares were mapped and photographs taken to form a photomosaic of the wreck. The grid maps were then transferred to a master site plan, which was digitized using AutoCAD (Watts and Bumpass, unpublished manuscript).

Throughout the project, artifacts were recorded and photographed in situ. Watts found that "the ceramics recovered from the site suggested a date nearer the end of the third or beginning of the fourth quarter of the 17th-century rather than mid-century" (Watts and Bumpass, unpublished manuscript). Also, the ship appeared to be English, rather than Spanish as Dethlefsen had reported in 1977 (Watts and Bumpass, unpublished manuscript).

Constellation: 1996

In 1996, the Maritime Archaeological and Historical Society returned to Bermuda to work with Richard Gould and the Bermuda Maritime Museum, to survey one of the most popular dive sites in Bermuda and to develop a dive slate for divers on the shipwreck. Constellation was a four-masted schooner built in 1918 and lost in 1943 on its way to Venezuela. When it sank, it was carrying a cargo of building materials and medical supplies (Cook, undated manuscript; Smailes, 1996).

To produce a site plan of Constellation, the wreck was divided into three sections and each mapped by setting a baseline down the center of the wreck. Teams were assigned a section and mapped the principle features of the ship by triangulation. The same process was used to record artifacts associated with the wreck. In addition, the site was videotaped and photographs shot (Smailes, 1996).

Sites Investigated: 1997

During the 1997 field season, students and staff from East Carolina University visited a variety of sites to note the change in ship construction over time. Students were trained in remote sensing and visual survey methods. Sites were located visually using towboards and by remote sensing with a proton precession magnetometer (Watts, personal communication, September 1998; Westrick, 1997).

Once discovered, a site's position was pinpointed along the western coral reefs with the Differential Global Positioning System. As a result of the group's work, three new wrecks were located: a 19th- to 20th-century schooner, an 18th-century wreck, and the "Iron Plate Wreck," which will be dated after more research is done (Watts, personal communication, September 1998; Westrick 1997).

UNDERWATER ARCHAEOLOGY IN BERMUDA: 1998

The Bermuda Maritime Museum's 1998 underwater field season started at the end of May and continued to October. During those four months, a variety of projects were undertaken, including moving a cannon, investigating isolated finds reported to the Museum, two wreck surveys, and excavation of a wreck. All these projects required help from many different groups, interns, and volunteers.

West Elbow Bay Cannon

In May, a cannon was reported to the museum offshore of the Coral Beach Club. Investigators thought it was one of two cannons that had belonged to West Elbow Bay Fort. Upon visual survey of the site a cannon was found partially exposed on the sandy bottom, showing signs of wear due to the surge of sand across its surfaces. To preserve it from further damage and to provide a new dive site, the cannon was relocated 500 yards offshore and set atop a reef outcrop. The project was conducted by the museum with a group of volunteers from the 3rd Royal Irish Regiment.

Manilla Wreck

June and July were devoted to investigation of a few reported isolated finds and final preparations for conducting underwater surveys slated to be completed in August. The first of these projects was the "Manilla Wreck," a mid-18th-century slave trader discovered by Harry Cox in 1975 at Northeast Breakers. There are no visible ship timbers on the site. The most prominent feature is a 14-m-long double row of cannons running along a rock breaker. To record this site, museum staff and volunteers from the Maritime Archaeological and Historical Society set in three 18-m-long baselines parallel to the cannons, and a detailed map of the site was established by triangulating from the baselines. All visible cultural remains were recorded on a master site plan and a videotape record made to document the site.

In September, students from East Carolina University joined the Manilla project for two days to produce a photomosaic of the site. Baselines were reset and each 1-m square of the site was defined using yellow nylon lines. A total of 280 photographs were shot to cover the 20 × 14 m area.

Dorothea and *Hunters Galley*

During their stay at the museum, students and staff completed two other shipwreck projects with staff from the Museum: *Dorothea* in St. George's Harbour and *Hunters Galley* off Pompano Beach.

During the last week of August, a preliminary survey of the *Dorothea* was undertaken to document the shipwreck's condition. A composite vessel, the ship was built with iron frames, copper fasteners, and wooden hull planks. Research on the wreck focused on the interaction between these components on the ship's rate of degradation.

To meet their research goals, the group surveyed the shipwreck to produce a site map of the site and took photographs and made a videotape to document the wreck's condition. This data can then be compared with research done on the ship in the early 1990s.

Once this project was completed, students and staff moved to *Hunters Galley.* Throughout September, students led by Watts conducted a survey and excavation of the wreck site. To map the wreck's remains, they established baselines and set grid frames over the hull and major timbers, then drew the major dearticulated timbers. They excavated test trenches at various points to establish the extent of salvage damage the shipwreck had suffered over the last 30 years. Unfortunately, the site was found to be picked clean and most of the ship's structure had been damaged by salvage.

CULTURAL HERITAGE: SALVAGE VERSUS UNDERWATER ARCHAEOLOGY

Throughout the Age of Discovery into the 17th and 18th centuries, through the American Revolution and Civil War and into the present century, ships have come to grief on Mount Bermuda. By the end of the World War II, which ushered in scuba diving, there was at Bermuda an extraordinary collection of underwater cultural resources, the legacy of sea disasters since the early 16th-century. Vessels of many nations and types were represented in this corpus of underwater sites, along with their knowledge-rich holdings of portable artifacts. Until the late 1990s, successive governments have squandered this part of Bermuda's national patrimony by making (as Throckmorton aptly said) the "world's worst investment" by allowing for the almost entirely unfettered dismemberment of many wreck sites by treasure hunters (1990).

Not only were shipwrecks destroyed as potential underwater diving exhibits and museum sites, their historical context and vast wealth of potential knowledge of seafaring, exploration, settlement, trade, and global communications of several centuries were summarily washed away. Previous visitors and local residents lacked the power of destruction unleashed after World War II; generally, they "took only photographs and left only bubbles." The scale of destruction of underwater heritage sites that followed was without precedent and, unfortunately, the dismemberment of Bermuda's underwater heritage continued apace throughout the 1960s, 1970s, into the 1980s, and to this day at Bermuda and in the Caribbean.

Damaged sites include shipwrecks of nearly every period, underwater cultural deposits associated with domestic dumping, and ships at moorings or berthings. Scant evidence has been displayed of any but the most rudimentary recording of these irreplaceable archaeological sites, and little has been published in the scientific press. Thus, after 50 years of destruction by salvage, the fight for the management and survival of Bermuda's underwater cultural resources remains a current process.

CONCLUSIONS

The effect of treasure hunters on Bermuda's cultural heritage can be noted in the harm salvors have inflicted on many shipwrecks examined by the museum during the last ten years. In the salvaged areas of the "Western Ledge Wreck," no articulated remains were found. Archaeological examination of *Nola* documented salvage damage to the ship's engineering space, boiler, and paddle wheels. The most powerful argument against wholesale looting of shipwrecks can be shown in the near-complete disturbance of *L'Herminie* by salvors and other divers.

Many research projects have presented both the underwater archaeological recovery of Bermuda's cultural history through a variety of sites, and the ultimate destruction of cultural history due to the unscientific recovery of artifacts, improper recording of wrecks, or absence of conservation. This unnecessary and unjustifiable destruction of Bermuda's underwater patrimony will continue without new legislation and the will of government to preserve the sites from further decline. Government leadership is essential, for institutions such as the Bermuda National Trust and the Bermuda Maritime Museum are doomed to fail in their attempts at preserving this national heritage without government resolve.

BERMUDA UPDATE

Throughout this chapter there has been a recurrent argument that the destruction of Bermuda's wreck sites, by salvors and treasure hunters, would continue unchecked unless the government were to take a legal stand to stop this behavior by passing new legislation to preserve and protect these sites. However, in November 2001, the government of Bermuda passed the Historic Wrecks Act 2001 "to preserve, protect and safeguard Bermuda's underwater cultural heritage by making provision for the classification of wreck and to control the archaeological and scientific examination of historic wrecks..." (HWA 2001).

This legislation more than meets the goals set by UNESCO for the protection of shipwreck cited in its 2nd November 2001 Convention on the Protection of the Underwater Cultural Heritage. The Historic Wrecks Act 2001 preserves and protects Bermuda's submerged cultural heritage by stating that "no person shall mark, remove interfere with, deal in or possess any wreck or historic artifact unless he is licensed... and authorized to do so." A person found guilty of an offense under the subsection is liable "to a fine of $25,000 or imprisonment for one year, or both" (HWA 2001). The Historic Wrecks Act 2001 limits the issuing of licenses only to those conducting archaeological research with an approved archaeological plan, using scientific methods, and affiliated with a maritime or archaeological organization. Anyone who fails to comply with these conditions is liable on conviction to a "fine of $10,000 or imprisonment for one year, or both" (HWA 2001). The fine is increased for any nonlicensed or unauthorized person who removes anything from a site, disturbs a site, or interferes with a site as they are liable upon "conviction to a fine of $25,000 or imprisonment for one year, or both" (HWA 2001).

Most important, protection and preservation of Bermuda's maritime heritage does not end at the water's edge. Ownership of "all wrecks and historic artifacts are vested in the Crown absolutely" (HWA 2001). There are no longer any compensation awards in Bermuda. All recovered materials now remain in the public domain as part of the National Collection to ensure access by the public.

Due care is also mandated for these recovered materials as the Historic Wreck Act 2001 requires any artifacts recovered must be stabilized in the field and then conserved. Gone are the days when artifacts could be pulled form a shipwreck and held without conservation and or sold to the highest bidder without any record of the transaction. License holders are now required to submit regular reports to the government and then publish the results of their archaeological work on these sites (HWA 2001).

Bermuda has turned an important corner in not only protecting its submerged cultural heritage but also the underwater patrimony of the world as found on its reefs. What will be required now is a long-term commitment by the Bermuda government and the local cultural institutions to enforce the legislation, to promote the archaeological investigation of Bermuda's maritime heritage, and to support the long-term conservation and exhibit of the recovered artifacts for the public.

REFERENCES

Askins, Adrian, 1992, ECU Field School. *Bermuda Maritime Museum Quarterly* 5(3):20–21.

Bream, Jonathan W., 1990, The Spanish Influence on Bermuda. *Bermuda Journal of Archaeology and Maritime History* 2:15–24.

Bermuda Maritime Museum Quarterly, 1989, Careful Excavation Yields Results: An Update on the 1992 Project and the Museum's Underwater Archaeology Programme, *Bermuda Maritime Museum Quarterly* 2(4):28–29.

_____, 1992, They Found *El Galgo* in Pieces. *Bermuda Maritime Museum Quarterly* 5(1):19–20.

Carpenter, Austin C., 1993, *Cannon: The Conservation, Reconstruction and Presentation of Historic Artillery.* Halsgrove Press, Tiverton.

Cook, William R., No Date, Unpublished files on Bermuda Shipwrecks. Manuscript on file at Bermuda Maritime Museum.

Fuller, Scott, 1993, Epitaph for a Lady. *Bermuda Maritime Museum Quarterly* 6(4):21–22.

Gould, Richard A., 1988, The 1988 Field Season on HMS *Vixen*. *Bermuda Maritime Museum Quarterly* 1(1):38–39.

_____, 1989, HMS *Vixen*: An Early Ironclad Ram at Bermuda. *Bermuda Journal of Archaeology and Maritime History* 1:43–80.

_____, 1990, Underwater Construction at the Royal Naval Dockyard, Bermuda. *Bermuda Journal of Archaeology and Maritime History* 2:71–86.

Gould, Richard A. and Souza, Donna J., 1995, History and Archaeology of HM Floating Dock *Bermuda*. *Bermuda Journal of Archaeology and Maritime History* 7:157–185.

Harris, Edward C., 1991, The Remains of HMS *Irresistible*. *Bermuda Maritime Museum Quarterly* 4(3):24–25.

Hoyt, Steven D., 1988a, Research into Early Ship Construction. *Bermuda Maritime Museum Quarterly* 1(1):32–35.

_____, 1988b, Archaeological Survey Update: The NOS Shipwreck. *Bermuda Maritime Museum Quarterly* 1(2):24–28.

Knepper, Dennis, 1993, Work on the Floating Dock *Bermuda*. *Bermuda Maritime Museum Quarterly* 6(4):22–24.

Lusardi, Wayne, 1996, East Carolina University's 1996 Season: Farewell to the *Stonewall*. *MARITimes: Quarterly Magazine of The Bermuda Maritime Museum* 9(4):11–13.

Malpas, Brian, 1991, Local Dive Team Assists Recovery of Shipwreck Timbers. *Bermuda Maritime Museum Quarterly* 4(4):12.

Morris, Kaea J., 1990, The 1577 Shipwreck Project: A Preliminary Report. *Underwater Archaeology Proceedings from the society for Historical Archaeology Conference*, edited by T. Carrell, pp. 63–66. Society for Historical Archaeology, Tucson.

_____, 1988, A Day in the Life of a Marine Archaeologist. *Bermuda Maritime Museum Quarterly* 1(2):18–20.

Smailes, Jim, 1996, MAHS Surveys the Schooner *Constellation*: Star Attraction. *MARITimes: Quarterly Magazine of The Bermuda Maritime Museum* 9(4):14–15.

Throckmorton, Peter, 1990, The World's Worst Investment: The Economics of Treasure Hunting with Real-Life Comparisons. *Underwater Archaeological Proceedings*, pp. 6–10.

Walker, Wayne, 1993, *A Castle and Her Ship: Results of the 1993 Underwater Survey of Castle Island including the Wreck of* HMS Cerberus. Manuscript On file at Bermuda Maritime Museum.

_____, 1996, HMS *Cerberus* and The Royal Naval Dockyard. *Bermuda Journal of Archaeology and Maritime History* 8:30–40.

Waters, Sarah, 1996, The Wreck of *L'Herminie*: A Preliminary Report. *MARITimes: Quarterly Magazine of The Bermuda Maritime Museum* 9(1):16–18.

Watts Jr., Gordon P., 1988, Bermuda and the American Civil War: A Reconnaissance Investigation of Archival and Submerged Cultural Resources. *International Journal of Nautical Archaeology* 17(2):159–171.

_____, 1990, Update on the IMHA 3 Shipwreck Investigation: The East Carolina University/Bermuda Maritime Museum Field School Programme, 1990. *Bermuda Maritime Museum Quarterly* 3(4):26–29.

_____, 1993a, A Decade of Shipwreck Research in Bermuda. *Bermuda Journal of Archaeology and Maritime History* 5:12–57.

_____, 1993b, The Western Ledge Reef Wreck: A Preliminary Report on Investigation of the Remains of a 16th-century Shipwreck in Bermuda. *International Journal of Nautical Archaeology* 22(2):103–124.

_____, 1994, 1994 Investigation of the Stonewall Wreck: A Preliminary Report. *Bermuda Maritime Museum Quarterly* 7(4):22–24.

Watts, Gordon P. Jr. and Bumpass, Kelly, No Date, *Reinvestigation of the 17th-century "Stonewall" Shipwreck in Bermuda.* Manuscript in possession of the author.

Watts, Gordon P. Jr. and Krivor, Michael C., 1995, Investigation of an 18th-century English Shipwreck in Bermuda. *International Journal of Nautical Archaeology* 24(2):97–108.

Westrick, Robert, 1997, In Search of Shipwrecks, *MARITimes: Quarterly Magazine of The Bermuda Maritime Museum* 10(3):18.

Chapter 20

Water
A New Field in Argentinean Archaeology

DOLORES CAROLINA ELKIN

INTRODUCTION: ARCHAEOLOGY AND ARCHAEOLOGISTS IN ARGENTINA

To better understand the context of underwater archaeology in Argentina it is useful to have some general information about the discipline of archaeology in the country, together with clarifying the meaning of terms that will be frequently used in this chapter.

Aside from a couple of universities that have a specific department of archaeology, this specialty has normally been included, together with social anthropology, within the department of anthropology or anthropological sciences. Although the study of archaeological remains and the creation of museums and institutions dealing with archaeology had started several decades before (Politis, 1992; Fernandez, 1980), it was not until 1958 that the department of anthropology was created at the Universities of Buenos Aires and La Plata.

Today there are eight universities in Argentina that offer a specialty in archaeology. All of them are free of charge, and they are run by the national government. It takes about five years of study, plus writing and defending a thesis, to obtain what is called a *Licenciatura* degree. Upon becoming a *Licenciado* in anthropology with a specialty in archaeology, one is formally considered an archaeologist. Some students continue their

Dolores Carolina Elkin, CONICET, Universidad Nacional del Centro de la Provincia de Buenos Aires, and Instituto Nacional de Antropología, Buenos Aires, Argentina 1378.

International Handbook of Underwater Archaeology, edited by Carol V. Ruppé and Janet F. Barstad. Kluwer Academic/Plenum Publishers, New York, 2002.

studies into a doctoral program. This involves several more years of original research and graduate courses, in addition to the final stage of writing and defending a dissertation.

In this chapter, the term "archaeologist" is applied only to (a) those who have a university-level (either *Licenciatura* or doctorate) degree in archaeology, either as a specialty of anthropology or not, and (b) those who took university studies either at times or in places where the career did not exist, and therefore studied some related career (typically history), and whose professional activities consists of the study, with scientific standards, of past human life through material remains.

In Argentina, then, we can view archaeology as a scientific discipline carried out by archaeologists.

According to the records of the Argentinean Association of Professional Archaeologists and the Argentinean Society of Anthropology, there are over 250 archaeologists in Argentina. There has always been a strong research emphasis on New World (and mostly Argentinean) prehistoric archaeology. This is reflected in the high percentage of papers corresponding to these geographic and temporal frames that have been presented at the National Congresses of Argentinean Archaeology, which has been held every two or three years since 1970.

Historical archaeology has had far less dedication (Zarankin and Senatore, 1996). As this chapter will show, underwater archaeology was nonexistent until the mid-1990s.

A BRIEF HISTORY OF ARGENTINA'S WORK WITH SUBMERGED REMAINS

In 1978, archaeologist Jorge Fernandez supervised the extraction of a logboat from Lake Nahuel Huapi, by the town of Bariloche in the Patagonian Andes (Fernandez, 1978; 1998).

The 4.7-m-long boat was partly buried at 12 m in the lake sediment. It was in a good state of preservation. Its recovery was carried out by a group of divers, directed by Franciso Requelme. They found no other archaeological material.

The logboat had been constructed out of a single trunk of a local beech tree known as *coihue* (*Nothofagus dombeyii*), and there was evidence that metal tools had been used for its manufacture. This fact, together with the presence of some small hollows filled with iron oxides (possibly the remains of metal nails), led Fernandez to state the boat's age should be placed between the mid-17th century, which is when European exploration introduced iron in the region, and the end of the 19th century, when timber for naval construction became so popular that it is highly improbable that someone would take the trouble of hollowing a tree trunk. A radiocarbon analysis applied to a wood sample did not clarify this chronological hypothesis.

Fernandez mentions that at least 15 monoxile canoes have been recovered by different people (none of them archaeologists) from Patagonian lakes, and that this important material evidence complements the ethnohistorical records of navigation across the Andes (Fernandez, 1998).

Some authors regard this canoe extraction as the first example of underwater archaeology in Argentina (García Cano, 1997a:396; Fernandez, 1998:1).

Although the lack of archaeological standards, at least in the underwater aspects of this study, leads me to disagree with such view, Fernandez certainly deserves much credit for being the first archaeologist to demonstrate concern and care about underwater cultural remains—something that would not happen again for about 15 years.

Aside from Fernandez's isolated action regarding our underwater cultural heritage, the activities by the Argentinean committee of the International Council of Monuments and Sites (ICOMOS) should be mentioned.

In 1970, UNESCO asked ICOMOS to analyze the status of underwater cultural heritage in every country where the latter had national committees. In 1980, the Argentinian report, made by four architects, noted the lack of specialists and the potential of underwater archaeological remains in the region (Pernaut, 1998).

In 1983, the Argentinian committee of ICOMOS and the World Heritage organized two seminars on underwater archaeology lectured by the Italian architect Antonio Di Stefano. The seminars were taught at the schools of architecture of the Universities of Buenos Aires and Mar del Plata. Organized by architect J. Gazzaneo, they were directed by architects A. Schellenberg and C. Pernaut, who were president and vice president, respectively, of the Argentinean committee of ICOMOS. The Argentinean navy and diving clubs participated, and anyone who had shown interest in underwater archaeology, among them "university students, diving instructors, etc.," were specially invited (Pernaut 1998:26). The invited university students were from the school of architecture (C. Murray, personal communication).

In 1985, a third seminar on underwater archaeology was organized by the Argentinian committee of ICOMOS with the goal of "experimenting with and developing the discipline in a practical way" (Pernaut 1998:26). Lecturing at this seminar were architect J. Gazzaneo, professional diver F. Requelme, and archaeologist J. Fernandez.

The seminar led to the creation of the Underwater Archaeology Working Group (GTAS), coordinated by architect–diver J. García Cano (Libonatti, 1986). The organization later changed its name to GTPS (Underwater Heritage Working Group). Other group members included seven architects and two experienced divers. Later on, a museum curator joined.

The main tasks of GTPS were to experiment with underwater archaeological techniques in several locations, with the support of diving schools and archaeology avocationals, and to acquire bibliography (Pernaut, 1998). In 1986, GTPS took on an educational task when it began giving talks at diving schools and clubs. The organization wrote several recommendations that were intended to be used by any diver who came in contact with in situ archaeological material (Ansaldo and García Cano, 1986).

Between 1987 and 1989, and during four fieldwork seasons, the ICOMOS–GTPS group surveyed the wreck of H.M.S. *Swift* in Puerto Deseado (Port Desire), Santa Cruz province. This was a British sloop-of-war that sank in 1770 while exploring the coast of Patagonia. The wreck had been partially excavated by a group of local sport divers who had extracted around 80 objects that were in extraordinary preservation conditions. Despite the nonsystematic collection and excavation, these objects were taken to a local museum, where the preservation state of most of the pieces remains quite good.

The ICOMOS–GTPS work at the *Swift* has been described in several reports (GTPS–ICOMOS, 1987; 1988; 1989; 1992), and in a general publication coordinated by architect C. Murray (1993). The main task carried out during the four underwater field seasons was the mapping of structural remains of the ship.

In 1989, ICOMOS–GTPS surveyed an area in the Paraná river (Misiones province, NE Argentina) in search of remnants of nautical activities of the 19th century. After the field season, 11 sites from the 19th and 20th centuries had been located (García Cano, 1991; 1997a).

In the early 1990s, despite the intention of turning it into a more interdisciplinary group (Pernaut, 1998), ICOMOS–GTPS gradually disbanded. Instead, several underwater activities have been carried out by a nonprofit private organization, the Albenga Foundation for the Preservation of Underwater Cultural Heritage, which was created in 1991 (Bonel, 1998; García Cano, 1997a). Architect J. García Cano was designated its scientific director.

Albenga's first underwater project, in 1994, was a new survey and a documentary film on H.M.S. *Swift* (Carcía Cano, 1997b). Since then, the foundation has been in charge of underwater surveys and excavations that were directed by archaeologists who do not dive. Their work will be described in another section of this chapter.

A final comment concerning treasure hunters must be included here. Although to my knowledge, such activity has not taken place within Argentinean jurisdictional waters, the threat is quite close: Our lack of nationwide protective legislation and the fact that treasure hunters are already making commercial profit out of the Uruguayan underwater heritage, which is just around the corner, places us in a very vulnerable position. Moreover, two attempts have been made to exploit shipwrecks commercially (one is the aforementioned H.M.S. *Swift* in the province of Santa Cruz, and the other one is a historic wreck in Tierra del Fuego). Fortunately, provincial and national authorities stopped both attempts, and even initiated regulations that represent the first legal steps toward the specific protection of our underwater cultural heritage.

ARCHAEOLOGISTS APPEAR ON THE SCENE

In 1990, architect Cristian Murray, by then an active member of the ICOMOS–GTPS group, personally went to the National Institute of Anthropology (Instituto Nacional de Antropología or I.N.A.) in search of archaeologists willing to collaborate with or professionally advise the GTPS group about underwater archaeology. He stated he could not conceive of underwater archaeology without archaeologists.

His proposal was appreciated, but the I.N.A. archaeologists were focused on their own research and academic duties, and had no desire to devote volunteer time and energy to this totally new field with which they were not familiar.

Murray deserved support, and I decided to start collaborating with the GTPS group. I suggested, though, that they not continue to work at the Swift site until a new research design, based on archaeological standards, could be set forth.

Progress was slow. There were occasional meetings, exchanges of literature, and a gradual increase in the number of archaeologists and archaeology students who were interested in underwater archaeology.

In 1994, Argentinean underwater archaeology made a turning point when several important events took place. During the 11th National Congress of Argentinean Archaeology, underwater archaeology was included for the first time. It is worth noting, though, that out of a total of 279 presentations, only two were related to underwater cultural heritage (Elkin et al., 1994 and Flores et al., 1994).

A few months later the 8th National Congress of Uruguayan Archaeology took place, and a special session was dedicated to underwater archaeology (Martínez, 1995). It was a good opportunity for Uruguayan and Argentinean archaeologists to discuss topics of common interest (Olivera et al., 1995).

Early in 1995, the Uruguayan Comisión Nacional de Patrimonio (National Heritage Commission) invited Mexican archaeologist Pilar Luna Erreguerena to give a series of lectures in Montevideo. She spoke on underwater cultural heritage and on the need to protect it from treasure hunters, who were so active on the Uruguayan side of the Río de la Plata that hundreds of pieces had already been sold at famous auction houses (Sotheby's, 1993).

During that event, I met Luna Erreguerena, and we had a fruitful discussion about the possibility of organizing an underwater archaeology team in Argentina. After her stay in Uruguay, Luna Erreguerena was invited to the I.N.A. in Buenos Aires by its director, Diana Rolandi, to give another lecture and to meet archaeologists and archaeology students who were interested in underwater archaeology.

Therefore, Luna Erreguerena lectured in two countries before an audience that included cultural resources management people, members of the Prefectura Naval (National Coast Guard) and the navy, mass media reporters and the general public, as well as archaeologists and archaeology students. She gave us a new perspective of how to deal with our underwater cultural heritage.

For archaeologists, her most significant messages were that something urgently needed to be done about our underwater cultural heritage, and that we could indeed do it—even if we had to start from scratch and even though we were not working in First World countries. Luna Erreguerena's own experience (Luna Erreguerena, 1997) proved that it was possible, and this gave us the necessary strength to begin.

Creation of the Program "Investigation and Conservation of Argentinian Underwater Cultural Heritage" at the National Institute of Anthropology

In 1995, I.N.A. director Rolandi then became aware of several things: (1) the archaeological potential of the Argentinean underwater cultural heritage; (2) the lack of archaeologists working in this area; and (3) the urgent need to stop treasure hunters who could extend their activities into our jurisdictional waters at any time. Rolandi suggested that I direct a program in underwater archaeology.

At the beginning I found a lot of limitations to this idea. My research background was in Early Holocene, high altitude, desert archaeology, and was not much help with underwater, mainly historical, archaeology. I did not know how to scuba dive and, as far as I knew, neither did my colleagues. The archaeology libraries in Argentina had nothing on underwater archaeology. There were no national or provincial regulations which could legally protect our underwater cultural heritage. In addition, it was made clear no financial support was available, at least for the time being.

All I had was Rolandi's and my own enthusiasm for this groundbreaking and challenging project. I also had Luna Erreguerena's constant moral support from Mexico, plus an archaeologist and lawyer (María Luz Endere), an archaeology student (Mónica Grosso), a museum curator (Alberto Orsetti), a professional diver and scuba diving instructor (Eduardo Kremer), and architect and diver Cristian Murray ready to do volunteer work. It is worth noting that the last three professionals had previously worked for the ICOMOS–GTPS group.

By the end of 1995, I had obtained my first scuba diving license, a program called "Investigation and Conservation of Argentinean Underwater Cultural Heritage" had been officially created at the I.N.A. by the National Ministry of Culture. Despite the lack of money for the program, the institutional support was strong and the group of volunteer assistants was outstandingly enthusiastic.

The main goals and related activities within the program were the following:

1. Assemble an interdisciplinary team, with clear leadership of archaeologists, to work on different aspects of underwater archaeology
2. Create a library on underwater archaeology and related topics that could help us learn different aspects of the specialty
3. Encourage the passing of a national law for the protection of the underwater cultural heritage
4. Seek different sources (historical, ethnohistorical, cartographic, etc.) in order to assess the actual potential of our underwater cultural heritage
5. Start a national database on underwater archaeological sites and remains, complementing the database on terrestrial sites that was already being done at the I.N.A.
6. Learn to scuba dive, and train in the performance of underwater archaeological techniques (this applied mainly to archaeologists and archaeology students working in the program)
7. Train people in conservation of archaeological materials recovered from submerged sites
8. Perform archaeological research on underwater sites
9. Educate the general public on the significance of our underwater cultural heritage and on the importance of its preservation from any sort of destruction, dispersal, or nonscientific recovery
10. Gradually incorporate the specialty of underwater archaeology within the local scientific and academic community

In short, the idea was to cover different aspects related to underwater cultural heritage which were considered equally important. For instance, no matter how necessary it was to start doing professional archaeological research, it would not have much future if the general public and local communities did not become aware of the importance of our underwater cultural heritage.

STATE OF THE ART

The National Institute of Anthropology Program

Six years later, significant progress was achieved in the different aspects covered by the I.N.A. program.

The Team.   Organizing an interdisciplinary professional team integrating skills in the main fields related to the general subject under study (archaeology, legislation, scuba diving, conservation, and museology) was among the first tasks of the program.

The current I.N.A. underwater archaeology team is composed of four archaeologists–divers (Amaru Argüeso, Virginia Dellino, Damian Vainstub, and Dolores Elkin) plus one advanced archaeology student–diver (Mónica Grosso), one scuba diving instructor–professional diver (Francisco Requelme), one museum curator (Alberto Orsetti), and one architect–diver (Cristian Murray). Occasionally, other researchers from Argentina, Mexico, Uruguay, the United Kingdom, Chile, and the United States of America participate.

Finally, several archaeology students, mainly from the University of Buenos Aires, also assist in a diversity of laboratory, field, and office tasks.

The Library.   Literature on underwater archaeology was virtually noninexistent in Argentina's public resources (including university libraries) at the time the I.N.A. program began. Therefore, another primary task was to gradually organize a collection of bibliographic material that could be consulted not only by us but also by anyone else willing to read or learn about underwater archaeology.

In 1994, we started with a generous literature and video donation from Luna Erreguerena, and we now have more than 500 titles (including books, articles, and videos) at the I.N.A.

Legislation.   After reviewing international law and other countries' legislation on underwater cultural heritage, as well as Argentinean legislation (both on cultural heritage and on scuba diving), archaeologist–lawyer María Luz Endere prepared a proposal for a national law that would protect Argentina's underwater cultural heritage. Among other issues, this proposal stated the need for scientific standards in the recovery and study of submerged remains, as well as pointing out that underwater cultural heritage is public property and therefore cannot be sold or kept in private hands. Endere's recommendations were given to the Argentinean Parliament.

I.N.A. occasionally advises legislators working on law projects dealing with archaeological remains. Currently the Argentinean Parliament is evaluating a national law project on archaeological heritage which, for the first time, specifically states that archaeological sites can be on land or underwater. Though the inclusion of submerged remains is indeed progress for our national cultural legislation, this project has the tremendous drawback of defining archaeological sites as those dated prior to the European presence in the region (i.e., early 16th century), therefore leaving aside the vast majority of our submerged heritage: historical shipwrecks. Archaeologists from the I.N.A. and other institutions are trying to modify that situation, but because of external reasons (such as political interests and schedules), the outcome is unpredictable, as it is with the actual passing of this or any other law.

At an international level, the I.N.A. has periodically represented the Argentinean government at the development of the Convention for the Protection of the Underwater Cultural Heritage fostered by UNESCO. They have done so since the early stages of this important initiative, which was finally adpoted by UNESCO in 2001.

Education.   Education was another important goal within the program, since public awareness and care for our underwater cultural heritage could become the most powerful weapon to fight against treasure hunters. It also could gradually decrease the number of amateur archaeologists operating on their own. Their activities, though sometimes well intended, are usually harmful to the underwater cultural heritage.

Our first task in pursuing this goal was to send different types of mailings to scientific and academic institutions, government naval authorities, and scuba diving schools, spreading the news of the creation of the I.N.A. program and offering any assistance or further information.

The second stage was a more direct education plan through talks and courses for the general public, including school children and archaeology students; presentations at scientific and academic meetings; and publications (Elkin, 1997a; Elkin, 1998a,b; Elkin and Dellino, 1998; Endere, 1997). Newspaper and other mass media information was also distributed and published.

The most relevant outcomes of the education-oriented tasks developed so far are the following. First, after attending several courses at the I.N.A., the authorities of the Prefectura Naval (Argentinean Coast Guard) decided to include the subject "Historical Heritage" in their national scuba diving instructor course. In 1997, a four-month course began to be regularly taught by the I.N.A underwater archaeology team, in and it used a special text prepared for that course (Elkin et al. 1997). Second, in 1998 a semester-long seminar on underwater archaeology became an optional course for archaeology students at the University of Buenos Aires. This event happened for the first time in the history of all Argentinean universities that teach anthropology/archaeology. As the director of the I.N.A. underwater archaeology program, I conducted the seminar, but invited other specialists to lecture on special topics such as scuba diving, naval architecture, maritime history, and conservation. The seminar included, for those students who were certified scuba divers, a practice on underwater survey in a 10-m-deep tank where nonarchaeological objects were placed. It is hoped this seminar will continue to be taught at the University of Buenos Aires every two years.

Database of Underwater Cultural Sites.   Argentina's ocean shore extends along thousands of kilometers, and a high percentage of the country is covered by rivers and lakes. Naturally, the water was intensely used during pre-Hispanic times (the oldest coastal sites along the Atlantic shore date from the early Holocene) and between A.D. 16th and 19th centuries, the time of exploration and colonization of the region along the South Atlantic and the dangerous Cape Horn and Strait of Magellan route. Natural factors favoring good preservation of submerged remains, such as the low temperature of the Patagonian waters, make it logical to expect a rich underwater cultural heritage.

A computerized database allows for the assessment of the diversity, amount, and location (confirmed or potential) of underwater sites, and thus can serve as a basis for planning field work and conservation policies. Therefore, we are gathering and analyzing different types of sources which may provide information about underwater remains.

We started by consulting many types of data sources. We looked up (terrestrial) archaeological data, historical written records, ethnohistorical and ethnographic information, oral tradition, newspaper articles, present-day and past geographic, geologic, and hydrographic information, and the register of sunken ships kept at the Prefectura Naval headquarters.

As regards underwater survey, in 1995, two archaeologists, who occasionally collaborated with the I.N.A. program, worked along the southern coast of Buenos Aires province (Curtoni and Campos, 1995). In that area, two Early Holocene archaeological sites, Monte Hermoso I and La Olla, had been identified several years ago in the intertidal zone (Bayon and Politis, 1994; Politis et al., 1994; Zavala et al., 1994).

The archaeologists used several 200-m-long transects parallel to the shore to determine the underwater site extension. They looked for Pleistocene deposits that could possibly hold archaeological material. This first underwater survey yielded no results, partly because the diving conditions were difficult (Curtoni and Campos, 1995).

All the information obtained for each new site was gradually incorporated into a computer database using the Access 97 database software program. This program has several practical advantages for its users (Kohrn, 1998) and is the same one that the I.N.A. uses for its National Register of Archaeological Sites program.

Underwater Technical Training. As stated elsewhere (Elkin, 1998b), the Achilles heel of our interdisciplinary team at the beginning was that the archaeologists and archaeology students had little, if any, experience in scuba diving, and let alone in the application of underwater archaeological techniques. This hindered the specific underwater aspects of the project.

Since then, all archaeologists and archaeology students on the I.N.A. team not only hold diving licenses issued by the Argentinean Coast Guard but have also taken courses in underwater archeological techniques taught by specialists from institutions such as INAH (Mexico), Ships of Discovery (USA), the University of Southampton (UK), and the Nautical Archaeological Society (UK) with tutors from Canada. In addition, most of us have participated in underwater archaeology field seasons in different parts of the world.

Our own research carried out at the H.M.S. *Swift* site (see next section) has provided us with further training in diving and in underwater work.

Archaeological Research: The H.M.S. Swift *Project.* Shortly after the creation of the I.N.A program, authorities of the Museo Regional Provincial Mario Brozoski in Puerto Deseado asked us to conduct archaeological research at the *Swift*, the already-mentioned British sloop of war which sank in Patagonia in 1770 and now lay at a depth of 15 m. The I.N.A. team's archaeological research began in January 1998.

Our theoretical approach to historical archaeology considers that the written documents referring to our subject (in our case, Officer Gower's diary [Gower 1803], Captain Farmer's Court Martial [ADM 1/5304], the H.M.S. *Swift* Muster's book [ADM 36/7511], or the British navy plans of H.M.S. *Swift* obtained from the National Maritime Museum at Greenwich) are useful sources for generating hypotheses to be tested against the archaeological record, but they are not the true data about the past into which the archaeological record has to fit. Written history is not what happened in the past, but instead is the act of selecting, analyzing and writing about the past. In this way, archaeology can provide alternative questions and interpretations to history (Little, 1994) and the archaeological record becomes a powerful tool for generating information about the past independently of the possible existence of historical documents (Binford, 1983; Goñi and Madrid, 1996; Little, 1994; Senatore and Zarankin, 1996).

Within this framework, several hypotheses about the *Swift* shipwreck and pertaining to the following topics were set forth (Elkin, 1997b; Elkin and Dellino, 1998): possible contact between the British and the French in the Malvinas–Falkland Islands; reason for H.M.S. *Swift*'s trip to the Patagonian coast; aspects of life aboard the ship such as diet, cooking techniques, sanitary conditions, and social and military rank; technological advances in naval architecture and navigation techniques of the 18th century (Morell, 1984); natural site formation processes related to agents such as flora, fauna, sediments, and currents; and life of the shipwreck survivors on land.

The project's methodological and technical approach includes a critical review of historical documents and of past and modern coastal cartography, underwater archaeological survey, and excavation (the latter based on statistical stratified sampling), water and sediment sampling for physical and chemical analyses, gathering of biological data related to site formation processes, study and conservation of archaeological remains, and land coastal survey.

After seven fieldwork seasons, the *Swift* project is certainly progressing. The portion of the ship hull not covered by sediment has been surveyed and drawn by means of triangulation from a base line. The relative positions of all the structural remains, including cannons, anchors and the capstan, have been recorded. Figure 20.1 shows the plan view.

The architectural study of the ship is slow. There is a significant cover of botanical and faunal colonies (the former mainly of *Macrocystis* sp., the latter of *Sissurella* sp., *Patinigera magellanica*, and *Paramugula gregaria*) that has to be carefully removed before the underlying wooden ship structure can be recorded. In addition, there is low visibility (an average of 1 m), and most of the hull on the port side is still beneath the sea bottom sediment.

We are analyzing the in situ preservation condition of the ship and archaeological materials. We found there was an increasing loss of sediment cover in some portions of the site, especially the stern. Although the tidal currents in the estuary are strong enough to disturb the sediment matrix, there is another issue: West of the *Swift* wreck, there is a harbor that is undergoing enlargement, and both cause intense traffic of large ships, which pass close to the site. In addition, this site's preservation is affected by the action of marine borers (Bastida, personal communication; Elkin, 2000) and the high level of organic contamination (Bastida et al., 2000).

Dozens of objects lying on the sea bottom have been recorded, and most have been collected. These artifacts include two main types of glass bottles that vary in size, shape, and manufacturing technique. One is a cylindrical bottle type, usually called "English wine bottle," that is quite common for that time period (McKearin and Wilson, 1978). It has been found in other British land and wreck sites of similar chronology, such as the *Pandora* (Campbell and Gesner, 2000: fig. 148, Gesner, 1991: 8). It is coarsely handmade of dark ("black") glass, using sand pontils (Jones, 1971), and has a capacity of 750 cm^3. The other type of bottle, a case bottle commonly known as "gin bottle" (Moreno, 1997), is made of dark brown glass. It has a square cross-section and its capacity is about one gallon or a half-gallon (8 or 4 points).

Glass cups and different types of fine ceramic plates found in the stern area, such as other fine objects of similar technical and stylistic characteristics recovered by local divers of Puerto Deseado in previous years, must have belonged to the officers' tableware. These provide information about the social and military rank aboard H.M.S. *Swift*. The stern is the area where excavation has begun, currently covering an area of 8 m^2 (see Figure 20.1).

Other elements scattered throughout the whole site on the sediment surface (level 0) include artifacts in wood (mainly blocks of different types), metal (cutlery, buckles, coins), leather (shoe soles, belts), stone (gunflints, whetstones), glass (window panes, flasks, bottles, cups), and ceramics (different types of containers, especially earthenware cups and stoneware jars). All elements have been recorded and recovered along different field seasons between 1998 and 2001 (Elkin et al., 1999; Elkin and Dellino, 2000; Elkin et al., 2000).

All artifacts are being taken to the Museo Regional Provincial Mario Brozoski where they enter the conservation phase: salt removal, stabilization, and curation.

As for the terrestrial part of the project, the modern growth and development of Puerto Deseado has considerably modified the original landscape. For this reason, our chances of finding the remains of the *Swift* survivors' camp are almost nil. However, our own surveys along the coastal zone and the critical analysis of the historical documents enable us to

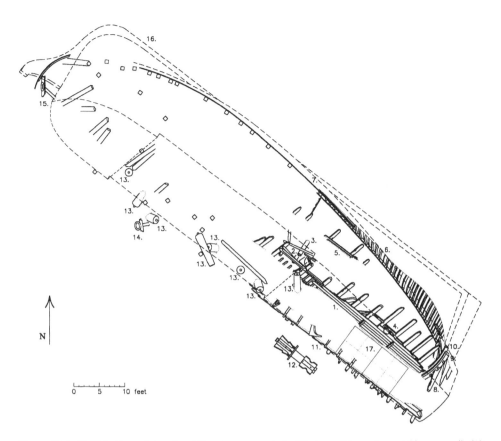

Figure 20.1. HMS Swift wrecksite plan. (1) main or upper deck; (2) place of the main mast (disappeared); (3) suction pump tube; (4) mizzen mast (broken); (5) lower deck; (6) starboard frames; (7) external planking; (8) stern post; (9) deck transom beam; (10) wing transom; (11) quarterdeck deck clamp of the port side; (12) capstan (collapsed); (13) cannons; (14) stream anchor; (15) bower anchor; (16) estimated position of the hull in the seabed; (17) current excavation zone, of 8 m^2 (Drawing by C. Murray).

evaluate areas that could have offered the best natural resources (drinkable water, rockshelters, high enough points with good visibility toward the ocean, etc.) for the nearly 100 people who lived in Puerto Deseado for a month. The first work carried out in that direction already has allowed us to discuss which areas could have best supplied the aforementioned resources for the *Swift* survivors back in 1770 (Acevedo and Grosso, 2000).

From Land to the Water

This section reviews other archaeological research projects that incorporate underwater surveys or excavations. In these cases, however, the archaeologists are project directors who do not dive.

Santa Fe La Vieja. The remains of *Santa Fe La Vieja* are located near the river San Javier (part of the Paraná river basin) in the province of Santa Fe, east-central Argentina. The town was founded in 1573 by Spanish explorer Juan de Garay, and it was abandoned a century later because of frequent flooding.

Excavations at this site reflect both Hispanic and aboriginal traditions and began in 1949 under the direction of A. Zapata Gollán. They are currently directed by archaeologist María Teresa Carrara from Universidad Nacional de Rosario. Since 1995, terrestrial excavations have been complemented by underwater work carried out by architect J. García Cano (Fundación Albenga) together with a group of archaeology students and scuba divers. The goals of the underwater work (García Cano and Valentini, 1996) are (1) to develop knowledge of the river dynamics and destruction of the bank; (2) develop archaeological methodology in waters with current and no visibility; and (3) train people in the specialty.

The specific aims pursued through underwater transect surveys and trench excavations were to confirm the presence of underwater remains in the San Javier river, to assess the potential of the submerged portion of the site, to evaluate the possible existence of redeposited material, and to develop a model to use to understand the collapse of the river bank in the original 16th-century settlement (García Cano and Valentini, 1996).

The authors state that the surveys and excavations allowed them to achieve most of the original goals. As for the recovered archaeological material, most of it consists of ceramic sherds, analogous to those recovered on land.

Las Encadenadas.   In the southcentral region of the province of Buenos Aires, 14 terrestrial sites are being investigated. Archaeologist Antonio Austral has been doing this since 1985. His chronological frame of reference is c. 2000–3300 years B.P. Particularly in the lagoon coastal site of Las Encadenadas (SA29LE), abundant archaeological material has been recovered along the shore during periods in which the lagoon water level decreased (Austral and García Cano, 1998). This situation, together with the later significant flooding of part of the terrestrial site, led to the 1996 inclusion of underwater archaeological surveys within the project. This was needed to obtain a more complete archaeological record by evaluating the magnitude of underwater remains and providing a better assessment of site formation processes and taphonomic aspects (Austral and García Cano, 1997, 1998).

The underwater survey, directed by Fundación Albenga, included several transects up to 70 m long, with a maximum depth of 1.80 m and zero visibility. The researchers state that in all cases the material (mostly lithic and ceramic remains) was found in a good state of preservation, without any fouling. Different lines of evidence led them to conclude that postdepositional natural processes were the main factors for the presence of underwater remains (Austral and García Cano, 1997; 1998).

Monje.   In the confluence of the rivers Coronda and Monje (Province of Santa Fe), in the Lower Paraná river basin, the material remains of a 17th-century aboriginal *reducción*, San Bartolomé de los Chaná, form a one-hectare archaeological site. European and native ceramic sherds are the most abundant finds there (Rochietti, 1997; Rochietti and Grandis, 1995–1996).

The water landscape that characterizes this site, which is partly submerged and affected by high mechanical and chemical dynamics caused by the riverine environment, led archaeologist Ana M. Rochietti to incorporate underwater archaeology methodology (Rochietti, 1997; 1998). The inclusion of underwater archaeology in this and other coastal sites fit in with the general goal of assessing site integrity and obtaining the greatest possible information from it (Rochietti, 1997: 2).

Rochietti (1997) believed there was a clear interdependence between the higher terrain of the river bank, adequate for human settlement, and the river bottom archaeological deposits, which are a consequence of the mechanical collapse of the river bank or an unusual rise of the river level. This close connection between both archaeological contexts requires a material and analytical integration, regarding the action of water in a site as something more than just an agent that destroys materials or puts them out of context. The possibility that the submerged deposits may have their own intelligibility, beyond representing the lost archaeological record, should be considered.

Rochietti proposed an island site model in which the main variables considered are size, setting, and type of spatial distribution of materials. She thought that because island sites have three sections, one of which is submerged, underwater archaeology becomes an unavoidable interpretive tool (Rochietti, 1997).

Cantón Tapalqué. In the central region of the province of Buenos Aires, archaeologist Miguel Mugueta and social anthropologist Marcela Guerci are carrying on an anthropological research program that includes the excavation of a 19th-century military settlement, actually a fortlet, called Cantón Tapalqué. It is located near the Tapalqué river (Mugueta and Gil, 1997; Mugueta et al. 1997).

The inclusion of underwater surveys in 1998, mostly carried out by archaeology students and sport divers, will provide information about several social and economic aspects of this settlement. One study is looking at irrigation technology; apparently the remains of a dam have been already located. The archaeological finds reported so far comprise varied materials, including glass, pottery, metal, bricks, and bones from extinct (Late Pleistocene/Early Holocene) and modern faunal taxa (Mugueta and Gil, 1997).

SUMMARY AND CONCLUSIONS

When we compare the present situation with that of only a few years ago, it is clear that significant progress has been made in underwater archaeology in Argentina: From my point of view, our most relevant achievement is that our archaeologists have become well-trained scuba divers and therefore can study submerged archaeological remains using current scientific standards. Though dealing with underwater cultural heritage certainly requires an interdisciplinary approach, the direction of the archaeological aspects of any project should obviously be in the hands of archaeologists. Moreover, I am convinced that the best scientific approach to an underwater site is for the archaeologists themselves to dive and get a personal idea of the in situ characteristics of materials and sediments (Elkin, 1998a). It is obvious, then, that I disagree with those colleagues who supervise or direct underwater work from land. However, their willingness to obtain information from underwater remains is surely a first and crucial step.

As regards other important progresses pertaining to Argentinean underwater cultural heritage, I think that among the nonacademic community there is a much greater conciousness of its importance and potential. For instance, close contact, exchange of experience, and cooperation between the I.N.A. and both the Prefectura Naval and the navy has proven that working together is possible and that this benefits our underwater cultural heritage. Among other advantages, the scarcity of money for archaeological research is being compensated by logistical support, experienced divers, diving equipment, and other resources provided by the two last institutions. Their participation in the field seasons of the *Swift* project has been extremely valuable.

Although there is still a long way to go and a lot to learn, Argentina is already on a good path. With better legislation and financial support, there is an enormous potential for the study of our underwater heritage in the years to come. This applies not only to the aboriginal communities in Argentina who had—and still have—a close contact with water, but also for those people of European origin. According to a popular saying, "Mexicans descend from the Aztecs, Peruvians from the Incas, and Argentineans from the ships."

ACKNOWLEDGMENTS. I would like to thank the many people and institutions who enabled us to be where we are now and who had faith in the future of Argentinean underwater archaeology. Pilar Luna Erreguerena (INAH-Mexico) and Diana Rolandi (I.N.A.-Argentina) were the first to believe that a dream that seemed impossible could come true. I will always be grateful to them for their help and their constant encouragement.

The archaeological research conducted within the I.N.A. underwater archaeology program has been funded by Fundación Antorchas, Secretaría de Cultura de la Nación, and the British Embassy in Argentina. The private companies Pérez Companc S.A., Pesquera Santa Cruz, Pesquera Santa Elena, and Dinar Líneas Aéreas have also provided funding for doing fieldwork and for diving and naval equipment.

The important discounts provided by the diving stores Rent a Diver S.A., Siete Mares Buceo, La Casa del Buceador, Todo Buceo S.A., and Astem Outek S.A., helped us make much more profitable use of our money.

The Municipalidad de Puerto Deseado always provided food, lodging, and logistical support for the *Swift* project, and a warm welcome every time we visit. Omar Juanola and Daniel Escobar helped a great deal in many underwater and surface tasks. The Asociación de Amigos del Museo Regional Provincial Mario Brozoski, formed by an enthusiastic group of people from Puerto Deseado, represent an important aspect of the *Swift* project—the active involvement of the local community. Biologists Esteban Frere and Patricia Gandini assisted us in the identification of flora and fauna from the *Swift* site before Ricardo Bastida became in charge of this aspect of the project.

The Prefectura Naval Argentina and the Armada Argentina (both in Buenos Aires and in Puerto Deseado) always help in many logistical aspects of the *Swift* project and also in the protection of our underwater cultural heritage.

Francisco and Norma Requelme provided a great deal of assistance for the I.N.A. team and the *Swift* project, besides being great diving instructors and trainers.

Jorge Manuel Herrera from the INAH of Mexico was the first to train us in specific underwater archaeological techniques and, like Pilar Luna, gave us time, dedication, advice, and, above all, friendship.

Many people have generously contributed to the I.N.A. underwater archaeology library by donating books, reprints, and other useful material.

María Ximena Senatore and Paula Moreno shared with us their respective knowledge of colonial pottery and glass.

Ana María Rochietti and Miguel Mugueta gave us recent articles and papers (some unpublished) that were useful for this chapter.

Last but not least, I extend my deepest thanks to all the members of the I.N.A. team and the *Swift* project for their optimism, their patience, their loyalty, their permanent good disposition, and their excellent work.

REFERENCES

Acevedo, G., and Grosso, M., 2000, *Informe de las prospecciones realizadas en la costa de Puerto Deseado en relación al campamento de los náufragos de la sloop Swift (1770)*. Postulado de probables modelos de uso del espacio. Desde el país de los gigantes. Perspectivas arqueológicas en Patagonia. Universidad Nacional de la Patagonia Austral, Río Gallegos, 673–682.

ADM 1/5304. Record of Martial Courts. *Public Record Office*, London.

ADM 36/7511. Muster's book (Record of the Crew on Board the *Swift* 1763-Feb. 1770). *Public Record Office*, London.

Ansaldo, C., and García Cano, J., 1986, Normas primarias de procedimiento. *ICOMOS Argentina – Boletín* 3 (January 1986): 3–4.

Austral, A., and García Cano, J., 1997, *La integridad arqueológica de los sitios costeros y la pertinencia de la arqueología subacuática*. Paper presented at the III Congreso Nacional de Arqueología Uruguaya. Colonia del Sacramento. Manuscript on file, Instituto Nacional de Antropología, Buenos Aires.

Austral, A., and García Cano, J., 1998, Un caso de arqueología en lagunas pampeanas. El sitio SA29LE, Las Encadenadas, en el partido de Saavedra, Provincia de Buenos Aires. Aplicación de técnicas de prospección subacuática. *Noticias de Antropología y Arqueología.- Revista electrónica de difusión científica* 21, Buenos Aires.

Bastida, R., Trassens, M., and Martín, J.P., 2000. *Informe preliminar sobre los sedimentos y bioclastos asociados con los restos de la corbeta HMS Swift (Puerto Deseado, Argentina)*. Manuscript on file, Instituto Nacional de Antropología.

Bayón, C., and Politis, G., 1994. Monte Hermoso I (Provincia de Buenos Aires).(Resumen extendido) *Actas y Memorias del XI Congreso Nacional de Arqueología Argentina (Resúmenes). Revista del Museo de Historia Natural de San Rafael (Mendoza)*, Tomo XIV (1/4):212–213, San Rafael.

Binford, L., 1983, Historical Archaeology: Is it Historical or Archaeological? *Working at Archaeology.* Academic Press, New York, 169–178.

Bonel, G., 1998, El aporte del sector privado a la arqueología subacuática. El caso de la Fundación Albenga. *Noticias de Antropología y Arqueología.- Revista electrónica de difusión científica* N. 21, Buenos Aires.

Campbell, J., and Gesner, P., 2000, Illustrated Catalogue of Artifacts from the H.M.S. *Pandora* Wrecksite Excavations 1977–1995. *Memoirs of the Queensland Museum – Cultural Heritage Series* 2 (1):53–159.

Curtoni, R., and Campos, F., 1995, *Primer acercamiento arqueológico a sitios prehistóricos sumergidos mediante técnicas subacuáticas*. Manuscript on file, Instituto Nacional de Antropología, Buenos Aires.

Elkin, D., 1997a, El proyecto Investigación y Conservación del Patrimonio Cultural Subacuático Argentino. *Actas del III Congreso Nacional de Arqueología Uruguaya*. Colonia del Sacramento.

Elkin, D.,1997b, *Proyecto Arqueológico Swift*. Presentado a la Secretaría de Cultura de la Nación y al Gobierno de la Provincia de Santa Cruz. on file, Instituto Nacional de Antropología, Buenos Aires.

Elkin, D., 1998a, Arqueología subacuática en el Instituto Nacional de Antropología. *Noticias de Antropología y Arqueología.- Revista electrónica de difusión científica* N. 21, Buenos Aires.

Elkin, D., 1998b, Underwater Archaeology in Argentina: State of the Art. *Common Ground – Archaeology and Ethnography in the Public Interest.* Summer 1999:12–15.

Elkin, D., 2000, Procesos de formación del registro arqueológico subacuático: Una propuesta metodológica para el sitio Swift (Puerto Deseado, Santa Cruz). *Desde el pais de los gigantes. Perspectivas arqueologicas en Patagonia.* Volumen I: 195–202. Universidad Nacional de la Patagonia Austral, Río Gallegos.

Elkin, D., and Dellino, V., 1998, *Protegiendo el Patrimonio Cultural Subacuático*. Paper presented at the Primer Congreso Virtual de Antropología y Arqueología. Internet (http//www.naya.org), October 1998. Manuscript on file, Instituto Nacional de Antropología, Buenos Aires.

Elkin, D., and Dellino, V., 2002, Underwater Cultural Heritage: The Case of Argentina. *Bulletin of the Australian Institute for Maritime Archaeology.* In press.

Elkin, D., Murray, C., and Vainstub, D., 1994, Arqueología Subacuática- Posibilidades de desarrollo en la Argentina. (Resumen extendido) *Actas y Memorias del XI Congreso Nacional de Arqueología Argentina (Resúmenes). Revista del Museo de Historia Natural de San Rafael (Mendoza)*, Tomo XIV (1/4): 367–368, San Rafael.

Elkin, D., Endere, M.L., Kremer, E., Murray C., and Orsetti, A., 1997, *El Patrimonio Cultural Subacuático - Una introducción a su estudio y preservación.* -Texto básico para la asignatura Patrimonio Histórico, Curso de Instructor Nacional de Buceo Deportivo. Escuela Superior de Salvamento y Buceo – Prefectura Naval Argentina. Manuscript on file, Prefectura Naval Argentina, Buenos Aires.

Elkin, D., Vainstub D., Argüeso, A. and Dellino, V., 2001. Proyecto Arqueologico H.M.S. *Swift* (Santa Cruz, Argentina). Memorias del Congreso Científico de Arqueología Subacuatica–ICOMOS (Pilar Luna Erreguerena y Rosamaría Roffiel, Coordinadoras) Coleccion Científica. Serie Arqueología. pp. 143–162. Instituto) Nacional de Antropología e Historia Mèxico, D.F.

Elkin, D., Vainstub, D., Argueso, A., and Murray, C., 2000, H.M.S. *Swift*: Arqueología submarina en Puerto Deseado. *Desde el país de los gigantes. Perspectivas arqueológicas en Patagonia* Volumen II: 659–671. Universidad Nacional de la Patagonia Austral, Río Gallegos.

Endere, M.L., 1997, *Quien protege al patrimonio arqueológico subacuático en Argentina?* Paper presented at the XII Congreso Nacional de Arqueología Argentina, La Plata, September 22–27, 1997.

Fernandez, J., 1978, Restos de embarcaciones primitivas en el lago Nahuel Huapi. *Anales de Parques Nacionales* XIV:45–77. Ministerio de Economía, Secretaría de Estado de Agricultura y Ganadería, Buenos Aires.

Fernandez, J., 1980, Historia de la Arqueología Argentina. *Anales de Arqueología y Etnología* XXXIV–XXXV. Universidad Nacional de Cuyo, Mendoza.

Fernandez, J., 1998, Canoas arqueológicas de un plao (huampus) recuperadas en lagos andinos del noroeste patagónico. *Noticias de Antropología y Arqueología.- Revista electrónica de difusión científica* N. 21, Buenos Aires.

Flores, R., Gaviorno, A.M., and García Cano, J.,1994, El problema de la legislación. Proyecto de Ley sobre la defensa, preservación, conservación y acrecentamiento del patrimonio cultural subacuático. *Actas y Memorias del XI Congreso Nacional de Arqueología Argentina (Resúmenes). Revista del Museo de Historia Natural de San Rafael (Mendoza)*, Tomo XIV (1/4):24–26, San Rafael.

García Cano, J., 1991. Arqueología subacuática. Prospecciones arqueológicas subacuáticas en Posadas. *ICOMOS – Argentina, Boletín* 19, Buenos Aires.

García Cano, J., 1997a, South America. In *Encyclopedia of Underwater and Maritime Archaeology*, edited by J. Delgado, pp. 395–398, British Museum Press, London.

García Cano, J., 1997b, Operación no intrusiva en un sitio de arqueología subacuática en Argentina. El caso de la sloop HMS *Swift. Anuario de la Universidad Internacional SEK* 2:45–65. Santiago de Chile.

García Cano, J., and Valentini, M., 1996, Arqueología subacuática en una fundación española del siglo XVI. Ruinas de Santa Fe la Vieja, un enfoque metodológico. *Anuario de la Universidad Internacional SEK*, Santiago de Chile.

Gesner, P., 1991, Pandora*: An Archaeological Perspective*. Queensland Museum, Brisbane.

Goñi, R. and Madrid, P., 1996, Arqueología sin hornear: sitios arqueológicos históricos y el Fuerte Blanca Grande. *Revista Intersecciones* No. 2:39–50. Facultad de Ciencias Sociales, UNCPBA., Olavarría.

Gower, E., 1803, *An Account of the Loss of His Majesty's Sloop Swift in Port Desire, on the Coast of Patagonia, on the 13th of March, 1770, and of Other Events which Succeded, in a Letter to a Friend.* Winchester and Son, London.

Grupo de Trabajo de Patrimonio Subacuático (GTPS) – ICOMOS, 1987, *Informe de campaña Proyecto Swift*. Manuscript on file, Instituto Nacional de Antropología, Buenos Aires.

Grupo de Trabajo de Patrimonio Subacuático (GTPS) – ICOMOS, 1988, *Informe de campaña Proyecto Swift*. Manuscript on file, Instituto Nacional de Antropología, Buenos Aires.

Grupo de Trabajo de Patrimonio Subacuático (GTPS) – ICOMOS, 1989, *Informe de campaña Proyecto Swift*. Manuscript on file, Instituto Nacional de Antropología, Buenos Aires.

Grupo de Trabajo de Patrimonio Subacuático (GTPS) – ICOMOS, 1992, *Informe de campaña Proyecto Swift*. Manuscript on file, Instituto Nacional de Antropología, Buenos Aires.

Jones, O., 1971, Glass Bottle Push-ups and Pontil Marks. *Historical Archaeology* V:62–73.

Kohrn, F., 1998, *Access 97 al máximo*. MP Ediciones S.A., Buenos Aires.

Libonatti, F., 1986. Arqueología subacuática. *ICOMOS Argentina – Boletín* 3 (January 1986):1–2. Manuscript on file, Instituto Nacional de Antropología, Buenos Aires.

Little, B., 1994, People with History: An Update on Historical Archaeology in the United States. *Journal of Archaeological Method and Theory* 1(1):5–36.

Luna Erreguerena, P., 1997, Stepping Stones of Mexican Underwater Archaeology. *Underwater Archaeology Proceedings from the Society for Historical Archaeology Conferenc*e, edited by Denise A. Lakey, pp. 50–53. Society for Historical Archaeology, Washington D.C.

Martínez, E., 1995, Problemática de la Arqueología Subacuática en el Uruguay. *Actas del II Congreso Nacional de Arqueología Uruguaya.* (Maldonado, Octubre 7–9 1994): 391–394, Montevideo.

McKearin, H., and Wilson, K.M., 1978, *American Bottles and Flasks and Their Ancestry*. Crown Publishers, New York.

Morell, F.D.L., 1984, La ciencia náutica de la época. In *Historia Marítima Argentina*, edited by L. Distefano, Tomo III, pp. 79–101. Departamento de Estudios Históricos Navales, Buenos Aires.

Moreno, P., 1997, *Botellas cuadradas de ginebra – Estudio de la forma y procesos de fabricación desde mediados del siglo XVIII hasta principios del XX*. Mariana Moreno, ed., Buenos Aires.

Mugueta, M., and Gil, C. 1997, *Cantón Tapalqué Viejo: Prospecciones subacuáticas en el Arroyo Tapalqué*. Paper presented at the 12th Conngreso Nacional de Arqueología Argnetina. La Plata, September 1997. manuscript on file, Facultad de Ciencias Sociales, Universidad Nacional del Centro de la Provincia de Buenos Aires, Olavarría.

Mugueta, M., Guerci, M., and Wagner, G. 1997, *Nuevos datos aportados por la arqueología subacuática en el Cantón Tapalqué Viejo*. Paper presented at the Primeras Jornadas Regionales de Historia y Arqueología del siglo XIX. Ms on file, Facultad de Ciencias Sociales, Universidad Nacional del Centro de la Provincia de Buenos Aires, Olavarría.

Murray, C., ed., 1993, *Corbeta de guerra H.M.S. Swift-1763-. Historia, naufragio, rescate y conservación*. Comité Argentino del ICOMOS, Museo Provincial Mario Brozoski y Municipalidad de Puerto Deseado, Buenos Aires.

Olivera, D., Elkin, D., and Murray, C., 1995, Punteo de la presentación: Patrimonio Cultural Subacuático - Situación actual y perspectivas en Argentina y Uruguay. *Actas del II Congreso Nacional de Arqueología Uruguaya*. (Maldonado, Octubre 7–9 1994): 393–394, Montevideo.

Pernaut, C., 1998. Los primeros pasos de la preservación del patrimonio cultural subacuático en la Argentina. La gestión no gubernamental del ICOMOS. *Noticias de Antropología y Arqueología.- Revista electrónica de difusión científica* No. 21, Buenos Aires.

Politis, G., 1992, Política nacional, arqueología y universidad en Argentina. In *Arqueología en América Latina Hoy*, edited by G. Politis, pp.70–87. Biblioteca Banco Popular, Bogotá.

Politis, G., Lozano, P., and Guzmán, L., 1994, Evidencias de la ocupación humana prehispánica del litoral bonaerense en el sitio La Olla. (Resumen extendido) *Actas y Memorias del XI Congreso Nacional de Arqueología Argentina (Resúmenes). Revista del Museo de Historia Natural de San Rafael (Mendoza)*, Tomo XIV (1/4): 240–241, San Rafael.

Rochietti, A.M., 1997, Integración de la arqueología subacuática a un modelo de sitio islero. *Conferencia. Arqueología Subacuática*. Archivo y Museo Histórico del Banco de la Provincia de Buenos Aires Dr. A. Jauretche. ICOMOS Argentina – Fundación Albenga, Buenos Aires.

Rochietti, A.M., 1998, Registro arqueológico integrado: Incorporación de la investigación subacuática en los sitios isleros. *Jornadas: Arqueología Subacuática en el Sur de Am*érica. 3 y 4 de septiembre de 1998. Archivo y Museo Histórico del Banco de la Provincia de Buenos Aires Dr. A. Jauretche. ICOMOS Argentina - Fundación Albenga, Buenos Aires.

Rochietti, A.M., and Grandis, N., 1995–1996, La boca del Monje: Un sitio reduccional pára indios isleros (siglo XVII). *VIII Reunion Cientifica de Arqueologia Brasileira – 12 al 15 de Septiembre de 1995*. Centro de Cultura y Ciencias de la Pontificia Universidad Católica. Asociación de Arqueología Brasilera, Porto Alegre.

Senatore, M.X., and Zarankin, A., 1996, Perspectivas metodológicas en arqueología histórica. Reflexiones sobre la utilización de la evidencia documental. *Páginas sobre hispanoamérica colonial. Sociedad y Cultura* 3: 113–122.

Sotheby's, 1993. *The Uruguayan treasure of the River Plate – El Tesoro Uruguayo del Río de la Plata*. March 24 and 25, 1993, New York.

Zavala, C., Bayón, C., and Barna, A., 1994, Procesos de formación de sitios de baja resolución en la costa sudoccidental de la Provincia de Buenos Aires. (Resumen extendido) *Actas y Memorias del XI Congreso Nacional de Arqueología Argentina (Resúmenes). Revista del Museo de Historia Natural de San Rafael (Mendoza)*, Tomo XIV (1/4): 252–254. San Rafael.

Zarankin, A., and Senatore, M.X., 1996, Reseña crítica sobre arqueología histórica colonial en la Argentina. *Páginas sobre Hispanoamérica colonial – Sociedad y Cultura* 3: 123–141. PRHISCO, Buenos Aires.

Europe and the Mediterranean

The *Handbook*'s European contributors have centuries of underwater culture to probe. From Scandanavia in the north to the British Isles and farther south to Portugal and Italy, Europe is a welter of diverse coastal and river environments with thousands of underwater archaeology sites to explore. We present here the status of European and Mediterranean research.

As Carl Olof Cederlund states, knowledge of Sweden's underwater landscape and material remains of human culture in this environment is so far quite limited. There is a need to develop cross-scientific information. Research should cover the environment of the sea bottom, coastal landscapes, and the ecology of lakes, river streams, marshlands, and bogs.

Christian Ahlström has chosen examples of archival records typical of their epoch to describe the rich underwater archaeology of Finland and the eastern Baltic. At this crossroads of northern Europe, ships of war or commerce from foreign countries provide an international aspect as seen in inscriptions and ceramics.

To introduce his chapter on the British Isles, Glenn Darrington states that the last 10 years have been most productive in cultural resource management, public awareness, and professional accreditation in England and Wales. When the work of English heritage is expanded, government support should be more than minimal, and predatory diving will be decreased.

Colin Martin reports that Scottish salvage law still favors the treasure hunter. Strong regulatory agencies together with strong programs in education, especially as produced at St. Andrews University, and public participation will prevail.

Colin Breen and Aidan O'Sullivan describe the abundant underwater resources that exist in the Republic of Ireland. Surrounded by water, with many rivers and lakes, Ireland is a natural setting for sites archaeological, both terrestrial and marine. Forthcoming is a lake settlement program; ongoing is riverine research from the Neolithic to historic periods. Recent coastal surveys of intertidal estuaries have expanded maritime heritage with its attendant shipwreck distribution.

Brian Williams states that since 1992, the Department of Environment for Northern Ireland has been responsible for maritime archaeology and guides for study of the seabed, intertidal zone and coastal interaction, and the offshore islands. The Maritime Record has documented 3000 wrecks and other submerged sites. A geomorphological map of the seabed around the coast of Northern Ireland is now in progress. The University of Ulster has created the Maritime Archaeology Department to develop research and education.

Max Guérout ably describes the contribution of the French in the underwater realm from 1948 to the present. The current status of work includes descriptions of work in Martinique and French Polynesia. Notable wrecks have been divided by century, a plus for those researching shipbuilding and artifact assemblages.

Carlo Beltrame portrays a dismal picture of nautical archaeology in Italian waters and shores. Lacking is the management and training in every aspect of the field. The richness of finds is described for more than 30 sites, but the overall scene is one of exploitation and neglect. Coordination and leadership are badly needed.

Jean-Yves Blot states that Portugal's submerged remains are primarily of the Roman period and from the late Middle Ages to modern times. Heavy silting and erosion have removed the presence of human activity along the coast. Shipwreck remains are "a scattered nonhomogeneous lot." Archival references have been a mainstay for nautical related research.

Chapter 21

Archaeology in the Marine Environment in Sweden

CARL OLOF CEDERLUND

TREASURE HUNTING, NATIONALISM, OR SCIENCE?

In Sweden, the established concept of and the term for archaeology directed toward the marine environment is "marinarkeologi"—in English, marine archaeology. Specialized fields are seen as "underwater archaeology," archaeology directed toward research in the underwater environment, as well as "boat and ship archaeology," dealing with recording, analyses, and interpretation of boat and ship remains. In this chapter, the term "archaeology in the marine environment" is used as the general term defining the kind of archaeology discussed.

Our way of perceiving archaeology in the marine environment, as well as other scientific fields within the humanities, has been influenced by strong evaluations, deeply embedded in our culture. These evaluations have influenced archaeology and its development. Seen in an overall perspective, the influence of these evaluations has given archaeology in the marine environment in Sweden, as well as in many other nations, a colossal tilt.

From an international perspective, archaeology in the marine environment deals about 80–90 percent with investigation and analysis of the wrecks of old boats and ships, for several reasons.

Carl Olof Cederlund, Marine Archaeology Program, University College of South Stockholm, Stockholm, Sweden.

International Handbook of Underwater Archaeology, edited by Carol V. Ruppé and Janet F. Barstad. Kluwer Academic/Plenum Publishers, New York, 2002.

Let us start far back in time, in myth and religion. Since the beginning of history, even prehistory, the ship has been loaded with strong symbolic value. It has had a central position in the economic system of many societies and has played roles in religion and myth. Ships carried the sun across the sky. Ships took the dead to the land of death. The ship was one of the magic assets of the gods, also magic in the respect that it could carry humans over water: It made humans able to "walk on water."

Perhaps the ship has a similar symbolic value and attraction today, both for archaeologists and others, as it had at the time when the sun was carried across the sky on a ship. Perhaps the ship is one of the strong, basic symbols in our time and has influenced interest in the ship and the wreck within archaeology in the marine environment.

Another type of evaluation with deep roots in time has had a decisive influence on the development of archaeology in the marine environment. To a high degree, our interest today in old, sunken ships comes from commercial interest in salvaging cargo and equipment from lost ships lying on the sea bottom. In earlier times, this was an occupation that offered great financial gain—and still can—and was one that developed great skills and an advanced technology to pursue, at least for a time. As time passed, an antiquarian interest was integrated into salvage. One could make money on old things salvaged from the deep. This antiquarian interest grew step by step and changed salvage enterprises to take the shape of scientific activities during the 20th century, developing within the humanities with its own approach to investigation, treatment, and analysis. This kind of archaeology thus emanates to a high degree from its counterpart: wreck loitering or commercial salvage.

Archaeology in the marine environment, so strongly directed toward ship remains, has limitations steered by certain ideologies. In our society, one is given really only two types of shipwreck of any archaeological interest: wrecks of large warships from the time of the older Vasa kings (16th and 17th centuries) and wrecks of ships from the Iron Age (especially from the Age of the Vikings) and from the Medieval Period. This inclination is evident in Nordic nations and exists in variations in other Western societies (Cederlund, 1997a).

THE REGAL SHIPS

The salvage of the warship *Vasa* in 1961 may be thought of as a *deus ex machina* event, but it was not. On the contrary, it was preceded by an extensive diving and salvaging activity on a series of wrecks of old warships, starting in the middle of the 19th century. The raising of other old warship wrecks was discussed long before the *Vasa* salvage. For example, when permission was requested to salvage the *Vasa* 40 years earlier, in 1921, it was denied by the harbor authorities. At that time, there was also salvaging performed on two other large warships or parts of them: *Riksäpplet* and *Gröne Jägaren,* which foundered at Dalarö in 1676. During the 1930s and 1940s, one wanted to raise the wreck of the "kravel" *Elefanten*, sunk in Kalmar Sound in 1564.

The Swedish navy has been especially interested in and has worked for the heightening of interest in old warship wrecks known as the Regal Ships. Salvaging objects from the wrecks of old warships began when the heavy diving suit was introduced in the navy in the middle of the 19th century. The navy trained divers to use the suit on the same wrecks; the divers needed tasks for training and exercise. A commercial aspect was supposedly integrated into early diving exercises, since one could sell ship timbers as "black oak" to furniture manufacturers and others. Some of the objects retrieved from the sea were offered or sold to naval and other museums, and exhibited there. Some were also sold to private collectors.

The ideology behind this interest is much older than the diving on wrecks of naval ships. So far, I have been able to follow it back to the beginning of the 18th century, but it may be be possible to trace it further back in time. It encompasses a certain set of imaginings around the large warships—the king's ships—and their roles in politically decisive and famous naval battles. This includes the king as a leader of the country and his officers, and the king's men as heroes on board the warships. This ideological interest, colored by symbolism, lives and thrives also today. Very similar stories, nearly myths, are woven into stories in history books, 100 or 200 years old, strongly ideological in character. In our day, the stories (or myths) are told time after time by the press and center around the localization or presentation of newly found wrecks of warships (Cederlund, 1994).

A certain type of representation or evaluation is forwarded in this context, not least by the press. This was clearly seen when the *Vasa* was salvaged in 1961 (Cederlund 1980; Franzen, 1974), and when the *Kronan* was located in 1980 (Johansson, 1985)— both so-called Regal Ships—and when a wreck, located in Nämdöfjärd Bay in the Stockholm archipelago and assumed to be King Gustav Vasa's ship *Lybska Svan*, was introduced worldwide in spring 1991. This was about the idealization of what is usually called the Era of Great Power during the 16th and 17th centuries in Swedish history, and about the kings and war heroes of this time, their national importance and courageous deeds.

The representations around the big, sailing warships and the remains of the same, especially of the 16–18th centuries, may be worth an analysis in the realm of psychology of religion. Basically it is the story of a holy quartet: *the King*, representative of *God on earth*, God's *Ship*, and *the King*'s *hero(es)* on board the ship. The "wreck salvage happenings," at which one "touches" (in other words, goes down to and salvages from) the wrecks of the Regal Ships, have now recurred at intervals of 10–15 years for at least 150 years in Sweden. The messages carried by these activities make it possible to see them as recurrent projections of an ideology, several hundred years old, around the big warships from the Swedish Era of Power: a ritual with nationalistic overtones (Cederlund, 1994).

THE VIKING SHIPS AND THEIR FOLLOWERS

A main trait or trend in Swedish and Nordic ship archaeology emanates from other nationalistic representations. This started a long time ago with the findings of Viking ships and other prehistoric vessels during the 19th century, especially in Norway and Denmark. These finds came during a period of strong nationalism and fitted well with evaluations then reigning. The Viking and the Viking ship are symbols of expansion and manly courage, which have been fostered to a conspicuous degree in Nordic culture. Once again, one finds in works on the history of the Swedish navy from the 18th and 19th centuries (mostly written by naval officers) the Viking as the precursor of naval officers, heroes on the warships of the Great Era in the 16th and 17th centuries—in other words, the precursors of the King's heroes.

Unlike the large postmedieval warship wrecks, the wrecks of Viking ships were not found in deep water but in soil or shallow water and investigated by archaeologists and ethnologists of the time. At the same time, these ships were also treated by scholars in the humanities. So it was that, early on, these ship remains were subjected to thorough scientific treatment according to the positivistic theory of the time.

I see the interest in Regal Ships and Viking ships in archaeology as parts of a modern-day myth of origin, intertwined (as such often are) with hero symbolism, and used as signals or symbols of Nordic identity and of the character of the Swedish national state as both have existed for several hundred years. Similar patterns of ideological identification, appearing in the field of archaeology of the marine environment, also can be seen in the other Nordic nations as well as in other European national states (Cederlund 1997a).

MEDIEVAL SHIP FINDS IN SWEDEN

In Sweden, few big Viking ship finds have been made, such as the ones discovered in Norway and Denmark. Perhaps this is because of a stronger cultural identification with the Viking concept there than in Sweden. As we know, one finds what one looks for. On the other hand, starting in the early 20th century, Sweden has executed several archaeological investigations of medieval ship finds. The most prominent excavations are more than 20 vessels in the harbor of Kalmar castle in the 1930s (Cederlund, 1980, pp. 80–81), and the excavation of 11 more at Helgeandsholmen in Stockholm, beneath the royal castle, in the end of the 1970s. The thorough presentation of the results of the Kalmar investigation, published by Åkerlund now nearly 50 years ago, is a good example of a sternly objective, scientific approach in this field (Åkerlund, 1951). A similar publication has been made on the Helgeandsholmen finds of 40 years later (Varenius, 1989).

Seen from an ideological perspective, it may not be a coincidence that the Kalmar and Stockholm excavations were performed at sites of central importance for the development of the Swedish state during the medieval period, and that they were both strongly supported by the state through the Central Board of National Antiquities.

ARCHAEOLOGY IN THE MARINE ENVIRONMENT ON THE EVE OF THE 21ST CENTURY

The trends just described constitute deep furrows in the archaeological field of the marine environment in Sweden. Extensive and important research material has come to be situated between the two main trends and thus has been treated to a much lesser degree, into our time. This is relevant for the hundreds of wrecks of big merchant ships of the 17th century and onward that have been located in coastal waters during recent decades or since scuba diving became common. These wrecks were not of any scientific interest or research before the 1970s—a remarkable situation, not the least because these ship remains constitute the most extensive research material under Swedish waters (Ahlström, 1997; Cederlund, 1980; 1983; 1987; 1997b; Rönnby and Adams, 1994).

And still this large, untouched research field is only one part of what has been forgotten or left behind. I maintain that Swedish underwater archaeology has not yet started to see and define its areas of research. This is a major structural problem, which should have high priority among archaeologists.

THE ARCHAEOLOGICAL STUDY OF MARINE AND CULTURAL ENVIRONMENTS: A HOLISTIC APPROACH

If we look past the old wrecks that hitherto have been of such interest for archaeologists working with the marine environment, there appear many and differentiated archaeological remains under water, on the beach, and in the soil near the coasts. Properly studied, these may give important insights in human and societal relations to the sea, the coast, the river, and the lake through time.

We sometimes praise ourselves for having a good understanding of our geographical–topographical surroundings. This assumption is not applicable for areas under water. In Sweden, this is about 20–30 percent of Swedish territory, partly the bottom of coastal waters out to the territorial boundary, partly the bottom of inland waters such as lakes, streams, and rivers. It was not until recent times that humans began to make the first systematic investigations of this underwater world. This has given us knowledge of ecological, geological, and biological conditions there. On the other hand, our knowledge of the topography or the underwater "landscape" and the material remains of human culture beneath the water is so far quite limited.

Modern archaeology in the marine environment should avoid the nationalistic and commercial motives which hitherto have influenced the subject to such a high degree, and instead formulate new and more general research approaches and perspectives. There is a great need for basic, archaeological research with the intent to widen our general perspectives of the whole research field of the marine environment. This implies, among other things, that one must apply archaeological research of a general scope and in a systematic way to the archaeological source material of the marine environment. It is important that this kind of archaeology, as general archaeology has done, develops the possibilities of cross-scientific cooperation in the subject, with marine geophysicists for the study of the underwater environment by systematic search and survey, and with marine ecologists for the study of preservation of archaeological remains, to mention just two examples.

Archaeological research under water must reach out from a theoretical and critical awareness. It is a science of the humanities whose aim is to widen our insight and expand our existence and role in the marine setting.

By enhancing one sector of society that often has been bypassed in favor of the rural and the urban, namely the maritime sector, archaeology in the marine environment may give a meaningful contribution to general humanistic research and social analysis (Cederlund 1980; 1997a).

RESEARCH CONDITIONS AND PRIORITIES

It is of primary importance to study and understand three types of conditions in the marine environment in order to develop a holistic approach to marine archaeology and its source material—the topographical and cultural character of the landscape and the influence of natural and cultural factors on material remains of human activities in the differing marine environments.

Three major research topics need to be developed in order to achieve the holistic perspective: (1) The survey, study, and analysis of the cultural environments in the underwater world, and their characteristics; (2) the study and definition of archaeological remains as physical objects in those underwater environments; and (3) the study and the evaluation of underwater environments and archaeological remains as cultural assets.

The study of these topics may offer perspectives on our ways of seeing and appreciating marine environments and cultures, and help to renew our approach to this subject. One general motive for such an approach may be the development of our historical awareness of maritime matters in society.

Our research must cover three basic types and two subtypes of marine environments (Figure 21.1):

1. Marine environment of the sea bottom, in Sweden's case especially the Baltic Sea and parts of Kattegat

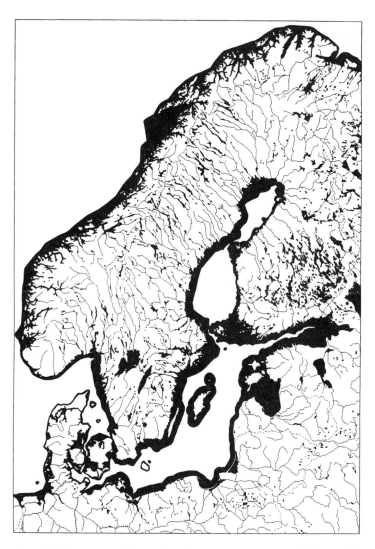

Figure 21.1. Water-covered areas of northern European nations including Sweden.

2. Coastal landscape, under and above water, a marine landscape, which is constituted by a series of variations along our very long coast
3. Inland marine environment of Sweden, again under and above water, which in turn, can be divided into subtypes, each creating a basic type:
   A. Marine environments of the more than 90,000 lakes
   B. Marine environments of the thousands of rivers and streams, thousands of km long.
   C. Marshlands and bogs, often partly dry lakes.

Each of these basic types of marine environments can be divided into special types of marine cultural environments. The latter may be defined with the help of the environmental factors which constitute them and the human factors which have influenced them: Both factors create the topographical and cultural structures which characterize the different types of marine cultural environments. They influence decisively the quality and state of preservation of the source material and all the types of cultural remains existing in the different environments.

A time factor is inherent in this structure: The passage of time makes evident changes in the environment, supporting the development of new environmental patterns due to natural or cultural effects. This means that our understanding of marine environments must integrate the study of changes through time so we can understand the environment's development and character.

Our present research can be divided into two kinds of research activity: *general research,* in which we study basic factors in natural as well as cultural environments, which constitute and influence the development of the special marine environments I discuss here, and *environmental research* directed toward studies in the special marine environments, by which we learn to define both the natural and the cultural characteristics, not the least the archaeological remains.

If our research, or even science in general, had been as well structured as we sometimes imagine it to be, we would begin by structuring this giant research field on the general level and proceed into studies of special marine environments. Scientific life is not so well ordered; instead, one must anticipate a research process which will consist of studies of both kinds, performed not only in parallel but also interwoven with each other. The scholar studying special marine environments should be encouraged to draw conclusions from general research. Also encouraged should be studies of a more general character of the interaction between the archaeological material and basic natural and cultural factors working in the marine environment, so as to create the set of tools necessary to do both general and specialized studies.

We should recognize the fact that we as archaeologists stand at a starting point in a race down into the underwater world during the coming century. One of our major aims will be to create insight in and understanding of archaeological situations in the marine environment, either at a depth of 500 metres at sea or in a shallow stream in a northern *fjell* area—and stressing the point that we are carrying out a commission in the humanities. In this we will need to listen hard to what the natural sciences have to teach us on these matters. Much of what we have to learn about the creation and operation of marine environments we will have to learn from quaternary geologists, ecologists, marine geophysicists, and marine botanists. Botanists have been working in the marine environment longer than archaeologists, and have a more systematic approach to their task. It might be valuable to learn about and to adapt the general approaches often used by the natural sciences.

A SPECTRUM OF RESEARCH TOPICS

Since we are dealing with subjective conceptions of human culture, there are few possibilities for offering an overarching explanation of the directions archaeology in the marine environment should choose in the future. On the other hand, from a personal standpoint, one may discuss and name such research subjects that seem to be little exploited and that may make important contributions to knowledge in our science in the future (Cederlund, 1996).

Basic Research Tasks

Archaeological remains under water or in the marine environment are physically influenced by a series of natural and other factors, which may be geological, chemical, biological, climatic, or human. The understanding of the interaction between these parts of nature and underwater and onshore archaeological remains constitute a group of important basic research tasks. We still have little understanding of the conditions of interactions between archaeological remains and the natural environment.

The sedimentation on the sea bottom and in lakes, rivers, and streams is in itself important archaeological information. The study of stratified sedimentation layers on a larger scale offers possibilities to understand the changes of surrounding land and its botanical, cultural and other circumstances. Such studies might be accomplished by sampling and analysis of sediment cores: quaternary geology or pollen analyses, searching for different sorts of macro- and micro-material, and chemical substances in the sediments that emanate from human activities in the past in the marine environment.

Further Development of Traditional Research Areas

The study of shipbuilding techniques of old vessels is traditional research in archaeology in the marine environment, often called boat-and-ship archaeology. At the same time, research on other subjects within the same realm have been ignored almost completely. One such area is the study of shipyards as archaeological sites, a type of archaeology that could prove very valuable for the understanding of ship technology of earlier periods.

Another important area of research also has had a low priority: study of prehistoric shipbuilding traditions and sea communications during the period from the Mesolithic to the early Iron Age. The main reason for this "white patch" on the map of ship archaeology is a decisive one: Few remains of vessels from this period have been found. Superficially, this is a good explanation for the lack of research in this area.

An opportunity to study original prehistoric ships would certainly augment interpretations of prehistoric seafaring and sea communications. It is important to begin research to locate remains of prehistoric vessels, as well as their building and landing places. As a first step, there should be a systematic search and survey especially in the sediments around prehistoric coastal trading sites. In this search, one should start from the conditions created by topography, quaternary geology, and archaeology.

One traditional and dominant research area deals with the remains of warships from the post-medieval period, research that may take new directions such as the location and study of remains of late medieval naval ships. It is evident that, during the 15th century in the Baltic Sea, there existed large warships carrying hundreds of men. Their design, as well as their cultural attribution (for example the symbolism they mirrored) has rarely been studied (Adams and Rönnby, 1996).

Wrecks of merchant ships from the post-medieval period, their cargoes, the equipment of the ships and their crews, constitute today the largest known group of identified underwater archaeological remains. They contain vast amounts of information and research potential. Although the wrecks of merchant ships are about 90 percent of the total number of larger wrecks from the period, only in the past three decades have archaeologists had the possibility to work with them to any extent. This research field may be expanded considerably. These wrecks can tell much about early sea trade and ship types, building techniques, types of cargoes and methods used for packing and stowing, and about living and working conditions of the men who sailed them. These are just a few of the primary possibilities for the study of sea trade in earlier phases of Western society (Ahlström, 1997; Cederlund 1980; 1983; 1987).

New Research Areas

The underwater landscape, the shore, and settled areas are locations of remains of structures and buildings of different types and functions once belonging to the part of society which turned towards the water. These remains cover a wide spectrum, from those created through sedimentation, to those built in the water, on the bottom, or on land, and later inundated or sunk. To these archaeological remains belong deposits of human activities in land settlements later inundated, or of debris once thrown from a nearby shore settlement. Also included in the same category are remains of hunting, or fishing traps, parts of communications, or transport systems, for example installations for transport routes on inland waters, river crossings and primitive bridges, water-based defense installations, and working places from prehistoric and historic times (Beier, 1990; Bergenblad, 1980, 1985; Cederlund, 1996; Larsson, 1983; Norman 1988; Rönnby, 1975; Westerdahl, 1987, 1989). Within this category might exist the largest amount of not yet ascertained or recognized archaeological remains under water, from the early Stone Age to recent times.

The major portion of known archaeological remains in the marine environment—wrecks—has been located in coastal waters. This is supposedly due partly to the fact that diving activities seem to concentrate on the coast, especially at the more densely populated areas where divers live and dive today. Coastal areas have also housed important seafaring routes and harbors. Of course, there is a connection between seafaring and the frequency of wrecking. Another reason for the concentration of diving exploration in coastal areas is that visibility is much better there than in many inland waters, which makes the diving enterprise more alluring and productive.

Because visibility in coastal waters is better, we know much less about submerged cultural remains in the inland waters of lakes and streams. We have in Sweden some 90,000 lakes, with an area larger than 0.01 km^2 (Svenskt sjöregister, 1983), as well as a huge number of streams and rivers, from the large rivers in the North to the smallest streams (Vattendrags-registret, SMHI, 1985). With a few outstanding exceptions, these waters have hardly been investigated at all.

Another area of future scientific exploitation is the deep-sea environment. Sweden is surrounded by relatively shallow seas, the Baltic Sea and the Kattegat, so in this part of the world deep-sea archaeology, in its true sense, will not exist. On the other hand, future finds on the seabed beyond the Swedish coast may make important contributions to our understanding of past maritime society. One example is the possibility of finding remains of the vessels which, in the Mesolithic period, were used to travel to and from the big islands far out in the Baltic Sea, for example the island of Gotland, which has rich archaeological remains of early Stone Age fishing and hunting settlements.

Marine Archaeology: "Communications Archaeology"

One vast and largely untouched research area is sailing, navigation, and sailing-route archaeology. Studies have been done of ancient sea routes and remains of installations along them, such as sea marks, lighthouses, and pilot stations. To this category belongs evidence of navigation or sailing techniques, such as navigation instruments. This area also includes interpretation of sailing and navigation techniques of former periods, since these can be tested along still existing, age-old sailing routes (Cederlund, 1989; Cederlund, 1995a).

There are border areas between archaeology on land and in the marine environment. To this category belongs harbor archaeology, which touches both land- and water-based research material. A common factor of old harbors is that they are made up of archaeological remains of maritime activities (Carlsson, 1987; Hansson, 1967; Lundström, 1981).

Another vast and untouched research area is the thousands of natural anchorages along the coast, whose bottoms often contain rich deposits of debris from ships and shore. The shores at these sites usually contain remains of former settlements at the anchorage.

Settlement on Swedish land during the prehistoric period and later always has had a strongly maritime inclination due to the many inland waters, the long coasts, and the vast archipelagos. Hunting, gathering, fishing, cattlebreeding, and transport over vast areas and long distances played a prominent role in human activities.

Transport in the roadless inland country passed over the water or ice of long lake systems and streams and over the land between them. This type of society and its ways of communication, existing for thousands of years, has deposited many different types of objects and structural remains on the bottom of the thousands of lakes and streams (Cederlund, 2000). So far, this material seems to have been left in peace by the archaeologists. Few people dive in and explore these waters.

Care and Preservation of Submerged Cultural Resources

Finally, a pivotal task for underwater archaeologists, both today and in the future, must be to augment their understanding of submerged cultural resources so they can preserve them. It might seem strange, especially to land archaeologists, to talk in earnest about systematic search and survey and the care of archaeological remains under water. On the other hand, there is a fast-growing need for such care. Leisure divers continue to damage shipwrecks several hundred years old and the rate of damage is increasing quickly. Today is supposedly only an "idyllic" beginning. There is reason to anticipate that the erosion of archaeological remains under water will increase even more strongly in the future, if nothing is done to protect them (Cederlund, 1998).

Sweden took on an international pioneer role in preservation in the 1950s, by introducing the technique of preserving waterlogged wood with polyethylenglycol; the technique was proven with the preservation of the warship *Vasa* (Barkman, 1968). The method has since been used in several international large ship projects and today is used all over the world. Yet, to ensure stable preservation results, several problems still need to be solved in this methodology. It is important, especially from an economic point of view, to solve these successfully. Polyglycol treatment is usually an expensive procedure.

Preservation techniques belong to the sector of the natural sciences. As an archaeologist, I would like to see an integration of archaeology in the marine environment and the business of preservation in education. Professionals in these two fields are separate groups in society and have created two different establishments with partly differing evaluations. It would be of value to have a bridge over the knowledge gap between them, through education.

THEORETICAL ASPECTS OF ARCHAEOLOGY IN THE MARINE ENVIRONMENT

Our theoretical structure is closely connected to the ideological ideas on which we stand as scientists. It is for the development of the latter that theoretical aspects are discussed continuously. Inherent in this process should be the multiplicity of voices and thoughts.

Basically, the theoretical basis for general archaeology, as well as archaeology of the marine environment, is the same. At the same time one can see, in the perspective of the history of science, that archaeological researchers who early on became interested in Sweden's maritime culture had a similar research profile. They often had a strong connection with social sciences, directed toward later periods than that of prehistoric archaeology. Professionally, most were both archaeologists and ethnologists (Cederlund, 1996; 1997a).

One reason for the inclination toward ethnology is that archaeology in the marine environment in Sweden works mostly with source material from later times than prehistory, the same time periods in which traditional ethnology worked. It is not unrealistic to state that this kind of archaeology developed an ethno-archaeological approach quite early, using studies of maritime folk culture and traditional boat-building (Hallström, 1910; Hasslöf, 1958, 1972; Humbla and von Post, 1937; Jonsson, 1988; Klein, 1932).

WHICH ATTITUDE TO CHOOSE TOWARD GENERAL ARCHAEOLOGY?

Scholars in the maritime field, among them archaeologists, have long debated the issue of the general role of maritime studies, including archaeology. It has been necessary to underline the special character of the maritime sector of society and the need to enlarge and deepen scientific studies in the field. In so doing, we have often stressed the importance of creating a freestanding, formalized discipline designed for specialized archaeological research.

I have often asked where the highest potential of a renewal of archaeology in the marine environment really lies. Is it as a separate science, as a branch of general archaeology, or as an integrated part of the latter? Development certainly might rest on different conditions and follow separate tracks in unique cultural settings. For Sweden, a strong potential lies in an independent development of the archaeology of the marine environment, within the scholarly society, created by researchers in this field, combined with an integration of the field with general archaeology. The main argument underlying my standpoint is that the theoretical basis for archaeology generally is the same in whatever field one works. It is thus essential that archaeological scholars in the maritime field continue their work to enlarge our understanding of maritime culture and society without isolating themselves or their results from general archaeology. It is of great importance to present the results of archaeological studies in the marine environment to the auditorium of general archaeology as often as possible.

By integrating with general archaeology, archaeology of the marine environment can then turn away from the ideologically steered course it so evidently has been following for a long time. This may mean a greater differentiation of studies, for example through an increased interest in the habitation remains, working places, and defences in the marine environment. The same approach would also work for a higher degree of differentiation of archaeology in general.

REFERENCES

Adams, J., and Rönnby, J., 1996, *Furstens fartyg. Marinarkeologiska undersökningar av en renässanskravell.* Uppsala.

Ahlström, C., 1997, Looking for leads. Shipwrecks of the past revealed by contemporary documents and the archaeological record. *Annales Academiae Scientiarium Fennicae.* The Finnish Academy of Science and Letters. Helsinki. (Also published in Swedish, 1995.)

Åkerlund, H., 1951, *Fartygsfynden i den forna hamnen i Kalmar.* Uppsala.

Barkman, L., 1968, On Resurrecting a Wreck. Att Bota Vrak. Some technical observations about the preservation exhibition 1967. Wasa Dockyard, *Vasastudier 6. Statens sjöhistoriska museum.* Stockholm.

Beijer, A., 1990, *Pålar och spärrar – en jämförande studie med utgångspunkt från Slätbakenanläggningarna.* Stockholms Universitet.

Bergenblad, H., 1980, Vättern—ett arkiv för geologi och arkeologi. In *Medd. från Marinarkeologiska Sällskapet,* edited by Harry Bergenblad, pp. 32–36.

_____, 1985, 3000-årig fornlämning på Vätterns botten: märkligt fynd i Huskvarnatrakten: förhistoriska studier, åttonde avdelningen av Harry Bergenblad. In *Vår hembygd: årsbok.*

Carlsson, D., 1987, Äldre hamnar: ett hotat kulturarv. In *Fornvännen* 82, pp. 6–18.

Cederlund, C.O., 1980, Background to the Baltic; Medieval ships in Kalmar; Wasa, the big warship; Recording wrecks in Baltic waters; Identifying the Älvsnabben ship; Maritime archaeology in the Baltic. In *Archaeology under Water. An Atlas of the World's Submerged Sites,* edited by Keith Muckelroy. pp. 78–89, New York.

_____, 1983, *The Old Wrecks of the Baltic Sea. Archaeological Recording of the Wrecks of Carvel-built Ships.* B.A.R. International Series 186, Oxford.

_____, 1987, A Systematic Approach to the Study of the Remains of Old Boats and Ships. In *Aspects of Maritime Archaeology and Ethnography in Northern Europe,* edited by Monograph Series pp. 173–209, National Maritime Museum.

_____, 1989, A Medieval description of searoutes along the Swedish and Finnish coasts, ending in Reval (Tallinn), Estonia. In *Marine Archaeology: Development of Research and Conservation. Seminar in the city of Kotka 29.–30.7.1988.* Publication number 13 in the series of Provincial Museum of Kymenlaakso. Kotka, pp. 3–25.

_____, 1992, The Sailing Route of King Valdemar. In *Medieval Europe 1992. Maritime Studies, Ports and Ships. Preprinted Papers.* Volume 2, pp. 81–86.

_____, 1994, The Regal Ships and Divine Kingdom. In *Current Swedish Archaeology.* Vol. 2. 1994. The Swedish Archaeological Society, pp. 47– 85. Also in Acerra, M., (ed.) 1997, *L'invention du vaisseau de ligne 1450–1700.* Kronos Marine. Editions 24, S.P.M., Paris, pp. 75–134.

_____, 1995a, Ship archaeology—communications archaeology. Archaeological ship remains from the medieval period as research material. In *Medieval Ship Archaeology. Documentation—Conservation— Theoretical Aspects—The Management Perspective,* edited by C.O. Cederlund, pp. 103–106. SMAR, Stockholm Marine Archaeology Reports No. 1. University of Stockholm. Published in association with the Nautical Archaeology Society, Edsbruk.

_____, 1995b, Marine Archaeology in Society and Science. *International Journal of Nautical Archaeology and Underwater Exploration* 24(1):9–13.

_____, 1996, Marine Archaeology on the Eve of the 21st Century. In *PACT European Network of Scientific and Technical Cooperation Applied to Cultural Heritage.* 47, Rixensart, pp. 11–28.

_____, 1997a, *Nationalism eller vetenskap? Svensk marinarkeologi i ideologisk belysning.* Stockholm.

_____, 1997b, Archaeological Excavation, Documentation and Interpretation of Postmedieval Wrecks of Carvel-built ships at the Swedish Coast of the Baltic Sea. In *Vyborg and Maritime Archaeology (The Perspectives of Investigations and Methodology).* pp. 19–35. Russian Academy of Sciences. The Institute of the History of Material Culture. The Centre of Maritime Archaeology. The Viborg Museum, St Petersburg.

_____, 1998, Developing the Care of Submerged Cultural Resources—Proposal and an Appeal. The Marine Archaeology of the Baltic Sea Area. *Newsletter of the Baltic Sea Area* 1:34–44.

_____, 2000, The structure of inland transportation in early Swedish iron production; types of vessels in the same; its relation to general transport and communications routes. In *Proceedings of the 8th meeting of the International Symposium on Boat and Ship Archaeology in Gdansk, Poland, September 1997,* pp. 245–250.

Franzén, A., 1974, *The Warship* Vasa. *Deep Diving and Marine Archaeology in Stockholm.* Stockholm.

Hallström, G., 1910, Båtar och båtbyggnad i ryska lappmarken. In *Fataburen* 1909, pp. 85–100.

Hansson, H., 1967, Gotländska tingshamnar. Föredrag i Vitterhetsakademien den 7 februari 1967. *Gotländskt Arkiv,* pp. 29–34.

Hasslöf, O., 1958, Arkeologiska båtfynd och levande tradition. In *Västerbotten Årsbok,* pp. 45–67.

_____, 1972, Maritime Ethnology and Its Associated Disciplines. In *Ships and Shipyards, Sailors and Fishermen. Introduction to Maritime Ethnology.* Copenhagen, pp. 9–20.

Humbla P., and von Post, L., 1937, *Galtabäcksbåten och tidigt båtbyggeri i Norden.* Göteborgs Kungl. Vetenskaps—och Historie—samhälles Handlingar. Femte följden. Ser. A. Band 6. No 1. Göteborg.

Johansson, B., (ed.) 1985, *Regalskeppet.* Ktonan, Höganäs.

Jonsson, G., 1988, Sjöliv. Valda delar av sjömanskulturen på nordisk botten sedda ur etnologisk synvinkel. In *Gotländskt Arkiv.* Visby, pp. 179–220.

Klein, E., 1932, Vikingaskeppens ättlingar i svenska farvatten. In *Fataburen,* pp. 139–158.

Larsson, L., 1983, Mesolithic Settlement on the Sea Floor in the Strait of Öresund. In *Quaternary Coastlines and Marine Archaeology. Towards the Prehistory of Land Bridges and Continental Shelves,* edited by P.M. Masters and N.C. Flemming pp. 283–301.

Lundström, P., 1981, *De kommo vida. . . Vikingars hamn vid Paviken på Gotland.* Uddevalla.

Norman, P., 1988, *Sjöfart och fiske. De kustbundna näringarnas lämningar.* Fornlämningar i Sverige 3. Riksantikvarieämbetet. Borås.

Rönnby, J., 1995, *Bålverket. Om samhällsförändring och motstånd med utgångspunkt från det tidigmedeltida Bulverket i Tingstäde träsk på Gotland.* Studier från UV Stockholm. Riksantikvarieämbetet. Arkeologiska undersökningar. Skrifter nr 10. Stockholm.

Rönnby, J., and Adams, J., 1994, *Östersjöns sjunkna skepp.* Stockholm.

Svenskt Sjöregister SMHI, 1983, Svenskt Vattenarkiv.

Varenius, B., 1989, *Båtarna från Helgeandsholmen.* Central Board of National Antiquities and the National Historical Museums. Rapport UV 1989:3.

Vattendragsregistret. SMHI. 1985.

Westerdahl, C., 1987, *The Norrland Sailing Route II. Description of the Maritime Cultural Landscape. Report from a Survey in Norrland and Northern Roslagen, Sweden, in 1975–1980.* Arkiv för norrländsk hembygdsforskning XXIII.

Westerdahl, C., 1989, *The Norrland Sailing Route I. Sources of the maritime cultural landscape. A handbook of marine archaeological survey.* Arkiv för norrländsk hembygdsforskning XXIV 1988–89.

Chapter 22

Aspects of Maritime History of Finland and the Eastern Baltic

CHRISTIAN AHLSTRÖM

INTRODUCTION

This chapter reviews the main lines of current underwater research on the coast of Finland. Since most finds have been dated to the historical period and have a contextual background documented in both physical and written evidence, arguments frequently will be supported by facts from both types of sources. It should be understood that no exhaustive quantitative analysis was possible within the available space. Though the number of underwater finds on the shores of Finland is much greater than those discussed here, each one chosen for the present study is typical of its epoch. I hope to give the reader a general view of the historical processes that have produced the current underwater finds.

Finland is situated beside the northwestern corner of Russia, the largest country in the world (Figure 22.1). Fate has placed Finland in a region from which navigation to the great trade centers of the world was far easier than from Russia for at least five centuries. Of course, the Baltic Sea during the days of sail was almost entirely isolated during winter. The southern coast of Finland is roughly on the 60th parallel, the same meridian

Christian Ahlström, International Congress of Maritime Museums, Helsinki, 00140, Finland.

International Handbook of Underwater Archaeology, edited by Carol V. Ruppé and Janet F. Barstad. Kluwer Academic/Plenum Publishers, New York, 2002.

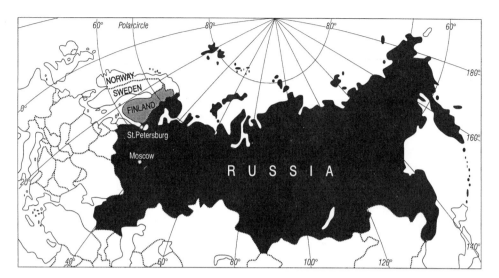

Figure 22.1. Finland and its location on the Baltic Sea, between Sweden and Russia.

cutting across southern Alaska. But the distance from the Baltic to the great commercial ports of the world was far less than from any of the traditional Russian ports.

Until Peter the Great founded the Russian capital of St. Petersburg in 1703, Arkhangelsk, on the coast of the Arctic Sea, was almost the only international port in that immense country from which the British, Dutch, and other Europeans could trade with Moscow. According to some sources, at the close of the 17th century Arkhangelsk was the site of about 30 Western trading houses. With the founding of St. Petersburg, however, the importance of Archangelsk was sharply reduced.

In the days of sail, Russian coasts were not navigable for the major part of the year. This partially explains why, almost throughout history, there has been Russian political and military pressure on the eastern Baltic area, not only on Finland but also on Sweden and the Baltic region of Estonia, Latvia, and Lithuania (which was held by Sweden from the late 16th century until 1721, when it had to be ceded to Russia). Russia's historical struggle toward the sea is not hard to understand in light of the insignificance of her coasts, disproportionate to her tremendous land area. From the Finnish point of view, however, this has meant that most of the historical development of the country has taken place in an atmosphere of continuous tension between east and west.

The history of Finland can be divided chronologically into four periods of varying length:

1. *Before* A.D. *12th century:* the country was pagan and lacked any form of central power or national center.

2. *c. 1100–1809:* At the beginning of this period, Christianity was introduced to Finland, probably following activities of peaceful missionaries but also through a series of crusades by Swedish troops until about the middle of the 13th century. The country gradually was incorporated into the Swedish realm. The seat of the government was in Stockholm, and the legal and administrative system was almost identical with Sweden's. The rights and privileges enjoyed by Finns were, at least in theory, the same as those of Swedes. This period was characterized by considerable tension between Sweden and Russia.

3. *Autonomy, 1809–1917:* Sweden was forced to cede Finland to Russia after a long series of armed conflicts. Subsequently, the country belonged to the Russian empire as an autonomous grand duchy, the Russian tsar being the grand duke of Finland during this period. Swedish laws were at least partly valid until 1899, when, during a Russification period, Finland had to accept incorporation into the Russian legal system.

4. *Independence, 1917 to the present:* As a Republic, caught in the clash between Russia and Germany, Finland had to fight hard to preserve her freedom. In the present account, we do not treat this period, since it deserves a treatment of its own. Too many complicated issues are involved in connection with World War II to justify an attempt at such a narrative.

No significant underwater finds date from the first period except for a few small rowing boats, most of which have been found on land. Historical sources tell us that budding contacts with other Nordic countries already existed during this era of Finnish history. Swedish Vikings who used the big Russian rivers to travel down to the south of Russia, the Black Sea, and now and then the Mediterranean, passed the south coast of Finland on their way to the mouth of the Neva River. Along their way, they must have had some contacts with the local population, but whether warlike or peaceful ones is not known. At least one Viking grave has been found on an island off the south coast (Cederlöf, 1986).

Finnish archaeologist Matti Huurre considers it possible that the Swedes had more or less permanent forts or strongholds in Finland during the Iron Age, although archaeological finds supporting such a theory have yet to be found.

EARLY MARITIME HISTORY

Norwegian Visit to Finland

Norwegian as well as Swedish Vikings went ashore in Finland. The future Norwegian King Olaf the Holy (995–1030) visited Finland in his younger days during his raids along the shores of the Baltic. Olaf's chronicle, dated to the early 10th century, describes the guerrilla tactics of the Finns:

> Olaf then sailed to Finland, went ashore and ravaged the country there, but all the people fled to the woods and took their property with them. The king went far into the wilderness pursuing them. There were glens, which were called the Har valleys. Some goods were taken there, but no men. When the day began to turn towards evening, the king went back towards the ships. But when they came into the woods, they were attacked and shot at from all directions. The king told his men to take cover, but before he had come out of the woods he had lost many men and several were wounded. In the evening they reached the ships. Using their witchcraft the Finns raised a storm and caused bad weather at sea. But the king gave the command to weigh anchor and set sail, and they cruised back and forth off the coast (Huurre, 1979).

This brief excerpt gives the first glimpse of what can be called the earliest maritime history of Finland. Lit like a lone lantern in a dark and stormy autumn night, and soon extinguished, the chronicle gives us at least some notion of the contacts between foreigners and local population during the later Iron Age.

The Danish Itinerary

A similar glimpse comes from a document written about 300 years later, which appears in a Danish cadastre (a register of real property) called *Kong Valdemars Jordebog*, in which more than two pages are devoted to a detailed description of the coastal route used by contemporary shipping. It names 101 locations, beginning at the southeastern tip of Sweden, reaching northward to the approximate latitude of Stockholm, east toward the Åland Islands and the archipelagos in the southwestern corner of Finland, east again to the Porkala Peninsula, and crossing over to Estonia. Most of the localities mentioned are in Sweden, but 14 are in Finland and four in Estonia, where Tallinn (Reval) is the terminus of the route. The exact dating of the document, written in Latin, is still debated (Breide, 1995).

By this time, Finland not only had been conquered by Sweden but also had been permanently integrated with the realm in the west, of which she was to be a part for nearly seven centuries. Local communities subordinate to Stockholm began to develop, and a central power residing in that city began levying taxes in Finland. But shipping along the coasts of Finland probably went on as usual, consisting mostly of small medieval peasant vessels in local traffic, as far as is known (Flink, 1995).

The Anchorage at Gäddtarmen

Until actual archaeological finds began to shed light on the maritime history of Finland, we had to rely on inscriptions carved in granite. Two islets enclosing the small, narrow sound of Gäddtarmen, on Finland's south coast near the town of Hanko, are literally covered with inscriptions originating from early sailors waiting at this anchorage for fair winds to carry them to their destinations. To pass time, they hacked at the rock, making inscriptions without knowing they would provide future historians and archaeologists with valuable material. These graffiti (for example, Figure 22.2) contain hymn verses, names, beautiful crests of noble families, simple initials, and pictures representing varying motifs, most of which can be dated. Numbering more than 400, they include Finnish, Swedish, and Baltic inscriptions whose dates vary from medieval times to a Russian inscription from World War II. Most originate from the 16th and 17th centuries (Boström, 1968).

There are also several other places in the vicinity with similar graffiti. In some of these places there were inns at the time, where sailors could buy tankards of beer or ale.

THE 17TH CENTURY

Pottery as Merchandise

A 17th-century wreck, perhaps one using the anchorage at Gäddtarmen, lies close to the city of Tammisaari (Ekenäs) on the south coast. It carried a cargo of ceramic pots, frying pans, and storage jugs, a total of 28 unbroken ones and a few fragments. The ship is relatively small and possibly of Baltic (Estonian) origin. It has not been possible to date her except with the aid of the cargo, which ceramic experts believe to have been manufactured between 1550 and 1600 (Edgren, 1978).

It is possible that this ship came originally from a Baltic country. Tallinn, Estonia, a former Hanseatic town, was a lively commercial center even after the dissolution of the Hansa league. The distance between the wreck site and that Estonian city is no more than

Figure 22.2. Inscriptions, including an escutcheon, on the cliffs at the Gäddtarmen near Hanko (Hangö), Finland (Photo courtesy of Finnish Maritime Museum).

50 km, and it is known that vigorous trade was carried on across the gulf separating the two countries. Of note is the fact that Helsinki, capital of present-day Finland, was founded by Swedish King Gustav Vasa as a competitor and counterbalance to Tallinn. The king's scheme did not succeed, since Tallinn already had achieved too strong a position to be influenced, still less to be driven out of business by her Finnish contender. The mercantilist trade doctrine, in its Swedish form, excluded the northern part of the Baltic (by royal decree) from most international trade activities, which were reserved for certain privileged ports in the south.

The Bell Wreck

A few kilometers west along the south coast lies one of the oldest wrecks so far found and investigated in Finland, lying at a depth of 14 m, about 50 m from the island of Mulan close to the mainland. In all probability, it is a small, open Swedish transport ship in military service, equipped with oars and a small sail, and probably a *lodja*, a ship type that may originate from Russia, considering that the Swedes may well have had some ships of this type built in Finland. *Lodjas* existed in two sizes, but none were made too large to make portages inpracticable. During this period, Sweden met little resistance in the Eastern Baltic, and there was hardly any point in sending bigger ships there.

The ship's cargo seems to have consisted mostly of booty from the war against the Russians in progress at the time the ship was lost. In addition, a large number of bricks have been found, but it is not certain whether these were part of the booty.

The ship is a remnant of one of the many armed conflicts between Sweden and Russia through the centuries. During this war, the king of Sweden appointed 25-year-old Jacob de la Gardie commander-in-chief. De la Gardie marched into Moscow but had to pull back his troops after Poland sent forces to side with the Russians. The situation was complicated by Swedish involvement in the ongoing struggle over the Russian throne, a consequence of the death of Russian Tsar Boris Godunov a few years before. Through an intrigue of foreign policy, Swedish Crown Prince Gustav Adolphus was among the pretenders to the throne.

This is a brief summary of the confused background and the mysterious doings of this small, clinker-built Swedish warship in Finnish waters. At present, the length of the wreck is no more than 15 m and the beam about 4.7 m; the ship was probably about 20–22 m long, and her beam may have been about 7 m. The exact position of the mast could not be ascertained, because the bricks had shifted and destroyed the mast-step.

Much attention was attracted by two bronze church bells found on top of the bricks. The larger of the two is 44.5 cm high excluding the suspension device, and its mouth is 53 cm in diameter, Encircling the rim is a Russian device reading:

> This bell was cast in the 7106th month (1596) the 2nd of June in honour of the birth of Christ at the monastery of Derevianitsky, in the reign of His Majesty Boris Feodorovich (Boris Godunov), in the time when he was the monarch of all Russia (Sammallahti, 1989–1990).

During the military occupation of the Russian city Novgorod (1611–1617), Jacob de la Gardie taxed the neighboring villages and settlements, including the nearby monastery of Derevianitsky. The taxes, mostly paid *in natura* and accounted for in an archive from the period, are kept at the National Archives in Stockholm (Ockupationsarkivet från Novgorod, Riksarkivet, Stockholm). The smaller of the bells has no text, and its mouth is somewhat more narrow in diameter. The thickness of the material in both bells is about 5 cm.

Among the finds were some personal belongings: a pair of eyeglasses—unusual for this period (Figure 22.3), a plate-warmer (a similar one was found in the regal ship Wasa, lost in 1628 at Stockholm), and great numbers of barrels.

Of considerable interest is a Swedish coin bearing the date 1611, that was found lodged in the ship's bottom. It is presumed that it had been placed in the mast-step when the ship was built, thus probably dating the year of the launching of the ship (Sammallahti, 1989–1990). The ship's rudder was discovered during recent investigations.

COURT RECORDS AS DOCUMENTARY MATERIAL

A form of documentary research useful for the study of historical archaeology has been developed for Finnish maritime history. An interesting source is the large collection of old court records, which yield a rich harvest of informative material to researchers. Sifting the extensive basic material has been simplified by means of an index to the cases, grouping records together according to subject. Aided by the records, Finnish historian Marja Pelanne has been able to create an illustrative picture of the maritime past of the

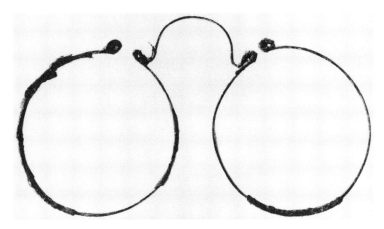

Figure 22.3. War booty: a pair of spectacles, unusual for the early 17th century, from the wreck of a Swedish military transport sunk near Hanko (Photo courtesy of Finnish Maritime Museum).

Kymi district in eastern Finland, concentrating on peasant shipping in the area and including topics such as size and types of ships, losses, channels, and salvaged goods (Pelanne, 1989–1990).

THE GREAT WRATH

The Russian Fleet of Galleys

Our chronology of Finnish underwater finds now takes us to a dramatic and tragic period in Finland's history, the war of 1713–1721, which in Finland bears the name of "The Great Wrath." These seven years of war and occupation were a part of the Great Nordic War of 1700–1721, in which Russia was Sweden's main enemy. During the first years of the war, Finland was left in relative peace, although Finnish troops took part in war operations. After 1714, when Russia invaded the entire country, the Swedish administration collapsed completely. Part of the population fled over the Gulf of Bothnia to Sweden, and some were taken to Russia as prisoners.

In 1715, the Russians made a few raids with detachments of galleys along the south coast of Finland, then turned north along the western coast. Some galleys even extended the raid into Sweden proper, burning and destroying everything in their way. Detachments traveling up Finland's west coast, intending to attack the town of Umeå on the Swedish side, had the misfortune to enter a zone of bad weather and were wrecked. At three points on the northern part of the Finnish west coast, great amounts of war matériel, Russian and Swedish coins, icons, and certain artifacts of Dutch origin have been found. The presence of Dutch artifacts may be explained by the fact that Peter the Great had close relations with the Netherlands and had imported Dutch workmen with various skills, among them sailors (Toivanen, 1984–1985).

ST. PETERSBURG AND NAVAL STORES

In 1703, Peter the Great founded the new Russian capital of St. Petersburg on a group of islands in the easternmost Gulf of Finland, close to the Russian mainland. It has been said, only half in jest, that 1703 is actually the most important in Finnish history, so influential has the position of St. Petersburg been for practically all aspects of the country's history. The impression the city has left on the Finnish maritime past is no exception.

Maritime traffic between St. Petersburg and Western Europe had to pass through the Gulf of Finland, since St. Petersburg and the other Baltic ports formed the most important source of naval stores in Europe during the heyday of the sailing ship. The Russian capital was one of the most important sources of immense amounts of timber, tar, pitch, hemp, iron, sailcloth, and other commodities needed by the British Admiralty for the upkeep of its large fleets (Albion, 1926; Ahlström, 1979).

During the sailing-ship era, naval stores of this kind had a strategic importance strongly resembling that of oil today. The same realities that decided the British stance regarding St. Petersburg and the Baltic in general also applied to the rest of Europe, at least to countries that had to maintain a navy of any size. It was naturally necessary to find products suitable to fill the holds of the ships sent out to obtain the naval stores. Here the large size of St. Petersburg was helpful, since it is clear that, even in pre-industrial times, the material needs of the city were considerable: The thirst for colonial and manufactured goods from Western Europe such as textiles, implements, and luxury items of various kinds, was hardly less so. By the late 18th century, the population of the young Russian capital had reached a figure that made the city rank third among the seats of government in the Europe of that day. In 1790, the 220,000 inhabitants gave St. Petersburg an important position (Bater, 1976).

The British handled traffic mostly under their own sail, while the Dutch—those indefatigable, omnipresent, business-minded transport experts—handled their part of Russian commerce partly on the account of others. St. Petersburg was by no means the only port of interest for Western European commerce in the Baltic area, but the Russian capital was the only large city in the Baltic.

The British and the Dutch were the only sizable extra-Baltic merchants specializing in foreign trade in the Russian capital. Their role was enhanced by the fact that the Russians themselves possessed an insignificant fleet of commercial ships, which could handle only a fraction of the import and export needs of St. Petersburg. In the 1770s, their commercial ships numbered no more than 12 or 15, according to the French ambassador to St. Petersburg (Marbault, 1777). The result was that the maritime commerce of St. Petersburg was almost entirely in the hands of foreigners, most of whom lived in the Russian city.

What, one may ask, has the commerce of the Russian capital to do with the underwater archaeology of Finland? It is simply explained by the fact that the last leg (or, for ships sailing out of St. Petersburg, the first leg) of the route ran past 400 or 500 km of Finnish coast, and many wrecks from that traffic will therefore certainly be found in Finnish waters.

CUSTOMS REGISTERS OF THE SOUND (DENMARK)

We possess a convincing documentary source that allows us to estimate the number of commercial ships of different nationalities entering and leaving the Baltic. It also tells us what cargoes they carried, the names of their skippers and, finally, the ports of departure and destination of each ship. This information applies to the period 1497–1856 and includes, among other things, hundreds of customs books kept at the National Archives of

Denmark in Copenhagen. With individual entries for each ship, the books document that the Danes demanded a toll from all ships entering or leaving the Baltic. The reason for this and (according to the contemporary view) the justification for it, was that the only channel leading into the Baltic went through Danish territorial waters. However, many attempts at customs evasion and smuggling by ships at the Danish Sound make caution and careful source criticism advisable when using this source (Ahlström, 1997).

St. Mikael

A commercial ship of the 18th century, the *St. Mikael* intended to sail to St. Petersburg. It now rests as a wreck in Nauvo (Swed. Nagu) parish in the archipelago of southwestern Finland. Site depth is 42 m, and the well-preserved wreck, a three-masted galliot (Figure 22.4) is 24.9 m long with a beam of 6.2 m. The finds on board give the impression that the galliot was Dutch. The vessel was unusual in that there were a great number of luxury items among its cargo: gold, silver, and enamel French snuffboxes, parts of fans inlaid with jewels, golden ornaments intended for the manufacture of snuffboxes, and English pocket watches. Recent finds consist of several pieces of Meissen porcelain from the 1740s. The passengers were distinctly upper-class, judging by the quality of their personal belongings.

Among the ship's navigational equipment was a cross-staff, an early instrument for determining the altitude of the sun, which was probably obsolete at the time the ship was lost. In the records of the customs house of the sound, correspondence was found regarding a collapsible carriole, (a light horse-drawn carriage) and the duties paid for it,

Figure 22.4. The well-preserved wreck of the St. Mikael. Watercolor by Henry Forsell (Photo courtesy of Finnish Maritime Museum).

which passed the customs station on board a Russian ship going to St. Petersburg in autumn 1747. The carriole was an interesting discovery, since a similar vehicle was found on the deck of the wreck. The skipper of the ship in question was Carl Poulsen Amiel (who may have been of either Russian or Dutch nationality since he gave both, but to different authorities: When he passed the sound on his way to Amsterdam from St. Petersburg, he claimed to be Russian, but on arriving in the Dutch port, he professed to be Dutch). The Dutch document verifying the arrival of the ship in Amsterdam also disclosed her name, the *St. Mikael* (Galjootsgeld Registers, 19 June 1747, Gemeentear- chief, Amsterdam). The skipper, returning to St. Petersburg on the fatal voyage when his ship was lost, flew the Russian flag when passing the sound.

Later, Count Nikita Panin, Russian ambassador to Copenhagen, wrote to the king of Denmark for a refund of the customs money the captain had paid for the carriage. The vehicle belonged to Empress Elizabeth of Russia (1709–1762) and was therefore exempt from fees by the king, who generally allowed the personal belongings of other monarchs to pass his customs stations without charge.

The customs books' entries regarding the rest of the cargo were also found, but they contained only ordinary items such as tobacco, brown sugar, vermilion, cotton, turkish yarn, boards, wine, and dried fish. In addition, valuables worth 1322 rixdollars (Danish, Dutch, and German silver coins) were carried in a separate part of the hold (Ahlström, 1997).

Among recent finds are high-quality ceramics manufactured around 1740 at a factory in Meissen, Germany, and containing porcelain ware of Strohblumenmuster, Alt-Ozier, and Deutsche Blumen types, as well as a Blanc de Chine bowl. They are considered unusual and valuable and have been thoroughly analyzed by the ceramic expert of the Finnish Board of Antiquities, Heikki Hyvönen (1997).

Recent discoveries have included several small porcelain figurines depicting a flute-player, a hunter, and a shepherdess. At the time of this writing, underwater research is continuing, but these latest objects have not yet been analyzed properly.

Vrouw Maria

In 1771, Russian Empress Catherine the Great ordered Prince Gallitzin, her ambassador to the Netherlands, to buy an art collection at the famous Braamcamp estate auction in Amsterdam. We do not know how much the empress bought, but she may have bought almost everything that was for sale. The collection contained paintings by 16th-century Dutch masters, furniture, sculptures, porcelain, and other collectables. The empress intended to have the pieces added to her large collections at The Hermitage, her palace in the Russian capital.

Once purchased, the art collection was placed on a Dutch ship bound for St. Petersburg. During the voyage, the ship ran into a storm and struck a rock in the Finnish archipelago. The crew escaped to a small nearby island. After a few days, the badly damaged ship sank.

The Russians naturally were keen on retrieving their valuable cargo. Since the accident happened in Swedish territorial waters, an extensive diplomatic correspondence ensued between the Foreign Office in Stockholm and the Swedish Embassy in St. Petersburg. Letters were also sent from the Russian foreign minister to the authorities in Stockholm. Local authorities in Finland were also contacted (Ahlström, 1979). The search for the sunken ship was conducted during most of the summer of 1772, but the primitive equipment of the 18th century naturally yielded no results, and eventually the matter was forgotten (Ahlström, 1979).

Extensive archival research has produced documentary evidence giving almost the whole picture of the historical events, so that it is more or less known where the 18th-century searches were conducted. A search with modern side-scan sonar equipment was carried out and turned up the wreck of a wooden sailing ship. On June 28, 1999 (the first day of the search), the wreck was found at a depth of 41 m, and she could be identified as the *Vrouw Maria*. Her cargo was complete. See the Appendix for a full discussion of the discovery.

Russian Brig *Graf Nikita*

Another example showing the value of documentary research is the identification of a shipwreck dating from the late 18th century, situated near the island of Jussarö near the small town of Tammisaari (Ekenäs) on the southwestern coast of Finland.

The pinewood hull is about 28 m long with a beam of about 7 m. According to local tradition, the wreck was plundered by Estonian helmet-divers in the early 20th century, and the aft deck was blown up to facilitate salvaging what was left of the cargo.

Thirteen Russian coins were found on board, the oldest bearing the year 1731, while the latest was minted in 1779. In addition, a gaming marker bearing the image of Louis XVI of France was discovered. At first, the marker was thought to be a coin, but the error was corrected by specialists of the Board of Antiquity.

According to 18th-century Swedish laws, which were also valid in Finland, it was compulsory to sell all salvaged goods, cargoes, and parts of wrecked ships at public auctions and to announce each auction in at least three nearby churches or other prominent places. There are valuable records of these auctions from different places on the coast, which facilitate to a considerable degree the identification of anonymous wrecks.

Finds on the Russian brig *Graf Nikita* established that the wreck had been lost some time between 1781 and 1788. During these years, 13 ships had been lost outside the town; in all probability, one of them was the wreck now being investigated. The ships had various destinations: St. Petersburg in Russia, Cadiz in Spain, Hamina in eastern Finland, Stettin in Poland, Setubal in Portugal, and Tallinn in Estonia. By comparing the cargoes of the different vessels with that remaining in the wreck (most of it seemed to have been removed), it was possible to exclude 11 ships, since their holds had contained goods different from those found on board. Two ships, Russian brig *Graf Nikita* and British barque *Constant Trader*, were still question marks. Either could be the wreck being researched.

A few attempts were made to use parts of the cargo to identify the wreck: mustard pots bearing the name of a French manufacturer, the Maille Company in Paris which is still in existence (Figure 22.5), and a number of oyster shells (*Ostrea edulis*) found in the ballast sand. These attempts were unsuccessful.

Finally, the investigators resorted to diatom analysis. By analyzing the wreck's ballast sand, it was established that most of the diatoms were of a type which thrive exclusively in brackish or fresh water. This fact made it probable that the ship came from the Baltic Sea (Ahlström, 1997).

As Elisabeth Harder, (1961) has shown, there was brisk trade between the north German town of Lübeck and St. Petersburg. In the Lübeck archives, customs records

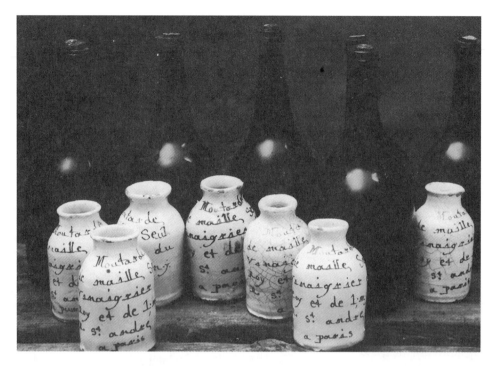

Figure 22.5. *From the Graf Nikita*, ceramic pots once containing mustard made in a factory that still operates near Paris (Photo courtesy of Finnish Maritime Museum).

showed that skipper Stephan Cornilsen left the port of Lübeck in ballast on October 16, 1784, carrying some small amount of goods (Archiv der Nowgorodfahrer, Contorgeld Bd. 13). In the contemporary local newspaper, *Lübeckische Anzeigen*, an advertisement was found telling local readers that Stephan Cornilsen was leaving for St. Petersburg with his ship *Graf Nikita* and had empty space in the hold of his ship, which he hoped local businessmen would fill. Added to all the other accumulated scraps of knowledge, this meant that the wreck off Jussarö was the *Graf Nikita* of St. Petersburg (Ahlström, 1995).

Ship-of-the-Line *Kronprins Gustaf Adolf*

In 1788, four years after the loss of the Russian brig, another war between Sweden and Russia broke out, begun by Swedish King Gustav III. He dressed Swedish soldiers in Russian uniforms with forged Russians coins in their pockets (the pieces are now in the coin cabinet of Stockholm) and ordered them to attack Swedish forces in Finland. War soon broke out, and naval forces from both sides took part. As usual, the Russians used many hired foreign officers—British, German, and French—in addition to their own. Two wrecks of naval ships are known from this war: Swedish ship-of-the-line *Kronprins Gustaf Adolf* off Helsinki, and the Russian frigate *Nikolai* off Kotka in eastern Finland (a city that did not exist in the 18th century).

During a skirmish near Helsinki, a few Russian ships chased the *Kronprins Gustaf Adolf*, which tried to escape into the nearby naval fort Sveaborg and almost succeeded.

The ship hit a rock, stuck, and was unable to move off the shoal. She lost her mainmast and had to lower her colors. The Russians overtook their helpless victim, captured her crew, and took the men away in the ship's boats.

A young Swedish lieutenant, Gustaf af Klint (later an admiral and a well-known cartographer), described this incident in his unpublished diary of August 1788. The action was clearly visible from the fort, and af Klint was ordered to go to the assistance of the ship in distress but was driven away. Later, back in the fort, he and Duke Charles, the king's brother, who happened to be at the fort, watched the Russians through binoculars. The following day, the Russians set the ship afire. When the fire reached the gunpowder compartment, the vessel exploded.

This find was discovered by the Finnish navy during echo-sounding practice in 1995. So far, little has been done to investigate her. Only two 24-pound guns, each weighing 1800 kg, have been recovered, although there are probably at least 70 more of varying calibres in the wreck. After the 1788 explosion, of course, there is not much hope of finding anything unbroken except the guns. The shoal had been called "Gustaf Adolf" ever since, but until recently no one knew why, since the incident had been totally forgotten.

Russian Frigate *Nikolai*

On July 9, 1790, 500 Russian and Swedish vessels with crews totalling 30,000 men clashed at Ruotsinsalmi (Svensksund) near the present-day industrial city of Kotka, in an area Sweden ceded to Russia in 1743. The Russians were led by the prince of Nassau-Siegen, a German aristocrat turned Russian admiral. The Russians were defeated, their losses overwhelming. Dozens of ships, most of them Russian, still cover the seabed. The majority of the wrecks were shot to pieces and are probably of little scientific value.

The wreck of the frigate *Nikolai*, a Russian vessel used in the battle, was found a few years after World War II. It contained a rich harvest of guns and other weapons, kitchen utensils, icons, book-covers (Figure 22.6), and personal belongings from officer's cabins, as well as a total of 677 coins (Sarvas, 1977). Unfortunately, the wreck is situated close to the channel leading in and out of the busy modern port of Kotka, and the wakes of ships have damaged the wreck. It has yet to be fully investigated.

Swedish Brig *Nordstiernan*

The Swedish merchant brig *Nordstiernan* lies at the island of Borstö on the southwestern Finnish coast. In 1809, on her way home to Sweden with a cargo of hemp and flax from St. Petersburg, she was surprised by foul weather and struck a rock so near the island that most of her crew could walk ashore dry-shod. The ship has been only partly investigated. As an interesting sidelight, in the days when she was lost, Swedish ships visiting Finland did not have to pay any duties, although in reality they were sailing to a foreign country. Close to the same island is the wreck of the *St. Mikael*, considered a much more interesting and valuable object.

THE ERA OF AUTONOMY

After 1809, a new era dawned in the history of Finland, the so-called period of autonomy when the country found herself transferred to the Russian Empire and forced, at least partly, to cut her ties to Sweden and traditions of more than 600 years standing (ties not

Figure 22.6. Bronze book cover from the Russian frigate *St. Nicholas* (Photo courtesy of Finnish Maritime Museum).

broken entirely even today). At that point, Finland enjoyed a century of relative peace and prosperity, which had a positive influence on economic and cultural development.

The maritime aspect of the Swedish era was characterized by the relationship of Finnish shipping to the government in Stockholm, which resembled that of a subordinate apprentice to his master. This was due to the age-old existence in Sweden of several prerequisites for the development of shipping: a long coast with good ports and, most important, relatively abundant supplies of capital to be invested in seafaring, far superior to those of Finland. This situation changed completely when Finland became a part of the large Russian Empire with its agrarian traditions. The Finns suddenly were considered the best shipping experts in the empire. Finnish skippers became responsible for most of the Russian merchant fleet, and many young Finns studied at the Russian Naval Academy. Some were successful enough to climb to high positions in the Russian navy: Several admirals, officers of the General Staff, and even a naval minister were Finnish (Pikoff, 1938).

Since 1721, the Baltic border states of Estonia, Latvia, and Lithuania also belonged to the Russian Empire. Socially, culturally, and economically, however, German influence in these countries was very strong (Thaden, 1981). With the conquest of Finland, the Russians were in control of both sides of the Gulf of Finland, with the result that their warships had free access to this part of the Baltic Sea and its ports.

Only once did they withdraw into the protection of Cronstadt, the naval fort off St. Petersburg. During the Crimean war, the summers of 1854 and 1855 saw attacks of combined Franco–British naval forces into the two arms of the Baltic bordering on Finland, the Gulf of Bothnia and the Gulf of Finland. These forces also bombarded the coastal defenses of Finland including the Aland Islands (for a more detailed account, see Greenhill and Giffard, 1988), battles that led to the destruction of the fortress of Bomarsund. The following year, the British and the French proceeded to the fortress of Sveaborg at Helsinki, but their cannonade had no particular effect. Russian fire had effects of still smaller proportions, since the defenders' artillery had a shorter range than that of the attacking forces, which naturally stayed out of reach.

As mentioned, Russian naval forces used the Gulf of Finland as a training ground. Russian tsars, with their families, often cruised with their yachts in the beautiful Finnish archipelago. Since Russia controlled both northern and southern coasts of the gulf, it was possible after 1809 to add another Russian naval base to the one in Tallinn (Estonia), which had existed there since the 18th century. The old Swedish fort of Sveaborg in Helsinki (Finland) now became Russian and added to the coastal defences of the Empire. The distance between Tallinn and Helsinki is slightly more than 80 km.

Due to the Russian domination of the Gulf of Finland in the 19th century—the era of Finnish autonomy—no naval operations of any importance took place there except the Franco–British naval expedition. Commercial traffic to St. Petersburg grew as the city's population rose. Ships and their cargoes also grew larger, so that the wrecks from this period are comparatively few.

Russian Monitor *Rusalka*

Two Russian naval ships, the monitor *Rusalka* and the small, old minelayer *Tutchka*, left Tallinn for St. Petersburg in September 1893, with orders to go to the Russian capital via Helsinki. They proceeded without problems during the beginning of the voyage, but when they reached the open sea the wind began to rise quickly and a storm set in.

In addition to her engines, *Tutchka*, the smaller of the two ships, was equipped with sails. Thanks to their stabilizing effect, she had no great problems in the storm. But the *Rusalka*, with her heavy armor, two turrets and low freeboard, lay dangerously deep in the water. She was designed to carry heavy artillery and to participate in coastal defense, but her seaworthiness was unsatisfactory. According to one theory, some distance south of the lighthouse at Harmaja off Helsinki, water found its way into the engine room through the funnels, put out the fires and stopped the engines, and the ship turned side-on to the wind and capsized.

The little minelayer escaped safely to the harbour of the Sveaborg fortress, but the *Rusalka* disappeared, and the drowned sailors, broken lifeboats, and lifejackets found on the shores of nearby islands told a frightening tale of what had happened. The ship has never been found, but it is certain that the wreck is lying somewhere on the sea floor off Helsinki.

Finnish Steam Schooner *Salama*

In the 19th century, regular traffic was maintained along the Finnish coasts with small steam-schooners, many of which used either Stockholm or St. Petersburg as end-stations. Some had routes taking them into the extensive Finnish system of 60,000 lakes of various sizes. One of these packet steamers, the iron *Salama*, sank on lake Saimaa in eastern Finland as a result of a collision in 1898, when she was on her way back from St. Petersburg. In 1971, she was raised from a depth of 30 m, drydocked, repaired, and put on display in her former port of registry, the city of Savonlinna (Ericsson, 1978).

Russian Minelayer *Ladoga* (Originally Armored Steam-Frigate *Minin*)

In 1975, Turku divers located the wreck of an unknown warship in the archipelago of southwestern Finland. It was soon identified as the minelayer *Ladoga* (*ex Minin*), built in St. Petersburg in 1869. Russian defense principles were dominated by the idea of defensive

Figure 22.7. The 18th-century wreck of the *Vrouw Maria* in southwestern Finland investigated by divers of a research vessel. (Watercolor by Dr. Juha Flinkman)

mine-barriers and, lacking suitable vessels for mine-laying, the Russian admiralty decided to convert a number of old-timers. The *Ladoga* was one of these, originally an armored steam-frigate. Holds for 1000 mines were built, heavy guns and the frigate-rig of the original ship were removed, and the old vessel was renamed. In August 1915, she struck a mine in Finnish waters and sank to a depth of 40 m (Ericsson, 1978).

CONCLUSION

By looking at wrecks found in the Gulf of Finland and reflecting on what types can reasonably be expected to be found in this area in the future, it is possible to distinguish two main trends or processes in the series of historical events that take place here:

1. Wrecks of naval ships dating from the early 17th century and Swedish cession of Finland to Russia in 1809. Constant tension between Sweden and Russia at that time led to many naval battles in the area with considerable losses on both sides. These losses actually date from the 18th century, since the Russians began to build an effective navy only in 1705, when three small cruisers were built (Glete, 1993, vol. 2, appendix 2). On the other hand, the early modern Swedish navy was of the same magnitude as the British navy (Glete, 1993, vol. 1). The Russian navy later became the strongest in the Baltic.

In all probability, only some of the wrecked ships off Finland have been discovered to date. After 1809, when the Swedes had to give in as the smaller and weaker nation, finds resulting from naval battles cease and, during the period of autonomy, hardly any man-of-war wrecks can be expected except those which were lost to accident or foul weather.

2. Wrecks created by commercial shipping between the Russian capital of St. Petersburg and Western Europe: As already mentioned, there was shipping in the Gulf of Finland long before St. Petersburg was founded but on a minor scale. Traffic to and from Russia consisted mainly of foreign ships, primarily British, Dutch, and German but also some Swedish, Danish, and Finnish vessels. How large a percentage of these ships was lost is difficult to estimate, but a considerable number, possibly as many as a fifth of those sailing to varying Baltic destinations in the 18th century, can probably be found on the sea-floor, and some on the shoals of the archipelago of the Finnish southern coast, victims of the violent autumn storms in these waters.

In conclusion, underwater finds on the Finnish coast clearly illustrate what frequently makes marine archaeology of the historical period so fascinating: the international and multifaceted nature of the finds, and the traces of human life from distant and different cultures of the past.

APPENDIX: The *Vrouw Maria* of 1771: An Example of Documentary Research

There are two sets of circumstances pertaining to the Baltic that make this large inland bay of the northern Atlantic almost unique from the perspective of the underwater archaeologist. First, there is an unusually low degree of salinity in the seawater which, among other things, prevents the presence of the shipworm, *teredo navalis*, and has a number of other factors that positively influence the preservation of wooden wrecks. The only other place in the world where underwater archaeologists are equally lucky are the Great Lakes of North America where the waters are completely fresh but considerably smaller in area.

Second, there is the historic institution of the Sound Registers in Denmark. This is less well known and has so far been used mainly by economic historians but it is also relevant to underwater archaeologists. It allows us to study, by way of historical documents, almost the entire traffic of commercial ships through the Danish Sound, 1490–1856. In the 15th century, the Danes began levying a toll on each ship passing through their territorial waters on the way to or from the Baltic, a practice that brought a great deal of revenue to the Danish state treasury. By the 18th century this had gone up to 7–8 % annually. It continued as late as the beginning of 1857, when U.S. ships refused to pay the fees and other nations followed suit. Today, the ledgers of the customs officials are kept in the National Archives of Denmark and contain data on cargoes, skippers, destinations, ports of departure, etc.

In 1771, one ship that definitely paid its customs fees at the sound was the Dutch ship, *Vrouw Maria*, according to the ledgers in the National Archives of Copenhagen. The *Vrouw Maria* was under the command of Reynoud Lorenz of Amsterdam, who had left there with his ship carrying cargo which in part belonged to the Russian empress, Catherine the Great. The ship was destined for St. Petersburg with some art treasures, probably paintings, which the Russian empress had purchased in Amsterdam. She wanted to take them to St. Petersburg to include in the collections of the Hermitage.

In October 1771, the Russian foreign minister, Count Nikita Panin, sent a letter by courier to Stockholm (to the president of the Royal Chancellery) requesting the Swedish government and the king do everything in their power to help the Russians with an unusual problem. The Dutch ship headed for St. Petersburg and had foundered in a storm close to the archipelago of southwestern Finland (which had belonged to Sweden since the 13th century) taking what Panin called the "numerous crates of paintings belonging to the Empress" down with her. The ship, badly damaged, had anchored some distance from the island of Jurmo after which the crew had attempted to discharge part of the cargo on a small rocky island in the vicinity. Then, a new storm arrived, the anchor cables broke, and the ship disappeared. Aside from the paintings, there may have been other items of value on board the wreck: silver and lacquer works, bronze statues, ivory works, even furniture.

In the National Archives in Stockholm there is an extensive correspondence on the matter that took place in 1772, after the receipt of Count Panin's letter. Some letters date from 1773. The correspondents were Swedish government officials in Stockholm, local officials in Åbo (Turku), the provincial capital of Finland, and members of the Swedish Embassy in St. Petersburg. The Russians evidently used the Swedish ambassador, Count Ribbing, as their correspondent when they wished to communicate with the Swedes. In addition to these documents, the protest and declaration given August 26, 1771 by the Dutch captain and his crew are in the archives of the city court of Åbo (Turku). This document included the log book of the *Vrouw Maria*, which proved useful when researchers needed to establish an area to search for the wreck. It said the *Vrouw Maria* had lost her rudder after striking a rock. This piece of knowledge was later important after the right ship was found and had to be positively identified. Swedish local officials tried on several occasions during the summer 1772 to find the shipwreck but did not succeed. Considering how primitive tools were in those days, this is not surprising, because the wreck was 43 m down.

At the preparatory stage, documentary research was no help beyond localizing the probable site. In 1979, the echo-sounding technique was not developed enough to find the physical remains of the wreck. The results of my research were published (Ahlström, 1979). Years later, a diver and side-scan operator, Rauno Koivusaari, after reading the story, contacted me, and we decided to join forces to find the wreck.

The plan was to delimit an area, then systematically search through it with a side-scan sonar. The procedure may be likened to an airplane taking continuous pictures of the ground. The airplane corresponds to the search vessel, moving along the surface, the camera of the airplane is equivalent to the side-scan sonar and the ground is analogous to the seabed. Images made this way are clear and of high quality, being continuously stored in the memory of a sonar machine.

In summer 1998, an association of divers made an attempt to find the remains of the *Vrouw Maria*. We did find a shipwreck from the same period as the *Vrouw Maria*, but it was empty and the rudder was intact, so it was not the right ship. Although the campaign of 1998 scanned a large part of the search area, no *Vrouw Maria* was found.

As 1998 neared its end, we started planning the next summer's campaign. The main problem was, we knew little about the physical appearance of the Vrouw Maria, and this meant we would have difficulties identifying her should we find her. We decided to make another attempt to find new archive material. But this time we would have to check the archives of the Netherlands. We were particularly keen to find the main measurements of the *Vrouw Maria*—her length and beam, for instance—so we could distinguish her from any other wrecks we encountered.

The *Gemeente archief* of Amsterdam was the best one to consult. I had some documentary research experience and had even published a few books and a doctoral dissertation based on it, but my focus had been mainly on the Baltic area, making only occasional minor expeditions into French, Dutch, and German archives. To better research the *Vrouw Maria* would require intimate knowledge of the enormous collections of Dutch maritime documents, good knowledge of the 18th-century version of a foreign language, may be even knowledge of the local history of Amsterdam. Clearly this research would have to be done by a Dutch professional historian. The Dutch ambassador to Helsinki, Jacobus van der Velden, was consulted and he personally telephoned the archives in Amsterdam. The result was the head of the section of Maritime Manuscripts set to work finding information on the ship.

In June 1999, the side-scan operators set out from Helsinki in the Teredo, a former trawler. Upon reaching the search area a few days later, they began to work. After only three hours of a systematic study of the sea floor, a promising echo was found. Divers were sent down. They surfaced, reporting the wreck of a wooden ship had been found. She corresponded to the measurement in the historical records, and her rudder was missing. The ship was lying at a depth of 41–43 m in almost perfect condition and with the two lower masts still standing. It was also discovered that she carried an almost full load of crates, barrels, etc. with an unknown content. It was thought that one problem with unloading the cargo would be a possible shortage of space between the cargo and the deck.

One small kedge-anchor with a missing fluke was found hanging on the ship's side. Apparently the same kedge-anchor with the missing fluke was mentioned in an inventory of the ship's gear in a document dated August 18, 1766—five years before the loss.

As required by law, a report was radioed to the museum officials in Helsinki. Three finds were lifted from the ship's deck: a metal ingot, an ordinary 18th century clay pipe made in Gouda, and a lacquer seal that bore the initials of a textile manufacturer in Leyden, the Netherlands. Only the pipe could be reached through the hatch, which had been left open by the crew in 1771 when they attempted to bring as much as possible of the cargo ashore before the ship sank.

Before the *Vrouw Maria* could pass through the Danish channel of Öresund in September 1771, she had to pay a customs fee on most of the merchandise making up her cargo (Usually royal property was granted exemptions from the customs fees). One entry in the customs ledgers (September 23, 1771, Dutch ship no. 508) was the *Vrouw Maria*'s shipment of zinc. Metal ingot recovered from the wreck was sent to a metallurgist for analysis. The ability of documentary research to supplement the findings of postmedieval archaeology was demonstrated when the ingot was found to be zinc.

It is true that, as a rule, there is a correlation between the size of a lost ship and the number of documents giving information about the accident. This case is exceptional, the ship being comparatively small, but the importance of one of the cargo-owners makes the amount of gainable information considerable. We may not know much about the *Vrouw Maria* yet, but we do know at least something. We know her position, we know a good deal about her cargo, we know her type, and we know the circumstances leading to her loss, among other things. If it had been necessary to gather even this amount of information about her by solely archaeological methods, how much time would be consumed, and what would it have cost? Archaeology has gladly incorporated with her box of tools methods which really originate from the natural sciences. But the age-old, inexplicable animosity between history and archaeology has so far allowed only lukewarm relations between these two sciences. I do not, for obvious reasons, propose any cooperation between prehistorical archaeology and history. But in postmedieval archaeology, perhaps especially the submarine brand, it can be an invaluable and rich contributor.

REFERENCES

Albion, R.G. 1926, *Forests and Sea Power.*

Ahlström, C., 1979, *Sjunkna skepp.*

_____, 1997, *Looking for Leads.* Finnish Academy of Science and Letters, Humaniora 284. Helsinki.

Bater, J.H., 1976, *St. Petersburg, Industrialization and Change.* Studies in Urban History 4. London.

Boström, B., 1968, *Hangö udd, forntida hamnar och hallristningar.* Hangö.

Breide, H., 1995, Itinerariet. In *Kung Valdemars segelled*, edited by G. Flink.

Cederlöf, H., 1986, *Farleder och lotsplatser i Ekenäs skägård.* Hangö.

Edgren, T., 1978, The Pottery of the *Esselholmen Wreck.* Annual Report. *Maritime Museum of Finland,* Helsinki.

Ericsson, C.H., 1978, The Steam-schooner Salama restored. Annual Report. The Maritime Museum of Finland, Helsinki.

Flink, G., 1995, *Kung Valdemars segelled.* Stockholm.

Glete, Jan., 1993, *Navies and Nations I–II. Warships, Navies and State Building in Europe and America.* Stockholm Studies in History 48:2.

Greenhill, and Giffard, 1988, *The British Assault on Finland 1854–1855. A Forgotten Naval War.* Conway Maritime Press, London.

Harder, E., 1979, *Seehandel zwischen Lübeck und Russland im 17. und 18. Jahrhundert nach Zollbüchern der Nowgorodfahrer.* Zeitschrift des Vereins für Lübeckische Geschichte und Altertumskunde. Lübeck.

Huurre, M., 1979, *9,000 vuotta Suomen esihistoriaa.* Keuruu.

Hyvönen, H., 1997, The *St. Mikael and Meissen Porcelain.* Annual Report. Nautica Fennica: Maritime Museum of Finland, Helsinki.

Marbault, 1777, *Essai sur le Commerce de la Russie avec l'histoire de ses découvertes.* Amsterdam, Netherlands.

Pelanne, M., 1989–1990, The 17th Century Judgement Books as Sources for the Study of Peasant Seafaring. Annual Report. The Maritime Museum of Finland, Helsinki.

Pikoff, E., 1938, Landsmän i ryska marinen. *Genealogiska Samfundet i Finland, tom xiv.*

Sammallahti, L., 1989–1990, Investigations by the Maritime Museum of Finland on the Mulan Wreck in Hankö. Annual Report. Maritime Museum of Finland, Helsinki.

Sarvas, P., 1977, Coins from the Frigate *Nicholas.* Annual Report. Maritime Museum of Finland, Helsinki.

Thaden, E., editor, 1981, *Russification in the Baltic Provinces and Finland 1855–1914.* Princeton, NJ.

Toivanen, P., 1984–1985, Expedition to Ostrobothnia by the Russian Inshore Fleet in 1714. On the Russian Trail in the Maksamaa (Maxmo) Islands. Annual Report. Maritime Museum of Finland, Helsinki.

Zolotukhin, K., 1894, O sredstva predlozhennikh dja otiskania bronenosza *Rusalka. Morskoy Sbornikh* 4:1–74.

Chapter 23

England and Wales
Recent Issues in Maritime Archaeology

GLENN P. DARRINGTON

INTRODUCTION

The field of maritime archaeology in England, Wales, Scotland, and Northern Ireland has seen interesting developments during the last ten years. The list of protected wreck sites in the United Kingdom now includes 47 designated sites ranging from Middle Bronze Age artifact scatters to the wreck of Britain's first Class A submarine (Table 23.1). The field has made significant strides in the areas of cultural resource management, public awareness, and professional accreditation.

Maritime archaeology in this region is not without its problems. Several critical issues, especially those dealing with salvage and the rights of sport divers, must be resolved if further progress is to be made.

CULTURAL RESOURCE MANAGEMENT

Archaeological Diving Unit

One of the most positive influences on maritime archaeology as a whole has been the work of the United Kingdom's Archaeological Diving Unit (ADU). Under the direction of

Glenn P. Darrington, Scottish Institute of Maritime Studies, University of St. Andrews, Fife, Scotland, United Kingdom.
International Handbook of Underwater Archaeology, edited by Carol V. Ruppé and Janet F. Barstad. Kluwer Academic/Plenum Publishers, New York, 2002.

Table 23.1. Protected Wreck Sites in the United Kingdom.

Prehistoric	*Wrangels Palais* (1687)
Middle Bronze Age	*Anne* (1690)
Langdon Bay Site	*Dartmouth* (1690)
Moor Sand Site	*Coronation*—inshore (1691)
	Coronation—offshore (1691)
12th Century	
The Smalls Site (1100)	*18th Century*
	Northumberland (1703)
15th Century	*Restoration* (1703)
Grace Dieu (1436)	*Stirling Castle* (1703)
Gull Rock Site (15th or 16th century)	*Hazardous* (1706)
	Tearing Ledge Site (1707)
16th Century	*Royal Anne* (1721)
Studland Bay (1520s)	*Assurance* (1738)
St. Anthony (1527)	*Amsterdam* (1749)
Cattewater Site (1530)	*Invincible* (1758)
Mary Rose (1545)	*Hanover* (1763)
Girona (1588)	South Edinburgh Channel Site (18th century)
Church Rock Site (16th century)	
Brighton Marina Site (16th century)	*19th Century*
Bartholomew Ledges Site (late 16th century)	*Admiral Gardner* (1809)
Yarmouth Roads Site (16th or 17th century)	*Pomone* (1811)
Erme Estuary Site (16th–18th centuries)	*Iona II* (1864)
	Resurgam (1880)
17th Century	
Rill Cove Site (1606)	*20th Century*
Salcombe Cannon Site (1630–1640)	*A-1* (1911)
Duart Point Site (1653)	
Kennemerland (1664)	*No Date*
Dunwich Bank Site (1672)	Burntisland Wreck
Tal-y-bont (1677)	Erme Ingot Site
Mary (1675)	Pwll Fanog Site
Schiedam (1684)	Seaton Carew Site

Martin Dean at the University of St. Andrews in Scotland, ADU consists of a team of diving archaeologists contracted to the United Kingdom's Department of Culture, Media, and Sport (DCMS) to provide expertise and guidance to the Welsh Historic Monuments Executive Agency (CADW), the Secretary of State's Advisory Committee on Historic Wreck Sites (London), Historic Scotland, and the Department of the Environment for Northern Ireland. These government agencies hold primary responsibility for shipwreck archaeology in each of their respective home countries.

Since its creation in 1986, ADU assisted with the implementation of the 1973 "Protection of Wrecks Act" and the education of the sport diving community concerning shipwreck preservation. To this end, the unit frequently offers advice and assistance to organizations holding licenses to conduct investigations at a designated wreck site. It also monitors the investigations, to assess their integrity when completed.

The Secretary of State's Advisory Committee issues licenses to allow work at a designated wreck site and makes recommendations to the secretary of state concerning a wreck's possible designation under the 1973 Protection of Wrecks Act. The committee changed its membership in 1996 and appointed a new chair, Lady Maureen Merrison. The reorganization has had an overall positive effect on the current system of wreck management in the U.K., putting it more in step with modern attitudes about heritage preservation.

In the past, many maritime archaeologists were considered outside the mainstream and had some difficulty integrating their research into other fields of study. The ADU, working with groups such as the Nautical Archaeology Society, has made significant progress in promoting multidisciplinary research and integration with the wider research community. Its promotion of higher professional standards and ethics also encourages integration. In 1999, the Institute of Field Archaeologists (IFA), a U.K. organization formed in 1982 to promote professional standards and ethics in archaeology, produced a technical paper with the help of ADU, which outlines methods for appropriate treatment of marine archaeological sites (Oxley and O'Regan, 1999). These efforts have the added benefit of helping to reduce the influence of treasure hunting and inappropriate salvage practices. The SUBMAP Project, an archaeological investigation of the 19th-century submarine *Resurgam* initiated in 1996, is a recent example of how ADU is working toward these ends.

BRITAIN'S FIRST POWERED SUBMARINE, *RESURGAM*

During the latter part of the 19th century, the use of submarines in naval warfare was considered by most British naval commanders to be a dishonorable practice. It was even suggested by one Edwardian navy admiral, "Tug" Wilson, that submarine crews should be outlawed and, in the event of capture, should be hanged (Archibald, 1971). As a result of these chivalrous attitudes, when more pragmatic minds prevailed at the beginning of the 20th century, the British navy was compelled to purchase its first submarines from abroad.

While the "establishment" in the British navy was preaching the evils of submarine warfare, a Manchester curate working in Liverpool was creating the world's first powered submarine for the Greek, Ottoman, and Russian navies. *Resurgam* was designed by the Reverend George W. Garrett, a minister ordained in 1873. Work on the submarine began after Garrett became intrigued with the problem of thwarting steel chain nets that surrounded vessels to protect themselves against torpedo attacks (Gardiner, 1992). *Resurgam* was constructed at Britannia Engine Works and Foundry in Birkenhead near Liverpool and launched in November 1879 (Figure 23.1).

Powered by a Lamm "fireless" steam engine, the submarine could operate for approximately ten hours on power stored in an insulated tank (Murphy, 1987; Official *Resurgam* Website, 1997). It carried a crew of three and was designed to launch two spring-mounted Whitehead torpedoes. After its initial success, the British navy expressed interest in conducting additional sea trials near Portsmouth. The following year, plans were made for the *Resurgam* to make the 350-mile journey under its own power. After it stopped in the Welsh port of Rhyl, it was decided that a steam yacht should be used to tow the vessel the rest of the way to Portsmouth. Unfortunately for Garrett, as the submarine passed near the north coast of Wales, it was caught in a violent storm, broke its cable, and was lost.

Attempts to relocate *Resurgam* proved fruitless. Through the years, however, descendants of George Garrett never gave up the search. One of the most active participants was William Garrett, great-grandson of George Garrett and a resident of New Jersey. With help from ADU and Massachusetts oceanographer John Perry Fish of American Search and Survey Ltd., George Garrett helped to finance a 1996 project that finally succeeded in relocating the lost vessel.

Figure 23.1. *Resurgam* before its launch in 1873 at Birkenhead. (Photo courtesy of the Royal Navy Submarine Museum Archive).

Using a side-scan sonar, *Resurgam* was found lying on its starboard side about 50 ft deep. The detail of the side scan image of the wreck was such that it even recorded a gravel anomaly created by the wreck's influence on the local environment.

Once the site had been relocated, ADU carried out an official site assessment. Damage to the conning tower and hull suggested that the wreck had been struck and moved either by a large anchor or a trawler beam. Given the uniqueness and historical importance of the site, it was recommended to the Advisory Committee that it be designated for protection. An "Order of Designation" identifies the site and the boundary of its "restricted area," within which certain activities are prohibited except under authority of a license. The location of protected wreck sites is also noted on future admiralty charts so that all vessels in the area are aware of its presence.

In 1997, the ADU organized SUBMAP, a two-week archaeological investigation of *Resurgam.* The aim of SUBMAP was to gather detailed information for use in formulating a management plan for the wreck. The project also introduced and educated the wider diving community to the principles and techniques of underwater archaeology. The success of SUBMAP can be measured by the fact that more than 100 amateur divers and 40 professional archaeologists and scientists were involved.

An unfortunate development occurred with *Resurgam*, which underscores the dangers facing the historical maritime resources of England and Wales. In April 1999, ADU returned to the site to investigate reports from local divers that the wreck had moved. It was thought that the site was under threat of destabilization from its local tidal environment. When members of the unit arrived, they immediately noticed that the vessel had moved a considerable distance—several meters from its original location. Closer examination revealed that, at some time during the previous year, someone had tried to steal the submarine. ADU divers found the remains of a broken lifting cradle and recent crushing damage to the conning tower. The wooden cladding around the hull had been severely damaged, and much of it had disappeared. Inquiries are underway to identify the individuals who were responsible for the assault on the wreck. Once they are found, CADW will pursue prosecution to prevent future vandalism of other wreck sites.

SALVAGE AND ITS MODERN INFLUENCE

A problem still facing maritime archaeology in the United Kingdom is the structure and wording of current legislation regarding salvage, the "Merchant Shipping Act" (MSA) of 1995, a modification of the 1894 Act. The act is inconsistent with present historic preservation legislation and sends a mixed signal to the public concerning proper treatment of historical resources on the seabed. The act also has helped preserve an active salvage industry whose roots go back several hundred years.

Wracking

As early as the 17th century, the English had developed a profitable salvage industry commonly referred to as "wracking" (Muckelroy, 1980). One of the most successful English "wrackers" late in the century was Sir William Phips, a Boston sea captain who in 1687 found the remains of a 600-ton Spanish *nao* lost in 1641 off the coast of Hispaniola (Smith, 1988). He recovered more than 26 tons of metal ingots and coins from the wreck, which would later be identified as the *Concepcion*. His deeds were recorded in 1702 by Cotton Mather, author of the *Ecclesiastical History of New England, from its first planting in the year 1620, unto the year of Our Lord, 1698.*

Initially, the right to salvage a shipwreck was granted by royal commission. These commissions were based on the practice of "no cure, no pay." Two royal commissions granted to Sir William Phips, first by Charles II in 1682 and again by James II in 1685, are prime examples of the practice. At the time Phips sought permission to salvage a Spanish vessel from an English monarch, although maritime law addressed the rights of divers to claim compensation for salvaging lost cargo, commissions did not address the issue of ownership directly. Eventually, the responsibility of granting salvage rights was delegated to the admiralty board, which would receive a petition by the salvor to work on a particular wreck site.

Merchant Shipping Act

In 1854, the United Kingdom passed the "Merchant Shipping Act" (MSA). Part VII addressed the issues of wreck, casualties, and salvage. The MSA also granted Board of Trade Superintendents of Wreck the power to appoint Receivers of Wreck. In 1865, the Board of Trade issued *Instructions to Receivers of Wreck and Droits of Admiralty, and to Officers of the Customs and the Coast Guard, Concerning Their Duties in Respect of Wrecks, Casualties, and Salvage* (Eyre and Spottiswoode 1865. Rare Books Collection, University of St. Andrews). Issued under the MSA of 1854, the Merchant Shipping Repeal Act of 1854, and the Merchant Shipping Act Amendment Acts of 1855 and 1862, this historic account provides a description of the "main ingredients of a Salvage Service," which includes:

- Degree of danger the saved property was in
- Value of the saved property
- Risk incurred by the salvors
- Values of the salvors property which was exposed to danger
- Skill shown in rendering the service
- Time and labor

The current MSA is based on amendments passed in 1894 and 1906. Today, the Receiver of Wreck operates on behalf of the Department of Transport and is part of the Coast Guard Agency. Materials recovered from the seabed must be reported to the Receiver of Wreck, who will then investigate the ownership of these items. The owner has one year to come forward and prove title to the property; if no claim is made at the end of that period, the materials become the property of the Crown, and the Receiver of Wreck is required to dispose of them through sale or auction. In some cases, recovered materials may be given back to the finder in lieu of a salvage reward.

In 1994, the number of cases handled by the Receiver of Wreck was fewer than 50. Now the number of new finders alone is in the hundreds, an increase that can be attributed to the combined efforts of the Receiver of Wreck, ADU, DCMS, the Advisory Committee on Historic Wreck Sites, and the government-sponsored training program run by the Nautical Archaeology Society (NAS). These groups are working to educate the public about the MSA and its legal requirements. The majority of new cases involve sport divers, who now report what they find and recover on the seabed.

Historic wrecks are defined by the MSA as items more than 100 years old. An attempt is made to offer materials recovered from these types of wrecks to registered museums to promote public accessibility. For many years it was legal for anyone, trained archaeologist or not, to remove historic cultural materials from a submerged shipwreck if those materials were reported to the Receiver of Wreck. Vandalism of many historically important wreck sites in the early 1970s, such as *Association* and *Amsterdam*, highlighted the inherent flaw in this system of protecting the United Kingdom's cultural heritage. In 1973, the issue of preservation was addressed by the passage of the Protection of Wrecks Act. Unfortunately, this legislation is reactive instead of proactive and does not afford protection to historically important wreck sites that have not been formally designated. At the time of its introduction, it was supposed that the act would apply to only a small number of wrecks.

Because of the prospect of a salvage reward, the MSA actually encourages the removal of items from a wreck site without any concern for an item's specific provenience. This goes against the most basic of archaeological principles concerning depositional context and spatial integrity. MSA could be an effective mechanism for the reporting of wrecks and archaeological finds, but there has been little movement to make it so (Oxley, 1996). Although there has been a steady increase in the number of cases reported to the Receiver of Wreck, there remains a general lack of thorough reporting procedures in England and Wales.

Marine Insurance.   Connected with the passage of the MSA was the development of marine insurance, which appears to have encouraged the growth of the salvage industry, especially during the 19th century. Although Hanseatic merchants were the first to adopt an early system of insurance during the early Middle Ages, the first published code did not not appear until the 16th century when France published *Guidon de Mar.*

The first extant marine insurance policy dates from 1613 for the ship *Tiger*, which sailed from London to Zantes, Patras, and Cephalonia (McFee, 1951).

It is a historical curiosity that a London coffee house, started in the 1680s by Edward Lloyd, would evolve into a vast, worldwide organization. Initially consisting of a loose association of independent businessmen, by the early 18th century Lloyd's Coffee House became the center of maritime business in the city of London. In 1726, Lloyd's published the remarkable periodical known as Lloyd's List, which presented rates of exchange, current price of gold, stock prices, "Mr. Flamstead's Correct Tide Table," and shipping news (McFee, 1951). Eventually, Lloyd's gained a monopoly on the insurance market and developed Lloyd's Register of Shipping.

The effect of marine insurance on salvage cannot be underestimated. As the value and risk of shipping increased, so did the need for marine insurance policies. Eventually, the insuring of vessels became standard practice. When a policy was sufficiently large, underwriters would try to minimize losses by employing salvage operators. In this way, the growth of the salvage industry became interconnected with the growth of the insurance industry.

WHERE HAVE ALL THE EXPERTS GONE?

A disappointing development in maritime archaeology in the United Kingdom has been a decline in the number of professionally-organized research projects. In 1998, most shipwrecks were being mapped and studied by a host of amateur groups and diving clubs. In 1992, some 70,000 sport divers undertook 1.5 million dives around the United Kingdom coast (English Heritage, 1999), a sharp contrast to the number of paid professional diving archaeologists, who are fewer than 20. Fortunately, ADU has been successful in shifting many amateur projects away from excavation to survey and recording, which is much less intrusive (Oxley, 1996).

Why has this situation developed? If one looks at current regulations placed on professional diving archaeologists, one reason becomes apparent. The days of simply strapping on dive gear and working underwater are long gone for the professional archaeologist of either a university or research institute. Today's world of injury litigation and governmental bureaucracy has heaped the professional with a multitude of health and safety regulations, inhibiting any researcher who wants to conduct a project under water; whereas amateur, nonprofessional groups do not suffer from these restrictions and can undertake such projects more easily. The new code of practice for scientists and underwater archaeologists, issued in 1998 by the Health and Safety Commission, makes it easier for professional archaeologists to work alongside amateur divers on a project but has not much lightened the burden.

Another setback for U.K. underwater archaeology is the lack of adequate funding for underwater as compared to terrestrial projects. Because of higher costs for equipment, labor, and artifact conservation, a typical underwater excavation tends to cost considerably more than the usual land excavation; to date, the Duart Point wreck in Scotland is the only U.K. project to use funding normally marked for land projects. In fact, the lack of professionally-directed projects in the United Kingdom has forced ADU to send younger staff members to Australia to work on the wreck of *Pandora* for the training they need in underwater excavation techniques. Although there has been a slight rise in the number of universities providing professional underwater archaeology training, such as the programs at the Universities of Bristol, Liverpool, St. Andrews, and Southhampton, employment after graduation is still difficult to find. Apparently, large-scale projects such as *Mary Rose* are a thing of the past.

Nautical Archaeology Society

The Nautical Archaeology Society training program has been effective in educating the general sport diving community about the basics of underwater excavation techniques and the need to protect wrecks. More than 3000 divers have taken the preliminary training course (Part I), an excellent first step in creating understanding between archaeologists and divers (English Heritage, 1999). However, enrollment for upper-level training modules (Parts III and IV) has not materialized, because of competition with universities that offer higher degrees in underwater archaeology and maritime studies (why should someone interested in professional archaeology choose upper-level NAS training over a university degree, which is more professionally and academically portable?) The NAS upper-level training courses require a significant effort for completion; when compared to a university degree, the effort seems somewhat unrealistic.

While the basic NAS training program (Parts I and II) obviously benefits the avocational diver, the program is not suited for someone interested in professional archaeology, which is based on scientific research methods and principles that cannot be learned in a weekend training course. NAS courses are successful as training mechanisms for divers assisting an excavation or survey but do not qualify anyone to organize and conduct a professional excavation. Further, excavation, while an important component of archaeology, is only one small part of investigating the past. An effective archaeologist must possess other research skills and a basic knowledge of the cultural history of the site under investigation, something the NAS basic program does not provide. Still, despite current limitations of NAS' Part III and IV programs, its *Archaeology Underwater: The NAS Guide to Principles and Practice* (Dean et al., 1995) remains an invaluable resource for amateur and professional archaeologists alike, and there are plans for a new revision of this significant work (Martin Dean, personal communication, 1999).

Lack of professional archaeologists in underwater archaeology has created a unique situation. Many amateurs and a few commercial divers are leading the fight to preserve Britain's maritime past. The efforts of these groups and individuals are commendable. The recent listing of the *A-1* submarine is a positive case in which a commercial diver worked with ADU to seek protection of an important historical resource under threat from trophy-seeking sport divers.

A-1 SUBMARINE

As the 20th century ends and the recent past becomes part of history, interest in the relics of this last century is growing, especially the engines of war used during this historic and dynamic period. In England, this interest is represented by the youngest vessel to be designated for protection, the *A-1* submarine, fewer than 100 years old.

When the British navy finally decided to add submarines to its contingent of naval forces, it turned to the American designer, A.P. Holland, for its first generation of submarines. Five boats of the "Holland" class, constructed between 1902 and 1903, were small vessels by today's standards, carrying a compliment of only two officers and three crew. They were powered either by a gasoline or electric engine and had a top speed of

8 knots on the surface or 5 knots submerged (Archibald, 1971). Average displacement was about 150 tons.

Because the British needed to play catch-up with its submerged naval forces, the navy initiated design and construction of its own submarines at this same time, building 13 "A" class submarines. They were slightly longer than "Holland" class vessels, 100 ft long, with a displacement ranging from 165 to 180 tons (Archibald, 1971). Despite their slightly larger size, "A" class submarines were faster because they were propelled by a gasline engine that produced a surface speed of 11 knots and a submerged speed of 7 knots.

The first-ever wholly British designed and constructed navy submarine, *A-1*, was launched July 1902 (Figures 23.2 and 23.3). Fewer than two years later, she was run down by *Berrick Castle* while participating in naval maneuvers in the Solent, and all six crew members were lost. She was raised a month later and eventually used for antisubmarine practice. Then in August 1911, during an experimental antisubmarine operation, she was lost for good off Brackleshan Bay about 10 miles east of Portsmouth. Attempts to relocate the wreck failed, most likely because the area searched was actually eight miles west of the vessel's true location.

A-1 remained lost for the next 70 years, until a fisherman's net became snagged on her in 1989. The fisherman notified Martin Woodward, a commercial diver who operates Bembridge Maritime Museum on the Isle of Wight. Woodward took an active interest in the wreck and initiated a program to purchase the submarine from the Ministry of Defense, which took six years and required the new owner to submit periodic reports every six months on the status of the vessel's condition and what was being done to it.

During this time, attempts were made to secure funding to raise the wreck, but the effort did not net enough money. Despite this setback, Mr. Woodward remained an advocate for the *A-1*'s preservation and continued to monitor its condition. As the location of the wreck became more widely known in the local sport diving community,

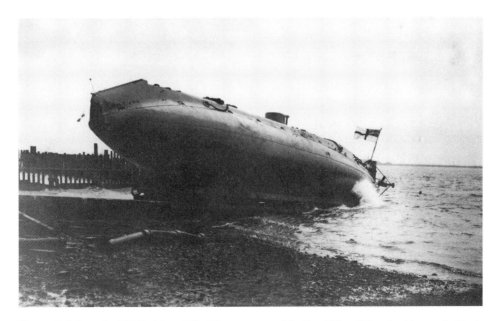

Figure 23.2. Launch of HMS *A-1* in 1902. (Photo courtesy of the Royal Navy Submarine Museum Archive).

Figure 23.3. HMS *A-1* in action. (Photo courtesy of the Royal Navy Submarine Museum Archive).

more divers started to visit the site. Some treated the find with respect and left it in the condition in which they found it. Others were not so benign and began to pull the submarine apart, to fill their trophy cases or sell what they took for scrap. Woodward tried to discourage this destructive behavior by posting a notice on the wreck so that divers would be aware of its historic importance; still, some ignored the notice and slowly destroyed the site. Some people believed that, if this were a Victorian church of historic significance, the local community would have mobilized to protect it, but few seemed to view what was happening to *A-1* with any concern.

A double standard seems to exist concerning the treatment of terrestrial sites and submerged sites. A possible explanation is that, unlike most land sites, shipwrecks lack a surrounding local community. Communities play an important role in site stewardship, and local pride is a strong motivating force for the active preservation of historic properties. As time passes, a historic landmark becomes a familiar part of the cultural landscape, an element which helps to define the community. Because submerged sites are not readily visible in the landscape, it is harder for people to identify with them, and the sites tend to be less well-known and more easily forgotten. It is easier to defend something that is widely seen every day than something rarely seen or seen by only a few. If archaeologists can increase the visibility of submerged wreck sites and present them to a broader audience, the public's drive to protect these properties may increase.

Eventually, the picking apart of *A-1* took its toll. The conning tower control panel was stolen, many exterior lights were removed, and a loading hatch was ripped open to reach the interior of the wreck. Woodward felt that the *A-1* needed additional protection and worked to have the site designated as a historic wreck. Through coordination with ADU, it was so designated in a few months. There are no formal plans for archaeological investigation of the wreck, but Woodward plans to create a video record of the site.

Because the site is now listed, ADU will make periodic visits to monitor its condition and generate its own record of site conditions.

OTHER RESEARCH PROJECTS

Seaton Carew Site

The Seaton Carew Site, designated on August 7, 1997, is another recent example of cultural resource management at work (Dean et al., 1998). The site was first located August 1996, by a local resident on the beach at Seaton Carew on England's east coast. Shifting sand levels in the foreshore revealed for the first time the outline of a wooden vessel, and the Archaeological Service for Teesside (AST) recognized it as being of some antiquity. Further analysis suggested that the vessel is probably the remains of a 19th-century collier brig, a common trading vessel along that coast. AST and NAS volunteers are recording the substantial exposed remains of the lower third of the hull.

Salcombe Cannon Wreck

A project highlighting weaknesses in current legislation is work being conducted on the Salcombe Cannon Wreck. The site was first described in 1992 by a member of the South West Marine Archaeological Group (SWMAG) as a cannon scatter with no visible structural remains. An examination in 1994 turned up gold artifacts exposed by changes in the seabed, and SWMAG immediately began a survey to plot the artifacts. It was decided that the objects posed too tempting a prize for treasure hunters, and the recorded items were removed. The recovered coins and jewelry were identified as Moroccan, dating from 1510 to 1636. Maker's marks found on a pewter bowl and a brass seal may shed some light on the identity of the Salcombe Cannon wreck. The site is of obvious archaeological importance, because it contains information about the nature of trade between Morocco and England, a trade originally established by Elizabeth I (Dean et al., 1998).

SWMAG and Annabel Lawrence of ADU are coordinating the site's future excavation and disposition of the artifacts. An agreement has been reached with the British Museum, which will purchase the items from the Receiver of Wreck; the money from the purchase will be passed on to members of SWMAG as a salvage reward. Naturally, the agreement has prompted questions about the actual value of the artifacts, a problem with no easy answers despite independent valuations.

More disturbing is a recent case in which two groups of divers were caught diving on the wreck site. Although the culprits were identified, no charges were brought. Local police were ignorant of the 1973 Protection of Wrecks Act and only formally "cautioned" the culprits. The apparent reluctance of DCMS to prosecute these individuals has angered licensees who follow the rules. The case has caused the wrong message to be sent to the public about the priority of maritime preservation and the perpetuation of the double standard at work in the treatment of terrestrial and submerged sites.

ASSESSMENT OF MARITIME ARCHAEOLOGY IN THE UNITED KINGDOM

The study of maritime archaeology is quickly approaching the end of its infancy and should no longer be considered a new research field. To do so limits the field's credibility in both the public's perception and in the research community as a whole. For almost five decades, professional archaeologists have studied humankind's relationship with the sea and have made significant strides in the scientific study of shipwrecks. In the United Kingdom, however, progress has been hampered by institutionalized salvage practices in direct conflict with the principles of historic preservation.

Within the general sport diving community of England and Wales, popular myths surrounding shipwrecks live on. Popular dive magazines contain many stories about dive clubs' latest visits to unprotected historic wreck sites and their recovery of dive trophies. Archaeologists must take most of the responsibility for losing this battle, since they have failed to meet critics in the popular press and convince the public about the real historic value of a shipwreck. In a fall issue of *Diver*, Britain's best-selling dive magazine, an article by Rex Cowan characterizes new UNESCO proposals, for regulating historic shipwrecks, as a threat to diver freedom. This statement, coming from a former member of the Secretary of State's Advisory Committee on Historic Wreck Sites, might seem credible, but it is not. UNESCO's *Draft Convention on the Protection of the Underwater Cultural Heritage* clearly is not an infringement on divers whose intent is to enjoy a dive on a historic wreck site. It is designed to discourage the destruction of submerged sites by those who wish to claim a bit of history at the expense of others.

Through the efforts of the ADU and organizations such as the NAS, attitudes of the sport diving community are starting to change, with the realization that shipwrecks are an important, nonrenewable, cultural resource and not simply a treasure trove waiting to be plundered for dive trophies. It is possible that the diving community will play the largest role in preserving the maritime past of the United Kingdom and of other countries around the world.

A key element in the success of any historic preservation program is governmental support. Underwater archaeology is an expensive undertaking and requires a substantial commitment of resources. As the number of protected wreck sites grows, so will the workload of ADU. If the current increase in the number of protected wreck sites continues, the governments of England and Wales will have to increase their funding substantially in the near future. To date, however, the government's attitude toward preserving the United Kingdom's maritime heritage can best be described as minimal.

The good news is that England is moving forward, albeit slowly, to improve the situation. In the near future, the responsibility for maritime heritage in England, and the management of the archaeological diving contract held by the ADU, will be removed from DCMS and given to English Heritage. The change requires primary legislation to extend the authority of English Heritage to below low-water mark and will bring England more in line with shipwreck management in Scotland, Wales, and Northern Ireland (English Heritage, 1999). This transfer of responsibility from uninterested civil servants to experienced heritage professionals should help alleviate many current problems facing underwater archaeology in England.

English Heritage is already investigating ways to integrate marine archaeology into the terrestrial mainstream and has commissioned several papers that examine how this might be done. It has recognized that there is a high number of historically significant sites around the United Kingdom The Royal Commission on Historic Monuments of England alone has generated a Maritime Record with a listing of more than 30,000 shipwrecks and areas of archaeological importance (Oxley, 1996). If these sites are to be protected, the scope of the archaeological diving contract must be expanded. The number of designated wreck sites will only increase in the future. ADU is doing an exemplary job, but it is unrealistic to assume that the unit can keep up with the pace of newly added sites, given its current resources. It is hoped that, when English Heritage reviews ADU's work, it will expand the archaeological diving contract.

English Heritage also has recognized that current salvage law in the United Kingdom is not consistent with the best management of the marine cultural resource, and it will give high priority to the establishment of formal protocols with the Coast Guard Agency to improve the law. What is really needed, however, is revision or amendment of the current version of the MSA, to make it more compatible with the goals of marine preservation.

The state of maritime archaeology in England and Wales can be characterized as good, given the positive influences of ADU. ADU's work during the last 13 years has been one of the most positive factors contributing to the improved development of underwater archaeology in Britain. Given three decades of professional growth, the field still falls short of higher goals. Positive change has been slow, taking years and decades. If the sport diving community seems reluctant to embrace a maritime heritage "green movement," lately there has been some growth in this area.

ACKNOWLEDGMENTS. The author thanks the members of the United Kingdom's Archaeological Diving Unit for their assistance in providing information for this publication, especially Director Martin Dean, and Steve Liscoe, Mark Lawrence, and Annabel Woods. Additional thanks are extended to the Bembridge Maritime Museum and the Royal Navy Submarine Museum.

REFERENCES

Archibald, E.H.H., 1971, *The Metal Fighting Ship in the Royal Navy 1860–1970*. Blandford Press Ltd., London.

Dean, Martin, Ferrari, Ben, Oxley, Ian, Redknap, Mark, and Watson, Kit, 1995, *Archaeology Underwater: The NAS Guide to Principles and Practice*. Archetype Press, London.

Dean, Martin, Lawrence, Mark, Liscoe, Steve, and Woods, Annabel, 1998, *Guide to Historic Wreck Sites*. Archaeological Diving Unit Web Site http://www.st-and.ac.uk/institutes/sims/deswreck.html, University of St. Andrews, St. Andrews.

English Heritage, 1999, *Towards a Policy for Marine Archaeology: An English Heritage and RCHME Discussion Paper*. London.

Eyre G.E., and Spottiswoode, W., 1865, *Instructions to Receivers of Wreck and Droits of Admiralty, and to Officers of the Customs and the Coast Guard, concerning their Duties in Respect of Wrecks, Casualties, and Salvage*. Issued by the Board of Trade, London.

Gardiner, R., 1992, *Steam, Steel, and Shellfire: The Steam Warship 1815–1905*. Conway Maritime Press, London.

McFee, William, 1951, *The Law of the Sea*. Faber & Faber Ltd., London.

Muckelroy, K., 1980, *Archaeology Under Water: An Atlas of the World's Submerged Sites*. McGraw-Hill Book Company, New York.

Murphy, William Scanlon, 1987, *Father of the Submarine, The Life of the Reverend George Garrett Pasha*. William Kimber & Co. Ltd., London.

Official *Resurgam* Website, 1997, http://members.aol.com/marknewell/index.html.

Oxley, Ian, 1996, The Development of an Integrated Approach to Field Archaeology in the UK and the Role of the Archaeological Diving Unit (ADU). *Bulletin of the Australian Institute of Marine Archaeology* 20(2): 41–53.

Oxley, Ian, and O'Regan, D.R., 1999, *The Marine Archaeological Resource*. IFA Technical Paper No. 2, Institute of Field Archaeologists, Reading.

Smith, R.C., 1988, Treasure Ships of the Spanish Main: The Iberian–America Maritime Empires. In *Ships and Shipwrecks of the Americas: A History Based on Underwater Archaeology*, edited by G.F. Bass. Thames and Hudson Ltd., London.

Chapter 24

Shipwreck Archaeology in Scotland

COLIN J.M. MARTIN

INTRODUCTION

Early Seafaring in Scotland

The inhabitants of Scotland probably have been seafarers since the first human groups penetrated the post-glacial landscape some time after about 10,000 B.P. (Morrison, 1983). Between 8000 and 6000 B.P., mesolithic occupants of a seasonal camp at Morton on the northeast coast of Fife were catching deep-sea fish, which implies the use of floating craft (Coles, 1971). Mesolithic activity at Oban and elsewhere in the Western Isles suggests that water transport played a major part in the lives of these island-hopping communities of hunter–gatherers (Wickham-Jones, 1994). The craft they used were almost certainly dugouts or skin boats, forms which have been used by traditional societies since prehistory and are still found in many places today (McGrail, 1998).

Dugout craft were not well-suited to the open sea and were probably confined mainly to estuaries and inland waters. The remains of many such vessels, dating from the prehistoric to medieval periods, have survived in Scotland, usually at the bottoms of lochs (Mowat, 1996). On the other hand, skin boats can be wonderfully seaworthy vessels, as their still-functioning descendants, the tarred-canvas curraghs of Western Ireland, amply

Colin J.M. Martin, Honorary Reader, Centre for Environmental History, University of St. Andrews, St. Andrews, Fife, KY16 9AJ, Scotland, United Kingdom.

International Handbook of Underwater Archaeology, edited by Carol V. Ruppé and Janet F. Barstad. Kluwer Academic/Plenum Publishers, New York, 2002.

testify. There are several early historical references to such craft in Scottish waters. It was in a skin craft that the 6th-century missionary, St. Columba, sailed from Ireland to Iona (Hornell, 1973). However, the light, hide-covered frameworks rarely survive in archaeological contexts, though the "ghost" of one has been recognized in a Bronze Age burial at Dalgety Bay, Fife (Watkins, 1980).

What vessels other than dugouts and skin boats were used by the prehistoric peoples of Scotland and their Dark Age successors is not known. The few representations of boats in Pictish art give little clue as to how they were constructed. However, there was much Roman activity in Scottish waters between the late A.D. 1st and early 3rd centuries (Martin, 1992). The Flavian governor Agricola, in his campaigns beyond the Forth in the early A.D. 80s, made extensive use of a fleet which, on at least one occasion, appears to have circumnavigated Scotland. According to Tacitus, vessels of the fleet included liburnians, two-banked oared warships of Mediterranean type. Also, river craft probably were used widely in Roman Scotland. At the fort of Newstead on the Tweed, a steering oar has been found (Curle, 1911).

During the middle of A.D. 2nd century, a Roman frontier system flourished briefly between the Forth and Clyde estuaries. It appears to have been supported by harbors at each end. From A.D. 208–211, the emperor Septimius Severus and his son, Caracalla, engaged in a series of massive campaigns along the northeastern coastal plain of Scotland, which evidently were provisioned by sea. For all this maritime activity, however, no traces of Roman shipwrecks have yet been found in Scottish waters.

The Scandinavian technique of building boats by creating "shells" of overlapping planks, edge-jointed with iron rivets ("clinker" technique) probably was brought to Scotland by Viking raiders and settlers. The technique has remained the traditional method of small-boat construction ever since. As yet, we know of no Viking wrecks in Scottish waters, although ships were sometimes buried with their owners. These can be recognized by surviving rows of iron fastenings even when all trace of the wooden structure has gone. A fine example recently was discovered at Scar in Orkney (Ritchie, 1993).

Parts of early Scottish clinker-built vessels occasionally turn up in the archaeological record. In the 19th century, two roughed-out end pieces for a clinker vessel were discovered in a bog on the island of Eigg, where they probably had been buried for seasoning (McPherson, 1877). Excavations in Perth High Street in the 1970s revealed, in a 12th century context, dismantled clinker boat components reused as parts of domestic houses. The same site has produced numerous examples of the distinctive rivet-and-rove iron boat fastenings, including unused strips of roves which suggest that boat building or repair had been practiced in the vicinity (Martin, 1998). A clinker boat of probable medieval date was revealed in 1934 when Loch Laggan was partially drained for a hydroelectric scheme. Unfortunately, the boat was neither preserved nor adequately recorded (Maxwell, 1950).

No examples of late medieval West Highland galleys have come to light so far, though they are familiar as representations on grave slabs (Steer and Bannerman, 1977). On the east coast, the medieval period saw the creation of many coastal burghs and the opening up of trade with the continent. Such records as we have show that ships and their cargoes frequently were lost, particularly in the approaches to the Forth and Tay, those great esturial highways into the heart of Scotland. Wrecks remain elusive, although the occasional recovery of medieval artifacts in fishing nets suggests that sites are there to be discovered.

Scottish maritime activity intensified in the 16th and 17th centuries, when ships voyaged regularly to Norway, the Baltic, Holland, France, and Spain and, occasionally, to the Mediterranean. Coastal trade within Britain itself was always extensive. Later, from the west coast and particularly Glasgow, Scottish shipping became active in transatlantic trade. Nor should we forget the countless small vernacular craft which, from earliest times, have provided Scots with a ready means of communication, transport, fishing, war and, on occasion, even pleasure.

Archaeological Potential

In light of the foregoing, it might seem surprising that historic shipwrecks so far discovered in Scottish waters are almost wholly unrepresentative of the continuous and widespread maritime activity which has been conducted along these shores for at least 8000 years. But such is the case. All known wrecks are foreign, of postmedieval date, and are either state-owned warships or large armed merchantmen that belonged to powerful European trading interests.

Several factors explain this skew. First, almost all sites so far discovered by divers lie in exposed locations on the western seaboard or among the Northern Isles. From the 16th century onward, these were hazardous sectors on northern Europe's main path of access to the world's oceans. Wrecks in such places are often broken up and widely scattered, though significant parts may remain unburied and visible on the sea floor. This is especially true in the case of large postmedieval armed vessels, where cannons and anchors provide obvious and unmistakable markers of their presence. Finally, these exposed but largely silt-free littorals provide the best underwater visibility and diving conditions, so that it is here that most exploration has taken place.

A vast resource of shipwrecks from all periods undoubtedly lies on the eastern seaboard, along the North Sea margin, and particularly around the approaches to the Forth and Tay. But there the water is silty, and much of the sea floor is covered with deep sediments into which wreckage naturally penetrates, rendering it invisible but providing excellent conditions for preservation. These waters, with their poor visibility and generally featureless seabeds, do not encourage sport diving. We may presume that the wrecks are there and in abundance, but we do not know where they are. At present, little is to be gained by actively seeking them, since the best-preserved sites are probably buried in anaerobic environments which will ensure almost indefinite survival. Their most effective protection, at least for the present, will be to remain undiscovered.

DEVELOPMENT OF UNDERWATER ARCHAEOLOGY IN SCOTLAND

Scotland's historic shipwrecks first attracted the attention of salvors and treasure hunters who were driven by uncomplicated and often self-deluding motives of gain. A classic example is *San Juan de Sicilia*, a Spanish Armada vessel that exploded and sank in Tobermory Bay off the island of Mull in 1588 (McLeay, 1986; Martin, 1998). Within a few years, an erroneous belief had sprung up that the wreck, variously misnamed *Florencia*, *Florida*, or *Florencion*, contained vast treasure. The misconception prompted a succession of abortive but destructive salvage ventures that have continued into recent times. As a result, little intact archaeology is now likely to survive on what otherwise might have been an extraordinarily rich site, though the well-documented endeavours of salvors extending from the 17th into the 20th centuries provide a remarkable chronicle of the development of diving and salvage techniques and demonstrate the philistine and almost invariably futile nature of treasure hunting.

Early salvors in Scotland also were active in the legitimate and generally more successful business of recovering cargoes from contemporary shipwrecks. The most notable was Captain Jacob Rowe of London who, with his associates, used a patented diving "engine" on several wrecks among the western and northern isles, including the Tobermory ship, in the 1720s and 1730s (Martin, 1992). Much of their work focused on outward-bound East Indiamen that contained rich consignments of specie with which to purchase their return cargoes of spices, porcelain, and, from the 18th century, tea. The extensive documentation generated by such ventures, often through acrimonious and lengthy court actions over the division of spoils, has inspired a number of modern researchers to relocate the remains of these wrecks.

Many such attempts, particularly during the 1960s and early 1970s, were privately funded expeditions based on the principle of recouping expenses by selling the finds, but an element of serious if misguided archaeological motivation lay behind some of them. The first recorded episode was in 1964, when the site of a Dutch East Indiaman, *de Liefde*, was found off the Out Skerries in Shetland, where she had been wrecked in 1711 (Bax and Martin, 1974). Several seasons of salvage-driven excavation followed. In the early 1970s, four more wrecks were located and excavated in Shetland waters by Robert Sténuit. These included *Lastdrager*, a Dutch East Indiaman of 1654 (Sténuit, 1974); *Curaçao*, a Dutch warship of 1729 (Sténuit, 1977a, 1977b); *Wendela*, a Danish Asiatic Company ship of 1737 (Sténuit, 1988); and *Evstafii*, a Russian naval transport of 1780 (Sténuit, 1976). Other salvors have carried out work in the same region on the remains of the Swedish Indiamen *Svecia* (1740) and *Drottningen af Swerge* (1745).

In 1973, a research institute was established at the University of St. Andrews to develop and foster maritime archaeology. Since then, the university has been at the forefront of the discipline in Scotland and further afield. St. Andrews is now the base of the Archaeological Diving Unit, a state-funded team that assesses and reports on sites throughout the U.K. in support of the government's historic shipwreck legislation (Delgado, 1997). Today, Scotland is the first of the U.K. countries to administer underwater archaeology as an integral part of the wider archaeological heritage, through its regulatory agency, Historic Scotland.

EXCAVATIONS

Three wreck excavations may be singled out for detailed description, reflecting both their intrinsic interest and their significance in the development of underwater archaeology. They are described in the following sections. In addition, serious archaeological work has been carried out on the Spanish Armada wreck *El Gran Grifón* off Fair Isle (Martin, 1972, 1975), the 18th century Dutch East Indiaman, *Adelaar*, off Barra (Martin, 1992, 1998), and the late 17th-century Danish warship *Wrangels Palais* on the Out Skerries of Shetland (Bound and Sharpe, 1995).

Kennemerland (Dutch East Indiaman, 1664)

On December 20, 1664, *Kennermerland* (Figure 24.1) struck the rock outcrop of Stoura Stack, close to the mouth of the wide natural harbor of the Out Skerries in Shetland. Her

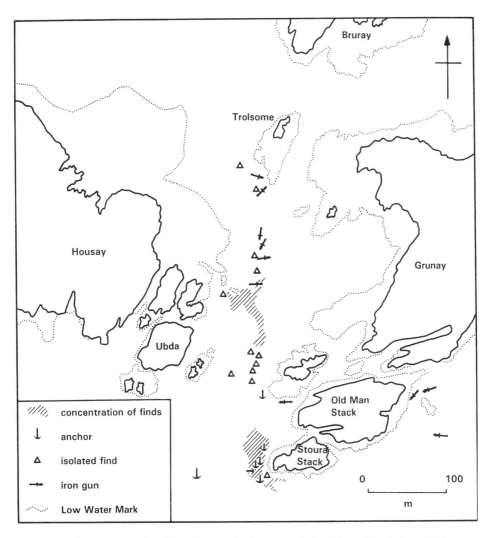

Figure 24.1. General plan of the *Kennemerland* wreck site (after Price and Muckelroy, 1974).

foremast fell against the stack allowing three lookouts, the wreck's only survivors, to scramble ashore. The ship, with more than 200 people on board, broke in half. As the forepart foundered in deep water beside the stack, spilling its ballast of bricks and lead ingots, the lightened stern portion was carried by the storm to Bruray Island, a kilometer away, where much wreckage was cast on shore. Salvors later recovered most of the ship's consignment of silver coins.

The remains of *Kennemerland* were located in 1971 by a team of divers from the Aston University Sub-Aqua Club (Foster and Higgs, 1973). Between then and 1987, six further seasons of archaeological work were conducted on the site, coordinated by Richard Price (Price and Muckelroy, 1974, 1977, 1979; Price et al., 1980).

During the 1970s, *Kennemerland* was investigated as a type-site for discontinuous wrecks by Keith Muckelroy in his pioneering work on formation studies (Muckelroy 1975, 1976, 1978). Muckelroy's interest focused on the complex interrelationships between underwater archaeological depositions and their environments, which he rightly saw as keys to understanding the processes of wrecking. This work has been continued more recently by Christopher Dobbs of the Mary Rose Trust (Dobbs and Price, 1991).

Muckelroy's "Filters."   Muckelroy's research was based on concepts which he labeled "extractive filters," which remove or destroy archaeological material, and "scrambling devices," which rearrange what remains.

Extractive Filters.   Extractive filters may be divided into three categories. The first operates during the physical event of the shipwreck, when much material is lost through the influences of wind, waves, and currents. What reaches the seabed is then exposed to a second extractive filter: chemical and biological degradation. Human interference, whether by salvors or archaeologists, constitutes a third filter which may remove material from the site.

These filtering processes, though often complex and difficult to interpret, are relatively straightforward to comprehend. It is harder to identify and quantify the nature and effects of the scrambling devices. The first is the process of the wrecking itself. In the case of the *Kennemerland*, a broad outline can be deduced from the disposition of wreck material on the seabed. The impact area around Stoura Stack is characterized by a spill of thousands of bricks and more than 100 lead ingots, which dropped from the lower hold when the ship broke apart. Six anchors have also been found in this area.

Scrambling Filters.   Much of the upper structure of the vessel and its contents was then carried across the bay by a southerly gale, grounding where the rocky seabed rises to within 10 m of the surface, about 150 m from the initial impact. Here a secondary break-up occurred, depositing more bricks and a concentration of other cargo. Even so, enough structural integrity was still retained by parts of the hull to carry six iron guns further toward the shore, dropping them in a linear scatter as far as the islet of Trolsome, 200 m away. According to a traditional account, much wreckage was finally thrown up on the main island, Bruray, although no archaeological evidence of this has yet been noted.

A second scrambling factor is the post-depositional movement of wreck material across the seabed or within its sediments. Tidal regimes within the bay and across its mouth are complex and, at times, powerful. It is possible that segments of the broken ship, after entering the bay, subsequently were swept out of it, as is suggested by the find of two isolated guns in deep water to the south of the primary impact point. Within the main depositions, moreover, current movements over the seabed have had the effect of burying objects and rearranging them over time. Marine flora and fauna may have contributed in various ways to the movement of artifacts within and across the sea floor. These aspects of formation processes have been the focus of several recent studies.

Most investigative work on *Kennemerland* has concentrated on the extensive deposits that lie just inside the bay, where much of the ship's cargo appears to have dropped. Excavation was conducted on a systematic grid designed to facilitate Muckelroy's calculations of distributive processes.

The finds provided a rich sampling of the ship's varied cargo. Among the most remarkable was a salt-glazed Rheinish flagon which proved to contain 18 kg of mercury. This heavy liquid metal is notoriously difficult to package, and it is likely that the flagon had been wrapped in straw or some similar material and contained within a box.

Other types of pottery were scattered widely across the wreck site, as were the remains of bottles. Most of the latter were of the square "case" variety associated with Dutch gin that were fitted with pewter screw-tops, many of which have been found on the wreck.

Clay pipes were another common find, although the variety of forms recorded suggests that they were not part of the cargo but more probably the property of individual crew members, either for personal use or private trade (Martin, 1987).

Private trade was almost certainly the purpose of a remarkable group of finds recorded in the same area, which includes decorated tobacco boxes, cheap brass rings, pewter pendants and brass janglers, brass bodkins, lace bobbins, thimbles, two pocket sundials, and five pewter golf-club heads.

Such mass-produced items from the cheap end of the luxury market are not the kinds of things that usually appear in East Indiamen's cargo manifests, and their discovery as a discrete group suggests that they may derive from an individual seaman's trading chest. A box-load of such light and relatively inexpensive European baubles would have yielded high profits to an enterprising private trader in Eastern markets. In modest ventures of this kind may be seen, in microcosmic form, the economic rationale of Europe's East India companies in the early modern period. This particular instance also underlines the high level of concomitant risk, in this case to life as well as to investment.

Almost none of the ship's fabric has survived in the exposed seabed around Stoura Stack, although some fragments of timber and rope have been preserved in protected pockets or within concretions. Several objects relate to activities aboard ship. Navigation is represented by dividers, sounding leads, and part of a backstaff. Two pewter syringes and a brass trepanation wimble indicate that quite complex surgical procedures could be performed on board. Of the ship's more perishable provisions, little has survived, apart from some plum and peach stones, bones from cattle and sheep, and a few peppercorns. It may be supposed that the latter were on their second voyage halfway round the world, for they originally must have been brought to Europe in the hold of a homeward-bound Indiaman.

Dartmouth (Fifth-Rate Warship, 1690)

On October 9, 1690, the English naval vessel *Dartmouth* (Figure 24.2) sank in the Sound of Mull off the west coast of Scotland. The admiralty in London barely noted the loss of this small, old, and unimportant vessel in England's rapidly developing navy. To modern scholars, however, the wreck has provided a unique microcosm of the events in which *Dartmouth* played so modest a part, for her very ordinariness makes her a wide and revealing exemplar of matters relating to contemporary nautical technology, warfare, and shipboard life.

Dartmouth was built at Portsmouth in 1655 by John Tippets, who later became surveyor to the Navy. She was an early member of a small, lightweight class of warships loosely called frigates, designed for dispatch and reconnaissance work. These ships were fast, maneuverable, and well-suited to operations in confined waters. Much of the influence behind their design appears to have come from Scandinavia by way of the Low Countries (Martin, 1978, 1998b).

In the 1670s, Willem van de Velde the Younger made a drawing of a fifth-rate, generally believed to represent *Dartmouth* (Robinson, 1958). It is known from

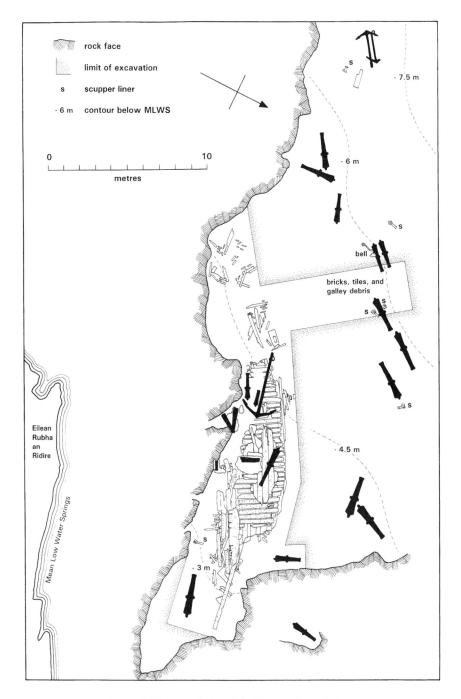

Figure 24.2. General plan of the *Dartmouth* wreck site.

documentary sources that the ship underwent a major refit in 1678, when her keel and lower planks were replaced. It may well be that the artist sketched her then. In the drawing she appears mastless, without a bell, and without her guns.

Dartmouth's long service career was varied if rarely spectacular. She played a minor role in several general engagements against the Dutch and undertook antipiracy patrols in the Mediterranean and Caribbean. In April 1666, in company with two other ships, she captured three Dutch merchantmen off the Irish coast and a few days later assisted in the destruction of a Flushing privateer. A notable incident occurred in 1686, when the ship fought her way out of Puerto Rico harbor to avoid being detained by the Spanish garrison, Spain then being a nominally friendly power. The ship's greatest moments came in the naval war which followed the dynastic settlement of 1688, during which she fought on the side of William and Mary. In 1689, *Dartmouth* participated in the battle of Bantry Bay, off southwest Ireland; later that year, she engaged Jacobite batteries at the entrance to the River Foyle, allowing victualling ships *Mountjoy* and *Phoenix* to break the boom across the river mouth and relieve Londonderry (Powley, 1972).

By 1690, *Dartmouth* was an old ship at the end of her useful life. Based at Carrickfergus and Greenock under the command of Captain Edward Pottinger, she was employed in patrol work off northern Ireland and western Scotland, carrying the writ of the new monarchs to their less enthusiastic subjects (Hopkins, 1986). The ship was long overdue a major refit or final scrapping: Her hull was worm-eaten and leaky and her rigging badly worn. Only a few weeks before she was wrecked, Pottinger wrote despairingly of the *Dartmouth*'s many defects, adding presciently that "our best bower cable with often anchoring, is so extremely worn as not to be trusted."

This was the cable that parted as the ship lay at anchor in the Sound of Mull on October 9, as it sheltered from a southwesterly gale. Thrown on her beam-ends and running stern-first, she was driven across the sound and wrecked on the small islet of Rudha an Ridre. Some contemporary salvage was carried out, and the site of the wreck was remembered locally until the mid-19th century. Thereafter, it was forgotten—until 1973, when the ship's remains were discovered by a group of divers from Bristol who subsequently, in association with the University of St. Andrews, carried out a limited program of excavation (Adnams, 1974; Holman, 1975; McBride, 1976; P. Martin, 1977 and 1987; C. Martin 1978, 1998a, 1998b).

Apart from the value of this investigation as a study in its own right, *Dartmouth* became one of Muckelroy's key type-sites in building up his classification of "continuous" wrecks (Muckelroy, 1978). All recoveries, including substantial elements of the hull structure, are now in the National Museum of Scotland, which partly sponsored the project.

Excavation revealed a run of articulated structure from the lower hull together with numerous associated components, ship's fittings, and other objects. Systematic investigation of the archaeological features within their environmental contexts has allowed an understanding of the wreck formation processes to be built up, which in turn has informed archaeological interpretations of the site as a whole (Martin, 1978; Muckelroy, 1978).

One extremity had wedged into the shoreward end of a triangular gully, where it collapsed and stabilized independently of the other half from which it had separated about midships. The seaward end then rolled down the slope onto its side, to lie along a slightly different alignment matching the seabed contour. As it disintegrated, the collapsing structure deposited its contents, which stabilized along a linear axis.

Meanwhile, during the wrecking process, the ship's inshore end had rocked from side to side on the fulcrum of its keel, digging deeply into an abrasive clay and pebble substratum. During this process a thick mat of wood splinters from the abrading keel, together with organic material from the fabric and contents of the ship, became incorporated beneath and around the hull remains. The keel trench acted as a gravity trap for a substantial deposit of metal and ceramic objects. This suggests that the ship broke up in a continuous and fairly rapid sequence, allowing structural components and other objects falling from the disintegrating vessel's upper parts to accumulate at the bottom of the trench before it became sealed by an infill of mobile shingle. Much of the collapsed structure, including 5 m of the keel, then stabilized beneath a stratum of mobile shingle.

No part of either extremity survives in the structural remains, and the orientation of the wreck was established by an analysis of artifact distributions over the site. This clearly identified the inshore end as representing the collapsed stern. Objects connected with the ship's executive management, such as navigational instruments, were reliable indicators of an association with the after part of the vessel. This hypothesis was reinforced by finds, in the same area, of personal items of a quality commensurate with the higher living standards enjoyed by the captain and his officers relative to individuals berthed elsewhere in the ship.

Distributions of correspondingly lower-quality personal and domestic objects were noted at the other end of the site. A final and compelling indicator of the after area was a group of mica glazing pieces cut in triangular or rhomboidal shapes, which can be associated unequivocally with the stern cabin windows.

Between the two extremities, a discrete group of bricks and tiles, burnt debris, animal bone, and coal indicated the whereabouts of the galley. These remains were topped by the ship's bell, which would have been positioned originally in an open wooden belfry on the forecastle deck just above the galley. A concentration of clay pipes was also noted in this area, while a more scattered distribution of pipes, most of which were of markedly higher quality than those associated with the galley, was recorded around the stern. These distributions prompt an interpretation that casts light on an aspect of shipboard life and discipline. Contemporary regulations confined smoking to the galley area, where the tile-lined cubicle around the hearth provided the only safe place on board in which to strike a light. The distribution of pipes on the *Dartmouth* wreck suggests that, though this sensible stricture was followed by the men, apparently it was not observed by their officers.

Although the surviving articulated structure represents only some 10 percent of the total hull, it has provided a basis for investigating several aspects of the ship's construction and design. The point at which the remains fitted into the axis of the hull was determined by a critical comparison of the archaeological evidence with documentary sources. About 5 m of the keel was preserved, including an elegant horizontal scarf joint with a faced overlap of 1.3 m. This keel was a replacement, fitted during an extensive rebuild of the ship at Rotherhithe on the Thames in 1678, for which extensive documentation survives. The first entry in the shipwright's invoice itemizes the new keel, which involved the supply of an 88 ft 6 in (27 m) linear run of elm 13 in (0.33 m) square. Yet the *Dartmouth*'s keel, as other descriptive specifications confirm, was only 80 ft (24.38 m) long. The discrepancy is twice the measured scarf overlap, indicating that the new keel was made up in three sections. Assuming these to have been of equal length and this to be the aftermost joint, a fixed point in the structure's longitudinal axis is obtained. The surviving timbers, and their curvature, can then be used to project the after part of the ship's original underwater shape. This exercise has confirmed the fine run of *Dartmouth*'s hull.

For a ship designed for speed and good sailing qualities such a conclusion was scarcely unexpected. Much more surprising is the apparently unconventional nature of her construction. As normal, the frames are arranged in pairs, with overlapping chocked joints. But the paired frames are not themselves fastened to one another transversely and could not therefore have been pre-erected as part of a skeleton in the manner traditionally associated with English shipwrightry of the period (McKee, 1976). Instead, it appears that framing and planking were introduced turn and about, working upwards from the keel, in the manner associated with a Dutch method of shipbuilding (Hoving, 1988: 216–217). This may serve to remind us that contemporary information about shipbuilding techniques derives, in the main, from theorists rather than practicing shipwrights. Many of the latter were illiterate, or nearly so. John Evelyn, after attending the launch of the 1200-ton first-rate *Charles* at Deptford in 1668, noted in his diary that she was "built by Old Shish, a plain honest carpenter, master-builder in this dock, but one who can give very little account of his art by discourse, and is hardly capable of reading, yet is of great ability in his calling." Such men worked by rule of thumb, and their methods are recorded not on paper by study-bound theorists but in the timbers of the ships they built.

Another unconventional feature of *Dartmouth*'s construction is that the surviving frames do not span the keel but end just short of it, where they are clamped in place by a massive and continuous chock of elm. This may be seen as a deliberate measure to reduce the number of sharply curved grown timbers required, although perhaps more probably it is connected with the replacement of the ship's keel and lower runs of planking in 1678. If these components were rotten, the central portions of the frames were no doubt affected, too, and what we may be seeing is an ingenious improvization whereby these sections were chopped out and replaced sequentially without the longitudinal integrity of the structure being compromised in the process.

An examination of the outer strakes raises further points of interest. As might be expected, the fastenings closely follow the locations of the frames within the hull, two treenails normally being applied to each joint. Viewed longitudinally, however, the treenails appear haphazardly placed, with no attempt to align them in neat rows. But this was clearly a deliberate policy, intended to avoid setting up lines of weakness along the grain of the planks. The use of secondary treenails is also notable. These sometimes impinge on existing ones, and were presumably intended to tighten up primary fastenings that had worked loose.

Even displaced single components can yield significant information. A lodging knee, found pinned beneath *Dartmouth*'s lower hull, can be identified as part of the main deck assembly, now collapsed. But the nature of that assembly can be deduced from the knee's dimensions, fastening holes, angles of set, and recesses for mating components. This evidence shows that the main deck construction was based on a series of 5 ft (1.52 m) modules. Once the possibility of modular construction was recognized, moreover, it was observed that, though the individual widths of the futtocks varied considerably, the hull framing conformed to a remarkably consistent centerline spacing of 1 ft (0.305 m).

The aforementioned does no more than touch on the potential of even fragmentary and insubstantial structural remains such as those encountered on the wreck of *Dartmouth*. Significant in their own right, such studies may bear on wider issues. The considerable ingenuity expended in repairing and squeezing a little more service from the ship's aging and ramshackle hull speaks of a navy under pressure from a parsimonious government (a circumstance well borne out by documentary sources), while the use of building techniques which minimized the need for complex or wastefully derived components patently reflects the timber-supply crisis of the mid-17th century (Albion, 1952).

Dartmouth's status as a source of information about contemporary technologies and activities, and as a microcosm of everyday life, is evident in the wide variety of small finds recovered from her wreck. Examples of three types of cast-iron guns, nine, six, and three pounds in calibre, provide valuable information about the ship's armament. The ship's bell carries the date 1678, indicating that a replacement had been provided during the refit of that date. Worn rigging fittings, some bearing evidence of makeshift repair, testify to the pressures which beset her hard-pressed crew during the final months of the ship's life. Navigation is represented by dividers, a protractor, a log-slate, and part of a backstaff. The work of the barber–surgeon is attested by pewter syringes, drug pots, apothecary's mortar, and a cut-throat razor. Weights and measures reflect the daily struggle of the purser to keep account of the ship's provisions. Craft tools include a folding two-foot rule (the inch units are indistinguishable from modern ones) and a remarkable boxwood calculator for working out volumes and prices of timber in various sizes. Weapons are represented by a small flintlock pistol, a musket stock, many thousands of musket balls, and several cast-iron hand grenades.

Most of the small finds are domestic in character and include several types of pottery, glass bottles, wooden vessels of various kinds, and a substantial collection of clay pipes, some of which bear initials which identify them as the products of known workshops (Martin, P., 1977, 1987).

Swan (English Warship, 1653)

Thirty-seven years before the loss of *Dartmouth*, another small English warship, *Swan* (Figure 24.3), wrecked in the Sound of Mull (Martin, 1995, 1998). Scotland's situation at the close of the Civil War was confused and complex. Following the execution of Charles I in 1649 and the temporary establishment of republican government in Britain, Oliver Cromwell embarked upon a brutal subjugation of Ireland. The following year Charles' exiled son, Charles II, landed in Scotland to reclaim his inheritance. Cromwell marched north with his New Model Army and, at Dunbar on September 4, inflicted a crushing defeat on the Scots. Nonetheless, Charles was crowned King of Scotland on January 1, 1651. Cromwell's response was delayed by illness, but in July his army crossed the Forth to decimate the Royalist forces at Inverkeithing on the 20th before marching through Fife to capture Perth. In a desperate countermeasure, Charles led his depleted army into England where, on September 3, he was decisively defeated at Worcester and fled back into exile on the Continent. Scotland was placed under firm government control, with major garrisons at Ayr, Perth, and Leith, and 20 smaller strongholds gripping the rest of the country, including the Highlands.

Royalist resistance continued through 1652 and into 1653, with a rebellion in the west led by the Earl of Glencairn. Although the revolt was sporadic and ill-organized, Cromwell was determined to nip it in the bud, and dispatched a task force to the Western Isles whose objective was to capture Duart Castle, medieval seat of Glencairn's principal supporters, Clan Maclean. In September 1653, a flotilla of six ships anchored in Duart Bay, carrying 1000 hard-bitten infantrymen of the New Model Army, commanded by Colonel Ralph Cobbett. The troops stormed ashore with their siege artillery only to find the castle deserted, the Macleans prudently having fled. Thus far the operation had been an outstanding success, achieved without firing a shot.

What followed is recorded in a report sent to Cromwell a few days later:

> . . . there hapned a most violent storme, which continued for 16 or 18 houres together,
> in which wee lost a small Man of Warre called the *Swan* that came from Aire, the

Figure 24.3. General plan of the *Swan* wreck site.

Martha and Margrett of Ipswich, wherein was all our remayning stores of ammunition and provision, only the Great Guns and Morterpeeces were saved. But that which was most sad was the loss of the *Speedwell* of Lyn, where all the men that were in her, being 23 seamen and souldiers (except one) were drowned. The rest of the Men of

> Warre and others in the fleete were forced to cutt their Masts by the board, and yet hardly escaped ... and all this in the sight of our Men att land, who saw their freinds drowning, and heard them crying for helpe, but could not save them.

In February 1979, John Dadd, a naval diving instructor, came upon the remains of an armed wooden sailing ship at a depth of about 10 m to the east of Duart Point. A number of recoveries, including a Frechen stoneware flagon of 17th-century date, were made during this and subsequent visits, but Dadd was unable to undertake extensive work on the site. In 1991, concerned that the wreck might be found and plundered by treasure hunters, he reported its location to Historic Scotland. The Archaeological Diving Unit was sent to investigate the find. In due course, the wreck was designated as a protected site but, since its remains appeared to be safely encapsulated within the drifted shingle piled against the rock face sloping down from Duart Point, no plans were made to excavate or recover them.

Within a year, the situation had changed radically. Shifts in the local seabed environment, not yet fully understood, began to sweep away the deposits of silt within which wreck material had been buried. When a group of amateur divers unintentionally came upon the site in the course of a training dive, they found the seabed littered with partially exposed objects. Some were raised and handed over to the National Museum of Scotland for identification and conservation.

Among the finds were wooden carvings from the vessel's decorated stern, various domestic items, a grindstone, a hoard of silver coins, and part of a snaphaunce pistol. The artifactual evidence suggested a date around the middle of the 17th-century, and documentary research identified the 1653 Cromwellian expedition as the most likely context. Soon afterward, the Archaeological Diving Unit returned to survey the site to rescue items still in danger of being washed away. These included an ornate sword, a pocket watch, and more wooden carvings. Among the latter was part of the coronet and ostrich feather device with the motto *Ich Dien*, which is the badge of the heir to the English throne.

This find identified the wreck beyond all reasonable doubt. Of the three ships lost in the 1653 incident, two were hired victuallers from East Anglia, *Speedwell* and *Martha and Margaret*. Neither would have carried the insignia of the royal heir. The third vessel, however, was the warship *Swan*, which had been built for Charles I in 1641. In 1645 she was captured by the Parliamentarians and in due course became part of the Commonwealth navy. Such a vessel certainly would have carried the trappings of a royal ship, and the presence of the heir's badge on the wreck site thus confirms its identity. This conclusion was later reinforced by the discovery of the thistle and harp emblems of Scotland and Ireland, countries over which Charles I once held dominion.

Swan's origins go back to the early years of Charles's reign, when the high-charged galleons he had inherited from his father's navy proved incapable of protecting shipping in the channel and its approaches from the depredations of North African pirates and, particularly, Dutch and Flemish privateers whose ships had been built to a radically new design based on lightness and flexibility. These fast and manueverable vessels were based in channel ports such as Flushing and Dunkirk. They could run rings round a front-line warship, complained an English naval expert, because the latter was like a clumsy giant, "strong and invincible at a close and grappling, but for all that so weak and impotent in his legs that any active and nimble dwarf, keeping out of reach, may affront and scorn him."

In 1635, one of these nimble dwarfs fell into English hands. She was a single-decked Flushing frigate, equipped with oars as well as sails and, according to a contemporary observer, went "like a sprite." Phineas Pett, the king's master-shipwright, was ordered to build two frigates on similar lines. These, *Greyhound* and *Roebuck*, were duly built, but the propensity of conservative English shipwrights to add unnecessary strength and weight prevailed, and their performance did not live up to expectations. The 120-ton *Roebuck* was later described as "not a good goer," although she was "strong and able to indure any sea."

The lack of fast frigates to engage in antipirate operations was of particular concern in Ireland, whose waters were infested with corsairs from as far afield as Algiers. In 1637, Lord Deputy Thomas Wentworth (later Earl of Strafford), personally acquired a 160-ton Dutch-built pinnace, *Confidence*, with which to combat them. Described as "an extraordinarily good sailer," she gave excellent service until 1641 when Strafford was impeached for treason and beheaded. His ship was sold, but the king immediately ordered the building of a replica to replace her. The new ship was to be called *Swan* (Thrush, 1991).

During 1643 and 1644, *Swan* provided a vital link between the Royalists in Ireland and North Wales, running the blockade of an increasingly strong Parliamentary navy. In 1645, she was captured off Dublin by subterfuge and thereafter fought for Parliament against Royalist and pirate shipping in the Irish Sea and off the west of Scotland. By 1653 the ship had been assigned to the naval base at Ayr, south of Glasgow, under Captain Edward Tarleton. From there, she joined Colonel Cobbett's expedition to Mull.

Swan's wreck has proved to be one of Scotland's most remarkable archaeological discoveries of recent times. When threats to the site became apparent in 1992, Historic Scotland and the National Museums of Scotland combined with St. Andrews University to seek ways of preserving this unique but fragile heritage resource. A long-term project was initiated to survey the wreck, assess its future stability, consolidate the areas under threat and, if necessary, excavate, recover, and conserve archaeological material that could not be protected any other way.

Work began in 1993 and has continued since then (Martin, 1995, 1998a). The site has been fully surveyed, and much of it is now secured by a covering of sandbags. Studies have been made into the site's morphology, sedimentation, and biological regimes. Experiments into corrosion and biological degradation have contributed to an assessment of the site, and to wreck formation studies in general (Gregory, 1995, 1999; MacLeod, 1995). An investigation of the complex currents influencing the site, and the patterns of sedimentation and erosion they engender, has revealed that the eastern part of the wreck has become destabilized in a way that cannot be reversed effectively. It has been decided to excavate this area to research standards and to preserve its contents as an intact collection in the care of the National Museum of Scotland.

One of the first items to be found was part of the ship's binnacle (Martin, 1999), a wooden, box-like construction divided into three compartments, one at each end for a compass and the center one for a night light. The component parts of the binnacle are fastened with oak pegs, as the contemporary nautical expert Sir Henry Mainwaring prescribes, to avoid causing magnetic deviation. Two compasses were necessary, because the steersman had to sweep his whipstaff (a long lever coupled to the tiller head via a fulcrum below deck) from one side of the deck to the other, and therefore required clear sight of a compass from either side. The naked candle constituted a fire hazard: on at least one occasion an inattentive steersman allowed it to burn a hole through the top of *Swan*'s binnacle. This had been carefully patched by the ship's carpenter, though inappropriately he used iron nails for the job.

The base of a mariner's compass was found in one of the binnacle compartments. A second compass, almost intact and retaining its brass gimbals, was discovered nearby; fragments of the broken glass face lay beneath it.

Further excavation has confirmed that this end of the wreck contains parts of the ship's collapsed stern. Ornate framing and elaborate panel work reveal an unexpectedly high standard of fitting-out, with a strong emphasis on status and luxury, at least as far as the captain's quarters were concerned. Molded timbers with decorative embellishments, and even a complete panelled door, are among the finds. This goes against received naval wisdom of the period, which cautions against lining the interiors of small vessels like *Swan*, for not only did the practice add unnecessary weight, but it deprived the hull of the flexibility essential to a fast and weatherly performance.

It has long been known that Charles I, along with other contemporary European monarchs, saw his larger ships as instruments not just of war but as manifestations of royal prestige. This policy led to decorative and other excesses of his celebrated 100-gun three-decker, *Sovereign of the Seas*, launched in 1637. Evidence from the wreck of *Swan*, built just four years later, now suggests that this pretentious and irrational policy of prestigious embellishment extended down to the smaller vessels of his navy.

As the excavation progresses (it is scheduled to continue until 2002), many new finds are being made. Some are overtly nautical: pieces of rope, sheaves, and parts of pumps. Elements of surviving structure, pinned beneath two mounds of stone ballast, suggest that the ship is quite heavily framed and may, as in the case of earlier copies of Continental privateers, have been misguidedly "beefed up" by conservative English shipwrights.

Other finds are concerned with shipboard routines: wooden lanterns, barrel staves, and an intact naval guncarriage. A 4 lb lead merchant's weight bears the monogram of Charles I and authenticating marks that guarantee its accuracy, shown by a modern controlled weighing to be correct within four places of decimals (Martin, 1998c). Personal possessions include a wooden chest, textiles, leather shoes, pottery, stave-built and turned wooden utensils, and a wooden spoon. The more lavish lifestyles of the captain and his officers is reflected by a large pewter plate, while clay pipes speak of a recreational habit indulged in by all ranks.

About a third of a single, disarticulated human skeleton has now been recovered and subjected to expert examination, which has revealed much about the individual concerned. He was a young man of between the ages of 23 and 25, about 5 ft 4 in (1.66 m) tall, (and would have been a couple of inches taller had not rickets badly bowed his legs in childhood). Apart from this slight deformity, his lower body was unremarkable. The same can not be said of his upper body and limbs, which were extraordinarily well developed, with the muscle groups of the shoulders, arms, and wrists quite exceptionally strong. These are the limbs and muscles required to work a sailing ship. There is also evidence of a repetitive injury to the hip joints, indicative of shock stresses such as might be induced by straining at a capstan bar or regular jumping from heights.

This seaman was well-fed, robust, and healthy. He clearly enjoyed a calorific intake commensurate with his strong physique and the heavy work demanded of him. He would not have fared so well, however, had he survived into later life. A congenital spinal abnormality would have caused severe back problems within a few years, while his teeth, though intact, were being progressively ground down by grit from the stone-ground flour which made up a substantial part of his diet. Severe tooth decay and its consequent agony lay not too far in the future (Black, 1999).

HERITAGE MANAGEMENT, PUBLIC ACCESS
AND PARTICIPATION, AND THE FUTURE

Through a combination of good fortune and good management, Scotland has been spared the excesses of treasure hunting that has dogged the development of underwater archaeology in other regions. Although many early ventures were driven by commercial motives, these were often tempered by at least a measure of archaeological sensitivity and sometimes by the active participation of local museums. This has been especially true in Shetland, where so many historic shipwrecks have been found. Since the 1960s, the County Museum at Lerwick has been highly effective in collecting and conserving shipwreck material.

Following the Protection of Wrecks Act of 1973, which allows specified sites in U.K. waters to be designated and controlled by statutory government agencies, various official bodies have played enlightened and significant roles in managing Scotland's historic shipwreck resource. The National Museums of Scotland partially sponsored work on *Dartmouth* in the 1970s, taking responsibility for conservation and curation of all recoveries from the site. A similar arrangement is now in place with respect to the *Swan* project.

Since 1992, Historic Scotland, which looks after the country's historic buildings and archaeological sites, has been responsible for underwater archaeology and has established the milestone principle (as yet not followed by the other U.K. countries) that underwater sites are to be managed by the same criteria as apply on land. The Royal Commission on the Ancient and Historic Monuments of Scotland, which maintains a nationwide Sites and Monuments Record, is now routinely inputting maritime data, including information on shipwrecks.

These encouraging leads by the regulatory agencies are underpinned by strong programs of education and public participation. St. Andrews University, in addition to its long-running participation in underwater archaeological projects in Scotland and elsewhere, has offered postgraduate training in this field since 1984. The training of avocational divers through the Nautical Archaeology Society's international program is centered at Lochaline, a popular diving resort close to two protected historic wrecks, *Dartmouth* and *Swan*. The Nautical Archaeology Society (NAS), through the Lochaline Dive Centre and in conjunction with Historic Scotland, now runs open days on these wrecks so that interested amateur divers can visit them under supervision.

This popular scheme has gone a long way to negate the hostility felt by many sport divers at being excluded from protected sites. Local dive operators are beginning to regard the preservation of all wrecks, not just protected ones, as a key element in ensuring the future of underwater ecotourism, an activity of increasing economic importance in areas such as the west of Scotland. Museums are now exploiting the potential of shipwreck material as a tourist attraction and educational resource. Access to information on historic shipwrecks in Scotland is available on the Internet through the Scottish Cultural Resources Access Network (SCRAN) scran.ac.uk.

These positive if modest achievements must be viewed with a measure of caution. As it now stands, salvage law still favors the treasure hunter, and there have been some close calls. An alleged (and still unlocated) treasure wreck has generated much local interest and good intentions, but this in turn has attracted frenzied publicity and the unhelpful attentions of international scam-operators. Public funding, though welcome, will always be limited, and innovative ways of utilizing and presenting the shipwreck heritage must be found without compromising its archaeological integrity. Scotland, like other small maritime countries with rich underwater archaeological resources, has challenges to face and problems to solve if these resources are to be exploited constructively and responsibly for the common good.

REFERENCES

Adnams, J., 1974, The *Dartmouth*, A British Frigate Wrecked Off Mull, 1690. *International Journal of Nautical Archaeology* 3(2):269–274.

Albion, R., 1952, The Timber Problem in the Royal Navy. *Mariner's* Mirror 38:4–20.

Bax, A., and Martin, C., 1974, *De Liefde*: A Dutch East Indiaman Lost on the Out Skerries, Shetland, in 1711. *International Journal of Nautical Archaeology* 3(1):81–90.

Black, S., 1999, *Preliminary Report on Human Bones from the Duart Point Wreck.* Unpublished manuscript.

Bound, M., and Sharpe, T., No Date, The Wreck of the Danish Man-of-War *Wrangels Palais* (1687) off Bound Skerry in the Out Skerries (Shetland Islands). In *The Archaeology of Ships of War*, edited by M. Bound, pp. 45–51. Anthony Nelson, Oswestry.

Coles, J., 1971, The Early Settlement of Scotland: Excavations at Morton, Fife. *Proceedings of the Prehistoric Society* 37(2):284–336.

Curle, J., 1911, *A Roman Frontier Post and Its People.* McLehose, Glasgow.

Delgado, J., editor, 1997, *Encyclopaedia of Underwater and Maritime Archaeology.* British Museum Press, London.

Dobbs, C., and Price, R., 1991, The *Kennemerland* Site. The Sixth and Seventh Seasons, 1984 and 1987, and the Identification of Five Golf Clubs. *International Journal of Nautical Archaeology* 20(2):111–122.

Foster, W., and Higgs, K., 1973, The *Kennemerland*, 1971: An Interim Report. *International Journal of Nautical Archaeology* 2(2):291–300.

Gregory, D., 1995, Experiments into the Deterioration Characteristics of Materials on the Duart Point Wreck Site: An Interim Report. *International Journal of Nautical Archaeology* 24(1):61–65.

_____, 1999, Monitoring the Effect of Sacrificial Anodes on the Large Iron Artifacts on the Duart Point Wreck, 1997. *International Journal of Nautical Archaeology* 28(2):164–173.

Holman, R., 1975, The *Dartmouth*: A British Frigate Wrecked off Mull, 1690. 2. Culinary and Related Items. *International Journal of Nautical Archaeology* 4(2):253–265.

Hopkins, P., 1986, *Glencoe and the End of the Highland War.* John Donald, Edinburgh.

Hornell, J., 1973, *The Curraghs of Ireland.* National Maritime Museum, Greenwich.

Hoving, A., 1988, A 17th-century Dutch 134-foot pinke, Part 1. A Reconstruction after Aeloude en Hedendaegse Scheepbouw en Bestier by Nicolaes Witsen 1671. *International Journal of Nautical Archaeology* 17(3):211–222.

McBride, P., 1976, The *Dartmouth*: A British Frigate Wrecked off Mull, 1690. 3. The Guns. *International Journal of Nautical Archaeology* 5(3):189–200.

McGrail, S., 1998, *Ancient Boats in North-West Europe.* Longman, London.

McKee, E., 1976, Identification of Timbers from Old Ships of North-western European Origin. *International Journal of Nautical Archaeology* 5(1):3–12.

McLeay, A., 1986, *The Tobermory Treasure.* Conway Maritime Press, London.

MacLeod, I., 1995, In situ Corrosion Studies on the Duart Point Wreck, 1994. *International Journal of Nautical Archaeology* 24(1):53–59.

McPherson, N., 1877, Notes on Antiquities from the Isle of Eigg. *Proceedings of the Society of Antiquaries of Scotland* 12:594–596.

Martin, C., 1972, *El Gran Grifón*: An Armada Wreck off Fair Isle. *International Journal of Nautical Archaeology* 1:59–71.

_____, 1975, *Full Fathom Five: The wrecks of the Spanish Armada.* Chatto and Windus, London.

_____, 1978, The *Dartmouth*: A British Frigate Wrecked off Mull, 1690. 5. The Ship. *International Journal of Nautical Archaeology* 7(1):29–58.

_____, 1987, A Group of Pipes from the Dutch East Indiaman *Kennemerland*, 1664. In *The Archaeology of the Clay Tobacco Pipe. X. Scotland*, edited by P. Davey, pp. 211–224. BAR British Series 178, Oxford.

_____, 1992a, Water Transport and the Roman Occupations of North Britain. In *Scotland and the Sea*, edited by T.C. Smout, pp. 1–34. John Donald, Edinburgh.

_____, 1992b, The Wreck of the Dutch East Indiaman *Adelaar* off Barra in 1728. In *People and Power in Scotland*, edited by R. Mason and N. Macdougall, pp. 145–169. John Donald, Edinburgh.

_____, 1995a, The Cromwellian Shipwreck off Duart Point, Mull: An Interim Report. *International Journal of Nautical Archaeology* 24(1):15–32.

_____, 1995b, Assessment, Stabilisation and Management of an Environmentally Threatened Seventeenth Century Shipwreck off Duart Point, Mull. In *Managing Ancient Monuments: An Integrated Approach*, edited by A. Berry and I. Brown, pp. 181–189. Clwyd County Council, Mold.

_____, 1998a, *Scotland's Historic Shipwrecks*. Batsford/Historic Scotland, London.

_____, 1998b, *Dartmouth*: The Archaeology and Structural Analysis of a Small Seventeenth Century English Warship. In *Excavating Ships of War*, edited by M. Bound, pp. 110–119. Anthony Nelson, Oswestry.

_____, 1998c, A Caroline Merchant's Weight from the Wreck of the *Swan*, 1653. *International Journal of Nautical Archaeology* 27(2):166–168.

_____, 1999, A 17th-century Binnacle and Mariner's Compasses from Duart Point, Mull. *International Journal of Nautical Archaeology* 28(1):60–69.

Martin, P., 1977, The *Dartmouth*: A British Frigate Wrecked off Mull, 1690. 4. The Clay Pipes. *International Journal of Nautical Archaeology* 6(3):219–223.

_____, 1987, Clay pipes from the Wreck of HMS *Dartmouth*, 1690. A re-assessment. In *The Archaeology of the Clay Tobacco Pipe*. X. Scotland, edited by P. Davey, pp. 225–232. BAR British Series 178, Oxford.

Maxwell, S., 1950, Discoveries in 1934 on King Fergus' Isle and Elsewhere in Loch Laggan, Inverness-shire. *Proceedings of the Society of Antiquaries of Scotland* 85:160–165.

Morrison, I., 1983, Prehistoric Scotland. In *An Historical Geography of Scotland*, edited by G. Whittington and I. Whyte, pp. 1–23. Academic Press, London.

Mowat, R., 1996, *Logboats of Scotland*. Oxbow Monograph 68, Oxford.

Muckelroy, K., 1975, A Systematic Approach to the Investigation of Scattered Wreck Sites. *International Journal of Nautical Archaeology* 4(2):173–190.

_____, 1976, The Integration of Historical and Archaeological Data concerning an Historic Wreck Site: The *Kennemerland*. *World Archaeology* 7(3):280–290.

_____, 1978, *Maritime Archaeology*, Cambridge University Press, Cambridge.

Powley, E., 1972, *The Naval Side of King William's War*. John Baker, London.

Price, R., and Muckelroy, K., 1974, The Second Season of Work on the *Kennemerland* Site, 1973. *International Journal of Nautical Archaeology* 3(2):257–268.

_____, 1977, The *Kennemerland* site. The Third and Fourth Seasons, 1974 and 1976. *International Journal of Nautical Archaeology* 6(3):187–218.

_____, 1979, The *Kennemerland* Site, the Fifth Season. *International Journal of Nautical Archaeology* 8(4):311–320.

Price, R., Muckelroy, K., and Willes, L., 1980, The *Kennemerland* site, a Report on the Lead Ingots. *International Journal of Nautical Archaeology* 9(1):7–25.

Ritchie, A., 1993, *Viking Shetland*. Batsford/Historic Scotland, London.

Robinson, M., 1958, *The van de Velde Drawings*. A catalogue of drawings in the National Maritime Museum, Cambridge.

Steer, K., and Bannerman, J., 1977, *Late Medieval Monumental Sculpture in the West Highlands*. RCAHMS, Edinburgh.

Sténuit, R., 1974, Early Relics of the VOC Trade from Shetland: The Wreck of the Fluit Lastdrager Lost off Yell, 1653. *International Journal of Nautical Archaeology* 3(2):213–256.

_____, 1976, The Wreck of the Pink *Eustafii*: A Transport of the Imperial Russian Navy Lost off Shetland in 1780. *International Journal of Nautical Archaeology* 5(3):221–243.

_____, 1977a, The Wreck of the *Curaçao*: A Dutch Warship Lost off Shetland in 1729. *International Journal of Nautical Archaeology* 6(2):101–125.

_____, 1977b, *La Flute Engloutie*. Plon, Paris.

_____, 1988, *Ces Mondes Secrets ou J'ai Plongé*. Robert Laffont, Paris.

Thrush, A., 1991, In Pursuit of the Frigate. *Historical Research* 64:29–45.

Watkins, T., 1980, A Prehistoric Coracle in Fife. *International Journal of Nautical Archaeology* 9(4):277–286.

Wickham-Jones, C., 1994, *Scotland's First Settlers*. Batsford/Historic Scotland, London.

Chapter 25

Underwater Archaeology in the Republic of Ireland

COLIN BREEN AND AIDAN O'SULLIVAN

INTRODUCTION

Ireland is a damp country. Its temperate climate, high effective precipitation, topography, and extensive low-lying, waterlogged soils mean that its landscape abounds with lakes, rivers, and estuaries. In some parts of the island, water is the dominant topographical feature of the physical landscape, and there can be almost as much water as dry land. The Irish coastline is similarly extensive, indented and complex, a fractal landscape of bays, inlets, and shorelines. Since early postglacial times, Ireland has been a small Atlantic island situated several days sailing off a continental coastline, with all that means for its culture and identity.

Yet underwater archaeology is a perspective that is new to Irish archaeology. For many years, the tendency among the historical and archaeological community of a newly emerging nation had been to look inward, both in theoretical and practical terms. Ireland, the common perception had it, was a society with its origins in the rural landscape, with cows and green fields the most common poetic metaphor for an ethnic identity. In contrast with other island nations, there was no perception that it was the seas around us and the watery seaways between us and the rest of the world that had shaped our society.

Colin Breen, Centre for Maritime Archaeology, University of Ulster, Coleraine, Northern Ireland. **Aidan O'Sullivan**, Department of Archaeology, University College Dublin, Republic of Ireland.

International Handbook of Underwater Archaeology, edited by Carol V. Ruppé and Janet F. Barstad. Kluwer Academic/Plenum Publishers, New York, 2002.

In recent years, archaeological research has shown that the maritime environment has always been a significant factor in the shaping of the Irish social landscape. The sea was a facilitator for contact and trade, a provider of abundant resources central to survival. The same view can be adopted for the inland waterways with lakes and rivers, which served since earliest times as the focus for settlement and provided a means of communications through a wooded and boggy country and an alternative means of food and industrial resources. It is hoped that, through research and management programs, an increased awareness of the potential of the maritime and freshwater cultural resource will help overturn research biases and correct existing prejudices during the coming years.

LAKE ARCHAEOLOGY

History of Research

The archaeology of Irish lakes has always been a subject of interest in Ireland, stretching back to the origins of the discipline itself. In the later 19th century, there was an astonishing spate of discoveries, when large numbers of Irish *crannogs* (artificially-built islands used as lake-dwellings from the early medieval to the early modern periods) were described, excavated, and synthesized, along with contemporary work on prehistoric and early medieval lake settlements in Scotland and Switzerland. Unlike other European countries, however, Ireland made no attempt to carry out underwater investigations of any form. Most crannogs were brought to antiquarian attention because of drainage from inland waterways (Wood-Martin, 1886; Coles and Coles, 1989; O'Sullivan, 1998). Irish crannogs were also a subject of great interest in the 1930s, when the American-funded Harvard Archaeological Expedition, led by Hugh O'Neill Hencken, excavated a number of Bronze Age and Early Medieval crannogs in the midlands (Hencken, 1936, 1942, 1950).

These excavations introduced scientific techniques into Irish archaeology. Moreover, the wealth of artifactual material produced from waterlogged settlement sites enabled Irish archaeologists to begin serious typological and cultural historical studies from comparatively well-dated sites. Ironically, this wealth of evidence also put Irish archaeologists off from further investigations, so intimidating were the apparent resources needed for lake settlement digs. Not until the mid-1980s did Republic archaeologists become actively involved in underwater research.

Largely, this involvement came about with the realization that archaeological sites in lakes were being rapidly plundered by treasure hunters armed with cheap and widely-available metal detectors. The National Museum of Ireland and other Irish authorities reacted both by providing strict government legislation designed to protect this cultural heritage and by doing underwater surveys of their own (Kelly, 1993, 1994). Victor Buckley of the Archaeological Survey of Ireland and Eamonn Kelly of the National Museum of Ireland were heavily involved in the surveys. These archaeologists also collaborated in the late 1980s with the Crannog Archaeology Project (CAP) team, a research project carried out between the State Institutions in the Republic and Cornell University in the United States (Farrell, 1989, 1990; Farrell and Buckley, 1984; Farrell et al., 1989).

The Archaeology of Ireland's Lakes

The archaeology of Ireland's lakes remains largely un-investigated and barely understood. Certainly, Ireland's lake shores provide some of the earliest archaeological evidence for human settlement in Ireland. An Early Mesolithic (c.7000 B.C.) hunter–gatherer campsite was excavated in 1978 on the shores of Lough Boora, County Offaly (Ryan, 1980), producing four fire hearths. Stone axes, chert cores, and tiny flint blades were scattered about the site. Faunal evidence indicated that the inhabitants hunted red deer, wild pig, hare, birds, and fish.

Late Mesolithic (c. 4500 B.C.) lithic scatters and artifacts also have been found on the shores of Lough Derravarragh, Lough Kinale, Lough Iron, Lough Allen, and Lough Gara. Most of these artifact sites were not seriously investigated. More recently, archaeological excavations at Moynagh Lough, County Meath, have produced Late Mesolithic Bann flakes and chert blades from a possible occupation horizon that remains to be fully investigated (O'Sullivan, 1998).

Late Bronze Age (1200–600 B.C.) lake settlements also are an important aspect of Irish archaeology (O'Sullivan, 1998). Excavated sites include a Middle Bronze Age lakeshore settlement at Cullyhanna Lough, industrial sites at Lough Eskragh, County Tyrone, and rich domestic settlements at Moynagh Lough, Knocknalappa, Clonfinlough and Ballinderry crannog 2.

Bronze Age lake settlements vary greatly in size, construction, siting, and complexity, but they have tended to be interpreted in simple terms as the domestic settlements of families, with some measure of isolation and need for defense in their siting. However, the variation in the structures and finds indicates a range of social, economic, and cult functions for these sites (O'Sullivan, 1998b). Some may have been temporary farmsteads of pastoralists who herded cattle on the summer marshes. It is also true that some Bronze Age lake settlements produced a wider array of domestic equipment, which would seem to argue for more long-term settlement. This seems to contrast greatly with contemporary drylands settlements, so these sites should be considered as high-status or elite centers. It is also possible that material was gathered for cult practices into these settlements at certain times of the year.

The crannog is the most common form of lake settlement in Ireland, with at least 1200 known examples widely distributed across the lakelands of northern and western Ireland. These sites usually appear today as tree-clad islands and rocky cairns in lakes and are one of the most evocative surviving features of the ancient Irish landscape (Wood-Martin, 1886; Kelly, 1991; O'Sullivan, 1998, 2000). Crannogs in Ireland are islands, wholly or largely artificially built, usually circular (typically 15–30 m in diameter), built-up of layers of dumped peat, brushwood (often woven), heavier timbers, stones, soil, and rubbish—whatever material was most readily available. The crannog's chief characteristic is that it was originally surrounded by a retaining ring of close-set vertical timber piles.

Crannogs typically date to the Early Medieval period (A.D. 5th–11th centuries), but many are known to have been occupied and used in prehistory until A.D. 17th century (O'Sullivan, 1998c). Typically, archaeological excavation has revealed well-preserved houses, pathways, fences, and working areas, metal, bone and wooden artifacts, food and industrial debris, and a wide range of environmental evidence in the waterlogged deposits.

Crannogs are generally interpreted as the homesteads of strong farmers, lower nobility, or as "royal centers." There is little doubt that many crannogs were the latter, used as summer lodges, strategic refuges, and military strongholds by the many kings of Early Medieval Ireland (each local territory or *tuath* had its own king). Lagore, Cro-inis and Island MacHugh are all historically attested royal sites, while Moynagh Lough crannog produced a massive central house, an array of high-status finds, and abundant metalworking evidence, which seems to indicate that it, too, was a royal center.

Early Medieval crannogs also were used as centers for craft production and the recirculation of goods through a pre-urban landscape. Moynagh Lough crannog had extensive evidence for the spatial organization of bronzeworking; two metalworking areas with their pits and furnaces were excavated. There were also numerous crucible fragments for brooches, mounts, studs, and other decorated items. A range of other crafts practiced on crannogs included glassmaking, boneworking, and woodworking. Several crannogs have produced high-status imported goods, such as E-ware and glass, which presumably was brought into Ireland from continental Europe by coastal traders.

Crannogs also were used as locations for ironworking. Unprocessed iron ore, slag, and iron bloom was found at Lough Faughaun, iron slag at Ballinderry 2, and iron furnace bottoms at Lagore. Bofeenaun is highly unusual in that it was used solely for iron production and could be considered an entirely industrial rather than a domestic site. It is possible that many small stone cairns situated adjacent to larger crannogs were used as iron-working sites, thus safely removing the threat of fire from the main site.

Much needs to be investigated about Irish crannogs. Although we have some knowledge of their dates, construction, function, and role in early Irish society, we have barely started to explore their origins, their role in the settlement landscape, how long they were occupied, by whom, and for what reasons.

Forthcoming Research Projects

An Irish government-funded research institute, The Discovery Programme, embarked on a major program of research on the archaeology of lake settlement in Ireland (O'Sullivan, 1998a), because of the growing interest in underwater archaeology in Ireland. The program, directed by Eoin Grogan, will adopt underwater geophysics, survey, and excavation techniques to explore a type of archaeology that has seen little investigation in recent years. The lake settlement project will operate as a multiperiod, regional landscape study focused on many aspects of the subject. Particular regions and study areas will be chosen, while thematic studies will explore the archaeology of allied subjects.

The project's first phase will concentrate on establishing available archaeological, historical, and environmental knowledge of the various study areas. The second phase will be one of large-scale fieldwork, including both intensive and extensive archaeological survey linked to dendrochronological and radiocarbon dating. Underwater archaeological investigations will be a major part of this survey. An integrated program of palaeoenvironmental research will be aimed at modeling past landscapes and relating environmental change to social and economic change in both local and regional terms. The archaeological and palaeoenvironmental data will be used within a geographical information system to enable reconstruction of past landscapes and to investigate settlement patterns. The third phase will include archaeological excavation, ranging in scale and resources from test trenching to open-area excavations of wetland occupation horizons. These excavations should aim to adopt the full battery of multidisciplinary techniques employed on modern wetlands excavations. Even at this early stage, it is obvious that the Discovery Programme's research on lake settlement archaeology will have a major effect on a subject close to the heart of Irish archaeology.

RIVERS

History of Research

The Irish landscape is dissected by many large rivers, which flow in all directions into bays and estuaries around the country's coastline. The rivers have always served as nautical routeways up into the country, as physical and territorial boundaries to drylands communications, and crossings at nodes where fording points and bridges channeled routeways through particular locations. Historically, rivers and river mouths have been common sites for rural and urban riverbank settlements.

Since the late 19th century, when extensive government-funded arterial drainage works began, Irish rivers have produced large amounts of Neolithic, Bronze Age, Iron Age, and historic-period artifacts that were uncovered by dredging. The Rivers Boyne, Shannon, and Barrow, as well as several other large rivers, also have extensive sacred and secular landscapes associated with their river valleys.

Riverine archaeological remains were not investigated by Irish underwater archaeologists until the late 1980s, when a number of fording points were systemmatically surveyed for the National Museum of Ireland, namely the River Suck and the River Boyne (Kelly, 1993b). Contract (CRM) archaeologists also have been active in recent years in landscape and underwater surveys for Environmental Impact Assessments in advance of river dredging operations and flood relief development.

Underwater Archaeological Excavations at Clonmacnoise Wooden Bridge

Underwater archaeology in rivers has leapt into public prominence in Ireland in recent years as a result of the Clonmacnoise bridge excavations. This large wooden structure, which crosses the River Shannon and dates to A.D. 804, was discovered by underwater archaeologists in 1994. Between 1995 and 1998, it has been the subject of detailed underwater survey and excavation by Management for Archaeology Underwater, in a project directed by Aidan O'Sullivan and Donal Boland (O'Sullivan and Boland, 1999) and funded by the National Monuments Service. The site has been the subject of much national media interest, thus introducing the Irish public to the results of underwater archaeology. It has also led to a more receptive view among the Irish archaeological authorities toward underwater archaeology.

Clonmacnoise Bridge is situated on a relatively narrow part of the River Shannon (about 160 m wide), in the heart of the Irish midlands. Its location is likely to have been caused by proximity to the well-known monastic town of Clonmacnoise, County Offaly. The bridge is situated on a natural routeway across the island, a glacial esker that runs up to the bank of the river and has served as a routeway throughout historic times. The river itself is fairly shallow at Clonmacnoise, although it never could have served as a natural ford, since the riverbed is composed entirely of soft silty clay.

The bridge was constructed by driving two parallel lines of posts vertically into the river clays to a depth of 3.5 m. This was accomplished by arranging the posts in pairs, the upstream and downstream posts being about 4–4.5 m apart and each pair spaced at 5–6 m intervals across the river. The discovery of several narrow, sharpened, roundwood posts beside these massive verticals indicates that the alignment of the bridge was first marked out by quickly driving in a line of hazel and alder saplings across the river. The large vertical posts were all of roundwood oak about 40 cm in diameter, which had been hewn to a square cross-section and with sapwood left sapwood along the edges. The verticals were sharpened to a blunt point with iron axes, and the tips had two augur holes drilled through them, for reasons still unknown. The posts were kept from sinking into the deep, semiliquid clays by an ingenious system of individual base-plates.

Reconstructing the upper structure of the bridge is a slightly more difficult interpretative task. Few remains of the upper portions of the vertical posts are lying on the riverbed. However, it seems certain that the upper part of the structure had a plank or wattle walkway. The posts probably projected high above this walkway, and there may have been a simple handrail. There appears to be little evidence for repair or the construction of a second bridge at this point. The lifespan of exposed timber bridges is typically about 50 years; without repair, their lifespan is even shorter. Major repairs are often required after 10–15 years, mostly confined to the upper deck. After about 25 years, the structure is generally considered unsafe. The vertical posts typically rot after 20–40 years. Whatever the arguments about these details, it seems likely that the Clonmacnoise wooden bridge was out of use by A.D. mid-9th century.

Dugout Boats and Other Finds. The underwater surveys and excavation at Clonmacnoise have uncovered a range of other finds on the riverbed. There are at least nine dugout boats along the line of the bridge, both upstream and downstream. Originally carved with axe and adze from whole roundwood trunks, the dugouts vary in form. Several are found in close association with the bridge timbers and probably also date to the Early Medieval period. Their length varies from 5.5 m to 3 m, with a typical width of 60 cm.

There are also some interesting details. One dugout boat found beside a vertical bridge post had repair patches at its end, where the boat cracked in antiquity and was fixed by nailing small carved oak planks into the internal floor. Another, found by a vertical post, had two separate wooden ribs nailed and doweled into the floor. A third, also found by a vertical post, contained two Early Medieval woodworking axes (a felling axe and a general-purpose carpentry axe) lying in the floor, with parts of the wooden handles still in the sockets. Another dugout boat produced an Early Medieval iron axe on the floor, and yet another had a whetstone for sharpening axes. Iron was common in another form on the riverbed, as large blocks and fragments of slag. This was probably dumped into the river from nearby ironworking areas.

Perhaps the most exciting artifactual find was a large decorated bronze basin of an A.D. 8th–9th century date. It was found lying in the river silts beside a vertical post of the bridge and may have had some function in the liturgy of the early Irish church, such as holding wine, or in the washing of the hands. It is damaged along its sides, evidently from a series of violent blows. The archaeologist is tempted to reach for documents on raids on the monastery by Irish kings and by Viking pillagers in the 9th century, as a means of explaining the loss of this valuable item in the river.

Historical Context of the Bridge. In A.D. 804, the monastery of Clonmacnoise was under the patronage of the overlords of Connaught. In later years, it came under the hegemony of the Clann Cholmain kings of the southern Ui Neill. Like Hiberno–Norse Dublin, Clonmacnoise was strategically placed on the border between provinces. However, it was primarily a Connaught monastery and perceived as the entrance to that province. A bridge was an obvious construction, given that it is technically in the territory of Mide.

In A.D. 8th and 9th centuries, the monastic town was expanding. Domestic structures and industrial working areas have been found in the vicinity of the modern graveyard by Heather King and elsewhere by Con Manning. The monastery was becoming a center for learning and art, with the production of such manuscripts as *Lebor na hUidre*, the high crosses, church building, and fine metalwork. The bridge may have been part of this confident expansion in population and works, with the added important role of physically linking the monastery with its political hinterland. It is also possible that it was built as a military venture, to provide access by the Connacht kings to neighboring rival territories. It is highly likely that geophysical surveys and underwater investigations planned for the near future will open up the archaeology of Ireland's rivers.

COASTAL ARCHAEOLOGY

History of Research

The archaeology of the coast and its associated wetlands has become a subject of interest in Ireland only recently, even though the coast was an area of concentrated settlement from earliest times. This is even more surprising given that Ireland is an island nation in an important location in northwestern Europe, and much of its history has been dominated by the sea. Vikings established major trading settlements at Dublin, Waterford, Wexford, Cork, and Limerick, towns that in turn became an integral part of the settlement pattern of the Anglo–Normans in the 12th and 13th centuries.

Shannon Estuary

While these towns have been the subject of much study and excavation, the rest of the coastline has been neglected. Pioneering research on the Shannon Estuary in the southwest of the country has begun to redress this imbalance. Between 1992 and 1995, the North Munster Project of the Discovery Programme has carried out several seasons of intertidal archaeological surveys in the estuary, revealing an astonishing array of prehistoric and medieval archaeological landscapes buried under the mudflats. The study has produced evidence of intensive cultural activity dating from early prehistoric times to the modern industrial era (O'Sullivon 2001).

Neolithic Occupation Site and Forests on the Shannon Estuary. The foreshore near Carrigdirty Rock is producing a range of early prehistoric material. A potential Early Neolithic occupation site is being exposed over a 45 m stretch of foreshore. A number of finds are emerging from a band of estuarine clays: ancient remains of reeds, wood fragments, twigs, and shells, suggesting that the site was originally located near reed beds or by the marshy banks of a tidal creek.

The most important find is a large fragment of basketry, tightly woven from narrow reeds using a complex twill-like technique. This basket has produced an Early Neolithic radiocarbon date of 4880 ± 50 B.P. (3780–3531 cal. B.C., Beta-102087). A single fragment of human skull also was found in the clays and has been identified as the frontal-parietal part of the cranium from an adult aged at least 25–35 years. It, too, has been dated to the Early Neolithic at 4730 ± 60 B.P. (3673–3360 cal. B.C., Beta-102086).

Neolithic submerged forests of Scots pine and oak have been recorded at nine separate locations on the estuary (O'Sullivan, 1996a). These submerged forests are potentially useful for the ecological reconstruction of ancient woodlands and the calibration of sealevel rise in the Shannon estuary. At Meelick Rocks, County Limerick, on the upper foreshore, the trunks and root systems of an oak–alder woodland have been dated to the Late Neolithic 4160 ± 20 B.P (2883–2623 B.C., GrN-21930). Submerged roots in peats at the lower part of the foreshore have been dated to the Mesolithic at 6240 ± 25 B.P. (5312–5077 cal. B.C., GrN-21929).

Bronze Age Marshland Huts, Platforms, and Trackways.   Bronze Age archaeology on the Shannon estuary foreshore generally comprises wooden trackways and hut structures associated with both organic peats and estuarine clays (O'Sullivan, 1995a, 1996b). At Carrigdirty Rock, County Limerick (800 m west of the possible Neolithic site described above), several wooden structures have been recorded on an eroding shelf of organic peats at −0.20 m OD. The peats are rich in woody fragments, and macrofossil studies indicate the presence of Cyperaceae and *Phragmites*. The peats have in situ vertical and bedded stems and rhizomes of reeds, suggesting that they were laid down in reed-swamp and saltmarsh, with carr woodland found on slightly drier ground.

An unusual wooden structure has been recorded on the peat shelf, a concentration of at least 22 vertical roundwood posts forming an oval structure measuring approximately 4.70 m × 3.50 m. A single piece of immature calf-bone was recovered within the group of posts, and a sample of sharpened post has provided a radiocarbon date of 3330 ± 25 B.P. (1687–1527 cal. B.C., GrN-20976), in the Middle Bronze Age. To the west, a second structure is represented by another cluster of vertical wooden posts with similar toolmarks on the sharpened ends, and a spread of large stone slabs among which were scattered the mandible, tibia, and femur bones of cattle (*Bos taurus* L.) between two and four years old.

A shallow, oval pit measuring 80 × 50 cm was recorded among the trunks and roots of an adjacent submerged carr woodland. The pit was packed with disarticulated red deer bone and pink-footed goose bone. Chopped pig bone and mature deer antler has been recovered from the neighboring foreshore. Other finds from the Bronze Age peats include a number of large split oak planks laid horizontally and at irregular orientations on the peat. One plank measured nearly 5 m long × 1.2 m wide. The planks were tangentially cleft from large oak trunks, cut across and possibly burned at the ends. It is still unknown what they were used for, but they appear too large for use as a trackway. It seems likely that more planks will be found in the peats. It is worth noting that large planks in Bronze Age coastal wetlands typically have been found to be associated with plank-boat construction.

The Carrigdirty Rock structures can be interpreted as the remains of small conical or dome-shaped huts constructed by bending over and tying together saplings with a thatch of reeds. Such huts could have provided shelters for herders tending cattle on the summer marshes in the manner of early medieval Irish "booleying". The calf bone may be important in this regard, since historically calves were born in spring. The presence of a young calf on the marshes would therefore place the Carrigdirty Rock occupation activities in the summer or early autumn.

Middle and Late Bronze Age wetlands occupations are an important component of the settlement record in later prehistoric Ireland, but few coastal sites have been investigated (O'Sullivan, 1996b).

A Late Bronze Age wooden structure has been recorded in estuarine clays on the upper Fergus Estuary at Islandmagrath, County Clare, a complex construction of woven hurdle panels laid between two parallel rows of posts. Wattle rods are woven through the posts. The structure measures at least 35 m long, disappearing inland into the clays of the upper foreshore. It is at least 2 m wide, but it is clear that more wood lies buried in the foreshore clays. A single find from this site was a length of twisted withy tie or rope. The structure drops at least 1.5 m down the shore, suggesting that it originally sloped down steep mudflats. A sample of narrow hazel rod provided a radiocarbon date of 2540 ± 20 B.P. (Cal. 799–602 B.C., GrN-20974).

Environmental evidence indicates that the structure was laid on tide-deposited estuarine clays, probably to create a stable surface on the soft mudflats or to make a waterfront structure by the channel. Its function is unclear, but it can be interpreted as either a "hard" or complex wooden jetty for beaching and unloading boats or as a well-built trackway providing access to the lower part of the shore. If it is interpreted as a trackway, it probably was situated on a routeway between two former islands, Island-magrath and Carnelly, in the coastal marshlands.

Medieval Fishtraps

By the early medieval period, it is clear that the local communities settled along the estuary were constructing and using tidal fishtraps to provide food for the table and fish for urban markets. These fishtraps typically were ebb-weirs, designed to guide fish, moving down with the falling tide, into traps. Post-and-wattle fences leading to woven baskets and nets typically were constructed across the narrow creeks that dissect the mudflats.

The earliest fishtrap is represented by a post-and-wattle fence on the upper Fergus Estuary, County Clare (O'Sullivan, 1994a), dated to the Early Historic period at 1495 ± 35 B.P. (A.D. 447–637 cal., GrN-20139). The structure measured at least 8.5 m long and was composed of narrow roundwood hazel, willow, and birch posts driven vertically about 70 cm deep into blue–grey estuarine clays. There is some evidence for Early Historic period settlement on the estuary, represented by three earthen ringforts on the dryland edge. Ringforts are known to have been constructed between A.D. 6th and 10th centuries as the homesteads of wealthy farmers and their families.

Medieval fishtraps have been discovered on the mudflats of the Deel Estuary, off the site of a known medieval castle at Ballynash, County Limerick (O'Sullivan, 1995b). This complex is particularly interesting in that the structures seem to have been repaired and then replaced with successive phases of construction. Deel 1, dated to 900 ± 20 B.P. (A.D. 1037–1188 cal., GrN-21932) is a V-shaped fishtrap, oriented to catch fish on the flooding tide with two converging post-and-wattle fences measuring more than 30 m long. A cluster of posts at the apex of the two fences may be the remains of a trap. Immediately to the south lies the remains of a second structure, Deel 2, similar in construction and orientation, a line of stout posts also erected on a northeast–southwest orientation and measuring up to 8 m long before it disappears into a clay bank. It has been radiocarbon-dated to 740 ± 15 B.P. (A.D. 1261–1278 cal., GrN-20975). A third, similar wooden fence (Deel 3) is situated yet farther to the south and has been dated to 640 ± 20 B.P. (A.D. 1282–1391 cal., GrN-21931). The evidence suggests the construction and renewal of fishtraps in the area between A.D. 12th and 14th centuries.

A dense concentration of medieval fishtraps has been recorded on the Shannon estuary mudflats, adjacent to the site of the Anglo–Norman borough of Bunratty, County Clare, one of the most important medieval settlements in the region. Established by the

Anglo–Normans in A.D. early 13th century, by A.D. 1287 the borough had a substantial population of about 1000 persons, with a harbor, seigneurial castle, parish church, markets, watermill, fishpond, and rabbit warren. It was also an important port: 14th-century texts refer to it as "Bunratty of the wide roads, oared galleys and safe harbour."

Intertidal surveys have revealed a further important economic element to Bunratty. There are at least 15 fishtraps in the vicinity, located both on the River Owenogarney channel and on the narrower mudflat creeks which drain into the Shannon estuary.

Other Intertidal Surveys. Since the inception of the Shannon Estuary survey, there have been several other intertidal surveys, notably on the Boyne estuary, County Meath, in Waterford Harbour, County Wexford–Kilkenny, Bannow Bay, County Wexford and, most recently, in Bantry Bay, County Cork. These surveys were carried out either as Environmental Impact Assessments (EIAs) or as research programs. Interestingly, each survey has produced its own type of evidence, indicating that intertidal survey is a useful means of revealing past regional and local identities. These intertidal archaeological discoveries give a first insight into the settlement and exploitation of Ireland's coastal wetlands and their surrounding landscapes.

THE ARCHAEOLOGY OF WRECK

History of Research

Ireland's first underwater shipwreck investigations took place in the late 1960s and early 1970s on the sites of two 1588 Spanish Armada wrecks off the north and west coasts. In 1967, Sid Wignal and his dive team located the wreck of *Santa Maria de La Rosa* after three years of searching in Blasket Sound, County Kerry. The wreck was found in 38 m of water in a high energy area with strong currents and pronounced tidal movement. Excavations on the wreck's ballast mound, the only section standing proud of the seabed, revealed a portion of the lowermost section of the ship's hull and exposed a section of the keelson and a mast step. A number of anchors and smaller artifactual material were recovered, but no armaments were found.

A number of years later, the City of Derry Sub-Aqua Club located the wreck site of a second Armada ship, *La Trinidad Valencera*, at Kinnaego Bay in County Donegal. Anxious to ensure that the site was dealt with scientifically, the club invited Colin Martin of the University of St. Andrews to direct excavations. The work uncovered a wealth of organic and artifactual material. Unfortunately, no coherent wreck structure survived.

Although investigation of these wrecks highlighted the wealth of archaeological information that can be obtained from such sites, contemporary mainstream Irish archaeology was not impressed. Indeed, there was a prevalent perception within the community that these sites were not part of our national heritage but were rather accidentally deposited on our shores and were unrelated to the national development of this island.

A number of other important wreck discoveries were made during the early 1980s. Seabed clearance operations in Bantry Bay, following the explosion of the oil tanker *Beetlegeuse* in 1979, located the remains of the French frigate *La Surveillante*, scuttled north of Whiddy Island in January 1797. The frigate was part of an ill-fated French invasion of Ireland meant to topple English rule, led by Wolfe Tone of the United Irishmen and the famous French naval leader La Hoche. As with similar campaigns throughout Ireland's history, the attempt failed for a variety of reasons, including poor preparation and management, terrible weather, and the dispersal of the invasion fleet. *La Surveillante* limped into Bantry Bay in December 1796 in poor shape. It was scuttled a few days later.

The wreck currently lies in 34 m of water, partially buried in silt and mud. Recent, integrated marine research involving diving archaeologists, geophysicists, and geomorphologists indicates that the vessel is upright on the seabed with up to 2 m of the vessel's lowermost surviving hull structure buried in the mud (Breen and Barton, 1998; Breen, 2001). When it was scuttled, the vessel appears to have hit the bottom bow-first and settled onto the seabed. The stern section sits on a hard gravelly substrate and stands to a height of more than 4 m proud of the seabed. Most of the original copper sheathing remains in situ, but much of the framing and planking has eroded away. Thirteen 12-pounder iron cannon were found on the vessel, as well as the brick foundations of the galley structure and a wide assortment of artifactual material.

Other major wrecks have been discovered throughout the last 20 years. A section of clinker planking from a double-ended 13th-century vessel caulked with moss was located by divers from a magnetic anomaly in Dublin Bay. The planking was similar in type and date to the many medieval timbers recovered during land excavations in Dublin's Viking town medieval waterfront.

A large stem post from a medieval vessel also was subject to investigations by the state's underwater unit in Waterford Estuary. Local fishermen had recovered the timber from the seabed after it had become snagged in the lines during net clearance on an upstanding fish weir. Three possible 1588 Armada wrecks were found by a team of English divers at Streedagh Strand in County Sligo in 1985. The divers uncovered a large rudder, gun carriage, and other artifacts from one site, which they have interpreted as the wreck of the *Juliana*. Numerous other wrecks have been located and explored, and their investigation has served to highlight the potential and extent of Ireland's wreck resource.

National Maritime Sites and Monuments Records

Fundamental to the successful management of the archaeological resource is an understanding of the nature and extent of that resource. Central to this understanding has been the establishment of Sites and Monuments Records (SMR). County SMRs of dryland sites have been active on this island since the 1960s, their range defined by the research interests of archaeologists at that time. While the SMRs slowly evolved to take account of all archaeological sites, they failed to record intertidal or subtidal sites. This was not a deliberate policy of exclusion but reflected the lack of awareness of the potential extent of the submerged resource.

Only in recent years, through the work of individual researchers, has the potential of the marine environment been highlighted. State bodies have in turn recognized this potential and initiated survey programs. In February 1997, the National Monuments Service, in the then-Department of Arts, Culture and Gaeltacht, established a national maritime survey, essentially an extension of the existing land SMR that extends the survey into the culturally dynamic intertidal and subtidal environments that surround this island.

The survey's first stage is an exhaustive, desk-based exercise that assesses the potential resource. A comprehensive computerized and paper-based record is being assembled that eventually will be incorporated into the National SMR Archive. The survey is also involved in extensive geophysical surveys of sections of the Irish coast, in an attempt to develop comprehensive mapping programs and landscape studies of the maritime archaeological resource. These programs are driven by landscape research agendas that attempt to establish a seamless view of our maritime heritage. All personnel employed on the survey are archaeologists with commercial diving qualifications who are fully equipped to carry out underwater surveys and operations.

Preliminary analysis of the SMR wreck data allows a number of observations on the nature and extent of the wreck resource around this coast. However, the observations are based almost exclusively on a desk-based assessment and should be treated accordingly. Only after a dedicated program of field mapping and research will a more concrete analysis be forwarded.

Not surprisingly, the wreck record is heavily biased toward the postmedieval period. This is largely due to the nature of documentary sources that began to record annual ship loss only in the 1740s. Eleven percent of the records date to the period 1751–1800, while only three percent are dated earlier. Twenty-seven percent are datable to 1801–1850, marking more systematic recording, while 39 percent date to 1851–1900. This high percentage marks not only a concerted effort by authorities to record ship loss, it also marks the large upsurge in shipping and coastal trading activity in the second half of the 19th century. Much of this activity is associated with the movement of goods and raw materials associated with the new industries developing in this industrial period. The movement of coal cargoes from Britain to Ireland was particularly active.

Whereas 20 percent of Irish wrecks date between 1901–1945, 32 percent of English wrecks date to the same period. The only exception to this in Ireland is the coast of Donegal, where nearly 35 percent of ships lost off that county were lost after 1901, many while participating in Atlantic convoys during wartime. Convoys passed along this coastline to and from the United Kingdom and were prime targets of German submarines, which patrolled these waters incessantly.

The extent of loss around the English coasts at this time can be explained by the large amount of loss during both world wars, while the decrease in Irish wrecks can be attributed to an increased awareness of safety at sea and improvements in ship and boat technology. Many wrecks lost in Irish waters during this 45-year period occurred during World War I, while neutrality during World War II helped to reduce loss considerably but not totally, as a number of merchant ships found out.

An analysis of wreck references supplies an indication of the distribution of wrecks around the coast. The majority are located on the south coast, with 42 percent in waters off Wexford and Cork (each with 21 percent). The east coast counties have 25 percent of wrecks, with Dublin accounting for 14 percent of the references, while the west coast, including the counties from Kerry to Donegal, accounts for 25 percent of the wrecks.

That the shorter east coast has more wrecks than the entire western seaboard is not a surprise. Throughout history, there has been far more shipping traffic in the Irish Sea than along the western coast. This is especially true of traffic between the east coast ports and the harbors of Britain. Concentrations of sites in Dundalk Bay and at the entrances to the ports of Drogheda and Dublin testify to this traffic. A number of these vessels would have traded with the ports of Limerick and Galway, but sea traffic on western waters must have been dominated by smaller, more localized craft engaged in fishing and coastal trade.

The number of wrecks around Wexford can be explained by the sheer density of traffic in the southern Irish Sea and the nature of the waters off Wexford. Shallow shoals, banks, and rocks have always posed a major threat to shipping. Spots such as Tuskar Rock and the Saltees are surrounded by hundreds of wrecks. Similarly, the coastline of

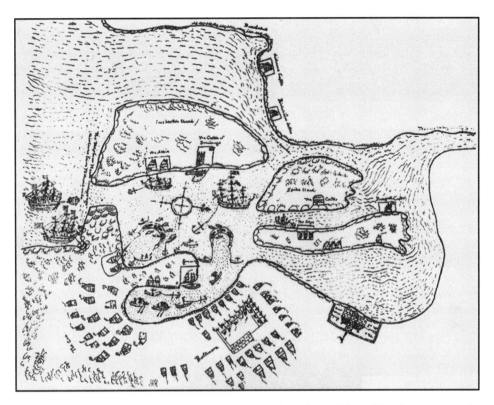

Figure 25.1. An early plan of Baltimore, County Cork, dated to about 1615 A.D. This plan epitomises the nature of maritime archaeology in Ireland, illustrating the four primary facets of coastal archaeological studies: settlement, defense, communications, and exploitation.

Cork has prominent medieval harbors with extensive shipping, including Youghal, Cork, and Baltimore (Figure 25.1). The waters off Cork are prime fishing grounds that have attracted fleets for centuries, but the county's coastline poses its own threats, being rocky and unforgiving, and with few established landfalls.

Wreck distribution is probably higher on the east and southern coasts, with increased rates of survival and better preservation of wreck material; the nature of the bottom and lower energy levels of the east coast's marine environment in particular should lead to increased levels of preservation. On the other hand, the exposed shores of the west coast militate against large- scale survival. Each section of the coast and its individual environmental attributes must be treated separately.

The weather is the biggest single contributor to shipping loss and loss of life at sea. This is borne out again and again in official records and enquiries into wreck instances. Statistics from the records support this: 53 percent of all recorded wrecks were lost in the four winter months of November through February, with 15 percent of the total lost in January alone. This percentage contrasts sharply with the figure of 10 percent of wrecks lost during June, July, and August. A closer examination of this 10 percent show that about five percent were lost as a result of conflict, further highlighting the role of the weather during the winter months, when conflicts were at a minimum. The effect of the weather is also greatly exaggerated when a vessel is not seaworthy and is incapable of dealing with the stresses of storms or strong winds.

A certain amount of economic information can be gleaned from the wreck data. By examining the ports of origin and destination of the wrecks lost in Irish waters, as well as cargoes carried, one gets a general idea of the nature of marine mercantile trade and activity. One striking statistic is the number of English vessels wrecked: Available port-of-origin data show that 29 percent of wrecks originated in England, highlighting the extent of cross-channel trade; yet only 21 percent with cargoes were destined for England, showing Irish dependence on imports. Where cargo data were available, 16 percent of wrecks lost were carrying coal, a major import commodity in the postmedieval period. Most of the coal was destined for the ports of eastern Ireland, indicating the more industrial nature of east coast industries; the western ports imported far less. Foodstuffs and livestock were the most common cargo, and building materials and coal accounted for 16 percent each of the overall total. Nine percent of wrecks were engaged in fishing, while six percent carried passengers. Only four percent were military, pointing to the expertise of naval crews making nonconflict passages.

LEGISLATION AND MANAGEMENT

Archaeological monuments and landscapes under water pose management and conservation problems that cannot be solved with existing land management strategies; they require independent solutions. The primary problem is the physical environment of the sites, which can be hugely dynamic but visually very beautiful. It is important to realize that these monuments are an integral part of their environment and should not be divorced from it. For example, one cannot address the conservation of a shipwreck site without understanding the site's interaction with the underwater biological ecosystem its submergence has created, and its overall landscape context in the underwater environment. The oceanographic factors of any site need to be addressed, as do the geomorphological processes active in its vicinity. These issues can be addressed only in an integrated, multidisciplinary manner with the participation of as many interests as possible.

Most archaeological sites eventually will reach some form of equilibrium with their environment, after which their natural rate of decay will slow markedly. However, many development-driven factors can upset this natural equilibrium with the surrounding environment and hasten site destruction. Erection and subsequent dredging of harbors, laying of cable and pipelines, gravel and sand extraction, and intensive fishing methods can all negatively affect an underwater site.

As a fragile, nonrenewable resource, archaeological sites require protection from these and many other effects in the waters of the Irish State. The primary tool used by the state to protect the archaeological resource has been protective legislation. The Republic has opted for blanket protection of sites, a system whithatch attempts to afford protection to all sites and objects which lie under water.

The relevant pieces of legislation are the *National Monuments Amendments Acts* of 1987 and 1994 and the *Merchant Shipping Salvage and Wreck Act* of 1933. The provisions of these acts include some of the most comprehensive pieces of heritage legislation anywhere in Europe. The acts aim to provide full protection for all underwater sites and limit all activities carried out on them. For example, the High Court Judgment in the Streedagh Strand Armada Case, in which a group of English divers attempted to lay salvage claims on a number of wreck sites at Streedagh in Sligo, recognized that wreck sites should be treated under the National Monuments Acts as opposed to the Merchant Shipping Act (Moore, 1995).

In the past, this comprehensive system of protection has been mistakenly interpreted as draconian by diving organizations and other marine users, a view that shows a fundamental lack of understanding of the acts and a failure to recognize their purpose: to protect a fragile and diminishing resource.

The provisions of the acts can be summarized as follows:

- All archaeological sites and archaeological objects over 100 years old are protected. The National Monuments Acts also protect wreck sites of major historical importance under 100 years of age. To date, the *Lusitania* has been so designated, and the *Aud*, a German ship involved in gunrunning for the 1916 Rising and scuttled off Cork Harbor, is being considered for this designation.
- All activities on underwater sites are subject to a licensing system: Any person wishing to dive on an archaeological site that is *"lying on, in or under the seabed or on or in land covered by water,"* or who interferes with a site in any way, must apply for a license. This is a straightforward procedure; only in very rare cases is a dive license refused.
- Any archaeological site or object found under water must be reported to the authorities. The National Monuments Amendment Act of 1994 notes that the finding of archaeological objects must be reported to the Director of the National Museum, while wreck sites and other such monuments must be reported to the Commissioners of Public Works. This reporting policy ensures that sites are recorded into the SMR and that protective and management measures can be implemented.

The Merchant Shipping Act requires that, regardless of age, all objects removed from the seabed must be reported to the Receiver of Wreck. A network of receivers is based along the coasts.

The acts also provide for the involvement of the director of the National Museum in the disposal of wrecks that come under salvage law (Kirwan, 1995). In the event of a salvage claim on a wreck, where no claim of ownership is present, the director can decide whether the wreck is important, in which case he may take delivery of the wreck and compensate the receiver for any expenses incurred.

Besides national legislation, an increasing number of European Union directives take account of environmental protection. In particular, European Community Directive 85/337 requires environmental assessments for many coastal developments, specifying that archaeology and architectural heritage be recognized as an integral part of the environment and be treated as such.

Although comprehensive legislation is in place, a problem remains with the actual policing of the act. The creation of an archaeological diving unit and the use of inshore mobile national customs units on many occasions has countered this problem to some extent, but it is only through local community education and vigilance that coastal policing can be effective.

Much work has been done on the protection of underwater sites, on paper, through legislative means. However, there has been little research or work on physical preservation of seabed sites. In situ preservation recognizes that many underwater sites are not stable and are actively undergoing erosion from a number of sources. In the past, the only way of dealing with active erosion was either to ignore the problem or excavate the site. Now more informed methods of site management are being introduced.

The introduction of protective membranes onto a site is one solution. Several types of membranes have been used. Colin Martin has experimented with the placement of sandbags on the site of the Armada wreck, *Trinidad de la Valencera*, off Ireland's north coast. This method has been used on a number of sites around the world but must be approached with caution. Placement of such a "hard" membrane could result in further erosion scouring under the site or could introduce a whole new set of erosive activities in the area directly surrounding it. Softer membranes, such as nets that take account of the fluid and mobile nature of underwater sediments, can be pinned to the seabed.

The United States and Australia have experimented with the introduction of sacrificial anodes onto iron and metal wrecks. This process attempts to stabilize archaeological material on the seabed so that researchers do not have to use the expensive process of raising material to the surface through the traumatic air–water interface.

The recent removal and reburial of seven threatened dugout canoes from the river at Clonmacnoise is an example of proactive conservation measures undertaken by the state. This strategy has been adopted at other sites, including the removal and reburial in deeper water of a Iron Age wooden boat built in the Mediterranean tradition, which was found at Lough Lene in County Westmeath.

CONCLUSION

The study of underwater archaeology is now firmly established in Irish archaeological research agendas. There has been a determined effort to guide the subject along the "landscape" route, moving away from the tradition of treating sites such as wrecks as single structural entities in their environment. On the other hand, underwater archaeology in Ireland has attempted to contextualize sites in their physical and cultural landscape and has tried to interpret these sites from an integrated and multidisciplinary perspective. This approach has gone some way toward a recognition of Ireland's island identity and maritime past.

ACKNOWLEDGMENTS. We would like to thank our archaeological colleagues, both north and south of the border in Ireland, who have contributed greatly to this subject: Donal Boland, Claire Callaghan, Eddie McPhilips, Fionnbar Moore, Wes Forsyth, Moira Ni Loingsigh, Tom McErlean, Rosemary McConkey, Paul McCooey, Declan Hurl, Brian Williams, Eoghan Kiernan, Karl Brady, Ed Bourke, Aisling Collins, Kevin Barton, Eoin Grogan, Rory Quinn, Andy Wheeler, and Tom Condit.

REFERENCES

Boland, D., and O'Sullivan, A., 1997, An Early Medieval Wooden Bridge at Clonmacnoise. In *The Quaternary of the Irish Midlands*. Field Guide No. 21, edited by F.J.G. Mitchell and C. Delaney, pp. 14–21. Irish Association for Quaternary Studies, Dublin.

Breen, C., 2001, *Integrated Marine Investigations on the Historic Shipwreck 'La Surveillante,'* Centre for Maritime Archaeology Monograph Series No. 1, University of Ulster.

Breen, C., 1996, Maritime Archaeology in Northern Ireland: An Interim Statement. *International Journal of Nautical Archaeology* 25(1):55–65.

_____, Forthcoming, *The archaeology of boat and ships in Ireland: an Introductory Study*. Government of Ireland Stationary Office.

Breen, C, and Barton, K., 1998, Mapping the French Man, *La Surveillante* re-visited. *Archaeology Ireland* 44:3.

Coles, B.J. and Coles, J.M., 1989, *People of the Wetlands*: *Bogs, Bodies and Lake-dwellings*. Thames and Hudson, London.

ECOPRO, 1997, *Environmentally Friendly Coastal Protection*: *Code of Practice*. Government of Ireland, Dublin.

Farrell, R., 1989, The Crannóg Archaeological Project (CAP), Republic of Ireland II: Lough Lene—offshore island survey. *International Journal of Nautical Archaeology and Underwater Exploration* 18(3):221–228.

_____, 1990, The Crannóg Survey Project: The Lakes of the West Midlands. *Archaeology Ireland* 4(1):27–29.

Farrell, R. and Buckley, V., 1984, Preliminary Examination of the Potential of Offshore and Underwater Sites in Loughs Ennell and Analla, County Westmeath, Ireland. *International Journal of Nautical Archaeology and Underwater Exploration* 13(4):281–285.

Farrell, R., Kelly, E.P., and Gowan, M., 1989, The Crannóg Archaeological Project (CAP), Republic of Ireland I: A preliminary report. *International Journal of Nautical Archaeology and Underwater Exploration* 18(2):123–136.

Hencken, H., 1936, Ballinderry Crannóg no. 1. *Proceedings of the Royal Irish Academy* 43C:103–239.

_____, 1942, Ballinderry Crannóg no. 2. *Proceedings of the Royal Irish Academy* 47C:1–76.

_____, 1950, Lagore Crannóg: An Irish Royal Residence of the Seventh to Tenth Century A.D. *Proceedings of the Royal Irish Academy* 53C:1–248.

Kelly, E.P., 1991, Observations on Irish Lake-dwellings. In *Studies in Insular Art and Archaeology*. American Early Medieval Studies 1, edited by C. Karkov and R. Farrell, pp. 81–98.

_____, 1993a, Treasure-hunting in Ireland—Its Rise and Fall. *Antiquity* 67:378–381.

_____, 1993b, Investigation of Ancient Fords on the River Suck. *Inland Waterways* 20(1):4–5.

_____, 1994, Protecting Ireland's Archaeological Heritage. *International Journal of Cultural Property* 2(3):213–225.

Kirwan, S., 1995, The Department of Arts, Culture and the Gaeltacht and Underwater Archaeology. In *The Future of Underwater Archaeology in Ireland*, pp. 32–36. IUART (unpublished conference proceedings).

Moore, F., 1995, The Role of the Office of Public Works in Underwater Archaeology with Reference to Past Activities, Current Policies and the Law. *The Future of Underwater Archaeology in Ireland*, pp. 39–43 IUART (unpublished conference proceedings).

O'Sullivan, A., 1993, Intertidal Survey on the Fergus Estuary and the Shannon Estuary. *Discovery Programme Reports* 1:61–68.

_____, 1994a, An Early Historic Period Fishweir on the Upper Fergus Estuary, County Clare. *North Munster Antiquarian Journal* 35:52–61.

_____, 1994b, Harvesting the Waters: Fishtraps in Early Ireland. *Archaeology Ireland* 27:10–12.

_____, 1995a, Marshlanders: Bronze Age People and Landscape on the Shannon Estuary. *Archaeology Ireland* 31:8–11.

_____, 1995b, Medieval Fishweirs on the Deel Estuary, County Limerick. *Archaeology Ireland* 32:15–17.

_____, 1995c, Intertidal Archaeological Surveys in the Estuarine Wetlands of North Munster. *International Journal of Nautical Archaeology* 24(1):71–73.

_____, 1996a, Exploring Ancient Woodlands. *Archaeology Ireland* 36:14–15.

_____, 1996b, Later Bronze Age Intertidal Discoveries on North Munster Estuaries. *Discovery Programme Reports* 4:63–72.

_____, 1996c, Medieval Fishtraps at Bunratty, County Clare. *The Other Clare* 21:40–42.

_____, 1996, Last Foragers or First Farmers? *Archaeology Ireland* 40:14–16.

_____, 1997, Neolithic and Bronze Age Discoveries on the Shannon Estuary, Ireland. *Past: Newsletter of the Prehistoric Society* 26:6.

_____, 1998a, *The Archaeology of Lake Settlement in Ireland*. Discovery Programme Monographs 4. Royal Irish Academy, Dublin.

_____, 1998b, Interpreting the Archaeology of Bronze Age Lake Settlements. *Journal of Irish Archaeology* 8:15–21.

_____, 1998, Crannogs in Contested Landscapes. *Archaeology Ireland* 44:14–15.

_____, 2000, *Crannogs*: *Lake-dwellings in Ireland*. Town House and Country House, Dublin.

Ryan, M., 1980, An Early Mesolithic Site in the Irish Midlands. *Antiquity* 80:46–47.

Wood-Martin, W.G., 1886, *The Lake-dwellings of Ireland or Ancient Lacustrine Habitations of Erin commonly called Crannogs*. Dublin.

Chapter 26

Maritime Archaeology in Northern Ireland
A Holistic Approach

BRIAN WILLIAMS

INTRODUCTION

Government has been responsible for the protection and promotion of archaeology in Ireland since 1882, but it was not until 1992 that the Department of Environment for Northern Ireland agreed to take responsibility for maritime archaeology. For its professional staff, the initial years of involvement led to an almost vertical learning curve in an area of archaeology for which there was little knowledge in this country, until a working knowledge of methodology, sources, and skills could be achieved. This chapter aims to record the history and current position of the discipline. While other chapters in this book may look simply at underwater archaeology, this chapter takes a more inclusive perspective: In Northern Ireland, the approach has been to study the interaction of coastal archaeological sites on land, in the intertidal zone, and on the seabed.

Brian Williams, Senior Inspector, Environment and Heritage Service, Belfast, BT1 2LA, Northern Ireland.
International Handbook of Underwater Archaeology, edited by Carol V. Ruppé and Janet F. Barstad. Kluwer Academic/Plenum Publishers, New York, 2002.

BACKGROUND TO THE STUDY OF MARITIME
ARCHAEOLOGY IN IRELAND

Searching through archaeological journals from the late 18th century up to recently leads to the conclusion that archaeologists have had no unified concept of maritime archaeology as a distinct field of study. Despite living on a North Atlantic island, Irish archaeologists have largely ignored the maritime aspects of our past. This section will attempt to outline some issues which have been considered by archaeologists.

Adolph Mahr, in his 1937 presidential address to the Prehistoric Society, advocated a systematic bathymetric survey of the Irish seabed to obtain maps of the land configuration at thousand-year intervals throughout prehistory (Mahr, 1937). Sea level change was considered simply in relation to its effect on the Irish Mesolithic by P.C. Woodman (1973–1974), who envisaged minimal effects, particularly on the hard rocky east Antrim coast in Belfast Lough, where there was little change after 7000 B.C., and in Strangford Lough, where he interpreted the rising sea level as resulting in a change from river estuary to a seashore (Woodman, 1973–1974).

The subject of land bridges is related to sea level change, and it was again in relation to the Mesolithic that this was discussed. Mahr dismissed the concept (Mahr, 1937). Woodman considered the matter from the viewpoint of biologists, who saw the restricted mammalian fauna as arriving in Ireland by a land route (Savage, 1966; Mitchell, 1964), but he found their arguments unconvincing (Woodman, 1973–1974). Raised beaches also have been of interest in relation to the Mesolithic, and papers have been written on the subject since the 1870s, most notably on the County Antrim sites (Praeger and Coffey, 1904–1905).

The coast has been considered in relation to some specific aspects of prehistoric cultures in Ireland. The dense coastal distribution of Mesolithic material led Movius to coin the term *Larnian* to describe Mesolithic coastal culture with his major studies of Curran Point, near the town of Larne on the east Antrim coast, the type site of the Irish Mesolithic (Movius, 1953–1954).

Neolithic culture must have arrived in Ireland by sea. The preponderance of megalithic court tombs in the County Down region led to the concept of the *Carlingford Culture*. This belief held that Carlingford Lough was a main point of entry for the builders of court tombs, who crossed the Irish Sea from southwest Scotland. Similar concentrations around west coast areas such as Sligo and Killala Bays, discovered in the 1950s by R. de Valera, were taken to indicate main landing places on the west coast (de Valera, 1960).

The first targeted approach to coastal archaeology was directed by renowned Ballymena antiquarian W.J. Knowles, who established the Sandhills Committee of the Royal Irish Academy in 1889. He studied prehistoric sites on the coast from Dublin around the eastern, northern, and western coasts, including Counties Donegal, Sligo and Mayo. In this pioneering study, Knowles met with a lack of understanding from other antiquarians and first had to locate and map the sandhills and their archaeology. The term *Sandhills Culture* came into currency in a series of papers in the Royal Irish Academy and the Royal Society of Antiquaries of Ireland from the 1880s to the 1930s (Knowles, 1888–1891).

The unique discovery of the Broighter Hoard in County Londonderry in 1896 included a small gold model of a boat complete with oars, mast, and other equipment (Figure 26.1), which gave a rare insight into the type of vessel in use during the Iron Age

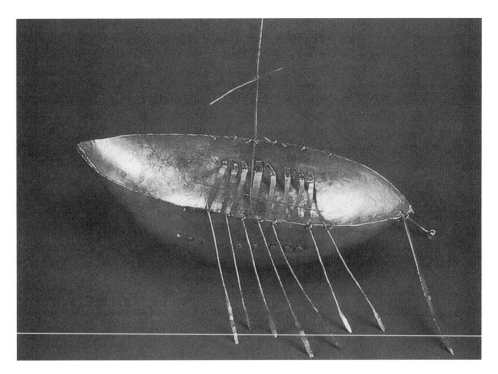

Figure 26.1. Broighter Boat.

(Evans, 1897). The discovery was the subject of a major legal battle between the Royal Irish Academy and the British Museum over treasure trove. The nautical aspects of the model boat were later considered in a review paper (Farrell and Penny, 1975).

The Romans did not colonize Ireland, but hoards of Roman coins and silver have been found at Balinrees, County Londonderry, and Flower Hill, County Antrim. A possible interpretation was that, from A.D. late 3rd century until the 5th century, booty was brought into Ireland by Irishmen returning from raiding expeditions, or perhaps by Irish mercenaries returning from colonies founded in Wales (Bateson, 1973).

Despite the highly popular profile of the Vikings, relatively little has been written about them in major journals relative to the north of Ireland, reflecting the lack of actual archaeological evidence. Some evidence exists for a Viking burial ground in Church Bay on Rathlin Island, in which a Hiberno-Norse silver brooch was found (Warner, 1973–1974). Viking burials have been recorded at Larne, County Antrim (Smith, 1840–1844) and Ballyholme, County Down (Milligan, 1906). A distribution of Viking Age silver hoards in Ireland shows coastal distribution in the north of Ireland, though not to the same extent as elsewhere on the island (Briggs and Graham-Campbell, 1976). Excavations in Dublin have determined the massive wealth of archaeological evidence for settlement of this period at Woodquay and has led to the discovery of quaysides and ships timbers (McGrail, 1993).

The Spanish Armada was the subject of archaeological discussion long before the 1960s and 1970s excavations. In a series of papers mainly in the late 19th century, ships lost on the coast of Clare (Westropp, 1889) were considered, while Green (1927) published the Armada ships of the Kerry coast. A letter from a surviving Spanish Armada sailor, Captain de Cuellar, was published in the Ulster Journal of Archaeology in 1895 and as a book in 1897 (Allingham, 1895, 1897). Biggar published papers on the Armada in Ulster and Connacht (Biggar, 1896), with a reference to an Armada wreck at Dunluce (Biggar, 1904).

Specific types of coastal sites and monuments have received attention in the literature. Most notable are promontory forts, which are fortified coastal headlands as yet of uncertain date. Westropp made a detailed survey of promontory forts along the western seaboard in a series of papers published in the *Journal of the Royal Society of Antiquaries of Ireland* from 1906 through to 1922 (Westropp, 1906). Specific excavations have been conducted at such sites as Carrigillihy, County Cork (O'Kelly, 1952–1953) and Larrybane, County Antrim (Proudfoot and Wilson, 1961–1962).

Fortified rock outcrops known as *Doons* are found in the coastal zone on the northeast coast of Ireland. Only one, at Fair Head, County Antrim, has been the subject of archaeological excavation. It revealed evidence for what was interpreted as an Iron Age and Early Christian period defended settlement (Childe, 1938).

Coastal caves have received relatively little attention, with the exception of an early report on antiquities found near a cave at Cushendall, County Antrim (Jones, 1847–1850) and the excavation of Portbraddan Cave (May, 1943).

Coastal castles are a defensive type of site in the archaeological record and have been the subject of much study. Anglo–Norman settlement of east Ulster in the late 12th century had a major coastal component, a network of castles from Greencastle on the shores of Carlingford Lough through Dundrum (Jope, 1966) and Carrickfergus (McNeill, 1981). Gaelic castles of the period A.D. 1350–1600 have been published for Inishowen, County Donegal (Davies and Swan, 1939), the Antrim coast (McNeill, 1983), and Dunluce Castle, County Antrim (Figure 26.2) (Lynn, 1905, Biggar, 1905). The tower houses of the 15th and 16th centuries have a particularly strong coastal distribution, most notably in the Strangford Lough region (Jope, 1966).

The archaeology of Ireland's offshore islands has excited some interest in the profession. The history and antiquities of Tory Island were the subject of an early study (Getty, 1852), as was Rathlin Island (Morris, 1911), but the most intensive island study came with a survey of Clare Island in 68 parts by the Royal Irish Academy, in which part 2 dealt with history and archaeology (Proceedings of the Royal Irish Academy, 1931). The archaeology of a deserted village on Achill Island has been the subject of recent study (McDonald, 1998), and a conference on the archaeology of islands was held in 1998 (Cooney, forthcoming).

The Ordnance Survey Memoirs, which did so much to record land archaeology in the 1830s, reported the discovery of a buried clinker-built boat in a bog in the parish of Ballywillin, close to Portrush on the north Antrim coast (Ordnance Survey Field Memoirs, 1838). Throughout the 19th century, many logboats were found in freshwater contexts in rivers, lakes, and bogs (McDowell, 1983; Gregory, 1997; Fry, 2000). Vernacular craft have been recorded and discussed (McCaughan, 1970, 1982, 1984; Wilkinson and Williams, 1996), and E.E. Evans, in an article on the curraghs of Sheephaven, County Donegal, introduced the subject of skin boats (Evans, 1939).

There are almost no references to archaeological remains of ships. The exception was a 17th-century vessel, known as the *Cedar Wreck*, at Tyrella (Graves, 1845–1847; Anonymous, 1905). Despite recent searches for the vessel, described as a Guinea slaver with a cargo of elephant tusks and gold dust, it has not been located. The first major archaeological paper on boats was on evidence from ships' timbers from excavations at Dublin (McGrail, 1993).

Figure 26.2. Dunluce Castle.

Economic exploitation of the coastal zone has left its mark on the archaeological record. Shellfish have provided a significant protein supplement to the Irish diet throughout history, so that shell middens have been the subject of some study, and specific species of shellfish are mentioned in the literature. Cockles and limpets were found in a *souterrain* at Cloughcorr, County Antrim (Harper, 1972), mussels and oysters were recovered from the raised rath at Rathmullan, County Down (Lynn, 1981–1982), and a cache of winkle shells was found in the Neolithic court tomb at Ballinran, County Down (Collins, 1976). Historical notes on the oyster fishery of Ireland were published in the Royal Irish Academy (Went, 1962). Shell middens were studied in the north of Ireland (Windle, 1911). A specific site was excavated near Groomsport, County Down (Young, 1898) and more recently at Minnis North, County Antrim (Simpson et al., 1993). Shell middens are central to a Emily Murray's doctoral thesis on the economy of Irish coastal settlement sites during the Early Christian period, A.D. 500–1200.

Until recently, Ireland's northeast coast was one of the richest fishing grounds in Europe, and fishing has been of major significance from earliest times. Excavations at Mountsandel, County Londonderry, found evidence for offshore and estuary fishing in the Mesolithic period (Woodman, 1985). Cod, salmon bones, and whalebone were found on the Early Christian settlement at Rathmullan, County Down (Lynn, 1981–1982), and a whale vertebrae was found as part of the paving of an Early Christian period surface at Cathedral Hill, Downpatrick (Brannon,1989). Papers have been published on the Ling in Irish commerce (Went, 1948), on the salmon fishery at Carrick-a-Rede (Went, 1958), on fishing for basking shark (Went and O Suilleabhain, 1966–1967), and on whale fishing off the coast of Ulster in the 18th century (Buckley, 1908). Irish fishing weirs were documented in a series of papers (for example, Went, 1946). Went described fish traps or fixed engines for the capture of salmon from 1800 (Went, 1963).

Despite the importance of seaweed exploitation to the Irish economy, little appears in the journals. Geographer Estyn Evans was among the first to understand the economic significance of seaweed and record its production techniques in *Mourne Country* (Evans, 1951). Ronald Buchanan estimated that seaweed was the second most valuable crop in the barony of Lecale in the 18th century (Buchanan, 1958).

Voyages and navigation, while not strictly archaeological subjects, were published in papers on the mythical voyages of Bran (Meyer, 1898), and the great medieval epic tale on the voyages of St. Brendan (Olden, 1891). Navigational charts were of interest as early as the 18th century, when a paper on Ptolemy's Map of Ireland was published (Beauford, 1789), with a subsequent paper (Orpen, 1894) and later in a paper on Greek geographic tradition and Ptolemy's evidence for Irish geography (Tierney, 1976). A general paper on charts, maps, and plans in Trinity College Library (Hardiman, 1821–1825), early Italian maps of Ireland from 1300–1600 (PRIA, 30 C, 361), a map of Agrippa (Tierney, 1963), Rathlin Island on the Portolan Charts (Andrews, 1925), and George Semple's Charts of Dublin Bay 1762 (Daly, 1993) attest to the interest in early navigational charts.

DIVING PROJECTS IN IRELAND IN THE 1960s AND 1970s

Ships of the Spanish Armada

During the 1960s and 1970s, there was no state-sponsored action to record or excavate submerged archaeological sites. Finds relied on chance discoveries and isolated instances of determined searches, usually by individuals and nongovernmental groups. The most significant investigations relate to the Spanish Armada. Twenty-four vessels of the Armada were wrecked around the Irish coast in 1588. Three, *Girona*, *Trinidad Valencera*, and *Santa Maria de la Rosa*, were subjects of directed diving investigations.

The location of the wreck of *Girona* was identified from place name and cartographic evidence by Robert Stenuit, a Belgian diver who undertook preliminary investigations in June 1967, at Lacada Point off Port na Spaniagh in County Antrim. During the dive, finds of Armada material prompted further excavation in 1968 and 1969, when ordnance, handguns, navigation equipment, coins, and decorated silverware were recovered. Of particular interest was Renaissance jewelry, gold coins, and pendants. None of the ship's structure appeared to remain on the sea floor (Stenuit, 1972). The entire assemblage of artifacts was acquired by Ulster Museum and conserved in the newly established Archaeological Conservation Laboratory in Belfast, where the nature of the finds prompted development of novel restoration techniques (Rees-Jones, 1972).

Diving investigations on *Santa Maria de la Rosa* located the wreck site in Blasket Sound, County Kerry. Dublin-based diver Desmond Brannigan led a preliminary search in 1963, without finding the site. In 1968, a diving team led by English diver Sidney Wignel, assisted by John Grattan and a team of service divers, located the first real clue: an iron anchor 4 m long. Since the vessel was a vice-flagship, it was thought a great treasure was a possibility, however this was never found. The finds from the wreck are in the collection of Ulster Museum by agreement with the Irish Government (Wignell, 1968).

The third Armada ship to be excavated, a refurbished Venetian merchantman named *Trinidad Valencera*, was wrecked in Kinnego Bay, County Donegal, on September 16, 1588, and discovered by members of the City of Derry Sub-Aqua Club in February 1971. Colin Martin of the Institute of Maritime Archaeology, University of St. Andrews, was appointed archaeological director of the ensuing excavation. Great guns in bronze and iron were recovered, together with organic remains such as wooden barrel staves, bungs for casks, stoppers for wineskins, wooden pegs for musical instruments, a campaign tent, and an anchor warp. Also present were wool, velvet, and silk textiles, along with leather shoes, which gave a remarkable insight into late 16th-century life (Martin, 1979). The Ulster Museum, having established title with the government of the Republic of Ireland, undertook the enormous task of conserving the artifacts.

In 1985, the Streedagh Armada Group, a team of Leicester-based divers, located three wrecks in shallow water on the sandy seabed of Streedagh Strand. Two bronze *pederos*, specially constructed to fire stone shot, and a bronze saker were raised. An intact wooden rudder, some 12 m long with iron pintles, was also located.

The 400th anniversary of the Spanish Armada was marked by a major international exhibition in Ulster Museum in Belfast, and a conference was held in Sligo on the west coast of Ireland (Gallagher and Cruikshank, 1990).

PRESSURE ON GOVERNMENT TO CARE FOR MARITIME ARCHAEOLOGY

Despite the Protection of Wrecks Act of 1973, government offered little action in protecting and promoting maritime archaeology. The Joint Nautical Archaeology Policy Committee (JNAPC), was established in England in 1988 as a public pressure group. Its membership is made up of individuals and representatives of various bodies with an interest in preserving Britain's underwater heritage. The committee sought to highlight perceived inadequacies in the treatment of submerged archaeology and to produce concrete proposals to address these problems. In 1989, JNAPC launched Heritage at Sea in the House of Commons (JNAPC, 1989). This document set out a number of recommendations underpinned by the principle that submerged archaeology should receive the same protection as archaeological remains on land. Recommendations covered legislation, inventories of submerged archaeology, treatment of finds from the seabed, reporting of finds, diver training, public administration of archaeology in the territorial sea, and the inclusion of archaeology in predevelopment impact assessments.

Response from Government

Faced with an informed and influential pressure group, the United Kingdom agreed to take responsibility for identifying and protecting archaeological remains on the seabed (Firth, 1992). The Department of the Environment for Northern Ireland (DOE [NI]) signed an agency agreement with the Department of the Environment for England (DOE) in April 1992, in which it undertook responsibility for underwater archaeology in Northern Ireland waters and an inventory of submerged sites. DOE agreed to maintain and pay for an Advisory Committee on Historic Wrecks (ACHWS) and, through the Archaeological Diving Unit (ADU), to provide an expert and technical service to DOE NI. Of some 40 sites designated under the Protection of Wrecks Act, only the site of the

Spanish Armada vessel, *Girona*, has been designated in Northern Ireland waters (Archaeological Diving Unit, 1994). Considerable effort was made by DOE (NI), in consultation with the archaeological profession, to develop a strategy for maritime archaeology (Williams, 1994, 1997).

THE MARITIME RECORD

A knowledge base was required for management of the maritime resource. Environment and Heritage Service funded a senior fellowship in The Queen's University of Belfast to create a maritime record (Breen, 1994, 1996a), in a computerized database form, of all archaeological sites in Northern Ireland's coastal waters. The first stage of the record was completed, accumulating all the available data from three source types: documentary, cartographic, and illustrative.

The main documentary sources included wreck lists, harbor plans, and shipping information from Commons Sessional Papers, and annual proceedings of Parliament published since 1800. Shipping information from this source was supported by Lloyds Register and Lloyds List, published since 1740. Wreck information was also extracted from Northern Ireland's local newspapers serving coastal communities. Even medieval texts and annalistic sources were searched. One of the more interesting references comes from the Annals of Ulster for the year A.D. 924, which refers to a great fleet of Viking ships foundering in Dundrum Inner Bay.

The Hydrographic Office of the British Admiralty has been producing charts of Northern Ireland's waters since the early 19th century. These charts record the position of numerous wreck sites as well as coastal landing places. Ordnance Survey maps and supporting early 19th-century memoirs, Royal National Lifeboat charts and estate maps have proved valuable sources. Work will be undertaken to catalogue the considerable body of paintings, drawings and photographs of maritime subjects.

The maritime record has now largely completed its documentary phase and contains evidence of some 3000 wrecks as well as a large archive on other maritime sites. While this is a useful starting point, the maritime record, as it stands does not fully reflect the potential of maritime archaeology in Northern Ireland. Information covers only the years A.D. 1740–1945, although there has been human occupation of the island for at least 9000 years. An additional problem is that the locational evidence for wrecks is often poor.

GEOPHYSICAL SURVEY

Net-fastening data donated by local fishermen has gone some way to provide non-time-bound information that is well located; the thousands of possible sites on disk have yet to be integrated into the record. Environment and Heritage Service now funds research at the University of Ulster to conduct a geophysical survey over a three-year period around the coast of Northern Ireland. This project will produce a geomorphological map of the seabed, including cultural data using side scan sonar, magnetometer, and subbottom profiler with plotted locational information from a single-frequency GPS mapping system. Since most wrecks lie in shallow water, a program of research on shallow water prospecting is being supported in the Department of Oceanographic Science, University of Southampton, England. Ground-truthing of the geophysical evidence will be undertaken at a later date.

ARCHAEOLOGICAL EXCAVATIONS

Taymouth Castle

The first underwater archaeological excavation of *Girona* took place in the 1960s. It was not until 1995 that a second shipwreck was excavated. The *Taymouth Castle*, bound from Glasgow to Singapore, left Broomielaw, Scotland, January 3, 1867 carrying a valuable general cargo of 738 gallons of wine and spirits, 74 barrels of beer, £42,370 worth of cotton, £511 worth of earthenware, £2926 worth of iron and metal building materials, £110 worth of saddlery, and £2000 worth of sundry articles. Built July 1865 at Glasgow by the Connell Company and registered with Lloyds in August as A1, *Taymouth Castle* was a fully-rigged ship with three masts and square sails, an experimentally-built, composite ship with iron framing and wooden planking, sheathed in yellow metal. Shortly after leaving port, the vessel met with severe gales that swept across the North Channel on January 5. It wrecked that night on Ireland's northeast coast.

The wreck site lay undisturbed for more than 100 years, until sport divers started looting it in the 1990s. As a result of the threat, Environment and Heritage Service conducted its first underwater excavation, in September 1995. The investigation recorded the surviving structure of the vessel and excavated two trenches across the cargo mound. Iron framing was found, which conformed to the known dimensions of the vessel. A large windlass of iron and wood was located with a taut chain still in position, indicating that an attempt had been made to anchor the ship to keep it offshore. Excavation of the cargo mound recovered piles of iron cooking bowls that had rusted and helped form a concretion, which preserved much of the cargo. Much evidence of bottles of alcohol, with makers' marks on the bottles, indicated a Scottish origin. In addition, pottery, of which there was a profusion on the seabed, was all Glasgow sponge ware (Breen, 1996b). The project marked the beginning of licensed underwater excavation by government in Northern Ireland.

Intertidal Archaeology

Faced with interesting studies of the archaeology of the intertidal zone elsewhere in Ireland and Britain, Environment and Heritage Service responded by conducting a pioneering survey of Strangford Lough from 1995 to 1998. Strangford Lough, a large sea lough, 30 km long and up to 8 km wide in the drumlin landscape of eastern County Down, has been designated a Marine Nature Reserve by Environment and Heritage Service. Surrounded by agricultural land, much of good, productive quality, the lough is renowned for the richness of its flora and fauna and particularly for its wildfowl. Since their arrival in Ireland some 9000 years ago, people have been drawn to the lough's mild and fertile shores, and a rich heritage of sites of archaeological and cultural interest has been left imprinted on this landscape. The intertidal survey has been richly rewarded with the discovery of a range of features that fall into the broad groups of submerged landscapes, communications, farming, and fishing.

Submerged Landscapes

Sea level fluctuated considerably in the postglacial period, and archaeological evidence for inundated landscapes has been found in the intertidal zone. Submerged forests are deposits of trunks, roots, and branches found in peats or clays and have been recorded at

Ballyurnanellan, Chapel Island, Greyabbey Bay, and Kircubbin. Radiocarbon dating for a tree stump at Greyabbey Bay has provided a date of 7035–6686 B.C. Geophysical survey of the seabed on the north Antrim coast and in Belfast Lough showed evidence for sea level some 30 m lower than present levels; it is estimated around 10,000 B.C., and it is clear from both these studies that there may be substantial archaeological landscape and settlement evidence on the seabed.

Communications

Remains of three large sailing ships and a smaller vessel of 19th and 20th century date were found. The schooner *Fanny Crossley*, abandoned and largely broken up at Ringneill Quay in 1939, had only a few remaining fragments. Another vessel of similar proportions survived as a stern fragment close to an old lead mine at Castleward Bay. Better preserved was the coal schooner *Hilda*, which caught fire and was abandoned at Quoile Quay in 1922. From the Maritime Record, it is known that the remains of the brig *Nimble* and several other vessels lie on the seabed at Ballyhenry Bay, where there was a breaker's yard.

Slipways, piers, and jetties of different periods have been encountered. The simplest form was the cleared slipway created by clearing boulders off a rocky beach to make a safe approach for small boats. These features are difficult to date; in some cases, they were adjacent to old buildings but often not associated with them. A substantial waterfront of uncertain date has been found in association with the Early Christian-period monastery at Nendrum with a similar complex waterfront at Mahee Castle. At Ringhaddy, stone footings of a jetty beside a cleared slipway was found in association with a late medieval castle; pottery and musket balls were found in deep water off the end of the jetty. A drystone-built pier, known as *The Seneschal's Quay*, was found near the Anglo–Norman motte and medieval tower house at Ardkeen, headquarters of the Savage family, seneschals of Ulster. Large, well-built stone quays were recorded at Strangford, Castleward, Audleys Castle, and Killyleagh; although some are shown on 17th-century maps, the date of their original construction is not known and could be considerably earlier. Large piers of the 19th century have been recorded at Castle Espie and Walshestown.

Farming

Harvesting and processing of seaweed was an important economic activity for Irish coastal communities. Historically, brown seaweed (wrack and oarweed) was gathered for use as an organic fertilizer or for burning to provide "kelp" rich in salts and to be used in glass-making.

Seaweed grows well on the stony shores of Strangford Lough. Walls unassociated with nearby fields were encountered in these weed-rich areas that may represent wrack ownership boundaries. Kelp kilns were recorded in a number of cases; a group on Chapel Island is of particular interest, surviving as boulder-built round "cairns" with central circular chambers. On muddy shores where seaweed is less common, boulders were laid out in wrack grids to provide a root attachment for the plants. At Greyabbey Bay, there is evidence for a stone fish trap that was dismantled and reused as a wrack grid. Documentary sources for the 18th and 19th centuries indicate that kelp production was a major part of the economy of the region.

Fishing

Fishing from boats was a major activity in the past. Strangford Lough was considered the best fishery on the east coast of Ireland in the 18th century and, although fishing fleets were maintained at Kircubbin, Portaferry, and Strangford, little evidence exists for the survival of this activity in the intertidal zone.

Fishtraps are barriers of wood or stone built across channels in the intertidal zone to trap fish on the ebbing tide. More than 20 fishtraps have been discovered in the Strangford Lough survey, the range of their radiocarbon dates suggesting usage from 8th–13th century. Although it is not possible to know dates of the stone-built traps, there is a clear association with ecclesiastical sites. No visible remains exist of the reported 6th-century monastic site on Dunsey Island, but a stone trap, built on the seabed between two islands, survives nearby.

The main area of stone fishtraps was found in Greyabbey Bay on the eastern shore of Strangford Lough, an area best known for its late 12th-century Cistercian abbey. The stone traps, here and at Comber (another Cistercian abbey), are comparable to similar structures associated with Cistercian houses in Britain.

PROTECTING THE MARITIME ARCHAEOLOGICAL RESOURCE

The Protection of Wrecks Act 1973 empowers the government to designate the wreck of a vessel it considers to be of historical, archaeological, or artistic importance. Only one site, *Girona*, has been designated under this legislation. The Historic Monuments and Archaeological Objects (NI) Order 1995 extended legislative protection, for the first time, to archaeological sites and objects below High Water Mark and to 12 miles offshore. Other legislation not specifically designed to protect archaeology is used to good effect: The Merchant Shipping Act 1995 is used throughout the United Kingdom to report the discovery of archaeological objects on the seabed and to arrange for their conservation and acquisition by cultural institutions. A consultation process for maritime archaeology issues is provided for Environment and Heritage Service by The Planning (NI) Order 1991, The Food and Environment Protection Act 1995, which regulates dumping at sea, Department of Trade and Industry oil and gas exploration licensing, and Ministry of Defence sales disposal procedures for naval vessels; it also administers The Shellfish Act 1995.

FUTURE DEVELOPMENTS IN MARITIME ARCHAEOLOGY

Maritime archaeology is now clearly on the heritage agenda in Northern Ireland. A recent review lays out the direction the subject should take in the years ahead (McErlean et al., 1998). Although Environment and Heritage Service has made progress in maritime archaeology, a government service can provide only a program of recording and protection. With many research questions being raised by the recording program, the need has been established for a university to develop academic research for the subject, along with the education of a new generation of maritime archaeologists as a priority. With both these points in mind, Environment and Heritage Service, in partnership with the University of Ulster, has created the Maritime Archaeology Centre to provide a program of recording, protection, research and teaching of maritime archaeology in Northern Ireland.

REFERENCES

Allingham, H., 1895, The Spanish Armada: A Spanish Captain's Experiences in Ulster in 1588: A Reminiscence. *Ulster Journal of Archaeology*, 2nd series 1:178–1194.

_____, 1897, *Captain Cuellar's Adventures in Connacht and Ulster*. London.

Andrews, M.C., 1925, Rathlin Island on the Portolan Charts. *Journal of the Royal Society of Antiquities, Ireland* 55:31–35.

Anonymous, 1905, Shipwreck at Tyrella, County Down. *Ulster Journal of Archaeology*, 2nd series, 11:139.

Archaeological Diving Unit, 1994, *Guide to Historic Wreck Sites Designated under the Protection of Wrecks Act 1973*, Archaeological Diving Unit, St. Andrews, Scotland.

Bateson, D., 1973, Roman Material from Ireland: A Reconsideration. *Proceedings of the Royal Irish Academy* 73(C):21–97.

Beauford, W., 1789, Ptolemy's Account of Ireland. *Transactions of the Royal Irish Academy* 3:51–73.

Biggar, F.J., 1896, The Spanish Armada in Ulster and Connacht. *Ulster Journal of Archaeology*, 2nd series 2: 99–105.

_____, 1904, References to Armada Wreck at Dunluce. *Ulster Journal of Archaeology*, 2nd series 10:5.

_____, 1905, Some Historical Notes about Dunluce and Its Builders. *Ulster Journal of Archaeology*, 2nd series 11:154–162.

Brannon, N.F., 1989, Not Just a Load of Old Bones: The Human and Animal Remains from Cathedral Hill Excavations, Downpatrick. *Lecale Miscellany* 7:18–22.

Breen, C., 1994, Researching the Maritime Archaeological Resource in Northern Ireland. In *The Future of Underwater Archaeology in Ireland*, edited by F. Williams. Proceedings of a conference held in Belfast. Belfast.

_____, 1996a, Maritime Archaeology in Northern Ireland: An Interim Statement, *International Journal of Nautical Archaeology* 25:55–65.

_____, 1996b, The Excavation of the *Taymouth Castle*. *Ulster Local Studies* 18:50–58.

Briggs, C.S., and Graham-Campbell, J.A., 1976, A Lost Hoard of Viking Age Silver from Magheralagan, County Down. *Ulster Journal of Archaeology* 39:20–23.

Buchanan, R.H., 1958, *The Barony of Lecale, County Down: A Study in Regional Personality*. Ph.D. dissertation, Department of Geography, Queen's University, Belfast.

Buckley, J., 1908, Whale Fishing off the Ulster Coast from 1736 to 1769. *Ulster Journal of Archaeology*, 2nd series 14:16–20.

Childe, V.G., 1938, Doonmore, A Castle Mound near Fair Head, County Antrim. *Ulster Journal of Archaeology* 1:122–135.

Childe, V.G., and Swan, H.P., 1939, The Castles of Inishowen. *Ulster Journal of Archaeology* 2:178–208.

Collins, A.E.P., 1976, A Court Grave at Ballinran, County Down. *Ulster Journal of Archaeology* 39:8–12.

Cooney, G., editor, forthcoming, *The Archaeology of Islands*. Dublin.

Daly, G., 1993, George Semple's Charts of Dublin Bay, 1762. *Proceedings of the Royal Irish Academy* 93:81.

de Valera, R., 1960, The Court Cairns of Ireland. *Proceedings of the Royal Irish Academy* 60(C):9–140.

Evans, A.J., 1897, On a Votive Deposit of Gold Objects Found on the Northwest Coast of Ireland. *Archaeologia* 55:391–408.

Evans, E.E., 1939, Curraghs of Sheephaven. *Ulster Journal of Archaeology* 2:28–31.

_____, 1951, *Mourne Country*. Dundalk.

Farrell, A.W., and Penny, S., 1975, The Broighter Boat: A Re-assessment. *Irish Archaeological Research Forum* 2:15–28.

Firth, A., 1992, *A Preliminary Account of the Management of Archaeology Underwater in the UK*. Southampton.

Fry, M.F., 2000, *Coití Logboats from Northern Ireland*, Environmental and Heritage Series, Belfast.

Gallagher, P., and Cruikshank, D.W., editors, 1990, *God's Obvious Design*. Spanish Armada Symposium, Sligo, 1988.

Getty, E., 1852, The Island of Tory: Its History and Antiquities. *Ulster Journal of Archaeology*, 1st series 1:27–37.

Graves, 1845–1847, The Discovery of the Remains of a Cedar Ship, at Tyrella. *Transactions of the Royal Irish Academy* T(3):248.

Green, W.S., 1927, Armada Ships on the Kerry Coast. *Proceedings of the Royal Irish Academy* 27(C):249.

Gregory, N.T.N., 1997, *A Comparative Study of Irish and Scottish Logboats*. Ph.D. dissertation, Department of Archaeology, University of Edinburgh.

Harper, A.E.T., 1972, A Souterrain at Cloughorr, County Antrim. *Ulster Journal of Archaeology* 35:59–61.

Hardiman, J., 1821–1825, Charts, Maps, and Plans Relating to Ireland in Library Trinity College, Dublin. *Proceedings of the Royal Irish Academy* 14:57.

Joint Nautical Archaeology Policy Committee, 1989, *Heritage at Sea: Proposal for the Better Protection of Sites Underwater.* London.

Jones, H.D., 1847–1850, On Certain Antiquities Presented to the Academy, Found near a Cavern at Cushendall, in the County Antrim. *Proceedings of the Royal Irish Academy* 4:394.

Jope, E.M., editor, 1966, *An Archaeological Survey of County Down.* Belfast.

Lynn, C.J., 1981–1982, The excavation of Rathmullan: A Raised Rath and Motte in County Down. *Ulster Journal of Archaeology* 44, 45:65–171.

Lynn, W.H., 1905, Notes on the Ruins of Dunluce Castle, County of Antrim. *Ulster Journal of Archaeology*, 2nd series 11:97–107.

McCaughan, M., 1970, The Lough Erne Cot. In *Ulster Folk Museum Year Book 1969/1970*, pp. 5–8. Belfast.
_____, 1982, Ulster Boat Types in Old Photographs. *Ulster Folklife* 28:40–48.
_____, 1984, A Lough Neagh Replica Fishing Boat. *Ulster Folklife* 30:55–62.

McCaughan, M., and Appleby J., editors, 1989, *The Irish Sea: Aspects of Maritime History.* Belfast.

McDonald, T., 1998, The Deserted Village, Slievemore, Achill Island, County Mayo, Ireland. *International Journal of Historical Archaeology* 2:73–112.

MacDowell, U., 1983, *Irish Logboats.* M.A. thesis, Department of Archaeology, University College, Dublin.

McErlean, T., McConkey, R., McCooey, P., and Williams, B., 1998, *A Review of the Archaeological Resources of the Northern Ireland Coastline.* EHS management document, Belfast.

McGrail, S., 1993, *Medieval Boat and Ship Timbers from Dublin.* Royal Irish Academy, Dublin.

McNeill, T.E., 1981, *Carrickfergus Castle.* Belfast.
_____, 1983, The Stone Castles of Northern County Antrim. *Ulster Journal of Archaeology* 46:101–128.

Mahr, A., 1937, New Aspects and Problems in Irish Prehistory. *Proceedings of the Prehistory Society* 3:261–436.

Martin, C.J.M., 1979, La Trinidad Valencera: An Armada Invasion Transport Lost off Donegal. *International Journal of Nautical Archaeology* 8:13–38.

May, A. McL., 1943, Portbraddan Cave, County Antrim. *Ulster Journal of Archaeology* 6:39–60.

Meyer, K., 1898, *The Voyage of Bran, Son of Ferbal to the Land of the Living: An Old Irish Saga.* London.

Milligan, S.F., 1906, Danish Finds in Ireland. *Journal of the Royal Society of Antiquities, Ireland* 36:205–206, 450–454.

Mitchell, G.F., 1964, Moraine Ridges on the Floor of the Irish Sea. *Irish Geographer* 4:335–344.

Morris, H., 1911, Some Antiquities of Rathlin. *Ulster Journal of Archaeology*, 2nd series 17:39–46.

Movius, H.L., 1953–1954, Curran Point, Larne: The Type Site of the Irish Mesolithic. *Proceedings of the Royal Irish Academy* 56(C):1–195.

O'Kelly, M.J., 1952–1953, The Promontory Forts in County Cork. *Proceedings of the Royal Irish Academy* 54(C):25–69.

Olden, T., 1891, The Voyage of St. Brendan. *Proceedings of the Royal Irish Academy* 21(C):676–684.

Orpen, G.H., 1894, Ptolemy's Map of Ireland. *Journal of the Royal Society of Antiquities, Ireland* 24:115–128.

Ordnance Survey Field Memoirs, 1838, *Parish of Ballywillin, County Antrim.* Dublin.

Praeger R.L., and Coffey, G., 1904–1905, The Antrim Raised Beach: A Contribution to the Neolithic History of the North of Ireland. *Proceedings of the Royal Irish Academy* 25(C):143.

Proudfoot, B., and Wilson, B., 1961–1962, Further Excavations at Larrybane Promontory Fort, County Antrim. *Ulster Journal of Archaeology* 24–25:91–115.

Rees-Jones, S.G., 1972, Some Aspects of Conservation of Iron Objects from the Sea. *Studies in Conservation* 17:39–43.

Savage, R.J.D., 1966, Irish Pleistocene Mammals. *Irish Naturalists Journal* 15:117–130.

Simpson, D.D.A., Conway, M.G., and Moore, D., 1993, The Excavation of a Shell Midden at Minnis North, County Antrim. *Ulster Journal of Archaeology* 56:114–119.

Smith, H.J., 1840–1844, Account of the Larne Viking Burial. *Proceedings of the Royal Irish Academy* 2:40–42.
_____, 1857–1861, The Ancient Norse and Danish Geography of Ireland. *Proceedings of the Royal Irish Academy* 7:390–392.

Stenuit, R., 1972, *Treasures of the Armada.* Devon.

Tierney, J.J., 1963, The Map of Agrippa. *Proceedings of the Royal Irish Academy* 63(C):151–166.

_____, 1976, The Greek Geographic Tradition and Ptolemy's Evidence for Irish Geography. *Proceedings of the Royal Irish Academy* 76(C):257–266.

Warner, R., 1973–1974, The Re-provenancing of Two Important Pennanular Brooches of the Viking Period. *Ulster Journal of Archaeology* 36–37:58–70.

Went, A.E.J., 1946, Irish Fishing Weirs, I. *Journal of the Royal Society of Antiquities, Ireland* 76:176–194.

_____, 1948, The Ling in Irish Commerce. *Journal of the Royal Society of Antiquities, Ireland* 78:119–126.

_____, 1958, The Salmon Fishery of Carrick-a-rede and Larry Bane, County Antrim. *Journal of the Royal Society of Antiquities, Ireland* 88:57–66.

_____, 1961–1962, Historical Notes on the Oyster Fisheries of Ireland. *Proceedings of the Royal Irish Academy* 62(C):195–223.

_____, 1963, Notes upon Some Fixed Engines for the Capture of Salmon, Used in Ireland since 1800. *Journal of the Royal Society of Antiquities, Ireland* 93:151–159.

Went, A.E.J., and O Suilleabhain, S., 1966–1967, Fishing for the Sun-Fish or Basking Shark in Irish Waters. *Proceedings of the Royal Irish Academy* 65(C):91–116.

Westropp, T., 1889, Notes on Armada Ships Lost on the Coast of Clare. *Journal of the Royal Society of Antiquities, Ireland* 20:131.

Westropp, T.J., 1912, Early Italian Maps Of Ireland from 1300 to 1600, with Notes on Foreign Settlers and Trade. *Proceedings of the Royal Irish Academy* 30(C):361–428.

Wignell, S., 1968, *The Spanish Armada Salvage Expedition (1968): A Progress Report on Seven Years Research and Underwater Investigation into the Sinking of the Santa Maria de la Rosa.* Unpublished manuscript, Ulster Museum, Belfast.

Wilkinson, D., and Williams, B., 1996, The Discovery of an Early 18th-century Boat in Lough Neagh. *International Journal of Nautical Archaeology* 25:95–103.

Williams, B., 1994, The Role of Environment Service in the Promotion and Protection of Underwater Archaeology in Northern Ireland. In *The Future of Underwater Archaeology in Ireland*, edited by F. Williams. Proceedings of a conference held in Belfast in 1994, Belfast.

_____, 1997, The Development of Maritime Archaeology in Northern Ireland. In *Underwater Archaeology*, edited by F. Williams. Society for Historical Archaeology.

Windle, B.C.A., 1911, Note on Kitchen Middens in the North of Ireland. *Journal of the Royal Society of Antiquities, Ireland* 42:1.

Woodman, P.C., 1973–1974, Settlement Patterns of the Irish Mesolithic. *Ulster Journal of Archaeology* 36–37:1–16.

_____, 1985, *Excavations at Mount Sandel 1973–1977.* Belfast.

Young, R.M., 1898, Vestiges of Primitive Man in the County Down. *Ulster Journal of Archaeology*, 2nd series 4:44–47.

Chapter 27

France

MAX GUÉROUT

INTRODUCTION

Precursors

In 1948, *Elie Monnier*, the French navy support ship of Groupe d'Etude et de Recherche Sous-Marine (GERS), undertook a survey of the *Mahdia* wreck. This wreck was discovered in 1907 by Greek sponge divers and excavated by helmeted divers from 1908 to 1913. It was the first scientific approach to exploration of an archaeological site made by scuba divers, although the survey was short and the method still in its infancy. The experience gained on this occasion by two French navy officers, Jacques-Yves Cousteau and Phillippe Tailliez, allowed them to be involved in two archaeological excavations that marked a step in the history of underwater archaeology.

From 1952 to 1957, Cousteau organized dives on the *Grand Conglou*é wreck (actually two superimposed wrecks from the 2nd and 1st centuries B.C.) off Marseilles, France, under the direction of the archaeologist Fernand Benoit, who remained on the surface aboard the support ship. On this occasion, lifting bags inflated with air were used for the first time. In 1958, Tailliez led an excavation of the *Titan* wreck (1st century B.C.), where he carried on the first study of the hull of an ancient wreck.

Creation of the Direction des Recherches Archéologiques Sous-Marine

As early as 1966, France created the Direction des Recherches Archéologiques Sous-Marine (DRASM), a specialized department under the authority of the Ministry of

Max Guérout, Groupe de Recherche en Archéologie Navale, 75012, Paris, France.

International Handbook of Underwater Archaeology, edited by Carol V. Ruppé and Janet F. Barstad. Kluwer Academic/Plenum Publishers, New York, 2002.

Culture, based at Fort Saint-Jean in Marseilles and equipped with *Archéonaute*, a ship built and outfitted for underwater archaeology research. This department is in charge of administrative and scientific management of the underwater heritage in French territorial waters and the adjacent zone. Its mission is to carry on archaeological mapping of the territory and to inventory archaeological remains. In 1996, the authority of this service was extended to cover rivers and lakes and renamed Département des Recherches Archéologiques Subaquatiques et Sous-Marines (DRASSM).

Legislation

After the creation of DRASM, French legislation followed the evolution of the effect of sport divers on the underwater patrimony of France and the growing interest in a protection of this heritage. Several successive laws were adopted, ranging from the "Loi no 89–874 du 1er Décembre 1989 relative aux biens culturels maritimes," to the "Arrêté du 8 Février 1996 relatif aux biens culturels maritimes." The principles of the laws are: "Maritime cultural remains situated inside French waters and not claimed by their owner are the property of the State," and "Cultural remains cannot be moved before official declaration and authorization granted by DRASSM."

Research Organizations

DRASSM is composed of 28 people, including archaeologists as well as conservators, technicians, and administrative personnel. Other research organizations are either institutions such as the Centre National de la Recherche Scientifique (CNRS), whose most active underwater archaeology unit is the Centre Camille Julian in Aix en Provence, the archaeological commission of the Fédération Française d'Etude et de Sport Sous-Marin (FFESSM), or private nonprofit associations, among which the Groupe de Recherche en Archéologie Navale (GRAN) is the most active (Internet site address: archeonavale.org).

Execution and Control of Excavations, Axis of Research

Authorization for archaeological operations are made by a national commission after the submission of a program. Individuals in charge of an archaeological operation are supervised by DRASSM, and a report must be made available to them before the end of the project year. In the general context of archaeology, two priority research themes have been defined for underwater archaeology: (1) the organization of maritime trade, and (2) naval archaeology. In terms of chronology, the study of wrecks from ancient times to the 17th century are considered a high priority.

Publications

Several scientific publications are published in France:

- *Archaeonautica*, published since 1977 by CNRS, supported by the Ministry of Culture.
- *Gallia*, periodical supplements devoted to underwater archaeology, published by CNRS.

- *Bilan Scientifique*, the annual scientific report of DRASSM, published yearly since 1991 by the Ministry of Culture, reporting all underwater operations during the year.
- *Cahiers d'Archéologie Subaquatique*, published since 1970 by FFESSM, supported by CNRS.
- *Underwater Archaeology*, an Internet site in French and English created by the Ministry of Culture; its address is http://www.culture.fr/culture/archeosm/archeosm/.

FRANCE

Ancient Times

During the past ten years, the orientation of research on ancient maritime trade has encompassed the commerce in food (grain, wine, oil, fish sauce or *garum*), metals (iron, copper, lead), and building materials. The chronology of the discoveries span a period from the 6th century B.C. to A.D. 5th century. Among the large number of excavated wrecks of this period, we have chosen the most representative.

Commerce in Food

Wine.   In the past, researchers studied numerous wrecks of ships carrying wine in amphorae along the French Mediterranean coast. The most important was the *Madrague de Giens* wreck from Terracina south of Rome (1st century B.C.), which carried about 6000 amphorae (Tchernia, Pomey, Hesnard, 1978); wine from Italy bound for the western provinces of Gaul and Spain was usually carried in amphorae. At the end of the 1st century B.C., the direction of commercial routes changed, and goods were sent from the Roman provinces to Italy, although the better wines were still exchanged between Italy and its provinces.

An exception to this type of trade was the transport of wine in *dolia*, large earthenware jars with a diameter of 1.5–2 m and a capacity of 1500–2000 l. Amphorae were used only as a complement to cargo in this trade, which took place at the beginning of A.D. 1st century, for the exportation of wines produced near the harbor of Minturnes (80 km north of Napoli). Dolia were made by local families of potters; the name *Pirani* is often found on seals. Ships also may have been built in this port, which was situated at the mouth of the Garigliano River.

About 12 wrecks of this type are known: *Diano Marina* (Italy), *La Garoupe* (France), *Ladispoli* (Italy), *Ile Rousse* (Corsica Island, France), *Petit Congloué* (France), *Grand Ribaud D* (France), *Giraglia* (Corsica Island, France), *Gulf of Baratti* (Italy), and *Benat 2* (France).

The last wrecks of this type studied are:

- *Petit Congloué* wreck off Marseille, 60 m deep; excavation revealed a cargo of 15 dolia (Figure 27.1) spread over an area of 20 m long and 6 m wide; and amphorae from Tarraconensis, a Roman–Spanish province (Corsi-Sciallano and Liou, 1985).
- *Grand Ribaud D* wreck, which has a capacity of 60 tons, in the Hyères islands. Excavated in 1983 and 1984, it was a disturbed and looted site at a depth of 13 m. This was an exemplary excavation that produced much data and recovered

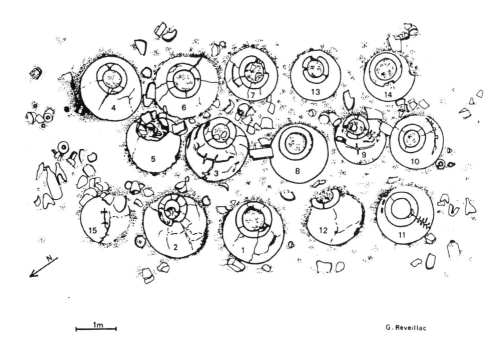

1m

G. Reveillac

Figure 27.1. Fifteen dolia, from *Petit Conglue* wreck near Marseilles.

a cargo of 11 dolia and 235 amphorae from Campania, Italy (Hesnard et al., 1988).

- *Giraglia* wreck off Cape Corse, lying at a depth of 20 m, was excavated by Martine Sciallano; the ship was carrying at least seven dolia of different sizes (a particularity already noticed on the *Diano Marina* wreck), as well as Spanish amphorae. The first excavation showed the presence of hull remains, and archaeologists expect to be able to observe the keel and the shape of the hull (Sciallano, 1995).

The disappearance of this type of trade, which seems to have lasted no more than about 50 years, is not yet well understood. Was its disappearance due to a change in the commercial terms of the trade, or to a structural defect of the ships—which might explain the number of wrecks?

Commerce in Metals

Iron. Luc Long conducted a survey for DRASSM off the delta of the Rhône River. Despite a difficult natural environment (strong current and poor visibility), numerous wrecks loaded with wrought iron ingots were studied. In a small area (3.5 × 1 nautical miles) off the city of Saintes-Maries-de-la-Mer, at least seven wrecks loaded with wrought iron bars or ingots were found either by divers or trawlers. The wrecks date from the second half of the 1st century B.C. to the middle of A.D. 1st century. Among the sites studied, the wreck *Saintes-Maries-de-la-Mer 2*, lying at a depth of 10.5 m and excavated between 1993 and 1996, furnished valuable data. Several iron concretions from *Saintes-Maries-de-la-Mer 2* lie scattered for a distance of 15 m; the cargo is estimated at 3000–4000 bars of different modules, with a total weight of 15–20 tons. The wrought iron bears different stamps, including the name *Lepidi*, thought to be the owner of the mine. It is difficult to work on such a site, not only because of environmental problems but also because the cargo of iron forms a compact mass of concretion, which cannot be studied until it is removed to the surface.

The presence of known amphorae from Tarraconensis, a Roman–Spanish province, dates the wreck to around the first quarter of A.D. 1st century. Even if the Spanish origin of the amphorae is certain, the origin and destination of the iron are not clear. However, the location of all wrecks in the area allowed us to draw a profile of the ancient shore of the Rhône River delta, and it is clear that the ships were attempting to enter an ancient arm of the river, Rhône Saint-Ferreol, now filled with sand. The discovery of similar wrought iron bars on the upper course of the Rhône River and on the banks of the Saone probably means the bars' destination may have been central Gaul (Long, 1997).

Lead.   In the field of the lead trade, there is the excavation of the *Ploumanac'h* wreck, found in the English Channel five nautical miles off the Brittany coast. *Ploumanac'h* is one of the area's rare ancient sites. Excavated from 1984 to 1986 by Michel L'Hour, the wreck was loaded with 271 lead ingots, each weighing between 27–150 kg; total weight of the cargo is estimated at 22 tons and seems to have consisted entirely of lead. A study of stamps and inscriptions on the ingots identified at least two Celtic tribes, *Brigantes* and *Icenes*, and dated the site between A.D. 2nd and 4th century. The *Ploumanac'h* wreck is an important material testimony of trade from England across the Channel (L'Hour, 1987).

Lead was usually only one part of a general cargo. Because of the metal's high density, ships could carry much weight in little space.

Two recently excavated wrecks were transporting such a cargo. *Sainte-Marie-de-la-mer 1* was found in 1989 off the Rhône River delta at a depth of 16 m and was studied the following year. One hundred lead ingots, without any ship's hull remains, lay in an area of 8 × 3.5 m. The weight of each ingot, expressed in Roman pounds, was etched on each ingot's surface and averaged 54 kg, making the total weight of the cargo around 5.4 tons. The ingots, 50 cm long with a trapezoidal section, carry several stamps that reveal the name of the probable mine owner. The inscription IMP.CAES, for *imperator caesare*, shows that the cargo can be considered an imperial tax. Several ingots also bear a large advertising stamp, FLAVI VERVCLA PLVMB GERM, which can be translated *true lead of Flavius Verucla*. The recovery of an amphora fragment from Baetica, a Roman–Spanish province, dates the site to A.D. 1st century. The origin and destination of the cargo are not yet known. (Long, 1997; Long and Domergue, 1995).

The *Sud Perduto* wreck was discovered in 1986 at a depth of 50 m in the Bouches de Bonifacio off the coast of Corsica. Excavated from 1986 to 1990 by Hélène Bernard, it was loaded with four layers of amphorae from Baetica; the amphorae were filled with oil, wine, and fish sauce (*garum*), dating the wreck precisely to A.D. the first 15 years.

Under the cargo of amphorae, 48 lead ingots were found lying over the mast step. They are between 460–490 mm long and weighing between 42–48 kg for the majority, and 27–32 kg for two series. Two shapes were observed: pyramidal and paraboloidal sections. The ingots can be classified in 10 series by their main stamp. Each ingot bears several types of perforations, marks, stamps, and inscriptions, some covering others, making it possible to establish a relative chronology between them. The perforations were likely made by nails used to fix the ingots on the floor of boats during their river trip from the mine to the sea harbor. Numeric inscriptions are etched Roman figures, indicating a weight in Roman pounds, the difference between the standard of one hundred pounds and the real weight of the ingots. Stamps bring to light a series of names; some are probable owners of mines, others collectors of lead ingots or merchants.

As already observed on lead ingots from the *Sainte-Marie-de-la-mer 1* wreck, two stamps are of the advertising type: EMPTOR.EME.G.AVI (buyer, buys [lead] of G. Au), and EMPTOR SALVE, (*Hello buyer*) (Bernard and Domergue, 1991). The probable origin of the lead is the mines of the Sierra Morena.

Commerce in Building Materials

Stone. The *Carry-Le-Rouet* wreck near Marseille was excavated in 1984 and 1985 and dates to the beginning of the 1st century B.C. The ship carried a cargo of stones extracted from a nearby quarry. Since the same Greek quarryman marks were found on excavated stones and on the Hellenistic wall of Marseilles, it is believed that the cargo was probably intended for building city walls (Pomey et al., 1988).

Marble. Two shipwrecks carrying marble also have been studied. The *Dramont I* wreck was discovered in 1991 off Cape Dramont near St. Raphaël, at a depth of 32 m. Three large marble blocks were found on the site, one measuring 2.2 × 1 × 1 m and the two others 3.8 × 1 × 1 m. The blocks have been identified as marble, usually called *africano*, from Teos in Asia Minor. The discovery of small pieces and powder of abrasive stones such as corundum (aluminium oxide) and pumice shows the ship board presence of workers in charge of polishing the marble. Artifacts found on the site date it to around the second half of the A.D. 1st century (Lopez, 1994).

The *Porto Novo* wreck, about 25 m long, was discovered off the Island of Corsica in 1991 and excavated in 1992. Five parallel-piped marble blocks ranging from 2–5 m long and 90 cm high, and four columns ranging from 2–5 m long and 150 cm in diameter, were found on the site, for a total weight of about 138 tons. The stone is a white marble from Carrara, Italy. The discovery of a golden coin struck during the reign of Tiberius dates the wreck to the beginning of A.D. 1st century. Nearly all the wrecks of ships carrying marble already known in the western Mediterranean are dated, at the earliest, to A.D. 3rd century and are associated with the use of eastern Mediterranean marble for the construction of monuments in Rome. The *Porto Novo* wreck, dated at two centuries earlier, evidences another type of trade, originating in Rome, to supply provinces with marble probably used for the construction of public monuments.

Another interesting facet of this wreck was the discovery of a number of tools: levers for handling marble blocks, hammers and chisels, and a set of tools used for working stone. The last were given to the Archéolyse International Laboratory for preservation treatment and the molding of replicas. As on the *Dramont I Wreck*, workers with these tools seem to have traveled on board the *Porto Novo Wreck* (Bernard and Chiapetti, 1993).

Other Types of Trade. All the wrecks cited above are linked to trade in the northwestern part of the Mediterranean between Italy, Gaul, and Spain. However, several wrecks are indicative of other types of trade. The *La Palud 1* wreck, found in 1980 on the shore of the Island of Port-Cros and studied in 1994 and 1995 by Luc Long and Giuliano Volpe, was loaded mostly with African cylindrical amphorae and with some amphorae from Syria and Palestine. Among the artifacts, a small precision balance with a set of copper weights was found in a very good state of preservation. Dated from A.D. 6th century, this wreck provides evidence of oil trade from North Africa, probably Tunisia (Long and Volpe, 1994).

The *Pointe Lequin 1 A* wreck was found mixed with three other ancient wrecks on the coast of Porquerolles Island and excavated by Luc Long between 1986 and 1992. Dating from 515 B.C., the ship was transporting amphorae from eastern Greece and also some 2500 ceramic tableware items from either Ionia or Attica. This wreck is a rare testimony of trade between eastern Greece and its colony of Phocea (Long et al., 1993).

Shipbuilding.   The study of ancient shipbuilding is especially well-developed in the Mediterranean. A better understanding of techniques and their evolution results from the study of a great number of wrecks; however, such study is often limited to ships' bottoms because the upper works are rarely preserved. Moreover, the period before 6th century B.C. is not well-documented; this is also the case for the Medieval period. No wreck of an ancient warship has ever been found in French waters.

In the context of the shell-first principle of shipbuilding used in ancient times, the importance and evolution of lashing techniques and pegged mortise-and-tenon joinery techniques have been enlightened by the 1993 discovery of two Greek wrecks, dating from 6th century B.C., in the Marseilles Underground. The first wreck is lashed with only cylindrical pegs used to maintain the boards during the building of the hull. The boards are lashed one to another by vegetal ties, and the frames are lashed to the boards. The hull's good preservation has allowed us to make a precise study of the methods used to strengthen and caulk the hull.

The second wreck is an illustration of a simultaneous use of the two techniques. If the building of the major part of the hull is made using the mortise-and-tenon technique, the extremities are stitched (Pomey, 1995), but observations made on five more recent wrecks show that, at the end of 3rd century B.C., the lashing technique was still used at the same time as the other technique. After a study of Roman shipbuilding techniques (Rival, 1991), a nautical history publication, *La Navigation dans l'Antiquité*, brought together all knowledge acquired on the subject (Pomey, 1997).

Other Themes

Dendrochronology.   A program of dendrochronology, applied to ancient wrecks excavated in recent years, has been underway since 1991. Its aim is to collect wood samples from the structures of wrecks whose dates are known approximately, in order to establish a chronological series and obtain a reference pattern for the western Mediterranean. The expected result is to obtain a reference pattern useful for about 10 species of wood for a period of 800 years beginning at the end of 4th century B.C. (Pomey and Guibal, 1995).

Study of Amphorae.   The study of amphorae has been active in recent years. An amphora typology has been published (Sciallano and Sibella, 1991) as well as several publications devoted to amphorae (Corsi-Sciallano and Liou, 1985) and their epigraphy (Liou, 1987, 1993; Liou and Gassend, 1990). The study of oil amphorae from Baetica is particularly interesting. At least five different painted inscriptions can be read on these amphorae, four of them now understood: a number indicating weight of the empty amphora, a number indicating weight of the oil, the name of the export trader, and a long inscription containing numerous data such as the names of the farm, owner, and person in charge of weighing, and the consular date. These data help clarify the organization of oil production in Baetica and describe more precisely the trade routes of this product.

Navalia. The remains of two buildings near the shore of the Gulf of Fos in Marseilles were discovered during air surveys in 1964 and 1973 and were studied from 1987 to 1994 by J.M. Gassend. This area is known as the Roman harbor of *Fossae Marianna*, now submerged. Harbor structures, a necropolis, and several wrecks have already been excavated and studied. Remains form two rectangular areas 100 × 36 m, identified by six parallel lines of stonework blocks, which measure 1.4 × 1.1 m and 0.6 m high. Each block includes a 0.45 × 0.55 m monolithic die with a 0.2 m-diameter mortise drilled in its center; the mortises were used to block the wooden posts supporting the building roof. The layout of these two buildings suggest that they could have been a shipyard or a shelter for ships, known in antiquity as *navalia* (Pomey, et al., 1992; Gassend, 1994).

The Middle Ages

The Batéguier Wreck. The Batéguier wreck was discovered off the harbor of Cannes in 1973. It was at a depth of 58 m and was first excavated in 1973 and 1974 by J.P. Joncheray. The site was disturbed by moorings and trawlers, and artifacts were spread over a large area. The most significant objects visible on the sea bottom were large earthenware jars, grindstones, iron anchors, and earthenware. All these artifacts, along with oil lamps, decorated plates, and Arabic graffiti, were characteristic of Muslim Spain and were dated from A.D. 10th century (Vindry, 1980). Twenty years later, another operation was undertaken on the site, to have a first look on the remains of the hull. A 11.35 × 4.3 m portion was examined and revealed a flat-bottomed ship with L-shaped futtocks, probably built following a skeleton-first principle. The nearest archaeological reference is the *Serçe Liman* wreck, found in Turkey and dating from A.D. 11th century. Earthenware, forming two homogenous series, was considered part of the cargo (Jezegou, et al., 1994).

The Aber Wrac'h 1 Wreck. This wreck was found in 1985 by R. Ogor, in the channel of l'Aber Wrac'h in Brittany at a depth of 15 m; it was excavated from 1987 to 1988 by M. L'Hour. Coherent ship's structures measuring 20 × 5 m were protected from a strong current by ballast stones. Our main interest in the wreck was the remaining portside structures. The ship was clinker-built, a technique observed for the first time in French waters. Surprisingly, clinker was associated with strong framing, which would have been more suitable for a carvel-built ship. A dendrochronological analysis of the wood failed to find a link with a known reference pattern, but the study of eight coins found among other artifacts (earthenware, animals bones) dated the site from the first half of the 15th century and showed a possible relation with a shipwreck that occurred in 1435, mentioned in a letter from Duke John V of Brittany. The northwestern European origin of the ship is quite certain (L'Hour and Veyrat, 1989).

The Cavalaire Wreck. Three separate elements of this wreck were discovered in 1987 and 1992 near the harbor of Cavalaire in the Mediterranean. The excavation, led by Marion Delhaye, lasted from 1994 to 1996. Our interest in this site was the simultaneous presence of elements of the hull either clinker-built or carvel-built. The main portion of the 15.3 × 3.3 m hull, identified as the bottom of the ship and her portside wall, was carvel-built; a second element was only clinker-built; the two methods were used simultaneously on a third portion. It is estimated that the hull was carvel-built below the level of the unique deck and clinker-built above. The ship had a calculated tonnage between 70 and 100 tons with a width of 5.75 m. The 4.18×0.65 m rudder was found in a perfect state of preservation.

In addition to a detailed description of the ship, this discovery allows an estimate of the height of the hull and the rake of the stern post. Another particularity of the site was the presence on board of eight wrought iron swivel guns found among other pieces of armament. Several rigging elements and earthenware were also found. Dendrochrono-logical analysis of the pine planking of the hold floor produced a date of 1479, but the oak used to build the hull structures could not be linked with a known reference pattern. An Atlantic origin of the ship is highly probable (Delhaye, et al., 1996).

The 16th Century

Lomellina. The wreck of a Genoese *nave* was discovered in the bay of Villefranche-sur-Mer near Nice in 1979 and excavated from 1982 to 1990. The ship, identified as *Lomellina* (Figure 27.2), capsized in the bay during a strong hurricane on 15 September 1516. Important hull remains were situated at a depth of 18 m, covered with sediment. The ship, under repair in the bay, had on board a cargo of guns and carriages, probably having to do with the Italian wars. The position of the wreck, leaning about 45° to port, made possible a study of two deck levels. The research design called for a study of ship's structures, ordnance, and equipment.

Lomellina has a 33.38 m long keel, is 14 m wide, and 4.4 deep. Overall estimated length is 46.5 m, and the calculated tonnage is 825 tons (Guérout, et al. 1989). Numerous important features and equipment were observed: a porthole still in position in the

Figure 27.2. Wreck of *Lomellina.*

portside wall (probably the most ancient ever observed); the lower part of the rudder; an intact capstan that was under repair; jeer bitts found dismantled in three parts in the hold, whose total length of 8.22 m gives the height of the missing third deck; an elm lateen mast-head, also found dismantled in the hold; feet and dales of pumps; and the location and structure of the powder hold and 21 associated powder barrels.

Besides giving a better understanding of shipbuilding principles and methods and a description of structures and timber work, *Lomellina's* main contribution was the remains of the main mast-step. Its structure, different from mast-steps of the shipbuilding tradition of the Atlantic Ocean, is similar to that of galleys and xebecs of the Mediterranean tradition, introducing evidence of a shipbuilding tradition of round ships that is not yet documented. These observations were supported by the study of shipbuilding contracts established in Genoa. In these documents, the terminology for building round ships was similar to the terminology for building galleys.

The excavation also helped to document the Genoese *nave*, a type of ship used for the transport of heavy cargoes through the Mediterranean Sea and to northwestern European countries. The study of weapons and gunnery improved our knowledge of 16th century ships' armament, although the cargo of guns and gunnery equipment was disturbed on several occasions either at the time of the sinking or in modern times.

Fifteen wrought iron breech-loading guns, some with their wooden carriages, were found and some were recovered. The chase is made of a stave-built cylinder reinforced by a series of iron rings, and the breech is a separate cylindrical container fitted with an iron ring for handling. Stone, iron, and lead shots were also brought to light, among them lead shots with an iron die inside. Several molds used to cast the lead shots were also found. Among the incendiary weapons are fire pots designed to be launched from the crow's nest down onto the enemy (Guérout and Rieth, 1997).

The Calvi Wreck.   This wreck was discovered at a depth of 9 m by DRASM during a 1979 survey in the harbor of Calvi, Corsica. A 9 × 5 m portion of the aft part of the hull was excavated by Pierre Villié from 1985 to 1988. The recovery of Ligurian and majolica ceramics dated the wreck from the end of the 16th century.

A detailed study and reconstitution were performed on the aft part of the ship, especially the framing and planking of the stern, a structure rarely preserved. The structure of the aft bottom portion of the hull and a portion of the port side, including a deck level, were also studied. The stern has a semicircular shape and unusually strong framing. The outside planking is made of diagonal boards inclined at an angle of either 30° or 60°. The inside planking is made of horizontal boards between the rails of the hull and, below them, is inclined at an angle of 30° on the horizontal. Two 43 × 43 cm-square, symmetrical stern-chase ports and a lateral porthole were documented (Villié, 1994). Although the shipbuilder is not known, the presence of a square stern is an important element for a better knowledge of the transition from round to square sterns in the Mediterranean and the Atlantic, a subject still not well-defined.

The 17th Century

La Hougue Wrecks.   The wrecks of Admiral Tourville's vessels, sunk in shallow waters in May 1692, are well known by local people. In 1985, the wrecks were precisely located by divers in the vicinity of the harbor of La Hougue. Twelve vessels, anchored near Saint-Vaast after the Battle of La Hougue, were attacked and destroyed by English launches and fire-ships. The study of five of these wrecks was conducted by Michel Cardin, and later by Michel L'Hour and Elisabeth Veyrat from 1990 to 1995, yielding important results. The study of the remains of these wrecks gave us a better knowledge of French navy shipbuilding under the reign of Louis XIV, and they allowed us to compare the rules laid down by Colbert for shipbuilding with the reality of shipyard work as well as the shipbuilding tradition of the different shipyards of the kingdom. The research also was especially interesting because few French navy shipwrecks of this period are known in the world.

Three vessels have been identified: the 84-gun *Saint-Philippe*, built by Rodolphe Gédéon at Toulon in 1665; the 86-gun *Magnifique*, built by Chapelle at Toulon in 1680; and the 92-gun *Ambitieux*, built by Malet at Rochefort in 1691. A complete study of the structural remains was made, and ceramics and wooden artifacts from the rigging were recovered (L'Hour and Veyrat, 1994).

Omonville La Rogue Wreck. The wreck was found in 1980 at the entrance of the small harbor of Omonville near Cherbourg, Normandy, at a depth of 10 m. The four-year excavation was conducted by Joe Guesnon from 1980 to 1983 and the results published in 1993 (Guesnon, 1993). Situated in a difficult natural environment (shallow waters, tidal current, poor visibility), the remains covered an area of 14 m × 3.5 m on a flat, sandy bottom. A remarkable excavation was done on this site, where only a portion of the starboard side of the hull had been preserved. A precise analysis of the hull remains indicated that it was a flat-bottomed ship with a calculated length of 21 m, a beam of 6 m, a draught of 2.6 m, and a tonnage of 150 tons. The hull was carvel-built according to the skeleton-first principle, with a mixed building method: shell-first for the bottom and skeleton-first for the top. This is a well-known Dutch shipbuilding principle, but Dutch origin for this wreck is not certain; it could have been of the *galiot* type. The recovery of one coin, pipes, and several ceramics from Normandy allowed us to date this site to near the end of the 17th century.

Cargo was composed of glass bottles and flat glass discs of about 1 m in diameter; the discs were raw material for window makers. The method of obtaining such a disc from an initial mass of glass originated in Normandy at the end of the 13th century and was still in use during the 18th century as a privilege for four families of the province.

The 18th Century

Slava Rossii. The wreck of *Slava Rossii* (Glory of Russia), a 66-gun Russian warship sunk November 3, 1780, was discovered off Levant Island in 1947. Excavation of the wreck took place in 1980 and 1981 and was first published in English in 1998. Among the artifacts found were a remarkable series of copper alloy icons, which contributes to a better knowledge of religious practices in the Russian Imperial Navy at the time of Catherine II. The discovery of a bronze gun called a unicorn, and three bronze Cohorn mortars, is testimony to Russian inventiveness in the field of gunnery: The unicorn is one of the first howitzer-type guns used at sea (Guérout, 1998).

The 19th Century

CSS *Alabama*. The Confederate raider CSS *Alabama* was sunk by the USS *Kearsarge* off Cherbourg, France, on June 16, 1864, after a war cruise of 22 months. The wreck was discovered with the use of sonar in October 1984, by the French navy mine hunter *Circé*, seven nautical miles off the harbor of Cherbourg, at a depth of 58 m. The wreck and its associated artifacts belong to the United States but, since *Alabama* lies in the French territorial waters, excavation is the responsibility of the French Ministry of Culture, advised by a Joint Scientific Committee created for the work. Site exploration and excavation was conducted from 1987 to 1995 by Max Guérout, with the assistance of Gordon Watts of East Carolina University.

The site's natural environment is difficult: Depth, poor visibility, cold water, and strong currents limit the dives to the period of slack tide. The research design concerns living conditions on board *Alabama*, mechanical propulsion and naval artillery, and evidence of the ship's operations. The most valuable contribution concerns the artillery, in particular the Rifled Muzzle Loaded (RML) Blakely gun. The recovery of the gun and of its pivoting platform, in a very good state of preservation, brought to light elements of this unique weapon designed by Alexander Theophilus Blakely and cast by the firm Fawcett & Preston. A shell found in place in the barrel (Figure 27.3) was first defused, then extracted, an operation that lasted a long time but allowed the recovery of the shell with its fuse, the lead sabot used to guide the shell into the grooves of the barrel, and remains of the cartridge. The shell apparently remained engaged in the barrel without being fired when the cease-fire order was given a few minutes before the order to abandon ship.

Parts of the propulsion system were studied: boilers, funnel, steam collectors, engine, and the propeller and its hoisting device. Two fire pumps were identified as Downton's patent pumps. Evidence of *Alabama*'s operations are given by a small number of artifacts: Brazilian 40-reis coins illustrate the stay of the *Alabama* at Bahia, Brazil, in May 1863; a sperm-whale tooth recalls the capture of whalers (14 were taken by the *Alabama*); and a crate with the inscription "Winchester Perfumed Saltwater Soap Boston Mass.", one of the raider's sixty-four prizes.

Operations on the *Alabama* site were stopped from 1995 to 1999 but are now being directed by G. Watts (Guérout, 1995).

Figure 27.3. Shell from CSS *Alabama*.

SS *Colombian*.   In 1985, the wreck of SS *Colombian* was found at a depth of 63 m in the channel of La Helle in Brittany. Property of the West India and Pacific Steam Ship Company Limited, *Colombian* was launched at Liverpool in 1864. This ship had a sail and steam propulsion, an iron-built hull, a length of 76 m and a tonnage of 1056 tons. Lost on January 17, 1864, during her maiden voyage from Liverpool to St. Thomas, Virgin Islands, she was carrying a general cargo of tableware, silverware, canvas, and leather and bronze harnessing. Excavation was conducted by Gilles Millot from 1986 to 1989. The difficult natural environment of the site limited the work to photographic coverage and artifact recovery, which gave an insight into general cargoes bound for South America. The tableware is represented by a large series of unusual Staffordshire Ironstone China made by Bodley & Harold at Burslem (Millot, 1990).

Magenta.   *Magenta*, a French navy ironclad frigate, exploded inside the harbor of Toulon in October 1875. In 1994, the frigate was discovered with the aid of a magnetometer, and its discovery brought to light a collection of antiquities from Tunisia. The antiquities were found in 1874 by archaeologist Pricot de Sainte Marie at Carthage and consisted of about 2100 Punic votive steles from the Tophet (the necropolis of Carthage), and a 2.1-m-high Roman marble statue of Empress Sabina, wife of Emperor Hadrian; they were loaded onto *Magenta* for shipment back to France. After the explosion, divers recovered 1500 steles, and major parts of the statue except a section of hip and the head. The wreck was destroyed with explosive charges to clear the harbor.

Excavation, led by GRAN from 1995 to 1998, recovered about 100 steles or fragments of steles and parts of the statue including the head. Votive Punic steles were dedicated to the gods, Tanit and Baal Hammon, on the occasion of the death of Carthage citizens.

Magenta herself, designed by naval engineer Dupuy de Lôme and built in Brest in 1860 after *Gloire*, belongs to a series of ironclad, wooden-wall vessels fitted with steam and sail propulsion and armed with rifled, breech-loading pivot guns. Her excavation was strictly limited by French authorities to structures and equipment found inside of the search area around the mizzenmast step. Two important elements of the structure have been observed and documented: the unusually large mizzenmast step, 3.30 m long and 0.90 m wide; and the stringer with indented joints linked to the diagonal lining, which was needed to reinforce the hull because of 800 tons of armour plating (Guérout, 1996).

FRENCH OVERSEAS DEPARTMENTS AND TERRITORIES

Martinique

A systematic survey of the coasts of Martinique has been underway since 1990, financed by the French Ministry of Culture, the Conseil Régional, and the Conseil Général of Martinique. The work is being conducted by GRAN under the direction of Marc Guillaume and encompasses different themes: the pre-Colombian period; discovery voyages; the struggle of European countries for the control of the West Indies; transatlantic trade; slave trade; and tramping in the West Indies and around the island. Excavations are not scheduled before the end of the survey. Only two test excavations have been undertaken on the wreck of the brig *Le Cygne* (1808) and the bark *Cato* (1893).

Nineteen wrecks were discovered around the island, and nine were identified:

- French bark *Notre Dame de Bonne Espérance*, lost in 1687 at the end of a voyage from Marseilles, while she was transporting convicts and Protestants;
- the 64-gun, ex-French HMS *Raisonnable*, stranded at the southwest end of the island in 1762, on the occasion of an attack of the island by an English fleet;
- French navy brig *Cygne*, sunk in 1808 by an English squadron blockading the island;
- French navy corvette *Caravane*, stranded on a coral reef during a hurricane in 1817;
- French bark *Edouard*, wrecked on a coral reef in 1845 while transporting spare parts for construction of the first sugar refinery of the "Usine centrale type" on the island;
- Schooner *Pigwidgeon* of Santa Lucia, wrecked on a coral reef in the south of the island in 1856;
- Norwegian collier bark *Cato*, with a cargo of coal from Cardiff, wrecked on a coral reef in 1893;
- French bark *Amélie*, stranded on a beach in 1902; and
- French bark *Biscaye*, with a cargo of cod from St. Pierre et Miquelon, sunk during the eruption of Mount Pelée in 1902.

Isolated, in situ artifacts were recorded as well as some on land, recovered by divers or fishermen. Among them were stones said to be Caribbean anchors, several ship bells, and a bronze minion cast under the reign of Henri VIII (Guérout and Guillaume, 1998).

French Polynesia

At the initiative of the government of French Polynesia, a program of inventory of French Polynesia's underwater heritage was undertaken. Data are being collected from archives and from inhabitants of the islands. Since 1992, this inventory has been the task of GRAN, under the direction of Robert Veccella. Main themes of research are pre-European Polynesian maritime activities, discovery voyages, control of the Pacific area by European countries, transpacific trade, whaling activities, and tramping between atolls and islands. Several sites have been surveyed:

- The sea bottom around the great *Marae* of Taputapuatea in Raiatea island, Society Islands, a primary Polynesian cult site destroyed by a tsunami.
- Channel entrances of several atolls, where fishing weights and Polynesian anchors were collected.
- The Dutch *Africaense Galley*, sunk in 1722 on the coral reef of Takapoto Atoll (Tuamotou); this wreck is one of the ships of the discovery expedition led by Roggeveen through the Pacific.
- American bark *Julia Ann*, sunk in 1854 on Manuae Atoll, also named Scilly, in the Society Archipelago; this site was discovered in 1997 in a joint operation of the Maritime Museum of Sydney and GRAN, under the authority of the Département d'Archéologie du Centre Polynésien des Sciences Humaines.
- Chilean ship (full-rigged) *Francisco Alvarez*, sunk in 1868 on Mangareva Island (Gambier Archipelago). Excavation was initiated October 2000 in cooperation with a Chilean archaeologist.

- Danish bark *Norby*, sunk in 1900 on Tepua reef, Raiatea Island, Society Archipelago.
- The four-masted *County of Roxburg*, sunk in 1906 during a hurricane on Takaroa Atoll (Tuamotou).

REFERENCES

Bernard, H., and Domergue, C., 1991, Les lingots de plomb de l'épave romaine Sud Perduto 2 (Bouches de Bonifacio, Corse). In *Bulletin de la Société des Sciences, Historiques & Naturelles de la Corse*, CXIème année, Fascicule no. 659, 1er Trimestre, pp. 41–64.

Bernard, H., and Chiapetti, J., 1993, Porto Novo. In *Bilan Scientifique 1992*, p. 61, *DRASM*, Paris.

Corsi-Sciallano, M., and Liou, B., 1985, *Les épaves de Tarraconaise à chargement d'amphores Dressel 2–4*, Archaeonautica, no. 5, CNRS, Paris.

Delhaye, M., Loewen, B., and Thirion, G., 1996, Epave médievale de Cavalaire. In *Bilan Scientifique 1995*, pp. 54–56, *DRASM*, Paris.

Gassend, J.M., 1994, Anse Saint-Gervais, Navalia. In *Bilan Scientifique 1993*, pp. 31–33, *DRASM*, Paris.

Guérout, M., 1995, CSS *Alabama*: Évaluation du Site (1988–1992). In *The Archaeology of Ships of War*, International Maritime Archaeological Series, Volume 1, edited by Mensun Bound, pp. 90–102. Nelson, Oswestry.

_____, 1996, Le Magenta. In *Bilan Scientifique 1995*, pp. 31–33, *DRASM*, Paris.

_____, 1998, The Wreck of the Slava Rossii. In *Excavating Ships of War*, International Maritime Archaeological Series, Volume 2, edited by Mensun Bound, pp. 194–202. Nelson, Oswestry.

Guérout, M., and Guillaume, M., 1998, The "Loup Garou" Bronze Gun from Martinica. *International Journal of Nautical Archaeology*, 27(2):150–159.

Guérout, M., and Rieth, E., 1998, The Wreck of the *Lomellina* at Villefranche sur Mer. In *Excavating Ships of War*, International Maritime Archaeological Series, Volume 2, edited by Mensun Bound, pp. 38–50. Nelson, Oswestry.

Guérout, M., Rieth, E., and Gassend, J.M., 1990, *Le navire gênois de Villefranche: Un naufrage de 1516?*, Archaeonautica, no. 9, CNRS, ed. Paris.

Guesnon, J., 1993, L'épave d'Omonville-la-Rogue (Manche). In *Archaeonautica, no. 11*. pp. 31–129. CNRS, Paris.

Hesnard, A., et al., 1988, *L'èpave romaine Grand Ribaud D (Hyères, Var)*. Archaeonautica no. 8. CNRS, Paris.

Jezegou, M.P., Joncheray, J.P., and Ximenes, S., 1994, Ile Sainte-Marguerite, Pointe du Batéguier. In *Bilan Scientifique 1993*. p. 52, DRASM, Paris.

L'Hour, M., 1987, Un Site Sous-marin sur la côte d'Armorique: l'épave de Ploumanac'h. *Revue Arch*éologique de l'Ouest 4:113–131.

L'Hour, M., and Veyrat, E., 1989, A Mid-XV Century Clinker Boat on the West Coast of France: The Aberwrac'h 1 Wreck. *International Journal of Nautical Archaeology* 18(4):285–298.

_____, 1994, The Wrecks of the Battle of La Hougue (1692): Evidence of Naval Construction in the 17th century. In *Proceedings of the 1994 Conference on Underwater Archaeology*, pp. 57–71. Vancouver.

Liou, B., 1987, Inscriptions peintes sur Amphores: Fos, Marseille, Toulon, Port-La-Nautique, Arles, Saint-Blaise, Saint-Martin-de-Crau, Mâcon, Calvi. In *Archaeonautica, no. 7,* pp. 55–139. CNRS, Paris.

_____, 1993, Inscriptions Peintes sur Amphores de Narbonnes (Port-La-Nautique). In *Archaeonautica, no. 11*, pp. 131–148. CNRS, Paris.

Liou, B., and Gassend, J.M., 1990, L'épave de Saint-Gervais 3 à Fos-sur-mer (milieu du Ier siècle AP. J.C.). Inscriptions peintes sur amphores de Bétique. Vestiges de la coque. In *Archaeonautica, no 10*. pp. 157–264. CNRS, Paris.

Long, L., 1997, Inventaire des épaves de Camargue. In *Crau, Alpilles, Camargue, Histoire et Arch*éologie. pp. 59–115. Groupe Archéologique Arlésien, Arles.

Long, L. et al., 1993, Ile de Porquerolles, Pointe Lequin 1A. In *Bilan Scientifique du DRASSM 1992*. p. 50. Ministère de la Culture, Paris.

Long, L., and Volpe, G., 1994, La scavo del relitto tardo antico della Palud (Isola di Port-Cros) Francia: prime note sulla campagna 1993. *Vetera Christianorum* 31:211–233.

Long, L., and Domergue, C., 1995, Le "véritable plomb de L. Flavius Verucla" et autres lingots, L'épave des Saintes-Maries-de-la-mer, In *MEFRA*, 107, 95, 2. pp. 801–867.

Lopez, A., 1994, Dramont 1. In *Bilan Scientifique du DRASSM 1993*. p. 51. Ministère de la Culture, Paris.

Millot, G., 1990, Le naufrage du vapeur anglais Colombian. *Le Chasse-Marée* 51:26–37.

Pomey, P., 1995, Les épaves grecques et romaines de la Place Jules Verne à Marseille. In *Compte-rendus de l'académie des Inscriptions et Belles Lettres*, avril-juin. pp. 459–484. Paris.

_____, 1997, Le navire. In *La navigation dans l'Antiquité*, edited by P. Pomey, pp. 60–101. Aix-en-Provence.

Pomey, P. et al., 1988, Avant-port de Carry. In *Gallia Informations, Recherches sous-marines 1987–1988*. pp. 9–11. CNRS, Paris.

_____, 1992, Fos-sur-Mer. In *Gallia Informations, Recherches sous-marines*. pp. 16–18. CNRS, Paris.

Pomey, P., and Guibal, F., 1996, Dendrochronologie et Dendromorphologie des épaves Antiques de Méditerranée. In *Bilan Scientifique du DRASSM 1995*. p. 56. Ministère de la Culture, Paris.

Rival, M., 1991, *La charpenterie navale romaine*. Paris.

Sciallano, M., 1995, Giraglia. In *Bilan Scientifique du DRASSM 1994*. p. 60. Ministère de la Culture, Paris.

Sciallano, M., and Sibella, P., 1991, *Les Amphores: Comment les Identifier?*. Edisud, Aix-en-Provence.

Tchernia, A., Pomey, P., and Hesnard, A., 1978, *L'épave romaine de la Madrague de Giens*, Supplement 34 de Gallia, Paris.

Villié, P., 1994, *Calvi 1*. De Boccard, Paris.

Vindry, G., 1980, Présentation de l'épave arabe du Batéguier. In *La céramique médiévale en Méditerranée occidentale Xéme-XIéme siècles, Valbonne, 1978*. pp. 221–226, CNRS, Paris.

Chapter 28

Italy

CARLO BELTRAME

INTRODUCTION

Management and Research in Underwater Archaeology

In Italy, both maritime and terrestrial archaeological affairs are under the authority of the Ministry of *Beni e Attività Culturali*. Sicily, an autonomous region, is an exception. Here all archeology lies within the competence of *Assessorato alla Cultura*. The ministry and the *Assessorato* use *soprintendenze archeologiche* (archaeological superintendencies) to supervise the territory. Each office controls the management of the inland waters and seas within its jurisdiction, but few have scientific staff who can dive, or specialist technicians and equipment. To overcome this gap, they finance private companies and professional underwater archaeologists on an *ad hoc* basis.

In 1986, the Ministry established a centralized operations group to provide technical support to the superintendencies that need help with problems relating to underwater archaeology. In practice, this service failed because of a lack of equipment and scientific programs and thus was shut down (Beltrame, 1995). Today the Ministry is restructuring its maritime archeology services through the creation of operative groups in each superintendency. In Sicily, the region formed a centralized group in 1999, called G.I.A.S.S., the group receives technical support from the police, Carabinieri, Capitanerie di Porto, and Guardia di Finanza. In Venice, a new office (NAUSICAA) became project coordinator for the superintendency of Veneto, Friuli Venezia Giulia, Emilia Romagna, and Marche regions.

Carlo Beltrame, Dipartimento di Scienze dell' Antichità e del Vicino Oriente, Università Ca' Foscari di Venezia, S. Polo 1977, 30125 Venezia, Italy.

International Handbook of Underwater Archaeology, edited by Carol V. Ruppé and Janet F. Barstad. Kluwer Academic/Plenum Publishers, New York, 2002.

Italian academic enterprise in the field of underwater archeology is rare. Foreign universities have undertaken some projects, though the most recent missions in Sicily of Mensun Bound (MARE-Oxford University) and A.J. Parker (University of Bristol) go back to 1988. The Germans of G. Martin's DEGUWA are currently the only foreigners engaged in underwater research in Italy.

Museums

Some small museums in Italy are completely or partly devoted to maritime archaeology: *Museo delle Navi* at Fiumicino (five boats and elements of a few others discovered on the site of the ancient harbor of Claudio during airport construction); *Museo delle Navi* at Nemi (two models of ships from Lake Nemi, burned during World War II, on display with objects salvaged from them); *Museo Navale Romano* at Albenga (finds from Roman wrecks of Albenga and Diano Marina); *Museo Archeologico Navale* at La Maddalena, Sassari (a monographic show of the Roman wreck of Spargi); *Museo di Capo Lilibeo* at Marsala (a gallery dedicated to the Punic Ship); *Museo Eoliano* at Lipari (an underwater section with many amphorae, anchors and other finds from various ancient wrecks); *Museo Nazionale Archeologico di Aquileia* (a gallery displaying a Roman boat); and *Museo del Mare* at San Vito Lo Capo (one room, dedicated to underwater archaeologist Fabio Faccenna, containing amphorae, cargo, and other finds from a wreck of the 12th century).

A national museum is opening at Grado (Gorizia). A suitable building was restored and the cargo and hull of Imperial wreck will be on display.

Training

Courses in underwater archaeology have recently begun to be taught at some universities, in the *curriculum* for the degree in Conservation of Cultural Resources (Conservazione dei Beni Culturali). Piero Alfredo Gianfrotta started the first course in Viterbo, and similar courses have also begun in Venice, Ravenna, Agrigento, Lecce, Naples, and Pisa.

Thanks to European Union financing, theoretical and practical courses for the training of technical operators have been organized at centers of professional training. These courses will enable staff to work with specialized companies. Often the courses are attended by archaeology students who wish to learn to work under water. Practical training is sometimes carried out at an archaeological site (see San Vito Lo Capo).

Scientific Debate and Popular Scientific Work

The annual review of underwater archaeology at Giardini Naxos in Sicily has become the key meeting for all those involved in this field in Italy, with some participation from abroad by invitation. The review is a clearinghouse for current research and news of salvage excavations. Every year, a distinguished scholar in the field is awarded a prize.

The first National Congress of Underwater Archaeology, organized by the Association of Underwater Archaeologists (A.I.A.Sub), was held in Anzio in 1996. The following year, the annual Summer School of Research in Archaeology was held at the *Certosa* of Pontignano (Siena) and dedicated to underwater archaeology. Teachers at this meeting were Italian, French, and Israeli scholars. The proceedings of these meetings have been published punctually, whereas the last edition of the review of the Naxos meeting was published in 1991.

The periodic review, *Archeologia Subacquea*: *Studi, ricerche e documenti*, edited by the University of Viterbo (Poligrafico—Libreria dello Stato), and the *Bollettino di Archeologia Subacquea* of the Ministero dei Beni Culturali e Ambientali, are also specialist publications. The latter is not for sale and has a very limited circulation. *Archeologia delle acque*, a review dedicated to wetland archaeology, and *Navis*, a periodical specializing in nautical archaeology, ethnography, and history, are new, edited publications.

Communication of ideas and new discoveries, review of publications in the field, and deontological debate takes place in the newsletter *L'Archeologo subacqueo*, edited by Edipuglia (Bari), a subscription quarterly.

Associations

A.I.A.Sub was established in 1993. The *Associazione degli Archeologi Subacquei*, based in Rome, was founded by individuals drawn from the staffs of superintendencies and academia, and self-employed professionals. Its aim was to establish professional standards and practices, protect the partners' interests, promote the image of maritime archaeologists, and develop a policy for preservation of the underwater cultural heritage. The organization promoted a bill on underwater archaeology which, after extensive amendments, was not approved by Parliament.

Volunteers

Amateurs work either in research or the training field, organizing theoretical and practical introductory courses in this subject. When volunteers are supported or supervised by serious researchers, as in the case of the surveying operations of submerged structures of ancient Baia, interesting scientific results can be obtained.

LEGISLATION

The law covering underwater cultural resources is the same that protects other historical assets of the state, Law 1089 of 1939. According to this law, when an archaeological find of interest (50 years or older) is discovered under water, it must not be removed from its context but must be reported to the authorities. The discoverer has a right to a reward, which must be equal to a quarter of the find's value.

Authorities can stop navigation and diving in some zones of the sea so that archaeological sites can be protected. Serious damage is caused to shipwrecks by the nets of fishing boats which, especially in the upper Adriatic, continuously "plow" the sea beds, mixing every sort of archaeological evidence. Despite the strictness of Law 1089, however, lack of any limit on underwater activity and the popularity of underwater sports have caused looting of a great part of Italy's submarine cultural resource. It is difficult to prosecute clandestine exporting, and today some masterpieces of ancient art discovered in Italian waters are in other countries. Prominent examples are the statue of the Fano athlete in the J. Paul Getty Museum, Malibu, California, and the bronze elm of Giglio, an archaic wreck now in a German bank. "Thanks" to technology, new dangers are looming:

the use of submarines cannot be controlled in any way. They can enter Italian territorial waters and illegally remove every artifact they find. There has been a big controversy over the recent explorations of Ballard's submarine along Italy's coasts.

PROBLEMS

After a good period in the 1960s and 1970s, Italian underwater archaeology now suffers from many problems which slow its development in comparison with other countries. First, in the ministry and in each superintendency, there is not enough specialized staff—that is, archaeologists able to work under water, experts in nautical and maritime archaeology, and trained specialists in the management of underwater cultural resources. Usually, the ministry ignores the specific training needed by its staff to deal with tasks in this field. It lacks its own equipped ship and must contract work out to companies with suitable craft.

In 1995, the Ministry tried to constitute a national commission of experts for planning underwater activities and for operating in the most pressing or scientifically interesting situations. Unfortunately, the commission had a short life. Now Italian underwater archaeology, except in a few situations, continues to show undue improvisation.

A specialized center for the conservation of underwater finds is necessary. Because resources are scarce, it probably should be a single center managed by a specialized staff well-informed in the most modern techniques such as freeze-drying. Today, this effort is the responsibility of the Central Institute for Restoration (ICR). At least in the conservation of wet wood, the ICR has found itself to be inadequately trained. Sometimes Italy has had to ask for help from foreign specialists (see the Punic Ship of Marsala).

Italy still lacks a school of underwater archaeology, and the establishment of a field-school is critical. Students who want such training must participate in foreign projects as volunteers. The university, as well as the Ministry B.A.C., is also absent from research, and scientific production comes largely from volunteers, students, or amateurs.

Private companies to which the superintendencies contract work are not always specialized, and sometimes they lack adequate experience. Obviously, such arrangement can jeopardize the scientific value of the operations.

Finally, in Italy there is still no sensibility for nautical archaeology in general or, in particular, for naval architecture. The discipline has no space in either the academic or in ministerial environment. This lack is unacceptable if we think of the role that Italy has played in the history of navigation and in ship construction in general.

PROGRESS

Positive signals are not entirely absent, and they come principally from young people. Those who want to specialize in the field go abroad, especially to France, where they can study special topics (such as naval architecture) and where they can train in underwater excavation.

The lack of a specialist review is now filled by the collection of the University of Viterbo, *L'archeologo subacqueo*, *Navis*, *Archelogia della acque*, and by the proceedings of congresses which are organized occasionally.

The new A.I.A.Sub brings together for the first time all Italian specialists in the field, with the aim of protecting the professional and scientific status of underwater archaeology. *L'Archeologo subacqueo* is an ideal venue for the expression of opinions and for the exposure of bad situations.

Finally, we no longer experience a total lack of dialogue between underwater and "land" archaeologists. After the death of Nino Lamboglia, the pioneer of underwater archaeology, land archaeologists gave our discipline a more "sporting" than scientific image, perhaps justly. Today, underwater archaeologists must be trained in the analysis of terrestrial deposits and must receive basic preparation in all scientific subjects applied to archaeology. These requirements, which abroad might seem an obvious prerequisite, are for Italy a recent and not fully completed conquest.

Important news comes from nautical archaeology. In 2000, Italy hosted the Ninth International Symposium on Boat and Ship Archaeology (ISBSA). This author in collaboration with the Dipartimento di Scienze dell'Antichità e del Vicino Oriente of Venice University, organized this important international conference on nautical archaeology. The theme was "Boats, Ships and Shipyards." This was an excellent opportunity to promote underwater archaeology in Italy where, at the moment, amateurs and junior researchers are the only specialists.

THE FUTURE

How can Italian underwater archaeology improve? In our opinion, five main steps should be taken by the Ministry of Culture:

1. It should engage young specialized archaeologists and form one or more teams to operate in the whole territory in collaboration with the superintendencies.
2. It should provide an equipped center and a ship with crew to operate on the seas.
3. It should engage divers specializing in archaeology, selecting some who are now working for private companies.
4. The Ministry of University should immediately introduce a course in "nautical archaeology," which must be assigned to foreign as well as Italian specialists in naval architecture, a course that will cover the history of ship in general. This course and underwater archaeology should be taught at the post-graduate level in the various schools of specialization.
5. Academic instructors must organize field schools for practical training.

SCIENTIFIC NEWS

Despite this rather gloomy view of the institutional situation of Italian underwater archaeology, there have been a number of scientific developments.

Technique

Coop. Aquarius has set up a new survey system, a rectangular metal frame with tubes having a square section. A bar slides in between the frame; one of the short sides is hooked to a steel cable with a spirit level in the center of an archaeological site. The structure is moved along the cable from one side of the site to the other, always

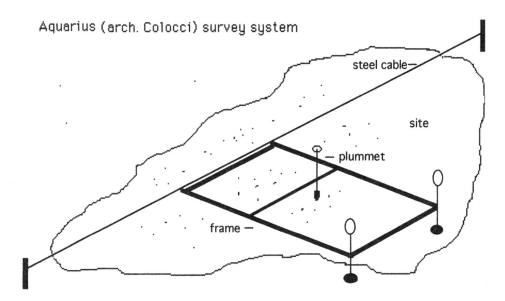

Figure 28.1. M. Colocci's survey system.

positioned with the spirit level. Two small buoys keep the frame level. The sector limited by the frame must be photographed, and the elements that must be surveyed are reproduced on a polyester sheet. The survey of the points registered on the drawing (which must be transported to the site) is by Cartesian coordinates read on the mobile bar and on the long sides of the frame, while the third dimension is measured by a plummet (Figure 28.1).

All data are recorded in a computer and elaborated by CAD software, which permits error checking and correcting of inaccuracies; the result is a 3-D graphic. This way, if only two points of an amphora (the lowest and the highest) are known, by vector analysis one can easily reconstruct the order of the cargo which has been mixed up during the wrecking of the ship. The system is quick and sharp and has been applied satifactorily on Grado, Porto Palo, and Sciacca wrecks.

The following sections discuss the main investigations along the Italian coasts, from 1989 to the present. They are presented in chronological order, dividing the ancient age from medieval and modern; and geographic order, along the littorals from Trieste to Sicily, from there to Liguria, then to the isle of Sardinia (Figure 28.2).

Ancient Wrecks

Grado. Off Grado, at 16 m deep, lies a Roman shipwreck that has been the object of an excavation and recovery project directed by the superintendency of Friuli Venezia Giulia. Aquarius, which carried out the work, surveyed, excavated, and salvaged the hull and the cargo, which was composed of at least one layer of amphorae. All the amphorae of the types Africana I A, Tripolitana I (Auriemma, 1997a), of Coan tradition, and the small amphorae Dressel 19 (Dell'Amico, 1997) held either fish sauce or small pieces of fish that were perfectly preserved. Because of the cargo's characteristics, dated at about the middle of A.D. 2nd century, researchers believe it could have been taken on board in an

Figure 28.2. Italy's archaeological sites mentioned in text. 1-Grado; 2-1 Caorle; 3-Eraclea; 4-Malamocco (Venice); 5-Pesaro; 6-Palodmbina (Ancona); 7-Torre S. Sabina, Punta del Serrone (Brindisi); 8-Catania; 9-Ognina (Siracusa); 10-Portopalo; 11-Camarina; 12-Gela; 13-Sciacca; 14-San Vito lo Capo; 15-Lipari; 16-Punta Mazza (Milazzo); 17-Capo Rasocolmo; 18-Punta Licosa; 19-"Flegrean area" (Baia, Bacoli, Nisida, Pozzuoli, Miseno); 20-Cala Rossano (Ventotene); 21-Ponza; 22-Anzio; 23-Capo Linaro (S. Marinella); 24-Golfo di Baratti; 25-Secche della Meloria; 26-Varazze; 27-Diano Marina; 28-Porto S. Paolo, Capo Coda Cavallo (Olbia); 29-Mal di Ventre; 30-Alghero; 31-Cala Reale, Capo Galera (Asinara).

Adriatic harbor. African and oriental amphorae could be reused for the fish (Auriemma, 1997a).

Part of the cargo, on the ship's prow, was a cask filled with broken glass vessels probably meant for recycling. There are many marked fragments, most unpublished, which may provide new information about glass production and commerce. This is the first real archaeological evidence of recycling of materials in antiquity (Giacobelli,

1997). In addition to a *dolium*, common and African pottery belonged to the vessel's outfit.

The wreck is interesting not only for the history of commerce but also for finds in the hold, which give an idea of shipboard life: games (a die, some game pieces), commerce (a scale), and religion (a bronze statuette of Poseidon). A large block with six pulleys and one "bilge pump" are unique. A lead tube protruding from the bottom of the vessel could have belonged to a piston-pump. If this is the case, it would be the first evidence of the use of this device on a ship (Dell'Amico, 1997).

Particulars of hull construction are interesting. This is one of the few Roman ships in which a wall is preserved up to the water line. One clearly can see how minor was the role of the frames in the shell first construction; in fact, the frames often are represented only by worked or peeled logs (Dell'Amico, 1997).

In 1998, researchers surveyed the hull with the aim of engineering a shell, supported by a metal frame, which would have permitted a complete salvage. The plans were to clean the hull and survey it in detail once it was out of the sea. This interesting salvage project, totally experimental, unfortunately did not run. Because of technical problems, the hull had to be rescued in pieces.

During 2000, individual pieces of wood were documented on a 1:1 scale. They are now being conserved in PEG (Beltrame and Gaddi, 2000). Study and reconstruction of the hull has begun. After restoration, the wreck will be reassembled and exhibited with its cargo in the museum. The Grado wreck is one of the few that has been excavated with good methods and has been studied and published almost entirely.

After every field season, the site was covered with a layer of sand and metal nets and kept on site by chains fixed to cement blocks, to protect it from theft. This system is also effective in preventing the devastating passage of fishing tools.

Also during 2000, another wreck was discovered off Grado. An initial survey led to the recovery of two lead anchor stocks and a few amphorae of southern Italian origin. These items are important because they are older than the foundation of the nearby city of Aquileia. This wreck dates to the first half of the 3rd century B.C., making it the oldest wreck found in the northern Adriatic Sea (Tortorici, 2000).

Caorle.   The Roman wreck of Caorle was found near international waters, at less than 30 m deep. The site, documented by the superintendency for Veneto through videos, appears to be a classic ellipsoidal tumulus of amphorae, covered by a layer of concretion 30 cm thick; through a crack, one can see that the amphorae have maintained their integrity and are still disposed on at least two levels. Visible amphorae are Lamboglia 2 and date to the second century B.C.

The site, already damaged by fishing boats, is now protected by a covering made of two layers of geotextile divided by a metal net; cement tetrapods have been placed around the site (Fozzati et al., 1995, 1997). Because of the extraordinary environment that "sealed" the wreck, and in spite of the clandestine removal of some containers, the cargo may be complete, and the hull seems to be in good condition. The wreck appears to be one of the more promising along the Italian coasts, but its distance from land makes investigation and supervision very expensive.

Venice-Lido.   Near the entrance to Malamocco harbor in Venice-Lido, researchers of the San Marco Diving Club have discovered numerous fragments of elm planks and an oak floor timber of a sewn boat. C-14 dates between A.D. 1 and 144 associate this wreck with other Roman hulls of the upper Adriatic zone built with the same technique. During the Roman age, this system of planking connection, typical of the Archaic age and alternative to the "mortise and tenon" type, is not present in other zones of the Mediterranean (Beltrame, 1996b; 2000).

Artifacts from the area of the wreck (amphorae, anchors, mill-stones, a clay *mortarium*, a lithic weight shaped like a truncated pyramid with lateral holds), and objects from the so-called "glass wreck" are evidence of many passages through the harbor during ancient times (Beltrame, 1993).

Palombina.   A Roman wreck investigated in the 1970s (Mercando, 1983) was the object of two seasons of excavation at the beach of Palombina (Ancona) by the archaeological superintendency for Marche. Amphorae found in the 1970s and initially classified as *brindisine* actually belong to the *ante 6B* kind of Altino (see Toniolo, 1991), which dates to the first half of the 1st century B.C. The wreck's hull awaits a good survey and study, but the waves and a thick layer of sand complicate operations. The ship lies between 4 and 5 m deep.

Torre S. Sabina.   In Torre S. Sabina Bay (Brindisi), parts of at least two hulls, at fewer than 3 m deep, are among scattered wrecks of Greek and Roman age (7th century B.C. to A.D. 6th century). The Greek and Roman wrecks were investigated by Lamboglia and Aquarius and, recently, their numerous pottery artifacts have been examined closely (Pietropaolo, 1997). One hull is especially interesting because of its foremast step, but it has no cargo (R. Auriemma, personal communication; Beltrame, 1996a).

Punta del Serone.   At Punta del Serrone (Brindisi), the most exciting discovery since the bronzes of Riace was made in 1992. One hundred fifty fragments of bronze statues were found, among which are seven heads and two busts. Because these works of art span a period from the Hellenistic age to about A.D. 3rd century, we believe they were a cargo of metal ready for recasting. The rocky bottom (fewer than 15 m deep) did not preserve any trace of the ship except a sounding-lead, some pieces of lead foil, and one lead ring. However, fragments of late Roman amphorae, probably from the cargo, suggest that it was a craft from the end of the Roman Empire.

Coast of Salento.   The Coast of Salento, in the context of a CNR "strategic project," has been the locale of the compilation of a detailed archaeological map by a Ph.D. student. Data for the Salento suggest a privileged relation with the opposite shore, emphasized by a quantitative relevance of Corinthian importation and, mainly in the late Hellenistic and Roman–Republican age, a prominent role in the Adriatic trade (Auriemma, 1997b). On the map is also an interesting cargo of Keay LII amphorae dating between A.D. 6th and 7th centuries, produced in Southern Italy (Auriemma, 1998).

Ognina.   Moving to Sicily, we report researches being carried out by the University of Catania along the coast of Catania, on wrecks and ancient anchorages. In Ognina beach (Siracusa), the university group is reexamining a cargo of Lamboglia 2 amphorae discovered in 1969 (La Fauci at Naxos 1997). DEGUWA (Berlin), directed by G. Martin, also operates in Ognina, studying wrecks of Corinthian amphorae (4th century B.C.).

Porto Palo.   In deep waters, at less than 45 m, lies the Hellenistic wreck of Porto Palo di Capo Passero (Syracuse). The site is composed of a cargo of Greek–Italic amphorae from the 4th to the 3rd century B.C., and by a *louterion*, a clay basin with stand (Basile, 1997). The excavation, carried out by Aquarius on behalf of the superintendency of Syracuse, is now on hold.

Camarina.   The bay under the ancient city of Camarina is one of the richest in archaeological evidence of the littoral zone. Here, at 50 m from the beach, are wrecks and many sporadic objects, which can be dated from the Classical to the Modern Age.
The most interesting ancient wreck is a cargo of two marble columns 6 m long. The site, surveyed by the University of Bristol, was the object of excavation and tests by Aquarius and directed by the Archaeological Museum of Camarina in 1989 and 1996. Part of the hull has been found under the columns. It seems that various kinds of bronze vases, three strigils, many *missiles* acorns (*glandes*), and three lance points also come from the site (Di Stefano, 1992). African and Oriental amphorae, as well as some African pottery, may date the wreck to the end of A.D. 2nd century (Di Stefano, Naxos 1996; Tortorella, 1981: 362).

Gela.   The most interesting wreck of the Greek age is certainly the Gela wreck, dated to the beginning of the 5th century B.C. The craft was constructed with the sewn technique, a system of planking junction alternative to the most common "mortise and tenon" and often used on hulls of Archaic age. The cargo was Greek–Oriental amphorae and figured pottery from various countries. Many artifacts, such as a bronze tripod, four small, clay altars, a bone flute and stylus, and eight vegetal fibers baskets also come from the wreck (Fiorentini, 1990; Beltrame, 1998). Lying at only 5 m deep, this wreck has been incompletely investigated, but an analysis would certainly contribute to the study of ancient shipbuilding techniques, redistributive commerce of Archaic age, and shipboard life. A few hundred meters from this wreck lies another, dated to the middle of the 5th century B.C. Preliminary investigations have shown it to be a hull constructed by the mortise and tenon technique (although there is probably at least one sewn repair), covered and protected by a heap of stones similar to the ballast of the first Gela wreck (Faccenna, 1997). Survey of the hull began during the 1997 field season, promoted by the superintendency of Caltanissetta (Benini and Panvini, Naxos 1997).

Sciacca.   The superintendency of Agrigento has investigated a 1st century B.C. wreck off Sciacca. Only the hull, some lamps and amphorae, and one lead anchor-stock survive from this ship, which lies at fewer than 25 m deep.

Trapani.   The G.I.A.S.S. Group coordinated the excavation of an A.D. 3rd century Roman wreck at Lido Marausa near Trapani. The ship, of which a section of the hull is preserved, carried African amphorae. The same group, with Marenostrum association, has begun surveying a 2nd century B.C. wreck in the sea of Porto Palo of Menfi (Agrigento). The ship carried both Punic (Mana z type) and Italic (Dressel 1 type) amphorae.

Porto Palo bi Menfi.   Between our index of wrecks, we report the finding of a bronze statue of a satyr and a bronze of an elephant leg off Trapani in 1998. In the past, one foot of the satyr statue was salvaged from the same zone. This exceptional discovery, made by a fishing boat, has had a negative effect on underwater archaeology, showing it as a simple salvage operation of works of art.

Punta Mazza.   Among the investigations carried out by Aquarius and various superintendencies in Sicily, in addition to the one at Lipari on a small late Roman cargo of tin ingots (Freschi, 1992), we report the excavation of a Roman wreck with oriental wine amphorae at Punta Mazza (Milazzo). Nine types of containers (Knossos 18, Dressel 30. . .) could date to the first half of A.D. 3rd century (Ollà, 1997).

Capo Rasocolmo.   The superintendency of Messina investigated a late Republican wreck of Capo Rasocolmo (Messina). Some nails are the only remains of the hull, while 15 elements of rotary millstones (part of the cargo or ballast) are preserved. The presence of melted lead and *glandes missiles* mean that it could be a military ship. Many coins were found at the site, including some Pompeo Magnos, and a small bronze plate carrying the name MAGNUS. These objects suggest a connection with military events involving Sicily during the triumvirate period (Bacci, 1994). If this is the case, it would be the first discovery of a military vessel of Roman age.

Punta Licosa.   Investigations by the superintendency of Salerno and the University of Viterbo have been conducted at Punta Licosa (Salerno) on a Dressel 1 amphorae wreck from the beginning of the 1st century B.C. On the site, which lies at fewer than 32 m deep, were a lead anchor stock and a lead tube.

Cala Rossano.   To the north, at Cala Rossano on the island of Ventotene, a wreck, partially looted, was excavated in 1990. It contained Dressel 8 and 9 amphorae and tin ingots. Amphorae preserved *tituli picti*, which identified the merchant's name and product (fish sauce). Only elements of the bilge pump remain from the hull. Analyzing the cargo and pottery, researchers deduce that the vessel left from a harbor of *Betica* and wrecked between A.D. 30 and 60 (Arata, 1993).

Ponza.   In the same archipelago, at Ponza, an emergency operation was mounted by volunteer Association A.S.S.O. on a Roman wreck in the harbor. Only disconnected elements of the hull, destroyed by the passage of motorboats, and bronze artifacts relating to the bilge-pump, still remain (Galli, 1995; 1996). The island also is famous for another wreck, well preserved, from the beginning of A.D. first century (Galli, 1993).

Capo Linaro.   One of the latest finds is a hull, dated to the middle of the A.D. 1st century, that was discovered a few meters from the beach of Capo Linaro at Santa Marinella. The hull is about 5 m long and in good condition. Survey operations, done by Istituto Centrale per il Restauro and still in progress (Petriaggi, Naxos 1997), unfortunately are not being overseen by a specialist in ancient naval architecture.

Golfo di Baratti.   Known from 1974 is the Golfo di Baratti wreck, on which excavation inexplicably stopped in 1989. From this site came many artifacts: glass cups, one precious bronze and two clay lamps, Dressel 1A amphorae, *lagynoi*, Campanian A, common and Oriental pottery, various metal vessels, one ink pot and one arm of a small wooden statuette. The most interesting artifacts were pieces that probably belonged to a doctor: a bronze cupping vessel, a lithic *mortarium*, a hooked tool, and 136 wooden and bone bottles containing essences or spices. Dates of the wreck extend from 140 to 120 B.C. (*Relitto del Pozzino*, 1990). We still await final publication of the excavation data, especially on the hull, of this important wreck.

Toscama Caladel Barbiere.   In 1998, the archaeological superintendency of Tosca began investigating an A.D. 1st–2nd century wreck in *Cala del Barbiere*, near Punta Ala (Grosseto). The ship, discovered by Nino Lamboglia in the 1970s, carried Dressel 20, Gauloise 4 and 5, Forlimpopoli B, and Dressel 2–4 amphorae. Mortise and tenons join the planks of the hull. The frames are connected to the planking not only by wooden pegs, but also by nails.

Secche Della Meloria.   Survey and study of two ancient ships wrecked at Secche della Meloria (Livorno) is being conducted by two enterprising students. One wreck, completely crumbled by waves, now appears as a group of ceramic blocks and amphorae cemented by concretions. The load was composed of Greco–Italic amphorae and black glazed pottery, which date to around the middle of the 3rd century B.C. (Bargagliotti et al., 1997).

Diano Marina.   Excavation of the Roman wreck of *Diano Marina* closed the long and profitable activity of the Centro Sperimentale di Archaeologia Sottomarina, created by Nino Lamboglia and, after his death, carried on by Francisca Pallarés). Between 1958 and 1991, the center dealt with all Italian maritime archaeology, thanks to a convention with the Minister B.C.A.

The *Diano Marina* ship carried wine in *dolia* and amphorae Dressel 2–4. Located at fewer than 40 m deep, the wreck's relatively good condition made possible the reconstruction of the order of the cargo in the hull. The ship, from the Iberian peninsula, probably wrecked during the half of A.D. 1st century (Pallarés, 1991; 1995–1996). This wreck was partially investigated during the center's final field season of 1991.

Olbia.   Moving on to the Island of Sardinia, we report investigations which the superintendency of Sassari and Nuoro are promoting along the northeast littorals of the island. During the investigation two hulls were discovered at Porto S. Paolo and Capo Coda Cavallo (Olbia), connected by the "mortise and tenon" technique (Riccardi, 1996).

Mal di Ventre.   The Isle of Mal di Ventre (Oristano) is the wreck site of a Roman ship carrying lead ingots. From Spain, the ingots carry the mark of the PONTILIENI family. Artifacts from the vessel, such as Dressel 1 amphorae and common pottery, date the site between 90 and 50 B.C. (Salvi, 1992). The ingots are of interest to the National Institute of Nuclear Physics because of the absence of radioactivity. Analysis of this cargo will contribute much to the study of metal exportation from Iberian mines and the people involved in this commerce.

Alghero and Cala Reale.   The discovery of a Dressel 2–4 amphorae wreck of *Flavii*'s age at Alghero, and another wreck at Cala Reale (L'Asinara) carrying Iberic amphorae containing fish are recent (P. Spanu, personal communication). The Iberic amphorae wreck can be dated to the 4th–5th centuries (Spanu, 1997).

Medieval and Modern Wrecks

Lake Garda.   In 1996, the galley liing in Lake Garda, already explored by the Natural History Museum of Verona, was videodocumented by the archaeological superintendency of Veneto (Bondioli et al., 1997). This is one of the few preserved galleys. It is 30 m long. The ship was probably a *fusta* that was deliberately sunk by loading with stones and setting a fire as the Venetians retreated from the lake in 1509.

Eraclea, Venice Lido, and Malamocco. About 500 m from Eraclea beach near Venice, the wreck of a 19th century military ship has finally seen the light of the day (Fozzati et al., 1997). Farther south, off Venice Lido, a 1997 investigation of a wreck carrying bricks, probably dating to the Renaissance, has been promoted by the superintendency for Veneto. Before the harbor of Malamocco, a site known as the "glass wreck" site was investigated, and found to have chronologically heterogeneous artifacts: one group is of Roman age (a bronze statuette of Hercules, the base of another small statuette, an iron anchor, a fragment of decorated moulding in Istrian stone, a lithic weight shaped like a truncated pyramid) while others, such as two swivel guns, date to the 16th century (see also D'Agostino, 1995–1996). Many artifacts are difficult to date: among these are five wooden vats filled with ferrous slag, and numerous blocks of rough green glass. The latter find, contrary to what has been written about it, could date to the Roman age because of the presence of natron (this melting was used until the late Middle Ages). The evidence of Roman cargoes of rough glass is quite rich. Also interesting is a brass masthead emblem of Ottoman design.

San Marco in Boccalama. Important evidence for the nautical archaeology of the Medieval period was found. When two ships were discovered in the submerged island of San marco in Bocca Lama, in the Southern lagoon of Venice. One is a galley 38 m long × 5 m wide and the other is a flat-bottom ship 24 m long × 6 m wide. They were used to strengthen the shore of the island, where a monastery stood. A document from 1328 could indicate when this operation was done. Excavation has already begun on the wrecks.

Pesaro Beach. The wreck of an 18th-century vessel is preserved about 200 m from Pesaro beach. The subclub Tridente, directed by an archaeologist, conducted the first excavations and discovered cannons, guns, pots, copper basins, and full bottles of rum. The hull is well preserved and lies partly under a breakwater, which was built without concern for the presence of the wreck (Spadoni et al., 1994).

Camarina Bay. Again from Camarina Bay, a few meters from the Roman wrecks, lies the hull of a long ship. The artifacts—helmets, horseshoes, blacksmith's tools, horse bones and pottery fragments—lead one to think that it is a 13th century *tarida* galley, used for the transport of horses (Di Stefano, 1991). The ship, which is the only one known, awaits documentation and study before the waves of the bay destroy it.

Sciacca. To the north, the sea of Sciacca conserves a site, recently discovered, composed of four French cannons, cannon balls, and carpenter's tools. Francis I's coat of arms dates the cannons at the beginning of 16th century (Purpura, Naxos, 1996).

San Vito lo Capo. At San Vito lo Capo (Trapani), the wreck of a 12th-century vessel, with a cargo of small amphorae of the same type as those recovered in another wreck near Marsala (Lido Signorino), was investigated during a professional course for scuba technicians (Faccenna, 1993).

Varazze. The small ship, wrecked off Varazze (Savona) and lying 46 m deep, dates to a more recent age: The cargo is composed of 16th to 17th century pottery. Only the bilge-pump area of the hull has been investigated (Riccardi, 1997).

Alghero.   The Alghero anchorage is exceptional. In a few centimeters of water, four beached crafts from the 16th to 17th centuries are preserved in very good condition; in one are barrels filled with sardines. Blocks, ropes, and nets were salvaged from the sand (Riccardi, 1994).

These wrecks and many others (see, for example, Palombina, Pesaro, Camarina, Capo Linaro, and Torre S. Sabina), demonstrate how the beach environment, in spite of strong hydrodynamics, is favorable for keeping crafts preserved in good condition. Immediately after the shipwreck, the vessel is quickly covered and protected by the sand, and hulls, organic finds, and precious artifacts are often well-preserved (Beltrame, in press).

Capo Galera.   Finally, at Capo Galera (Asinara), an Islamic wreck of the 12th to 13th century has been discovered. It carried jars with stamped decorations as well as glazed pottery, sandals, a silver pitcher, and a musical wind instrument (Spanu, Naxos, 1997).

Submerged Buildings

Italy has a solid tradition of research in the field of ancient submerged buildings, in contrast to the paucity of research in nautical archaeology. More closely connected to land archaeology and less complex from an operational point of view, academic research is quite active in this topic. The University of Viterbo has carried out the interpretation of harbor buildings from the Augustan age of the Flegraean area (Nisida, Pozzuoli, and Miseno) and those once covered by the modern pier of Ponza (Gianfrotta, 1996). The university recently investigated "Pilato's caves" of Ponza, where the discovery of parts of a statue, an altar, and lamps prove that this cavern was a nymphaeum of an imperial villa (P.A. Gianfrotta, personal communication). At Baia, surveys by volunteers of submerged remains of the Roman city are continuing. The volunteers are working on a villa attributed to the *Pisoni*, complete with fish tanks, and remains related to the coastal structures in *opus pilarum.* Analyses also are taking place in an urban sector, on thermal baths (perhaps associated with a villa), the channel, and the *Baianus lacus*, the *Stagnum Neronis*, the *Ostriaria*, and port structures (Scognamiglio, 1997).

Remains of a Roman maritime villa were identified during a survey in the bay of Marina Grande of Bacoli. Parts of the *thermae* and a bridge supported by arches, which connected the building to the promontory, are still preserved (Benini, 1997).

Nero's port at Anzio shows some building particulars that cast new light on Roman techniques of building concrete structures in water, thanks to careful work of survey and analysis (Felici, 1993). Research is ongoing into a previously unknown pier near the "main," which still conserves parts of the wooden molds (E. Felici, personal communication).

Finally, we report the detailed recording and study by a student of two Roman maritime fish tanks on the north coast of Rome (Pellandra, 1997).

We conclude with the project "The Harbours and the Anchorages in Antiquity from Prehistory to Early Middle Age," financed by the Ministry B.C.A. This project ended a few years ago. For three years, hundreds of harbors, anchorages, villas, and fisheries were surveyed and recorded along a good part of the peninsula (Pallarés, Naxos 1995).

REFERENCES

Arata, F.P., 1993, Il ritrovamento di Cala Rossano a Ventotene. *Archeologia subacquea. Studi, ricerche e documenti* 1:131–151.

Auriemma, R., 1997a, Le anfore africane del relitto di Grado. Contributo allo studio delle prime produzioni tunisine e del commercio di salse e di conserve di pesce. *Archeologia subacquea. Studi, ricerche e documenti* 2: 129–155.

_____, 1997b, Per la Carta Archeologica Subacquea del Salento. In *Atti del Convegno Nazionale di Archeologia Subacquea. Anzio 1996*, edited by A.I.A. Sub, 225–240. Edipuglia, Bari.

_____, 1998, Un carico di anfore Keay LII nelle acque dello Ionio. In *Ceramica in Italia: VI–VII secolo. Atti del Convegno in onore di John W. Hayes. Roma 1995*, edited by L. Saguì, 753–760. All'Insegna del Giglio, Firenze.

Bacci, G., 1994, Recenti esplorazioni a Capo Rasocolmo. In *VI rassegna di archeologia subacquea. Giardini Naxos 1991*, 115–122. P & M Associati, Messina.

Bargagliotti, S., Cibecchini, F., and Gambogi, P., 1997, Prospezioni subacquee sulle secche della Meloria (LI): alcuni risultati preliminari. In *Atti del Convegno Nazionale di Archeologia Subacquea. Anzio 1996*, edited by A.I.A. Sub, 43–53. Edipuglia, Bari.

Basile, B., 1997, Il relitto ellenistico di Portopalo di Capo Passero (Siracusa). In *Atti del Convegno Nazionale di Archeologia Subacquea. Anzio 1996*, edited by A.I.A. Sub, 147–152. Edipuglia, Bari.

Beltrame, C., 1993, Ancore antiche dai litorali di Venezia e Caorle. *Rivista di Archeologia* 17:42–45 and plates.

_____, 1996a, Archaeological Evidence of the Foremast on Ancient Sailing Ships. *The International Journal of Nautical Archaeology*, 25.2:135–139.

1996b, *La sutilis navis del Lido di Venezia. Nuova testimonianza dell'antica tecnica cantieristica "a cucitura" nell'alto Adriatico.* In *Navalia. Archeologia e storia*, edited by F. Ciciliot, 31–53. Savona.

_____, 1998, *Review of Atti del Convegno Nazionale di Archeologia Subacquea. Anzio 1996*, edited by A.I.A. Sub. *International Journal of Nautical Archaeology*, 27(2):180–181.

_____, 2000, *Sutiles naves* of Roman age. New Evidence and Technological Comparisons with PreRoman Sewn Boats. In *Down the river to the sea. VIIth International Symposium on Boat and Ship Archaeology. Gdansk 1997*, edited by J. Litwin, 91–96. Polish Maritime Museum.

_____, in press, The Case of Mediterranean Beach Wrecks in the Investigation of Wreck Formation Processes. *Archeologia subacquea, studi, ricerche e documenti* 3.

Beltrame, C., Gaddi, D., 2000, Iulia Felix. Documentazione e analisí degli elementi strutturali dello scafo della nave romana di Grado (GO). *Archeologia delle acque*, 4:99–102.

Benini, A., 1997, Una villa marittima nelle acque di Bacoli. In *Atti del Convegno Nazionale di Archeologia Subacquea. Anzio 1996*, edited by A.I.A. Sub, 193–202. Edipuglia, Bari.

Bondioli, M., D'Agostino, M., Fozzati, L., 1997, Lago di Gardo, Lazise (VR). Relitto di nave lunga veneziana. II relazione preliminare. *Archeologia Medievale*, 24:145–153.

D'Agostino, M., 1995–1996, Il relitto del vetro. *Bollettino di archeologia subacquea* 1–2: 29–89.

Dell'Amico, P., 1997, Il relitto di Grado: considerazioni preliminari. *Archeologia subacquea. Studi, ricerche e documenti* 2:93–128.

Di Stefano, G., 1991, Antichi relitti nella baia di Camarina. In *IV rassegna di archeologia subacquea. Giardini Naxos 1989*, 127–134. P & M Associati, Messina.

_____, 1992, Camarina 1990. Nuove ricerche e recenti scoperte nella baia e nell'avamporto. In *V rassegna di archeologia subacquea. Giardini Naxos 1990*, 175–206. P & M Associati, Messina.

Faccenna, F., 1993, Un relitto del XII sec. a San Vito lo Capo (Trapani). *Archeologia subacquea. Studi, ricerche e documenti* 1: 185–187.

_____, 1997, Indagini preliminari sul secondo relitto di Gela (Gela II). In *Atti del Convegno Nazionale di Archeologia Subacquea. Anzio 1996*, edited by A.I.A. Sub, 143–146. Edipuglia, Bari.

Fiorentini, G., 1990, La nave di Gela e osservazioni sul carico residuo. *Quaderni dell'Istituto di Archeologia della Facoltà di Lettere e Filosofia della Università di Messina* 5:25–39 and plates.

Fozzati, L., D'Agostino, M., and Toniolo, A., 1995, Il "Relitto delle alghe" di Caorle. Relazione preliminare (1992–1994). *Quaderni di Archeologia del Veneto* 11:48–53.

Fozzati, L., Bressan, F., and D'Agostino, M., 1997, Interventi di archeologia subacquea nel mare adriatico. *Quaderni di Archeologia del Veneto* 13:64–68.

Freschi, A., 1992, Il relitto con lingotti di stagno di Lipari (Messina). In *V rassegna di archeologia subacquea. Giardini Naxos 1990*, 227–235. P & M Associati, Messina.

Galli, G., 1993, Ponza: il relitto della Secca dei mattoni. *Archeologia subacquea. Studi, ricerche e documenti* 1:117–129.

_____, 1995, Relitto d'età romana dalle acque del porto di Ponza. *Archeologia Classica*, 47:329–341.

_____, 1996, Roman Flanged Pump Bearings: Further Finds in the Harbour of Ponza (Pontine Islands, Italy). *International Journal of Nautical Archaeology* 25(3,4):257–261.

Giacobelli, M., 1997, I vetri del relitto di Grado. In *Atti del Convegno Nazionale di Archeologia Subacquea. Anzio 1996*, edited by A.I.A. Sub, 311–313. Edipuglia, Bari.

Gianfrotta, P.A., 1996, Harbor Structures of the Augustan Age in Italy. In *Caesarea Maritima*, edited by A. Raban and K.G. Holum, 65–76. E.J. Brill, Leiden.

Mercando, L., 1983, Relitto di nave romana presso Ancona. *Forma Maris Antiqui*, 11–12:69–78.

Ollà, A., 1997, Osservazioni preliminari sul carico del relitto romano-imperiale nelle acque di Punta Mazza. In *Ritrovamenti Subacquei a Milazzo e il relitto di Punta Mazza*, 65–98. Milazzo.

Pallarés, F., 1991, Alcune considerazioni sui resti lignei dello scafo della xnave romana del golfo di Diano Marina. In *IV rassegna di archeologia subacquea. Giardini Naxos 1989*, 171–177. P & M Associati, Messina.

_____, 1995–1996, Il relitto a *dolia* del Golfo Dianese: nuovi elementi. *Bollettino di archeologia subacquea* 1–2:127–140.

Pellandra, D.I., 1997, Due poco note peschiere romane a Santa Severa e a Santa Marinella. *Archeologia subacquea. Studi, ricerche e documenti* 2:21–34.

Pietropaolo, L., 1997, L'approdo di Torre S. Sabina (Brindisi). Le ceramiche comuni di età romana. In *Atti del Convegno Nazionale di Archeologia Subacquea. Anzio 1996*, edited by A.I.A. Sub, 249–270. Edipuglia, Bari.

Relitto del Pozzino (B del Golfo di Baratti), 1990, Catalogo della Mostra, Edizioni Zeta, Firenze.

Riccardi, E., 1994, The Wrecks off the Camping Site "La Mariposa", Alghero, Sassari, Sardinia, Italy. In *Crossroads in Ancient Shipbuilding. VIth International Symposium on Boat and Ship Archaeology. Roskilde 1991*, edited by C. Westerdahl, 131–136. Oxbow, Oxford.

_____, 1996, Indagine preliminare sui frammenti di due imbarcazioni di epoca imperiale. In *Da Olbìa ad Olbia. 2500 anni di storia di una città mediterranea. L'età antica, I*, edited by A. Mastino and P. Ruggeri, 471–477. Chiarella, Sassari.

_____, 1997, The 1993 Season of Operations on the Varazze Wreck, Liguria, Italy. *International Journal of Nautical Archaeology* 26:300–305.

Salvi, D., 1992, Da Carthago Nova verso i porti del Mediterraneo: il naufragio di un carico di lingotti di piombo. *Bollettino di Archeologia* 16–18:237–248.

Scognamiglio, E., 1997, Aggiornamenti per la topografia di Baia sommersa. *Archeologia subacquea. Studi, ricerche e documenti* 2:35–46.

Spadoni, U., Profumo, C., Riccardi, E., Semenza, F., and Nastasi, G., 1994, Il "galeone" di Pesaro. *Archeologia Viva* 45:70–74.

Spanu, P.G., 1997, Il relitto "A" di Cala Reale (L'Asinara 1): note preliminari. In *Atti del Convegno Nazionale di Archeologia Subacquea. Anzio 1996*, edited by A.I.A. Sub, 109–119. Edipuglia, Bari.

Toniolo, A., 1991, *Le anfore di Altino*. Società Archaeologica Veneta, Padova.

Tortorella, S., 1981, Ceramica di produzione africana e rinvenimenti archaeologici sottomarini della media e tarda età imperiale: analisi dei dati e dei contributi reciproci. *Mélanges de l'École Française de Rome* 93:355–380.

Tortorici, E., 2000, Un nuovó relitto di etá repubblicana nel mare di Grado. *Archeologia delle acque* 4:91–98.

Chapter 29

New Courses in Maritime Archaeology in Portugal

JEAN-YVES BLOT

INTRODUCTION

Underwater archaeology in Portugal has faced a radical change in the last decade.

After past legal battles for underwater archaeology, Portuguese authorities opted at the last moment (and as a consequence of a national decision in late 1995) not to submerge Portugal's most controversial archaeological site, Foz Côa, a unique series of late Palaeolithic petroglyphs in a small river valley far from the sea. If the electors had not chosen otherwise, one of the largest set of open-air petroglyphs presumably would be part of the-sunken cultural heritage. Instead, a national archaeological park with guided tours has been created in the valley under the scientific control of prehistory specialists.

In the meantime, a more elusive but equally radical situation occurred for all of the country's underwater heritage, with the official birth of underwater archaeology as a scientific discipline.

How the years-long legal turmoil developed, climaxed, and receded is a still-to-be-written chapter of *Politics of the Past* (Gathercole and Lowenthal, 1994).

Jean-Yves Blot, Archaeologist, consultant for CNANS-National Center of Nautical and Underwater Archaeology, Portuguese Institute of Archaeology, Lisbon.

International Handbook of Underwater Archaeology, edited by Carol V. Ruppé and Janet F. Barstad. Kluwer Academic/Plenum Publishers, New York, 2002.

Background

If Portugal's nautical archaeological remains known to date in Portugal were condensed in one sentence, we might say that the whole lot divides roughly into two clusters, one concentrated in the Roman period, the other from the late Middle Ages to modern times, with early and mid-medieval periods scantily represented. This distribution may reflect the chronology of maritime activities off the Portuguese coast, as well as the size-effect phenomenon associated with the visual detection in an underwater environment of large and durable artefacts like *amphorae*, anchors, or cannons.

The specificity of Portuguese nautical territory comes from the general situation of the northern part of the country on the slopes of the continental Iberian *meseta* (tableland). The coastline of the past (Dias et al., 1991) has been heavily modified by alluvial (Moreira and Psuty, 1993) and marine silting drained by the rivers and coastal currents, evidencing on the marine façade the results of human transformations of inland soils (Rochette Cordeiro, 1992) and removing many physical traces of past human activities near the coast, especially near the mouths of rivers.

Portugal (Figure 29.1), on the outer edge of southwestern Atlantic Europe, is more than anything else a frontier that is easy to reach and cross. Its role and that of the Iberian Peninsula at the world crossroads begins in the early Paleolithic, with the ongoing debate regarding the 400-m-deep Straits of Gibraltar and its influence as a sea-barrier to diffusion of early humans from Africa (Raposo et al., 1986).

Although coastal finds were made decades ago at very low tide levels of unrolled Asturian (pre-neolithic) lithic materials at Carreço, in the Minho region in the country northern area (Breuil et al., 1962), the potential of the Portuguese continental platform for submerged traces of human presence since the last glacial maximum in late Würm remains to be explored (Blot and Blot, 1990–1992).

During river dredging in 1923 in Huelva, Spain, in 1923, near the Portuguese border, close to the sea, the potential of a single submerged site of the Atlantic Iberian southwest was revealed with the find of a late Bronze Age hoard of bronze spades, other weapons, and *fibulae* from the 8th century b.c. (Henkin, 1952). From this period on, Phoenician and Carthaginian sailors reached or settled the remote shores of Portugal and southwestern Spain, but the question of pre-Roman navigation is still under debate (Arruda, 1996; Blot, 2002).

Even though the archaeological debate at this stage is far from implementing the totality of the heuristic tools available from a "nautical" perspective, land excavations of coastal settlements have provided a wide spectrum of data for the analysis of those past maritime contacts. A small coastal settlement at Santa Olaia, on a low hill near the mouth of the Mondego River in central Portugal, revealed abundant traces of contact with the Phoenician world, namely from Gades (modern Cadiz, in southwestern Andalusia, Spain), from the 9th to the 6th centuries b.c. (Pereira, 1997). Here, a "wall near the water" has been identified, a rare trace of harbor structures of antiquity along the Portuguese coast (Correia, 1995). This fluvial site is now silted in.

Luxury "Phoenico–Oriental" ceramics and other Mediterranean-related products found at Santa Olaia fit the broad description proposed by Rouillard (1991), who situates in the 8th century b.c. the "rediscovery of the West by the Orient," the start of Mediterranean influence and commerce in the southern Europe Atlantic's "Far West."

At Cerro da Rocha Branca, a low elevation on the right bank of the Arade river near Silves, in Algarve, a Phoenician settlement with no previous occupation has been

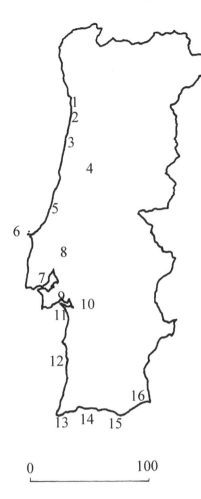

Figure 29.1. Map of Portugal. The numbers correspond to present-day place names cited in the text: 1=Porto; 2=Espinho; 3=Aveiro; 4=Coimbra; 5=Alfeizerão; 6=Peniche and Berlenga Island; 7=Lisbon; 8=Santarem; 9=Setubal; 10=Alcacer do Sal; 11=Troia; 12=Sines; 13=Sagres; 14=Portimão; 15=Faro; 16=Castro Marim.

identified. Three periods of occupation are apparent at Rocha Branca: Oriental (Phoenician) (7th–6th centuries B.C.), Punic (5th–3rd centuries B.C) and Ibero–Punic (3rd century B.C. to the Roman period) (A. Dias Diogo, personal communication, 2002). Forty percent of the fragments of Ibero-Punic *amphorae* at Rocha Branca were Pellicer D, a shape observed at an anchorage in the lower Arade river at Portimão (Silva et al., 1987). This feature suggests a seaward evolution in the use of the river after the 5th century B.C.

Another similar Phoenician presence, known since the early 7th century B.C. has been recognized at Abul, a former peninsula on the banks of the Sado River, presently some 23 km from the sea (Mayet and Silva, 1997). The site, now silted in, was partly occupied in the Roman period for ceramic production from A.D. 1st–3rd centuries, then abandoned until present times.

At Castro Marim, a former peninsula near the mouth of the Guadiana river (Portugal's southeastern border with Spain), recent excavations have revealed a similar impact of eastern Mediterranean commerce around the late 8th century B.C. Greek goods from Athens began to arrive in the mid-5th century B.C., a situation that lasted until the mid-4th century B.C. North African goods arrived after this time (Arruda, 1996).

A key factor in the control of maritime movement in southwestern Atlantic Iberia occurred in 206 B.C. in Andalusia, Spain. The town and harbor of Gades, a Carthaginian outpost on the Atlantic and one day by sea away from the straits of Gibraltar, became an ally of Rome. The nautical importance of the Straits from that point on is reflected by an abundance of lead anchor stocks found by local divers near the Spanish-Moroccan town of Ceuta. A study published in 1972 referred to 30 lead stocks with weights ranging 5.7–266.5 kg (Bravo Perez and Bravo, 1972).

High-amplitude tides strike ships and sailors coming out of the Mediterranean into the Atlantic. Aristoteles related the phenomenon to the steepness of the local coastal cliffs, an opinion later dismissed by Posidonius, who visited Gades in the late 2nd century B.C. Posidonius, quoted by Strabon in *Géographie* III 3: 3, argued that most of the shores of Iberia were low and sandy, with no coastal cliffs.

Modern geographer O. Ribeiro (1991) shows that the adjectives "flat and sandy" apply only to a limited part of the Portuguese coastline while steep cliffs occupy a major part of the Portuguese Atlantic façade. These contrasts in coastal geomorphology have influenced the regional shapes of traditional Portuguese ships up to the present day.

Atlantic Sailing

In the mid-1950s, writer and sailor Alan Villiers described with admiration the strong, flat-bottomed, moon-shaped fishing boats of northern Portugal's flat, sandy coast, fighting their way through the breakers. Trains of oxen and men and women waited on the beach to help pull the nets to land, while the heavy Atlantic surf sounded above the efforts of the mob. The influence of specific sea-conditions on the morphology of Atlantic boats had been commented long ago. In 56 B.C., Julius Caesar observed Venetic ships of northwestern Gallia and their differences from Roman naval technology:

> The Gauls' own ships were built and rigged in a different manner from ours. They were made with much flatter bottoms, to help them ride shallow water caused by shoals or ebb-tides (Handford translation, in Rule and Monaghan, 1993).

Strabon, a widely traveled writer born in 64 B.C., compiled many of the written sources available in his time. He refers to the skin boats used by mountain populations-the Callaics, Asturians, and Cantabres-of northern Iberia, in an often-quoted paragraph:

> Until Brutus conquest (2d C.B.C.), skin boats were used to cross the water expanses left by the tide and the swamps. To-day, on the opposite, even the boat dug-out from a single piece of wood are rarely seen (*Geographié* III,3,7, our translation from the French edition by Lasserre, Paris, 1966).

This text gives a strong feeling of the fast evolution of Iberian local boats at the end of the first millennium B.C.

When referring specifically to the coast of present Portugal, Strabon does not fail to mention the river network and its suitability for shipping, with special mention of the Tagus River, 20 *stades* wide near its mouth (*Geographié* III 2: 15) and deep enough to handle 10,000 *amphorae*-carriers, among the largest commercial ships of the time.

The most relevant traces of ancient navigation off the coast of Portugal have been found by scuba-divers. The sport of diving developed in the 1950s and led to the location of dozens of lead anchor stocks. Such finds, although isolated and lacking archaeological context in almost all cases, helped shape what would eventually prove to be the first crude but direct portrait of early maritime activity in Portuguese waters.

These finds focused on two locales, one off the southwestern coast of Sesimbra near the mouth of Sado river and town of Setubal, and another on the east side of Berlenga, a small, rocky island six miles off the mainland 50 miles north of Lisbon. Anchor stocks were found at more than 20 m depth at Berlenga and more than 50 m at off Sesimbra, resembling similar deep (45–50 m) anchorages of the Roman period in the Mediterranean (Blot and Pinheiro Blot, 1990–92).

Similar discoveries were made at other parts of the coast and in northwestern Spain: three lead stocks found at the entrance of Ria de Pontevedra (Galicia) in the early 1980s, each weighing nearly 200 kg (Santos, 1984). A systematic inventory was begun in the mid-1980s at Lisbon's National Museum of Archaeology, which led to the published documentation of 69 lead stocks (Alves et al., 1988–1989).

Variables of weight and dimension available for 56 of the 69 units cluster in two groups. The lighter stocks, less than 150 kg, are the most numerous, clearly different from a group of heavier stocks weighing up to a little above 400 kg. This later group corresponds to two coastal anchorages (Cape Espichel and Berlenga Island) and to a third point (Ponta da Galé); stocks' wooden cores are observable only in the second group.

Such groupings suggest a predominance of small boats, while the largest lead stocks, concentrated in specific open-water anchorages, are related to boats under 200 tons of displacement corresponding to medium-sized merchant vessels (Blot, 2002) (150 tons for a ship carrying 3000 *amphorae*, the largest-sized craft able to enter the shallow Tiber River before Imperial harbor works in A.D. 1st Century) (Pomey et al., 1997).

Haldane (1985), who has proposed a typology of ancient wooden anchors, connects the spreading of his type III (solid lead stock into which the end of the shank is inserted, the overwhelmingly dominant shape among lead stocks found to date in Portugal) to the sharp increase in lead production in Spain and Britain in the 2nd century B.C. From his observations on wreck sites data, Gianfrotta commented on the replacement of stone by lead stocks in wooden anchors in the 4th century B.C., and the relationship with the increasing availability of lead. On the basis of secure archaeological evidence, namely shipwrecks, Haldane gives a time-span of 200 B.C. to 300 A.D., for his type III, which covers most of the Roman presence in Iberia (Haldane, 1985).

C-14 dating of the burnt wooden core (*alma de madeird*) of a large lead anchor stock, found at Berlenga Island and now preserved at Peniche Museum, indicated an origin for the wood of late 5th to 4th century B.C. (Alves, Diogo, Cardoso, 2001). The dating of another lead stock's wooden core found in Algarve (Armação de Pêra) pointed to a 2nd-4th century B.C. date (*Correio da Arqueonautica*, 1995).

Two small lead stocks from Cape Espichel, part of the group of 69 anchor stocks referred to above (nos. 28 and 39 in Alves, Reiner et al., 1988–89), weighing 26 and 18 kg respectively, correspond to the simpler shape II defined by Haldane (lead-filled wooden stock): a solid, linear lead body with a triangular section (Haldane, 1985). The time-span given by Haldane for this shape II ranges 400–150 B.C. In 1995, ten more lead stocks were found by divers, adding to the 69 previously published (*Correio de Arqueonautica*, 2, 1995). More than eighty lead stocks are known at present (2002).

Single *amphorae*, mostly broken brought from the Berlenga Island area by fishermen and divers, cover a wide chronological spectrum: two 2nd century B.C. Dressel I, eleven from the middle of 1st century B.C. to the middle of A.D. 1st century (Haltern 70) (Diogo, Trindade, Venâncio, on press) and Lusitanian and African amphorae dating from

A.D. 3rd or 5th centuries (Diogo, 1999). Occasionally, single *amphorae* covering a wide chronological spectrum (Punic to Roman) are found in deep water (200–250 m) off Cape Sardão on the southwestern coast. Later finds by fishermen of amphorae in deep water (600 m+) off the coast of Algarve help to define ancient maritime routes in the first century A.D. (Diogo and Cardoso, 2000; Diogo and Martins, on press).

Nineteenth-century sources refer to the sea's exposure of a masonry structure (a *pier with large rings*) in 1715 at Boca do Rio in Algarve, a site used in the Roman period for the industry of fish products. Most of the area is normally covered with sand. Forty years after the discovery, as a consequence of a tidal wave associated with the earthquake that destroyed Lisbon in November 1755, the removal of large amounts of sand exposed a complex of ancient buildings. It was excavated in 1878 and corresponded to a factory for fish products (Santos, 1971).

In 1989, erosion along the north coast of Portugal near the present town of Espinho exposed remains of a wooden fish-trap consisting of two sets of wooden stakes (one sample proved to be *Quercus robur*) joined by wattling. C14 dating showed it to be from A.D. lst–2nd centuries (Alves et al., 1988–89). The find was related to a former coastal lagoon.

Even more intriguing is the discovery of an unidentified structure referred by fishermen of Algarve in the beginning of the 20th century. The structure, which routinely damaged the fishermen's nets, was dynamited by authorities in 1930. The diver commissioned to perform the task observed that the masonry structure included parts of ceramic jars which later proved to be ceramic pipes. The remains were relocated in September 1998, 700 m away from the coast and identified as part of a structure used in the Roman period, although none of the original surrounding sediments have survived. The depth (9–11 m depending on the tide) forced researchers to discard local tectonics in the spatial interpretation of the find. Later research explored the links between geomorphology and archaeology on this site which might have been a coastal structure in a lagoon along the inland side of a stretch of sand dunes later eroded away by the sea, a very active phenomenon in this area (C. Simplício, personal communication, 1998; Teixeira, 1999; Simplício et al., 2001).

An essential aspect of the mapping of archaeological remains of ancient navigation on the Portuguese coast for the last three millenium focuses on geomorphology and the progressive evolution from the originally highly river-indented coast to the almost linear north–south profile of today.

Huge expanses of today lagune waters behind coastal crests of sandy dunes (Aveiro Ria south of Porto) were a bare, open coast until the 10th century. Until the early Middle Ages, rivers such as the Mondego, flowing through the towns of Coimbra and Montemor), or even tiny river outlets to the south, were accessed through wide and sheltered fjord- or ria-like estuaries extending deep into the interior. A major consequence and one of the most innovative visions of the past sea-to-land network is provided by geographer S. Daveau.

Daveau's research (1995) shows how, two milleniurn ago, deep-river entrances running almost perpendicular to the Portuguese Atlantic coast were directly in touch with the main axis of terrestrial circulation developed in Roman times. They ran from the Lisbon River north along an inland route mostly parallel to the coast, with a narrow connection to the sea at every river junction. Those insights were ultimately extended to the archaeological and spatial context of ancient harbors of the southwest coast of the Alentejo. (Blot, M.L. Pinheiro, 1998) or to the lower Tagus River (Guerra et al., 2000) and to the whole Portuguese nautical territory (Blot, M.L., 2002).

In some cases, even single ceramic finds suggest a close association between harbor activity and the development of urban settlements. A set of *amphorae* (3rd century B.C. to A.D. 2nd century) found in the Sado River had a *terminus ante quem* coinciding with the full development of the neighboring town of Alcacer do Sal, a proto-historic settlement and Roman town named Salacia (Diogo and Alves, 1988–89). In another case involving the Sado river near Alcacer do Sal, several intact *amphorae* from A.D. first century, caught on several occasions in fishermans' nets, suggest the presence of a shipwreck (Diogo and Alves, 1988–89).

A similar occurrence is referred in the Tagus River near Mouchão da Póvoa, several km upriver from Lisbon. According to local informants, locally produced *amphorae* from A.D. 1st century to early 2nd century were associated with wooden remains that have since been lost. An older presence in the same area of the river is attested by other finds of *amphorae* dated between the 2nd and 1st centuries B.C. (Diogo, 1987).

Regarding this stretch of the Tagus River north of Lisbon, Strabo refers explicitly to the town of Moro, a pre-Roman settlement near present-day Santarem 500 *stades* or 92.5 km upriver. He also mentions the possibility of large vessels sailing upriver until being relayed by smaller river boats (*Géographie* III 3:1).

The pre-Roman town of *Olisipo* (Lisbon), situated near the Tagus estuary, was occupied in 138 B.C. by the Roman general Brutus, to protect maritime access to the Tagus River routes of central Portugal. Thanks to its qualities as a harbor and nucleus of fluvial and land circulation, *Olisipo* was able to expand dramatically as a commercial pole in the later period.

Atlantic Fishing

An obscure episode related to early fishing along the northern coast of Africa, narrated by Posidonius, leaves a clear image of the presence of fishermen from the Gades area along the coast of northern Africa in the 2nd century B.C. (Desanges, 1978).

Further north along the southwestern Atlantic Iberian coast, intense fishing, an industry of fish products, and a large distribution network into the Mediterranean are attested from A.D. 1st–5th century in the coastal zones of southern Portugal and the large estuarine complex of the Tagus and Sado Rivers. For many years, Portuguese divers have discovered single *amphorae* (Cardoso, 1978) (Sousa e Sepúlveda, 1997) from that period and earlier, starting with the 2nd century B.C. (Diogo and Trindade, 1998). The *amphorae* were located 30–32 m deep in the inshore estuarine area off Troia peninsula, where fish-derived industries are known from A.D. 1st–5th century along 2 km of flat, sandy coast. Local amphorae-producing centers (starting in the middle of the 1st century with Dressel 14 types, followed by Almagro 50 and Almagro 51 c) have been found on land on the bank of the river (Etienne and Mayet, 1997).

In the Arade River at Portimão in Algarve on the southern coast, 1983 dredging operations, and occasional finds of *amphorae* and ceramic materials by divers, cover a time-span ranging from 5th century B.C. to A.D. 5th century (Diogo, Cardoso, Reiner, 2000). Detailed study of the ceramic materials, from an area that was apparently an anchorage near the mouth of the Arade River, gives us a picture of maximum commercial activity from the 2nd century B.C. to A.D. 5th century (Silva et al., 1987). Diogo, Cardoso and Reiner (2000), give a general approach to the *amphorae* finds made during dredging operations in the Arade River.

In sharp contrast to the rarity of underwater finds off the coast of Portugal itself are several centers of *amphorae* production that were located and excavated on land, in the Tagus and Sado valleys, in Algarve and, very recently, in Peniche, a former island north of Lisbon. Decades of shipwreck discoveries and investigation in the Mediterranean have allowed archaeologists to shape an initial spectrum of distribution of Lusitanian fish products in the Mediterranean from the 1st to the 5th century, with concentrations on the southern coast of France, in the Baleares Islands, and in southern Sicily-only for the later period in this case- (Lopes and Mayet, 1988).

At Anse Gerbal, an A.D. late 4th to early 5th century shipwreck (Port Vendres I) contained a cargo of Almagro 50 and 51c *amphorae* in which 22–25-cm-long sardines (*Sardina pilchardus*) were found. Compared with modern (1959) statistics, this size corresponded to nine-year-old fish (Chevalier and Santamaria, 1971), far above present-day ages. Today, the highest figure for sardine fishing in Portugal appears to be a seven-year-old sardine weighing slightly less than 80 grams (Pestana, 1989). "What is evident," concluded Etienne and Mayet in their synthesis, "is that the Portuguese sardines-can finds its origin in the Almagro 51c amphora of the late Luso-Roman period"(Etienne and Mayet, 1997).

MEDIEVAL FRONTIERS

The role of the Atlantic Iberian coast as a maritime frontier is exemplified again in the early Middle Ages. Arab expansion began in the 7th century and reached the peninsula when Muslim general Tarik ibn Zyad disembarked at Gibraltar in A.D. 711. A six-centuries-long Islamic presence will follow in Portugal, affecting roughly two-thirds of today's territory. Islam's northern border was situated halfway between the latitude of present-day towns of Coimbra and Porto.

The importance of Islam in Portugal's nautical context is crucial on several levels, with lasting results namely in the field of nautical terminology. Words such as *almadia* (African or Asian small boat, generally a dug-out), *falua* (small, lateen-rigged, twin-masted river transport vessel), and *recife* (sunken or barely emerged rocks) all have an Arabic origin (Machado, 1997).

More disruptive to the history of naval techniques at the interface of northern Europe and the Mediterranean is the order issued by Andalusian Caliph Aláqueme in A.D. 859, instructing local shipwrights to replicate Viking ships for the use of Muslim naval forces. The aim was to feint and sail closer the enemy threatening the southern coast of Iberia (Borges Coelho, 1989).

Among rare, significant maritime artefacts is a bell-shaped sounding lead found during the dredging of Ria de Alvor, between Portimão and Lagos, in Algarve (*Correio de Arqueonautica*, 1995). Another similar sounding lead was later found in Algarve, again related with the Arade river near Portimão (CNANS *Carta Arqueológica*). Similar artefacts, with a distinctive hollow tallow-cup at the bottom and divided into geometrical sections, have been found in the Mediterranean. Their distribution and chronology (Greek, Roman, and Byzantine) are discussed by Oleson (1998, 1994), who, in his later work (Oleson, 2000), revised his previous classification. This recent article by Oleson (2000) on ancient sounding weights brings a wide geographical and historical scope to an otherwise very fragmentary aspect of the Portuguese nautical reality.

Modifications of Portugal's coastline since the Middle Ages are responsible for another scant but important find made on land. In 1973, a mechanical excavator recovered a Clinker-built ship's rib made of oak from the soil of Alfeizerão, in the lowlands of the central Portugal coast that provided shelter to marine navigation up to late Middle Ages and are now silted in. The rib was photographed but lost except for a small remaining fragment; the fragment was dated by C-14 techniques to 1010 ± 35 years before present (Alves, 1990).

The rib was a fragile piece of evidence but a strong indicator of the role of now-silted coastal areas in the spatial distribution of nautical remains from before and during the Middle Ages. Nearby was Alcobaça Monastery, a later Cistercian institution founded in the 12th century, which controlled a wide economic network along Portugal's central coast. Its proximity enhances the spatial significance of the find, since Alfeizerão was still under Muslim control in the early 12th century.

In another instance, one of two wooden ship remains, later called *Arade* II and located during dredging operations at the mouth of the Arade River in Portimão, Algarve, proved to be clinker-built. A useful background for the Portimão find is provided by the clinker-built remains of a small 15th century vessel, 10–12 m long, recently found at Urbieta in the Basque country on the Northern coast of Spain (Izaguirre et al., 1998). On the neighboring French Atlantic coast to the north (Aquitaine), the change from clinker-built to carvel-built shipbuilding techniques occurred in the last decades of 15th century (Rieth, 1998).

Diver and journalist Helder Mendes photographed the exposed underwater wooden remains in Portimão. In a letter to Mendes, Danish naval archaeologist Ole Crumlin-Pedersen (quoted in Alves, 1990) referred to the importance of *Arade* II for a better understanding of past relationships between different shipbuilding traditions in Europe.

In a recent edition of a classical work on Arab seafaring (Hourani, 1995), a commentator observed that a few medieval Islamic wrecks excavated on the southeastern coast of France have thrown light on the relationships between Arabs and previously existing local shipyards. French naval historian Mollat du Jourdain has shown how, in the 12th century Gelmirez, a bishop in northwestern Spain, ordered Italian shipbuilders from Geneva and Pisa to come to Galicia and build warships (Filgueiras, 1994).

The final campaigns that drove Islam from Portugal (A.D. 1230–1249) opened the way for a new maritime venture: convoys of Italian ships travelling to Northern Atlantic Europe, beginning in the second half of the 13th century soon after the fall (in 1265) of Islamic control in Cadiz. Soon afterward, Genoese merchants, ship masters, and pilots were invited to Portugal, and trade with northern Europe and Mediterranean countries was encouraged by the Portuguese crown (Waters, 1994). A century and a half later, in 1476, the young Chistophus Columbus, shipwrecked off the southern coast of Portugal, was heir to those late medieval Italian sea-voyages around southwestern Europe. So was the young Italian traveler, Luis de Cadamosto, when his convoy of *galés*, on its way to Flanders in August, 1444, was delayed by contrary winds at an anchorage off the cliffs of Sagres at the southwestern tip of Portugal.

A few years before, Portuguese shipbuilders built several ships, including a *galé*, two caravels, and a great *nave*, in Bruxels (1438–1439) and Antwerp (1439–1441). Accounting documents referring to these early Flemish caravels were published a number of years ago in Lisbon by Paviot and Rieth (1988–89).

Paviot and Rieth (1988–98) refer to an early mention of a *caravel* (the word and the corresponding vessel) in England in 1448 in a document, related to a Portuguese boat from the town of Porto. The name *caravela* is first mentioned in Portugal in a document from 1255 (Foral de Vila Nova de Gaia) (Pico, 1963). The origin of the *caravela* (both name and ship) appears to be Portugese (Barata, 1989) although early evidence of lateen-rig is found in the Eastern Mediterranean in the first millennium A.D. (Fonseca, 1978; Basch, 1991).

Although written treatises regarding Portuguese ships and shipbuilding in the late 16th and early 17th centuries had been known for some time, material clues were unavailable to Portugal's archaeologists until recently. This was deplored years ago by Pimentel Barata, a naval archaeologist who, relying mostly on written sources, published a series of essential papers (Barata, 1965, 1970, 1989). Recent finds, either accidental or related to dredging or dry-land urban works, altered this situation and bridged the methodological gap between artifactual evidence and a rich body of written works by Portuguese naval experts and shipbuilders of the late 16th and 17th centuries. These works include *Ars Nautica*, circa 1570, and *Livro da Fabrica das Naos*, circa 1580, both by Fernando Oliveira; *Livro Primerio da Architectura Naval,* by João Baptista Lavanha; and Livro de Traças de Carpintaria by Manuel Fernandes, 1616. These reference works range from a theoretical (F. Oliveira) to a purely practical approach (M. Fernandes). Although widely known among naval experts since the end of the last century, some of those works have become available only recently. *Ars Nautica* by Fernando Oliveira was mentioned in the printed catalogue of the Leiden University Library in 1716 but was identified and finally used only in 1960 by Portuguese historian Luis de Matos (Contente Domingues, 1997).

A detailed study by a naval engineer of the *caravela de onze rumos* described by Manuel Fernandes was published recently (Branco, 1994). Other publications, namely by Lisbon Academia de Marinha, have made these essential Portuguese works available to a broader public. A few texts still remain unpublished (Contente Domingues, 1998).

THE 1990S: TESTAMENTS IN WOOD

Evidence of late medieval shipbuilding was found in Portugal in 1996, during urban works at Largo do Corpo Santo in south Lisbon, a few hundred meters from the Tagus River. The area, which in Roman times was at the mouth of a small river outlet, was subjected to successive landfills that made the line of the river move south, by several hundred meters in places (L.F. Castro, personal communication, 1998). The 14th century *Corpo Santo* find (C-14 dating: 620 ± 40 years), cut away by heavy machinery 5 m below street level, is limited to the stern end of a small ship. The wooden remains (1.8 m x 1.6 m) include the ends of the two lower planks fitted to the sternpost; this sternpost, made from a single piece of wood; includes a skeg protruding backwards (Alves, et al., 2001).

A similar structure for a slightly later period was found among the partly burnt remains of another small vessel. The site, 10.4 m × 2.5 m, dated from the mid-15th century and later named *Aveiro A*, was located in 1992 within the closed inland water system of the Ria de Aveiro on the northern coast (Figure 29.2). The cargo of ceramics, laid in the hull over a thick layer (20 cm) of "interwoven brush, sticks, straw and mats," provided new insights on late medieval forms used in Portugal (Alves, 1998).

The wooden remains were from the bottom of a small ship and included framing, outer planking, more than 9 m of keel (12 cm × 12 cm in section), and a bolt-strengthened composite sternpost. Three longitudinal cavities on the upper part of the keelson

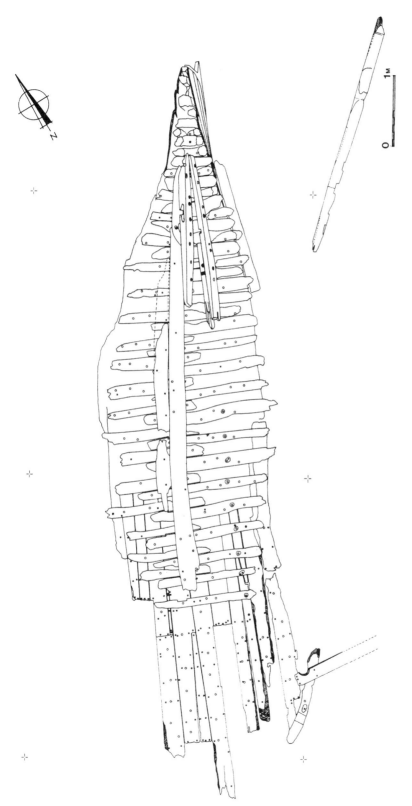

Figure 29.2. Lower section of a 15th-century vessel *Aveiro A*, on the northern coast of Portugal.

indicated that the ship was equipped with a deck. Several floor-timbers, some with Roman numeral markings (V, XII, and XV on floor-timbers 5, 12, and 15 respectively) displayed the characteristic dovetail joint with the corresponding vertical faces of the first futtocks. Average C-14 dating values for hull parts or fittings (hull plank, oar, keg stave) and cargo (walnut) indicated a period from 1424 to 1469 (Alves, 1998).

Another important discovery occurred in 1995 at Cais do Sodré, a Lisbon quarter well known to sailors for its bars, ship-chandlers, and shipping agencies. As in Corpo Santo a few hundred meters to the east, the area was built on landfills taken to the Tagus River bed in the last centuries. The wooden remains of *Cais do Sodré* were exposed; 5–6 m below street level by a huge drilling machine used in the extension of Lisbon's underground. The remains, 24 m × 5 m, belonged to the central part of the vessel and included 23 futtocks (22–24 cm wide) toward the stern and 19 futtocks from the main section toward the bow. According to the Portuguese sources of the period, the "gauged" futtocks defining the shape of the central part of the hull were identified by Roman numerals IIII to XVIII chiseled on the wood (stern futtocks) and the corresponding numbers for the gauged futtocks XVII and XVIII toward the bow. On this basis, the original keel length was computed as at least 18 *rumos* (27.72 m) (Rodrigues, 1998). The keel itself, 25 × 27 cm in section, was built in four parts.

Unlike *Corpo Santo* and *Cais do Sodré* (discovered and damaged beyond repair by driling machinery), the full-scale recording of wooden remains from one 16th-century vessel was made possible in the spring of 1998, during the survey of Angra do Heroismo harbor at Terceira Island in the Azores, where the building of a breakwater and marina were planned.

Besides the remains of blockade runner CSS *Run' Her*, lost in Angra in 1864, the survey soon targeted the remains of a lead-sheathed wooden vessel. Thirty-five meters long with a maximum width of 8.1 m, the wreck lay in 7 m of water 50 m from shore; it was labeled *Angra D* (Monteiro and Garcia, 1998). Schedules imposed by the planned harbor works made it necessary to remove the whole ballast in order to reach the wooden remains, which, once recorded, were dismantled with the help of consultants from abroad using techniques developed by Robert Grenier and his team at Red Bay.

The *Angra D* remains included 25.5 m of keel (full length unknown) with a large section (44 cm-sided by 40 cm-moulded). The presence of nine floor riders (40 cm moulded average "by 25 cm inside thickness"), a typical 18th century feature of warships, came as a surprise, although it is known on *Mary Rose*. The ship structure still included bow knees, keelson and main mast step, deck beams and sternpost assembly. The latter was lifted in one piece and deposited, with all other wooden remains, in deeper water, away from the planned harbor works (Monteiro and Garcia, 1998).

AIMING AT THE SUN

The majority of ship or shipwreck remains known along the coast of Portugal can be classified as "scattered non-homogeneous," following the late K. Muckelroy's (1975) approach. Many sites, inventoried since 1984, through a program launched by the National Museum of Archaeology and Ethnology, have been detected by fishermen or divers or during dredging operations. In one case, spear-fishermen at Carrapateira found several bronze cannons later related with the shipwreck of a Spanish vessel coming from West Indies in the mid-16th century. The site, on an open coast, is subject to strong movements of sand and has been partly surveyed. A nucleus of mid-16th century iron swivel guns has been locaLizéd in the vicinity and later charted during successive missions for CNANS in 2000 and 2001. Dozens of similar sites are referred within the existing inventory (CNANS *Carta Arqueológica*).

Development of direct sea routes to India in the late 15th century soon focused maritime commerce around Lisbon and increased the maritime presence of Portugal in northern Europe. In the period between November 1539, and August 1540, 328 Portuguese vessels arrived at Walcheren Island to feed the Antwerp market (Braudel, 1979). Even local traditional products such as wine, fruits, and salt kept a steady flow of ships heading to northern Europe. In the 17th century, the commerce of salt to Dantzig, Poland, mobilized 200 vessels. Two categories of Portuguese artefacts from the period, both durable underwater, discovered since the 1990s, are marine astrolabes and bronze artillery.

The first reference to the use of a marine astrolabe by Portuguese sailors occurred in 1481, during the voyage of Diogo de Azambuja along the western coast of Africa. Half a century later, astrolabes were found aboard even merchantmen and had evolved from a crude solid disk into a more refined and robust instrument. Around 1534, French privateers from Rouen seized a Portuguese vessel sailing from Madeira to Flanders with a cargo of sugar. An astrolabe and a *carta de marear* (nautical chart) were found on board the prize (Rau, 1984). Later in the century, the British privateer Francis Drake was known to throw these instruments overboard each time he seized them on an enemy vessel.

Whatever the causes, only ten marine astrolabes where known to exist in the mid-20th century. The later increase in the number of known instruments enhanced the role of past Portuguese craftsmen in the making of this particular kind of nautical instrument.

Until recent times, few of those marine astrolabes were known in Portugal itself, with the exception of one labelled Ericeira's, located in the early 20th century along the coast. Another, of proven Portuguese origin, was found in Japan in 1932 among the remains of the Portuguese vessel *Madre de Deus*, burnt in Nagasaki harbor in 1610 (Estácio dos Reis, 1998). A copy is on display at Lisbon Museu da Marinha.

Diving technology improvements in the second half of the 20th century profoundly modified the shape of the known population of marine astrolabes. In 1966, British expert D.W. Waters inventoried 21 such instruments. This number jumped to 28 in 1979, 32 in 1983, 48 in 1985 (Stimson, 1985), 65 in 1989, and 80 in 1997 (Estácio dos Reis, 1998). The number stood at 81, in the late 1990s, including finds in Brazil (Guedes, 1983) and, three in Portugal, found during the excavation of an early 17th-century Portuguese East-Indiaman near the fortress of São Julião da Barra in the Tagus estuary. This site was tentatively identified as part of the remains of *Nossa Senhora dos Martires*, wrecked in the vicinity in 1606 (Fig. 29.3). The site gained special visibility and logistical dimensions due to the financial support provided by the national organization Expo98, then in preparation. The three astrolabes, along with other finds from the site were put on display June–September 1998 during the international exhibit in Lisbon.

Aside from the increase in underwater exploration during the last few decades, the sharp increase in the finds of marine astrolabes has taken place because one single wreck yields potentially more than instrument. Five astrolabes were found on the Spanish ship *Nossa Senhora de Atocha* (1622); four were of Portuguese origin. Due to their value as collectables, these instruments have been in the center of a public turmoil in Portugal in the last few years. Authorities fired the situation in the 1980s, when they paid a high price for two Portuguese astrolabes from the *Atocha* at a U.S. auction. In 1994, the state bought

478   J.-Y. Blot

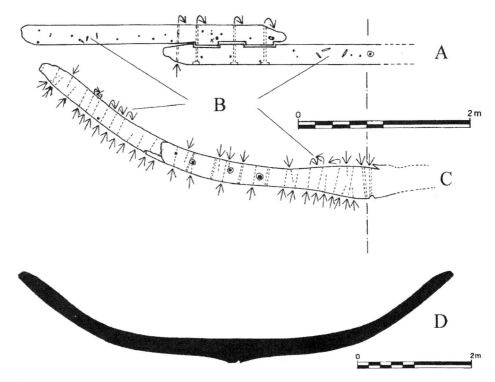

Figure 29.3. Frame n°3 from the early 16th-century Portuguese East-Indiaman at São Julião da Barra. A = horizontal section (flattened curvatures); B = nails with ends bent; C = vertical section; D = frame n°3 (floor timber and futtock). (SOURCE: Alves, Castro, Rodrigues, Garcia and Aleluia, 1998, Arqueologia de um naufrágio. In *Nossa Senhora dos Mártires: A última viagem*, edited by S. Alfonso Luz and R. D'Intino. Lisbon, p. 196)

another well preserved marine astrolabe found by a local diver in Ria de Aveiro in shallow inland waters and bearing the date 1575; a generous reward was given to the finder in the hope of promoting similar finds. However, the major interest of the São Julião da Barra' shipwreck, provisionally identified as *Nossa Senhora dos Martires* on the basis of several pieces of evidence including a cargo of pepper and Chinese porcelain from the Wanli period, are the wooden remains from the vessel itself (Alves et al., 1998; Castro, 1998a).

TO INDIA AND BACK

São Julião da Barra and similar sites are so interesting to Portuguese nautical archaeology because *naos da India*—East-Indiamen—were for several countries, the instrument of a long-distance monopoly and as such have their own story. On his first expedition, Vasco da Gama' made a huge profit on pepper brought with the ships. By itself, this single fact may have influenced the shape of future East-Indiamen.

Like Roman ships of A.D. 1st century, sailing through with the Indian Ocean monsoon toward Southern India and Ceylon to bring back ever larger cargos of pepper, Portuguese East-Indiamen increased in size over time. Inspired at the start by large merchantmen of Italian design, the Portuguese were the first to adapt their ship types to extremely long voyages. The size of the *naos da India* caused discussions at the Portuguese court and among seamen as early as the first decade of the 16th century, climaxing long after, in the 1620s. After heavy losses on the Indian route, state commissions in Lisbon then debated the advantages and inconveniences associated with the largest four-deckers, which had a huge draft but were better fit for military defense than the supposedly smaller three-deckers. Advocates of the three-deckers pointed out that four-decker *naos*, which cost 40,000 cruzados to build, were sold as firewood at 1500 cruzados after two Indian voyages (Barcelos, 1899). Among the major technical issues then debated were the relationship between the ship internal morphology, the crown's monopoly for pepper (volumes in the hold) and private ventures (volumes in upper structures), As such, those Portuguese debates of the 1620s echo the Spanish naval *Ordenanzas* of the early 1600s (Blot, Rodrigues, Lizé, in press).

Even with the doubts still surrounding its contaminated archaeological context, the São Julião da Barra shipwreck site fits into the crucial period of the early 17th century, following several decades of Spanish presence in Portugal (1580–1640).

The wooden remains of the São Julião da Barra' shipwreck, 12 m long and 7 m wide, were distributed along the keel. They include 11 pieces of framework and 26 rows of 11 cm-thick hull planking. The floor timbers (24.7 cm average width), connected to the keel with square iron nails nearly 2 cm × 2 cm in section, were united by a classical dove-tail mortise joint to the first futtocks, 21.5 cm average width (Castro, 1998a). The keel, composed of several sections with scarf joints, was only 12 cm thick; this thinness could be related to the initial presence of a false keel, which was not observed (Alves et al., 1998). Most of the wooden structure was left in situ. A comparison with Portuguese shipbuilding treatises of the period (Oliveira, Lavanha, and Manuel Fernandes) led researchers to interpret the remains as "from an area immediately forward of the main floors" (Castro, 1998a).

QUIET REBELS

One of the most lasting piece of evidence of Portuguese nationalistic reaction against Spanish dynastic presence during the period 1580–1640 is a detail in the configuration of some of the Portuguese bronze artillery manufactured in the late 16th and early 17th centuries (Santos, 1989). This phenomenon, well-known to artillery experts, was echoed once again on the 1993 recovery of eight bronze guns from the *Ponta do Altar B* shipwreck site in Algarve near the mouth of the Arade River and the harbor of Portimão. Scattered materials, such as lead pistol, musket balls, and lead seals, were found. The artillery itself included six *colubrinas bastardas* (half culverins); three were from the Spanish gun foundry of Fernando de Ballesteros including one bearing the date '1606'. Two other pieces were classified as *meias-esperas* (half-sakers?). On most of those guns, the Portuguese coat of arms was enclosed within the arms of the king of Spain (Alves, 1990–1992a), a reference to the dynastic presence of Spain throughout the period. Portuguese founders had been reluctant to work under Spanish rule and to comply with such symbols, so that earlier Portuguese artillery pieces, such as those produced in India in the last two decades of the 16th century, display decorative features which suggest at first glance a much earlier date.

The clue to this "dating trap" lies in the fact that under the reigns of Kings Manuel I (1495–1521) and João III (1521–1557), the identifying figures, including the Portuguese coat of arms, the royal arms and the foundry's initials, were all situated at the forward end of the chase of the gun, then moved backwards to the breech with the reign of Sebastião (1557–1578). However, late 16th-century bronze artillery made in Goa display markings on the forward half of the chase of the gun similar at first glance to those made under King Manuel, with no Spanish royal arms are visible on those 16th century pieces. The "trick" the Portuguese founders used was to represent, instead, the arms of the town where the gun was made. In the case of Goa, those arms were the armillary sphere already used more than half a century before by King Dom Manuel I, who died in 1521.

EUROPE IN PORTUGAL

With the end of the Spanish dynastic presence in Portugal, England, Portugal's oldest ally, recovered a prominent role in sea-transports from Portugal to the North. Out of a total of 2518 vessels, 690 ships (27 percent) that entered the harbor of Porto between 1657 and 1698 came from England (computed from data in Hanson, 1986). The British role in Portuguese commerce expanded still more in the 18th century, when more than 53 percent of all ships coming to Lisbon in 1774 were British. Average tonnage also increased, from 75 tons between 1715 and 1717 (230 ships/year) to 117 tons between 1771 and 1775 (161 ships a year) (Fisher, 1984).

Britist ships, at least in the late 18th century, had a specific shipyard facing Lisbon Customs. It was owned by an Englishman (*Gazeta de Lisboa*, Supl., 6/1/1784) and provides one more clue to the intricate network of European presence in the 18th-century shipbuilding industry in Portugal and Spain. Such technological interactions had predictable consequences on the morphology of the ships.

1100 vessels from all nations enter Lisbon harbor in 1788 (*Gazeta de Lisboa*, 6/1/1788). Finds made in modern times by dredging or drivers reflect nature and intensity of shipping at the entrance of Lisbon River and in the open waters of the huge harbor. These finds range from Roman *amphorae*, Islamic ceramics, a 15–16-century wrought iron falconet on display at Lisbon Museu da Marinha or to a 19th century wreck in 2 m of water at Trafaria on the southern bank of Tagus estuary (Alves, 1990). The copper-sheathed wreck, with copper or bronze nails and a cargo of skins, became exposed as a consequence of riverine works for the setting up of giant silos (A° Gil, personal communication, 1994).

Silting explains why most of the materials in the bed of the central Tagus River are generally unreachable: they are buried under thick layers of sediment. Records for the period 1939–1954 indicate sedimentation rates of 1.9 cm/year in the Torre de Belem and in the *thalweg* of the river, where the most intense deposition was observed. Later data indicate still higher sedimentation rates (3.4 cm/year) near the right bank (Castanheiro, 1986).

As far back as 1683, the inhabitants of Belem complained to the King about fast erosion caused by the sea (*mar*) and the constant waves (*ressacas*) on the right bank of the Tagus estuary and asked for a pier to be built-and soon destroyed by draining waters.

The role of Portugal on the route between the Mediterranean and northern Atlantic Europe was evidenced once again when spear fishermen located, in the 1960s, the scattered remains of a large man-of-war, which proved to be the French 80-guns *l'Océan*, burnt by British forces after running aground in 1759. The vessel, sailing with a small fleet from Toulon to join naval forces stationed in Brest, was attacked by a large squadron of British vessels from Gibraltar. It tried without success to find protection from the small forts on the coast of Algarve (Portugal was then a neutral power). The burnt remains were partly salvaged for their bronze artillery soon after the naval affair and again in the 1960s. The surviving wreckage, spread over a 3000 m^2 area, included a French bronze 36-pounder, two iron 18-pounders, and some wooden remains, which served as an exercise in underwater archaeology for a team from the National Museum of Archaeology of Lisbon (Alves, 1990–1992b). In 1987, a similar site, the French 74-gun man-of-war *Redoutable*, was the target of a magnetic survey. A strong magnetic anomaly was located in the area pointed by historical research.

In 1993, the non-profit association Arqueonautica, based in the National Museum of Archaeology, encouraged guided tours to *l'Ocean* remains for divers, after removing the most significant pieces of artillery (Alves, 1990–1992b).

TRACES FROM A REMOTE WORLD

The Position of Portugal on historical international sea routes, and the narrow links between land and underwater field-work for shipwreck coastal sites, were illustrated by a long-term investigation project started on land in 1985 with a magnetic survey by Kermorvant, Pratt, and Romero (1992) to locate the burial ground of the dead from the Spanish 64-gun man-of-war *San Pedro de Alcantara* lost in February 1786 on the coast of Peniche north of Lisbon. Undertaken from 1986 to 1988 with the support of the National Museum of Archaeology, the research has been following a dual land and underwater scope. After seven campaigns on land, the remains of 29 individuals connected to the maritime accident were located (Figure 29.4). Several individuals connected to the Tupac Amaru rebellion in Peru in the early 1780s, were among the 128 who died in the accident. A comparative study in collaboration with Universidade Catolica de Lima has been completed (Blot and Vivar, 2002).

The underwater site was first surveyed in 1988. Three ceramic sherds from a vase of the late Intermediate phase of the northern Peru Chimu culture were identified; they were interpreted as part of the collections lost by Spanish naturalists Ruiz and Pavon in a mission to Peru and Chile between 1778 and 1788 (Blot and Blot, 1991). The relationship between artefact scatter and navigation conditions after the ship left Peru led to further investigation underwater. Since 1996, the site has been the focus of a detailed underwater scatter study (Blot, 1998a,b). The pre-Hispanic archaeological materials known to exist on the *San Pedro de Alcantara* site raise broader methodological questions about South American artefacts within present-day Portuguese marine territory (Blot, J.-Y., 1994).

The question of underwater sites in the Portuguese Atlantic islands was brought forward in the early 1970s with surveys by two British teams of divers led by S. Wignall and J. Gratham. Among the sites targeted was Francis Drake's ship *Revenge*. One artillery piece recovered at the time is now preserved at the Angra do Heroismo' Museum. Another site, that of the Dutch East-Indiaman *Slot ter Hooge* (1724) was located and excavated in Porto Santo, near Madeira (Stenuit, 1975).

A broader chronological approach to the position of the Portuguese islands within the framework of ancient navigation was proposed by Monod (1973), Isserlin (1984), and Butler (Butler and Isserlin, 1990) for the Azores, in an attempt to interpret the reference to the 1749 discovery of buried ruins on Corvo Island. One ceramic vase was found, containing Carthaginian coins later examined by Spanish numismatist Henrique Florez. J.

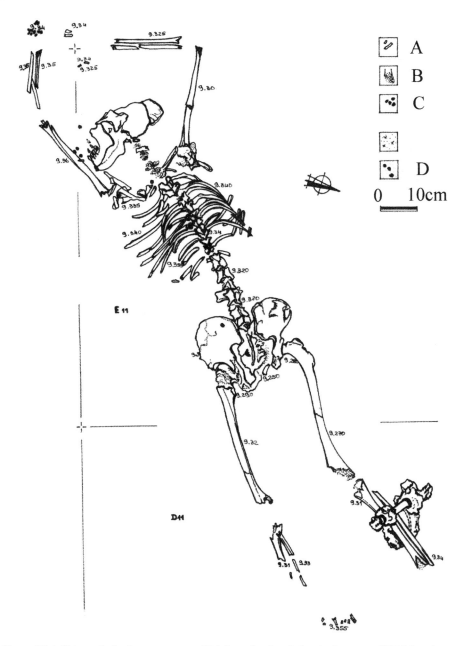

Figure 29.4. Shipwrecked prisoner: passenger X24 from the *San Pedro de Ancantara* (1786) burial site at Peniche, Portugal. The skeleton, which faces the soil, has a large shackle around its right leg and bears the marks of a long stay at sea. The skull as well as the pelvis bones are incomplete. The determination of sex and anthropological family will be possible only through DNA analysis. A = bones; B = spongy tissues; C = iron fragments from an undetermined object; D = shells (helix). (SOURCE: Maria Luisa P. Blot; 1994 archaeological campaign)

Podolijn reviewed and published on the subject in Sweden in 1778. A critical view of the question is proposed by Rouillard (1991).

The question of contamination was at the heart of a discovery made in the early 1970s at the mouth of the Arade River, where a dredge exposed a large wooden ship structure containing a Roman coin. The hull that protruded from the thick mud wall dug by the dredge was surveyed by J. Farrajota, J. Albuquerque and other sport divers, who found that 5 cm of thick external planking was fixed to the frames by treenails 3 cm in diameter. Frames, 13 cm × 16 cm in section, were spaced 16–35 cm apart (drawings by J. Albuquerque, in Blot and Blot, 1994). An initial C-14 dating placed the wood around the mid-16th century (Alves, 1990).

In 1987, the National Museum of Archaeology had promoted with researchers from Tours university, France, and La Rabida' Escuela Politecnica, Huelva, Spain, the testing underwater of electrical survey methods in the riverbed of the Arade river (Kermorvant et al., 1992). Later developments of electrical measurements underwater were implemented by Aveiro university researchers on the *Aveiro A* shipwreck site (Almeida, Moura, 1998; Pinheiro, 1998).

THE EARLY 1990s LEGACY

Until 1996, Portugal had no official structure to deal with underwater archaeology on a continuous and legal basis. Until 1994, most of the action was taken by individuals under the umbrella of the National Museum of Archaeology, thanks to the initiative of the museum's director and a handful of collaborators. The emergence of a radical new legal frame in 1993 led to promote separate actions through the nonprofit association Arqueonautica based at the National Museum of Archaeology, the local museum of Peniche and, since 1996, the Museum of Angra and related collaborators in the Azores.

The situation of domestic statu quo in which the discipline had been existing until the late 1980s suddenly worsened in the early 1990s when political circles close to the government management of cultural affairs started promoting a radically new legal framework. This channelled the initiative to private groups able to compete for legal concessions of the commercial exploration of underwater heritage areas in Portuguese waters. Because Portugal has a large legal zone of influence ($500,000$ km^2) due to the Atlantic archipelagos of Azores, Madeira, and Salvage Islands north of the Canaries (Ribeiro, 1992) and because the Azores part of the zone coincided with most of the return routes of vessels during the colonial period (Blot and Blot, 1992), there was a considerable inflation of the debate regarding deep wrecks and the related interest of private groups involved in deepwater slavage operations.

Who Cares?

The latest, best-known controversy of the period deals not with underwater archaeology but with the flooding of a lonely valley where numerous petroglyphs have been sighted. Initially, a group of scholars and enthusiasts militantly defended the integrity of the site, fighting against a project to build a dam in the valley. The "Foz Côa" affair, as it came to be called, took on a greater importance when high-level politicians joined the fray. During a visit by rubber boat to the most threatened petroglyphs of Foz Côa valley, the president of the Republic commented: "The engravings can't swim." This presidential sentence traveled all over the country, helping to fuel public discussion about archaeological heritage and its importance to society. Was the electricity produced by one more dam worth the flooding of a major and unique site of the late prehistory in

Europe? Could a small country like Portugal, last on the economic list of the European Community, afford to preserve such an archaeological treasure at such a high cost to the general public?

When Foz Côa reached the pages of England's *Times* newspaper, a new path was traced, bringing the small country to international attention-not strongly enough, however, to deter the Lisbon authorities from their project.

The breadth and intensity of the Foz Côa discussions, including the scientific dating of the petroglyphs, was a debate in which a young prehistorian and scholar, João Zilhão (1995), took a decisive part from the beginning. The Foz Côa affain left in the background, a still more radical debate where government circles brought their initial decision down to the last step: the 1993 adoption (in the middle of the summer holidays) of a legislative package regarding the management of the underwater heritage as a business affair.

Promoted by the Secretary of State for Cultural Affairs (a young politician under the personal leadership of the Prime Minister), the law of August 1993 was the result of consultations and lobbying by several salvage operators. At the cost of 1.2 million U.S. dollars, private groups would be given special lease to practice underwater archaeology in Portuguese waters. The commercial value of the artefacts, and the possibility of bringing archaeological finds to the antiquities market, served as an incentive to local and foreign investors. The groups selected by a government commission would be allowed to sell their leases to sub-operators as sublease concessions.

The Foz Côa affair started to boil soon after the law was passed, diverting everyone's attention from the fact that, by then, underwater archaeology had then been brought to a standstill.

This states of affairs brought intense and exclusive focus towards financially rewarding shipwreck sites of the four last centuries.

The position of Portugal in the geography and history of maritime contacts between the Mediterranean and Northern. Atlantic Europe gives a measure of the gap (not to say the crater) that the legislation of August 1993 blantly created in the management of the local underwater heritage, keeping in the shade the commercially unrewarding sites of the medieval and pre-medieval periods.

Francisco Alves, then director of the National Museum of Archaeology, became *persona non grata* in leading administrative circles. National elections in late 1995 led to the sudden promotion of a radically different orientation of cultural affairs.

The newly created Ministry of Culture took several steps toward the resolution of the anterior problems. The flooding of the Foz Côa petroglyphs was cancelled. The creation of the Portuguese Institute of Archaeology (I.P.A) followed, including a department (CNANS) specifically aimed at the management of underwater archaeology at the national level, and a new law promoting archaeology underwater as a purely scientific activity. The creation of this administrative structure, the first in the country, followed several actions started in the 1990s at the individual or collective level: the non-profit association Arqueonautica, the Peniche museum, and the CPAS (Portuguese Center of Underwater Activities, a founding member of the world-wide CMAS sport-divers organisation) to promote introductory courses to archaeology underwater (*Arqueonautica* 2, 1995). A decade before, in 1985, an international symposium of boat archaeology had been organized by naval archaeologist and ethnographer Lixa Filgueiras, professor of architecture in Porto.

In 1996, a new circle of archaeology students promoted another symposium with Lisbon University's Faculdade de Letras and CPAS, which brought land archaeologists into the debate for the first time (Arruda, 1996; Fabião, 1996; Oliveira and Almeida, 1996; C. Simplicio, personal communications, 1996, 1998). In September 1998, the Portuguese Institute of Archaeology, through its underwater branch CNANS, promoted an international symposium on several aspects of late medieval to early 17th-century ship remains, recently exposed either through archaeological excavations at Aveiro A, São Julião da Barra, or as a result of urban work along Tagus River's bank in south Lisbon.

PORTUGAL AND THE WORLD

The Lisbon Symposium, organized by Francisco Alves, director of CNANS, was opened by special guest and famed nautical archaeologist George Bass, and included a debate with UNESCO representatives on the coming international discussion of the legal framework for archaeological finds in international waters. The symposium, with participants from 18 countries, brought into focus the concept of "Ibero-Atlantic" construction, a group of common features found in several shipwreck sites from the 14th to 17th centuries which were discovered or excavated in recent decades.

Sixteenth-century sites recently exposed and investigated in Portugal were all characterized by the features at the center of the debate. A 17th-century wreck, *Angra C*, where the presence of wooden treenails and other features made researchers suspect a North European (perhaps Dutch) origin, was briefly commented by Dutch archaeologist Thijs Maarleveld at the public debate: "Angra C does not strike me as a dutch ship...It is still very much in the open".

Dutch shipbuilders provided ships to several European countries. Archival data indicate that most large vessels of a small, active harbor such as Rochelle, on the Atlantic coast of France, were provided by the Dutch (Trochmé and Delafosse, 1952), and the Dutch built ships for the French East-India Company during the first half of the 18th century.

The debate around Angra C suggests that it would be interesting to probe a possible relationship between wooden joinery, salt routes and salt-carrying vessels, in which wooden joinery would be preferred over iron nails and joinery.

The extensive maritime activity of Dutch commercial vessels during the 16th and 17th centuries provided opportunites for contact. Salt was an essential product for meat and fish industries of the northern Europe countries, and the Dutch network was extended in the late 16th and early 17th centuries to remote sources such as the Caribbean and Cape Verde Islands (E. Sluiter, quoted in Rau, 1984); therefore within the nautical hemisphere of the Azores. To non-Iberian vessels legally excluded from the Spanish colonial hemisphere, the Azores were the last officially accessible zone and a welcome source for goods smuggled from the prohibited American zones (Trochmé and Delafosse, 1952).

Portuguese Shipbuilding from Abroad

A ship, *Santo Antonio de Tanna* stands at the end of the shipbuilding time sequence in Portugal in the 16th and 17th centuries. Built in Bassein, India, in the early 1680s, this man-of-war was lost in Mombasa, Kenya, in 1697 during operations against troops controlled by Oman. The excavation of the ship's remains, under the direction of INA's R. Piercy, began in 1977. A small group of officers from the Portuguese Navy participated (Cardoso, 1978), making the experience an important step toward his future developments of underwater archaeology in Portugal. Some aspects of the wooden structure of the Mombasa wreck, such as the 20 cm × 20 cm frames overlapping "under the first bilge of stringers" (Piercy, 1977) will no doubt fuel interesting conclusions about the way Indian shipwrights implemented nonlocal shipbuilding techniques under Portuguese supervision.

By far the largest Portuguese archaeological project went mostly unnoticed by the archaeological community and culminated along the Expo98 wharf in the summer 1998: the floating and reconstruction of the frigate *Dom Fernando*, built in Damão, northwestern India, 1833–1843 under the direction of a Portuguese Navy officer, Gil José da Conceição, "and a local craftsman" (Brito, 1994). It was destroyed by fire in the mid-20th century. The wreck had been a familiar view on the left bank of the Tagus river for decades. In 1988, under new legislation favoring cultural sponsorship, the Portuguese Navy started a joint project with the government and several private entities, which in 1992 led to the consolidation and floating of the frigate's wooden structure, after the removal of nearly 600 m^3 of mud and some 75 tons of ballast (iron and bricks) from the inside of the hull. Many surviving parts of the copper-sheathed, all-teak original structure were found to be in good condition, including the keel; although the copper-sheathing was brittle and could not be maintained (Brito, 1994). A floating dock allowed the frigate to be brought by sea to Aveiro's shipyards a 100 miles voyage. White oak and yellow pine (*pinho manso*) 12 were used' to rebuild each frame, requiring 8–10 futtocks (Rubino, 1996). Twelve to 15 percent of her original materials were used to rebuild her, compared to 7 percent of the British *Victory* and 4 percent of the American *Constitution* (Brito, 1994).

The rebuilt 1800$^+$ ton frigate was launched in time to be re-rigged and displayed in the Tagus river, along a wharf at Expo98. A naval engineer in charge of rebuilding operations observed that some " anomalies" were spotted in the original construction: the orientation of the keel scarfs, in the opposite direction to what they " should have" been (Gonçalves de Brito, personal communication 1994). A draftman from the Navy shipyards who monitored the rebuilding process revealed during private discussions that most of the original wooden structure had in fact been recorded. Among the other "anomalies" thus observed were the joints between the six lower planks of the hull, all with a deep Z-shaped scarf obliquely nailed with a barbed copper spike, features uncommon to Portuguese shipwrights but which strongly suggest that the Indian shipbuilders from Damão had their say in the birth of the big "Portuguese" frigate.

Live Secrets

The wooden remains of *Cais do Sodré* and *Corpo Santo*, exposed and destroyed by machinery during urban works, are two more elements on the long worldwide list of important nautical finds made on land. They illustrate how such sites maintain a high potential for producing information, even badly damaged by machinery or exposure to air, and without proper excavation.

The morphological unity of the features of the five ships recently studied in Portugal fuels the debate regarding the very basis of the concept of "Ibero-Atlantic" shipbuilding tradition.

"It is useful to us", commented Robert Grenier at the last session in Lisbon, on September 9th, 1998, before adding: "But if we find next week it does not work anymore, we will throw it out and adopt a new one".

In the same Academia de Marinha, four years earlier, historian F. Castelo Branco (Branco, 1994) reminded his colleagues of the importance of inference and hypothesis in historical research, and quoted French historian Lucien Febvre: "Il faut savoir foncer dans le provisoire. A condition de ne pas oublier que c'est du provisoire".

The tentative identification of the São Julião da Barra wreck is such a case. As researchers have pointed out, this might be the Portuguese East-Indiaman (*nau*) *Nossa Senhora dos Martires* lost in 1606 in the vicinity at its arrival from Asia. However, the site, highly scattered and contaminated by numerous other finds, might prevent any further investigation to bridge the epistemological gap that separates pre-medieval anonymous shipwrecks from the sites for which archives might provide a positive identification.

Identification is more than a historical procedure and should be seen as a purely archaeological step. It took two carved teak planks bearing the Portuguese coat of arms to establish definitely the identity of the remains of the warship *Santo Antonio de Tanna* built in Bassein (late 1670s) and Goa (1681) and lost in Mombasa in 1697.

More than anything else, operations in Portugal in the last decade illustrate the sharpness of broader debates going on elsewhere on the question: Is (underwater) archaeology a science? This point was at the center of discussions in Lisbon when UNESCO delegates informed their listeners that archaeology was NOT among the list of scientific disciplines included in the international debate regarding the management of ocean resources. Several observers noticed the lack of representatives of the discipline at the international level. More lobbying was required from the archaeologists, said the UNESCO representatives.

The harsh debates launched years ago about the status of archaeology as a science, and the links between archaeology and other social sciences, was echoed in the present situation in Portugal, where the largest "archaeological" project in the country, the rebuilding of frigate *Dom Fernando*, was accomplished without the presence of any archaeologist. This came about because the main actors in the rebuilding process were professional shipbuilders who have worked in wood for their entire careers (Rubino, 1996). *Dom Fernando*, although built far abroad by foreign hands with foreign wood, was simply a larger ship, not too different from the last Portugese codfishing luggers used off Terra Nova until the early 1970s. Despite its large size, the huge Indo-Portuguese frigate fitted into a technical framework that Aveiro shipbuilders of the 1990s already knew. With a few exceptions such as the original exotic anomalies described above, Dom Fernando was simply a giant exercise in a dying knowledge now recorded in wood. The *Dom Fernando* experience helps focus on the late 20th-century living experience in a country where, half a century ago (1947), only 3877 of 9350 fishing boats were motorized, and with a population of 130,000 people who depended on fishing for a living (Ribeiro, 1991).

The September 1998 Lisbon Symposium was dedicated to the memory of O. Lixa Filgueiras, an architect from Porto who played a decisive role in recording the last moments of Portuguese traditional boats. Although his interpretations of the origins of boats strongly reflect a now-outdated reconstruction of the past, his work as an ethnographer will remain decisive. The fact that wooden shipbuilding has remained well alive in Portugal until late into the second half of the 20th century, with several shipyards still at work in Vila do Conde, Aveiro and Peniche, and the ease with which the huge rebuilding project of the frigate was achieved years ago, are strong indicators that hoards of archaeological information are still embedded in the present-day practice of Portuguese shipwrights.

Naval archaeologist John Sarsfield told the 1985 symposium of boat archaeology in Porto of his astonishing experience regarding the modern use of the old graminhos technique in a shipyard of Northern Brazil. It took a long time for Sarsfield to access the information, because the Brazilian shipbuilder kept it secret even from his own family. Four hundred years after the original writing of the *Livro da Fabrica das Naos* in which the Portuguese author, Fernando Oliveira, detailed the building and use of the *graminho*, the Brazilian shipbuilder had no idea about the historical origin of his professional secret.

YEARS AFTER

Much has happened in Portugal since this chapter was written. A few major questions are now outdated, and there are new expectations. A decisive momentum regarding the focus on the detailed interpretation of wooden ship remains has undoubtedly been gained with the September 1998 Lisbon symposium during which a Spanish participant privately commented:

"I don't know any other country where the remains of FIVE (Iberian-related) wooden vessels dating back to the 16th and 17th centuries have been exposed."

He added:

"And investigated."

The proceedings of the 1998 symposium on Ibero-Atlantic Shipbuilding have been printed, and several important articles have found their way to the public. Some decisive results have been gained through the 3rd Congress of Iberian Archaeology held in 1999. Researchers focusing on the Portuguese and Spanish realities brought new light into ancient questions, namely the submerged remains investigated off Quarteira, now clearly interpreted within a geomorphological approach focusing the several hundred meters long shorewards retreat of the coastline at that spot (Simplício, et al., 2002).

Several articles related with naval archaeology have found they way into the *Revista de Arqueologia* (Portuguese Institute of Archaeology) and concerned excavations in the Azores (Garcia et al., 1999) (Monteiro, 1999) (Crisman and Jordan, 1999), recent finds of amphorae at sea, among which A.D. 3rd–5th century, materials found in 25–26 m of depth in Algarve (Lagos) with varied origins (Lusitania, Betica and North-Africa) (Diogo, 1999). A general synthesis of the amphorae found in dredging operations in the Arade river at Portimão is now available (Diogo et al., 2000). Elephant tusks connected with the Punic presences on the coast of Portugal have been identified in the Arade estuary as well as in deep water, off Cape Sardão; in that case, the tusks were fished together with African amphorae fragments (Mañá A) (Cardoso, 2001).

The long-term project related with the *Aveiro A* ship is now in his final phase of study at the National Centre for Nautical and Underwater Archaeology (CNANS), where conservation facilities are being prepared. Short missions to Portugal from researchers, such as Eric Rieth from France, Brad Loewen from Cananda and Ian MacLeod from Western Australia, have helped create links which consolidate the direction of several fields of research which, years ago, could not have existed as such in the country. A Portuguese researcher L. F. Castro;who excavated the São Julião da Barra shipwreck site, has completed a Ph.D. dissertation on this subject at Texas A&M University. He knows teaches Iberian shipbuilding in the 16th and 17th centuries at INA (Texas A&M). Within a broader historical scope, another Ph.D. thesis on Portuguese shipbuilding was completed at Sevilla University (Martins, 2001). A decisive contribution to the discipline has finally been brought to its final academic term by historian F. Contente Domingues

(2000), who has focused on the major Portuguese manuscripts sources related with shipbuilding in the 16th and 17th centuries. Relying on reproductions of the manuscript deposited at CNANS, P. Monteiro has transcribed and annoted the manuscript of *Coriosidades* by Gonçalo de Sousa, an important text from the late 1620s. A masters thesis at Minho University does a general synthesis on the link between urban origins and ancient harbor activities in Portugal (Bolta, M.L., 2002).

An initial field-survey of the ancient anchorage of Mertola, on the Guadiana river, to the Southeast (Simplício et al., 1999) opens the way to future fluvial investigations on this important point of the ancient marine network during Roman and Islamic periods.

The repeated presence of INA archaeologists in the Azores has helped materialize the local presence of nautical archaeology as a discipline. The situation of the archipelago on the route from India back to Portugal in the colonial time is evidenced by the scattered remains of the Portuguese carrack *Nossa Senhora da Luz* (1615), recently surveyed in Fayal (P. Monteiro, personal communication 1999). Azores authorities have recently gained their autonomy for the management of their underwater heritage.

On the continent, the huge potential of the Portuguese waters has been demonstrated lately during a survey mission organized by CNANS with the collaboration of George Robb and his boat *Robo*. From a total of eight sites investigated, the CNANS/*Robo* mission helped to define the scatter pattern of a 1636 Portuguese carrack a dozen miles to the north of the Tagus mouth and to enhance the repeated presence, at an anchorage in Berlenga Island, of Haltern 70 *amphorae* (as identified by A. Dias Diogo within a previous framework already defined by this researcher) (Diogo, 1999). Side-scan sonar and Cesium magnetometer, combined in real time on board *Robo* were used for a preliminary survey of several sites, including the elusive *Faro A* (late 17th century ?) shipwreck site, previously mapped by trilateration during a CNANS mission in June 2000. The Spanish frigate *Mercedes*, is known to have sunk nearby, probably in deep water, in 1804 (Castro, 1998b).

Side-scan sonar and real time high-resolution DGPS positioning, available throughout the *Robo* mission, were used to survey a several km^2 of coastal area off the Alcabrichel river where Mesolithic (8500 B.P.) shellmidden were investigated at Toledo (Araújo, 1998). The nature of the shell population left by early Holocene hunter-gatherers who heavily relied on aquatic resources (as exemplified on the Toledo shellmidden) suggest profound differences between the present and the past morphology of the seashore from when it existed 8500 years ago. The spatial analysis of the side-scan data acquired with *Robo* are being analyzed by geographers from Lisbon Faculdade de Letras within the scope of the coastal geomorphology (Ramos, 1992) in the early Holocene in Portugal. A rare amphibolite was found during a dredging operation monitored by CNANS at the mouth of the Obidos lagoon (Lillios et al., 2000). A synthesis of the use of marine resources in the prehistory of southern Portugal has been proposed by Tavares da Silva and Scares, (1998).

In late 2000, the SEMAPP project, a joint pluridisciplinary mission by the University of Connecticut and the Luis de Camões Universidade Autónoma, Lisbon, launched an initial instrumental survey in deep water off Portimão, Algarve. Several archaeological remains possibly associated with Roman or later shipwrecks were spotted during the survey (A. Silveira Martins, personal communication 2001). In July 2001, side-scan sonar surveys of the Berlenga Island anchorage and off Ericeira, north of Lisbon, were undertaken by CNANS in collaboration with COMEX president Henri Delauze and the research vessel *Minibex*.

The broadness of the archaeological scope related with past Portuguese commercial and maritime networks leads the Portuguese archaeology of to-day to explore potential traces of such presence in remote contexts. Such was the case with some ceramics vessels with inlaid porcelain fragments found on the Spanish ship *San Diego* sunk off Manila, Philippines, in 1600 (Sardinha, 1999). The presence of south American among the victims of the San Pedro de Alcantra shipwreck (1786) in Portugal was investigated in 1999 as a result of a long-standing protocol with a physical anthropologist from Lima Universidad Catolica, Peru (Blot, and Vivar, 2002). A general synthesis of the theoretical approaches in maring archaeology has been lately proposed (Blot, 1999), starting with K. Muckelroy's approach to scattered shipwreck sites and including research orientations focused by Gould (1983, 1998), Gibbins (1990, 1995), McCarthy (1998) and others.

REFERENCES

Several of the original articles quoted in the text, referring to the *Pre-Proceedings of the International Symposium 'Archaeology of Medieval and Modern Ships of Iberian-Atlantic Tradition'* held in Lisbon in September 1998, have since then been developed by authors in the 2001 edition of the *Proceedings*. For more details, contact the coordinalor al **fa.cnans@ipa.min-cultura.pt**

Almeida, F.E.R., 1998a, Prospecção Geofisica Aplicada à Arqueologia Subaquática, *Al-madan*. Almada, 11,1, pp. 95–99.

Almeida, F.E.R., 1998b, Subaquatic Electrical Measurements. In *Proceedings of the IV meeting of the Environmental and Engineering Geophysical Society (European Section)*, Barcelona, edited by A. Casas, pp. 749–751.

Alves, F.J., 1990, Arqueologia Subaquática em Portugal. In *Memórias*, XIX, Academia de Marinha, 5–18. Lisboa.

_____, 1990–1992a, Ponta do Altar B – Arqueologia de um naufrágio no Algarve nos alvores do século XVII. *O Arqueólogo Português*, Série IV, 8/10:357–424. Lisboa.

_____, 1990–1992b, O itinerário arqueológico do Océan, *O Arqueólogo Português*, Série IV, 8/10:455–467. Lisboa.

_____, 1998, Ria de Aveiro A – a mid-15th century shipwreck from the west-central Portuguese coast, *Pre-Proceedings. International Symposium 'Archaeology of Medieval and Modem Ships of Iberian-Atlantic Tradition'. Hull remains, manuscripts and ethnographie sources: a comparative approach*, pp. 63–71. Lisboa.

Alves, F.J., Dias, J., Alveirinho, M., Rocha de Almeida, M.J., Ferreira, O. and Taborda, R., 1988–1989, A armadilha de pesca da época romana descoberta na praia de Silvalde (Espinho). *O Arqueólogo Português*, Série IV, vol. 6/7:187–226. Lisboa.

Alves, F.J., Reiner, F., Almeida, M.J. and Veríssimo, L., 1988–1989, Os cepos de éâncora de chumbo descobertos em âguas portuguesas. Contribuição para uma reflexão sobre a navegaçâo ao longo da costa Atlântica da Península Ibérica na Antiguidade. *O Arqueólogo Português*, Série IV., 6/7: 109–185. Lisboa.

Alves, F., Rieth, E. and Rodrigues, P., 2001, The Remains of the *Corpo Santo*, a 14th-century shipwreck and the remains of a shipyard at Praça do Município, Lisbon, Portugal, in Alves, F. (ed.), *Proceedings. International Symposium on Archaeology of Medieval and Modem Ships of Iberian-Atlantic Tradition. Hull remains, manuscripts and ethnographie sources: a comparative approach*. I.P.A. Trabalhos de Arqueologia, 18: 405–426. Lisboa.

Alves, F., Castro, F., Rodrigues, P., Garcia, C., Aleluia, M., 1998, Arqueologia de um naufrágio. In *Nossa Senhora dos Mártires. A última viagem*. Expo 98, edited by S. Luz Afonso and R. D' Intino, pp. 183–215. Lisboa.

Alves, F., Diogo, A.M. Dias, Cardoso, J.P., 2001, Considerações sobre os dois grandes cepos de âncora em chumbo com alma de madeira, do século V–IV a.C., provenientes do ancoradouro natural da ilha Berlenga (Peniche) e sobre os achados de ânforas de "tipo púnico" em águas portuguesas. In *Os Púnicos no Extremo Ocidente*. Actas do Colóquio Internacional (Lisboa, 27 e 28 de Outubro de 2000), Universidade Aberta, pp. 239–260. Lisboa.

Araújo, A.C., 1998, O concheiro de Toledo (Lourinhã) no quadro das adaptações humanas do Pós-Glaciar no litoral da Estremadura. *Revista Portuguesa de Arqueologia*, 1(2): 19–38. Lisboa.

Arruda, A.M., 1996, "Navegação atlântica em época pré-romana: uma realidade a confirmar". In *Arqueologia em meio Aquático*. Faculdade de Letras de Lisboa. Círculo de Estudos Arqueológicos. CPAS, March 11–13, 1996 (unpublished).

_____,1997, Os núcleos urbanos litorais da Idade do Ferro no Algarve. In *Noventa séculos entre a Serra e o Mar* (several authors). IPPAR, pp. 243–255. Lisbon.

Barata, J. da Gama Lobo Pimentel, 1965, O "Livro Primeiro da Architectura Naval", de João Baptista Lavanha. *Ethnos*, IV, pp. 221–298. Lisbon.

_____,1970, O traçado das naus e galeões Portugueses de 1550–1580 a 1640. *Revista da Universidade de Coimbra*, XXIV. Coimbra.

_____,1987, A Caravela. Breve estudo geral. *Studia*. Lisbon, 46: 157–192.

_____, 1989, *Estudos de Arqueologia Naval*, Lisboa, 2 volumes (a posthumous reedition of previous texts). Lisboa.

Barcelos, Senna, 1899, Construções de naus em Lisboa e Goa para a Carreira da Índia no começo do século XVII. *Boletim da Sociedade de Geografia de Lisboa*. 17ª série, 1898–1899 (l). Lisboa.

Basch, L., 1991, La fellouque des Kellia, *Neptunia*, pp. 2–10. Paris.

Blot, J-Y, 1994, Problemática americana em contextos histórico-arqueológicos fora do território americano: O interface história-arqueologia. In *Five Hundred Years After Columbus: Proceedings of the 47th International Congress of Americanists, Middle American Research Institute*, Publication 63: 157–161.

Blot, J-Y., 1998a, First Steps in the Analysis of Ship Overload, *Archaeological Computing Newsletter*, 51, Summer: 1–8. Oxford.

Blot, J-Y, 1998b, From Fera to Europe ,1784–86: Field and Model Analysis of a Ship Overload. In *The Maritime Archaeology of Long Distance Voyaging*, 17th International Conference, Bulletin of the Australian Institute for Maritime Archaeology.

Blot, J-Y, 1999, O Mar de Keith Muckelroy. O papel da teoria na arqueologia do mundo náutico. *Al-madan*, II , 8: 41–53. Almada.

Blot, J-Y, 2002, Elementos para a tonelagem dos navios na costa ibero-atlântica na Antiguidade: o testemunho dos vestígios de âncoras (cepos em chumbo). In *Terrenos da Arqueologia da Península Ibérica, sessão 35*, Actas do 3° Congresso da Arqueologia Peninsular, vol. VIII, pp. 571–594. UTAD. Vila Real.

Blot, J-Y. and Blot, M.L. Pinheiro, 1991, Le naufrage du San Pedro de Alcantara, *La Recherche*, 230: 334–342. Paris.

Blot, J-Y. and Blot, M.L. Pinheiro, 1990–92, De la glaciation de Würm aux derniers temps de la marine à voile: Eléments pour une carte archéologique du patrimoine immergé au Portugal. *O Arqueólogo Português*, IV,8/10 425–454. Lisboa.

Blot, J-Y. and Blot, M.L. Pinheiro, 1994, Arqueologia Subaquática. In *Síntese da Arqueologia em Portugal*. Atlas de Arqueologia, edited by Arnaud, J., pp. 380–381. Lisboa.

Blot, J-Y. and Blot, M.L. Pinheiro, 2001, Archives and Nautical Archaeology. Late 17th Century Portuguese Shipbuilding in India and the Fragata *Santo António de Tanna* (Bassein, 1678–Goa, 1681). In *Fourth Centenary Commemorative Volume (1595–1995)*, edited by S.K. Mhamai. Directorate of Archives, Archaeology and Museum, Goa, Panaji: 104–124. India.

Blot, J-Y, Rodrigues, P., and Lizé, P., 2002, Contributo do MS 4794f da biblioteca da Universidade de Harvard para o estudo da construção de naus de 3 ou de 4 cobertas no início do século XVII. *Revista Portuguesa de Arqueologia*, Lisbon. In press.

Blot, M.L. Pinheiro, 1994, The Skeletal Population of a Maritime Accident. *Paleopathology Newsletter*, 85: 11–12. Detroit.

Blot, M.L. Pinheiro, 1998, Mar, Portos e Transportes no Alentejo. *Arquivo de Beja*, 6/7 (3): 145–176. Beja.

Blot, M.L. Pinheiro, 2002, *Os Portos na Origem dos Centros Urbanos. Contributo para a Arqueologia das Cidades Marítimas e Fluvio-Marítimas em Portugal*. Lisbon. In press.

Blot, M.L. Pinheiro and Vivar Anaya, J., 2001, Arqueologia funerária de um naufrágio. Presenças humanas sul-americanas num depósito de náufragos da costa portuguesa (Peniche, 1786). *3° Congresso de Arqueologia Peninsular*, vol. VII, pp. 549–570. UTAD. Vila Real.

Borges Coelho, A., 1989, *Portugal na Espanha Árabe*. 2 vols. Lisboa.

Braudel, F., 1979, Le Temps du Monde, In *Civilisation Matérielle, Economie et Capitalisme, XVe-XVIIIe siècle*, 3 vols. Paris

Branco, J.N. Rodrigues, 1994, A Caravela de Onze Rumos do Livro de Traças de Carpintaria. In *A Engenharia Naval em Portugal*, X, edited by Guedes Soares, 1.11.35. Instituto Superior Técnico. Lisboa.

Bravo Perez, J. and Bravo Soto, J., 1972, Vestigios del pasado de Ceuta. In *Inmersion y Ciencia*, Barcelona, 4: 26–39 (as quoted by V. Cosma, in IJNA, 1975, 4 (1): 24)

Breuil, P., do Paço, A. and Zbyszewski, G., 1962, Les industries paléolithiques des plages quaternaires du Minho(la station de Carreço). *Comunicaçes dos Serviços Geologicos de Portugal*, 46: 53–131. Lisboa.

Brito,V.M. Gonçalves de, 1994, Projecto e Primeira Fase da Recuperação da Fragata *D. Fernando II e Glóri"*. In *A Engenharia Naval em Portugal*, X, edited by Guedes Soares, 2.1–2.17. Instituto Superior Técnico. Lisboa.

Butler, L.A.S. and Isserlin, B.S.J., 1990, Report on additional investigations at Corvo(Azores) in June, 1986. *IRivista di Studi Fenici*, XVIII, 1: 125–129, map.

Cardoso, A., 1978, Missão a Mombaça. Academia de Marinha. Lisboa.

Cardoso, G., 1978, Ânforas romanas no Museu do Mar (Cascais). *Conimbriga*, 17: 63–78.

Cardoso, J.L., 2001, Achados subaquáticos de defesas de elefante, prováveis indicadores do comércio púnico no litoral português. In *Os Púnicos no Extremo Ocidente*. Actas do Colóquio Internactional (Lisboa, 27 e 28 de Outubro de 2000), Universidade Aberta, pp. 261–282. Lisboa.

Castanheiro, J.M., 1986, Distribution,Transport and Sedimentation of Suspended Matter in the Tejo Estuary. In *Estuarine Processes: An Application to the Tagus Estuary*. December 13–16, 1982. Mem Martins.

Castelo Branco, F., 1994, Perspectivas da problemática das Navegações para Ocidente Pré-Colombianas. In *Simposio de Historia Maritima*, pp. 21–22. Academia de Marinha, Lisbon.

Castro, L.F.V., 1998a, The remains of a Portuguese Indiaman carrack at the mouth of the Tagus, Portugal (Nossa Senhora dos Mártires, 1606 ?). In *Proceedings. International Symposium Archaeology of Medieval and Modem Ships of Iberian-Atlantic Tradition*, pp. 79–87. Lisbon.

_____, 1998b, O naufrágio da fragata espanhola Nuestra Señora de las Mercedes afundada pelos ingleses ao largo do Cabo de Sta Maria em 1804. *Revista Portuguesa de Arqueologia* 1(2): 219–230. Lisbon.

Chevalier,Y., and Santamaria, C., 1971, L'épave de l'anse Gerbal à Port-Vendres. In *Forma Maris Antiqui*, VIII. Homenaje a Fernand Benoit. Separata from *Rivista di Studi Liguri*, XXXIII (1967)–XXXVII (1971), pp. 1–3.

Contente Domingues, F., 1997, Problemas e Perspectivas da Arquitectura Naval Portuguesa dos Séculos XV-XVII: a obra de João da Gama Pimentel Barata. In *Sessao de Homenagem à memória de Joao da Gama Pimentel Barata* 11–34. Academia de Marinha, Lisboa.

Contente Domingues, F., 1998, Documentation on Portuguese Naval Architecture (Late 16th–early 17th centuries): A general overview. *Pre-Actas. International Symposium on Archaeology of Medieval and Modern Ships of the Iberian-Atlantic Tradition-Hull Remains, Manuscripts and Ethnographie Sources: A Comparative Approach*. pp. 37–41. Academia de Marinha, Lisbon.

Correia, V.H., 1995, The Iron Ages in South and Central Portugal and the Emergence of Urban Centres. In *Social complexity and the development of towns in Iberia from the Copper Age to the Second Century* AD, edited by B. Cunliffe and S. Keay, pp. 237–262. Oxford. Oxford University Press.

Crisman, K., 1999, Angra B: The lead-sheeted Wreck at Porto Novo (Angra do Heroismo, Terceira Island, Azores– Portugal). *Revista Portuguesa de Arqueologia*. 2(1): 255–262. Lisboa.

Crisman, K. And Jordan, B., 1999, Angra A: The Copper-fastened Wreck of Porto Novo (Angra do Heroismo, Terceira Island, Azores–Portugal). *Revista Portuguesa de Arqueologia*. 2(1): 249–254. Lisboa.

Daveau, S., 1995, *Portugal geográfico*. Lisboa.

Desanges, J., 1978, *Recherches sur l'activité des Méditerranéens aux confins de l'Afrique*. Ecole Française de Rome. Paris and Rome.

Dias, A., Magalhães, F. and Rodrigues, A., 1991, Evolution of the North Portuguese Coast in the Last 18,000 years. *Quarternary Journal*, 9: 67–74.

Diogo, A.M. Dias, 1987, Ânforas provenientes do rio Tejo (Salvaterra de Magos), no Museu do Mar. *Arqueologia*. 16: 112–114. Porto.

Diogo, A.M. Dias, 1999, Ânforas provenientes de achados marítimos na costa portuguesa. *Revista Portuguesa de Arqueologia* 2(1): 235–248. Lisboa.

Diogo, A. Dias and Alves, F.J.S., 1988–1989, Ânforas provenientes do meio fluvial nas imediações de Vila Franca de Xira e de Alcácer do Sal. *O Arqueólogo Português*, Série IV (6/7): 227–240. Lisboa.

Diogo, A. Dias and Trindade, L., 1998, Uma perspectiva sobre Tróia a partir das ânforas. Contribuição para o estudo da produção e circulação das ânforas romanas em território português. *O Arqueólogo Português*, IV (16): 187–220. Lisbon.

Diogo, A. Dias, Cardoso, J.P. and Reiner, F., 2000, Um conjunto de ânforas recuperadas nos dragados da foz do rio Arade, Algarve. *Revista Portuguesa de Arqueologia* 3(1): 81–118. Lisboa.

Diogo, A.M. Dias and Cardoso, J.P., 2000, Ânforas Provenientes de um Achado Marítimo ao Largo de Tavira, Algarve. *Revista Portuguesa de Arqueologia*. 3.2: 67–79. Lisboa.

Domingues, F. Contente (2000), *Os Navios da Expansão. O Livro da Fábrica dos Naos de Fernando Oliveira e a arquitectura naval portuguesa dos séculos XVI e XVII*. Dissertação de Doutoramento em História dos Descobrimentos e da Expansão Portuguesa. 2 vols. Faculdade de Letras da Universidade de Lisboa. Lisbon.

Estácio dos Reis, A., 1998, Instrumentas de Navegação. In *Pavilhão do Conhecimento dos Mares*. Exposição Nacional de Lisboa de 1998, edited by R. Borges Martins and A. Nabais, pp. 104–115. Lisboa.

Fabião, C., 1996, De onde, para onde, como e quando: os naufrágios e a arqueologia clássica. In *Arqueologia em meio Aquático*. Faculdade de Letras de Lisboa. Círculo de Estudos Arqueológicos. March 11–13 (unpublished).

Filgueiras, O. Lixa,1994, A influência dos mestres construtores de Génova e de Pisa na reconversão da construção naval no séc. XII, na Galiza-base da técnica dos navios dos descobrimentos, In *I Simposio de Historia Maritima*. Academia de Marinha, pp. 341–349. Lisboa.

Fisher, H.E.S., 1971, *The Portugal Trade. A Study of Anglo-Portuguese Commerce*. Portuguese edition. Lisbon, 1984.

Fonseca, H.A. Quirino, 1978, *A Caravela Portuguesa*, 2 vols. Coleção Documentos. Ministério da Marinha. Lisboa.

Garcia, C., Monteiro, P. and Phaneuf, E., 1999, Os destroços dos navios Angra C e D descobertos durante a intervenção arqueológica subaquática realizada no quadro do projecto de construção d euma marina na baía de Angra do Heroismo (Terceira, Açores). *Revista Portuguesa de Arqueologia* 2(2): 211–232. Lisboa.

Gathercole, P. and Lowenthal, D., 1994, *The Politics of the Past*. London, New York. Routledge (1st ed. 1990).

Gianfrotta, P.A., 1977, First elements for the dating of stone anchor stocks. *International Journal of Nautical Archaeology*, 6(4): 285–292.

Gibbins, D., 1990, Analytical Approaches in Maritime Archaeology: a Mediterranean Perspective. *Antiquity*, 64, 243: 370–389.

Gibbins, D., 1995, What Shipwrecks can tell us. *Antiquity*, 69, 263: 408–411.

Gomes, M. Varela, 1993, O estabelecimento fenício-púnico do Cerro da Rocha Branca(Silves). In *Os Fenícios no Território Português*, *Estudos Orientais*, IV, edited by A.A. Tavares, pp. 73–108. Lisboa.

Gould, R., 1983, Looking below the surface. Shipwreck archaeology as Anthropology. In *Shipwreck Anthropology*, edited by R.Gould, Albuquerque. New Mexico Press, pp. 3–22.

Gould, R., 1998, Contextual Relationships. In *Enciclopedia of Undewater and Marine Archaeology*, edited by Delgado, J., British Museum, pp. 108–110. London

Guedes, M. Justo, 1983, Considerações sobre um Astrolábio assinado e datado, encontrado recentemente na Bahia. *Navigator*, 19: 3–11. Rio de Janeiro.

Guerra, A., Blot, M.L. Pinheiro and Quaresma, J.C., 2000, Para o enquadramento do sítio de Povos, um estabelecimento romano do curso inferior do Tejo. In *Senhora da Boa Morte, Mitos, História e Devoção*. Câmara Municipal de Vila Franca de Xira, 30–42.

Haldane, D., 1985, Recent discoveries about the dating and construction of wooden anchors. In *Thracia Pontica*, III, pp. 416–427, figures pp. 555–557.

Hanson, C.A., 1986, *Economia e sociedade no Portugal barroco*. Lisbon.

Henkin, 1952, The Huelva Hoard. In *Zephyrus* VII.

Hourani, G.F., 1995, *Arab seafaring in the Indian Ocean in ancient and early Medieval times*. Expanded edition by J. Carswell. Princeton.

Isserlin, B.S.J., 1984, Did Carthaginian Mariners reach the island of Corvo (Azores)? Report on the Result of Joint Field Investigations undertaken on Corvo in June, 1983. *Tartessos*, XII 1: 31–46.

Izaguirre, M., Valdés, L., Matés, J.M., Diez, A. and Pujana, I., 1998, State of the excavation works of the 15th century shipwreck in Urbieta (Gernika, Spain). In *Pre-Proceedings, International Sympo-sium "Archaeology of Medieval and Modem Ships of Iberian-Atlantic Tradition*, pp. 103–109. Lisboa.

Kermorvant, A., Romero, S. and Pratt, Fr, 1990, Desarollo de una técnica de deteccion geofisica aplicada a la exploracion arqueologica de medios humedos e subacuaticos. *Geociências*, 5(1): 123–134. Aveiro.

_____, 1992, Resultados da exploração por detector magnético efectuada numa superficie de 600 m2 no Porto da Areia Norte, Peniche, Junho 1992. In Blot J-Y and Blot M.L. Pinheiro, 1992, *O Interface História-Arqueologia: o caso do San Pedro de Alcantara (1786)*, pp. 36–38. Academia de Marinha, Lisboa.

Lenihan, D.J., 1983, Rethinking Shipwreck Archaeology: A History of Ideas and Considerations for New Directions. In *Shipwreck Anthropology*, edited by R. Gould, pp. 37–64. Albuquerque. New Mexico Press.

Lillios, K., Read, C. and Alves, F., 2000, The Axe of the Óbidos Lagoon (Portugal): An Uncommon Find Recovered during an Underwater Archaeological Survey (1999). *Revista Portuguesa de Arqueologia* 3 (1): 5–14. Lisboa.

Lopes, C. and Mayet, F., 1988, Commerce régional et lointain des amphores lusitaniennes. In *Les amphores lusitaniennes. Typologie, Production, Commerce*, edited by Alarcão, A. and Mayet, F., pp. 295–303. Paris.

Machado, J.P., 1997, Contribuição para o estudo do elemento arábico na terminologia naval portuguesa. In *Ensaios arábico-portugueses*, pp. 65–72. Lisbon.

MacLeod, I., 1998, In Situ Corrosion Studies on Iron Shipwrecks and Cannon: The Impact of Water Depth and Archaeological Activities on Corrosion Rates. *Metal 98*: Proceedings of the International Conference on Metals Conservation, pp. 116–124. James and James (Science Publishers), Draguignan.

Martins, A. Silveira, 1996, Fontes para o estudo daa Arqueologia Naval em Portugal do Século XIII a meados do século XVI. In *Memórias*. Academia de Marinha. Lisbon.

Martins, A. Silveira, 2001, *A Arqueologia Naval Portuguesa (Séculos XIII-XVI). Uma aproximação a seu estudo ibérico*. Universidade Autónoma de Lisboa.

Mayet, F. and Silva, C. Tavares, 1997, L'établissement phénicien d'Abul. *In Itinéraires Lusitaniens. Trente années de collaboration archéologique luso-française*, pp. 255–271. Paris.

McCarthy, M., 1998, The Study of Iron Steamship Wrecks: is it Archaeology?, *Bulletin of the Australian Institute for Maritime Archaeology*, 22: 99–106.

Monod, T., 1973, Les monnaies nord-africaines anciennes de Corvo(Açores). *Bulletin de l'Institut Français d'Afrique Noire*, 35, B, 3.

Monteiro, P., and Garcia, C., 1998, Angra D: A shipwreck from Angra Bay, Azores Islands. *Pre-Proceedings. International Symposium "Archaeology of Medieval and Modern Ships of Iberian-Atlantic Tradition*, pp. 93–102. Lisbon.

Monteiro, P., 1999, Os destroços dos navios Angra C e D descobertos durante a intervenção arqueológica subaquática realizada no quadro do projecto de construção de uma marina na baia de Angra do Heroísmo (Terceira, Açores): discussão preliminar. *Revista Portuguesa de Arqueologia*, 2, 2: 233–260. Lisbon.

Moreira, M. and Psuty, N., 1993, Sedimentação holocénica no estuário do Sado. Nota preliminar. *3ª Reuniao do Quaternário Ibérico*.

Muckelroy, K., 1975, A systematic approach to the investigation of scattered wreck sites, *International Journal of Nautical Archaeology*, 4.2: 173–190.

Oleson, J.P., 1988, Ancient Lead Circles and sounding-leads from Israeli Coastal Waters". In *Sefunim VII*, pp. 27–40.

Oleson, J.P., 1994, An Ancient Lead Sounding-weight in the National Maritime Museum. In *Sefunim VIII*, pp. 29–34.

Oleson, J.P., 2000, Ancient Sounding-weights: a Contribution to the History of Mediterranean Navigation. *Journal of Roman Archaeology* 13: 294–310.

Oliveira, P. and Almeida, M.J., 1996, Ilha da Berlenga e Foz do Douro: contribuição para o conhecimento das rotas comerciais na Antiguidade. *Arqueologia em meio Aquático*. Faculdade de Letras de Lisboa. Circulo de Estudos Arqueológicos. CPAS (unpublished).

Paviot, J. and Rieth, E., 1988–89, Un compte de construction de caravelles portugaises à Bruxelles en 1438–1439, *O Arqueólogo Português*, 4 (6/7): 307–331. Lisboa.

Pereira, A. Ramos, 1992, A Geomorfologia da Margem Continental Portuguesa e a Interdependência das Plataformas Continental e Litoral. Evolução do Conhecimento e linhas de Investigação. *Linha de Acção de Geografia Física. Relatório n° 30*. Centro de Estudos Geográficos. Lisboa.

Pereira, I.S., 1997, Santa Olaia et le commerce atlantique. In *Itinéraires lusitaniens (trente années de collaboration archéologique luso-française)*, edited by Etienne, R. and Mayet, F., pp. 209–253. Paris.

Pestana, G., 1989, Manancial ibero-atlantico de sardinha (*Sardina pilchardus*,Walb.) Sua avaliação e medidas de gestão. Instituto Nacional de Investigação das Pescas. Lisbon.

Pico, M.A.T. Carbonell, 1963, *A Terminologia Naval Portuguesa Anterior a 1460*. Lisbon.

Piercy, R., 1977, Mombasa wreck excavation. Preliminary report, 1977. *International Journal of Nautical Archaeology*, 6(4): 331–347.

Piercy, R., 1978, Mombasa wreck excavation. Second preliminary report, 1978. *International Journal of Nautical Archaeology*, 7(4): 301–319.

Piercy, R., 1979, Mombasa wreck excavation. Third preliminary report, 1979. *International Journal of Nautical Archaeology*, 8(4): 303–309.

Pinheiro, L., Almeida, F., Bernardes, C., Alves, F. and Teixeira, F., 1998, Geofisica e estratigrafia geológica do sítio dos destroços do navio dos meados do século XV Ria de Aveiro A. *Resuma estendido do Congresso Nacional de Geologia*, Lisboa.

Pomey, P., editor, 1997, *La navigation dans l'Antiquité*. Arles.

Raposo, L. and Carreira, J.R., 1986, Acerca da existência de complexos industriais pré-acheulenses no território português. *O Arqueólogo Português*, IV, 4: 7–90. Lisboa.

Rau, V., 1984, *Estudos sobre a história do Sal*. Lisbon.

Ribeiro, M. de Almeida, 1992, *A Zona Económica Exclusiva*. Lisbon.

Ribeiro, O., 1991, Portugal, o Mediterrâneo e o Atlântico. Sixth edition. Lisbon.

Rieth, E., 1998, Le cas de la France à la fin du XVIIe siècle: une même méthode de conception des navires au Ponant et au Levant. In *Pre-Proceedings. International Symposium "Archaeology of Medieval and Modern Ships of Iberian-Atlantic Tradition*, pp. 49–56. Lisbon.

Rochette Cordeiro, A.M., 1992, O Homem e o meio holocénico português. Paleoambientes e erosão. *Mediterrâneo*, 1: 89–109. Lisboa.

Rodrigues, P., 1998, Cais do Sodré-une épave de la deuxième moitié du XVème siècle/début du XVIème siècle à Lisbonne, Portugal. In. *Pre-Proceedings. International Symposium "Archaeology of Medieval and Modern Ships of Iberian-Atlantic Tradition*, pp. 72–78. Lisbon.

Rouillard, P., 1991, *Les Grecs et la Péninsule Ibérique du VIIe au IVe siècle avant Jésus-Christ*. Paris.

Rubino, T.C., 1996, *Dom Fernando II*. A fragata reborn. *Wooden Boat*, 1/2: 26–28.

Rule, M. and Monaghan, J., 1993, *A Gallo-Roman Trading Vessel from Guernsey. The Excavation and Recovery of a Third Century Shipwreck*. Guernsey Museum Monograph n°5.

Santos, M.L. Estácio da Veiga Affonso dos, 1971, *Arqueologia Romana do Algarve*. 2 volumes. Lisbon.

Santos, A.P., 1984, Primeras prospecciones arqueologicas subaquaticas en el litoral de la provincia de Pontevedra. *Pontevedra Arqueologica*, Pontevedra 1: 205–238.

Santos, N. Valdez dos, 1989, A representação das armas nacionais nas peças de artilharia. In *Memórias*, vol. XIX. Academia de Marinha. Lisboa.

Sardinha, O., 1999, Notícia sobre as peças pedradas do galeão San Diego (1600), *Arqueologia Medieval*, 6: 183–192. Porto.

Silva, C.T., Coelho-Soares, A. and Soares, J., 1987, Nota sobre material anfórico da Foz do Arade. *Setubal Arqueológica*, VIII: 203–219. Setúbal.

Silva, C.T. and Soares, J., 1998, Os Recursos Marinhos na estratégia da Pré-História do Sul de Portugal. *Al-madan* 7: 71–82. Almada.

Simplício, C., Braz Teixeira, S. and Costa Barros, P. 2002, Arqueologia e geodinâmica do litoral – O Caso de Quarteira (Algarve-Portugal), *3 Congresso de Arqueologia Peninsular*, vol. 8, pp. 609–622. UTAD. Vila Real.

Simplício, C., Barros, P.F. Da Costa, and Garcia, A.C.A., 1999, Prospecções no Rio Guadiana. *Al-madan* 8: 54–62. Almada.

Sousa, E.M. and Sepúlveda, E., 1997, A Colecção de contentores cerâmicos de Tróia de Setúbal conservada no Museu Municipal de Mafra. *Boletim Cultural* '97, pp. 143–158. Câmara Municipal de Mafra.

Stenuit, R., 1975, The treasure of Porto Santo. *National Geographie*, 148(2).

Stimson, A., 1985, The Mariner's astrolabe. A survey of 48 surviving examples. *Revista Universitária*, XXXII, pp. 573–605. Coimbra.

Teixeira, S. Brás, 1999, *Contribuição para o conhecimento da evolução do litoral entre Olhos de Água e Ancão; prospecção de ruínas submersas ao largo de Quarteira (Algarve-Portugal)*. Relatório. Ministério do Ambiente. Direcção Regional do Ambiente do Algarve. Faro.

Trochmé, E; and Delafosse, M., 1952, *Le commerce rochelais de la fin du XVe au début du XVIIe*. SEVPEN. Paris.

Waters, D.W., 1994, The originality of the Portuguese development of oceanic navigation in the XlVth and XVth centuries. In *I Simpósio de História Marítima*, pp. 71–97. Academia de Marinha. Lisboa.

Zilhão, J., 1995, The stylistically Paleolithic Petroglyphs of the Côa Valley (Portugal) are of Paleolithic Age: A refutation of their "Direct Dating" to Recent Times. In *Dossier Côa*, edited by Jorge, V. Oliveira, pp. 121–165. Sociedade Portuguesa de Antropologia e Etnologia, Porto.

The East, Australia, and Africa

In a category that includes the rest of the globe, the *Handbook* includes special representatives from four areas.

Israel is still in its infancy in deepwater research. Shelley Wachsmann and Dan Davis estimate there is evidence of a shipwreck for every 50 meters on the Mediterranean shore of Israel. Discoveries of the Athlit Ram, the Sea of Galilee Boat, and the harbor at Caesarea, with attendant preservation and publications, brings prominence to maritime archaeology in Israel.

Emad Khalil and Mohamed Mustafa present the latest activity in the waters of Egypt. A country of antiquities, Egypt is in the early stages of probing its wealth of submerged resources. The Egyptian Supreme Council of Antiquities has created an underwater archaeology department to regulate and supervise the work. Foreign nautical archaeological teams have contributed manpower and expertise. USESCO has helped to sponsor a workshop, and the University of Alexandria has plans to offer courses in marine archaeology. All bodes well for a rich future in preservation and recovery of Egypt's innudated world.

Growing pains in South Africa's underwater archaeology, writes John Gribble, mirror those of many countries. The wreckage is there. Legislative protection is there. The University of Cape Town has a program in place. Decreasing budgets have placed the most ambitious plans in limbo, but the discipline of underwater archaeology is gaining acceptance with state authorities and the diving community.

Jeremy Green has provided a summary not only of Australia's maritime archaeology programs but also those in place in Asia and the Indian Ocean. He highlights the Philippines and China and focuses on Far Eastern ship construction in Thailand, Vietnam, Sri Lanka, and Malaysia. In Australia, a national database is being developed for availability on the Internet.

Chapter 30

Nautical Archaeology in Israel

SHELLEY WACHSMANN AND DAN DAVIS

INTRODUCTION

Common wisdom has it that ancient mariners tried to hug coastlines for safety. In reality, probably the last place they wished to find themselves in any kind of a sea was directly opposite a rapidly approaching lee shore, from which there could be little chance of escape with their primitive rigs.

It is a truism that, even today in an age of motorized water transport, the vast majority of ships that wreck do so within several hundreds of meters of a coastal obstruction. Israel's Mediterranean shore is littered with the remains of wrecked ships and their cargoes, and it would not be an exaggeration to say that there is probably evidence of a wrecked ship for every 50 m of Israel's Mediterranean beachfront property. At Tantura Lagoon alone, remains of seven different ships have been documented in an area about the size of a regulation basketball court. This preponderance of shipwrecks is not the result of a biblical "Bermuda Triangle" but a statistical inevitability resulting from numerous ships plying these waters over many millennia.

Due to the long, straight profile of Israel's Mediterranean coastline, most ships that wrecked here are evidenced today by little more than scatterings of artifacts, found when sand covering the seabed is swept away by storms and currents. Only in areas where the

Shelley Wachsmann, Institute of Nautical Archaeology, Texas A&M University, College Station, Texas 77841. **Dan Davis**, RPM Nautical Foundation, Key West, Florida 33040.

International Handbook of Underwater Archaeology, edited by Carol V. Ruppé and Janet F. Barstad. Kluwer Academic/Plenum Publishers, New York, 2002.

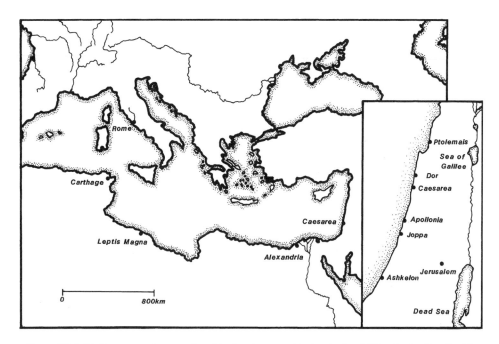

Figure 30.1. Mediterranean sites mentioned in the chapter, with sites in Israel (Drawing by Dan Davis).

coastline has some form of a geomorphologic change, such as islands, lagoons, or peninsulas, do ships seem to be buried by moving sands quickly enough to be protected from the vicissitudes of shoreline energy and biogenic degradation.

This chapter covers some of the most important hull and other submerged *wooden* remains in Israeli waters that have been found, studied, and published to date (Figure 30.1). It is important to emphasize that marine archaeology in Israel is extremely diverse and that many different types of sites other than those that will be described in this chapter have also been studied.

Marine archaeological research in Israel began in 1960, when Edwin Link surveyed underwater at Caesarea and in the Sea of Galilee. Since then, four research bodies have carried out marine archaeological work in Israel: the Underwater Exploration Society of Israel (now defunct), Haifa University's Recanati Centre for Maritime studies (CMS), Israel's Department of Antiquities and Museum (IDAM, now the Israel Antiquities Authority, or IAA), and the Institute of Nautical Archaeology (INA) of Texas A&M University.

MA'AGAN MICHAEL SHIPWRECK

In 1985, while teaching a dive course opposite Kibbutz Ma'agan Michael, kibbutz member Ami Eshel discovered waterlogged timbers, together with "nonlocal" stones, peeking out from a patch of seabed from which the sand covering had been scoured away. He notified Shelley Wachsmann (1995a: 287–289), then inspector of Underwater Antiquities for IDAM, who examined the site. The short probe excavation that followed revealed that the planking had been fastened with mortise-and-tenon joinery, typical of Mediterranean hull construction spanning a period from at least the Late Bronze Age

Uluburun Shipwreck to the Late Roman Period. An oil lamp and fragments of "basket-handle" jars found beneath the ballast immediately suggested a mid-first-millennium B.C. date for the hull. Subsequently, Elisha Linder and Field Director Jay Rosloff excavated the shipwreck for CMS.

The ship has been assigned a date in the late 5th century B.C. and is one of three from the period: two other late 5th-century B.C. shipwrecks currently are being excavated; one foundered off the southern coast of Alonnesos in the northern Sporades and was excavated by Elpida Hadjidaki (1997) for the Greek Department of Maritime Antiquities; the other sank near Sigaçik, Turkey, and its excavation, directed by George F. Bass (2002) for INA, began in the Summer of 1999. The Ma'agan Michael ship is a sailing merchantman about 13.5 m long, whose homeport remains elusive. The majority of some 70 ceramic artifacts found onboard come from Cyprus or the Lebanese–Israeli coasts, while a limited group is Greek in origin. The ship carried some 12.5 tons of ballast composed of three types of rocks; one type is thought to have come from the island of Evia in Greece, while another may have come from near the Kouris River in Cyprus.

The hull's rockered, 8.26 m-long keel is fashioned from a single timber, sided 10.5 cm and molded 16 cm. Its bottom was protected by an oaken false-keel. Most of the lower hull survived to a length of 11.15 m, a breadth of 3.35 m, and a maximum height of 1.5 m. Many planks reached nearly 7 m long, ranging 20–25 cm wide and 3.8–5.1 cm thick. Each plank is edge-joined to its neighbors with pegged mortise-and-tenon joints, 4–5 cm wide and spaced 12.1 cm apart. Mortises are 7.9 cm deep.

Other surviving hull parts include part of a wale, 14 widely spaced frames with futtocks in some cases, a stringer, and four center-line stanchions used, presumably, to hold up some form of deck structure forward and aft of the mast. A stout mast-step timber sat just forward of amidships.

The planking ends were *sewn* at the hull's extremities, in a manner known from other 7th- to 6th-century B.C. Mediterranean shipwrecks. Yaakov Kahanov (1999) notes that the closest parallels for the Ma'agan Michael hull's sewn construction are to the *Place Jules Vernes-7* and *Cesare-1* shipwrecks excavated by Patrice Pomey in Marseilles, France.

Additional finds of note recovered from the shipwreck include a full set of carpenter's tools and a one-armed wooden anchor carved from a single piece of oak and weighted with a lead-filled wooden stock (Rosloff, 1991). At present, the anchor is unique to the archaeological record, although Gerhard Kapitän (1973) had postulated the existence of this anchor type long before its discovery, based on a study of lead anchor fittings.

The Ma'agan Michael shipwreck bears many similarities to the 4th-century B.C. Kyrenia shipwreck. J. Richard Steffy's study of the latter hull and the construction of the *Kyrenia II*, a 1:1 sailing replica, demonstrated the advanced state of ship construction and sailing capabilities of such craft (Steffy, 1985; Katzev, 1989; Katzev and Katzev, 1986). The dimensions and presence of nearly every timber is repeated on both vessels. Pine was used throughout on both vessels with the exceptions of tenons and false keel. The differences in hull construction between the two ships are expressed in the framing configuration and the choice of fastening methods.

The Ma'agan Michael ship has completed its conservation process. At the time of this writing (Summer 1999), a museum was built at the University of Haifa, in which the hull is being reassembled and will be later exhibited.

ATHLIT RAM

The waterline ram served as the nautical weapon par excellence of the ancient world. In 1980, the late Yehoshua Ramon found the only ram known to date protruding from the sandy sea bottom north of the promontory at Athlit. The Athlit ram, as it has become known, ranks as one of the most significant discoveries of nautical archaeology (Figure 30.2; Casson and Steffy, 1991). Until this finding, information concerning ancient rams came solely from iconographical and textual sources.

The ram's maximum dimensions are 2.26 m long, 76 cm wide, and 96 cm high. The ram head is 41.1 cm high and 44.2 and 42.26 wide at its upper and lower fins respectively. It weighs 465 kg. Radiographic study indicates that it was probably cast in a sand mold and that at least 30 furnaces would have been needed to produce the amount of bronze required (Eisenberg, 1991). In consideration of some asymmetrical aspects of the casing, Steffy concluded that the ram was cast to the shape of the bow timbers rather than the opposite.

The ram encased 16 surviving timbers. The degree to which this discovery advanced our knowledge of ancient ship construction is perhaps best illustrated by the consideration that, when Steffy (1991) studied the ram, he had to invent terms to define several of the surviving timbers, since no current terminology existed to describe these constructional oddities.

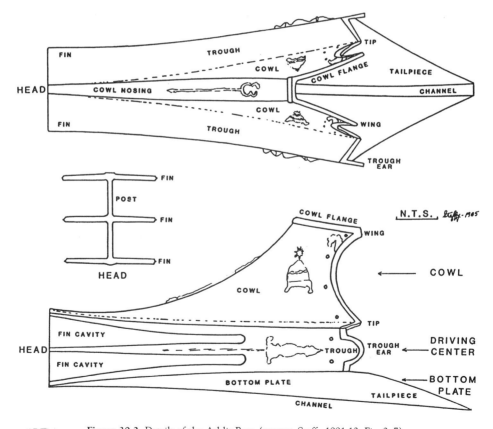

Figure 30.2. Details of the Athlit Ram (source: Steffy 1991:12, Fig. 2–7).

Shipwrights used at least four different woods to construct the ship: They chose cedar (*Cedrus*) for the stem and ramming timbers, elm (*Ulmus*) for the chock and nosing timber, pine (*Pinus*) for the keel, wales and planking, and oak (*Quercus*) for the tenons and tenon pegs.

Steffy established that contrary to common belief, ram-tipped ships required considerable mass in order to attain the momentum required to damage enemy ships. The ship itself was the weapon, with the ram serving as the spearhead that imparted the warship's momentum to its opponent in a concentrated and most useful manner.

Steffy observed that rams were not intended to pierce enemy hulls. Rather, their purpose was to crack open the planking seams by damaging the mortise-and-tenon joinery of their victims. With the wooden locking mechanisms spread apart, seawater would pour into the hull, incapacitating it. Indeed, piercing an enemy hull would have been extremely dangerous to the attacking ship, since it could become embedded in its victim and open itself to enemy attack. For this reason, the ram head was outfitted with three narrow, horizontal fins attached in their centers by a fourth, vertical fin, a design intended to *prevent* it from piercing an enemy hull.

The ram bears four decorations: a bird's head, a single wreathed helmet surmounted by an eight-pointed star, a decorative handle-device incorporated into the fins, and a herald's staff tied with a fillet, located on the cowl nosing.

With the reasonable assumption that the symbols represent the authority under which the ram was manufactured, William M. Murray (1991) studied the iconographic symbols to determine the ram's date and provenience. Murray argues that the government that produced the ram might be determined by finding a stylistically similar match for all four symbols on a coin or series of coins. The only known precise parallels to this grouping of symbols could be found on the silver and copper coins minted under Ptolemy V Epiphanes, although this same repertoire may have continued in use into the early years of his successor, Ptolemy VI Philometor. Thus, it appears that the ram was cast on Cyprus between 204–164 B.C. for use on a Ptolomaic warship.

In the Hellenistic period, galleys were usually described by numbers: "fours," "fives," and so on, up to Ptolemy IV's Brobdingnagian "forty." These terms are generally thought to represent the number of men assigned to superimposed levels of oars, with several men to each oar. The Athlit ram is so massive that it is easy to assume it belongs to one of the larger of the classes of Hellenistic warships.

Not so, observes Murray. Following the Battle of Actium, Octavian built his campsite memorial at the location where his tent stood during the Battle of Actium. On this retaining wall, he affixed the rams removed from Anthony's fleet (Murray and Petsas, 1989). Although the bronze rams themselves have long since disappeared, the sockets that supported them have survived. Surprisingly, all those presently visible are meant for rams larger than the Athlit ram, suggesting that it came from a fairly small class of warship, perhaps a "five" but more likely a "four."

SEA OF GALILEE BOAT (AKA *KINNERET BOAT*)

The Sea of Galilee (Hebrew: Yam Kinneret) is an inland lake that today serves as Israel's main freshwater reservoir. A devastating drought in 1986 caused the lake's level to plummet as waters were drawn off for agricultural and other needs. Vast expanses of seabed turned into mud flats, which became the setting for that year's discovery of one of the most significant archaeological discoveries for our understanding of the background to the Gospel stories relating to Jesus's ministry on the lake: a well-preserved fishing boat dating, within a century or younger, to the time of Jesus.

Yuval and Moshe Lufan, two brothers from nearby Kibbutz Ginosar, discovered the boat, buried entirely in the lake's sediment, north of the ancient site of Migdal Nunya, the home of Mary Magdalene ("Mary from Migdal") on the Sea of Galilee's western shore. A short IDAM probe excavation revealed that much of the lower part of the hull had survived in good condition. Its strakes had been edge-joined with pegged mortise-and-tenon joinery. Two ceramic artifacts suggested a more limited dating for the hull during the 1st centuries B.C–A.D.

The press soon learned of the discovery and termed it the "Jesus Boat," which started a cascade of events that threatened the vessel's safety. To parry this danger, IDAM undertook its excavation, which was directed by Wachsmann (1988; 1995a; Wachsmann et al., 1990). At the excavation's completion, project coordinator Orna Cohen developed an innovative method for moving the boat intact, by wrapping it in a cocoon of fiberglass frames and polyurethane. Protected in this manner, the vessel was floated to the Yigal Allon Center at Kibbutz Ginosar, where it underwent conservation with polyurethane glycol (PEG) in a specially-built pool, a process completed in mid-1995. At the time of this writing, work is underway on a museum wing at the Yigal Allon Center for the boat.

The boat's date—sometime between 100 B.C. and A.D. 67—is based on techniques used in the hull's construction, a battery of radiocarbon dates, ceramics found in and around the boat, as well as historical considerations.

Steffy (1987; 1990; 1994) studied the hull during the excavation (Figure 30.3). It survives to a length of 8.2 m, with a maximum breadth of 2.3 m and a surviving height of 1.2 m. The vessel was built with shell-based construction techniques, and its planks are edge-joined with mortise-and-tenon joinery. Its framing pattern follows the alternating floor and half-frame pattern of contemporaneous Mediterranean vessels.

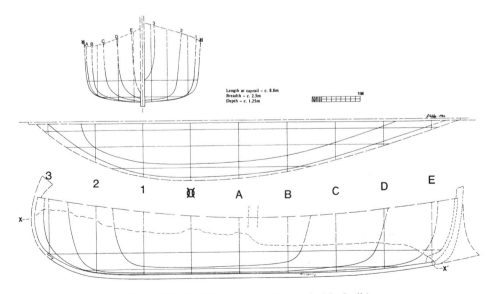

Figure 30.3. The Kinneret boat (Drawing by J.R. Steffy).

The Kinneret boat is constructed largely of recycled timbers, many of which appear to have seen previous service, probably on older hulls. A bizarre variety of timbers served in the hull's construction. Although the builder chose Lebanese cedar (*Cedrus*) primarily for the planks, and oak (*Quercus*) for the frames, five other wood-types were identified among the 41 timbers examined by Ella Werker (1990): Aleppo pine (*Pinus halapensis*), hawthorn (*Crataegus*), jujube—also known as siddar or Christ thorn (*Ziziphus spina-cristi*), redbud (*Cercis siliquastrum*), and willow (*Salix*). This mixture suggested either the owner's poverty or a regional situation of wood starvation.

From the numerous repairs evident in the hull, it apparently had a long working life. No doubt employed primarily for fishing—it was ideally suited for seine fishing—the vessel also could have transported passengers and supplies.

Years of toil eventually weakened the boat and, when it became clear that it was unlikely to withstand another season, its owner brought it to a site that seems to have been a center for the building and repair of local craft. There wreckers removed all reusable timbers including the bow assembly, stern post, mast-step, and several frames, before leaving it to disappear into the lake's sediment.

The Kinneret boat appears to be representative of the type of vessel used by the apostles (Mark 1:20; John 21:2–3) and may have been the type of boat in which Jews fought the Romans in the nautical Battle of Migdal of A.D. 67 (Josephus, *Jewish War* 3: 462–505, 522–542). However, no archaeological evidence connects this specific hull with any recorded events or persons.

CAESAREA

Introduction

In 31 B.C., King Herod the Great (c. 73–4 B.C.), ruler of Judea, found himself in a decidedly uncomfortable situation, having backed Antony against Octavian at the battle of Actium. Despite this mistake, Herod managed to ingratiate himself with the victor. Octavian, renamed Augustus Caesar, allowed Herod to keep both his life and his throne. This may explain Herod's subsequent decision to build a harbor city in Augustus's honor and name it *Caesarea Maritima*, "Caesarea on the Sea." He constructed it on a grand scale between 22–10 B.C. at the location of a more ancient settlement, known as Straton's Tower, with all the trappings of a large Graeco–Roman city. The site was well-chosen economically, for it served as a maritime outlet for the rich agricultural region south of the Carmel Range.

Along this coast natural harbors are few and far between, and those in use at the time offered only limited shelter. So Herod's ambitious plan also called for the construction of an artificial harbor, one using the most innovative building techniques of the Roman world. He named the port *Sebastos*, the Greek equivalent of the Latin *Augustus*.

Marine archaeologists have found fertile ground for ancient harbor research here. Since 1980, the site and its immediate vicinity has been intensively studied by a consortium of universities, archaeologists, and volunteers termed the Caesarea Ancient Harbour Excavation Project (CAHEP) and under the direction of CMS' Avner Raban (1989). Work has focused primarily on studying the foundations of Herod's port and the manner in which it was built. Additionally, a Roman-period merchant ship of unusually large proportions found nearby also has been studied in detail.

Herodian Caisons of Sebastos

Herod turned to Roman engineers and materials in the construction of the harbor of Sebastos. Despite severe logistical problems, the engineers succeeded in turning his dream into a reality. They constructed two breakwaters: a northern arm stretching 280 m west from shore perpendicular to the coastline, and a southern arm extending 800 m west, then north, in a long arc. Both arms had warehouses and ship berths. The harbor entrance, located in the northwest corner, faced north. The harbor's internal area amounted to 200,000 m^2 (20 ha). To prevent the enclosed basin from silting up, its builders incorporated sluice gates into the southern arm, which funneled sand out of the northern entrance channel using along-shore currents from the south.

In creating the arms of the harbor, Herod's engineers employed two types of cement-filled wooden caissons, which were studied by Raban (1989), John P. Oleson (1988; Oleson and Branton, 1992) and Chris Brandon (1996; 1997). Excavators discovered the first of these in 1982 in Area G, at the northwest tip of the northern breakwater flanking the harbor entrance (Raban, 1989). The caisson's top "surface" was badly eroded and nearly 4 m below sea level. Divers were surprised to discover the remains of the cement blocks' wooden frames. On plan, the Area G caisson measured 15 m × 11.5 m, with a height of 2 m. Stout sleeper beams of pine and fir composed the rectangular base of the structure, each 29 cm sided and molded. A double wall of pine planks, each 8 cm thick and 14 cm wide, ascended from each side and end. All planks were edge-joined to one another with pegged mortise-and-tenon joinery. This hallmark feature of ancient Mediterranean ship construction suggests that shipwrights built the caissons.

The lowest planks joined the sleeper beam. The resulting 23 cm-wide compartment between the double wall provided the necessary buoyancy to keep the caisson afloat for final positioning. No floor was discovered despite a thorough search. At the corners, spaced every 1.60 m, were 12 cm × 15 cm uprights; numerous crosspieces and struts strengthened the structure internally.

The current view is that engineers constructed these structures on shore, then towed them out to the site and lowered them to the sea bed by filling up the voids in the double walls with pozzolana-based concrete (Oleson, 1988; Oleson and Branton, 1992). The Romans had discovered that pozzolana ash (named after Puteoli, a modern town near the base of Mt. Vesuvius in southern Italy) made an excellent ingredient for hydraulic concrete. The earliest evidence for its use is at Cosa, a small Roman colony north of Rome, where similar caissons formed a breakwater as early as 2nd century B.C. Its use at Caesarea reinforces the view that Herod employed Roman engineers and materials to construct his harbor.

After the caissons sank to the sandy bottom, workers filled the main voids with stone and tufa aggregate and more pozzolana-based concrete. Stones placed at the base of each caisson prevented undercutting. The quay wall, promenade, and warehouses would have rested on the limestone blocks that topped the caissons.

Another type of caisson came to light when divers explored the northern, seaward tip of the southern breakwater in Area K. Here they found several caissons arranged side by side in an east-west orientation. At 14 m × 7 m, these caissons—barges, really— differ in plan only slightly from the Area G caissons. Their original height was 4 m, however, and, unlike the Area G caissons, each Area K caisson has a floor of 5.5 cm thick, edge-joined planking, with plank widths ranging 12–26 cm.

Thick pine chine girders, sided 26 cm and molded 20 cm, form the union between bottom and sides. End girders are mortised to receive the ends of the bottom planks. Here again, as in Graeco–Roman ship construction, pegged mortises and hardwood tenons were the rule throughout; they measure 8 × 10 cm and are spaced 20 cm center to center. Pegs are 1.1 cm in diameter.

Heavy uprights at the corners have two grooves each to receive plank ends from both side and end planks. Rough-cut pine floor timbers, sided 20–25 cm and molded 20 cm, rest loosely spaced atop the bottom planks, and frames of similar dimensions rise from the same station. Treenails join both floors and frames to the floor and side planking. Significantly, the floors are set into the chine girder with mortise-and-tenon joints, demonstrating that the floors were in place before the walls went up. At first, this would seem an unconventional procedure for shipwrights accustomed to shell-first construction. The Nemi ship's deck, however, also had been built in skeleton-first technique yet using edge joinery (Basch, 1972), suggesting that lack of evidence for this practice may be due to the rarity of finding intact deck structures in Roman ship excavations.

Notched stringers, 25 cm square and placed over the floors, provided additional longitudinal strength. Knees, joining the floor, chine girder, and walls by means of treenails and iron fastenings, served as further reinforcement, and diagonal braces contributed to overall stiffening.

Of all the caissons examined, only K2 had a central compartment, 6.5 m long and 2.5 m wide, which may have served as a "stabilizing chamber" during the sinking phase as the caisson was positioned on site (Brandon, 1997).

The barge would have weighed about 70 metric tons empty and had a .5 m draft. According to one scenario, it would have been filled with a half-meter of pozzolana-based concrete, increasing the draft to 1.5 m, which would have allowed for relatively easy towing while facilitating mooring operations once it was on site. Vessels would have come alongside and offloaded nonhydraulic lime mortar, tufa, and limestone aggregate until the barge sank to within a few centimeters of the surface. The caisson then would have been topped off with an additional meter of hydraulic mortar and aggregate (Figure 30.4).

The nonhydraulic core is puzzling and perhaps may be explained by a perceived lack of local sources for pozzolana ash. Although ash of similar quality could be found in the neighborhood of Caesarea, the Romans seem to have been unaware of it, and these deposits remained unexploited (Oleson and Branton, 1992). The poor state of the caissons apparently was the result of the dissolution of their cores, which weakened the entire structure.

The type-K barges at Caesarea are the earliest examples of such vessels. While the engineering of Herod's caissons may have had provincial influences, this particular usage was remarkably inventive and bold, remaining unparalleled until modern times.

A Roman Period Shipwreck

In 1980, during an IDAM underwater survey to determine the viability of plans for a marina north of the Herodian harbor at Caesarea, Shelley Wachsmann and Kurt Raveh found remains of a large hull with thick planking and staggered mortise-and-tenon joinery peaking out of the sand, a discovery that initiated the hull's excavation by CAHEP. Michael Fitzgerald (1994, 1995) studied and published his findings on the hull.

Excavations revealed the survival of a small portion of an enormous hull consisting of 16 strakes averaging 22 cm in width and dating to A.D. 1st century. The planks, more

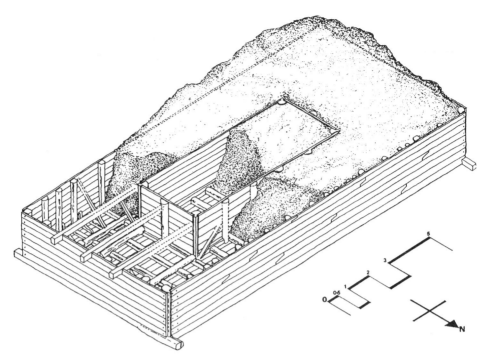

Figure 30.4. Artist's reconstruction of a type "K" caisson (SOURCE: Brandon 1997: 49, Fig. 3).

than 9 cm thick, are edge-joined to each other with pegged mortise-and-tenon joints. The lower part of the hull is double-planked.

Following traditional Graeco–Roman practice, half-frames alternated with floor timbers and floating futtocks. Robust pine frames, boasting naturally grown shapes, were quarter-cut at the heartwood; their sawn surfaces revealed virtually no axe or adz marks. No mast-step, stringers, or keelson survived. Two lines of Greek graffiti had been carved on the upper face of a futtock.

The Caesarea ship fits into a category of large Roman merchantmen that is well-documented in the archaeological, literary, and iconographical record.

TANTURA LAGOON

Introduction

Tantura Lagoon is situated on the Carmel Coast 25 km south of Haifa and is one of only three natural harbors along Israel's long and shallow Mediterranean coast. The cove has served as a harbor for Tel Dor and its immediate vicinity since the site's foundation c. 2000 B.C. (Figure 30.5). The lagoon is protected by a necklace of small islands and covered by a thick blanket of constantly moving sands, which tended to bury wrecked ships under a protective anoxic sand layer quite quickly. This resulted in the excellent preservation of numerous shipwrecks in shallow depths inside the lagoon.

INA and CMS created the Joint Expedition, directed by Wachsmann, which carried out three extremely productive seasons of exploration at Tantura Lagoon (1994–1996),

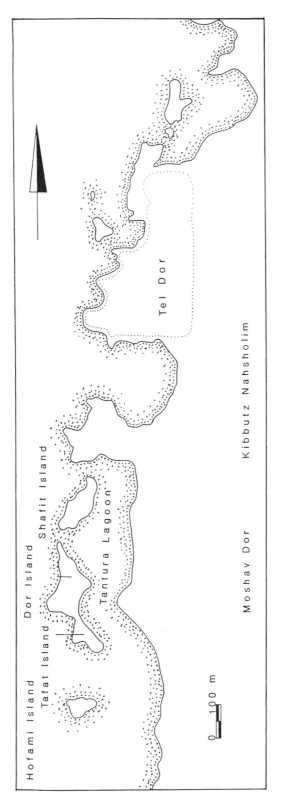

Figure 30.5. Tantura Lagoon and Tel Dor. (Drawing by S. Wachsmann)

recording in situ a series of significant *contributory* shipwrecks, a few of which are described below.

For recording purposes, Steffy (1994) defines shipwrecks as either *capital* or *contributory*. Capital shipwrecks are well-preserved, while their contributory sisters have only limited preservation. The significance of some contributory wrecks, including several studied at Tantura, lies in their uniqueness within the existent archaeological record. Steffy (1994) noted:

> It must not be assumed that capital reconstructions are always more important or provide more new information than contributory projects. If a sister ship to the Serçe Limani vessel were excavated and found to be in a similar state of preservation, its overall contribution to the historical record might be far less than that of the Athlit ram, which gave us a first limited look at the ramming structure of an ancient warship and changed so many of our theories. It does not matter that one vessel presented several tons of wood and the other only a few hundred pounds, nor do the number of drawings produced, the extent of research, or the size of the budget have any effect on the potential. The dominant factor here is that one wreck is a duplicate of another major project and may only confirm or complement the original discovery; as such it is essentially a contributory project in spite of its size. The 16 wood fragments of the Athlit ram, on the other hand, are so unique and have so much research value that the importance of this work borders on the realm of a capital project.

At least some of these ships had been literally ripped apart during their sinking processes. At first this seemed enigmatic, since they are now located inside a sheltered cove that is well protected from storms and waves. The most probable explanation for the manner of their destruction is that they seem to have been caught against a lee shore during storms. When caught in a storm, a sailing vessel or galley had little choice but to run before the wind until driven onto a lee shore. The only hope for survival of this destructive process lay in running the ship aground, a process graphically described in the wrecking of Saint Paul's ship off Malta (Acts 27).

Crews may have tried to reach the safety of Tantura Lagoon by maneuvering their ships between the islands. Instead of safety, however, they found destruction as hulls shattered on the unseen shallow rocks that are hidden between the islands. Once a ship received such a mortal blow, it would have been pushed by the crashing waves into the lagoon, hull torn and cargo spilling out. Soon afterward, the cove's moving sands buried the broken ships' remains, thus preserving them.

Tantura Lagoon's northernmost island is now connected to the mainland by a *tombolo*, or sand spit. During storms, water rushes in between the islands, creating a powerful southerly current that would have spread the cargoes and shipwrecked hull parts across the lagoon. The tombolo's existence in antiquity may be inferred by the fact that all hulls found by the Joint Expedition have a northwest-to-southeast alignment, to the degree that their plan looks almost like a parking lot for shipwrecks (Figure 30.6), presumably the result of the eastern part of each hull being buffeted by the southerly current caused by the tombolo to a greater extent than the other ends.

Tantura A Shipwreck (Trench VI)

In 1984, during an underwater IDAM survey dive in the lagoon, Wachsmann and Raveh discovered timbers of a ship that were covered with quantities of Byzantine ceramics. Due to concurrent discoveries and resultant time constraints, the site received only a

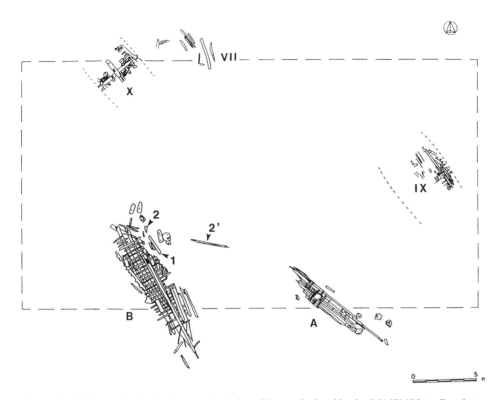

Figure 30.6. Like a parking lot for shipwrecks. A plan of the wrecks found by the INA/CMS Joint Expedition to Tantura Lagoon during three seasons of exploration. The expedition recorded parts of seven different shipwrecks, all located in an area no bigger than a regulation basketball court (28.65 × 15.24 m), represented here by a superimposed dashed rectangle (Drawing by P. Sibella).

preliminary study at that time. In 1985, IDAM carried out a short probe excavation in conjunction with CMS and a group of volunteers from the United Kingdom's Nautical Archaeology Society (NAS), led by Valery Fenwick. Again, due to logistical constraints, only a limited area of the site was explored.

Finally, in 1994 the Joint Expedition relocated the site and enlarged the excavation in its Trench IV. Only then did it become clear that the timbers were but few in number and that they, together with the Byzantine pottery and other artifacts, resulted from the break-up and spread of a ship and its cargo across the lagoon as it sank (Wachsmann, 1995b, Figure 30.3).

Where was the ship? Following the debris field north beneath 2 m of sand overburden, and using a systematic hydraulic probe, excavators located a large section of a hull, now termed the "Tantura B shipwreck," some 60 m north of the timbers found in 1984. In 1995, the Joint Expedition excavated the hull in its entirety in situ (Figure 30.7; Wachsmann, 1996; Wachsmann and Kahanov, 1997).

Yaakov Kahanov and Jeffrey Royal studied the hull, of which an estimated one-quarter of its bottom survives. The keel survives to 5.2 m. The vessel is believed to have been about 12 m long and approximately 4 m at its greatest breadth. Although the majority of the frames had been ripped away when the ship broke up, eight frames

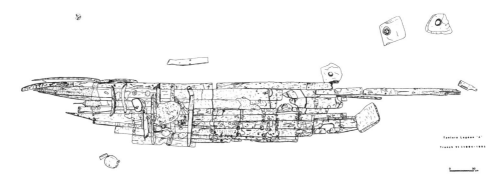

Figure 30.7. The Tantura A shipwreck (Drawing by P. Sibella).

remained with the hull, and various clues indicated a total of 24 framing stations extant on the remaining planks.

Charring found on the hull, and also concentrated at the hull's two extremities, continues *beneath* the framing stations, indicating that the planks were singed prior to their attachment to the hull. From these clues, Steffy concluded that the signs of burning represent "char-bending," a process in which water-soaked planks are bent to shape while heated over a fire. The charring is localized at the ends of the hull because these are locations where planks receive their strongest curvature as they turn in to meet the posts. *Tantura A* is the earliest hull for which the plank-bending technique has been recorded.

Because the date of the hull was securely assigned to A.D. mid-5th to mid-6th centuries, an intense search was undertaken to locate mortise-and-tenon joints which, common wisdom argued, should be found on a hull dated to this time frame. There were none found. Further, *Tantura A* is clearly "frame-based," making it the earliest recorded Mediterranean vessel to have been built with these innovative techniques. As such, it represents an important transition in the slow and gradual evolution of Mediterranean hull construction.

The hull apparently came to rest in its present location before breaking apart. This is indicated by the near-perfect alignment of the remaining strakes, although most of the frames securing them had been torn off when the ship's other sections parted from it.

Tantura B Shipwreck (Trench VIII)

The Joint Expedition discovered the Tantura B shipwreck in 1995 and completely excavated it in situ during the 1996 campaign (Figure 30.8; Wachsmann et al., 1997). Kahanov and Jerome Hall carried out the study of the hull, which so far is unique among Mediterranean medieval hulls in the continuity of its hull breadth, strongly suggesting a relatively long and narrow vessel, perhaps a galley. This is the first recorded example of a hull of this configuration from among known Mediterranean medieval shipwrecks.

The extant remains appear to be a relatively small part of the overall hull. Steffy estimated this section possibly represented less than 25 percent of the ship's bottom.

Dating to early A.D. 9th century, the hull was built in a skeleton-based tradition, indicated by planking joints located against frame stations and extensive use of caulking. The rockered keel is preserved for 9.8 m and contains two horizontal hook scarves. An imposing rockered keelson, now preserved for 7.48 m, is the most substantial longitudinal centerline timber, with a mast-step cut into its upper surface and notches in its

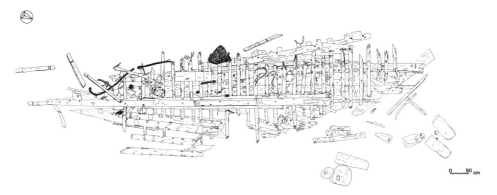

Figure 30.8. The Trench VIII site plan with Tantura B and Roman-period shipwrecks (bottom right) (Drawing by P. Sibella).

under-surface to seat the alternating floors and pairs of half-frames. The extant part of the keelson is composed of two timbers, attached by means of a hook-scarf covered by a timber attached to it by nails.

Longitudinal stringers lie on either side of the keelson. These are only lightly attached, suggesting that they served mainly as a base for the inner edges of ceiling planks aligned perpendicular to the keel, while the outer edges of these planks would have sat at the turn of the bilge. Three examples of such loose-fitting ceiling planks were found.

Seven strakes on the southwestern side of the hull survived, and six remained on the northeastern side. The sixth strake, apparently made of oak, is narrower yet thicker than the other strakes and is believed to be either a bilge-wale or a bilge-keel.

A single crenellate plank overlays the hull, its toothed (outer) side apparently intended to sit snugly over the frames at the turn of the bilge. It bears a single piece of graffiti—"HX"—when viewed from the ship's centerline.

This is a relatively flat hull, with a maximum beam of about 5 m. Unfortunately, its remains lack both its extremities, making it impossible to determine its length. If it was a single-master, it may have been 19 m long but, if it carried two masts, it could have reached a length of 30 m.

Its builders used pine (*Pinus*) for the keelson and one plank. Aleppo pine (*Pinus halepensis*) served for the stringers on either side of the keelson, a frame, a garboard, crunulate ceiling planking overlying the hull in the northwest quadrant, and a ceiling plank overlying planking in the southwest quadrant. The ship's keel and the longitudinal strengthening piece placed over the keelson scarf were made of oak (*Quercus*).

The ship's rigging can be inferred from the numerous ropes of varying dimensions found in it, as well as from four toggles.

Three wooden roundels, similar to one found on A.D. 7th-century Yassiada shipwreck, were found in the hull. One carried a Kufic inscription: "God has the purest judgment."

Roman-Period Shipwrecks at Tantura Lagoon (Trench VIII)

In 1995, the Joint Expedition found a plank fragment with two pegged mortise-and-tenon joints and associated Roman pottery in Trench VIII, intermingled with timbers from the

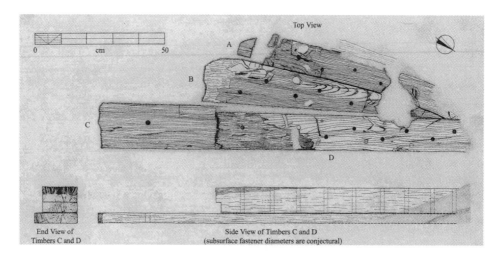

Figure 30.9. The Roman hull beneath Tantura B (Drawing by D. Davis).

Tantura B shipwreck, raising the possibility that another, earlier shipwreck existed in the vicinity (Wachsmann and Kahanov, 1997; Figure 30.8A). The following season, the expedition discovered an assemblage of hull timbers, jutting from beneath the Tantura B hull, also bearing Roman constructional features and covered with Roman-period pottery (Figures 30.8A and 9; Wachsmann et al., 1997; and Figure 3 [lower right]). To the east, team members also uncovered evidence for a third, apparently small, vessel in Trench VIII, including a disarticulated keel bearing mortise-and-tenon joinery and two frames. Dan Davis studied these hull remains. A summary of his research is published for the first time here.

Based on associated pottery, including a lamp boasting a Christian *tau–rho* symbol (Sibella, 1997), the assemblage protruding from beneath the Tantura B shipwreck is tentatively assigned to the Late Roman period, probably A.D. 4th century.

One of the planks was identified as cypress (*Cupressus*), making the hull one of only four recorded ancient hulls in which shipwrights employed cypress in their construction (Yassiada [A.D. 4th century], Port-Vendres I [A.D. 4th or 5th century], and Pantano Longarini [A.D. 7th century]) (Yassiada: van Doorninck, 1982; Port-Vendres: Rival, 1991, Table 11; Pantano Longarini: Throckmorton and Kapitän, 1968).

The recorded dimensions of the individual timbers were:

Timber A: 80 cm long, 10.5 cm wide, narrowing to 10 cm.
Timber B: 92 cm long, 16 cm wide, narrowing to a point, 9.3 cm thick.
Timber C: almost 1.5 m long, 16.5 cm wide, narrowing to 16 cm, 3.7 cm thick.
Timber D: 96 cm long, 13.2 cm narrowing to 11.8 cm wide, 9.3 cm thick.

The unusual notch cut into the end of Timber D gives a first impression of a weak scarf, altgough this may be due to damage caused during sinking and breakup. The peg pattern on Timbers A, B, and D indicates the presence of mortise-and-tenon joinery. No treenails are evident nor, oddly enough, is there any evidence of frames or frame fastenings: No nails or nail holes could be found, nor were any timbers discolored.

At first glance, the four planks might appear to be deck planking, either at the peak of the bow or stern; however, no evidence for nails appears anywhere on the timbers. Yet the preserved deck of the Roman-period *Anse des Laurons 2* shipwreck contained numerous bronze or copper nails, particularly at plank ends (Gassend et al., 1984) and, along 1.5 m of planking, there is no evidence of deck beams.

Two scenarios present themselves. First, the assemblage may be simply hull planking near the end posts, the location where strakes curve sharply inward and stealers appear. Most wrecks from the period exhibit this feature. In this case, Timber B would be a stealer joined to Timber C with mortise-and-tenon joinery (although this is not apparent). Timber D, then, might be a wale, a feature common in contemporaneous ship depictions.

The argument against this interpretation is overpowering: First, the peg pattern does not fit this solution, for Timber C has only one peg, although room for many more exists. Second, there are no other fastenings besides the pegged mortise-and-tenon joints, nor is there any discoloration of the wood to indicate where frames may have rested. Finally, Timber B's dimensions closely match those of Timber D, in effect constituting a never-before-seen double wale. If this was a hull-planking assemblage, we would expect its well-preserved surfaces to show indications of these features.

An alternate scenario, which seems preferable at present, is that this is a keel or lower end-post with false keel and garboard strake. Indeed, the shape of Timber B resembles a garboard strake falling out toward the ends of the hull, which would make Timber C a false keel lightly attached to the keel's bottom with pegs (although it is enigmatic as to precisely why the false keel would be wider than the keel it serves to protect).

False keels are attached lightly for good reason: They are used to protect a ship during beaching and grounding; hence, rigid physical attachment to the keel is undesirable. They were meant for everyday war and tear and for easy removal and replacement. Although the assemblage appears to represent a small, perhaps flat-bottomed trading vessel of indeterminate size, any conclusions as to the specific placement of these timbers within the larger whole, and the type of function of the vessel, must be reserved until more of its remains are uncovered and studied.

CONCLUSIONS

While other Mediterranean countries might boast greater numbers of known ancient shipwrecks, Israeli waters seem to be a repository for vessels otherwise unknown in the archaeological record. No doubt future exploration along Israel's shores will continue to contribute to our knowledge of a unique Mediterranean nautical heritage. Still in its infancy, deep-water research promises to contribute even more as it opens new areas for search and study.

ACKNOWLEDGMENT. We wish to thank J. Richard "Dick" Steffy for his invaluable comments.

REFERENCES

Basch, L., 1972, Ancient Ships and the Archaeology of Ships. *International Journal of Nautical Archaeology* 1:1–58.

Bass, G.F., 2002, Golden Age Treasures: A Fifth-Century B.C. Shipwreck off Turkey Shines Light on Greece's Finest Hour. *National Geographic* 201: 102–117.

Brandon, C., 1996, Cements, Concrete, and Settling Barges at Sebastos: Comparison with Other Roman Harbor Examples and the Descriptions of Vitruvius. In *Caesarea Maritima: A Retrospective After Two Millennia*, edited by E.J. Brill, pp. 25–40 Leiden. A. Raban and K.G. Holum.

_____, 1997, The Concrete-Filled Barges of King Herod's Harbor of Sebastos. In *Res Maritimae*: *Cyprus and the Eastern Mediterranean from Prehistory to Late Antiquity. Proceedings of the Second International Symposium Cities on the Sea, Nicosia Cyprus, October 18–22, 1994*, edited by S. Swiny, R.L. Hohlfelder, and H. Wylde Swiny, pp. 45–58. Scholars Press, Atlanta.

Casson, L., 1995, *Ships and Seamanship in the Ancient World.* Princeton University Press, Baltimore.

Casson, L., and J.R., Steffy, 1991, *The Athlit Ram.* Texas A&M University Press, College Station.

Eisenberg, S., 1991, Metallurgical Analysis of the Ram. In *The Athlit Ram*, edited by L. Casson and J.R. Steffy, pp. 51–66. Texas A&M University Press, College Station.

Fitzgerald, M., 1994, The Ship. In *The Harbours of Caesarea Maritima*: *Results of the Caesarea Ancient Harbour Excavation Project 1980*–1985, II, edited by J.P. Oleson, pp. 163–255. BAR International Series 594, Oxford.

_____, 1995, *A Roman Wreck at Caesarea Maritima, Israel*: *A Comparative Study of Its Hull and Equipment.* Ph.D. dissertation, Texas A&M University, College Station.

Gassend, J.M., B., Liou, and S., Ximénès, 1984, L'épave 2 de l'Anse des Laurons. *Archaeonautica* 4:75–105.

Hadjidaki, E., 1997, The Classical Shipwreck at Alonnesos. In *Res Maritimae*: *Cyprus and the Eastern Mediterranean from Prehistory to Late Antiquity, Proceedings of the Second International Symposium Cities on the Sea, Nicosia Cyprus, October 18–22, 1994*, edited by S. Swiny, R.L. Hohlfelder, and H. Wylde Swiny, pp. 125–134. Scholars Press, Atlanta.

Kahanov, Y., 1999, *Sewing System in the Hull Construction of the Ma'agan Mikhael Shipwreck*: *A Comparative Study with Mediterranean Parallels.* Ph.D. dissertation, in Hebrew, University of Haifa, Haifa. (in Hebren).

Kapitän, G., 1973, Greco-Roman Anchors and the Evidence for the One-armed Wooden Anchor in Antiquity. In *Marine Archaeology, Proceedings of the 23rd Symposium of the Colston Research Society held in the Univesity of Bristol, April 4–8, 1971*, edited by D. Blackman, pp. 383–395. Archon Books, London.

Katzev, M.L., 1989, Kyrenia II: Building a Replica of an Ancient Greek Merchantman. In *Tropis 1, Proceedings of the 1st International Symposium on Ship Construction in Antiquity, Piraeus, August 30–September 1, 1985*, edited by H. Tzalas, pp. 163–175. Hellenic Institute for the Preservation of Nautical Tradition, Athens.

Katzev, M.L., and S.W., Katzev, 1986, Kyrenia II: Research on an Ancient Shipwreck Comes Full Circle in a Full-Scale Replication. *INA Newsletter* 13(3):cover, 1–11.

Linder, E., 1992, Excavating an Ancient Merchantman. *Biblical Archaeology Review* 18(6):24–35.

Murray, W.M., 1991, The Provenience and Date: The Evidence of the Symbols. In *The Athlit Ram*, edited by L. Casson and J.R. Steffy, pp. 51–66. Texas A&M University Press, College Station.

Murray, W.M., and Petsas, P.M., 1989, Octavian's Campsite Memorial for the Actian War. *Transactions of the American Philosophical Society* 79, Part 4.

Oleson, J., 1988, The Technology of Roman Harbours. *International Journal of Nautical Archaeology* 17:147–157.

Oleson, J., and G., Branton, 1992, The Technology of King Herod's Harbour. In *Caesarea Papers: Straton's Tower, Herod's Harbour, and Roman and Byzantine Caesarea*, edited by R.L. Vann, pp. 49–67. *Journal of Roman Archaeology*, Supplementary Series 5, Ann Arbor.

Raban, A., 1989, *The Harbours of Caesarea Maritima*: *Results of the Caesarea Ancient Harbour Excavation Project, 1980–1985*, I. BAR International Series 491, Oxford.

Rosloff, J.P., 1991, A One-armed Anchor of *c.* 400 B.C.E. from the Ma'agan Michael Vessel, Israel. A Preliminary Report. *International Journal of Nautical Archaeology* 20:223–226.

Sibella, P., 1997, Light from the Past: The 1996 Tantura Roman Lamp. *INA Quarterly* 24(4): 16–18.

Steffy, J.R., 1985, The Kyrenia Ship: An Interim Report on its Hull Construction. *American Journal of Archaeology* 89:75–101.

_____, 1987, The Kinneret Boat Project, Part II: Notes on the Construction of the Kinneret Boat. *International Journal of Nautical Archaeology* 16:325–329.

_____, 1990, The Boat: A Preliminary Study of its Construction. In S. Wachsmann et al., *The Excavations of an Ancient Boat in the Sea of Galilee (Lake Kinneret)*, pp. 29–47 (*Atiqot* 19). Israel Antiquities Authority, Jerusalem.

_____, 1991, The Ram and Bow Timbers: A Structural Interpretation. In *The Athlit Ram*, edited by L. Casson and J.R. Steffy, pp. 6–39. Texas A&M University Press, College Station.

_____, 1994, *Wooden Ship Building and the Interpretation of Shipwrecks.* Texas A&M University Press, College Station.

Throckmorton, P., and G., Kapitän, 1968, An Ancient Shipwreck at Pantano Longarini. *Archaeology* 21:185–187.

van Doorninck, F.H. Jr., 1982, The Hull Remains. In *Yassi Ada: A Seventh-Century Byzantine Shipwreck*, edited by G.F. Bass and F.H. van Doorninck Jr., pp. 32–64. Texas A&M University Press, College Station.

Wachsmann, S., 1988, The Galilee Boat: 2,000-Year-Old Hull Recovered Intact. Biblical *Archaeology Review* 14(5):18–33.

_____, 1995a, *The Sea of Galilee Boat: An Extraordinary 2000 Year Old Discovery*. Plenum Press, New York.

_____, 1995b, The 1994 INA/CMS Joint Expedition to Tantura Lagoon. *INA Quarterly* 22(2): 3–9.

_____, 1996, Technology Before its Time: A Byzantine Shipwreck from Tantura Lagoon. *The Explorers Journal* 74(1): 19–23.

Wachsmann, S., et al., 1990, *The Excavations of an Ancient Boat in the Sea of Galilee (Lake Kinneret)*. (*Atiqot* 19). Israel Antiquities Authority, Jerusalem.

Wachsmann, S. and Y., Kahanov, 1997, Shipwreck Fall: The 1995 INA/CMS Joint Expedition to Tantura Lagoon, Israel. *Institute of Nautical Archaeology Quarterly* 24(1):3–18.

Wachsmann, S., Y., Kahanov, and J., Hall, 1997, The *Tantura B* Shipwreck: The 1996 INA/CMS Joint Expedition to Tantura Lagoon, Israel. *INA Quarterly* 24/4:cover, 3–15.

Wachsmann, S., and K., Raveh, 1984, A Concise Nautical History of Dor/Tantura. *International Journal of Nautical Archaeology* 13:223–241.

Werker, E., 1990, Identification of the Wood. In *The Excavations of an Ancient Boat in the Sea of Galilee (Lake Kinneret)*. (*Atiqot* 19), edited by S. Wachsmann, et al., pp. 65–75. Israel Antiquities Authority, Jerusalem.

Chapter 31

Underwater Archaeology in Egypt

EMAD KHALIL AND MOHAMED MUSTAFA

INTRODUCTION

Egypt's rich maritime history has left a variety of archaeological remains and has made a great impact on seafaring and shipbuilding traditions in the ancient Near East. Yet modern Egyptians and scholars around the world know little about the ships, ports, and trade routes that helped maintain Egypt's relationships with other lands and peoples. Egypt's lucky year was 1994 because of the revival of Egyptian interest in its maritime heritage, although interest in Egypt's underwater archaeology, especially in Alexandria, started much earlier (Figure 31.1).

In 1910, while studying the possibility of expanding and improving Alexandria's Western Harbor, Gaston Jondet discovered piers of an entire seaport west of Pharos Island, completely submerged at a depth of about 8 m. The seaport consisted of an outer and inner breakwater, each about 2500 m long, placed 200 m apart, and measuring 10 m in height, 60 m across, and 12 m thick. Jondet regarded his find as evidence for the existence of a seaport predating the modern city of Alexandria, founded by Alexander. It was the first time that such gigantic submerged structures had been found.

Emad Khalil, Assistant Lecturer, Archaeology Department, Alexandria University, Alexandria, Egypt.
Mohamed Mustafa, Archaeological Inspector, Underwater Archaeology Department, Supreme Council of Antiquities, Alexandria, Egypt.

International Handbook of Underwater Archaeology, edited by Carol V. Ruppé and Janet F. Barstad.
Kluwer Academic/Plenum Publishers, New York, 2002.

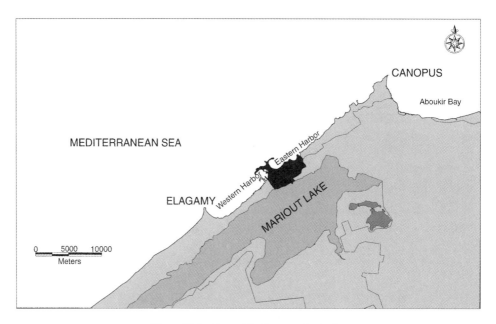

Figure 31.1. Alexandria, Egypt, and suburbs.

In 1933, accident again played a role in the discovery of a second underwater site, when a British Royal Air Force pilot saw a number of submerged ruins from his plane while flying over Abu-Qir Bay east of Alexandria. Prince Omar Tousson, a member of the Royal Archaeological Society in Alexandria, funded a research that led to the recovery of a larger-than-life-sized white marble head of Alexander the Great, now in Alexandria's Greco–Roman Museum. Prince Tousson published his work in the *Bulletin of the Archaeological Society of Alexandria.*

In 1961, Kamel Abu El-Saadat, a sport diver and spear fisherman who knew of hundreds of submerged archaeological remains in Alexandria's waters, drew maps of the Eastern Harbor, defining the site of Antirhodos Island and the archaeological remains around Cape Lochias outside the harbor (Figure 31.2). On a map of Abu-Qir Bay he defined the shipwrecks of Napoleon's fleet, sunk in 1798 during the Battle of the Nile against the British fleet under Admiral Nelson. In April and November 1962, Abu El-Saadat participated with the Egyptian navy in recovering a male statue east of Cape Lochias, and a 6 m-tall royal female statue thought at the time to be the statue of the goddess Isis Pharia, from the Pharos site off Fort Qaitbay. Both granite statues are now in the National Maritime Museum in Alexandria.

In 1968, the Egyptian government, via UNESCO, invited Honor Frost to examine the site believed to be the remains of the Pharos lighthouse. Frost and Abu El-Saadat examined it and gave a list of 17 different items located there. Frost noted that such evidence would be multiplied a hundred-fold through a complete survey.

Finally, in 1986, the French navy, in cooperation with la Société Française de Recherché Archéologique Sous-marines (SOFRAS) with funding from Electricité de France (EDF), salvaged the shipwrecks of Napoleon's fleet in Abu-Qir Bay. Objects such as cannons, military costumes, utensils for daily use, and coins were salvaged from the site. In the same season, the SOFRAS team defined the wreck of *Le Patriote*, a research vessel that accompanied Napoleon's expedition and sank off Al-Agami.

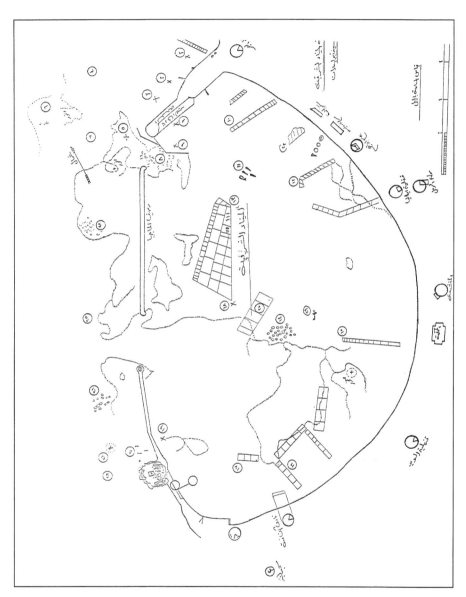

Figure 31.2. Abu El-Saadat's map of Eastern Harbor archaeological remains.

Following the SOFRAS expedition, the development of Egyptian nautical archaeology remained dormant until April 1994, when the Centre d'Etudes Alexandrines (CEA), directed by Jean-Yves Empereur, decided to complete the Pharos surveys begun by Abu El-Saadat and Frost. At the same time, the Institute of Nautical Archaeology (INA) established a permanent branch in Alexandria, under the direction of its research associates Cheryl Ward and Douglas Haldane. INA-Egypt, dedicated to the exploration, protection, and preservation of Egypt's maritime cultural heritage, started its first project, a coastal survey of the Red Sea, which led to the Sadana Island Shipwreck Excavation.

These two events mark the real beginnings of Egyptian marine archaeology. In response, in 1996 the Egyptian Supreme Council of Antiquities (SCA) established an Underwater Archaeology Department and certified Egyptian antiquities inspectors in scuba diving for advanced training in underwater excavation techniques with foreign missions working in Egypt.

ARCHAEOLOGICAL PROJECTS ON EGYPT'S MEDITERRANIAN COAST

Pharos

The ancient harbor of Alexandria was dominated by the Pharos Lighthouse, the Seventh Wonder of the World. Built on the eastern end of Pharos Island by Ptolemy II Philadelphus in 280 B.C., the lighthouse was more than 130 m high, and its light could be seen 50 km out at sea. For about 16 centuries, the Pharos light guided ships in and out of Alexandria's Portus Magnus, or Eastern Harbor. Writers and travelers from the Ptolemaic to medieval periods described the Pharos and the damage it received in successive earthquakes. It was completely destroyed in the earthquake of A.D. 1303 and, in 1477, Mamluk Sultan Al-Ashraf Abu Al-Nasr Qaitbay ordered a fort built on the ruins.

For many years in Alexandria, tales were told of fabulous statues and engraved blocks scattered across the sea floor just outside the Eastern Harbor. But the area was a military zone and considered off-limits to scientific investigation.

In 1993, the SCA stopped a project adopted by the Egyptian Coasts Protection Agency to protect Fort Qaitbay from waves and marine factors. The project called for throwing 20-ton concrete blocks off the fort to weaken wave action and protect the fort's walls. But the blocks were falling over hundreds of submerged archaeological remains near the fort. In fall 1994, a team of CEA archaeologists, in cooperation with the SCA, began an extensive survey to determine the extent of the Pharos site, and the number, size, and importance of the pieces.

As with any archaeological site, plotting a detailed, accurate map is a necessity. The mapmaking for Pharos has been a major undertaking for two reasons. The field of ruins extends over 2.25 hectares at a depth of 6–18 m, making it one of the largest underwater archaeological sites in the Mediterranean. In addition, pieces often lie on top of each other. To map the site effectively, the team created a detailed database, the like of which has never before been used in archaeology (Figure 31.3).

In addition to using the traditional method of triangulation for measuring the site, work depended on establishing a fixed Electronic Distance Measurement (EDM) using an electronic theodolite on shore to "spot" the underwater blocks, which were indicated by a reflector mounted on a floating mast. The mast was connected to a lead line placed against the four corners of the submerged block and held in position by a diver. Another

Blocks Lifted

Concrete wall

0   15   30
Metres

Fort Qaitbay

Figure 31.3. Pharos Site: Topographic plan of Qaitbay. Status as of July 1, 1998.

diver on the surface ensured that correct tension was maintained and that the floating mast did not move too much. Depending on sea conditions, this technique was accurate to between 10–30 cm. It was the sole option, given the need to relate the underwater site to other Alexandrian archaeological sites.

At the end of each day, information stored in the EDM's memory was imported into computers and combined with triangulation and Global Positioning System (GPS) data to plot the overall site map. Partial charts were given to divers the following day to orient them underwater and help them add complementary features of the blocks. This method has contributed enormously to the progress of the excavation and could be applied to other underwater sites around the world.

During 14-plus months of diving, more than 3000 artifacts were documented, from pharaonic, papyriform columns, obelisks, sphinxes, and lintels to an enormous collection of Greco–Roman columns, capitals, bases, and statues in granite, quartzite, diorite, basalt, and marble. Weights ranged from 100 kg to 75 tons. Forty pieces were raised and conserved and are now exhibited in the Roman Theater in Alexandria.

Empereur concluded that the site contained blocks (90 percent of which are granite) that once belonged to the lighthouse, and remains of some other buildings that existed on the island of Pharos, such as the temple of Isis Pharia. Most pieces were recycled from pre-existing structures in the Nile Delta and Heliopolis. There are clear signs of the application of Greco–Macedonian technology to thoroughly Egyptian architectural materials, throwing light upon both architectural styles and construction methods of the Pharos. It is likely that the Pharos was not built in purely Greek style but also depended on Egyptian technical expertise. On the other hand, the Pharos would not have been purely Egyptian, because the Greeks commissioned it. Significant amounts of statuary discovered and evidence of other complete structures underwater may lead to conclusions that the Pharos was part of a larger complex.

Architectural analysis of the Pharos site presents a formidable challenge. The only blocks that can be dated even approximately are those bearing decorations, such as moldings, inscriptions, and statuary, and there are relatively few of these. Because the major portion of the material was recycled, this, also, presents a challenge, since any traces of construction techniques could be from either the original structure or from the Pharos itself.

The project's main and continuing objectives are to advance a clear hypothesis about the arrangement of the site and to produce a hand-drawn and computer-generated architectural reconstruction of the buildings, whose elements now lie on the floor of the Mediterranean.

Alexandria Shipwrecks Survey

A number of ancient sources mention the hazardous entries to the Eastern Harbor of Alexandria as well as several shipwreck sites in the vicinity of the city or at the harbor entrance. But these sources do not define the exact location of shipwreck sites, and they often formulate the accidents in a literary manner.

In 1996, CEA/SCA undertook an underwater survey to locate shipwrecks outside the ancient harbor of Alexandria for a better understanding of Greco–Roman trade routes and international relations prevailing in the Mediterranean. The surveyed area extended from Fort Qaitbay on the west to Cape Lochias on the east and about 4 km to the north. Work began by combining the map drawn for the area by Abu El-Saadat in the 1960s with present marine charts. The combination enabled the team to relocate and record sites

Abu El-Saadat had mentioned earlier. Using the GPS, six points were confirmed, two of which were found to have concentrations of amphorae. The site was studied further during winter 1998.

The survey used two search methods. Initially, diving groups surveyed around the Diamond Rock at the entrance of the harbor between 2–16 m. The survey team located several sites.

Qaitbay 1.   One hundred meters north of Fort Qaitbay, at a depth of about 11 m, the site contains a large number of broken Lamboglia II, stamped Rhodian, and Cretan amphorae, and stone anchors. A detailed site map, made by triangulation, was put on the general map using GPS.

Qaitbay 1 East.   Lying about 50 m to the east of Qaitbay 1, Qaitbay 1 East has the same characteristics as the first site but with a lower concentration of artifacts. The two sites may belong to the same shipwreck; most discovered artifacts are utensils used daily by seamen and sailors.

Qaitbay 2.   Located about 650 m northeast of Fort Qaitbay on a submerged reef, at 15–18 m deep, the wreck contains scattered amphora fragments, about 100 mostly-intact, stamped Rhodian amphorae (2nd-to 1st-century B.C.), stone and iron anchors, and lead anchor stocks. The area with the highest concentration of artifacts was drawn, mapped, and added to the general map using GPS.

Qaitbay 3.   About 450 m north of Fort Qaitbay, Qaitbay 3 lies in 17–20 m of water. Divers discovered a large number of type LRI amphorae scattered over a wide area, along with a number of stone and iron anchors and lead anchor stocks.

The rocky seabed in these relatively shallow areas does not provide a good environment for hull preservation. Therefore, survey work shifted to deeper water, starting from 30 m depth, where the seabed consists of rocky hills separated by wide, sandy areas more suitable for preserving wood. In this area, the survey team used a Zodiac to tow divers who searched visually for shipwreck remains and located stone and iron grapnel anchors. The site will be explored further.

Portus Magnus

In the 1992 and 1996–1998 seasons, Franck Goddio, founder of the Paris-based l'Institut Européen d'Archéologie Sous–Marine (IEASM), surveyed and excavated in the Eastern Harbor. Goddio's discoveries confirmed that much of the Ptolemaic Royal Quarter of Alexandria, once east of the harbor within sight of the city center, was now in the Eastern Harbor. His team of French divers and Egyptian archaeologists rediscovered and mapped the outlines of the sunken royal quarters and the ancient shoreline of Alexandria (Figure 31.4).

Goddio's team confirmed Strabo's description of Antirhodos Island, on which stood Cleopatra's palace, as the only natural island in the harbor. However, they located it near the shore in front of the harbor mouth, as one enters the harbor, rather than to the left where later geographers placed the island. The island is about 350 m long and lies at 4.5 m depth southwest of the submerged royal quarter. Limestone and marble paving blocks mostly cover the island, which features in its center a large court measuring 6000 m^2. If, as Strabo says, the island was covered with buildings, the paving blocks must have acted as a foundation, since no building foundations have been found.

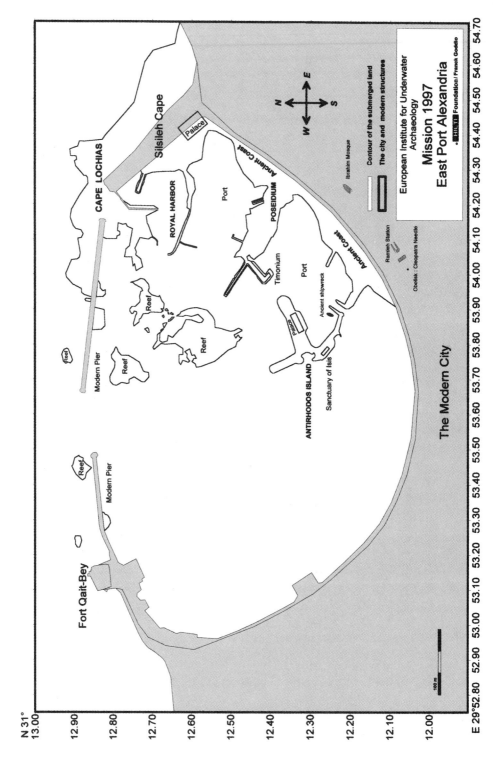

Figure 31.4. Eastern Harbor, submerged royal quarters.

However, wall foundations for marine constructions, and the peninsula bearing the Timonium of Mark Anthony, have been found connected to the ancient coastline.

Goddio made accurate drawings and maps of all discoveries using differential GPS, magnetometers, and side-scan sonar. The team located, identified, and cleaned 1065 artifacts and architectural features including pharaonic sphinxes, Greco–Roman columns, capitals, lintels, and blocks inscribed with hieroglyphs, which were submerged in a series of earthquakes and a tidal wave in A.D. 365, and through slow subsidence.

The IEASM team found concentrations of remains on Antirhodos Island and along the ancient shoreline. These artifacts fit descriptions in ancient sources of dazzling architecture and give a more complete picture of the Portus Magnus. Goddio's team also located four inner harbors, including the royal harbor, inside the Portus Magnus, and maps resulting from this mission will form the basis for future archaeological work in this zone.

Abu-Qir Bay

This ongoing IEASM project started June 1997 with plans to survey a 150-square-kilometer off Abu-Qir Bay, about 30 kilometers to the east of the Pharos site. The objective was to discover the submerged remains of the two long-lost cities of Menouthis and Heraclium, which disappeared more than 1000 years ago. These cities were renowned for their riches and lifestyle, as well as their temples dedicated to the gods Serapis, Isis, Anubis, and Hercules. IEASM conducted a geophysical bathymetric survey using the mapping techniques developed in the Eastern Harbor. Survey methods included side-scan sonar, subbottom profiler, and magnetometry.

In 1999, the discovery of Menouthis and Heraclium was announced. Several fractured columns and other architectural elements had been found submerged in silt fewer than 8 m below the sea surface. Many artifacts were discovered including several granite and marble statues ranging in date from the 25th pharaonic dynasty to the Byzantine period. In addition, a collection of jewelry, gems, and golden coins were found to date to Byzantine and early Islamic periods. In Menouthis, the remains of one of the famous Isis temples were discovered.

Earthquakes may be the prinicipal cause for the destruction and sinking of those two great cities. In Alexandria itself both historical records and archaeological evidence have shown that the city was devastated by several earthquakes from A.D. 8–14 century.

But still, Intensive research is being conducted in order to reveal the truth behind their demise. Moreover, studies attempt to determine the extent of the Canopic branch of the Nile, which passed to the east of Heraclium connecting the Nile to the Mediterranean Sea.

IEASM has also relocated the wrecks of Napolean's fleet sunk in 1798 and has added the discovery of the frigate *La Sérieuse*. In fall 1998 and 1999, IEASM worked to salvage the flagship *L'Orient*. So far, the IEASM team has recovered gold, silver, and bronze coins, ceramic, leather, wooden and metal artifacts from daily life, human and animal remains, weapons, and artillery. A large section of he ship's hull was uncovered and is being studied by measurement and data collection.

Northwest Survey

INA-Egypt's interest in the Egyptian Mediterranean coast has focused so far on the northwestern coastline. Directed by Douglas Haldane, in cooperation with SCA, INA-

Egypt conducted two shipwreck surveys, in March 1996, and April 1998. The surveys included an area 200 km long west of Alexandria between Sidi Abd Al-Rahman and Um el Rakham.

The survey teams investigated 17 reported sites, including six ancient harbors, for possible shipwreck remains. Some points have archaeological evidence on land such as the temple–fortress of Ramses II and Roman tombs at Um El-Rakham, 300 km west of Alexandria. Material evidence for seafaring discovered during the surveys ranges in dates primarily from the 4th century B.C. to A.D. 7th century.

At one site, Ras Gibesa, 130 km west of Alexandria, the team found a fragment of porcelain from a peony-scroll ware dish resembling many found on the 18th century shipwreck at Sadana Island in the Red Sea. The find indicates that the route followed by the Sadana ship also extended west to North Africa in addition to north to Istanbul. This information, together with the land sites, is datable evidence of seafaring. Since no shipwreck survey had been carried out on the Mediterranean coast previous to the INA-Egypt/SCA explorations, the earliest evidence for seafaring now based on survey results dates to the 4th century B.C.

However, the earliest archaeological evidence on land, Late Bronze Age Cypriot and Canaanite ware found at Marsa Matrouh and Um El-Rakham, and the Phoenician colonization of Carthage, all point to pre–Hellenistic seafaring in the area. Continued nautical archaeological exploration will push the boundaries of knowledge about seafaring along the Egyptian northwest Mediterranean coast to a much earlier period than the 4th century B.C.

Alexandria Conservation Laboratory for Submerged Antiquities

Conservation is an integral part of any archaeological research, especially since waterlogged artifacts require specialized conservation treatment. The existence of a laboratory devoted to the conservation of waterlogged artifacts was considered a priority and, in 1983, EDF donated a small metal conservation laboratory, located in the Roman Theatre (Kom El Dikka) in Alexandria, to the Egyptian Antiquities Organization for artifacts from the shipwrecks of Napoleon's fleet. The lab also conserves metal artifacts from land excavations.

When INA set foot in Egypt, it had conservation in mind. Before beginning any archaeological projects, INA-Egypt wished to ensure the existence of a conservation facility to receive all types of waterlogged artifacts from surveys and excavations. In October 1994, the group submitted a plan to SCA for permission to convert five deserted outbuildings in Alexandria's National Maritime Museum into a laboratory complex for conserving antiquities from INA-Egypt projects and for training Egyptian conservators. SCA granted permission in April 1995, and INA-Egypt began to create the Alexandria Conservation Laboratory for Submerged Antiquities.

The complex consists of two wet-artifact storage tanks, a main lab, a mechanical support building, a large artifact conservation area, illustration and photo documentation areas, and a storeroom. Creation and equipping of the lab was funded through grants from the Amoco, Bechtel, Chase Manhattan, and Mobil Foundations, the United States Agency for International Development-funded Egyptian Antiquities Project (administered through the American Research Center in Egypt), and private U.S. and Egyptian donors.

ARCHAEOLOGICAL PROJECTS ON EGYPT'S RED SEA COAST

Red Sea Survey

In June and July 1994, under the direction of Cheryl Ward, INA-Egypt conducted its first archaeological project, a shipwreck survey between Al-Quseir and Hurghada, and the tip of Sinai Peninsula. The survey team visited 26 sites along 160 km of Red Sea coastline, discovering and excavating the Sadana Island shipwreck. The 1994 survey was the first scientific shipwreck exploration ever conducted in the Red Sea and was designed to evaluate known sites for future excavations in the area.

Sadana Island Shipwreck Excavation

The 1994, the INA-Egypt–SCA Red Sea Shipwreck Survey located an Ottoman-period vessel off Sadana Island near Safaga, about 40 km south of Hurghada and excavated the wreck during the 1995, 1996, and 1998 seasons. Sport divers in the Red Sea have known of the shipwreck for more than 10 years, and some reported that the wreck was being looted. INA-Egypt decided to excavate the wreck to protect the information that was being lost and to draw attention to its importance to the Egyptian authorities. The Sadana Island Shipwreck Excavation also provided an opportunity to train archaeology students and SCA inspectors from the SCA's nascent Underwater Department on the aspects and techniques of nautical archaeology. The excavation's primary goals were to remove visible, portable, and attractive objects to discourage looting, to document the ship's structure, and to address questions related to number of objects of various classes, their stowage, and the ship's origin. All excavated objects have been transferred to the INA/ SCA Alexandria Conservation Laboratory for Submerged Antiquities in the National Maritime Museum.

During three excavation seasons, INA-Egypt–SCA logged slightly more than 4000 dives to depths of 22–45 m. Divers found that the Sadana ship is more than 50 m long and at least 15 m wide, and may have carried up to 900 tons of cargo. After the ship sank, it split open along its central longitudinal axis, making study of its interior construction relatively easy. The port side rests in sand 27 m deep at the base of the coral reef. Exposed frames along or near the keel mark where the starboard side broke away and fell downslope, and concerted frames mark the port side's upslope edge. Three 4-m-long, stacked grapnel anchors mark the bow, and thousands of earthenware juglets (*qulla* in Arabic) cover the stern (Figure 31.5). Clusters of large storage and transport jars (*zilla* in Arabic) lay amidships. The *zilla*, which may have carried stores of dry foods and water for the crew and passengers, were closed with wooden lids, some of which have been recovered.

In the 17th and 18th centuries, Egypt and the Red Sea lay at the end of a major branch of the porcelain trade network in the Indian Ocean. Once the cargo reached Suez, it was transferred by land to Cairo, where part continued by river to Alexandria. From Alexandria, Ottoman and European ships carried it throughout the Mediterranean. More than 600 porcelain artifacts of the Chinese Qing Dynasty's Kangxi period were excavated from the Sadana Island wreck (Figure 31.6). Because it was intended for the Middle Eastern Islamic market, the porcelain cargo is unique among Chinese export wares. The Sadana porcelains bear no human or figurative decoration, unlike porcelains found on a number of European ships excavated in the Pacific and Indian Oceans that bore cargoes

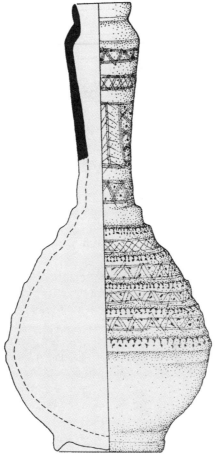

Figure 31.5. Qulla.

destined for western markets. In contrast, Sadana porcelains are decorated almost entirely with floral motifs (Figure 31.7). A coffee cup bearing a crane motif is the sole exception.

The ship's porcelain cargo included small and large bowls, white ware, peony-scrollware dishes, and a variety of handle-less coffee cups of about 20 different designs, including cobalt blue, celadon, blue-on-white, and monochrome brown-glazed examples. Besides the porcelain, more than 1500 earthenware objects were excavated and raised, including *qullas*, tobacco pipes (Figure 31.8), and bowls of different styles. Among the glass objects found onboard were three types of case bottles, a European-style liquor bottle, and a cut glass perfume bottle. More than 70 copper artifacts were excavated as well, including dishes, trays, basins, and cooking pots, one bearing an Arabic inscription dated to AH 1169 (A.D. 1755–56), thereby dating the ship to the second half of the 18th century.

The wreck also contained a rich variety of organic remains, including aromatic resin tentatively identified as frankincense, charcoal, rope, birds' bones, seeds, pepper, coriander, coffee beans, and cardamom. About 60 coconuts were found, including a 33-cm-long, bilobed *cocos de mer*, valued as an aphrodisiac, that grows only in the Seychelles Archipelago. About 20 percent of the excavated area contained tree branches

Figure 31.6. Porcelain plate. (Drawing by Neita Piercy).

intended either as firewood or cargo. The large amount of wood and its high position in the hull suggests that one of the Sadana ship's last ports-of-call had ample supplies of such wood.

Figure 31.7. Day-lily patterned porcelain bowl. (Drawing by Lara Piercy).

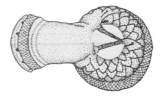

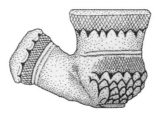

Figure 31.8. Earthenware pipes.
(Drawing by Lara Piercy).

Through the cargo's origins we can trace the ship's last voyage. Porcelain and spices originating in China and the East Indies were trans-shipped at Aden or Jeddah, where the incense was also available. Coffee came from Mocha in Yemen, and the *qullas* from some still-unknown location in the Red Sea region. Since no cannon were found on board, it is likely that the vessel did not leave the Ottoman-controlled Red Sea and so did not require protection against piracy. It is possible the Sadana ship was one of six Indian ships described by Danish traveler Carsten Niebuhr in the mid-18th century. These ships plied the Red Sea pilgrim and trade routes from their base in Suez.

The Sadana ship herself is one of the most important artifacts on the site, since the construction style is undocumented: We only know what she is not. The construction style is non-European, non-Arab and non-Mediterranean, and the large amount of timber used to build her assists in discovering her origins and equating her with Niebuhr's Indian ships. India was the closest source of the ample supplies of wood necessary to build a ship of such massive size.

The hull is characterized by large timbers joined with iron fastenings; no traces of sewing have been found. The iron fastenings have completely deteriorated, but measurements of their locations indicate that the ship was fastened rather lightly. Frames and floor timbers are widely spaced compared to other contemporary hulls, and stringers traversing the length of the hull from the keel to the upper deck are unusually robust. Three levels of knees indicate that the ship may have had three separate decks, but further study of the photodocumentation is necessary to clarify such construction details.

Through the study of the largest type of ship active in the Ottoman Red Sea in the second half of the 18th century, the Sadana Island Excavation has allowed a far better understanding of Red Sea trade, and it gives us a firm link for further exploration of this trade.

CONCLUSION

Seafaring along Egypt's Mediterranean and Red Sea coasts, her ancient Nile river traffic, her historically pivotal, regional role in ancient seafaring offer a unique opportunity for nautical archaeological exploration. In the 1960s, people did not believe Kamel Abu El-Sadaat when he said he had seen sphinxes and statues underwater. More than ten years ago, it was difficult to accept the idea of nautical archaeology and the possibility of retrieving more antiquities for a country with an abundance of archaeological remains. But times have changed, thanks to foreign nautical archaeological missions and a new, rising generation of Egyptian archaeologists convinced of the importance and value of Egypt's maritime heritage. In response, SCA has created an Underwater Archaeology Department to regulate and supervise nautical archaeological expeditions.

On the academic level, no nautical archaeology program exists at an Egyptian university so far, but the Archaeology Department of the University of Alexandria has shown great interest in cooperating with foreign missions offering field training in marine archaeology to its students. The university plans to offer an undergraduate level introductory course in marine archaeology and will require qualified Egyptian scholars to teach the course.

In April 1997, in response to public interest in Egypt's maritime heritage, UNESCO cooperated with the University of Alexandria and SCA to hold an International Workshop on Submarine Archaeology and Coastal Management. The workshop's objectives were to assess the pioneering efforts in surveying and studying archaeological sites in Alexandria's nearshore waters, to benefit from international experience in submarine archaeological detection, and to study the impact of urban development, pollution, erosion, and sediment accretion on submerged archaeological sites.

UNESCO currently is assisting with studies aimed at protecting Fort Qaitbay from wave damage, and in the creation of underwater archaeological museums at the Pharos site off Fort Qaitbay and in the Eastern Harbor. However, pollution in these areas remains a persistent problem. The Egyptian government is taking serious steps to remedy the situation.

Since its beginnings in 1910 with Jondet's study of Alexandria's harbors, nautical archaeology in Egypt has come through a series of stages, each building on the accomplishments of the last. We believe that in the next ten years, Egypt will take a role in the forefront of nautical archaeological exploration.

ACKNOWLEDGMENTS. The authors thank Douglas Haldane for his assistance in editing this chapter, Jean-Yves Empereur and Franck Goddio for their valuable support, and Lionel Fadin for supplying the CEA maps.

REFERENCES

El-Fakharany, F., 1963, *The Ancient Harbor of Alexandria*. Public Lecture in Arabic, University of Alexandria.
Empereur, J.Y., 1995, *Travaux menés en collaboration avec l'école française d'Athènes en 1994*. Les fouilles sous–marines BCH 119:756–760, Athènes.

_____, 1998, Alexandrie redécouverte. Fayard.

_____, 1998, *Le Phare d'Alexandrie, La merveille retrouvée*. Découvertes Gallimard, No. 352.

Frost, H., 1975, The Pharos Site, Alexandria, Egypt. *International Journal of Nautical Archaeology* 4:123–130.

_____, 1996, New Light from the Pharos of Alexandria. The Mariner's Mirror 82:3.

Goddio, F., et al., 1998, *L' Epigraphie Sous-Marine dans Le Port Oriental D'Alexandrie*. Zeitschrift Fur Paryrologie und Epigraphik, Band 120.

Grimal, N., 1996, Travaux de l'IFAO en 1995–1996, *Fouilles sous-marines à l'est de Fort Qaitbay*, 1995. BIFAO 96:563–570, le Caire.

_____, 1997a, Travaux de l'IFAO en 1996–1997, *Le site immergé a l'est de Qaitbay*: pp. 376–377, BIFAO 97, le Caire.

_____, 1997b, Travaux de l'IFAO en 1996–1997, *Les épaves au Nord du rocher du Diamant*. BIFAO 97:378–379, le Caire.

Haldane, C., 1993, The Promise of Egypt's Maritime Legacy. *INA Quarterly* 20(2):3–7.

_____, 1994, INA-Egypt's Red Sea Survey. *INA Quarterly* 21(3):4–9.

_____, 1995, Sadana Island Shipwreck Excavation 1995. *INA Quarterly* 22(3):3–9.

_____, 1996a, Sadana Island Shipwreck Excavation 1996. *INA Quarterly* 23(3):3–8.

_____, 1996b, Sadana Island Shipwreck, Egypt: Preliminary Report. *International Journal of Nautical Archaeology* 25(2):83–94.

Haldane, D., 1996a, Alexandria Conservation Laboratory for Submerged Antiquities. *INA Quarterly* 23(2):3–6.

_____, 1996b, *Mediterranean Shipwreck Survey*. Final Report.

Jondet, G., 1912, *Les ports antiques de Pharos*. Société Archéologique d'Alexandrie, Bulletin 14.

Morcos, S., 1993, *Submarine Archaeology and its Future Potentials: Alexandria Casebook*. Société Archéologique d'Alexandrie, Bulletin 45.

Toussoun, O., 1934, Les ruines sous-marines de la Baie d'Aboukir. *Société Archéologique d'Alexandrie Bulletin* 29:342–345.

Chapter 32

Maritime Archaeology in Australia, the Indian Ocean, and Asia

JEREMY N. GREEN

AUSTRALIA

Legislation

In 1963, following the discovery of two 17th-century Dutch East India Company (VOC) shipwrecks, Western Australia introduced maritime archaeological legislation. The government amended the *Museum Act* to include shipwrecks of archaeological significance, and later amended it to the *Maritime Archaeology Act 1973* with the capacity to protect all shipwrecks lost prior to 1900. The act included elements entitling finders to rewards and punitive measures against anyone who disturbed sites. Although it automatically protected sites, it required them to be proclaimed. The enactment of this legislation was the result of hard work by a group of public-spirited individuals who saw the need to protect sites they had found for the greater common good: At the time, there were reports of looting and destruction of sites. Following passage of the legislation, the Western Australian Museum was given the responsibility for administering the act.

Jeremy Green, Head, Maritime Archaeology and National Centre of Excellence, Department of Maritime Archaeology, Western Australia Maritime Museum, Fremantle, Western Australia WA6160.

International Handbook of Underwater Archaeology, edited by Carol V. Ruppé and Janet F. Barstad. Kluwer Academic/Plenum Publishers, New York, 2002.

Figure 32.1. Modern China Junk.

In the early 1970s, the museum embarked on an extensive maritime archaeological program, starting with a survey of the English East India Company ship *Trial* (1622), Australia's oldest known shipwreck. Following this survey, excavation began on the VOC ship *Vergulde Draeck* (1656), then moved to the more significant and complex *Batavia* (1629) site, which represents the largest maritime archaeological project the museum has ever undertaken.

At the end of the main part of the *Batavia* fieldwork, the Department of Maritime Archaeology established a program dealing with shipwrecks of the post-European settlement period and began work on two other VOC shipwrecks, *Zuytdorp* (1712) and *Zeewijk* (1727). The post-European settlement program included major excavations of *James Matthews* (1841), an ex-slave ship, *Rapid* (1811), an American China trader, and *Livley* (1818).

In 1977, the Western Australian legislation was challenged in the High Court of Australia. In the case *Robinson v. the Western Australian Museum* (1977), a decision was handed down that state government did not have the jurisdiction to legislate in this area, since it was the prerogative of the Commonwealth. The ruling made the *Maritime Archaeology Act 1973* invalid in any waters other than state waters.

Immediately following the ruling, the Commonwealth's *Historic Shipwrecks Act 1976* was proclaimed in Western Australia. This decision set the scene for a bipartite form of legislation in Australia. The *Historic Shipwrecks Act 1976* operates in areas legally defined as Commonwealth waters, and the state act operates in state waters. In Western Australia, the *Maritime Archaeology Act 1973* still is in operation.

Cultural Heritage Management in Australia

An interesting aspect of the implementation of state and federal underwater cultural heritage management is the differing perceptions held by state and federal agencies in exercising their roles. The federal *Historic Shipwrecks Act 1976* defines the cultural resource as a historic shipwreck or a historic relic and, for the purposes of the act, the remains of a ship or relic from a ship that are in the sea or have been removed from the sea. No definition of "historic" is made. Until recently, protection went into effect only after the minister declared the shipwreck protected; now, an amendment allows for "blanket protection," whereby all wrecks 75 years and older are automatically protected.

On the other hand, the Western Australian state *Maritime Archaeology Act 1973* deals with maritime archaeological sites including remains of ships, relics, or structures, either in the water, on land, or both. Sites are automatically protected—that is, they are protected from the moment of discovery. In most other states, state legislation is "mirror" legislation, meaning, it exactly duplicates federal legislation.

One of the most contentious issues of the implementation of the *Museum Act 1963* was that the Western Australian government chose not to reward the finders of sites discovered before passage of the legislation. Thus, the finders of the *Batavia*, *Vergulde Draeck*, *Zeewijk*, and *Zuytdorp*, and individuals who had given the material they recovered to the Western Australian Government, were not rewarded. This resulted in a long-standing perception by the general public and the diving community that the government had disadvantaged or treated these individuals badly.

These issues were reexamined recently, when in 1992 a Western Australian government select committee was established to investigate the question of rewards. In the foreword to the report (Select Committee on Ancient Shipwrecks, 1994iii), Chairman Hon. P.G. Pendal, MLA, stated: "two fundamental issues are addressed in this Report: firstly, whether a person should be rewarded for doing the 'right thing' by society; and secondly, if they *should* be so rewarded, how much is a fair thing?"

The Select Committee on Ancient Shipwrecks eventually recommended that four finders of the *Batavia* should each be paid an *ex-gratia* payment of $25,000, and it recommended rewards to finders of other sites and to "secondary" finders (individuals who, although not finding the site, were instrumental in its discovery). Thus, the Parliamentary Select Committee clearly believes in financial rewards for finding or discovering wreck sites of historic significance and is thus at odds with federal perceptions.

The *Historic Shipwrecks Act 1976* requires that the act be proclaimed in each state before it can become law. It further requires that each state nominate a delegated authority to administer the act. Thus, when the act was proclaimed in a particular state (not all states chose to proclaim the act at the same time), the delegation was usually to the state authority considered responsible for maritime archaeological sites. As a result, two different types of agencies have delegated authority: museums in Western Australia, Northern Territory and Queensland, and heritage management agencies in other states. To some extent, this has led to differing perceptions of how the management of underwater cultural heritage should be managed. However, such differing approaches by practicing professionals have tended to be constructive, and that has meant that the agencies have a more flexible attitude toward the subject.

Promoting Australia's Maritime Archaeology

Two issues have helped promote a sense of cohesiveness in Australia's maritime archaeology. In 1981, Curtin University, together with the University of Western Australia, Murdoch University, and the Western Australian Maritime Museum, initiated a graduate diploma course in maritime archaeology. The course was unique, because it was not run concurrently each year (a total of five courses have been given in the last 20 years). It involved a number of different universities, it covered both maritime archaeology, conservation, materials science, oceanography, and marine surveying, and it taught the subject at a highly practical level. At present, course graduates are employed in every state in Australia in institutions involved in maritime cultural heritage management. In addition, James Cook and Flinders Universities have introduced maritime archaeology as a core subject within the archaeology syllabus. Many universities teach the subject as a part of a general archaeology syllabus. It has been observed that in spite of the potential for personality and institutional conflict, maritime archaeologists in Australia have become an elite group with a strong sense of cohesiveness.

Another unifying feature in maritime archaeology is the Australian Institute for Maritime Archaeology (AIMA), which grew out of a combination of state agencies and state maritime archaeological associations that developed in the mid-1970s. AIMA was created as a forum for the disparate interests of state and federal issues related to maritime archaeological sites. Publication is an important aspect of the organization, which produces a quarterly newsletter, an annual *Bulletin* that has been published for 21 years, and occasional special publications. AIMA helped formulate guidelines for the management and practice of maritime archaeology. Designed by practitioners in each state, the guidelines express a group or national consensus on maritime archaeology management and are important for the development of archaeological standards in maritime archaeology. In addition, according to the *Historic Shipwrecks Act 1976*, it is required that a register of historic shipwrecks be maintained. AIMA has contracted to develop a national database of all known historic shipwrecks, which can be incorporated into a historic shipwreck register and which is available for researchers, historians, and archaeologists via the Internet.

Today, each state has its own maritime archaeological program, and individual agencies are developing interesting and varied programs. One of the most significant programs is in Queensland, where the wreck of the *Pandora* has been under investigation for nearly two decades. This site is well preserved and of considerable historical and archaeological significance; however, it is also remote, located in an area subject to tropical cyclones, logistically difficult to operate, and lies at an intermediate depth of 31 m, creating decompression problems.

ASIA AND THE INDIAN OCEAN

Treasure Hunting

The Indian Ocean, Southeast Asia, and East Asia region includes a wide cultural and economic diversity. From the maritime archaeology perspective, the region has suffered from the treasure-hunting industry, which started with the notorious *Geldermalsen* case. A VOC shipwreck was salvaged in Indonesian waters (Exclusive Economic Zone), and the collection, mainly of ceramics, was exported through Singapore to Amsterdam where it was auctioned for enormous profit. When material from the *Geldermalsen* sold at two or three times the normal price expected, this added an inducement for the exploitation of sites. It showed that "treasure" in Asian waters was not just gold and silver but could be ceramic material as well.

Today, considerable variation exists in the countries' treatment of their cultural heritage. Some countries exclude treasure hunting and maintain an underwater archaeological program. Others allow treasure hunting, and the government keeps a share of the profit. Still others have both a department of maritime archaeology and accept treasure hunters, with the result that archaeologists are mainly observers, or they police large-scale operations.

It is difficult to assess the situation in this region. While countries have the right to dispose of their heritage as they see fit, their decisions often are driven by misconceptions of what they will receive from treasure hunters. From experience in other parts of the world, many know that, although investors have been promised huge profits, these promises are rarely kept. In Asian regions as well, profit-sharing comes after all costs have been defrayed and, given that working persons' yearly salaries can be as low as the weekly wage of equivalent Westerners, the opportunity for bribery and corruption is obvious.

Treasure hunters usually target European vessels, since information on their location is easily accessible through European archives. For many countries, such vessels represent examples of past colonialism, and while they may be considered of general interest, they are not part of the country's cultural heritage and are often considered insignificant. However, that attitude is changing, as countries begin to assess their underwater cultural heritage resources in the light of potential cultural tourism. Such sites may well be of interest to a wide range of overseas visitors.

Regional Maritime Archaeology

This section highlights some of the more interesting aspects of maritime archaeology in the Asia/Indian Ocean region, but is by no means a comprehensive review of the region.

The Philippines and the Butuan Boats.   The Philippines has an old maritime tradition. It is probably through the Philippines and the Molluccas that the Austronesian migration into the Pacific began. Early contacts with China and other parts of Southeast Asia, prior to the arrival of the maritime Europeans, are well-documented. In the 16th and 17th centuries, the Philippines was the base of Spanish operations in Asia: Large Manilla galleons carried Asian trade to the West over the Pacific to Central America and on to Spain. The Philippines National Museum has been involved in maritime archaeology, although the government does license treasure hunters to search for and survey sites. A number of major excavations of European vessels, including *Griffin* (1761) and *San Diego* (1600), have been undertaken by the National Museum in partnership with the European group World Wide First, a noncommercial organization that is not involved in the sale of material from the excavation.

The Butuan Boats represent an important part of the understanding of Southeast Asian shipbuilding technology. These vessels have a lashed-lugs construction which has parallels in other parts of Southeast Asia, particularly Malaysia and Sumatra. The technique is still found in the Moluccan and Solar Archipelago and the Solomon Islands and has parallels in Europe.

The National Museum has discovered and investigated nine boat sites around Bancasi, Libertad, and in the Butuan area of Mindanao. Three have been excavated: Butuan 1, on display in Libertad City, Mindanao; Butuan 2, in the National Museum, Manila; and Butuan 5, in the Butuan Region X Museum, Mindanao.

The remains of Butuan 1 comprises a keel, a wing stem, two strakes on one side, one strake on the other, and some fragments. The dowels are counter-pegged at every alternate dowel, except at the wing stem where they pegged at every dowel. The strakes are broad at the center and the overall length of the remains is about 13 m. The keel plank is interesting because, except at the narrow end, it has lugs in sets transversely in threes, the outer two having been drilled to take the lashings and the middle one apparently to act as a support. All other strakes have single lugs. There are three lashing holes in nearly all of the lugs, two equidistant from the ends of the lug, and the third spaced at an equal distance to the separation of the symmetrically placed holes.

Butuan 2 is the best preserved of the three vessels. The remains, consisting of a keel and two strakes on one side and five strakes on the other, suggest there were at least 14 sets of lugs cut into each strake and into the keel, and set in rows across the vessel. The lugs were rectangular except for the keel lugs, which were double. Each lug had two pairs of lashing holes and, in many cases, the original fiber could still be seen in the holes. There were some small remains of a frame or frames, but these were badly degraded. The dowels were set about 129 mm apart without locking pins. A complex scarf joint system at one end of the ship ended in a complex stem or stern post. It is still uncertain which was the bow and which was the stern of these vessels. At the other end, the strakes taper to a fine point. The lugs on the strakes were aligned across the hull, although there was much variation in the size of the lugs and their separation. The doweling pattern for all the strakes showed that the dowels were arranged in a pattern of six, possibly meaning that a template was used to mark the holes.

The remaining timbers of Butuan 5 are degraded, with only a few planks in good condition. The remaining frames are generally in better condition than the planking. The vessel was probably about 13 m in length, though the keel, the longest remaining portion, is about only 11.5 m. There are remains of eight planks on one side of the vessel and seven on the other, which vary in thickness from 30–45 mm. Maximum thickness at the lugs is sometimes 80 mm but is usually about 60–75 mm. The planking is edge-joined with dowels of approximately 12 mm diameter spaced about 200 mm apart. The dowels extend more than halfway through the width of the plank, and their relative positions on opposite sides of the plank strakes are staggered slightly. The dowels on each side of the lugs are counter-pegged with hardwood locking pins, square in section, and slightly tapered. In the midships part of the boat, where there is a large space between lugs, every third dowel is pegged.

On plank number 8, the lugs are different from the others, being carved in a triangular cross-sectional shape. Unlike the other lugs, these triangular section lugs have no lashing holes. This was the last, or highest, strake remaining on the site, but the presence of dowels on the upper edge indicates this was not the highest strake. Most lugs show slight compression of the timber at the frame-lashing positions. In some lugs, a slightly raised ridge running across the lug about midway between the lashing holes was noted.

Remains of another unusual plank, thought to be number 7, were also noted. This strake has a continuous raised portion, similar to the keel but off-center, and lugs were pierced with lashing holes. The strake also has a series of notches cut between the lugs, perhaps to hold beams or uprights. The continuous raised portion certainly could have functioned as a whole but may have been a beam shelf.

The keel is a narrow plank with a raised lug running its full length. This carinate or ridged keel is different from keel planks found on Butuan boats 1 and 2. Presumably, this continuous raised lug not only serves as a frame- lashing structure but also—and primarily—increases the stiffness of the keel and decreases any tendency for the vessel to hog.

Shipwreck Sites in China. A series of papers were published in Chinese by the Museum of Overseas Communication, describing excavation and subsequent analysis of the Quanzhou Ship, but surprisingly little has been published in non-Chinese literature.

The hull has been completely rebuilt, with some minor modern additions to the damaged bow section and bulkheads. The remains, measuring 24 m long by 9 m wide, consist of the keel, part of the transom, 12 bulkheads, and the ship's sides, up to and sightly beyond the turn of the bilge (14 strakes on the port and 16 strakes on the starboard side). It is thought that the ship was originally 34 m long and 11 m wide, with a displacement of around 380 tons.

The keel is constructed of pine in three parts. The fore and aft parts slope upward (the fore part more than the aft) and are scarfed longitudinally to the central part. In the vertical faces of both scarf joints, seven bronze coins and a bronze mirror were found. This is a *baosongkong* or longevity symbol: The coins were placed to represent the constellation of Ursa Minor, and the mirror is thought to represent the moon. The *baosongkong* have Daoist significance, bringing either good luck and fair winds, or representing the Seven Star Ocean where there are many dangerous rocks. The mirror is present to reflect light and ensure a safe journey. Apparently this tradition is continued today in modern shipbuilding, the stars represented by nails and the moon by a silver coin. A square-sectioned rabbet is cut on either side of the keel to accept the garboard strake.

The hull is double-planked up to the beginning of the turn of the bilge, where it becomes triple-planked. Made of cedar, the planking is complex, a mixture of carvel and clinker design. In order to describe this structure adequately, some liberties have been taken with conventional Western shipbuilding terms:

Inner or *inside* refers to the surface or side facing the interior of the hull; conversely, *outer* or *outside* refers to the side facing the water. *Upper* refers to the part (edge or strake) away from the keel, and *lower* refers to the part toward the keel.

A *carvel joint* (conventional definition), the edge-joint between two adjacent strakes, is a flat butt-joint cut at right angles to the surface of the strakes, producing a smooth (carvel) surface on the inside and outside of the hull. A *rabbeted carvel joint* (unconventional definition), the edge-joint between two adjacent strakes, is rabbeted along the whole of the strake joint by a type of lap-joint.

In a *clinker joint* (conventional definition), the strakes overlap one another, so that the upper strake overlaps the lower strake on the outer surface; the jointing surface is between the outer and inner faces of the strakes. This type of joint produces a discontinuity in both the inside and outside surfaces of the ship's hull. In a *rabbeted clinker joint* (unconventional definition), a rabbet is cut in the inside of the lower edge of the strake; the upper, uncut edge of the lower strake in this rabbet gives an external appearance of a clinker joint, but the thickness of the step between the strakes at the surface is reduced by the depth of the rabbet. A similar type of joint was found on the Shinan ship, but the rabbet was cut out of the inside upper strake, and the upper surface of the lower strake was cut square and fitted into the rabbet.

The inner planking, made of cedar, is 80 mm thick. The lower edge of the garboard strake is rabbeted so that the strake lies against the horizontal surface of the keel rabbet and a short part of the vertical face of the keel. Starting from the garboard strake of the inner planking, the first three strakes have carvel joints, the rabbets being cut in the outer edge of the lower strake and the inner edge of the upper strake. The third and fourth strakes are joined with a rabbeted clinker joint. This system of two rabbeted carvel and one rabbeted clinker joints continues for 16 strake joints. Each rabbeted clinker joint on the hull's inner surface has a strip or lath of wood set over the top of the joint, to seal it. The outer planking is 50 mm thick and is carvel-joined, the planking being irregularly nailed to the inner planking with light nails. The garboard strake of the outer planking butts up against the keel, with an additional plank attached to the vertical surface of the keel, forming a type of sheathing. The rabbeted clinker joint on the inner planking is cut so that the thickness of the projection of the strake on the outside is 50 mm. This allows the strake edge of the outer planking to form a carvel joint. The next strake of the outer planking is then attached with a clinker joint. It could be said that the outer planking becomes the inner planking, and that the whole arrangement is a type of mixed clinker–carvel construction.

At the fourth clinker joint on the outer planking, at the turn of the bilge, a third layer of planking is applied to the hull, 25 mm thick and carvel-joined, continuing for five strakes to the edge of the hull remains. The author's impression is that this planking was the same thickness as the second layer of planking, although it was not possible to measure this.

Twelve bulkheads create 13 compartments roughly equal in size, the two aftermost compartments slightly smaller than the rest. The bulkheads are formed by a series of cedar planks, edge- joined with a similar type of rabbeted carvel joint as the inner hull planking. A waterway cut into the lowest plank of every bulkhead except the aftermost and forwardmost bulkheads. All bulkhead joints were sealed with luting. Some longer planks in the bulkhead's upper sections are made in two parts, with a scarf joint.

On the aft sides of the bulkheads forward of the mast step, and on the forward sides of the bulkheads aft of the mast step, are heavy wooden frames. These are half frames, not floors, and they extend up to about the 14th strake. It is not known if there were subsequent futtocks, nor is there any clear evidence for scarfs on the frames. A waterway is cut into the frames to match the bulkhead waterways. They are in a much poorer state of preservation than the rest of the hull so that it has not been possible to identify the species of wood used to make them.

The transom is flat, inclined outward, and constructed in two layers, the inner consisting of horizontal planks and the outer a series of thick camphorwood blocks into which is cut a round, vertical groove which takes the missing axial rudder. This method of mounting the rudder allows it to be raised or lowered without affecting its operation, a common Chinese tradition. The outer layer of triple planking extends outward beyond the transom, indicating that there was a type of counter projecting over the stern.

The foremast and mainmast steps were set on the keel against the forward side of a bulkhead, the foremast against the first bulkhead, the mainmast against the sixth bulkhead. Both steps had two square sockets to take the partners of a tabernacle mast housing. The mainmast step was braced against the forward bulkhead by two beams running parallel to and on either side of the keel.

A square section was cut out of the upper remaining (fifth) bulkhead plank forward of the mainmast step (bulkhead five). It has been suggested that this allowed the mast to be lowered. If so, where did the mast pivot? It could have been either at the step or on the deck. If it pivoted at the step, the mast, which would lower forward, could not be lowered completely, because it would rest on the bulkhead's cut-out section. If it pivoted on the deck, it could be lowered completely to the aft. From a simple inspection of the plan, it is clear that the former situation was the case, because the mast's height, from the step to the deck, is more than twice the width between the bulkheads.

Iron appears to have been the main fastening material; wooden treenails were not been reported. The edge joints of the rabbeted inner planking were nailed diagonally from the outside through the joint. The outer layers of planking were nailed onto the inner planking. The rabbeted joins on the bulkheads were also nailed diagonally; it was also reported that they were edge-joined with round iron dowels, but there appears to be evidence only for diagonal nailing. The strakes were nailed to the edges of the bulkheads with iron nails, and the bulkheads were attached to the hull by an unusual type of iron fastening, a flat bar bent at right angles at one end to form an L-shape, mounted through the inner planking and set against the opposite side of the bulkhead to the frames. The strap had four or five holes on its long side, through which it was attached with nails to the bulkhead. The short angle, flush with the outside of the inner planking, had a single hole through which it was fastened with a nail to the hull. These straps or *ju*-nails appear to be placed so that they were centrally located on each bulkhead plank.

In addition to the Quanzhou ship, another site was excavated at Fa Sui, near the city of Quanzhou. The Fa Sui site is constructed with unusual wooden stiffeners, which seem to duplicate the function of the iron *ju*-nails used in the Quanzhou ship. They also appear in the Shinan Ship, which will be described in Section 2.2.3. The Fa Sui site was partially excavated, the remaining unexcavated section lying under a modern house.

Another buried ship was found at the wharf site at Ningbo. The vessel, whose stern part is missing, was originally about 13 m long and is thought to date from the Song Dynasty. It consists of seven bulkheads, a main and foremast step, eight strakes on the port side, and four strakes on the starboard. The keel is comprised of three parts scarfed together with an attached stempost, and with *baosongkong* or longevity holes with coins similar to the Quanzhou ship.

Shipwreck Sites in Korea.   The excavation and finds of the Shinan Ship have been discussed by a number of authors, the discussion centering mainly on the immense ceramic collection that numbers some 16,000 items to date. Excavation took place between 1976 and 1982; by that time, the main part of the cargo had been recovered, and work had begun on excavation of the hull. Since then, the whole ship has been dismantled and raised and is now undergoing conservation treatment at the Mokpo Conservation and Restoration Centre of the Cultural Property Research Institute. The Shinan Ship site was dated to A.D. 1323 by a wooden cargo tag. Along with the ship were 26.8 tons or more than seven million brass-bronze coins, which bore the earliest date of A.D. 14 and the latest of A.D.1310.

The ship's remains include the keel, about 14 strakes of the starboard side and six strakes of the port side, part of the transom bow, and a small section of the stern transom.

The vessel has seven internal bulkheads, creating eight compartments. There is a fore and mainmast step, and a structure that is possibly part of the decking of the ship. The bulkheads forward of the mast step are supported on the aft side with frames and on the forward side with stiffeners. The stiffeners are pointed wooden pegs that penetrate each strake from the outside of the hull planking, thus locating the opposite side of the bulkhead to the frames. They are attached to the face of the bulkhead (these stiffeners serve the same function as the *ju*-nail described in the Quanzhou and the Fa Sui sites). Aft of the mainmast step, the reverse situation occurs. The strakes are butt-jointed, in most cases a lap joint butt, on the garboard strake and at least one other place, a mortice and tenon joint. On the internal face of the butt-joints are butt plates lying over the top of the joints, clamping them together. In some cases, the butt plates are set under a frame, indicating that the frames were placed after the completion of the planking. The strakes are rabbeted clinker construction, the rabbet cut out of the lower inside edge of the uppermost plank. The bulkhead floor and planks have a rebate set in the joint to locate the edge of the bulkhead. In the fore part of the ship, this arrangement gradually changes to a rabbeted carvel or shiplap construction, which allows a flush rabbeted joint onto the transom bow.

A research model of the ship was built by the Mokpo Conservation and Restoration Centre at a scale of 1:5, based on measurements made of the hull timbers. Although the model raises a number of complex and interesting problems, it has some limitations: (1) Because of the poor visibility on the wreck site, it was not always possible to establish the exact orientation of the pieces, so that in some cases their relationship was uncertain; and (2) the plans of the timbers were made from individual measurements of the timbers but were not direct 1:1 tracings. In spite of these drawbacks, the model is one step toward a complete understanding of the structure.

A major, unresolved problem is that the keel has a distinct hog: The center is 220 mm higher than the fore and aft ends over the length of the keel. It is not certain if this is a feature incorporated in the construction of the ship or a result of forces on the hull structure after the sinking. Further work on the research model may resolve this problem. The scarf joints in the keel have a similar arrangement to the Quanzhou ship but with coins and a mirror placed on the sloping horizontal face of the joint rather than the vertical faces.

The mast step shows the arrangement of the step and the three-part mast. It is possible that the mast's orientation is wrong. The foremast is arranged to lie against the bulkhead, and it appears that the bulkhead has been specially angled so that is aligned with the rake of the mast. A pin was used to fix the base of the masts.

The way the transom bow is attached to the keel is not absolutely certain, but it is double planked. A single cant frame is unusual, because it has a series of semicircular holes cut from the upper through to the side face of the frame, holes whose purpose is unclear. The arrangement of the upper part of the ship's side is also not clear. The structure projecting into the body of the ship may be a sort of deck, but it has also been suggested that it may have been a coaming, so that it is not certain if the associated were separated from the main part of the hull. The bulwark associated with the "coaming" has been cut with 150 mm circular holes of unknown purpose. They may have been scuppers or possibly holes for oars. Until the position of the bulwark on the hull section is known more precisely, the function of the holes will remain unclear.

The Wando ship was discovered in southwestern Korea in 1984. The cargo of 30,000 celadon pieces originated from a kiln in Haenam Province are thought to date from around the second half of the 11th century. The vessel's distinctive construction and timber species indicate that it was built in Korea. Its original length would have been about 9 m. There is no keel, rather there are five heavy longitudinal timbers (180–200 mm thick and 300–350 mm wide) pinned together with a complex series of mortice and tenon joints. The center three planks have six mortice and tenons that run through the three planks; the two outer planks also have six mortice and tenon joints, but these penetrate through the outer plank, only partially into the outer edge of the second strake. The side planking is attached to the bottom with chine planks, L-shaped planks rebated into the upper edge of the outer bottom plank and fastened with mortice and tenons. Five strakes of the ship's sides are arranged in rabbeted clinker fashion. The upper edge of each strake has a rebate cut in the outer edge, and the strakes are attached with mortice and tenons, the tenon being driven through the upper strake and partially into the lower. There is evidence that the third strake was penetrated with a thwart beam. All these features are associated with Korean ship construction.

The Jindo Logboat, a dugout vessel originally about 19 m long and 2.3 m broad, was excavated by the Mokpo Conservation Institute of Maritime Archaeological Finds in 1992. Built in three parts and described as a three-piece logboat, it had six bulkheads with a mast step in front of the third bulkhead. The vessel is thought to be Chinese because the timber is camphorwood, which is indigenous to South China, and it has the *baosongkong* with coins in the holes. The coins date from A.D. 1111–1117; a carbon date for the timber and putty is of A.D. 1260–1380. The bow and stern sections were attached to the main body of the hull in rabbeted joints with a brace in the form of a longitudinal beam set over the joints.

Japan.   In 1982, a search was conducted for the remains of Kublai Khan's fleet, destroyed in 1282 by a typhoon in and around the Bay of Imari, Kuyushu. Under the leadership of Professor Mozai, Merchant Marine Department, Tokai University, Tokyo, a wide variety of ceramic material was recovered from the seabed, together with examples of projectiles thought to be associated with *P'ao*, a type of fireball or projectile fired form, either a trebuchet or early cannon. An illustration by an unknown artist exists of an exploding device, in the scroll *Moko shurai ekotoba* (Illustrative narrative of the Mongol Invasion of Japan), a work written in about 1292 by the Japanese warrior Takezaki, who took part in the campaign of 1282. The scroll describes his battle experiences and shows him being dismounted by an exploding device, perhaps the afore-mentioned projectile. The scroll is one of the oldest contemporary illustrations of Japanese and Chinese ships.

Shipwrecks off the Gulf of Thailand.   In 1975, a wreck site was discovered near the island of Ko Khram in the southeastern section of the Gulf of Thailand. The site's excavation was the beginning of Thailand's underwater archaeology program. Since then, a number of sites have been examined in the Gulf of Thailand. Some were completely excavated, and some have only surveyed.

The Ko Khram site was excavated by a joint Thai–Danish team from 1975 to 1977, during which more than 5000 pieces of Thai ceramics were recovered. Sukhothai and Sawankhalok ceramics account for 60–75 percent of the total cargo; the remainder are probably Vietnamese, and there are some of unknown origin. Sisatchanalai celadons include plates and bowls with tubular support marks on the base, jarlets, eared bottles, potiche, and small bowls. Earthenware rice pots and unglazed stoneware storage jars and basins are thought to have been produced at kilns northwest of Lopburi. The underpainted fish and floral designed plates and bowls were produced in the Sukhothai kilns. Green glazed bowls with an unglazed ring in the inside center are thought to be Cham. A blue and white jarlet and a saucer are perhaps Vietnamese. In a number of places, the ceramic material was still stacked in rows. In 1987, when the site was visited to obtain timber and ceramic samples, it was still remarkably intact, with no evidence of looting. The site is one of the largest and best preserved in the region and certainly warrants further investigation at some future date.

The Ko Kradat Wreck in Trat Province can be dated definitively by a blue and white porcelain-base sherd bearing the inscription *Da Ming Jiajing Nian Zhi*, which translates to "Made in the Jiajing reign of the Great Ming Dynasty," between 1522 and 1566. Other porcelain sherds suggest a date from the Wanli period, 1573–1619. These Chinese ceramics clearly date the Sawankhalok products encapsulated with the porcelain at the time of the wreck; they indicate that the Sawankhalok kilns must have been producing in the mid-16th century, with strong evidence for the latter half of the century. Ceramics that can be definitely attributed to Sawankhalok include small cover boxes with a thin glaze fusing the base to the lid, indicating that the article had never been used and had probably come straight from the kiln.

The Pattaya site consists of a 9 m length of hull with a maximum width of 4.5 m, and six bulkheads together with eight strakes on either side of the keel. The hull profile has a marked V-shape next to the keel, which flattened out and ended in an upward curve at the turn of the bilge. Here the continuing sides of the ship obviously had broken away and disintegrated. The keel was a large, apparently single timber 300 mm wide with 45° bevels on the upper edges, giving an upper keel surface of 200 mm. The planking consisted of three layers, the inner 70 mm thick and the second and third 40 mm thick. The garboard strake of the inner layer was attached to the bevel on the upper part of the keel by a series of dowels 20 mm in diameter and spaced 160 mm apart. The strake–scarph joints all occurred under bulkheads and show no logical system. Traces of six bulkheads found on the site consist of two components; the bulkheads themselves, and a lightly constructed, bevelled frame, locating and securing the bulkhead to the hull. In all cases, the bulkhead frames were on the side of the bulkhead nearest the midships. The bulkhead consisted of a number of parallel planks 70 mm thick, dowelled together with round pegs in the same manner as the strakes of the hull planking. The ends of the planks were shaped so that they fitted flush with the hull planking and appeared to be lightly nailed to the planking at the narrow ends. There was no evidence of dowels being used to join the bulkheads to the hull. The lowest bulkhead plan is regular in section, lying symmetrically over the keel. The extreme ends of the planks were trimmed in the same way as the scarph-joint of the planks. Waterways consisted of two circular holes, 110 mm in diameter, lying on either side of the keel. The frames lodge against the side of the bulkhead nearest the midships. The central frame was a floor in all cases except for bulkhead 3, where it was a half-frame. In this case the two half frames were clamped with chocks. In all other frames, the first futtocks were scarphed to the floors. A mast step was located on the southern side of bulkhead 6. Two large, rectangular holes, 110 mm by 260 mm, are cut 90 mm deep and equidistant from the mid-line, which was the recess for the tabernacle of the mast. On the west side is a round hole 110 mm in diameter, inclined at about 50° towards the center, possibly a pump hole. Two more small notches, 90 mm by 80 mm, are located on the southern edge of the top surface, possibly for longitudinal braces. The mast step has two waterway holes similar to the others in the other bulkheads.

The Ko Si Chang 1 Wreck, Chonburi Province, can be dated by a Chinese blue and white porcelain bowl bearing the inscription *Da Ming Wanli Nian Zhi*, meaning "Made in the Great Ming Year Wanli," who reigned 1573–1620. Nonceramic items from this site include lacquer-ware with a dragon motif, pyramide-shaped lead ingots (as found on the Ko Si Chang 3, Pattaya and *Risdam* sites), a copper bowl, a lidded copper lime container complete with lime remains and a stirrer, wooden bungs, sappanwood, (also recovered from the *Risdam* site), a musket stock, and a grindstone.

The Ko Si Chang 2 site ceramics are complex and include material thought to originate from Thailand and Southern China. Also present is a small group of uncertain origin. Researchers recovered a portion of an Oriental style oven and metal objects that included a square lead ingot and a Chinese cash coin.

The survey of the Ko Si Chang 2 site hull showed some unusual features not previously encountered on vessels in the Gulf of Thailand. The ship's planking is joined with iron nails driven diagonally from about the middle of the inside of the hull planking downwards through the abutting surfaces into the next strake. This method of fastening is unknown in the region; Southeast Asian fastenings of adjacent strakes are usually edge-joined dowels, and Chinese and Korean are diagonal iron nails from the outside. On the Ko Si Chang 2 site, there is no doubt that over the strakes remaining, the nails are driven from the inside, unusual because hull cross-sections are invariably concave, and the angle the nail is driven will be more difficult from the inside than the outside. There may be an advantage to fastening in this manner, but it is not immediately obvious.

It is unfortunate that the site has suffered badly from the effects of trawler activity and from looters. During a brief inspection of the site in 1985, it was reported that timbers were projecting from the seabed at an angle of about 20°, almost certainly the result of a trawler net snagging and ripping up the end timbers. So it is impossible to determine what happened on the strakes further up the hull. One possibility is that the vessel was flat-bottomed and that this method of fastening was used in the region but changed at the chine. The two remaining outer strakes of the inner planking are narrower than other planks, and the nails are driven into the plank at the outer edge.

The Ko Si Chang 3 Wreck, Chonburi Province, excavated by a joint Thai–Australian–SPAFA team in 1986, has not suffered at the hands of looters. Even though trawling activities had disturbed the surface to some extent, an accurate estimation of the quantity and placement of cargo could be made. The hull structure consisted of the keel, the planking (at most, six strakes on the starboard side and five strakes on the port), the remains of nine bulkheads, and the mast step. It is evident that the site, especially the hull structure, was damaged by bottom-trawlers, and that the stern part of the structure has collapsed. The keel appears to have separated at the scarf joint, causing the stern part of the keel to drop, so that the garboard strakes separated from the keel. At the stern on the port side, the remains of six planks were discovered lying below the main planking, running at an angle to the keel and perhaps part of the outer planking, which was detached from the inner planking. Three unusual blocks, sitting on the keel, may be associated with the keel's complex scarfing arrangement.

The ship would have been slightly more than 20 m long with a beam of about 6 m. Compartments were about 1.2 m wide, suggesting that there were about 16 over the length of the ship. Apparently the ship was quite old at the time of the loss, from the evidence of repairs. In particular, the scarf on strake 3 (starboard), between bulkheads 51 and 52, shows evidence of repair, and strake 2, on the port side, has two scarf joints very close together (between bulkheads 45–46 and 46–47) less than a metre apart.

The Rang Kwien site was excavated by the Fine Arts Department between 1978 and 1981. It had been extensively looted by sports divers; nonetheless, the excavation team recovered 200 kg of artifacts such as copper coins, copper ingots, ceramics, gongs, bells, and elephant tusks. A large section of the ship's hull survived, including the keel, which had an unusual waterway cut out of the center. In 1987, when the survey group visited the site to recover timber samples for dating and analysis, the keel was found to be exposed, so a series of cross-sectional measurements were made to record the keel waterway.

In February 1992, the Royal Thai navy detained a salvage vessel operating in Thailand's Exclusive Economic Zone. Much ceramic material was confiscated, and the vessel was ordered out of Thai waters. This was the first time a country in the region has detained a vessel involved in large-scale looting.

Vietnam.   A number of sites have been salvaged by treasure hunting groups with permits issued by the Vietnamese government. A late 17th-century vessel was recovered off Con Dao. From the design of the vessel it was concluded that it was probably a *lorcha*. In addition, there has been a report of a shipwreck off Phu Quock. In all cases, the findings in Vietnam support the work in Thailand. The vessels seem to be traditional to this particular region.

Sri Lanka.   In March 1992, and January 1993, three-week maritime archaeology training and research programs were conducted in Galle under the auspices of Sri Lanka's Archaeology Department in conjunction with the Post-Graduate Institute for Archaeology. The courses were intended to provide an introduction to maritime archaeology and conservation to a range of archaeologists and conservators. The research program involved a survey of Galle Harbour and concentrated on a number of sites. One site around a large iron wreck had produced a range of material (mostly local, Chinese and European ceramics) dating from about the 14th century to modern times. The survey's objective was to determine the origins of this material and to determine if the site represented harbor jettison or a number of discrete shipwreck sites.

Since Galle has a long history as a port, and ships were unloaded by lightering, there were an array of alternative hypotheses. Surface sampling from 1 m grid squares was made at distances up to 30 m from the site at selected points around the main iron wreck. The data are being analyzed and, at present, it is too soon to draw any firm conclusions. A detailed description of this work will be presented by Vosmer.

In addition, two wooden wrecks, both early 19th century European, and one cannon site were examined and recorded. The latter site is of great interest, because a large bronze bell was found with the inscription "AMOR VINCIT OMNIA ANNO 1625." (Love conquers all, 1625). This is almost certainly a ship's bell and probably belongs to an early-17th century Dutch East Indiaman.

Malaysia.   In 1985, a project to survey the VOC fluit *Risdam* off Mersing was carried out in conjunction with the Museum Negara. The project was of particular interest because the ship, which was wrecked in 1727, was involved in trade with Ligor and Ayutthaya and carried a cargo of mainly Southeast Asian material. In addition, a large section of the hull structure survived.

REFERENCES

Abinion, O.V., 1989, The Recovery of the 12th Century Wooden Boats in the Philippines. *The Bulletin of the Australian Institute for Maritime Archaeology* 13(2):1–2.

Atkinson, K., Green, J.N., Harper, R., and Intakosai, V., 1989, Joint Thai-Australian Underwater Archaeological Project 1987–88. Part 1: Archaeological survey of wreck sites in the Gulf of Thailand, 1987–1988. *International Journal of Nautical Archaeology* 18(4):299–315.

Bell, H.C.P., 1940, The *Maldive Islands: Monograph on the History, Archaeology and Epigraphy.* Ceylon Government Press, Colombo.

Block, G., 1992, Island Craft, Gus Block Looks at Traditional Boatbuilding in the Maldives. *Classic Boat* February:22–26.

Brown, R., 1975, Preliminary Report on the Ko Khram Sunken Ship. *Oriental Art* 24(1):356–370.

_____, 1977, *The Ceramics of Southeast Asia, Their Dating and Identification.* Oxford University Press, Kuala Lumpur.

Burningham, N., 1993, Bajau Lepa and Sope: A Seven-part Canoe Building Tradition in Indonesia. Beagle 10(1):193–222.

Burns, P.L., and Green, J.N., 1989, A New Maritime Archaeological Training Programme in China. In Shipwrecks and Their Environments. *The Australian Institute for Maritime Archaeology VIIIth Annual Conference, Perth, Western Australia, September 1989,* edited by M. Stanbury, pp. 4–10. Australian Institute for Maritime Archaeology, Fremantle.

Clark, P., Conese, E., Green, J.N. and Nicholas, N., 1989, Philippines Archaeological Site Survey, February 1988. *International Journal of Nautical Archaeology* 18(3):255–262.

Clark, P., Green, J.N., Vosmer, T., and Santiago, R., 1993, The Butuan Two Boat Known as a Balangay in the National Museum, Manila, Philippines. *International Journal of Nautical Archaeology* 22(2):143–160.

Conservation Science Research Department, 1986, *Component Analysis of the Shinan Coins.* Cultural Properties Research Institute, Cultural Property Maintenance Office, Ministry of Culture and Publicity, Seoul.

Cultural Property Maintenance Office, 1984, *Shinan Seabed Relics (information data No. 2).* Cultural Property Maintenance Office, Ministry of Culture and Publicity, Seoul.

Cultural Property Research Institute, 1986, *Annual Report Mokpo Conservation and Restoration Centre, 1985.* Cultural Property Maintenance Office, Ministry of Culture and Publicity, Seoul.

Evans, I.H.N., 1927, Notes on the Remains of an Old Boat Found at Pontian. *Journal Federated Malay States Museum* 12:93–96.

Folkard, H.C., 1854, *The Sailing Boat: A Description of English and Foreign Boats, Their Varieties of Rig, and Practical Directions for Sailing.* Hunt and Son, London.

Forbes, A.D.W., 1941, Southern Arabia and the Islamicization of the Central Indian Ocean Archipelago. *Archipelago* 21:55–92.

Gibson-Hill, C.A., 1952, Further Notes on the Old Boat Found at Pontian, in Southern Pahang. *Journal (Malay Branch) Royal Asiatic Society* 25(1):111–113.

Gray, A., and Bell, H.C.P., 1887, The Voyage of François Pyrard of Laval to the East Indies, the Maldives, the Moluccas and Brasil. Hakluyt Society.

Green, J.N., 1981, Further Light on the Koh Khram Wrecksite. *Transactions of the S.E. Asian Ceramic Society* 8:18–26.

_____, 1983a, The Song Dynasty Shipwreck at Quanzhou, Fujian Province, People's Republic of China. *International Journal of Nautical Archaeology* 12(3):253–261.

_____, 1983b, Two Season's Excavation of the Ko Kradat Wrecksite, Thailand: Conclusions. *Oriental Art* 29:59–68.

_____, 1983c, The Shinan Excavation: An Interim Report on the Hull Structure. *International Journal of Nautical Archaeology* 12(4):293–301.

_____, 1983d, The Ko Si Chang Excavation Report, 1983. *Bulletin Australian Institute for Maritime Archaeology* 7(2):9–37.

_____, 1983e, In Search of Khubila Khan's Lost Fleet. *Geo Magazine* 5(4):58–69.

_____, 1986, The Survey of the VOC Fluit *Risdam,* Malaysia. *International Journal of Nautical Archaeology* 15(2):93–104.

Green, J.N., and Devendra, S., 1993, Interim Report on the Joint Sri Lanka–Australian Maritime Archaeology Training and Research Programme, 1992–3. *International Journal of Nautical Archaeology* 22(4):331–343.

_____, 1994, *Maritime Archaeology in Sri Lanka*: *The Galle Harbour Project 1992*. Central Cultural Fund, Colombo, Sri Lanka.

Green, J.N., and Harper, R., 1982, The Excavation of the Ko Kradat Wreck site, Thailand. *International Journal of Nautical Archaeology* 11(2):164–171.

_____, 1983a, *The Excavation of the Pattaya Wreck Site and Survey of Three Other Sites, Thailand 1982*. Australian Institute for Maritime Archaeology, Special Publication No. 1, Fremantle.

_____, 1983b, Maritime Archaeology in Thailand—Seven Shipwrecks. In *Proceedings of the 2nd Southern Hemisphere Conference on Maritime Archaeology*, edited by W. Jeffery and J. Amess, pp. 153–174, South Australian Department of Environment and Planning and Commonwealth Department of Home Affairs and Environment, Adelaide.

_____, 1987, *The Maritime Archaeology of Shipwrecks and Ceramics in Southeast Asia*. Australian Institute for Maritime Archaeology Special Publication No. 4.

_____, 1995, Management of Maritime Archaeology under Australian Legislation. *Bulletin of the Australian Institute for Maritime Archaeology* 19(2):33–44.

Green, J.N., and Intakosai, V, 1983, The Pattaya Wreck Site Excavation, Thailand. An Interim Report. *International Journal of Nautical Archaeology* 12(1):3–14.

Green, J.N., and Kim, Z.-G., 1989, The Shinan and Wando Sites, Korea. Further information. *International Journal of Nautical Archaeology* 18(1):33–41.

Green, J.N., Henderson, G., and McCarthy, M., 1981, Notes and News, Maritime Archaeology and Legislation in Western Australia. *International Journal of Nautical Archaeology* 10(2):145–160

Green, J.N., Harper, R., and Intakosi, V., 1986, The Ko Si Chang One Shipwreck Excavation 1983–1985. A Progress Report. *International Journal of Nautical Archaeology* 15(2):105–122.

_____, 1987, *The Ko Si Chang Three Shipwreck Excavation*, 1986. Australian Institute for Maritime Archaeology Special Publication No. 4.

Green, J.N., Millar, K., and Devendra S., 1992, *Maritime Archaeology in Sri Lanka, the Galle Harbour Project—1993*: *an Interim Report*. Report — Department of Maritime Archaeology, Western Australian Maritime Museum No.64.

Green, J.N., Vosmer, T., Clark P., Santiago, R., Alveres, M., 1995, Interim Report on the Joint Australian–Philippines Butuan Boat Project, October 1992. *International Journal of Nautical Archaeology* 24:117–188.

Haddon, A.C., and Hornell, J., 1975, *Canoes of Oceania*. B.P. Bishop Museum Special Publications 27, 28, and 29 (first printed 1936–1938), Bishop Museum Press, Honolulu.

Henderson, G., 1986, *Maritime Archaeology* in Australia. University of Western Australia Press.

Hoffmann, P, Choi, K.-N and Kim, Y.-H., 1991, Technical Communication, the 14th-century Shinan Ship: Progress in Conservation. *International Journal of Nautical Archaeology*, 20(1):59–64.

Hornell, J., 1920, The Origins and Ethnological Significance of Indian Boat Designs. Memoirs of the Asiatic Society of Bengal, No. 7.

_____, 1943, Fishing and Coastal Craft of Ceylon. *The Mariner's Mirror* 29(1):30–53.

_____, 1946, Constructional Parallels in Scandinavian and Oceanic Boat Construction. *Mariner's Mirror* 21:411–427.

Horridge, G.A., 1982, *Lashed-lug Boats of the Eastern Archipelagoes*. National Maritime Museum Monographs No.5, Greenwich.

_____, 1987, *Outrigger Canoes of Bali and Madura, Indonesia*. Bishop University Press, Honolulu.

Howitz, P.C., 1977, Two Ancient Shipwrecks from the Gulf of Siam: A Report on Archaeological Excavations. *Journal of the Siam Society* 65:1–22.

_____, 1978, *The Research into the Old Sailing ShipWrecks which are Found in the Gulf of Thailand* (in Thai). Special publication, Bangkok.

_____, 1979, *Ceramics from the Sea, Evidence from the Ko Kradat Shipwreck Excavated 1979*. Archeaeology Division, Silpakorn University, Bangkok.

Intakosi, V., 1983, Rang Kwien and Samed Ngam shipwrecks. *SPAFA Digest* 4(11):000–000.

Kentley, E., and Gunaratne, R., 1987, The *Madel Paruwa*: A sewn Boat with Chine Strakes. *International Journal of Nautical Archaeology* 16(1):35–48.

Kinney, S.F., 1981, *Skene's Elements of Yacht Design*. Dodd, Mead and Co., New York.

Li Guo-Qing, 1989, Archaeological Evidence for the Use of "Chu-nam" on the 13th century Quanzhou Ship, Fujian Province, China. *International Journal of Nautical Archaeology* 18(4):277–283.

Lin Shimin, Du Genqui, and Green, J.N., 1991, Waterfront Excavations at Dongmenkou, Ningbo, Zhe Jiang Province, PRC. *International Journal of Nautical Archaeology* 20(4):299–311.

Manguin, P.-Y., 1984, *Sewn-plank Craft of South-East Asia.* A preliminary study. Second International Conference on Indian Ocean Studies, Perth, Western Australia. Section E, Maritime studies: Shipping, Trade and Port Cities.

_____, 1985a, Late Medieval Asian Shipbuilding in the Indian Ocean. *Moyen Orient & Ocean Indien* 2(2):1–30.

_____, 1985b, Sewn-plank Craft of South-East Asia: A preliminary survey. In *Sewn Plank Boats*, edited by S. McGrail and E. Kentley, pp. 319–43. British Archaeological Reports, International Series 276, Oxford.

_____, 1985c, *The Pontian and Butuan Finds. In Sewn Plank Boats*, edited by S. McGrail and E. Kentley, British Archaeological Reports, International Series 276, Oxford.

_____, 1993, Pre-Modern Southeast Asian Shipping in the Indian Ocean: The Maldives Connection. In *New Directions in Maritime History Conference*, International Commission of Maritime History, Fremantle, December.

McGrail, S., 1974, *The Gokstad Faering, Building the Replica. Part 1: Maritime Monographs and Reports.* Greenwich.

Millar, K., 1993, Preliminary Report on Observations made into the Techniques and Traditions of Maldivian Shipbuilding. *Bulletin Australian Institute for Maritime Archaeology* 17(1):9–16.

Mokpo Conservation Institute, 1993, *Report on the Excavation of the Jindo Logboat.* Mokpo Conservation Institute for Maritime Archaeological Finds, Mokpo, Korea.

Mookerji, R.K., 1957, *Indian Shipping: A History of the Sea-borne Trade and Maritime Activity of the Indians from the Earliest Times.* Orient Longmans, Bombay.

Mozai, T., 1982, The Lost Fleet of Kubali Kahn. *National Geographic* 162(5):635–649.

Museum for Overseas Communication History, 1987, *The Excavation and Research of the Shipwreck of Song Dynasty in Quanzhou Bay.* (In Chinese.) China Ocean Press, Quanzhou.

Paris, E., 1841, *Essai sur la Construction Navale des Peuples extra-Europeens.* Paris.

Peralta, J.T., 1980, Ancient Mariners of the Philippines. *Archaeology* 33(5):41–48.

Prins, A.H.J., No Date, *A Handbook of Sewn Boats.* Maritime Monographs and Reports No. 59. National Maritime Museum, Greenwich.

Ronquillo, W.P., 1987a, Highlights of Philippine Prehistory: 1986. *SPAFA Digest* 8(1):22–26.

_____, 1987b,. The Butuan Archaeological Finds: Profound Implications for Philippines and Southeast Asian Prehistory. *Man and Culture in Oceania* 3 (special issue):71–78.

Salmon, C., and Lombard, D., 1979, Un vaisseau du XIIIème s. retrouvé avec sa cargaison dans la rade de "Zaitun." *Archipelago* 18:57–67.

Scott, W.H., 1981, Boat-building and Seamanship in Classic Philippine society. *Philippine Studies* 30:335–376.

Skjølsvold, A., 1991, Archaeological Test-excavations on the Maldive Islands. *The Kon-Tiki Museum Occasional Papers* 2:1–202.

Song Shipwreck Committee, 1975, The Song Dynasty Shipwreck Excavated at Quanzhou Harbour: i. The Excavation; ii. History of the Port of Quanzhou; iii. Naval Construction during the Song Dynasty; iv. The Reconstruction of the Ship after Recovery. *Wen Wu* 10:1–34.

Varadarajan, L., 1994, *Seafaring and Shipbuilding Technology of Lakshadweep.* International Seminar on Techno-Archaeological Perspectives of Seafaring in the Indian Ocean, February 28–March 4, 1994, New Delhi.

Vincent, R.K., and Green, J.N., 1990, A Reconnaissance along the Coast of Oman. *INA Newsletter* 17(1):8–11.

Vitharana, V., 1992, *The Oru and the Yatra: Traditional Out-rigger Water Craft of Sri Lanka.* Sridevi Printers, Dehiwala.

Vosmer, T., 1993a, The Boats of Khawr Kumzar. *Indian Ocean Review* 6:2.

_____, 1993b, The *Yatra Dhoni* of Sri Lanka. *Bulletin Australian Institute for Maritime Archaeology* 17(2):37–42.

_____, 1994a, Traditional Boats of Oman, Links Past and Present. *Proceedings of the Conference on Techno-Archaeological Perspectives on Shipbuilding in the Indian Ocean*, February 28–March 4, 1994, New Delhi.

_____, 1994b, *Traditional Boats of Oman*, Ministry of National Heritage and Culture, Muscat.

Vosmer, T., Margariti, R., Tilley, A., and Godfrey, I., 1993, *The Omani Dhow Research Project, Final Report, Fieldwork 1992.* Western Australia Maritime Museum Report No. 69.

Xu Yingfan, 1985, Origin and Technique of "Gua-ju" (Iron Cramp) Connections in Wooden Craft Construction. *Special of ship Engineering Marine History Research Transactions of CSNAME—Marine History Research Group No.1*, Shanghai.

Chapter 33

Past, Present, and Future of Maritime Archaeology in South Africa

JOHN GRIBBLE

INTRODUCTION

Maritime archaeology in South Africa is a fledgling discipline that has enjoyed official recognition for a little more than a decade. That the discipline should have received such scant attention until relatively recently may seem surprising, given the importance of maritime influences on the last five centuries of South African history and the profusion of historical shipwrecks in our coastal waters. To be understood fully, the development of South Africa's maritime archaeology must be considered in conjunction with a variety of circumstances. This chapter will attempt to trace the birth and growth of the field, discussing the historical, economic, and political factors that account for both the development of the discipline and for its relatively late arrival. Possible future directions for the development of the discipline also will be considered.

DEFINING THE RESOURCE

In 1498, Portuguese explorer Vasco da Gama finally pioneered the elusive sea route around Africa from Europe to the East. Since then, the southern tip of the African

John Gribble, South African Heritage Resources Agency, Cape Town, 8000, South Africa.

International Handbook of Underwater Archaeology, edited by Carol V. Ruppé and Janet F. Barstad. Kluwer Academic/Plenum Publishers, New York, 2002.

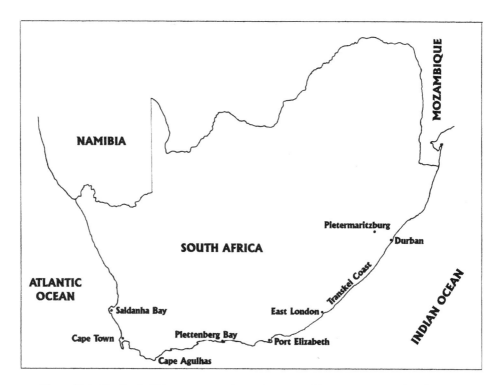

Figure 33.1. The South African coast, showing major ports and locations mentioned in the text.

continent has played a vital role in global economic and maritime affairs and, until the opening of the Suez Canal in 1869, represented the most viable route between Europe and the markets of the East. In the intervening years, thousands of vessels from a host of countries have passed around the Cape of Good Hope en route to and from the East. The geographical position of the South African coast on this route and the physical conditions mariners could expect to encounter in this area have been responsible for the large number of maritime casualties, which today form part of South Africa's underwater cultural heritage.

The South African coast, which stretches some 2954 km from the mouth of the Orange River on the Namibian border in the west to Ponto Do Ouro on the Mozambique border in the east, is rugged, and the seas are unpredictable (Figure 33.1). Rocks and cliffs are interspersed with sandy beaches pounded by heavy surf. The long fetch and the deep surrounding waters mean that the force and size of the seas are considerable, a situation often exacerbated by prevailing seasonal winds. These physical conditions become important when considering the routes used by vessels sailing to and from the East. No matter what course was chosen in the Atlantic or Indian Oceans, all vessels were forced to sail close inshore when rounding southern Africa, a geographical necessity that proved fatal in many cases. Some of the worst sea and weather conditions anywhere in the world, combined with the poor physical condition of many vessels and their crews by the time they reached these waters, has left South Africa with a legacy of more than 2200 historical shipwrecks, 1914 of which are protected. This list is by no means complete, and it is anticipated that further research in local and foreign archives, together with physical surveys to locate the remains of historical shipwrecks, will produce a final tally of more than 3000 wrecks.

Historically, the earliest known South African wrecks are Portuguese, dating to the 16th century when that country held sway over the route to the East. Due to the later, more prolonged ascendancy of first the Dutch and then the British in European trade with the East, the majority of wrecks along the South African coast are Dutch and British. However, at least 36 other nationalities are represented among the other wrecks, making this a diverse and cosmopolitan resource of great comparative value.

SHIPWRECK EXPLORATION: THE EARLY YEARS

Historical shipwrecks in South Africa have been the object of interest and exploration since vessels were first wrecked on this coast. Initially, much of the interest focused on the opportunistic recovery of cargos and contents of vessels at the time of their loss. By the early 18th century, however, more ambitious attempts were being made to salvage the contents of earlier or more inaccessible wrecks.

The first recorded salvage operator in South African waters was John Lethbridge, an Englishman hired by the Dutch East India Company (VOC) in 1727 to recover goods from some of their vessels lost in the disastrous Table Bay gale of 1722 (Burman, 1976). Lethbridge used a wooden diving bell supplied with air from the surface to recover cannon, anchors, silver ingots, and substantial quantities of silver specie from the wrecks of the *Rotterdam* and *Zoetigheid* (Ellerton, 1986; Speight, 1956; Turner, 1988).

Although the Siebe Gorman Closed Diving Dress was available after 1837, there is no record of its early use in South Africa. Henry Adams was still using a diving bell in 1851 to recover from wrecks "a quantity of very old china, tea sets and smelling bottles," which he then offered for sale at his house. Captain William Lea worked on wrecks in the Table Bay area in 1876 and is credited with locating the *Het Huis te Craijestein*, a Dutch East Indiaman wrecked at Oudekraal on the Cape Peninsula (Liebenberg, in press) in May 1698. During the late 18th and early 19th centuries, successful attempts were made to recover material from the wreck of the Dutch East Indiaman *Middelburg*, burned and scuttled in Saldanha Bay in 1791, while the cargos of tin aboard the *Jupiter T* (1875) and *L'Aigle* (1850), and copper and chrome ore on the manifest of the *Hypatia* (1929) attracted the attention of divers early in the last century (Turner, 1988).

The growth of a salvage industry during the 19th century generated what appears to be the earliest South African attempt to legislate protection for historical wrecks. In 1884, Jan Steyn and John Courtenay carried out salvage work on two wrecks near the mouth of the Salt River in Table Bay, reputed to be the Dutch East Indiamen *Haarlem* (1647) and *Jonge Thomas* (1773). They recovered large quantities of specie and organized a treasure show, which resulted in a rival salvage operation by a Captain Teague. Shortly afterward, Steyn and a rival diver met underwater and had an altercation. According to Liebenberg (in press), this prompted the government to intervene by issuing a proclamation in the *Government Gazette*, which read: "No person is at liberty, without the sanction of the Government, to remove or appropriate any wreckage found in the waters of Table Bay, and any person who may be discovered so doing after the publication of this notice will be prosecuted."

While some salvage undertakings were relatively successful, others were less so but had the effect of perpetuating the popular myth of shipwrecks as treasure troves. A classic example is the British East Indiaman *Grosvenor*, lost on the Transkei coast in 1782. Since shortly after she was wrecked, expeditions have been mounted to search for her remains and salvage a treasure she was purported to carry. Historical evidence, strongly suggesting that the stories of treasure are unfounded, has not deterred adventurers and investors, and fortunes continue to be lost on these endeavours (Kirby, 1960).

TREASURE AND TRIBULATION

Increased access to scuba equipment after the 1950s, and the growing number of South Africans venturing underwater, resulted in an upsurge of interest in wreck hunting and the discovery and salvage of a number of historically important, high-profile shipwrecks before the mid-1980s. A contributing factor to the interest was the lack of physical and legislative control over activities on wrecks. With legislative protection for wrecks as a heritage resource still some distance in the future, divers had free rein on these sites and could do as they wished, provided they paid proper customs and excise dues on material recovered.

Among the wrecks located and salvaged during that period were the 17th-century wrecks of Portuguese sister ships the *Santissimo Sacramento* (Allen and Allen, 1978a) and *Nossa Senhore Da Atalaia de Pinheiro* (Warriner, 1990), both lost in 1647 and located in the Eastern Cape. The *Sacramento* carried a cargo of Chinese bronze and iron cannon from the famous Bocarro foundry in Macao. After her discovery, a number of these cannon were raised (Allen and Allen, 1978a). Fortunately, the best examples found their way to the Port Elizabeth Museum, but others were sold for scrap, as were many of the 23 bronze ship's cannon, weighing more than 50 tons, recovered from the *Atalaia*.

In the hunt for more conventional treasure, large quantities of silver specie were recovered from the wrecks of the outward-bound Dutch VOC vessels *Merestijn* (1702) (Marsden, 1976) and *Reijgersdal* (1747) on the Western Cape coast. Renewed salvage work on the wreck of the *Middelburg* (1781) produced limited quantities of Chinese porcelain (Turner, 1988). The Danish East Indiaman *Nicobar*, lost on the Cape South coast in 1783 while carrying large quantities of Swedish copper plate money, was also located and most of this cargo removed (Herbert, 1991).

Another shipwreck of note investigated in the early 1980's was the HMS *Birkenhead*, an early paddle-wheeled steamship which sank with the loss of 445 men after striking an unmarked pinnacle off Danger Point on the Cape south coast in February 1852 (Bevan, 1989, 1998). In 1983, the Depth Recovery Unit, led by Allan Kayle, worked on the wreck, which lies at a depth of 30 meters. The depth of the site and dangerous diving conditions meant that the extent of recording and control of excavations of the wreck were perhaps not as thorough as could have been desired. Furthermore, although the wreck was in reasonable condition at the time, the divers argued against the need to accurately record the hull and machinery because original plans for the vessel existed. Subsequent reports indicate that the wreck has deteriorated alarmingly in recent years, and many of these structural remains no longer exist. Needless to say, none of the gold bullion the *Birkenhead* was reputed to have been carrying was found, although a significant collection of historical artifacts, including regimental insignia and many identifiable personal belongings, were recovered (Kayle, 1990).

During the early 1970s, two Port Elizabeth divers, David Allen and Gerry van Niekerk, began searching for wrecks in the Eastern Cape. Apart from locating the *Santissimo Sacramento*, they were particularly interested in the wreck of the British East Indiaman *Dodington*, lost in 1755 and reputed to have been carrying the personal fortune of Lord Robert Clive (Clive of India). Extensive archival research paid off when, in 1977, they located the *Dodington* off Bird Island in Algoa Bay (Allen and Allen, 1978b). Although not an archaeological investigation, their work on the site proved to be methodical and thorough, and many of the artifacts recovered were donated to the Port Elizabeth Museum, with which the two divers maintained a good working relationship.

With few exceptions, activity on historical shipwreck sites during this period was nonarchaeological, motivated instead largely by commercial considerations. Although some divers paid lip-service to archaeology, they thought archaeology simply meant working within a rough grid laid over the site. Acceptable archaeological standards of excavation and recovery generally were not employed, nor were detailed records such as excavation logs, artifacts registers, or site plans generally kept. Thus, while a great deal of the shipwreck material recovered was subsequently donated to museums, much is of questionable provenance and is of little or no use other than for display. Furthermore, no meaningful, published scientific results have yet been produced by these projects, or for a number of other wrecks investigated according to "archaeological principles." The only exceptions have been a short paper by Clackworthy (1989) regarding a forged coin recovered from the *Sabina* (1842), and a paper by Meltzer (1984) on specie from the *Reijgersdal* (1747); however, both papers relate only indirectly to the excavation of these sites. The result of much of the interest in historical shipwrecks during the last 30 years has been little more than an unquantifiable loss of archaeological or historical material and information, as sites fell victim to often indiscriminate commercial salvage.

CROSSING THE RUBICON: ARCHAEOLOGY WADES IN

In 1988 the Department of Archaeology at the University of Cape Town and the South African Cultural History Museum (SACHM) created a joint post for a maritime archaeologist—the first of any kind in the country—and in so doing formalized the establishment of the discipline in South Africa. Historically, most South African archaeological research has focused on the long, precolonial archaeological record, with historical archaeology—and by association maritime archaeology—receiving little attention. Another possible reason South African maritime archaeology lagged behind the rest of the world is the academic isolation experienced during the international cultural boycott of the 1980s. Whatever the reason, prior to 1988 South African maritime archaeology was largely virgin territory.

The Early Years: Getting Our Feet Wet

There were a few notable exceptions; early instances of terrestrial archaeologists involved in shipwreck-related projects. In 1982, Dr. Tim Maggs, an archaeologist based at the Natal Museum in Pietermaritzburg, published the results of a collaborative project with a group of amateur divers to investigate the wreck of the *São Bento* (1554) on the Transkei coast (Auret and Maggs, 1982). Maggs later studied material from the wreck of *São João* (1552) (Maggs, 1984).

In the southern Cape, Professor Andrew Smith of the University of Cape Town (UCT) excavated a portion of the survivors' camp from the wreck of the Portuguese *nao*, *São Gonçalo*, lost in Plettenberg Bay in 1630 (Smith, 1986). The importance of this site, which was occupied for eight months while the survivors built two new boats, is that it represents the first well-recorded and prolonged settlement by Europeans on South African shores (Storrar, 1988).

Figure 33.2. The "Civic Centre Ship" being excavated.

Perhaps the most technically outstanding project of this period, from a maritime archaeological perspective, was the investigation in 1971 of the so-called "Civic Centre Ship" on the Cape Town Foreshore, an area of Table Bay's historical anchorage reclaimed over the last century (Lightley, 1976). In 1970, during construction of the Cape Town Civic Centre on the Foreshore, contractors uncovered the remains of a vessel. When no archaeological interest was shown in the discovery, the exposed timbers were ripped out and dumped. In April 1971, further remains were uncovered. Bob Lightley, an internationally renowned ship model builder and then an employee of the Cape Town City Council, was given the opportunity to excavate and record an undisturbed section of the wreck (Figure 33.2).

Although the excavation of the wreck was carried out by untrained volunteers, the work was highly professional. Investigators have concluded that the vessel was deliberately grounded, broken up, and filled with a ballast of reject cannon shot to keep her on the bottom. Archival research has suggested that the remains may be those of the Dutch East Indiaman *Nieuw Rhoon*, towed into Table Bay after breaking its back when it struck Whale Rock off Robben Island in January 1776 (Lightley, 1976).

The first South African project on a submerged wreck to which were applied strict maritime archaeological principles was the investigation of the British troopship *Arniston*, wrecked east of Cape Agulhas with appalling loss of life in 1815 (Jobling, 1982; Turner, 1988). In 1982, the National Monuments Council (NMC) issued a permit to UCT's Department of Archaeology to investigate the wreck, which at the time was a declared national monument. The project, initiated by members of the commercial salvage company Seabed Enterprises who wished to promote the practice of maritime archaeology in South Africa, and the team included UCT archaeology student, Jim Jobling.

According to Jobling (1982), the project's primary goal was to conduct an underwater survey of the site, followed by a small test excavation. Because none of the other participants had any real maritime archaeological experience, and because there were limited conservation facilities and expertise available in South Africa, it was decided to keep activities as simple as possible and excavation to a minimum.

Although the wreck lies at a depth of only 5–6 m, poor visibility and strong wave action on the site made diving difficult. Despite these constraints, the team managed a comprehensive survey, which was translated into an accurate and detailed site plan. The small test excavation was accomplished using an airlift, a modified diamond gravel pump (Gericke, 1982), and a deflected propwash blower. Most of the artifacts recovered, including coins, jewelry and organic remains, were donated to the Bredasdorp Shipwreck Museum.

More recently, large pieces of what may be the *Arniston*'s hull structure have been exposed on the beach near the site, and NMC and South African Maritime Museum initiated a joint project to investigate and record them (Figure 33.3).

The Later Years: Learning to Swim

The growth of South African maritime archaeology since 1988 has been relatively modest but has been placed on a firm foundation by the creation of several permanent

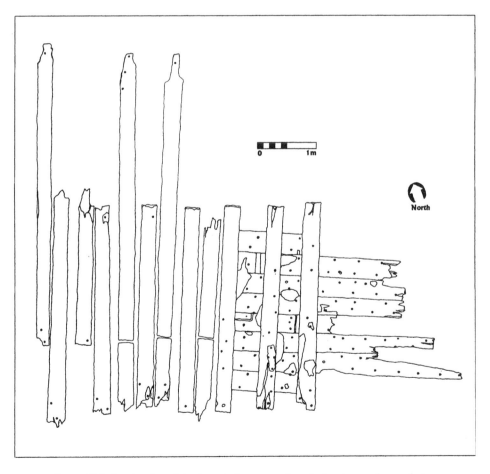

Figure 33.3. Interim plan of *Arniston* timbers exposed on the beach near the wreck site.

professional posts. Shortly after the creation of the UCT post, the South African Maritime Museum was established in Cape Town as part of the South Africa Cultural History Museum, with a post for a maritime archaeologist that was filled in 1991. This was followed in 1993 by the temporary appointment of a maritime archaeologist at the National Monuments Council. The post was made permanent in 1996.

Spurred on by the establishment of a professional capability, a number of maritime archaeological projects have been initiated in the last ten years. In 1993, the NMC began to compile an inventory of historical shipwrecks in South African waters, using information from mainly archival sources and the South African Library. Although not yet complete, this database is an important tool in the management of the resource and is continually updated with information received from other historical sources, divers' reports, and NMC site inspections (Gribble, 1996).

The management of historical shipwrecks in the area now defined as the Robben Island Museum and World Heritage Site in Table Bay is likely to be facilitated in the future by a major interdepartmental underwater survey of the island coast undertaken in 1990–1991. Code-named Operation Sea Eagle, the project took place under the joint auspices of the various government departments then responsible for management of the island and aimed to provide an assessment of underwater cultural resources around the island at a time when the island's future was being decided. The project successfully located 15 of 22 known wrecks, 10 of which were identified with reasonable certainty as specific vessels (Werz and Deacon, 1992; Werz, 1993b).

In 1988, a project was begun to excavate the Dutch East Indiaman *Oosterland*, wrecked in Table Bay in 1697. The wreck was discovered by three local divers, who reported it to Bruno Werz, maritime archaeologist at University of Cape Town. A joint project between UCT and the divers was established, and an agreement was drawn up regulating the conduct of the project. An important aspect of the agreement was that the archaeologists would have an opportunity to study all material recovered before its division between the museum and divers took place (Werz, 1992a, 1993a, 1997). The excavation is still in progress and has produced a postgraduate dissertation on the application of GIS technology to shipwrecks site recording and artifact mapping (Sharfman, 1998).

In 1993, participants in the first Nautical Archaeology Society course to be presented in South Africa stumbled upon an unidentified wreck in Simon's Bay near Cape Town while engaged in the practical surveying component of the course. Such was their enthusiasm and excitement at the discovery that, in collaboration with the archaeologist at the South Africa Maritime Museum, they initiated a comprehensive site survey and carried out some limited excavations (J. Boshoff, personal communication). The wreck's location in a sheltered bay, well-preserved hull sections, and a maximum water depth of 7 m made the site ideal for such a recording project. Sandalwood logs and other artifacts found on the site have since aided in the identification of the vessel as the British East Indiaman *Brunswick*, lost in Simon's Bay in 1805 (Fawcett, 1995). This project has been important in South African maritime archaeology not only for being our first avocational work but also for being the only project thus far with no commercial incentive or component.

Another NAS-related project is the ongoing investigation of the wreck of the *Philia* (1880) at Mossel Bay by an NAS graduate, and a linked initiative to establish a shipwreck route in the area (J. Cilliers, personal communication).

Further afield, Jenny Bennie of the Port Elizabeth Museum is investigating the 1817 wreck of the Dutch man-o-war *Amsterdam*, large portions of which are periodically exposed on the beach at Bluewater Bay near Port Elizabeth (J. Bennie, personal communication; Neethling, 1974). In 1993, the East London Museum surveyed a substantial section of ship's timbers that washed ashore at Bonza Bay. The timbers are believed to be the remains of the Portuguese galleon, *Santa Maria Madre de Deus*, which burned and sank in 1643 (D. Smit, personal communication).

Shipwreck-related projects have included the rescue excavation of two burials believed to be the remains of victims of the *British Peer* (1896) (Wilson and Van Rijssen, 1994). UCT's Department of Archaeology recently analyzed bone isotope ratios in a collection of human skeletal material from a shallow mass grave uncovered near the remains of Fort Knokke on the south-eastern shore of Table Bay in the early 1950s (Singer, 1953). Opinion was that these were the remains of slaves drowned when the Portuguese slaving brig, *Pacquet Real*, was wrecked in 1818. The analysis by Cox and Sealy (1997) confirmed this opinion.

A research area currently being pursued is the archaeology of sealing and whaling, which began with documentation of seal hunting sites on South Africa's sub-Antarctic Prince Edward Islands (J. Boshoff, personal communication; Boshoff et al., 1997). It is anticipated that this project will be expanded in the future to include a survey of coastal whaling sites within South Africa.

Finally, another sphere in which maritime archaeology has grown in recent years is cultural resource management. Whereas dredging operations, harbor construction, offshore prospecting and mining, and other maritime developments in the last 30 years have destroyed significant quantities of shipwreck material with little or no opportunity for prior archaeological investigation, recent environmental legislation requires environmental impact assessments ahead of developmental activities. The legislation will prevent future indiscriminate destruction of shipwreck remains.

Large-scale land reclamation in port cities such as Cape Town and Port Elizabeth in the last century protected much historical shipwreck material by burying it. Increasing pressure for space in these cities is precipitating the development or redevelopment of tracts of this reclaimed land and will allow maritime archaeologists an opportunity to investigate these buried sites in the future.

THE REGULATORS: THE COMPLIANCE AGENCY AND THE COASTAL MUSEUMS

When Allen and Van Niekerk discovered the wreck of the *Sacramento*, they did their best to keep the discovery quiet, but word of the find leaked out, and they soon found themselves fighting off rival groups intent on salvaging bronze cannon for their scrap-metal value. Their subsequent discovery of the *Dodington* led them to approach John Wiley, a Cape Town Member of Parliament interested in historical shipwrecks, with their concerns about the lack of legal protection for shipwreck sites. Wiley took up the cause and, in an address to Parliament in May 1977, called for legislation to protect historical shipwrecks (Hansard, 1977).

Indicative of the low profile of historical shipwrecks, at the time of Wiley's speech South Africa's relatively new heritage legislation, the National Monuments Act (Act No. 28 of 1969), contained no mention of shipwrecks and made no provision for their protection as part of the nation's cultural heritage. Wiley's intervention, combined with pressure from the South African Museums Association (SAMA), representing the coastal museums that were becoming increasingly alarmed by salvage activities on these sites (Bell-Cross, 1980), led to the first legal measures to protect historical wrecks and control the activities of divers and salvors.

Protection took the form of an amendment to the Act in 1979, which gave the National Monuments Council power to declare as a national monument any shipwreck in South African territorial waters more than 80 years old. Once declared, it was an offense to destroy or damage such a wreck. For reasons discussed elsewhere (Deacon, 1993; Gribble, 1998), this legislation was not particularly successful, and there were two further amendments to the Act, both of which were attempts to improve protection for historical wrecks. In 1986, the second of the later amendments extended blanket protection to all shipwrecks and shipwreck material over the age of 50 years and in South African territorial waters and made it an offense to disturb such a shipwreck or remove anything from a site except under the terms of a permit issued by the NMC. The NMC established a permit system to manage historical shipwrecks and drew up criteria under which work on wrecks could be carried out that stressed the archaeological nature and importance of these sites (Gribble, 1998).

The first permit for a historical shipwreck was issued in 1982, for the investigation of the wreck *Arniston*. Prior to April 2000, the NMC had received 140 permit applications, of which 103 were approved. Applications received, and the number of shipwreck permits issued, peaked in 1986, the year in which permits to investigate historical wrecks became mandatory. Since then, there has been a steady decline in applications and permits. While it is always possible that divers simply ignored the requirement of obtaining a permit, indications were that this practice was not widespread and that the decline in permit numbers represented a real decline in particularly commercial salvage interests on these sites. After 1998 most NMC permits were issued in two phases: an initial predisturbance permit, followed by an excavation permit once the predisturbance survey was completed satisfactorily. This allowed the NMC and collaborating museums to assess the commitment and abilities of permit holders before any damage was done to sites.

The 30-year-old National Monuments Act was finally repealed on April 1, 2000 and replaced by the National Heritage Resources Act (Act No. 25 of 1999). The new legislation established a new legal compliance agency, the South African Heritage Resources Agency (SAHRA) and ushered in a new era for the protection and management of the country's underwater cultural heritage. Although similarities exist between the two pieces of legislation (such as the concept of blanket protection for historical wrecks), there are critical and fundamental differences in how wrecks are written into the new legislation.

A potential legal shortcoming of the National Monuments Act was that because their protection had been written into the Act as amendments, wrecks were not defined as archaeological sites and thus did not receive the additional protection this status promised. By contrast, Section 2 of the National Heritage Resources Act defines any wreck older than 60 years as an archaeological site. It is hoped that this language will clear up the ambiguity about the exact legal status of historical wrecks that existed under the National Monuments Act by removing them from the realm of wrecks perceived to be commercially salvageable.

Closely related to the issue of definition is a second important divergance from the past. The National Heritage Resources Act states that all archaeological material, including historical wrecks and their contents, is state property. This provision makes explicit what was considered to be the case under the National Monuments Act but never expresssly stated. With wide new powers and a fundamentally different approach to heritage management in general, the National Heritage Resources Act, through SAHRA, is likely to have a major effect on future management of historical wrecks in South Africa.

Besides the legal compliance agencies, other major players in promoting maritime archaeology have been the coastal museums, whose involvement with historical ship-wrecks long predates that of the NMC and SAHRA. Because divers offered shipwreck artifacts to museums and approached them for assistance with historical research, coastal museums were the first public institutions to be aware of the marked increase in the discovery of and activity on shipwreck sites. In the absence of legislative protection or any other responsible authority, museums were forced to develop strategies to cope with the upsurge of interest in shipwrecks (Bell-Cross, 1980). As early as the 1950s, some institutions attemped to work with the diving and salvage community to ensure the preservation of at least some of artifactual material recovered from these sites, although they were powerless to insist on application of archaeological standards for excavation and recording. The lack of standards and, most important, the lack of legislative protection was an issue of concern for museums, and a number of representations were made to government to introduce protective legislation.

Museums continued to play a central role in shipwreck management after the introduction of the National Monuments Act, because the Act required the collaboration of a suitable institution on any shipwreck project (Gribble, 1998). Furthermore, although amendments to the National Monuments Act established legal control over historical shipwrecks, they were not accompanied by an increase in the capacity to manage a resource strung out along nearly 3000 km of coastline, or to control the activities of divers at a local level. Although the situation has improved somewhat during the last decade, the compliance agency continues to rely heavily on coastal museums for the *de facto* enforcement of shipwreck legislation and conservation through local policing, education, and liaison.

TOWARD A PUBLIC ARCHAEOLOGY

Historically, there has been and sadly remains a lack of awareness among the South African public of the importance and archaeological potential of their underwater cultural heritage. It has been suggested elsewhere that this lack of awareness is unusual for a country whose recent history has been so intimately connected with the sea (Gribble, 1998), but that it may stem from the inward-looking national psyche that has been a feature of the last 200 years of South Africa's history, manifest in recent times in the apartheid system, and in South Africa's thumbing its nose at world opposition to these policies.

The fact that historical shipwrecks are essentially hidden from view—a case of "out of sight, out of mind"—has probably also contributed to public ignorance of their cultural heritage worth. Popular perceptions of historical shipwrecks based on tragic tales of human loss and suffering, or the inspiring stories of heroism that often accompany a wreck, and because these vessels came from far-off places carrying exotic and often valuable cargos, have imbued shipwrecks with a special romance and allure that in recent years has been entrenched by the activities of treasure hunters and salvors.

Archaeologists continue to face great difficulties in weaning public opinion away from these attractive traditional perceptions of historical shipwrecks and persuading them that the real value and importance of sites and objects lies in their archaeological and scientific potential. While legislation can offer legal protection, this alone will not alter public perceptions. In recent years, efforts have been made to change attitudes through education and participation, and appear to be bearing fruit, particularly among the younger generation of divers who have grown up in the milieu of increasing environmental awareness, a feature of the last decade throughout the world. Recent trends which emphasize the interconnectedness of all aspects of the environment, whether natural or humanly derived, offer new hope that we will be able to prise divers away from the outdated notion that wrecks are simply objects of salvage.

One of the tools South African maritime archaeologists have used to change public perceptions is the press. Wherever and whenever possible, work is publicized in the press, generally evoking a strong and positive public interest. The result has been that members of the public have reported wreckage on beaches at Plettenberg Bay (Werz, 1992b), Amsterdamhoek (J. Bennie, personal communication) and Bonza Bay in the Eastern Cape, and at Bloubergstrand (Werz, 1996), Milnerton (Boshoff, 1997), and Yzerfontein in the Western Cape. Members of the public also have reported instances of looting or damage to wreck sites, which has prevented loss of valuable shipwreck material.

A major public relations challenge facing maritime archaeologists in South Africa has been to win over the diving community, many of whom consider shipwrecks their exclusive preserve, for the historical reasons outlined above. It is not necessarily the salvage divers who do the most damage to wreck sites but sport divers, who are often ignorant of the sites' protected status and archaeological importance. Unlike commercial salvors, divers generally collect only the odd souvenir to take home; however, given their numbers and the regularity with which they dive, many of the better-known wreck sites will soon be stripped bare unless this practice is stopped.

South African maritime archaeologists have attempted to address this problem with a proactive educational approach, based on an affiliation by the NMC (continued by SAHRA), and the South Africa Maritime Museum with the British-based Nautical Archaeology Society (NAS). Since 1993, NAS courses have been offered throughout the country, introducing divers to shipwreck legislation, basic archaeological theory, and the fundamentals of underwater archaeological survey, recording and excavation practice (Boshoff, 1998; Dean et al., 1992). So far, more than 200 divers have obtained the NAS Part 1 qualification, and the addition in 1998 of the NAS Part 2 course had proved equally popular (Oxley, 1999). The ongoing process of education is changing divers' attitudes towards shipwrecks by offering them basic skills and the opportunity to participate in and, in some cases, initiate archaeological work on historical wrecks. Participation in NAS courses by divers currently holding NMC and SAHRA permits also has resulted in greatly improved standards of excavation, recording and reporting.

Another initiative to stimulate public interest in the archeological importance of historical wrecks is the establishment of a shore-based and underwater shipwreck trail around the Cape Peninsula. An abundance of suitable sites and spectacular scenery make this an ideal prototype for a concept which will, if successful, be extended to other areas of the coast in the future.

FINAL WORDS

In the two decades since Allen and Van Niekerk's discovery of the *Dodington* and *Sacramento*, there have been sweeping changes in official attitudes to historical ship-wrecks. A heritage resource that enjoyed no legal protection whatsoever at that time is now covered by blanket legislative protection, and the replacement of the outdated National Monuments Act by the National Heritage Resources Act in April 2000 offers new and exciting opportunities to strengthen and develop the legal protection for historical wrecks.

Considering too that when historical shipwrecks were given legislative protection in 1986 there was not a single trained maritime archaeologist in the country, South Africa's maritime archaeological capacity has increased dramatically in the last decade. It is clear, however, that the existing professional capacity is by no means adequate given the number and distribution of historical shipwrecks along the coast and external pressures on the resource. It is an unfortunate reality, too, that the prospects for increasing this capacity in the short term are not rosy. Although the number of qualified professionals in the field has been increased by graduates from the maritime archaeological program at the University of Cape Town, South Africa's economic realities mean that the heritage sector is facing ever-decreasing budgets, effectively putting the brakes on the creation of new maritime archaeological posts at both SAHRA and coastal museums. Furthermore, the teaching of maritime archaeology at UCT, the only tertiary institution to offer this subject nationally, has been discontinued, thereby setting a ceiling on the number of trained professionals locally available, at least for the present.

Despite this possibly gloomy prognosis, however, successes in the last 10 years have demonstrated that maritime archaeology does have a future in South Africa. It has shown a steady if slow growth and is gradually gaining acceptance as a legitimate archaeological discipline with authorities and institutions, and within the diving community. The support of both these groups is critically important for its survival and growth. Governmental authorities and institutions have the responsibility of underwriting maritime archaeology and shipwreck conservation in the future, and it is pleasing to note that provision has been made in the new organizational structure of SAHRA for the creation of a second maritime archaeological post. At the same time, because wrecks historically have been the almost exclusive preserve of sport and salvage divers, acceptance by this group of maritime archaeology and archaeologists is of paramount importance for the survival of the discipline and the conservation of historical wrecks.

South Africa's maritime archaeological potential is huge, and the wrecks around the South African coast represent many lifetimes of work. The challenge for South African maritime archaeology is to manage successfully manage the pressures on this resource and to pass on to future generations as rich and exciting a resource as exists today.

REFERENCES

Allen, G., and Allen, D., 1978a, *The Guns of Sacramento*. Robin Garton, London.
_____, 1978b, *Clive's Lost Treasure*. Robin Garton, London.
Auret, C., and Maggs, T., 1982, The Great Ship *Sao Bento*: Remains from a Mid-16th-Century Portuguese Wreck on the Pondoland Coast. *Annals of the Natal Museum* 25(1):1–39.
Axelson, E., editor, 1988, *Dias and His Successors*. Saayman & Weber, Cape Town.
Bell-Cross, G., 1980, Research Policy on Shipwrecks. *South African Museums Association Bulletin* 14(1/2): 39–44.
Bevan, D., 1989, *Drums of the Birkenhead*. The London Stamp Exchange, London.
Bevan, D., 1998, *Stand Fast*. Traditional Publishing, New Malden.
Boshoff, J.J., 1997, *Investigation of an Exposed Shipwreck on Milnerton Beach*. Unpublished Report to the National Monuments Council.
_____, 1998, NAS Courses in South Africa. *Bulletin of the Australian Institute for Maritime Archaeology* 22:133–136.
Boshoff, J.J., Hart, D.G., and Loock, J., 1997, *Survey of Historical Sites on Marion Island*. Unpublished report, Cape Town.

Burman, J., 1976, *The Bay of Storms: Table Bay 1503–1860*. Human and Rousseau, Cape Town.

Clackworthy, G., 1989, A Forged Silver Coin Recovered from the Shipwreck *Sabina*. *South African Archaeological Bulletin* 44(149):44–45.

Cox, G., and Sealy, J. 1997, Investigating Identity and Life Histories: Isotopic Analysis and Historical Documentation of Slave Skeletons Found on the Cape Town Foreshore, South Africa. *International Journal of Historical Archaeology* 1(3):207–224.

Deacon, J., 1993, Protection of Historical Shipwrecks through the National Monuments Act. In *Proceedings of the Third National Maritime Conference, Durban 1992*, University of Stellenbosch, Stellenbosch.

Dean, M., Ferrari, B., Oxley, I., Redknap, M., and Wilson, K., 1982, *Archaeology Underwater: The NAS Guide to Principles and Practice*. Nautical Archaeological Society and Archetype Publications, London.

Ellerton, J., 1986, Lowering Experiences: Early Diving Machines. *Country Life* March 20, 1986: 726–727.

Fawcett, N., 1995, The Wreck of the H.E.I. Co. Ship *Brunswick*. *Simon's Town Historical Society Bulletin* 18(3):118–120.

Gericke, I.H., 1982, Grids and Pumps for Underwater Archaeological Work. *International Journal of Nautical Archaeology* 12(2):171–173.

Gribble, J., 1996, National Databases on Monuments and Sites. In *Monuments and Sites of South Africa*. ICOMOS 11th General Assembly, Colombo, Sri Lanka,

————, 1998, Keeping Our Heads above Water: The Development of Shipwreck Management Strategies in South Africa. *Bulletin of the Australian Institute for Maritime Archaeology* 22:119–124.

Hansard, 1977, *Republic of South Africa House of Assembly Debates*. 68 (April 18–May 20) Column 7869–7872.

Herbert, J., 1991, Biggest Hoard of Swedish Plate Money ever Discovered. *Underwater* 16:42–46.

Jobling, J., 1982, *The Arniston—1815*. Unpublished Survey and Excavation Report. National Monuments Council Library, Cape Town.

Kayle, A., 1990, *Salvage of the Birkenhead*. Southern Book Publishers, Johannesburg.

Kirby, P.R., 1960, *The True Story of the* Grosvenor, *East Indiaman*. Oxford University Press, Cape Town.

Liebenberg, N., 1999, *Knights of the Deep*. In press.

Lightley, R.A., 1976, An 18th century Dutch East Indiaman, found at Cape Town, 1971. *The International Journal of Nautical Archaeology* 5(4):305–316.

Maggs, T., 1984, The Great Galleon *Sao Joao*: Remains from a 16th-century Wreck on the Natal South Coast. *Annals of the Natal Museum* 26(1):173–186.

Marsden, P., 1976, The *Meresteyn*, Wrecked in 1702, near Cape Town, South Africa. *The International Journal of Nautical Archaeology* 5(3):201–219.

Meltzer, L., 1984, The Treasure from the Shipwreck, *Reijgersdal* (1747). *Bulletin of the South African Cultural History Museum* 5:5–19.

Neethling, E.M., 1974, The History of Swartkops and Amsterdam Hoek. *Looking Back: Quarterly Bulletin of the Port Elizabeth Historical Society* 14(4):107–118.

Oxley, I., 1998, South African First for NAS Training. *Nautical Archaeology* (3):2.

Sharfman, J., 1998, *The* Oosterland *GIS: Applying Aspects of Geographical Information Systems to a Maritime Archaeological Project*. Masters dissertation, University of Cape Town.

Singer, R., 1953, Artificial Deformation of Teeth: A Preliminary Report. *South African Journal of Science* 50: 116–122.

Smith, A.B., 1986, Excavations at Plettenberg Bay, South Africa of the Camp-site of the Survivors of the Wreck of the *São Gonçalo*, 1630. *The International Journal of Nautical Archaeology* 15(1):53–63.

Speight, W.L., 1956, *Swept by Wind and Wave*. Howard Timmins, Cape Town.

Storrar, P., 1988, *Drama at Ponta Delgada*. Lowry, Johannesburg.

Turner, M., 1988, *Shipwrecks and Salvage in South Africa—1505 to the Present*. C. Struik, Cape Town.

Warriner, C., 1990, The Wreck of the *Atalaia*. *Underwater* 15:94–95.

Werz, B.E.J.S., 1992a, The Excavation of the *Oosterland* in Table Bay: The First Systematic Exercise in Maritime Archaeology in Southern Africa. *South African Journal of Science* 88:85–89.

————, 1992b, *Report on the Survey of a Wreck, Plettenberg Bay Beach: 25–27 October 1992*. Unpublished Report to the National Monuments Council.

————, 1993a, Maritime Archaeological Project Table Bay: Aspects of the First Field Season. *South African Archaeological Society Goodwin Series* 7:33–39.

————, 1993b, Shipwrecks of Robben Island, South Africa: An Exercise in Cultural Resource Management in the Underwater Environment. *The International Journal of Nautical Archaeology* 22:245–256.

_____, 1996, *Excavation of a Shipwreck on the Table View Beach*. Unpublished Report to the National Monuments Council.

_____, 1997, *Diving up the Human Past: Perspectives of Maritime Archaeology, with Specific Reference to Developments in South Africa until 1996*, Cape Town.

Werz, B.E.J.S., and Deacon, J., 1992, *Operation Sea Eagle: Final Report on a Survey of the shipwrecks around Robben Island*. Unpublished report. National Monuments Council, Cape Town.

Wilson, M.L., and Van Rijssen, W.J.J., 1994, Two Victims of the Wreck of the *British Peer*. *Southern African Field Archaeology* 3:10–14.

Part III

Issues in Underwater Archaeology

Culture and Law

The first section in this part deals with culture and law. Anne Giesecke leads off with her summary of the Abandoned Shipwreck Act as well as a report on UNESCO meetings on the "Convention for the Protection of the Underwater Cultural Heritage." She takes the reader through the maze of legalities necessary to preserve the world's underwater cultural heritage.

Sheli Smith follows with her chapter on how to get the public involved in underwater archaeology through education. Programs produced via cyberspace and programs that create "hands-on" sites are just two examples that departments, museums, and schools can provide to educate both children and adults about their relationship to the underwater environment.

Mather and Watts state in their all-encompassing chapter on ethics "only professionals with strong and confident codes of ethics can defend and protect submerged cultural resources." Member organizations and legislative bodies must continue to refine and enforce management and preservation of this one-of-a kind heritage. Salvors must give up their greedy destruction for private investors.

In their second chapter in the section the Watts and Mather team provide a splendid overview of public programs. Organized state by state for the United States and including the United Kingdom, the chapter represents a synthesis on which others can build.

Chapter 34

Wrecked and Abandoned

ANNE G. GIESECKE

INTRODUCTION

In the early morning hours of July 31st, the wind suddenly shifted to the east–northeast, and the hurricane struck with all its fury. The ships, gripped in the incredible force of the crashing waves and mighty winds of nature's most awesome phenomena, were lifted like matchsticks on mountainous crests to be plummeted in the next instant into deep troughs of the ocean. Tons of seawater crashed over railings of the galleons and, with the shriek of the wind, drowned out the screams of the seamen washed overboard to their death. (Cobb Coin, Inc. The Unidentified Wrecked and Abandoned Sailing Vessel. 525F. Supp. 186 [S.D. Fla. 1981])

So begins U.S. District Judge James Lawrence King's decision concerning the fate of artifacts recovered from shipwrecks of the 1715 Spanish Plate fleet off the Florida coast, a decision that challenged the law of Florida and other states of the United States.

The intense human drama of a storm and a shipwreck captures everyone's imagination. Today, after two decades of bad weather, shipwreck enthusiasts of all stripes are finding themselves with more technology, less money, and a very mixed legal weather forecast for the future. To help navigate the foggy legal coastline of today, this chapter will describe the shipwreck resource and the interested groups, and it will provide a brief chronology of selected events in the legal history of shipwrecks. The chapter will frame the three core legal issues: definition of the resource, who owns the resource, and who owns the bottomland where the resource is located.

Anne G. Giesecke, Institute for Heritage Administration, Washington, D.C. 20016.

International Handbook of Underwater Archaeology, edited by Carol V. Ruppé and Janet F. Barstad. Kluwer Academic/Plenum Publishers, New York, 2002.

One of the greatest scientific texts of the 19th century, Lyell's *Principles of Geology* (1832), made this important speculation: "It is probable that a greater number of monuments of the skill and industry of man will in the course of ages be collected together in the bed of the oceans, than will exist at any one time on the surface of the Continents."

Shipwrecks as cultural resources provide valuable information about historical changes in vessels and about changes in warfare and commerce. About the ship's place in history, moreover, people learn not only about the cargoes, but also from the utensils and other artifacts of daily life that the ships carried and that sank with them: plates, glassware, cutlery, and clothing.

Shipwrecks can be understood as potential museums of behavioral context, preserving a collection of items frozen in time as well as a narrative segment of history that the routes, logs, and wreckage present to the archaeologist as a unique challenge to preserve. In some cases, shipwrecks may provide extremely rare evidence, as with the history of smuggling.

Shipwrecks are the primary focus of legal discussions about underwater cultural heritage, because government control of prehistoric sites has not been challenged. However, the legal discussion does include other vehicles, such as railroad locomotives, airplanes, and spacecraft.

Historic values are not the only values that must be considered when discussing the bottomlands of the lakes, rivers, coasts, and oceans. Population pressure has put these areas in high demand. Ocean dumping, for example, is a habit from the past that is continuing into the future with serious negative implications. Miners and drillers are recovering sand and gravel, oil and gas, phosphates, sulfur, other minerals, diamonds, and gold. Commercial fisherman demand undisturbed nursery areas for fish and beds for shellfish, areas for

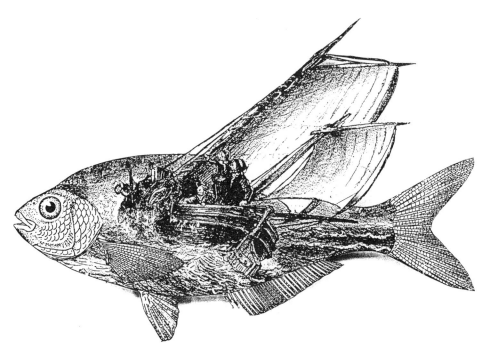

Figure 34.1. Collage pen and ink by John Digby.

aquaculture, as well as areas where they can drag multiton trawls along the bottom, and areas where nets can be pulled unobstructed through the water. Port development along the coast is increasing in scale, and artificial islands further offshore are expanding the need to dredge and shape the bottomland. Underwater hotels are increasing in number.

This intense development must be managed with care. Myopic economic exploration of the wilderness during the settlement of the New World—and the search for gold—proved destructive to civilizations, animals, and plants. The equally myopic exploration of bottomlands will also prove self-destructive. Cries of individual rights, free enterprise, and available resources are unconvincing. After all, creation of national parks and government regulation of clean air and water have allowed everyone to benefit from the strength and bounty of the natural and cultural environment, without diminishing the creation of high-tech industrial economies throughout the world.

WHO IS INTERESTED IN SHIPWRECKS?

From a legal perspective, groups with an interest in underwater cultural heritage, particularly the shipwreck resource, are sport divers, archaeologists, treasure salvors, administrative governing bodies, and courts.

Sport Divers

The largest group interested in shipwrecks is the sport diving community, with approximately two million members in the United States alone. Sport divers are defined here as that group of divers whose primary source of income is not from the diving industry. They are machinists, dentists, salesmen, lawyers, and others who enjoy recreational activities using scuba equipment.

For the sport diver, wrecks are an important focus for recreational activity. Some divers like marked underwater trails explaining the wrecks. Some like to photograph wrecks undisturbed by the modern world. Some value wrecks that attract fish for spear fishing. Some like to collect artifacts. Around the world, most of the work to locate and evaluate shipwrecks is done by sport divers with the support of archaeologists and government administrators, for the benefit of the general public.

Preservationists

The next largest group is the several thousand members of the archaeological and historic preservation communities. There are 200–300 underwater archaeologists around the world—archaeologists who have formal higher education in archaeology *and* archaeological field experience underwater. To these archaeologists, shipwrecks are an integral part of the total material cultural resource base. Certain social, economic, and technological systems of the past are reflected in the patterned pieces of ship and cargo spread across the ocean floor. This information is recovered for the general public good. The historic preservation community is a large and diverse group of professionals and interested citizens who value a broad range of cultural resources.

Treasure Salvors

The third group is composed of a small number of treasure salvors. Here "treasure salvors" refers to those people who derive their primary source of income from forming investment organizations for the purpose of recovering shipwrecks for profit. The treasure salvor's goal is primarily economic: He wants to minimize the cost of recovering gold, silver, or artifacts that have a maximum commercial value. The minimization of recovery costs can mean the loss of archaeologically valuable information and artifacts. The private ownership of sites and of artifacts from these operations limits sport diver and other public access to the material and information. Treasure salvors sometimes operate within the legal structure of the admiralty court system.

ADMIRALTY SYSTEM

The admiralty court and admiralty system have their roots in English history and common law from about 1236, a time when commerce and piracy had reached points of significant economic impact, and the admiral was the law of the sea. The admiralty system was developed to reward salvors who recovered ships, cargoes, and lives from peril at sea with a payment from the owner of the vessel.

All countries have systems of laws and courts to address maritime and admiralty issues. In this chapter, the United States system will be used as an example, although it is recognized that each country's system will be different. Notably, the U.S. court has made decisions about shipwrecks beyond the U.S. territorial waters, including the *Titanic* in the north Atlantic, *Luisitania* off Ireland, *Atlantic* off Canada, and SS *Central America*, 180 miles off the Atlantic coast of the U.S.

According to Article III, Section 2, of the United States Constitution, the federal court is given the responsibility over "all cases of admiralty and maritime jurisdiction." The federal court has interpreted this responsibility through the district court structure. When the court hears a case concerning maritime affairs or admiralty, the court applies the precedents of previous case law and makes an award to the salvor.

For example, in a landmark decision in 1869, Justice Clifford in a U.S. Supreme Court case concerning *The Blackwall* (77 U.S. 10 Wall 1, 19L.Ed.870 [1869]) is credited with setting the precedent ruling for salvage awards. Justice Clifford stated that a salvage award determination should consider:

1. Marine peril—that is, was the ship in danger of being destroyed?
2. Voluntary service—did the salvor volunteer?
3. Success in recovering the vessel or cargo.

Further, the court will consider the degree of danger to the salvor present in the rescue, the value of the property recovered, and the time and labor expended by the salvor. In the case of abandoned property, the salvor may receive the property or the proceeds from the sale of the property (Benedict on Admiralty, 1980). The courts have handled only a few dozen cases of abandoned shipwreck property worldwide. Traditionally, a shipwreck is considered abandoned if a considerable amount of time has passed and the owner has made no attempt to recover the material.

Three important administrative features of the court system are time, cost, and a case-by-case approach based on the judge's discretion. First, when considering time, there may be a delay of as much as two years before a case is heard; then the appeal process may postpone a decision for as many as ten years. Second, cost is important to individuals filing a claim for an award, because the complex procedures require the services of a lawyer and, if there are counterclaims by other parties, states, or the federal government, legal fees and court costs can rapidly escalate. Third, the court takes a case-by-case approach: each judge in each district makes an independent decision based on precedent after a case is brought to court. In the realm of maritime affairs where there is little statutory law, there is much room for interpretation by the judge. The task of interpretation becomes even more difficult where conflicting uses that are not part of the court's tradition are involved, such as endangered species habitat or oil and gas drilling. The judges' independence resulted in seven conflicting U.S. federal court decisions concerning abandoned shipwrecks between 1982 and 1988 (Giesecke, 1988).

Also critical is the concern that a wreck must be located and efforts made to recover property before there is an award claim to file with the court. A major concern is that the conflict of use concerning the bottomland often comes during attempts to locate buried shipwrecks. Shipwreck treasure hunters have set off dynamite to look for wrecks and have destroyed ecologically vital coral reefs. They have used prop-wash to blast away sand, causing severe devastation to fishery nursery areas, and dredged habitat and recreational beaches, imperiling already endangered species as well as small children. Judges are not in a position to act as land managers.

ABANDONED SHIPWRECK ACT

Like many nations, states of the United States manage many submerged resources, including major sectors of the economy such as fishing, oil and gas drilling, and tourism. Management of shipwrecks is part of a state's multiple-use land management responsibilities. Since the 1950s, U.S. states have managed historic shipwreck archaeological sites as part of their historic preservation programs and, since 1966, have applied minimum national standards to their management efforts. The standards of the National Historic Preservation Act define what is historic, set forth management procedures, incorporating public participation on decision-making boards and a public hearing and appeals process. Although there have been problems with some state permits and contracts, these conflicts have been resolved by the state courts, so that citizens have always had an impartial forum for conflict resolution.

The state's claim is supported by its Constitutional property rights under Article IV and Amendment 10, that is, Congress power to dispose of property to the state's and the state's reserved rights. Wrecks governed by the Abandoned Shipwreck Act are those no longer in the stream of commerce. Because the function of the ship has changed, from a means of transport to a time capsule that can tell us much about our past, these vessels are no longer the ships that the framers of the Constitution had in mind when they established federal admiralty courts.

The Abandoned Shipwreck Act of 1987 affirmed the state's role by declaring that the states are owners of all abandoned shipwrecks that are: (1) embedded in state submerged lands; (2) embedded in coralline formations on state submerged lands; or (3) on state submerged lands and are either included or determined eligible for inclusion in the National Register of Historic Places. For the state to have clear authority to control the excavation of state land, the act includes a broad range of wreck sites: some considered historic, some to be removed as hazards to navigation, some that are environmental hazards because of fuel leaks or toxic cargoes, and some to be protected as part of coral reefs.

From 1988 to 1998, the improved condition of U.S. state shipwreck management programs has become readily apparent. In 1988, only 27 states had laws specifically addressing their underwater cultural resources. By 1998, all states had evaluated their legal systems as they apply to underwater resources and where necessary have modified their laws; now all states include underwater resources in their historic preservation plans. In 1988, only 36 underwater sites were listed in the National Register of Historic Places; by 1998, 579 sites were listed. In 1988 only Florida had a state underwater park; by 1998, several states had underwater parks. Finally, rather than facing 30 to 40 salvor court claims in a given year, as had been the case prior to passage of the Abandoned Shipwreck Act, for the last eight years the courts have dealt with four wrecks: one in California, one in Michigan, and two in Illinois (Giesecke, 1999). Progress to protect underwater cultural resources in most countries has been positive and impressive.

The complex interaction of interest groups, sport divers, archaeologists, treasure salvors, courts, and government administrators has been increasing for 40 years. During the 1960s, improvements in scuba equipment made underwater areas accessible to a broad range of people. At the same time, George Bass and Peter Throckmorton began their efforts to have shipwrecks recognized as archaeological sites because of their value to tell stories about human culture. In 1960, they published articles about their work on a Bronze Age wreck located off the coast of Turkey. In 1960–1961, sport divers succeeded in having two sites in Lake Champlain in the northeast U.S. put on the list of National Historic Landmarks: the Revolutionary War ships sunk at Valcour Bay and the British warships of the War of 1812 sunk at Plattsburg Bay. Shipwrecks were increasingly understood as historic resources.

In 1963, Colorado became the first state to pass a law specific to the ownership of abandoned shipwrecks on state submerged lands as part of a review of its water rights legislation. In the same year, gold coins washed up on a beach in Florida led to discovery of the 1715 Spanish Plate Fleet. In 1967, Florida passed its shipwreck management law. Indeed, states west of the 98th meridian (approximately the Mississippi river) generally have considered shipwrecks in the context of their water rights regimes while states east of the line, such as Florida, have developed laws and programs in response to specific finds and projects. State programs are based on property law (state title to state land and what is buried in state land) and are part of the state's historic preservation legal regime.

In 1971, after four years of searching, Mel Fisher and his company, Treasure Salvors, Inc., discovered the *Atocha* from the Spanish Plate Fleet of 1622 and in 1975 filed an ownership claim with the admiralty court. In 1978, Cobb Coin, Inc., another of Mel Fisher's companies, went to federal court to claim ownership of the Spanish Plate Fleet of 1715. Thus, treasure salvors and admiralty courts joined sport divers, archaeologists, and states as groups interested in shipwrecks.

In 1979, bills were introduced in the U.S. Congress to give the federal government ownership of shipwrecks buried in state land and on the Outer Continental Shelf. Archaeologists largely settled their internal debate over the scientific merits of nautical archaeology and refocused their attention on the fight with salvors over cultural values and lifestyle issues.

In July 1982, the U.S. Supreme Court awarded ownership of the *Atocha* to Treasure Salvors, Inc. (Florida Department of State v. Treasure Salvors, Inc., 458 U.S. 670 [1982]) because it was sunk beyond Florida state waters. In August 1982, the federal court for the southern district of Florida awarded ownership of the 1715 Plate Fleet to Cobb Coin, Inc. (Cobb Coin Co. v. Unidentified, Wrecked and Abandoned sailing Vessel, 549 F. Supp. 540 [S.D. Fla. 1982]). Because of the threat the Cobb Coin decision posed to the viability of state law, the author of this chapter drafted the Abandoned Shipwreck Act to resolve the conflict of jurisdiction between the federal admiralty courts and state governments, in favor of the states.

Consequently, in 1983, when bills were introduced in the U.S. Congress affirming states' title to abandoned shipwrecks, Congress became the forum for resolution of the federal–state conflict. A series of House and Senate bills and hearings continued through sequential sessions.

Archaeologists and salvors continued their debate but did not control or own the resource as did the court and states. The author brought sport divers into the debate separate from salvors and archaeologists. Testimony was collected from all interested groups.

In 1984, Council of Europe discussions, begun in 1977, resulted in a "Draft Convention for the Protection of the Underwater Cultural Heritage." Continuing the process, in 1988 the International Law Association began work on what became its 1994 "Draft Convention on the Protection of the Underwater Cultural Heritage." Academic and administrative maritime lawyers led many of the discussions in Europe in cooperation with government administrators, sport divers, and archaeologists.

Meanwhile, in 1985, Robert Ballard proved new technologies by locating HMS *Titanic*, which had sunk in the North Atlantic in 1912. Concerns were expressed about the management of shipwrecks in international waters in an era of deep-water technology and discovery. As a result, Congress in 1986 passed the "Titanic Maritime Memorial Act of 1985" in an effort to respect the integrity of the shipwreck and those who had lost their lives. Bilateral international negotiations continue to address management of *Titanic*, and the U.S. admiralty court continues to make decisions about the wreck.

In 1987, SS *Central America*, sunk in 1857, was discovered by another deep-water technology effort, and concern was raised about the management of shipwrecks in the waters of the United States beyond state waters.

The Abandoned Shipwreck Act sailed through the U.S. House of Representatives in the early evening of April 13, 1988, with a final roll-call vote of 340 to 64. Three amendments were offered, debated, and defeated. The bill, which had passed the Senate on a voice vote on December 19, 1987, was signed into law by President Ronald Reagan on April 28, 1988. The passage of the Abandoned Shipwreck Act was a long process of balanced and open public debate. The legislative debate served the important function of educating many people about the shipwreck resource base. As directed by the act, the National Park Service in 1990 published guidelines for the management of shipwrecks.

In litigation between the salvors and the insurance companies over *Central America*, the federal court in 1992 determined that abandonment can be found only on the basis of an express renunciation of ownership, affirmative abandonment, and valid technological possession of the wreck rather than physical possession. In 1998, the Supreme Court remanded a case over *Brother Jonathan* "with clarification that the meaning of 'abandoned' under the Abandoned Shipwreck Act conforms with its meaning under admiralty law," which means that this refers to the passage of time and the level of effort applied to recovery of the shipwreck as measures of abandonment (California et al. v. Deep Sea Research, Inc. et al., U.S. No. 96-1400 S. Ct. [Decided April 22, 1998]).

Meanwhile, in 1996, the United Nations Educational, Scientific, and Cultural Organization (UNESCO) built on the International Law Association's work by beginning meetings on a "Draft Convention for the Protection of Underwater Cultural Heritage," meetings which continue today.

This historical review briefly outlines the introduction of several interest groups to the developing regime for the management of historic shipwrecks. As is shown by the legal history, shipwrecks are the focus of conflicting and evolving principles of maritime, property, and historic preservation laws. Protection of the underwater cultural heritage faces one of the greatest integrative legal challenges in modern times.

DEFINING THE RESOURCE

Before laws can be written about a particular resource, that resource must be defined. To focus the discussion of how to define underwater cultural heritage (a broad range of resources including sites, structures, buildings, artifacts, and human remains together with their archaeological and natural contexts), shipwrecks will be used in examples as the object and site to be considered. Also, shipwrecks are the primary subject of legal challenge in maritime law. The term "shipwreck" will be used to refer to the ship, cargo, and other contents of the vessel and the site of the deposition. As with other examples of material culture, not all shipwrecks are created equal; some are old wet debris, and some are significant historical treasures. Each cultural resource management system must have a way to identify the class of materials to be treated in a special way.

Site Age

Many countries use site age to distinguish sites of historical significance that will be managed with special care from those sites that will be managed differently. The United States, in general, uses 50 years old, but 75, 100, and 150 years old are common. Age often must be further defined, for example as the age when the ship was built or when the ship sunk. When a site is completely buried, age may be difficult to determine without substantial impact to the site.

Site Significance

The concept of "significant" is also common in defining a resource. This concept may be used alone or in combination with age. Whether or not something is of significance is a relative value, determined against a cultural background of time and place. What is considered significant at one time by one group of people may not be considered significant at another time or place. As other countries have done, the United States has developed a process for making decisions about what is significant.

In the United States, the process begins when anyone identifies a resource as having historic potential. That person prepares a document requesting an evaluation by the state administrator and the state board. The state review board membership includes professionals in the fields of architecture, history, and archaeology, and other private citizens. The state administrator makes a recommendation, and the board votes on the significance of the resource. The evaluation is based on published criteria.

The National Register of Historic Places in the United States uses five criteria: the first concerns the resource's integrity of location, design setting, materials, workmanship, feeling, and association. In addition to integrity, resources are (a) associated with events that have made a significant contribution to the broad patterns of history; (b) are associated with the lives of persons significant in the past; (c) embody the distinctive characteristics of a type, period, or method of construction, or that represent a significant and distinguishable entity whose components may lack individual distinction; or (d) have yielded, or may be likely to yield, information important in prehistory or history. A provision is also available for including sites of less than 50 years of age if they are exceptional.

These criteria are generally consistent with the UNESCO "Convention for the Protection of the World Cultural and Natural Heritage 1972," which includes the World Heritage List. Unlike the U.S. National Register, inclusion on the World Heritage List places special responsibilities for protection of the site on a country. The "Draft Convention for the Protection of the Underwater Cultural Heritage" has for some time considered the age criteria of 100 years under water, with a provision for special consideration of heritage under water less than 100 years.

Physical State

In addition to age and significance, the physical state of the shipwreck may be considered. The U.S. Abandoned Shipwreck Act attempted to define the shipwreck resource by the physical condition of being embedded. A ship that is firmly affixed to the land and has not moved for some time, although it may have been more or less exposed at any point in time, is captured by the act. On the other hand, some countries have considered shipwrecks as movable heritage and treat material that is movable differently from material that is not movable.

The shipwreck resource has been defined by age, by significance, and by physical state. The next issue to be addressed is ownership of the resource.

OWNERSHIP OF THE RESOURCE

In the Abandoned Shipwreck Act, the physical state of being embedded also defines the shipwreck as abandoned. The owner of the ship and subsequent shipwreck is recognized in all legal regimes. However, at some point in time, if no effort has been made to recover the property, the original owner or subsequent insurance company owner or salvor may be considered to have abandoned—given up ownership of—the shipwreck, cargo, and other contents of the vessel.

The unavailability of technology has been considered a criterion for abandonment. However, late in the 1990s, the availability of technology for the discovery and recovery of shipwrecks reached a sufficient level of development and became accessible to a broad enough range of people that the availability of technology was effectively dropped as a criterion for defining the resource or ownership of the resource.

Warships and other noncommercial ships owned by a government are a special category of shipwreck. These wrecks are often war graves. Government-owned ships and shipwrecks are considered abandoned only if they are *affirmatively* abandoned: The government must take affirmative action and give notice that a shipwreck is no longer its property. The principle of sovereign prerogative or sovereign immunity refers here to government ownership and evolved as kings consolidated their power. The United States is adamant in support of sovereign immunity as applied to any warship, naval auxiliary, or other vessel, to aircraft owned and operated by a State and sued, at the time it sank, for government, noncommercial purposes, and to their associated contents.

Most nations apply the principle of sovereign prerogative to a broad range of property, onshore and offshore, that the government claims and owns. In most countries, shipwreck material and other cultural resources are the property of the government. In the United States, the finder of the shipwreck material may claim the property against the original owner in admiralty court.

U.S. admiralty courts are awarding ownership of title and intellectual property rights on shipwrecks around the world, potentially coming into conflict with the rights of other nations. Further, the admiralty courts have not been consistent in their interpretation of abandonment, two courts requiring affirmative abandonment and others holding with traditional elements of time and effort. Litigation on the definition of abandonment, and on the ownership of property and intellectual property rights of shipwrecks, and legislative debates in Congress are expected to continue for some time before the issue is resolved. Whoever owns or controls the shipwreck material has the right to sell the material. The application and evolution of maritime law (often called salvage law and which, in the United States, includes the law of finds) to cultural resources is a subject of international debate.

The UNESCO "Draft Convention for the Protection of the Underwater Cultural Heritage" is not expected to address the ownership issue in general but may include language specific to ownership of government shipwrecks. Notably, ownership is determined in part by where the shipwreck is located.

The issue of who owns the bottomland where the shipwreck is located is the subject of national legislation and international conventions or treaties.

Countries as sovereign nations have exclusive right to exercise authority in their internal waters, archipelagic waters, and the territorial sea. The bottomlands of rivers, lakes and other waters are internal waters. Archipelagic waters surround groups of islands. The territorial sea was historically three miles out from shore. The Convention on the Law of the Sea 1982 recognizes the territorial sea of a country as 12 miles. In the territorial sea, a country can apply its domestic legislation in the same way it can apply the law to dry land. Counties can claim ownership of shipwrecks in their territorial sea. The contiguous zone is from the coast to 24 miles out, and coastal country authority is internationally recognized for control of customs, pollution and immigration. Enclosed or semienclosed seas are often the subject of special regional agreements.

From the coast to 200 miles offshore is the "exclusive economic zone," in which the coastal state has control of natural resources for its exclusive economic use. The "outer continental shelf" is a coastal geographic feature where a country can exploit natural resources to its technological capability. The outer continental shelf can extend a few miles to hundreds of miles offshore. The waters beyond the exclusive economic zone and the outer continental shelf are international waters known simply as "the area". Some countries claim territorial sea rights out into the exclusive economic zone. Freedom of navigation is a critical value in all jurisdictions beyond the territorial sea.

The "Convention on the Law of the Sea" recognizes the importance of underwater cultural resources but does not have specific requirements for management of the resource. The current UNESCO meetings on the "Convention for the Protection of the Underwater Cultural Heritage" are addressing management alternatives for the waters beyond the territorial sea. There is precedent for considering coastal state management practice to the limits of the contiguous zone, 24 miles, but the waters beyond have multiple-nation interests. The Convention on the Law of the Sea Article 149 identifies the interested parties as the country of origin, country of cultural origin, and country of historic and archaeological origin. The descriptors recognize that ships are built, captured, and rebuilt, and that they pick up crews and cargoes in one place and travel to another many times before reaching a home port. For ancient shipwrecks, the country of origin may no longer have a modern nation identification.

MANAGEMENT OF SHIPWRECKS AND OTHER CULTURAL RESOURCES

The management of shipwrecks and the other underwater cultural resources is a difficult subject. The International Council on Monuments and Sites (ICOMOS) "Charter for the Protection and Management of Underwater Cultural Heritage" is a critical reference in the development of national and international management regimes. The principles of the charter include in-place preservation where possible, public access, archaeological investigation including a research objective and documentation, and that human remains be treated with respect. Once the jurisdictional questions are answered, the implementation of management systems by separate nations will determine the fate of the shipwrecks.

In summary, historic shipwrecks and underwater cultural heritage are a recently discovered and appreciated resource. Different interest groups have different values and priorities for the resource. These differing values are reflected in the contradictory elements of the laws that govern human behavior on the resource. Although society can only create legal systems to manage behavior and cannot legislate values, for laws to work there must be rule and order. Consequently, the laws are in the process of evolving.

Groups interested in shipwrecks include sport divers, archaeologists, and the historic preservation community, treasure salvors, courts, and administrative governing bodies that are local, national, and international. Sport divers are recreationalists who appreciate and explore the bottomlands. Sport divers discover, report, and preserve many important shipwreck sites. Artifact collecting by some sport divers may be incompatible with ordered collection by archaeologists and exclusive ownership by salvors.

Archaeologists are the archivists for the future. Working with the historic preservation community, they preserve artifacts, archives, and stories for people in the future to study and interpret. Treasure salvors are often dreamers who use finance to structure a lifestyle of adventure and have a goal of vast wealth. Much of the contextual information collected by the archaeologists is not of value to, and so not collected by, the treasure salvor.

Government administrators attempt to manage multiple use demands on public land. Shipwrecks are part of historic preservation programs, and cultural values must be balanced with habitat, fishing, drilling, mining, and other uses. Courts have jurisdiction over ships in modern maritime commerce, and some have claimed jurisdiction over ships that ceased to function as ships many years ago. Government administrators and court systems are sometimes in conflict over control of historic shipwrecks.

The core legal issues being debated are the definition of the resource, who owns the resource, and who owns the bottomland where the resource is located. The parameters of the discussion have been outlined but no conclusions are offered. Historic shipwrecks and the underwater cultural heritage are often defined by age; 50 years old, 75, 100, and 150 years old are common. A determination of significance may define a resource. Significance is relative to a culture and may change over time. A decision process using written criteria is often developed to determine significance. The physical state of "embedded" or "movable" may be used to define the resource.

The ownership of the shipwreck resource is determined by the owners' continued interest in the site. Nations use a principle of sovereign prerogative and immunity to maintain the ownership of warships and other vehicles and, in many countries, to hold for the public good a variety of cultural resources. Technology allows access to shipwrecks almost anywhere by almost anyone.

Warships and other noncommercial ships owned by a government continue to be owned by that government anywhere they wreck until they are affirmatively abandoned. The validity of affirmative abandonment as applied to nongovernment shipwrecks is the subject of current litigation. The ownership of intellectual property rights is also being litigated.

A coastal nation has exclusive rights in the territorial sea and can enforce those rights out to 12 miles. UNESCO international negotiations may result, in that exclusive authority over the underwater cultural heritage being extended to 24 miles. The multination interest in shipwreck sites beyond 24 miles is the subject of the same international negotiations and of decisions by the U.S. admiralty court. UNESCO meetings on the "Draft Convention for the Protection of the Underwater Cultural Heritage" are the current forum for discussions. The role of the U.S. admiralty court may be subject to challenge by foreign nations and the U.S. Congress.

The emotionalism of the debates about ownership and management of shipwrecks and underwater cultural heritage often reaches the fury of the storms that sunk ships and crews. Unfortunately, in carelessly destroying the past, people destroy part of their present and part of the future. One can only hope that the legal and management decisions now being made will reflect the same ingenuity and skill required for the successful building and sailing of a ship.

REFERENCES

Benedict on Admiralty, 1980, pp. 1–2. Mathew Bender, New York.

Giesecke, Anne G., 1999, The Abandoned Shipwreck Act through the Eyes of its Drafter. *Journal of Maritime Law and Commerce* 30:1–7.

_____, 1991, *Historic Shipwreck Resources and State Law: A Developmental Perspective*. Ph.D. dissertation, Catholic University of America (Washington D.C.). University Microfilms, Ann Arbor.

_____, 1988, The Abandoned Shipwreck Act: Affirming the Role of States in Historic Preservation. *Columbia-VLA Journal of Law & the Arts* 12:379–389.

_____, 1987, Shipwrecks: The Past in the Present. *Coastal Management Journal* 15:179–195.

_____, 1987, The Future Underwater. In *The Sea Remembers*, edited by Peter Throckmorton, pp. 226–227. Weidenfeld & Nicolson, New York.

Gould, Richard, 1983, *Shipwreck Anthropology*. University of New Mexico Press, Albuquerque.

Prott, Lyndel V., and O'Keefe, P.J., 1984, *Law and the Cultural Heritage*. Vol. I, *Discovery and Excavation*. Professional Books Limited, Great Britain.

Shallcross, D., and Giesecke, A., 1983, Recent Developments in Litigation Concerning the Recovery of Historic Shipwrecks. *Syracuse Journal of International Law and Commerce* 10:371–404.

Throckmorton, Peter, 1960, Thirty-three Centuries Under the Sea. *National Geographic* 117:682–703.

Chapter **35**

Education
The Power Tool of Underwater Archaeology

SHELI O. SMITH

INTRODUCTION

Education is the mightiest tool archaeologists possess. More than any other facet of the discipline, how we wield the tool defines the level of archaeological professionalism for any site. No longer is educational interpretation relegated to the afterthought category. The power of underwater archaeology has always been and will continue to be defined by the strength of our ability to reach out and touch the public—young and old—with fascinating discoveries and sound interpretations. Thousands of tourists visit the *Vasa* (www.vasamuseet.se/lankar/links.html), *Mary Rose* (England) (www.maryrose.org), and *Roskilde* (Denmark and Norway) ships (vikingskipshuset@iakn.uio.no) each year, while hundreds of tourists veer off the beaten path to see the reconstructed hull of the fourth-century Kyrenia merchantman on the island of Cypress, and the reconstructed stern of the Dutch East Indiaman, *Batavia*, in Freemantle (Australia) (www.ma.wa.gov.au/Museum/march/hartog/hartog-intro.htm). All of these archaeological finds are on exhibit for the world to see and a number of fine educational programs are presented by the host institutions. The fact that underwater archaeologists have always sought out a public forum for our endeavors may explain why 98 percent of the world's maritime museums have underwater archaeologists on staff. The encouragement is that alternative edu-

Sheli O. Smith, Long Beach City College, Maritime Archaeology Certificate Program, Long Beach, CA 90808.
International Handbook of Underwater Archaeology, edited by Carol V. Ruppé and Janet F. Barstad. Kluwer Academic/Plenum Publishers, New York, 2002.

cational programming is one of a number of global trends that have spurred new innovative educational programs for archaeology.

"PARALLEL SCHOOLS"

The world is growing smaller because of real-time communication, while the amount of information we need to pass on to our children is growing by leaps and bounds. It has been evident for years that learning needs to be spread out across several formats and not just be limited to classrooms. Museums, already known as the touchstones of a culture, were natural formats to enlist in the growing educational demands on global societies. By the early 1980s, the Association of American Museums noted that museums were often cited as the "parallel schools" of more traditional academia (www.aam-us.org/index.html). Subjects such as history, art, and music were rapidly disappearing from the curricula of primary and secondary educational institutions. Museums and interpretive centers picked up the slack, creating innovative ways to inculcate children of all ages with the wonder and excitement that these subjects can generate. By moving history outside the mainstream curriculum, museums and centers have been able to blend material culture, historical documents, and the processes of archaeology to present fuller, more multidimensional packets or units of information.

This need has been a boon for the public, museums, and the history and anthropology professions. Because of the educational needs of our country, and indeed the whole world, medium-sized and small museums have flourished around the globe. These new institutions and the older, established centers have made gigantic strides to become more interactive, more educationally inclined, and more user-friendly. This is also true of professional historians and archaeologists. More and more archaeological sites and their historic components are being interpreted and presented the moment the expedition gets underway. Museums and centers are dedicating more staff and resources to the explanation of archaeological and interpretive processes. Professional organizations, such as the International Congress of Maritime Museums (www.icom.org), the Society for American Archaeologists (www.saa.org), the Council of American Maritime Museums, the National Maritime Museum Association (www.maritime.org) and the Society for Historical Archaeologists (www.sha.org) regularly present symposia focused on education. The Society for American Archaeologists has a highly active educational caucus. Numerous publications now available through the Internet provide resources and programs on archaeology. This concentrated effort brings a multidimensional approach to exhibits and programming, making them more alive, more imaginative, and more likely to leave a lifelong impression on a visitor.

EDUCATION, ARCHAEOLOGY, AND THE INTERNET

Even a quick search of museum web sites provides a huge list of educational programs for maritime museums and interpretive centers around the globe. Some list units for teachers to down-load and use in their classrooms. Two of the easiest web sites to locate are Archaeology on the Net (www.serve'com/archaeology) and Archaeology Resources for Education (www.interlog.com/~jabram/elise/archres.htm). And don't miss the local institutions that often list their schedules. South Street Seaport Museum (New York) (www.southstseaport.org) lists all its youth programs well in advance, as does the

National Maritime Museum at Greenwich (England) (www.nmm.ac.uk). Even the floating complex museum of HM *Bark Endeavour* has an extensive educational web site (www.winthrop.webjump.com/cooklink.html).

INNOVATIVE EDUCATIONAL PROGRAMMING

The size of an institution and its ability to promote itself via cyberspace are not the sole criteria for use in judging quality educational programming. Some of the most innovative exhibits and classroom units were created by small or medium-sized institutions. In a few cases, whole communities have put their collective weight behind creating rich and complex exhibits. Such was the case in the small community of Mendocino in Northern California where three museums, the community college, the town paper, the local theater group, and even the local brewery joined together to present the whole story of the California Gold Rush wreck of the *Frolic*. The results were spectacular and awed even the largest of sister institutions. In most instances, these presentations are exciting not simply because of the overwhelming use of new technologies, but rather because of a new way of looking at and interpreting data with which we are already familiar.

Many of these new presentation formats rely on age-old formulas that combine touching, listening, and observing. Simple means of presentation sometimes bring highly technical tools and complicated processes to an accessible level of understanding for the general visitor. Climbing up to stand within a cutaway, deep-diving Newt Suit at Vancouver's Maritime Museum (www.vmm.bc.ca), allows visitors a moment of common experience with the scientist who actually climbed into the suit and sank into the great depths of the ocean. Donning empty soda-pop bottles for pretend scuba tanks at Texas' Corpus Christi Science and History Museum (www.thc.state.tx.us/journeys/museums.html), transforms youthful visitors into full-fledged scientific argonauts. Running down to the surf to help shipwrecked survivors at the Florida State Museum's Interpretive Center transports students back in time (www.dos.state.fl.us/dhr/musuem/c_r.html). In each case the key to success was interaction. The technology and processes were not laid out in long, tedious text panels. Rather, each exhibit set up a moment of common experience that simply required the participation of the visitor to turn it into a reality. If a picture is worth a thousand words, then an experience is of exponential value.

CREATING THE EXPERIENCE

Since their inception, interpretive centers have capitalized on the use of "hands-on" learning or *creating the experience*. Archaeologists of North Carolina's Kure Beach Unit (www.ah.dcr.state.nc.us) have taken advantage of the state's plethora of beached hulks. Mud, kids, and old shipwrecks are a potent mix. Utilizing the "real thing" to create an enjoyable learning experience turns kids into archaeological sleuths who work their way through the math of measuring, the language of yesteryear's documents, and the geography of trade networks. These types of experiences go well beyond a simple history or they blend all the disciplines and classroom lessons into a worldly experience. Yet, hands-on learning is not limited to resource-rich environments. Not all places have the spectacular resources of North Carolina at their back doors. Many have created sites. Vermont's maritime museum at Lake Champlain (www.lcmm.org) buried a small

Figure 35.1. LBCC students learn to map underwater.

rowboat outside the center and set up an excavation program for visiting groups. Students are moved through all the phases of an excavation, from dirt to lab to interpretation. Once the site has been excavated—presto!—it can be reburied and readied for the next group. Indiana University's underwater education program (www.indiana.edu/~scuba/artificial.html) created a shipwreck in the college swimming pool. Everything is present except the sediment. Each of these projects are interactive. The visitor does not stand apart from the processes. Instead, each participant is given a role, and the common experience of the professional archaeologist is forged with the public. The students get a chance to feel the exhilaration of having successfully unraveled the mystery. The feeling of success enfranchises the youth of our nations, giving them ownership of their own histories and stewardship of our fragile past (Figure 35.1).

PACKAGED PROJECTS

Even in institutions where large-scale projects may not be possible or practical, a number of packaged projects have been successfully launched, many of which were created outside the institution that utilizes them. South Australia's State Archaeology Office (www.flinders.edu.au) created a program that can be crated and shipped to participating schools. Tom Oertling (OertlingT@aol.com) created both a scale-model hull puzzle and a wreck site puzzle that have been successfully employed by museums around the United States. Another creative entrepreneur of educational programs for middle-school level is Marco Meniketti, who created the "shipwreck in the fish tank" and utilized common computer programs like Hypercard™ to help students easily create databases about shipwrecks. Bill Lees of the Oklahoma Historical Society (www.ok-history.mus.ok.us)

developed "Dig Bingo" to encourage students in the identification of site features. Again, the key to success in each program has been interaction: Students are drawn into the mystery or the puzzle and shown the way to solve the problem.

COMPUTER TECHNOLOGY

Museums are also moving into the technological realm of computers. Interactive multimedia programs in museums allow in-depth information presentation. Newport Harbor Nautical Museum (www.newportnautical.org), uses still images, videos, and sound to explore the histories of each model on display. Underwater archaeology is well-suited to this medium of presentation, since there are so many facets to an archaeological expedition. Both touring exhibits, *The Wreck of the Julia Ann* and *Pandora*, travel with touch-screen interactive computer programs that encourage visitors to explore the subjects in depth, presenting collaborative information different from what is displayed in the cases or on the panels.

In addition to programs available at museums, a number of computer programs can be taken home. Widely distributed is the game Yukon™ that focuses on the 1890s gold rush of Alaska. Another popular computer quest is Trading Game™, produced and distributed through the Australian National Maritime Museum (www.anmm.org.au). Both games are trade-network oriented and valuable tools in the understanding of shipping and cultural contact. These games can be explored at the museum, in school and at home, giving them a lasting versatility and an appeal to all ages. For the more traditionally inclined, there is always Iron Men and Wooden Ships™, a board game for the ages.

ADULT EDUCATION

Luckily for all of us, learning does not end at graduation from primary and secondary school. Numerous courses at museums around the world teach the fundamentals of underwater archaeology at the adult or continuing education levels, and many are directed toward scuba divers. South Carolina (www.clas.sc.edu) has one of the largest and best organized "hobby diver" programs in the world. On the same scale is the Sub Aqua Clubs of British Columbia and South Africa, where enthusiastic divers assist local museums in finding and studying shipwrecks. Also, recreational scuba training programs of the world promote education about shipwrecks and underwater archaeology. Professional Association of Diving Instructors (www.padi.com), Scuba Schools International (www.ssiusa.com), National Association of Underwater Instructors (www.naui.com) and British Sub Aqua Club (www.ukdiving.co.uk) have continuing curricula that explore archaeological shipwreck sites as nonrenewable resources. Probably the best known and most widely used is the multilevel program developed in England by the Nautical Archaeology Society (naspon@aladdin.co.uk). All these programs combine education with hands-on experience, and academic or government representatives combine their knowledge with the talents of recreational divers to explore, understand and enhance their nation's fragile underwater archaeological resources.

COLLEGE AND UNIVERSITY PROGRAMS

Students who want to pursue the field of underwater archaeology can find a number of college and university programs around the globe. Some present maritime courses

Figure 35.2. Professors use underwater video to help students understand underwater tasks and procedure.

embedded in existing history or anthropology programs, while other institutions provide full accredited maritime programs. Europe has a number of colleges that provide courses in underwater archaeology, most notably that of St. Andrews in Scotland (www.st-and.ac.uk/intitutes/sims/courses.htm), where students can obtain both masters and doctoral degrees. North and South America also have numerous programs in the subject, with the best known programs at Texas A&M University (www.nautarch.tamu.edu), which provides both masters and doctoral degrees, and East Carolina University, (www.ecu.edu), which offers masters degrees. Australia boasts several programs, with the most active at Flinders University (www.flinders.edu.au). In the Middle East, Haifa University in Israel has led the way in maritime studies.

Each of these institutions produces students who move into museums and interpretive centers, bringing with them new and innovative ways to promote underwater archaeology (Figure 35.2).

CONCLUSION

In this brief survey, it is easy to see that education regarding underwater archaeology is all around us. It exists at all levels of formal education and is neatly woven into the curricula of the parallel schools represented by museums and learning centers. It has the potential to reach young and old. It is pervasive and it is powerful. It is there for the asking.

However, we have only just begun to explore the potential of this powerful tool. There is a great deal more to do. If we hope to protect the remaining fragile resources of our maritime past, we must seize this powerful tool and use it to the advantage of everyone, encouraging people to explore the past, enhancing our explanations of the archaeology we expose and enriching the historical interpretations we present. We must lay out our educational tools on the planning boards of every archaeological site. We must include educators in an already extended family of specialists. By following this recipe we will succeed in giving our rich maritime heritage its just due.

Chapter **36**

Ethics and Underwater Archaeology

IAN RODERICK MATHER
AND GORDON P. WATTS JR.

INTRODUCTION

Professional ethics play a defining role in underwater archaeology and submerged cultural resource management. Ownership, preservation, management, access, and investigative obligations associated with the resource base are problems at the heart of professional ethics. Ethical dictums are not stagnant but change and evolve in the face of current archaeological issues and challenges. Archaeological ethics are also influenced, if not defined, by state and federal legislation, regulation, and, frequently, litigation.

As pressures on a finite resource base increase, issues of professional ethics, legislation, regulation, education, and public benefit will become even more critical. Therefore, it is important to examine the interface between archaeological ethics and the issues and laws that help define them. Although ethical questions affect underwater and terrestrial archaeologists throughout the world, the primary focus of this chapter is on archaeological ethics in the United States.

Ian Roderick Mather, Assistant Professor, Maritime History and Underwater Archaeology, Department of History, University of Rhode Island, Kingston, Rhode Island 02881. **Gordon P. Watts Jr.**, Institute for International Maritime Research, Inc. Washington, North Carolina 27889.

International Handbook of Underwater Archaeology, edited by Carol V. Ruppé and Janet F. Barstad. Kluwer Academic/Plenum Publishers, New York, 2002.

ETHICS

Archaeologists operate under a code of ethics, variations of which are prescribed by virtually all major archaeological societies and professional organizations in the United States. These codes are outlined in a single document or incorporated within an organization's bylaws. The American Anthropological Association (AAA) made the first significant step in developing ethical criteria for American anthropologists: In 1971, the association published a code of ethics, Principles of Professional Responsibility (PPR), which identified ethical responsibilities of archaeologists and anthropologists to the people they studied, the public, students, other anthropologists, sponsors and employers, and governments. Although the PPR identified a number of ethical guidelines, it failed to address some specific, critical archaeological issues (American Anthropological Association, 1971).

Since then, other professional organizations have developed similar ethical guidelines. The Society of Professional Archaeologists (SOPA), which later was reconstituted as the Register of Professional Archaeologists (ROPA), has a Code of Ethics and a separate Standards of Research Performance. First published in 1976, SOPA's Code of Ethics defines members' responsibilities to the public, colleagues, employees, students, employers and clients (Society of Professional Archaeologists, 1991a).

The Archaeological Institute of America (AIA) also has a brief code of ethics, developed in 1991, and a more substantial Code of Professional Standards that defines members responsibilities to the archaeological record, the public, and colleagues (Archaeological Institute of America, 1991). The Society for Historical Archaeology (SHA) includes a code of ethics within its bylaws that specifically covers archaeological work both on land and underwater (Society for Historical Archaeology, 1990).

But it is the Society for American Archaeology (SAA) that has conducted the most recent inquiry into professional ethics (Wylie, 1994; Wylie and Lynott, 1995). Since 1961, the SAA has required members to adhere to a brief published statement of professional ethics. Its executive board did not approve a more comprehensive document until 1996. That document, entitled Principles of Archaeological Ethics, was divided into sections on stewardship, accountability, commercialization, public education and outreach, intellectual property, public reporting and publication, records and preservation, training, and resources (Society for American Archaeology, 1996).

Dozens of other archaeological societies and organizations in the United States and elsewhere have codes of ethical behavior. The Institute of Field Archaeologists (IFA), in Great Britain, for example, has a Code of Conduct constituted under five principles: ethical behavior, conservation/preservation, methods, dissemination, and treatment of others (Institute of Field Archaeologists, 1985). Professional organizations outside archaeology but with related interests also have codes of professional ethics. The International Council of Museums (ICOM) has a code that includes sections dealing with collections, directly relevant to the archaeologist's work (International Council of Museums, 1986).

Archaeological codes of ethics are certainly not uniform. They vary in length, detail and, to some extent, content. A few central common elements, however, identify the main principles and features of these order. These are equally applicable to both terrestrial and underwater research.

Professional archaeologists recognize that archaeological sites are finite and vulnerable. They concede that archaeological resources are diminishing as a consequence of both deliberate and accidental damage and destruction and, to a lesser extent, archaeological investigation. Professional archaeologists and many amateur archaeologists feel an ethical responsibility to conserve and preserve the archaeological resource base, to argue publicly for the investigation of sites using acceptable archaeological methods, and to disturb sites only when armed with appropriate research questions, equipment, personnel, and funding.

Archaeologists generally accept that the knowledge acquired from sites is part of society's common heritage and that the benefits and knowledge derived from investigating our past should, therefore, be made available to everyone. From this, they extract an ethical responsibility to disseminate data, to share it with their colleagues and the public, to publish reports and present papers in a timely manner, and to ensure long-term access to data and collections for future generations. This generally means conserving and curating artifacts to ensure access to the collection in perpetuity. For this reason, archaeologists oppose dissemination of collections and commercialization of artifacts. Private ownership limits public and academic access to archaeological finds. They generally point to the 1970 UNESCO *Convention on the Means of Prohibiting and Preventing the Illicit Import, Export and Transfer of Ownership of Cultural Property* as a minimal standard for preventing the commercial exploitation of archaeological finds (United Nations Education, Scientific, and Cultural Organization, 1970).

Archaeology is the study of people, their society, culture, and behavior as evidenced through physical remains. Archaeologists feel an ethical responsibility to treat those remains with respect and dignity and to consult with the descendants of the people being studied.

Archaeological codes of conduct invariably include ethical responsibilities that are not specifically archaeological in nature—for example, an obligation to work within the law. That responsibility, however, says little about archaeology as a discipline. Presumably, all scholastic endeavor should operate within these parameters. Similarly, codes of conduct invariably contain statements about professional interpersonal relationships: an obligation, for example, to treat colleagues with respect, advance the interests of students, and be nondiscriminatory in dealings with others. Again, these say little about archaeology as a discipline. They are, at the very least, standards that should apply to all academicians.

Allied to codes of archaeological ethics, most professional organizations also subscribe to standards for professional research. Professional ethics and professional standards, however, should be kept separate. In general, professional standards should be confined to the practice of such things as correct methodology, archaeological procedure, conservation, and dissemination, rather than the moral basis for these procedures. Because of its development as a response to the problems associated with contract archaeology in the United States, SOPA's/ROPA's Standards of Research Performance is one of the most extensive documents concerning professional standards. SOPA's standards require members to investigate previous research thoroughly, develop a research design, ensure the availability of expertise and facilities, and comply with the law. They also require members to execute a research plan in accordance with appropriate archaeological methods, identify and record the provenience of finds, document features, keep intelligible records, conserve recovered materials, and publish findings in a timely, professional manner (Society of Professional Archaeologists, 1991b).

In general, underwater archaeology has adopted the ethical guidelines established by investigators on land. The principles behind the discipline apply equally to either environment. Nevertheless, underwater archaeologists do place special emphasis on several principles. Most professionals strongly oppose the commercialization of finds and division of artifact collections. In addition, underwater investigators keenly feel the need for preservation, conservation, and protection of the underwater cultural heritage. The reasons are clear, in that these are the issues and challenges most commonly faced by field professionals. The relationship between ethics and current issues is critical in defining and understanding the ethics of archaeology.

ETHICS AND ISSUES

Principles of Professional Responsibility

It would be wrong to think of archaeological ethics as stagnant. Many moral precepts evolve over time, primarily in response to new cultural and political environments, and to different issues affecting the discipline from one decade to the next. The major archaeological organizations' codes of ethics illustrate this phenomena, none more so than the American Anthropological Association's Principles of Professional Responsibility (PPR), the first comprehensive statement governing archaeological ethics in the United States.

The PPR is a direct product of issues raised by the Vietnam War era. During the 1960s and early 1970s, the press reported, and anthropologists feared, that various United States governmental agencies (particularly the Department of State, Central Intelligence Agency, and Pentagon), were funding and contracting with universities and anthropologists to conduct clandestine research in Southeast Asia and South America. The alleged purpose of this work was to support United States intelligence gathering, insurgency or counterinsurgency operations. Anthropologists feared for their discipline's reputation and for the possibilities of future research abroad. They were also concerned about the ethics of governments that tried to change the cultures and political environments of the peoples being studied, and about the element of secrecy involved. Many anthropologists feared that the resulting research would be clandestine in nature and closed to public scrutiny and peer review (Hill, 1987; Woodall, 1994).

Camelot Project. These concerns were first raised in 1965, most notably in relation to the so-called Camelot Project, a project that arose from fears that Chile was moving toward a Marxist government—fears that were eventually realized in 1970 with the election of Salvador Allende Gossens, the first democratically elected Marxist leader in the western world. In response to this perceived threat, the United States Army developed a working relationship with American University in Washington, D.C., to study Chilean society and culture. Many scholars identified this as a thinly veiled attempt to gather data designed to support the existing Chilean government.

Vietnam War. The Vietnam War, particularly the period of most direct United States involvement from 1964–1973, exacerbated these fears. It was widely believed that anthropologists were used in Southeast Asia to gather intelligence data and spy for the United States. In addition, a number of researchers working in Thailand in 1970 were supposedly implicated in counterinsurgency operations designed to support the Royal Thai government (Hill, 1987; Woodall, 1994).

The respective merits of these fears and accusations need not concern us here. Whether or not the allegations can be substantiated, the American Anthropological

Association's PPR was in large measure a direct result of the ethical debates, fears, and issues raised by the Vietnam War era. Those issues drove the archaeological ethics agenda. The proof is not hard to find. A reading of the PPR reveals a profession deeply troubled by secret and clandestine research. The document states that "no reports should be provided to sponsors that are not also available to the general public"; that "anthropologists should not communicate findings secretly to some and withhold them from others"; that "anthropologists should undertake no secret research or any research whose results cannot be freely derived and publicly reported"; that "anthropologists should avoid even the appearance of engaging in clandestine research, by fully disclosing the aims and sponsorship of all research"; and that "anthropologists should attempt to maintain such a level of integrity and rapport in the field that, by their behavior and example, they will not jeopardize future research there." Clearly the PPR is a product of its times (American Anthropological Association, 1971).

Pot-Hunters and Native Peoples' Concerns. The Vietnam War was not the only issue that helped define anthropological and archaeological ethics in the 1970s. The collection and marketing of artifacts by rapidly increasing numbers of "pot-hunters" also caused great alarm. The scale of this activity varied, as it still does today, from small-time individual collectors to large-scale, organized commercial operations. The damage to sites and the sale of artifacts caused great concern among archaeologists and anthropologists. Since then, archaeologists have tried to stop pot-hunting by supporting the passage of protective legislation, appealing to courts of law, and influencing public opinion. They also have declared the practice abhorrent to their discipline's moral code.

But it was not just archaeologists that decried pot-hunting. At about the same time, the latent objections of Native Americans to this activity came to the fore. Much pot-hunting in the United States was directed against the burial places of Native Americans, and the aim was to rob graves of funerary goods, many of which carried considerable commercial value. Naturally, the living descendants of these ancient people found the collection of funerary goods objectionable. The problem, for archaeologists, was that Native American groups also objected to the excavation of grave sites by archaeologists. For much of archaeology's history, professional researchers had enthusiastically excavated and recovered the remains of indigenous peoples and their funerary goods. In their objections to this activity, Native Americans were joined by groups elsewhere, especially indigenous Australians. The living descendants of those people being studied soon started to demand that both the human remains and associated artifacts be returned to the descendants for reburial. The increasing sensitivity to this issue by archaeologists resulted in changes of the archaeological codes of ethics and ultimately improved relations with indigenous peoples. The SAA's Principles of Archaeological Ethics states that "Native Americans and other ethnic, religious, and cultural groups...find in the archaeological record important aspects of their cultural heritage" (Society for American Archaeology, 1996).

Perhaps more significantly, the World Archaeological Congress (WAC), at its meeting in 1990, adopted the Congress' First Code of Ethics: Members' Obligations to Indigenous Peoples (World Archaeology Congress, 1990; Zimmerman, 1994). Without doubt, pot hunting and reburial issues have affected and will continue to affect archeological codes of ethics.

Ethical Issues in Underwater Archaeology

Underwater archaeology has its own set of ethical issues, some of which are extensions of debates conducted by our colleagues on land, others more uniquely defined by the marine environment. Underwater archaeologists face their own pot-hunters: commerical salvors and treasure hunters. If there is one issue that has shaped the ethics of underwater archaeology, it is the rights of the commercial salvor and treasure hunter. The exploration, investigation, and recovery of artifacts from historic shipwrecks are philosophically contentious. For many years, the two leading groups of shipwreck investigators, underwater archaeologists and professional treasure salvors, have vied for jurisdiction over the cultural material deposited in the world's rivers, lakes, and oceans. Each group comes armed with its own philosophical justification, and, as we shall see later, legal defense.

Underwater Archaeologists vs. Salvors.   Underwater archaeologists generally contend that archaeological and historic shipwrecks and their associated material must be protected and preserved, and sometimes retrieved and studied. Any investigation should be accompanied by an appropriate research design and should be carried out in accordance with strict archaeological standards. Qualified personnel responsible for sharing their findings with their professional colleagues and the public at large should supervise fieldwork. In addition, artifacts must be conserved and curated to permit further study. Archaeologists favor federal or state jurisdiction over vessels lost in territorial waters.

Professional treasure salvors generally see attempts to limit the recovery of artifacts from historic shipwrecks as a bureaucratic infringement on private enterprise. Salvors invariably claim that the archaeologist's "normal" work is dependent on government funding, and they question whether hard-pressed taxpayers should sponsor research that private investors are willing to undertake. In any case, they argue, government funding will never be sufficient to locate, excavate, and curate all the world's shipwrecks. In short, there are sufficient wrecks to go around.

In recent years, some salvors have become interested in recruiting archaeologists and replicating their scientific methodology. Archaeologists, they argue, have a moral obligation to help salvors document, recover, and conserve legally acquired artifacts.

Archaeologists worry about such an arrangement, which they see as being fraught with ethical and practical dangers. For the most part, professional archaeologists doubt that their work can be accomplished in an intensely profit-driven environment. They fear, justifiably, that the first casualty in such efforts would be their scrupulous scientific methodology, jettisoned to save a project in peril just as mariners throughout history have thrown cargo overboard to save their vessels. Many archaeologists also object to the sale of artifacts and the destruction of the collection, which has been the inevitable consequence of commercial salvage operations (Goodheart, 1999; Koerner, 1999).

Some observers have argued for a common sense solution to this impasse, based on consensus and compromise. Such a solution would require the interested parties to come together and settle their differences; each would have to give a little ground in order to reach an understanding and agreement. There is a precedent for cooperation between archaeologists and those who threaten the resources. Archaeologists routinely work for construction companies and recover archaeological data prior to building and development. In fact, this is the basis of rescue or contract archaeology conducted in the United States and elsewhere. Archaeologists work alongside construction companies, even though the companies' activities damage archaeological sites. However, many archaeologists fail to see a parallel with treasure hunting. Unlike commercial salvage, development plans are not based on realizing a profit specifically from the location and destruction of archaeological resources.

Although there have been some well-meaning attempts to develop a constructive dialogue between archaeologists and treasure hunters, the two groups still appear to be oceans apart. Underwater archaeologists see a distinction between construction and salvage. At the heart of treasure salvage are violations of the archaeological code of ethics: the failure to keep the collection together, the sale of artifacts, and the destruction of the resource base.

It must be remembered that salvage operations can be one of the most destructive actions imposed upon historic shipwrecks. Parties interested in salvaging a vessel or its cargo are sometimes unconcerned with the vessel's historic value and the archaeological record that a shipwreck preserves. The use of cutting tools and explosives can completely destroy a vessel and eliminate any possibility of documenting the archaeological record preserved in the vessel's remains. Furthermore, even the most "responsible" treasure salvage damages the resource base in the interests of private enterprise rather than public good. In short, the danger presented by construction and development, presumably for the good of society and the economy, justifies rescue archaeology, whereas the danger presented by treasure salvage, for the good of private individuals and investors, does not warrant any abrogation of professional ethical responsibilities.

There is little reason to believe that tension between archaeologists and salvors will subside. Whereas once the competing groups directed their attentions only to shallow-water and coastal sites, the contest now has moved onto the high seas and into deeper waters, where there is less possibility of monitoring and regulation.

Advances in Technology.   Advances in deep-ocean technology have propelled this trend. Deep-sea tow vehicles, submersibles, and remote operated vehicles (ROVs) are forcing the ocean to give up deep water secrets. But among shipwreck investigators, it is the salvors who have generated the financial resources, skills, and perhaps even inclination, to use this technology.

The professional archaeologist, to some degree already left at the dock, clearly has to respond to these ethical and practical problems. For in the stable cold waters of the ocean depths undoubtedly lie some of the world's most precious submerged archaeological sites. Each site salvaged without consideration of its archaeological context is one more site lost to the scientific community and the public forever (Dumas, 1962; Bascom, 1976). Archaeologists have responded to these threats by calling for an international convention on the protection of the world's underwater cultural heritage. A draft UNESCO convention already has been circulated, aimed at removing cultural resources from salvage law and protecting deep-ocean archaeological sites (United Nations Education, Science and Cultural Organization, 1998).

On November 2, 2001, the UNESCO General Conference adopted the UNESCO Convention on the Protection of Underwater Heritage. While it seems likely that the Convention will be ratified, there is little chance that it will significantly help protect cultural resources in deep water. A number of nations either voted against the Convention or abstained. The Convention remains controversial and probably unenforceable.

Underwater archaeologists also face another ethical and technological dilemma. While sophisticated deep-ocean technology remains tantalizingly out of reach, the equivalent tried and tested shallow-water systems are becoming ever more accessible to other searchers, including small-time treasure hunters and sport divers. Small- and medium-sized operators can now acquire new or used side scan sonars, magnetometers, and positioning systems that were once prohibitively expensive. This undoubtedly increases the pressure on the world's finite shallow-water archaeological sites (Mather, 1999). Within this commercial and ethical quagmire, underwater archaeologists grapple with yet more moral problems. For example, how much public access should there be to underwater sites? Should sports diving be permitted?

Vandalism.   Vandalism constitutes an important threat to submerged cultural resources. Many important wrecks lie in shallow waters within easy reach of the diving public. Small-time collectors of portholes, bottles, and other artifacts frequently recover objects from the seabed with little or no concern for provenience or context. Relic hunters often use highly destructive techniques. There have been numerous confirmed and unconfirmed reports throughout the world that relic hunters have pillaged shipwrecks, completely destroying the archaeological and historical evidence they preserve. In 1994, relic hunters who recovered and marketed artifacts from the USS *Congress* in Hampton Roads, Virginia, were prosecuted by the U.S. government. However, successful prosecution of such cases is often difficult and expensive. Without outside pressure from archaeologists and others interested in the preservation of our cultural heritage, some federal and state agencies are hesitant to investigate or prosecute such cases. It seems unlikely, for example, that the relic hunters who stole two cannon from an 18th century wreck being investigated by Southern Oceans Archaeological Research in Pensacola, Florida, will ever be found and prosecuted.

Volunteers and Public Participation.   While damage to archaeological sites by some sport divers is indisputable, it is also true that others have generously volunteered their time and energy to many archaeological projects. Many amateur organizations have adopted codes of behavior that promote conservation and management of submerged cultural resources.

The fact that archaeological codes of ethics require public participation and access to the archaeologist's work presents field professionals with both practical and ethical dilemmas. While public access is required and mandated, that same access also facilitates damage to irreplaceable cultural resources.

One solution is the development and use of public programs to monitor, regulate, and redirect sport diving. For example, Florida, North Carolina, Wisconsin, Michigan, and New York permit and encourage access to historic shipwrecks through underwater parks, with moorings, trail lines, signs, and guidebooks. Sport divers are invited to visit the wrecks but not to touch or remove artifacts. In Rhode Island, the Rhode Island Marine Archaeology Project even trains sport divers to take part in archaeological projects. The uses and extent of these and other public programs are described elsewhere in this volume.

The extent of protection as well as the definition of an archaeological site is also controversial. How old should a site be before it becomes part of our collective cultural heritage? Are logs containing 19th-century saw marks worthy of protection? Questions such as these reflect upon the archaeologist's moral obligations but are not easily answered. Nevertheless, archaeologists have an ethical responsibility to address them and inform the public what they believe constitutes an archaeological site. They also have an moral obligation to identify resources that are most in need of protection, and to target their efforts accordingly. As a profession, archaeologists should, perhaps, identify their priorities, explain the basis for those priorities, and ensure the protection and investigation of relevant resources.

Philosophical Approaches

A series of ethical issues face any underwater archaeologist about to begin an on-site investigation. The philosophical approaches of archaeologists are by no means uniform. Not all archaeologists approach sites with the same theoretical premises. In North America, archaeology is generally taught and practiced within an anthropological framework: Archaeological sites are approached with specific questions about broad and general problems. For these researchers, the questions and problems are crucial, providing both the context and the justification for disturbing a site.

But the anthropological framework and tradition is by no means universally accepted. Some archaeologists, particularly those working in the classical world and some working underwater, approach sites as unique historical entities. All data from the site, not just data relevant to answering a particular anthropological question, is deserving of careful consideration and retrieval. These investigators, sometimes referred to as historical particularists, fear that the questions asked of a site will change from one investigator to another, from one generation to the next. Only if archaeologists recover all archaeological data to the best of their abilities will sites be preserved for future generations (Gould, 1983).

The intellectual jousting over philosophical approach between anthropological generalists and historical particularists will undoubtedly continue. At the extremes, some generalists seem to suggest that their approach is ethically acceptable, while the other is not; that their theoretical framework is mandated by a moral imperative, while the other represents a violation of professional ethics. Guarding the other outpost, some particularists claim to recognize the folly that can be associated with grandiose research designs formulated without a sound basic knowledge of history, the specific details of technological evolution and the impacts of practical patterns of human behavior. Without a basic understanding of the specifics that fortunately attract the interest of particularists, they argue, it would be difficult to develop or evaluate a hypothesis that relates those issues to broad patterns of human behavior.

As archaeologists prepare to excavate, they frequently face another hotly debated issue: whether a particular site *should* be investigated. Is the site worth disturbing and ultimately destroying in order to gather the archaeological data? Should the site be left alone in anticipation of future improved questions, techniques, and technology?

These questions are especially acute when the site is in no imminent danger. It is certainly logical and ethical to preserve sites for future generations of archaeologists, but taken to its logical conclusion, this argument would dissuade archaeologists from ever beginning an excavation. If we always wait for improved techniques and technology, the archaeological information contained within important sites might never be retrieved. Each generation would postpone excavation in deference to the next. In the meantime, some sites may be lost and the development of more effective methodologies and techniques of data recovery could be stifled. Until recently, nondisturbance work at *Monitor* National Marine Sanctuary, for example, only presided over the natural degradation of the site.

Anthropological archaeologists are particularly cautious about disturbing a site, while historical particularists feel less restricted. The latter's methodological framework calls for the recovery of all archaeological data, not just what is necessary to answer predetermined, specific questions. For the historical particularist, the whole site is preserved on paper and in the conservation lab to the best of the archaeologist's ability and is, therefore, capable of contributing to all manner of research questions in subsequent years.

Even assuming the archaeologist decides to excavate, further ethical problems invariably arise. How strict is the archaeologist's moral imperative to curate all finds? Is it necessary that all artifacts be conserved and curated, or can some be redeposited on the site? What about museum collections? Innumerable maritime museums have artifacts in their collections that have been recovered without archaeological provenience. Can such artifacts be used for comparative analysis, or would that simply legitimize the destruction of archaeological sites (Johnston, 1993)?

Contract Archaeology. Some archaeologists are even nervous about contract or rescue archaeology. They fear that the time limits and constraints associated with this kind of work will inevitably lead to an erosion of archaeological standards and scientific methodology. In such circumstances, the discipline becomes weaker, and precious archaeological resources are undermined. Others see in contract archaeology the fulfillment of an archaeologist's obligation to rescue and preserve archaeological data in peril. Since contractors have a legal and ethically justifiable obligation to impinge on the resource base, it would be foolish for archaeologists not to mitigate the damage.

Nevertheless, there are practical and ethical problems associated with contract archaeology. Because contract archaeology is driven by developmental priorities rather than historical or archaeological issues, archaeologists often conduct research under considerable pressure. While the standards for research and professional qualifications are well-defined by professional organizations, the essential issue becomes one of balancing the requirements of legislation and regulations, the standards defined and adopted by the Department of Interior, and the economic realities of a competitive capitalist system. Although legislation and regulations promulgated to protect archaeological resources are specific, they represent minimum standards. Contract archaeologists must compete within the system to provide services that meet the minimum standards at the most competitive price. Perhaps not surprisingly, that can create serious problems.

In spite of the standards for personnel and research and the strong commitment to ethical standards shared by most professional archaeologists, economic priorities and inadequate oversight has contributed to the acceptance of less-than-ideal research and management activities. One factor in the quality of research and management activity is the level of interest, knowledge, and commitment of federal and state government agency staff responsible for identifying and managing submerged cultural resources, which can vary widely from agency to agency and from state to state. While many federal agencies and states have personnel and programs to manage submerged cultural resources, others have not made that commitment.

Many federal and state bureaucrats take their historical and archaeological responsibilities seriously, but others find it more difficult to justify the expense and commitment to protecting the surviving physical remains of our past activities. It is not unusual for their staffs share, or be required to share, those sentiments. In some cases, personnel responsible for primary oversight of an agency's historical and cultural resource responsibilities have little or no education or training in the field. That makes it difficult for them to provide adequate oversight and review. Although there is a review process for contract activities that involves many well educated, trained, and committed professionals, politics, economics, and even interest can play a role in determining if research and management activity meets minimal standards.

The quality and reliability of research and management activity can also be a factor of the level of education, training, and ethical commitment of contract field personnel. Like the federal and state bureaucrats who supervise their activities, archaeologists undertaking contract research and management projects have varying perspectives on the quality of work that must be performed.

Although most firms maintain high standards for both personnel and contract research, others weigh economic and political factors more heavily and are willing to justify compromises that fail to provide adequate protection for and treatment of historical and cultural resources. In all but the most blatant cases, it is difficult to take to task those willing to conduct substandard work. Professional organizations rely on peer commitment to enforce their standards. Disciplinary action could cause retaliatory legal action that might consume a great deal of time and expense. Although the system provides considerable latitude for diverse opinions and varying levels of ethical commitment, it functions reasonably well within the confines of politics and economic reality.

ETHICS, ISSUES, AND THE LAW

Questions having to do with the law and litigation provide yet another context for viewing archaeological ethics. The relationship between the law, professional morality, and archaeological issues is central to any discussion of professional ethics. While the law has helped define archaeological ethics, archaeological ethics have also helped determine the nature and scope of cultural resource legislation. Professional ethics, archaeological issues, and the law, therefore, are all interrelated.

The archaeologist sometimes makes a distinction between what is legal and what is ethically acceptable. The two do not necessarily dovetail. One can easily imagine a series of on-site activities conducted by archaeologists or others that are totally legal but also might be morally reprehensible. Nevertheless, protective legislation is absolutely crucial to archaeology. Outlawing destructive activities facilitates the protection of cultural resources and helps marshal public opinion. Conversely, the failure to make reprehensible activities illegal makes it more difficult to protect important archaeological sites.

Federal legislation pertaining directly or indirectly to archaeological and historic resources spans a period of more than 80 years. Taken as a whole, this legislation shows a steady trend toward placing responsibility for preserving and conserving the archaeological and historical heritage of the United States under the umbrella of federal control. The most important laws pertaining to the protection of cultural resources are described elsewhere in this volume, but they include: the Antiquities Act of 1906; Historic Site Act of 1935; Submerged Lands Act of 1953; Reservoir Salvage Act of 1960; Historic Preservation Act of 1966; National Environmental Policy Act of 1969; Archaeological Resource Protection Act of 1979; and the Abandoned Shipwreck Act of 1987.

Archaeological issues and problems undoubtedly have contributed to the passage of much of cultural resource legislation. The problems associated with pot-hunting and looting, for example, contributed to the passage of the 1906 Antiquities Act and more recently to the Archaeological Resources Protection Act of 1979. While only superficially related to underwater sites, the hotly debated issues of reburial and repatriation contributed to the Native American Grave Protection and Repatriation Act of 1990.

Just as topical issues have contributed to the making of laws, laws have certainly contributed to the making of issues. Existing laws, whether new or ancient, have contributed significantly to a number of contentious archaeological issues. The structure of admiralty law, for example, has shaped the treasure-salvage debate. Admiralty law includes the law of salvage and the law of finds. Salvage law has a rich and important history of its own dating back to the ancient world: It rewards mariners for rescuing vessels in marine peril and returning the ships and their cargo to the stream of commerce. The rescuer or salvor is entitled either to a maritime lien on or ownership of the vessel and its cargo, depending on whether or not the owners have abandoned the vessel. In this way, property and life at sea are protected. The law of finds—"finders, keepers"—in which ownership of an abandoned vessel passes to the first person to take possession, supplements salvage law. Neither law, however, makes a distinction between vessels lost recently and those of historic and archaeological importance. If unrestricted by other legislation, treasure salvors can legally "rescue" and salvage historic shipwrecks and sell off the associated cultural material with no regard for the archaeological significance of their finds (Sweeney, 1999).

Archaeologists and others have sought ways to remove historic shipwrecks from salvage law. Such efforts have an ironic twist, for to a large extent the roots of archaeology underwater lie in the modern salvage of material from shipwreck sites. Collectors, museums, historians, and, ultimately, archaeologists were attracted to shipwreck salvage projects by the exciting nature and scope of material recovered from sunken vessels. That initial interest in shipwreck material fostered the realization that the remains of sunken vessels could also preserve an important archaeological record associated with life on board the vessel, its cargo, the technology and cultural preferences that produced it, and the architectural and construction record associated with the vessel itself. With the systematic investigation of a Bronze Age shipwreck at Cape Gelidonya, Turkey that began in 1960, George F. Bass, then a student of classical archaeology at the University of Pennsylvania, demonstrated that archaeologists could work as effectively underwater as they could on any terrestrial site.

The realization that shipwreck archaeology really could contribute significantly to our better understanding of the past corresponded with the passage of state and federal legislation and litigation designed to control salvage activity. Initially, that salvage activity was associated with material from Spanish Plate Fleet wrecks in Florida and Civil War shipwrecks in North Carolina.

Federal attempts to control unrestricted salvage of historic shipwrecks took several forms. In the first instance, the federal government attempted to assert ownership of vessels lost in waters within its control. In 1978, however a landmark case destroyed the federal government's claim to ownership of shipwrecks beyond immediate coastal waters. In *Treasure Salvors, Inc. v. The Unidentified Wrecked and Abandoned Sailing Vessel*, 569 F.2d 330 (5th Cir., 1978) the federal government tried to assert its ownership of the Spanish treasure ship *Nuestra Senora de Atocha*. Although the *Atocha* was 40 miles off the coast of Florida, the government argued that the Outer Continental Shelf Lands Act (OCSLA) gave the United States control over the seafloor in that region, and that the Antiquities Act protected artifacts located on lands owned and controlled by the federal government. The Fifth Circuit ruled against the federal government, stating that OCSLA applied only to mineral rights and did not give the government the necessary control as required under the Antiquities Act (Zander and Warmer, 1996).

Abandoned Shipwreck Act

The failure of the government to assert ownership over historic shipwrecks in this case, and its limited success in others, led to calls for new legislation and a new strategy. In 1987, Congress passed the Abandoned Shipwreck Act (ASA). This legislation placed under governmental control historic shipwrecks located within territorial waters. The legislation first asserted federal ownership over the wrecks, then transferred title to the states. Only those vessels abandoned and embedded in the seabed fell under the legislation. The framers of the ASA were clearly motivated by archaeological ethics and the need to protect submerged cultural resources. Under the Abandoned Shipwreck Act, the Department of the Interior and National Park Service were required to issue a set of guidelines to help states manage shipwrecks in their waters (Giesecke, 1999).

The ASA should have ensured the removal of historic vessels from the jurisdiction of admiralty courts, but litigation in the 1990s has threatened to undermine the act's intentions. The decision by the Fourth Circuit Court in *Columbus America Discovery Group v. Atlantic Mut. Ins.*, 974 F. 2nd at 472 (4th Cir., 1992) introduced the possibility that an owner might have to abandon a vessel actively and expressly before it could pass to the state's control under the ASA. This threat to the act's intentions and to submerged cultural resources intensified with *Deep Sea Research, Inc. v. The Brother Jonathan*, 883 F. Supp. 1343 (N.D. Cal. 1995), aff'd, 89 F.3d 680 (9th Cir., 1996); here, not only was the notion of express abandonment applied, but the constitutionality of the ASA came into question. The case eventually went to the Supreme Court, which, by taking a narrow definition of the case, excused itself from deciding many of the crucial issues (Pelkofer, 1996; Giesecke, 1999; Jones, 1999).

Set against the long standing traditions of admiralty law, acts of Congress, the briefs of highly experienced lawyers, and the judgments of courts up to and including the Supreme Court of the United States, the archaeologist's code of ethics appears humble and insecure. As Chief Justice O'Connor penned the unanimous decision of the Supreme Court in the *Brother Jonathan* case (a decision that could have set back the protection of submerged cultural resources at least 20 years), she certainly did not pick up something akin to the American Anthropological Association's PPR. Archaeologists should not be misled into overestimating the power of their codes of ethics or into underestimating the significance of the law and litigation. The primary safeguards must be: (1) clear cultural resource legislation that minimizes the chance of misinterpretation by the courts; and (2) effective public education programs.

For the archaeologist, one of the most important implications of salvage law is that treasure salvage can be conducted in a way that is totally legal but which categorically violates the archaeologist's code of professional ethics. Some states and archaeologists have responded positively to these challenges and in one case have used salvage law to their own advantage. Driven by D.K. Abbass, Ph.D. of the Rhode Island Marine Archaeology Project, and with guidance from state underwater archaeologist Charlotte Taylor, the state of Rhode Island recently used salvage law, the ASA, and state historic preservation legislation to claim title to all wooden, nonmotored shipwrecks in a 2 × 3 mile section of Newport Harbor. Archaeologists may soon wish to add an ethical obligation to hire a good admiralty lawyer to the list of moral imperatives.

The law, particularly changes to the law, can influence archaeological ethics. The creation of SOPA is a case in point. By the mid-1970s, demands for archaeological investigation, spawned by federal legislation, created a dimension in archaeology that expanded rapidly outside the traditional scholarly academic field and outside the bounds of its censure. The influx of new "archaeologists" and the volume and quality of work related to federal legislation created demands for more specific standards for research and clearly defined ethics. In 1974, SAA formed a committee to address the pressing issues associated with standards and ethics in archaeology. The committee recommended establishing a National Registry of Professional Archaeologists. After consideration by the membership, and upon the advice of council, SAA determined that a registry would have to be a separate entity.

Therefore in 1976, the members of that committee formed SOPA (Society of Professional Archaeologists) to establish and enforce professional standards. That same year, SOPA produced a code of ethics that it enforced through a formal grievance procedure. SOPA, which later became the Register of Professional Archaeologists (ROPA), also developed a program of professional certification for archaeologists.

CONCLUSIONS

Archaeological ethics are protective by nature. They lay down patterns of acceptable practice that protect the good name of the discipline, shield academic and field professionals, and defend archaeological resources. The physical remains of our maritime heritage are nonrenewable: unless they can be preserved and scientifically documented, they are lost. Only professionals with strong and confident codes of ethics can defend and protect submerged cultural resources.

This is not to say that archaeological ethics are unresponsive to change. For many years, the archaeologist's code of ethics changed and evolved in response to the discipline's debates and issues. Through member societies, archaeologists should continue to refine and enforce the ethical cannons of the profession.

Archaeological ethics and issues are also tied to legislation and litigation. Federal, state, and international law have helped to define archaeology's moral precepts, just as archaeology has helped shape some of the current cultural resource legislation. Archaeological ethics and the law, however, do not live in complete harmony. Archaeologists still consider some legal behavior to be morally reprehensible. Archaeologists should continue to lobby lawmakers and inform the public of the need to protect the physical remains of our past. The ultimate goal must be to eliminate the gap between what is legal and what is right.

Imposing sanctions on archaeologists who violate codes of ethics is difficult. As a result, personal integrity among professionals is critical. All archaeologists should carefully weigh the impact of their activities on the resource base in terms of state of the art in scientific investigation, contribution of research to enhancing our understanding of the past, and preservation of the physical evidence of our heritage for future generations. If we are to receive the maximum benefit from the physical evidence of our past, we must be effective in preserving and managing those resources. Archaeological ethics will continue to be a central component of this task.

REFERENCES

American Anthropological Association, 1971 [adopted] 1986 [amended], *Statement on Ethics, Principles of Professional Responsibility.* Washington, D.C.

Archaeological Institute of America, 1991, Code of Ethics. *American Journal of Archaeology* 95:285.

Bascom, Willard, 1976, *Deep Water, Ancient Ships: The Treasure Vault of the Mediterranean.* Doubleday, Garden City.

Dumas, Frédéric, 1962, *Deep Water Archaeology.* Routledge and K. Paul, London.

Giesecke, Anne G., 1999, The Abandoned Shipwreck Act through the Eyes of Its Drafter. *Journal of Maritime Law and Commerce* 30(2):167–173.

Goodheart, Adam, 1999, Into the Depths of History. *Preservation.* 51(1):36–45.

Gould, Richard A., editor, 1983, *Shipwreck Anthropology.* University of New Mexico Press, Albuquerque.

Hill, James N., 1987, The Committee on Ethics: Past, Present and Future. In *Handbook on Ethical Issues in Anthropology*, edited by Joan Cassell and Sue Ellen Jacobs. Special Publication No. 23, American Anthropological Association, Washington, D.C.

Institute of Field Archaeologists, 1985 [ratified], 1997 [revised], *By-Laws of the Institute of Field Archaeologists, Code of Conduct.* IFA, University of Reading, Reading.

International Council of Museums, 1986, *ICOM Code of Professional Ethics.* International Council of Museums, Paris.

Johnston, Paul Forsythe, 1993, Treasure Salvage, Archaeological Ethics and Maritime Museums. *International Journal of Nautical Archaeology* 22(1): 53–60.

Jones, John Paul, 1999, The United States Supreme Court and Treasure Salvage: Issues Remaining after Brother Jonathan. *Journal of Maritime Law and Commerce* 30(2):205–227.

Koerner, Brendan I., 1999, Race for Riches. *U.S. News and World Report* 4 (October):45–50.

Mather, Roderick, 1999, Technology and the Search for Shipwrecks. *Journal of Maritime Law and Commerce* 30(2):175–184.

Pelkofer, Peter, 1996, A Question of Abandonment. *Common Ground* 1(3/4):64–65.

Society for American Archaeology, 1996, *Principles of Archaeological Ethics.* Washington, D.C.

Society for Historical Archaeology, 1990, *Article VII, Society for Historical Archaeology Bylaws.* Society for Historical Archaeology, Tuscon.

Society of Professional Archaeologists, 1991a, Code of Ethics. In *Guide to the Society of Professional Archaeologists.* Society of Professional Archaeologists.

_____, 1991b, Standards of Research Performance. In *Guide to the Society of Professional Archaeologists.* Society of Professional Archaeologists.

Sweeney, Joseph C., 1999, An Overview of Commercial Salvage Principles in the Context of Marine Archaeology. *Journal of Maritime Law and Commerce* 30(2):185–203.

United Nation Education, Scientific, and Cultural Organization (UNESCO), 1970, *Convention on the Means of Prohibiting and Preventing the Illicit Import, Export, and Transfer of Ownership of Cultural Property.* Cultural Heritage Division, UNESCO, Paris.

_____, 1998, *Draft Convention on the Protection of Underwater Cultural Heritage.* Doc. CLT-96/Conf. 202/5. UNESCO, Paris.

Woodall, J. Ned, 1994, Comments on Archaeological Ethics: Past, Present, Future. *Public Archaeology Review* 2(1):9–10.

World Archaeological Congress, 1990, *World Archaeological Congress: First Code of Ethics (Members' Obligations to Indigenous Peoples).* World Archaeological Congress, Barquisimeto, Venezuela.

Wylie, Alison, 1994, Principles of Archaeological Ethics: A Preliminary Report on the Reno Workshop Ethics in Archaeology. *Public Archaeology Review* 2(1):11–13.

Wylie, Alison, and Lynott Mark J., 1995, Overview: The Work of the SAA Ethics in Archaeology Committee. In *Ethics in American Archaeology: Challenges for the 1990s*, edited by Mark J. Lynott and Alison Wylie, pp. 25–28.

Zander, Caroline M., and Varmer, Ole, 1996, Closing the Gaps in Domestic and International Law. *Common Ground* 1(3/4):61–70.

Zimmerman, Larry J., 1994, Indigenous Peoples and the World Archaeological Congress Code of Ethics. *Public Archaeology Review* 2(1):5–8.

Chapter 37

Public Programs

An Overview

GORDON P. WATTS JR.
AND IAN RODERICK MATHER

INTRODUCTION

Archaeologists recognize that archaeological sites are an integral part of our collective heritage. Professional archaeologists also acknowledge that the privilege of investigating an archaeological site carries with it certain obligations, which include conducting state-of-the-art research, publishing the results, and preserving the data and cultural material generated by investigation. Professional archaeologists also recognize that the privilege of investigation carries responsibilities to the public. Those obligations include publishing in nonacademic journals, supporting education and training programs for the avocational, and providing opportunities for the public to have controlled access to the archaeological record and the cultural material that it comprises.

One of the most important commitments professional archaeologists should adopt is to support public education and training programs. Such programs provide important public access to resources that are indeed our common heritage and include those designed to accommodate individuals and amateur organizations, provide access to precollegiate school groups, and disseminate information to the public at large. Although never adequately supported, public education has long been recognized as a critical element in preserving resources and securing support for cultural resource protection, management, and research.

Gordon P. Watts Jr., Institute for International Maritime Research, Inc. Washington, North Carolina 27889. **Ian Roderick Mather**, Assistant Professor, Maritime History and Underwater Archaeology, Department of History, University of Rhode Island, Kingston, Rhode Island 02881.

International Handbook of Underwater Archaeology, edited by Carol V. Ruppé and Janet F. Barstad. Kluwer Academic/Plenum Publishers, New York, 2002.

Figure 37.1.

Most states with submerged cultural resource programs have allocated some of their available resources to public programs, a major portion of which is used to educate the general public or to coordinate diver education, training, and underwater activity. In virtually every state where personnel are responsible for the management of submerged cultural resources, they have developed formal and informal presentations designed to promote resource preservation, protection, and management. Several federal agencies have presentations and public programs associated with their submerged cultural management responsibilities.

Unfortunately, few agencies have resources or personnel to develop and maintain a highly organized, systematic program of public education. Equally unfortunate is the fact that underwater archaeologists and submerged cultural resource managers have not developed successful and influential educational programs such as those produced by terrestrial archaeologists, museologists, and educators. With a few exceptions, we have not cultivated a powerful public interest in archaeology under water.

UNDERWATER SHIPWRECK PARKS AND PRESERVES

One excellent example of that interest is the public support for and use of shipwreck parks and preserves. Several state and federal agencies have established underwater parks, preserves, and sanctuaries to protect shipwreck remains and encourage their educational and recreational use by the diving public.

Florida

John Pennekamp Coral Reef State Park.   In Florida, where underwater archaeology frequently has been confused with treasure salvage during the past three decades, several public programs provide a recreational and educational interface with shipwrecks and underwater archaeology. The first underwater park in the United States was established in the Florida Keys: John Pennekamp Coral Reef State Park was created in 1960 to preserve a large section of the coral reefs off Key Largo. Although shipwrecks in the park originally were not a major consideration, today they are an important part of the Pennekamp educational and recreational diving program (Miller, 1989).

Urca de Lima Preserve.   Underwater Archaeological Preserves, established by the Florida Division of Historical Resources in Tallahassee under the direction of state underwater archaeologist Roger C. Smith, Ph.D. provide divers with opportunities to visit and learn about several historic shipwreck sites. Preserves are nominated by local citizens and developed by local community support organizations working with division staff and local governments.

The first underwater archaeological preserve was established in Fort Pierce, Florida, on a vessel from the 1715 Plate Fleet identified as *Urca de Lima*. Although the wreck site had been disturbed extensively by salvage activity, and cannon associated with the vessel had been recovered in 1928, remains of the lower hull and ballast survived. In 1986, St. Lucie County Historical Commission and Florida Division of Historical Resources worked together to have replica concrete cannons placed on the wreck along with a buoy and a bronze plaque identifying the site as a preserve. The wreck was opened to divers the following year. Divers visiting the site are not permitted to disturb the wreck or recover material associated with the vessel. An illustrated brochure available locally and from the Division of Historical Resources provides an interpretation of the vessel's history and archaeological significance (Miller, 1989; Smith 1991).

San Pedro Preserve.   The success of the *Urca de Lima* Underwater Archaeological Preserve led the Division of Historical Resources to develop additional shipwrecks for public access. The second was another Spanish Plate Fleet wreck, a vessel from the 1733 fleet wrecked off the Florida Keys. A survey of 11 of the 1733 wrecks was carried out by students from Florida State University and Indiana University, who ranked the *San Pedro*, a Dutch-built vessel wrecked off Islamorada, as the most appropriate candidate for a new preserve. Like the *Urca de Lima*, the *San Pedro* wreck site contained both intact hull structure and ballast. Cement cannons were used to replace previously salvaged gun tubes, and moorings and a historical plaque were placed near the wreck. An illustrated brochure interprets the vessel's history and the significance of shipwrecks and their archaeological importance for visitors. Since the park was opened in 1989, the wreck has been visited by hundreds of divers and has been used by Boy Scouts and area students and teachers in educational programs (Smith, Finegold, and Stephens, 1990; Smith, 1991).

Five additional wrecks also have been developed as Florida underwater archaeological preserves. The *City of Hawkinsville*, a late-19th-century sternwheel steamer sunk in the Suwannee River, became the third preserve, and the USS *Massachusetts*, a Spanish–American War battleship sunk off Pensacola Bay, was developed as the fourth. The remains of the steamer *Copenhagen*, lost off Lauderdale-by-the-Sea, and the steamer *Tarpon*, sunk off Panama City, became the fifth and sixth preserves (Smith, 1991; Smith, 1997). A seventh preserve was established in 2000 around the *Half Moon*, formerly the ocean racing yacht *Germania*, which lies in shallow water off Key Biscayne (FDHR, 2000b).

City of Hawkinsville Preserve. *City of Hawkinsville* was developed in conjunction with the staff and students from nearby Bronson High School. They helped map the well-preserved remains and prepare literature to provide the public with a historical background for the vessel and an interpretation of the history of steam navigation on the Suwannee River (Smith, 1991).

USS Massachusetts Preserve. Pensacola-area divers nominated the hull of USS *Massachusetts* (BB-2) as a candidate for a preserve. The *Massachusetts* lies off the entrance to Pensacola Bay where the 350-foot ship was sunk in 1921 to serve as an artillery target. The exposed remains of the battleship have been mapped, and historical research has been carried out to facilitate interpretation of the wreck and its history. An underwater guide to the site makes it easy for divers to identify features of the vessel and navigate along the wreck (Smith, 1991).

Copenhagen Preserve. The wreck of the steamer *Copenhagen* was cosponsored as a preserve by the Division of Historical Resources, Department of Environmental Protection, Broward County Department of Natural Resource Protection, and Marine Archaeological Council of Broward County. The *Copenhagen* was enroute from Philadelphia to Havana with a cargo of coal when the 3279-ton ship stranded on the reef off of Pompano Beach in 1900. Although the cargo was salvaged, the vessel was declared a total loss, and the hull eventually broke apart. Today, the remains of the *Copenhagen* lie on a sand bottom adjacent to a limestone ledge in 16–31 ft of water (FDHR, 1993).

Tarpon Preserve. The remains of the steamer *Tarpon* lie in the Gulf of Mexico west of Panama City. The *Tarpon* operated between Mobile and several Florida ports on the gulf including Pensacola, Panama City, Apalachicola, and Carrabelle. In August 1937, the heavily loaded steamer cleared Pensacola for Panama City. As weather deteriorated during the night, the 50-year-old vessel took on water; just before dawn, it finally sank. Today, its remains lie in 95 ft of water. The Department of Environmental Protection, Bay County government, and the Museum of Man in the Sea sponsored the *Tarpon* preserve. Brochures for the *Copenhagen* and *Tarpon* enhance diving on the wrecks by providing insight into both the history of the vessels and the nature of material surviving at each site (FDHR, 1996).

Half Moon Preserve. *Half Moon*, formerly *Germania*, was a chrome nickel-steel ocean racing yacht built in 1908 by the Krupp Germania-Werft in Keil, Germany, to compete in the annual races there and in the international regatta at Cowes in England. Taken as a prize of war by Great Britain in 1914, the vessel led a series of different lives, ending up in Miami as a floating saloon and later as a fishing barge before it was sunk off Key Biscayne. Nominated by a local Miami diver, *Half Moon* is the latest of Florida's underwater archaeological preserves (FDHR, 2000a).

North Carolina

USS Huron Preserve. In North Carolina, the Underwater Archaeology Unit (UAU) of the Division of Archives and History has developed one shipwreck park and is considering several others. The first park encompasses the wreck of the USS *Huron*, built in 1874; it sank off Nags Head on North Carolina's Outer Banks in 1877, during a fierce storm. Because the wreck was accessible from the beach, it has been frequented by divers for many years, and much of the cultural material associated with its remains has disappeared (Friday, 1991).

In 1987–1988, Joe Friday, a lifeguard for the town of Nags Head and a graduate student in the Program in Maritime History and Nautical Archaeology at East Carolina University, explored the wreck, mapped the exposed remains and recovered loose material associated with the vessel. This work was carried out in conjunction with UAU Director Richard Lawrence and the UAU staff and with assistance from Sandy Sanderson, director of ocean rescue at Nags Head. Historical research associated with Friday's thesis on the USS *Huron*, his map of the wreck remains and material recovered from the site have been used in developing educational exhibits associated with the wreck that are on display locally and in a beachfront gazebo. The site map and a brief history of the ship have been presented in a brochure distributed to divers and the general public in the Nags Head area and can be obtained from UAU. The brochure carries a message about submerged cultural resource preservation and an invitation to explore the remains of the USS *Huron* without disturbing the wreck (Friday, 1991; Lawrence, 1989).

Fort Fisher State Historic Site.   From 1994 to 1997, the authors, students of ECU, and staff of UAU investigated Civil War shipwrecks in the vicinity of Fort Fisher State Historic Site. The survey, funded by grants from the National Park Service Battlefield Protection Program, was designed to locate, identify, and document vessels associated with maintaining and running the blockade of Wilmington.

Fort Fisher, a massive earthwork fortification adjacent to New Inlet, served as the most effective deterrent to Union efforts to close the Cape Fear River to Confederate commerce until it was captured by an amphibious assault in January 1865. Because Fort Fisher and other fortifications kept the port of Wilmington open, swift steam-powered blockade-runners could carry valuable military and civilian cargoes into the Confederacy from neutral ports including Halifax, Bermuda, Nassau, and occasionally Havana. Although the Union blockade failed to eliminate Confederate maritime commerce, the risks of blockade-running were high, and more than 30 steam-powered blockade runners were lost while attempting to run into Wilmington. Several are within a mile of the remains of Fort Fisher. Today, the remains of these shipwrecks represent unique features of one of the most significant battlefields of the American Civil War (Watts, 1985).

Researchers initiated reconnaissance investigations of the blockade-runners *Condor*, *Modern Greece*, *Stormy Petrel*, and *Arabian* as well as USS *Aster*, USS *Flambeau*, and USS *Peterhoff* during the summers of 1995–1997. Each shipwreck was relocated, and material exposed on the bottom surface at each site was documented. Documentation consisted of mapping and, where possible, photographing sites. Data generated by the survey provided new insight into the nature and scope of the archaeological record associated with each vessel. The condition of these wrecks and the wreck-site environments have been assessed to determine their potential for development as additional underwater parks. Development of the wrecks of the blockade-runners *Modern Greece* and *Condor* and the blockade ships USS *Peterhoff* and *USS Aster* as underwater park preserves is currently being considered.

Modern Greece, run ashore in 1862, and *Condor*, lost in 1864, represent both the slow, traditional transoceanic steamers first employed to run the undeveloped blockade early in the war and the faster, highly specialized steamers built to run the more effective steam blockade developed late in the war. Considerable hull structure and machinery of the screw-propelled *Modern Greece* and the paddlewheel-equipped *Condor* survive intact and exposed on the bottom.

The remains of USS *Aster* lie in the same general area as *Modern Greece* and *Condor*, but *Aster*'s wood hull has disappeared, leaving only the boiler, engine, propeller and shaft, anchors, and a windlass. The remains of USS *Peterhoff* lie almost three miles offshore and southeast of Fort Fisher; like *Modern Greece*, most of its hull survives along with the boilers, engines, propeller and shaft, anchors, and a steam capstan.

Although visibility is often limited on all of the Fort Fisher sites, there are excellent days to explore the wrecks. Using data from the NPS-funded survey, UAU is considering developing underwater slates with a plan of the wreck, information about each significant feature, and a historical synopsis of the vessel. Because the wrecks of USS *Aster* and USS *Peterhoff* belong to the U.S. Navy, a decision about the development of these sites for public access will be made in conjunction with the Naval Historical Center. All Fort Fisher shipwrecks are protected by state and federal legislation, and disturbance or removal of material without a permit is illegal.

South Carolina

South Carolina Institute of Archaeology and Anthropology. In South Carolina, one of the earliest organized public programs was designed to regulate the recovery of submerged cultural resources by sport divers. South Carolina's Underwater Antiquities Act of 1976 provided the South Carolina Institute of Archaeology and Anthropology (SCIAA) with authority to regulate divers recovering natural and cultural material from state-owned bottomlands. Under the direction of Alan Albright, SCIAA developed a hobby license program permitting divers to conduct small scale, noncommercial artifact and fossil collecting and required periodic reports on their activities, and it prohibited all powered mechanical dredges, lifting devices, or remote sensing equipment.

Hobby diver reports provided SCIAA with valuable information on the nature and location of submerged cultural resources. Bob Densler reported the Mepkin Abby wreck to SCIAA in 1970, and a decade later SCIAA and volunteers documented the wreck remains (Wilbanks, 1982). Hampton Shuping reported the historic 18th-century Browns Ferry vessel that subsequently was excavated, recovered, and preserved. Both SCIAA director Albright and Ralph Wilbanks maintained close contact with hobby license divers, which led to the identification of a group of volunteers who worked with SCIAA on research and management projects (Albright, 1985).

By 1987, SCIAA personnel, working under the direction of Christopher Amer, determined that South Carolina's Underwater Antiquities Legislation needed revision. After an internal review, SCIAA introduced three types of artifact recovery licenses, each with specific restrictions (South Carolina Antiquities Act of 1991 -S.C.C.L 54-7-210).

Sport Diver Archaeology Management Program. In addition, a Sport Diver Archaeology Management Program (SDAMP) was established to extend the program's educational–recreational component and to facilitate a more structured and extensive role in supervision of the hobby license diver activity. The program's staff was to serve as a quick-response field team to make initial assessments to SCIAA of sites located by sport divers. Sport divers continued to discover and report many more sites to SCIAA through the 1980s and 1990s, but SDAMP provided them with more guidance in mapping, recording, and interpreting sites. Hobby reports were more closely scrutinized for useful and accurate information (Harris, 1996a, 1996b).

In 1989, Lynn Harris took over responsibility of SDAMP through the Charleston field office of SCIAA and addressed the need to offer underwater archaeology field training courses and workshops to the public. Harris developed an educational program that introduced training courses focusing specifically on South Carolina's local resources, legislation, and management needs (Harris, 1996, Part II) and offered an option of dual certification through the British Nautical Archaeology Society (NAS). Harris helped create an avocational underwater archaeology manual and then developed a newsletter to keep the public informed about educational opportunities (Harris, 1991; Harris and Naylor, 1996-revised edition). Completion of the educational program qualified divers to work with SCIAA personnel on research projects. Other SCIAA trained divers have initiated their own predisturbance projects that were supervised by SDAMP (Amer, 1994; Amer and Steen, 1988; Harris, 1991; Harris, Moss, and Naylor, 1993).

Ashley and Cooper Rivers Underwater Heritage Trails.   As part of South Carolina's public education mandate, two interpretive trails accessible by divers or paddlers have recently been created under the direction of SDAMP. The trails, on the Ashley and Cooper Rivers, showcase remnants of the state's riverine and coastal heritage and are comprised of the remains of sailing ships and steamboats, ferry and plantation landings, and a modified environment associated with colonial rice agriculture and other water-control devices. The sites represent the period from the early English colonial period, from the 1700s to the early 20th century. The trails traverse the low-country ecology of swamps and marsh, with river denizens including ospreys and bald eagles, alligators, and an abundance of fish. The initiative to create these trails occurred through SCIAA, but the construction of each trail relied heavily on volunteers, local businesses, and other state agencies (Harris, 1999a; Harris and Spirek, 2000).

Most of the wrecks on the Ashley River Trail are visible only at low tide. Eight sites, including examples of colonial-period sailing boats, a 19th-century steam tug, and early 20th-century motorboat, form part of the trail and illustrate diverse aspects of maritime history on the Ashley River as well as settlement patterns and transportation networks. Wharves and workboats form an integral economic connection between the land and the inland waterway. Steamboats link the rivers to estuarine and coastal trade. The canoe trail interpreters focus on shipbuilding technology, architectural adaptations to the inland environment, frontier settlement, and local economy, such as fur trade and phosphate mining. The trail is self guided, although ranger-guided tours can be arranged through Old Dorchester State Historical Park and Middleton Place situated on the riverbanks. Information slates are available from both these locations. Canoe trails are combined with tours to two historic sites: Dorchester, a colonial village, and Middleton, a rice plantation. Both link history on land with the waterway (Harris, 1996c).

For four centuries, the Cooper River provided a major avenue of inland trade and transportation for the coastal city of Charleston. One of the most complex plantation systems in colonial and antebellum America developed along the shores of the Cooper and relied on the river to ship out agricultural products and naval stores and bring in manufactured goods imported through Charleston. During the American Revolution and Civil War, the Cooper was the scene of considerable military activity.

As a consequence of the intensity of trade, transportation, and fishing activity, the Cooper River contains one of South Carolina's richest collections of submerged cultural resources. The Cooper River Underwater Heritage Trail was sponsored by SCIAA, National Recreational Trails Program in cooperation with South Carolina's Department of Parks, Recreation and Tourism, U.S. Department of Transportation, Federal Highway Administration, and several local agencies, firms, and organizations. Despite black water diving conditions, it is also one of the most popular sites for recreational diving (Harris, 1990; Harris, 1999b).

Currently, six sites comprise Cooper River Underwater Heritage Trail, including a British Revolutionary War shipwreck burned at Strawberry Ferry by American Colonel Wade Hampton, the Mepkin Plantation vessel, the remains of a large sailing vessel, a barge, a ferry landing, and a dock (Harris, 1999b).

To facilitate diving on the trail, mooring buoys have been placed on each of the sites. Private and dive charter vessels are encouraged to tie up to the buoys and avoid the hazard of anchoring and damaging wrecks. Divers enter the water at the buoy and follow a guideline leading to the underwater site marker and the vessel remains or other features. Waterproof slates with maps of the shipwrecks and historical information about the Cooper River are distributed by area dive shops and charter operations. As with most states, submerged cultural resources in South Carolina waters are protected by state law (Harris, 1999a; SCIAA, 1999; Spirek and Harris, 2000).

Maryland

Maryland Maritime Archaeology Program.   In Maryland, responsibility for submerged cultural resource management lies with the Maryland Maritime Archaeology Program (MMAP), established by the Maryland Historical Trust in 1988. Under the direction of Susan Langley, MMAP has worked with volunteers to establish one shipwreck preserve and is working on a second. MMAP personnel also work with volunteers and individuals interested in avocational training in underwater archaeology. Much of the education training program is tied to MMAP field research objectives, and participation frequently must be based on available space (Langley, 2000).

Black Panther (U-1105).   One of the more complex projects carried out by MMAP personnel and volunteers was to develop the wreck of the World War II German submarine U-1105, *Black Panther*, for recreational diving. *Black Panther*'s remains are U.S. Navy property, so the project was carried out in conjunction with the Naval Historical Center and with support from the Department of Defense Legacy Resource Management Program. Because *Black Panther* was fitted with a rubber coating that absorbed sound to allow it to avoid acoustic detection, it was brought to the United States for testing and evaluation after being surrendered to the Allies. After testing, it was sunk near the mouth of the Potomac River. In conjunction with MMAP personnel, local volunteers mapped the vessel, and the Piney Point Lighthouse Museum partnered with the navy to produce a brochure providing divers with insight into the history of the warship and the present condition of the wreck. The brochure encourages divers to leave the site undisturbed for others to enjoy (Shomette, 1997; Langley, 2000).

USS *Tulip.*   Investigation of U.S. Navy shipwrecks in Maryland waters has included the Civil War gunboat USS *Tulip*. The 240-ton gunboat originally was built as the *Chi Kiang* for the Chinese navy but was purchased by the United States shortly after its completion in 1863. After commissioning, *Tulip* became part of the Potomac Flotilla created by union secretary of the navy Gideon Welles to patrol the Potomac River and Chesapeake Bay. Throughout the war, the flotilla's ships exchanged fire with Confederate batteries and troops on the Potomac and Rappahannock Rivers. Although no Union vessels were lost in action, the *Tulip* sank in July 1864 after its boiler exploded (Thompson, 1996; Langley, 2000).

Divers discovered *Tulip*'s remains in the 1960s. During the following decade, hundreds of artifacts were recovered from the wreck site. With funding from the U.S. Department of Defense Legacy Resource Management Program, Bruce Thompson of MMAP began to relocate and recover collections in 1995. In conjunction with the Naval Historical Center, management authority for all United States Navy shipwrecks, MMAP personnel and volunteers from the Maritime Archaeological and Historical Society (MAHS) also mapped the wreck remains and inventoried the recovered collections (Langley, 2000).

The Maryland Historical Trust is working with other state and Charles County agencies to develop Mallow's Bay as another shipwreck preserve. Although shallow, Mallow's Bay contains the remains of more than 150 vessels. While most of these date to World War I, some date to World War II, and historical research suggests that even Revolutionary War vessels could have been lost in Mallow's Bay (Shomette, 1996). The proposed preserve ultimately may include terrestrial remains associated with a Civil War encampment, a sturgeon caviar cannery and a Depression era marine railway (Langley, personal communication).

Michigan

Michigan has 38,000 square miles of bottomlands and more than 1300 shipwrecks. Management of these submerged cultural resources has been the responsibility of the Office of the State Archaeologist, Michigan Department of State, and the Land and Water Management Division, Michigan Department of Environmental Quality. While the state has not developed a formal underwater archaeology program, many educational and management objectives of the state archaeologist have been accomplished through cooperative endeavors with other state agencies and institutions, volunteers, dive organizations, and private enterprise (Halsey, 1982; Halsey, 1989; Pott, 1999).

As a consequence of legislation in 1980, Michigan has established several underwater preserves to foster shipwreck preservation and recreational diving, efforts in part developed and widely supported by Michigan sport divers. Eleven preserve areas include the Alger Underwater Preserve, Detour Passage Underwater Preserve, Keweenaw Underwater Preserve, Manitou Passage Underwater Preserve, Marquette Underwater Preserve, Sanilac Shores Underwater Preserve, Southwest Michigan Underwater Preserve, Straits of Mackinac Underwater Preserve, Thumb Area Underwater Preserve, Thunder Bay Underwater Preserve, and Whitefish Point Underwater Preserve. Some preserves contain natural resources, and all have shipwreck sites dating from the 19th and 20th centuries (Halsey 1990, 1994). The preserves also have been the subjects of academic analysis of shipwreck allocation, accessibility, and management practices (Vrana and Halsey, 1991, Vrana and Halsey, 1992; Vrana and Mahoney, 1993).

Thunder Bay Underwater Preserve. Michigan's first preserve was at Thunder Bay, where 288 square miles of Lake Huron bottomland contain a rich collection of shipwreck remains. One of the most popular sites is the wreck of the

German steamer *Nordmeer*, which sank in 1966. Other interesting sites include the 128-foot schooner *Lucinda Van Valkenburg*, which sank in 1887, and the *Montana*, a 235-foot sidewheel steamer that burned and sank in 70 ft of water in 1914. In October 2000, Thunder Bay was designated as a National Marine Sanctuary. The National Oceanic and Atmospheric Administration (NOAA) and the state of Michigan will jointly manage the sanctuary. The 113-square-mile Alger Underwater Preserve on Lake Superior contains a number of popular shipwreck sites: *Bermuda*, a schooner that sank in Murray Bay in 1870 with a load of iron ore, and the steamer *Smith Moore*, which sank after colliding with another ship in 1889 and today lies largely intact and upright in 100 ft of water. The Straits of Mackinac, which include 148 square miles of bottomland, also contain one of the oldest and most recent shipwrecks in the Michigan preserve system: the well-preserved *Sandusky*, a 110-foot sailing ship that sank there during a September gale in 1856 and now sits upright in 90 ft of water. *Cedarville*, a 588-foot self-unloading freighter that sank after a collision in 1965, lies in 110 ft of water east of the straits (Ring, 1999).

Literature associated with the Michigan shipwreck preserves is available locally and from the Michigan Historical Center at the Department of State, and an Internet website provides an excellent introduction to the shipwreck preserves. Divers visiting the preserves are encouraged to explore Michigan's shipwrecks but are cautioned not to disturb them. State law protects all Michigan shipwrecks, and the penalties for illegal removal of wreck remains and artifacts are substantial. As a consequence of cooperation between the state and the Michigan diving public, the underwater preserves provide divers with access to some of the best-preserved shipwreck sites in the Great Lakes (Halsey, 1996; Harrington, 1998). To broaden the reach of its historic marker program even further, Michigan Historical Center placed an official marker at the wreck of the tug *Sport*, 1873–1920, which has been listed on the National Register and identified as the earliest steel-hulled ship in the Great Lakes (Schmitt, 1989; Peters and Ashlee, 1992). The marker, placed beside the largely intact and accessible wreck, has made the site highly popular with divers (Stayer and Stayer, 1995).

Wisconsin

State Historical Society of Wisconsin. The State Historical Society of Wisconsin (SHSW) is responsible for the management of Wisconsin's submerged cultural resources. The society's inventory of shipwrecks was initiated by Dave Cooper in 1987; it has mapped and documented more than 600 identified wrecks in conjunction with other state and federal agencies, educational institutions, avocational organizations, and interested divers. In partnership with the University of Wisconsin's Sea Grant Institute, SHSW has produced guides for seven of the numerous vessels lost on Lake Superior. The guides, on waterproof slates, contain site maps, interpretive information, historical background data, and site-specific dive information. The research, protection, and management activities of the historical society are currently directed by Jeff Gray and supported by the Wisconsin Underwater Archaeological Association, a nonprofit organization formed by a group of volunteer divers contributing time and efforts to preserve Wisconsin shipwrecks (Cooper, 1994; Cooper, 1996).

Apostle Island Shipwrecks. One of the most important concentrations of Wisconsin shipwrecks lies in the Apostle Islands area of Lake Superior. Several Apostle

Island shipwrecks are popular dive sites, and information about those vessels has been developed by the SHSW underwater archaeology program. The remains of the schooner *Lucerne* and the steamer *R.G. Stewart*, both popular dive sites, lie within the boundaries of the Apostle Islands National Lakeshore and are managed jointly by the National Park Service and the State Historical Society of Wisconsin. The 728-ton *Lucerne* lies off Long Island and was run ashore during a gale in November 1886. The wreck lies in 24 feet of water, and a substantial portion of the hull survives largely intact. The wreck of the steamer *R.G. Stewart* lies off Michigan Island. *Stewart* ran aground in June 1899 while heading for Bayfield in a fog. During efforts to get the vessel off the next day, the ship caught fire and burned to the waterline. Little of the *R.G. Stewart* survives; the wreck remains consist of a large scatter of fasteners, hardware, and tools.

Additional Apostle Island sites where recreational diving is encouraged include the steamer *Coffinberry* and tug *Ottawa* at Red Bay, the steamer *Fedora* near Chicago Creek, and the steamer *Sevona* on Sand Island Shoals. Plans of each vessel were developed by staff members and students during an East Carolina University field school (Cooper et al., 1991).

Minnesota

Minnesota Historical Society.   The well-preserved remains of ships, boats, and a variety of other small vessels can be found in many of Minnesota's 15,000 lakes, the headwaters of the Mississippi and other Minnesota rivers, and Lake Superior. The Minnesota Historical Society (MHS), managed by Scott Anfinson, has responsibility for the protection, investigation and management of Minnesota shipwrecks. Following passage of the Abandoned Shipwreck Act in 1988, the State Historic Preservation Office (SHPO) of the Historical Society received funding from the Legislative Commission on Minnesota Resources to survey the submerged cultural resources and develop a plan for their management (MHS, 1999).

Although the historical society has limited resources for putting elements of the management plan into effect, the SHPO has a slide show on Minnesota shipwrecks available to help inform divers and other interested groups about the historical and archaeological value of shipwrecks and the legislation that protects them. Much of the work illustrated by the slide program has been the result of sport divers and organized preservation societies such as the Great Lakes Shipwreck Preservation Society, whose activities have contributed significantly to the preservation of Minnesota's submerged cultural resources.

Put-It-Back.   One program developed and organized by the sport diving community is called Put-It-Back (PIB), which encourages divers to return recovered artifacts to their original shipwreck location. Returned artifacts are inventoried by the SHPO and permanently labeled with a PIB number to discourage removal (MHS, 1999; GLSPS, 1999).

Although there are no shipwreck preserves in Minnesota waters, the Minnesota Historical Society is studying the possibility of developing underwater parks. One site under consideration is offshore Split Rock State Park. It is the remains of the iron steamer *Madeira* lost at Gold Rock. Recent public acquisition of waterfront access at Gold Rock could make the Split Rock underwater park concept practical (MHS, 1999).

New York

Lake George Submerged Heritage Preserves. In New York, the nonprofit avocational group Bateaux Below, Inc., has a memorandum of understanding with the New York State Department of Environmental Conservation to establish and monitor submerged heritage preserves in Lake George, New York. Established by sport diver Joe Zarzynski in 1993, Bateaux Below has developed three underwater preserves. Unique is the *Land Tortoise* radeau, a 52-foot-long by 18-foot-wide floating gun battery built and sunk during the French and Indian War. The unusual vessel, located in 1990, was designated a submerged heritage preserve in 1994 (Zarzynski et al., 1994).

Other sites in the Lake George shipwreck preserve system associated with the French and Indian War include seven bateaux at the Wiawaka site. Like the *Land Tortoise*, these vessels are from the fleet of British warships scuttled on Lake George by the British in 1758 to prevent their capture by the French. The 1906 launch *Forward* makes up the third underwater preserve shipwreck.

New York's State Department of Environmental Conservation manages wrecks in the Lake George Submerged Heritage Preserve system. Buoys mark the site of each wreck and brochures provide information on the nature of each vessel, its history, guidelines for diving in the Lake George preserves, and a bibliography for those interested in finding out more about Lake George history. The diving public is invited to attend an annual Shipwreck Weekend at Lake George, sponsored by Bateaux Below, Lake George Historical Association, and New York Sea Grant. The Shipwreck Weekend's goal is to educate the diving public about the need to protect and preserve submerged cultural resources such as those in the Lake George Submerged Heritage Preserve system (Zarzynski et al., 1994).

Vermont

Division of Historic Preservation. Vermont's Division of Historic Preservation is responsible for management of the state's submerged cultural resources. In response to public pressure, state archaeologist Giovanna Peebles developed a policy and set of guidelines for underwater research activity in Vermont waters. In addition, the division worked with Champlain Maritime Society, which in 1986 merged with the newly formed Lake Champlain Maritime Museum to develop an active program of maritime education and underwater archaeology.

Lake Champlain Maritime Museum. The Lake Champlain Maritime Museum (LCMM), a private, nonprofit organization, works with the states of Vermont and New York to organize and fund historical and archaeological research projects associated with Lake Champlain. In addition, the museum features a variety of educational exhibits and public participation programs designed to enhance awareness of and appreciation for Lake Champlain's maritime heritage (Peebles, 1985; Lake Champlain Maritime Museum, 1999). The museum's underwater archaeology program has focused attention of professional archaeologists and volunteers on a variety of projects designed to locate, investigate, preserve, and manage the lost vessels of Lake Champlain. Their efforts, in conjunction with Vermont and New York officials and the Underwater Preserve Advisory committee, enabled the designation of six shipwreck preserves administered by the state of Vermont and one administered by the state of New York.

The steamboat era is represented by *Phoenix*, launched in 1815 and sunk in 1819, and *Champlain II*, launched in Burlington as the *Oakes Ames* in 1868 and wrecked on the shore at Westport New York in 1875. Other preserves include a rare horse-powered ferry and several vessels that document the region's bustling trade and commerce, including standard canal boats *A.R. Noyes* sunk while transporting a cargo of coal; and, because of its location and its cargo, the so-called Diamond Island Stone Boat. The preserves include the remarkably intact *General Butler* and *O.J. Walker*, both sailing canal schooners constructed on opposite shores of Lake Champlain in 1862 and now sharing a common resting place in Burlington Harbor (Cohn, 2000).

Shipwrecks in the underwater historic preserve system are marked by buoys and identified by underwater signs. Annual registration is required, and brochures are provided with information on each wreck, diving conditions, and regulations that prohibit disturbance of material at underwater sites (Peebles, 1985; Cohn, 1987; Crisman, 1996; Lake Champlain Maritime Museum, 1999). In 1993, the Underwater Preserve Advisory Committee was formed to provide a forum for current preserve issues and make management recommendations to the division. During the summer, preserve managers actively educate divers about the history of shipwrecks in the preserves. Non-divers can explore the wrecks through the maritime museum's variety of exhibits, including "Shipwrecks: A Porthole to History," and the touch-screen "Virtual Diver" (Cohn, 2000).

In 1996, in response to the newly discovered infestation of zebra mussels, LCMM launched a landmark Lake Survey, an eight-year sonar mapping program of the lake bottom. The survey located dozens of previously unidentified shipwrecks, including one of Benedict Arnold's Revolutionary War gunboats. The LCMM, states of New York and Vermont, and Naval Historical Center are cooperating to develop a management plan for the historic gunboat on behalf of the public. A new study begun in 1999, defining effects of zebra mussels on Lake Champlain shipwrecks, is the museum's unique project (Lake Champlain Maritime Museum, 1999; Cohn, 2000).

LCMM also has an active nautical archeology education program that reaches students of all ages and has sponsored Nautical Archaeology Field Schools since 1987. Working with the University of Vermont and Texas A & M University, LCMM provides graduate and undergraduate students practical experience in the technical analysis of submerged cultural resources and teaches site documentation and conservation techniques. More than 120 students have participated in the field schools and have produced more than a dozen master's theses and doctoral dissertations.

LCMM's educational programs for school groups, Elderhostel, and Summer Programs for Kids are richly intertwined with the Museum's archaeological fieldwork and research. The most recent efforts on its Lake Survey have sparked development of new summer programs, new winter outreach programs, and more diverse on-site field trips. Current research projects and artifacts provide unparalleled opportunities to teach visitors of all ages about history, artifact conservation, and issues regarding cultural resource management (Cohn, 2000).

Massachusetts

Massachusetts Board of Underwater Archaeological Resources.   Responsibility for protecting and managing submerged cultural resources in Massachusetts falls on the Massachusetts Board of Underwater Archaeological Resources and its director,

Victor T. Mastone. State law and board regulations permit the diving public to interact with submerged sites in a number of ways. The board issues reconnaissance permits to sports divers and avocational archaeologists to conduct nonintrusive work on Massachusetts' shipwrecks and other submerged cultural resources. In addition, the board has the authority to establish underwater archaeological preserves that allow public access to specific sites. Although no underwater archaeological preserves have been established to date, a number of proposals are currently under consideration.

Massachusetts's law allows removal of artifacts by sports divers from certain sites identified on a "List of Exempt Sites." This somewhat problematic list, created in and unaltered since 1985, contains 40 sites supposed to have been disturbed by salvage or judged to have little archaeological or historical significance (Mastone, 2000).

NATIONAL MARINE SANCTUARIES

USS *Monitor* National Marine Sanctuary

Federal agencies also have developed shipwreck sites to focus public attention on and provide public access to submerged cultural resources. Historic USS *Monitor* sunk off Cape Hatteras, North Carolina in 1862 became the first National Marine Sanctuary under the National Oceanographic and Atmospheric Administration (NOAA) in 1975. Sanctuary protection, management, and research activities are directed by John Broadwater.

Although the wreck lies in 230 ft of water, NOAA permits limited public access to the site. Dive organizations, dive charter operators, and individuals can make proposals to NOAA for organizing expeditions that help accomplish sanctuary management objectives. Organizations such as the Cambrian Foundation, a technical diving society, have worked with NOAA on several projects in the *Monitor* National Marine Sanctuary (Watts, 1987; NOAA, 1999a).

The purpose of designating *Monitor* as the nation's first National Marine Sanctuary was to protect and manage the wreck. Permits for scientific research on the ironclad have been granted to organizations since 1977. Proposals for research in the sanctuary have been approved if the research was deemed beneficial to management of the wreck and facilitated achieving sanctuary goals and objectives. A critical consideration has been the potential effect on the wreck or its environment. From 1976–1978, the *Monitor* Research and Recovery Foundation of Beaufort, North Carolina, was granted research permits to carry out environmental testing and site mapping. Jacques Cousteau obtained a permit in 1979, and his personnel made two dives to *Monitor* to videotape the wreck (Watts, 1987).

Sport divers also have made dives on *Monitor*. In the wake of a successful suit in 1989, NOAA was forced to open the wreck to the diving public on a limited basis. NOAA reviews applications from sport divers, and acceptable proposals are approved annually. Sport diving activities in the *Monitor* National Marine Sanctuary are carried out under the supervision of NOAA personnel to ensure that the wreck site is not disturbed or damaged.

The first avocational group to dive on *Monitor* was organized by Rod Farb in 1990 (Farb, 1992), when four expeditions were organized to videotape and photograph areas of the wreck for NOAA. Since 1990, permits have been issued regularly to other commercial dive operations carrying sport divers to the wreck site (NOAA, 1992).

The most successful and productive expedition to *Monitor* occurred in 1998. The project was designed to accomplish objectives identified in a 1997 long-range comprehensive plan for management, stabilization, preservation, and recovery of artifacts and materials from the ironclad, as mandated by the U.S. Congress. Objectives included mapping and documenting the wreck and its environment and recovering the propeller and propeller shaft. Two operations were carried out in May and June 1998, the first aided by the U.S. Navy and nonprofit Cambrian Foundation, the second with support from the Cambrian Foundation, National Undersea Research Center, and Mariners' Museum. Although successful recovery of the propeller and propeller shaft was the most visible evidence of the operation's success, much mapping and documentation also was completed during more than 106 hours of diving, and 30 artifacts and samples were recovered (Broadwater, 1997; NOAA, 1998).

In addition to protecting and managing the *Monitor*, NOAA has developed an educational program to make the historic shipwreck more accessible to the public. Under the direction of educational coordinator Dina Hill, materials include brochures, posters, publications, and slide and video programs designed to enhance understanding of the vessel's role in American Civil War history and to promote appreciation of its value as an archaeological resource. In addition, NOAA personnel worked with the education division of the Mariners Museum to develop and distribute a *Monitor* curriculum for teaching middle and high school students, with an outreach kit to support the curriculum. A traveling exhibit developed by the North Carolina Maritime Museum at Beaufort, North Carolina, makes the history of the ship and the sanctuary available for display. As much as possible, NOAA supports public and professional staff presentations on *Monitor*, and the newsletter, *Cheesebox*, conveys periodic information about *Monitor* National Marine Sanctuary activities to the public (NOAA, 1999a).

Florida Keys National Marine Sanctuary

Shipwreck Trail. In 1990, Congress designated the coral reefs of the Florida Keys a national marine sanctuary. To enhance recreational diving in the Sanctuary and provide opportunities for the public to learn about American maritime heritage, NOAA developed a shipwreck trail. Working with university graduate programs, private contractors and volunteers, the staff of the Florida Keys National Marine Sanctuary identified and documented nine wreck sites for inclusion in the trail: the state of Florida's *San Pedro* preserve, remains of the 19th-century vessels *North American* and *Adelaide Baker*, and a variety of 20th-century shipwrecks including Coast Guard Cutter *Duane* and destroyer escort *Amesbury*.

NOAA produced an underwater guide for each vessel, identifying the location of site mooring buoys, a short history of the vessel, a site plan, and a description of the wreck and marine life in the area. Divers are encouraged to visit the sites to examine and photograph the wrecks, but disturbance of wreck remains or marine life is not permitted (Lynch, 1999; NOAA, 1999b).

Channel Islands National Marine Sanctuary and Channel Islands National Park

NOAA cooperates with the National Park Service, state of California and U.S. Navy to manage submerged cultural resources of Channel Islands National Marine Sanctuary and Channel Islands National Park. In the more than 1000 square miles that make up the sanctuary and park, there are more than 100 documented shipwrecks, many of which are popular dive sites. In Biscayne National Park and the Tortugas National Park in Florida, NPS personnel from the Submerged Cultural Resources Unit in Santa Fe, New Mexico, cooperate with the State of Florida to inventory, record, and interpret shipwreck sites.

Pictured Rocks National Lakeshore, Sleeping Bear Dunes National Lakeshore, Alger Underwater Preserve, and Manitou Passage Underwater Preserve, established by the state of Michigan offshore of national parks of the same name, provide additional examples of Federal and state cooperation in submerged cultural resource management. Submerged cultural resource studies have been completed for both parks and preserves (Labadie, 1987; Vrana, 1995).

While NPS issues permits and encourages recreational diving on shipwrecks in the waters of many national parks, unauthorized disturbance of vessel remains is strictly prohibited.

Isle Royale National Park

One of the best examples of NPS shipwreck resource management can be found in Lake Superior. At Isle Royale National Park on Isle Royale in Lake Superior, the National Park Service manages a variety of shipwrecks associated with navigation on the Great Lakes. At least 20 vessels dating from the late 19th century to post-World War II have been identified; the remains of 10 were documented during a five-year survey and assessment project carried out by NPS' Submerged Cultural Resources Unit between 1981 and 1985. Diving and recovery of material from the wrecks was relatively unregulated until the mid-1970s. Because of the intensity of diving activity and the extent of salvage and damage to the wrecks, NPS determined that regulation was required to protect them (Murphy et al., 1982; Lenihan, 1987).

Today, Isle Royale is one of the most popular diving sites on the Great Lakes. Shipwrecks at Isle Royale provide divers with the opportunity to examine a cross section of historic Great Lakes steamships in a variety of environments.

America. One of the most heavily visited sites is the 1898 steamer *America*. The steel-hulled *America* was wrecked in 1928, and its largely intact remains lie in a readily accessible and protected area on the west end of the island. The site is in relatively shallow water, and the bow remains are visible from the surface.

Henry Chisholm and Cumberland. West of the *America*, wrecks of the wooden steamers *Cumberland* and *Henry Chisholm* lie on a reef several miles offshore. The 1775-ton *Henry Chisholm* was built in 1880 to carry bulk freight. It ran onto Rock-of-Ages Reef 18 years later. The Canadian-built, 629-ton *Cumberland*, designed to carry passengers and freight, was launched in 1871 and ran onto Rock-of-Ages Reef in 1877. Both wrecks are broken up, but large sections of hull structure and machinery litter the bottom from 25–140 ft.

Monarch. Off the east end of the island, the remains of the wooden steamer *Monarch* lie adjacent to impressive Palisades Cliff and provide another popular dive site. The Canadian-built steamer was constructed in 1890 to carry bulk freight. During heavy weather in December 1906, *Monarch* steamed into the solid wall of Palisades Cliff. Today, fragmentary remains of the hull lie in 20 to 70 ft of water below Palisades Cliff (Murphy et al., 1982; Solutions, 1999).

NPS encourages diving on these and other shipwrecks at Isle Royale. However, activity is strictly regulated, and diver registration is required. Only licensed sport diving operators are permitted to carry divers for charter within the boundaries of the Isle Royale National Park. Disturbance of the wrecks and removal of material associated with the vessel remains are prohibited. Some sites such as *Monarch* have interpretive trails and brochures to help identify sections of the wreck and convey the history associated with the vessel.

OTHER PUBLIC EDUCATION AND TRAINING PROGRAMS

In addition to state and federal shipwreck preserves that provide an outlet for recreational divers and promote the protection of submerged cultural resources, several state agencies, institutions, and organizations have developed diver and public education and training programs. These programs generally are designed to promote submerged cultural resource protection and public participation in resource-related research and management. Although limited by funding, the programs provide a step in the direction that submerged cultural resource management programs must inevitably take to be effective.

Florida

Orientation to Underwater Archaeology for Sport Divers. The Florida Division of Historical Resources selected the Pensacola area to test a training program for sport divers. The Orientation to Underwater Archaeology for Sport Divers program was designed by Della Scott to acquaint Pensacola-area divers with the essentials of underwater archaeological research. The workshop was designed around criteria identified by the Advisory Council on Underwater Archaeology and the National Association of Underwater Instructors. Using a workbook developed specifically for the course, Division of Historical Resources personnel led interested divers through three stages of instruction, progressing from the classroom to confined water, and finally to open water. Topics included local history, underwater archaeology and ship construction, ethics, legislation and regulations, and artifact preservation (Scott, 1994).

Maple Leaf Documentation and Excavation. Documentation and test excavation of the Canadian-built steamer *Maple Leaf* generated equal interest in Florida's Civil War history. *Maple Leaf* was a captured blockade-runner employed as a Union transport when it was sunk on April 1, 1864. As it was returning to Jacksonville from Palatka, the steamer hit a Confederate torpedo near Mandarin Point in the St. Johns River and sank immediately. The vessel was loaded with the personal effects, camp equipage, and suttlers' stores associated with Union army units dispatched to Florida to counter a Confederate victory at Olustee, Florida (Holland et al., 1993).

After a lengthy search, the wreck was located in 1984 by Keith Holland and members of St. Johns Archaeological Expeditions, Inc. Their work and subsequent investigations were carried out under grants from the state of Florida, with the assistance of staff and students from the Program in Maritime History and Underwater Archaeology at East Carolina University, and produced an impressive collection of data and material from the wreck.

Besides conserving material for public display in the Museum of Science and History in Jacksonville, St. Johns Archaeological Expeditions joined the Duval County

School Board in producing a half-hour video on the *Maple Leaf*, its discovery, and investigation. The video also was used to produce an interactive computer program for visitors to the Museum of Science and History. The exhibits, interactive program, and video convey a message of preservation and responsible management of submerged cultural resources to the general public and area students (Holland et al., 1993).

Lighthouse Archaeological Maritime Program.   The Lighthouse Archaeological Maritime Program (LAMP) is an archaeological research program of St. Augustine Lighthouse and Museum, which conducts its primary field research during a four-month field season, from July through September. In conjunction with the field season, LAMP offers several educational opportunities for students from high school through graduate school, as well as projects designed for public participation and education. Results of LAMP's research, as well as the educational projects and volunteer activities, are fully interpreted for the general public through the dynamic exhibits at the museum. Public presentations by archaeology staff members, and a lecture series featuring visiting scholars hosted by the museum, bring the results of archaeological research directly to the community (Morris, 2000).

During the summer field season, LAMP includes graduate students as part of the full-time archaeology staff. Students work with archaeologists in all aspects of field research, conservation, archival research, exhibit preparation, and report writing. During the remote sensing portion of the field season, LAMP has worked with several students under the direction of Gordon Watts, Ph.D., of East Carolina University. During the spring semester, two graduate students from the History Department of the University of North Florida also work as interns for the program.

In addition to time spent working directly with program and museum staff, students conduct research that will contribute to the ongoing investigation of shipwreck sites currently under investigation and also will contribute to the student's individual academic requirements. In one case, a thesis topic was provided by research associated with one of the most significant sites known to be offshore of St. Augustine (Morris, 2000).

To provide a broader base of educational opportunities for students in the area, LAMP works with high school students in marine research classes and programs. In the spring, students work with LAMP to learn basic field methods and research techniques. Currently, students are working on a project to create an underwater park at a 19th-century shipwreck site located offshore. They learn to map and record under direct staff supervision and with their own dive safety officer and scuba instructor. As part of their academic curriculum, they research the vessel and work toward nomination of the site as an underwater archaeological preserve in the system established by the Florida Division of Historic Resources; this will create the first fully interpreted shipwreck site for sport diver visitation in northeast Florida (Morris, 2000).

At the end of the field research season, LAMP will offer a marine archaeology field seminar for qualified sport divers, which will include instruction in basic research, field methodology, archaeological ethics, exhibit design, and conservation. The program allows local divers to participate in examination and documentation of historic shipwrecks under professional direction and emphasizes the need to record and protect the fragile, tangible remains of St. Augustine's maritime past. In spring 2000, LAMP worked with city archaeologist Carl Halbirt and the St. Augustine Archaeological Association to record the base of the previous lighthouse structure, now partially submerged. LAMP also worked with the field school from the University of Florida under the direction of Kathleen Deagan, Ph.D. Although this is a terrestrial field school, LAMP has provided expertise for the underwater work directly associated with the site, located near Nombre de Dios and the Fountain of Youth (Morris, 2000).

Encouraging and facilitating public participation and providing educational opportunities are two of the key components of LAMP. Public interpretation through the museum's ongoing exhibits ensures that all aspects of marine archaeology in St. Augustine are brought to the community and museum visitors. Research archaeology, public involvement, and multilevel educational opportunities combine to make LAMP a unique program, a key component in the St. Augustine Lighthouse and Museum's interpretation of the maritime history of the nation's oldest port. LAMP and the museum will continue to expand the professional staff and program capabilities. Within five years, the museum and LAMP will have a complete marine archaeological research center and conservation lab to facilitate ongoing research in the waters off St. Augustine (Morris, 2000).

Henrietta Marie Investigation.   Investigation of the remains of the *Henrietta Marie*, sunk near Key West, has attracted international attention to the slave trade and stimulated the development of two sets of educational materials, one developed by the Mel Fisher Maritime Heritage Society, the other by Prentice-Hall Publishing Corp. The package developed by the Mel Fisher Maritime Heritage Society contains posters, maps, illustrations, and activity sheets that focus student attention on the shipwreck and the slave trade. Hypothetical narratives by three children in England, Africa, and Jamaica provide insight into the social implications and impacts of the slave trade. The material assembled and distributed by Prentice-Hall includes a teacher's manual, a student workbook, and an associated reader. This material was designed to focus on the history of the *Henrietta Marie* and the methods that underwater archaeologists employ to investigate shipwrecks (Barringer, 1996; Prentice-Hall 1997).

North Carolina

"Hidden Beneath the Waves."   In addition to developing wreck sites for sport diver access, Mark Wilde-Ramsing of the Underwater Archaeology Unit of the North Carolina Division of Archives and History along with the Museum of the Cape Fear at Wilmington started a program called "Hidden Beneath the Waves" for public schools. The program is based on a multicomponent kit that includes a shipwreck model, videotapes, and copies of historical and cartographic resources. It introduces local maritime history and underwater archaeology and challenges students to use artifacts and historical and cartographic evidence to identify the model wreck. Teachers must participate in a one-day orientation before using the popular "Hidden Beneath the Waves" kit in their classrooms (Wilde-Ramsing, 1995).

Louisiana

El Nuevo Constante Package.   A similar educational kit was created around the wreck of the late-18th-century Spanish galleon *El Nuevo Constante*, lost off the coast of Louisiana. Discovered in 1979, the wreck was excavated and recorded under the supervision of the Louisiana Department of Culture, Recreation and Tourism. The educational package utilizes real and replicated artifacts associated with the wreck, historical and archaeological illustrations, and documents to support student interpretation of the ship and its cargo and to draw conclusions about shipboard life (Nobles et al., 1995).

Texas Educational Programs

La Belle.   The Texas Historical Commission and Texas Seaport Museum in Galveston built educational programs related to ships and shipwrecks that convey a message of resource and heritage preservation. Texas Historical Commission capitalized on the media attention generated by the discovery of La Salle's ship, *La Belle*, by developing and distributing lesson plans and other resources associated with the wreck (Arnold, 1995, 1996). *Journeys*, an electronic newsletter, provides information on the ship's history, discovery, excavation, conservation, and subsequent public display. The newsletter format is designed for teachers, providing classroom activity ideas and an e-mail link for student, teacher, and public inquiries. Special workshops also are offered to teachers wishing to include the La Salle Shipwreck Project in their curriculum (Texas Historical Commission, 2000).

"Maritime Mystery."   Texas Seaport Museum offers a half-day program for secondary-level students, "Maritime Mystery," designed to provide an introduction to seafaring and underwater archaeology. Program activities are initiated with a videotape introduction to the program and a tour of the sailing ship *Elissa*. Then students are engaged in the documentation of a shipwreck site recreated in the museum. Documentation activities include mapping, recording, artifact identification, and analysis of the wreck site. From data associated with the wreck, students are challenged to develop hypotheses about the identity of the ship, its cargo and crew, and the investigation of shipwrecks using underwater archaeology methods (Smith, 1998).

Several organizations have been formed to preserve maritime history, conduct research, and protect submerged cultural resources. Four of the most active are the Maritime Archaeological and Historical Society (MAHS) of Virginia, Rhode Island Marine Archaeology Project (RIMAP), Great Lakes Shipwreck Preservation Society (GLSPS) of Minnesota, and Coastal Maritime Archaeology Resources (CMAR) of California; all are nonprofit organizations offering members a combination of education, training, and field research opportunities.

Maritime Archaeological and Historical Society.   One of the most active organizations working with state and federal submerged cultural resource management programs is the Maritime Archaeological and Historical Society (MAHS), formed in 1988 to "enhance public awareness and appreciation for the preservation of historic shipwrecks and the science of maritime archaeology." The organization has a strict code of ethics, and acceptance of that code is a condition of membership (MAHS, 1999).

MAHS membership involves education and training. MAHS developed an introductory course in underwater archaeology, "Diving into History," designed around field exercises and a series of lectures presented on videotape. The popular video series, funded by Maryland Historical Trust, features several professional archaeologists lecturing on topics presented during the course, for which MAHS has published a curriculum and an instructor guide. The recommended text is *Archaeology Underwater: The NAS Guide to Principles and Practice*, published by the Nautical Archaeological Society in the United Kingdom.

Once members have completed an introductory course in underwater archaeology, they can participate in field research projects organized or cosponsored by MAHS. During the past ten years, MAHS members have worked on surveys and site-specific investigations with the National Park Service, Maryland Maritime Archaeology Program, Bermuda Maritime Museum, East Carolina University, and University of Maryland (Howard, 1998).

Rhode Island Marine Archaeology Project

The Rhode Island Marine Archaeology Project (RIMAP) has been very active in recent years. Formed in 1993 by D.K. Abbass, Ph.D., the project trains sport divers to interact in its research programs. Members take a series of courses on nautical archaeology and historic ship construction before taking part in fieldwork. Sites are managed by professional field directors who coordinate volunteer activities. To date, RIMAP has conducted preliminary investigations of a series of warships and transports sunk during the Revolutionary War, a possible slave ship, *Gem*, two unidentified vessels designated Alpha and Beta, the rum runner *Viola*, and several other identified and unidentified wrecks and inundated sites (see Abbass, this volume; Zarzynski et al., 1994).

HMB *Endeavour*. Recently, RIMAP announced the search for the remains of Captain James Cook's vessel, HMB *Endeavour*, a Whitby-built collier purchased in 1768 by Britain's Royal Navy for Cook's first scientific voyage to the southern hemisphere. After the Royal Navy sold *Endeavour*, the vessel was renamed *Lord Sandwich* and served as a transport ship during the Revolutionary War. It was scuttled during a naval blockade of Newport in 1778. RIMAP staff and volunteers currently are working with the Rhode Island Historical Preservation Commission to investigate its possible remains (Ground Truth, 1999).

RIMAP Public Outreach and Education Programs. RIMAP's public outreach and education programs have been highly innovative. In July 1999, with assistance from the Naval Undersea Warfare Center (NUWC), the University of Rhode Island and the Institute for International Maritime Research, RIMAP conducted a special education program for high school students and their teachers who were participating in a maritime history program run by the National Maritime Historical Society (NMHS) on board the replica British Revolutionary War frigate *Rose*. RIMAP's day-long program centered on archaeological investigations of HMS *Cerberus*, a British warship lost in Narragansett Bay in August 1778.

The day started with the *Rose* coming to anchor adjacent to the *Cerberus* site. On board, Rhode Island state underwater archaeologist Charlotte Taylor and RIMAP director Abbass lectured on underwater archaeology and maritime history, and other RIMAP instructors discussed scuba diving and dive safety. In the afternoon, students were invited to participate in an interactive "telepresence" tour of *Cerberus*. Archaeologists working on the *Cerberus* used a wireless video and audio link, developed by scientists at NUWC under the direction of Roy Manston, to communicate with the students, so that they could see, hear, and talk to the researchers who were working under water. Afterward, the archaeologists came aboard *Rose* for further discussion and commentary.

In July 2000, RIMAP and NUWC, the PAST Foundation, and the University of Rhode Island created a real-time video link of on going work at the site of HMS Cerebrus. In order to make the live coverage meaningful, these partners organized an education and outreach program that would allow students and the general public in special prearranged centers to access this link over the Web. Archaeologists at the various venues would be on hand to help answer questions and provide the crucial interpretive framework. The largest venue was at the Burns Telecommunications Center at Montana State University in Bozreman, where Dr. Annalies Corbin and their PAST Foundation hosted approximately 170 children for an hour-long broadcast from Narragansett Bay (Mather, 2000).

Minnesota

Great Lakes Shipwreck Preservation Society.   Although the underwater archaeology program in Minnesota has suffered for lack of adequate funding in recent years, the Minnesota Historical Society receives valuable assistance from members of the Great Lakes Shipwreck Preservation Society (GLSPS), a nonprofit, tax-exempt organization formed in May 1996 to stabilize and restore deteriorating shipwrecks of the Great Lakes. GLSPS members have helped stabilize the remains of the schooner S.P. *Ely*, sunk at Two Harbors. The schooner's surviving hull was slowly collapsing; GLSPS members reinforced it with rods positioned and tightened to bring the sides of the hull and deck beams back into position (Merryman, 1999; GLSPS, 1999). When initial attempts at stabilization were not entirely successful, GLSPS members installed a heavier system, to help the hull resist the dynamic Lake Superior environment more effectively. During the winter of 1999–2000, GLSPS also worked to develop a comprehensive plan for documentation and preservation of the S.P. *Ely* (Merryman, 1999, 2000; GLSPS, 1999).

The group also has been trying to document and stabilize the remains of the steamer *America*, sunk at Isle Royale inside the Isle Royale National Park. Diving activity on the *America* has accelerated deterioration of interior features, and GLSPS members have been restoring damaged structural elements in the surviving hull. One of the most important aspects of GLSPS work on the *America* has been documentation of the surviving wreck structure. Results of the work were published in a book of drawings sold by the society, whose proceeds support GLSPS shipwreck preservation activities.

GLSPS members also developed a shipwreck exhibit for the Isle Royale Windego Visitor Center, complete with ship models and preserved artifacts from Isle Royale wrecks. Information about the S.P. *Ely* and *America* is shared with State Historical Society of Wisconsin Underwater Archaeologist Jeff Grey, to help stabilize the remains of a Lake Michigan wreck (Merryman, 1999 and GLSPS, 1999).

In conjunction with the Minnesota Historical Society, GLSPS members monitor shipwreck sites and place buoys at wreck sites so that recreational divers will not damage the sites with boat anchors. They also have initiated a program to sink vessels that will offer divers an alternative to historic shipwrecks. This unique organization conducts programs to educate divers about submerged cultural resource conservation (Merryman, 1999; GLSPS, 1999).

A new facet of the GLSPS educational program currently under development is a course to train divers in Low Impact Wreck Diving, a concept designed to teach divers how to explore shipwrecks without having an adverse impact on vessel remains. Shipwreck diving ethics is an integral part of the program.

The success of GLSPS provides an excellent example of the positive impact that can be made when submerged cultural resource managers, professional archaeologists, and members of the diving community work together (Merryman, 2000).

California

Coastal Maritime Archaeology Resources.   In California, Coastal Maritime Archaeology Resources (CMAR) was formed in 1993 to "advance the understanding and preservation of...maritime heritage through...partnerships with the National Park Service, NOAA's Sanctuaries and Reserves Division and other institutions with similar agendas." Although CMAR does not offer regularly scheduled field schools or other structured programs, members can participate in research and field projects in conjunction with agencies with maritime as well as submerged cultural resource protection and management mandates. To date, CMAR members have supported projects in the Channel Islands National Park and NOAA's Olympic Coast National Marine Sanctuary (CMAR, 1999).

United Kingdom

Nautical Archaeological Society.   In 1985, the Nautical Archaeological Society (NAS) was formed in the United Kingdom to organize and educate sport divers interested in protecting and investigating shipwrecks. NAS offers instruction in shipwreck research and underwater archaeology that qualifies divers to participate in research projects throughout the United Kingdom. The organization has produced, and is currently revising, a text on underwater archaeology that supports its instruction program. In 1990, a branch of NAS was formed in Florida. NAS instruction also has been offered in South Carolina by personnel from the South Carolina Institute for Archaeology and Anthropology (Dean et al., 1992).

Although many federal and state agencies have developed programs that promote public education and encourage public participation in submerged cultural resource protection, investigation, management, and recreational use, only a few of these programs are mandated. Similarly, only a few receive more than nominal support for their operations. Many programs are the product of one or a few individuals' interest and enthusiasm.

When these programs are unique and responsive to public interest, there has been a high degree of success. Underwater parks designed to protect resources and cultivate public interest have proven a highly popular outlet for sport diving activity. These programs provide important public access to resources that are indeed part of our common heritage. However, access is not enough. Programs must be dynamic, well organized, and effectively supported to maintain interest and support.

As former Wisconsin underwater archaeologist David Cooper pointed out, "Developing public support for underwater archaeology will ultimately hinge on how well we translate the fascination of our past into responsible public attitudes and public stewardship for the future" (Cooper, 1994). Because historically significant submerged cultural resources are finite, effective programs for protection, management, and investigation will become increasingly critical. Through public education and volunteer programs, and the popular and professional dissemination of information, archaeologists should continue to influence legislation, in order to protect important cultural resources and make them accessible to the general public. Only through public education programs designed and run by professionals will submerged cultural resources be recognized for what they are and be given the protection and scientific consideration they deserve.

REFERENCES

Albright, Alan B., 1985, *Take the Cash and Let the Credit Go*. Underwater Archaeology Proceedings from the Society for Historical Archaeology Conference, edited by Paul F. Johnston, pp. 146–150, Boston.

Amer, Christopher F., 1994, *Legislation and the Management of South Carolina's Historic Shipwrecks and Submerged Cultural Resources: From Something to Something Else*. Underwater Archaeology Proceedings from the Society for Historical Archaeology Conference, edited by Robyn P. Woodward and Charles D. Moore, pp. 164–167, Vancouver.

Amer, Christopher F., and Steen Carl, 1988, The South Carolina Hobby Diver Program. *South Carolina Antiquities* 20(1,2):41–44.

Arnold, Barto, 1995, *Underwater Archaeological Survey of 1995*. Report on file with the Texas Historical Commission, Austin.

_____, 1996, Preliminary Report on the *Belle*, La Salle's Shipwreck of 1686. *Historical Archaeology* 30(4):66–87.

Barringer, Tonia, 1996, The Wreck of the *Henrietta Marie*. Mel Fisher Maritime Heritage Society, Inc., Key West, Florida.

Broadwater, John D., 1985, *Rescuing the Monitor: Stabilization and Recovery Efforts at the Monitor National Marine Sanctuary*. In Underwater Archaeology Proceedings from the Society for Historical Archaeology Conference, edited by J. Barto Arnold, pp. 55–59, Baltimore.

Coastal Marine Archaeology Resources, 1999, Coastal Marine Archaeology Resources Internet web site at weber.u.washington.edu/nailgun/cmar.

Cohn, Arther B., 1987, *Underwater Research on Lake Champlain*. In Underwater Archaeology Proceedings from the Society for Historical Archaeology Conference, pp. 7–11. Alan B. Albright, editor, Savannah.

Cooper, David J, ed., Megan A. Partlow, Bradley A. Rodgers, Gregory T. Smith, and Gordon P. Watts, Jr., 1991, *By Fire, Storm and Ice: Underwater Archaeological Investigations in the Apostle Islands*. State Historical Society of Wisconsin, Madison.

Cooper, David J., 1994, *"Come All Ye Gentlemen Volunteers": Perspectives on Avocationalists in Underwater Archaeology*. Proceedings from the Society for Historical Archaeology Conference, pp. 145–149. Robyn P. Woodward and Charles D. Moore, editors, Vancouver.

_____, 1996, *Building Bridges in the Badger State: Partnerships in Wisconsin Underwater Archaeology*. Proceedings from the Society for Historical Archaeology Conference pp. 105–111. Stephen R. James, Jr. and Camille Stanley, editors. Cincinnati.

Crisman, Kevin J., 1985, *The Nautical Archaeology of Lake Champlain: Research from 1980 to 1995*. Proceedings from the Society for Historical Archaeology Conference, pp. 105–111. Stephen R. James, Jr. and Camille Stanley, editors. Cincinnati.

Dean, Martin, Ben Ferrari, Ian Oxley, Mark Redknap and Kit Watson, editors, 1992, *Underwater Archaeology: The NAS Guide to Principals and Practice*. Nautical Archaeology Society, Institute of Archaeology, 31–34 Gordon Square, London WC1H 0PY.

Farb, Roderick M., 1992, *Computer Video Image Digitization on the* USS Monitor. *A Research Tool for Underwater Archaeology*. Underwater Archaeology Proceedings from the Society for Historical Archaeology Conference, pp. 100–104. Donald H. Keith and Toni L. Carroll, editors. Kingston, Jamaica.

Friday, Joe D., 1991, *The History, Archaeology and Current Status of the Wreck of the USS Huron*. Underwater Archaeology Proceedings from the Society for Historical Archaeology Conference, pp. 51–53. John Broadwater, editor. Richmond.

Florida Division of Historical Resources, 1985, SS Copenhagen *Underwater Archaeological Preserve*. Florida Division of Historical Resources, Tallahassee, Florida.

_____, 1996, SS Tarpon *Underwater Archaeological Preserve*. Florida Division of Historical Resources, Tallahassee.

_____, 2000a, *A Short History of* Half Moon. Florida Division of Historical Resources, Tallahassee.

_____, 2000b, Florida Underwater Archaeological Preserves, Internet Website: http://dhr.dos.state.fl.us/bar/uap.

Great Lakes Shipwreck Preservation Society, 1999, Great Lakes Shipwreck Preservation Society Internet Website: www.glsps.org.

Ground Truth, 1986, *Ground Truth*: The Newsletter of the Rhode Island Marine Archaeology Project, Rhode Island Marine Archaeology Project, Newport.

Halsey, John R., 1989, *Nine Years Before the Mast: Shipwreck Management in Michigan Since 1980*, Underwater Archaeology Proceedings from the Society for Historical Archaeology Conference, pp. 43–48. J. Barto Arnold, editor. Baltimore.

_____, 1990, *Beneath the Inland Seas: Michigan's Underwater Archaeological Heritage*, Bureau of History, Michigan Department of State, Lansing.

_____, 1985, *Freshwater Refractions*, Underwater Archaeology Proceedings from the Society for Historical Archaeology Conference, pp. 108–113. Robyn P. Woodward and Charles D. Moore, editors. Vancouver.

_____, 1996, Twenty Years On: Shipwreck Preservation in Michigan. *Common Ground* 1(3,4):26–33.

Harrington, 1998, Divers Guide to Michigan. Maritime Press, in association with Great Lakes Diving Council, St. Ignace.

Harris, Lynn, 1987, *Future Plans for Sport Diver Management in South Carolina*. Underwater Archaeology Proceedings from the Society for Historical Archaeology Conference, pp. 132–134. Toni L. Carroll, editor, Tucson.

_____, 1990, *Future Plans for Sport Diver Management in South Carolina*. Underwater Archaeology Proceedings from the Society for Historical Archaeology Conference, pp. 132–134. Toni L. Carroll, editor, Tucson.

_____, 1990, *An Underwater Archaeology Manual For South Carolina Sport Divers*. South Carolina Institute of Archaeology and Anthropology, University of South Carolina, Columbia.

_____, 1991 *The Waccamaw-Richmond Hill Waterfront Project 1991: Laurel Hill Barge No. 2*. South Carolina Institute of Archaeology and Anthropology, Research Manuscript Series No. 214, University of South Carolina, Columbia.

_____, 1996a, *South Carolina's Underwater Archaeology Public Education Program and International Outreach Initiatives; Part I*. South Carolina Institute of Archaeology and Anthropology Research Manuscript Series No. 218, University of South Carolina, Columbia.

_____, 1996b, Database Management Report on the South Carolina Hobby Licensing System and Submerged Resources Inventory. Part 11, South Carolina Institute of Archaeology and Anthropology Research Manuscript Series No. 218, University of South Carolina, Columbia.

_____, 1996c, *Survey of Submerged Cultural Resources in the Ashley River, Dorchester County, South Carolina*. Institute of Archaeology and Anthropology, Stephenson Award Publication Series.

_____, 1997, Public Education and Submerged Smallcraft Documentation in South Carolina. *Museum Small Craft Association Transactions* 3:46–53.

_____, 1999a, Flowing Timelines. *Sandlapper*, Summer 1999. The Sandlapper Society, Lexington, South Carolina.

_____, 1999b, *Slaves, Swamps, and Shipwrecks: Blending Archaeology with Heritage Tourism*. World Archaeology Conference 1999, Cape Town, South Africa.

Harris, Lynn and Carleton Naylor, 1996a, *South Carolina's Submerged Heritage: An Underwater Archaeology Field Manual*. South Carolina Institute of Archaeology and Anthropology, University of South Carolina, Columbia.

_____, editors, 1996b, *South Carolina Maritime Archaeology Proceedings 1996*. South Carolina Institute of Archaeology and Anthropology, University of South Carolina, Columbia.

Harris, Lynn, Moss, and Carleton Naylor, 1993, *The Cooper River Survey: An Underwater Field Manual*. South Carolina Institute of Archaeology and Anthropology, University of South Carolina, Columbia.

Holland, Keith V., Lee B. Manley, and James W. Towart, editors, 1993, The Maple Leaf: *An Extraordinary American Civil War Shipwreck*. St. Johns Archaeological Expeditions, Inc., Jacksonville.

Howard, Brenda A., 1998, *Diving into History: An Introductory Course in Underwater Archaeology*. Maritime Archaeological and Historical Society, Washington.

Hulse, Charles A., 1982 *The Management of Shipwrecks in the Great Lakes: A Michigan Case Study*. Underwater Archaeology Proceedings from the Society for Historical Archaeology Conference, pp. 151–157. Gordon P. Watts, Jr., editor. New Orleans.

Labadie, Patrick, 1989, *Submerged Cultural Resource Study: Pictured Rocks National Lakeshore*. Southwest Cultural Resources Center Professional paper No. 22, National Park Service, Santa Fe.

Lake Champlain Maritime Museum, 1999, Lake Champlain Maritime Museum Website: www.lcmm.org.

Lawrence, Richard W., 1986, *Current Underwater Archaeological Research in North Carolina*. Underwater Archaeology Proceedings from the Society for Historical Archaeology Conference, pp. 55–59. J. Barto Arnold, editor, Baltimore.

Lenihan, Daniel J., editor, 1987, *Submerged Cultural resources Study: Isle Royale National Park*. Southwest Cultural Resources Center Professional paper No. 8, National Park Service, Santa Fe.

Lynch Marika, 1999, Trail of Shipwrecks Laid Out for Divers. *Miami Herald*, 8 July 1999.

Maritime Archaeological and Historical Society, 1999, *Maritime Archaeological and Historical Society*. Maritime Archaeological and Historical Society, P. O. Box 44382, L'Enfant Plaza, Washington, D.C. 20026.

Mather, Ian Roderick, 2000, *Continuing Research on HMS Cerberus and a Special Education Program*. Paper presented to the Society for Historical Archaeology, Conference on Historic and Underwater Archaeology, Quebec, Canada, 4–9 January, 2000.

Miller, James J., 1985, *Managing Florida*'s Historic Shipwrecks. Underwater Archaeology Proceedings from the Society for Historical Archaeology Conference, pp. 53–55. J. Barto Arnold, editor, Baltimore.

Minnesota Historical Society, 1999, Minnesota's Historic Shipwrecks. Internet Website: www.mnhs.org.

Murphy, Larry. Dan Lenihan and Toni Carrell, 1982, *Underwater Archaeology of Isle Royale National Park*. National Park Service, Submerged Cultural Resources Unit, Southwest Cultural Resources Center, Santa Fe.

National Oceanic and Atmospheric Administration, 1987, *Charting a New Course for the* Monitor. *A comprehensive long-range plan for the preservation, management and exhibition of the* Monitor. Sanctuaries and Reserves Division, National Oceanic and Atmospheric Administration, U.S. Department of Commerce, Washington.

National Oceanic and Atmospheric Administration, 1999a, Welcome Aboard the *Monitor*. Internet Website: *monitor.nos.noaa.gov.*

National Oceanic and Atmospheric Administration, 1999b, *Florida Keys National Marine Sanctuary Shipwreck Trail*. Florida Keys National Marine Sanctuary.

Nobles, Connie H., Connie H., Laurie T. Eddy, 1995, *Teaming Up to Teach Archaeology*. Underwater Archaeology Proceedings from the Society for Historical Archaeology Conference, pp. 140–143. Paul F. Johnston, editor, Boston.

Peebles, Giovanna, 1985, *The Management of Vermont's Underwater Resources: A Model for Shared Responsibility*. Proceedings from the Society for Historical Archaeology Conference, pp. 153–156. Paul F. Johnston, editor. Boston.

Peters, Scott M., 1999, *Underwater Archaeology in Michigan. Retrieving Michigan's Buried Past: The Archaeology of the Great Lakes State*. Bulletin No. 64, John Halsey (editor), Cranbrook Institute of Science, Bloomfield.

Peters, Scott M. and Laura R. Ashlee, 1992, Working for a Living. *Michigan History Magazine*, 76(6):47–51.

Prentice-Hall, Inc., 1997, *The Wreck of the* Henrietta Marie. Interdiciplinary Explorations Series. Prentice-Hall, Inc., Upper Saddle River.

Ring!On Line, 1999, Diving Michigan's Underwater Preserves. Internet Website: www.ring.com.

Scott, Della, 1994, *Florida's Experimentation with Sport Diver Work Shops*. Underwater Archaeology Proceedings from the Society for Historical Archaeology Conference, pp. 164–167. Robyn P. Woodward and Charles D. Moore, editors, Vancouver.

Scott-Ireton, Della, 1996, *The Role of Historic Preservation and Public Interpretation in Shipwreck Management: The Pensacola Partnership*. Proceedings from the Society for Historical Archaeology Conference, pp. 29–34. Stephen R. James, Jr. and Camille Stanley, editors, Cincinnati.

Shomette, Donald, 1996, *Ghost Fleet of Mallows Bay*. Tidewater Publishers, Centerville.

_____, 1997, The U.S. Navy Shipwreck Inventory Project in the State of Maryland. Underwater Archaeology Proceedings from the Society for Historical Archaeology Conference, pp. 164–167. Denise C. Lakey, editor, Corpus Christi.

Smith, K.C., 1991, *From Dugouts to Doubloons: A Maritime Education Program for Youths*. Archaeology Proceedings from the Society for Historical Archaeology Conference, pp. 27–30. John Broadwater, editor, Richmond.

_____, 1998, *Luna's Legacy in the Classroom: The Emanual Point Ship Resource Packet*. Archaeology Proceedings from the Society for Historical Archaeology Conference, pp. 122–127. Lawrence E. Babits, Catherine Fach, and Ryan Harris, editors, Atlanta.

Smith, Roger, 1991, *Florida's Underwater Archaeological Preserves*. Underwater Archaeology Proceedings from the Society for Historical Archaeology Conference, pp. 43–46. John Broadwater, editor, Richmond.

Solutions, 1999, *Wreck Scuba Diving, Isle Royale, Lake Superior*. Internet Website: www.solutions.net/ aqualand/royale.

South Carolina Institute of Archaeology and Anthropology, 1999, *A Black Water Diving Experience in South Carolina: Cooper River Heritage Trail*. South Carolina Institute of Archaeology and Anthropology, Columbia.

Spirek, Jim and Lynn Harris, 2000, *Maritime Heritage on Display: Underwater Examples from South Carolina*. Society for Historical Archaeology Conference. Quebec.

Stager, Paul and Jim Stager, 1995, *Shipwrecks of Sanilac*. Out of the Blue Productions, Lexington.

Texas Historical Commission, 2000, *Welcome to the La Salle Shipwreck Project*. Internet Website: www.thc.state.tx.us/belle/

Thompson, Bruce F., 1996, Legacy of a Fourth-Rate Steam Screw. *Naval History* 10(3):36–39.

Vrana, Kenneth J., 1995, *Inventory of Maritime and Preservation Resources of the Manitou Passage Underwater Preserve*. CMURM Management Series MS-1995-01. Center for Maritime and Underwater Resource Management, Department of Parks, Recreation and Tourism Resources, Michigan State University, East Lansing.

Vrana, Kenneth J. and John R. Halsey, 1991, *Why 5% Wasn't Enough*. Archaeology Proceedings from the Society for Historical Archaeology Conference, pp. 40–42. John Broadwater, editor. Richmond.

_____, 1992, Shipwreck Allocation and Management in Michigan: A Review of Theory and Practice. Advances in Underwater Archaeology. *Historical Archaeology* 2(4).

Vrana, Kenneth J. and Edward Mahoney, editors, 1993, *Great Lakes Underwater Cultural Resources: Important Information for Shaping Our Future*. Proceedings of the Great Lakes Regional Conference on Underwater Cultural Resource Policy, 3–4 February 1993. Department of Park and Recreation Resources, Michigan State University, East Lansing.

Watts, Gordon P. Jr., 1985, *Towards Establishing Research and Significance Criteria for Civil War Shipwreck Resources*. Proceedings of the Sixteenth Conference on Underwater Archaeology. Paul F. Johnston, editor, Boston.

_____, 1986, *A Decade of Research: Investigation of the* USS Monitor. Underwater Archaeology Proceedings from the Society for Historical Archaeology Conference, pp. 128–139. Alan B. Albright, editor, Savannah.

Wilbanks, Ralph, 1986, *Preliminary Report on the Mepkin Abby Wreck, Cooper River, South Carolina: An Early 19th Century River Trading Vessel*. Underwater Archaeology Proceedings from the Society for Historical Archaeology Conference, pp. 151–157. Gordon P. Watts, Jr., editor, New Orleans.

Wilde-Ramsing, Mark, 1995, Hidden Beneath the Waves. North Carolina's Underwater Archaeology Educational Program. *Public Archaeology Review* 3(1,2):27–29.

Wisconsin Historical Society, 1985, *Archaeology*. Internet Website: www.shsw.wisc.edu.

Zarzynski, Joseph W., D.K. Abbass, and Russell P. Bellico, 1994 *Strange Bedfellows: Research and Politics of the* Land Tortoise, *Lake George's 1758 Radeau Shipwreck*. Proceedings from the Society for Historical Archaeology Conference, pp. 74–79. Robyn P. Woodward and Charles D. Moore, editors, Vancouver.

Technology

The field of underwater archaeology has benefitted greatly from advances in technology during the last 10 years. No aspect of the study of submerged resources can be accomplished without the use of highly sophisticated equipment, recording devices, and preservation techniques. The following chapters present these advances.

The use of side scan sonar is aptly described by its inventor, Martin Klein. This tool's contribution is unfathomable. The examples Klein provides in his chapter are mere tokens of its overall success.

Computer-based geographic information systems (GIS) are well described by the team of Ian Mather and Gordon Watts. GIS is a tool that can organize and analyze data and has the capacity to update existing information as needed. As usage of these systems grows, the more accurate the interpretation of the data will be.

Ian MacLeod presents a most definitive chapter on the long-term rate of deterioration of a shipwreck site. A key issue is how to rate decay due to excavation or natural processes associated with storms. The detailing of corrosion potential of metal objects through on-site measurements is invaluable.

Site management with its attendant goals and strategies are prerequisite for achieving the potential of underwater research. Ian Oxley and David Gregory describe examples of methods now in use and how to analyze conditions presented. Since only limited data is now available on the subject of site management, Oxley and Gregory provide information on how to increase the database in this area.

Preservation and its partner, conservation, are keys to follow-up by underwater archaeologists. Donald Keith explains by examples the methods and innovations being used in saving underwater materials either in situ or on land. Expert conservationists, especially with training in the "hard sciences," are in demand. Keith also asks the difficult question of what should or should not be preserved.

Chapter 38

Digging Deeper

Deepwater Archaeology
and the *Monitor*
National Marine
Sanctuary

JOHN D. BROADWATER

INTRODUCTION

Deepwater Archaeology: New Interest, New Controversy

"*Titanic* found!" was a major headline in 1985. Although worldwide excitement over the discovery and the blockbuster film may have subsided, the controversy continues. RMS *Titanic*, hands-down the world's most famous shipwreck, lies in international waters nearly 2.5 mi (4 km) beneath the stormy surface of the North Atlantic. Exploitation of the final resting place of the *Titanic* and its hundreds of passengers has created a storm of debate and legal actions that still pummels the historic preservation community and threatens the very survival of submerged cultural resources in deep water. Although it was the discovery of *Titanic* that brought public attention to these issues, professional oceanographers and archaeologists have been fending off this onslaught for years. Rapid improvement in ocean technology during the past two decades has enabled, for the first time in history, deepwater shipwrecks and other archaeological sites to come within reach

John D. Broadwater, Manager, Monitor National Marine Sanctuary, National Oceanic and Atmospheric Administration, Newport News, Virginia 23606.

International Handbook of Underwater Archaeology, edited by Carol V. Ruppé and Janet F. Barstad. Kluwer Academic/Plenum Publishers, New York, 2002.

of investigators. Unfortunately, deepwater technology is extraordinarily expensive, and those with commercial interests, usually not archaeologists, often are the ones who can raise the necessary funds for deepwater exploration. In spite of a recent United Nations convention intended to protect submerged cultural resources, it may be years before it becomes fully effective.

Since archaeology in the deep oceans represents only a tiny fraction of a percentage of the archaeology currently taking place, it is legitimate to ask, "Why all the fuss?" For one thing, the potential stakes are almost unimaginably high. William J. Broad, in his comprehensive and fascinating book *The Universe Below*, describes "the deep" as that region of the seabed "which lies beyond the shallows that border the continents and in total accounts for about 65 percent of the Earth's surface." Broad nicely captures the current concerns, saying, "the seabed is a vast repository of failed ambition that contains... millions of ships and treasures, arms and artifacts... and it is opening rather suddenly as people use deep technologies to uncover a wealth of human worlds that had been presumed gone forever" (Broad, 1997).

In January 1999, these concerns were aired at a conference titled "Technology and Archaeology in the Deep Sea: Toward a New Synthesis." Sponsored by the Massachusetts Institute of Technology and the Institute for Exploration, this conference was the first such meeting ever held. The conference's purpose was to "bring together a small number of respected scholars from various academic fields to articulate and discuss the intellectual foundations of this emerging science." Among the invitees were field and theoretical archaeologists, cultural resource managers, engineers, and ocean scientists. The stated goal was to "allow archaeological research in the deep sea to continue to evolve as a truly integrated scientific practice." As word spread about this unique conference, it soon became clear to the organizers that there existed an intense and widespread interest in deepwater archaeology, and this would require rethinking the original boundaries of the agenda. Thus the number of formal presentations was kept to the original manageable 12 papers, 4 commentators, and 26 panelists, but the number of invitees was tripled to include representatives from as many potential stakeholder groups as possible, as well as from the press. This meeting is likely to be remembered as the first comprehensive attempt to define the issues of deepwater exploration and to make initial suggestions for possible resolution of those issues (Stone, 1999; Wiseman, 1999).

Before the newly-emergent specialty of deepwater archaeology can be placed in its proper perspective, it is necessary to summarize briefly the subfield of underwater archaeology and its relationship to the overall discipline of archaeology.

Underwater Archaeology or Archaeology under Water?

It is generally agreed that underwater archaeology as a scientific pursuit began in the 1960s, particularly with the Mediterranean excavations of George F. Bass, University Museum, University of Pennsylvania (Bass, 1966, 1972). Bass and others effectively argued that archaeology under water differed little in planning, methodology, and cost from its terrestrial counterpart. The basic goals and methodologies of archaeology may— and should—always be employed, regardless of the surroundings, and results should always meet accepted professional standards. Nevertheless, it is seldom possible to transfer terrestrial methods and personnel directly to a site immersed in a liquid that alters human senses and requires specialized equipment for maintenance of basic life functions. The deeper the site, the more challenging the environmental differences become.

Difficulties in Working under Water

Theoretically, one can survey and excavate an archaeological site under water using essentially the same techniques as those employed on "dry" sites. In practice, however, most underwater sites present formidable obstacles, particularly turbidity, rough seas, strong currents, and cold temperatures. These obstacles, coupled with the necessity for wearing cumbersome breathing equipment, mask, and other dive gear make investigative tasks much more difficult for the archaeologist working under water. A dry-land colleague, after his first underwater archaeology dive in Virginia's murky, swift-flowing Chickahominy River, described the experience as "like trying to excavate in a blizzard while wearing a blindfold, gas mask, heavy parka, mittens, and snowshoes!"

As any terrestrial archaeologist will attest, archaeology is a hands-on science. On a typical dry-land excavation, the archaeologist slowly removes soil, noting changes in sediment color and texture, and takes care not to overlook artifacts within the various strata. Notes, measurements, and sketches are kept in a journal; on a nearby table lies the site plan, drawn to scale and referenced to one or more permanent datum markers so that the site can be positioned accurately on a geographical map. The site is recorded in three dimensions using simple equipment. Usually, a single archaeologist can oversee a fairly large excavation crew. The site supervisor strolls around the site to inspect progress, discuss methodology, answer questions, observe soil stratigraphy, and participate in the examination of especially significant features. Underwater, however, these relatively simple and straightforward tasks become much more difficult. Frequently, the job of directing a large crew of excavators is impractical if not impossible.

These relatively obvious (at least after a few dives) impediments often are compounded by more subtle pitfalls of underwater work, including disorientation, anxiety (even fear), inability to communicate effectively, difficulty in discerning stratigraphy and features, and dramatic reduction in dexterity and short-term memory. The last two impediments may come as a surprise, even to experienced divers. However, in controlled dexterity tests, subjects required an average of 28 percent longer to complete a specified exercise in 10 ft (3 m) of water compared to their times on the surface; at 100 ft (30 m), the tasks took 49 percent longer! Tests also suggest that sentence comprehension, time estimation, and memory suffer similarly (Muckelroy, 1978) as does visual response time (Haseltine, 1999). Therefore, the archaeologist must take into account that any task takes longer to perform underwater than on land and that mistakes in observation and recording are more likely—what Muckelroy (1978) calls the "mental retardation effect."

In other words, numerous diving-related factors interact to create an unfamiliar, inhospitable, and sometimes even hostile environment with which archaeologists must contend in order to conduct high-quality underwater research. Consequently, working in the underwater environment is costly in terms of both time and money. For instance, assume that a terrestrial site supervisor oversees six excavators. Allowing for several breaks during an eight-hour day, these seven people each will probably excavate for about six hours per day. Therefore, six hours times seven persons equals 42 person-hours of excavation per day. On a relatively shallow underwater site—say 33 ft (10 m), where decompression is not a factor—the underwater team would probably average about four hours of underwater excavation each, the remaining time being occupied in tending the active divers, operating compressors, boats, and other equipment, and handling other above-water activities. This team would produce four hours times seven people or 28 person-hours of excavation, a decrease of 14 hours or a third less excavation time each day. This statistic does not take into account evidence that the aforementioned environmental factors make diving archaeologists less efficient than their terrestrial counterparts or that the lack of adequate supervision necessitates excavators with higher skill levels.

Another factor adding to costs for underwater archaeology is safety. Scientific and commercial divers must observe strict safety requirements involving tenders, standby divers, decompression chamber operators, equipment technicians, and possibly others.

Up to this point, the facts presented are more or less "old hat" to experienced recreational and archaeological divers alike. However, one of the most important factors affecting divers is yet to be factored in: water depth. Almost all diving problems are exacerbated by increasing depth.

Problems Associated with Working in Deep Water

As a diver descends into deeper water, there is a corresponding decrease in ambient light and water temperature, while at the same time there is a rapid increase in pressure—one atmosphere (14.7 lb/in^2) for every 33 ft (10 m) of depth in seawater. Because this extraordinary increase in pressure on the diver's body brings on physical and mental impairments, dive time is severely limited by depth. A major culprit is increased nitrogen in the bloodstream, which causes a narcotic effect commonly referred to as "nitrogen narcosis." This condition can be severely debilitating and can even induce fatalities at depths below about 130 ft (34 m).

Nitrogen constitutes a proverbial two-edged sword: At depth, it can induce a diver to hand his regulator to a passing fish. And on the diver's return to the surface, it can injure or kill as well. Surfacing too rapidly from a deep dive can cause nitrogen dissolved in the blood to form bubbles, resulting in decompression sickness, or "the bends." Slightly deeper, around 200 ft (61 m), even oxygen becomes toxic and can cause convulsions and death. Even when a diver has followed all the rules of safety, evidence shows that prolonged deep diving may cause long-term adverse changes in the brain, nerves, joints, and bones (Bennett and Elliott, 1982).

The costs associated with deepwater work escalate rapidly with depth. If the team of six excavators and one supervisor move from a shallow-water site to one at 240 ft (73 m), they will be severely limited by the requirement for decompression. Each diver will be limited to one 30-minute dive a day, and each dive will require the support of three to six people. Therefore, even if the entire 30 minutes is counted as work time, the day's output will be seven divers times 30 minutes each, or 3.5 hours total—only 12.5 percent of the work time logged at the shallow-water site and just over 8 percent of that accomplished on land! These figures are optimistic, since actual work time on a 30-minute dive averages only 20–25 minutes, reducing work output by another third. The accomplishment-to-cost ratio is further reduced by related support costs: The team of seven must be augmented by at least an equal number of nondiving support staff, as previously mentioned, and the equipment and logistics required for deepwater work are considerably more costly.

Beyond a depth of about 660 ft (200 m), there really are no options for hands-on archaeology. At such depths, costs and hazards of underwater work become unjustifiably severe. It is true that as early as 1977, commercial divers conducted a working saturation dive at 1644 ft (501 m) (Earle and Giddings, 1980), but even in the offshore oil industry such projects are infrequent, and the number of archaeologists with the budget for such an operation are even more rare. As will be discussed, technology is providing ever-improving means for reaching extremely deep sites, but the costs are still very high. In short, the costs and human risks are so great that an archaeologist should have a very solid justification for pursuing research on a deepwater site.

Why Work in Deep Water?

Faced with such an array of formidable and life-threatening hazards, and given that a majority of submerged archaeological sites lie in coastal waters shallower than 100 ft (30 m), why would a sane, sensible underwater archaeologist deliberately seek a deepwater site? In some instances, it is because the site of interest happens to lie in deep water, as is the case with the RMS *Titanic*, *Hamilton and Scourge*, CSS *Alabama*, and USS *Monitor*, which this chapter will examine.

Another reason for seeking sites in deeper water is the potential for locating undisturbed, well-preserved cultural resources. Many, if not most, shallow-water archaeological sites have been disturbed by natural forces (storms, erosion, and biological action), human action (dredging, trawling, vandalism, and salvage), or both. Deeper sites have been relatively inaccessible until recently, so most have been immune to human disturbance—with the glaring exception of deep trawling. In addition, the deep-water environment tends to support preservation of organic and metallic objects because of reduced water movement, lower oxygen content, lower temperature, and fewer destructive organisms (Bascom, 1976).

The decline in the number of relatively intact shallow-water archaeological sites has forced researchers and salvors to turn their attention toward deeper water, where technology is providing more effective and affordable access. Just as the invention of the demand regulator breathing system in 1943 made it possible for average swimmers to venture beneath the waves, technology has, in the past several decades, produced a dazzling array of new devices and vehicles that provide scientists with the means to conduct research hundreds or even thousands of meters beneath the surface of the oceans.

The history of deepwater archaeology is inseparable from that of the ocean technology that makes it possible. Although basic methodology of underwater archaeology has not changed appreciably since the 1960s, equipment and techniques for gaining access to deeper sites have improved dramatically. A brief history of diving technology will underscore the progress that has been made and will provide a basis for speculation on the incredible future for deepwater archaeology.

HISTORY OF DIVING TECHNOLOGY AND UNDERWATER EXPLORATION

By the time the first modern humans walked the earth, most likely their ancestors had long since ventured into the sea. However, it has been only in the recent history of our species that we invented the means for remaining beneath the surface for extended periods of time and at great depths. Diving developed along several technological paths: breath-hold diving, self-contained diving, diving bells, submarines, and armored suits (see Chapter 2 for Timelines).

Evolution of Diving Systems

Some of the earliest written records include descriptions of diving activities. Herodotus recorded the use of divers for military operations as early as 480 B.C. (Davis, 1936; Dick, 2002). In Japan, divers have harvested pearl oysters for centuries without the aid of even the simplest equipment. These early divers were limited to the time they could spend underwater on a single breath of air. Since breath-hold divers can remain underwater for only two or three minutes, it was not long before they discovered ways to extend their dive times.

Open Diving Bells.   Aristotle wrote that, by the 4th century B.C., sponge divers were able to extend their stay under water by using an inverted "cauldron," a forerunner of the diving bell (Bachrach, 1998; Davis, 1936). The earliest reliable record of a diving bell in actual use dates to A.D. 1535, when Guglielmo de Lorena employed a diving bell in Italy to investigate sunken Roman barges (Davis, 1936; Dick, 2002). In 1691, a bell designed by Sir Edmund Halley (the astronomer of comet fame) reportedly carried several divers to depths of 60 ft (18m), where they could remain for an hour or more. In 1779, John Smeaton refined the diving bell by adding a crude air pump (Dick, 2002).

Diving bells continued to be employed successfully for many years, but they were limited in their usefulness, since they restricted divers to short-duration excursions of a few meters from the bell. What divers needed was a device that would allow them to work underwater without those restrictions. This need led to the development, in the early 18th century, of a variety of diving suits that supplied air from the surface.

Surface-Supplied Diving.   In 1715, an Englishman named Andrew Becker purportedly built a leather dive suit, which had a metal helmet and used air supplied from a bellows. In England in 1754, a well-documented dive operation was conducted by helmet divers apparently with air supplied through a hose connected to a pump on the surface (Davis, 1936). Diving suits gradually improved, especially with the invention of effective air pumps. Finally, in 1840, German inventor Augustus Siebe began producing his "closed dress" diving suit, which employed a seal between helmet and suit that allowed pressurization of the entire suit. The Siebe system is generally credited as the first modern diving suit (Davis, 1936; Leaney, 2002). In 1915, the U.S. Navy introduced the venerable MK V Diving Helmet, which was soon integrated into a sealed helmet–suit system that remained the navy's standard dive dress until finally replaced in 1980 by the MK-12. The MK-12 was replaced by the MK-21 in December 1993 (NAVSEA, 1999).

Surface-supplied diving with newer, lightweight helmets is still the primary system for commercial and military diving, mainly because of a solid history of safety and versatility combined with good communications with the working diver. However, the majority of scientific and recreational divers utilize less expensive and more versatile "self-contained" diving gear.

Self-Contained Diving

Open-Circuit Systems.   In 1825, Englishman William James developed the first "self-contained" dive system that employed a container of compressed air (Jackson,

1997). One of the most successful early self-contained dive systems was developed in 1865 by two French inventors, Benoît Rouquayrol and Auguste Denayrouse, whose system was featured in Jules Verne's famous novel *Twenty Thousand Leagues under the Sea* (Bachrach, 1982; Davis, 1936; Jackson, 1997). This line of development culminated in the 1943 invention of the "aqua-lung" breathing system by Jacques-Yves Cousteau and Emil Gagnon (Earle and Giddings, 1980). Cousteau and Gagnon's system differed from the others in that it utilized a simple, reliable "demand" regulator that supplied air to the diver on an as-needed basis, thus conserving the compressed air supply and making diving practical. The system was soon marketed around the world, leading to today's popular scuba (self-contained underwater breathing apparatus), the system used in most of today's recreational and scientific diving. Conventional scuba designs are known as "open-circuit" systems, because the exhaled air is vented into the water. In the late 19th century, dive systems were developed that conserved breathing gas even further by recycling exhaled gas.

Closed-Circuit Systems. The first "closed-circuit" system appeared in England in 1879, when Henry Fleuss developed a "rebreather" unit employing a reservoir of compressed oxygen coupled with a carbon dioxide absorbent that permitted the exhaled gas to be replenished with oxygen, cleaned of carbon dioxide, and recirculated to the diver (Davis, 1936; Earle and Giddings, 1980). Modern rebreathers utilize the same principle but have been improved significantly and now employ computerized control and monitoring systems to ensure that the diver receives the proper gas mix regardless of ambient pressure. These systems, such as the U.S. Navy's MK15 and MK16 and several commercial systems, permit divers to reach depths of hundreds of feet and remain for several hours. These units are generally reliable but can be unforgiving; a high level of training and maintenance is required to prevent serious mishaps or death.

One-Atmosphere Systems

Throughout the development of diving systems for individual divers, there was a parallel effort to develop systems for exploring the depths without being subjected to the pressure of seawater—that is, for keeping the occupants at surface pressure, or one atmosphere.

Closed Bells and Bathyspheres. As early as 1774, John Day successfully descended to a depth of 30 ft (9 m) in Plymouth Sound, England, in a closed bell made of wood. In 1930, off Bermuda, William Beebe descended to the incredible depth of 1426 ft (435 m) in a thick-walled steel ball known as a bathysphere (Davis, 1936). Bathyspheres reached great depths but, because they had to be lowered on a cable, they had limited depth and usefulness. Closed bells are still in regular use for transferring saturation divers between work site and chamber, as Deck Chamber, Bell Transfer System section describes.

Atmospheric Diving Suits. In 1715, Englishman John Lethbridge first tested an ingenious rigid diving suit consisting of a wooden barrel with a glass viewport and armholes sealed with leather cuffs. Because the barrel was sealed, the interior remained at surface pressure. Although the suit was not fitted with an air supply, Lethbridge was able to work a depth of 70 ft (21 m) long enough to carry out simple tasks (Davis, 1936; Earle and Giddings, 1980; Nuytten, 2002). Little more than a century later, in 1838, an American, William Taylor, developed the first successful armored suit, made of metal and fitted with articulated joints that permitted the diver to move about and perform work while remaining inside at one atmosphere (Davis, 1936). It was nearly another century, 1913, before Neufeldt and Kuhnke developed the first modern form of armored one-atmosphere suit. This steel suit was fitted with ball-and-socket joints that were flexible at greater depths (Davis, 1934). Modern one-atmosphere suits, some fitted with thrusters and nimble mechanical arms, are capable of very sophisticated tasks to depths of 1000 ft (305 m) or more (Nuytten, 2002).

From at least as early as the 17th century, other inventors pursued a different approach for venturing beneath the sea: the development of underwater boats that could provide protection from water pressure for its occupants while offering excellent mobility. Thus, the submarine was born.

Submarines. The first record of a functional submarine was a wooden-hulled vessel powered by 12 oars, built by a Dutchman, Cornelius van Drebbel, who tested two such submarines in the River Thames in 1620 (Davis, 1936; Earle and Giddings, 1980). In 1776, an American, David Bushnell, built the *Turtle*, a small wooden submarine that became the first such craft to be employed in warfare (Davis, 1936; Earle and Giddings, 1980). Submarine technology continued to improve throughout the 19th century until 1886, when the *Gymnote* became the French Navy's first operational submarine and the world's first modern submarine boat (Davis, 1936; Earle and Giddings, 1980). By World War I, submarines had evolved into powerful, effective weapons, reaching a new peak in 1955 when the United States launched the world's first nuclear-powered submarine, USS *Nautilus* (Earle and Giddings, 1980).

In 1953, Swiss inventor Auguste Piccard launched the *Trieste*, a strange craft which he called a bathyscaph, an underwater vessel that was part submarine and part dirigible. In 1960, Auguste's son, Jacques, and U.S. Navy Lt. Don Walsh descended in *Trieste* to the Challenger Deep, the deepest known spot in the oceans: 35,820 ft (10,916 m), where the pressure on their small cabin was 200,000 tons! The early 1960s also saw the emergence of several small submarines designed for research, such as Cousteau's "diving saucer," capable of reaching depths of 1000 ft (305 m), and John Perry's *Cubmarine*, which had a 150 ft (46 m) capability (Earle and Giddings, 1980).

Then, in 1963, the U.S. Navy suffered a major blow: America's most advanced nuclear submarine, *Thresher*, went missing off the coast of New England in 8400 ft (2561 m) of water. The navy had no means of conducting a rescue or recovery at that depth (Broad, 1997; Earle and Giddings, 1980). The *Thresher* disaster had at least one positive effect: It motivated the navy to develop deepwater rescue capability. The result was a flurry of research projects and the proliferation of a new type of underwater vehicle known as the submersible. These were primarily designed for scientific research in deep water (Broad, 1997).

Submersibles. Submersibles are specialized submarines designed for short-duration scientific or rescue missions. In 1964, the *Alvin* was christened at the Woods Hole Oceanographic Institution on Cape Cod. Funded by the U.S. Navy, this versatile and rugged craft is still one of the most active underwater vehicles in use today. Joining *Alvin* in the 1960s were dozens of submersibles of varying sizes and capabilities, many built by major defense contractors on the speculation that deep-ocean research would receive huge government contracts. The navy also launched two deep submergence rescue vehicles designed specifically for submarine rescue. One of the most remarkable of the new vehicles was the U.S. Navy's *NR-1*, still the world's only nuclear-powered research submersible

(Broad, 1997). Because research submersibles are designed to transport human occupants to extreme ocean depths, they are expensive to build and operate. As a result, other design efforts have been directed at unmanned "robot" vehicles that can conduct deep research at a fraction of the cost of manned submersibles and at no risk to humans.

Robotic Underwater Vehicles

Robotic vehicles are the primary workhorses of today's deepwater research, small enough to be launched and recovered by one person, or huge systems weighing several tons. They vary widely in function, payload, and depth rating; most are tethered to a surface ship from which they receive power and guidance commands, while others roam the seas independently, carrying out preprogrammed instructions and returning when those instructions have been completed. Those in the first group are generally referred to as remotely operated vehicles (ROVs), while the latter are called autonomous underwater vehicles (AUVs). At the January 1999 MIT conference, Gordon Watts predicted that robots would become "the archaeologists' trowels of the future" (Stone, 1999). As discussed below, robotic vehicles have already proven themselves in oceanographic and archaeological research. In fact, these underwater marvels of technology are actually beginning to *wield* the trowels!

With the availability of one-atmosphere and robotic systems, many have begun to ask, "Why use divers at all?"

HUMANS OR ROBOTS?

Some scientists believe that there is no longer a valid reason for humans to subject themselves to the hazards of deepwater diving. This same argument has raged for years in the U.S. space program: Humans or robots? Clearly, it is more costly to send humans to Mars or to the bottom of the ocean, but are there advantages that outweigh those costs? The answer, for space and the deep oceans, is that there are justifications for both humans *and* robots. For deepwater archaeology at moderate depths, there are viable options.

Additional Depth-Related Considerations

Regardless of the type of equipment worn, divers have always been limited to relatively short excursions into the depths. Of primary concern is the threat of complications from subjecting their bodies to ever-increasing pressure as they dive deeper. The weight of seawater causes the pressure on a diver's body to double every 33 ft (10 m) of depth, which elicits a complex series of physiological reactions. As the diver descends, water pressure increases and inhaled gases, especially nitrogen, begin to dissolve in the bloodstream in ever-increasing concentrations. Then, as the diver ascends and the surrounding pressure decreases, dissolved gasses attempt to escape through the lungs. If the ascent is too rapid, nitrogen cannot diffuse into the lungs rapidly enough and bubbles may form in the bloodstream, a condition that can create serious and even life-threatening symptoms, including decompression sickness ("the bends") and embolism.

In 1906, John Haldane developed for the British navy the first "decompression tables" for depths to 200 ft (61 m), consisting of a schedule for returning to the surface in timed stages in order to avoid pressure-related complications (Earle and Giddings,

1980: 104). Today, there are numerous sets of published decompression tables and even computer programs that automatically calculate decompression for a wide range of dive profiles and gas mixes. Regardless of the decompression method, divers making excursions from the surface are limited to relatively short dive times, which decrease rapidly with increasing depth. Saturation diving, a relatively recent innovation, makes it possible to extend dive times by orders of magnitude, although at increased cost and risk.

Saturation Diving

During saturation diving, divers are pressurized in a gas-filled chamber to the ambient pressure of the intended dive site, then kept at that pressure for several days or weeks. By remaining under pressure, the divers' blood and tissues become "saturated" with dissolved gasses, reaching an equilibrium state for a given pressure. At the end of the saturation cycle, the divers are slowly returned to surface pressure in a protracted decompression phase. Such dives generally, but not always, involve the use of gas mixes other than air. In 1960, the U.S. Navy conducted the world's first saturation dives, pressurizing divers in a chamber to a simulated depth of 200 ft (61 m), keeping them at that pressure for 14 days (Earle and Giddings, 1980). There are two principal modes of saturation diving: habitat diving and bell-transfer diving.

Habitat Systems. A habitat is essentially a pressure chamber permanently moored on the seabed, in which divers live for days or weeks at a time without decompression. Some habitats are simple cylinders, while others can be quite elaborate underwater laboratories and dormitories.

The world's first undersea habitat was a private venture. In 1962, American inventor and entrepreneur Edwin Link deployed his Man-in-Sea habitat. Link's success was followed later the same year by another private habitat, Cousteau's Conshelf One. In 1964, the U.S. Navy launched the first of its Sealab habitats, where divers remained at 193 ft (60 m) for 11 days (Earle and Giddings, 1980). Habitat research was lively during the 1960s but is now almost nonexistent, due primarily to the high costs of maintaining adequate levels of safety and logistical support. One of the few remaining habitats where research is conducted on an annual basis is *Aquarius*, operated by the National Oceanic and Atmospheric Administration (NOAA, 1991).

Deck Chamber, Bell Transfer Systems. In this saturation system, divers live in a large pressure chamber situated on the deck of a ship or oil platform. For each dive, the divers are transported from the chamber to the dive site in a closed diving bell, also pressurized to the working pressure. When the bell reaches the dive site and the pressures inside and outside the bell equalize, the hatch can be opened and the divers can exit the bell for up to several hours of work time. At the end of the dive, they return to the bell and are transferred back to the surface chamber where they can eat and sleep in relative comfort. Although this method is used extensively in the world's oil fields, it is rarely employed for scientific projects due to the high costs and risk factors.

All of the previously described dive systems, which include shipwreck discoveries and surveys by snorkelers, have been used by archaeologists. A brief review of the relatively new field of underwater archaeology reveals that archaeologists have been remarkably resourceful in acquiring access to new technology.

PROGRESS IN THE TECHNOLOGY OF UNDERWATER ARCHAEOLOGY

Early Search and Salvage Operations

In reviewing the early history of diving, one cannot fail to note a conspicuous and ever-present motivation for diving innovation: shipwreck salvage. Evidence suggests that many noteworthy inventions in diving were developed for the primary purpose of recovering valuable cargoes from sunken ships. As early as the 5th century B.C., Herodotus recorded that Scyllias, a Greek diver, recovered treasure from wrecked Greek vessels (Davis 1936). As sea trading in the Mediterranean began to burgeon, so, apparently, did the salvaging of wrecked ships. According to Livy, divers in the Levant, especially in Rhodes, were so adept at recovering valuables from sunken wrecks that a law was passed for the regulation of the distribution of finds (Davis, 1936; Marx, 1998). Rhodian sea law was the seed from which developed modern admiralty law that even today dictates the fates of many shipwrecks.

The first reported application of diving equipment to a shipwreck site was in Italy in A.D. 1535, when a bell designed by Guglielmo de Lorena was used to locate and explore Emperor Caligula's barges at the bottom of Lake Nemi (Earle and Giddings 1980; Marx, 1998). In 1664, a bell was used in Stockholm Harbor to recover most of the guns from the *Vasa*, which sank in 110 feet (33.5 m) of water in 1628 (Earle and Giddings 1980; Franzen, 1974). In the New World, Sir William Phipps used a diving bell in 1685 to salvage treasure from a Spanish ship in the Caribbean (Marx, 1998). The Spanish, too, conducted extensive recovery operations on ships sunk in the Americas on their way back to Spain with cargoes of New World gold, silver, and other valuables. Techniques and equipment developed during those early salvage attempts eventually contributed to the conduct of more effective scientific investigations.

Early Underwater Archaeology Efforts

Possibly the first attempt at underwater archaeology occurred in Italy in 1775 when English antiquarians sponsored an expedition to recover artifacts from the Tiber River near Rome. A diving bell was used in this operation, which was not successful because of the thick silt that blanketed the riverbed (Marx, 1998). The first major underwater excavation in the Western Hemisphere began in Mexico in 1904, where U.S. Consul Edward Thompson recovered Mayan artifacts from the cenote of Chichén Itzá in the Yucatán Peninsula. At first he used only a dredge, but in 1909 he briefly employed a Greek sponge diver (Delgado, 1997). Although thousands of artifacts were recovered, little if any archaeological information was recorded. Neither project can be classified as an archaeological excavation, but both hinted at the potential for underwater archaeology.

The first effort to conduct a professional archaeological study under water probably took place in 1900, when divers recovered objects from a Roman wreck, c. 75 B.C., near the Greek island of Antikythera. Helmet divers, under the direction of a nondiving archaeologist, recovered a variety of Greek art and a rare navigational computer. However, the wreck lies at a depth of 180 feet (55 m), which made the site difficult and dangerous, and the excavation was never completed (Bass, 1966; Delgado, 1997; Throckmorton, 1987).

During the first six decades of the 20th century, numerous underwater excavations were attempted, particularly after the demand regulator became widely available in the late 1940s. Most of these early excavations took place in the Mediterranean. Not until the 1960s, however, was the potential for underwater archaeology fully realized.

During summer 1960, graduate student George Bass directed the excavation of a Late Bronze Age shipwreck at a depth of 90–95 feet (27–29 m) near Cape Gelidonya, Turkey. Every day, Bass and other archaeologists dove to the site, where they personally conducted the excavation, applying proven practices of land archaeology and adapting their methodology as needed to the underwater environment. Bass soon published his research on the Cape Gelidonya wreck, setting a new standard for underwater archaeology and demonstrating that archaeology under water could be—and should be—conducted in the same detailed, rigorous manner of terrestrial excavations (Bass, 1966; Delgado, 1997).

Since the Cape Gelidonya project, Bass and others have conducted many additional scientific underwater archaeological investigations that have contributed significant new information on ancient trade routes and commerce, shipboard stowage and life, nautical technology, and other topics. Advances in diving technology have contributed to improvements in the efficiency and effectiveness of underwater archaeology and allowed archaeologists to investigate sites in deeper water.

Deepwater Exploration

The Antikythera wreck was not only the first wreck to be excavated under the direction of an archaeologist but also was the first deepwater wreck excavation. At a depth of 180 feet (55 m), the wreck lies near the safe limit for divers breathing compressed air. The need for decompression was poorly understood in 1900, and few Mediterranean divers had access to any form of decompression tables. One diver died during the project (Bass, 1966). Nevertheless, early in the 20th century salvors and ocean engineers began to apply new technology to the problems of accessing deepwater shipwrecks.

In 1935, the wreck of the *Lusitania* was located at a depth of 330 feet (100 m) with an early echo-location device that rapidly evolved into the sonar systems that would play a major role in antisubmarine warfare during World War II. Modern sonars, particularly side-scanning sonars, have become a primary tool for locating and mapping shipwrecks and other submerged cultural features.

Soon after the *Lusitania*'s discovery, Jim Jarrat became the first to explore the wreck, diving inside a special one-atmosphere suit called the "Iron Man" because of its thick, pressure-resistant, steel form. One-atmosphere "armored" suits have improved tremendously, and current models allow excellent mobility and dexterity; they also allow the operator to remain at surface pressure, thus making possible almost unlimited dive time with no need for decompression.

The *Lusitania* was revisited in the 1960s and 1980s by scuba and helmet divers. In 1993, a team led by Robert Ballard, documented the wreck in detail with still and video photography, utilizing three ROVs and a manned submersible (Ballard, 1995; Delgado, 1997). The progression of technology on this one site is impressive, demonstrating the ever-increasing capabilities for conducting deepwater shipwreck research.

In 1964, George Bass employed state-of-the-art technology in mapping a Late Roman shipwreck in the Mediterranean Sea with a stereophotogrammetric system mounted on the research submersible *Ashera*. Launched in May 1964 by the Electric Boat

Division of General Dynamics of Groton, Connecticut, *Ashera* was the first submarine built specifically for archaeological survey and mapping and was capable of descending to 600 feet (183 m). Less than one hour of underwater stereo photography, followed by 56 hours of laboratory processing, produced a three-dimensional site map that would have required a dozen archaeologists diving for several weeks to complete (Bass, 1966).

In 1973, the wreck of the United States Civil War ironclad USS *Monitor* was discovered off the coast of North Carolina at a depth of 240 feet (73 m). The following April *Monitor* was thoroughly mapped using a two-ton instrument pod deployed from the R/V *Alcoa Seaprobe*. From hundreds of 35 mm still photos the U.S. Naval Research Laboratory produced a photomosaic, showing the wreck from above, in excellent detail. In 1979, specially trained archaeologists conducted an excavation within the *Monitor*'s hull, the deepest "hands-on" excavation yet conducted by professional archaeologists (Broadwater, 1998). Research at this site is ongoing and is described in the next section.

With improvements in diving technology during the 1970s, deepwater research reached for new limits. The 1980s and 1990s brought a remarkable series of discoveries and new recovery techniques. Academic and governmental institutions and numerous commercial companies demonstrated their ability to locate deepwater wrecks and to recover data and material.

One of the most famous modern salvage projects occurred in 1981, when divers using saturation diving techniques recovered $67 million (U.S.) in gold from HMS *Edinburgh*, a ship that sank in 1942 in 800 ft (244 m) of water (Delgado, 1997). In 1985, RMS *Titanic* was discovered and extensively photographed at a depth of 12,500 ft (3810 m) using manned submersibles and ROVs. Subsequently, several expeditions have been made to the site, some documenting the site on film, others recovering artifacts. The California Gold Rush steamer *Central America*, which sank in 1857, was discovered in 1987 at a depth of 8000 ft (2439 m) by the Columbus-America Discovery Group. In 1991, a six-ton ROV, *Nemo*, was used to raise gold from the wreck. Uncirculated gold coins were successfully encapsulated in a rubber compound to protect them during recovery (Delgado, 1997; Kinder, 1998). In 1994, the Au Company located the wreck of the Japanese submarine *I-52* off Africa in 18,000 ft (5500 m) of water, making it the deepest shipwreck yet discovered (Delgado, 1997; Hamilton-Paterson, 1998).

In 1989–1990, Seahawk, a private company, conducted what was probably the world's first remote, deepwater excavation, using ROVs and employing archaeological methodology. The specially designed ROV, *Merlin*, conducted the excavation, mapping, and recovery at a depth of 1500 ft (457 m) (Delgado, 1997; Marx, 1998).

In 1989, Robert Ballard, the *Lusitania* investigator and a discoverer of the *Titanic* and other deepwater wrecks, began a series of deepwater investigations in the Mediterranean Sea, searching for ancient shipwrecks. A wreck dating to the 4th century B.C. was located on Skerki Bank, off Sicily, in 2950 ft (900 m) of water, the first wreck to be located, photographed and mapped using newly designed deepwater remote electronic mapping equipment and robotic vehicles. A few dozen artifacts, recovered from this and other nearby wrecks, have provided valuable information on the vessels' ages, origins, and routes. Ballard is continuing his explorations of the Mediterranean Sea floor and expanding into studies in the Black Sea and elsewhere. On these expeditions, Ballard has collaborated with respected archaeologists who have conducted post-expedition research, conservation, and publication.

Deepwater exploration has now developed into a viable, active and specialized discipline that is changing the way archaeologists and salvors view the potential for shipwreck discovery and investigation. New technology not only permits location of wrecks that had heretofore been considered "lost" but also provides the means for studying, mapping, and even recovering such wrecks.

Most deepwater shipwrecks lie outside territorial seas, in ocean areas where few if any laws can be used to protect them. These wrecks often fall victim to the interpretation of admiralty courts, which are not always sympathetic to archaeological principles and guidelines. One small program in the United States has proven successful at protecting and managing deepwater cultural resources: the National Marine Sanctuaries Program administered by the National Oceanic and Atmospheric Administration. The *Monitor* National Marine Sanctuary, one of the world's first marine protected areas and the first to protect a shipwreck, can serve as a model for submerged cultural resources inside or outside the world's territorial seas.

THE *MONITOR* NATIONAL MARINE SANCTUARY: A CASE STUDY IN DEEPWATER CULTURAL RESOURCE PROTECTION AND MANAGEMENT

USS *Monitor*: Dawning of a New Age of Warships

Launched on January 30, 1862, the Civil War ironclad warship USS *Monitor* was quite unlike any other vessel afloat. Her hull was almost completely submerged—only 13 in (33 cm) of freeboard when in battle trim—and her only superstructure an armored gun turret amidships and a small raised pilot house forward. *Monitor* was constructed primarily of iron, although her main deck and armor belt consisted of wood plated over with iron. Instead of a conventional "broadside" of cannon, *Monitor*'s armament consisted of only two 11-in (27 cm) Dahlgren smoothbore cannon mounted side by side in a unique, armored, revolving turret (Figures. 38.1 and 38.2).

On March 9, 1862, USS *Monitor* and the much larger Confederate ironclad CSS *Virginia* (ex-USS *Merrimack*) fought to a draw at Hampton Roads, Virginia, in one of the

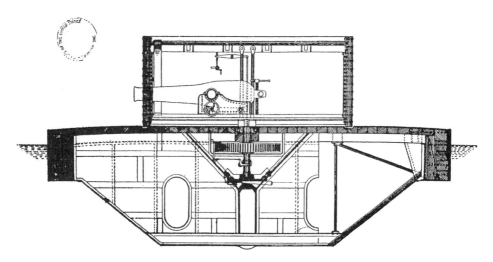

Figure 38.1. Transverse section through the turret of the original *Monitor*, 1862. (SOURCE: U.S. National Archives)

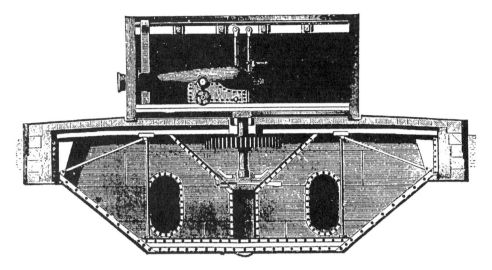

Figure 38.2. Transverse section of the *Monitor* through the center of the turret. (SOURCE: The Century Company)

most celebrated sea battles in history, the first between ironclad warships. The result, repeated around the world, was the rapid abandonment of conventional wooden, sail-powered warships and an escalation of naval weaponry and armor. In spite of her resistance to cannon fire, however, the *Monitor* was not designed for the high seas. On New Year's Eve, 1862, while being towed south along the North Carolina coast, she foundered in a severe storm off Cape Hatteras, with a loss of 16 lives.

The prototype for a new class of warships, the *Monitor* was followed by more than 60 *Monitor*-type vessels, some of which were in service well into the 20th century. Because of its international significance, *Monitor* was listed on the National Register of Historic Places and was designated a National Historic Landmark.

Managing and Protecting *Monitor*

When the wreck of the USS *Monitor* was discovered in 1973, lying off the coast of North Carolina at a depth of 240 ft (73 m), there was first elation, then concern. Her remains had long been sought because of her legendary reputation; however, her discovery left her vulnerable to exploitation by souvenir hunters and professional salvors. Because of her location, some 16 nautical miles off the coast of the United States—well beyond the three-nautical-mile territorial seas of the U.S. at that time—there were grave concerns that this internationally-significant historic ship would become the subject of unwanted looting and salvage. An examination of relevant U.S. legislation revealed that only the recently enacted Marine Protection, Research and Sanctuaries Act of 1972 conferred the authority for protecting resources out to the 200 nm. Exclusive Economic Zone (EEZ). This act provided for the designation of discrete areas as national marine sanctuaries and provided for their protection and management (16 U.S.C. 1431 et seq.). As a result, on January 30, 1975, *Monitor* was designated the first National Marine Sanctuary, to be managed by the National Oceanic and Atmospheric Administration (NOAA), an agency of the United States Department of Commerce.

The management role is carried out by NOAA's National Marine Sanctuaries Program (NMSP), which manages 13 National Marine Sanctuaries throughout the continental U.S., Hawaii, and American Samoa. NOAA published a management plan for *Monitor* in 1982 and revised the plan in 1992 to reflect the results of management policies and scientific research since the wreck's discovery (NOAA, 1982, 1992).

Monitor's inaccessibility, because of her remoteness, depth, and harsh environment, is a major factor influencing protection, management, and research. She lies on a flat, featureless, sandy bottom at a depth of 240 ft (73 m). She rolled over as she sank, causing her turret to pull free and sink to the bottom, upside down. Then the hull settled to the seabed, where it landed on the turret. The inverted hull now lies partially buried in sediment, with the stern port quarter suspended above the bottom by the displaced turret. The lower hull, now the highest part of the wreck, has collapsed forward of the midships bulkhead, and the stern armor belt and associated structure is badly deteriorated. The position of the turret under the port quarter elevates the stern and port side, producing a list to starboard and creating severe stresses on the hull.

Monitor suffers from extensive deterioration and structural damage as a result of three factors: (1) damage that occurred at the time of sinking; (2) deterioration caused by more than a century of exposure to a dynamic seawater environment; and (3) damage resulting from human activities. The wreck has suffered from the natural effects of corrosion and the action of strong currents. Several researchers have hypothesized that *Monitor* was inadvertently depth-charged during World War II, resulting in part of the visible damage to the lower hull and, possibly, to the stern armor belt. In addition, evidence exists that the wreck has been damaged by recent anchoring and fishing activities. In 1991, despite efforts at protection, a private fishing vessel anchored illegally on *Monitor*, apparently initiating a chain reaction of deterioration and collapse that is still underway. Fishing gear and nets have been found on the wreck on almost every site visit, suggesting that these illegal fishing activities have done additional damage. The U.S. Coast Guard assists NOAA in the protection of *Monitor*; however, the remoteness of the site makes continual surveillance impossible.

One of the most effective protection strategies in the National Marine Sanctuary Program is education. NOAA subscribes to the belief that most people will support a program of resource protection if they understand what they may lose if the resources are damaged or destroyed. This strategy of promoting better public understanding of and appreciation for the underwater environment and the beautiful and fragile resources that lie within has been very successful. Most sanctuaries now have public advisory committees and nongovernmental organizations that support and assist NOAA with sanctuary management programs and activities.

NOAA also operates on the assumption that sanctuary resources are to be both protected and enjoyed; as a result, the Sanctuary Program Plan includes provisions for promoting nondisturbance visitation to the reefs, kelp beds, shipwrecks, and other sanctuary resources. Education programs include a wide range of informational brochures, organized school programs, publications, diving and whale-watching charters, and narrated beach walks. The Florida Keys National Marine Sanctuary has a "Shipwreck Trail" containing a variety of sunken vessels, for which educational brochures are available. Even though *Monitor* lies at a depth of 240 ft (73 m), since 1990 she has been visited annually by recreational divers using advanced scuba equipment and techniques generally called "technical" diving. Many, but not all, use "tri-mix" gas (oxygen, nitrogen, and helium) rather than air, in order to increase dive safety and enjoyment.

The third major component of sanctuary management is scientific investigation. Through staff projects, grants, and cooperative research programs, NOAA conducts research aimed at a better understanding of each sanctuary which, in turn, leads to better management and conservation practices and policies.

Scientific Investigations of *Monitor*

Since its discovery in 1973 and its designation as a National Marine Sanctuary in 1975, *Monitor* has been the object of numerous scientific expeditions, many sponsored by NOAA. Since 1975, NOAA has gathered a considerable amount of data at the Sanctuary through the application of a wide range of ocean technologies. A major expedition was conducted in August 1979 by NOAA, the state of North Carolina and the Harbor Branch Foundation. A team of archaeologists surveyed and photographed *Monitor*'s hull and conducted a test excavation in the captain's stateroom. The archaeologists and their Harbor Branch tender divers, "locked out" of a dive chamber on the *Johnson-Sea-Link* submersible, breathing a helium–oxygen mix supplied by a hose from the submersible (Figures 38.3 and 38.4). As mentioned in the previous section, this may still be the deepest shipwreck excavation ever conducted by professional archaeologists.

Monitor's anchor was located and recovered in 1983, using the same equipment and many of the same diving team members. During the 1980s, NOAA also conducted several remote-sensing and submersible operations at the sanctuary.

Observations during the early 1990s revealed a serious increase in the rate of deterioration of *Monitor*'s hull. NOAA recognized that additional site data were needed in order to make effective long-range management decisions. Thus in July and August 1993, the agency conducted the *Monitor* Archaeological Research and Structural Survey (MARSS) expedition. Their principal goals were to map and videotape the hull in order to quantify and document site changes and deterioration, deploy a permanent mooring, locate, map and recover exposed, threatened artifacts, and conduct test excavations and mapping of the turret to assess the feasibility of recovery.

During the expedition, NOAA divers moved to and from the wreck in an open bell, breathing "tri-mix." This was the first time NOAA had ever approved tri-mix for deepwater scientific dives. Because the proportion of gasses (18 percent oxygen, 32 percent nitrogen, and 50 percent helium) was optimized for the depth and desired dive times at the *Monitor*, this mixture was called "*Monitor* tri-mix." Bad weather severely hampered operations, resulting in the completion of only nine submersible dives and three bell dives. In spite of these problems, several major objectives were met and the new diving methodology tested.

Two years later, in August and September 1995, the *Monitor* Archaeological Research, Recovery, and Stabilization Mission (MARRS '95) was conducted. Among the participants were NOAA, U.S. Navy, The Mariners' Museum, National Undersea Research Center at the University of North Carolina at Wilmington, and Key West Diver, Inc. MARRS '95 consisted of two segments: a NOAA diving reconnaissance operation, and a major effort to partially stabilize *Monitor*'s stern by removing and recovering its iron propeller, which had been displaced by a boat anchor.

After an interruption by Hurricane Felix, NOAA divers returned to Hatteras, where the navy salvage ship USS *Edenton* (ATS-1) joined them. *Edenton* established a four-point moor over the *Monitor* and diving operations began. On August 24–25, both NOAA and the navy conducted initial reconnaissance dives. As the final step in a program of extensive preparation and training, the NOAA team conducted a series of self-contained

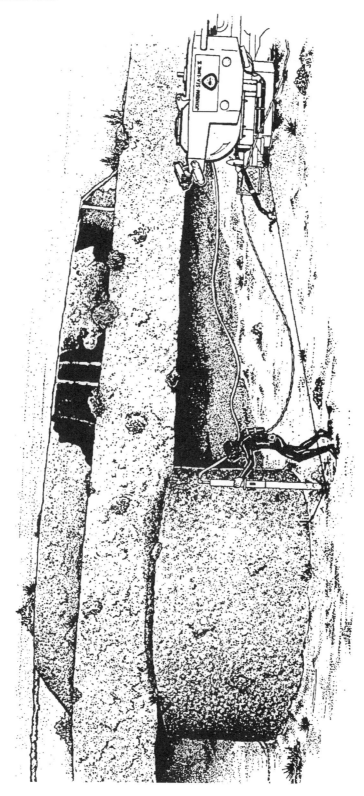

Figure 38.3. Artist's rendering of installation of datum casings at *Monitor's* turret (From the *Monitor* Collection).

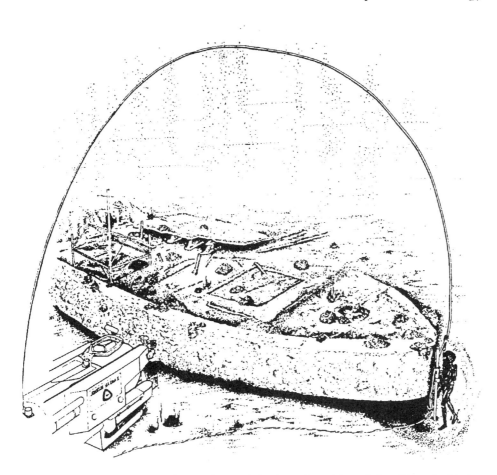

Figure 38.4. Artist's rendering of diver working with leveling tube at *Monitor*'s bow (From the *Monitor* Collection).

(untethered) dives, the first such dives ever approved by NOAA. These experimental dives, conducted for assessment and evaluation purposes, used open-circuit scuba equipment especially configured for redundancy and safety and once again utilized "*Monitor* tri-mix" for the bottom gas. Decompression was accomplished using tables developed specifically for the mission.

Navy divers initiated a carefully planned series of tasks designed to recover the *Monitor*'s propeller. Work progressed steadily until the threat of additional hurricanes and tropical storms forced the mission's early termination. It was three years before another attempt to stabilize the hull could be organized and funded.

Throughout this period, NOAA attempted to obtain an up-to-date image of the *Monitor* site to define an archaeological and engineering baseline site description. During 1996 and 1997, two imaging surveys were conducted at the *Monitor* Sanctuary with laser line scanners, a relatively new type of imaging device. Both expeditions were hampered by heavy seas, strong winds, swift currents, and poor visibility. Although the laser imaging surveys did not provide sufficient data for a complete mosaic of the *Monitor*'s hull, the images did provide extensive high-resolution documentation of the *Monitor*'s present condition and a baseline for comparison with future survey imagery.

Charting a New Course for *Monitor*

In 1995, in response to the challenging problem of *Monitor*'s disintegration, NOAA began to develop a comprehensive, long-range plan to document the problem, to present and discuss options for preserving *Monitor*, and to propose an aggressive course of action. Entitled "Charting a New Course for the *Monitor*," the plan was submitted to Congress in April 1998. The plan described each major option and planning element in detail and addressed all aspects of management, protection, and possible recovery. It discussed resources for planning, funding, and coordination with governmental and nongovernmental agencies with expertise in diving, salvage and marine engineering, conservation, exhibition, and other specialties.

The comprehensive plan addressed a range of management and research options for the immediate future, including the needs for recovery, conservation, curation, interpretation, and exhibition of the artifacts selected for recovery from the site. Six major phases of on-site research and recovery operations were identified:

- Preshoring mapping and archaeology
- Shoring beneath the hull
- Removal of skeg, propeller, lower hull, and engine
- Removal of armor belt/hull above the turret
- Removal of turret and contents
- Post-removal survey and stabilization

Implementation of the *Monitor* Preservation Plan

In 1998, a research expedition to the *Monitor* National Marine Sanctuary, whose primary purpose was to complete all tasks that must necessarily precede stabilization of the hull and recovery of hull components, was conducted to complete the first phase of the long-range preservation plan. The expedition's major goals were to map and document key areas of the hull, particularly in the stern and near the turret; to map and recover exposed artifacts; to recover the propeller (if deemed feasible at the time); to recover environmental data; and to complete an assessment of self-contained deepwater diving methodology and equipment. The expedition consisted of two phases, the first conducted jointly with the U.S. Navy and the Cambrian Foundation, the second a cooperative effort of the National Marine Sanctuary Program, NOAA Diving Center, National Undersea Research Center/University of North Carolina at Wilmington, Cambrian Foundation, and The Mariners' Museum. The groups worked from May 24 to June 25, 1998, with a one-week overlap between the two dive operations.

This expedition was extremely successful. Ninety dives were conducted on 27 of 30 possible dive days, 55 by the U.S. Navy and 35 by the combined NOAA team. The expedition logged a total of 106 hours cumulative bottom time, nearly twice the total (55 hours) of all five previous NOAA diving expeditions; counting lengthy decompression, the cumulative dive time was 625 hours. The group raised *Monitor*'s four-bladed iron propeller on June 5, along with an 11-foot section of shaft. On June 10, the propeller assembly was transported aboard the salvage vessel *Kellie Chouest* to Newport News Shipbuilding and transported to The Mariners' Museum, where it is undergoing conservation.

The expedition logged almost twice as much time on the wreck than in all previous NOAA expeditions, and it recovered data essential to the upcoming effort to stabilize *Monitor*'s hull and recover key components for long-term preservation and exhibit. In addition, 30 artifacts and samples were recovered, including wood and metal samples from the hull, core samples, and geotechnical data from the seabed.

In June and August 1999, NOAA, the U.S. Navy, National Undersea Research Program, University of North Carolina at Wilmington, Cambrian Foundation, and Mariners' Museum conducted two additional, highly successful *Monitor* expeditions: further survey and assessment of the lower hull above the engineering space in order to develop a recovery plan for the engine, and completion of the survey and assessment of the deck and armor belt on the port side in order to develop a stabilization plan. The mission completed all primary objectives and recovered a few small artifacts. U.S. Navy combat photographers recorded unprecedented video and still photographic images of the areas that were exhibiting dramatic changes: the stern, the engine and boilers, and other areas aft of the midships bulkhead.

Contributions by Private Researchers

Since 1990, NOAA has issued permits to private-sector divers to conduct research at the *Monitor* National Marine Sanctuary. While research by private groups has contributed to the growing body of knowledge on *Monitor*, the groups also have stirred controversy. In the beginning, nearly all made their dives breathing compressed air which, at *Monitor*'s 73 m depth, is considered by dive training organizations and most recreational divers to be unsafe. NOAA always has been concerned that air divers, impaired by an advanced level of nitrogen narcosis, pose a risk of damage to the wreck from inadvertent contact, both by the divers and their bulky equipment. In recent years, however, more divers have begun diving with mixed gasses and "technical diving" techniques suitable for *Monitor*'s depth, thus improving dive safety and increasing the quality and quantity of research results. NOAA encourages partnerships with private organizations for the conduct of *Monitor* research, but only under conditions that provide maximum safety for everyone and that will not result in adverse effects on the wreck.

In recent years, NOAA also has issued several nonresearch permits to allow recreational divers to visit *Monitor* before it collapses or is removed. These divers are not allowed to make contact with the wreck, but they can swim freely around the entire site and take still and video pictures. The response from these expeditions has been positive, and NOAA plans to resume the nonresearch permits when the hull has been stabilized.

Future of *Monitor*

NOAA believes that *Monitor*, a National Historic Landmark, deserves to be protected and, to the fullest extent possible, preserved for the future. Ocean technology appears to be the only means of achieving that goal. If no action is taken, the hull will collapse and eventually disintegrate completely. The comprehensive long-range plan now in effect will help determine which options can be carried out, given realistic constraints on funding and other resources. NOAA's present plans are to proceed with recovery of the engine, guns, and turret and to shore up the remaining hull. Once stabilized, *Monitor* will provide a deepwater archaeological site that can be excavated over a period of many years, and will involve NOAA, the U.S. Navy, The Mariners' Museum, and the private sector. NOAA will continue to encourage on-site research, documentation, publication, and exhibition to insure that *Monitor* will never be forgotten and that her story will continue to be told through educational and museum programs.

THE FUTURE OF DEEPWATER ARCHAEOLOGY

The field of deepwater exploration is still in its infancy, but the pace is quickening. As William Broad (1997) reported:

> The sea may cover 71 percent of the planet. But what dominates…is the deep, which lies beyond the shallows that border the continents and in total accounts for about 65 percent of the Earth's surface. This domain is so wide and so deep that by some estimates it comprises more than 97 percent of the space inhabited by living things on the globe, dwarfing the thin veneer of life on land.
>
> Human eyes have glimpsed perhaps one-millionth of this dark realm. Perhaps a thousandth or a billionth. No one knows….The truth is that our planet has managed to remain largely unexplored, until now.

Exploration Pushes Deeper

During the second half of the 20th century, humankind began to venture far out onto the continental shelf. In 1963, pioneer explorer Edwin A. Link mused:

> If man could find a way to work [on the continental shelf] in safety and relative comfort, he would at once possess the key to more than 10,000,000 square miles of sea bed. He could tap the scientific secrets…of these immense submerged plains… (quoted in Earle and Giddings, 1980).

Fewer than two decades later, Earle and Giddings (1980) were able to state, "Today the entire continental shelf area of the world—the region that extends from shore to about 600 feet down—is accessible to divers." Now, with the passage of another two decades, commercial divers work routinely at such depths, and deeper. Even more remarkable is that scuba divers are beginning to explore these previously forbidden realms. Carrying four or more cylinders pressurized with a variety of special gas mixes and following custom decompression tables generated by sophisticated, yet widely-available computer programs, these "technical divers" routinely explore caves and shipwrecks 300 or more ft (91 m) down, sometimes into the 500–600 foot (152–183 m) range. Those with the necessary funds are shedding their bulky scuba cylinders and donning lightweight, high-tech rebreathers that can automatically supply the appropriate gas mix for several hours of diving, regardless of depth. Technical diving, developed primarily by recreational divers, has proved so safe and efficient that it is being adapted for scientific research.

Researchers are now reaching new ocean frontiers, in person and via robotics and remote sensing. Each methodology has its advantages and disadvantages, its supporters and detractors; each will have its niche in underwater archaeology of the future.

Human Intervention. "Human intervention" is the term used by the commercial sector to denote a diving task conducted by humans. In commercial underwater services, divers typically are employed to depths of 450 ft (137 m), although they can go much deeper. Beyond 1500 ft (457 m), machines are the only means of intervention at this time, and they are often more economical than divers at depths below 500 feet (152 m) (Sea Technology, 1999). Because of the high cost of mounting diving operations at great depths, few archaeologists have attempted deepwater surveys or excavations, and those have remained shallower than 250 ft (76 m).

Humans also can reach extreme depths using submarines and submersibles. Such vehicles can descend thousands of feet, and a handful are capable of visiting almost all of the world's seabed. Humans can work in deep water using armored suits that maintain an interior pressure of one atmosphere. However, submersibles and armored suits are expensive to operate. Few are in service, and those are generally available only to large institutions that compete with other institutions for available time. Therefore, many researchers are relying more and more heavily on robots.

Robotic Intervention.   The field of robotics has expanded rapidly in recent years, primarily because of advances in computer technology but also because of the commercial oil industry's need for robotic tools for use in water depths below safe and economical limits for human divers. From simple instruments suspended on cables to sophisticated autonomous vehicles that can conduct complex tasks without human operators, robots are evolving rapidly into capable and cost-effective tools.

These tools are becoming widely accessible to scientists, including underwater archaeologists. ROVs with high-resolution color video cameras can be purchased or leased at reasonable costs, some small enough to be placed in the water by one or two persons in a small boat. Larger, more complex ROVs can even conduct archaeological mapping, excavation, and artifact recovery! Because ROVs can give an operator the feeling of being on the dive—similar to the experience of playing a high quality "virtual reality" video game—this heightened ability is referred to as "telepresence."

AUVs, equipped with sonar, global navigation receivers, and other instruments, can conduct complete surveys and return to specified locations. Some can even surface periodically, transmit data to a satellite, then resume their survey. Advances in computer artificial intelligence suggest that AUVs will soon be able to make independent decisions on what types of targets to investigate and which equipment and methods are best for each.

Ballard, for years an enthusiastic proponent of robotics and telepresence, conceded that humans will never allow robots to conduct all deepsea exploration. "Nor should they," he added (Earle and Giddings, 1980). "There is no completely satisfactory substitute as yet for the combined dexterity, perception, and decision-making capability of an on-the-spot human being. But for general observation, as well as for well-defined specific jobs, machines are at least as good, sometimes better." The rapid development of these machines during the late 20th century makes this statement all the more valid.

Survey and Positioning Equipment.   Before archaeologists can extract information from underwater sites, they must first find the sites. Remote-sensing equipment has become so essential to underwater archaeological survey that almost all experienced researchers can operate basic instruments or at least can choose appropriate equipment and operators for any given survey task. The capabilities of these instruments are improving rapidly.

Modern, digitally based, side-scan sonar can map a quarter-mile swath of seabed at a boat speed of several miles per hour, displaying real-time, spatially corrected bottom topography on a computer screen. Simultaneously, a bottom-penetrating sonar can probe within seabed sediments to map buried objects while a cesium magnetometer detects ferrous material. All survey data are recorded on digital media, along with precise geographic locations, so that located objects and features are spatially related. Computers "post-process" the data, providing the survey archaeologist with a wide range of information on potential sites of interest. While the capabilities of integrated survey systems are increasing rapidly, their costs are dropping, making them more accessible even to small, modestly funded archaeological surveys.

Until recently, archaeologists often discovered that their survey targets could not be relocated and "ground-truthed" by divers because of inaccuracies in their positioning equipment. Satellite technology has virtually eliminated that problem. The U.S. global positioning system (GPS), and a similar satellite-based Russian system, have significantly reduced positioning errors. Using GPS and a "differential" reference signal (DGPS), one can return to the same spot on the ocean to within a few yards (meters).

These advances in diving and instrumentation have made it possible for underwater archaeologists to reach ever-increasing depths in their quest for well-preserved clues to our past.

Deepwater Archaeology Becomes a Reality

Although archaeology has been conducted in deep water since the beginning of the 20th century, the average underwater archaeologist's definition of "deep" is quite different from that of an oceanographer, to whom the term implies thousands of feet below the surface. At present, only a few underwater archaeology projects are taking place at depths below 200 ft (61 m), and these few are intermittent investigations. But the potential for deepwater archaeology has already been demonstrated. At the *Monitor* National Marine Sanctuary, NOAA-sponsored dive teams have extended the boundary of scientific diving, and U.S. Navy divers have conducted precise recovery operations at the *Monitor*'s depth of 240 feet (73 m). The Institute of Nautical Archaeology is conducting excavations at depths of 180 feet (55 m) and deeper, and a multinational team is investigating the remains of CSS *Alabama* at 200 ft (61 m).

Submersible and robotic operations, unconstrained by the limitations of human divers, have ventured much deeper. The *Titanic* has been extensively mapped and photographed, as have ancient shipwrecks in the Mediterranean; excavations have been conducted by ROVs on shipwrecks lying thousands of feet beneath the surface; dozens of famous shipwrecks in deep water have been located by remote-sensing instruments. During a single deepwater recovery dive on the 19th-century steamship *Central America*, the six-ton ROV, *Nemo*, worked for more than 100 hours (Kinder, 1998).

Although the technology exists to reach and explore the deepest realms of the oceans, little funding is available for such efforts. Most deepwater technology has been developed by the military and the oil industry, most of it concentrated on depths of a few thousand feet or less. No one can provide accurate information on military undersea capabilities, but a recent *Sea Technology Buyers Guide* provides some interesting statistics on current deepsea capabilities (Table 38.1).

Deepwater Archaeology in the Future

Although predictions for the future of deepwater exploration may sound to some like the dreams of science fiction writers, many researchers are confident that we will soon be able to explore the remotest ocean depths in person. For underwater archaeologists, the possibilities are endless and exciting.

Table 38.1. Deepwater capabilities at the start of the 21st century.

Work-class ROVs (worldwide)	400+
Firms building/supplying ROVs/AUV/UUVs	79
Firms producing/distributing equipment/apparel	48
Diving service companies	65
Firms producing/distributing sonar systems	100+

SOURCE: *Sea Technology Buyer's Guide,* 1999.

The underwater archaeology project of the future will probably be a collaboration between humans and machines. Let us speculate on the possibilities by imagining a hypothetical future project. First, the archaeologist conducts an underwater survey by programming an AUV, telling it to cover a specific area of sea bottom and to look for specific types of archaeological sites. The torpedo-shaped robot is released to complete the assignment on its own. Days or weeks later, the AUV returns, slides into a docking station, and downloads its data into a computer. The computer reads the instructions given to the AUV and examines the collected data. Based on the information available, the computer then analyzes the data and prepares a survey report for the archaeologist. The report includes locations, site plans, and interpretation of all data, including analyses of the age, origin, and identity of each located site and recommendations on which sites warrant further investigation. The archaeologist then conducts the excavation from the surface, using an ROV to map and excavate the site and recover the artifacts.

Further into the future, archaeologists may inspect deep sites in person, breathing oxygenated liquid or possibly wearing artificial gills. By swallowing a pre-dive pill containing a chemical antidote to the bends, divers may avoid the need to follow old-style decompression tables on ascent. Alternately, they might don thin, comfortable dive suits capable of generating force fields that provide protection from the pressures of the deep.

These future sites might even be excavated as if they were on dry land. The archaeologist might place on the site a large box that, upon activation, would create a powerful force field that forms a protective dome from which all water is purged to allow the archaeologist to work at surface pressure. Under the watchful eye of the archaeologist, small robots could conduct excavation and mapping, and send artifacts to the surface in special sealed containers that pass through a special gateway in the pressure dome.

Following our futuristic dig, artifacts probably will be documented by a holographic camera, then processed in an automated laboratory to insure that the objects will not deteriorate. Not to be left out of the scientific process, our archaeologist now studies the excavation results and the artifacts and writes an interpretive report that is richly illustrated by three-dimensional site plans and artifact images. Even with the anticipated array of future technology, interpretation and reporting of archaeological sites will still require trained professional archaeologists!

Competing Interests in the Deep Oceans

Unfortunately, underwater archaeologists and other scientists do not have the ocean depths to themselves. Commercial and military interests often compete for access or control of the deep. Some fishing activities, especially deep trawling operations, can pose a threat to deepwater archaeological sites. Gibbons (1991) reported that Ballard's teams found much of the seabed they have surveyed—even at depths of hundreds of meters—scoured by trawl nets. Deepwater resource recovery projects such as oil drilling and manganese nodule dredging also can damage or destroy cultural resources.

Of even more concern to underwater archaeologists is the specter of commercial salvage. The October 4, 1999, issue of *U.S. News & World Report* featured the cover headline, "Gold Rush: Salvage teams and scientists battle over sunken treasure and priceless artifacts." The accompanying article (Koerner, 1999) reports that treasure hunters now have "unfettered access" to the latest high-tech equipment. In fact, many commercial projects are much easier to fund than traditional scientific expeditions, since speculators are lured by the twin incentives of adventure and possible return on investments. In the past, treasure hunters often did not produce scientific data or reports, a situation that appears to be changing.

Many commercial salvage companies now employ archaeologists and conservators and attempt to conduct their recovery operations to acceptable professional standards. Some salvors have come to appreciate and prefer a high level of scientific investigation; others make the effort because it is good business: They have discovered that artifacts are worth more to serious collectors when their provenience is well documented and accompanied by detailed stories of the ships that carried the objects. Cultural resource managers are not mollified by the current salvage situation, most preferring to protect underwater archaeological sites in situ whenever possible. Since most deepwater sites have heretofore been beyond the range of scientists and salvors alike, archaeologists did not have to worry about deepwater treasure hunters.

Most laws intended to protect shipwrecks and other submerged cultural resources are limited to coastal waters, and even there they are often ineffective or inadequate. In the United States, the Abandoned Shipwreck Act only applies out to the three-mile limit of state waters. In November 2001, the United Nations Educational, Scientific, and Cultural Organization (UNESCO) adopted the Convention on the Protection of Underwater Cultural Heritage by a vote of 94 to 5. The first principal of the UNESCO Convention is to "preserve the underwater cultural heritage for the benefit of humanity" (UNESCO, 2001). The Convention discourages the commercial exploitation of cultural sites, recommends in situ preservation whenever practicable, and appends a set of professional archaeological standards. However, several of the major industrialized countries with capabilities for deepwater recovery either voted against the Convention or abstained. (The United States is not a member of UNESCO, so could not vote on the convention.) Therefore, it remains to be seen if sufficient countries will ratify the Convention in order for it to become international law. Even more problematic is whether the world's nations will work together to enforce this sensible doctrine and ensure that submerged archaeological sites will be properly studies, documented, and reported to other professionals and to the public at large.

In 1980, Sylvia Earle (Earle and Giddings, 1980) wrote, "The time has come to combine the wisdom of science and the sensitivity of art to mold attitudes that will transcend written laws. Needed is an ocean ethic." Later, Earle (Earle and Henry, 1999) wrote with an increased urgency: "There is a window in time, now, when we could forever lose a priceless ocean wilderness heritage—or develop the foundation for an enduring legacy of natural and historic treasures, an inspired gift from the 20th century to all who follow."

William Broad (1997) described archaeological sites lying in deep water as an international "archive" of our world culture. Broad also cautioned us to manage that archive wisely, lest we lose significant and nonrenewable cultural resources:

> Done right, the excavation of this archive will strengthen us as a species and give us new depths of self-knowledge....If it is done wrong, we will miss a unique opportunity that is never to be repeated. The wave breaks but once.

The UNESCO Convention has created an international wave of concern for the preservation of our underwater archaeological resources. Let us hope that the world's political leaders and resources managers will catch this wave and support the long-term preservation of our maritime heritage.

REFERENCES

Allen, Thomas B., 1999, The Battle of Midway, *National Geographic* 195(4):80–103.

Bachrach, Arthur J., 1982, A Short History of Man in the Sea. In *The Physiology and Medicine of Diving*, edited by P.B. Bennett and D.H. Elliott. Best Publishing Co., San Pedro.

_____, 1998, The History of the Diving Bell. *Historical Diving Times* 21 (Spring).

Baker, Nick, 1997, William Thompson: The World's First Underwater Photographer. *Historical Diving Times* 19:Summer.

Ballard, Robert D., 1987, *The Discovery of the* Titanic. Madison Press Books, Toronto.

_____, 1990a, *The Lost Wreck of the* Isis. Madison Press Books, Toronto.

_____, 1990b, *The Discovery of the* Bismarck. Madison Press Books, Toronto.

_____, 1995, *Exploring the* Lusitania. Madison Press Books, Toronto.

_____, 1998a, *Explorations: My Quest for Adventure and Discovery under the Sea. Hyperion*, New York.

_____, 1998b, High Tech Search for Roman Shipwrecks. *National Geographic* 193(4):32–42.

Balter, Michael, 1999, Bible's Bad Boys Weren't Such Philistines After All. *Science* 285:36–37.

Bascom, Willard, 1976, Deep Water, *Ancient Ships*. Doubleday & Company, Garden City.

_____, 1987, Deepwater Salvage and Archaeology. In *The Sea Remembers*, edited by Peter Throckmorton, pp. 222–225. Weidenfeld & Nicholson, New York.

Bass, George F., 1966, *Archaeology under water*. Thames and Hudson, London.

_____, editor, 1972, *A History of Seafaring Based on Underwater Archaeology*. Thames and Hudson, London.

Beebe, William, 1939, *Half Mile Down*. Harcourt, Price, New York.

Bennett, Peter B. and Elliott, David H., editors, 1982, *The Physiology and Medicine of Diving*. Best Publishing Co., San Pedro.

Broad, William J., 1997, *The Universe Below*. Simon & Schuster, New York.

Broadwater, John D., 1997, Rescuing the Monitor: Stabilization and Recovery Efforts at the *Monitor* National Marine Sanctuary. *Underwater Archaeology*, Society for Historical Archaeology.

_____, 1998, Managing an Ironclad: Research at the Monitor National Marine Sanctuary. In *Excavating Ships of War*, edited by Mensun Bound, pp. 287–293. International Maritime Archaeology Series, Volume II, Oxford University. Anthony Nelson Press, Oswestry.

Broadwater, John D., Hill, Dina B., Johnston, Jeffrey P., and Kozlowski, Karen, 1999, Charting a New Course for the *Monitor*: Results from the 1998 Research Expedition to the *Monitor* National Marine Sanctuary. In *Underwater Archaeology*, Society for Historical Archaeology.

Cain, Emily, 1977, *Ghost Ships*. Beaufort Books, New York.

Cousteau, Jacques-Yves, and Dugan, James, 1963, *The Living Sea*. Harper & Row, New York.

Cousteau, Jacques-Yves, and Dumas, Frederic, 1953, *The Silent World*. Harper & Brothers, New York.

Davis, Robert H., editor, 1936, *Deep Diving and Submarine Operations*. Published for Siebe, Gorman and Co. Ltd., by The Saint Catherine Press, London.

Deacon, G.E.R., editor, 1962, *Seas, Maps, and Men: An Atlas-History of Man's Exploration of the Oceans*. Doubleday & Company, Garden City.

Deacon, Margaret, 1971, *Scientists and the Sea, 1650–1900: A Study of Marine Science*. Academic Press, London.

Delgado, James P., editor, 1997, *Encyclopaedia of Underwater and Maritime Archaeology*. British Museum Press, London.

Dick, Peter, 2002, Historical Diving Society USA, presonal communication.

Diole, Philippe, 1954, *4000 Years Under the Sea: The Story of Marine Archaeology*. Julian Messner, New York.

Doyle, Howie, 1995, Man and Machine: Divers, ROVs and High-Tech Solutions to Undersea Missions. *UnderWater Magazine*: Winter, 1994.

Dugan, James, 1956, *Man Under the Sea*. Harper & Brothers, New York.

Dumas, Frederic, 1976, *30 Centuries Under the Sea*. Translated by Ph. A. Facey. Crown Publishers, New York.

Earle, Sylvia A. and Giddings, Al, 1980, *Exploring the Deep Frontier*. National Geographic Society, Washington, D.C.

Earle, Sylvia A. and Wolcott Henry, 1999, *Wild Ocean: America's Parks under the Sea*. National Geographic Society, Washington, D.C.

Ellis, Richard, 1996, *Deep Atlantic: Life, Death, and Exploration in the Abyss*. Knopf, New York.

Franzén, Anders, 1974, *The Warship Vasa*. P.A. Norstedt and Söners Förlag, Stockholm.

Frey, D.A., Hentschel, F.D., and Keith, D.H., 1978, Deepwater Archaeology: The Capistella wreck Excavation, Lipari, Aeolian Islands. *International Journal of Nautical Archaeology and Underwater Research* 7(4):279–300.

Gibbons, D., 1991, Archaeology in Deep Water: A Preliminary View. *International Journal of Nautical Archaeology and Underwater Research* 20(2):163–168.

Gilliam, B., and Von Maier, R., 1992, History of Diving. In *Deep Diving: An Advanced Guide to Physiology, Procedures and Systems*. Watersport Publishing, San Diego.

Hamilton-Paterson, James, 1998, *Three Miles Down: A Hunt for Sunken Treasure*. The Lyons Press, New York.

Haseltine, Eric, 1999, Slow Pain Coming. *Discover Magazine* August: 88.

Jackson, Peter, 1997, Development of Self-contained Diving Prior to Cousteau-Gagnan. *Historical Diver* 13:34–36.

Kinder, Gary, 1998, *Ship of Gold in the Deep Blue Sea*. Atlantic Monthly Press, New York.

Koerner, Brendan I., 1999, The Race for Riches, *U.S. News & World Report* October 4, pp. 45–50.

Larson, H.E., 1959, *A History of Self-Contained Diving and Underwater Swimming*. National Academy of Sciences, National Research Council, Washington, D.C.

Leaney, Leslie, 2002, Historical Diving Society, USA, personal communication.

Link, Marion Clayton, 1973, *Windows in the Sea*. Smithsonian Institution Press, Washington, D.C.

Marx, Robert F., 1971, The Early History of Diving, Part 1. *Oceans* 4(4):67–74.

_____, 1971, Early History of Diving, Part 2, *Oceans* 4(5):25–34.

_____, 1998, *Deep, Deeper, Deepest: Man's Exploration of the Sea*. Best Publishing Co., Flagstaff.

McCann, Anna M. and Freed, J., 1994, Deep Water Archaeology: A Late Roman Ship Sailing from Carthage. *Journal of Roman Archaeology*, Supplementary Series No. 13.

Muckelroy, Keith, 1978, *Maritime Archaeology*. Cambridge University Press, Cambridge.

_____, 1980, *Archaeology under Water: An Atlas of the World's Submerged Sites*. McGraw-Hill Book Company, New York.

National Oceanic and Atmospheric Administration, 2001, *NOAA Diving Manual: Diving for Science and Technology*. U.S. Department of Commerce, Washington, D.C.

Nuytten, Phil, 2002, Historical Diving Society, Canada, personal communication.

Penzias, Walter, and Goodman, M.W., 1973, *Man beneath the Sea: A Review of Underwater Ocean Engineering*. Wiley-Interscience, New York.

Risso, Gianni, 1999, Gianluca Genoni is the New "King of the Abyss." *Skin Diver Magazine* March: 11.

Stone, Richard, 1999, Researchers Ready for the Plunge into Deep Water. *Science* 283:929.

Throckmorton, Peter, editor, 1987, *The Sea Remembers*. Weidenfeld & Nicholson, New York.

_____, 1972, Romans on the Sea. In *A History of Sea-faring, Based on Underwater Archaeology*, edited by George Bass, Thames and Hudson, London. pp. 65–86.

_____, 1970, *Shipwrecks and Archaeology: The Unharvested Sea*. Little, Brown, Boston.

UNESCO, 2001, Convention on the Protection of Underwater Cultural Heritage, United Nations Educational, Scientific, and Cultural Organization, November 6, 2001.

U.S. Navy, Naval Sea Systems Command, 1999, *U.S. Navy Diving Manual (Revision 4)*. U.S. Government Printing Office, Washington, D.C.

Wiseman, James, 1999, Challenge of the Deep. Archaeology. May/June:10–12.

Chapter 39

Side Scan Sonar

MARTIN KLEIN

INTRODUCTION

Side scan sonar is the most commonly used remote sensing tool for detecting shipwrecks, artifacts, and other cultural resources of archaeological interest.

On land, the primary "tool" for archaeological search is human vision. Underwater, there are severe limitations to optical visibility. The maximum range of optical detection, even in ideal conditions, is approximately 30 m; in many situations, turbidity reduces optical detection range to less than 1 m. Turbidity may vary on a diurnal or seasonal basis, and it is often prevalent in shallow areas or near highly populated regions. These areas of reduced visibility often have the highest potential for archaeological discovery.

Yet, compared to light, sound is able to travel underwater with reduced attenuation. Sound Navigation And Ranging (sonar) uses underwater sound in a variety of applications. The earliest sonar equipment was used in warfare to detect midwater submarines. A sound was transmitted in the water, and a trained operator with headphones listened for the echoes of enemy targets. Headphone detection was later supplemented by electronic detection. Cathode-ray-tube (CRT) displays gave a visual indication of the range and bearing of targets. Other sonars were developed to determine water depth below the keel of a ship. These echo sounders were first used for safe navigation and later for hydrographic and geologic mapping of underwater terrain. The sinking of the RMS *Titanic* in 1912 sparked research into using sonar to detect icebergs. Other developments were made in specialized applications such as fish finding and seismic prospecting for oil.

Side scan sonar is a specialized technique in which short pulses of acoustic energy are transmitted along the seabed in fan-shaped beams (narrow in the horizontal plane and

Martin Klein, Consultant, 4 Old South Lane, Andover, Massachusetts 01810.

International Handbook of Underwater Archaeology, edited by Carol V. Ruppé and Janet F. Barstad. Kluwer Academic/Plenum Publishers, New York, 2002.

Figure 39.1. Artist's concept of side scan sonar with subbottom profiler (courtesy Klein Associates, Inc.).

wide in the vertical plane) from a moving vessel or an underwater towed vehicle. Figure 39.1 shows an artist's conception of the side scan sonar technique, and Figure 39.2 the launching of a towfish from the stern of a survey vessel. The return echoes from any objects in the path of the beams are continuously recorded on a graphic display to create an image called a sonograph, which frequently resembles a large-scale aerial photograph.

Figure 39.2. Launch of a side scan sonar towfish (Photo by Martin Klein, courtesy Klein Associates, Inc.).

In a way, human vision is still used, but sonar produces an image which the eye can interpret.

Originally developed for the military in the latter part of World War II, side scan sonar was first used for academic research in the late 1950s. Systems were developed at academic institutions such as the British National Institute of Oceanography, Hudson Laboratories of Columbia University, Bath University, and Scripps Institution of

Oceanography. In 1960, Kelvin Hughes introduced "Fisherman's Asdic," which could be used as a side scan sonar, followed in 1966 by "Transit Sonar," a single-channel side scan sonar with a transducer mounted on a pipe off the side of a ship.

Early side scan sonars displayed results on mechanical graphic recorder mechanisms developed in the 1940s by companies such as Hogan, Finch, Times Facsimile, Alden, and Muirhead, for weather map transmission and early newspaper facsimile. These recorders utilized a rotating drum or a mechanical stylus to move an electrical point of contact on chemically treated recording paper. The recorders improved over the years, but they were still subject to reliability and stability problems. In the 1980s, digital thermal recording systems appeared, resulting in significant popularization of facsimile instruments. The new mechanisms allowed simpler and more reliable electronically scanned thermal graphic recorders and were soon adapted by all side scan sonar manufacturers.

In modern side scan systems, sonar signals are converted to digital form, allowing for a wide variety of signal enhancements. In addition to "hard copy" sonographs, sonar records may be displayed on computer CRTs, and color may enhance appearance and assist interpretation, although the color is false—not the actual optical color of the target. Side scan sonar images once were highly distorted, but recent developments in digital processing allow the images to be presented in a more geometrically correct fashion.

Modern side scan sonar systems may now be integrated with electronic global positioning systems (GPS) so that targets may be accurately located and relocated. Sonar survey information may now be stored on digital storage devices for later retrieval, analysis and processing. The huge processing capability and relatively low cost of personal computers have allowed for the development of powerful systems that use the computer's CRT for the sonar images.

Side scan sonar systems are typically portable, so they can be deployed on "ships of opportunity" anywhere in the world. Some systems are small, lightweight, and battery-powered and can be operated on small boats. Lightweight cables are available for shallow-water operations, while high-strength, steel-jacketed cables are used for deep tow operations. Systems are now able to operate in the deepest parts of the ocean. Towing sonar often involves peripheral equipment such as winches, slip rings, depressors, cable fairing (to minimize cable drag and vibration), and safety devices.

Harold Edgerton: Strobes, Pingers, and Mud Penetrators

During the 1950s, Professor Harold E. Edgerton of the Massachusetts Institute of Technology, famed for his inventions that improved the strobe light, teamed with Jacques Cousteau to take pictures of the ocean depths, as deep as 12,000 m. Edgerton developed specialized cameras and strobe lights and utilized a precision 12 kHz sonar "pinger" to position the camera precisely near the sea floor. When he observed that the pinger was penetrating the ocean floor and graphing shallow sediment layers, he went on to develop a high-resolution, acoustic subbottom profiler he called a "mud penetrator."

Edgerton's device had been adapted from an old 12 kHz U.S. Navy echo sounder that utilized a wide, cone-shaped sound beam. The device normally pointed vertically toward the ocean floor. However, in 1961, Edgerton experimented with tilting the unit sideways and found that he was able to detect shipwrecks (Yules and Edgerton, 1964).

GREAT DISCOVERIES

The Search for *Thresher*

In 1963, the submarine *Thresher* sank in 2560 m of water. During the search for the submarine in 1963 and 1964, much deepwater technology was developed. The U.S. Navy Electronics Laboratory (NEL) built a deepwater sled carrying a magnetometer, sonar, underwater cameras and strobe lights, and a long-baseline acoustic positioning system. The bathyscaphe *Trieste*, which had made the first and only dive to the deepest known part of the ocean, was refurbished and called into service for the search. Two sonars were used on *Trieste*. One was a continuous-transmission-frequency-modulated (CTFM) sector-scanning sonar from Straza Industries; the other was a side scan sonar designed by Martin Klein of E.G.&G. International, which used the 12 kHz conical-beam technique. Neither sonar had the appropriate resolution to find the ill-fated submarine, which had imploded into a huge field of pieces of small debris. The sub was found with a magnetometer, then photographed in detail by the *Trieste* and the NEL camera sled.

Vineyard Lightship

In 1964, the *Vineyard Lightship* was found in Buzzards Bay, Massachusetts by Edgerton, Edward P. Curley, and John Yules, using the 12 kHz conical beam echo sounder transducer aimed sideways—an arrangement that was successful if the target was a large intact ship lying on an uncluttered ocean bottom (Figure 39.3). As side scan sonar developed over the years, sonograph quality improved dramatically. Figure 39.4 shows a detailed record of the *Vineyard Lightship* made 15 years later, when Klein introduced a 500 kHz high-resolution system.

After the *Thresher* search, a team led by Martin Klein of E.G.&G. International of Bedford, Massachusetts, continued to develop a side scan sonar that used a high frequency (100 kHz), a much narrower horizontal beam angle of 1°, and a streamlined towfish. In 1967, the team introduced the first commercial dual-channel towed side scan system (Klein, 1967). Although the system was intended for other research and commercial applications, it found some of its earliest use in assisting marine archaeologists.

An Ancient Find in Turkey

The year 1967 proved to be a watershed in the use of the new sonar technology in the nascent field of underwater archaeology. In August of that year, George Bass used an experimental system from Scripps, then the new E.G.&G. system, to locate a 2000-year-old ship in an area 92 m deep off the coast of Turkey (Bass, 1968). The ship, an ancient craft in which all exposed timber was gone and only a pile of amphorae and other artifacts remained visible, showed up on the original sonograph as only a blob—a blob, however, that has important historical significance as being the first remote-sensing discovery of an ancient ship.

Mary Rose

Two months later, Edgerton, John Mills, and Robert Henderson used side scan sonar in combination with a subbottom profiler to help Alexander McKee locate King Henry

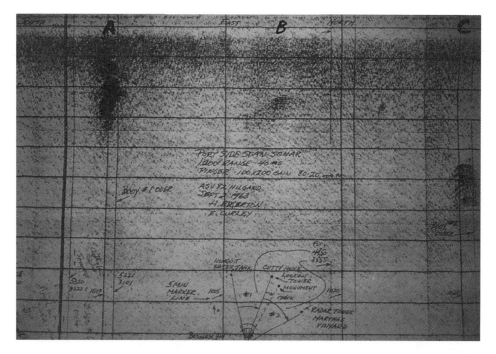

Figure 39.3. Side scan sonar record of *Vineyard Lightship*, 1964 (courtesy E.G. & G., International, Inc.).

VIII's flagship *Mary Rose*, which sank in 1545 (McKee, 1982). In November, Edgerton and Klein worked with Elisha Linder, using the older 12 kHz sonar and subbottom profiler to survey the ocean floor off the coast of Israel, in the ancient harbor near Ashdod (Edgerton et al., 1974). The expedition located a number of stone anchors and amphorae as well as a large outcropping suspected to be part of the ancient harbor works.

USS *Monitor*

In August 1973, Duke University mounted an expedition under the direction of John G. Newton to find the famed Civil War ironclad, USS *Monitor*, that sank off Cape Hatteras in 1862 (Newton, 1975). After first locating a possible target on the ship's "fish-finder," Edgerton lowered a side scan sonar and made an image that looked promising. A video camera lowered to the wreck revealed that the ship was lying upside down on its turret. After studying the video images, marine archaeologist Gordon Watts decided *Monitor* had been found. In 1975, the *Monitor*, an important American icon, was designated the first National Marine Sanctuary of the United States.

Hamilton and *Scourge*

In 1975, a team from the Royal Ontario Museum and Canada Centre for Inland Waters, under the direction of Daniel A. Nelson, used side scan sonar to search for two War of 1812 American-armed schooners, the *Hamilton* and the *Scourge*, in Lake Ontario (Cain, 1983). The ships sank August 8, 1913 after being overwhelmed in a sudden violent squall. After covering some 110 km^2, the team found the vessels about 550 m apart in

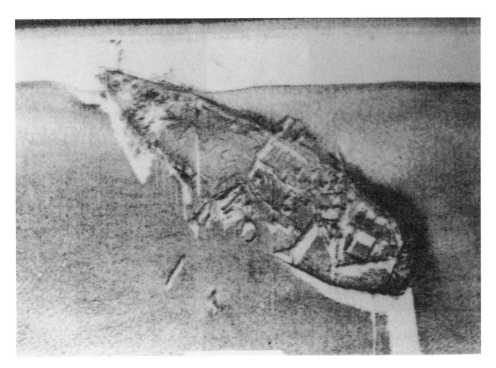

Figure 39.4. 500 kHz side scan sonar record of *Vineyard Lightship*, 1979 (courtesy Klein Associates, Inc.).

90 m of water. Both vessels were upright with hulls intact, masts, topmasts, and bowsprits in place and guns and even bones on deck (Nelson, 1983). Because of their unusually fine condition, the *Hamilton* and the *Scourge* have been the subjects of much archaeological research over the years. The ships were even commemorated by Canadian government stamps in 1987. Figure 39.5 shows a sonograph of the *Hamilton*.

The "Loch Ness Wellington"

Side scan sonar also has been used to find old aircraft. Of course, an "old" plane is not as old as an ancient shipwreck. Still, these finds can be important. On New Year's Eve 1940, an aging Wellington bomber ditched in Loch Ness in Scotland. In 1976, during a side scan sonar survey in the Loch, Martin Klein and Charles Finkelstein detected a twin-engine airplane. Told that a twin-engine PBY Catalina had been lost in Loch Ness, Klein and Finkelstein announced the discovery of the PBY. In 1978, Klein returned to Loch Ness with Garry Kozak and Thomas Cummings to make an improved sonar image of the aircraft (Figure 39.6). Cummings observed that the image looked like a Wellington. Investigations by a team led by Robin Holmes of Heriot-Watt University of Edinburgh determined that the aircraft was indeed *R for Robert*, RAF N2980. It was raised, restored, and put on display at the Brooklands Museum in Weybridge, England, where it had been built. Designed by famed Barnes Wallis, it had a unique, cloth-covered geodesic construction that allowed it to continue to fly even when riddled with gunshot holes. Known forever afterward as the "Loch Ness Wellington" (Holmes, 1981), the aircraft is the only known survivor of the many that served in World War II.

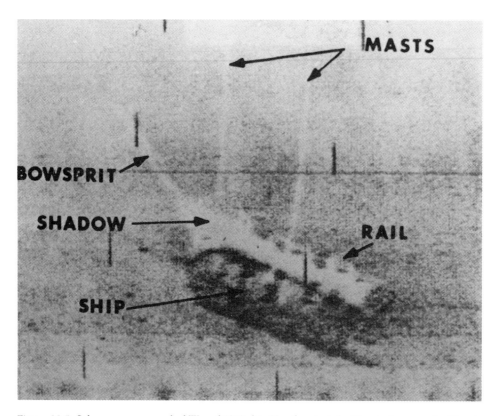

Figure 39.5. Side scan sonar record of War of 1812 ship *Hamilton* in Lake Ontario (courtesy the Canada Centre for Inland Waters and the Royal Ontario Museum).

Breadalbane

In 1845, Sir John Franklin set forth from London with the *Erebus* and *Terror* to search for the Northwest Passage. Franklin's journey was doomed, and the *Erebus* and *Terror* were lost. Of several ships that set out to find Franklin, the *Breadalbane* sailed in May 1853, only to sink near Beechey Island in Resolute Bay on August 21, 1853. In 1980, Joe MacInnis, Ph.D. led an expedition sponsored by National Geographic Society to locate the *Breadalbane* (MacInnis, 1983, 1985). Using a side scan sonar operated by Garry Kozak, the ship was found sitting upright in 100 m of water (Figure 39.7). Two masts were standing, and the hull was substantially intact. The *Breadalbane* was commemorated by a Canadian government stamp in 1987.

Lake Champlain and Lake George

For many years, Lake Champlain Maritime Museum, under the direction of Arthur B. Cohn, has used side scar sonar and other techniques to map Lake Champlain. Museum researchers have located and documented scores of shipwrecks and marine artifacts, including 525-year-old Native American canoes, ships from the French and Indian War, and a brig from the War of 1812. In 1997, the team accelerated its mapping program in

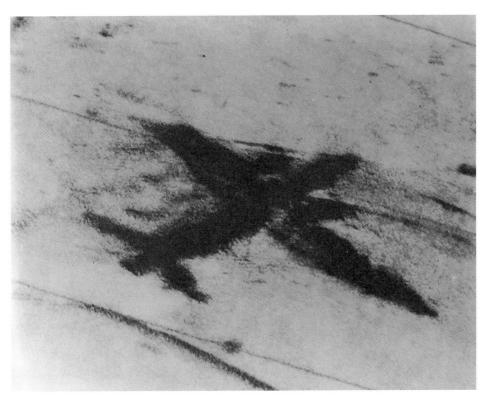

Figure 39.6. Side scan sonar record of twin-engine bomber "*R for Robert*," Loch Ness, Scotland (courtesy Klein Associates, Inc.).

response to a serious infestation of zebra mussels, worried that the lake's collection of shipwrecks would soon become encrusted and impossible to document.

During this effort, the researchers discovered Benedict Arnold's last missing gunboat: a gondola, intact and upright. Built during the summer of 1776, the gunboat was part of Arnold's fleet that engaged the British at the Battle of Valcour Island, October 11–13, 1776. It was sunk during the Americans' retreat from the battle, as they attempted to return to the safety of Fort Ticonderoga.

Another significant side scan sonar find in Lake Champlain was the discovery of the Horse Ferry wreck by James Kennard and Scott Hill in 1983 (Shomette, 1989). The ship was mapped in detail by Cohn's team the following year (Crisman and Cohn, 1998). Cohn said, "The archaeological significance of the ferry wreck was, for us, beyond question: It was the only horse-powered boat ever found in Lake Champlain. Indeed, to the best of our knowledge, it is the only known example of an intact horseboat in the world."

During the 1980s, the Lake George Bateaux Research Team (later know as Bateaux Below, Inc.) led by Joseph W. Zarzynski, used side scan sonar to survey Lake George in New York State. The group located a number of Colonial ships called *bateaux* (singular: bateau), flat-bottomed, double-ended wooden vessels pointed at bow and stern. In 1990, the expedition located the 1758 radeau *Land Tortoise*, an unusual seven-sided floating gun battery (Figure 39.8). This British warship from the French and Indian War, North

Figure 39.7. Side scan sonar record of *Breadalbane* (courtesy Klein Associates, Inc.).

America's oldest "intact" warship, was listed as a National Historic Landmark in August 1988.

HMS *Titanic*

In September 1985, side scan sonar played an important role in the location of the British luxury liner RMS *Titanic*, whose story is so well-known today. The Woods Hole Oceanographic Institution expedition, led by Robert D. Ballard, Ph.D. used the deep-towed vessel Argo, which was equipped with sophisticated television, lights, sonar, and underwater navigation. The Argo was similar to the vessel used by the Navy Electronics Laboratory in 1964 to locate the wreckage of the submarine *Thresher* except, of course, with much more advanced equipment. In an interview with the Titanic Historical Society, Captain Richard J. Bowen of the Research Vessel Knorr (Childs, 1985) noted

> that was the Argo, that also had a side-scan sonar on it. That pings out on either side of the sled a couple of hundred metres on each side. It gives you a shadow graph. If you shined a light over this thing here, in back of it would be a shadow and that is what you see. Where the shadow is dark, the object shows up light but like a silhouette. They were getting objects on this thing so they maneuvered over to look at them. The side-scan is important because it allows you...if you get into the neighborhood of debris, you can get up to it and estimate the height, width, length, whatever before you actually get the camera into it...The better part of (the next) day was spent towing the

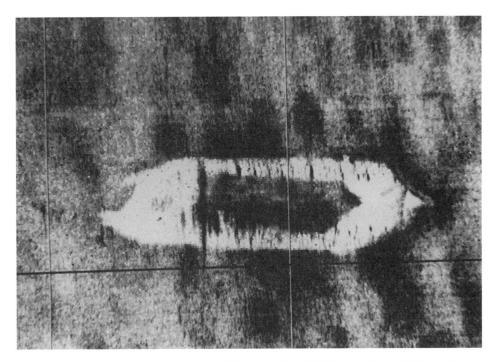

Figure 39.8. Side scan sonar record of *Land Tortoise* radeau, 1990 (courtesy Joseph W. Zarzynski).

Argo around and using the side scan to map the area. Not necessarily looking for stuff with the tv but looking for objects with the side scan because that, remember, gives you a big swath. Maybe a couple hundred meters on each side…So this side scan gives you a big, big scan and allows you to locate and map objects without actually getting up on them with a camera…I think the latter part of the second day…they were able to get down and find the hull with the side-scan and start getting video images on, I believe, the port bow.

After the *Titanic* expedition, Ballard founded the Jason Foundation and continued his pioneering work in locating deepwater shipwrecks of extraordinary archaeological interest.

CONCLUSION

These brief anecdotes illustrate only a small fraction of the shipwrecks and other underwater cultural resources found with the help of side scan sonar. In the future, we can expect side scan sonar and other sonar technology to evolve and become much more sophisticated and more within the financial reach of the archaeological community. This will present many possibilities to extend the world's knowledge of ancient ships and maritime civilizations. According to Crisman and Cohn (1998):

> The raising of shipwrecks has all but ceased in recent decades, but the number of underwater discoveries has greatly increased due to the development of a new and effective array of electronic underwater survey technologies. Side-scanning sonars,

magnetometers, sub-bottom profilers, remotely operated vehicles (ROVs) and navigational control systems have allowed us to find shipwrecks, no matter where or how deep they may lie. The issue at hand is not how to locate underwater archaeological sites, because we have the capability to find nearly all of them, but rather what to do with shipwrecks after they are found. The way we answer this question, and the decisions we make at this time, will directly determine what we preserve for the knowledge and enjoyment of future generations.

REFERENCES

Bass, G.F., 1968, New Tool for Undersea Archaeology. *National Geographic* 134:403–423.

Bruce, Roger R., editor, 1994, *Seeing the Unseen: Dr. Harold Edgerton and the Wonders of Strobe Alley*, pp. 59–67. George Eastman House, New York.

Cain, Emily, 1983, *Ghost Ships*. Musson Publishing, Toronto.

Childs, Karen, 1985, An Interview with Captain Bowen of the R/V Knorr. *The Titanic Communicator* 9(3):12–36.

Crisman, Kevin J., and Cohn, Arthur B., 1998, *When Horses Walked on Water: Horse-powered Ferries in Nineteenth-Century America*. Smithsonian Institution Press, Washington, D.C.

Dean, M., Oxley, I., Redknap, M., and Watson, K., editors, 1992, *Archaeology Underwater: The NAS Guide to Principles and Practice*, pp. 136–146. Nautical Archaeology Society, Dorset Press, Dorset.

Edgerton, Harold E., 1986, *Sonar Images*. Prentice-Hall, Englewood Cliffs.

Edgerton, Harold E., Linder, Elisha, and Klein, Martin, 1974, Sonar Search at Ashdod, Israel. *National Geographic Society Research Reports, 1967 Projects*. National Geographic Society, Washington, D.C.

Fish, John P., and Carr, H. Arnold, 1990, *Sound Underwater Images*. Lower Cape Publishing, New Orleans.

Flemming, B.W., 1976, Side Scan Sonar: A Practical Guide. *International Hygrographic Review* 53(1).

Fox, P.A., and Denbigh, P.N., 1983, Electronically Focussed, Multibeam Side Scan Sonar. In *Acoustics and the Seabed*, Conference Proceedings, pp. 347–355.

Franzen, A., 1981, *HMS Kronan: The Search for a Great 17th Century Swedish Warship*. Royal Institute of Technology, Stockholm.

Haines, Gregory, 1974, *Sound Underwater*. David and Charles Ltd., Devon.

Holmes, Robin, 1991, *One of Our Aircraft: The Story of R for Robert, The Loch Ness Wellington*. Quiller Press Ltd., London.

Klein, M., 1967, Side Scan Sonar. *Undersea Technology* 8(4):24–36, 38.

Klein, M., and Edgerton, H.E., 1968, Sonar: A Modern Technique for Ocean Exploitation. *IEEE Spectrum* June: 40–47.

Mazel, C., 1985, *Side Scan Sonar Training Manual*. Klein Associates, Inc.

McKee, Alexander, 1982, *How We Found the Mary Rose*. Souvenir Press Ltd., London.

MacInnis, Joe, 1985, *The Search for the Breadalbane*. David and Charles Ltd., Devon.

MacInnis, Joseph B., 1983, Exploring a 140-year-old Ship under Arctic Ice. *National Geographic* 164(1):104A–104D.

Nelson, D.A., 1983, *Hamilton* and *Scourge*, Ghost Ships of the War of 1812. *National Geographic* 163(3):288–313.

Newton, John G., 1975, How We Found the *Monitor. National Geographic*. 147(1):48–61.

Sands, John O., 1983, *Yorktown's Captive Fleet*, pp. 152–163. Mariners' Museum, Newport News.

Shomette, Donald G., 1989, Heyday of the Horse Ferry. *National Geographic* 176(4):549–556.

Trabant, Peter K., 1984, *Applied High-Resolution Geophysical Methods*. International Human Resources Development Corp., Boston.

Chapter 40

Geographic Information Systems

IAN RODERICK MATHER
AND GORDON P. WATTS JR.

INTRODUCTION

Spatial relationships between artifacts, features, and sites are at the heart of archaeology. The traditional way archaeologists recover, represent, and store spatially referenced data is through analog (printed) maps and site plans, which use lines, polygons, points, color, shading patterns, symbols, scale, and a key to preserve and present the information. In essence, the map and its key form a spatially related database. Although a resourceful investigator can present a variety of thematic maps, scatter plots, and site plans in this way, the archaeologist's analog chart has intrinsic limitations. Invariably, archaeological data must be generalized to prevent the map from becoming cluttered and incomprehensible. Limitations of space and clarity mean that analog maps must display only a minute fraction of the available data. Underwater archaeologists work in a new and nascent discipline, but the volume and variety of professionally produced, spatially referenced data is already difficult to calculate.

Within the last two decades, highly complex computer programs have been developed to manage voluminous, spatially related data. The more sophisticated programs permit the production of maps or site plans with electronic pathways that tie the map's graphic features to specific database information. Computer-based systems that

Ian Roderick Mather, Assistant Professor, Maritime History and Underwater Archaeology, Department of History, University of Rhode Island, Kingston, Rhode Island 02881.   **Gordon P. Watts Jr.**, Institute for International Maritime Research, Inc. Washington, North Carolina 27889.

International Handbook of Underwater Archaeology, edited by Carol V. Ruppé and Janet F. Barstad. Kluwer Academic/Plenum Publishers, New York, 2002.

store, display, and mathematically analyze spatially related data in this way are collectively referred to as Geographic Information Systems (GIS).

In this chapter, we examine the uses of GIS in underwater archaeology, first by outlining the essential elements of GIS, then by describing its applications to our discipline. Although archaeologists in general and underwater archeologists in particular are only just beginning to recognize the potential of computer-based spatial databases, this chapter describes a number of completed GIS projects. These case studies demonstrate the practical benefits of GIS for both submerged cultural resource managers, and research or contract archaeologists working underwater.

GEOGRAPHIC INFORMATION SYSTEMS

Geographic Information Systems are computer-based systems that store, update, edit, display, and analyze spatially referenced (map) data. GIS software packages link graphic and rational databases together, so that graphic images such as maps, site plans, drawings, photographs, and even video can be cross-linked to tabular and text data. A GIS is like a "smart map" in which most graphic features have associated database information stored in the computer that can be accessed by users almost instantaneously.

Geographic Information Systems were conceived as long ago as the mid-1960s. In 1966, Roger Tomlinson constructed the Canadian GIS, the first computerized system to use the name GIS. Other early pioneers included Howard Fisher at Harvard Laboratory for Computer Graphics, Jack Dangermond at Environmental Systems Research Institute, and David Bickmore at the United Kingdom's Experimental Cartography Unit. In the 1970s, United States regional and national mapping agencies sponsored and promoted emerging GIS technology. Until the mid- to late-1980s, GIS was available only to researchers with high-powered work-stations capable of storing massive amounts of data and running memory-intensive software. Within the last decade, as powerful personal computers have become more widely available, GIS usage has become more broad based (Coppock and Rhind, 1991; Caswell, 1992).

Because of the speed and efficiency with which computerized data can be recovered, the use of GIS has grown rapidly in recent years. It has become a principal tool for planners and managers, who must store, centralize, organize, update, and access data necessary to facilitate effective decisionmaking. It has also become useful for academic researchers from a variety of disciplines who must maintain, retrieve, update, combine, generalize, organize, analyze, and share their spatially referenced data. Even archaeologists have broken through their traditional reluctance to embrace new technology and have recognized the usefulness of GIS. Today, GIS is being developed to assist both submerged cultural resource managers and contract and research archaeologists in storing, organizing, and analyzing data effectively (Allen et al., 1990).

Data

GIS data sets are invariably presented in one of two forms: raster data and vector data. Raster data is arranged in a regularly-spaced grid or matrix, each cell carrying an associated data value. Any gridded information can be presented in this form, including elevation, bathymetric, acoustic, magnetic, and sedimentary data. Photographs and scanned images, which comprise pixels of different colors arranged in a grid, are also included within raster data. Vector data is linear in character and consist of points, lines, and polygons constructed from nodes and vertices. CAD drawings are the most commonly utilized forms of vector data and can be used to represent coastlines, archaeological sites, site plans, survey areas, targets, dredge channels, underwater cables, pipe lines, and any number of other linear, area, or point features.

GIS data is stored in "coverages," similar in appearance and principle to "layers" in CAD systems. What sets GIS coverages apart from CAD layers, however, is that each coverage has an associated, spatially referenced database. Coverages can be interrelated—combined, generalized, and reorganized—and new data sets created from information already within the system. GIS coverages enable researchers to present complex data and analysis in a visual form that is readily understood by nonexperts. It is this capacity to interrelate, analyze, and display multivariate spatial data sets in a meaningful way that renders GIS such an important tool for submerged cultural resource managers and underwater archaeologists.

Hardware and Software

As a computer-driven system, GIS relies on a combination of hardware, software, and peripherals. Today, most high-end computers are capable of running GIS programs and come equipped with high-capacity disc drives for data storage. Display of GIS data is generally handled by the system's monitor but can also be reproduced using plotters, printers, and projectors. GIS-ready data can be generated by a variety of peripherals and equipment. Digitizing tablets, scanners, digital cameras, GPS (Global Positioning Systems), side scan sonar, and magnetometers all generate data that can be included in GIS development. To a degree, the development and availability of these and other components and equipment has driven the development of GIS (Marble, 1990). For example, the first GIS computer software packages could handle either raster or vector data but not both, whereas today's programmers produce software that can use both types of data. As we enter a new era for spatially related databases, scores of manufacturers now produce high quality GIS software packages. Environmental Systems Research Institute Inc. (ESRI) is one of the leading manufacturers, particularly of software for IBM-compatible machines. ESRI produces a variety of programs, including ArcInfo, ArcCAD, and ArcView, that can be employed in developing and querying a GIS. While ESRI has abandoned its commitment to develop software versions for Apple Computers, other software developers certainly target this market. ComGrafix, Inc., for example, produces a software program identical as MapGrafix GIS specifically for use with Apple Computer's Mac-based systems.

Applications

Although underwater archaeologists have started to use GIS only recently, the tool's potential for both research and management is already clear. The application of GIS in underwater archaeology can be divided into four broad areas: survey, cultural resource management, site specific investigations, and predictive modeling and exploratory data analysis.

Survey.   Much of the 71 percent of the earth's surface that is underwater remains undocumented and unexplored. As scientists from various disciplines map these regions, GIS will become an increasingly important and essential tool. It can be used in variety of ways to facilitate underwater archaeological remote sensing survey work. Post-processed data from magnetometers, side-scan sonars, and positioning systems can be overlaid in a GIS to permit rapid visual and mathematical analysis. Other coverages such as archaeological sites, areas of resource sensitivity, zones of historical activity, bathymetry, dredged channels, underwater pipe lines, modern obstructions, and aerial photographs can be added so that remote sensing targets can be located, analyzed, and placed into context even more readily.

In recent years, GIS technology has emerged to facilitate the real-time acquisition and display of spatial data. It is now possible to log and update remote-sensing and positional data as it is acquired. That data can be transferred to the GIS computer via serial port connections or over an ethernet network. Acquisition of data in this way offers great potential for the underwater archaeologist. It provides researchers with a way to ensure that all necessary data is collected, and that any additional work is completed before the survey crew leaves the water. A GIS that updates information from the sea floor in real time could also be used to drive a monitoring and control system that would greatly enhance search efficiency. The foundation of real-time GIS data acquisition is good positioning; without it, spatially referenced data is meaningless. Modern Differential Global Positioning System (DGPS) can provide the submeter accuracy that makes real-time GIS data acquisition viable. Software extensions that effectively link GPS and GIS already are available.

Few if any underwater archaeological remote sensing surveys incorporating real-time GIS data acquisition have been attempted to date. A system developed by the Submerged Cultural Resources Unit (SCRU) of the National Park Service for surveying submerged cultural resources in the Dry Tortugas off Key West, Florida, may be the closest example. In other disciplines, however, scientists have progressed much further along these lines. Oceanographers, environmental scientists, and ocean engineers have employed GIS to collect, assess, store, and present a wide range of data about the ocean environment and resources (Dzurenko, 1997).

Cultural Resource Management.   Cultural resource managers have been among the first to recognize the usefulness of GIS in underwater archaeology. In the United States, Sections 106 and 110 (f) of the National Historic Preservation Act of 1966 require that agencies assess the effects of federal, federally assisted, or federally licensed projects on properties included in or eligible for inclusion in the National Register of Historic Places. The Section 106 review process has been developed to facilitate the identification of historic and archaeological resources and address the necessities for historic preservation associated with mitigation of developmental impacts on those resources.

GIS can provide a highly effective vehicle for geographically identifying known submerged cultural resources, areas of potential resource sensitivity, historic and cartographically identified patterns of human activity, and waterway development and maintenance impact areas. Ready access to those data can be a critical factor in the effectiveness of the Section 106 review process. By opting to preserve Section 106-related data in GIS format, cultural resource managers can store, arrange, manage, and access vast amounts of crucial archaeological and historical data. By entering proposed improvements or construction projects into the GIS, the manager can instantly ascertain the potential effect on known cultural resources and determine whether predisturbance archaeological surveys are appropriate. In addition, the manager can require that the results of all future work include GIS-ready data. In this way, survey, assessment, excavation, and site documentation data can be added to the existing GIS. This capacity to update data and to present it in an efficient and understandable manner has made GIS one of the most useful tools for cultural resource managers. As Larry Murphy of SCRU has stated, "It is difficult to overstate the importance of cumulative databases whose variables can be easily manipulated; they have revolutionized the management of land in the National Park Service. Seaborne GIS inventory programs promise the same for submerged sites" (Murphy, 1996).

Five examples of GIS designed for submerged cultural resource managers follow. With one exception, the Bermuda Shipwreck GIS, the systems were constructed using software developed by ESRI.

James River Historic Properties Treatment Plan GIS.   The United States Army Engineer District, Norfolk, Virginia, is responsible for maintaining and developing navigation channels in one of the most historically sensitive waterways in the United States. Since the first permanent English settlement was established at Jamestown in 1607, the James River has been one of the most important navigation systems in the eastern United States. Continuous development, extensive maritime commerce and transportation, and military activities associated with the American Revolution, the War of 1812, and the Civil War have made the James and its tributaries an important repository of submerged cultural resources, which preserve a significant physical record of national, regional, and local maritime activity.

The submerged cultural resources in the James River are protected by a variety of regulations and orders designed to guide the activities of all federal agencies and federally permitted projects. To coordinate their historic preservation responsibilities more effectively, the U.S. Army Corps of Engineers (USACE), Wilmington and Norfolk Districts, cooperated in the development of a long-term Historic Properties Treatment Plan for the James River Navigation Project.

Objectives of the Historic Properties Treatment Plan for the James River Navigation Project were to provide both a historical and cultural background for the James River and an inventory of known historic and archaeological resources. The plan also addressed identification of priorities and methodologies for remote sensing survey and archaeological research designed to locate and assess submerged cultural resources that could be affected by continued maintenance dredging activity. The overall project goal was to identify and develop effective Section 106 procedures for the Norfolk District. Those procedures would assist the agency in the responsible implementation of submerged cultural resource obligations associated with its maintenance-dredging program on the James River. In order to formulate a functional plan, the project design identified a series of priorities, including the development of a submerged cultural resource management document and a computer-based GIS for the James River.

Tidewater Atlantic Research (TAR) of Washington, North Carolina, developed the James River Historic Properties Treatment Plan and GIS to provide resource managers with a quick and efficient means of gaining access to computerized data associated with the river's submerged cultural resources (Figure 40.1). Rather than performing manual searches, the GIS allows users to query computerized site information by selecting on-screen symbols displayed against a series of digitized United States Geological Survey (USGS) 7.5-minute topographic maps (quad sheets). The user may explore the GIS for information on archaeological and historic sites, past and present channel alignments,

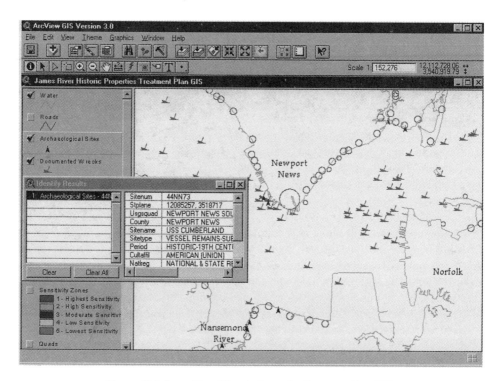

Figure 40.1. James River Historic Properties Treatment Plan GIS.

dredge cuts, known wrecks and obstructions, archaeological surveys, remote sensing targets, and submerged cultural resource sensitivity zones.

Twenty USGS 7.5-minute quad sheets served as the cartographic base maps for the James River GIS. Coverages representing the quad sheets, the river, and all major highways in the region were extracted from these maps and displayed in real-world coordinates (Virginia State Plane Coordinates, NAD 83). Researchers also developed two data sets associated with channel alignments and dredged cuts. First, Norfolk District's channel alignment data was converted into a GIS coverage representing the currently maintained James River channel. Second, TAR archaeologists digitized channel cuts from historic charts, topographic maps, navigation charts, and USACE survey charts to form a coverage representing previously dredged channels.

An intense program of historic, cartographic, and archaeological research resulted in the development of three more GIS data sets. The first comprised 264 historic sites. Using the direct historical approach, historic maps and charts were analyzed for areas of cultural activity, particularly in relation to shipbuilding, shipping, and other activities affecting the scope and nature of the submerged archaeological record. Included in those historic areas were plantations, landings, shipyards, ferry crossings, forts, redoubts, derelict vessels, and shipwrecks. A comparison of historic maps with present-day USGS 7.5-minute quad sheets revealed a striking similarity between physiographic aspects of the project area's rivers and streams. Landmarks such as river bends and tributaries, coupled with written historical records, permitted researchers to employ the computer-assisted design program (AutoCAD) to identify historic areas on the digitized USGS 7.5-minute topographic maps. These areas of historic activity were developed into a GIS coverage of historic sites. In its final form, the GIS permitted end-users to select a graphically displayed symbol for each historical area and obtain database information such as name, description, and reference data.

The second data set comprised 139 known archaeological sites and regions preserved along the banks or within the sediments of the James River. Site locations, derived from published and unpublished archaeological reports and from the Virginia Department of Historic Resources site files, were entered into CAD drawings and used to create a GIS coverage for known archaeological sites. The resulting database allowed end-users to query individual sites for specific information such as location, site name, cultural affiliation, type, and National Register of Historic Places significance.

The third data set comprised 204 charted or documented wrecks and obstructions. For more than 400 years, humans have been mapping America's river systems. As a result, charts of the James River contain the locations for hundreds of wrecks and obstructions. Through detailed cartographic research, TAR archaeologists recorded the location of these documented wrecks from historic maps and overlaid them on modern digitized charts. This data was used to create a GIS coverage of documented wrecks and obstructions. Researchers also included the location of wrecks and obstructions from modern navigation charts and information derived from the National Oceanic and Atmospheric Administration's (NOAA) Automated Wreck and Obstruction Information System (AWOIS). The database information accessible to the end-user varied with the cartographic source for the wreck or obstruction. For example, where wrecks had been derived from historic maps, the end-user could obtain name, description, location, and cartographic reference. Where the documented wrecks or obstructions came from the AWOIS database, all information from that database became accessible to the end-user.

Archaeologists have conducted a number of submerged cultural resource surveys along the James River. TAR researchers delineated, digitized, and developed data from these surveys into a GIS coverage. They also created a second data set containing all potentially significant magnetic and acoustic remote-sensing targets identified within those survey areas. Norfolk District personnel could then locate both tabular and textual data associated with survey areas and targets. Access to textual data, taken directly from archaeological reports, was made possible by an ESRI software function known as "hotlinking." By using the "hotlink tool" and selecting an entity, end-users were able to view a descriptive passage associated with a survey area or target.

One of the most controversial uses of GIS in archaeology has been in the field of predictive modeling (Maschner, 1996). Although a predictive model of shipwreck losses in the James would have been extremely useful for the Norfolk District, the high degree of mobility associated with vessels created a major obstacle to prediction of shipwreck location. Without a fairly specific documentary record, our ability to develop accurate predictive models for shipwreck locations is extremely limited. Given the historically high usage of the James River, researchers could not eliminate the possibility of intact shipwrecks in any unsurveyed or undisturbed area.

As an alternative to predictive modeling, TAR researchers divided the river into a series of sensitivity zones. By using GIS map overlay techniques, TAR personnel examined the spatial relationship between the system's data sets. By overlaying various historic, archaeological, dredging, and remote sensing survey coverages, researchers examined the relationship between areas of historic significance, the level of possible site disturbance, and the level of archaeological survey, then divided the river system into zones and assigned a sensitivity rating to each area. This significance and submerged cultural resource analysis was not an exact but rather a general analysis. While the random nature of vessel loss associated with storms and other unpredictable catastrophes cannot be fully quantified, an examination of the historical record associated with settlement patterns, regional economics, and the environment provided insight into areas of potentially high sensitivity for associated submerged cultural resources.

Sensitivity ratings assigned to various parts of the river system included: (1) highest sensitivity (National Register-eligible sites), (2) high resource sensitivity, (3) moderate resource sensitivity, (4) low resource sensitivity, and (5) lowest resource sensitivity (areas that had been surveyed and reliably demonstrated not to contain potentially significant submerged cultural resources). End-users were then able to query the GIS for zone specific information, such as sensitivity rating, USGS quad, body of water, previous survey activity, known archaeological sites, documented wrecks, and historic activity along the waterway.

Charleston Harbor Project GIS. For more than 300 hundred years, Charleston, South Carolina, has been one of the most important seaports and maritime centers in the South. As a result, Charleston Harbor and the surrounding river systems have become an important repository of submerged cultural resources, which preserve a significant physical record of American and Southern maritime history. To preserve that record, submerged archaeological resource managers must work within state and federal legislation and a variety of regulations and orders designed to guide the activities of all federal agencies and federally permitted projects.

The Charleston Harbor Project was a five-year Special Area Management Plan developed to focus management attention on the effect of development on the Charleston Harbor estuary system, which included the harbor itself, the Ashley, Cooper, Wando, and Stono Rivers, their natural resources, and adjoining lands. Goals of the project were to enhance the quality of the environment while maintaining the many uses of the waters and natural resources, and to anticipate and act on potential problems before they harmed the harbor system. To formulate a comprehensive plan, the project staff identified a series of priorities, including development of a submerged cultural resource management plan for the Charleston Harbor Project study area.

Tidewater Atlantic Research worked with the Charleston Harbor Project to develop a GIS-based, submerged cultural resource management plan for the study area. The plan included the GIS, analysis of known submerged cultural resources, and identification of potentially sensitive archaeological areas (Figure 40.2). The GIS provided resource managers with a quick and efficient means of accessing computerized data regarding submerged cultural resources in the project area.

The Charleston Harbor Project GIS was constructed along lines similar to the James River Historic Properties Treatment Plan GIS. The cartographic foundation of the Charleston GIS was derived by digitizing seven USGS 7.5-minute quad maps and developing the resulting shorelines and riverbanks into a GIS coverage. TAR personnel used historical records of river and harbor improvements, particularly in relation to U.S. Army Corps of Engineers dredging activities, to create GIS data sets that identified previously disturbed bottomlands as well as currently maintained channels.

A vigorous program of historic, archaeological, and cartographic research resulted in the development of GIS coverages for archaeological sites, historic sites, and previously documented wrecks and obstructions. The inclusion of GIS data for

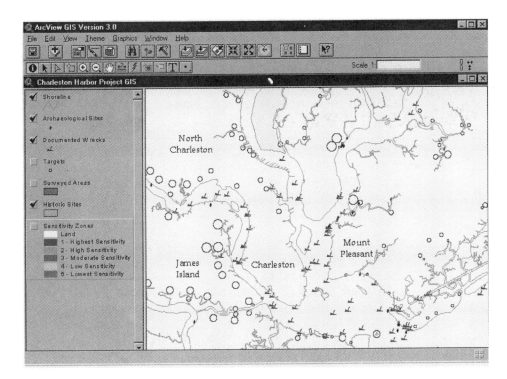

Figure 40.2. Charleston Harbor Project GIS.

submerged archaeological sites was an important element of the project, as was the development of GIS coverages for historic sites and areas of historic activity along the waterways. Previous research had demonstrated that settlement in the Charleston area developed near waterways, especially along the Cooper, Ashley, Wando, and Stono Rivers. Identification of areas of historic activity such as brickyards, plantations, and landings aided researchers and resource managers to define high-probability areas for submerged cultural resources. Based on previously documented submerged sites in the Charleston project area, researchers found that submerged archaeological sites are frequently an extension of, or associated with, terrestrial sites (Errante, 1993). The historic sites coverage enabled TAR archaeologists to develop a geographic framework for settlement and maritime activities along the project area's waterways. Previously surveyed areas and remote-sensing targets also were delineated, digitized, and developed into GIS coverages. Those survey areas were then laid over areas of historic and channel maintenance activity to assist with subsequent sensitivity analysis.

As researchers constructed the Charleston Harbor Project GIS, they encountered the familiar problems of predictive modeling for underwater sites. Due to a dearth of information regarding historic site predictive modeling, particularly for submerged sites, and the sometimes random nature of vessel losses, researchers determined that a GIS-based predictive model for Charleston's submerged archaeological resources would be unreliable and possibly misleading. However, a sensitivity analysis seemed to offer greater potential for facilitating effective management and decision-making. To prepare the sensitivity analysis, TAR personnel examined the spatial relationship between the various system coverages. By overlaying historic site, dredging, and remote sensing survey coverages, archaeologists were able to examine the relationship between areas of historic significance, level of possible site disturbance, and level of archaeological survey. TAR personnel also utilized a methodology previously employed by South and Hartley (1980), Hartley (1984), and Ferguson and Babson (1986) to locate 17th-, 18th-, and 19th-century terrestrial sites in the Charleston area. By examining historic maps and hypothesizing that the settlers desired "deep water and high ground," South, Hartley, and Ferguson successfully located numerous historic terrestrial sites illustrated on historic maps. Using GIS overlays along with the "deep water and high ground" methodology, TAR researchers divided Charleston Harbor and its river systems into five sensitivity zones corresponding to areas of highest, high, moderate, low, and lowest sensitivity. The result was a system that permitted users to query the GIS for zone specific information such as sensitivity rating, USGS quad, body of water, previous survey activity, known archaeological sites, and historic activity along the waterway.

Bermuda Shipwreck GIS.   During the first decade of the 16th century, Spanish Captain Juan Bermudez discovered Bermuda during a voyage from the New World back to Spain. To take advantage of the Gulf Stream and Atlantic trade winds, Spanish *flotas* sailed through the Bahama Channel and up the southeast coast of North America before turning northeast out into the Atlantic for Europe. That course brought Bermudez' vessel into first contact with the mid-Atlantic volcanic atoll that bears his name. After his discovery, the islands became a last point of reference for vessels sailing from the Americas for Europe.

Because of the extensive complex of reefs that surround the islands, Bermuda occasionally proved to be dangerous. The first ships lost on the islands' reefs were Spanish and Portuguese. French and English vessels also came to grief in Bermuda as their navigation in the western Atlantic increased. While the Spanish never settled the islands, they charted the reefs and released pigs on the islands to provide a source of food for shipwreck survivors. In 1609, almost a century after Bermudez' discovery, the English vessel *Sea Venture*, enroute to the new settlement at Jamestown, Virginia, was wrecked off the northeast end of the archipelago. After building two smaller vessels from the *Sea Venture*'s timbers and the abundant cedar growing on Bermuda, the colonists finally reached Virginia. Shortly afterward, Sir George Somers returned to Bermuda with a number of colonists and established the first of the island's settlements.

The Bermuda colony would play an increasingly important role in British colonization of North America and, after the American Revolution, became the Royal Navy's most important base in the western Atlantic.

As a consequence of Bermuda's geographical position adjacent to the trade routes of the western Atlantic, more than 200 ships, and perhaps twice that many, have been wrecked on the island's reefs during the past five centuries. Those shipwrecks represent vessels that supported virtually every period of exploration, colonization, and development of the New World, as well as the vessels of every nationality involved in those activities. Today, the shipwrecks of Bermuda preserve a rich, valuable, and irreplaceable archaeological record associated with the entire spectrum of European navigation in the western Atlantic. In addition to representing a major source of income associated with the recreational and tourist industry, Bermuda shipwrecks preserve an important source of information about our collective international maritime heritage.

The Bermuda Maritime Museum, in the old Royal Navy Dockyard at Ireland Island, was established in 1974 to preserve and interpret the nation's rich maritime heritage. Since 1983, the Program in Maritime History and Nautical Archaeology at East Carolina University in Greenville, North Carolina, has co-sponsored shipwreck research projects with the Bermuda Maritime Museum. Graduate students in the program have participated in field and archival research projects designed to locate, identify, scientifically investigate and preserve Bermuda's shipwreck resources. During this long-term association, university and museum personnel and students have identified and documented more than 50 shipwreck sites. In addition, site-specific investigations have been carried out on wrecks from the 16th, 17th, 18th, and 19th centuries. Data generated by the research is stored at the museum, making it the largest repository of shipwreck archaeological information in the country. In conjunction with the government office of the Receiver of Wreck, the museum plays a role in approving permits for exploration, research, and salvage activities on Bermuda wrecks.

To facilitate effective management of historical and archaeological shipwreck data, the Bermuda Maritime Museum decided to develop an in-house GIS, whose primary objective is to produce an updatable and electronically accessible database that provides interfaces with known archaeological and salvage shipwreck geographical data and historical, literature, graphic, and photographic records. Because the museum uses an almost entirely Apple-based system of computers, MapGraphix was selected as the software.

The GIS was developed as a thesis project by Kimberly Yeaman, an East Carolina University graduate student. Working independently under the supervision of a graduate advisor and the director of the museum, she produced a detailed, digitized map of Bermuda and the surrounding reefs to serve as the primary coverage. Known shipwrecks with accurate geographical coordinates were included in the GIS as an additional coverage. Historically referenced shipwrecks with and without accurate geographical coordinates were also included as a coverage. A database was developed to contain a combination of historical, literature, graphic and photographic records associated with historical and archaeological sites identified in the GIS. Database information was generated by research in the Bermuda Maritime Museum's archive and library, records in the Bermuda Archives, and microfilm and secondary source materials of Hamilton Public Library.

Although the Bermuda Maritime Museum GIS provides the most comprehensive access to shipwreck data in Bermuda, it is far from complete. New historical and archaeological data will be included in the system regularly. This capacity to update the system makes it a powerful tool for supporting future research and management activities. Because old and new data can be obtained almost instantaneously, those activities can be carried out quickly and with a high degree of reliability. Development and maintenance of the Bermuda Shipwreck GIS is an important part of the Bermuda Maritime Museum's long-term commitment to preserving and scientifically investigating the shipwreck resources of the Bermuda reefs.

U.S. Navy Resource Management Program.   The Naval Historical Center (NHS) in Washington, D.C., has been charged with responsibility for the identification, protection, and management of U.S. Navy shipwrecks and naval aircraft. Consequently the center has compiled one of the largest inventories of submerged cultural resources. To date, the worldwide inventory includes more than 2000 shipwrecks and more than 2000 aircraft. Those resources are associated with every aspect of the Navy's two-century history.

To facilitate management of the database information associated with those resources, the Naval Historical Center has contracted for the development of model GIS coverages for two significant geographical areas: the State of Virginia and the State of South Carolina. The South Carolina GIS is being developed by the South Carolina Institute for Archaeology and Anthropology (SCIAA), and the Virginia GIS is being developed by the Institute for International Maritime Research, Inc. (I^2MR). Both the South Carolina and Virginia coverages are being designed to tie historical, archaeological, and cartographic data included in the NHS database into a statewide geographic coverage. Development of a GIS for South Carolina and Virginia will provide NHS personnel with an expandable, ArcView-based management tool that will ultimately include all of the resources under its management.

Dry Tortugas and Key Biscayne Shipwreck and Natural Resource Survey System and GIS.   The islands and seabed associated with the Dry Tortugas National Park off Key West, Florida, and the seabed associated with the Biscayne National Park off Miami are managed by the National Park Service. Both the Dry Tortugas and Biscayne parks preserve fragile, coral-based ecosystems and historic shipwreck resources lost on those reefs. SCRU of Santa Fe, New Mexico, has carried out a number of surveys to identify and assess submerged cultural resources in the Dry Tortugas National Park that fall under NPS jurisdiction. SCRU also has surveyed in Biscayne National Park to identify and assess both submerged cultural and natural resources. To control the data generated by these surveys, SCRU employed a GPS-based Archaeological Data Acquisition Platform (ADAP). ADAP generates magnetic and acoustic data that can be channeled into GIS coverages.

The ADAP system was developed to facilitate identification, assessment, and management of cultural resources in underwater areas within the jurisdiction of the National Park system. To be effective, ADAP had to be mobile enough to be shipped and adaptable enough to utilize vessels of opportunity. The "off-the-shelf" system hardware included DGPS, proton precession magnetometer, side scan sonar unit, subbottom profiler, survey fathometer, and RoxAnn bottom classification equipment. ADAP system software included a variety of programs available commercially. Survey positioning was controlled by Hypack hydrographic data collection software produced by Coastal Oceanographics, and data was logged by GPSLOG developed by Sandia Research Associates. AutoCAD from Autodesk and QuickSurf from Schrieber Instruments provided pre- and post-processing capabilities. A GIS module for AutoCAD, ArcCAD from Environmental Systems Research Institute, provided access to data in ARC/INFO and AutoCAD. Raw field data was post-processed by Hypack and imported into QuickSurf as ASCII files for contouring. Magnetic, hydrographic, RoxAnn, and other processed data could be imported into ArcCAD as distinct coverages associated with environmental conditions, natural and cultural resources, aerial photography, or other geographic considerations. Site-specific data generated by surveys, photography, video, convergent photographic documentation and historical and cartographic data could be associated with GIS coverages by hotlinks and databases. Themes associated with different types and specific resources in the Dry Tortugas National Park were included in the comprehensive GIS. ArcView provided researchers and NPS resource managers with easy access to the entire spectrum of Dry Tortugas data.

Although natural and cultural resource surveys had been carried out in Biscayne National Park, NPS personnel attempting to assess the effects of Hurricane Andrew realized that there was no comprehensive and readily accessible data to support assessment of the storm's damage. In 1994, SCRU initiated a comprehensive survey designed to generate digital bathymetric and environmental data that could be used as a baseline for future research and assessment. The major difference between the survey initiated by SCRU in 1994 and previous surveys was the areal extent of the investigation, the method employed for defining the bottom surface environment, and data compatibility with GIS. To conduct the survey, SCRU employed the ADAP portable remote-sensing system first employed in the Dry Tortugas.

The Biscayne survey employed a proton precession magnetometer to facilitate identification of submerged cultural resources. To develop a chart of the bottom environment that accurately differentiated between bottom surface conditions, SCRU used RoxAnn, which generates data by processing the first and second echoes from a single beam survey fathometer through a dedicated parallel receiver operating between the transducer terminals. By processing both echoes using a formula developed to identify bottom surface environment conditions based on an index of hardness, rock, sand, grass, mud, coral, and other features can be charted with considerable accuracy. Because magnetic and RoxAnn data collection was controlled by GPS, GIS coverages could be developed to include magnetic contours and anomalies that could represent submerged cultural resources, as well as a chart of natural bottom surface features. Data collected by the ADAP and included in the Biscayne National Park GIS provides a baseline for preserving and protecting both natural and cultural resources.

Site-Specific Investigations

A GIS can be used to store and access the entire spectrum of data generated by site-specific research. Virtually all archaeological site data can be stored in GIS format including architectural and construction features, stratigraphic profiles and artifact provenience, photographic documentation, and historical or literary references essential to archaeological interpretation. Once the site-specific GIS becomes a more universal product of research, it will undoubtedly be used to support various forms of comparative analysis, of which comparisons of artifact and feature data from different sites are the most obvious examples. The increasing use of GIS for site specific investigations also promises to facilitate the exchange of archaeological data between scholars. Although there are relatively few examples of an underwater site-specific GIS, one of the few systems thus far developed *(Monitor* National Marine Sanctuary GIS) does demonstrate the utility of the technology in this area.

Monitor National Marine Sanctuary GIS.   The remains of USS *Monitor*, the first ironclad warship to be tested in combat, lie off the coast of North Carolina. After successfully engaging the Confederate ironclad CSS *Virginia* at Hampton Roads, Virginia, on March 9, 1862, the John Ericsson-designed warship sank in a gale off Cape Hatteras on December 31, 1862. In 1973, the remains of *Monitor* were located and identified by a research team operating from the Duke University research vessel *Eastward*. Two years later, *Monitor* was designated as the nation's first Marine Sanctuary. Consequently, NOAA assumed management responsibility for the wreck.

I^{2}MR developed the *Monitor* National Marine Sanctuary GIS for NOAA (Figure 40.3). It represents one of the first attempts to realize the potential of GIS technology for site-specific underwater archaeological research. The system was designed

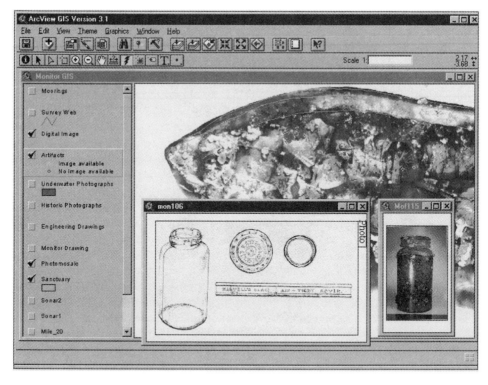

Figure 40.3. *Monitor* National Marine Sanctuary GIS.

to store and display archaeological and historic data associated with the remains of USS *Monitor* and to assist managers with planning research and preservation of the vessel.

Institute researchers used a digital map of North Carolina as the cartographic foundation for the *Monitor* GIS, providing geographic context data against which end-users could access both sanctuary specific and site-specific information. The *Monitor* National Marine Sanctuary GIS included two sanctuary-specific coverages, the first a circle representing the 1-n.mi.-diam. sanctuary boundary with the circle's center located in accordance with the sanctuary coordinates established by Congress; the second was a sonar mosaic of the sanctuary compiled in 1985. When institute personnel scaled and oriented the sonar mosaic and aligned it correctly, the image covered all but the most northern part of the sanctuary. All manipulation of raster images—scaling, orientating, and rubber-sheeting—was accomplished using the Hitachi image-processing software packages V/Image Plus and Tracer.

I^{2}MR developed a total of 10 site-specific vector and raster image coverages for the *Monitor* National Marine Sanctuary GIS, the first a high-resolution, closeup view of the 1985 sonar mosaic. Institute personnel scaled, orientated, and aligned the sonar mosaic with the wreck. I^{2}MR personnel digitized a photomosaic of the wreck constructed in 1974 to generate a GIS coverage and plan view of *Monitor*. When scaled and rotated, the resulting CAD drawing was used to develop a GIS coverage of the wreck and its main features. To locate the wreck in real-world coordinates, the institute used data supplied by NOAA. In the absence of an overall measurement for the wreck, historic engineering drawings, and known dimensions of features such as the turret and armor belt, were used to scale and manipulate the raster image. Scale, location, and orientation of all subsequent GIS vector and raster coverages of *Monitor* were controlled using the same coordinates and assumptions. NOAA provided I^{2}MR with two digital images of the wreck: the 1974 photo mosaic and an archaeological illustration of the vessel. Institute personnel scaled, rotated, and aligned both images in accordance with the established coordinates and wreck's orientation. Both digital images contained some distortion, which was corrected using the 24-point rubber sheeting capabilities of the image-processing software.

The locations of NOAA and navy moorings in the vicinity of *Monitor* were grouped together to create their own GIS coverage. By using the mooring's database, end-users were able to identify each mooring and its associated GPS coordinates. In addition, control points for future recording and data recovery were identified in a survey web coverage. Once replicated on the site itself, these reference stations provided a spatial control for future research activities at the site.

A key element in the *Monitor* National Marine Sanctuary GIS was the development of a spatially related artifact inventory. This coverage identified the location of all artifacts recovered from the wreck since on-site investigation began in 1973. The location of each recovered artifact was entered into the GIS and represented by a symbol. By selecting the symbol, the end-user could tap into database information including provenience, condition, date recovered, associations, and drawings and photographic images pertinent to the artifact.

To demonstrate the further potential of GIS for managing site-specific data in the *Monitor* National Marine Sanctuary, I^{2}MR personnel developed coverages linking engineering drawings, historic photographs, underwater photographs, and video to appropriate features of the wreck. As the *Monitor* GIS is developed further, the entire spectrum of data associated with the vessel's historic career, archaeological investigation of the wreck site, and engineering efforts to recover material from the wreck will be stored within the framework that has been established.

Predictive Modeling and Exploratory Data Analysis

One of the earliest and most controversial uses of GIS in archaeology has been in the area of predictive modeling. The concept of a predictive model was first developed by terrestrial archaeologists, who wanted to identify the location of human habitations based on analysis of environmental conditions in a particular region. They reasoned that, because human behavior in locating sites was strongly determined by environment, analyzing conditions around sites could lead to a set of variables that, when applied elsewhere, would help locate new sites in uninvestigated areas.

Many who still see predictive modeling as an important tool also recognize GIS as the ideal instrument for conducting their research. Digital databases can be used to overlay known sites with multiple environmental variables to develop a statistical model of environmental conditions around the site that can then be applied elsewhere (Maschner, 1996).

Predictive modeling is not without its critics. Some archaeologists believe that all models will have severe limitations, and they argue that regulatory agencies will use predictive models to authorize disturbance and development of substantial areas under the potentially erroneous assumption that they contain no significant archaeological sites.

If predictive modeling on land is contentious, it promises to be even more so underwater. The location of shipwrecks is clearly not behaviorally based in the same way as human settlement. The human decision-making component for underwater sites is considerably more limited: a captain's choice about where to sink is marginal at best. Neither do we know all the factors that determine shipwreck locations. Many stretches of water are dynamic and change over time. Ships are mobile. Also, there may be a considerable array of random factors such as storms, fires, and battles that help determine the patterns of vessel losses. Given the historically high usage of some stretches of water, it may be difficult to eliminate the possibility of shipwrecks in any unsurveyed or undisturbed areas. Viewed from this perspective, GIS predictive modeling may be immensely complex, expensive, and of limited use to underwater archaeologists and submerged cultural resource managers until more data about the temporal and spatial distribution of shipwrecks can be used in model development.

Despite these criticisms and limitations, scholars and managers will undoubtedly attempt to construct GIS-based predictive models for shipwreck losses. Such models certainly will include a number of environmental data sets such as prevailing winds, currents, hydrography, channel alignments, and bottom sediments. It will almost certainly include human factors such as known archaeological and historical patterns of human settlement and bottom disturbing activities. Data generated by other scientists such as oceanographers, marine biologists, and ocean engineers probably will be added to archaeologically gathered data. All this information will then be entered and overlaid in a GIS and spatial analysis routines developed, in order to try to establish the probabilities of finding shipwrecks in uninvestigated waters. If successful, such a model would be a highly significant development.

The completed GIS also could be used to determine the most likely sailing routes or drift patterns for vessels in distress, given certain variables such as prevailing winds and tidal sequence. Such a calculation would require the use of a technique called optimum path analysis. Armed with a series of variables, the GIS can be used to calculate the ease with which a vessel could pass from one raster cell to another—in other words, the path of least resistance between two points.

As an alternative to predictive modeling, researchers, and in particular cultural resource managers, should consider GIS-based archaeological sensitivity analysis. By overlaying data such as historic and archaeological sites, hazards to navigation, dredging activity, and remote sensing data, researchers can divide water systems into sensitivity zones. The advantage of archaeological sensitivity analysis is that it correlates directly with known data. Areas of highest sensitivity incorporate known archaeological sites; areas of lowest sensitivity have been surveyed by reputable researchers and are known to contain no archaeological sites. The unknown remains unknown, and no probability ratings are assigned to areas as a result of archaeological sensitivity analysis. Nevertheless, sensitivity zones are extremely useful for cultural resource managers, who can be alerted to potential effects on historical and archaeological resources, and who instantly can identify unsurveyed areas that will be affected by any proposed bottom-disturbing activities.

The capacity and analytical capability of GIS encourages researchers to gather substantial amounts of data, then display, analyze, and explore that information, whether they are interested in predictive modeling, archaeological sensitivity analysis, site specific investigations, management issues, or survey. Graphic and visual representations of thematic maps and overlays often will show relationships between data sets with startling clarity. This form of exploratory inductive research is commonly called exploratory data analysis (EDA) and stands in contrast to the more hypothesis-driven deductive research with which most archaeologists are familiar. As an increasing number of underwater archaeologists adopt GIS, they might consider adopting EDA to explore their data and the relationships between variables. Then it may become possible to develop more fruitful hypotheses and theories that can be tested by augmenting the same GIS with additional data sets.

CONCLUSIONS

Geographic Information Systems have proven to be valuable tools for both cultural resource managers and site-specific investigations. The systems are being used to preserve, store, display, and analyze multivariate spatial data sets and instantaneously access information that was hitherto difficult or cumbersome to acquire. It is now possible to use GIS to gather real-time data from a typical underwater archaeological remote-sensing survey. It may be possible also to develop GIS-based predictive models for shipwreck losses.

Yet the potential uses for GIS in archaeology far exceed any goals thus far realized. As with any technological advancement, user adaptation has been slow. Through continued development and research, however, GIS implementation will prove to be extremely beneficial. One of the most important aspects of GIS is that design, implementation, and maintenance are part of an ongoing process that constantly expands and updates the system. Once the geographical foundation has been developed, the amount of data that can be associated with specific features is limited only by ever-expanding computer capacity. In the immediate future, GIS will doubtless be adopted as the primary reference for Section 106 decision-making.

While GIS probably will never entirely replace hard-copy site documentation, continued development and use of this technology in site-specific research appears inevitable. Excavation and documentation records lend themselves to coverages that can be sufficiently complex to build an electronic image or reconstruction of the entire site. Specific diagnostic features can be linked to detailed drawings, photographs, historical records, literature references, and data from comparative sites. Artifacts, samples, and other material associated with on-site features can be catalogued in association with those features. Artifact photographs, drawings, and historical and comparative analytical data can be tied to specific symbols associated with layers of the master site plan.

As more archaeological sites are preserved in GIS format, and increasing numbers of cultural resource managers turn to spatial databases as a way to enhance their effectiveness, so the opportunities for intersite comparative analysis and widespread dissemination will grow. As more resource managers and research archaeologists adopt GIS, however, so the need for a nationwide database and standardized system of analysis will become more pressing. If archaeologists fail to preserve data in a way that can be shared with their colleagues, the power of GIS to assist the discipline will be greatly curtailed.

REFERENCES

Allen, Kathleen, M.S., Green, Stanton, W., and Zubrow, Ezra, B.W. 1990, *Interpreting Space: GIS and Archaeology*. Taylor and Francis, London.

Arnoff, S., 1989, *Geographic Information Systems: A management perspective*. WDL Publications, Ottawa.

Caswell, D.A., 1992, GIS: The Big Picture in Underwater Search Operations. *Sea Technology* 33(2):40–47.

Coppock, J., and Rhind, D., 1991, The History of GIS. In *Geographical Information Systems*: *Principles and Applications*, edited by D. Maguire, M. Goodchild, and D. Rhind, pp. 21–43. John Wiley and Sons, New York.

Dzurenko, Stephen Michael Jr., 1997, *Development of a Real-Time Geographic Information System Toolbox for Oceanographic Survey Data Acquisition, Monitoring and Processing*. M.S. thesis, University of Rhode Island, Kingston.

Errante, James, 1993, Waterscape Archaeology: Recognizing the Archaeological Potential of the Plantation Waterfront. In *Historic Landscapes in South Carolina*: *Historical Archaeological Perspectives of the Land and Its People*, edited by Linda F. Stine, Lesley M. Drucker, Martha Zierdan, and Christopher Judge, pp. 56–60. Council of South Carolina Professional Archaeologists.

Ferguson, Leland, G., and Babson, David, 1986, *Survey of Plantation Sites along the East Branch of Cooper River: A Model for Predicting Archaeological Site Location*. Manuscript on file, Department of Anthropology, University of South Carolina, Columbia.

Hartley, Michael, O., 1984, *The Ashley River: A Survey of Seventeenth Century Sites*. Research Manuscript Series 192, South Carolina Institute of Archaeology and Anthropology, Columbia.

Marble, D., 1990, The Potential Methodological Impact of GIS on the Social Sciences. In *Interpreting Space*: *GIS and Archaeology*, edited by Kathleen M.S. Allen, Stanton W. Green, and Ezra B.W. Zubrow, pp. 9–21. Taylor and Francis, London.

Maschner, Herbert, D.G., editor, 1996, *New Methods, Old Problems: Geographic Information Systems in Modern Archaeological Research*. Center for Archaeological Investigations, Southern Illinois University, Carbondale.

Mather, Ian Roderick, and Watts Jr., Gordon, P., 1998, Geographic Information Systems for Cultural Resource Management and Site Specific Investigations. In *Underwater Archaeology 1998*, edited by Lawrence Babits, pp. 3–12. Society for Historical Archaeology, Tucson.

Murphy, Larry, 1996, Shipwrecks, Satellites, Computers: An Underwater Inventory of Our National Parks. *Common Ground*, 1(3/4):47–51.

South, Stanley, and Michael Hartley, 1980, *Deep Water and High Ground: Seventeenth Century Low County Settlement*. South Carolina Institute of Archeology and Anthropology, Columbia.

Chapter 41

In Situ Corrosion Measurements and Management of Shipwreck Sites

IAN D. MACLEOD

INTRODUCTION: CORROSION PHENOMENA AND IRON SHOPWRECKS

The overall impression of an iron shipwreck site is often dominated by the remains of the boiler, engine, and frames that once gave the vessel its form. In warm tropical to subtropical seawater, corroding iron and steel rapidly become encapsulated by encrusting organisms such as coralline algae and bryozoa (North, 1976). This encapsulation begins the process of separating the anodic and cathodic sites of the corrosion cell, with oxygen reduction generally happening on the outer surface and oxidation of the metal occurring underneath the marine growth (MacLeod, 1989a). Under such conditions, the cathodic reduction of dissolved oxygen is the rate-determining step in the overall corrosion process.

The main environmental parameters controlling the level of dissolved oxygen are salinity and water temperature. Colder sites, and those with lower salinity, will normally have greater amounts of dissolved oxygen in the waters surrounding the wreck. Since

Ian D. MacLeod, Director, Museum Services, Western Australian Museum, Fremantle, Western Australia WA 6160.

International Handbook of Underwater Archaeology, edited by Carol V. Ruppé and Janet F. Barstad. Kluwer Academic/Plenum Publishers, New York, 2002.

metal ions are produced during the corrosion process, the positive charges released into the immediate environment of the metal surface attract chloride ions through the marine growth. The buildup of chloride ions, from inward diffusion or from the sea, leaves the excavated artifacts at great risk of subsequent corrosion.

Embayed waters and those in cooler regions are dominated by different colonizing marine organisms. In the absence of calcareous colonizing organisms, a corroding iron wreck generally will be covered with a matrix of corrosion products and marine organisms such as algae, barnacles, and tunicates. The wreck *City of Launceston* (1865) in Port Phillip Bay, Australia, typifies such sites. The only major difference in the corrosion processes are the less dense the marine cover, the less the underlying metal is protected from the ravages of dissolved oxygen (MacLeod, 1993a, 1999). Studies on submerged and riparian sites on the River Murray have confirmed that cathodic reduction of dissolved oxygen is the dominant process in determining the overall rate of corrosion (MacLeod, 1994).

Naturally, corrosion rates are dependent on a range of microenvironmental parameters. For iron materials lying above or on the seabed, the primary cathodic reaction is the reduction of dissolved oxygen. For metal totally buried in the sediment and not electrically connected to iron exposed to oxygenated waters, the major cathodic reaction is the reduction of water and the associated evolution of hydrogen. Under such circumstances, the corrosion process is often dominated by microbiological activity (Fischer, 1983) since the presence of dehydrogenase enzymes will often control the rate of hydrogen evolution (Sequeira and Tiller, 1988).

Since the concretion acts as a semipermeable membrane, 100 years of corrosion results in the establishment of a substantially different microenvironment around the metal itself, compared with the surrounding sea. For example, chloride concentration can be increased by a factor of 3 above the mean seawater levels, and pH can fall from the normal value of 8.2 to as low as 4.2 (MacLeod, 1989b). If the matrix of corrosion products and calcareous deposits is accidentally removed, the increased access to oxygen results in accelerated corrosion of iron in a chloride-rich, acidic microenvironment and the loss of archaeological values (MacLeod, 1981, 1987).

On an iron wreck, any nonferrous materials electrically connected to metallic iron will be protected by galvanic coupling. As a result, all copper, brass, and bronze fittings become covered with a thin, adherent, white calcareous concretion (MacLeod, 1982). Once the concretion has formed, the surface is no longer biologically toxic; it is then subject to the normal colonization mechanisms associated with the particular marine ecology of the area.

A novel form of corrosion has been observed on historic shipwrecks where the deleterious effects of galvanic coupling on the corrosion of iron materials are observed where there has been no direct physical contact. This phenomena is now known as *proximity corrosion* and has been observed on the historic shipwreck sites of *Rapid* (1811) and *Hadda* (1877) in Western Australia. These wrecks are in shallow waters at depths of 7 m and 4–6 m respectively. Initial research into the nature of this type of corrosion and its implications for structures has been reported by North (1989).

CORROSION SURVEYS

Routine measurement of electrochemical parameters such as the surface pH of degrading artifacts and the corrosion potential, E_{corr}, of metal objects on wreck sites has a recent

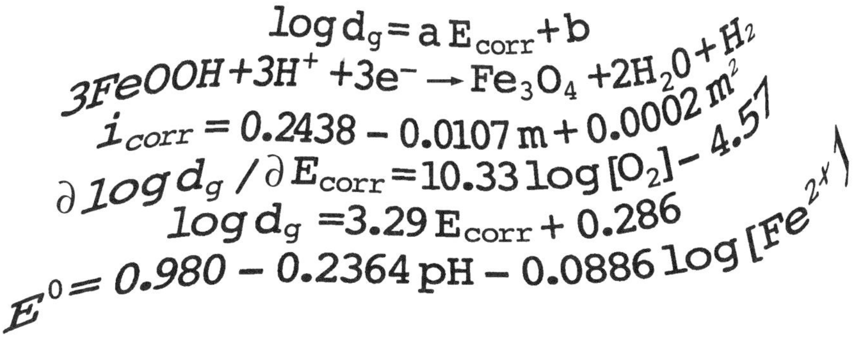

$$\log d_g = a\, E_{corr} + b$$
$$3FeOOH + 3H^+ + 3e^- \rightarrow Fe_3O_4 + 2H_2O + H_2$$
$$i_{corr} = 0.2438 - 0.0107\,m + 0.0002\,m^2$$
$$\partial \log d_g / \partial E_{corr} = 10.33 \log [O_2] - 4.57$$
$$\log d_g = 3.29\, E_{corr} + 0.286$$
$$E^0 = 0.980 - 0.2364\,pH - 0.0886 \log [Fe^{2+}]$$

Figure 41.1. Corrosion measurement equations.

history (Lenihan, 1989; MacLeod 1981; North, 1982). Corrosion scientists have found that knowledge obtained through these on-site measurements is an invaluable aid in understanding the corrosion mechanisms and modes of deterioration of materials on archaeological sites.

Corrosion potentials are measured by noting the voltage difference between a platinum electrode in contact with the corroding metal and an appropriate reference electrode. For practical reasons, the digital multimeter is normally housed in a waterproof case, with the electrodes connected via insulated wires sealed through the box with O-rings. A suitable reference electrode for working in open sea water is a silver/silver chloride (Ag/AgCl). If work is done in sediments or in waters subject to sulphide contamination, this double-junction Ag/AgCl electrode is necessary to prevent contamination of the electrode, which would change the standard voltage. Platinum is used as the working electrode because it is chemically inert; the measured voltages refer to the object itself and are not due in part to the nature of the electrode material.

Corrosion potential measurements are made by drilling through the marine growth and placing the platinum electrode into the hole with the reference electrode adjacent to the point of measurement, then reading the voltage. Correct determination of the corrosion potential is normally indicated by a very steady voltage, i.e. a reading that varies by only 1–2 mv over several minutes. The significance of the corrosion potential is that it is a readily measurable parameter sensitive to the rate of metal corrosion. The primary corrosion product occurring underneath the concretion is ferrous chloride ($FeCl_2$), which subsequently undergoes hydrolysis to $\{Fe(OH)_2 \cdot FeCl_2\}$. As the ferrous chloride solution diffuses out through the concretion matrix and undergoes hydrolysis, the resulting increase in acidity causes dissolution of calcium carbonate in the encapsulated marine organisms. Reprecipitation of iron carbonate follows with concomitant oxidation of the iron II (Fe^{2+}) corrosion products to iron III (Fe^{3+}).

SITE-SPECIFIC CORROSION RATES AND USE OF E_{corr}

Archaeologists have a strong desire to determine the long-term rate of deterioration of a shipwreck site. Secondary to this key issue is the desire to understand how the rate of decay changes with the effect of excavation activities or with natural scouring processes associated with heavy storms. Fortunately, historic shipwrecks generally have a unique record of the effect of corrosion preserved in corroded cast iron objects. For wooden ships, the presence of cast iron cannon provides a source of such data, while for iron shipwrecks, the massive cast iron bollards, capstans, and engine mountings provide a site-specific corrosion database. Because of its elemental composition and associated microstructure, cast iron corrodes to leave behind the original surface dimensions of an object because of its high carbon content. This change results in a composition profile that leaves graphite on the original surface, followed by a mixture of graphite and cementite (Fe_3C, iron carbide), pearlite (a phase consisting of lamellae of cementite and pure iron, or ferrite), and ferrite itself. By drilling into the corroded metal, perpendicular to the exposed face, the researcher can obtain a corrosion profile of the vessel since it was immersed in sea water. Once the drill bit encounters solid material, in the form of uncorroded metal, the penetration depth can be recorded with a micrometer. Penetration depth, or graphitization, of cast iron is a good indicator of the net effects of exposure to the corrosive environments over past centuries.

Previous work has established a direct relationship between the logarithm of the annual rate of corrosion rate of cast iron artifacts and their in situ corrosion potential (MacLeod, 1989a). Annualized corrosion rate is determined by dividing the depth of graphitization d_g by the number of years of the object's immersion; corrosion rates are reported in mm/year. It is desirable to have a number of sets of measurements of depths of graphitization and E_{corr} so that a measure of the variability of data across the site can be determined. Sufficient data has been recorded from a number of sites to ascertain that objects that do not "lie on the straight line" relationship are more than likely to be indicators of significant changes in the nature of the microenvironment since the initial wrecking event.

Site-specific corrosion equations take the general form of Equation 1:

$$\log d_g = a \, E_{corr} + b \tag{1}$$

where a is a constant for the site at the time of measurement, and b is another constant relating to the general corrosivity of the site. The value of the slope a has been found to be sensitive to temperature and salinity, since these are the two parameters that ultimately determine saturation values of dissolved oxygen in the water. The units of a are volt^{-1}, the reciprocal of this slope provides a measure of the number of volts or millivolts needed per tenfold change in corrosion rate. The higher the dissolved oxygen values, the greater the increase in corrosion rate per unit increase in the value of the corrosion potential.

GENERAL CORROSION PHENOMENA AND USE OF IN SITU CORROSION MEASUREMENTS TO ASCERTAIN RATES OF DECAY

Corrosion potential (E_{corr}) data collected from a number of wreck sites show that archaeological iron is often in strongly reducing conditions, with Eh values at -0.290 ± 0.015 volts at a mean pH of 4.8, or just below the hydrogen evolution potential for that acidity level. Hydrogen has been identified as a major component of gases released when concretions are penetrated for the first time in centuries (MacLeod, 1988). Among the other gases were carbon dioxide (from acid dissolution of calcite and aragonite as a result of hydrolysis reactions) and methane. Analysis of the carbon isotope ratios of $^{13}C/^{12}C$

in the methane gave an isotope shift of −4.7 ppt, showing that the methane was inorganically derived via reactions such as those shown in Equation 2:

$$CO_2 + 4H_2 \rightarrow CH_4 + 2H_2O \qquad (2)$$

Since bacteria effectively fractionate carbon isotopes in favor of ^{12}C, an isotope shift ($\delta^{13}C$) with a value in the range of −55 to −75 ppt (relative to standard limestone, PDB) would be observed for bacterially-produced methane (Hunt, 1979). Inspection of the carbon Pourbaix diagram shows that methane is the thermo-dynamically stable form of carbon under the lower portion of the range of Eh and pH (Pourbaix, 1974) recorded on wreck sites at depths to 22 m.

EFFECTS OF CORROSION PROCESS

Dissolved Oxygen

The equation connecting dissolved oxygen content of seawater and values of a was developed empirically from the following observations. The wreck of the *Lively* (c. 1820), in the warm tropical waters of the Rowley Shoals some 400 km off the Western Australian coast, had a slope of 2.84 (Carpenter and MacLeod, 1993); the average slope of more temperate Australia sites was 3.05; and the much cooler Scottish waters in the Sound of Mull (Ellett and Edwards, 1983) gave a slope of 3.70. Concentration of dissolved oxygen increases as both temperature and salinity fall (Riley and Skirrow, 1975). From a knowledge of salinity and temperatures of wreck sites, it is possible to gain typical values of dissolved oxygen concentration. When the values of the slope a are plotted as a function of the O_2 concentration, the observed slopes were related by Equation 3:

$$\partial \log d_g / \partial E_{corr} = 10.33 \ \log[O_2] - 4.57 \qquad (3)$$

where the concentration of oxygen is recorded in $cm^3 \cdot dm^{-3}$. Once the salinity and temperature of the seawater and hence the dissolved oxygen concentration is known, Equation 3 can be used to calculate the a value for Equation 1. This means that it is now possible to determine the differences in the rates of corrosion for artifacts in similar chemical environments. At least one set of data on $\log d_g$ is needed to determine the value of the constant b in Equation 1 to allow a quantitative calculation of corrosion rates.

As already noted, it is possible to use the shift in E_{corr} values to determine the extent to which a corrosion environment has changed. Once the value of a is known, it is possible to see how many millivolts difference in the value of E_{corr} is needed for a tenfold change in corrosion rates. The *Tafel* slope is the number of millivolts that equates to a tenfold change in corrosion rate (Kiss, 1988). Changes in E_{corr} values, as measured in volts, can then be multiplied by the value of the slope a, and the "multiplier effect" on the corrosion rate is determined by taking the antilogarithm of this value. To determine when any changes in the values of E_{corr} are significant, it is vital to know the reproducibility of data over several seasons. Repeated visits to the SS *Xantho* site showed that the corrosion potential measurements of the boiler were reproducible within ±2 mV (MacLeod, 1992). If there are larger differences in corrosion potentials, it is possible to state that a change occurred. A change of 3 mV in the value of E_{corr} equates to a variation of 2.5 percent in the cooler Scottish waters off the Isle of Mull, to 1.6 percent in the tropical waters at the *Lively* site in tropical Western Australia.

Cyclic Burial and Exposure

The effects of cyclical burial and exposure of wreck materials and effects on corrosion mechanisms is best illustrated by analysis of SS *Xantho*, which sank off Port Gregory, Western Australia in 1872. A copper wire in an engine room water cooling device showed a number of corrosion layers. When the logarithm of the spacings between the layers was plotted against the number of growth rings, a series of linear relationships showed that the corrosion phenomena on the SS *Xantho* site can be described in terms of *liesegang* phenomena, i.e., of periodic precipitation (MacLeod, 1986). Precipitation of copper sulphides as corrosion products occurs with the change of the microenvironment from aerobic, when the object was exposed to strongly flowing seawater, to anaerobic, when 2 m of sand were deposited on the site. During periods of exposure to open seawater, the fitting was in a passive corrosion state and suffered negligible corrosion. Under anaerobic conditions, the passivating nature of the Cu_2O film was rendered inactive, and significant corrosion took place each time the site was reburied. With 16 corrosion bands over the 113 years since the vessel sank, the data strongly supports a seven-year cycle of burial and exposure. This phenomena readily explains the "newness" of the biological environment on the wreck site, compared with the surrounding reef that was noted during the predisturbance survey (MacLeod et al., 1986).

Water Depth

During the initial corrosion surveys on the wreck site of HMS *Sirius* (1790) on Norfolk Island, it was noted that the cast iron ballast pigs were much more extensively corroded in shallow waters than in the deeper part of the site (MacLeod, 1989a). These differences occurred over the range of water depth from 1.5 to 3.5 m at the high-water mark. Any diver working the site can vouch for major differences in the degree of difficulty of working in the strong surge in the extremely shallow site. Since water depth made such a huge difference to the divers, it is not surprising to find such issues reflected by the degree of degradation of the artifacts. For many years, the search for a model was fruitless, until a larger number of wrecks had been surveyed and their corrosion characteristics noted.

One of the most direct corrosion indices is the annualized depth of corrosion as measured by the mm/year of graphitization of cast iron; this has been plotted as a function of water depth across the site. This research is entirely empirical in nature, and the interpretation of data is subject to change as more sites are examined and the model is refined.

Despite these limitations, some general comments can be made. The shallowest vessel from which data was collected is that of the breastwork monitor HMVS *Cerberus* (1876) in Port Phillip Bay in Victoria, which was sunk as a breakwater in 1926. The deepest vessel is *City of Launceston* (1865) at a depth of 22 m in the middle of the west shipping channel in Port Phillip Bay. The zero water depth for corrosion measurements on *Cerberus* related to the former splash zone, which subsided a few years ago to lie 1 m below its previous level. The annual corrosion rate of 0.242 mm/year at zero water depth relates to the armor plating on the outerdecks of the vessel (MacLeod, 1996a).

Since previous studies had shown that E_{corr} steadily decreased with water depth, the corrosion rates from the iron shipwrecks were plotted according to average water depth.

The best fit for the regression analysis was a quadratic equation (see Equation 4), with the square of the correlation coefficient being 0.9985, a strong indicator that the relationship has a high degree of validity.

$$i_{corr} = 0.2438 - 0.0107 \text{ m} + 0.0002 \text{ m}^2 \tag{4}$$

where i_{corr} is in units of mm/year and water depth m is in meters. This equation can be used to calculate the long-term corrosion rate of an iron shipwreck in the open ocean waters of southern Australian latitudes with only water depth being known. The benefit of this relationship is that it can be used by anyone to calculate the expected corrosion rate for vessels when the only archaeological information known is the date of wrecking and water depth. If the original thickness of metal ribs, frames, and plates are known, Equation 4 can be used to estimate how much of the materials is likely to remain on the site (MacLeod, 1998b).

Since corrosion rate decreases in a primarily linear fashion with depth but is corrected for this by a smaller positive term associated with the square of water depth, there comes a point where the corrosion rate will be independent of depth. This minimum, or point of independence from depth, can be determined by differentiation of Equation 4 with regard to the water depth m which gives Equation 5:

$$\partial I/\partial m = 0.0004 \text{ m} - 0.0107 \tag{5}$$

The minimum value is reached when the slope is equal to zero; this occurs at a water depth of 26.8 m. This observation is profound, implying as it does that, once an iron wreck is in water of greater depth than 26.8 m, the overall effect of the increased depth is limited. *It must be emphasized that these observations are limited to the data collected and that the deepest site measured was 22 m.*

The other implication is that the minimum corrosion rate of iron shipwrecks is 0.100 mm/year, the average long-term corrosion rate of marine iron in an exposed location (La Que, 1975). More experimental data needs to be obtained from deeper water sites to determine how this relationship applies. Given that the general mixing of ocean waters becomes significantly less at depths greater than 35 m (Riley and Skirrow, 1975), other variables are likely to affect the amount of water movement, such as deep ocean currents, that would begin to play a significant role in the supply of dissolved oxygen to the corroding metal surfaces.

Shelter from Prevailing Weather

The effect on overall corrosion rate of an iron shipwreck lying in the lee of an island can now be calculated using Equation 4 to predict the annual rate of decay and by comparing it with the in situ data. A convenient case is that of *Songvaar* (1912), which lies in the lee of Wardang Island in Spencer Gulf, South Australia. The actual corrosion rate of the iron clipper is some 30 percent less than would be anticipated on the basis of the water depth. Another possible factor that may have lowered the historical corrosion rate of *Songvaar* is that, when it sank on its own anchor, the vessel was fully laden with wheat. As the wheat swelled, it would have begun to undergo marked biodeterioration, which would have rendered the waters on the inside of the vessel anaerobic and so reduced the initial corrosion rate. More data from other protected wreck sites is needed before the relative effect of the cargo and the shelter of the island can be quantified.

Explosives

Management of historic shipwrecks without the assistance of enacted protective legislation is made much more difficult by the activities of would-be salvors who attack vessels with explosive charges. Reasons for such vandalism are many but include those of recovery of nonferrous metal fittings for scrap value. An example of the effect of explosives on an historic iron shipwreck can be judged from the wreck of *Clan Ranald* (1909), which sank off Troubridge Point, Gulf St. Vincent, South Australia. If Equation 4 is used to calculate the anticipated corrosion rate, actual data shows an increase of 33 percent above the level based on water depth of 18 m. The increased corrosion rate is probably due to extensive blasting of the site during a series of salvage operations. Shock waves from the exploding charges tend to strip the protective concretion from the hull and other fittings and give the dissolved oxygen direct access to the degraded metal. Observations of the rapid increase in corrosion potential of several hundred millivolts when an iron artifact has its protective concretion accidentally removed during archaeological excavations testifies to the effect of such activities (MacLeod, 1987).

Another shipwreck subjected to explosives during salvage operation was *Pareora* (1919), which shows an elevation of some six percent. Most of the blasting on this site took place during initial salvage operations, and much of the effect also could be due to stresses imparted to the vessel during blasting operations. In contrast, most of the blasting on *Clan Ranald* took place some 50 years after the vessel had foundered. Clearly, the effect of stripping of the protective concretion has a much larger effect on the vessel after the iron has been subjected to decades of corrosion activity.

Trawling Operations in Closed Waters

Shortly after the initial in situ corrosion survey of the Australian wreck *City of Launceston* (1865) in Port Phillip Bay in Victoria, a moratorium was placed on scallop dredging. The site is still littered with the remains of scallop dredges that became entangled with the wreck. *City of Launceston* lies on a shingle bottom, surrounded by a silt mound several meters deep at the midpoint of both port and starboard sides of the hull, but the vessel is still intact. The primary reason for the dredging ban was the diminishing resource (local fishermen were not staying within the bag limits imposed by the Fisheries Department). The presence of the wreck and the damage the fishermen were doing had no effect on the enactment of the ban.

When the site was reassessed six-plus years later, it was noted that the apparent corrosion rate had fallen by approximately 21 percent, and that the extent of marine growth was much greater than it had been during the first season. A subsequent set of measurements one year later confirmed that the lowered corrosion rate was maintained. Although the amount of suspended sediments in the bay varies significantly (Cowdell et al., 1985), normal peaks in this indicator occur in the warmer late spring and summer months. Thus, the improved visibility noted in November and December is not simply a reflection of better timing in the cycle of visitation, since November visibility should be expected to be lower than April values. It appears that cessation of dredging this silty bottom sediment has assisted in the support of a more developed marine ecology; this in turn has led to a lowered corrosion rate.

Salinity

Iron's overall corrosion behavior changes markedly with chloride ion concentration but not unduly over the normal range of salinities associated with natural variations in seawater. Once chloride concentration rises above 2 ppm, overall kinetics do not change appreciably until 500 ppm (salinity of 1 ppt), then up to normal seawater at 18,500 ppm or salinity of 35 ppt. In the Great Lakes of Canada and the United States, the corrosion behavior of iron is dominated by the natural alkalinity of fresh water. Although only a few ppm of chloride are present, this amount still corrodes iron objects in much the same way as in Australian riverine systems such as the River Murray, which is 100 times more salty. During a study of submerged barges and paddle steamers in South Australia's River Murray, a gradual increase in salinity from 113 ppm to 520 km upstream, to 410 ppm chloride near the river mouth, does not seem to have had a major effect on the corrosion mechanism (MacLeod, 1993b, 1994).

A series of measurements on seven shipwrecks in the Fathom Five National Park of Lake Huron has shown that this approach works as a sensitive indicator of microenvironment for the iron fastenings in this alkaline freshwater lake. Because of the alkalinity, iron fastenings holding together the wooden vessels are covered in dense and thin layers of calcium carbonate (MacLeod, 1999b).

EFFECTS OF METAL COMPOSITION AND RATE OF CONCRETION GROWTH

Analysis of the metal composition of iron objects and the thickness of concretion has shown that there is a direct relationship between thickness of the marine concretion and weight percent of phosphorous in the metal (MacLeod, 1988). If the rate of corrosion is partly dependent on the thickness of the concretion (on the electrical resistivity of that pathway), the artifacts containing a greater percentage of phosphorous might be expected to corrode at a slower rate, owing to the increase of resistance due to a greater concretion thickness. It should be noted that too little data exists to check this supposition readily.

Other biological factors also can be important. An example of this has been found on Norfolk Island, at the wreck site of HMS *Sirius*. One cause for differences in corrosion potential of similar materials appears to lie in the presence of the black long-spined sea urchin, *Heliocidaris tuberculta* (Lamarck, 1816), which burrows into the marine growth on the artifacts, thereby shortcircuiting one rate-determining parameter in the corrosion cell: the electrical resistance of the concretion layer. Inspection of HMS *Sirius*' carronade and ballast pigs' surfaces shows that hemispherical depressions in the cast iron are due to the burrowing of marine organisms.

EFFECTS OF WATER DEPTH ON E_{corr}

A function of the encapsulating concretion that forms on iron objects of a wreck site is to act as a buffer zone between the immediate physical environment of the sea and the artifact. It also serves to separate dissolved oxygen from corroding metal. In the warm tropical to subtropical waters of Australia, marine growth is dominated by coralline algae and bryozoa as primary colonizers. E_{corr} values fell by 21 ± 3 mV/m in both the ocean and in the River Murray (MacLeod 1989a, 1994). Since all the metal was covered with a thin and dense layer of accretion, the physical separation of anode and cathode of the corrosion cell is similar to that of sea water. The combination of pH and E_{corr} data for 10 riverine sites indicate that pH is controlled by the equilibrium between magnetite, Fe_3O_4, and Fe^{2+} ions, whereas in sea water it is dominated by the equilibrium between Fe^{2+} and $Fe(OH)_2 \cdot FeCl_2$. In the absence of such dense concretion layers, depth dependence of E_{corr} is less in the cooler waters of Gulf St. Vincent in South Australia, where E_{corr} fell by only 3 mV/m, and in the adjacent Spencer Gulf, where E_{corr} fell by 5 mV/m of water depth (MacLeod, 1998).

VOLTAGE DIFFERENCES BETWEEN WROUGHT AND CAST IRON

Correct interpretation of corrosion potentials requires that the measurements relate to the same type of metal in the same chemical environment. If this is not the case, errors of interpretation most likely will occur. Since all the forms of iron encountered on a wreck site have corroded in an essentially similar fashion, it is possible to interpret the data with a reasonable degree of confidence. Although iron artifacts are often difficult to conserve because of the way in which chloride ions have permeated the metal's microstructure, collections of hull plates, boilers, cast iron fittings, and anchors all behave in similar fashion. Under conditions generally found on the seabed, iron corrodes in a film-free state in an active corrosion zone of the Pourbaix diagram (Pourbaix, 1974). Thus, a more anodic voltage is a measure of an increased corrosion rate, whereas if the metal was in a passive state with a protective film over the metal, the reverse could be the case. However, in the initial study of the effects of water depth on E_{corr} on the HMS *Sirius* site, such complications were not present, and systematic differences in E_{corr} between wrought and cast iron of approximately 70 mV occurred at the same water depth (MacLeod, 1989). More anodic voltages of cast iron are due to the much higher carbon content of cast iron. Since the graphite form of carbon in the microstructure of alloys is inert, cast iron objects have less negative E_{corr} values, yet corrode at the same rate as wrought iron fittings at 70 mV more cathodic voltages.

With less dense layers of marine growth on the surface of the corroded iron objects, such as in South Australian waters, separation between the characteristic voltages of cast iron and wrought iron are less and vary between 12 mV and 20 mV, depending on the local site differences in marine biology and overall physical oceanography. Clearly, less dense concretions do not support such a large diffusion gradient in pH. They also provide less of a physical barrier to oxygen. In turn, this leads to less of a differentiation between carbon-rich and lower carbon sources in cast iron and wrought iron objects. For similar water depths and similar chemical microenvironments, cast iron fittings will have higher, less negative E_{corr} values than corresponding wrought iron and steel objects.

EFFECT OF ARCHAEOLOGICAL ACTIVITY ON LATER CORROSION OF RESIDUAL DEPOSITS

Analysis of corrosion data collected in the predisturbance survey of the *Xantho* site led to the installation of aluminium sacrificial anodes on the engine and propeller shaft (MacLeod et al., 1986) to minimize further corrosion damage. During recovery operations, corrosion potential measurements were used to gauge the effect of excavation on the stern's remaining parts. The quantification of the differences in E_{corr} values observed during the various stages of archaeological intervention on the site can be made with the knowledge that a tenfold increase or decrease in corrosion rate is indicated by a 370 mV change in the value of E_{corr} (See Section 5.1. Dissolved Oxygen). The data show that application of anodes to the propeller shaft caused a 37 percent reduction in the corrosion rate of the drive train. At the end of the life of the anode in May 1986, the corrosion rate had increased by 14 percent above the predisturbance level, or a 57 percent increase above the previously protected level. This clearly indicates that the removal of the engine did have an initial adverse effect on the corrosion rate of downstream areas. The attachment of new anodes in 1986 caused the predisturbance corrosion rate to be cut in half. The E_{corr} of the stern plating increased to 48 mV four days after the removal of the engine, which indicated an increased degree of water turbulence; this amounts to a 35 percent increase in corrosion rate.

Although the relative corrosion rate for the stern section fell by 12 percent after a year, as increased sand coverage began to correct the effects of the engine removal, it was not until new anodes were attached directly to the stern section that the initial effect of archaeological intervention was corrected. The stern section's present condition is that the corrosion rate has been reduced by 91 percent compared with predisturbance values (MacLeod, 1998b).

CORROSION POTENTIALS AS AN IDENTIFICATION TOOL IN ZERO-VISIBILITY CONDITIONS

River Murray was the major trading route for much of the inland areas of Victoria and South Australia in the 19th century. One consequence of this extensive riverine traffic was the deposition of a substantial number of submerged and partially submerged wrecks over a period of many decades. Since the river's turbid waters preclude visual inspection methods, a study of the corrosion potentials of metals on the sites can act as a set of sensitive "remote sensing" eyes. It is proposed to use E_{corr} measurements as a database for monitoring changes in site conditions; this is the first time corrosion data has been used for this purpose under "black water" conditions. E_{corr} data was recorded on board the support vessel and communications were via a tethered life line and "comms" setup. Voltages were read on board, and the diver was instructed to hold the electrodes in particular configurations once good electrical contact was made. The electrodes were connected with 15-m lengths of insulated cable clipped to the lifeline to keep them from becoming snagged on the wrecks, submerged trees, and other debris.

By plotting the average corrosion potentials for the iron frames and engine components from different sites on a Pourbaix diagram, it is easy to see the varying degrees of corrosion activity that characterized each site. The average E_{corr} values for all sites where solid metal is present show that all the wrecks are in the region of active corrosion. Equilibrium reactions appear to be related to the corrosion of iron to produce Fe^{2+} ions, which are in equilibrium with magnetite, Fe_3O_4 according to the following reactions 6 and 7:

$$Fe \rightarrow Fe^{2+} + 2e^- \tag{6}$$

$$3Fe^{2+} + 4H_2O \rightarrow Fe_3O_4 + 8H^+ + 2e^- \tag{7}$$

The pH of the microenvironment associated with this equilibrium is given by the relationship

$$E^0 = 0.980 - 0.2364\,\text{pH} - 0.0886\log[\text{Fe}^{2+}] \qquad (8)$$

which for the pH of 6.46 observed on the concreted sections on *Uranus* at Goolwa gives a ferrous ion concentration of 3.9×10^{-5}M or roughly 2.2 ppm Fe^{2+} in equilibrium with magnetite. All these data are consistent with a slow corrosion rate. Assuming that this pH value is typical, average corrosion potentials on *Jolly Miller* correspond to approximately 200 ppm Fe^{2+} ions in the immediate vicinity of the corroding metal.

Some individual E_{corr} measurements on the extensively corroded iron materials of *William Randell* and *Cobar* are in the region where FeOOH is the stable form of iron. These data also are consistent with the observation that the fittings appeared to be extensively degraded and that there is essentially no solid metal remaining in them. The diver indicated several times that he believed the solid iron-stained beams were "real," but the voltage measurements were typical of iron (III) corrosion products such as FeOOH impregnated into wooden timbers. Thus, the E_{corr} measurements confirmed the presence of wooden beams on the *J.G. Arnold*, *William Randell*, and *Ventura* sites. Since many areas of the river have iron wrecks and wooden wrecks on the same spot, such measurements are a vital part of determining what part of the site belongs to a particular wreck.

A summary of average corrosion potentials for iron fittings and iron structural material on the vessels is found in Table 41.1. Only one of each of the pairs of vessels at each of the main sites at Goolwa, Morgan, and Waikerie is listed, since they all had similar corrosion potentials. Where the vessels were at a similar depth, the more corrosive environments closely correlated with increased water flow over those wrecks. More negative E_{corr} values for the vessels upstream of Waikerie, Loxton, and Berri are dominated by greater water depth. Burial in the silt mounds on the site of *Jolly Miller* gave partly-buried iron fittings an E_{corr} 82 mV more negative than values obtained on similar iron sections floating above the river bed. Any parameter that increases water movement in the area of the wrecks will increase the rate of deterioration of metals. Banning water skiing would help the wrecks by removing the effects of the wash from speed boats.

USE OF IN SITU CORROSION STUDIES TO DETERMINE ORIGINAL METAL THICKNESS

Maritime archaeologists often are presented with the problem of trying to determine the nature of the vessel from measurements of original metal thickness, since records often denote the construction details of ribs, frames, and metal plate thickness. In the past, this

Table 41.1. Corrosion parameters for iron and wooden wrecks in River Murray, South Australia.

Wreck	Miles from Sea	Town	Cl ppm	pH (river)	E_{corr} volts vs. NHE
Uranus	5	Goolwa	410	7.90	-0.163 ± 0.007
Crowie	199	Morgan	185	7.86	-0.150 ± 0.019
J.G. Arnold	224	Waikerie	168	7.67	-0.229 ± 0.025
Jolly Miller	298	Loxton	154	7.67	-0.282 ± 0.033

was estimated by using the preserved form of the object encapsulated in the calcareous concretion. This approach has great limitations, not the least of which is that the method is essentially destructive: It involves smashing open and cleaning out the concretions. A novel way to use in situ corrosion data to estimate the original metal thickness of such fittings is to use a combination of residual metal thickness and an estimate of amount of metal lost from the time of shipwreck.

Residual metal thickness data can be obtained using devices such as a Cygnus digital meter, which provides a readout of the solid metal retained in the structure. Once a site-specific corrosion equation has been established for a wreck site, this relationship can be used to determine total amount of metal lost during the time of immersion in seawater. An example of this approach was used initially on the wreck of HMVS *Cerberus* to establish the method, since the original specifications were at hand. The corrosion equation for the site is given by the relationship shown in Equation 9:

$$\log d_g = 3.29 E_{corr} + 0.286 \qquad (9)$$

This equation can then be used to determine what the current E_{corr} data corresponds to in terms of how fast the metal is corroding, expressed in terms of mm/year of immersion.

Data on residual metal thickness presented a large spread, from 20 mm to as low as 3 mm, along the length of the vessel and between the upper works to the bottom of the vessel. Ultrasonic metal thickness measuring devices report on the thickness of solid metal bounced back from the interface between solid metal and degraded material. Given that the original armor plating was between 8–10 in (203–254 mm), it is readily apparent that our experimental method did not pick up massive plating, and that data related to an outer zone of metal that lay on top of the original armor. The supposition that the outer upper skin was an addition that took place after construction was shown to be correct: Inspection of the wreck's starboard side shows a clear line of extra plating that ends about 3 m below the original deck height. It is apparent that the data relates to secondary cladding over the armor belt and to the degraded values of plating and frames and ribs.

When thickness data is plotted in order of increasing residual material, four subsets of solid metal thickness appear. The data, summarized in Table 41.2, indicated that *Cerberus* used a range of metal thicknesses which generally was incremented by 1/8 in and that the vessel's upper works have suffered greater corrosion than the middle. The amount of corrosion of the upper section is similar to that of the frames and ribs at the interface between the sea bed and the vessel.

The implications of this study for underwater heritage managers are significant. Field measurements of residual metal thickness, in association with on-site depth of corrosion data from cast iron, can provide a method of determining the original dimensions of the scantlings. Many wrecks contain only a series of iron ribs and frames,

Table 41.2. Average metal thickness for iron on the HMVS *Cerberus* site.

Mean thickness (mm)	Corrosion loss (mm)	Calculated original (mm or in)	Number of samples
3.77 ± 0.46	8.9	12.7 mm or 1/2 in	23
7.60 ± 0.79	8.3	15.9 mm or 5/8 in	16
11.7 ± 0.95	7.4	19.1 mm or 3/4 in	7
18.2 ± 2.40	8.8	27.0 mm or $1^1/_{16}$ in	7

which could have come from a number of vessels known to have been lost in the general vicinity. Given that most wrecks at the same site came from different-sized vessels and from different periods of history, this new approach of using the corrosion measurements as a diagnostic tool has major implications for maritime archaeology.

The method has been applied to the wreck of *Clan Ranald* (1909) in South Australia to determine the original specifications for the thickness of the donkey boilers and the main boilers, since this data was not to be found among Lloyd's specifications or among the ship's drawings. The method accurately determined the correct scantling thicknesses as laid down in the Lloyd's tables for turret-style vessels (MacLeod, 1998a).

IN SITU CONSERVATION OF CORRODED IRON OBJECTS

A number of treatments have been performed on extensively corroded iron objects using sacrificial anodes to reverse the effect of hundreds of years of corrosion from the effects of dissolved oxygen in aggressive site conditions. Although experiments are currently underway on the site of *Swan* (1653) in Scotland and *Resurgam* (1867) off the Welsh coast (Gregory, 1998; MacLeod, 1999), the only completed works have been done on materials recovered from the wreck of HMS *Sirius* (1790) on Norfolk Island in the South Pacific Ocean.

HMS *Sirius* bow anchor

A section of concretion cover was accidentally removed from the shank of the bow anchor during excavation. The concomitant increased corrosion rate was monitored four days before the decision was made to attach an anode. After a year of treatment with an aluminium anode, the area of concretion loss was covered by a calcareous scar (MacLeod, 1987). If 50 percent current efficiency is assumed, the loss of 7 kg of anode material should have provided complete cathodic protection (Fischer, 1983). The effectiveness of the treatment can be gauged from the final E_{corr} value of −0.430 volts vs the Normal Hydrogen Electrode (NHE), which has an equivalent pH of 7.43, assuming the surface is in equilibrium with hydrogen discharge. Copious amounts of hydrogen escaped when the concretion was cracked at the end of the treatment program. The increase from a pH of 5.6 to 7.4 indicates a major reduction of hydrogen ion activity as a result of the cathodic current flowing into the anchor. The other principal effect of the cathodic current is that chloride ions diffuse through the concretion into the surrounding sea water (MacLeod, 1988).

After being removed from the sea, the anchor was given follow-up treatment of gentle electrolysis for over two years. On final examination, the anchor was shown to have retained large areas of the original surface (Carpenter, 1986; MacLeod, 1989). The normally encountered friable surface that characterizes zonal corrosion of wrought iron was replaced by a solid but fragile matrix (Chilton and Evans, 1955). The best-preserved surfaces were those that had suffered no damage to the concretion during the excavation process. One of the main reactions that probably takes place under the concretion layer is the electrochemical reduction of iron (III) corrosion products to form magnetite and hydrogen, as shown in Equation 10:

$$3FeOOH + 3H^+ + 3e^- \rightarrow Fe_3O_4 + 2H_2O + H_2 \tag{10}$$

Table 41.3. Corrosion parameters for the HMS *Sirius* carronade.

Date	E_{corr} volts vs. NHE	pH	Object condition
10/15/88	−0.240	5.82	Predisturbance
10/24/88	−0.379	not measured	anode attached
3/20/90	−0.300	7.16	anode lost
3/26/90	−0.485	8.19	anode attached

In the absence of corrosion, and under the influence of cathodic current, chloride ions will diffuse out of the matrix. The reduction in acidity will tend to promote redeposition of calcium/magnesium carbonates (magnesium calcites) and deposition of the iron carbonate siderite ($FeCO_3$). Slag inclusions are retained in a complex matrix, which results in replication of surface detail, such as manufacturing stamps. The one year of pretreatment was equivalent to one year of land-based treatment.

HMS *Sirius* Carronade

Following the successful treatment of the anchor, a similar approach was applied to the second *Sirius* carronade (Stanbury, 1994). Predisturbance data and three other measurements over three years led to a much clearer understanding of the changes that occur during seabed electrolysis. Predisturbance data showed that the gun was in a highly corrosive microenvironment, hardly surprising since the gun lay in 1.5 m of water in the full surf zone on top of a reef platform. Treatment progress can be seen by the changes in the E_{corr} values and pH (Table 41.3).

On connecting the first anode, the 140 mV decrease toward more negative potentials showed that good electrical contact had been made and that the cathodic current was flowing into the carronade. It was necessary to replace the first anode because of a violent storm, which moved a 1.5 ton concrete plinth several hundred meters across the seabed and ripped the first anode from the carronade (Henderson, 1989).

After three more years of cathodic protection, the carronade was excavated from the depression in the reef and freed from the encapsulating coral. During the excavation process, some of the concretion was accidentally dislodged from the breech end at the cascable. Despite this direct exposure to oxygenated sea water, there was no sign of flash rusting during the final four days of excavation work, indicating clearly that the carronade had undergone significant stabilization. Although the final E_{corr} was measured, a sudden deterioration in site conditions precluded recording pH. If pH is in equilibrium with hydrogen at the same voltage as the corrosion potential, it can be seen that the calculated final pH of 8.2 is the same as the surrounding sea water, which means the treatment was essentially complete. During excavation, large volumes of gas evolved from small fissures in the concretion layer, which is consistent with hydrogen evolution. The alkalinity and lowered chloride content of the metal both increase the degree of safety for recovery and transport to conservation facilities for the extensively degraded object.

The carronade was deconcreted eight months after recovery, revealing a wooden tompion that had kept the bore sealed for 200 years. The tompion's inner surface was covered with a brown, waxy–oily layer containing elemental sulphur, which probably came from gun powder residues. A massive ball of wadding was attached by a rope to the tompion; the organic materials were quickly treated with neutral citrate solutions to prevent damage due to oxidation and precipitation of iron corrosion products (MacLeod et al., 1991).

The total amount of chloride removed during the laboratory phase of the treatment of the carronade was 4.22 kg, a small amount indicating that a significant mass of chloride had been removed during in situ treatment. Since it was not possible to determine directly the initial amount of chloride removed, it was necessary to resort to a series of comparative measurements in order to estimate the efficiency of the treatment.

The first method involves a comparison of the composition of the *Sirius* bore solution and the bore solution from a similarly plugged gun from the wreck of *Zuytdorp* (1712). The chloride ion concentration of the 1.4 liters of bore solution trapped by the tompion gave a concentration of 8366 ppm, less than half the amount of chloride ions found in local sea water. Thus the chloride ions had diffused through the concretion into the sea. Given that the *Sirius* gun had corroded for only 200 years compared with 275 years for *Zuytdorp*, the initial chloride content of 54,593 ppm found inside the bore of the *Zuytdorp* gun may have been as high as 54,593 × (200/275) or some 39,704 ppm in the *Sirius* ordnance. This may mean pretreatment reduced chloride levels in the bore solution by 78.9 percent during the time on the seabed.

A second way of estimating amount of chloride released is to compare mass losses of the two HMS *Sirius* carronades. The first carronade, SI 58, suffered a weight loss of 26.88 percent with a corrosion depth of 25 mm, while the second carronade lost only 20.7 percent but had a much greater depth of corrosion, at 39.5 mm. Since the guns have the same shape, it is reasonable to assume that, with an open bore, the mass loss from corrosion should be related directly to their depths of corrosion. After correcting for immersion of five years longer for the second gun, the calculated mass loss might have been expected to be (200/195) × 39.5/25 × 26.8wt percent. or 43.4 percent. This figure may seem extraordinarily high, but a cast iron ballast pig from the same part of the wreck site as the second carronade lost 57.9 percent of its weight for a corrosion depth of 35.5 mm. Another ballast pig, with a corrosion depth of only 27.6 mm, had lost 43.8 percent of its original weight.

Details of the methods for calculating original chloride content of the carronade can be found in the primary reference, but the data indicates that somewhere on the order of 80 percent of the chlorides were removed before excavation (MacLeod, 1996b). Typical surface chloride activity measurements on freshly exposed marine iron artifacts are of the order 40,000 ppm chloride, whereas the surface under the concretion layer was 4100 ppm immediately after the recovery of the gun. Surface chloride activity fell to only 0.4 ppm at the end of the two years of electrolysis, which showed the treatment was finished.

GLOSSARY

ppm: Parts per million or μg/gram
ppt: parts per thousand
PDB: PeeDeeBelemite. PDB is the acronym for the mineral that is a reference sample of a Cretaceous belemnite, *Belemnitella americana*, from the Pee Dee formation in South Carolina. The carbon dioxide evolved from the reaction of the limestone, with 100 percent phosphoric acid at 25.2°C, is used as a standard in carbon isotope measurements for determining $^{13}C/^{12}C$ ratios. Details are found in Craig, 1957.

REFERENCES

Carpenter, J., 1986, *Conservation of an Anchor from the Wrecksite of* HMS *Sirius (1790)*. Unpublished report, Australian Bicentennial Authority.

Carpenter, J., and MacLeod, I.D., 1993, Conservation of Corroded Iron Cannon and the Influence of Degradation on Treatment Times. *ICOM-Committee for Conservation, Preprints 10th Triennial Conference*, Washington, D.C., Vol. II, pp. 759–766.

Chilton, J.P., and Evans, U.R., 1955, Corrosion Resistance of Wrought Iron. *Journal of the Iron and Steel Institute*, 113–122.

Cowdell, R.A., Gibbs, C.F., Longmore, A.R., Theodoropolous, T., 1985, *Tabulation of Port Phillip Bay Water Quality Data between June 1980 and July 1984*. Internal Report No. 98, Marine Science Laboratories, Ministry for Conservation, Fisheries and Wildlife Division, Queenscliff, Victoria.

Craig, H., 1957, Isotopic Standards for Carbon and Oxygen and Correction Factors for Mass-spectrometric Analysis of Carbon Dioxide. *Geochimica et Cosmochimica Acta* 12:133–149.

Ellett, D.J., and Edwards, A., 1983, Oceanography and Inshore Hydrography of the Inner Hebrides. *Proceedings of the Royal Society of Edinburgh* 83B:143–160.

Fischer, K.P., 1999, *Microbial Corrosion*. Metals Society, London.

Gregory, D., 1999, Monitoring the Effect of Sacrificial Anodes on the Large Iron Artifacts on the Duart Point wreck, 1997. *International Journal of Nautical Archaeology* 28(2): 164–173.

_____, 2000, In situ Corrosion on the Submarine *Resurgam*: A Preliminary Assessment of Her State of Preservation. *Conservation and Management of Archaeological Sites Volume 4* pp. 93–100.

Henderson, G., and Henderson, K.J., 1988, *Unfinished Voyages 1851–1880*, p. 57. University of Western Australia Press, Nedlands.

Henderson, G.J., 1989, *1988 Expedition Report on the Wreck of* HMS *Sirius (1790)*. Unpublished report to the Australian Bicentennial Authority, pp. 1–95.

Hunt, J.M., 1979, *Petroleum Geochemistry and Geology*. W.H. Freeman, San Francisco, p. 178.

Kimpton, G., and McCarthy, M., 1988, The Freeing of the SS *Xantho* engine. In *Papers from the First Australian Institute for Management of Iron Ships and Steam Ship Wrecks*, edited by M. McCarthy, pp. 73–74. Australian Institute for Maritime Archaeology Conference Series No. 1.

Kiss, L., 1988, *Kinetics of Electrochemical Metal Dissolution, Studies in Physical and Theoretical Chemistry*, Vol. 47, p. 60. Elsevier, Oxford.

La Que, F.L., 1975, *Marine Corrosion*. John Wiley and Sons, New York.

Lenihan, D.J., 1989, *Submerged Cultural Resources Study, USS Arizona Memorial and Pearl Harbor National Historic Landmark*. Southwest Cultural Resources Center Professional Papers No. 23, pp. 1–192, Santa Fe.

MacLeod, I.D., 1981, Shipwrecks and Applied Electrochemistry. *Journal of Electroanalytical Chemistry* 118:291–304.

_____, 1982, Formation of Marine Concretions on Copper and Its Alloys. *International Journal of Nautical Archaeology & Underwater Exploration* 11(4):267–275.

_____, 1986, Conservation of the Steamship *Xantho*. *ICCM Bulletin* 12(3/4):66–94.

_____, 1987, Conservation of Corroded Iron Artifacts: New Methods for on-site Preservation and Cryogenic Deconcreting. *International Journal of Nautical Archaeology* 16(1):49–56.

_____, 1988, Conservation of Corroded Concreted Iron. *Proceedings of Conference 28*, Australasian Corrosion Association, Perth, pp. 2–6.1, 2–6.9.

_____, 1989a, Electrochemistry and Conservation of Iron in sea Water. *Chemistry in Australia* 56(7):227–229.

_____, 1989b, Marine Corrosion on Historic Shipwrecks and Its Application to Modern Materials. *Corrosion Australasia* 14(3):8–14.

_____, 1989c, The application of corrosion science to the management of maritime archaeological sites. *Bulletin of the Australian Institute for Maritime Archaeology* 13(2):291–304.

_____, 1992, Conservation Management of Iron Steamships: The SS *Xantho* (1872). *Transactions of Multi-Disciplinary Engineering* GE 16(1):45–51.

_____, 1993a, Metal Corrosion on Shipwrecks: Australian Case Studies. *Trends in Corrosion Research* 1:221–245.

_____, 1993b, Conservation Assessment." In *Historic Shipping on the River Murray. A guide to the terrestrial and submerged archaeological sites in South Australia*, edited by Sarah Kenderine, pp. 273–282. State Heritage Branch, Department of Environment and Land Management, Adelaide.

_____, 1994, Report on the Corrosion of Iron Shipwrecks in South Australia with Particular Reference to the River Murray. In *Muddy Waters: Proceedings of the First Conference on the Submerged and Terrestrial Archaeology of Historic Shipping on the River Murray*, Echuca, September 1992, pp. 1–14. State Heritage Branch, South Australia Department of Environment and Natural Resources, Adelaide.

_____, 1995, In situ Corrosion Studies on the Duart Point Wreck 1994. *International Journal of Nautical Archaeology* 24(1):53–59.

_____, 1996a, An in situ study of the corroded hull of HMVS *Cerberus* (1926). *Proceedings of the 13th International Corrosion Congress*, Paper 125:1–10.

_____, 1996b, In situ Conservation of Cannon and Anchors on Shipwreck Sites. In *Conservation of Archaeological Sites and Its Consequences*, IIC, edited by Ed Ashok Roy and Perry Smith, pp. 111–115. London.

_____, 1998a, In situ Corrosion Studies on Iron and Composite Wrecks in South Australia Water: Implications for Site Managers and Cultural Tourism. *Bulletin of Australian Institute of Maritime Archaeology* 22:81–90.

_____, 1998b, In situ Corrosion Studies on Iron Shipwrecks and Cannon: The Impact of Water Depth and Archaeological Activities on Corrosion Rates. In *Metal 98 Proceedings of the ICOM—CC Metals Working Group Conference*, edited by W. Ed Mourey and L. Robbiola, Draguignan-Faginere, France 1998, James & James, London pp. 116–124.

MacLeod, I.D., and North, N.A., 1980, 350 years of marine corrosion in Western Australia. *Corrosion Australasia* 5:11–15.

_____, 1987, *Corrosion of Metals*. In *Conservation of Marine Archaeological Objects*, edited by C. Pearson Butterworths, pp. 68–72. London.

MacLeod, I.D., North, N.A., and Beegle, C.J., 1986, The Excavation, Analysis and Conservation of Shipwreck Sites. In *Preventative Measures during Excavation Site Protection*. ICCROM Conference, Ghent, 1985, pp. 113–131.

MacLeod, I.D., Brooke, P., and Richards, V.L., 1991, Iron Corrosion Products and Their Interactions with Waterlogged Wood and PEG. *Proceedings of the 4th ICOM Group on Wet Organic Archaeological Materials Conference*, Bremerhaven, 1990, edited by Per Hoffmann, pp. 119–132.

McCarthy, M., 1988, SS *Xantho*: The Pre-disturbance, Assessment, Excavation and Management of an Iron Steam Shipwreck off the Coast of Western Australia. *International Journal of Nautical Archaeology and Underwater Exploration* 17(4):339–347.

Martin, C.J.M., 1995, The Cromwellian shipwreck off Duart Point, Mull: An Interim Report. *International Journal of Nautical Archaeology* 24(1):15–32.

Microbial Corrosion, 1983, *Proceedings of the Conference Sponsored and Organised Jointly by the National Physical Laboratory and the Metals Society and held at NPL Teddington 8–10 March 1983*. The Metals Society, London.

North, N.A., 1976, The Formation of Coral Concretions on Marine iron. *International Journal of Underwater Archaeology and Underwater Exploration* 5:253–258.

_____, 1982, Corrosion Products on Marine Iron. *Studies in Conservation* 27:75–83.

_____, 1989, Proximity corrosion in Seawater. *Corrosion Australasia* 14(5):8–11.

North, N.A., and Pearson, C., 1978, Recent Advances in the Stabilisation of Marine Iron. In *Conservation of Iron Objects Found in a Salty Environments*, pp. 26–38. Chief Conservators Office. Historical Monuments Documentation Centre, Warsaw.

Pourbaix, M., 1974, *Atlas of Electrochemical Equilibria in Aqueous Solutions*, 2nd edition. NACE, Houston.

Rhead, E.L., 1945, Chemical Reactions of Blast furnaces. In *Metallurgy*, pp. 148–150. Longmans, London.

Riley, J.P., and Skirrow, G., editors, 1975, *Chemical Oceanography, Vol.1*. Second Edition, Academic Press, London.

Sequeira, C.A.C., and Tiller, A.K., editors, 1988, Microbial Corrosion. In *Proceedings of the First European Federation of Corrosion Workshop on Microbial Corrosion*. Elsevier Applied Science, London.

Stanbury, M. 1994, HMS *Sirius 1790. An Illustrated Catalogue of Artifacts Recovered from the Wreck Site at Norfolk Island*. Australian Institute of Maritime Archaeology Spec. Pub. 7:74–78.

Strommel, H., Stroup, E.D., Reid, J.L., and Warren, B.A., 1973, Transpacific Hydrographic Sections at Lats. 43°S and 28°S: The *Scorpio* Expedition—I Preface. *Deep Sea Research* 20:1–7.

Chapter **42**

Site Management

IAN OXLEY AND DAVID GREGORY

INTRODUCTION

Trends in submerged cultural resource management are moving away from recovery, to management of sites together with their constituent structures, artifacts and deposits, in the environments in which they are found. Although the subject is not well-researched or published (no comprehensive, comparative studies of in situ management strategies for shipwreck site deposits have been carried out), conservation strategies often have been implemented as short-term, stopgap measures. Further, the variety of factors involved in deterioration processes, as well as the complexity of their relationships, are not widely understood or accepted. The recommended conditions for protecting one type of archaeological material or context will not necessarily be conducive to preserving another, and the real effects of even simple stabilization strategies are not fully understood. Finally, inappropriate strategies that do not take account of the actual factors governing the site will inevitably fail.

All sites require management in one form or another. However, management cannot be seen as being synonymous with preservation: It cannot eliminate change but can only put forward procedures that might reduce the detrimental effects of recognized effects. Deterioration cannot be completely avoided; therefore, *absolute* preservation in situ is not achievable. All sites are dynamic, continuing to form in the sense that degradation processes keep on altering the material remains albeit at slow, often imperceptible, rates. Extra materials also can be added to sites as part of formation processes and will themselves start to deteriorate as soon as they are deposited. On the

Ian Oxley, Department of Civil and Offshore Engineering, Heriot-Watt University, Edinburgh, Scotland, United Kingdom.   **David Gregory**, Centre for Maritime Archaeology, National Museum of Denmark, DK-4000 Roskilde, Denmark.

International Handbook of Underwater Archaeology, edited by Carol V. Ruppé and Janet F. Barstad.
Kluwer Academic/Plenum Publishers, New York, 2002.

715

Figure 42.1.

positive side, effective management can facilitate wider appreciation and access to submerged sites and the information potential that they contain (Cuthill, 1998; Kaoru and Hoagland, 1994).

In this chapter, most examples referred to are shipwreck sites, because many more of these types of site have been discovered, and because they form the most visible part of the underwater archaeological resource. However, other submerged cultural heritage remains such as caves, artifact scatters from all periods, and drowned landscapes exist in all parts of the world. Some of the strategies outlined here also may be suitable for such diverse site types.

APPROACH

The overall approach to any site management project should be one of careful consideration of all relevant factors in order to develop, in well-researched stages, an appropriate strategy that will reach the management objectives. Objectives should include aiming for the highest quality information about the site and the processes affecting it. It is important to remember that a site includes both the archaeological components (physical remains such as structures, artifacts, and deposits) and their spatial relationships.

Each assessment stage should be designed to capitalize on data derived from preceding steps. Examples of the types of assessments that should be carried out include: oceanographic survey of the surrounding area; recording of visible archaeological remains; detailed determination of physical, chemical, and biological conditions on the site; identification of threats; and evaluation of potential for visitor access and interpretation for public enjoyment.

The next step is to consider the goals of any specific management program for the site. It may be that a site has been excavated and structural timbers are to be reburied as part of a long-term storage plan (Stewart et al., 1994); or that temporary stabilization may be required between excavation seasons (Martin, 1995); or that the site is to be left in situ without archaeological intervention but monitored to safeguard its future (Elliget and

Breidahl, 1993). Possible management strategies might include concentrating on measuring potential effects, defining environmental changes to be induced on the site through specific intervention, or establishing a monitoring and evaluation program to track the condition of the site.

What Is There?

A fundamental starting point is to determine what is present on the site. Assessment of specific components and characteristics of archaeological remains must be made, to the highest standard achievable. Visible remains should be mapped, together with an estimation of the nature and condition of buried items (Clarke et al., 1993). It is important to understand that underwater investigation of upstanding archaeological remains involves excavation and can cause erosion and collapse of wooden wreck structures. Further, one must consider which components are to be specifically managed, perhaps through stabilization, reinforcement, or in situ conservation treatment, and what are the principle material types (i.e. wood, metal), since certain parameters relevant for the preservation of each category are quite different (Weier, 1973).

Site Environmental Assessment

Which environmental parameters will affect the site? Those parts of a wreck that lie above the seabed will be affected by water current, sedimentary regime, and a whole range of micro-, macro- and mega-flora and fauna that may increase or lessen the stability of a site, depending on their nature. The integral strength of wood usually will have been compromised by the deteriorating effects of natural organisms and chemical attack. In open water marine environments, boring mollusks such as species of the shipworm *Teredo* and the crustacea species *Limnoria*, will cause rapid deterioration of wood. Dissolved oxygen content, temperature, and salinity should be monitored in order to investigate the potential for future colonization. However, while biodeterioration and corrosion of artifacts are important factors for long-term site management, the immediate problems may be the physical forces of water currents and tides, or destabilizing sedimentary regimes.

The state of preservation of all artifacts and structures on the site, in their various burial or immersed environments, must be investigated. This is a vital step, which will establish baseline data for any subsequent investigation plans.

Wood can be characterized by chemical methods (usually on samples recovered from the site) to determine which components of the cell structure remain, i.e., lignin and cellulose (Grattan and Mathias, 1986). Further, microscopic study can identify biological deterioration by wood-boring fauna, and fungal and bacterial microorganisms (Blanchette et al., 1990).

The remains of iron ships in the marine environment suffer much more decay than wooden ships because of the relative instability of the metals in seawater. Unless they are of massive construction, metal structures exposed to the effects of free running seawater are commonly degraded, whereas wooden elements appear better preserved, particularly in anaerobic environments. Iron and steel wrecks may not achieve the same state of equilibrium expected from their wooden counterparts. It is doubtful whether recent wrecks of iron vessels will last thousands of years, as wooden sites in anaerobic environments have done.

Sedimentary Environments.   In the short term, marine fungi and bacteria, which can digest lignin and cellulose, are less degrading than wood-boring organisms. A growth-limiting factor for marine fungi is the presence of oxygen: Levels below 0.42 mg/l have been reported to be sufficient to suppress their growth. Since cellulolytic bacteria can survive in both oxic (aerobic) and anoxic (anaerobic) environments, lack of oxygen will not stop deterioration. However, burial depth should limit their activity: Only the first few centimeters of sediment are oxygenated, and the sediment depth limit for most aerobic and anaerobic bacteria is 50–100 cm.

Assessing the environment within a sediment is more problematical, due to the logistical difficulties of collecting viable data by in-situ measurement or by sampling (Guthrie et al., 1995). Furthermore, research into what is important to measure is lacking. However, measurement of the dissolved oxygen content of sediment pore water is important. A method to determine this parameter is to place in the sediment a sealed plastic tube that will admit only water from the sediment and to analyze the sample on the surface, using a dissolved-oxygen meter.

The Redox potential of a sediment can indicate whether the environment is oxidizing or reducing. These states affect the stability of certain chemicals, as well as bacterial activity. Abundant oxygen controls the oxidizing and reducing (Redox) reactions involved. Where oxygen concentration is low, the contribution of minor oxidizing and reducing agents is important. The Redox potential of a sediment sample or sediment pore water is determined by measuring the electrical potential difference between the sample and a standard reference system, and the sediments may be then be characterized as shown in Table 42.1.

Artifacts and wooden structures usually will be well-preserved in sediments whose Redox potential is of a reducing nature.

Water Quality.   Analysis of various compounds within the sediment will also indicate processes of deterioration. Water can be sampled as for the dissolved oxygen measurements described above, or a sediment sample can be taken and various chemicals extracted and analyzed. For example, the presence of certain nitrogen and sulphur compounds will indicate the mechanisms of deterioration prevalent in the sediment. During decomposition of nitrogenous organic material, ammonia is readily oxidized to nitrite and nitrate by the bacteria *Nitrosomonas* and *Nitrobacter*. Thus, high levels of ammonia together with low levels of nitrate and nitrite would indicate that the environment is anaerobic, since it will not permit oxidation of the ammonia.

Sulphur compounds can be examined similarly. Sulphate is the second most abundant anion in circulating seawater; thus, high levels of sulphate and low levels of sulphide found within a sediment indicate oxic conditions. If the sediment is suboxic, sulphate will be reduced to sulphide by sulphate-reducing bacteria, which survive in anaerobic conditions.

Table 42.1. Redox environments of sediments.

Environment	Millivolts (mV)
Oxidizing	+700 – +400
Moderately reducing	+400 – +100
Reducing	+100 – 100
Highly reducing	−100 – 300

Metals

Corrosion of iron artifacts is the biggest problem on underwater archaeological sites. After an initially rapid rate of deterioration during the first few years of immersion, most iron artifacts develop some form of protective coating, commonly called concretion, on their surfaces. Concretion limits availability of dissolved oxygen to the corroding surface, and the corrosion rate falls to low levels. In seawater, this protective layer is normally calcareous in origin and, in warm water, and iron artifacts can be covered with a thick encrustation of organisms after several centuries. (MacLeod, 1995).

The basic construction of a concreted artifact is such that an acidic and chloride-rich microenvironment is established around the corroding metal. The acidity results from hydrolysis of metal ions and, as corrosion proceeds, chlorides from surrounding seawater diffuse through the marine growth and corrosion products to the corroded metal interface, to achieve electrical neutrality of the corrosion products. Thus, measuring various parameters in open seawater, sediment, or sediment pore water is not necessarily useful in determining the state of preservation or deterioration rate of concreted metal artifacts: The microenvironment around the surface of the degraded artifact itself must be investigated. Electrochemical parameters, such as the the object's surface pH and corrosion potential, can be invaluable tools in understanding corrosion mechanisms (see MacLeod; Chapter 41 in this volume).

Corrosion potential is the voltage of the corrosion cell that exists between oxidation of the iron and reduction of dissolved oxygen in oxygenated seawater. Corrosion cell voltage refers to the difference in electrical potential of a reference electrode such as silver/silver chloride in seawater, and a working electrode such as platinum, which must be in contact with the corroding metal surface. If the pH at the metal surface is known, it is possible to plot it and the corrosion potential onto a Pourbaix diagram (a thermodynamic stability map for metals in an aqueous solution). This analysis will help determine the nature of the processes controlling the stability of metal objects in their own particular environments.

Site Decay Modeling

An understanding of degradation and related effects (e.g. fishing trawls, ships' anchors, and even icebergs) may be gained from modeling site deterioration (Vrana and Mahoney, 1995). Recent research into quantification of site formation processes has explored innovative ways to depict such processes on the scale of the whole site. In land archaeology, Mathewson (1989) proposed a concept of archaeological site decay adapted from models of forest succession—accepting the fact that forests are renewable and archaeological sites are not. The archaeological model shows a uniform decay rate for a specific site component. External effects can either increase or retard this rate. The positive or negative effect of an induced change in the site environment for each site component and spatial relationship also can be estimated.

SITE MANAGEMENT STRATEGIES

In-situ conservation represents a viable and increasingly acceptable alternative to the essentially destructive practice of excavation. In the past, various strategies have been tried to achieve aims of in-situ conservation, allowing some archaeological sites, or parts thereof, to be protected from deterioration processes. On-site artifact deterioration can be slowed by remedial actions based on knowledge of physical, biological, and chemical processes that can be reduced or eliminated. As discussed in previous section, a limiting parameter for colonization and deterioration of wood is oxygen; bacteria and fungi will not attack below the sediment surface; therefore, burying wood to limit the supply of oxygen to bacteria and fungi is the best way to control their attack (on a large, upstanding, three-dimensional wreck structure, however, this strategy may not be feasible).

Physical Stabilization

The physical condition of the burial environment around a site should be considered first. Mitigation strategies will often involve physical stabilization—methods that are usually relatively unsophisticated and involve simply the pinning down of unstable archaeological contexts and features. Covering an archaeological site is not a new phenomenon, since the natural burial of sites in the past is common: Dramatic examples include the sealing of Herculaneum and Pompeii by volcanic activity.

Solutions involving the deposit of imported sediment (often sands or gravels) onto the site from the sea surface have been attempted in the past (McCarthy, 1986). These strategies may appear initially attractive because of their relatively low cost, but they must be accompanied by extensive environmental assessment of the site to understand the implications, and considerable forward planning to ensure that the sediment is deposited in the right place. It is recommended that a suitable barrier layer (e.g., an inert textile) be placed between the stabilization material and the site surface, both to provide a marker (should reexcavation be necessary) and to prevent unnecessary contamination of the original deposits.

Informal site management techniques often have involved reburying the excavated or exposed site with the original overburden (i.e., sediment removed during the archaeological excavation process). Once this material has been disturbed, however, it is rarely as impervious to marine organisms and oxygen as before (Gesner, 1993; Guthrie et al., 1995), and this strategy may actually contribute to the acceleration of deterioration of the archaeological materials that were to be protected.

Allowing natural deposition to occur is likely to be a long, unpredictable process and might leave certain areas of the site exposed to increased deterioration. Intentional encouragement of sediment deposition, perhaps by causing a local slowing of current speed, can be employed to promote the settling out of suspended sediment.

Artificial seagrasses with extended fronds, designed to remain upright in strong currents and reduce the velocity of the water, have been employed in this context. The fronds can be fabricated into mats and located in strategic positions on the site, according to prevailing current patterns (Elliget and Breidahl, 1993). However, such systems are very sensitive to environmental change. For example, the effectiveness of artificial seagrass mats is severely compromised when the fronds are colonized by marine organisms such as mussels. The weighted-down fronds collapse and cease to function as sediment traps, so that currents regain their original velocities. Alternatives to the use of natural seagrass species require careful research and planning, to match the target species and planting methods to the particular characteristics of the site and its environment.

Other artificial constructions may be used to alter site environmental conditions, such as the employment of artificial barriers to divert current flow as well as encourage deposition. Such strategies will succeed only if their development is based on high-quality information about the site environment.

Various sources of information about stabilization methods and materials exist (e.g. Thorne, 1991; U.S. Army Corps of Engineers, 1992; Oxley, 1998). It also may be useful to consult coastal and marine engineering literature.

Reinforcement

In marine environments, traditional types of ship-fasteners, such as the iron bolts in wooden ships, may degrade before the structure itself. Collapse can be prevented by inserting new, artificial pegs into the voids created by such degradation. Or, hull structures of wrecks may be supported by the insertion of braces to replace missing elements. "Jacks" or "Acro-props" also have been widely used, normally on a temporary basis (Adams, 1987).

Covering

A degree of stability on a submerged site may be achieved by covering over the archaeological deposits or structures, thereby inhibiting aerobic agents of deterioration by reducing their access to oxygen in free-running seawater.

The physical covering of archaeological deposits, often with polyethylene sheeting, is common, although there are problems with the establishment and maintenance of an effective covering. This is most true of extended, high relief, three-dimensional sites such as wooden wreck structures. Such an exercise may also have substantial financial and practical problems. Geotextiles have been available for many years in the construction industries, especially of roads. Geotextiles, synthetic and resistant to erosion, can be moulded around irregular surfaces, and permeability can be controlled to some degree by careful fabric selection. It is important to recognize that environments that promote deterioration rather than preservation can be created underneath impervious membranes. Although they are useful in the right circumstances, geotextiles and other humanmade fabrics are relatively expensive and have a finite useful life.

Since unit costs are low, sandbagging often has been used in the past although, when used in great numbers, sandbag costs can rise, along with problems in identifying a suitable source material. For small applications, material to fill the bags (often gravel or sand) usually can be found locally. Since the method is under-researched, it can be considered only as a temporary site-stabilization method. Since sandbags are readily colonized by local flora and fauna, well-designed stabilization can assimilate into the local environment and, to casual observation, become indistinguishable from the surrounding seabed. This can be an advantage in cultural resource management, in that exposed areas are less likely to attract inappropriate attention from divers.

Intentional Reburial

In some instances, intentional reburial is an important technique for the recovery of information from archaeological sites without incurring the substantial costs of conservation and storage (Stewart et al., 1994). The method entails reburial of archaeological material, in an appropriate environment, after suitable archaeological recording has been carried out. It is likely that variations on this resource management method will become increasingly popular in the future. However, its effectiveness depends on how well the reburial environment mimics the original burial conditions, and it clearly depends upon how precisely the preservation conditions of the site are known. Further, intentionally reburied material must be monitored and action taken as appropriate if the strategy is seen to be not working. For organic materials in marine deposits, it is imperative that anoxic conditions be achieved in as short a period of time as possible.

The long-term effect of reburial on archaeological site components is largely unknown, yet it must be acknowledged that removing objects from their environment and uncovering structures, even for the briefest time, exposes sites and features to some environmental changes. Any exposure is sufficient to restart the process of deterioration, which may continue for some time after the object has been reburied, even in its original sediment type, before gradually decreasing again as near-equilibrium is reached.

Cathodic Protection and Sacrificial Anodes

One way to slow corrosion of iron objects and structures is by cathodic protection (British Standards Institute, 1991), which consists of inhibiting one or more of the four requirements of the corrosion cell (cathode, anode, electrolyte, and a metal). It can be achieved by reducing the environment's conductivity as well as eliminating cathodic reactants. Alternatively, a coating system that separates the metal surface from its environment will prevent cathodic reactions. Sacrificial anodes or impressed current can be used to ensure that the entire metal surface (which previously included anodic and cathodic areas) remains cathodic relative to a remotely located anode.

In the case of sacrificial anodes, potential differences exist between electrically connected, dissimilar metals, which can provide the driving force for the cathodic protection—providing materials are carefully selected (MacLeod, 1995). Sacrificial anodes must be more active than the metal they are to protect; they must not be allowed to passivate (form a protective oxide layer), and they must corrode actively for their entire life in order to function satisfactorily. Metals suitable for protecting steels and wrought irons are zinc, magnesium, and aluminium—although aluminum can passivate in stagnant environments and may not be effective in estuaries and harbors. Zinc anodes tend to be chosen for stagnant conditions. Selection of alloy composition and assessment of the electrolyte (e.g., water quality and movement, temperature, dissolved oxygen) is critical to the success of this corrosion protection strategy.

Monitoring

All sites should be monitored regularly in order for management to be effective, to allow for unexpected effects to be identified at an early stage and mitigation strategies to be implemented. Details of the monitoring program will depend on management aims for the site and environmental conditions affecting it. Examples of parameters that might be important can be found in cultural resource management texts such as those issued by the Australian Institute of Marine Archaeology and Australian Cultural Development Office (Australian Institute of Marine Archaeology and Australian Cultural Development Office, 1994; Lenihan, 1989; USS *Monitor* National Marine Sanctuary, 1997) or other research reports (Herdendorf, 1995; Oxley, 1998).

Monitoring is not a one-off event. Sites should be periodically reviewed. Review results can be useful even if monitoring is carried out only infrequently, but this strategy is unlikely to lead to a full understanding of processes such as sedimentation and erosion cycles.

Cost–Benefits

Some in-situ preservation strategies, such as sandbags, can be implemented on underwater environments for relatively modest sums, but they should be employed in the full knowledge that their effectiveness may be only short-term, probably measurable in years rather than decades. Depending on the scale of intervention, some methods may represent significant barriers to any future archaeological research or survey. Access will be reduced, and the site will be less visible for heritage appreciation, because many physical protection methods will significantly reduce the amenity value of a site by masking areas of interest. A further disadvantage is the cost of removing material from sites where further investigative work is planned in the future. There also may be adverse effects on the natural environment, particularly from methods such as sandbagging and artificial layers such as polyethylene, which alter underlying and adjacent marine ecosystems. It should be remembered that submerged archaeological sites have significant economic, recreational, tourist, social, and educational potential as well as scientific and archaeological ones (Kaoru and Hoagland, 1994).

STATE AND GOVERNMENT INITIATIVES

Useful examples of government and state management initiatives from various parts of the world (AIMA and ACDO, 1994) are excellent models of the management development process and illustrate the recommended stages and categories required in an effective management plan. They include highly significant sites such as USS *Arizona* and *Monitor*, which have required detailed research designs and comprehensive management plans that pay specific attention to site formation (Lenihan, 1989; *Monitor* National Marine Sanctuary, 1997).

CONCLUSIONS

The continued existence and cultural resource potential of many submerged archaeological sites can be threatened by deteriorating processes and destabilizing factors. Therefore, effective site management has a place in protecting and conserving archaeological potential, whatever its environment. On underwater sites, in freshwater or in the sea, a wide variety of site management strategies are available that can be used to protect the submerged archaeological resource for the benefit of present and future generations.

In approaching site management, the quantified assessment of the site to an accepted scientific standard is required, followed by design and implementation of mitigation strategies as appropriate. Ensuring that protective measures are effective requires baseline data capable of supporting rigorous research, analysis and comparison in the future.

All new site management strategies and solutions should be published widely. Throughout the whole discipline of underwater archaeology, there is a distinct lack of established, well-proven methodologies for the planning and installation of site management strategies. The suggestions made here are based on the limited data available. Little research has been undertaken to assess the actual long-term implications of in situ management, and most methods are likely to involve significant expenditure. Without comprehensive research in advance of protective measures (and clearly there is some experience of specific methods that could be collated and analyzed as part of this effort), there is a risk of endorsing methods with highly unpredictable results.

REFERENCES

Adams, J., 1987, Hull reinforcement. In *Amsterdam Project: Annual Report of the VOC-ship Amsterdam Foundation 1986*, edited by J.H.G. Gawronski, pp. 12–15. VOC-ship *Amsterdam* Foundation, Amsterdam.

Australian Institute of Marine Archaeology and Australian Cultural Development Office, 1994, *Guidelines for the Management of Australia's Shipwrecks*. Australian Institute of Maritime Archaeology Inc. and Australian Cultural Development Office, Canberra.

Blanchette, R.A., Nilsson, T., Daniel, G., and Abad, A., 1990, Biological Degradation of Wood. In *Archaeological Wood Properties, Chemistry and Preservation. Advances in Chemistry Series 225*, edited by R.M. Rowell and R.J. Barbour, pp. 158–161. American Chemical Society, Washington, D.C.

British Standards Institute, 1991, *BS 7361: Cathodic Protection. Part 1. Code of Practice for Land and Marine Applications*. British Standards Institute, Milton Keynes.

Clarke, R., Dean, M., Hutchinson, G., McGrail, S., and Squirre, J., 1993, Recent Work on the R. Hamble Wreck near Bursledon, Hampshire. *International Journal of Nautical Archaeology* 22(1):21–44.

Cuthill, M., 1998, Managing the Yongala Historic Shipwreck. *Coastal Management* 26:33–46.

Elliget, M., and Breidahl, H., 1993, *A Guide to the Wreck of the Barque William Salthouse*. Victoria Archaeological Survey, Melbourne.

Gesner, P., 1993, Managing *Pandora*'s Box: The 1993 *Pandora* Expedition. *Australian Institute of Marine Archaeology Bulletin* 17(2):7–10.

Grattan, D.W. and Mathias, C., 1986, Analysis of Waterlogged Wood: The Values of Chemical Analysis and Other Simple Methods in Evaluating Condition. In *Somerset Levels, Paper Number 12*, edited by J.M. Coles, pp 6–12. Somerset Levels Project, Hereford.

Guthrie, J.N., Blackall, L., Moriarty, D.J.W., and Gesner, P., 1995, Wrecks and Marine Microbiology Case Study from the Pandora. *Australian Institute of Maritime Archaeology Bulletin* 18(2):19–24.

Herdendorf, C.E., Thompson, T.G., and Evans, R.D., 1995, Science on a Deep-ocean Shipwreck. *Ohio Journal of Science* 95.1:4–212

Kaoru, Y. and Hoagland, P., 1994, The Value of Historic Shipwrecks: Conflicts and Management. *Coastal Management* 22:195–213.

Lenihan, D.J., 1989, USS Arizona *Memorial and Pearl Harbor National Historic Landmark*. Submerged Cultural Resources Study, Southwest Cultural Resources Center Professional Papers No. 23, Santa Fe.

MacLeod, I.D., 1995, In Situ Corrosion Studies on the Duart Point Wreck, 1994. *The International Journal of Nautical Archaeology* 24(2):53–59.

Martin, C.J.M., 1995, The Cromwellian Shipwreck off Duart Point, Mull: An interim report. *The International Journal of Nautical Archaeology* 24(1):15–32.

Mathewson, C.C., editor, 1989, Logic-based Qualitative Site Decay Model for the Preservation of Archaeological Sites. In *Inter-disciplinary Workshop on the Physical–Chemical–Biological Processes Affecting Archaeological Sites*, pp. 227–238. Environmental Impact Research Program Contract Report EL-89-1, US Army Corps of Engineers, Waterways Experimental Station, Vicksburg.

McCarthy, M., 1986, Protection of Australia's Underwater Sites. In *Preventive Measures during Excavation and Site Protection*, edited by ICCROM, pp. 133–146. ICCROM, Rome.

Monitor National Marine Sanctuary, 1997, *Charting a New Course for the* Monitor: *Comprehensive, Long Range Preservation Plan With Options for Management, Stabilization, Preservation, Recovery, Conservation, and Exhibition of Materials and Artifacts from the* Monitor *National Marine Sanctuary*. Monitor National Marine Sanctuary, Newport News. Draft.

Oxley, I., 1998, The In Situ Preservation of Underwater Sites. *In Preservation of Archaeological Remains In Situ*, edited by M. Corfield, P. Hinton, T. Nixon, and M. Pollard, pp. 159–173. Proceedings of Conference held at the Museum of London, April 1996. Museum of London Archaeology Service, London.

Stewart, J., Murdock, L.D., and Waddell, P., 1994, Reburial of the Red Bay Wreck as a Form of Preservation and Protection of the Historic Resource. In *Materials Issues in Art and Archaeology IV*, edited by P.B. Vandiver, J.R. Druzik, J.L.G. Madrid, I.C. Freestone and G.S. Wheeler, pp. 791–805. Materials Research Society Symposium Proceedings Volume 352. Materials Research Society, Pennsylvania.

Thorne, R.M., 1991, *Site Stabilization Information Sources*. U.S. Department of Interior, National Parks Service Archaeological Assistance Program Technical Brief No. 12 ISSN 1057–1574.

U.S. Army Corps of Engineers, 1992, Bibliography of Corps of Engineers Research Related to Cultural Site Protection and Preservation. In *The Archaeological Sites Protection and Preservation Notebook*, Section ASPPN XII-1. Environmental Impact Research Program, Waterways Experiment Station, Vicksburg.

Vrana, K.J., and Mahoney, E.M., 1995, Impacts on Underwater Cultural Resources: Diagnosing Change and Prescribing Solutions. In *Underwater Archaeology Proceedings from the Society for Historical Archaeology Conference, Washington, D.C., January 1995*, edited by P. Forsythe Johnston, pp. 176–180. Society for Historical Archaeology, Tucson.

Weier, L.E., 1973, The Deterioration of Inorganic Materials under the Sea. *Bulletin of the Institute of Archaeology* 11:63–163.

Chapter 43

Heritage or Hazard?
The Oil Tanker *Montebello* and Its Potentially Dangerous Cargo

JACK HUNTER

What lies at the bottom of the ocean and twitches? A nervous wreck.
ASHLEY BRILLIANT

INTRODUCTION

On December 23, 1941, just 16 days after the Imperial Japanese navy's bombing of Pearl Harbor in Hawaii and the entry of the United States into World War II, Union Oil Company's tanker *Montebello* departed California's Port San Luis, bound north for Vancouver with a cargo of crude oil. At dawn off Estero Bay, the ship was going about eight knots when lookout Dick Quincy saw a submarine surface (Quincy, personal communication, 2001). He gave the alarm. Everyone on the bridge saw the wake of a torpedo as it streaked toward them from the Imperial Japanese submarine *I-21* (Browning, 1966). *Montebello* could not evade the onrushing torpedo, which slammed into the hull near the bow of the hapless vessel. Fortunately no one was on the foredeck at this early hour because of heavy seas.

Captain Olaf Eckstrom ordered the ship abandoned. The 38-man crew scrambled into lifeboats and pulled away as the submarine used its deck gun to pump more rounds into the sinking tanker. The crew was grateful but a bit mystified that the crude oil wasn't ignited by the torpedo's explosion.

Jack Hunter, Underwater Archaeologist, California Department of Transportation District 5, San Luis Obispo, California 93401.

International Handbook of Underwater Archaeology, edited by Carol V. Ruppé and Janet F. Barstad. Kluwer Academic/Plenum Publishers, New York, 2002.

Montebello settled quickly. At 6:45 a.m., the tanker went down bow first in 880-ft (268 m) of water, six miles (10 km) off the coast of San Luis Obispo County, with a cargo of 75,346 barrels of crude oil (Dewberry, 1991) and an additional 8400 barrels of bunker fuel stored onboard for its own engine use, a total of some 3.5 million U.S. gallons (by comparison, the 1989 Exxon *Valdez* oil spill in Prince William Sound, Alaska, was estimated at 11.2 million gallons (Environmental News Network, 1999).

Two small Morro Bay tugboats, *Alma* and *Estero*, rescued three lifeboats containing most of *Montebello*'s crewman; the fourth lifeboat came ashore in rough surf near the seacoast community of Cambria. No lives were lost, and injuries were minor.

Montebello was not the first vessel lost off the California coast at the beginning of World War II. That dubious distinction belongs to SOCONY oil tanker *Emidio*, which broke in half when torpedoed several days earlier some 200 miles north of San Francisco (Browning, 1966).

HISTORY OF AN OIL TANKER

The shelter-deck oil tanker SS *Montebello* (Figure 43.1) was launched in 1921 by Southwestern Shipbuilding Company in San Pedro, California, for Union Oil Company of California (UNOCAL), Federal Enrollment No. 221100. The steel-hulled, 440-ft (134 m) vessel had a beam of 58.2-ft (18 m) and depth of 32.8-ft (10 m). The ship was divided by bulkheads into compartments that included 10 liquid-product storage tanks, each 28.5 ft in length and running the width of the vessel (Figure 43.2). Since *Montebello* was not double-hulled, her hull plates and tank walls were one and the same. Her displacement was 8272 tons gross. The average useful life of a steel vessel of the period was more than 25 years (Westcott, 1948). *Montebello* was 20 years old at the time she was lost.

Although there was a government-ordered blackout of news coverage of war losses, *Montebello*'s sinking was widely reported in the newspapers of the maritime communities that knew her. The loss of *Montebello* has remained San Luis Obispo County's most memorable casualty of World War II (Harth, Krieger and Krieger 1991). Rarely a year goes by that the story of her sinking is not retold in the local media. After 55 years at the bottom of the sea, the time had come to examine the site of her repose, the appearance of her structure, and the condition of her cargo of crude oil.

Eligibility for National Register of Historic Places

Montebello's location off the west coast of the United States placed the vessel outside the normally accepted three-mile (4.8 km) territorial waters limit. However, assertion has been made that the U.S. government may have reimbursed *Montebella*'s owners (UNOCAL) under the War Reparations Act after World War II, which conceivably could have placed her ownership with the U.S. government. Since the government does not automatically relinquish title to a vessel of its ownership regardless of its location of loss, a reasonable case might be made that the U.S. government, UNOCAL, or the *Montebello*'s marine insurance underwriters may still hold legal claim.

Notwithstanding, the *Montebello* may be eligible under three criteria of the U.S. National Historic Preservation Act of 1966, National Register of Historic Places 36 CFR 60.4:

Figure 43.1. Oil tanker SS *Montebello*. (Undated photo courtesy UNOCAL Museum of Oil, Santa Paula, CA)

(a) ...Association with events that have made a significant contribution to the broad patterns of our history [World War II], or

(b) that embody the distinctive characteristics of a type, period, or method of construction, or that represent the work of a master, or that possess high artistic values, or that represent a significant distinguishable entity whose components may lack individual distinction; or

(c) that have yielded or may be likely to yield information important in history or prehistory.

The *Montebello* may be eligible for listing as a California Heritage Site and an underwater landmark in San Luis Obispo County environs. But her value to local and national history begins a not uncommon dilemma. Like many other cargo vessels lost at sea, *Montebello* represents both a historic resource and (by virtue of her burden of crude oil and bunker fuel) a potential hazard to the local and regional environment. The tanker rests just south and within easy reach of the Monterey Bay National Marine Sanctuary.

A RESEARCH SUBMARINE DIVE

As with many impromptu enterprises, a serendipitous chain of events led to a one-day reconnaissance of the wreck site of *Montebello*. The story of *Montebello*'s loss was well

730   J. Hunter

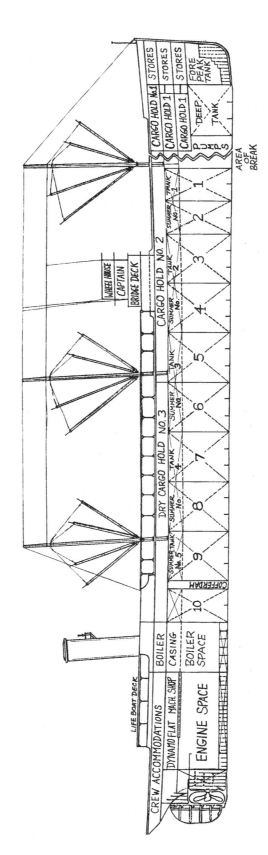

Figure 43.2. Structural profile of the SS *Montebello* showing principal engineering, cargo, and living spaces, and where broke when the ship hit the sea floor. (Modified from a drawing in the UNOCAL Museum of Oil, Santa Paula, CA)

known to the Central Coast Maritime Museum Association in San Luis Obispo County. The local commercial fishing communities of Port San Luis, Morro Bay, and San Simeon knew her location based on her value as a deep-sea artificial fishing reef. All that remained for resolution was a method of investigating the wreck site in nearly 900 ft (274 m) of water in the open sea.

The West Coast National Undersea Research Center (WCNURC), an activity of the National Undersea Research Program (NURP) of the National Oceanographic and Atmospheric Administration (NOAA) operating out of the University of Alaska in Fairbanks, was able to provide this support. WCNURC did not have a deep-tow side scan sonar system, which was initially envisioned as the best way to obtain a preliminary look at the *Montebello* site. What the center could offer, if the research season's concluding schedule allowed, was a day of diving in the well-known research submersible, *Delta*.

This 16-ft (5 m), two-person undersea diving craft is operated by Delta Oceanographies of Oxnard, California. It is familiar in underwater exploration for the investigation of the HMS *Lusitania*, torpedoed off Ireland in 1915, and for the examination of such wrecks as *Edmund Fitzgerald* in Lake Superior and *Brother Jonathan* off Northern California.

On the morning of November 7, 1996, *Delta* cast off from its temporary mother ship R/V *Cavalier* and descended into the depths of the Pacific Ocean. Ambient light diminished steadily, until at about 600 ft (183 m), darkness enveloped the tiny submersible. Pilot David Slater switched on some of the 12 lamps positioned around the outside of the submersible, and the descent continued within the sub's own sphere of light. Onboard depth gauges hinted the bottom was near, and the sub's two occupants strained to catch sight of it as it came into view. At this place the sea floor is fine silt punctuated with periodic pits, tracks, and trails of benthic life. The pilot adjusted the buoyancy of the submersible to be slightly positive so it would rise rather than sink, an obvious safety factor in case of a power failure. The depth of the sea floor at this location is 880 ft (268 m). The mother ship "live-boated" overhead (under power, no anchors out) while watching the submersible and its objective on her fathometer. The *Cavalier*'s crew gave a vector to the wreck and within 10 minutes the sub was near a great gray wall looming out of the darkness. The tanker's presence was heralded by increasing biological disturbance of the sea floor and a sparse but noticeable debris field consisting primarily of pieces of fishing gear and small bits of *Montebello*'s superstructure that had been pulled away or drifted off the wreck over the years.

INITIAL OBSERVATIONS

The *Delta* approached slowly and found *Montebello* sitting upright on the sea floor as though she were tied to the dock. If the tanker were listing slightly off center either way, *Delta*'s crew could not detect it. Cautious at first because of fishing nets and commercial fishing tackle hanging from her, the crew performed the first of what would be a total of 14 circumnavigations over four separate, two-hour sub dives made that day. A fifth and last dive briefly explored the sea floor downslope of the tanker.

Delta moved slowly along the side of *Montebello* at a speed of less than one knot, equivalent to a slow walk. This was done for safety and documentation. Whether researchers document by still photography or videocamera, motion blurs detail and results in diminished documentation quality, not to mention the potential for hurtling incautiously into a trap for little submarines. Looking inboard from the main deck railing, the research sub's lamps don't quite illuminate the pipe-bridge, a structure that runs longitudinally down the vessel's midship deck from the bridge house to the stern house. One can sense that it is still there and upright just beyond the reach of the lights. Evident on the midship main deck, besides the arrays of piping and valves that belong there (White, 1927), is debris broken loose from above and aft of this area by the ship's impact on the sea floor and from 50 years of commercial fishing. Among the identifiable fallen items were the ship's single smokestack with the formerly attached steam whistle lying separately nearby. Air funnels and tangles of cable rigging were strewn around. The main deck railing was evident by its uprights, the connecting cables missing entirely or seen loosely curled without tension.

Forward of the wheelhouse, the foredeck was a jumble of fallen rigging and debris from the bridge as well as crumpled and bent steel plates, apparently from the explosion of the torpedo. The fallen foremast with attached ladder was prominent upon this deck. The crew saw this topple when the torpedo struck.

Suddenly the submersible had run out of ship . . .

The bow is gone. The interior of *Montebello's* construction lay open and exposed to view. The bow's location went unnoticed until the fourth dive of the day because its distance was outside the reach of the sub's lamps, and the observers were more attentive to the striking view of the ship's interior in the area of the break. Broken approximately at the location of the pump room forward of the No. 1 tank, about 60 ft (18 m) aft of the stem, the bow is 100 feet (30 m) or more forward of the break. It is partially buried under a huge wave of sediment pushed forward by impact. It looked as though it had struck the sea floor at a steep angle; such was exactly *Montebello's* attitude in sinking. It would seem that the tanker's streamlined design kept her oriented upright all the way to the sea floor. Then the tanker struck bow first and recoiled backwards from the impact, the buried bow breaking off in the bottom sediments, with the major portion of the vessel settling not far behind.

A Deep Sea Biological Reef

Biologically, the wreck of *Montebello* is a magnificent, deepwater, artificial reef sustaining a significant biological community (Kim and Ljubenkov, personal communication). A distinct difference exists between the fauna of the wreck and that of the immediate surroundings. The water column around the wreck is alive with small swarms of mysids attracted to the lamps of the submersible. Waves of the jellyfish *Mitrocoma cellularia* and the comb jelly *Pleurobranchia* drift through the water. Larvaceans, swimming polychaetes, and the market squid *Loligo opalescens* reduced distance vision in the sub's lights.

An ecotone occurs at the juncture of the tanker's hull and the mud bottom. A distinct boundary area with dense aggregations of the galatheid crab *Galathea californica* is in a band fewer than 2 m wide around the base of the ship. Up to 1000 individuals/m^2 were observed. Their size ranged from 5 mm to 5 cm in length. Outside of this galatheid zone, the biota is dominated by polynoid polychaetes, probably *Chloeia pinnata*, in densities up to 25/10 cm^2. Also common are colonies of unidentified branching bryozoans in densities of 1/2 m^2. Less frequent are large slugs, *Pleurobranchaea*

Figure 43.3. Weather deck covered passageway with large *Metridium farcimen*, stanchion, fishing and net cordage draping down to left side of view.

californica in mating groups of 2–6 individuals, and translucent pink sea cucumbers. Shrimp, rays, and anemones are more rarely seen in this area.

At the level of the main deck, Chilipepper rockfish (*Sebastes goodei*) predominate over schools of widow rockfish (*Sebastes entomelas*), Bigfin eelpouts (*Lycodes cortezianus*), and lingcod (*Ophiodon elongatus*), while torpedo rays (*Torpedo californica*) orbit the ship and its structures.

The tanker itself provides a hard substrate in an otherwise soft bottom habitat and gives an attachment point to many sessile and encrusting organisms. The dominant sessile organism is the anemone (*Metridium farcimen*), which proliferated on some of the ship's horizontal surfaces (Figure 43.3). These animals occur grouped in aggregate clones up to 50 cm high and in appearance suggest small forests of giant white satin mushrooms. The densities of these animals vary around the vessel but in some places are on the order of 10/m^2. It would be difficult to move among them without causing them damage. Populations of the crab *Paralithodes rathbuni* seemed to increase with each trip around the wreck; snagged fishing nets continued to trap fish startled whenever the *Delta* suddenly appeared, and their squirming attracted the crabs from their lairs. The hull itself has small patches of epifaunal growth but is still remarkably clean, due at least in part to the effectiveness of lead-based paints with which the vessel was coated many times during its years of service.

Structural Integrity

Montebello was built at a time when the American shipbuilding industry was experimenting with welding techniques to replace rivet fasteners in specified structural locations. *Montebello*'s exact place in this evolution is not known, since her construction drawings or other assembly details have not been located. Dick Quincy (personal communication, 2001) remembers only rivets in the parts of the ship in which he personally spent his time. A good bead of painted weld however, may not attract much casual attention. All seams adjoining exterior hull plates, whether fastened by rivets or welds, are free of any signs of the metal and joint deterioration that expected might be after a half-century underwater. This must be due in part to the protective outside hull paint still in place. *Montebello* was painted completely gray as part of war preparations immediately prior to her doomed voyage. The inside of her hull would be protected where in direct contact with oil within tank locations. Many interstitial spaces within the ship's structure also may be protected by the migration of those oil-based liquids that all vessels carry and which invariably became uncontrolled during the dynamics of a shipwreck.

The wood decking originally in place throughout the ship has deteriorated and disappeared. Examination of a model of *Montebello* in the collection of the San Diego Maritime Museum revealed that wood decking (probably teak) was utilized on the fantail behind the stern house, on the boat deck forming the top of the stern house, and variously higher up within the bridge area of the wheelhouse. The loss of this organic material leaves steel floor supports and stanchions protruding eerily into the water column. Much of the upperworks of the wheelhouse structure are damaged or missing due possibly to original sea floor impact, but more probably to deterioration and decades of commercial fishing impacts on the wreck. The galvanized mounting assembly of the port-side navigation lamp was given to the Central Coast Maritime Museum Association in 1999 by a commercial fisherman after it was snagged off the wreck by a trawl net.

The Cargo

Montebello's cargo is "Grade A" Santa Maria crude oil. This asphalt-base petroleum has a high viscosity and must be heated so it will flow when pumped. The tanker was equipped with steam pipes in its tanks to keep the cargo warm so that it could be pumped off at its destination without delay. Water temperature on the sea floor at the wreck site is 8 °C (46 °F). Within hours of *Montebello*'s sinking, the cargo of crude oil undoubtedly reached ambient sea floor temperature and further congealed. If it were loaded at 27 °C (80 °F), the shrinking volume of oil as it cooled would have created a partial vacuum in each tank and potentially pulled seawater in through tank pressure vents. Tank vents were attached to the nearest mast. The specific gravity of the crude oil would cause it to float above the incoming seawater and shrink in volume to nearly half of its volume at loading (Zamboni, 1936). The proportion of crude oil and water by volume and percentage of tank space occupied is speculative.

There is no local memory of an oil slick associated with *Montebello* at the time of her loss, later during the war, or in subsequent years (Giannini, 1999; Molinari, 2001). Based on the reconnaissance team biologists' observations, if there were small leaks of oil still ongoing, *Beggiatoa*, a bacteria which feeds on hydrocarbons, would be discerned as pale, white thread wisps in the area of a leak. None were noted.

A single torpedo is thought to have struck the vessel in the area of the forward pump room and hence caused no fire, much to the relief of the crew. The bow appears to have broken at this weakened location when she struck the sea floor. Overall, the visual impression obtained by direct observation of *Montebello*, and subsequent review of the videotapes obtained on each dive, is that her hull, main deck, and lower portions of the two deckhouses are in surprisingly good condition. A resulting preliminary impression of *Montebello*'s 10 onboard liquid product storage tanks strongly suggest that they are intact and still contain their crude oil allotments.

What future can be predicted for the crude oil cargo and subsequently the affected local and regional environment? Scenarios range from slow leaks as the hull ages and eventually deteriorates, through the prospect of sudden catastrophic failure in the case of an earthquake, underwater landslide, or cumulative impacts from commercial fishing activities.

What are the risks of removal versus monitoring? Should the cargo be removed or allowed to leak at a controlled rate within the capacity of the ocean to absorb it without denigration? There is no solid national policy in place that recognizes that such environmental dangers exist. No national research and monitoring program exists to assess the pollution potential, predict the time frame for release of the hazardous cargo into the environment, or monitor the site against unpredicted adverse forces.

PREPARATION FOR FUTURE INVESTIGATION AND MONITORING

Obvious reasons for locating and studying this kind of shipwreck range from expanding our knowledge of history to assessment and remedy of the potential for pollution of the environment. Many historical details of *Montebello* already have faded into obscurity. The company who built her has long been out of business. Files documenting her construction, voyaging history, repairs, and other details kept by her owner, UNOCAL, have been lost or discarded, so that differences between her museum model and actual structure seen during reconnaissance remain unexplained. Over the intervening years, stories of her sinking change as participants and witnesses pass on or memory fades.

Future investigative methodology is based on data need and available resources. Suitability of remote sensing versus direct human observation needs to be determined. Each has advantages, and ideally both can be logically employed. It is a rare tool of investigation that can provide data at varying scales. An instrument such as a deep-tow, side-scan sonar system that can view the entire site in one image is currently unable to resolve details sufficiently to monitor *Montebello*'s structural integrity. Advantage may be taken of the cargo's accessibility behind the hull plating by using acoustic reflection to determine the presence, location, and quantity of remaining oil. An instrument can be packaged that measures reflections based on the differing densities of oil and water in the tanks. Small leaks could be monitored by hydrocarbon sensors set at detection thresholds, which trigger a signal to the U.S. Coast Guard, the agency charged with managing oil spill response coordination. How this response would counter the onset of leaking aboard a ship 270 m underwater has yet to be addressed officially.

A preemptive strategy to remove the cargo using current technology is regularly suggested. Since the crude oil would need to be heated in order to pump it, this would require injection of steam or hot water. The effect of such pressure on *Montebello*'s tanks is open to theoretical discussion. The hoses to the surface would probably require additional heating to prevent the crude oil from congealing in them on the trip to the surface. The U.S. Coast Guard's policy of "passive monitoring" may suffice in the present, but decisive action may someday be necessary to avert a potential sea floor catastrophe.

ACKNOWLEDGMENTS: *Montebello* investigation team members, in addition to the author, were Robert Schwemmer, Roy Pettus, Stacey Kim, Patrick Smith, John Ljubenkov, Steven Maddex, and Robert Pavlik. Submersible pilots were David Slater and Chris Ijames of Delta Oceanographies. Additional individuals, and institutions figuring prominently in the reconnaissance of SS *Montebello* were Brent Roberts; Frederick G. Novy III, Henry Silka, and Larry Newland, all of the Central Coast Maritime Museum Association, NOAA's West Coast National Undersea Research Center, Fairbanks, Alaska; California State Department of Transportation (Caltrans), San Diego Maritime Museum, Monterey Bay National Marine Sanctuary, and UNOCAL Museum of Oil in Santa Paula, California.

REFERENCES

Abell, Westcott, 1948, *The Shipwright's Trade*. Conway Maritime' Press Edition of 1981.

Browning, Robert M. Jr., 1996, *S. Merchant Vessel War Casualties of World War II*. Naval Institute Press, Annapolis.

Dewberry, Suzanne, 1991, Perils at Sea: The Sinking of the SS Montebello. *Prologue*, Quarterly of the National Archives 23(3):260–265.

Environmental News Network, 1999, *Legacy of an Oil Spill*: *Ten Years after the Exxon* Valaez. A conference sponsored by the *Exxon Valdez* Oil Spill Trustee Council and the Alaska Sea Grant College Program. March 23–26.

Harth, Stan, Krieger, Liz, and Krieger, Dan, editors, 1991, *War Comes to the Middle Kingdom, California's* Central Coast Enters World War II. San Luis Obispo County Historical Society, EZ Nature Books, San Luis Obispo.

Kim, Stacy and John Ljubenkov, 1997, Personal communication on biological observations of the wreck of the SS *Montebello*, in *Reconnaissance of the Shipwreck of the* SS *Montebello*. By Hunter, Jack, and Robert Schwemmer, Roy Pettus, Stacy Kim, John Ljubenkov, Pat Smith, and Robert Pavlik for West Coast National Undersea Research Center, University of Alaska, Fairbanks.

Molinari, Merle, 2001, personal communication.

U.S. Coast Guard, No Date, *Area Contingency Plans for the Eleventh Coast Guard District*. U.S. Department of Transportation, Long Beach.

White, Herbert John, 1927, *Oil Tank Steamers*: *Their Working and Pumping Arrangements Thoroughly Explained*. Brown, Son and Ferguson, Ltd., Glasgow.

Zamboni, G.A., 1936, *Motor Oils and Their Application*. Educational Institute, Los Angeles.

Chapter 44

Preservation

DONALD H. KEITH

OF TIME AND CHANGE

We measure time by change and divide it broadly into past, present, and future. With the possible exception of folklore, humanity's past exists only to the extent that the artifacts it created and the landscapes it modified survive into the present.

All humankind feels a need to have contact with the past—and the desire to preserve it for the future. Unfortunately, this is in direct opposition to the universal and natural force of entropy, the degradation over time of matter and energy to randomness, disorder, and chaos. The very antithesis of preservation, this tendency is a blessing in disguise. If every object produced by the humanhand survived, we would be smothered by our own artifacts. Given today's global population of approximately six billion people and the attendant problems of waste disposal, that prospect does not seem too far-fetched. But in the past, just as today, most material evidence of humankind's presence was ephemeral. The greater the passage of time, the greater the degree of loss; and over the millennia a great deal indeed was thrown, fell, or sank beneath the waters that cover nearly three-quarters of the earth's surface.

The Value Concept

Why are we curious about the past, and why should we preserve it? What are the costs and what are the benefits? Given the limited resources available to devote to the preservation of our common past, it behooves us to be highly selective about what we try to save. This dilemma lies at the heart of the preservation debate. What is one person's

Donald H. Keith, Ships of Discovery, Corpus Christi Museum of Science and History, Corpus Christi, Texas 78401.

International Handbook of Underwater Archaeology, edited by Carol V. Ruppé and Janet F. Barstad. Kluwer Academic/Plenum Publishers, New York, 2002.

Figure 44.1.

treasure is another's trash. Obviously, not everything can or should be preserved. From pyramids to pins, most artifacts go through one or more value cycles. Created for a specific purpose, they have value while fulfilling that purpose, but value declines with use and the passage of time. When finally worn out or outmoded, they are discarded. Attrition takes its toll. Objects made of durable materials such as stone and ceramics may last for millennia; most other materials rapidly disintegrate. Rediscovered centuries or millennia later, these remnants of the past regain value in direct proportion to their novelty and rarity, and the cycle is complete.

Preservation Strategies

Preservation is a many-faceted concept. In everyday speech, it means "to protect from injury or peril, to maintain intact, or to treat so as to prevent decay." In archaeological parlance, preservation refers to how artifacts fare in nature, without human interference. The condition in which they are found is their "state of preservation." "Conservation," on the other hand, is the practice of cleaning and stabilizing artifacts using a set of specialized techniques. Sweden's miraculously intact royal ship *Vasa*, sunk in 1628, provides perhaps the best example of a traditional strategy for preserving the past: total excavation of a site, conservation of the finds, and analysis followed by a final report and creation of a landmark museum exhibit (Kvarning, 1993).

Increasingly, this approach is the exception rather than the rule. Test excavations such as those conducted on USS *Monitor*, lost off Cape Hatteras in 1862, are more common (Watts, 1985). Digging a site to save it from destruction by development, as was the case with the Ronson ship, an early 18th-century merchant vessel found beneath the streets of New York City (Steffy, 1988), and placing the artifacts in a safe repository is a common "dig now, study later" preservation strategy used in "rescue" or "salvage" archaeology.

An approach virtually unheard of in the not so distant past but now quite popular, is the archaeological park, such as the Lake Champlain Underwater Historic Preserve, which the public may visit for recreational and educational purposes. Simply leaving a site alone is another way to preserve it, although being an inherently inquisitive and impatient species, humans seldom exercise this option. A notable exception is the remarkable restraint shown in the case of the *Hamilton* and *Scourge*, two cargo ships converted to military duty during the War of 1812 and sunk in Lake Ontario by a sudden violent squall (Cassavoy and Crisman, 1988). In-situ preservation of underwater sites is the latest refinement in the preservation struggle and one that can be considered a good first step in any case, as well as one that can be combined with the park strategy (Oxley, 1996).

Site Preservation Under Water

There are as many equivalent types of archaeological sites under water as there are on land: paleolithic rock art, such as the paintings found in Cosquer Cave, France; prehistoric human remains such as those found in Warm Mineral and Little Salt Springs, Florida; inundated prehistoric dwelling sites such as those found in the crannogs of Scotland and in many lakes in central Europe; sunken cities such as Gythion, seaport of ancient Sparta, and Port Royal, Jamaica; and sacred lakes and sinkholes into which offerings were cast such as Laguna de Media Luna and Chichén Itzá in Mexico. Still, shipwrecks predominate the field of underwater archaeology. Producing hundreds of thousands of artifacts in addition to the remains of the ship itself, they are the most prolific of underwater sites, frequently requiring the creation of museums to curate and exhibit the finds. Such sites have become national shrines, the very symbols that spring to mind when one hears the name of a country: Henry VIII's *Mary Rose*, found in Portsmouth harbor, England (Rule, 1982); the 4500-year-old Cheops Boat, found in a special tomb at the foot of the Great Pyramid outside Giza, Egypt (Lipke, 1984); or the Gokstad and Oseberg Viking ships found in burial mounds near Oslo, Norway (Brøgger and Shetelig, 1951).

Preservation of Waterlogged Artifacts

Artifacts can survive long immersion in water apparently intact. But appearances are deceiving. Although objects may look much the same as they did before immersion, they are often subtly but profoundly changed. When Capt. Jacques-Yves Cousteau and his colleagues began the first underwater excavation involving an archaeologist in 1952, little thought was given to how to preserve the artifacts they would raise. The subject of the excavation was a Roman shipwreck from about 180 B.C., lying in water 90 ft deep at the foot of a sheer cliff at Grand Congloué, near Marseilles, France. Many of the techniques and tools used by the excavators are virtually unchanged today, including underwater television cameras!

But diving technique and equipment was far in advance of the investigators' ability to conserve the finds or even understand how long immersion had changed them. Cousteau (1954) wrote, "When divers found the sunken argosy's main deck surprisingly firm, hope grew that the entire ship might be raised intact. Fragments brought to the surface, however, shriveled and crumbled." Artifacts that had the appearance of perfect preservation dried, shrank, warped, and crumbled—sometimes in a matter of hours—while archaeologists looked on helplessly. It became apparent that any benefit from the remarkable and unique discoveries being made under water would depend wholly and entirely on the highly specialized and nascent art of archaeological conservation.

Given the twin facts that it is much easier to find and recover artifacts than it is to treat them, and that for every qualified conservator who enters the job market there are many field archaeologists, it is not surprising that from the beginning, conservation of waterlogged finds has been the bottleneck of underwater archaeology. Today, conservation of waterlogged finds is regarded as an important specialization within the universe of archaeological conservation. Many gains have been made, but the rate at which finds are made and objects are raised has always kept ahead of the discipline's ability to produce both effective treatments and practitioners.

Perhaps the principal difference between a "good" project and a "bad" project is the extent to which attention is paid to preservation. At the low end of the spectrum are the many ill-conceived and often highly destructive examples of the present feeding off the past: salvage attempts guided primarily by the principal of instant gratification, such as the one that destroyed *De Braak* (Shomette, 1996). At the opposite end are examples of the present contributing to a better future, such as the methodical terrestrial and underwater excavation of Saddle Island and the Basque whaling vessel *San Juan*, projects for which the principal of preservation was the always the guiding light (Grenier and Tuck, 1988).

An Embarrassment of Riches

Thirty years ago, archaeologists could only speculate about what might lie on the bottom of the sea, what condition it might be in, and what it might tell us about the past. Now, after literally thousands of discoveries in lakes, rivers, bays, estuaries, and seas the world over, the question is, "What do we do with it all?" Underwater archaeologists are well and truly mired in an embarrassment of riches, almost all of which have been recovered in the last three decades.

As the rate at which underwater sites are being discovered and exploited increases, new questions are being asked: Which ones should we preserve? Why? Can we preserve them in situ? Should we wait until better techniques are available? Should some sites be allowed to monopolize the preservation resources of a nation, possibly at the expense of others? Are there alternatives to full-scale excavation? When is it appropriate to raise the entire ship's hull? Which preservation techniques are best, fastest, and least expensive? *Is it worth it?*

PRESERVING THINGS, PLACES, AND KNOWLEDGE

Different approaches to preservation are required by what is being preserved: things, places, or knowledge. Obviously, there are things—personal possessions such as the leather-bound trunk of clothing belonging to John Dement, found on SS *Central America*, sunk in 1857 (Herdendorf, 1995); items of shipboard equipment, such as the cannons and anchors recovered from two ships that wrecked on the coast of Padre Island, Texas in 1554 (Arnold and Weddle, 1978); artifacts that were once cargo, such as the thousands of pieces of celadon ware and tons of copper coins raised from the early 14th-century Sinan Gun shipwreck in South Korea (Keith, 1980); or even a complete hull, e.g., the 14th-century *Bremen Cog* (Lahn, 1990). Each contributes to the telling of the overall story of a site. While the ultimate objective of conservation is to extend the life of artifacts, in the process of doing so the archaeologist has an opportunity to gain knowledge of how things were made and used, as well as what they were made of (Keith, Carlin, and deBry, 1997).

Things

There is some evidence to suggest that excavation does not "save" the things in a site, but rather accelerates their loss. Important ancient ships excavated before World War II were destroyed during the conflict (e.g., two Roman pleasure barges from Lake Nemi, Italy, and three Bronze Age sewn boats found in North Ferriby, England). More recently, the 4th-century B.C. Greek Kyrenia ship came close to annihilation during the 1974 Cyprus War, and government policy prevented one of the two 3rd-century B.C. Punic warships found in Sicily from being conserved. Almost perfectly preserved for four and a half millennia, the Cheops Boat has deteriorated dramatically since it was disinterred fewer than 50 years ago (Jenkins, 1980). The inability of conservators to maintain this, the oldest and best-preserved vessel in the world, may have been one of the reasons why other similarly entombed ceremonial boats have not been disturbed. Concern for the vast quantity of exquisitely preserved artifacts recovered from the Civil War steamboat *Maple Leaf*, sunk in Florida's St. John's River, caused excavators to halt the project after removing only an estimated 1 percent of the ship's cargo of personal belongings and camp equipment (Holland et al., 1993).

Places

Taking a broader view, there are also places, "super sites" containing many shipwrecks resulting from a single event such as a battle or storm, or from a slow accretion over time in the vicinity of a menace to navigation. General Cornwallis' fleet of ships, trapped and sunk in the York River, Virginia, in the last battle of the American Revolution in 1781, is an example of the former (Sands, 1988), as are Kublai Khan's fleet sent to the bottom of the sea by a typhoon during his abortive invasion of Japan in 1281 (Mozai, 1982) and the Spanish Armada wrecks scattered across the northern coasts of the British Isles (Martin, 1975). Fathom Five National Park in Georgian Bay, Ontario, and Isle Royale National Park in Lake Superior (Lenihan, 1987) are examples of the latter. It is desirable to protect, preserve, and study such super sites intact, because the overall context is more important than its individual constituent parts.

A basic fact of underwater archaeology is that once something is discovered, it cannot be un-discovered. People are inherently impatient and curious, and as soon as a new discovery is made or a new site found, they feel that something should be done with it *now*! With proper legislation and enforcement, continuous, disruptive human intervention can be minimized. Even when no formal parks or preserves exist, it may be possible to preserve sites, in situ, under water. The greatest impediment at the moment is lack of information: baseline data on the forces controlling overall site stabilization, and on-site preservation across the spectrum of commonly encountered materials. In addition to continuous human intervention, we know at least some of the variables on which site stabilization depends: physical variables such as currents, sedimentation, depth, and temperature; electrochemical variables such as salinity, and proximity of dissimilar metals to each other; biological variables such as wood-boring organisms, burrowing animals, fungi, and kelp; and chemical variables such as pH and oxygen content.

Underwater sites are often discovered as a result of exposure following a natural event or resulting from large-scale human disruption. Perhaps the most striking example of the former is the spectral emergence in 1979 of what may have been the 17th century third rate HMS *Stirling Castle* from Goodwins Sands "with guns in position, stores in the hold, and a huge copper kettle lying on deck" (Fenwick and Gale, 1999: 96–98). The well-preserved mid-18th-century Dutch East India Company ship *Amsterdam* is an example of the latter. Buried in sand beneath the tidal flats of Pevensey Bay, it was rediscovered in 1969 during the laying of a sewerline (Gawronski, 1990).

Following initial disruption of a site's equilibrium, accelerated disintegration often occurs until a new equilibrium is reached. Underwater archaeologists are now testing ways to stabilize and preserve historical and archaeological resources in situ. Oxley (1996) describes efforts by licensed teams to protect sites from the impacts of fishing nets and anchors, attack by microorganisms, erosion, human interference, structural collapse, and electrochemical dissolution, as well as site stabilization techniques during and following excavation, and site reburial.

Pioneering studies on the physical and chemical changes that take place in artifacts during long submergence are beginning to generate baseline data that may be useful in the future to predict the rate at which different materials decompose. Studies on actual shipwreck sites in Australia (e.g., *Santiago* and SS *Xantho*), Norfolk Island (HMS *Sirius*) and Scotland (the Duart Point wreck) appear to indicate that proper installation of sacrificial anodes on wreck sites can help stabilize—and perhaps even partially conserve—target artifacts in situ (MacLeod, 1993; Gregory, 1999).

Knowledge

Nothing lasts forever. Conservation science may extend the life of artifacts by decades or even centuries, and developing technology may enable us to preserve entire sites on the seabed, but sooner or later all material objects will yield to corrosion, decomposition, war, fire, earthquake, flood, or asteroid bombardment. Therefore, preserving knowledge in the form of *data* is probably the most important part of preservation. A good example is the case of the Dutch East Indiaman *Hollandia*, which was lost with all hands in 1743 near the Scilly Isles. Badly ravaged by the sea and poorly preserved, the site was sporadically salvaged over a 20-year period following its discovery in 1971. About 80 percent of the collection, some 3500 items, was acquired by the Rijksmuseum in Amsterdam, where it was methodically studied. The result is the *Hollandia Compendium* (Gawronski, Kist, and Stokvis-Boetzelaer, 1992), a systematic catalog of the surviving artifacts according to functional classification, complemented by exhaustive historical documentation. Such efforts deserve applause. The editors and staff of the *Compendium* saved a tremendous amount of data that would normally have been lost, and made it accessible to their colleagues in an exemplary fashion.

The knowledge of what—and how—to do in the field is preserved and continuously upgraded in such publications as *Archaeology Underwater: The NAS Guide to Principles and Practice* (Dean et al., 1992). Up-to-date information on the conservation of artifacts is available in such journals as *Canadian Conservation Institute Publications and Notes* (CCI), the *Journal of the American Institute for Conservation* (AIC), *Studies in Conservation* (IIC) and the *International Council of Museum Papers* (ICOM), as well as the *International Journal of Nautical Archaeology.*

THE REVELATIONS OF UNDERWATER ARCHAEOLOGY

A pattern has emerged in the last 30 years: The types of artifacts found on shipwrecks are often substantially different from those found on terrestrial sites, offering a different perspective on society, trade, and technology. The fact that ships carried artifacts in the form of equipment, personal possessions, and cargo rarely, if ever, found on terrestrial sites was born out early in the 20th century, when Mediterranean sponge divers located and raised Classical Greek bronze statues such as the Zeus statue found near Cape Artemisium, Greece (Rackl, 1968).

Unique Objects

Sponge divers made an important discovery in 1900 when they stumbled onto a Roman shipwreck off the coast of the Aegean island Antikythera. Working with the Greek Archaeological Service, the divers raised the ship's cargo of marble and bronze statues. They also raised, but took little notice of, a curious concretion containing a collection of metallic wheels of some sort. Not until the late 1950s was the object finally radiographed, studied in detail, and recognized for what it is: a mechanical device for computing sun and moon calendrical relationships (Price, 1997), the earliest such device ever discovered by far. Nothing like it has been found before or since.

Taking note of remarkable discoveries such as these, archaeologists began to appreciate the historical and technological importance of seafaring. Although it was the cargo and equipment carried aboard ships that initially attracted salvors and archaeologists alike to shipwreck sites, archaeologists took the process a step further by initiating the careful study and reconstruction of the ships' hulls (Steffy, 1994). Marine archaeologists are fond of saying that the largest and most important artifact on any shipwreck site (when it survives) is the hull of the ship itself. The study of the wooden hulls of ships led to the revelation that nautical technology worldwide can be divided into several distinct traditions of ship design and construction. It is fascinating to contemplate the reasons behind the similarities and differences in these traditions, as well as their gradual blending over time.

Vessel Design and Construction

Ancient ships built in the Mediterranean tradition, such as the Kyrenia Ship, were assembled "shell first": The hull planks were bent to shape and joined edge to edge, often using thousands of mortise and tenon joints (Throckmorton, 1972). A different tradition in northern Europe produced clinker-built ships of an entirely different design and appearance, such as the rowed and sailed open longboats on display in the Viking Ship Museum in Oslo, Norway (Greenhill and Manning, 1988). Farther to the east in the Indian Ocean, the dominant tradition joined planks of ships' hulls edge to edge as in the Mediterranean technique, but the planks were sewn together rather than doweled or nailed. The hull of the Cheops Boat is connected in this manner, as is the hull of the modern-day East African boat type *Mtepe* (Gilbert, 1988). That the tradition was once more prevalent is attested by Marco Polo's revelation that the hulls of the Arab ships on which he traveled at the end of the 13th century were sewn together rather than nailed.

Archaeology is just beginning to reveal the secrets of Chinese and Southeast Asian ship-building traditions. Analysis of the well-preserved hull of the late 13th century Chinese ship discovered in Quanzhou, China, is revealing peculiar construction features characteristic of Chinese sea-going vessels (Green and Burningham, 1999) such as the use of bulkheads to divide the hold into many compartments, the double-planked hull utilizing "rabbeted carvel" joinery, and the movable stern rudder. The Pacific boat-building tradition is known mainly from accounts of the first Europeans to make contact with Polynesian, Micronesian, and Melanesian seafarers, and from traditions that exist to the ethnographic present (Allen, 1980). Archaeology has yet to contribute much to understanding where and how this tradition evolved, but it is apparent that the multihulled and masted catamaran designs used by the inhabitants of Oceania were some of the most innovative and successful of all time, enabling people possessing only stone-age technology to explore and colonize the largest ocean on earth (Haddon and Hornell, 1975).

STRATEGIES FOR THE FUTURE

There is little point in preserving the past if we do not take its lessons to heart. Without question, much of the archaeological record has been eradicated by people with good intentions and abundant (if only temporary) enthusiasm but insufficient knowledge and experience in the realm of conservation. Tragic and unnecessary mistakes were made in the past, the transformation of the ironclad gunboat USS *Cairo* from perhaps the best-preserved Civil War era shipwreck to compost being a case in point (McGrath, 1981). North (1987) summed up a more common conservators' lament:

> The first introduction that many people have to marine archaeological conservation happens when a local group of underwater enthusiasts raise an anchor from a locally important shipwreck. The aim usually is to place the anchor, after cleaning, in a local park whence it will commemorate the fortitude, heroism, or possibly stupidity of the area's progenitors. It is usually only after the concreted and seaweed-encrusted anchor is finally dragged ashore that the problems of cleaning and conservation are considered.

Cases like this beg three questions: What should come up? What should be done to it after it comes up? And what will happen to it once it comes up?

Recognizing the Resource

The first step in any systematic approach to preservation is to ascertain the size of the resource. Cultural resource managers cannot make informed decisions without knowing the limitations of the resource for which they are responsible. Because responsibility for action taken as well as benefit from its results is most likely to be a local phenomenon, resource surveys are usual regional, such as The National Inventory of Maritime Archaeology in England being undertaken by the Royal Commission on the Historical Monuments of England, and the Australian National Historic Shipwrecks Database. Other types of less formal but equally useful surveys are less regional and more thematic, such as Classical shipwreck sites (Parker, 1992), and East India Company ships (Redknap and Smith, 1990).

Because there is often a disparity between where the resources for preservation exist and where the rarest, most deserving sites are found, a corollary to this approach is the need to cultivate a feeling of global responsibility for the preservation of world heritage-class sites, wherever they may be found. A current case in point is HMS *Swift*, which sank in Puerto Deseado, Argentina, in 1763. Test excavations conducted at the site by ICOMOS Argentina revealed a very well-preserved mid-18th century corvette. The nascent status of maritime archaeology in Argentina has necessitated a slow approach to excavation of the site while project leaders accumulate the necessary skills, technology, and equipment (Murray, 1993). The maritime archaeology community should work hard to provide the resources and expertise necessary to preserve truly significant discoveries in developing countries or anywhere the discipline is in its formative stages. Under normal circumstances, such sites fall prey to elements motivated by the promise of a quick return from a "blast and grab" salvage scheme. The failure to keep abreast of and assist in the preservation of new discoveries, wherever they may be found, leaves the resource open to exploitation by the prominent but unscrupulous, the curious but ignorant, and the law-abiding but unethical.

Conserving the Resource

The conservation of underwater finds is a new field, still in its infancy. There is a similarity between the state of conservation science now and that of medicine 2400 years ago. The first rule of the Oath of Hippocrates, to which all physicians are sworn is to "do no harm." In addition to its value as a reassurance to the patient (you probably won't get any worse), this rule acknowledges that medicine does not always diagnose the problem correctly or have the cure, and therefore a conservative approach is less likely to result in disaster. The medical analogy also holds true in another important way. All the skill and knowledge of the physician merely postpones the inevitable: Eventually the patient will die. Nothing lasts forever.

Most laboratories for treating artifacts from underwater sites are ad hoc affairs, created specifically for the materials from one site and closed immediately upon completion of the project. If a certain treatment has been demonstrated to work, it is followed over and over again with little refinement or elaboration. Under such conditions, there is little incentive or even opportunity for conservators to experiment with new techniques. Consequently, there is enormous potential for improving the efficiency of existing techniques. It would be optimistic indeed to presume that all treatments currently in use need no refinement.

Most treatments in common use today are relatively new, and no one really knows how "good" they are, meaning how efficient, how protective, how long-lasting. Conservators sometimes disagree over basic concepts. Some are convinced that it is always preferable to strip iron artifacts to bare metal, removing all corrosion products (Armstrong, 1997). Others believe that there are good reasons to preserve and pacify an artifact's "rind" as well as its metallic core, because that is where all markings and potentially important surface detail reside (Carlin and Keith, 1996). One dictum of artifact conservation has been that every treatment must be "reversible." This is a desirable concept: If the first treatment doesn't work for some reason, you can undo it and start over. Unfortunately, in the real world few treatments are truly reversible, and the conservation community is finally beginning to hedge on that requirement.

The vast majority of archaeologists are accustomed to working with small budgets, which usually necessitates finding low-tech, low-cost solutions to their problems. This is also true of the laboratory phase of any project. Conservation budgets are generally inadequate to promote the simultaneous treatment of many artifacts at the same time so that, once they enter the laboratory, they may remain there for many years. During that time, they are out of the sight and minds of the general public which *had been* fascinated by the field work. By the time the objects re-emerge, they and the site they came from are old news. Therefore, conservators specializing in artifacts from marine environments must look for better, faster, and cheaper conservation methods and strive to understand the factors affecting degradation of materials underwater.

No less important is the training of professional conservators who will do this work in the future and instilling in them an enthusiasm for conservation and preservation. It is not obvious to most underwater archaeologists that the real excavation takes place in the laboratory, not in the field. Nor is it clear to them that knowledge of conservation science is the only reliable job security in underwater archaeology. Field work is exciting, visually attractive, and virtually the only part with which the public is familiar. But the fact is that the lion's share of the total energy, resources, and time expended on any legitimate project goes into documentation, conservation, and analysis efforts of the laboratory phase.

Many archaeological conservators come into the field through archaeology, history, or anthropology rather than from strong backgrounds in the hard sciences. As a result, they have a tendency to practice conservation more as an art than a science, in the sense that the treatments they design tend to be slow, cautious, one-on-one artifact-to-conservator affairs. Lamenting the fact that many volunteers offer their training and experience in diving as adequate credentials for participation in an excavation, underwater archaeologists sometimes say, "It's easier to train an archaeologist how to dive than it is to teach a diver how to be an archaeologist." Such would seem to be the case with the conservation of finds from submerged sites. It should be easier to train a research chemist in artifact conservation than to train an archaeologist in chemistry. In any case, the recruitment rate is abysmal. Courses in conservation of artifacts from the sea have been offered at one university in the United States for more than 20 years, yet the number of graduates doing conservation professionally is less than 5 percent of the total.

How Much Time Is Left?

We must recognize and slow down the rate at which underwater sites are being consumed. There is evidence that the cornucopia of material culture from the past preserved under water is not without limit. There is quantitatively-based reason to suspect not only that the resource is finite, but also that in certain areas we have, in fewer than 40 years, discovered—and in about 10 percent of cases completely removed—more than half of it (Keith and Carrell, submitted). When we will "run out" of shipwreck sites depends both on how many are left and how rapidly they are being depleted. Refinements in technology, such as the ability to recover objects from abyssal depths, may make more sites available, but the rate of consumption in areas where sites are still plentiful continues to increase. If we are interpreting the indications properly, maintaining the present rate of use will exhaust the potential for new shipwreck discoveries, within four decades, in those areas of the world where heavy exploitation has already taken place: Australia, the Mediterranean coast of Europe, Great Britain, Canada, the United States, and much of the Caribbean.

But the news is not all bad. Many countries in these same areas now have legislation regulating their remaining underwater cultural heritage and curtailing the pell-mell rush to squander it to complete exhaustion. Additionally, a large proportion of discovered sites are "in reserve": examined and in some cases partially excavated but still sufficiently intact to be of interest to archaeologists in the future. Currently, shipwreck resources in developing countries are at the greatest risk because they are taking the full brunt of experienced, well-equipped and financed North American- and European-based commercial salvage operations spreading out across the globe to look for rich, new hunting grounds in the Philippines, Melanesia, Cuba, and Southeast Asia. Sadly, many sites will be discovered and extracted before the nations in whose waters they lie are aware of their existence or of alternatives to simple commercial salvage (Carrell, 1996).

Making the Most of It

Finally, we should make the most of what we have already preserved. Sites that seemed insignificant in the past should be re-investigated. Museums are full of collections that have never been studied adequately. Furthermore, museum policies can make it difficult to sample and study collections or even individual artifacts. Now that the potential importance of shipwreck hull remains is universally appreciated, and increased amounts of data are available for comparative studies, shipwrecks with only scanty hull remains should not be slighted on that account. Similarly, it is apparent that the presence of a valuable cargo has in the past often eclipsed the potential value of hull remains and, indeed, all other artifact categories. That the re-examination and study of ignored but still surviving hulls and orphaned artifacts may be worth while is confirmed by Skowronek's (1984) study of artifacts salvaged from a fleet of ships that wrecked on the coast of Florida in 1733. Representing the "state's share" of various salvage contract splits, the artifacts were turned over to the Research and Preservation Laboratory of the Florida Bureau of Historic Sites and Properties for conservation.

The alternative of leaving hull remains on the bottom should be considered when optimum conservation and reconstruction facilities are not available. The shipwreck archaeologist should be aware that past performance indicates that the raising of hull remains from underwater sites actually reduces their potential for survival. While the conservation of hulls has been very successful in Scandinavia and northern Europe, the record for hulls in the Mediterranean, East Asian, and Caribbean regions has been poor. A good model for the future is the "raise, record, and rebury" strategy embraced by Parks Canada archaeologists during the excavation of the Basque whaling ship found in Red Bay, Labrador (Waddell, 1996). The archaeologists completely disassembled the ship under water, raised each piece to the surface, recorded it, then transferred it to a carefully prepared underwater storage area. Provisions were made for monitoring the chemical and physical condition of the re-interred wood.

THE FOES OF PRESERVATION

What are the foes of preservation?

First and foremost: humans. We break up and recycle materials—the fate of the Colossus of Rhodes, one of Herodotus's Seven Wonders of the Ancient World. We bury and burn things such as the Library of Alexandria, said to contain the accumulated knowledge of the ancients. We cover old cities and ports beneath new ones: The Roman port of Ostia is buried beneath Rome's airport at Fiumicino (Shaw, 1972), and Roman and medieval ships and harbor works lie beneath the streets of London (Marsden, 1994). We lose things again, a few years after finding them the first time, such as the site near Cape Artemisium, Greece, that yielded two Classical bronze statues. More often than not, when we do happen upon well-preserved remnants of the past, we treat them as an Easter egg hunt, or the focus of get-rich-quick schemes, or merely the sources of baubles and curios, rather than treating them with the respect they deserve.

The hand of Nature takes care of the rest. Biological activity attacks and breaks down everything organic as well as many inorganic materials such as metals. Iron artifacts, completely covered in marine concretion or buried in anaerobic sediments, can be completely consumed by bacteria. Coastlines are particularly susceptible to catastrophic change. The sea lures us to the coast, then destroys our ships, flimsy quays, piers, and docks.

Time turns tragedies into troves. Volcanoes bury under ash and mud whole populations such as the Roman town of Pompeii and its port of Herculaneum. Earthquakes cause cities such as Port Royal, Jamaica, to sink beneath the waves (Link, 1960). Sea level change and siltation inundate and cause the abandonment of coastal cities and ports: Leptis Magna in Libya and Ostia in Italy (Shaw, 1972). Rivers change course, trapping vessels such as Columbus' caravel *Gallega* behind sandbars (Keith et al., 1990), and leaving steamboats such as *Arabia* in abandoned streambeds (Hawley, 1995). All this is fortunate indeed for archaeology, the "handmaiden to history." If nothing disappeared over time, the past would not hold the same fascination for us, and archaeology—the study of the past through its material remains—would not exist.

REFERENCES

Allen, O., 1980, *The Pacific Navigators*. Time-Life Books, Alexandria.

Armstrong, D., 1997, A Wrought Iron Gun for 16th Century Sea Service. *Journal of the Ordnance Society* 9:27–48.

Arnold III, J. Barto, and Weddle, R., 1978, *The Nautical Archaeology of Padre Island*. Academic Press, New York.

Brøgger, A., and Shetelig, H., 1951, *The Viking Ships*. Dreyers Forlag, Oslo.

Carlin, W., and Keith, D., 1996, An Improved Tannin-based Corrosion Inhibitor-coating System for Ferrous Artefacts. *International Journal of Nautical Archaeology* 25(1):38–45 and 26(1):65–74.

Carrell, T., 1996, Mutate, Migrate, Adapt or Die. *Common Ground: Archeology and Ethnography in the Public Interest*, 1(3–4):72–75.

Cassavoy, K., and Crisman, K., 1988, The War of 1812: Battle for the Great Lakes. In *Ships and Shipwrecks of the Americas*, edited by G. Bass, pp. 169–188. Thames and Hudson, London.

Commonwealth Government of Australia, n.d., *Australian National Historic Shipwrecks Database*. National Centre for Excellence, Western Australia Maritime Museum, Freemantle.

Cousteau, J-Y., 1954, Fish Men Discover a 2,220-Year-Old Greek Ship. *National Geographic* 105(1):1–36.

Dean, M., Ferrari, B., Oxley, I., Redknap, M., and Watson, K., 1992, *Archaeology Underwater: The NAS Guide to Principles and Practice*. Nautical Archaeology Society and Archetype Publications. Henry Ling Ltd. at the Dorset Press, Dorchester.

Delgado, J., editor, 1997, *Encyclopaedia of Underwater and Maritime Archaeology*. British Museum Press, London.

Fenwick, V., and Gale, A., 1999, Historic Shipwrecks Discovered, Protected & Investigated. Tempus, Gloucestershire.

Gawronski, J., 1990, The *Amsterdam* Project. *International Journal of Nautical Archaeology* 19(1):53–61.

Gawronski, J., Kist, B., and Stokvis-Boetzelaer, O., 1992, *Hollandia Compendium: A Contribution to the History, Archaeology, Classification and Lexicography of a 150 ft. Dutch East Indiaman (1740–1750)*. Elsevier, Amsterdam.

Gilbert, E., 1988, The Mtepe: Regional Trade and the Late Survival of Sewn Ships in East African Waters. *International Journal of Nautical Archaeology* 27(1):43–50.

Green, J. and Burningham, N., 1999, The Ship from Quanzhou, Fujian Province, People's Republic of China. *International Journal of Nautical Archaeology* 27(4):277–301.

Greenhill, B., and Manning, S., 1988, *The Evolution of the Wooden Ship*. Facts on File, New York.

Gregory, D., 1999, Monitoring the Effects of Sacrificial Anodes on the Large Iron Artefacts on the Duart Point Wreck, 1997. *International Journal of Nautical Archaeology* 28(2):164–173.

Grenier, R., and Tuck, J., 1988, *Red Bay, Labrador: World Whaling Capital 1550–1600*. St. John's, Newfoundland.

Haddon, A., and Hornell, J., 1975, *Canoes of Oceania*. Bishop Museum Press, Honolulu.

Hawley, D., 1995, *Treasures of the Steamboat Arabia*. River Salvage, Inc., Kansas City.

Herdendorf, C., 1995, Science on a Deep Ocean Shipwreck. *Ohio Journal of Science* 95(1). Special Issue.

Holland, K., Manley, L., and Towart, J., 1993, *The Maple Leaf: An Extraordinary American Civil War Shipwreck*. St. Johns Archaeological Expeditions, Inc., Jacksonville.

Jenkins, N., 1980, *The Boat Beneath the Pyramid*. Holt, Rinehart and Winston, New York.

Keith, D., 1980, A Fourteenth-Century Shipwreck at Sinan-gun. *Archaeology* 33(2):33–43.

Keith, D., Carrell, T., and Lakey, D., 1990, The Search for Columbus' Caravel *Gallega* and the Site of Santa María de Belén. *Journal of Field Archaeology* 17(4):123–140.

Keith, D., Carlin, W., and de Bry, J., 1997, A Bronze Cannon from *La Belle*, 1686: Its Construction, Conservation and Display. *International Journal of Nautical Archaeology* 26(2):144–158.

Keith, D., and Carrell, T., Underwater Archaeology. In *Handbook of Historical Archaeology*, edited by T. Majewski and C. Orser. Plenum Press, submitted.

Kvarning, L-Å., 1993, Raising the *Vasa*. *Scientific American* 269(4).

Lahn, W., 1992, *Die Kogge von Bremen. Band I, Bauteile und Bauablauf*. Earnst Kable, Hamburg.

Lenihan, D., 1987, *Submerged Cultural Resources Study: Isle Royale National Park*. National Park Service Submerged Cultural Resources Unit, Santa Fe.

Link, M., 1960, Exploring the Drowned City of Port Royal. *National Geographic* 117(1):151–183.

Lipke, P., 1984, *The Royal Ship of Cheops*. British Archaeological Reports International Series 225. Oxford University Press, Oxford.

Marsden, P., 1994, *Ships of the Port of London: First to Eleventh Centuries A.D.* London.

Martin, C., 1975, *Full Fathom Five: Wrecks of the Spanish Armada*, The Viking Press, New York.

McGrath Jr., T., 1981, The Eventual Preservation and Stabilization of the USS *Cairo*. *International Journal of Nautical Archaeology* 10(2):79–94.

Mozai, T., 1982, The Lost Fleet of Kublai Khan. *National Geographic* 162(5):634–649.

Murray, C., 1993, *Corbeta de Guerra* H.M.S. Swift, *1763*. Museo Regional Provincial Mario Brozoski, Buenos Aires.

North, N., 1987, Conservation of Metals. In *Conservation of Marine Archaeological Objects*, edited by C. Pearson. Butterworths, Boston.

Oxley, I., 1996, The In-Situ Preservation of Underwater Sites. In *Proceedings of the Preservation of Archaeological Remains In Situ (PARIS) Conference*, London.

Parker, A., 1992, *Ancient Shipwrecks of the Mediterranean and Roman Provinces*. BAR International Series 580. Hadrian Books, Ltd., Oxford.

Price, D., 1997, An Ancient Greek Computer. *Origins of Technology*, special publication of Scientific American, pp. 96–103. Reprinted from *Scientific American*, June 1959. Scientific American, New York.

Rackl, H-W., 1968, *Diving Into the Past*. Charles Scribner's Sons, New York.

Redknap, M., and Smith, R., 1990, Introduction to Ships, Cargoes and The East India Trade: The English East India Company and Its Competitors. *International Journal of Nautical Archaeology* 19(1): 1–3.

Royal Commission on the Historical Monuments of England, 1996, *The National Inventory of Maritime Archaeology in England*. Royal Commission on the Historical Monuments of England, National Monuments Record Centre, Swindon.

Rule, M., 1982, *The Mary Rose: The Excavation and Raising of Henry VIIIs Flagship*. Conway Maritime Press, London.

Sands, J., 1988, Gunboats and Warships of the American Revolution. In *Ships and Shipwrecks of the Americas*, edited by G. Bass, pp. 149–168. Thames and Hudson, London.

Shaw, J., 1972, Greek and Roman Harbourworks. In *A History of Seafaring*, edited by G. Bass, pp. 87–112. Thames and Hudson, London.

Shomette, D., 1996, HMS *De Braak*. In *Encyclopaedia of Underwater and Maritime Archaeology*, edited by J. Delgado, pp 125–126. British Museum Press, London.

Skowronek, R., 1984, Trade Patterns of Eighteenth Century Frontier New Spain: The 1733 *Flota* and St. Augustine. *Volumes in Historical Archaeology*, edited by Stanley South. South Carolina Institute of Archaeology and Anthropology, University of South Carolina, Columbia.

Steffy, J., 1988, The Thirteen Colonies. In *Ships and Shipwrecks of the Americas*, edited by G. Bass, pp.107–128. Thames and Hudson, London.

_____, 1994, *Wooden Ship Building and the Interpretation of Shipwrecks*. Texas A&M University Press, College Station.

Throckmorton, P., 1987, *The Sea Remembers*: *Shipwrecks and Archaeology*. Weidenfeld and Nicholson, New York.

Waddell, P., 1996, The Disassembly of a 16th-century Galleon. *International Journal of Nautical Archaeology* 15(2):137–148.

Watts Jr., G., 1985, Deep-water Archaeological Investigation and Site Testing in the Monitor National Marine Sanctuary. *Journal of Field Archaeology* 12(3):315–332.

Chapter 45

Underwater Archaeology and the Internet

Navigating a Web of Challenges and Opportunities

ANDREW W. HALL

INTRODUCTION

The emergence of the Internet is probably the most visible sign of what has come to be called the "Information Age." Despite the hype and superlatives that often surround it, the Internet has made a fundamental change in the way most scholars do their work.

This short chapter will not discuss in great detail the origins of the Internet or the pedagogical implications of its use; there are many book-length volumes that cover those topics. Nor will this chapter offer detailed evaluations of specific software applications or Internet tools, since any described will likely be superseded by the time this volume goes to print. Rather, it will attempt to provide an overview of the Internet's most important attributes and propose a few staple guidelines for those who want to establish an Internet "presence" for their own projects.

Andrew W. Hall, Faculty Associate, Director of Grants and Publications, and Manager, Office for Nursing Research and Scholarship, University of Texas School of Nursing at Galveston, Galveston, Texas 77550.

International Handbook of Underwater Archaeology, edited by Carol V. Ruppé and Janet F. Barstad. Kluwer Academic/Plenum Publishers, New York, 2002.

What the Internet Is

When most people use the word "Internet," they are referring to electronic mail, the World Wide Web, or a combination of the two. The Internet is actually a much larger network of computer systems that use a common way of sending and receiving electronic information, and e-mail and the Web are the two most significant forms of communication that make use of the medium.

The Internet most of us know today is an outgrowth of ARPANET, a Cold War project of the U.S. Defense Advanced Research Projects Agency that linked major military commands and institutions doing heavy-duty computing for the military—primarily universities—in a way that might conceivably survive a nuclear war. ARPANET officially went online in fall 1969 with only two sites, Stanford University and the University of California-Los Angeles (Keating and Hargitai, 1999).

The system grew quickly, but for years it was limited primarily to basic research in computer science and physics, and its main users were a handful of scientists and graduate students. Although a variety of other applications subsequently were developed that increased the network's utility, including file transfer protocol (FTP), Telnet, and Usenet newsgroups, it was the creation and growth of electronic mail in the 1970s and the World Wide Web in the 1990s that have created a fundamental overhaul, a true sea change, in the way scientists, scholars, and ordinary people exchange ideas and information in the industrialized world.

For most of us, e-mail and the Web are synonymous with the Internet and likely to remain so. They are Internet applications we use nearly every day, and the ones that would handicap us the most if we were left without them. For that reason, and because e-mail and the Web seem likely to retain their central importance as our means of Internet-based communication for the foreseeable future, those two applications are this chapter's main focus.

ELECTRONIC MAIL

The use of electronic mail, or e-mail, has become a basic element in the daily routine of most professionals, scholars, and university students. One recent study suggests that about two-thirds of the U.S. workforce and about half of U.S. homes now use e-mail on a regular basis. It is estimated that, by the end of 1999, there were about 569 million e-mail accounts worldwide, with that number expected to top one billion by 2002. The largest share of that growth is expected to take place outside the U.S. A 1999 Reuters survey suggested that among users in the U.S. and the United Kingdom, access to e-mail was the primary reason for going online (NUA Internet Surveys, 2000a; NUA Internet Surveys, 1999).

A number of years ago, when access to e-mail was becoming commonplace among people outside major research universities, some pundits argued that the new communications medium, by partially supplanting the telephone, might lead to a rebirth of elegance and precision in written communication. That notion, as any e-mail user today can testify, was wrong. Electronic mail is frequently ungrammatical, peppered with spelling and punctuation errors, and often shows a complete disregard for the rules of capitalization. Nevertheless, these cluttered and sometimes confusing messages have a genuine value, because they are perceived and used as an entirely new medium, one that values spontaneity over reflection, and timeliness over deliberation. Electronic mail is cheap and fast, combining the immediacy and informality of a personal conversation with the ability to preserve the message for future reference (Keating and Hargitai, 1999).

One useful application of e-mail is the mailing list, also known as LISTSERVs after the popular software used to manage them. Mailing lists allow the user to "subscribe," usually by e-mailing a typed command to a specific address. Every time someone sends a message or inquiry to the list, that message is forwarded to all the other members on the list. Replies are similarly passed along, so that many mailing lists become extended, informal discussions on specific topics of interest. Frequently, several discussions will be going on at once. Mailing lists may be "moderated," meaning that the list manager screens incoming messages for content and relevance before passing them on to the list, but many are not. Some lists are open to anyone who cares to join, while others are by invitation only. Unmoderated lists occasionally become rather raucous, with vigorous (and sometimes inappropriate) arguments going back and forth, but after a time these disputes die out.

There are many thousands of publicly accessible mailing lists, devoted to every imaginable topic. The original LISTSERV software was estimated to control more than 70,000 lists with more than 20,000,000 subscribers by the end of 1997 (Keating and Hargitai, 1999). There are even more options today for those who want to create mailing lists. Some Internet-based companies allow users to create and run their own mailing lists for free, making their revenue by inserting small text advertisements in each message that passes through their systems.

Numerous mailing lists are devoted to nautical archaeology and maritime history. The following list includes several English-language public mailing lists that have a general or wide-ranging focus. Information about these mailings lists is current as of summer 2000; all URLs, e-mail addresses, and subscriber numbers are subject to change.

Underwater Archaeology Discussion List

The Underwater Archaeology Discussion List (SUB-ARCH) is owned and managed by Anita Cohen-Williams and hosted by Arizona State University. SUB-ARCH is probably the best-known and longest-standing list of its type, with a current membership of about 450. Topics discussed range from specific research inquiries to ethical issues, international legislation, and regulations affecting archaeological projects. Exchanges on SUB-ARCH are frequently spirited and occasionally contentious. To subscribe, send a message reading "subscribe SUB-ARCH" to listserv@asu.edu, or visit the SUB-ARCH website at http://lists.asu.edu/archives/sub-arch.html.

Marine History Information Exchange Group

The Marine History Information Exchange Group (MARHST-L) is sponsored by the Marine Museum of the Great Lakes at Kingston, Canada, and managed by Walter Lewis and Maurice D. Smith. Although MARHST-L is not strictly an anthropology list, a significant amount of material is discussed that would be of interest to nautical archaeologists working in the historical period. The membership of MARHST-L, which runs to about 400 subscribers, includes a number of respected and widely published authors as well as professional mariners. MARHST-L is a relatively high-volume list, occasionally exceeding 50 messages per day. To subscribe, send a message reading

"SUBSCRIBE MARHST-L [Your Name]" to LISTSERV@Post.Oueensu.ca, or visit the MARHST-L website at http://www.marmus.ca/marmus/marhst.html.

Network for Underwater Archaeology

Established in 1998, the Network for Underwater Archaeology (NUA) is an interdisciplinary group of institutions actively involved in research on the underwater archaeology on the island of Ireland. NUA's mailing list is hosted by the Irish National Information Server and is managed by Kevin Barton of the Applied Geophysics Unit, National University of Ireland, Galway, and Rory Quinn of the Centre for Maritime Archaeology, Coastal Research Group, University of Ulster, Coleraine. To subscribe, send a message reading "subscribe NUA" to listserv@listserv.heanet.ie, or visit the NUA list archives website at http://listserv.heanet.ie/lists/nua.html.

Sea-Site

Sea-site is a multidisciplinary discussion list that explores the wide range of factors that affect preservation of underwater archaeological sites. Sea-site is owned and maintained by Ian Oxley of the Scottish Institute of Maritime Studies at the University of St. Andrews and the Department of Civil and Offshore Engineering at Heriot-Watt University. Sea-site currently has about 200 subscribers. To subscribe or obtain more information, visit the Sea-site website at http://www.mailbase.ac.uk/lists/sea-site/.

Coast–Arch

Coast–Arch is a multidisciplinary mailing list that explores archaeological issues unique to coastal sites, both underwater and terrestrial. The Coast–Arch list is owned and managed by Deanna Groom, project manager of the Maritime Record of the National Monuments Record of Scotland. Current membership is about 65 subscribers. To subscribe or obtain more information, visit the Sea-site website at http://www.mailbase.ac.uk/lists/coast-arch/.

THE WORLD WIDE WEB

Increasingly, the Internet is synonymous with the World Wide Web. The invention of the "Web," as it is often called, is usually credited to physicists working at the European Particle Physics Laboratory (CERN) in Geneva, Switzerland. In fact, the concept of *hypertext*—written material that can be linked electronically to other related materials— had been around for years. Apple Macintosh's HyperCard, introduced in the late 1980s, allowed developers to create sophisticated hypertext applications but was limited to running on individual computers and local networks.

Academic Publishing on the Web

Established, recognized venues for publishing within the profession may shift increasingly toward the electronic medium. Several journals, including the *International Journal of Nautical Archaeology* (www.apnet.com/ijna) and *Historical Archeology* (www.sha.org), already publish contents and abstracts electronically, while a few journals have eschewed paper altogether and are entirely Web-based. The latter represent a small but growing part of the academic publishing community. For example, the peer-reviewed, U.K.-based, online journal *Internet Archaeology* (intarch.ac.uk), had more than 26,000 registered readers by the end of 2000. Although it is unlikely that electronic-format-only journals and books will supplant their traditional models (the bound, printed page retains a sensuous appeal no website can match), they will become an increasingly important part of the way archaeologists share information with each other, their sponsors, and the public.

One other area in which electronic publishing can make a significant difference in the dissemination of research findings is in the area of so-called *gray literature*—works not widely published but representing a substantial proportion of current work by professional archaeologists and historians. The volume of this material has expanded tremendously in the last two decades, due largely to the increasing complex legislative requirements for cultural resource management activities (Bastian and Bergstrom, 1993). Individually, the reports generated tend to be focused, practical, and direct. They do not aspire to be definitive works in their areas. Nevertheless, taken as a whole, they can provide a strong, wide-ranging assessment of a given geographical area or period. Unfortunately, much of their value to the profession is lost by their limited distribution: Sometimes file copies go only to the agency or governmental entity that sponsored the work. The Web provides an opportunity for sponsoring agencies to publish these materials electronically at minimal cost, making them immediate available to researchers over a wide area.

Role of the Web Designer or Webmaster

The web site designer or webmaster has to perform a fairly complex task and must bring multiple skills to the job. Technical skill with computers and the Internet is important, of course, but it is arguably of secondary consequence to either the web designer's ability to synthesize and present a complex subject to a variety of audiences. This is difficult because archaeology, more than most fields of study, is always a multidisciplinary endeavor. Just as shipwrecks represent a microcosm of the cultures that created them, their study, analysis, and dissemination demand a solid working base in fields as disparate as history, ethnology, economics, botany, and geology.

It is not surprising, then, that the role of the web designer has been likened to that of a weaver, bringing together varied strands of a complex story into a coherent whole (Lawrence, 1996; McDavid, 1998). In many respects, "weaver" seems a more appropriate title than "webmaster," since the latter implies mere authoritative control over a website, without any reference to skill or creativity required to establish it in the first place.

Website Structure: Deep versus Wide

"Deep" sites represent problems, for shipwrecks and websites alike.

Everyone who uses the World Wide Web will occasionally encounter a "deep" website—that is, one in which the information provided is broken into sequences of individual pages that restrict the user's options in navigating the site. The organization of the site, as defined by its internal links, is hierarchical and rigid. The web designer has constructed the links between elements of the website in a way that forces the user to follow through a specific sequence of pages to find a given bit of information. Individual

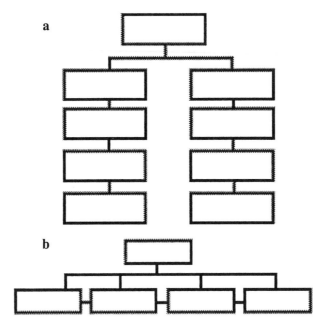

Figure 45.1. (a) On a deep website, the user must proceed through a narrow, rigidly sequenced series of web pages to find the information desired, which makes it difficult to find specific information quickly. (b) On a wide website, information is arranged so that any given document can be reached from any other; this organizational style, though preferable, can overwhelm users not familiar with the subject or who are not seeking specific information.

pages within the sequence are not extensively linked with others, so that users who look for that desired bit of information in another location must retrace their electronic steps back to the top of the website, then follow a different path in the hope of finding the elusive information elsewhere. This sort of website structure (Figure 45.1a) becomes tiresome to use and is rarely necessary.

While such a fixed, highly directed website structure might be desirable where a strict sequence is essential to understanding the subject (such as an online exhibit of successive images or essays whose meaning or significance is lost if viewed in random order), it works to confound and hamper anyone trying to find specific information quickly. It also ignores the one real advantage that the Web offers over other more traditional media: that any document can be linked directly to any other.

A far better approach is to create a site that is as "wide" as possible, with each page linked either to all the others (on a small website), or linked to an index from which other parts of the website can be accessed quickly (Figure 45.1b). This makes navigating the site much easier and quicker, immeasurably improving its utility as a source of reference and information.

Not every web designer chooses the "wide" approach over the "deep," or recognizes its merit. Indeed, one well-known author not long ago condemned hypertext linking as "a kind of video game. . . Jumping from one document to another baffles me even more than watching someone channel-surf. . . Hypertext documents lack unity: One page may be dense with information; another may be a vacuum. . . As a result, the author's logic, structure, and reasoning disappear. You get random fact..." (Stoll, 1995).

This is a valid enough complaint as far as it goes, but the very thing the author complains about is the one strength the Web has over other media: It allows the user to take his or her own path through the material. And if the web designer has done the job properly, there is no reason why the user should be baffled or confused.

DEVELOPING AN ARCHAEOLOGICAL PROJECT WEBSITE

Basic Guidelines

It would be less than useful to make overly specific recommendations about how an archaeological project's website should be designed. Every project is different, and there are far too many variables (not the least of which is the constantly changing technology and capabilities of the World Wide Web itself) to make it practical to offer more than general guidelines for use in building a website. Nonetheless, in the present author's experience of developing websites for archaeological projects and other organizations, several basic principles should apply to any website that focuses on a specific project or scholarly endeavor. While the principles are offered here in the context of nautical archaeology, they apply equally well to terrestrial archaeology or even to disciplines outside anthropology. In addition, the reader should note that several principles are closely related.

The Website Should Be as Comprehensive as Possible. When publishing in a traditional medium—a book or a journal article, for example—there is almost always some outside element that limits the volume of information that can be presented at one time. The limit may be specific and arbitrary, such as a page or word limit prescribed by an editor; or practical, as when a tome becomes too large and expensive to publish. Fortunately, neither of these types of limitations apply to publishing on the Internet via the World Wide Web.

This gives the website developer the opportunity to do something almost impossible to do in anything short of a book-length publication: to create a genuinely comprehensive information resource. While any competent website developer will provide specific and accurate information about a project, it is only when the website's scope is expanded to include the historical and anthropological context of the archaeological site that the potential of web-based publishing comes into play.

This opportunity to include "all the good bits" has its pitfalls. When given the opportunity to hold forth without reservation on a subject that interests them, many authors will gladly drone on at great length, finally coming to a conclusion several pages beyond which the most dedicated reader has since given up the whole endeavor.

A good editor will not let an author get away with "drone" in a journal, and an equally fatal mistake is to allow it in web publishing. Keep things short and to the point. Get an editor, be it a professional editor or a colleague with a critical eye and a stack of red pens, to go over a printout of the website's content. As with printed publications, the best editors are sometimes the most ruthless.

Keep It Simple. Some website designers seem compelled to include as many "bells and whistles" as possible on their websites: animated logos, complex programming routines, and material in file formats that require users to have additional software on their machines. While these features may be viewed as evidence of the web designer's skill and technological sophistication, they are often counterproductive to the web designer's first and most important objective: presenting as much information to as many people as easily as possible. Many high-tech features are not strictly necessary and sometimes cause more trouble than they are worth. File formats or designs that require additional software "plug-ins," as they are known, or the latest version of web browser should never be used to convey essential information about a project. If used at all, they should be restricted to supplemental or complimentary material that the user can do without while still finding the essential information.

Keep It Up to Date.   There are few things more frustrating to web users than sites that are rarely (or never) updated. The frequency of needed updates depends on the nature of the project and should, in general, match the level of activity on the project. On a large project, nothing of particular significance may happen for weeks or months at a time. As the pace of the project picks up during the field season, so should the frequency of updates to the website. Weekly updates from the field, describing general activities, new findings, or interesting events, take some time to prepare but are appropriate in many cases. Regular updates serve to remind the archaeologist's multiple constituencies (public, professional community, and project sponsors such as governmental agencies, universities, or private donors who pay the bills) that the project is active and accomplishing its goals (Figure 45.2).

Make It Easy to Navigate.   The web designer's goal should be to break up the information to be presented into manageable chunks that can be readily accessed and understood by the reader. Any user interested in the description of polychrome ceramics found at a certain site, should not have to wade through extended narratives on the economic significance of maritime trade in that period. Both of these subjects are important to an understanding of the site in all its complexities, but the site should be designed to make it easy to find a particular bit of information. This can be accomplished by including on each web page a link to a site index, a pull-down menu listing other pages, or a series of direct links at the bottom or side of every page.

Integrate!   In some respects, integrating the website into the project is difficult because it requires a shift in thinking. If an "online presence"—a website—is going to be part of an ongoing archaeological project, it must be planned and executed in parallel with the multitude of other logistical and operational elements of the endeavor. Ideally, the project's website should grow and develop as do the scope and knowledge base of the project itself.

In practical terms, this means, first and foremost, that the development of a project website should be anticipated and planned from the early stages of a field project, and that appropriate resources should assigned to it. That means devoting the technical and personnel resources needed to do the job.

Technical resource needs usually can be met without too much difficulty. Numerous software packages exist that can be used to create web pages. These vary considerably in purchase cost and ease of use. Most organizations that sponsor archaeological efforts, such as universities or governmental agencies, already have a web presence of some sort, so getting the project online should not present much problem.

Meeting the personnel needs of a website development project is more complex. Skill in website development is easy enough to come by, particularly among university students, and it seems likely that someone on the crew will be willing, even eager, to take on the task. As with anything else, website development takes time and should be an assigned job within the project organization as preparing crew meals, drafting site plans, and maintaining diving equipment. If the compilation of web material is not made part of the field project, that activity is liable to be one of the first to be dropped when other needs arise, as they invariably do.

Develop Partnerships. If the archaeological project is one that generates a high degree of public interest, it should be feasible to develop a partnership with the local media that includes providing both fixed and updating content via the Internet. Such a partnership benefits both parties: the project, by providing web design, graphic arts, or other skills useful for developing a comprehensive site, while the media outlet (a newspaper, for example) benefits by having extensive, direct access to the project, its personnel, and activities (Figure 45.3).

The Internet offers all of us—archaeologists, historians, and the public alike—an unprecedented range of opportunities and challenges for the future. For those who are prepared to use it wisely, the Internet represents a chance to reach a wider audience and share knowledge quickly and effectively.

Figure 45.2. Nautical archaeologists serve many constituencies, including sponsors, academic administrators, public agency chiefs and, ultimately, the general public. The Internet provides an unparalleled opportunity to present relevant information to all these audiences quickly and effectively. One of the fastest-growing ways to do this is through the use of "webcams" at archaeological sites and laboratories. These allow website visitors to follow archaeological and conservation work in real time, as they happen. Here, workers at the Conservation Research Laboratory, part of the Nautical Archaeology Program at Texas A&M University, reassemble the hull of La Salle's ship *Belle*, lost in Matagorda Bay in 1686 (Image courtesy Conservation Research Laboratory, used with permission).

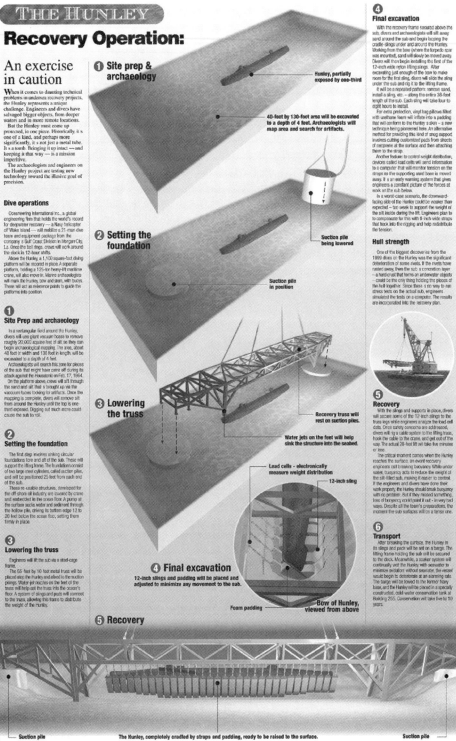

THE HUNLEY
Recovery Operation:

An exercise in caution

When it comes to daunting technical problems in underwater recovery projects, the Hunley represents a unique challenge. Engineers and divers have salvaged bigger objects, from deeper waters and in more remote locations.

But the Hunley must come up protected, in one piece. Historically, it s one of a kind, and perhaps more significantly, it s not just a metal tube. It s a tomb. Bringing it up intact — and keeping it that way — is a mission imperative.

The archaeologists and engineers on the Hunley project are testing new technology toward the illusive goal of precision.

Dive operations

Oceaneering International Inc., a global engineering firm that holds the world's record for deepwater recovery — a Navy helicopter off Wake Island — will mobilize a 21-man dive team and equipment package from the company s Gulf Coast Division in Morgan City, La. Once the bell rings, crews will work around the clock in 12-hour shifts.

Above the Hunley, a 1,100 square-foot diving platform will be anchored in place. A separate platform, holding a 125-ton heavy-lift maritime crane, will also move in. Marine archaeologists will mark the Hunley, bow and stern, with buoys. These will act as reference points to guide the platforms into position.

❶ Site Prep and archaeology

In a rectangular field around the Hunley, divers will use giant vacuum hoses to remove roughly 20,000 square feet of silt so they can begin archaeological mapping. The area, about 40 feet in width and 130 feet in length, will be excavated to a depth of 4 feet.

Archaeologists will search this zone for pieces of the sub that might have come off during its attack against the Housatonic on Feb. 17, 1864.

On the platform above, crews will sift through the sand and silt that s brought up via the vacuum tubes looking for artifacts. Once the mapping is complete, divers will remove silt from around the Hunley until the top is one-third exposed. Digging out much more could cause the sub to roll.

❷ Setting the foundation

The first step involves sinking circular foundations fore and aft of the sub. These will support the lifting frame. The foundations consist of two large steel cylinders, called suction piles, and will be positioned 25 feet from each and of the sub.

These re-usable structures, developed for the off-shore oil industry, are owered by crane and embedded in the ocean floor. A pump at the surface sucks water and sediment through the hollow piles, driving its bottom edge 12 to 20 feet below the ocean floor, setting them firmly in place.

❸ Lowering the truss

Engineers will lift the sub via a steel-cage frame.

The 55-foot by 10 foot metal truss will be placed atop the Hunley and afixed to the suction pilings. Water-jet nozzles on the feet of the truss will help set the truss into the ocean's floor. A system of slings and pods will connect to the truss, allowing this frame to distribute the weight of the Hunley.

❶ Site prep & archaeology

Hunley, partially exposed by one-third

40-foot by 130-foot area will be excavated to a depth of 4 feet. Archaeologists will map area and search for artifacts.

❷ Setting the foundation

Suction pile being lowered

Suction pile in position

❸ Lowering the truss

Recovery truss will rest on suction piles.

Water jets on the feet will help sink the structure into the seabed.

Lead cells - electronically measure weight distribution

12-inch sling

❹ Final excavation

12-inch slings and padding will be placed and adjusted to minimize any movement to the sub.

Foam padding

Bow of Hunley, viewed from above

❺ Recovery

❹ Final excavation

With the recovery frame secured above the sub, divers and archaeologists will sift away sand around the sub and begin looping the cradle-slings under and around the Hunley. Working from the bow (where the torpedo spar was mounted), sand will slowly be moved away. Divers will then begin installing the first of the 12-inch wide nylon lifting slings. After excavating just enough of the bow to make room for the first sling, divers will slide the sling under the sub and drag it to the lifting frame.

It will be a repeated pattern: remove sand, install a sling, etc. — along the entire 38-foot length of the sub. Each sling will take four to eight hours to install.

For extra protection, vinyl bag pillows filled with urethane foam will inflate into a padding that will conform to the Hunley s skin — a new technique being pioneered here. An alternative method for providing this kind of snug support involves cutting customized pads from sheets of neoprene at the surface and then attaching them to the strap.

Another feature: to control weight distribution, devices called load cells will send information to a computer that will monitor tension on the straps as the supporting sand base is moved away. It s an early warning system that gives engineers a constant picture of the forces at work on the sub below.

In a worst-case scenario, the downward-facing side of the Hunley could be weaker than expected — too weak to support the weight of the silt inside during the lift. Engineers plan to compensate for this with 8-inch wide straps that hook into the rigging and help redistribute the tension.

Hull strength

One of the biggest discoveries from the 1999 dives on the Hunley was the significant deterioration of some rivets. If the rivets have rusted away, then the sub s concretion layer — a hard crust that forms on underwater objects — could be the only thing holding the pieces of the hull together. Since there s no way to run stress tests on the actual sub, engineers simulated the tests on a computer. The results are incorporated into the recovery plan.

❺ Recovery

With the slings and supports in place, divers will secure some of the 12-inch slings to the truss legs while engineers analyze the load cell data. Once safety concerns are addressed, divers will rig a cable system to the lifting truss, hook the cable to the crane, and get out of the way. The actual 28-foot lift will take five minutes or less.

The critical moment comes when the Hunley reaches the surface, an event recovery engineers call breaking buoyancy. While under water, buoyancy acts to reduce the weight of the silt-filled sub, making it easier to control. If the engineers and divers have done their work properly, the Hunley should break buoyancy with no problem. But if they missed something, loss of buoyancy could point it out - in very bad ways. Despite all the team's preparations, the moment the sub surfaces will be a tense one.

❻ Transport

After breaking the surface, the Hunley in its slings and pads will be set on a barge. The lifting frame holding the sub will be secured to the deck. Meanwhile, a soaker system will continually wet the Hunley with seawater to minimize oxidation without seawater, the vessel would begin to deteriorate at an alarming rate. The barge will be towed to the former Navy base, and the Hunley will be placed in a specially constructed, cold-water conservation tank at Building 255. Conservation will take five to 10 years.

Suction pile

Suction pile

The Hunley, completely cradled by straps and padding, ready to be raised to the surface.

Sources: National Park Service, Naval Historical Center, S.C. Institute of Archaeology and Anthropology, Oceaneering International Inc.   Post and Courier Graphic by Gill Guerry

Figure 45.3. Most archaeology projects have limited resources dedicated to disseminating information about the project to the general public. At the same time, many media outlets have very sophisticated resources, especially in the areas of graphic design and illustration, that can be applied to archaeological endeavors that may be of interest to their audiences. A partnership between archaeologists and media organizations, whether formal or informal, can significantly enhance a project's visibility in print, broadcast, and web-based media. This image, produced by the *Charleston* (South Carolina) *Post and Courier* newspaper, shows the techniques used in raising the American Civil War submarine *H.L. Hunley* in 2000. This image appeared both in the newspaper and on the newspaper's website (Courtesy *Charleston Post & Courier*, used with permission).

REFERENCES

Bastian, Beverly E., and Bergstrom, Randolph, 1993, Reviewing Gray Literature: Drawing Public History's Most Applied Works out of the Shadows. *The Public Historian* 15 (2):63–77.

Keating, A.B.,. and Hargitai, Joseph, 1999, *The Wired Professor: A Guide to Incorporating the World Wide Web in College Instruction*. New York University Press, New York.

Lawrence, J., 2000, Going Beyond Default: Constructing Alternative Families. World Wide Web document, September. http://staffweb.lib.uiowa.edu/jlawrence/old/Family/Writing Research.html.

McDavid, Carol, 1998, Archaeology and "the Web": Writing Multi-linear Texts in a Multi-centered Community. Presentation to the 1998 Conference on Historical and Underwater Archaeology, Society for Historical Archaeology, Atlanta, Georgia. Archived at: http://www.webarchaeology.com/Html/carolsha.htm.

NUA Internet Surveys, 2000, Messaging Online: One Billion E-mail Accounts by 2002. World Wide Web document, http://www.nua.ie/surveys/?f=VS&art_id=905355701&rel=true

NUA Internet Surveys, 1999, E-mail now Primary Reason People Go Online. World Wide Web document, http://www.nua.ie/surveys/?f=VS&art_id=905355315&rel=true.

Government Agencies

Government agencies play an important role in monitoring national historical treasures. Guidebooks, public education, and funding are necessary segments for the agencies' operation. The role they have played in the development of underwater archaeology can been seen in these three chapters, as well as in the chapters of the Geography section, where chapter authors detail the involvement of many governments around the world.

Robert Neyland presents the recovery of military vessels and planes by the U.S. Navy, which has been so important to the history of the United States. He discusses the overall picture of what has been found submerged but also the gaps, of which there are many. What has been investigated needs quality reporting to make the contribution known and useful. After inventories, assessment, and management are put in place, priorities for selective research should go forward.

The National Marine Sanctuary Program is the main theme of Bruce Terrell's chapter on the National Oceangraphic and Atmospheric Administration (NOAA), which now manages 12 sanctuaries. The national sanctuaries (the first of which was the Monitor NMS) protect and preserve historical properties in federally-managed areas. Working with state governments, NOAA will be able to bring into existence even more sanctuaries. Funding is, as always, the all-important issue. Budgetary constraints are many.

Calvin Cummings presents the work of the Submerged Cultural Resource Program of the Department of Interior's National Park Service. The program has grown and matured in a relatively short time. He concludes that historic shipwrecks and inundated prehistoric remains are our most neglected resource.

[*Editor's Note*: Cal Cummings wrote and submitted the chapter on the National Park Service for the *International Handbook of Underwater Archaeology* before he died September 2, 2000.]

Chapter 46

Preserving and Interpreting the Archaeology of the United States Navy

ROBERT S. NEYLAND

INTRODUCTION

Interpretation of naval archaeological sites is more than a study of military strategy, technology, or transmission of culture. Through time, naval victories and defeats have been pivotal to the fate of nations: Ramses II's defeat of the Sea People, the Battle of Lepanto, destruction of the Spanish Armada, and the Battle of Midway, all of which were turning points in history. The archaeological remains of the United States Navy lie buried in the silts of U.S. rivers and harbors, beneath the tides and sands of foreign beaches, in clear Caribbean and Mediterranean waters, and in the vast canyons of the Pacific Ocean. The Navy's history, evidenced in its submerged ship and aircraft wrecks, is the history of the United States, from its birth to its rise to global leadership. Ships and people were lost both at home and abroad in events that shaped U.S. and world history, global culture, and technology. The navy's goal is to develop policies and programs to preserve and, as time and funding allow, study and interpret these military sites as a functional category.

Robert S. Neyland, Head, Underwater Archaeology Branch, Naval Historical Center, Washington Navy Yard, Washington, DC 20374.

International Handbook of Underwater Archaeology, edited by Carol V. Ruppé and Janet F. Barstad. Kluwer Academic/Plenum Publishers, New York, 2002.

Table 46.1. Navy Ship Losses during War and Peace.

Years	Conflict	Losses	Military unit	
1714–1775		0	U.S. Navy	2353
1776–1783	American Revolution	41	U.S. Army	19
1784–1811		10	Continental Navy	41
1812–1815	War of 1812	72	Confederate State Navy	244
1816–1860		38	Confederate States Army	77
1861–1865	American Civil War	210		
1866–1916	Spanish-American War	53		
1917–1918	World War I	76		
1919–1940		179		
1941–1945	World War II	948		
1946–present		726		
Total		2353	*Total*	2734

There are potentially as many as 3000 U.S. naval shipwrecks worldwide, although the majority lie within United States waters. World War II losses represent the largest number, with 1084 wrecks. Those sunk shortly after the war are the second highest group, with 740 wrecks, and the third largest group are those from the American Civil War, a listing of 564 that includes 320 confederate naval losses (Table 46.1).

Thus, U.S. Navy wrecks begin with those of the Continental Navy and extend through World War II. Numbers include ships lost while under the jurisdiction of the U.S. Army and under the Maritime Administration. Potential naval aircraft wrecks are far more extensive than shipwrecks and may exceed 12,000 worldwide. Although these numbers seem large, they are but an approximation made from the historical records. Actual numbers may be lower, since time, current, dredging, and salvage have taken a toll.

POLICY AND ADMINISTRATION

These wrecks have not been abandoned by the passage of time. The Navy retains custody of its ship and aircraft wrecks by the principle of "sovereign immunity," and wrecks remain United States property unless the government takes a specific formal action of disposal. Naval wrecks are immune from the law of salvage unless appropriate Navy authorization is given. Immunity is founded in historic principles of maritime law. Sovereign ownership was recognized in the Abandoned Shipwreck Act of 1987 (43 USC 2101-6), which excluded transfer of ownership of naval wrecks to the states. Establishing that right, title, and ownership of United States government property is not lost with the passage of time or by neglect or inaction, is the property clause of the United States Constitution (Article IV, Section 3, Clause 2), Articles 95 and 96 of the United Nations Convention on the Law of the Sea (1982), and precedents of International Maritime Law. This doctrine has been upheld in United States case law, such as Hatteras Inc. vs. the USS Hatteras, her engines, etc. *in rem* and the United States of America, *in personam* (1984 A.M.C. 1094, aff'd, 698 F.2nd 1215, 5th Cir. [1982]), and U.S. vs. Richard Steinmetz (763 F.Supp. 1293, 1294, [d.n.j. 1991]; aff'd, 973 F.2nd 212, [3rd Cir. 1992] cert. Denied, 113 S. Ct. 1578 [1993]. This doctrine was also upheld in an October 4 1996 admiralty decision, Historic Aircraft Preservation, Inc. (HAPI) vs. One Wrecked and Abandoned F4F-4 Wildcat Fighter Airplane, *in rem*, and United States of America (In Admiralty,

Figure 46.1. USS *Kearsage* sinking CSS *Alabama* off Cherbourg, France.

Civil No. C95-0795Z, presided over by the Honorable Thomas S. Zilly, Entered October 4, 1996).

The Naval Historical Center (NHC) is responsible for managing sunken United States properties. NHC and the Office of the Judge Advocate General, Admiralty Division, have been involved for some time in protecting historic navy shipwrecks on a case-by-case basis. One of the most significant and problematic of wrecks was CSS *Alabama*, a confederate warship sunk by USS *Kearsarge* six miles off the coast of Cherbourg, France. In November 1984, *Alabama* was discovered by the French navy and excavated by a French archaeological team (Gúerout, 1995). Although the warship lay in the territorial waters of France, negotiations between the two nations led to a diplomatic note providing that the wreck and its artifacts were the property of the United States, the successor government to the Confederacy, but that the laws of France applied to the excavation (Dudley, 1995).

In 1993, underwater archaeologist David Cooper came to the NHC on loan from the state of Wisconsin's Office of the State Historic Preservation Officer (SHPO) to assist the NHC in developing management plans for shipwrecks such as *Alabama* and the navy's ship and aircraft wrecks. Cooper initiated a draft management plan and a naval wreck database and tackled the difficult issue of treating naval aircraft as properties of potential national register eligibility. In 1994, the author replaced David Cooper as underwater archaeologist and, in 1996, the NHC established an Underwater Archaeology Branch (UAB).

NHC's UAB organized an underwater archaeology program within the Navy by developing management policies and procedures and by inventorying all wrecks potentially under navy jurisdiction. The branch encouraged partnerships with state agencies and universities for preservation and research, and most recently developed its own archaeological field capabilities (Table 46.2).

Table 46.2. Navy Ship Losses by State.

Alabama	28	Mississippi	54
Alaska	37	Nebraska	1
Arkansas	12	New Hampshire	5
California	122	New Jersey	20
Connecticut	4	New York	68
District of Columbia	6	North Carolina	134
Delaware	9	Ohio	1
Florida	97	Oregon	5
Georgia	31	Pennsylvania	7
Hawaii	36	Rhode Island	31
Illinois	2	South Carolina	96
Louisiana	72	Tennessee	30
Massachusetts	45	Texas	22
Maryland	43	Virginia	211
Maine	12	Vermont	1
Michigan	4	Washington	13
Missouri	2	*Total*	1261

SUCCESSION TO THE CONFEDERATE NAVY

During the Civil War, the Confederate navy and army lost some 320 vessels, most resulting directly from military action. These include such famous warships as CSS *Alabama* and *Florida* and the earliest attempts at submarine warfare, *American Diver* and *H.L. Hunley*. *Pioneer*, the predecessor of Confederate submarines, is not the property of the United States: It carried a Letter of Marque and was thus a true privateer, distinguishable from Confederate navy commerce raiders such as *Alabama* and *Florida*. *Pioneer* was scuttled April 1862, prior to the fall of New Orleans.

Confederate naval vessels are under the Administrator of the General Services Administration (GSA), a responsibility GSA inherited from the Department of the Treasury (Neyland, 1996). An 1870 Joint Resolution of Congress provided for the secretary of treasury to collect "moneys, dues, and other interests lately in the possession of or due to the so-called Confederate States, or their agents, and now belonging to the United States" (Forty-first Congress, Session II, Res. 75, 1870). On June 2, 1965, the resolution was incorporated into 40 U.S.C. 310, so that the administrator of GSA is responsible for these sunken vessels.

The United States Supreme Court developed the doctrine of succession concerning Confederate property in an 1872 Supreme Court decision, *United States, Lyon, et al. v. Huckabee* (83 U.S. 414 1872), in which the court ruled that property purchased and owned by the Confederacy passed to the conqueror, the United States, which became the "absolute owner." This continued to be the prevailing opinion; in *Williams v. Bruffy* (96 U.S. 176 1877: 188), the court made a similar decision: "... the Confederacy failed and in its failure its pretensions were dissipated, its armies scattered, and the whole fabric of its government broken in pieces. The very property it had amassed passed to the nation."

The principle of succession was applied to shipwrecks of the Confederacy with *Leathers v. Salvor Wrecking etc., Co.* (15 Fed. Cas. 116, No.8164 1875: 116). The court stated in regard to the wreckage of the steamboat *Natchez* (pressed into Confederate service and burned and sunk during that service) that "... whatever was left of her hull and machinery belonged to that government, and, by consequence, became the property of the United States." The principle has been extended even to the present day in *United States v. Steinmetz*, which considered ownership of the bell of CSS *Alabama*. The wreck of CSS *Alabama* was not considered abandoned by the mere passage of time. The court applied the doctrine of sovereign immunity to property formerly owned by the government of the Confederacy and held that the United States rightfully succeeded to the property of the former. In so doing, the court recognized that, despite the rhetoric used during the Civil War to describe Confederate raiders as pirates and the citizens of the rebelling states as traitors, the federal government had in its prosecution of the war dealt with the Confederacy as a sovereign nation, although an adversarial one (Poser and Varon, 1995). This case also interpreted United States' ownership as unaffected by the passage of time or by failing to salvage the property.

NAVY AIRCRAFT WRECKS

Aircraft are machines of our recent past. Navy and Army Air Corps aircraft were mass-produced in the thousands during World War II. Once plentiful, they are becoming increasingly rare as their historical significance grows. Military aircraft wrecks, particularly those known as "Warbirds," from World War II, are highly sought after by museums, collectors, and salvors and are extremely threatened wreck sites. The navy, represented by NHC, has become a leader in aviation archaeology and the preservation of historic aviation resources.

It is difficult to calculate the total number of navy aircraft wrecks. The navy has more than 35,000 "Aircraft Crash Cards" for World War II. However, many crash reports refer to aircraft repaired, removed, scrapped for parts, or otherwise eliminated, and each of these records requires scrutiny. After many grueling hours, NHC personnel estimate that about 12,000 Crash Cards might represent extant terrestrial and submerged Navy aircraft wrecks.

Developing Policy for Submerged Navy Aircraft

In developing its underwater archaeology program, NHC believed that its primary focus would be shipwrecks. Requests from salvors and museums alike made it apparent that naval aircraft from World War II and earlier were hunted intensely and that they rivaled shipwrecks as management concerns (Cooper, 1994). Reports of aircraft recoveries, both real and imagined, came from numerous locations in the United states and the distant Pacific. The NHC was forced to actively pursue the archaeology of naval aviation by the competing demands of aviation museums, salvors, and the resulting immediate threats to the preservation of the underwater remains of navy aircraft (Whipple, 1995).

Before World War II aircraft reached the 50-year threshold date for National Register consideration, navy aircraft wrecks were dealt with as surplus equipment that must satisfy legal requirements for disposal of federal property, demilitarization of weapons systems, munitions, and human remains. A Naval Air System Command Fact Sheet of May 1987 (United States Navy [USN], 1987), states that navy aircraft belong to the government of the United States until the navy determines their disposition, which, as defined in the fact sheet, can be "recovery, loan or donation to a qualified organization, or sold either intact or as scrap." The fact sheet provided the possibility of public sale through the Defense Reutilization and Marketing Service (DRMS) but stipulated there were no assurances that any located and identified aircraft would be offered for public sale.

The 1987 memorandum illustrates that the navy was already engaged in defending title over wrecked aircraft well before the NHC became involved. Two examples include a TBF Avenger recovered off the Florida coast in the mistaken belief it was from the lost Flight 19, and a stripped and burned Helldiver recovered from Lake Washington. Also in the 1980s, two part-time salvors found navy aircraft in Lake Michigan, lost during World War II-era carrier qualification training. A Douglas SBD Dauntless dive-bomber and a Grumman F4F Wildcat fighter were first recovered for loan to Patriots Point Museum in Mount Pleasant, South Carolina. Captain Bob Rasmussen, director of the navy's National Museum of Naval Aviation (NMNA), heard of the recoveries, of which his museum did not have examples, and realized the cold waters of Lake Michigan had preserved a wealth of Navy World War II aircraft. He also discovered that these submerged aircraft might be used in trade for aircraft recoveries, restoration services, or even as items to trade with museums for other aircraft (U.S. law allowed military museums to exchange one item for another). In 1988, Congressman Earl Hutto helped NMNA by sponsoring legislation making it possible for military museums to exchange equipment for services, including salvage and restoration. NMNA used this mechanism to trade title to two Wildcats and a Dauntless for the services of A&T Recovery. In return, A&T Recovery salvaged a Vought Vindicator, a Dauntless, and a Wildcat for the museum. To date, NMNA has sponsored more than two dozen aircraft recoveries from Lake Michigan and credits the trading program with supplying half of its collection (Hoffman, 1998). Its trading policies also encouraged the creation of a market for navy aircraft, thereby fostering a climate of exploitation.

As NHC became involved in underwater archaeology, it was faced with ensuring that other navy commands followed NHPA guidance. This was applied to the Lake Michigan and other aircraft recoveries proposed by the museum. An SBD-3 Dauntless, veteran of the Battle of Midway and Pearl Harbor and eligible for listing on the National Register, was the most significant navy aircraft recovered from Lake Michigan waters (Wills, 1997) (Figure 46.2).

A Grumman F6F-5 Hellcat was the first contest NHC fought over aircraft over both ownership and historic preservation. In 1993, an aircraft wreck was spotted on the seabed off Martha's Vineyard, Massachusetts, during a U.S. Coast Guard aerial security patrol. The wreck was investigated and identified as World War II vintage, and more research revealed it was an aircraft attached to a Night Air Combat Training Unit headquartered at Charleston, Rhode Island. On April 3, 1945, the aircraft ditched due to engine failure; the pilot escaped from the sinking aircraft but perished in the 42-degree water. Of the 7869 Hellcats built during World War II, only 20 are now extant, and this specific Hellcat was found to be an early production variant, of which only 1404 were built (Weekly, 1994).

Quonset Air Museum, a fledgling air museum in Rhode Island, was immediately interested in adding this aircraft to its collection and proceeded with recovery. Initial recovery efforts failed because of a lack of removal of sediments. Publicity about these efforts alerted the Naval Historical Center, which contacted Quonset Museum, which requested the loan or donation of the aircraft. In response, the NHC requested a submission of plans for recovery, conservation, and restoration, and warned Quonset that it must first obtain the Navy's permission before recovery. Damon Ise, president of Quonset Museum, agreed not to proceed further without the Navy's approval. This promise was soon forgotten, however, and on December 5, 1993, Quonset recovered the Hellcat without notifying the navy (Weekly 1994:13–14). Although the recovery was lauded in local press accounts, the Hellcat suffered significant damage from the recovery, losing the tail section, wings, and engine.

Figure 46.2. SBD-2 being pulled from the Lake Michigan.

This breach of faith forced the navy's hand, and the Judge Advocate General, Admiralty Division, requested Naval Criminal Investigative Service to initiate an investigation. In an effort to deter others from similar salvage attempts, the navy asked that the aircraft be turned over and transported to the National Museum of Naval Aviation in Pensacola, Florida, at Quonset's expense. In reality, this course of action was a disadvantage for NMNA, which already had a Hellcat in its collection. The new acquisition would force reallocation of scarce resources to pay for restoration and conservation.

Quonset sued for ownership of the aircraft and eventually spent several thousand dollars on legal fees. The navy responded by defending government ownership. Both sides took a beating in the newspapers: The navy was portrayed as the schoolyard bully and Quonset as a looter of war graves and taker of federal property. The press made more than a few David-and-Goliath comparisons. Eventually, an out-of-court settlement was reached whereby Quonset Air Museum obtained the aircraft on loan, and the aircraft remained navy property and would be conserved and restored according to navy standards. In this agreement, replacement of parts would be minimal, and the aircraft would be stabilized and exhibited as an artifact from the seabed.

This was not the only issue over ownership of navy aircraft. As the Hellcat incident was resolved, two other legal cases were developing. One confrontation occurred over a rare navy aircraft 20 miles off the coast of Florida in 500 feet of water, the other over an aircraft pulled from the Indiana waters of Lake Michigan. The former was a Douglas TBD Devastator discovered in 1991 by New York-based treasure hunter Robert Cervoni, who first offered to sell the coordinates to the National Museum of Naval Aviation for $25,000. After the Navy did not immediately purchase the coordinates, Cervoni sold the coordinates for $75,000 to Doug Champlin, a collector of World War II aircraft, who had a museum in Arizona. Champlin attempted to trade the coordinates to NMNA for one or two Wildcats recovered from Lake Michigan. In early 1994, he hired a submarine to recover a portion of the aircraft's canopy and directed his attorney to arrest the aircraft as abandoned property in a Miami court. When NHC discovered that an admiralty arrest had been made in federal court, it requested JAG-Admiralty Division and Department of Justice-Civil Division (DOJ) take immediate action. DOJ, after investigating the merit of the case, threatened civil and criminal sanctions if the admiralty arrest of the aircraft were not dropped and the canopy immediately turned over to the navy. The canopy was delivered to NMNA, and the admiralty suit was dropped. However, this was far from the end of attempts to gain control of the TBD or receive money or other aircraft in trade from the navy in exchange for recovery or coordinates (Hoffman, 1998). There would be continued attempts to overturn navy policies through court precedent and congressional legislation.

As the Department of Justice was resolving the TBD case, Naval Criminal Investigative Service (NCIS) was pursuing Florida salvor Peter Theophanis for his taking of a Douglas Dauntless SBD aircraft in 1993. Theophanis originally was searching for an aircraft he hoped to sell to the NMNA. Unable to find that aircraft, he offered to recover another navy aircraft for the museum but was rejected. Unknown to the navy, Theophanis later brought up this Navy aircraft from Indiana waters and delivered it on the dock to a middleman buyer, who then resold it to a private collector. The recovery, which took place at night, was discovered by a reporter listening to a marine radio, and reported in a local paper. A&T Recovery, a rival salvage firm, informed on Theophanis, and the NMNA requested the NCIS investigate. Theophanis failed to turn over the aircraft as requested; perhaps he no longer knew where it was. The U.S. Attorney's Office issued a warrant for his arrest on charges of theft of government property. During the trial, it was discovered that the identifying bureau number of the aircraft was mis-identified, and the case was dismissed on this technicality (Hoffman, 1998).

Shortly afterward, a civil court case in the state of Washington was initiated against a navy aircraft located on the bottom of Lake Washington. The Washington federal court may have been chosen intentionally for a 1984 court ruling against the navy. In this earlier case, the judge ruled in his 1985 decision that the navy had shown evidence of abandoning a specific Curtis Helldiver (*United States of America, v. Jeffrey Kenneth Hummel and Matthew W. Mc Cauley*, U.S. District Court, Western District of Washington at Seattle, Case No. C84-1058C), which the navy had stripped, burned repeatedly in fire-fighting practice, and finally taken out in Lake Washington and sunk. In his 1984 decision, the judge ruled that navy abandonment applied only to this specific aircraft and did not apply to any other navy aircraft in Lake Washington. Regardless of the limitations of this court ruling, the plaintiff, Historic Aircraft Preservation Inc., chose to arrest a navy Wildcat on May 24, 1995. In the resulting 1996 decision, the court ruled in favor of the navy and ordered that the Warrant of Arrest of the aircraft be vacated. In addition, the court stipulated that the plaintiff was prohibited from conducting salvage operations or any other activities that interfered with the United States ownership interest in the aircraft and ordered that any pieces of the aircraft be turned over to the navy (*Historic Aircraft Preservation Inc. v. One wrecked and Abandoned F4-F-4 Wildcat Fighter Airplane*, U. S. District Court, Western District of Washington At Seattle, Civil No. C95-0795 Z).

The ruling in favor of the navy may have inspired Doug Champlin (who still maintained his interest in the TBD aircraft and who is a constituent of Senator John McCain of Arizona) to attempt to obtain the senator's support for a proposed navy Warbird Act, which would formally abandon all navy aircraft lost prior to November 19, 1961. The NHC and Navy JAG denounced this act as a self-serving attempt to benefit financially a few salvors, collectors, and their attorneys at the expense of the American public. The navy's review of the proposed legislation found it to be in conflict with the Federal Property Act, 40 U.S.C. 512. Not only was the legislation unnecessary, but if it had passed, it would have encouraged disturbance of war graves, fostered commercial exploitation, depleted a finite resource, and harmed the public's interest in these historic aircraft. The saga of the TBD continues, for attempts were renewed in 1998 to place the wreck under Admiralty Court arrest.

Why the intense interest of salvors in navy aircraft? Dollars, real and anticipated, are the principle motive. The Hellcat recovered by Quonset Air Museum, though badly damaged, had an estimated value of $200,000. Two Lake Michigan Wildcats recovered by A&T Recovery were reported to have been sold for $250,000 apiece. The rare TBD was estimated to have a value of $1–2 million once it was restored. In the crush to build collections, aircraft museums have been an impetus for recoveries and have been instrumental in creating a market value for historic aircraft. This is a familiar pattern with museums, for it is similar to how the acquisition practices of many museums of fine arts and archaeology stimulated looting of archaeological artifacts and illegal collecting of stolen art (Herscher, 1998).

POLICIES OF THE U.S. AIR FORCE AND THE U.S. NAVY

Air Force

The U.S. Air Force's policy differs strikingly from that of the navy's. Air Force policy is provided in a 1994 Air Force manual (United States Air Force, 1994):

> Aircraft that crashed before 19 November 1961 (when a fire destroyed pertinent Air Force records), and that remain wholly or partially unrecovered, are considered formally abandoned. The Air Force neither maintains title to nor has property interest in these aircraft. The authority for access to and recovery of these aircraft, as well as liability for damages associated with their recovery, are matters to be resolved between persons seeking recovery and landowners of the wreckage sites.

In 1996, the Air Force added the following caveat:

> if any human remains are discovered at the site, recovery personnel should immediately contact the nearest United States Embassy or United States military installation. To assist in proper identification of remains, recovery personnel should refrain from further operations at the site pending removal of the remains by United States experts (United States Air Force, 1996).

Air force records lost in a fire may be found elsewhere. According to the web site for the Air Force Historical Research Agency (AFHRA), its agency "maintains individual records for all aircraft once or presently in the United States Air Force inventory. These records begin in 1924 and continue to July 1990 and appear to be about 98 percent complete" (United States Air Force, 1998). Aircraft salvors dispute the air force's claim that the records were lost. One career aircraft salvor created his private database from approximately 67,000 individual Army Air Corps and Air Force accident records (Hoffman, 1997). Perhaps as many as 44,000 of these records are aircraft lost in accidents. Potential wreck sites represent possibly half this number.

Air force abandonment was the basis for attempting to force the navy to abandon its aircraft in the recently proposed Warbird Act. The navy has not disputed the Air Force's claim of abandonment, but other agencies have not recognized the Air Force's assertion as legitimate abandonment (Pelkofer, 1998).

Navy Leadership

Since 1993, NHC has significantly advanced the cause of historic aircraft preservation. By undertaking NHPA, Section 106 compliance, NHC has used the same measuring sticks applied to other historic properties. Applying NHPA to aircraft, however, has not been as straightforward as its application to historic buildings, archaeological sites, and ships. Because of the ambiguities about aircraft wrecks, in 1993 NHC sponsored the development of a National Register Bulletin, *Guidelines for Evaluating and Documenting Historic Aircraft Properties* (Millebrooke, 1998). This bulletin provides guidance for federal agencies in managing historic aviation properties, including aircraft and aircraft wrecks. Another ongoing NHC project is an inventory of navy aircraft wrecks and recommended guidelines for documenting them.

The navy maintains ownership of its historic aircraft in order to preserve the nation's heritage in naval aviation. In a letter from the Advisory Council on Historic Preservation, Deputy Executive Director John M. Fowler, commented on navy policy:

> By continuing to claim ownership we believe that the navy is in a good position to advance the causes of preservation of those aircraft that are historic, i.e., that meet the criteria for inclusion in the National Register of Historic Places. . .we believe the navy's ownership position is consistent with the stated goals of the National Historic Preservation Act (16 U.S.C. 470 as amended). Sections 110 (a)(1) and (d) of the Act require that Federal agencies assume responsibility for the preservation of their historic properties, and carry out programs which further the purposes of this Act. By maintaining jurisdiction over their downed aircraft, and by supporting the restoration, education, and display of those historic properties significant to the Navy in particular and the history of aviation in general, the Navy is taking a reasonable and responsible role in the field of aircraft historic preservation (Fowler, 1994).

WAR GRAVES

The Memorial in Pearl Harbor, rising over the wreck of USS *Arizona*, epitomizes the sense that the site of a "war grave" should be treated with dignity, respect, and honor (Lenihan, 1989). Surprisingly, the term "war graves" does not have a legal definition in United States law. Nonetheless, navy policy is clear where the remains of deceased service men are concerned. In the case of salvage of U.S. warships, the navy does not easily, if at all, grant permission for salvage to wrecks that contain the remains of service men. Although there are exceptions to this policy, it has been in force for some time, as the example set by USS *Tecumseh* illustrates.

Exploded by a mine in 1864 during an assault on Mobile, Alabama, the ship sank with 93 men on board. No attempt was made to recover *Tecumseh* until 1873, when it was sold for salvage (West, 1995). When the relatives of the men who died learned that the salvor proposed to blast the wreck into portions with explosives, they protested to Congress to stop the salvage, and Congress complied. The money was returned to the salvor, and the wreck was turned over to the Secretary of the Navy. In Joint Resolution No. 23, Congress further stipulated that any salvage must provide for the removal and proper burial of the crew's remains.

The Civil War gunboat USS *Tulip*, most of whose crew were killed in a boiler explosion, is another example. Correspondence in navy files, dating to 1929, 1951, and 1967, provided continued concern over the remains of both the crew members buried ashore and those carried down with the ship. (Ellicott, 1929, Hefferman, 1951; [Eller], 1969). In the latter case, the Navy refused a 1967 request from a diving club for salvage rights to *Tulip*, primarily on the basis of "non-desecration of crew members entombed in sunken naval vessels."

A more famous example can be found with the War of 1812 vessels, *Hamilton* and *Scourge*. When these vessels were transferred to the government of Canada, a principal consideration was the treatment of the remains of the service men on board. These remains were to be transferred back to the United States for burial (Claytor, 1979).

PARTNERSHIPS AND RECIPROCITY

Unlike other federal land managers, the navy only occasionally owns the river, lake, or seabottom on which its submerged wrecks lie. This means that some other federal, state, or foreign agency has jurisdiction over the wreck site. In addition, the Navy's wrecks are spread over a broad geographic area, making it logistically difficult for the navy to monitor them. With overlapping state and federal jurisdictions, there is also room for conflict. The Abandoned Shipwreck Act clearly provided that sovereign vessels are not abandoned and were not transferred to the states with the passage of the act. However, naval wrecks are frequently some of the most historically significant resources within state waters, sites that generate intense public interest and local, state, and national pride. They are often part of local lore, a part of the historic landscape and local identity.

Realizing that any real preservation depends upon the support of the public, NHC UAB has sought from the beginning to create partnerships with states and local groups. One way to accomplish this was to help states inventory and assess naval wrecks within their respective state waters and thus create a navy–state framework for more effective partnering and management. These projects also proposed to evaluate which wrecks had been affected by environmental and human action, to rank the wrecks from most to least threatened, to rank those most important for archaeological research, and to determine which should be developed for recreational diving. navy–state partnerships also were designed to build bridges between federal and state agencies and reduce the possibility of conflict.

Funding from the Department of Defense Legacy Resource Management Program enabled the creation of naval wreck inventories and management plans on a state and regional basis. This approach is similar to the way the services pursued cultural resource management on military bases with Integrated Cultural Resource Management Plans (ICRMP). In 1995, NHC initiated such projects with North Carolina, Texas, Florida, and the Lake Champlain region, soon followed by Rhode Island, Washington, Maryland, Massachusetts, South Carolina, and Virginia. Inventory and management plans are being followed up with programmatic agreements for coordination between the state and navy and for partnering for effective management.

The Navy is contemplating this strategy of reciprocity for wrecks outside the United States that lie in foreign waters, or with the navies of countries having wrecks in United States waters. Nations under consideration for partnering are France, Great Britain, Germany, and Spain. French waters contain 91 U.S. Navy shipwrecks, most from World Wars I and II, and including the Civil War wreck CSS *Alabama*. A smaller number of French naval shipwrecks lie in United States waters but, like their British and Spanish counterparts, they are a significant group of archaeological sites in the United States. These include many wrecks of exploration, the colonial era, and the American Revolution. Effective management of naval wrecks in foreign waters is dependent upon the cooperation of the nations and the willingness to reciprocate in managing the others' wrecks. To accomplish this, NHC, Navy JAG Admiralty, and the Department of State are working together to initiate agreements of reciprocity between the aforementioned nations.

The Pacific Ocean contains a large number of navy wrecks. Midway Atoll, Guam, the Philippines, and the Solomon Islands contain significant numbers of wrecks, many of which are threatened by salvors and recreational divers. For a small island chain far removed from the United States, the Solomon Islands initiates numerous communications to NHC, related to salvors' attempts to recover and sell navy aircraft wrecks located in their waters. NHC has denied salvage right to salvors in the Solomon Islands and Philippines. Closer to home, the Bahaman government withdrew a salvor's permit at the request of the director of the Naval Historical Center. This affected the Civil War-era wreck of USS *Courier*, a sailing ship carrying supplies lost on a reef in 1864. This set an encouraging precedent for protecting U.S. Navy wrecks from salvors operating in foreign waters.

LOOKING TO THE FUTURE OF RESEARCH

The NHC UAB is encouraging research on naval shipwrecks and is developing capabilities for research and field archaeology. As with state and regional management projects, NHC has used DOD Legacy money to encourage research on significant wrecks, projects that include survey work for the remains of the War of 1812 Chesapeake Flotilla, archaeological surveys of the War of 1812 gunboats *Allen* and *Linnet*, and survey for the American Revolution fleet lost in Maine's Penobscot River. NHC participated in or initiated surveys on the shipwreck believed to be the 1820 United States Schooner *Alligator*, a 1996 survey on the Confederate submarine *H.L. Hunley*, and an unidentified late-18th century vessel located on navy property in Key West, Florida. NHC and NPS–SCRU have actively partnered on various projects to further both of their programs and the quality of archaeological research on naval wrecks. NHC's mission is research and analysis of the navy's history, as well as the preservation and interpretation of that history.

Orser and Fagan (1995), in their text *Historical Archaeology*, point out a number of site types that are studied by function; a prominent example is military sites. For some time, terrestrial archaeologists have focused on military sites, forts, and battlefields as deserving special consideration.

Warships, smaller combat craft, military transports, auxiliary craft, privateers, and naval aircraft from our recent past are our primary naval sites. Naval shipyards, smaller structures (such as caissons or floating gun emplacements), and sites of naval battles should not be excluded from study. It should be kept in mind that, while armies put their resources into forts and camps, navies put theirs into ships (Neyland, 1998).

Warships as well as the small naval craft are highly specialized structures, designed to convey men and supplies, to conduct missions of war, exploration or diplomacy, and to provide a home at sea. They contain communities made up of individuals with dissimilar backgrounds (frequently multiethnic) organized in a hierarchy to function as a unit. Warships are monumental structures and can represent the product of the best construction techniques, skills, and materials of their time. Warships can also be the opposite of deliberate and expensive constructions. An arms race occurs in times of conflict, resulting in hurried and expedient constructions. Naval shipwrecks thus offer a wealth of technical and architectural information.

The decisions of individuals are evident in the archeological remains of navies. Unlike archaeological sites from prehistory or the wrecks of unknown merchantmen, the effect of individual decisions in producing the archaeological record and the course of history can be considered with the remains of naval vessels. The decisions also reflect the naval and military strategy of their time. Naval victories and defeats have been pivotal to the fate of nations.

Research methodology on navy shipwrecks may not differ dramatically from other archaeological research. However, with naval and other state-owned vessels, there is often more documentation than exists on merchant ships and calls for a thorough use of documents as well as archaeological materials. Warships, besides protecting a nation's interests at sea, were built as a national symbol, to make a political statement, and perhaps even to express the nation's world-view. Kevin Crisman, an underwater archeologist who studied the naval vessels of Lake Champlain, put it this way: "A warship is not just a ship, but a statement." How sovereign ships portray military strategy and national characteristics is a relevant issue for research and analysis.

The most immediate and significant contributions of naval archaeology have been to our understanding of the history of ship construction, studies that fill in gaps in our technical knowledge. The most obvious benefits are in the excavations of ancient and medieval warships. Evidence of ancient warships such as the Athlit Ram found off Israel (Casson and Steffy, 1991), the remains of two warships found off the coast of Sicily (Freschi, 1995; Riccardi, 1995), and the late Roman river warships of Mainz, Germany (Höckman, 1985), have increased our understanding of the construction of ancient oared warships, rams, and early naval strategies.

Our profession has learned much from investigations on warships such as Henry V's 15th-century *Grace Dieu* (Hutchinson, 1995) and the 16th-century Tudor warship *Mary Rose* (Rule and Dobbs, 1995). These excavations taught us a vast amount about late medieval warship construction and gave us insights into the waning of clinker construction in large warships and the transition from clinker to carvel construction.

Contributions to the history of ordnance parallel those to the history of ship construction. Likewise, the knowledge of small arms and their use aboard ships has grown accordingly and made possible improved typologies.

An important use of naval shipwrecks is the use of their artifact assemblages to provide more accurate dating and complete typologies. Shipwrecks represent sites with known dates; thus, their ceramic assemblages are used to improve ceramic typologies that are used as tools for the dating of less well-documented sites. Typologies for other artifacts can be improved with the use of artifact collections from naval shipwrecks that are accurately dated. This is especially true for artifacts that rarely survive on terrestrial sites due to their fragility or, in the case of metals, recycling.

Naval shipwrecks can be studied as social sites: how their assemblages reveal life on board, communities of differing classes, organization of shipboard space, nutrition and hygiene. Artifacts from the Swedish warship *Kronan*, the English *Mary Rose*, and the

British army transport *Betsy* have been used to infer class distinctions aboard ships (Einarsson, 1997; Hildred, 1997; Broadwater, 1995). In a Dutch shipwreck, Vlierman (1997) contrasts a merchantman outfitted for war with commercial counterparts and their assemblages to illustrate the increases in manning of the former. Likewise, Broadwater's (1995) study of the British transport *Betsy* shows us the selection and conversion of a merchant vessel to naval auxiliary service.

Some researchers have shown how our knowledge of a specific battle or military strategy can be increased through analysis of archaeological finds. The provenance of weapons found on board *Mary Rose* has been used to interpret spatial organization of small weapons and may reveal shipboard strategies and battle readiness (Hildred, 1997). Colin Martin's research showed that a confusing multiplicity of gun sizes, ammunition and gunners' rules hindered gunnery performance of the Spanish Armada (Martin, 1997). Recovery and study of the Blakely cannon from CSS *Alabama* revealed that the gun was underweight and thus substantiated Captain Semmes's complaints of the Blakely's poor performance (Guérout, 1995).

No one has reinterpreted a naval battle by locating spent munitions, as was done by Fox and Scot with the battle site of Little Bighorn. Don Shomette (1995), did hypothesize that the Chesapeake Flotilla's naval engagements in the War of 1812 might be interpreted using this analysis.

Archaeology is used both to support and contradict the documentary record. A number of studies have compared and contrasted ships' manifests with artifact assemblages from wrecks. Gawronski (cited in Kleij, 1997) favorably compares artifacts from Dutch shipwrecks with extensive Dutch East Indies Company records. Faunal remains of sheep bones recovered from the Spanish wreck *Trinidad Valencia*, however, contradicted the documentary record on the meats used to provision the ship (Martin, 1997). Likewise, faunal remains from *Betsy* indicated supplementation of the ship's stores with fresh provisions (Broadwater, 1995).

Status, Obstacles, and Future Research on U.S. Naval Shipwrecks

Except for a few well-done works, we have not accomplished a great deal more than producing site reports. Quality final, comprehensive reports and analytical articles are lacking. This is especially true about Civil War naval wrecks, since this seems to be a period from which there has been extensive archaeological survey and recoveries of large inventories of artifacts. Collections of Civil War naval artifacts include approximate 16,000 from CSS *Neuse*, 534 from USS *Florida* and *Cumberland*, 220 from CSS *Alabama*, and more than 1000 from USS *Tulip*. Other significant collections include those from the confederate ships *Chatoohoochi*, *Jackson*, and USS *Monitor*. These collections offer opportunities for comparison and analytical studies of Civil War cultural material.

When considering future investigations, thorough and professional archaeological documentation is the key to producing an archaeological record against which future analytical questions can be tested. Caution may be needed in issuing authorizations to excavate navy shipwrecks if there are not adequate resources to insure quality reporting or if the individuals involved have a poor track record in finishing their reports. It also might be possible to hold periodic conferences dedicated to research in naval shipwrecks. Then there is the issue of finding funds or other resources to assist with publication. Federal agencies, focused on only minimal compliance with NHPA, will not use public money to pay for this aspect unless legislation changes.

There is a vacuum of careful and detailed archaeological research into navy shipwrecks. Chief among them are naval shipwrecks from the American Revolution and War of 1812, especially capital ships, since as yet none have been studied by archaeologists. The smaller combatants, sloops and schooners, are important to study, since there is little information on them. Privateers, although not navy-owned, played a dominant role in the American naval strategy both in the American Revolution and the War of 1812. Little has been done on French and Spanish naval efforts in support of the American Revolution.

Vessels built between the War of 1812 and Civil War are of interest. The small swift schooners built for the suppression of the slave trade and piracy, which are a significant step above the Jeffersonian gunboats, reveal a great deal about developing American ship construction both from a naval aspect and an understanding of clipper ship development. Certainly, more could be done with Civil War wrecks, but first, completion of some meaningful analysis with the extant artifact collections of Civil War shipwrecks would be prudent.

Nothing has been done on vessels from the Spanish American War or World War I. Although these and World War II wrecks are our most recent past, something new can always be added. Wrecks off the landing beaches of Normandy, for example, could be interpreted as an invasion site. Only a few naval aircraft have been investigated archaeologically; certainly much awaits us in this area, particularly in the study of wartime construction, modification, and interpretation of battle damage.

Other periods of interest are those of technological change, and transition from one class of ship or mode of propulsion to another. Transition from sail to steam and the last of the wooden-hulled navy also should be considered, since technological transition can accompanied by periods of social change. Interpretation of artifact assemblages can also shed light on class distinctions within the U.S. Navy and may identify the presence of different ethnic and religious groups on board.

The immediate focus of the NHC is to finish the naval shipwreck inventory and the partnerships with states for assessment and management before initiating extensive field research. Inventory, assessment, and management is the foundation for making wise decisions in selecting research priorities on navy shipwrecks. Once this is accomplished, great potential will exist for more profound investigations into the U.S. Navy's archaeological record.

REFERENCES

Broadwater, John D., 1995, In the Shadow of Wooden Walls: Naval Transports during the American War of Independence. In *The Archaeology of Ships of War*, International Maritime Archaeology Series, edited by Mensun Bound, Vol. I, pp. 58–63. Anthony Nelson, Ltd., Shropshire.

Carrell, Toni L., editor, 1991, Submerged Cultural Resources Assessment Micronesia. *Southwest Cultural Resources Center Professional Papers Number 36*. Sante Fe, New Mexico.

Casson, Lionel, and Steffy, J. Richard, editors, 1991, *The Athlit Ram*. Texas A&M University Press, College Station.

Claytor, W. Graham Jr., 1979, *Letter from Secretary of the Navy to the Chairman of the Board of Trustees, Royal Ontario Museum*. April 27. Naval Historical Center, Washington, DC.

Cooper, David, 1994, In the Drink: Naval Aviation Resources and Archaeology. In *Underwater Archaeology Proceedings from the Society for Historical Archaeology Conference 1994*, edited by Robyn P. Woodward and Charles D. Moore, pp. 134–139. Vancouver.

Dudley, William S., 1995, Submerged Cultural Resources in Peril: A Naval Perspective. In *Underwater Archaeology Proceedings from the Society for Historical Archaeology Conference*, edited by Paul F. Johnston, pp. 111–114. Washington, DC.

_____, 1996, Submerged Resources in Peril. *Common Ground* 1(3/4): 52–58.

Einarson, Lars, 1997, Artefacts from the Kronan (1676): Categories, Preservation and Social Structure. In *Artefacts from Wrecks: Dated Assemblages from the Late Middle Ages to the Industrial Revolution*. Oxbow Monograph 84, edited by Mark Redknap, pp. 209–218. Oxbow Books. Park End Place, Oxford, UK.

Eller, Ernest M., 1969, *Letter from Director of Naval History to the Judge Advocate General*, February 28. *USS Tulip* file.

Ellicot, J.M., 1929, *Letter to the Secretary of the Navy*, September 16. USS *Tulip* file, Ship's History Branch, Naval Historical Center, Washington, DC.

Forty-first Congress, Session II, Resolution 75, 1870, Joint Resolution to enable the Secretary of the Treasury to collect wrecked and abandoned property, derelict Claims, and Dues belonging to the United States. *Statutes at Large and Proclamations of the United States of Large and Proclamations of the United States of America, from December 1869 to March 1871*, edited by George P. Sanger, Vol. 26. Little, Brown, Boston.

Fowler, John M., 1994, *Letter to Commander Kevin P. McMahon (USN)*. August 24. Underwater Archaeology Branch Files. Naval Historical Center, Washington.

Freschi, Alice, 1995, An Ancient warship in the Waters off Capo Rasocolmo, Sicily. In *The Archaeology of Ships of War*, International Maritime Archaeology Series, edited by Mensun Bound, Vol. I, pp. 10–12. Anthony Nelson, Ltd., Shropshire, UK.

Guérout, Max, 1995, *CSS Alabama*: Evaluation du Site (1988–1992). In *The Archaeology of Ships of War*, *International Maritime Archaeology Series*, edited by Mensun Bound, Vol. I, pp. 90–102. Anthony Nelson, Ltd., Shropshire.

Heffernan, John B., 1951, *Letter to Captain Riddle, Commandant, Naval Gun factory, Washington, D.C.*, October 31. *USS Tulip* file, Ship's History Branch, Naval Historical Center, Washington, D.C.

Herscher, Ellen, 1998, Tarnished Reputations: Museum Acquisition Policies Remain Mired in Scandal and Controversy. *Archaeology* 51(5): 66–78.

Hildred, Alex, 1997, The Material Culture of the Mary Rose (1545) as a Fighting Vessel: The Uses of Wood. In *Artefacts from Wrecks: Dated Assemblages from the Late Middle Ages to the Industrial Revolution*. Oxbow Monograph 84, Mark Redknap, pp. 51–72. Oxbow Books, Oxford, UK.

Höckman, Olaf, 1985, Late Roman River Craft from Mainz, Germany. In *Local Boats: Fourth International Symposium on Boat and Ship Archaeology, Porto*. BAR 438: 23–34. Oxford, UK.

Hoffman, Carl, 1997, Gary and the Pirates. *Air & Space/Smithsonian* 12(1): 26–35.

_____, 1998, Whose Planes Are They, Anyway?" *Air & Space/Smithsonian* 13(4): 37–43.

Hutchinson, Gillian, 1995, Henry V's Warship *Grace Dieu*. In *The Archaeology of Ships of War*, International Maritime Archaeology Series, edited by Mensun Bound, Vol. I, pp. 22–25. Anthony Nelson, Ltd. Shropshire, UK.

Kleij, Pieter, 1999, The Identification of a Ship's Place of Departure with the Help of Artefacts. In *Artefacts from Wrecks: Dated Assemblages from the Late Middle Ages to the Industrial Revolution*. Oxbow Monograph 811, edited by Mark Redknap, pp. 181–190.

Lenihan, Daniel J., 1989, *USS* Arizona *Memorial and Pearl Harbor National Historic Landmark*. Southwest Cultural Resources Center Professional Papers No. 23. Sante Fe, NM.

Martin Colin, 1997, Ships as Integrated Artifacts: The Archaeological Potential. In Artefacts from Wrecks: Dated Assemblages from the Late Middle Ages to the Industrial Revolution. *Oxbow Monograph 84*, Mark Redknap, pp. 1–14.

Millibrooke, Ann, Patrick Andrus, Jody Cook, David B. Cook, and David B. Whipple, 1998, *Guidelines for Evaluating and Documenting Historic Aviation Properties*. National Register Bulletin. United States Department of the Interior National Park Service. National Register of Historic Places.

Neyland, Robert S., 1996, Sovereign Immunity and the Management of United States Naval Ship-wrecks. *Underwater Archaeology 1996*, edited by Stephen R. James Jr. and Camille Stanley, pp. 98–104.

_____, 1998, The Archaeology of Navies: Establishing a Theoretical Approach and Setting of Goals. *Underwater Archaeology 1998*, edited by Lawrence E. Babits, Catherine Fach, and Ryan Harris, pp. 14–19.

Orser, Charles E., and Brian M. Fagan, 1995, *Historical Archaeology*. HarperCollins College Publications, New York.

Pelkofer, Peter, 1998, *Letter to Robert L. Bridge*, April 29. Underwater Archaeology Branch Files. Naval Historical Center, Washington, DC.

Poser, Susan, and Elizabeth R. Varon, 1995, *United States v. Steinmetz*: The Legal Legacy of the Civil War Revisited. *Alabama Law Review* 46(3): 725–762.

Riccardi, Edwardo, 1995, An Ancient Warship Near Marsala, Sicily. In *The Archaeology of Ships of War*, International Maritime Archaeology Series Volume I, edited by Mensun Bound, pp. 19–21. Anthony Nelson, Ltd. Shropshire, UK.

Rule, Margaret H., and C.T.C. Dobbs, 1995, The Tudor Warship Mary Rose: Aspects of Recent Research. In *The Archaeology of Ships of War*, International Maritime Archaeology Series, edited by Mensun Bound, Vol. I, pp. 26–29. Anthony Nelson, Ltd. Shropshire, UK.

Shomette, Donald, 1995, *The Chesapeake Flotilla Project Design: A Cultural Resources Study and Management Program for the War of 1812 Fleet in Patuxent River, Maryland*. Manuscript on file, Naval Historical Center. Washington, DC.

_____, 1996, *Air Force Manual* 23–110, 6(9.10.1): 104. October 21.

United States Air Force, 1998, *Frequently Asked Questions*. Web page for U.S. Air Force History. 1994 *Air Force Manual* 23–110, 6(9.10): 104. November 14.

United States Navy, 1987, *Policy on Submerged Naval Aircraft*. NAVAIR Fact Sheet, Congressional and Public Affairs Office, Naval Air Systems Command. Washington, DC.

Vlierman, Karel, 1997, The Galley, Galley Utensils and Cooking, Eating, and Drinking Vessels from an Armed "Tjalk" Wrecked on the Zuiderzee in 1673: a Preliminary Report. In *Artefacts from Wrecks: Dated Assemblages from the Late Middle Ages to the Industrial Revolution*. Oxbow Monograph 84, edited by Mark Redknap, pp. 157–156.

Weekly, Howard Jr., 1994, Presidential Hellcat. *Warbirds International*. May/June: 10–17.

West, Wilson E. Jr., 1995, USS Tecumseh *Shipwreck Management Plan*. Report prepared by National Park Service-Maritime Initiative, submitted to Naval Historical Center, Washington, DC.

Whipple, David, 1995, Aircraft as Cultural Resources: The Navy Approach. *Cultural Resource Management* 18(2): 10.

Wills, Richard K., In press, *Dauntless in Peace and War: A Preliminary Archaeological and Historical Documentation of Douglas SBD-2 Dauntless BuNo 2106, Midway Madness*. Prepared by Naval Historical Center, Underwater Archaeology Branch, and submitted to United States Navy, Washington, DC.

Zehner, Michael W., 1994, *Letter to Frank P. Carchedi*, April 6. Underwater Archaeology Branch Files. Naval Historical Center, Washington, DC.

Chapter 47

The National Oceanic and Atmospheric Administration

BRUCE G. TERRELL

PROGRAM DESCRIPTION

The National Oceanic and Atmospheric Administration (NOAA) directs the National Marine Sanctuary Program (NMSP), through its Office of Ocean and Coastal Resources Management (OCRM). There are presently 13 national marine sanctuaries, most of which are known or believed to contain both submerged prehistoric archaeological remains and historic shipwrecks.

Congress passed the National Marine Sanctuaries Act in 1972 to promote the comprehensive management of special ecological, historical, recreational, and aesthetic marine resources. Sanctuaries may be designated in coastal and ocean waters, in submerged lands, and in the Great Lakes.

In addition to harboring numerous species and historic properties, the sanctuaries also are home to many human users. Commercial industries carried on in sanctuary waters include fishing, boating, whale watching, and tourism. Part of NOAA's mandate is to balance multiple uses of the resources but at the same time protect these resources.

Bruce G. Terrell, Maritime Archaeologist, National Oceanic and Atmospheric Administration, National Marine Sanctuary Program Silver Spring, Maryland 20910.

International Handbook of Underwater Archaeology, edited by Carol V. Ruppé and Janet F. Barstad. Kluwer Academic/Plenum Publishers, New York, 2002.

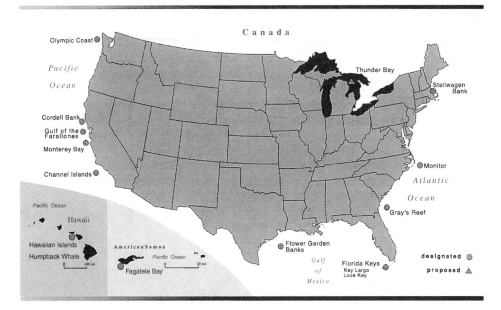

Figure 47.1. National Marine Sanctuaries.

This work is conducted in partnership with states adjacent to the protected waters. The sanctuaries often share boundaries and jurisdictions between states and other federally protected areas such as national parks. Unlike some submerged national parks, NOAA does not own submerged bottomlands; rather, it serves as trustee for the bottomland resources.

Although the sanctuary act was passed primarily to protect natural resources, it is significant that the first designated sanctuary was the site of the USS *Monitor*. The site was discovered in 1973 and the *Monitor* National Marine Sanctuary designated in 1975. The national marine sanctuaries presently include:

- Stellwagen Bank National Marine Sanctuary, Cape Cod, Massachusetts.
- *Monitor* National Marine Sanctuary, North Carolina
- Gray's Reef National Marine Sanctuary, Georgia
- Florida Keys National Marine Sanctuary, Florida
- Flower Garden Banks National Marine Sanctuary, Gulf of Mexico, Texas/Louisiana
- Fagatele Bay National Marine Sanctuary, American Samoa
- Channel Islands National Marine Sanctuary, Santa Barbara, California
- Monterey Bay National Marine Sanctuary, Central California
- Gulf of Farallone National Marine Sanctuary, Marin County, California
- Cordell Bank National Marine Sanctuary, in the Gulf of Farallones NMS
- Hawaiian Humpback Whales National Marine Sanctuary, coastal Hawaiian waters
- Olympic Coast National Marine Sanctuary, Northwest Washington coast

In addition to these sites, the program is currently to designated the Thunder Bay National Marine Sanctuary and Preserve off Alpena in Lake Huron. This sanctuary is

NOAA's second all-cultural resource sanctuary, designated for its collection of significant historic shipwrecks.

As with all federal land management agencies, the sanctuary program is responsible for the protection of historical and archaeological properties within its managed lands. The sanctuary act directs the program to comply with the Federal Archaeological Program (FAP) (federal laws and regulations pertaining to management of cultural heritage on federally managed lands, administered by the National Park Service) to the maximum extent possible. These laws include the National Historic Preservation Act of 1966 (NHPA), the Antiquities Act of 1906 (AA), and the Abandoned Shipwreck Act of 1987 (ASA).

Unlike most other federal agencies, the sanctuaries are not clearly accorded the considerable protections offered by the Archaeological Resources Protection Act of 1979 (ARPA). ARPA pertains primarily to lands which federal agencies either own or to which they hold fee title. NOAA is only a trustee, since it only manages federal bottomlands either in conjunction with state partners or as stewards for the U.S. government. As this chapter will show, this has hobbled the sanctuary program's ability to protect archaeological resources in some areas.

The FAP law that most directly applies to the sanctuary program is NHPA. NHPA assigned federal agencies the responsibility of protecting historical and archaeological properties on the public lands they manage. Section 106, in particular, requires that an agency take into account the effects of federal actions on known or potential archaeological and historical resources. Section 110, which most influences the sanctuary program's management of submerged cultural resources (SCRs), requires inventory of historic and archaeological properties and their assessment for eligibility for the National Register of Historic Places.

Before 1988, the sanctuary program's cultural resources management program primarily involved the *Monitor* NMS. In 1988, a single archaeologist position was created to bring the agency into compliance with federal preservation law. Federal budget shortfalls have kept the cultural resources management program small, but it has gradually grown in an attempt to meet its mandate.

In 2001, the NMSP instituted a new cultural resources initiative designed to enhance the NMSP's management of cultural resources. NOAA and the Mariners Museum in Newport News, Virginia, began working together to incorporate a NMSP submerged cultural resources center into a new USS Monitor center. The NMSP also initiated several nationwide workshops to build partnerships and identify resources to strengthen submerged cultural resource management in state and federal agencies.

The NMSP consults many partners in its management of archaeological resoures. The program partners with the National Park Service and coordinates with several volunteer avocational archaeological organizations. The Coastal Maritime Archaeological Resources team (CMAR), Sanctuary Resource Inventory team (SRI), and Submerged Cultural Resources Assessment Project (SCRAP) assist sanctuaries with site inventories in compliance with NHPA's Section 110. Volunteers provide an important source of labor in these times of poor government funding, and the sanctuary program views their participation as an opportunity to provide a unique educational experience for local communities. The program is committed to expanding and enhancing the archaeology program's volunteer component.

NOAA's cultural resource management policy states a preference for in-situ preservation except in cases of clear public interest or when archaeological remains are threatened with harm. In compliance with Section 106 of NHPA, the agency has prepared archaeological research guidelines to be used by applicants desiring a permit to recover archaeological material from a sanctuary. The guidelines comply with the FAP by requiring a qualified overseeing archaeologist, research design, explanation of methodology and final project report. Applicants also must show fiscal responsibility and develop comprehensive conservation, curation, and education plans. Since the sanctuaries are generally not equipped with artifact storage space, an applicant must arrange for artifact storage at repositories that satisfy federal guidelines and regulations.

The main activities of the sanctuary program's SCR management efforts involve Section 110 inventory and assessment. In accordance with the Secretary of Interior's Standards and Guidelines for Archaeology and Historic Preservation, NOAA published a historical contexts publication, "Fathoming Our Past," which develops a series of historical classifications around discreet time periods and cultural and economic phases. The contexts are used to consider the historic activities that occurred within and near the National Marine Sanctuaries, so that sanctuary sites are placed within contexts of larger national and world events and cultural patterns. In addition to serving as an educational tool for sanctuary personnel and sanctuary users, the document begins the process of predicting locations and numbers of historic shipwreck and prehistoric archaeological sites, which is essential to the inventory process.

Also in coordination with the Secretary of Interior's guidelines, the sanctuary program has developed NOAA's National Marine Sanctuaries Archaeological Site Database (NOAA's ARCH), presently a data-only database. The agency is currently pursuing plans to bring it up to the GIS standards being developed by the National Park Service.

While NOAA's goal is to inventory the submerged archaeological resources of the sanctuaries, the sanctuary program has been hampered by reductions in the federal budget. Recognizing that spending may never increase, the program has sought alternative ways to meet its mandate. As previously noted, the program seeks alliances with avocational archaeological groups. Volunteers are playing a significant part in site survey in the Florida Keys, the Channel Islands, and the Olympic Coast. Volunteer teams also assist with public education by speaking in various forums about their activities in support of the sanctuaries.

NOAA also seeks to meet its goals through partnerships with state and federal agencies. The program coordinates with various state historic preservation offices in developing its archaeological site data base, and enlists technical assistance of such federal agencies as the National Park Service in developing management plans as well as site inventory.

By virtue of NOAA's orientation towards ocean issues, the agency's OCRM office is a lead agency in international SCR management issues. The Titanic Memorial Act of 1986 was enacted to encourage the development of an international agreement designating the wreck site as an international maritime memorial, and to address the threat of unguided salvage of the wreck site. The act directed NOAA, through the Department of State (DOS), to consult with the appropriate parties (United Kingdom, Canada, and France) in developing guidelines for exploration, research and, if deemed appropriate, salvage of the *Titanic*. NOAA is also a prominent U.S. agency in the formulation of U.S. policy for UNESCO's "Draft Convention on Underwater Cultural Heritage."

SANCTUARY ISSUES

"Fathoming Our Past: the Historical Contexts of the National Marine Sanctuaries" establishes the probability of historical and cultural resources within the sanctuaries. Virtually all the sanctuaries, except for Flower Garden Banks, are believed to contain submerged prehistoric sites, and most may contain historic shipwreck sites. The unifying theme common to most sanctuaries is their proximity to historic shipping lanes as well as to submerged navigational hazards. This is a commonality in many areas with large numbers of shipwrecks. The sanctuary program has attempted to initiate inventory programs in the sanctuaries, using resources of the partner states and local communities. Some successful programs are described in the following sections.

Florida Keys National Marine Sanctuary

Established in 1990 to provide comprehensive protection of the marine environment, the Florida Keys National Marine Sanctuary (FKNMS) spans both the Atlantic and Florida Bay sides of the Florida Keys chain of islands. The region holds potential for inundated prehistoric sites as well as several hundred reported shipwrecks ranging from the Spanish Colonial era to the 20th century. The keys have been at the center of American treasure hunters' focus because of the high concentration of Spanish treasure flota wrecks. Salvors' past depredations have resulted in the near-total destruction of many sites from prop-wash deflectors or "mailboxes."

The sanctuary signed a programmatic agreement with the state of Florida for the management of FKNMS's submerged cultural resources, which called for an archaeological recovery permit system as well as research, volunteer, and education plans. Acting on the sanctuary act's mandate for multiple usage (as well as the state's demand), the management plan allowed treasure salvors the right to request transfer of certain classes of artifacts into private hands. A three-tiered permit system, complying with FAP's laws and regulations, requires that applicants must comply with each level of permit before moving on to the next level. Permit types are the Survey/Inventory, Research/Recovery, and Deaccession/Transfer. Each permit type requires the presence of a qualified marine archaeologist, in compliance with the Secretary of Interior's Standards and Guidelines for Archaeology and Historic Preservation. Permitees must submit research plans, proof of ability to complete work, conservation and curation plans, and a comprehensive final report of their work. The final Deaccession/Transfer permit, in accordance with ARPA, provides for the transfer into private hands of certain artifacts determined to be no longer of archaeological significance.

Although the programmatic agreement reinforces NOAA's responsibility, under Section 110 of NHPA, to inventory the sanctuary's submerged cultural resources, the sanctuary is presently unable to pursue a comprehensive inventory program due to budgetary restraints. In the absence of a staff sanctuary archaeologist, SCR plan mandates are met by coordination between NOAA's Marine Sanctuary Division Archaeologist, Florida's Department of Historic Resources (FDHR), and the SCRAP team.

A shipwreck database has been compiled from the Florida State Site Files and is enhanced by information received from SCR permit applications. Site survey and inventory is conducted by the avocational volunteers, coordinated by the SCRAP team. SCRAP team volunteers have been trained in the National Park Service's Submerged Cultural Resource Unit's (SCRU) program, and their field skills are of professional caliber.

The centerpiece of the FKNMS SCR educational program is the Shipwreck Trail program. Working with the state DHR, the sanctuary has selected ten historic shipwreck sites for their educational values. Buoys have been placed at the sites and brochures and diver information cards created to interpret the sites for the diving public. The sanctuary plans to add sites in the future and, eventually, to integrate an interpretive center for nondivers.

In 1977, the government successfully prosecuted a site-looting case in the FKNMS against treasure-hunter Mel Fisher's company, Motivation, Inc. The federal court upheld NOAA's right to protect sanctuary resources from unregulated treasure salvage in *U.S.A. vs. Salvors, Inc.* Defendant Kane Fisher was found guilty of using mailbox propwash deflectors to blow over 600 holes in the bottom, destroying ecologically sensitive seagrass beds, and of recovering artifacts from two historic shipwrecks. The case is significant because it determined that admiralty laws of salvage do not apply in national marine sanctuaries. The decision is presently under appeal by the salvors.

Channel Islands NMS

Channel Islands NMS (CINMS) lies 20 miles off the coast of Santa Barbara, California, and encompasses 1252 nautical m^2 surrounding the islands. The waters hold great potential for inundated prehistoric sites, Chumash Indian sites, and historic shipwreck sites. Among the many known shipwrecks is the SS *Winfield Scott*, a Gold Rush-era steamer on the National Register of Historic Places.

The sanctuary manages its shipwrecks in coordination with the Channel Islands National Park (CINP), which has conducted the bulk of the inventory activities to date. The sanctuary recently contracted with a cultural resources coordinator to work with the park and the new Santa Barbara Maritime Museum, to conduct further SCR surveys and to enhance interpretation of sanctuary cultural resources. The park and sanctuary work in partnership with the avocational archaeological dive team from the Coastal Maritime Archaeological Resources group (CMAR). CMAR divers, trained to National Park Service's SCRU team standards, have provided technical assistance to the park's archaeological standards. The team documents, records, and reports on historical shipwrecks.

The wreck of the SS *Winfield Scott* was the focus of a significant court case involving the illegal recovery of archaeological material from CINMS: In 1987, divers were arrested in the act of removing artifacts from the wreck at the National Register site. The court assessed civil penalties, and the case confirmed NOAA's ability to protect historic resources within the sanctuaries.

Olympic Coast National Marine Sanctuary

Olympic Coast National Marine Sanctuary (OCNMS) encompasses 2500 nautical m^2 off the Olympic Peninsula of Northwest Washington. Most of the shoreline is owned either by Olympic National Park or by several Native American tribes, the Makah, Quinault, Quilleutte, and Hoh. The sanctuary wraps around the treacherous rocky shoreline of Cape Flattery at the mouth of the Strait of Juan de Fuca, extends south almost to Gray's Harbor, and reaches out nearly 30 miles to the edge of the continental shelf.

The sanctuary region is rich in the history of navigation by seafaring whaling tribes. It also is the site of much western seafaring, ranging from 18th century Spanish exploration to the explosion of coastal navigation in the late 19th and early 20th centuries as a result of the Puget Sound lumber industry. Perilous submerged pinnacles and dramatic weather changes have caused numerous shipwrecks in the sanctuary region.

The sanctuary's submerged cultural resource initiatives rely on public volunteers. The Westend Shipwreck Project is an education project coordinated between the town of Forks, Washington, the Clallam County museum system, and the sanctuary. Its participants interview neighbors about local shipwreck and maritime lore. The project also sponsors an annual Shipwreck Weekend and invites historians and archaeologists to speak on wide-ranging topics.

Together with the Shipwreck Project, the sanctuary coordinates with the California CMAR team and the sanctuary program to conduct inventories and assessments. CMAR members assisted the sanctuary by compiling an extensive database of the region's historic ship losses amd by helping with the four-year Cape Flattery Survey. The survey assessed the effects of dynamic regional storms on shallow-water wrecks at Cape Flattery, Tatoosh Island, and the inside of the mouth of the strait. Of some 14 reported historic 19th- and 20th-century shipwrecks, only two sites were identified, both fragmentary and scattered, a testament to the severe environment.

In 1997, a beach survey was conducted at Ozette Beach near Cape Alava along the Pacific coast. Organized to cooperate with a public education workshop, an archaeological team mapped the fragmentary remains of the medium clipper *Austria*, which sank in 1887 at the foot of Ozette, a now-abandoned Makah village. Evidence of *Austria*'s iron and bronze fittings and rigging was found in the village's trash middens, indicating potential adaptive re-use of shipwreck elements by the villagers.

USS *Monitor* National Marine Sanctuary

The site of the remains of the Civil War ironclad ship *Monitor* was NOAA's first national marine sanctuary, designated in 1975. Alarmed by the rapid deterioration identified by sanctuary-sponsored surveys, NOAA initiated the *Monitor* Archaeological Research and Recovery Surveys in 1990.

In an attempt to arrest the decomposition of the ship's hull structure, the sanctuary embarked on an innovative initiative to recover significant historic elements of this singular warship, and to stabilize the rest of the hull remains.

During summer 1998, the John Ericsson-designed propeller was recovered, and in 2001, the side lever action engine was recovered by many divers coordinating with the sanctuary. Future plans include the recovery of the ship's turret and guns. Future proposed work includes recovery of parts of *Monitor*'s engineering space and engines and possibly the turret, which contained the vessel's guns.

Gray's Reef National Marine Sanctuary

Gray's Reef NMS, 17 miles off the mouth of Georgia's Savannah River, is a live hardbottom that may contain inundated remains of prehistoric living sites. Located near the edge of the outer continental shelf, this region was above sea level 10,000–12,000 years ago, during the shallower sea levels of the Pleistocene era.

Inspired by fishermen's reports of prehistoric camel and other megafauna remains snagged in fishing nets, scientists from the University of Georgia, under Ervan Garrison, are conducting research to locate evidence of human habitation, an ongoing research project supported by sanctuary staff and vessels.

FUTURE OF CULTURAL RESOURCES MANAGEMENT
IN THE SANCTUARY PROGRAM

As a prominent federal agency managing seabed resources, NOAA recognizes its responsibility to manage the submerged cultural resources on its public lands. To date, the agency has attempted to put its house in order by developing a SCR policy, as well as by establishing a foundation that includes a permit system and a usable resource database.

Like most government agencies of the late 1990s, NOAA has felt the squeeze of the federal budget shortfalls and has attempted to meet its responsibilities by using volunteers, avocational organizations, and partnerships with federal and state agencies that share each sanctuary's mandate of resource protection. In 1999, the sanctuary program prepared a comprehensive evaluation of its SCR program to determine its strengths and weaknesses. Based on that evaluation, the National Marine sanctuary program renewed its commitment to the protection of submerged cultural resources by creating a new program-wide initiative. It is anitcipated that this support will enhance NMSP's ability to protect and manage submerged cultural resources.

Chapter 48

The National Park Service Submerged Cultural Resources Program

CALVIN R. CUMMINGS

BACKGROUND

In 1916, the United States Congress created the National Park system and formed the National Park Service (NPS) to be the only federal agency with a "primary preservation mandate" (United States Congress, 1916). This act set the parameters, defined the objectives and purpose, shaped the philosophies, and guided the operation of the NPS for more than 80 years. Within the 1916 law is the category "historic objects," which includes the thousands of historic and prehistoric archaeological sites and their contents located within the boundaries of the more than 375 parks that now comprise the national park system. The category also includes all the submerged cultural resources and underwater archaeological sites and remains located in all national park areas.

The National Park Service's stewardship role in preserving America's cultural heritage is the ideal forum to address its most threatened and neglected class of historical remains: submerged cultural resources. Inherent in this stewardship is the concept of a "conservation ethic." All historic and prehistoric remains, including those cultural resources occurring in the underwater environment, are fragile, finite, and nonrenewable.

Calvin R. Cummings, Senior Archaeologist, Late of the National Park Service, Golden, Colorado 80401.

International Handbook of Underwater Archaeology, edited by Carol V. Ruppé and Janet F. Barstad. Kluwer Academic/Plenum Publishers, New York, 2002.

Figure 48.1. Illustration taken from cover of Don P. Morris and James Lima, 1996, *Channel Islands National Park and Channel Islands National Marine Sanctuary Submerged Cultural Resources Assessment*, Intermountain Resource Centers Professional Papers, No. 56, National Park Service, Santa Fe. Original drawing by Jerry Livingston.

Such resources occurring in national park areas have the best chance of surviving because of the protected status for these areas.

Both the legal mandates of the NPS and the organizational structure of the agency work in favor of preserving these submerged cultural resources.

Beginning in the 1960s and continuing through the 1970s, NPS developed the experience and capability in the new specialty of underwater archaeology. By 1980, NPS underwater archaeological activities had moved into the more broad-based concepts of submerged cultural resource management. Project by project, concepts and philosophies evolved. Today, the "conservation ethic" developed by NPS archaeologists is applied to all archaeological resources, both terrestrial and submerged, in all national park areas. These archaeologists have developed new, nondestructive technologies and approaches, and the concepts of resource management and conservation are stressed.

While NPS's primary focus in underwater archaeological activities has been on the submerged cultural resources in national park system areas, the effect of those activities is worldwide. As NPS developed experience and expertise in underwater archaeology and created the concept of submerged cultural resource management, others began to seek its professional advice and technical assistance. Colleges and universities, local organizations and state governments, other federal agencies, and even other countries, made numerous requests for help. NPS provided advice and assistance, ranging from a simple reference to building entire cultural resource management programs. Through three decades, it has been both a national and a world leader in the development of highly specialized activities of underwater archaeology and submerged cultural resource management.

EARLY EFFORTS: 1934–1965

The first documented underwater archaeological work in North America was undertaken at Colonial National Historical Park, Virginia, in 1934 and 1935, sponsored jointly by the Mariners' Museum at Newport News, Virginia, and the NPS. Hard-hat divers recovered artifacts from several British Revolutionary War ships, part of the Cornwallis fleet sunk in the James River at Yorktown (Ferguson, 1939; Mariners' Museum, 1939). In 1939, Colonial National Historical Park, Virginia, investigated the remains of an old ship found on Bodie Island, North Carolina, in Cape Hatteras National Seashore (Borresen, 1939). In 1949, additional work was done on the Yorktown wrecks, a cooperative effort by the Mariners' Museum, U.S. Army hard-hat divers from Fort Dixon, and NPS (Mariners' Museum, 1950).

In 1952, U.S. Navy divers conducted an underwater search in the river for remains of the Colonial Period Fort Caroline at Fort Caroline National Historical Park, Florida (Fairbanks, 1952).

In 1956, Edwin C. Bearss, Warren Grabau, and M.D. Jacks at Vicksburg National Military Park, Mississippi, used historical documents to plot and locate the wreck of the Civil War ironclad USS *Cairo*, sunk in the Yazoo River by a electrically activated Confederate torpedo. The *Cairo* was one of seven ships in the "City Series" built by James B. Eads and was among the first ironclad warships in the Western Hemisphere, predating USS *Monitor* (Bearss, 1965, 1966).

In 1965 and 1966, NPS and the Council of Underwater Archaeology (first council, 1959–1967) sponsored a test magnetometer survey at Point Reyes National Seashore, California, to obtain information on the existence of historic shipwrecks in Drakes Bay. The project's objective was to locate the wreck of the 1595 Spanish Manila Galleon *San Agustin* and to find evidence of the visit of Sir Francis Drake (Breiner, 1965).

PRESENT BEGINNINGS: 1966–1975

In the late 1960s, NPS began the slow process of building in-house capacity to accomplish underwater archaeological projects. At the same time, NPS employees carried the service's message about conservation of submerged cultural resources to the archaeological community, the American public, and the world.

The conceptualization and early development of NPS's underwater archaeological program began through the efforts of two NPS archaeologists, George R. Fischer and Calvin R. Cummings. They saw the critical need for and great benefits of a specialized program to deal with the underwater archaeological remains in national park areas.

During the ensuing years, an NPS underwater archaeological program gradually emerged. The belief, dedication, perseverance, hard work, and accomplishments of a few NPS employees led directly to today's highly successful program. Equally, the vital concepts of "professional," "conservation ethic," and "leadership" were implanted in all submerged cultural resources functions and activities, resulting in today's undisputedly successful model. The program, along with the many achievements, received both national and international recognition and acclaim.

In fall 1968, NPS conducted its first underwater archaeological reconnaissance project, using only NPS employees, at Montezuma Well, part of Montezuma Castle National Monument, Arizona (Fischer, 1974).

In 1968–1969, the NPS Midwest Archeological Center in Lincoln, Nebraska, excavated the 1865 Missouri River steamboat *Bertrand* at the DeSoto National Wildlife Refuge near Omaha. This was the first scientific excavation of an entire historic shipwreck in the United States, probably in the New World (Petsche, 1974).

Fort Jefferson National Monument, some 70 miles into the Gulf of Mexico beyond Key West, Florida, was the focus of NPS's first major underwater archaeological endeavor. During the summer of 1971, its Office of Archaeology and Historic Preservation in Washington, D.C., conducted a shipwreck survey and excavations in the moat (Fischer, 1973).

In 1973, the NPS Southeast Archeological Center (SEAC) did a second major underwater project: a shipwreck survey at Gulf Islands National Seashore (Lenihan, 1974). In 1975, SEAC's, third large-scale project was a shipwreck survey at Biscayne National Park, Florida (Fischer, 1975).

NATIONAL RESERVOIR INUNDATION STUDY: 1976–1980

The National Reservoir Inundation Study extended January 1976–September 1980, under the direction of Daniel J. Lenihan, NPS Southwest Cultural Resources Center, Santa Fe, New Mexico. This five-year, multiagency effort was supported and funded by four federal agencies: Soil Conservation Service, Bureau of Reclamation, Army Corps of Engineers, and National Park Service. Research was undertaken across the entire United States, both by the NPS team and by individuals and institutions under contract. The study utilized systematic research problems and test parameters to define the impact of reservoir inundation on archaeological remains (Lenihan et al., 1981).

NPS SUBMERGED CULTURAL RESOURCES UNIT

The National Reservoir Inundation Study served as a long-range mechanism for developing the staff, experience, and equipment necessary for a future NPS underwater archaeology team. In 1980, upon completion of the National Reservoir Inundation Study, the core researchers became the nucleus of the new team and moved into a broad, service-wide role under Daniel J. Lenihan, chief of the new unit (Cummings, 1978).

ISLE ROYALE PROJECT: 1980–1986

In 1980, Isle Royale National Park became the focus of a prototype five-year research program. The park was selected because of its known significant resource base and established sport diver use patterns. This provided the newly established Submerged Cultural Resources Unit with a management-oriented archaeological research project, emphasizing documentation and evaluation of known sites. A separate research strategy was developed for each phase of the project before entering the field. This was accomplished using nondestructive methodology: the mapping of exposed wreckage, photography, artistic perspective drawings, and videotape footage. Archival work was also initiated to obtain primary source references on each vessel investigated in the field.

Social, economic, and technological questions were addressed as thematic issues throughout the field research (Lenihan, 1987).

THE DEVELOPMENT YEARS: 1976–1985

From 1976 to the present, NPS archaeologists have actively promoted worldwide
preservation of submerged cultural resources, especially shipwrecks. Much of their early
work resulted in today's underwater archaeology professional ethics and scientific
standards. They became heavily involved in promoting underwater archaeology as a
scientific activity, presenting papers at archaeological conferences, providing aid and
advice to state and federal agencies and other nations, and participating in state and
federal projects. They hosted a number of annual conferences on underwater archaeology, joined national and international advisory boards, councils and committees, and
published numerous scientific publications on completed work accomplished. (Cummings, in press).

Through the efforts of Lenihan (NPS Submerged Cultural Resources Unit), in May
1981 the School of American Research (Santa Fe, New Mexico) hosted an advanced
seminar, "Shipwreck Anthropology," a critical effort to begin applying basic anthropology principles to the study of shipwrecks (Gould, 1983).

In 1982 and 1983, NPS conducted a submerged cultural resources survey in Point
Reyes National Seashore and Point Reyes-Farallon Islands National Marine Sanctuary,
California, to provide baseline information on potentially significant historical shipwreck
sites in portions of Drakes Bay. A second objective was to locate the remains of the
Spanish Manila Galleon *San Agustin*. The vessel had been engaged in the Manila–
Acapulco trade, and historical documents indicated that the ship wrecked near Drakes
Estero in 1595 (Murphy, 1984).

MICRONESIA: 1981–1992

In 1981, the Submerged Cultural Resources Unit was asked to conduct a field assessment
of the remains of a copper-clad wooden vessel in Utwa Harbor, Kosrae (Kusaie),
presumed to be the wreck of the brig *Leonora*, lost in 1874. This "by chance" opportunity
opened the door to a vast new area, the Pacific Basin, for the unit's scientific efforts
through the next decade (Lenihan, et al., 1981).

The unit worked at War in the Pacific National Historical Park, Guam, in 1981,
1983–1988, and 1992, conducting shipwreck surveys, site mapping, evaluations, and
training (Carrell, 1991). During the decade of the 1980s, the unit also conducted
shipwreck surveys, site mapping, and evaluations on Chuuk (Truk), Kosrae (Kusaie),
Belau (Palau), and Pohnpei (Ponape) in the Caroline Islands; Rota, in the Mariana
Islands; and Majuro in the Marshall Islands (Carrel, 1991).

The next major project undertaken by the National Park Service after the
completion of the Isle Royale Shipwreck project was the USS *Arizona* project. The
Submerged Cultural Resource Unit conducted investigations, mapping, and evaluation at
Pearl Harbor on the USS *Arizona* and the USS *Utah* from 1983 to 1988 (Lenihan, 1989).
In 1989 and 1990, the unit conducted investigations of naval vessels sunk in Bikini
Lagoon, Marshall Islands, during the Able and Baker atomic bomb tests of July 1 and 25,
1946 (Delgado et al., 1991).

PROJECT "SEAMARK"

Research on the USS *Arizona* and the USS *Utah* involved a partnership between the U.S. Navy's Mobile Diving and Salvage Reserve Unit One (MDSU) and NPS by way of "Project SeaMark," conceived by U.S. Navy Commander James "Otto" Orzech. The navy provided personnel, boats, ships, and heavy equipment for the research as part of active duty training for its Mobile Diving and Salvage Reserve Units. By 1988, almost the whole naval mobile diving and salvage community spent part of its active-duty training with the National Park Service, documenting historic shipwrecks from Guam, Hawaii, and the Republic of Palau to Cape Cod National Seashore, Golden Gate National Recreation Area, and the Statue of Liberty National Monument (Lenihan, 1989).

NOAA MARINE SANCTUARY PROGRAM: 1985–1987

The National Marine Sanctuaries Program of the National Oceanic and Atmospheric Administration (NOAA), U.S. Department of Commerce, requested assistance from the National Park Service to build a complete submerged cultural resources management program. NPS produced regulations, policies, standards, guidelines, and procedures for NOAA, as well as specialized documents related to the management of the USS *Monitor* and the RMS *Titanic* (Cummings, in press).

DRY TORTUGAS PROJECT: 1985–1998

With the completion of the USS *Arizona* project, a new major research effort began at Fort Jefferson National Monument (renamed Dry Tortugas National Park in 1993), which lies 70 miles into the Gulf of Mexico beyond Key West, Florida. In 1985, NPS started a long-term inventory, documentation, and evaluation of the historic shipwrecks, using a GIS-based, remote-sensing survey, for site testing, mapping, documentation, anomaly investigation, and test excavations. The 1988 field season was conducted with U.S. Navy (USN) Mobile Diving and Salvage Unit 2 Detachment 506, as a "Project SeaMark" effort; the 1990 field season included members of the Maritime Archaeological and Historical Society (MAHS) of Arlington, Virginia, and a team from Brown University of Providence, Rhode Island, under the direction of Richard Gould, (Murphy, 1993).

WORLD-WIDE ACTIVITY: 1986–PRESENT

In addition to research in national park areas, NPS archaeologists participated in several important projects and activities around the world. Since the late 1980s, for example, NPS has participated in efforts to protect the wreck of the Confederate raider CSS *Alabama*, which sank after a battle with the USS *Kearsarge* about seven miles off the Normandy coast near Cherbourg, France, on July 19, 1864 (Lenihan, 1993).

In 1989, the Submerged Cultural Resources Unit conducted another SEAMARK project in the Aleutian Islands, Alaska, to investigate World War II remains at Attu Island and in Kiska Harbor (Murphy and Lenihan, 1995). In 1990 and 1998, NPS participated in a joint Mexican and United States project on the wreck of the brig USS *Somers* (1842–1846), located off the coast of Veracruz, Mexico (Delgado, 1992).

In 1994, Daniel J. Lenihan was elected to the Advisory Council on Underwater Archaeology (ACUA), continuing the tradition of NPS involvement on the council. NPS employees have served on the council continuously since the organization's founding in 1970: Fischer (founding member, 1970–present), Cummings (1978–1984), Carrell (1985–present), and Lenihan (1994–1998). Since 1992, Lenihan has served as the official United States representative on the International Committee on the Underwater Cultural Heritage of the International Council on Monuments and Sites (ICOMOS).

In 1995, Larry Murphy (NPS Submerged Cultural Resources Unit) was project archaeologist for a Farb investigation of the USS *Monitor* under a NOAA Research Permit. In 1997, he served as a member of the International Congress of Maritime Museums Committee to evaluate the methodology of artifact salvage from the shipwreck RMS *Titanic*, in association with IFREMER and the Greenwich Maritime Museum.

In 1996, NPS conducted a remote sensing survey, assessment and evaluation, and site documentation of H.L. *Hunley*, the famous Confederate submarine in Charleston harbor, South Carolina (Lenihan, 1996).

CONCLUSIONS

The National Park Service Submerged Cultural Resources program has grown and matured in a relatively short time. A surprising number of underwater archaeological and submerged cultural resources management projects have been accomplished, and the service's capabilities were built and developed in the process.

Since 1966, NPS has conducted underwater archaeological and submerged cultural resources projects in the following National Park System areas:

American Memorial Park, Saipan
Apostle Islands National Lakeshore, Michigan
Arkansas Post National Memorial, Arkansas
Assateague Island National Seashore, Maryland
Biscayne National Park, Florida
Buck Island Reef National Monument, Virgin Islands
Cape Canaveral National Seashore, Florida
Cape Cod National Seashore, Massachusetts
Cape Hatteras National Seashore, North Carolina
Cape Krusenstern National Monument, Alaska
Castillo de San Marcos National Monument, Florida
Channel Islands National Park, California
Chickasaw National Recreation Area, Oklahoma
Dry Tortugas National Park (Fort Jefferson National Monument), Florida
Fire Island National Seashore, New York
Fort Frederica National Monument, Georgia
Fort Matanzas National Monument, Florida
Glacier National Park, Montana
Glen Canyon National Recreation Area, Arizona
Golden Gate National Recreation Area, California
Gulf Islands National Seashore, Florida
Hawaii Volcanoes National Park, Hawaii
Isle Royale National Park, Michigan
Jean Lafitte National Park, Louisiana
Kalaupapa National Historical Park, Hawaii

Kaloko-Honokohau National Historical Park, Hawaii
Montezuma Castle National Monument, Arizona
Moores Creek National Battlefield, North Carolina
Ozark National Scenic Riverways, Missouri
Padre Island National Seashore, Texas
Point Reyes National Seashore, California
Puukohola Heiau National Historic Site, Hawaii
Salt River National Historic Park and Ecological Preserve, Virgin Islands
Sleeping Bear Dunes National Lakeshore, Michigan
Statue of Liberty National Monument, New York
USS *Arizona* Memorial, Hawaii
Vicksburg National Military Park, Mississippi
Virgin Islands National Park, Virgin Islands
War in The Pacific National Historical Park, Guam
Wrangell–St. Elias National Park, Alaska
Yellowstone National Park, Wyoming

Significant historic shipwrecks and prehistoric remains are still the most neglected class of resources and are still threatened with destruction. The preservation of underwater archaeological remains still requires a great amount of attention. It is sincerely hoped that these important shipwreck and prehistoric sites will survive for future generations through the continued efforts of the National Park Service Submerged Cultural Resources Program.

REFERENCES

Arnold, J. Barto III, and Weddle, Robert S., 1978, *The Nautical Archaeology of Padre Island: The Spanish Shipwrecks of 1554*. TAC Publication Number 7, Studies in Archaeology, Academic Press, New York.

Bearss, Edwin C., 1965, Saga of the *Cairo*. In *Man Under Water*, edited by J. Dugan and R. Vahan, pp. 194–201. Chilton Books, Philadelphia.

_____, 1966, *Hardluck Iron Clad: The Sinking and Salvage of the* Cairo. Louisiana State University Press, Baton Rouge.

Borresen, Thor, 1939, *Final Report on the Remains of an Old Ship Found on Bodie Island, Dare County, North Carolina (Within Cape Hatteras National Seashore)*. National Park Service, Colonial National Historical Park, Yorktown.

Breiner, Sheldon, 1965, The Rubidium Magnetometer in Archaeological Exploration. *Science* 150 (3693):185–193.

Carrell, Toni, editor, 1991, *Micronesia: Submerged Cultural Resources Assessment*. National Park Service, Submerged Cultural Resource Unit, Southwest Cultural Resource Center Professional Paper No. 36, Santa Fe, New Mexico.

Cummings, Calvin R., 1978a, The Southwest Regional Model for National Park Service Cultural Resources Management. *Proceedings of the Annual Meeting of the Society for Applied Anthropology*, April 2–9, 1978, Merida, Yucatan, Mexico; and

_____, 1978b, *Proceedings of the Annual Meeting of the American Anthropological Association*, November 14–18, 1978, Los Angeles.

_____, 1998, *National Park Service Underwater Archaeology and Submerged Cultural Resources Management: Contributions by NPS Employees*. National Park Service, Submerged Cultural Resource Unit, InterMountain Cultural Resource Center Professional Papers, Santa Fe.

Delgado, James P., 1992, U.S. Brig *Somers*, Preliminary Report, 1992. Documentation of the U.S. Brig *Somers* (1842–1846), Veracruz, Mexico, in cooperation with the Government of Mexico and National Park Service Submerged Cultural Resources Unit, Santa Fe.

Delgado, James, and Lenihan, Daniel J., guest editors, 1988, Special Maritime Issue. *Courier* 33(8).

Delgado, James P., Lenihan, Daniel J., and Murphy, Larry E., 1991, *The Archaeology of the Atomic Bomb: A Submerged Cultural Resources Assessment of the Sunken Fleet of Operation Crossroads at Bikini and Kwajalein Atoll Lagoons*. National Park Service Submerged Cultural Resources Unit and National Maritime Initiative, Southwest Cultural Resources Center Professional Paper No. 37, Santa Fe.

Fairbanks, C.H., 1952, *Archaeological Explorations at Fort Caroline National Historical Park Project, Florida.* Manuscript on file. Southeast Archeological Center, National Park Service, Tallahassee.

Ferguson, H.L., 1962, Salvaging Revolutionary War Relics from the York River. *William and Mary College Quarterly Historical Magazine*, Series 2, 19(3).

Fischer, George R., 1973, *New World Underwater Archaeology 1972.* National Park Service Division of Archaeology and Anthropology, Washington, D.C.

_____, 1974, Underwater Archeological Survey of Montezuma Well. In *Underwater Archaeology in the National Park Service: A Model for the Management of Submerged Cultural Resources*, edited by Daniel J. Lenihan, National Park Service, Southwest Regional Office, Santa Fe.

_____, 1975, Archeological Assessment of Biscayne National Monument. Manuscript on file. National Park Service, Southeast Archeological Center, Tallahassee.

Gould, Richard A., editor. 1983. *Shipwreck Anthropology.* A School of American Research Book, Advanced Seminar Series. University of New Mexico Press, Albuquerque.

Lenihan, Daniel J., 1974, Preliminary Archeological Survey of the Offshore Lands of Gulf Islands National Seashore. In *Underwater Archaeology in the National Park Service: A Model for the Management of Submerged Cultural Resources*, edited by Daniel J. Lenihan, National Park Service, Southwest Region, Santa Fe.

_____, 1993, *CSS* Alabama *Project 1993*. Report to the American Scientific Committee. Manuscript on file, National Park Service Submerged Cultural Resources Unit, Santa Fe.

_____, 1996, Surprises Uncovered in *Hunley* Probe. *Proceedings of the United States Naval Institute.* 122:64–65.

_____, editor, 1987, *Submerged Cultural Resources Study: Isle Royale National Park.* National Park Service Submerged Cultural Resources Unit, Southwest Cultural Resources Center Professional Paper No. 8, Santa Fe.

_____, 1989, *Arizona Memorial and Pearl Harbor National Historic Landmark.* National Park Service Submerged Cultural Resources Unit, Southwest Cultural Resources Center Professional Paper No. 23, Santa Fe.

Lenihan, Daniel J., Carrell, Toni L., Fosberg, Stephen, Murphy, Larry, Rayl, Sandra L., and Ware, John A., 1981, *Final Report of the National Reservoir Inundation Study.* Vol. I, Summary, and Vol. 2. Technical Reports, National Park Service, Southwest Cultural Resources Center, Santa Fe.

Lenihan, Daniel J., Toni, Carrell, and Murphy, Larry, 1981, The Utwa Harbor Wreck Site: A Shipwreck Evaluation and Management Report. In *Of Wooden Ships and Iron Men: An Historical and Archaeological Survey of the Brig* Leonora, edited by Scott Russell, Micronesian Archaeological Survey Report No. 15. Trust Territories of the Pacific Islands, State Historic Preservation Office, Saipan.

Mariners' Museum, 1939, The Mariners' Museum Clipping Book: *Richmond Times-Dispatch*, Sunday, May 7, 1939, Hulk Of Ancient Ship at Manteo Identified; Monday, May 15, 1939, Ancient Hulk to Be Checked In Laboratory. *Newport News Daily Press*, Sunday, May 7, 1939, Mariners' Museum Staff to Explore Old Vessel; Tuesday, May 9, 1939, Holzback Studies Hulk of Old Ship. The Mariners' Museum, Newport News, VA.

_____, 1950, *The Mariners'* Museum: *A History and Guide*. Museum Publication No. 20. Vol. Relics: 1. Revolutionary War: 61–63. The Mariners' Museum, Newport News, VA.

Murphy, Larry, editor, 1984, *Submerged Cultural Resources Survey: Portions of Point Reyes National Seashore and Point Reyes—Farallon Islands National Marine Sanctuary: Phase I——Reconnaissance, Sessions 1 and 2, 1982*. National Park Service Submerged Cultural Resources Unit, Southwest Cultural Resources Center Professional Paper No. 1, Santa Fe, NM.

_____, editor, 1993, *Dry Tortugas National Park: Submerged Cultural Resources Assessment*. Southwest Cultural Resources Center Professional Paper No. 45. National Park Service Submerged Cultural Resources Unit, Southwest Region, Santa Fe, NM.

Murphy, Larry, and Lenihan, Daniel J., 1995, Recent Archeological Investigations of World War II Materials in Kiska Harbor, Aleutian Islands. In *Alaska at War, 1941–1945: The Forgotten War Remembered*, edited by Fern Chandonnet, pp. 353–357. Proceedings of Alaska at War Symposium, November 11–13, 1993. The Alaska at War Committee, Anchorage.

Petsche, Jerome E., 1974, *The Steamboat* Bertrand: *History, Excavation and Architecture*. Office of Archaeology and Historic Preservation, National Park Service, Publications in Archaeology No. 11, Washington, DC.

United States Congress, 1916, *An Act to Establish a National Park Service, and for Other Purposes*. The National Park Service Organic Act, August 25, 1916 (39 Stat. 535).

Afterword

Archaeology in the 21st Century

GEORGE F. BASS

The second half of the 20th century saw remarkable feats of exploration that can never be repeated, even if our species survives for thousands of millennia. During a period of fewer than 50 years, humans for the first time reached the highest point on Earth, for the first time descended to the deepest point on Earth, and then, for the first time left Earth altogether to set foot on another celestial body.

Those last five decades also saw the creation of a new field of exploration, the exploration of our past in the beds of seas, lakes, and rivers. Of course there were earlier, pioneering efforts—in Swiss and Italian lakes, in a sacred Guatemalan cenote, in American waters from Lake Champlain to Virginia's York River, in Lebanese ports, and by Greek sponge divers around the Mediterranean. Everything changed, however, with the development of modern scuba equipment by Jacques–Yves Cousteau and Emile Gagnan in the 1940s. By 1952 Cousteau had demonstrated off the French island of Grand Congloué that divers could use this new device to work delicately in the fragile remains of ancient ships. Within a decade, scuba-equipped divers had begun white-water archaeology in the rapids of Minnesota and Canada and had excavated Bronze Age and Byzantine wrecks off the Turkish coast. They had explored drowned sites from Port Royal, Jamaica, to the Roman port of Caesarea in Israel and had discovered a scuttled fleet of Viking ships in Denmark. And they were diving on sites ranging from a 1715 Spanish treasure fleet off Florida to a Maya cenote in Mexico and medieval lake-dwellings in Germany. Although not dependent on scuba, divers elsewhere were helping to raise lost vessels as disparate in time and place as the 17th-century Swedish warship

George F. Bass, Institute of Nautical Archaeology, Texas A&M University, College Station, Texas 77843.

International Handbook of Underwater Archaeology, edited by Carol V. Ruppé and Janet F. Barstad. Kluwer Academic/Plenum Publishers, New York, 2002.

Vasa in Stockholm Harbor and the Civil War ironclad *Cairo* in the Yazoo River, Mississippi. Sessions of international conferences were devoted to the new field of "underwater archaeology".

The chapters of this book, written by many of the very people who shaped a mature and respected branch of research from those early beginnings, show the immense strides already taken in the second half of the 20th century. Some were based on technical advances, allowing the use of sonar, magnetometers, and even a submersible to locate new sites, or the use of stereo photography to speed accurate plans of those sites. The most important technical advances, however, were probably those in the conservation of waterlogged or salt-impregnated materials. Today, more time, effort, and money are usually devoted to the conservation of underwater sites than to their excavation, with well-equipped conservation laboratories springing up around the world. Strangely, diving did not change much during those 50 years. The common use of submersible pressure gauges, buoyancy compensators, one-hose regulators, oxygen decompression, and improved wet and dry suits made diving safer and more comfortable, but these were not revolutionary changes; although mixed-gas and saturation diving became common in the offshore oil industry, neither was regularly used in archaeology.

Perhaps the most crucial advance made in underwater archaeology between 1950 and 2000 was not technical, but philosophical. Archaeologists themselves began to dive and direct underwater projects. Within a few years, the new academic field of nautical, or marine, or maritime archaeology was born. Universities in the United States, United Kingdom, Denmark, Israel, and Australia established departments or programs specifically designed to train archaeologists to excavate, conserve, interpret, and publish shipwrecks, harbors, and drowned terrestrial sites. The list of such programs expands yearly.

Public appreciation for any field of research is necessary for its survival. Museums devoted to shipwrecks have become major tourist attractions around the world, sometimes inspiring young visitors to pursue careers in shipwreck archaeology. The press discovered that magazine articles and television programs about underwater archaeology are enormously popular. This popularity led to the funding of an increasing number of national, state, and private agencies and institutes devoted solely to the field. Sadly, the press frequently does not distinguish between treasure hunting and archaeology, blurring public comprehension and appreciation. Almost any diver who salvages artifacts is still identified as "underwater archaeologist so and so," whereas the person who uses a bulldozer to loot a site on land is not similarly identified as any kind of "archaeologist."

So far we have talked about how far underwater archaeology advanced in the 20th century. Now we have stepped over the threshold of a new millennium. What does the future hold?

More academic programs will be formed, more maritime museums established. More state and national agencies around the world will have specialists in underwater archaeology. I would even hazard a guess that the most important archaeological discoveries of the first half of the 21st century will be made under water.

Yet I hope that our field does not remain in some academic minds outside the mainstream of archaeology. There are archaeologists who clearly do not read reports of ship excavations, no matter how important to their interests. Handbooks of classical and Near Eastern archaeology still do not treat ships equally with architecture, coins, sculpture, and pottery, although ships were no less important to the ancients, and many of these ships are now as fully documented and published as sites on land. I hope that within a few decades we will all be known not as "underwater archaeologists" but simply as the archaeologists we all are.

In those decades, technical advances will continue. The United States Navy's nuclear research submarine *NR-1* has revealed beautifully preserved Phoenician wrecks far too deep to be explored by divers using current equipment, but Robert Ballard and colleagues like David Mindell have shown that such deep wrecks can be mapped quickly and accurately. As I write, Ballard and his colleagues are designing a robotic device to excavate with care wrecks a thousand feet and more deep. That careful work can be done at such depths has already been demonstrated by treasure salvors working on a Spanish galleon in the Caribbean and on the 19th-century *Central America*. Ballard has also shown that, as predicted by oceanographer Willard Bascom in *Deep Water, Ancient Ships* (New York 1976), organic remains in the deep, anaerobic layers of the Black Sea are well preserved, with timbers of Byzantine hulls lying exposed on the sea floor.

Technical advances are needed in other areas, especially in conservation and site location. More stable and cost-effective means of preserving ships' wooden hulls are a priority. Experiments with silicone oils for organic remains are promising but costly. Conservation of iron hulls remains prohibitively expensive except for national icons such as the Civil War submarine *H.L. Hunley*. Will electrolysis ever seem old-fashioned?

Similarly, better methods of finding lost ships are required. Although wrecks of more recent vintage have been located in extreme depths after sonar/magnetometer searches covered hundreds of square miles, not a single ancient wreck I have excavated over the past four decades would have been found by remote sensing. Until sonar can produce images of photographic clarity, only the eye can spot nearly buried, nonmetallic artifacts lying among sea-floor boulders, sometimes on steep slopes. The Institute of Nautical Archaeology at Texas A&M University (INA) has shown that *Carolyn*, its two-person submersible, can find wrecks in diving depths. *Carolyn* carries its occupants inside a clear acrylic dome over the sea bed at a speed of two knots. INA also is working with a professional sea-lion trainer to discover whether these aquatic mammals can be taught to identify, say, amphoras, as they have been taught to identify lost naval hardware.

The difficulty of predicting technical advances, however, was brought home to me vividly a little over a decade ago when I was asked to write an article for *Archaeology* magazine on what classical archaeology would be like in the year 2050. After speculating on futuristic and nondestructive devices for terrestrial site examination, I concluded:

> I am probably too conservative in predicting technical developments. I remind myself that the two devices I use most often, a personal computer for work and a video laserdisc player for relaxation with operas, are things I had not imagined just 15 years ago.

Of course that computer has long since been replaced by a more modern one, and laserdiscs are not even made today! I remind myself that I crossed the Atlantic by ship 28 times before flying across, yet today there is not a single scheduled transatlantic passenger liner; in a future world history, the eras of transatlantic passenger liners and even transatlantic propeller planes will scarcely register. It seems that it is virtually impossible to anticipate progress.

So perhaps the future in the deep sea will lie less in robotics than with divers, either wearing strong but flexible one-atmosphere suits, or using startling breakthroughs in diving physiology. Cousteau once speculated on true "fish-men." Are there wreck-produced ions in sea water that could lead searchers to pottery or metal from great distances?

One area in which deep-water archaeology is bound to create increasing controversy is ownership of wrecks in international waters. Suggested extension of territorial waters up to 200 miles off Mediterranean shores is not the answer for ancient wrecks. Why, for example, should Greece or Italy any more than Lebanon or Syria have ownership of a Phoenician ship that happened to sink within a couple of hundred miles of their coasts? Suggested laws requiring the return of artifacts to their land of "cultural origin" are simply silly. More than four decades after my excavation of a Bronze Age shipwreck at Cape Gelidonya, Turkey, scholars still argue in print over whether it was Greek, Canaanite, or Cypriot. Can a lay jury decide if its contents should be returned to the land of Canaan, and if so would that be in modern Syria or Israel? International treaties are contemplated that would prohibit entry into ports of signatory nations by ships engaged in looting of historic wrecks, but what international agency could be entrusted to issue the right permits to the right groups, and to monitor activities worldwide? National lobbying for permits would be highly politicized on the international scene.

These have been some thoughts on where we have been, where we are, and where we are going. Ours is an exciting field, bound to become even more so.

Glossary

anaerobic: living, active, occurring, or existing in the absence of oxygen.

anomaly: something different, abnormal, peculiar, not easily classified; term used for possible sources of material from under water found by probing with various technologies.

birchbark canoe: canoe made wherever paper birch trees (*Betula papyrifera*) grow (Canada, Alaska, and northern United States); lightweight and maneuverable but fragile and easily damaged.

bull boat: skin boat with a framework of willow rods covered with buffalo hides, used by North American Indian tribes for crossing rivers; circular or oval in shape, lightweight, similar to British coracle. See *coracle*.

buoyant hull: term used to describe a Great Lakes trading vessel.

caloric sailing ship: ship driven by hot air, whose construction was similar to mid-19th-century ocean-going ships.

caravel: small to medium-sized lateen- or square-rigged trading vessel that evolved around Spain and Portugal starting in 14th century; superceded by the carrack. See *carrack*.

carrack: merchant vessel with various types of rigging used especially by Mediterranean countries in 15th and 16th centuries.

coracle: small, round, or broad boat made of wickerwork or interwoven laths covered with a waterproof layer of animal skin, canvas, tarred or oiled cloth, or the like; used in ancient times in Wales, Ireland, and parts of western England.

chine logs: heavy beams.

come-along: chain.

corrosion: see *corrosion potential*; *proximity corrosion*.

corrosion potential: corrosion cell voltage between the oxidation of iron and reduction of oxygen in seawater.

crannog: artificial island used as lake dwelling from early Middle Ages to early modern periods in Ireland, Scotland, and Switzerland; constructed of layers of peat, brushwood (often woven), heavy timbers, stones, and rubbish; usually circular, 15–30 m in diameter, originally surrounded by a retaining ring of timber pilings.

diatom analysis: system of analyzing ballast sand based on the fact that diatoms found in the sand (unicellular algae in marine, fresh and brackish water) have silica-containing cell walls highly resistant to deterioration; structure and ornamentation of cell walls are used in locating origins of wrecks.

dolia: large earthenware jars used for wine transport, usually bearing a seal with the name of the family of potters who made them.

downeaster: generic American wooden-hulled, deepwater cargo carrier of late 19th century.

E_{corr}: factor in corrosion potential equations.

edge-fastened construction: method of stacking thick wooden planks and fastening them with long iron bolts inserted through holes drilled in their edges; this method saved timber and hold space.

edutainment: television program, movie, book, etc., that is both educational and entertaining, especially one primarily for children in elementary grades; also called *infotainment*.

Exclusive Economic Zone: area from the coast to 200 miles offshore in which the coastal state has control of natural resources for its exclusive economic use.

extractive filter: see *filters*.

fall boat: see *Petersburg boat*.

filters: terms used by Keith Muckleroy to describe types of action upon shipwrecks and their artifacts, which "filter" information from them; *extractive filters* operate during the physical event of a shipwreck, when much material is lost because of high waves and currents; *scrambling devices* are secondary extractive filters of biological and chemical degradation when material reaches the seabed; a third type of filter is *human interference*, when sailors, archaeologists, salvors, or others remove material from a shipwreck site.

galiot: small galley or type of brigantine moved by both sails and oars. Also galliot.

galleon: large sailing vessel of the 15th–17th centuries used as a fighting or merchant ship, usually square-rigged on foremast and mainmast and generally lateen-rigged on one or two after masts.

garum: fish sauce widely used as a condiment by ancient Greeks and Romans, made by soaking pieces of fish in brine with aromatic herbs.

Global Positioning System (GPS): system of 24 U.S. Army satellites that transmit latitude and longitude coordinates to a hand-held device, which then gives its exact position on Earth.

gondola: in the United States, a river barge with a high, curved bow and large lateen mainsail set on a short mast; small offshore fishing schooner of Maine with a high stern; small wooden warship propelled by oars and carrying a single gun in the bow, built in large numbers on Lake Champlain during the American Revolution. Also *gundalow* or *gundelo*.

ground-truthing: relocation of survey targets; on the ground or underwater; difficulty of relocating targets has been much reduced with the introduction of GPS. See *Global Positioning System*.

gunboat: light patrol vessel of less than 2000 tons, armed but unarmored; used in shallow water.

gunboat, ironclad: gunboat armored with iron plates.

horseboat: unique ferry powered by on-board horses; used on eastern U.S. lakes in the 19th century. Also called *teamboat*.

hotlinking: use of ESRI software to allow computer user to view a descriptive passage of text associated with a survey area.

human intervention: diving task conducted by humans, as used by commercial entities.

in ordinary: in storage; "mothballing" of ships.

ironclad: see *gunboat, ironclad*.

lake sailor: schooner with bowsprit, two hatches, raised quarterdeck, and small housing over the companionway at the forward end of the quarterdeck; mainstay of regional trade in northeastern lakes of the United States from 18th to early 19th century.

leister: three-part fish spear, a variation of the gass hook or harpoon.

lightship: "floating lighthouse," a vessel used on the U.S. Great Lakes for nearly a century. Also called a *light vessel*.

List of Exempt Sites: list in Massachusetts law that identifies certain underwater sites from which sport divers may remove artifacts.

lodja: Russian ship built in two sizes, both of which can be portaged.

log canoe: historic vessel of the Chesapeake region, made of one to five logs and shaped to form the hull of a larger craft.

log boat: boat made from a hollowed-out tree trunk; used mainly on larger rivers and in coastal and interisland regions; in existence for about 4000 years.

low impact wreck diving: instruction for divers on how to explore shipwrecks without causing adverse effects on vessel remains; shipwreck diving ethics are an integral part of such a program.

mental retardation effect: in diving, the effect induced by being underwater that causes any task to take longer to perform than it would on land, thus facilitating mistakes in observation and recording.

monitor: low-freeboard, shallow-draft ship mounting one or two guns for coastal bombardment; name derived from famous ironclad of the American Civil War.

monoxile canoe: canoe from 17th-century Argentina, when iron was introduced; constructed from a single beech tree with metals tools and metal nails.

mud-pinger: subbottom profiler invented by Harold Egerton, Ph.D.

nao: 14th-century square-rigged ship with two, three, or four masts; beamier and heavier than caravels, its contemporary.

nave: large sailing ship in the Mediterranean during the Middle Ages; no term available in modern languages.

package freighter: freighter carrying product packaging on the Great Lakes in the late 19th and early 20th centuries.

packet boat: small wooden-hulled boat used for carrying freight, mail, and passengers on a regular schedule.

Panama route: route established at beginning of California Gold Rush by mail steamship companies for regular travel between Panama City and San Francisco; provided impetus for Panama Railroad, later the Panama Canal.

patrimony: the waters under the sovereign jurisdiction of a nation or state, including marginal sea and inland waters.

Petersburg boat: wooden river craft that carried cotton bales and other cargo; about 80 ft long, drew 1 1/2 ft when loaded.

plantation flat: barge of southern U.S. rivers.

Pourbaix diagram: thermodynamic stability map for metals in an aqueous solution.

Project SEAMARK: National Park Service–U.S. Navy cooperative project to document war remains of the Aleutian Islands, Pearl Harbor, Guam, and Palau.

proximity corrosion: a novel form of corrosion of historic shipwrecks in which the deleterious effects of galvanic coupling on the corrosion of iron materials can be seen where there has been no direct contact.

radeau: from French "raft," a seven-sided, floating gun battery or small floating fort; the radeau *Land Tortoise* of 1758, found in Lake George, New York, is the oldest intact war vessel in North America.

red paint people: a prehistoric people of Maine.

ROV: Remotely Operated Vehicle; used in deepwater exploration.

row galley: shallow-draft gun boat.

sampan: any of various small boats of the Far East, as one propelled by a single scull over the stern and provided with a roofing of mats; Hawaiian type was originally Japanese with features of yamato-gata-style vessel, its square sail replaced by diesel-powered engine.

scatter pattern: integration of archaeological data with an interdisciplinary assessment of wave and current patterns, beach erosion and accretion, and other natural processes, as seen from disintegrated wooden ships on a beach.

scow-ended: square-cornered deck, a feature of canal boats.

seagoing canoe: canoe such as the Hawaiian *vaka*, which has an outrigger or double hulls and upper splashboards for the bow section and carries no ballast; the Hawaiian canoe is made from a solid tree trunk. Also called *voyaging canoe*.

shell construction: overlapping planks, edge-joined with iron rivets; a "clinker" technique.

squaw town: frontier village of traders, hunters, and Native Americans.

store ship: a ship scuttled to form a stable platform for a dock.

steam corvette: combat patrol sailing vessel; smaller than a sailing frigate.

steamboat: river or coasting vessel propelled by steam power, as distinct from an ocean-going steamer.

steam schooner: steam-operated schooner that evolved from two- and three-masted sailing vessels; used primarily for hauling lumber along the west coast of the U.S.

technical diver: diver who uses four or more cylinders pressurized with variety of special gas mixes and who follows custom decompression tables generated by a sophisticated computer program; diver also uses a lightweight, high-tech rebreather.

telepresence: television cameras on an ROV that give the operator a heightened feeling of being on a dive. See *ROV*.

trimix: gas supply of oxygen, nitrogen, and helium that replaces air in dive tanks to increase diver safety and enjoyment.

try works: brick oven on a whaling ship used for processing blubber for oil.

try pot: pot used on try works.

unicorn: one of the first howitzer-type guns used at sea; of Russian origin.

voyaging canoe: see *seagoing canoe*.

waterlot: a California Gold Rush ship scuttled to fix title to a water lot; the ship was later buried by landfill.

windjammer: nonnautical name often used for a square-rigged sailing ship.

wracking: British slang term for its salvage industry.

Author Index

Subject Index

Chiapas, Mexico, 272
Chicago, Illinois, 178
Chicago Creek, Wisconsin, 617
Chicago Maritime Society, 178
Chichén-Itzá, Mexico, 22, 269, 271, 647, 737
Chickasaw, 149
Chih Kiang, 111
Chile, 9, 480–481
    Camelot Project in, 595
Chimu culture, 480–481
China, shipwreck sites in, 539–541
China Trade, shipwrecks associated with, 227–228
Chinese, shipbuilding techniques of, 539–541, 742
Chinese fishing village, Rincon Point, San
        Francisco, California, 232–233
Chinese shipwrecks, Pre-Columbian, 241
Chippewa, 195
Chitales Reef, Bahía de Mujeres, Mexico, 274
Chittenden, Hiram, 200
Chloeia pinnata (polynoid polychaete), 730–731
Chloride, in corrosive environments, 696, 709, 710
Chronology, of underwater archaeology, 17–24
Chronometers, 299
Chubb Head, Bermuda, 302, 305–306
Chudskoye Lake, 14
Chumash Indians, 783
Chuuk (Truk), 791
Circé, 443–444
Cistercian abbeys, 429
Cities, submerged, 461–462, 737, 746
City of Ainsworth, 236–237, 241
City of Annapolis, 109
City of Derry Sub-Aqua Club, 410, 425
City of Hawkinsville, 162, 609, 610
City of Launceston, 696, 700, 702
City of Naples, 173
City of Rio de Janeiro, 241
City-states, ancient Greek, 12–13
"Civic CentreShip," Cape Town, South Africa,
        555–556
Civil War (American), shipwrecks of, 775
    Alabama, CSS, 443–444, 641, 660, 763, 764, 765,
        772, 774, 792
    artifact inventories from, 774
    Aster, USS, 611, 612
    in Bermuda, 304–305
    blockade runners, 120, 121, 122, 211, 304–305,
        476, 623
    Cairo, 742, 789, 799–800
    in Caroline Islands, Micronesia, 255
    Condor, CSS, 611, 612
    Eastern Carolina Civil War Shipwreck District,
        122–123
    Ella, 122
    Flambeau, USS, 611
    in Florida, 147–148, 151, 152–153, 623

Civil War (American), shipwrecks of (*cont.*)
    Fort Fisher State Historic Site, North Carolina,
        611–612
    in French waters, 443–444
    Georgia, CSS, 210
    in Gulf of Mexico, 210
    gunboats, 122
    H.L. Hunley, CSS (submarine), 5–6, 20, 130,
        137–139, 764, 772, 793, 801
    Maple Leaf, 144, 152–153, 623, 739
    in Maryland, 111
    Modern Greece, CSS, 119–120, 611–612
    Monitor, USS, 119–120, 122, 670, 721, 774, 789,
        793
        battle with CSS *Virginia*, 650
        cultural resources management program for,
            792
        deepwater environment of, 641
        as deepwater site, 648–649, 650–657, 660
        deterioration of, 652, 653, 655
        discovery of, 648, 651
        documentation and mapping of, 620–621
        educational programs related to, 621
        Geographic Information System assessment of,
            689–691
        launching of, 650
        mapping of, 648–649
        as National Historic Landmark, 651
        as National Marine Sanctuary, 600, 620–621,
            648–649, 650–657, 689–691, 780, 781, 785
        National Register of Historic Places listing of,
            651
        photographs of, 22
        preservation plan for, 655–656
        private researchers' access to, 656
        public access to, 620
        scientific investigations of, 652–655
        structure of, 650, 651
        test excavation of, 737
    Neuse, CSS, 119–120, 774
    in North Carolina, 120, 121, 122–123, 603
    Peterhof, USS, 611
    Ranger, 122
    Run' Her, CSS, 476
    Shenandoah, CSS, 255
    in South Carolina, 131, 133
    Stormy Petrel, CSS, 611
    in Texas, 211
    transport ships, 623
    Tulip, USS, 111, 614–615, 771, 774
    Underwriter, 122
    in Wisconsin, 174
Civil War (English), shipwrecks of, 392–394, 395
Claesson, Stefan, 39
Clallam County, Washington, 784
Clamor, Myrna, 261–262
Clan Maclean, 392